A HISTORY OF WESTERN POLITICAL THOUGHT

A History of Western Political Thought is an energetic, engaged and lucid account of the most important political thinkers and the enduring themes of the last two and a half millennia. J.S. McClelland traces the development and consolidation of a tradition of Western political thought from Ancient Greece through to the development of the modern state, the American Enlightenment, the rise of liberalism and the very different reactions it engendered. He discusses how a tradition beginning before Socrates might be said to have played itself out in the second half of the twentieth century.

McClelland's aim is to tell a complete story: his definition of politics encompasses both power wielded from above and power threatened from below, and the sustained pursuit of this theme leads him to present an original and often controversial view of the theorists of the received canon and to add to that canon some writers he feels have been neglected unjustly.

A History of Western Political Thought will inform, challenge, provoke and entertain any reader interested in what people have had to say about politics in the last two and half thousand years, and why it matters.

J.S. McClelland is Senior Lecturer in Politics at the University of Nottingham. He has held visiting posts at the University of Indiana at Bloomington and Sacramento State University, California. His previous publications include *The French Right: From De Maistre to Maurras* and *The Crowd: From Plato to Canetti*.

A HISTORY OF
WESTERN POLITICAL THOUGHT

J.S. McClelland

London and New York

First published 1996
by Routledge
11 New Fetter Lane, London EC4P 4EE

Simultaneously published in the USA and Canada
by Routledge
29 West 35th Street, New York, NY 10001

Routledge is an International Thomson Publishing Company

© 1996 J. S. McClelland

Typeset in Perpetua and Optima by
Keystroke, Jacaranda Lodge, Wolverhampton
**Printed and bound in Great Britain by
T. J. Press (Padstow) Ltd.**

British Library Cataloguing in Publication Data
A catalogue record for this book is available from the British Library

Library of Congress Cataloguing in Publication Data
A catalogue record for this book has been requested

ISBN 0–415–11961–8 (hbk)
ISBN 0–415–11962–6 (pbk)

CONTENTS

CONTENTS

Part V Enlightenment and the development of the modern state

Part VI The rise of liberalism

Part VII Reactions to liberalism 1: Hegel – the state and dialectic

Part VIII Reactions to liberalism 2: socialism

Part IX Reactions to liberalism 3: irrationalism and anti-rationalism

BIOGRAPHIES

BIOGRAPHIES

FOREWORD

This is an old-fashioned history of political thought. It gives an account of great texts. These texts are chosen either because they are great in themselves or because they have influenced other texts or the world. I have no particular story-line. I did try to keep one going, but it refused to work except intermittently. I began to try to write a history of political thought from the bottom up, so to speak, concentrating on the ruled as well as upon rulers. It has always struck me that there has never been enough attention paid to the nature of the people – sometimes the crowd, sometimes the mob – who are to be ruled. A particular thinker's view of the raw material of government is bound to affect what that thinker thinks rule can and should be like. However, I found that line of approach difficult to sustain, because the views of particular thinkers about the human raw material of political communities are often so deeply buried in their texts that those texts would have to be put on the rack to yield up their secrets. And, as everybody knows, secrets revealed on the rack are notoriously unreliable.

This book is the product of many years as a teacher of what used to be called 'political theory', and I have many debts. Richard King, Dennis Kavanagh and David Regan kindly read chapters and offered good advice. Robert Markus was, as ever, the soul of generosity, and the range of Peter Morris's wit and wisdom is a constant surprise and delight to me. Mrs April Gibbon displayed her usual intelligence and patience with the typescript. I would like to thank two of my former students. Mr Lee Steptoe invented in a seminar the idea of a 'bourgeois tank', and this made me wonder whether there are any genuinely socialist *means* towards socialist ends, and Ms Elizabeth Walters turned my flank in a tutorial by showing that a rather complex argument of mine (and one of which I was rather proud) about the Guardians in Plato's *Republic* was completely unnecessary.

Finally, I would like to acknowledge the debt I owe to Tom Paulin. This book would never have been written if he had not encouraged and consoled me on Monday evenings over several years.

John McClelland,
Nottingham

Part I

THE GREEKS

1

ANCIENT GREEK POLITICAL THOUGHT

THE CONTEXT

The ancient Greeks are said to have invented political theorising, but the sense in which they *invented* it is frequently misunderstood. Systematic reflection about politics certainly did not begin with Plato, and Plato himself certainly did not wake up one day, find that he had nothing much on his hands, and begin to write the *Republic*. Equally, it appears to be the case that politics were not the first thing that the ancients reflected systematically about; nor was it the case that when they did begin to think about politics they had nothing else in their heads. Speculation about the gods, about how a properly conducted household should be run, about what moral instruction the Homeric poems contained, about the nature of the natural world, about the duties and limits of hospitality, and about many other things was already far advanced before anything like political theorising began. That list of things could no doubt be extended almost indefinitely, and perhaps we should extend it, even if we would have to extend it by guesswork, because what we do in fact know about what the ancients did think about is largely the result of the accidents of the historical survival of manuscripts, and it is perfectly possible that what has come down to us is a distorting fragment which gives us a very misleading picture of what was going on inside the heads of ancient Greeks. And *which* ancient Greeks? Some ancient Greeks were very ancient indeed (the Homeric poems were probably already being recited around 800 BC), and some lived very far from the borders of the modern state of Greece, in southern France and Italy, for instance, or in Asia Minor, or Egypt. Those calling themselves Greeks did not even agree about what it was that made them Greek. The Greek world had its great centres: Delphi for its oracle; Olympia and Corinth for their games; Athens for its wealth, its empire and its learning; and Sparta for the longevity of its peculiar institutions, but myriads of people thinking of themselves as Greek had never been near any of those places, though they would have heard of them and might have felt their influence. Nobody knows now what all of these people thought, just as nobody did then.

If the business of trying to empty a typical Greek mind of its contents is a fruitless exercise, we can still ask the important question of how the mind was organised. The list of things which the Greeks had thought about before they began to think systematically about politics gives us a clue to how their minds worked. That list could be extended but we would have no reason for ordering it in any particular way. The ancients were pragmatic; they always asked: How? before they asked: Why?, and in the pre-classical period they do not appear to have distinguished between different kinds of 'how?'-questions. How a stranger should be treated, how a sacrifice to the gods should be conducted, how war should be waged, or how the work of a farm should be organised did not seem to them to be different kinds of questions. We are so accustomed to thinking that questions which involve morality are different from technical questions about the best way to do things, that it is very easy to slip into the error of supposing that the ancient Greeks must have been very simple folk because they could not see the difference. There can be little doubt that they did not see the difference, or if they did, the difference did not seem very remarkable to them, but the reason they did not was far from simple. The pragmatism of the ancients originally stemmed from so close a connection between thought and action that thinking about

4

anything was thinking about the proper or the best way of doing it. It is almost as if they thought that thinking without a view to action was not worth the trouble, and no ancient Greek thinker ever thought that in some sense thinking was worth it for thinking's sake any more than any Greek artist did art for art's sake. Questions about how to do something always implicitly contained the question: How ought we to do something?, and the question: How ought we to do something? always contained the implicit assumption that anything which was worth doing was worth doing well.

Thinking about how things can be done well, how they ought to be done, has to start somewhere, and the ancients were fortunate to have at their disposal the Homeric poems, the *Iliad* and the *Odyssey*, which, if properly read, could answer almost any conceivable question about how a man should act towards his fellow men and towards the gods. The poems also contain a good deal about how the gods act towards men. The anger of the gods with men, or with each other, frequently results in what we would call 'natural' disasters, plagues, thunderstorms, storms or contrary winds at sea, for Zeus rules the land and Poseidon the ocean, so that the Homeric poems contain a good deal about how the natural world works as well. These three worlds, the world of nature, the world of men and the world of the gods, exist in the poems in very close harmony, so that it would not be stretching the term 'system' too far to say that there is a Homeric system which explains and justifies almost everything that goes on in the world and which answers almost any questions that someone living in the world would care to ask. It was this Homeric world-picture which in classical times was becoming less and less satisfactory as a universal explanation of what went on in the world, at least to philosophers, but it was also a world-picture which never lost its appeal entirely as the source of a code of conduct, and some classical philosophy can best be understood as an attempt to resurrect the certainties of the Homeric world on the basis of rational argument, so that these certainties could still retain the loyalty of rational men. In particular, what attracted political philosophers to the enterprise of restating Homeric truths was the sense of order and symmetry which pervades the poems, an order which was never complete but which seemed to survive all the vicissitudes to which it was subjected. A world which was always threatened by disorder but out of which order always eventually came was bound to be attractive to political thinkers as a mirror and image of their own world of politics, where the alternation of order and disorder could easily lead to a sense of despair unless an order could be discerned prior to and beyond the everyday messiness of the affairs of cities.

The order of the Homeric world was a hierarchical order, and it was an order with an ancestry. The great gods who ruled the world and the underworld were not the first. In the beginning Chaos reigned, a void, or shapeless matter. Chaos begot five children: Erebus, the dark; Nyx, the night; Tartarus, a prison as far under Earth or Hades as Heaven was above; Eros, and Ge, Mother Earth. Ge married Uranus, the god of the Sky. Uranus imprisoned most of their children in the bowels of the earth except Chronos and the Titans, who rebelled against Uranus and castrated him with a sickle. Chronos then ruled the world on the condition that he had no son. He therefore ate his male children, but his wife Rhea preserved Zeus, and perhaps others, by substituting a dressed-up stone which Chronos swallowed and eventually spewed up. Zeus led a revolt of the other surviving sons against

Chronos (who ruled from Mount Ida in Crete), took Mount Olympus, and blinded Chronos at the moment of victory because a god, being immortal, could not be killed. The victorious brothers then took to quarrelling, as brothers will, and to prevent the fruits of the victory going sour they divided what they had conquered into three, Zeus taking the land to rule, Poseidon the Sea and Hades the underworld. These events are supposed to have happened a long time before the Trojan War began, and the gods we hear about in the poems are Zeus and his companions who get into the story because they are interested in the fates of the Achaeans and the Trojans, and in the fates of individual heroes. To be a hero, which means to be mentioned by name and to have your hero's death recorded, means that you have an Olympian patron who looks after you in the war, but it must never be forgotten that these godly patrons are as unequal as the heroes whom they strive to protect. A hero's chances of survival increase the higher up the Olympian hierarchy his patron is, or the more in favour his patron is with one of the gods who really matters. Gods, like the men embattled against each other and engaged in internecine quarrels on the plain before Troy, sometimes fall out with each other. Zeus reigns over all, but he has favourites, and these favourites have rivals. Being immortal, there is a limit to the harm gods can do to each other, but a god could always deal death by proxy to another god by contriving the death of a hero in whom his rival took a particular interest. The gods took their own politics seriously, and that politics was deadly serious for the heroes whom the gods made their battleground.

This tale of the gods is not altogether a happy one. Cannibalism, incest and parricide are the most horrific of crimes, but they are to be regarded as incidents, not regular occurrences, and we are given to understand that they are crimes. The fact that the gods are immortal does not put them above some kind of law, even though what that law is and where it came from are questions beyond human understanding. All is certainly not sweetness and light in heaven, but heaven's disorders always seem to dissolve themselves into a new order which keeps the hierarchy of the gods substantially intact.

In the Homeric poems, the hierarchy of the gods is mirrored in the hierarchy of men. Every man, kin, hero or ordinary warrior, has some tutelary deity who watches over him. The names of the Olympians do not exhaust the roll-call of the gods but, living on the sacred mountain, the Olympians can see further and can oversee the affairs of important men wherever they are, at home or at Troy. Every man has somewhere he calls home, where he calls on his own local gods in troubled times and to whom he pays back what is due when times are good. These local spirits inhabit a wood, keep a spring running, or guard the fertility of a particular field and must have seemed very far away to the unnamed warriors at Troy. There was nothing to stop them calling on the great gods who see everything, but the Olympians, like earthly kings, are accustomed to being pestered by the petitions of the many, and, like earthly kings, have become used to listening only to the great ones. So what kept the warriors at Troy for ten years with only the very occasional murmur of discontent? The *Iliad* makes it clear that the fall of Troy is by no means a foregone conclusion, and it is also clear that the lion's share of any booty is going to go to the heroes, who alone are entitled to wrangle over who gets what. We are not even told what the obligations and loyalties were that made the assembly of the Achaean force possible in the first place, though it is plainly a temporary alliance for the duration only, and it is equally plain that there is some kind of pecking order among the great ones. What is clear is that a complicated grading of esteem orders the relations between the warriors, and because esteem comes from rank and from prowess, it can cause trouble, as it does right at the beginning of the poem where Agamemnon claims the girl by right of kingship and Achilles claims her by right of his achievements in the war. There is no scale on which these incommensurate rival claims can be measured. Agamemnon claims what is due to a king and Achilles claims what is due to the best of the heroes; each acts out the role in which he is cast. Achilles loses out, sulks famously, and the Achaeans have to suffer at the hands of man-slaying Hector, and Patroclus has to fight and die in the armour of Achilles, before the matter is set to rights and Achilles rejoins the battle. What is remarkable is that while everyone can see that the quarrel threatens to bring disaster on the Achaeans, there is so little murmuring in the ranks.

So why do they put up with it? If we assume that the poet wants us to see the affairs of the heroes through the eyes of the warriors, that we see what they saw, then we can make sense of what might otherwise seem to be a rather childish quarrel. Agamemnon acts his part as he does because he has no option. There is no man behind the mask. Agamemnon does what any king would do in the circumstances, and Achilles does what any hero would do in the circumstances, and the warriors are there to see that each plays his part properly. There is a notion of legitimacy buried in there. The fact that the more important gods are interested in the fates of the more important heroes creates a sense of dramatic distance between heroes and ordinary warriors, so that it is not supposed to occur to the ordinary warriors to be jealous of the heroes, let alone that they should try to usurp their place. That sense of distance reconciles each man's obedience to his self-respect. The heroes are a different order of men, and to compete with them would be a kind of *hubris*, unfitting and absurd when the fate of heroes is not in their own hands but in the lap of the gods. There is implicit agreement about this between gods, heroes and men; each is there to make sure that the others act out roles which they have not chosen and with which everyone is familiar. The story is known in advance, so to speak, and the drama of the poem lies in the possibility, which is only a possibility, that one of the actors will fail to live up to his own part in the story. Achilles must kill Hector, and the warrior-audience enjoys watching Hector squirm a little.

These predetermined roles allow very little room for manoeuvre, though there is more room in the *Odyssey* than in the *Iliad*. That is why there is so little condemnation of the actions of heroes, and why they can seem so childish to us, Agamemnon and Achilles as brats in the playground, both saying 'I want' without ever considering what effect their quarrel might have on the outcome of the Trojan War. They never question their desires, and the warrior-audience does not condemn them for it. What would be condemned would be a failure to pursue the paths to a collision in an attempt to avoid the consequences. The heroes are god-like, but to try to prevent what the gods have in store would be to attempt to be gods, and that must not be. The heroes are touched by the divine, but there still must be a dividing line between them and the Olympians, the more so because the gods moved so easily in the company of men. Religion could hardly be separate from everyday life when the gods took such a detailed interest in, and played so important a part in, human affairs. Religion was everyday life before the divine was alienated from the human, and the life of this world could not be so bad if the immortals themselves consented to share it.

The Homeric gods controlled the natural world on the same hierarchical principle. Zeus the thunderer naturally had the most frightening natural phenomenon in his power; a less important but still influential god like Apollo could send plagues, while a local deity could cause a stream to dry up; lesser gods could cause storms in tea-cups, but only Poseidon could make the whole sea rage. The greater gods could encompass the ruin of a great man, or a great number of men, while a malignant spirit could only ruin a man of no importance at all. Every god, every man, and every natural event had its place in the scheme of things, and that scheme of things explained everything that had to be explained. What finally distinguished the gods from men was death, and a good human life consisted of giving every man his due by treating him in the way demanded by your status and his, honouring the gods, putting up with misfortune, and meeting your own death in the way appropriate to a warrior or a hero. This was not necessarily a recipe for human happiness but neither was it a recipe for despair. Given reasonable luck, and a fair wind, the Homeric world contained within itself everything that a man could possibly want. It was a world fit to live in.

Heroic values survive in more complex societies because they are values of order; the less plausible they become, the more attractive they are. The world of the classical Greek *polis* was as different from the world of heroic kingship as the world of modern democracy is from the medieval kingdom. Even in Homer's day the Greek world was divided into a large number of different political communities ('Across the wine-dark sea lies Crete, an island populous beyond compute with ninety cities'), and if you had asked a Greek of classical times how many different *polises* there were, he would probably have said a thousand, meaning a very large number indeed. Some were very large, like Athens in her heyday with about 400,000 inhabitants, while others could count their numbers in hundreds, and they lived under a bewildering variety of political systems. Aristotle thought it worthwhile to have descriptions made of 158 different political constitutions, and, while only the Constitution of Athens has survived, it is a safe guess that those 158 constitutions were worth describing because they were all different. Just to go on a journey in ancient Greece was to provide yourself with the opportunity to do comparative government. Superimposed on the variety of political regimes was the tendency of those regimes to change. The ancients tried to impose some kind of intellectual order on this puzzling political world by dividing types of regime into three broad classes, depending on whether rule was by the One, the Few, or the Many, but the width and the slipperiness of the categories tell us that they are being stretched very far indeed to cover all the different cases. Aristotle sensibly settles in the end for the continuum Few/Many to classify states, a rough enough guide to contemporary political practice and pointing to the age-old division in Greek cities between the oligarchs and the democrats.

The ancients were frank about the class nature of politics. Oligarchy was a conspiracy of the rich to rob the poor and democracy a conspiracy of the poor to rob the rich. Along with this frankness about class went an equal frankness about power. Power was there to be used to further one's own interests or the interests of the group to which one belonged. The Greeks expected to get something out of politics; power was not there just to be occupied in the way some modern governments seem content to hold office without doing anything very much. The divisions within cities made them hard to govern, and there was never any certainty that the future was going to be like the past. Part of the cause of the unruliness of the *polis* stemmed from the fact that there was nothing much to rule it with. Whatever economic prosperity there was was extremely modest, which meant that cities could not afford to spend much of a hard-won agricultural and trading surplus on government. There was never much in the way of professionalisation of the functions of war and government, which makes the politics of the Greek cities seem makeshift and amateurish when compared to the civilised despotisms of the East or to the succeeding empires in the West. For cities to be largely self-running and self-policed, legitimacy was essential. Citizens had to be able to feel that on the whole they ought to obey the law, do what their rulers told them, and defend their city in time of war. Legitimate power is power on the cheap, power which does not have to be backed up by the expensive threat of official force. (Herodotus contrasts the voluntary military service of the Greeks with the soldiers of the Great King driven to battle by whips.)

Legitimate power is not the same as force. Force has only natural limits, while legitimate power is subject to the formal limitations of law. From very ancient times, the Greeks had an idea of law (*nomos*) which they contrasted with the arrogance of power (*hubris*). *Hubris* was the cause of chronic uncertainty and instability (*stasis*) in cities because, being the ally of the instability of character which the possession of power is likely to bring out or even to cause, hubristic behaviour was unpredictable. In the Homeric world, men were as accustomed to the unsettling effects of the anger of kings as they were to the effects of the anger of the gods. The law which can be inferred from the Homeric poems is unwritten law, where unwritten law means both a moral law (perhaps emanating from the gods), a set of ancestral customs, and a set of expectations about how particular kinds of men should behave. The unwritten law sets limits to the conduct of the great ones, but it is clear that the great ones are in fact expected to flout these expectations, and it is also clear that not all of the parts of the unwritten law mesh well with each other. Agamemnon persists in his disruptive course of action at the beginning of the *Iliad* despite the fact that the Achaeans showed by acclamation that they thought he should return the girl to her father, and Apollo also wants him to give her up. Such action is hubristic, but we have already noted the sense in which it is not surprising that Agamemnon acts as he does; kings can be expected to act like that. Agamemnon's actions are still well within the framework of expected, if not exactly acceptable, behaviour, and the Achaeans do accept it, some less willingly than others, as part of the world and its problems in which they have to live. It is also clear that the unwritten law expects very different things from different orders of men, and a select few have a licence to cause *stasis*. What is missing is any idea of a law before which troublemakers can be brought to book, or of a law which can be applied to everyone (*isonomia*).

Law made the *polis* possible by enabling large numbers of people to live cheek by jowl without having to look over their shoulders the whole time for dangers attendant on mere force. The early heroes of the *polis* were all law-givers who mapped out what the relations between men should be. Part of that law was what we would call constitutional law because it dealt with what the arrangements for holding public office should be, part of that law dealt with religious observations, and part of that law was what we would call the ordinary law of the land. There was still no idea of 'equality before the law' because the laws of most cities spelled out different political rights and duties according to gradations of wealth, and if there was to be equality it was equality among equals; rather, what was aimed at was that everyone (even in some cases slaves) had access to law and that everyone was accessible by law. No Greek city had a system of public prosecution. All prosecutions were brought by individuals against individuals, and the nearest the Greeks got to equality before the law was to stipulate that nobody was immune from prosecution and that nobody was so low on a scale of public esteem that he could not have the law on a fellow citizen. (Solon said that in the best city an individual citizen would bring a lawsuit against those who harmed others when he himself had not been harmed.) Of course, 'fellow citizens' was the key term. Many cities contained large numbers of residents, in some cases the majority, who were not citizens at all. Slaves, foreigners (*metics*) and women were typically excluded from the exercise of political rights, which made citizenship a privilege worth defending.

The law of the *polis* was a facility rather than a system of regulation. Even where it could appear repressive to an outsider, as at Sparta, the law was always *for* something beyond the timid acquiescence required by an eastern despot. The *polis* was supposed to provide its citizens with the opportunity to live a good life, and keeping out of trouble in the lawcourts no more made a man a good citizen than avoiding courts-martial makes a good soldier. Citizens were expected to oversee each other's conduct and to have enough civic virtue to go to law about it if it became overweening and unlawful, but the good life did not just consist of avoiding the censure of one's neighbours. Rather, the good life meant to practise those virtues which were held in high esteem in the scale of public values in your city, and to be held in high esteem for doing so. For the Greeks, free competition within the law was not a market but a moral principle. The law, except in special cases like Sparta, was essentially negative. The law ruled out some of the ways to steal a march on one's fellows, murder, for instance, or wife-theft, or cheating in business deals; and law was usually strict about religious observance because failing to give the gods their due was always a sign that worse was to follow. But beyond that, men were expected to compete for those things which men called good: wealth, physical strength, wisdom, courage, self-control, justice, and fame.

The problem of the *polis* was the difficulty of reconciling the agonistic striving of self-assertive men with the universally recognised need for moderation if they were to live comfortably together. The calls for moderation from all the sources of moral authority from the Delphic Oracle downwards testify to the existence of men who were disinclined to do anything by halves, and this accounts for a certain distaste that we have for the Greeks if we judge their characters through the Sermon on the Mount. Brought up as we are in a moral tradition which invites us to see virtue in poverty, modesty, and simplicity of soul, it is easy to see ancient Greeks as loud and boastful when they tell us about the nobility of their birth, their wealth, and the extent of their achievements in the service of their country, but we have to set against that their lack of all hypocrisy. They did not pretend to admire poverty while secretly admiring wealth, or publicly commend the virtues of an obscure private station while privately longing for fame. What men called good *was* good, and it was the job of philosophers to show how these goods could be pursued without *stasis* in the *polis*, and not to try to show that their goodness was illusory. Plato will try to show that most of the things men call good are not what they seem, and so will the Stoics, the Cynics and the Christians, but by then the *polis* had had its day.

Moderation had to come from the characters of individual men because, no matter how hard they pretended otherwise, the Greeks knew that *polis* law was man-made, and being man-made it could be altered. Law was always the law of a regime, regimes change overnight and a disgruntled oligarch or democrat could always find a regime that suited him by walking up the road to a more congenial *polis*. The use of exile as a punishment meant sending a political opponent to another city where his political opinions would mean no trouble for you and less trouble for him: oligarchs to Thebes, democrats to Athens. Any set of political arrangements is vulnerable to questions about who made them, especially when they have become old, and old can mean only a generation or two in societies where history is the writing of contemporary history or the heroic tittle-tattle of poets now becoming quaint. Any constitution which is the product of the mind of one man, or a group of men, who can be identified by name is open to charges of class bias, and charges of class bias lead naturally to an undermining of the idea of the antiquity of a constitution as a reason for still living with it. A man might say that what my ancestors made is good enough for me, but the idea that what someone else's ancestors made for me is good enough for me is ridiculous, and to say that a constitution made in the past, by a group which has nothing to do with me, should command *my* loyalty *now*, when that group of constitution-makers' descendants might be my political enemies, is laughable. The Greeks did understand that one of the ways of getting round the problem of the vulnerability of a constitution on account of its age and its political bias was to pretend that it was very ancient indeed. That meant mystifying the origins of a constitution to the point where it had no origins at all. The way to do that was to make the constitution immortal by the simple expedient of making it the product of an immortal mind, and the only immortal minds were possessed by gods, or, as a second-best, by supremely god-like men. Cities with constitutions which lasted tended to have *legendary* founders, and when they planted colonies, as many of them did, it was always convenient for the colonists to take the constitution of their mother-city with them to provide continuity with legendary origins and avoid the asking of awkward questions about why the constitution of the new city should be a copy of the old. Cities did get new and reconstructed constitutions, and the philosophers were attracted to the business of constructing ideal constitutions because it was god-like.

The constraints which a properly constituted *polis* based upon law were supposed to put on the more outlandish tendencies of human greed and ambition are easily confused with ideas of constitutional constraint and limitation which since the eighteenth century inform the Western European and American traditions of liberal constitutionalism, and the ease of

11

that confusion is compounded by the fact that modern constitutional theory is in part based on a particular reading of ancient constitutional thought and practice. Montesquieu and the Founding Fathers who wrote the American Constitution found constitutional checks and balances, separation of powers, and a limited sovereignty in the ancient world because they went looking for them in the first place. What did they get wrong? They certainly found political institutions and practices which appeared to put limits on sovereignty, but the mistake they made was in thinking that the ancients had any clear idea of sovereignty at all. Montesquieu and the Founding Fathers came from political cultures and from states where it was difficult to think of the state at all without assuming that the state's chief characteristic was sovereignty. Modern states all claim to be sovereign, and it is in the name of their sovereignty that they make law and engage in relations with other sovereign states. When eighteenth-century constitutionalists looked back to the independent cities of the Greek world, it was natural that they should see in them the exercise of that free and independent sovereignty which seemed to be the hallmark of states in their own day. What eighteenth-century liberals forgot when they looked at the ancient world was that to think about sovereignty in any very precise way at all was to begin to think about the *limitations* of sovereignty. No modern state, not even the France of Louis XIV or the Russia of Stalin, has ever claimed an absolutely unlimited sovereignty over the bodies and souls of its members, though liberals think that in both these cases too great a sovereignty was claimed in fact. The basis of the liberal claim that the sovereignty of the state is limited in principle is that the state is only one sovereign body among many. Individuals and groups also have an equally legitimate claim to be sovereign, so that the state's sovereignty has to negotiate a *modus vivendi* with the equally legitimate sovereignty of the individuals and groups who go to make up its citizen body. The articles of the treaty agreed to by the contending parties, individuals, groups and the state, go to make up a constitution which wisely limits the power of each party, and one of the ways the liberal constitution does this is by putting limits on sovereignty, both of a procedural kind, making the business of legislation complex, and of a kind which we have come to think of as being 'typically' constitutional, reserving certain kinds and areas of conduct for the exercise of the individual, sovereign right of free choice. Of course, behind all the negotiations lies a fear of sovereign power; individuals and groups fear the state's sovereignty and the state fears unlimited personal sovereignty or the unlimited sovereignty of groups. Hence the distinction between private and public, each wary of the other; a theory of limited sovereignty, and a constitution in which sovereignty is limited, is the connecting link and the compromise between the two.

The ancient Greeks did not think about sovereignty in that way because a distinction between public and private in our sense was not available to them. The *polis* based on law was above all other things designed to judge and control the characters of its members in the widest sense. The *polis* was always concerned about what kinds of men its citizens were. In the *polis* it was very difficult to hide, and the Greeks had not the faintest notion of a decent, law-abiding man, who keeps himself to himself, and is a model for others. Quite the reverse. Greek, and especially Athenian, political experience stressed the idea of the *polis* as collective action; the *polis* was *ours* or it was nothing, and an ancient law attributed to Solon even made it illegal to remain neutral in a civil war. There was to be no staying at home while *they* decided the fate of the regime; no trimming; you were either with the regime or against it, and there was no in-between. The *polis* gave its members the opportunity to see what they could make of themselves, so that what a man became could hardly be a matter of public indifference.

The opportunity to perform on the public stage required leisure away from the business of getting a living, and this always caused problems because on the face of it only the rich could be citizens because only they had the time to spare. The virtues could only be practised publicly, so hard luck on the cobbler who had to stick to his last and to the money-maker who made money into an obsession. When Aristotle summarised ancient wisdom about the good life, he decided that a man would do best to be a soldier when young, a man of affairs in middle age, and a priest when old. That was the standard oligarchic view. The presumption was always bound to be in favour of inherited landed wealth because it had only to be well-managed, not made; wealth for use, not capital for accumulation. Aristotle must have known when he said this in the middle of the fourth century in Athens that he was already being old-fashioned. Athens was an industrial and commercial city by ancient standards whose empire, by then nearly over, had relied on forced tribute from nominal allies. Under the leadership of Pericles, Athens had become the richest and most famous city in Hellas, but she was defeated by Sparta in the Peloponnesian War (ended in 404 BC). Thoughtful men like Thucydides, who wrote a history of the war, wondered why, and the conclusion they came to was that Athens had overreached herself. Ever since the mainly Athenian army had beaten the hosts of the Persian king at Marathon, the Athenians had come to think that there was nothing they could not do. The Athenians had lost all sense of the proper limits to human action; its democracy had almost casually decided to invade Sicily, failed disastrously to take Syracuse, and the long road to defeat ended with a Spartan garrison on the acropolis at Athens.

In the part of Thucydides' history of the Peloponnesian War which we call the Melian Dialogue, the Athenian envoys point out to the Melians, who are trying to get out of their alliance with Athens in the middle of the war, that the choice before them is either to give way to superior force or to be crushed by it. That is the way things are in the world. Nothing could be more natural than that the strong should inherit the earth, and the weak had better get out of the way. There is something Homeric about that sense of power, yet the *polis* was supposed to be tempered by the restraints of *nomos*; law was supposed to map out the acceptable boundaries of conduct.

So what was it about the *polis* which threatened to leave the promise of *nomos* unfulfilled? In one sense the idea of the *polis* based on law was a victim of its own success. There was no doubt a time when *nomos* was considered a liberating force because it freed men from brute force's more extravagant caprices. A law that was fixed, knowable and known, or which at worst changed only slowly, and after proper public deliberation, as the decision of the *polis* itself, must at one time have seemed to be the way to impose order and justice on men's conflicting wills, or at the very least law would have appeared to be the basis upon which a just and orderly community could be built. During the centuries of the *polis*'s existence, there was to be huge disagreement about what the law should contain and about who should in fact make it, but law there had to be. Towards the end of the fifth century, there was enough *polis* experience in the past, and enough variety of *polis* experience in the present, for thinkers to begin to wonder what all the fuss about law had once been about when it seemed so obvious that law was just another of the things that men made. Like other human artifacts, laws were subject to the vicissitudes of fashion and taste; constitutions came and went (except at Sparta); men in one *polis* called good what men in others called wicked; and there were other civilisations which the Greeks knew which called good things of which the Greeks had never previously heard. Laws, constitutions, types of regime, sets of public values, beliefs about the gods (and even their names) must therefore be matters of conventional agreement among men. Law, therefore, cannot be part of the nature of things (*physis*), but is more or less arbitrarily invented out of people's heads. The rules of proper social living could even be seen as being against nature. In Socrates' day, the Sophists were saying that law was irksome, intolerable to strong natures, setting undue limits to what those strong natures could achieve if they were allowed their natural sway. In the rest of nature, the strong preyed on the weak, so why should this not also be the rule in the world of men?

The Sophists' argument was made stronger by the facts which they drew from the world of politics to support it. The laws of different cities were plainly the inventions of those cities, and, while it was true that a great variety of types of law existed, there was none the less some kind of perceptible order. If you looked at the types of law which did in fact exist, and at the types of regime which those laws supported, then it was very obvious that the laws of each city were made by that city's strongest party. Philosophers debated the question of whether the One, the Few or the Many ought to rule, and that was an interesting enough question, but it tended to obscure the important truth that the One, the Few or the Many did in fact rule where each was strongest, and the laws of each city and its system of public values proclaimed it loudly to the world. Nature was bound to win out against *nomos* in the end, and only a fool could fail to see it. The Sophists were sceptical about the claims made for laws, but they were not anarchists. They did not think that, because law was convention, it was any the less law. Their argument was not meant to encourage crime; nor was it an invitation to ordinary human wickedness. Rather it was an incitement to very grand larceny indeed: you and your friends could try to take over a whole *polis* if you felt your strength was up to it; otherwise, you had better stick to the rules of the *polis* in which you happened to live because those rules had been made and were administered by the strong.

A refutation of that doctrine of power is the starting point of Plato's *Republic*, which is a search for a kind of order different from the hard-nosed worldly wisdom of the Sophists. The Sophists' case amounted to no less than the denial that there were any political values worth standing up for. How could there be when, according to the power doctrine, everything was up for grabs? It has to be remembered that when the Sophists said that justice was the interest of the stronger, they meant something very broad by justice. It would include legal justice, how the law courts should behave, and it would include ideas about morality, the right thing to do, but it would also include what we have come to call a lifestyle and the values and attitudes which go with it. The *polis* was supposed to produce particular kinds of men leading a particular kind of life. The whole *feel* of an oligarchic *polis* was supposed to be oligarchic; a disgruntled Theban we call the Old Oligarch once complained that Athens was no place for a gentleman because it was dangerous there to lash out at a slave in the street in case you hit a free citizen by mistake. Athenian democratic manners made the citizens dress so scruffily that it was hard for a stranger to tell the difference between slaves and free men. Contrast Sparta, where the citizens lived in a state of perpetual war with the subject helots whom they plundered, so that to kill a helot who got above himself was no crime. The problem with the Sophist argument was that it offered no grounds for thinking which was the better way of life.

Plato often seems to link the Sophists with democracy, which might seem odd when we consider that the Sophist argument could be used equally well as a justification for monarchy or oligarchy. Besides, Plato's teacher, Socrates, was widely considered to be just another Sophist (otherwise why would Plato deny that he was?), and Socrates himself was tried and executed on a charge of impiety by the restored Athenian democracy in 399. Plato probably thought that democracy was the ideal culture for the Sophist bacillus. The Sophists taught their wisdom for pay, and as always when wisdom is on sale, people had to know that they were getting value for their money, and this the Sophists provided in the form of rhetoric, something half way between what we would call the art of public speaking and the forensic art. The Sophists taught their pupils how to be persuasive, how to speak on both sides of a question, sometimes to a time limit and always with indifference about which side was right. The obvious place in which these skills would be marketable would be a democratic *polis* where there would be large popular juries and popular assemblies worth persuading. Mob oratory would be useless in a monarchy and out of place in an aristocracy; you do not harangue kings, and the appropriate mode among aristocrats is conversation. The Sophists' skills would be useful only to agitators of the people in cities where there was a people allowed to assemble in order to be agitated. (It is no coincidence that the Spartans were laconic.) Fear of the people as a mob is at the back of Plato's distaste for Sophism. He never doubts that mob oratory can be taught. It is a very inferior science, but it is based on a psychology of the common man which is in all respects essentially true. The common man cannot think things out for himself and is therefore incapable of judging whether others have thought anything out properly; he does believe he can understand public affairs and will only listen to those who tell him that he can; he likes things put to him simply, and he likes simple answers to complex questions because he is really bewildered underneath his own self-confidence. *En masse* the common man is a great beast who needs to be stroked, fed, flattered and led by the nose.

The common man's lack of a sense of his own limitations, and the demagogue's ability to exploit it, means that a democratic *polis* is always likely to get out of control. The demagogue and the *demos* corrupt each other because the demagogue knows that he can only propose what the people are already predisposed to believe is right, and the people will only listen to those who tell them that they are right to want what they already want. Men such as these are the first in the world's history to have nothing between their this-I-want and their this-I-will-do. The Homeric heroes were at least constrained by their roles and by the expectations of the multitude, aristocrats were subject to *noblesse oblige* and even tyrants had to watch their step; only *demos*, by universalising itself, found that it could do anything, provided only that it had a will to do it.

NOTES ON SOURCES

As you might expect, there is a vast literature on Ancient Greece, and that literature keeps on increasing at an alarming rate. Perhaps surprisingly, there is not that much on the Homeric poems as they make their presence felt in the formal Greek political theory that has survived. Easily the most accessible account, aimed mainly at Aristotle, is Ch. 1. of J.B. Morrall, *Aristotle* (1977). All recent discussion of the world of the Homeric poems begins from M. Finley, *The World of Odysseus* (1977). Finley has written a series of sparkling books on Ancient Greece. His *Democracy: Ancient and Modern* (1985), *Ancient Slavery and Modern Ideology* (1987), and *The Ancient Greeks* (1991), are especially recommended. A.H.M. Jones, *Athenian Democracy* (1957), is a classic, as is V. Ehrenberg, *The Greek State* (2nd edn, 1969). The Homeric poems are available in decent prose translation in the Penguin Classics series, though I have a lingering fondness for some of the cod couplets in Chapman.

2

SOCRATES AND PLATO

PLATO

Plato was born in 427 BC into an Athens which had already been engaged in the Peloponnesian War (430–404) with Sparta for three years. Pericles, the great aristocratic leader of the Athenian democracy, had died the previous year. Plato therefore grew up in interesting times, and he came of age while the war was ending disastrously for Athens with the humiliation of a Spartan garrison on the Acropolis and some vicious political infighting between the oligarchic and democratic factions for control of the city's politics. Plato had family connections with both the oligarchic and democratic parties, and, as a well-born youth with a foot in both camps, it was natural for him to consider a political career. The politics of a city at war was no doubt the staple of conversation in his youth. Contemporary witness suggests that the Athenian democracy changed its nature as the war went on. Pericles took Athens and her allies into the war because he thought Athens had no option, and his control of the popular assembly meant that he could confine Athenian strategy and expenditure within the bounds of the possible. After Pericles, the Athenian assembly began to listen to ill-bred demagogues who were willing to tell the assembly only what it wanted to hear. Athens became less cautious in its policy towards its own allies, whom it began to treat as part of an Athenian empire, and much less cautious in strategy, which eventually led to the débâcle of the expedition to take Syracuse. The rich saw themselves as being bled white to pay for a badly conducted democratic war, while their democratic enemies began to suspect that the oligarchs might be moving towards defeatism because victory against aristocratic Sparta would be a victory for the Athenian *demos* and its leaders.

The last years of the Peloponnesian War were years of bitter party strife in Athens, oligarchy alternating with democracy, but the problem was virtually impossible to solve while the Athenian army consisted of the better-off hoplites and the equally important navy relied on the poor for its manpower as rowers. Athens lost the war, and an oligarchic government of the Thirty came to power partly with the help of Spartan arms. The government of the Thirty was vicious to its democratic enemies but it did not last long, democracy being quickly restored. In 399 it executed Plato's mentor, Socrates, on a charge of impiety and corrupting the young, and this despite a famous pronouncement by the Delphic Oracle that he was the wisest man in Greece.

The political experience of the Athens of his youth and early manhood appears to have sickened Plato. As he says in the (possibly spurious) autobiographical Seventh Letter, 'I was forced, in fact, to the belief that the only hope of finding justice for society or for the individual lay in true philosophy, and that mankind will have no respite from trouble until either real philosophers gain political power or politicians become by some miracle true philosophers.' Plato travelled widely after the death of Socrates (there are rumours that he dabbled in the olive oil business in Egypt), made an unsuccessful attempt to convert a tyrant of Syracuse into a philosopher-ruler, and eventually founded the Academy in Athens in 386 where he taught for the rest of his life. He died in 347.

Besides the *Republic* Plato wrote two other books on politics, *The Statesman* and *The Laws* (this latter is often taken to be an account of Plato's 'second best state', and is said to contain the first account of the doctrine of mixed government). His famous account of a drinking party, *The Symposium*, celebrates homosexual love in a way once thought to be mildly scandalous.

Plato says in the *Republic* that there are people living in his own day who still believe that all aspects of life should be regulated according to precepts derivable from the Homeric poems. This tells us that there are also people living in Plato's day who thought nothing of the kind. The world view of Homer still commands the loyalty of some men but not of others. Men cannot live without a value system which orders their lives, so it follows that Plato's own world is one in which a number of different value systems compete for the attention of thinking men. That plurality of possible value systems easily led to the Sophist position that value systems are matters of convention only in a world where it was strength which really counted. Of course, none of this might be very obvious to ordinary men, who would try to continue to live according to the values which they had always lived by, though they might be discomfited by whispers that what they had always thought of as values no longer counted for much in advanced circles.

This plurality of value systems caused Plato trouble from the beginning. If there were a number of value systems on offer, they obviously could not all be right. Therefore most of them would have to be dissolved in moral scepticism in order to see what survived, but the sceptical temper was ill-suited to the construction of the kind of absolute value-system which Plato thought was the only antidote to the moral, and therefore political, instability which surrounded him. Plato solved his problem by inventing a double Socrates, a sceptical Socrates and a Platonic Socrates. The historical Socrates undoubtedly existed, but he did not write anything, so that what we know about his opinions comes to us at second-hand and largely through admiring friends, the chief among whom is Plato. What was it that led Plato to write so much of his philosophy through the mouth of Socrates? Socrates was an extraordinary man, capable of arousing fierce loyalty and irritated enmity. According to his friends he was wise, courageous, self-controlled and just, the best man of his time, exactly the kind of man least likely to survive in a society in which injustice was getting the upper hand. Perhaps there is something too mannered in this description of Socrates: wisdom, courage, temperence and justice are the conventional catalogue of the ancient virtues, but, on the other hand, perhaps Socrates did possess them all. What seems beyond dispute is that Socrates had an extraordinary presence, almost a stage presence in our sense. He was one of those people whom, once you have met them, you never forget. Socrates earned his own living, though he never took a penny-piece for his teaching, but he seemed to exercise a kind of fascination over well-born youths like Plato and Alcibiades. Socrates played the game of philosophy in a way so new that we call his predecessors pre-Socratic.

Those predecessors had left knowledge in a mess. The certainties of the Homeric world of natural hierarchies were undermined from any number of different directions, but because those three interlocking hierarchies stand or fall together, a sustained and successful attack from any direction would have been fatal to all three. The hierarchy of the gods, the hierarchy of men and the hierarchy of nature paid a high price for their card-castle elegance; all three would tumble down at the removal of a single card. Among the first to remove a card was Democritus with his brilliant guess at atomic theory. In essence, what Democritus had to say about atoms was simple, but it had very far-reaching consequences. Democritus said that the whole of nature could be explained as the

19

behaviour of very small particles acting in ways which were in principle predictable but which men were in fact incapable of predicting. Everything was made of the same stuff, and every happening was simply the result of that stuff moving around. The implication for the Homeric view of nature was obvious. How could nature be hierarchical if everything was made up of everything else? Some events are bigger than others, a storm at sea bigger than a storm in a tea cup, but that was just the way things turned out; a sliding-scale of events of infinitely graded magnitude made much more sense than different classes of events clearly differentiated from each other. And it was hardly reassuring for a king to be told that he was made of the same clay as the meanest of his subjects, or his slaves, or even his domestic animals. If the events which concerned kings and nobles were not qualitatively different from the events which concerned ordinary men, then there was no need to introduce into the world a special class of gods important enough to account for the greatness of great men's deeds. Now only their scale is greater, not their nature.

The world posited by Democritus was a world of constant change. It was Heraclitus who most famously characterised that inconstant world as a world in flux. Democritus and Heraclitus between them fashioned a world about which it was very difficult to say anything very positive at all, beyond saying that it was like what they said it was like. For knowledge to be true, it had to be true always, so perhaps, as Parmenides was to say, it was not worth the trouble to try to find knowledge in the world at all because what would be true of the world today was bound to be untrue tomorrow. For those who took Parmenides at his word, the only honest conclusion to be drawn was that the business of trying to find knowledge should be wound up almost before it had begun. That was the intellectual world in which Socrates lived and died, and, Plato wrote, a world in which all dogma – moral, political and religious – had had its day. No doubt there was a good deal of dogma still around; dogma does not die the day it is shown to be baseless (any more than all the machines constructed on the basis of Newtonian physics stopped working on the day that Einstein discovered the principle of Special Relativity). Plato had his work cut out as a philosopher because he believed that it was still possible to find true knowledge, so he had to face the preliminary task of uncluttering men's minds of the baseless opinion which still passed for knowledge in the world after Parmenides. By Plato's account, Socrates was the past master in the art of showing that what men thought of as knowledge was nothing of the kind. The most pleasing image we have is of Socrates stopping people in the Athenian *agora* (the public square) – a famous Sophist, a politician, a noted humbug – and asking them about their beliefs about how men should live, dominating them by his questions, and cornering them in self-confessed absurdity. What made the whole business maddening, and may have led to his trial and execution, is that Socrates always claimed that he himself knew nothing. We can only guess that the historical Socrates was really like that, but we can easily see why, if the invention of Socrates the gadfly is an invention of Plato's, it is a necessary invention. He stands for the instrument needed to clear away all outmoded doctrine before the true job of philosophy could begin.

Socrates made his living as a stonemason, and he is reputed to have said that the only men who knew anything at Athens were the craftsmen. For Socrates, there was always more than an analogy between knowing something and a technical skill (*techne*). What a craftsman knows is the reverse of dogmatic; a craft is not a set of principles to be put into operation; that is not what a craftsman does when he practises his craft, and the learning of a craft certainly does not consist of learning a set of principles and then putting them into practice. It is not even clear that a set of principles could usefully be extrapolated from a craft, and most craftsmen, when asked what they are doing, would be hard put to it to explain beyond saying: 'Any fool can see I'm doing carpentry.' The questions which can sensibly be asked of someone practising a skill are not about what the skill is like but about how the skill was acquired. Someone practising a skill would be able to propose a training programme for skill-learning much more easily than he would be able to describe the end-product of that training. The relationship between master and pupil would be central to the enterprise. A craft does not exist apart from its exercise, so a pupil has to see the master practise the craft before he can begin to learn, and the whole purpose of the training is to produce a master. That is not to say that all of the training would be on-the-job training. A certain amount of 'theoretical' work might be useful, in mathematics, say, and there might be room for physical exercise to cultivate desirable physical attributes, like strength and dexterity, but these too would be learned from a master. Being a master also requires its own forms of in-service training, because a master is only a master in so far as he actually practises his craft. Skills can become rusty; fitness for anything means keeping fit; practice does not always make perfect, but lack of practice always leads to degeneration.

Socrates may have thought that goodness was a kind of skill, being good at doing good. Goodness always had an active quality about it for the ancient Greeks. Goodness was not a passive condition of the soul, like innocence; nor was it simply to be well-intentioned. To be good was to do good things, and to be considered good was to be seen to be doing them. Men would be known by their works. The question was how to train a man to do good. If goodness was a skill, being good at doing good, then a moral training would have to go far beyond posting up a list of things to do and things to avoid: tell the truth, help friends, harm enemies, pay debts, husband inheritances, avoid self-indulgence, and so on. These might well be the things that good men would do, and the list could no doubt be extended almost indefinitely, but there is nothing in that list which guarantees that they will in fact be done. Doing them requires practice so that they become second nature, and no amount of diligent study of the list will produce men like that. And, as with all lists of rules, there will always be exceptions because on occasions rules will conflict. Plato deals with one such conflict in the *Republic*, Book I. The old man Cephalus suggests that two of the rules of justice are helping friends and paying debts. Socrates points out that it could not be justice to return a knife borrowed from a friend if the friend had gone mad in the meantime. That would be paying the debt, but it could hardly be called helping a friend. Cephalus confesses that he is stumped by that objection. He could have said that justice is helping friends and paying debts, but not in that case. Plato does not allow him to say that for the obvious reason that a list of exceptions to the rules of justice would make for a very long list indeed. Not only would the list have to contain all the rules which a just man would follow, but it would also have to contain a complete list of the exceptions. This list of the exceptions would almost certainly have to be much longer than the list of rules because the exceptions would always depend on circumstances, and there is in principle no limit to the number of possible circumstances that could arise in which the rules of justice could come into conflict. And even if the list of rules and exceptions could be made exhaustive, there is still nothing in the list which would guarantee that a particular man would order his life and his conduct in strict accordance with it.

Much better, then, to approach the problem from another direction. Why not devise a training programme to produce just men? Here the idea of justice as a skill really helps. If there is a man somewhere who is just, then he is the master and the rest are naturally his pupils. The pupils will themselves become just men by going through the same training programme as he did and by attending to his example. It does not much matter if the master cannot tell the uninstructed what the end-product of the training will be like beyond saying: 'You will end up by being like me and doing what I do.' Plato may have thought about Socrates like that and Socrates may have meant that he could not produce a set of rules of justice when he said that he knew nothing. His questioning of those who said they knew what justice was may have been meant to demonstrate that justice could not be a set of rules for conduct which only had to be memorised for justice to follow. What Socrates obviously had was a disposition to be just, and Plato thought that the cause of justice could best be served by devising ways in which the Socratic disposition could be cultivated in others. Of course, this can only be a guess because we know practically nothing about the young Socrates, and we certainly do not know enough to know how Socrates came to be just.

Plato knows that there is still one difficulty to be overcome. Just as there is nothing in a list of rules for just conduct which would necessarily compel anyone to follow them (why should I?), so there is no very compelling reason why I should want to be just like Socrates. I might want to be like Socrates, but I might not. Plato has to find a readily intelligible motive for wanting to be like Socrates, and for being prepared to go through a course of training to become like Socrates. Training implies sacrifice of present inclination for future benefit, so what would make it *worth it*? Plato has to compete in a market in which the Sophists are the market leaders offering success in public life as the bait to potential customers. Plato never denies that the Sophists can deliver the goods on their prospectus, and, being Greek, he knows that nobody does anything for nothing, so he undertakes to show that the just man is always happier than the unjust man. Plato takes it as axiomatic that most successful men in corrupt societies cannot be all good. This applies particularly to men who have had to make their own way – exactly the market that the Sophists aimed at. Plato is straightforward about what he means by the happiness of the just man; he means what everybody means by happiness. The lucky or the successful man in a corrupt society may have everything he wants, and his contemporaries may envy him as the happiest of men, but he really is unhappy. Likewise, the just man in an unjust society may appear to be the most miserable of men, always doing good and always suffering calumny and worse from his contemporaries, but he really is happier even if he is hounded to death. Happiness is the motive for justice: happiness now, not happiness in some state of future bliss after death, and not happiness defined out of existence as something else.

That is a tall order. Plato has to convince his audience that justice really is what he says it is and then he has to show that audience that we have good reasons for wanting justice.

Justice is obviously a very odd virtue, different in kind from wisdom, courage and self-control, which, with justice, go up to make the catalogue of the virtues. The difference between justice and the other virtues is that the other virtues are worth practising even though others do not practise them. It is to my advantage to be wise if others are foolish, brave (though not foolhardy) if others are poltroons, and temperate if others are profligates. At the very least, these virtues do not make me vulnerable and they might also enable me to protect myself from others; at best, they might help me to a position of dominance on the principle that in the kingdom of the blind the one-eyed man is king. Justice holds out no such promise. The good fare badly among the wicked, and the worst position of all would be to be the only just man left. The conclusion might be drawn that wisdom, courage and temperence are obviously *political* virtues in a sense that justice is not. These virtues are directly and positively related to the power relations between men, while justice can hardly be recommended as a course of life and as a prescription for happiness. In the *Republic* Plato argues the reverse. He argues that justice is a political virtue in a sense in which the others are not. The other virtues are certainly worth having, and Plato will end up by showing that the just man will in fact possess all the other virtues, but he wants us to believe that justice is the central political virtue, useful in politics in a way the others are not.

Justice is necessarily a political virtue because it has to be widely practised for the just to survive. The just have an interest in the spread of justice, in making others in the image of themselves. Wise men may want others to be wise, but a selfish man who was also wise might well want to restrict wisdom to himself and a few friends for the advantages it brings. A just man in an unjust society would always be at risk unless he could persuade others to share his justice, but problems immediately begin to arise when one begins to ask whether or not all men are capable of being just. If the answer is that all men *are* capable of being just, then the additional question has to be asked: If that is so, why is it the case that so few are just in fact? If justice is so generally accessible, why is it so rare? Wisdom, courage and temperance, if not exactly common, are spread fairly wide, so why is the same not true of justice? (Lots of people *think* they know what justice is, profess it themselves, and affect to admire it in others, but that is not the same thing.) Partly, no doubt, the rarity of justice is to be explained by the fact that it is usually inexpedient to be just, but it might also be that being just is in itself harder than practising any of the other virtues (and it will be even harder after Plato has made justice include all the other virtues as well). Justice is the most difficult of all the virtues because justice is practised by the whole man. In Plato's view of it, justice *is* the whole man.

An inferior virtue like courage, while admirable in itself, fails to engage the whole personality. Plato divides the human personality (*psyche*) into three faculties (reason, passion and appetite), and he thinks that there are virtues appropriate to each. Courage is a passionate virtue, and has as its object military honour, and the passionate virtues in general are directed towards everything which concerns a good reputation. The pursuit of a good reputation is admirable because it requires the sacrifice of inclination; honourable men do not break the line by running away from the battle, and they are prepared to forego self-indulgence to maintain the state of physical fitness required by the military life. Base

23

appetite is therefore controlled for some higher good. Plato believes that courage is a limited virtue because the man of honour has a limited understanding of his own virtue. The courageous man is not always very clear about why he pursues honour, and the proof of this is that he is kept to the path of honour by the opinion of others with whom he competes for honour's prize. This leads to a certain moral emptiness, especially when the courageous man is away from the censuring gaze of his peers. He is likely to be self-indulgent in secret, and to be jealous of others' fame and so he hides this jealousy. He is also prone to admiration of the other things which men do in fact admire, like wealth, but he also conceals this admiration because the soldierly character is supposed to care only for honour. The secret life of the man of honour means that he is never really at peace with himself. There is always something puzzling to him about his life which he does not wish to examine too closely. This can make the man of honour appear to be unreflecting, and it explains the attractions of the battlefield; there the call of duty is pure and simple: at war with his enemies, he finds that he is at peace with himself.

There is also a subordinate virtue associated with the appetites. By appetites Plato means desires directed towards things which are neither true nor good in themselves. That definition is negative but it is not meant to be evasive. Plato deliberately refuses to give a list of the appetites beyond the most obvious – food, drink and sex – because he thinks that the desires multiply, and the more they multiply the more difficult they are to satisfy and the worse they become. A taste for this leads to a taste for that, until the man dominated by his appetites finds himself in a state of siege, surrounded by clamouring desires each yelling out to be satisfied. He cannot satisfy them all, and he might not even know which to satisfy first. (The only way out of the dilemma is to become a tyrant. He would then have all the resources of his state to satisfy his desires.) If a man can only live a life of appetite then the best thing he can do is to subordinate as many different appetites as possible to a single appetite – say the love of money. Miserliness is about the best that the appetites can offer. The miser denies himself other indulgences so he can indulge his love of money to the full. He does not care who knows that he is a miser; in fact he might take a perverse pride in it; unlike the honourable man, he does not need the good opinion of others, and he could easily spend his life in lonely contemplation of his hoard. It never occurs to him to ask himself why he wants more money; he simply does, and finds it odd that not everybody else does too.

Reason in Plato's sense is not involved in the lesser virtues of courage and self-control. This is not to say that the lesser virtues can be practised without some kind of knowledge. A courageous man has to be good at being a soldier, which involves training in a skill and in the kind of knowledge which comes from knowing the dangers to be faced in war. Likewise, the moneymaker must know something, otherwise we could not distinguish between those who make money and those who try to but don't. In Plato's view, reason is directed towards true knowledge. By reason he sometimes means what we mean by reasoning, or judgement, or contemplation, but reason is to be thought of as unitary because it is directed towards a single object. Of course, not everything we call knowledge is true knowledge in Plato's special sense, and not all knowing is done by those who possess true knowledge. There is a rough, everyday knowledge, which Plato does not always despise in the way he despises moneymaking – a craftsman's knowledge for instance – but that is not the true knowledge which reason seeks. That everyday knowledge, while not despicable, can easily get in the way of the acquisition of true knowledge and can even be mistaken for it. Much more insidious are the bastard claims to true knowledge peddled by Sophists. The mind's search for true knowledge is made that much easier by emptying the mind of these other kinds of knowledge at the start. Part of this mistaken knowledge is about justice; at Sparta, courage was reckoned the supreme good, and at Carthage, wealth. Part of true knowledge is the recognition of the limitations of other views of justice. The practice of the virtues is supposed to bring happiness, but the happiness which courage and self-control bring is always incomplete. The courageous man has his self-doubt and the miser always wants more. Only reason can complete the happiness of the other virtues, and reason does this partly through its relationship with the other faculties and partly through the pursuit of the true knowledge which is its own. Reason supplies a kind of control to the other faculties which they cannot provide for themselves. The self-control exercised by the lower faculties, while useful, only tells a man how to control himself, and never why. Only reason can tell us why control of the other faculties is good. Reason's first job is therefore self-knowledge, an awareness of the right ordering of the soul.

Like the other faculties, reason is active. It works out what the soul's order should be and it is also the guarantor of that order. Reason's knowledge is its title to rule the rest of the self, and that knowledge, together with the rule which it justifies, makes up the kingly science. What is true for each man within himself is also true for the relations between men. The man who is himself properly self-controlled is fit to command others unlike himself. His relations with others like himself will be friendly and co-operative, but his relations with others unlike himself will be relations of rulership. Plato sees a very close connection between instability of character and political instability. An unstable character is one where the naturally ruling part is not in control, and an unstable state is one where men who are not naturally in control of themselves control public affairs. In both cases, an inherent instability will cause unhappiness sooner or later; much better to get things properly organised at the outset. The *Republic* is largely an attempt to show how just men can be produced and how advantageous it would be if they were to rule a *polis*.

THE *REPUBLIC*: SETTING THE SCENE

The *Republic* is written in the form of a long conversation between Socrates and others. The tone becomes less conversational as the work goes on, and by the end it has virtually become a Socratic monologue. Some commentators have concluded that the *Republic* as we have it must be a composite of two works because the first at least of its ten books is so unlike the rest; but no-one denies that there is a single connecting argument which goes right through it. Perhaps the best way of looking at the relationship between the beginning of the *Republic* and the rest of it is to see the first and second books as setting the scene for the arguments which follow. 'Setting the scene' is meant in a straightforwardly dramatic sense. The *Republic* opens with Socrates walking back from the Piraeus to Athens after a religious festival when he is persuaded by Polemarchus, the son of Cephalus, to come home with him and meet a gathering of friends. Socrates is greeted by Cephalus, who seems to have aged since Socrates saw him last, and the talk quickly turns to the question of what it is like to be old. In the course of that discussion Plato allows us to find out a good deal about Cephalus and about the way he looks back on his own life. Cephalus has lived a good life according to his lights. He has told the truth and paid his debts; unlike the other old men of his acquaintance he does not regret the passing of youth and its pleasures, and he does not take a jaundiced view of the young. He has been a businessman (there is a historical Cephalus who was a shield manufacturer). He inherited a diminished family capital and increased it, which enables him to look forward to leaving his sons more than his father left him, though less than his grandfather left his father. He has been able to make money without having to struggle; he has never been tempted to lie and cheat for it, and he has not become over-fond of money. He has heard tales about the punishments which might be visited upon the wicked after death, but when he looks back on his life he sees no cause for alarm. Socrates finds his serenity in the face of death admirable.

Cephalus' goodness lies in his consistency. His is a businessman's ethic, giving every man what he is owed. He has done his duty by his fellow men and by his own sons. When Socrates meets him he has been sacrificing to the gods, for Cephalus will leave no debts unpaid. If he has a fault, it is that he is not very reflective about his own ethic, though Socrates does not chide him for that. Socrates does ask him what he thinks goodness is, and Cephalus answers that it is telling the truth, helping friends and paying debts. Socrates suggests very gently that there may be cases where that definition might cause a problem or two, as when a friend has lent you a knife and gone mad in the meantime. Would it be just to return the knife in these circumstances? Well, probably not, because that would hardly be helping your friend, though it would certainly be paying your debt. Cephalus can see no way out of the difficulties; Socrates does not press him, and anyway Cephalus has more important things to do because he hasn't finished his sacrificing yet. Obviously there is more to be said. He bequeaths the argument to the young men and quietly shuffles off the scene, never to be heard again. We are to assume that a properly conducted sacrifice is not a trifling matter, so at least during a part of the action on-stage (perhaps while Thrasymachus is talking because he is in many ways the opposite of Cephalus) religious rites are still being practised off-stage.

The scene is charming, but at the same time puzzling. One of the pleasures of old age that Cephalus mentions to Socrates is a delight in intelligent conversation, yet Plato does not keep Cephalus in the dialogue very long. Plato has even prepared us for his exit right at the beginning of the scene where Cephalus is found resting in a chair with a garland round his neck; plainly Cephalus has unfinished business on hand. Cephalus is dismissed because his is not an example to be followed. The *Republic* is a book about justice, and Plato could have said: Being just is being like Cephalus; his life is admirable, so imitate him. When Cephalus leaves the scene the moral authority of a lived life leaves too; justice is to be found elsewhere, in the present, not the past. Perhaps the dismissal of Cephalus is also meant to tell us that the gods can no longer be relied on to provide answers to questions about how we ought to organise our lives. Religion is no longer centre-stage; it has lost the moral authority it once had. What old men and the gods have to say is still worth listening to, but what is said has to be examined on its merits. Nothing is to be taken at face value.

Cephalus is replaced by the Sophist Thrasymachus, and the scene has been carefully set for him too. The rejection of ancestral wisdom and the wisdom of the gods is meant to tell us that the world has lost its way. Moral authority is no longer adequate; everything is questionable and there are no obvious answers. The great danger in a world like that is the man who peddles easy answers to complex questions, and the greatest danger of all is the man who has only one answer to a host of different questions. Thrasymachus stands for both. Justice is the interest of the stronger and injustice pays; remember that and life becomes simple; you'll get through and you will never have to think again. Thrasymachus gets a real drubbing from Socrates. What happens when the strong tell you to do something which is obviously not in their interest? Is it then right to do what they tell you? Thrasymachus wriggles by saying that rulers *as* rulers never make mistakes. We do not call a mathematician a mathematician by virtue of his mistakes and the same is true of rulers: they are called rulers to the extent that they get things right. This is the moment when Socrates begins to duff Thrasymachus up. On Thrasymachus' own account of it, ruling is a skill like other skills. Socrates has no trouble in showing that skills like medicine are practised for the good of the patient, not for the good of the practitioner. The relationship between doctor and patient is one between superior and inferior (doctor's orders), but the doctor has the good of the patient's health at heart and not his own. It follows from this that all skills are practised for the good of their object; ruling is a skill, therefore its purpose is the good of the ruled, not the ruler. Therefore justice is the interest of the weak, not the strong. Thrasymachus does not give up easily, although in the end he concedes defeat; but unlike Cephalus he is not dismissed from the dialogue. He is tamed and allowed to remain, but to remain in silence. It might have made more sense to keep Cephalus and let Thrasymachus go. Thrasymachus is exactly the kind of false philosopher that Plato despises. After Socrates has finished with him he really ought to go off in a huff. Cephalus ought to stay, not perhaps following all the stages of Socrates' subsequent argument very closely, but nodding a kind of distant approval as Socrates expounds true justice to the young men. Yet Cephalus goes and Thrasymachus stays.

Why? The answer is probably age. The theory of justice which Socrates will eventually offer in the *Republic* is a theory of self-control. Cephalus is a man with all passion spent. One of the advantages of old age that Cephalus mentions to Socrates is the freedom from the tyranny of desire. That is what makes Cephalus unteachable; there is nothing left to be controlled. Thrasymachus is still vigorous. We are to assume that there is still something there worth controlling, and the whipping-in of Thrasymachus is meant to tell us that it is controllable. Thrasymachus cares about money and will not tell the company what justice is until he has been paid. Socrates has no money and the others agree to pay for him. Thrasymachus is worthy of his hire. He has a reputation as someone worth listening to and we can assume that he has done well in this kind of discussion before. Thrasymachus is worldly. He makes a claim to an expertise which looks as if it is based on experience of the political world: no matter where you go you will find that all states are in fact divided into the powerful and the weak, no matter how that fact is disguised. Thrasymachus' expertise is something like the expertise of political science, seeing beyond the appearances to what really is the case. Thrasymachus' claim to his expertise is never seriously disputed. Socrates' refutation of Thrasymachus is purely formal. Plato wants us to think that the knowledge possessed by Thrasymachus is inferior to the knowledge possessed by true philosophers, but Thrasymachus' claim to knowledge is left substantially intact. Plato probably wants us to think that what Thrasymachus has to tell us about the world of politics is substantially correct, and Plato in fact returns to a power theory of politics in Book IX of the *Republic* where he discusses imperfect forms of rule. His objection to Thrasymachus is not just that Thrasymachus is dangerous because like all Sophists he peddles false ideas about justice. Rather, it is the claim of Thrasymachus to have seen beyond the appearances to the reality of politics. Thrasymachus says that justice is always the interest of the stronger, and that would be the case even where the interest of the stronger is publicly proclaimed as the interest of everybody. Thrasymachus claims a knowledge which is worldly knowledge, but not everyday knowledge. In the *Republic* Socrates is also laying claim to knowledge beyond the appearances, and so it is important for Plato to distinguish between 'real' real knowledge beyond the appearances and bogus real knowledge beyond the appearances of the kind that Thrasymachus possesses. This makes for a certain complication, and it is well to understand clearly that knowledge for Plato is divided into three classes, not two: first, ordinary knowledge as it appears to men living ordinary lives in the world; second, knowledge of the Thrasymachus kind which avoids the deceptions practised by the world on the perceptions of ordinary men; and third, a true knowledge which sees beyond what Thrasymachus has seen.

Perhaps inadvertently, Thrasymachus has put his finger on something which always causes trouble in states. Things are not always as they seem to be; the strong do not always proclaim openly that what they say justice is, is really only their own self-interest. Ways can always be found of softening the message. Ideological forms can easily conceal the reality of power, and power itself can always find proxies. It can be difficult in states to get to the bottom of the question: Who rules? We sometimes forget that the oppressiveness of government is not the only thing about it which causes discontent. Often a sense of alienation arises from not knowing who it is who really does call the tune. If those who apparently rule are in fact the agents of others, then discontent can be compounded with frustration: I am being badly treated *and* I do not even know by whom. Political science since Thrasymachus, and especially modern political science, has importantly concerned itself with questions of this kind: Who really rules? The Ideal State of Plato's *Republic* is designed to bring the realities of power out into the open. Plato's Guardians rule and are seen to be doing so. There is no place in the *Republic* for informal oligarchs of wealth and influence. Guardians rule, and that's it. Plato knows that family, caste, and class based on wealth, are often the bases of disproportionate power in states, and the purpose of the political engineering in the *Republic* is to neutralise them. Rulers are denied wealth and family life so that they can control the deleterious effects of wealth and family loyalty in others on the state, and the military caste in his Ideal State is kept in strict subordination. In Plato's Ideal State, politics in the sense of naturally arising conflict, or as caused by conflict, has no place. He is not trying to stop family life, or to prevent people from loving honour; rather he devises arrangements which will make them a source of unity, not of division.

The final problem which Thrasymachus leaves unresolved is the problem of divided states. The state as it exists in the world is not one state but two. All cities are divided. Plato could either try to construct a state in which the causes of those divisions were eradicated or try to construct a state in which the causes remain but the effects are not divisive. Plato takes the second course by making sure that the causes of division, where they operate at all, always have the effect of dividing the ruled and not the rulers. He has at least as sure a grasp as Aristotle of the principle that the cause of political instability and changes of regime is disunity in the ruling group, and he adds the twist that the ideal recipe for political stability is unity above and disunity below. If all the material wealth in a society is possessed by the ruled class, then they can quarrel about it to their hearts' content provided only that wealth is not concentrated in too few hands. The same is true of honour. Provided that competition for honour is confined to a military caste who are kept from the highest positions in the state, then the military are unlikely to compete with their rulers, who are above such things, and they are unlikely to be united as a group except on the battlefield. The problem then becomes one of finding a principle which can keep the ruling group itself united, and this Plato thinks he has found in the principle of justice.

3

THE GUARDIANS OF THE STATE AND JUSTICE

Justice is the integrating principle in Plato's Ideal State. It both binds the classes to each other and is the basis for unity in the ruling group. In the *Republic* Socrates changes over from trying to find out what constitutes justice in a single man to trying to find out what constitutes justice in a whole community. It is only when he has given an outline of state justice that he returns to the question of justice in individuals from which the *Republic* began. The reason Socrates gives for this alteration in procedure is that justice is easier to find in the state because there, being public and a quality of the whole thing, it will be easier to recognise, but it will be the same justice. Being a quality of the whole, justice cannot inhere in a part of the whole, in a legal system for instance, administered by wise and learned judges. Justice must touch everybody. We already know that justice is not a set of do's and don't's, and so we are already in a position to guess that justice will be a characteristic of a certain kind of arrangement in which everyone has his proper place. We already know that Plato is concerned to distinguish between different kinds of knowledge, and that for him knowledge is closely related to the idea of a skill, so we should not be surprised when Socrates suggests that a properly organised state is one in which people are assigned to their places according to what kinds of skills they are capable of developing.

One of these skills, the art of managing others, will be the basis of the ruling group's claim to rule the rest. Therefore, we would be right to expect that the most important institutional arrangements in Plato's state would be those devoted to the training, and so to the perpetuation, of the ruling group. There would always be Guardians-in-training in Plato's state, and preserving that training unchanged would be the state's first priority. The aim of that training is to produce just men in the double sense that Plato understands justice: men who are in fact just and who know what justice is. The training of Guardians, like all training, is a process of selection. Plato does not actually tell us whether everyone in his state will begin the training process, but his concern that there will be no wastage of talent makes it a reasonable inference that nobody will in principle be excluded, and certainly not women. During the education of Guardians a good deal has to be taken on trust because the end is very far away from the beginning. It is not until Guardians are over fifty that they emerge from the training process as fully-fledged rulers in their own right, and we are to assume that only a few make it right to the end. The selection process also provides the state with its structure, because each person remains in the highest class that his own talents will take him to. Promoting a person beyond his capacities is neither good for him nor good for the whole.

The training programme proceeds from lower to higher stages. The less difficult subjects of literature, mathematics, music and gymnastics are followed by the most difficult subject of all, dialectic, or training in philosophy. The whole of Plato's *Republic* is itself an exercise in dialectic, which has led some commentators to suggest that the *Republic* is a textbook for the Philosopher-Ruler's training in the double sense that it contains an account of what that training should be like using the dialectical method of reasoning to show that the training prescribed is the best possible training method for ruling. Being able to understand fully what the arguments are for the training is itself evidence that you are yourself suitable training material. (And perhaps even Thrasymachus could in the end be made to see the truth of the arguments and so be rescued for true philosophy.) Perhaps the character of the *Republic* as a dialectical excercise explains why Plato is so careful to set up the dialogue in such a dramatically formal way. Easy definitions of justice have to be formally dismissed to show that philosophy is a serious business. The early refutations of Cephalus and Thrasymachus, and the long formal re-statement of Thrasymachus' position in Book II, are meant to prepare the young men for a long discussion before justice is finally reached. Only those who stay the course are capable of understanding what justice is, just as there are no short cuts to the training of Philosopher-Rulers.

Dialectic works through statement and contradiction. A position is stated by one speaker in the dialogue, and somebody else offers qualifications or objections. These qualifications or objections can be of two kinds: either they can hold that the originally stated position is unclear, perhaps because it contains contradictions, or objections can be raised to a stated position on the grounds that it is inadequate because it leaves something out. The original position is then restated by ridding itself of its own contradictions and by taking into account the objection that it was inadequate. The process is one which produces increasing coherence both in the sense that what is being proposed becomes internally more coherent as the contradictions are ironed out, and in the sense that it incorporates what seems sensible from the criticisms which are offered against it. It is easy to see that this is ideally how ordinary argument should proceed. It is essentially co-operative despite the dialectical form the argument takes. The protagonists offer positions and objections to positions, but they agree about the rules of the dialectical game, and their competition has the common purpose that both want to get to the end to find out what the truth about something really is. In the case of the *Republic*, truth about justice will have been reached when a description of justice is offered which contains no internal self-contradictions and to which no other objections on the grounds of inadequacy can be made. Truth exists without contradictions.

What might not be so obvious about dialectic is the number of different things which have to be agreed to before dialectic can proceed. There are at least six aspects of dialectical argument which have to be agreed to before true dialectic can begin. First, because dialectic is a process, its stages are necessary; at any stage of dialectical argument positions are put forward as if they were truths and are only seen to be partial truths when objections do in fact arise; you have to be committed to waiting to see whether objections do arise; thinking through implies patience. Second, nothing in dialectic is ever wasted; nothing is wholly true until the end is reached, so nothing is wholly false; a position needs its contradiction to move to a higher stage of synthesis. Third, it follows that in a truly dialectical argument nothing is ever completely destroyed; rather, ideas are incorporated by having their independent existence negated; positions offered as truths or as objections to truths are gathered into truths which become truer by becoming more comprehensive. Fourth, it must follow that what truth will eventually be comes from the dialectical process itself; truth cannot be a *deus ex machina* or a blinding flash of inspiration; therefore we are being asked to distrust all truth claims which themselves claim that everying which came before was false. Fifth, because truth comes out of the process of dialectic it is not so much invented as discovered, not so much created but grasped. Truth emerges, is at first dimly perceived, and only at the last is it there for all to see. And finally, anybody who does not

33

wait the process out to the end goes away with something inferior, and anybody who thinks he can see through to the end before the end is reached is at best guessing and at worst cheating. Small wonder, therefore, that Plato is careful to set the scene for the dialogue about justice in the *Republic*. We might find the Are-you-sitting-comfortably-then-we-can-begin aspects of the *Republic* irritating, but Plato means us to take them very seriously indeed. We have to commit ourselves to a very long process if we are to understand what justice is and to grasp the necessity of the procedure which gets us to it.

The way that Plato uses the dialectical argument in the *Republic* is also meant to point up the difference between dialectic and other forms of argument with which it might possibly be confused. The kind of fast table-tennis that Socrates plays with Thrasymachus looks like dialectic but is in fact what the Greeks called eristic, show-off stuff, sometimes played to a timetable and always played for applause. Socrates wins. The question is: Why does Plato allow Socrates to play the eristic game in front of the young men when the point of the ensuing dialogue about justice is to show that dialectic is superior to eristic? Socrates is better than Thrasymachus at eristic, so is there not a danger that the young men will think that Socrates is a better man *because* he is better at eristic? Something must make that risk worth taking, but Socrates takes a long time before he tells us what it is, and then only after the audience has already got a hefty slice of dialectic under its belt. Eristic is part of the armoury of Sophistry, where Sophistry is seen as the essential equipment for success in a democratic *polis*. The young men of the dialogue's audience are exactly the sort of people who might do well in democracy through the corruption of their good qualities. Like all the Greeks, Plato knew that the *polis* would be difficult to govern, and one of the things that made it so was the tendency of men to choose the wrong kind of government when they were in a position to choose at all. The Athenian democracy had had notable aristo-cratic leaders, truly superior men, who had done nothing to educate the people, so that nothing had been done to prevent the *demos* choosing to be ruled by a man who was one of themselves; where Pericles was, there shall Cleon be. The hint of deference towards superiors is only a hint; aristocratic leaders of the democracy are a stage on the downward path towards the democracy finding leaders of its own.

So where does dialectic eventually lead? Plato's answer is that the dialectically trained mind strains after the vision, or the Form, of the Good. Being able to see the Form of the Good is the highest kind of philosophical knowledge. Plato also claims that true knowledge *begins* with the Form of the Good. So how can the Form of the Good be the end to which all knowledge strives and at the same time the beginning of all knowledge? Plato thinks that the Form of the Good illuminates all the other Forms of knowledge in the way that the sun illuminates all the other objects of sight as well as giving the power of seeing to the eye: no sun, no sight and no objects to be seen. All other Forms which are not the Form of the Good have something of the Good in them, just as everything that we see has something of the sun in them which enables them to be seen. Of course, this clever analogy does not actually tell us what the Form of the Good is. Plato is merely saying that, once seen, the Form of the Good could no more be forgotten than we could forget the sun; nor, once we have seen the sun, would we be likely to mistake anything else for it, and once the sun is up, everything else looks different, so that we can say that the sun enables us to look at everything else in a different way. Seeing other Forms in the Form of the Good's light is to see them for the first time as they really are. Everything which has one of these Forms, an intelligible essence, is an object of true knowledge. Forms appear in the world of experience amid clusters of appearances which attach themselves to Forms in much the same way that the soul can only exist in the everyday world by putting up with the grossness of its enclosing body which anchors it to imperfect human societies. Justice has its own Form which, like every other Form, can only be perceived when the Form of the Good throws its effulgent light upon it. Therefore Philosopher-Rulers must attain the highest form of knowledge before they can know the first thing about their business, which is the preservation of justice in the state. Justice has first to be seen before it can be defended.

Plato's contention that his Philosopher-Rulers must be able to see the Form of the Good before they can even begin to learn the practical skills of ruling under the wise tutelage of an experienced Guardian, may look odd at first sight. Why cannot Guardians be taught the art of ruling direct, by imitation for example? Why cannot they be told by a fully trained Guardian: Do what I do? That question is especially pertinent when we consider that the training in practical skills is that kind of apprenticeship anyway. After the period of philosophical training it takes a further fifteen years before full mastery of ruling is achieved. The obvious answer is that the philosophical training is designed for the benefit of the ruling class itself, and only indirectly for the benefit of the ruled. Plato, like all the Greek political thinkers, believed that political instability was caused by divisions within the ruling elite, and he realised that a common system of education is one of the ways that an elite can be bound together. All Plato's Guardians would have been to the same elite school, and some of the characteristics of a particular kind of school are preserved through-out a Guardian's life, for example the common meals and the barracks life in general. They would all know each other and would continue to live and work together in each other's company. This close proximity has its dangers, especially as the system of education which Guardians go through is selective and therefore competitive. What is to prevent Guardians continuing to compete with each other after their education is over? Would that not threaten the solidarity of the Ideal State's ruling group? Plato believes that his education system would in fact lead to elite solidarity, but he is well aware of the dangers of intra-elite competition and goes to some lengths to explain why he thinks that it would not happen. Men compete to outdo each other in the things they call good. On the face of it, therefore, it appears to be the case that there is no end to competition because there is no reason why competition should ever stop.

However, Plato thinks there is a limiting condition on competition which is obvious when you actually look and see what happens when men compete. Musicians, for instance, tend to be competitive, and this is at its most obvious when they tune their instruments. Tuning a lyre by altering the length of its strings is a tricky business requiring a lot of practice, so that in those days tuning the instrument correctly would be an important part of musicianship. A musician whose ear could not recognise perfect pitch and who lacked the dexterity to tune his lyre probably would not really know what to do. His ear would not tell him what to aim at and his incompetent hands would not be very helpful in achieving what he thought he was aiming at. With these handicaps, all the incompetent musician could do would be to try to do what he was doing better than other musicians. He would make a hash of it, but trying to tune his lyre better than other musicians were tuning theirs would be the only way he could proceed. Lacking skill, and lacking knowledge of perfect pitch, he would find himself competing with others like himself and also with those musicians who have perfect pitch and the skill to tune their lyres to it. He would not know he was competing with the good musicians because, lacking knowledge of perfect pitch, they would all seem to be much the same to him: natural competitors. Plato then considers the case of the good musician, the lyrist who knows what perfect pitch is and has the skill to tune his instrument to it. He would try to tune his lyre better than the incompetent musician but he would only be trying to tune his lyre as well as the other good musicians. The good musician, unlike the incompetent musician, only competes with others unlike himself. Plato thinks that just men will be like good musicians. They will not compete with other just men but only with unjust men. By 'compete' he means strive to overcome, to dominate, by which he means rule. Just men do not try to outdo each other in the thing which is most important to them, therefore a ruling group of just men would be solid.

Plato thinks that men are to be judged by the way they treat each other. Guardians are expected to treat other Guardians differently from the way they treat those whom they rule. Perhaps Plato means this to be a test of whether those who make it through the Guardians' training really are fit to be Guardians. The account in Book IX of the *Republic* of the process by which the Ideal State could degenerate shows that Plato thinks that the most likely cause is a mistake in the training programme for rulers. Guardians only have their knowledge to distinguish them from non-Guardians. That knowledge is the product of a certain inner condition of the soul and there is always the possibility of a fake. One of the ways of detecting a fake who had somehow slipped through the selection process would be to watch the way he acted towards his fellows. There would be something forward about the false Guardian; he would be trying just a bit too hard; he would always go an inch beyond what was considered proper by the others. It is easy to see what form this would take. The true Philosopher-Ruler is a reluctant ruler. His heart is set on the Good, and he accepts the burdens of rulership because the Good can only survive and prosper in a city which is ruled by just men. Rule by Guardians is an attempt to universalise justice in so far as that is possible, and the end is happiness because the just are happier than the unjust. Ruling is not exactly a chore for Guardians, but, not being their first love, it is certainly a duty. The almost-but-not-quite Guardian would betray himself because he was too keen to command; he would want to show how good he was at it and insensibly he would begin to compete with his fellow rulers. This second-best Guardian would thus show his timarchic character, fit to be a member of the military Auxiliary class and promoted beyond his competence.

Real Guardians, unlike pretend Guardians and all other ruling groups or individuals, have to be persuaded to rule. In all other regimes the ruling part obviously gets something out of ruling: wealth, fame, ease or anything else that men call good. Guardians, on the other hand, get none of the things men normally call good from the exercise of their function; indeed, most of the things that men do call good are excluded from their lives.

They are forbidden gold and silver; sexual life is strictly controlled through mating festivals, their food is eaten in frugal common messes and what fame there is that is available to them would accrue to the group, not to individuals. And ruling is not made easy for Guardians because they do not have a system of law to guide them. Decisions have to be made by thinking things out from first principles, not by reference to rules and precedents. What, then, is to prevent Guardians from leaving decisions to other Guardians? Why could not each Guardian say to himself: 'Let someone else suitably qualified do the work. Leave me to my philosophy. I know that it is important for decisions to be made by those qualified to make them, but why should I make them? Provided they are made by someone *like me* they will be good decisions.' The arguments for rule by philosopher-kings fail to be convincing as arguments about why a particular Guardian should engage in the work of ruling. It could easily be that the disinclination of each individual Guardian from the business of ruling could introduce an element of competition into the ruling group which is analogous in reverse to the element of competition which would arise if a mildly timarchic character was to make his way by accident into the Guardian class. The unsuitable Guardian would compete with others in his eagerness to command; suitable Guardians might insensibly begin to compete by avoiding the distracting duty to rule by putting the burden on others.

This is no small objection to Plato, who is anxious above all else to keep the ruling group solid, yet here is the possibility of Guardians competing with others like themselves, something Plato says should never be. Perhaps Plato never thought that there would be more than one philosopher-king. One would certainly be enough, and in his case there could be no question of his leaving rule to others like himself because there would be none like himself to leave it to. However, the elaborate educational arrangements in the Republic can leave us in very little doubt that they are designed to produce a group of rulers. Otherwise, why devise such a system at all if it is only ever likely to produce a single kingly man? If a single kingly man, why not none? None is just as likely as one, and it is hardly likely that Plato would design a whole state on the off-chance that it might occasionally produce a man capable of ruling it. So even though Plato never comes clean about the likely numbers of his ruling class we are entitled to suppose that it would in fact be a group. So the question still arises: What would a particular Guardian's motive be for ruling himself rather than leaving it to other Guardians to rule? (Plato might have said it would be fair if Guardians took it in turns, but he does not.) Perhaps the answer lies in the idea of justice itself. Justice is the proper relationship between the parts in a whole, where proper relationship means something like a working relationship. Rule has a dynamic quality about it; it is something which has to go on the whole time. Rule is not conquest. Reason in an individual does not overcome the lesser faculties of spirit and appetite once and for all; it establishes a proper relationship with the lesser faculties and has to keep that relationship in good working order. Reason has to be trained to form that relationship and has to keep in training by maintaining it in much the same way that to keep fit you have to keep on training. What is true of the rational part of the individual personality is also true of the state. The rational part, Guardians, do not just have to *become* Guardians; they have to keep up their fitness as Guardians, and the only way they could do that would be to keep on doing what a Guardian does, which is to rule. It would not be enough just to keep their eyes fixed on the vision of the Good and let the rest go hang. That would be the equivalent of the trained athlete who thought he could maintain his fitness by keeping the *idea* of fitness constantly in his mind. Justice is illuminated by the Form of the Good, but being just also requires the exercises which justice requires, one of which is ruling.

The absence of a system of law also makes these exercises in justice necessary. Each Guardian really has to think each decision out. Even sympathetic critics of Plato have been unsettled by the absence of law in the *Republic* on the grounds that without law there would be nothing to act as a control on the ruling activities of Guardians. *Quis custodiet ipsos custodes?* If there is no body of men to keep Guardians in control there should at least be the constraining force of law. The sympathetic critics of Plato turn to his work the *Laws* with relief because there rulership is hemmed in by law and the prime duty of rulers is to keep the laws unchanged and to obey them. The criticism of the lack of any system of law in the *Republic* is based on Plato's own worry that the Guardians' system of internal self-control might fail, and that failure is always a possibility at least in principle, but what the criticism fails to take account of is the positive benefits which the absence of law brings to Guardians themselves. The test of the rightness of a ruling decision would always be that it was the same decision that any other Guardian would make in the circumstances, and it is by no means fanciful to suppose that faced with making a decision, each Guardian would see himself as going through the same thought process that any other Guardian would. Every Guardian is present when each decision is made in the same sense that each penitent confronts the whole priesthood at his confession. Every Guardian guards every other Guardian. Something like this is also implicit in the division of the state into classes. A class relationship between two members of different classes means that a member of one class would treat every member of the other class in exactly the same way that any other member of his own class would treat him, and the obvious test of the rightness of the treatment would be to ask: How would anybody else like me treat him? The advantages of that mode of operation for class solidarity are obvious; being designed to promote solidarity, it also acts as a check on the behaviour of any particular member of a class.

The other great advantage of the absence of a legal system is that it would make the lower class much easier to rule. We have become so used to the idea that law is the obvious way to regulate behaviour that we have come to associate behaviour in the absence of law with anarchy. Plato's *Republic* points to a very different conclusion. Imagine yourself in the position of one of the ruled class in Plato's state. How would you know how you were supposed to behave? The law would not tell you, but the fact that a Guardian class existed would tell you that certain things were permitted and certain things forbidden. You would in fact be in the position of someone in a country whose manners and morals were not your own. You would tend to be cautious, and the only way to proceed would be to imitate the people around you in much the same way that people at a service in a strange church tend to stand at the back; to stand right at the front with no-one to imitate would be to risk solecism. Imitation, doing what others are already doing on the assumption that it is permitted, is a perfect image of law-abiding behaviour in a society which has rulers but no laws. Where there are no rules, the ruled would make their own.

If there were to be a challenge to the rule of Guardians in Plato's Ideal State, it would be much more likely to come from the Auxiliary class than from the class of the ruled. The class of Auxiliaries comprises those who were selected for Guardianship but who do not quite make it. Plato has already alerted us to the fact that he expects trouble from this group of slightly disappointed superior men. The Auxiliary class has a kind of group solidarity which the ruled class lacks. It is the military and police power of the state, its strong arm. It is not clear how many Auxiliaries there will be in Plato's state because Plato is not precise about numbers, but we can be sure that there will be more Auxiliaries than there are fully fledged Guardians and we can also be sure that there will be fewer Auxiliaries than there are members of the ruled class. What is not clear is how the Auxiliaries are going to be satisfied with their lot. They have all the disadvantages of Guardians with none of their compensations. Auxiliaries are to share the highly disciplined barracks existence of Guardians with its denial of family life and wealth, but Auxiliaries would never be quite sure about why their life should be organised in that way. Not having access to a vision of the Good, they would have to be content with their own *esprit de corps*. Plato compares them to watchdogs, gentle with friends and terrible against enemies, but they are watchdogs who might in fact have very little to do. Plato wants his state to be as isolated as possible. Economic autarky means that there will be very little contact with the outside world; being far from the sea, there will be no trade, and especially no trade in ideas which might lead to questions being asked about the desirability of the Ideal State's existence. Plato probably had Sparta in mind, notoriously difficult to provoke into war, and whose dependence on its hoplite army contrasted with the Athenian dependence on its navy manned by the common people. Athens had been commercial, imperialist and democratic, and Plato wanted his state to be none of these things. So what would the Auxiliary class actually spend its time *doing*? Snooping perhaps, and training for wars which would rarely happen; not a recipe for a very satisfying life. Satisfaction by doing is, according to Plato, the key to all fulfilment, and that would be particularly true of active Auxiliary types. No amount of make-believe battle could work indefinitely as a substitute for the real thing. Either Auxiliary morale would eventually slump or pressure would build up for a real war, and with that pressure would come the danger of a military *coup d'état*.

It is hard to see what Guardians could do in these circumstances. They are few and the Auxiliaries many. Guardians would have to rely on the respect of young warriors for older and senior soldiers to curb Auxiliary discontent. Guardians have been Auxiliaries themselves, and perhaps Plato thought that the respect which comes from seniority would continue. And it might work. Modern governments sometimes appoint very senior officers to positions of civilian authority when soldiers are more than ordinarily involved in the business of rule. During colonial uprisings, for instance, when the possibility exists that the army will take matters into its own hands, the firm hand of an old soldier may be used to strengthen government's authority with its own forces. Auxiliaries might also be reconciled to their position in Plato's scheme of things by the state religion. Plato's state is to be sustained by a noble myth which holds that all men are the children of the same mother who has produced men of gold, silver and bronze corresponding to the three different classes into which Plato divides his ideal community. Mixing of the metals would be sacrilege, and, because the division of the state is division of function, seeking to usurp a function to which one was not suited would itself be sacrilege.

The introduction of a state religion has led some critics of Plato to question how seriously he means us to take the claim that the Ideal State of the *Republic* is founded on reason. The myth of the metals looks uncomfortably like an exercise in political propaganda, and Plato appears to damn himself by saying that the state would be well served if everyone were to believe in the myth, Guardians included. If that is so, then what is the point of the long and rigorous education of Guardians so that they can come to see the vision of the Good? Would not inculcation of the state religion have the same effect? Put that way, it becomes obvious that, in the case of Guardians, belief in the myth of the metals could never be a substitute for the vision of the Good, because without knowledge of the Good they would not know that the myth of the metals itself enjoined belief in something which was itself good. All Plato means by saying that Guardians too must believe in the myth is that they would have to know that the division of the state into three classes was good, and that there exist in the state large numbers of people whose access to that truth can only be through the myth. Why that should be especially sinister is not clear, unless one is to take the position that all belief in the truths of religion is sinister. Like most Greeks, Plato believed that a man without a religion was something less than a whole man, just as a city without its own civicly recognised religion was something short of a whole city.

The question: How literally does Plato want us to take the religious provision in his Ideal State? really shades into the general question: How literally did the ancient Greeks as a whole take their religion? This is a question fraught with difficulty, because the way the question can be answered can easily depend on the answer to yet another question: What kind of religion could *anybody* take seriously? Atheists would say that no religion could be taken seriously and Christians would say that only a serious religion could be taken seriously, by which they would mean Christianity. The case for Christianity would be that it was theologically consistent, was grounded in proof, and therefore it was capable of gaining the consent of rational men. Ancient Greek religion falls on all three counts. It was a religion of public observance, not inward conviction, and it had no rational system of theology. But that view of Greek religion fails to take account of what it was *for*. The Greeks had no idea of the separateness of religion from government. Religion to them was just one aspect of the order which was meant to guide and control men's lives. What this meant in practice was that what could not be done in one way could be done in the other. Religious observance was a form of social control which did not require the socially expensive use of force. Most Greek cities lived close to the breadline by modern standards, and few cities could afford to professionalise the function of rule. Greek cities had ruling classes in a sense which is literal, and, faction-divided as most of those cities were, there was always bound to be something grating about the way rule was exercised. The rules were made and enforced by the same ruling group, and rule enforcement could not be softened by an appeal to an impartial state. In these circumstances, any form of social control for which some extra-personal authority could be cited was bound to be attractive to a ruling group as a way of sweetening the pill. Perhaps Plato's state religion is best seen in this light. He may have thought that the milder forms of social control which a shared religion made available were less likely to be resented than the overt exercise of power by a ruling class.

Above all other things, Plato's Ideal State was meant to last, and it is easy to underestimate how difficult it must have been in the ancient world even to begin to think of a state as being able to exist for ever in the same form. The miracle of Sparta apart, the founding and destruction of cities was the rule rather than the exception when even whole nations could appear and disappear. Plato was one of the first to see the connection between the domestic arrangements of a state and foreign policy. Chronically divided cities would be divided about peace and war as they would be divided about everything else. The war party would look around for allies in cities with war parties like themselves, fight a war with a similarly constituted league of other cities, and if victorious, return with the help of their allies to settle accounts with the enemy at home. Oligarchs and democrats both played that game, so that foreign policy compounded domestic class war. Most Greeks could see no way out of a vicious circle of changes of regime, and it is no wonder that Plato says in the *Republic* that each city as we find it in the world is best described not as one city but as two. In Book IX of the *Republic* ('Imperfect Societies') Plato shows that he thinks it is possible to begin to generalise about the causes of changes of regime and to suggest that those changes follow a distinct pattern.

THE THEME OF POLITICAL DEGENERATION

In Book IX of the *Republic* Plato discusses timarchy, oligarchy, democracy and tyranny as degenerations from his own Ideal State. He imagines the Ideal State as once having existed and states as they exist in his own contemporary world as degenerate copies. He also means us to see that process of degeneration as the danger to be guarded against if the Ideal State were to be set up at some time in the future. We have already seen what Plato thought the destabilising effects would be if a timarchic character found his way by accident into the ruling Guardian class. In the section of the *Republic* on Imperfect Societies Plato uses the idea of instability of character as a way of showing how all states except his Ideal State are unstable, and he works out a sliding scale of instability, with timarchy the most stable of the imperfect forms and tyranny the least; oligarchy and democracy come somewhere in between.

Plato's approach to the problem of political instability through the idea of the instability of individual character can easily seem naive to us because we are so used to seeing the political and social values associated with a political system as mediating between individuals and the political arrangements with which they live. Excuses are sometimes made for Plato on the grounds that individual character mattered much more in the Greek *polis* because it was so small by subsequent standards. The character of individuals and the character of a *polis* are supposed in some sense to be 'closer' than is possible in large states. Excuses like these are in fact unnecessary because the *polis* was there to mould the characters of individual men. Plato's interest in individual character stems from the straightforward perception that men are difficult to rule. He accepts that there are three different character types depending on which faculty of the soul – reason, spirit or appetite – predominates, but it would be misleading to say that this classification is merely the result of soul-surgery; rather, the classification already corresponds to different political types moulded by different types of *polis*. Plato is the last theorist who should be accused of a simple nature *or* nurture view of human personality or attainment. Nor is Plato's classification of character types to be thought of as a form of prediction about what the characters of particular men and women will turn out to be like. A character has to occur in the right circumstances and have access to the right training before it can develop in its natural direction. On Plato's view of the world as it is, it is highly unlikely that any state as it is constituted is the right place for the natural development of the rational character which is the type of the Philosopher-Ruler. Plato is pessimistic about character: when the best becomes corrupted it becomes the worst. His idea of character, especially his idea of the best character, is far removed from that idea of character which means 'able to resist temptation', and it is precisely because he is so pessimistic about the capacity of the Greeks to resist life's cruder blandishments that he attaches so much importance to character *building*.

Ancient Sparta had the greatest reputation for building the character of its citizens. Plutarch's *Life of Lycurgus*, who is credited with founding the Spartan Constitution, dwells long on the programme for training the young men in war, and Plato's own account of timarchy is so closely modelled on Sparta that we are justified in inferring from it that it is Plato's view that even so well-constituted a training system as Lycurgus' is bound to fail in the end because it falls short of the ideal. Timarchic society degenerates into oligarchy because the timocrat does not really know what to admire until others point the way. Military training is discipline forced on him from the outside; no doubt its code of self-denial and contempt for riches in favour of honour is meant to be internalised, but the very fact that the timocrat is easily led in war means that he could be easily led in other directions too. There is always something brittle about timarchy, and Sparta's own collapse is its object lesson. When Sparta gained an empire with all its opportunity for self-enrichment, Spartan self-control gave way before the treasure house, and competition for military honour converted itself overnight into the undignified scramble for wealth.

It is not difficult to explain how timarchy, as long as it lasts, is able to maintain itself. As long as luxury is avoided monopoly of armed forces easily extracts the means of life from a subject population. The population would not have to be exploited economically in the managerial sense, and neither would it be cannon fodder; provided the serfs paid their tribute in kind and did not get ideas above themselves they would at the very least be secure. Oligarchy, the natural degeneration from timarchic society, is unstable from the beginning because it cannot offer security to the ruled class. The oligarchs are to be thought of as timocrats who have gone off war. Loving money, they are too mean to pay for the preparations for war so that when war comes they are at a loss. Being few, they cannot defend the city by themselves, and having neglected military exercises in the pursuit of wealth, they and their sons are ridiculous in the eyes of the lean and mean lower classes whom they have been forced to arm in the emergency. In its ideal character, an oligarchy consists of misers and their fat brats. Oligarchs are moneymakers, and the easiest way to make money is to lend it out at high rates of interest. No sensible oligarch would allow himself to become the victim of usury, but every oligarch is vulnerable through his sons. Every oligarch dreams of the day when his son will take over the business, but, to show that he is fit to take it over, the son has to show that he too can subordinate all his other appetites to the single appetite for wealth. The sons know they will be wealthy when they inherit, but why should they wait? And they might have to wait a very long time. Misers die notoriously old because they sacrifice all other forms of self-indulgence to the supreme appetite for money. It might easily occur to a young oligarch that he will be too old to enjoy the wealth when his father dies. This would be especially true if the young oligarch had taken his father's advice and kept to the straight oligarchic path towards miserliness because he would already be an oligarch by the time he inherited.

None of this would go unobserved by other oligarchs on the lookout for opportunities to put money out at interest. They would encourage the profligacy of oligarchic sons with 'poisoned loans' effectively on the security of their fathers' deaths, which is not exactly an ideal basis for family life either in the case of the borrower or the lender. The borrower would have a reason to look forward to his own father's death and the lender would live in continual fear that some other oligarch would do to his own sons what he was doing to the sons of others. The corruption of sons puts the whole system of oligarchy at risk. Plato believes that it is solidarity in a ruling group which enables a type of government to last, and his account of oligarchy shows just how disunited a ruling group of oligarchs would be. Sons are pitted against fathers, and those same fathers are the cause of the corruption. Each oligarch sees the sons of other oligarchs as fair game while trying to protect his own sons, while knowing that every oligarch is thinking in exactly the same way that he is. Oligarchy begins to look like a crabbed and miserable existence, and the unhappiness of oligarchy is Plato's other test for injustice. The just are happier than the unjust and the extent of oligarchic unhappiness is the measure of how far oligarchy falls off from the justice of the Ideal State.

It is when Plato comes to consider democracy, which is the next stage downwards from oligarchy in his scheme of political corruption, that the measurement of justice and injustice in terms of happiness and unhappiness begins to cause him problems. There is something obvious, perhaps even commonplace, in Plato's picture of miserly fathers afraid that their sons will squander the family wealth. Nobody would find it easy to regard that as a recipe for human happiness. Democracy as Plato describes it is different. The problem of democracy for Plato is that, at least at first sight, it appears to be such an attractive way of life, attractive both to the leaders of the democracy and to the people themselves. Plato is very honest about this. In a democracy everybody can choose what kind of life he wants to live, and he can change his mind about that from day to day. Oligarchy, while it lasts, does at least require the single-mindedness and avoidance of self-indulgence necessary for the accumulation and preservation of wealth, but democratic man 'lives for the pleasure of the moment. One day it's wine, women and song, and the next bread and water; one day it's hard physical training, the next indolence and ease, and then a period of philosophic study. Next he takes to politics and is always on his feet saying or doing whatever comes into his head. Sometimes all his ambitions are military, sometimes they are all directed to success in business. There's no order in his life . . . ' We have already seen that Plato means us to take literally the idea that the just man is happier than the unjust man, and he means by happiness what we ordinarily mean by happiness, so he knows he is on dangerous ground when he begins to argue that democracy is less just that the Ideal State, timarchy or oligarchy. The free and easy style of life in a democracy, where people pursue their self-chosen ends, might easily seem to promise more ordinary human happiness than the austere and disciplined forms of *polis* which precede democracy in Plato's scheme of degeneration. To argue against democracy, therefore, Plato has to ask us to take very seriously the possibility that democracy cannot last. Democracy is the least stable of his forms of rule.

What democracy gains by its attractiveness it loses by its instability. Plato's treatment of democracy is different from his treatment of other forms of rule because he has a very clear grasp of the stages of its political development. Unlike oligarchy, which disappears overnight as a result of its unfitness for war, democracy goes through a series of well-defined phases before it finally sinks into the mire of demagogic tyranny. The establishment of democracy is the easiest of its stages: either in war, or from some other cause which Plato does not specify, the people realise that it was their own cowardice which allowed the oligarchs to rule them. They kill or exile the oligarchs, proclaim that henceforward all offices are open to everybody by lot (election was an oligarchic principle in ancient Greece) and that from now on everybody is free to live as he pleases. An assembly of all the citizens will now decide all the important matters which affect the life of the city. Democracy's first leaders will obviously come from the ranks of the discontented under the oligarchy. No doubt those profligate, debt-ridden sons of oligarchs would have had a hand in the rebellion against the oligarchy, and they are the natural leaders of the democracy. Most of the people do not have much time for politics because they have to earn their living and are content to leave the direction of affairs to the spoilt youths who keep the mass of the people sweet by robbing the rich, keeping most for themselves, and distributing the rest among the poor. Demagogic leadership requires just that kind of knowledge which Plato thinks the Sophists peddled at Athens. Sophist training was training in the psychology of the crowd. Plato sometimes talks as if democratic leaders are themselves Sophists, natural crowd-pleasers, superior men with a capacity for real philosophy, who are corrupted by the crowd, but more often he talks of the Sophists as trainers of demagogues. Plato does not doubt that crowd psychology can be taught. It is not a true science, like statesmanship or medicine; it is more like learning to control a large and powerful animal; you could teach demagogy to yourself by observation and practice because it is not very difficult, though it would take time; however, the Sophists can pass on their knowledge of the passions and pleasures of the mass of the common people much more quickly.

In this first stage of democracy, the crowd and its leaders are accomplices. Rich and superior young men have just those qualities – intelligence, good memories, courage, generosity, perhaps good looks and noble birth – which make them attractive to the crowd. Men like these cannot be expected to resist the crowd's plaudits. In this it is the crowd itself which is really the Sophist on a grand scale, turning these golden youths into just the sort

44

of people the crowd wants for its leaders. Given these qualities and that training, there is no reason why a natural leader of the crowd should not, like Alcibiades, aspire to lead the whole of Hellas and to conquer the world. This lack of moderation in the character of its leaders is the beginning of the ruin of democracy. We have to assume that the corruption of the demagogue's character was incomplete before the transition from oligarchy to democracy. The would-be democratic leader would have been brought up as an oligarch, quarrelling with his father (who might have made the mistake of buying him a Sophist's education), exposed to the poisoned loans of the moneylenders, thinking himself a hell of a fellow and finding the restraints upon him irksome. None the less, restraints there would have been; Plato thinks that all education has some effect, and while the oligarchy lasted the soul of the young oligarch would have been disciplined to some extent. Oligarchic parsimony would be in conflict with the desires which clamoured for satisfaction. With the change to democracy, paternal precept and example would no longer exert any external control on the crowd leader's character. The only surviving force for moderation would be the extent to which the leader of the crowd had internalised the values of his oligarchic upbringing, but the principle of oligarchic self-discipline would have the clamouring desires to contend with inside the demagogue's own personality. Plato's account of the internal conflicts of the demagogic character in the process of corruption is a brilliant image of what happens in the first stage of democratic politics. As crowd pleasers, democratic politicians have to listen to the crowd in the assembly bawling for what it wants. The only way the demagogues would know what to do in these circumstances would be to give in to the section of the crowd which shouted the loudest or to give the crowd what it shouted loudest for. The crowd's own character is already democratic, following the desire of the moment. Being undisciplined, the democratic character fails to order its desires. It sacrifices the one which at the moment is the most importunate. Popular leaders are exposed to the clamouring multitude at exactly the moment when their character has thrown off all external constraint and demands are being increasingly made upon it by its own desires. The demagogue finds the same thing happening both in his political and in his private life. Wherever he looks, both outside and inside himself, he sees desire demanding to be satisfied; he gives in to both, satisfies both himself and others, and so is dragged down to the crowd's own level.

At first, the crowd is flattered to find that it has a leader who professes to be no better than themselves, but the people need something more than flattery to remain convinced that their leader has a care for their welfare. Despoiling vanquished oligarchs will keep them happy for a time; so will cancelling debts and redistributing cultivated land, but this is harder to do. Democracy is also the ideal breeding ground for a new class of money-makers now that the old rich have gone or have gone underground, so the demagogue begins to rob them. The easiest way to do this is to invent oligarchic plots, and there follows a spate of denunciations of enemies of the people followed by treason trials during which the democratic leader begins to get a taste for blood. The strategem of inventing conspiracies can easily backfire. The surviving oligarchs and the *nouveaux riches* take to real plotting; some plot in voluntary or enforced exile, so that the demagogue finds that he now has real internal and external enemies. The next expedient the demagogue on the way to becoming a tyrant tries is war. War reinforces the people's conviction that they need a ruler; it serves the ruler well because he can now begin to tax the people to supply the war-chest and this would send the idlers among the people back to work in order to be able to pay the taxes. There has already been some grumbling, and the discipline of regular work is a useful antidote against the grumblers turning to plotting. It is easy to see what the grumbling would have been about. The people originally followed the demagogue for an easy ride; they expected to live off the spoils of a democratic victory and they did not mind too much that the demagogue took a disproportionate amount of the spoils because the crowd were doing well enough. Besides, democratic leaders did not pretend to be better than their following and were only doing what each member of the *demos* would do himself if he had the chance. Now things were beginning to change. Insensibly, being a member of the *demos* becomes less a matter of collective self-interest in the distribution of the good things of life and more a matter of self-sacrifice in the interests of the *demos*'s leader. Taxation and war were not the reason why the crowd followed its leader, and it would be at the moment when both appeared on the political agenda that it would begin to be frequently remarked that, after all, the demagogue has done much better out of the democracy than the people, and that in the coming war the leader is probably not going to be found in the forefront of the battle.

The third stage of democracy follows in which the democratic leader degenerates into tyranny. The treason trials have already given him a taste for blood. He begins to see that wherever he looks he is surrounded by real or potential enemies. Dispossessed oligarchs plot at home and abroad, and the people's enthusiasm is turning into sullen acquiesence. It is about time that the demagogue looked to his own safety, so he equips himself with the badge of tyranny, a foreign guard loyal to his own person for pay. These would be men like the tyrant himself, discontented sons of the rich from other cities, who would become the companions of his debauches and they would make it their business to see that the tyrant's character combined to be dominated by the low desires which they share. Theirs is a bought friendship, and they would live in the fear that the tyrant might reform, regain his people's love, and make them redundant. The praetorians feed the tyrant's desires so that he is mastered by them, and it is the tyrant's taste for blood which gives them the clue to their best strategy. Plato speaks of a master passion which is the most deeply embedded and secret of all the desires. It is of the kind which is normally allowed out only in the dreams which follow the sleep of debauch. It shrinks at nothing – not incest, not bestiality, not rape of the gods – and it feeds on murder. The tyrant's guard sees to it that the tyrant can live out in his waking hours the darkest and most repressed wishes of the human soul. Once he has been mastered by them, the tyrant is the most slavish of men and, all other courses of human action now being closed to him, he can only go forward in blood.

Plato's account of the degeneration of the oligarchic character through democracy to tyranny completes the elegant symmetry of his whole argument about the connection between human character and forms of rule. The character of the Philosopher-Ruler was dominated by the single faculty of reason and the Ideal State was dominated by the single vision of the Good; now the tyrant is dominated by the single master passion and the tyrannical state is dominated by the absolute inversion of the Good. Plato never wavers from his contention that the character of a city is determined by the character of its rulers. Guardians are well-adjusted men who have been trained to acquire that internal right ordering of the faculties which alone can bring that strength and peace of mind which brings true happiness, and they impart that strength, peace and happiness to the state. The tyrant's is a disturbed personality, and his state is weak and unhappy as his retinue of armed guards turns the people into slaves to service evil. Just as the perfectly just man is always the happiest of men even in the worst of societies, where he will be reviled, tortured and killed, so the tyrant is the most wretched of men even in a society which he can bend to his own will because he is a slave to the master passion which controls him. This provides Plato with a good reason for banning the poets from his Ideal State. The poets present tyrants as happy and god-like, and it is no wonder that tragedians like Euripides prosper in democracies and tyrannies.

The description of the descent from democracy into tyranny completes Plato's account of the degeneration of human character and of states into abject misery. Right at the beginning of the *Republic* he had promised to show that, despite appearances, states ruled by the One and the Few were happier than states ruled by the Many, just as he promised to show that individual characters were happy to the extent that they were able to control the unruly multitude of the desires. On its own terms we can accept Plato's contention that the Philosopher-Ruler is the happiest of men and that the tyrant is the least happy, but these are plainly extreme cases. The account of timarchy is equally plainly modelled on Sparta, and so is a special case. Most Greek cities hovered between the polarities of oligarchy and democracy, and it is on his treatment of these that any claim for Plato as an analyst of the nature of political change and its relationship to human happiness must be based. It has been remarked before that Plato knows that he is on sticky ground here because the democratic way of life is so attractive. Those busy rich oligarchic misers with their pleasure-loving sons straining at the paternal leash are not very obviously happy men, and they are certainly not happy in comparison with the versatile democrats who do a bit of everything and nothing for long. Plato recognises this and that is why he breaks up the democratic stage of political degeneration into different periods to show that, while democracy might well be an attractive proposition in the short run, its long-term prospects are very bleak indeed. Plato never in fact argues that the democratic character in its early stage is unhappier than its oligarchic predecessor, so his only case against it, and against those who in general favour democracy, is short-sightedness.

This is a matter of some importance, because commentators on Plato's *Republic* have sometimes said that the scheme of political degeneration is not to be taken seriously as history on the grounds that, because the Ideal State has never actually existed, Plato cannot mean us to take literally the idea that the imperfect forms of state are degeneration from it, and this in its turn has tended to reinforce the view that Plato's political thought is in general divorced from the real political world. Yet the obvious care with which Plato sets out the argument about political degeneration, and the real or imagined detail he puts into it, makes it hard to believe that what he says about political change is not based on a reading, if only a very partial reading, of ancient Greek political experiences. His treatment of democracy bears this out. If Plato means us to take his argument that it is the tyranny which eventually comes out of democracy which is the chief case against it, then he must mean us to take at least that part of the degeneration scheme seriously as history. Of course, taking the developmental connection between democracy and tyranny seriously as Plato does, entitles us to ask how seriously we are prepared to take it, and how seriously we are prepared to take other parts of the historical scheme. One very obvious thing can be said at the outset. If it is short-sighted to prefer oligarchy to timarchy, because oligarchy leads to democracy and democracy leads to tyranny, why is it not short-sighted to prefer timarchy to the Ideal State, because timarchy leads to oligarchy, oligarchy leads to democracy and democracy leads to tyranny? And finally, why would it not be short-sighted to set up the Ideal State, because degeneration from the Ideal State begins the process which leads through all the intervening stages to tyranny? From Plato's account of degeneration it simply is not clear why the charge of short-sightedness applies only to the first, relatively happy days of the democracy.

It could be argued for Plato that it is all a question of time. Any form of government which lasted any length of time would have the advantage of putting off the fatal day on which tyranny, the worst of all governments, at last emerged from democracy. Spartan timarchy and Theban oligarchy stood as examples of very long-lived non-democratic regimes. However, if Plato means us to take his scheme of political degeneration seriously as a gloss on the political practice of the Greek cities, then the longevity of the democracy at Athens has to be put on the other side of the balance. Athens had some kind of working democracy from the time of the Constitution of Cleisthenes (end of the sixth century) until the oligarchic *coup d'état* towards the end of the Peloponnesian War, a period of two centuries, and the democracy re-emerged and survived intermittently until Philip of Macedon destroyed all independent Greek political life at the battle of Chaeronea in 338. It must be stressed that the democratic regime at Athens corresponds to the early stage of the democracy in Plato's scheme, the period in which democracy appears attractive on Plato's own account of it and the period which, also on Plato's own account of it, cannot last, so that to favour the democracy is to be fatally short-sighted. Yet where in the *Republic* is there a mention of the short-sightedness of Cleisthenes?

There is no quibble. Plato wants it both ways in his attack on democracy. He wants on the one hand to display his fairmindedness by showing that he understands why democracy is attractive, at least to minds unused to giving much consideration to the future, and on the other hand he wants to argue that democracy is the least stable of all the political regimes with the horrors of tyranny waiting at the end. To do this, he has to make his account of democracy a historical, that is, a developmental account. Of course, Plato had to argue something like that, because his account of human character demands it. If the democratic character is the least stable of the four types of human character, then the democratic regime has to be the least stable of the four types of regime. If he had admitted that democratic regimes can be stable, then he would have had to modify his account of the types of human character, just as, if he had modified his account of human characters, he would have had to modify his account of different types of regime. The bedrock of Plato's political theory being the identification of types of regime with human character types, it follows that Plato's whole political theory begins to look shaky if his historical account of democracy can be undermined in those same historical terms Plato himself uses. Plato's political theory is nothing if not architectonic; everything in it stands or falls together. If the account of human character, or a part of it, falls, then everything else falls; if the account of the types of political regimes, or a part of it falls, then everything else falls.

There is a notable irony here. It was remarked right at the beginning of the opening chapter on the Greeks that the old Homeric account of the world was vulnerable because its three interlocking hierarchies of gods, men and nature stood or fell together. It was also pointed out that Plato's own political theory can be seen as an attempt to remake the hierarchy of men on a rational basis in a world in which it was becoming increasingly difficult for rational men to justify the way they ordered their political relationships by appeals to ancestral wisdom. Plato's own political theory turns out to have something of the card-castle quality of the world view which it was intended to replace.

NOTES ON SOURCES

Plato has attracted a mound of learned commentary since antiquity. His *Republic* (Penguin Classics) is only one of his political works, the other two being *The Laws* and *The Statesman*, both of which exist in various editions. All students of Plato ought also to treat themselves to the delights of *The Symposium* (Penguin Classics). In the English-speaking world, modern commentary begins with Plato's enemies, R.H.S. Crossman, *Plato Today* (revised 2nd edn, 1959), and Karl Popper, *The Open Society and its Enemies*, Vol. 1. *The Spell of Plato* (revised edn, 1962). These two works have to be watched every inch of the way. Ernest Barker's *Greek Political Theory: Plato and his Predecessors* (5th edn, 1960) and *The Political Thought of Plato and Aristotle* (1959) are more balanced, though Barker has a tendency to regard Plato as a Jacobin and Aristotle as a sound Victorian liberal. R.L. Nettleship, *Lectures on the Republic of Plato* (1901, reprint 1968), has great staying power. A.D. Winspear, *The Genesis of Plato's Thought* (2nd edn, 1952), and Alexandre Koyre, *Discovering Plato* (1960), deserve a mention.

4

ARISTOTLE AND THE SCIENCE OF POLITICS

ARISTOTLE

Aristotle was born a subject of the king of Macedon at Stageira in Thrace in 384 BC. His father was a doctor who attended king Amynatas, whose throne was later occupied by the Philip who was father to Alexander the Great. Philip made peripheral Macedon the most powerful state in Greece, and Alexander conquered the world. Aristotle came to study at Plato's Academy at Athens when he was seventeen, and he remained there as student and teacher until he was nearly forty. Aristotle's Macedonian court connections may have made him slightly suspect in an Athens that saw its own rather complicated foreign policy being undermined by Macedonian success. Athens still regarded itself in important ways as the centre of Hellas and could be expected to look askance at the threat to Greek city-state autonomy posed by Macedon's rise to hegemony, first in Hellas and then in the whole world. We shall probably never know for certain how far Aristotle was 'involved' in Macedonian politics. Some have seen only the detached scientist in Aristotle, while others have seen him as the cultural wing of Macedonian imperialism (or even as a Macedonian spy). The evidence for the latter is not much more than ancient tittle-tattle, though the extended treatment of monarchy in *The Politics* has sometimes been seen as a defence of Macedonian kingship.

Whatever the truth of the Macedonian connection, Aristotle had to leave Athens on account of anti-Macedonian feeling at least twice, though his first exodus was probably also bound up with the question of the succession to Plato as head of the Academy, a job Aristotle failed to get. Aristotle went to Assos in the territory of the tyrant Hermias of Atarneus, whose daughter he married. This is the period of Aristotle's studies in marine biology. He also went to Macedon to become tutor to the young Alexander for a year or two, and he was back in Athens in 336. By this time, Philip of Macedon had established himself as *hegemon* of the Greek cities. He was assassinated in 336, and it was Alexander who became 'the Great'. Aristotle founded his own school at Athens, the Lyceum, with its famous covered walk (*peripatos*), hence the name Peripatetics for the followers of the Aristotelian philosophy. The curriculum at the Lyceum contained biology, theology, metaphysics, astronomy, mathematics, botany, meteorology, ethics, rhetoric and poetics as well as politics, so that Aristotle has a much better claim than Plato to being the founder of the first real university.

Athens was divided into pro- and anti-Macedonian parties, roughly oligarchs against democrats, and Aristotle had well-born friends (he was a snappy dresser and affected the aristocratic lisp). There was a renewal of anti-Macedonian feeling at Athens when news reached the city of Alexander's death at Babylon in 332, and Aristotle sensibly took up residence at Chalcis in Euboea, where he died ten years later at the age of sixty-two.

THE PROBLEM OF ARISTOTLE'S *POLITICS*

Much is usually made of the fact that Aristotle was Plato's pupil. Plato, being the great man he is, must have been an inspirational teacher, and Aristotle, being the clever man he is, must have been a model student, therefore Aristotle must have learned much from Plato and have come a good deal under his influence. Plato spent his life trying to design the Ideal State, so that any mention of ideal states in Aristotle's work on politics must reflect the influence of Plato. However, Aristotle's conception of what political theorising consists of contains many things that are not very conspicuous in Plato, so there must have come a time when Aristotle chose to break with Plato and branch out on his own. Because Plato was bound to have been so influential, Aristotle's break with Plato must have been difficult to make, even painful, comparable with Marx's break with Hegel, or J.S. Mill's with Bentham (which took the form of a much-publicised nervous breakdown). Therefore, so the argument runs, the break can never have been really complete, which brings the argument back full circle to Plato's own greatness as an influence on Aristotle. Various possible reasons have been canvassed for the necessary influence of Plato on Aristotle. For some, Plato's 'greatness' is enough; he would have influenced anybody, so that it is to Aristotle's credit that he should have sloughed off even a part of Plato's influence. This tendency to patronise Aristotle from the Platonic heights is at its most pronounced in the view that Aristotle, not being quite Greek (he was born in Stageira in Macedonian Thrace) and being an Athenian only by adoption, must have been wonderfully impressed by a philosophical Athenian aristocrat like Plato. The young Aristotle was probably pathetically grateful for any attention the great man could spare him after finishing the education of the gilded Athenian youths for whose benefit the Platonic Academy had been founded.

This picture of Aristotle the outsider is used to explain some of the fundamentals of Aristotle's political thought. By origin the subject of a king and living in Athens as a resident foreigner (*metic*) without political rights, Aristotle came to overvalue the idea of citizenship; coming from the fringe of the Greek world, he made too much of the distinction between Hellene and barbarian; and like all outsiders wanting to belong, he cried up the virtues of the *polis* and took too rosy a view of its faults. Aristotle may even have done this for entirely self-interested motives. It was the rise of Macedon under Philip and Alexander which put an end to the free and independent *polis*, and Aristotle himself may have come under suspicion as some kind of Macedonian agent, as the philosophical wing of semi-barbarian military kingship, and so had to cover his tracks by always arguing that life in a properly constituted *polis* was the best life that Greeks could aspire to. Aristotle's own father was probably court physician at Pella when Philip was king, and there is a tradition that Aristotle was tutor to the young Alexander. There is something too pat about that tradition. Of course the greatest ruler of his day had to have the greatest philosopher of his day as tutor, and of course the greatest philosopher of his day had to have the greatest pupil. The most poignant image we have of Aristotle is of the old man anxiously waiting in Athens for news of the progress of Alexander's eastern conquests, worrying about the orientalisation of Hellas which is its inevitable result, and hurriedly putting together in the *Politics* everything that was worth saying about those little Greek states before they disappeared into the world empire which was to be the standard political unit for the next two thousand years. Greeks and those whom the Greeks called barbarians were going to be living on terms of rough equality in these new-fangled empires. Best to get down on papyrus what the *polis* at its best was like while the *polis* was still a living memory, while there was still time, and while it still made sense. Aristotle's cousin, Callisthenes, accompanied Alexander to the east, ostensibly to compose the official campaign history and to recite Homer to Alexander when he was drunk and thought he was Achilles; but Callisthenes, in one version of the story, was really Aristotle's spy, planted on Alexander to report back what he was up to and to put a halt, as far as he was able, to Alexander's admiration for the Persian king Cyrus turning Alexander into the kind of oriental despot which it had been Greece's greatest triumph to stop in his tracks at Marathon, Salamis and Plataea. Callisthenes was eventually executed for complicity in a plot against Alexander's life, though the details of what happened are obscure. In one version, Callisthenes died as a martyr to Hellenism because he refused to bow and scrape before Alexander in the eastern manner, and after this the rot set in because there was no-one to stop Alexander's ascent into mystical kingship and his companions' descent into subjecthood.

The event which really sent a shudder through all right-thinking Hellenes was the banquet at Opis in 324. By this time, Alexander was leading a multi-racial army. The supply of Greek mercenaries was never enough, and Alexander had recruited large numbers of Persians. The Macedonians mutinied in the camp at Opis. Their grievances seem to have been racial: Alexander had allowed Persians into the elite Companions of Alexander and into the decent regiments, had taken to wearing Persian dress, and had begun to greet his Persian commanders with a kiss. Alexander confronted the Macedonians, threatened to pension them off back to Macedon, and distributed all the commands among the Persians. When the Macedonians had sobered up, they kissed and made up with Alexander, and Alexander ordered a banquet to celebrate the reconciliation. The occasion was skilfully used by him to effect a reconciliation between the Persians and the Macedonians. We are told that the priests of the Macedonians and the magi of the Persians shared in the religious rites, and that Alexander persuaded 10,000 of his Macedonian veterans to marry their Asiatic concubines. He made a remarkable speech in which he pleaded for *omonoia*, concord and co-operation, between the races. From that time onwards it was to be recognised that the multi-racial empire was the coming political unit. This was the supremely anti-Aristotelian moment, when the distinction between Hellene and barbarian, free and slave, naturally at war with each other, so carefully made by reason, was obliterated by the sword of Alexander. And on this occasion, the true Greeks appear to have been ominously silent about the question of racial mixing.

Perhaps it was the speed of Alexander's conquests which accounts for the form of Aristotle's *Politics* as we have it. All of the commentator's agree that the book is a mess, and the most charitable view we can take of it is that it was put together in a hurry. There is no evidence that this was in fact the case, just as there is no evidence available to tell us that Aristotle himself wrote the book as it has come down to us. (One view of the *Politics* is that it is a compilation of notes taken by pupils from Aristotle's lectures on politics at the Lyceum.) Aristotle has a great reputation as a systematiser of knowledge, and the *Politics* is on the face of it so unsystematic that it appears to be impossible that Aristotle himself could have been responsible for the finished product. Another, equally plausible, view is that the order of the *Politics*'s eight books has become jumbled during the course of the centuries, and several scholarly careers have been made out of the business of rearranging them. The most convincing case for rearranging the books has been made out by Werner Jaeger in his *Aristotle: Fundamentals of the History of his Development*, though Jaeger's case depends on the basic premise that Aristotelianism took the distinctive form it did as a result of a painful break with Platonism. Jaeger argues that there is a distinction to be made between what he calls 'the Original Politics' (Books 2, 3, 7 and 8) and the truly 'Aristotelian Politics' (Books 4, 5 and 6), with Book 1 written the latest of all as a general introduction. The Original Politics is Platonic in inspiration and deals with the construction of the Ideal, or best possible, State, while the Aristotelian Politics contains a much more empirical grasp of how politics works in the real political world.

Aristotle's political science is empirical in the way that Aristotelian biology is empirical. On Jaeger's view of it, Aristotle's chief contribution to political science is to bring the subject matter of politics within the scope of the methods which he was already using to investigate other aspects of nature. Aristotle the biologist looks at the developments in political life in much the same way that he looks at the developing life of other natural phenomena. This rooting of political life in nature contrasts strongly with Plato's tendency to write off most of what actually happens in the life of cities as a hindrance to true political knowledge, as useless in theory and dangerous in practice. For Aristotle, part of political experience is what men have thought of that political experience. It is natural that political experience has a meaning for those whose experience it, and so Aristotle has a tendency, again markedly absent in Plato, to give common or received opinion about politics a sympathetic hearing.

Aristotle often begins a subject of enquiry by reviewing current opinion about it, and it is easy to think that Aristotle does this merely because he has to start somewhere, or because he is modest and fair-minded, and does not want to exclude opinion just because it is received. Aristotle's purpose is rather different. He wishes us to understand that men have not lived for nothing. Men differ from the animals because they are capable of understanding the kinds of lives which they live, and it would be absurd to pretend that all previous understanding had understood nothing at all. Aristotle does in fact think that common opinion (common, that is, among Greeks) and other philosophers have got things wrong, have been confused, or have offered a limited understanding of politics, but it is inconceivable to Aristotle that they have nothing at all to teach us. An important part of systematic reflection about politics will consist of sifting through this received opinion and explaining how its errors arose. Even the mistakes of the past can be instructive. Of course, Plato had not in fact ignored received opinion. The *Republic* borrows from Spartan practice for instance, but Plato borrows from Sparta because he approves of Sparta and not because Sparta as a piece of political experience must have something important to teach us. (Aristotle will even allow the non-Greek city of Carthage a place in political science because it has a reputation for being well-governed.)

The naturalistic approach to politics is far from simple-minded. Aristotle does not think that everything which just happens to happen in the world is natural. The processes of nature are subject to endless vicissitudes. Aristotle preserves Plato's distinction between the world as it is and the world as it is meant to be. Political science is meant to be useful, and political science's function as Aristotle sees it is to identify those aspects of political life which operate as nature intended ('Nature does nothing without a purpose'), with a view to removing or amending those aspects of political life which frustrate nature's own purposes. This is an extremely ambitious undertaking. It means that nothing political is in principle outside its concern, and it involves developing a sense of judgement about what is in fact possible. Aristotle sees nature eternally striving to reach its fulfilment in a hostile world, and those who strive with it must often settle for its partial fulfilment. This has often been misunderstood to mean that Aristotle is the political theorist of the second-best, or of the mediocre, on the grounds that Plato went straight for the ideal while Aristotle was content for the best possible in the circumstances, but that view of Aristotle misses the point about the usefulness of political science. The informed gardener who makes the best of his own tools, his own seed and his own soil really has got the best out of nature. The fact that tools, seed and soil could all be improved does not detract from his achievement, and thinking about how they could be improved, possibly even to perfection, might or might not improve his performance. In thinking this, Aristotle is not in fact very far from the Plato of the *Republic* who says that in any case practice always falls short of theory.

A MAP OF THE *POLITICS*

Perhaps the best way to approach the *Politics* is through a kind of traveller's guide to the text as we have it because nobody is very likely to read the book in the order that Jaeger suggests it was composed. This can be done in a fairly schematic way, though how the various themes relate to each other is more of a problem.

Book 1 contains:

1 Aristotle's defence of the *polis* against the Sophist view that the *polis* exists through convention only. Aristotle distinguishes the *polis* from other forms of human community because its 'end' is different. Everything in nature has one of these ends, so the *polis* must have one too. There is a distinction to be made between the cause of something and the end to which it naturally develops. The causes which make a *polis* come into being may be economic (only a *polis* can be economically self-supporting, for instance), but the end to which it strives is moral (only in a *polis* can men live what Aristotle calls 'the good life').

2 A justification of slavery as part of a well-managed household, and therefore natural.

3 A discussion of the relationship between the acquisition of wealth and the management of a household (the original meaning of 'economics'). Wealth has as its end provision for a household, and must be limited by its end, so 'making money for its own sake' is

unnatural. Aristotle also discusses the forms of relationship which naturally occur in a household on the basis of the possession of 'reason' (the capacity to direct one's own life and so the lives of others), so free men in whom the directive faculty naturally rules, rule over others, including wives (because the directive faculty, while existing in women, is 'inoperative'); slaves, having no reason, are ruled as tools or beasts of burden.

Book 2 contains:

1 A discussion of ideal communities.
2 A discussion of the community of wives and children among the Guardian class in Plato's *Republic*.
3 A discussion of the best arrangements for the holding of property. Aristotle tries to have it both ways, arguing that property can be held privately but used in common through gifts and hospitality which impart 'friendship to the state'.
4 A discussion of whether property held in common would decrease wrongdoing which concludes that common ownership would not prevent crime because men steal more than the necessities of life.

Book 3 contains much definitional matter, including:

1 The answer to the question 'What is the *polis*?' The *polis* must be its constitution (the arrangements for the holding of public office, the way it is governed) because the constitution provides the *polis* with its identity over a period of time. The *polis* cannot be defined as its citizens, because they die and are replaced; nor can it be its territory because territory expands and contracts.
2 The answer to the question 'What is it to be a member of a '*polis*?' States are composed of citizens, and citizens are those who have a share in public affairs, which means holding office, taking part in the administration of justice and membership of a governing assembly. The exact meaning of 'citizen' will of course vary from *polis* to *polis* because citizen is a genus, not a species. Those directly engaged in the business of getting a living with their own hands are excluded from citizenship because they haven't the leisure for virtue.
3 A classification of different types of constitution, probably borrowed from Plato's *Statesman*. Aristotle divides constitutions into two groups of three, what we have come to call the 'good' and the 'corrupt' forms. The good forms are monarchy, aristocracy and *politeia* (Aristotle's best state) and their analogous corrupt forms are tyranny, oligarchy and democracy (which is really rule by the mob, what the historian Polybius was later to call 'ochlocracy'). Aristotle reminds us that this is a broad-meshed classification because in the natural world there are many more species than genera, so that it is convenient to class constitutions on the continum Few/Many, democratic/oligarchic. Like Plato, he thinks that different types of regime are based on different ideas about justice.

4 A discussion of five different types of monarchy, which leads to the more general question of whether man or law should be supreme. Aristotle comes up with the dubious-sounding formula that law should be supreme in general, but men in particular cases. Kingship, he concludes, is not unnatural, provided the king rules in the interest of all and is truly a kingly man. (In Aristotle there are no queens.)

Books 4, 5 and 6

These are the books which, according to Jaeger, represent a new departure in the study of politics. It is here that Aristotle is at his most biological, discussing the morphology of states and their pathology. So far he has only discussed monarchy and aristocracy, and he goes on to consider *politeia*, tyranny, oligarchy and democracy. These books contain:

1 A discussion of oligarchy in opposition to democracy and of *politeia* in opposition to tyranny.
2 An answer to five main questions:
   (a) How many kinds of constitution do in fact exist?
   (b) What constitution is best suited to normal circumstances, and which is best after the ideal constitution?
   (c) Which of the inferior kinds of constitution are suited to each kind of population?
   (d) How are the various forms of constitution to be organised? (Part of Book 4 and part of Book 5.)
   (e) How are constitutions preserved and destroyed? (Book 5.)
3 *Book 5*. Aristotle on political pathology and preventive medicine. This book contains much historical detail and much sound political wisdom which has worn remarkably well over the centuries. (This is the 'real political world' that Thrasymachus claimed to understand at the opening of Plato's *Republic*.) Points worth noting are the following:
   (a) In a democracy men should be equally wealthy because they are equally free.
   (b) In an oligarchy men should be unequal in all things because they are unequal in wealth.
   (c) The cause of disaffection is desire for wealth and honours, or the desire to avoid poverty and dishonour.
   (d) The causes which lead men to change a regime are:
      • Indignation at the monopolisation of wealth and honours by others.
      • Insolence, fear and the undue prominence of individuals.
      • A disproportionate increase in a particular class.
      • Intrigues at election time.
      • Carelessness in allowing disloyal persons to hold office.
      • Neglect of apparently insignificant changes.
   (e) Regimes are preserved by:
      • A spirit of obedience to the laws (Aristotle at his most obvious).
      • Not relying on being able to fool all of the people all of the time.

- Aristocrats and oligarchs would do well to cultivate the people.
- The ruling group must on no account allow a split to develop in its own ranks.
- Those who rule must not appear to be profiting from office too obviously.
- Most importantly, the education system must be well adapted to the forms of government. Aristotle adds the twist that oligarchs should be educated democratically and democrats must be educated oligarchically, because bringing up young democrats in complete freedom and young oligarchs in luxury and ease is asking for trouble in the future.
- Tyrants may preserve their power by appearing to act like kings.

Books 7 and 8 – Aristotle on the best state

These are 'Platonic' books in Jaeger's sense because they have little to say about the real political world and are largely concerned with the question of what kind of state would be the best. The best *polis* looks something like this:

1 The question of population is not a matter of numbers so much as a question of how many are needed 'to do the work of a city', and the minimum number would be that which was required for self-sufficiency where self-sufficiency means both self-defence and economic autarky. Aristotle does not think that more means better. The *polis* should be small enough to be 'seen at a single view'. Perhaps the ideal number would be a *polis* of adult male citizens who could hear the voice of a single herald in peace and of a single general in war.
2 The question of territory is resolved in much the same way as the question of population. It must be large enough to secure a leisured life for its citizens but not so large as to provide luxury. Aristotle considers a position by the sea, because sea-power is a factor in war and commerce by sea is useful in providing those necessities of life which might not easily be provided by one's own territory.
3 Only Greeks are fit to be citizens.
4 A *polis* obviously needs craftsmen and labourers, farmers, soldiers, a leisured class, priests and judges. The important question is the extent to which these roles can be merged into a single person, and Aristotle makes a division between those roles which are appropriate to a free man and those which are not.
5 The best life for a free citizen would be to be a warrior when young, a ruler in middle life and a priest when old. When young, a man should defend his city, in middle age he should busy himself about its affairs, and in old age he should make sure that the gods are on its side.
6 Agricultural workers, artisans and slaves form separate classes (though they are not cannon fodder), and so do women.

It is clear that only the warriors, rulers and priests are really part of the *polis* in Aristotle's original terms in Book 3. The rest of the *Politics* is taken up with a discussion of education. The *polis* exists for 'the good life' of its citizens, and the good life depends on nature, habit and a 'reasoned course of life'. Education is concerned with the last two. The end of man, what he has got it in him to be, is found ultimately in his reason. Reason is divided into two kinds, speculative reason concerned with 'the life of mind' and practical reason, which fits a man for the business of a city – politics and war. Education should be primarily directed towards citizenship in peace, and it is importantly a moral education because the *polis* exists to enable men to practise those virtues which go to make up the good life.

THE NATURALNESS OF RULERSHIP

Fundamental to everything that Aristotle thinks about politics is the idea that some ways of ordering human life are natural and others not. Aristotle's teleological biology informs his view that only some kinds of human relationship are as nature intended them to be and his treatment of rulership is largely concerned with untangling the natural forms of the ruler–ruled relationship from the unnatural. In the *Politics* Aristotle establishes the criteria for naturalness in the context of his treatment of slavery in Book 1. Aristotle begins the discussion by identifying what he calls 'natural pairs', one half of which rules the other. Rulership, he thinks, exists in any relationship between superior and inferior. Rulership includes commanding, but it also includes directing, guiding and educating. Aristotle thinks that masters and slaves, husbands and wives, fathers and children, and rulers and ruled, are all natural pairs for the straightforward reason that each needs the other to be what it is. This is more than a matter of definition; of course, fathers cannot be fathers without children and children cannot be children without fathers, but Aristotle also means that neither can begin to be self-sufficient without the other, and neither can perform its function without the other. The ruling of one of a natural pair by the other must be in the interest of both. The rule of men over animals qualifies as natural. Men are naturally at war with wild animals, as they are with wild men, so it is highly advantageous for animals to become domesticated. They are then fed and watered, are protected by their owners, and, most importantly, are protected from other men. Domestic animals have the stamp of ownership on them, so that men who are not their owners have no reason to fear them because the animals, being at home somewhere, can be assumed to be tame. The same goes for men. Strangers are greeted with the question: Where do you come from? because the answer they give tells us something about what we can expect from them. The man who has a home acknowledges the authority of a set of manners and morals which we might know about, so we can feel safe in our dealings with him; even the stranger very far from home is at least domesticated somewhere. The most unsettling man is the 'man from nowhere', 'the war-mad man who has no morals and no home' that Homer mentions. It is probably best to kill him to be on the safe side.

Rulership is exercised in different ways. Aristotle gives two illuminating examples: mind over body and intelligence over the desires. The rule of mind over body is absolute or despotic in the interests of both, while the rule of intelligence over the desires is constitutional and royal. By this Aristotle means that the mind does not negotiate with the body. If I say to my legs 'go that way' and the legs begin to argue, life begins to be difficult; if I say to my legs 'run away from the battlefield' because everybody else is running away and the legs wish to discuss the matter, then life itself is put in danger; therefore the mind demands instant obedience from the body. The desires are a different case. The desires arise naturally, and some, like the desires for food, drink and rest, have to be satisfied sometimes or the body would die and the desires would die with it. The desires are best thought of as subjects petitioning a king. They ask to be satisfied, but the king decides if and when. Constitutional monarchy for Aristotle is kingship exercised through laws, and a wise king would outlaw some desires as being too unruly, and would establish some kind of orderly programme for the satisfaction of the reasonable desires, say three meals a day, none in excess, and regular hours of sleep. The desires would then know where they stood, like the subjects of a king ruling through law. Like Plato, Aristotle does not think that the desires are fixed, either in number or in intensity. New desires arise, or old desires assert themselves with a new intensity; a wise mind considers the first kind on their merits and puts down the rebellion of the second. Endless self-indulgence kills desire (the cult of the aperitif), dulls the intelligence and threatens the body. Much better for all that matters to be in the control of a moderating kingly intelligence.

All forms of rulership are limited by the end for which rulership is exercised. Rule is not domination for its own sake; abuse of power for Aristotle means something very close to what we mean by 'drug abuse', the use of something which has no end and which can only lead on to disaster because it has no end. Husbands must remember that sexuality is for procreation and not for mere enjoyment (though they are allowed to smile), fathers must remember that children will one day be like themselves, and masters of slaves must remember that slaves are for use and not for exploitation. Slaves exist to free masters from the menial (*banausic*) occupations. Free men need the leisure for virtue and so have not got the time to get their own living. Aristotle is careful to say that slaves are a part of wealth and not a means towards the increase of wealth, by which he means that it is no part of a master's business to squeeze the last ounce of labour out of his slaves. Some commentators think that in making this distinction Aristotle was already being a little old-fashioned in his treatment of slavery, defending a traditional form of 'household' slavery in the face of a new kind of slavery which saw slaves as an investment on which their masters demanded the highest possible return. (There is a parallel between what Aristotle has to say about slavery here and American defences of slavery before the Civil War. What was always considered most defensible was the aristocratic household slavery of Virginia ('slaves are practically members of the family') and not the ruthlessly exploitative field slavery, particularly of the sugar plantations in the deep South ('being sold down the river').) Aristotle says that a slave is like a bed, not a shuttle. In principle, there is no limit to the use of a shuttle, which could be used to weave day and night; beds are for sleeping in, not for sleeping in all day, and the bed does not produce anything else. Likewise the slave. He is not for increasing his master's wealth; he must, of course, reproduce his own kind, but slave-breeding for profit would be ruled out.

The ends of human relationships have their places in a hierarchy of ends. Nature's pattern is a pattern of subordination, otherwise no form of rule would itself be natural and men would not even rule over animals by nature, and this hierarchical pattern extends to the ends for which forms of rule exist. The relationship between husband and wife makes the continuation of the species possible; the rule of the head of a household over wife, children and slaves has as its end the social unit which, together with others like itself, goes to make up economically self-sufficient village communities, and it is a group of these self-sufficient communities which makes up the supreme community, the *polis*, which has as its end not just self-sufficient life but the good life. The end of the family and the village lead naturally to the supreme end which is life in a properly constituted *polis*.

Aristotle's theory of ends is called the doctrine of the priority of ends, and on the face of it can appear to be puzzling on the grounds that it is difficult to see how the *end* of a process can be *prior to* the process itself. It is important to realise, however, that Aristotle does not mean *prior to* in the sense of time but *prior to* in the sense of understanding a process. No natural process is capable of being fully understood until it is complete. It is the end of a process which gives meaning to a process as a whole. Aristotle sometimes speaks as if the end of a process pushes or pulls the process to its completion, and has some- times been accused of mysticism as a consequence, but that is just Aristotle's manner of speaking. There is a metaphorical sense in which the idea of the oak either pushes or pulls the acorn into becoming an oak, just as there is a literal sense about the end determining the process of the formation of the *polis* among men. Men differ from the rest of nature because they alone can have a say in what the processes of their life should be like, and Aristotle thinks that it is difficult to know what life should be like in all its subordinate stages unless we have a clear idea of where the whole process is leading. It is not until we have an idea of what a properly constituted *polis* looks like that we can form any just idea about how the subordinate communities within the *polis* should themselves be organised. Above all, Aristotle's teleology is not prediction. Natural processes are accident-prone; acorns are often eaten by pigs. Aristotle has a tendency to shrug his shoulders when this happens. Everything has its natural place but, the world being what it is, things are frequently misplaced.

Aristotle's doctrine of natural places grates on the liberal ear because it justifies slavery. No doctrine, so the argument goes, which justifies slavery can be taken seriously. None the less, Aristotle himself plainly takes his argument for slavery seriously, though to say as some commentators do that he is especially 'worried' by slavery is to take the matter too far. A rational account of slavery is necessary, just as a rational account is necessary of any other kind of relationship between rulers and ruled; Aristotle is 'worried' about slavery only in the sense that he is 'worried' about all possible abuses of power. There is no special worry about slavery, though there is a special technical difficulty. Nature has made the difference between men and animals, male and female, children and adults, very clear, and it is this clarity which enables Aristotle to speak of nature's 'intentions'. Nature does nothing without a purpose, and there must therefore be a purpose in these distinctions. In the case of the distinction between free men by nature and slaves by nature a clear-cut distinction is not so easily made. The problem is compounded by the obvious fact that in the world of the Greek cities some obviously superior men ended up by being slaves and some obviously inferior men ended up as the masters of slaves, and the clever slave who outwitted and manipulated his dull master was to become one of the stock figures of ancient comedy. Who, then, is fit to be a master and who a slave? Aristotle says that those who are fit to direct themselves are fit to direct those who are incapable of self-direction. The ability to rule a household is part of intelligence; being good at running a household is part of goodness, so the claims of masters to rule slaves are partly managerial and partly moral. Ideally, the master's intelligence should take the place of the absent intelligence of the slave, but unfortunately slaves, even slaves by nature, are not always entirely stupid. There is *something* in the slave which corresponds to intelligence in the master, and the fact of the matter is that slaves are treated differently from tools or from beasts of burden. Masters talk to slaves and give them orders, and slaves are capable of being trained to do fairly sophisticated jobs.

So what is the proper relationship between the slave's intelligence and the master's intelligence? The master is fit to rule the slave because he is himself self-directed. This would be true of the master even if he had no slaves. He is capable of a rational course of life; he is a man who knows what his life should be and is capable of sticking to what he knows it should be like. Not so the slave. Left to his own devices he would probably descend to a level of swinish idleness; much better for him to be part of a well-run operation under a master's direction. These generalities are not really very helpful in deciding who should be a slave, and Aristotle provides a sliding scale of suitability from nobly born Greeks, who are the least suitable, to base-born barbarians, who are the most suitable. Base-born Greeks and nobly born barbarians come somewhere in between, and Olympic victors should probably not be made slaves. Barbarians make the best slaves because they have never known the rational liberty which only a *polis* can provide. The classification is meant to show that it does a master no favours to have as his slave someone who is unsuitable, and a master who has a better man than him for his slave would look ridiculous. Aristotle knows that slaves are frequently slaves by accident, and he has heard the Sophist argument that all power relations are the result of more or less arbitrary convention. What bothers Aristotle about the Sophist position is that if every ruler–ruled relationship is conventional only, then nobody would ever have cause for complaint. Nothing would ever be unnatural. If there are no slaves by nature, then there are no free men by nature and the world becomes meaningless, fit only for those capable of a stoical indifference.

Aristotle's arguments about slavery have been called embarrassingly bad, but it is not always clear on what grounds. If slavery is just another form of rule, then there is no reason in principle why it should not be examined along with the other forms of rule. Of course, slavery, especially if it is slavery for ever, is open to horrible abuses, but Aristotle seems to be saying that the existence of a bad master no more vitiates the idea of mastery than a bad father vitiates the idea of fatherhood. It is irrational for a master to treat his slave badly, but there are no guarantees for the slave. The master's desire for the good opinion of other masters might keep him in check. Ill-treatment of slaves, like any other form of domineering, would be shameful. Aristotle just accepts slavery as one of life's facts. Where his argument is weak is in the form it takes. Aristotle is so convinced that the good life must be provided with the leisure for virtue that slavery becomes a necessity. He can then treat the question: Who should be a slave? as a subordinate, technical, question, a problem of identification. Identification is sometimes difficult in nature, and it is only Aristotle's prior certainty that slaves by nature do exist that enables him to identify them in nature. If he had gone about the enquiry the other way round and first asked: Does Nature in fact distinguish clearly between free men and slaves? then the fact that nature does not distinguish clearly between them might have led to the conclusion that there *are* no slaves by nature. If there are no slaves by nature, then slavery cannot be a necessity and then the *polis* cannot itself be natural, and that Aristotle will not have.

THE NATURALNESS OF THE *POLIS*

Ends exist in nature as a hierarchy. Plants exist for animals, animals for men, slaves for free men, but at the level of free men special problems arise. If the citizens of a *polis* are to be free and equal, how is the *polis* then to be governed? No natural order can be said to exist among citizens. So how can the *polis* be natural? Does the *polis* not stand outside the order of nature? Perhaps the Sophists were right after all. The natural groups are families, or as the Epicureans were later to say, groups of friends. Aristotle approaches the problem with some caution, because he can feel both the Sophists and Plato breathing down his neck, interest against justice. Aristotle cannot believe that forms of government are simply matters of taste or indifference, but he cannot believe that the *polis* exists for the convenience of a very few just men. Plato's vision of the state ruled by experts in justice already casts its shadow over Aristotle as it will cast its shadow over almost every other political thinker. The sheer plausibility of Plato's argument is the problem for all subsequent thinkers. Stated baldly, Plato's argument is this: Only a fool would fail to get the best advice he could when faced with a difficulty. If I am ill I consult a doctor; in an emergency *any* doctor will do. If I look at the way I live my life, I find that I consult experts the whole time, and the more serious the business in hand is, the more care I take to consult the right expert, emergencies apart. The most serious business of all is the life of the *polis*, a matter of life and death on a public scale. It follows, therefore, that political matters should be the first to be subject to expert advice and treatment. Not all experts are equally adept and some claims to expertise are bogus. The most pressing political business is therefore to find out what real political expertise is, and to devise a programme to train people in the kingly science; hence Plato's *Republic*.

Plato's is a hard argument to meet on its own terms, and Aristotle meets it by altering the ground. If the question: Who is the best for ruling? keeps being asked, then the answer: 'experts' will keep being given, because the question itself contains its own answer. Aristotle begins with a very different kind of question: What kinds of men would they be who could make a good life for themselves? What kind of wisdom would *they* need? Not, to be sure, the highest conceivable form of wisdom (*sophia*) but practical wisdom (*phronesis*). *Phronesis* is not easy to pin down. It is wisdom where being wise recognises its own limitations, because *phronesis*, not being founded on a knowledge of the nature of things, is always aware that it could make a mistake. *Phronesis* is decision-making wisdom in a world which is always partly contingent; it deals with problems of the kind which require a grasp of essentials and grip on a situation. Free men choose the kind of life which they are going to lead in a world of imperfect information and rationality. Choose they must, and *phronesis* is the accumulation of the experience of having made good choices in the past, informed by reflection. Aristotle thinks the wise man will interest himself in cities which have a reputation for being well-governed because such an interest will increase the range of possible experience available to decision-makers.

Choices about how we should live our lives are frightening choices to make. Choices of this kind are not to be made every day; nor are they to be made for light and transient causes. Aristotle is particularly interested in the forms which these decisions are to take, and when they are properly made he calls them laws. Laws rule in cities which are uncorrupted. Law has as its end the good of those who are asked to obey, not the good of those who make it. Kingship is therefore the rule of one man through law for the benefit of all; aristocracy is the rule of the best, where the best are few, through law for the benefit of all; and *politeia* is the beneficent rule of the many (where the many are not the many-too-many). The corrupt forms rule through force for the benefit of the ruling part only. Aristotle will not trust even wise and moderate rulers with executive power, always preferring that ruling decisions take the form of law. Laws rule when intelligence rules without the passions, and by intelligence he means an accumulated intelligence, the register of past decisions which have been found to be good. Everybody cannot take part in the decision-making process all of the time. Even in the best-constituted *polis*, the *politeia*, there have to be certain arrangements, which Aristotle sometimes calls laws and sometimes constitution, which lay down who is to make what decisions on what occasions, on the assumption that no citizen may be excluded entirely and for ever from the exercise of *phronesis*.

It is with this almost prosaically sensible formula that Aristotle solves the mystery of the place of the *polis* in the order of nature. There is no natural hierarchy among free and equal men, so on the face of it a *polis* of equal citizens could not govern itself. All of the other relationships in nature constitute natural pairs, one part of which governs the other by nature, but this cannot be true about the way citizens organise their relations with each other. The arrangements for holding office solve this problem: because there is no naturally ruling part in a *polis* of free and equal men, they must take it in turns, ruling and being ruled. Life in a properly constituted *polis* must be according to nature because there nature ends in equality.

Aristotle thinks that taking it in turns to rule will have a moderating influence on the *polis* as a whole when it is done through law. His citizens are consumers of rule as well as producers; they will be both men of judgement and very good judges of the judgements of other citizens. Judging and being judged binds the *polis* together. No man will hold office for ever; and he knows that his stewardship will be the talk of his equals. He would avoid arrogance and would act with a certain caution; he would also watch his back. This caution in the business of law-making would tend to make law negative, perhaps a list of sensible prohibitions against those things which would make the good life impossible. The law would have a good deal to say about theft and about the breaking of promises, and it would regulate the religious life of the city. Law would provide life's framework and also life's preparation, so it would concern itself with education. Beyond that, it would probably not do very much. Aristotle is very clear about the two fundamentally different expectations that men have of a legal system, that it should be at once fixed and at the same time that it should change. Unchanging law lets us know where we stand, and knowing the law would be no fiction in an Aristotelian *polis* where all citizens would take part in making and enforcing law. On the other hand, laws which never change become an embarrassment. Aristotle's way out of the difficulty is to say that laws should change only slowly, by which he means not all at once, and should contain within themselves enough flexibility to deal with unexpected cases. Good men would try to deal lawfully with each other wherever that was possible, and it might be that in referring to unusual cases Aristotle is pointing to the necessity for ingenuity in rule through law which deals with difficult cases, another sense in which intelligence can rule without the passions.

Aristotle's rather modest claims for the rule of the law leaves a great deal in the hands of citizens. If law's claims on men's conduct are modest, then obedience to the law can only be one aspect of what it is to be a good citizen. Aristotle's citizens are to be provided with the leisure for virtue, and it would be very odd indeed if he were taken to be saying that men who do not have to make their own living only have to obey the law to be good men. The making of law and its enforcement do have an important educative effect in promoting those virtues which are essentially co-operative. *Phronesis* accepts that mistakes can be made; where there is the possibility of error there is bound to be disagreement, and so it follows that where choices have to be made about what the good life entails there has to be agreement that the best way to proceed is always to seek out what is in fact agreed upon. Relation between citizens are to be conducted on the basis of civility. They are not to be always on the lookout for what divides them. The last man Aristotelian citizens would want among them would be the supremely clever man who would always be able to see the faults and difficulties in any proposed line of conduct. That might paralyse the will to act or to choose, which is the function of a body of free men. Civility is not dialectic, not agreement to wait out an argument to the end to see what we ought to think. Rather, free men would begin from what was already common amongst them.

But what would it be, exactly, which would be common amongst them? That would vary from *polis* to *polis*, and Aristotle does not make up recipes for the formulation of good public policy, but he is very clear what all free men would bring to the consideration of public policy. The qualification for being a policy-maker is that each free citizen is already successful at making decisions in the families and other subordinate communities which go up to make the *polis*. The *polis* is already implicit in those subordinate communities because heads of households are already used to making the decisions which determine the smooth running of their own establishments. As the head of a family, the citizen already knows how to exercise different kinds of authority as a father, a husband and a master of slaves; as the head of a household he already knows how to manage a common enterprise for the benefit of all. When he meets others like himself in the public assembly he sees his *equals*, men not to be domineered over. Aristotle's is no assertion of equality in general, but of equality among equals. Free men like his would no more seek to dictate to each other than they would expect to be dictated to; civility would come naturally to them. There is always the possibility that one man among them would be outstanding, a really kingly man in something like Plato's sense. What should be done about him? Aristotle would say: exile or kill him, because he has no place in the city. Subjecting the kingly man to the rule of his inferiors, however good, is an insult to him, and subjecting good men to the kingly man, however superior, is an insult to them. The *polis* cannot exist for one man only, and to make the *polis* subject to one man would not stop at the public affairs of the city, for in the *polis* there are no private affairs in the modern sense. Everything is of public concern, so the rule of a kingly man would extend right through all the subordinate institutions of the city. Plato saw that very clearly when he said that rule by Guardians meant that everything had to be ruled by them. Rule by one man would extend to the villages and households in the Aristotelian *polis*, so that there would be no free citizens at all.

This is an important *theoretical* point for Aristotle, because to hedge about the kingly man would be to deny his own doctrine of the naturalness of the state. The thrust of Aristotle's argument is intended to proceed from what we can easily agree about, to matters which are less easy to agree about. Nobody would deny that families are natural communities, groups of families make up villages, and so it is easy to agree that self-sufficient communities are natural. The difficulty comes at the level of the *polis* itself. It is about the naturalness of the *polis* that there is disagreement among rational men. The case of the Sophists that the *polis* is merely accidental cries out to be answered in a Hellas dominated by the Macedonian Regent, Antipater, from the fortress of Acrocorinth while the Greeks are gawping with wonder at the empire which Alexander made, and when it is beginning to dawn on the Hellenes that the events which will dominate their lives are taking place not in Europe but in Asia. An imperial world is being created where all that will be required is obedience. Aristotle's claim for the naturalness of the *polis* depends on his being able to integrate communities which everyone might agree were natural into the supreme community, and one important way he does that is by showing that the subordinate communities of the family and the village produce heads of households of the kind who would naturally rule themselves on the basis of ruling and being ruled by turns. The truly kingly man is an embarrassment in the *polis* because he has a claim through his excellence to control every institution in the *polis*, and that being true, the naturalness of the progression from family to *polis* in Aristotle's scheme of things is undermined. Again, it is important to remember that 'progression' does not mean *temporal* progression here. A free citizen does not become the head of a household and *then* a full member of the *polis*; he becomes both at once. Each role feeds on and feeds the other, so that diminution in the role of free and equal citizen would diminish the role of head of a household. How could a man who is bossed about by another in the public square carry natural authority at home? He would be more likely to become a domestic tyrant, taking it out on the members of his household to pay himself back what his self-esteem had paid in public subservience, and so he would begin to unpick the carefully integrated but differentiated forms of rule which Aristotle thinks constitute properly conducted domestic life. Abuse of power in the family would take the place of authority exercised for limiting ends. Rule by even a philosopher-king would cause what power was left to other men to be exercised against nature.

NOTES ON SOURCES

In Aristotle's *Politics* everything lies in the definitions and in the details, so the text is the thing. There is an excellent, updated edition in the Penguin Classics series, and a good, new translation by Carnes Lord (1984). The body of Aristotle's work ranges very widely, and anyone wishing to take Aristotle at all seriously ought to read a version of his *Ethics* and his *Constitution of Athens (Aristotle and Xenophon on Democracy and Oligarchy*, ed. J.M. Moore, 1975). There is about two millennias' worth of learned commentary on Aristotle, most of which is best avoided because it was based on what, by modern standards, were very corrupt texts, many of them in bad Latin. Modern discussion of Aristotle's *Politics* begins from Werner Jaeger's *Aristotle* (1934, reprint 1962). See also the works of Barker and Morrall (see Chs 1 and 3, Notes on Sources). D. Ross, *Aristotle* (2nd edn, 1934), is a good example of an older tradition of Aristotle commentary, and Alasdair McIntyre, *After Virtue* (1981), is a virtuoso performance of what can still be done with Aristotle's ethics and politics.

Part II

ROMANS AND ROMAN CATHOLICS

5

FROM *POLIS* TO *COSMOPOLIS*

STOIC THINKERS

The ancient world was tolerably well stocked with Stoic sages. It has become the custom to divide the Stoa into Early, Middle and Late. We know relatively little at first hand about the earlier, and perhaps more important, Stoic philosophers, and we know a lot at first hand about the later, and perhaps less important, ones. I take Zeno to stand for the former and Cicero and Marcus for the latter, though the distinction is rough and ready. I choose Cicero, though he was not *only* a Stoic as a thinker, because everybody has heard of him, and Marcus because his *Meditations* are so easily available in English.

ZENO

Born in the Greek and Phoenician city of Citium in Cyprus in *c.* 330 BC, Zeno was already twenty-four when he made the philosophically obligatory journey to Athens. His merchant father is said to have brought home Greek books for his son, and it was enthusiasm for these which turned the boy's mind towards the philosophical life. At Athens he appears to have listened to teachers of all the current philosophical schools, in turn becoming something of a Platonist, learning something of Aristotelianism, and then 'converting' to Cynicism. He eventually taught his own philosophy in Athens in the Stoa Poikile (the Painted Colonnade), from which the name Stoicism comes. All his works are lost, and all we know of them for certain are some of their titles and references to them in later philosophical treatises. We know that Zeno taught that only the Good is really good, that nothing can take away the goodness of the wise, and that only the good man is always happy.

We know that Zeno had good Macedonian connections (through the blunt and soldierly king, Antigonus Gonatus, who, like many of the supposedly rough kings of Macedon, took an interest in philosophy), did not always suffer fools gladly despite his Stoicism, and, though never an Athenian citizen, he was enough of an object of admiration to the Athenians for them to pass a resolution in his honour when he died in 262. They also set up inscriptions in praise of Zeno to be read by the young men in the gymnasia, so in Athens he was plainly thought of as a good influence on her youth.

CICERO

Cicero's letters have survived (as he meant them to) in such numbers that we know more about him than we do about almost any other ancient worthy. We don't always like what we see, because there is very little in Cicero of that self-abnegating modesty which the rise of Christianity was to make compulsory a century or two later. Still, Cicero is not modest even by the forgiving standards of the ancient world. He always thought that he had saved the republic once, in the affair of Cataline, and that that he could do it again despite Pompey and Caesar.

Born in 106 BC, the young Marcus Tullius acquired an early familiarity with the Epicurean and Platonic philosophies. He was also heavily influenced by the blind Stoic philosopher Diodotus, who lived in the family house after 87 BC. Cicero saw some military service, met all the great men of his day and made his name as a lawyer-politician after a series of successful prosecutions in state trials, notably against Verres, the corrupt and rapacious governor of Sicily. Cicero went on to hold high offices (consul in 63). He was in the muddled and murderous politics up to his neck, and he found himself leaning against the popular party of Caesar and Crassus.

Cicero tried to retire from politics and return to the law in 57, while attempting to occupy a middle ground, which did not really exist, between Caesar and Pompey, but he submitted to Caesar after Caesar's victory at Pharsalus in 48. Perhaps he once really believed that Caesar would rule according to the constitution of the republic, but Cicero must have changed his mind pretty quickly, because word soon got round that he approved of Caesar's murder, thus earning the hatred of Antony, to whose hatred Octavian (the future Augustus) sacrificed him in the proscription of 43.

Most of the philosophy of the ancient world went through Cicero's head at one time or another. Perhaps his own philosophical development can be best explained psychologically, as the reluctant (and late) transformation, under the pressure of events, of an enthusiastic Platonist into a Stoic consoling himself with philosophy while he waited for death.

MARCUS AURELIUS

Marcus was the ideal (and idealised) philosopher-emperor, a man who would rather have spent his time at his books than at ruling the world. He was never a popular emperor; neither did he court popularity, spending his time at the Games dealing with official correspondence while the Roman *plebs* bawled for the blood of the gladiators. Marcus was so good that in *On Liberty* J.S. Mill comes close to apologising for Marcus's persecution of the Christians.

Born in AD 121, the young Marcus attracted the favour of the emperor Hadrian, the great patron of the Athenians, and Hadrian made sure than his protégé was taught by the best masters of grammar, rhetoric, philosophy and law. Antoninus Pius adopted the frank, serene and sensitive young man, who, before he was twenty-five, served in the usual high offices of a potential emperor. Marcus and Antoninus Pius were virtually co-emperors until the latter's death.

Marcus was ascetic by temperament and training (though his health was never good), a 'natural' for the Stoic philosophy of which he became an adept long before he became emperor in 161. At first, Marcus ruled with his fellow consul, Verus, who proved to be something of an embarrassment, especially as a general (his troops, returning from the East, spread the clap half-way round the Roman world). The Germans came accross the Danube frontier about the year 166, and they were well contained by Marcus, who showed himself to be a more than competent general. His aim was to stabilise the Germanic breeding-grounds north of the river, and it was when he was campaigning on the Danube that he is supposed to have written much of the famous *Meditations*. Marcus also had to cope with revolts in Syria and in Egypt, so the most famous philosopher-emperor who ever lived spent most of his imperial life making war. His duty done, he died in AD 80.

Phrases like 'the twilight of the city-state' do not do much for our understanding of what the *polis* meant in the era of Macedonian world conquest. While there has always been something touching about the idea of Aristotle's *Politics* as a kind of memorial notice for the classical city-state, we must always remember that the city-state experience did not come to an abrupt end the moment Alexander won his first battle in Asia. The Macedonian Empire is supposed to mark the end of the classical city-state because the city-state lost its autonomy once Macedonia began to dominate the affairs of Hellas. The problem with that view is that only a very idealised *polis* could have lost its autonomy because most city-states most of the time had not been imperfectly autonomous at all. It may be true that every *polis* dreamt of political, economic and moral autarky, but that perfect autarky is hard to find outside the pages of Aristotle's *Politics*. Over-concentration on the apparent freedom of action of the big states like Athens, Sparta or Thebes can lead us to ignore the frequent and effective dependence of humbler cities on the great. There was a difference, of course, between the dependence of an obscure *polis* on a famous one, and the dependence of all the city-states on an outside empire like the Macedonian, but that difference would be felt more keenly in Athens than in a *Polis* whose name nobody now remembers.

What was undeniably lost was the sense of wholeness which *polis* life provided. The *polis* gave answers to all questions about how you should live your life. In the *polis* you knew who you were. You had an identity within the *polis* and an identity in relation to members of other cities. The city-state was far from being a recipe for universal human happiness, but being miserable in the *polis* meant having missed out on something which the *polis* had to offer. The *polis* came in all shapes and sizes, and they didn't always guard the right of citizenship very jealously, so the chances were that you could always find a *polis* to fit. That was what Thrasymachus meant in the *Republic* when he said that everywhere justice was the interest of the stronger. If you did not like what the strongest party was doing in your own city, you could always try another city likely to grant citizenship to foreigners. Transfer of allegiance was a way of increasing life's opportunities, and it was those opportunities which the *polis* existed above all to provide. The *polis* was a stage for role-playing, and it could serve as a platform on the way to playing greater, pan-Hellenic roles. The Greeks came together through athletics, religion, artistic competition and war. (It was considered improper, for instance, to enslave Olympic victors who were captured in war, and nobody would lay a hand with impunity on a priest from Delphi. Sophocles ended his days in Macedon.) The *polis* catered for every possible level of human happiness and fulfilment, but it offered no guarantees. The classical Greeks knew that happiness could lie within the self, but only if all else failed.

The world empire of the Macedonians offered new kinds of opportunity. Philip and Alexander dominated Hellas, and so did some of the successor kings. They garrisoned the strategically important cities, recruited mercenaries (especially from the Peloponnese) and controlled foreign policy. In effect, the Macedonians decided who would fight whom, when. The *polis* could easily survive for a long time as a social and cultural unit within the loose framework of the Macedonian Empire. Part of the reason for this survival was that the *polis* had never been entirely itself. The *polis* was only a caricature of itself in the era of world empire if it is considered as a caricature of the truly developed *polis* of Aristotle's imagination. *Polis* life in most cities was probably not all that different from what it had always been like, and it was this continuing imperfection which enabled the *polis* to survive so long in a changing world.

The Macedonians had good reasons for keeping the Greek cities sweet – the last thing Alexander wanted was trouble back in Hellas when he was on his way to Nepal. This involved some very serious play-acting on the part of Alexander and the successor kings. Some of the Greek cities had a great reputation in the world, and their sensibilities could easily be outraged by too naked a display of Macedonian power. It was always going to be in Macedon's interest to treat prickly cities as if nothing had really changed. Alexander himself founded Greek cities everywhere. They were populated willy-nilly, but Alexander always garrisoned them with Greeks if he could (Macedonians were carefully husbanded for use as shock-troops on the battlefield). If we didn't know better, we could easily assume from their ruins that these cities had been the centres of classical city-states. Alexander took a nephew of Aristotle's with him on his conquests, partly to recite Homer to him when he was drunk and really believed he was Achilles. (This is known as Alexander's Hellenising mission in the East.) The Macedonians did not see themselves as rough pike-men from the hills, half-Greek and half-barbarian as their Greek enemies claimed. Archaeology has only recently revealed how Hellenic the Macedonian capital was in the days of Philip.

None the less, things like the survival of the blood-feud among impeccably classical columns, or the co-existence of barbarian chivalry with the latest Aristotelian learning, give some idea of what conservative and self-consciously Hellenic Greeks must have thought of as puzzling about the Macedonian character. Macedonians were not really Greek at all because they lacked the Greek senses of rationality and moderation. It must therefore have been the barbarian side of Alexander's character which succumbed to the tinsel wiles of oriental kingship. Alexander was not the first conqueror in history to fall victim to the culture of the country he conquered, and falling victim was always a sure sign of the cultural inferiority of the invader. No true Greek would have allowed himself to fall in the way Alexander did. A true Hellene would have kept his distance from barbarian Asiatics, treating them 'like plants and animals'. Nobody minded Alexander taking Asiatic concubines (or boys), but marriage to an Asian woman was quite another thing. The ancient histories make a good deal out of Alexander's adoption of eastern customs, especially *proskynesis*, the Persian prostration before the great king. This appears to have caused trouble between Alexander and Aristotle's nephew. Callisthenes is supposed to have angered Alexander by ostentatiously refusing to follow Persian custom and to have died a martyr to Hellenism. The details of the story are obscure, but what is telling is that stories like this were put about to discredit Alexander despite the obvious fact that Alexander spread the Greek language and Greek manners and morals wider than any other man.

'Hellenistic' is the word we use to refer to the culture of the world that Alexander made. No culture can exist without its element of political culture, and the political culture of Hellenistic civilisation was undoubtedly royal. For a long time, to please the Macedonian core of the army, Alexander stuck to calling himself king of the Macedonians, but nothing could disguise the fact that he was king of a great deal more. So much more, that he enrolled himself among the gods to help him keep what he had conquered. Perhaps Alexander always believed that he was of divine origin. There was no love lost between him and Philip his father, and there was not much love lost between Philip and Alexander's mother. She probably encouraged Alexander to believe that some god and not Philip was his real father. The oracle at Siwah in Egypt is supposed to have revealed to Alexander that he was sprung from the gods. As the son of Zeus, Alexander was called to do great things and this confirmed his early identification with Achilles. According to some, it was downhill all the way after Siwah for Alexander's character, so that by the time he died at Babylon in 323 at the age of thirty-two he had come to be seen as an object lesson for anyone tempted to follow his megalomaniacal path towards tyrannical domination of the world. Alexander, it has always been said, died because there were no more worlds to conquer. Therefore he must have died unhappy, and, by implication, he made others unhappy too, especially the Greeks, because their world would never be the same again.

We can never be certain about what was actually true about Alexander and what is later malicious embroidery. The case for Alexander is that he made certain political ideas possible which had never stood a chance within the morally confining walls of the *polis* classically conceived. Prominent among these is the idea of a multi-racial state. The idea comes down to us not from any self-conscious 'theory' but from a story about a mutiny in Alexander's army at Opis on the Tigris, and it is a story worth the re-telling. Discontent among the Macedonian veterans had come to a head for reasons we do not know, but their grievances were clear enough: non-Macedonians, that is Persians, had been let into the crack cavalry regiment the Companions of Alexander, had been given commands which involved ordering Macedonians about, and had been granted the (Persian) favour of greeting Alexander 'with a kiss'. The Macedonians formed up and stated their grievances, whereupon Alexander lost his temper, threatened to pension them off back to Macedonia, and distributed the vacant commands among the Persians. When both sides had simmered down, the soldiers came back to their allegiance, Alexander granted the Macedonians the favour of the kiss, and he promised to forget about the mutiny. But not quite. Alexander ordered up a feast to celebrate the reconciliation, and the religious honours were done by the priests of the Macedonians and the magi of the Persians. Alexander himself prayed for *omonoia*, concord, and persuaded 10,000 of his Macedonian veterans to marry their Asiatic concubines. And so the story ends.

The plea for *omonoia* has come to be recognised as a kind of turning point in the history of the way men thought about politics in the Greek world, and, by extension, in the western world in general. The ancient Greeks were racist in theory and practice in something like the modern sense. They divided the world, as Aristotle did, between Greeks and the rest, and their fundamental category of social explanation was race. Race determined at bottom how civilised a life a man was capable of living. The civilised life was, of course, only liveable in a properly organised city-state. Only barbarians could live in a nation (*ethnos*) or in something as inchoate and meaningless as an empire. The Greeks also seem to have had the modern racist's habit of stereotyping, which simply means going from the general to the particular: barbarians are uncivilised, therefore *this* barbarian is uncivilised. The race question was inevitably tied up with slavery, though it is by no means clear that the ancient Greeks had a 'bad conscience' about slavery, as some have claimed. From time to time, they may have felt badly about enslaving fellow Greeks, and that was probably the reason why thinkers like Aristotle troubled themselves with questions about who was most suitable for slavery and who the least. Low-born barbarians born into slavery were always at the top of the list of good slave material. Most Greeks probably believed that without ever thinking about it much.

The Macedonians may have lacked the subtlety of the Hellenes, but Alexander was no fool. Whatever the Macedonians might have thought to themselves about the races of the East, Alexander would have been asking for trouble if he had arrogantly proclaimed Macedonian racial superiority over conquered peoples, and it would have caused a snigger or two back in Hellas. What better way for the conqueror of a multi-racial empire to conduct himself than in the name of human brotherhood? Imperialism then becomes a gathering-in of the nations rather than the imposition of one nation's will upon another and this thought follows from the empire-builder's real desire: secretly, he expects to be obeyed for love. This was Alexander's way of showing that he was not a tyrant.

The idea of the tyrant had made a deep impression on the minds of the Greeks. The word 'tyrant' was itself ambiguous in the ancient world. It appears first of all to have meant someone who came to supreme power in a city by unconstitutional means, but the idea of overweening and scandalous exercise of power was soon added to the original meaning of usurpation. Aristotle tried to attach a technical meaning to the word by defining tyranny as the exercise of supreme power by one man in his own interest, by force not law. Tyranny is a degenerate form of kingship, which he defines as the rule of the best man, in the interests of all, through law. These definitions should make us pause. Aristotle does in fact spend quite a lot of time in the *Politics* discussing the various forms of kingship and, on the face of it, this may seem out of proportion granted the very low incidence of kingship in the classical *polis*. Explanations vary as to why Aristotle has so much to say about kings. Some say that Aristotle speaks of kings in the way that Samuel does, not to praise them but to warn against them. It would have been almost impossible to be a true king in Aristotle's sense. Where would such a man be found, and where was the city modest enough and rational enough to accept the claim of rulership of outstanding virtue? Others see Aristotle's treatment of kingship as a direct critique of Plato's *Republic*. The most obvious criticism of Plato's plan for rule by philosopher-kings has always been that such outstandingly talented men and women are only likely to be found in very small numbers. Is the *polis*, then, to exist simply for the sake of being ruled by the very fortunate very few? And Lord Acton has nothing to teach Aristotle about the corrupting effects of absolute power. By 'rule in his own interest' Aristotle means that the tyrant will use all the resources of his city to further his own happiness. Tyrants expected to be the happiest of men because they could do what other men could only dream of doing. (Tyrants of Syracuse were sometimes drunk as lords for months on end.)

It is, then, possible to read an anti-kingship bias into Aristotle's treatment of kingship, whether that treatment is regarded as being very wary of kingship in general or as being an attack of Plato's *Republic*. But Aristotle's contemporaries, aware as they must have been of Aristotle's Macedonian connections, might have taken a different view of what he has to say about kings. Aristotle was, after all, enough of a Greek and enough of a Platonist to believe that it was possible for a political community to produce a single outstanding man. The central place of the *agon*, the competition, in Greek political and cultural life is testimony to the fact that the ancients were interested above all in winners. There were no second and third prizes at ancient Olympia. Aristotle also believed with most Greeks that virtue was not its own reward. Unrecognised virtue was an insult to its possessor, and, in political terms, it was degrading to be ruled by men who were worse than oneself. The truly outstanding men had a real claim on the recognition of their fellows, and the outstanding men were not notorious for concealing their own light. Like Plato, Aristotle knows that outstanding talent is a political menace if it goes to the bad, but that might be all the more reason for putting talents to good use in ruling the state to prevent them going to the bad. Aristotle is careful to say that all forms of government are attended by risks. Governments of the Few and the Many are just as liable to go wrong as governments by the One. Aristotle's *Politics* can easily be read as an apology for monarchy, or at the very least for the idea that monarchy is simply another available form of rule which, like oligarchy and democracy, has its good and its bad sides.

Perhaps Alexander has an inkling of this, or perhaps he was told it all by Callisthenes. Perhaps the plea for *omonoia* was Alexander's way of showing the world that there was more to him than military prowess, that the Macedonian empire had more to offer the world than the example of successful violence. It had a mission; in the Aristotelian sense, it was *for* something. On the other hand, the mystical and ceremonial aspects of Macedonian kingship are easy to explain but very hard to explain away. We do not need the increasing megalomania of Alexander's character to account for his assumption of the attributes of oriental kingship. What better way to govern the Persians than in the manner to which they had become accustomed? (Napoleon said that if he were governing Jews he would rebuild the temple of Solomon.) The orientalisation of Macedonian kingship may have been a matter of straightforward calculation, but that is not how contemporaries saw it. What was particularly galling to some sensibilities was that Alexander and his successor kings went around pretending to be gods. This was supposed to be un-Greek, which might at first seem odd. The Greeks had always lived on familiar terms with their gods, whom they saw as sharing the world with men. The gods assumed the shapes of men and animals (and even plants) at will, and the attribution of divine characteristics to men was not all that uncommon. The heroes of Homer are god-like, occupying a place midway between the gods and men, and many cities honoured their founders as demi-gods. Why, then, was there all the fuss about the divine kingship of the Macedonians? The Greeks thought that as far as they were concerned kingship was in the past. All their thinkers agreed that kingship deriving from the headship of the family must have been the first form of rule which human beings lived under. Kingship might be appropriate to peoples still at a relatively primitive stage of their development into free and rational men, and it would always be appropriate to barbarians. But kingship was asking free and equal men to swallow too much. Either there was a man so much better than anybody else or there wasn't. Either way, the king would be a threat. If he was better than anybody else, then free citizens would be obliged to surrender their right to self-rule voluntarily to the king, an act of collective civic suicide, or the king was no better than ordinary men, in which case he ought not to be king at all. Whichever way you looked at it, kingship spelled disaster for the *polis*.

The idea of divine kingship fed on and was fed by the cult of personality carefully cultivated by Alexander. Alexander had great virtues, and he made sure that the world knew about them. Even his vices were the vices of military life long ago described by Plato: love of plunder (though he gave a lot of it away), drunkenness and an insatiable appetite for glory. Alexander was a hard act to follow, and this probably accounts for the elements of royal ritual and symbolism developed by the later Macedonian kings. The rituals which we ordinarily associate with kingship originated in an attempt to convince subjects that the powers which Alexander had by good fortune belonged to his successors by right of their kingship. All ritual separates the man from his office, implying that the virtues which do not appear in the man inhere in the office. In some mystical way, the virtues rub off onto the man who is king. Hence the magnificence of courts, and ceremonies like coronations and royal funerals. Some of this can be put down to human vanity, no doubt, but it was also designed to send out important legitimising signals. Nor should we underestimate the legitimising ties of royal blood in an age which knew nothing about genetics but which knew a good deal about horse-breeding. A king sprung from a line of kings who could be taught to act like a king was always likely to be mistaken for the real thing. The later Macedonians tried very hard to establish the hereditary principle. The successful generals who made themselves into the first generation of successor kings could claim to have a share of the *mana* of Alexander himself. Through heredity they could pass some of it on to their sons.

Ancient thinkers knew very well that kings would try to found dynasties. This was a fact of human nature as it applied to kings, and it required no special explanation. Equally obvious was the flaw in the dynastic principle. Reigning kings could not sire winners every time, and one day an absolute dud would lose the kingdom. It did not seem to matter much theoretically whether the dud was useless by nature or made useless by the corrupting temptations of power. Kingship was one of the forms of rule which would not be expected to last. This was a perception shared by Romans as well as Greeks. Yet the successor kingdoms of the Macedonians lasted until Rome took over the whole of the Mediterranean littoral, and they were the scenes of flourishing Greek culture, something which in original Greek terms they could not be. According to the best ancient authorities, only the equal members of a free citizen body were ever likely to achieve anything noteworthy. The freer the city, the greater the achievements of its citizens were likely to be. Sparta and Thebes left behind very little except memories, whereas the Athenian investment in the muses still pays dividends. The Greeks never forgot that they fought as free men against the subjects of the Persian kings, yet the Hellenistic kingdoms everywhere contained Greek subject cities which took great pride in their Greek constitutions and whose citizens thought of themselves as Greeks. And these kingdoms lasted. So what happened to the idea that the *polis* was the only form of government which could possibly accommodate the turbulent and innovating spirit of the Greeks?

The obvious answer to this question is probably the correct one: Alexander gave the Greeks opportunities on a scale hitherto unknown. Alexander's own identification with

Achilles is the clue; fame was won abroad, at Troy, and not in Hellas. At home, the heroes were little more than barnyard cocks. Odysseus's journey back to Penelope in Ithaca is so full of wonders that we are being asked not to ask what it is, exactly, that he is going back to. Penelope's suitors are going to make things tough for Odysseus, and he is going to have to be very heroical indeed to overcome them, but after that all he can do is sit in his own armchair by the fire and relive the deeds in far-away places which made him the talk of Hellas. The *polis* was too small for real deeds of fame. Everybody knew everybody else too well for anyone but the very greatest to acquire the unfeigned admiration of their fellow citizens. Prophets with honour practise their trade away from home. Private lives came under close scrutiny in the claustrophobic world of the *polis*. Everyone was everyone else's valet. The *ad hominem* attack was second nature in city politics because everyone knew what everyone else was like. What was lacking was the sense of a distance between the great ones and the rest. And if one were truly great, there was always Aristotle's warning that a man who could live outside the *polis* was either a beast or a god. (Think of the Athenian who voted for the ostracism of Aristides because he was sick of hearing Aristides called 'the Just'.) The world that Alexander made was not the end of the *polis* but its fulfilment. Greeks now had the choice of staying at home in their familiar world or of taking their chances outside. It was the difference between provincial rep and Hollywood, modest success and stardom. The extended multi-racial states created by Alexander and his successors were the safety-valves of the Greek cities, and failures could always return to them, sadder but wiser men. There was no particular reason why any but the most politically and culturally conservative should find the semi-independence of their city particularly galling, provided always that the Macedonian kings kept up appearances. Philip of Macedon's domination of Greece was covered with the fiction that he was the chosen leader of a league of independent Greek cities, for which there was ample ancient precedent. Alexander saw no reason for stripping his own power naked, sometimes posing as leader of the Greeks taking revenge on Persia, sometimes calling himself king of the Macedonians, and sometimes calling himself king of everything, king by rank, so to speak, everybody's superior.

The Greeks were hard-headed enough to accept Macedonian power as a fact in the world, and the divine honour paid to Macedonian kings even by Athens helped the Greeks to preserve some of their self-respect. What better way to reconcile yourself to overwhelming power than to say that the overwhelming power is more than human? Nobody minds being beaten by the gods nearly so much as being beaten by other men. No doubt there was a certain amount of sniggering behind the backs of saviour gods, as they tended to be called, but then the Greeks had not always taken all of their gods equally seriously. Empire had its own effect on the gods. All monarchs are monotheists at heart. If one god rules the whole universe then some of his glory rubs off onto universal kings. A very great king needs a very great god, and a very great king does a very great god no harm. This would be especially true in a world where the gods were already anthropomorphically conceived.

The Greeks had never thought of their gods as living in a *polis*. Zeus had always been king of Olympus. Like all kings, he sometimes had trouble with his subjects, and the lesser gods could sometimes frustrate his wishes by cunning. The politics of Olympus was the politics of a court. The favour of Olympian Zeus was never quite satisfactory as a support for earthly kingship because the gods were always divided over which human kings and heroes should be specially favoured. The gods took different sides in the Trojan War. The favour of the gods was almost evenly divided, and both sides knew that it was the really important gods who would decide the victory. The favour of a god was one of the things which made a king a king, but real kingship needed either one god ruling alone in the heavens, or one god before whom all the other gods and spirits would bow down. What would a god who could do these things be like? Remote, perhaps, the opposite of the intense locality the Greeks were used to attributing to their gods, but at the same time everywhere, in the same way that a great king's power was supposed to reach into the far corners of his kingdom. The best way for a god to be everywhere, while at the same time not being in any particular place, was for him to dwell in men's hearts. What king would not want to be loved by all his subjects and to be constantly in their thoughts? If god as some mysteriously universal spiritual being dwells in everybody, and if one of the things he tells everybody is to love and honour the king, then kingship is well on the way to ideological security, and the king is equipped with sound ideological motives for making sure that god's worship is never neglected.

Sceptical Greeks were never going to accept such views all at once. Even the despised orientals had never gone so far as actually to worship their kings as gods, though they had long since been accustomed to thinking of their kings as god-like. It was probably easier for the Greeks to think of kings as gods than it was to think of god as a spiritual principle ruling everywhere. Plato's Philosopher-Rulers were supposed to be in touch with divine ideas which were unchanging, but that was an exceptional view and it began late in the experience of the *polis*. The Macedonian kings knew that Greek scepticism was a force to be reckoned with. No king ever commanded a Greek city in the name of his own divinity. It was the reality of power which whipped the cities into Macedonian hegemony. The Macedonians had the sense never to try to install a cult of themselves as gods in Macedonia itself. The idea of elective warrior kingship was still useful long after Alexander was dead, and a time would come when the words 'the Macedonians' simply meant 'the army', or crack troops, no matter what their ethnic origins.

We can easily see that the emasculated *polis* still made sense in the Hellenistic world. Living in a Hellenestic *polis*, with a Greek constitution – popular assembly, council, lawcourts and all the rest – was the only way of being at home in kingdoms of millions of square miles. The kingdoms which were founded when Alexander's empire broke up lacked the organic unity which had allowed Aristotle to see the *polis* as the crowning part of nature. Crudely, the cities ruled themselves and the kings ruled the land. It was impossible to feel part of a whole in this vast world. The state became *them*, not *us*. What it meant to be Greek changed. There was no loose talk after Alexander about Persians or other foreigners sharing the rule of kingdoms with Greeks. The Greeks became a more or less closed ruling caste, the price of entry into which was Hellenisation – that is to say, complete identification with the aims and culture of conquerors. However much they might try to disguise it for reasons of prudence, the kings of the Macedonian kingdoms never forgot that Alexander had won his empire by the sarissas of the phalanx. The Ptolemies could claim to be the legitimate successors of the Egyptian pharoahs; other Macedonian rulers could invent genealogies to show that they held their kingdoms by a right derived from the gods; the diadem, the sceptre and the signet ring might dazzle some, and elaborate court ceremonial might fool others, but at bottom the kings ruled by right of conquest. That meant that it was kingship which held the state together. The body of state consisted of the king, the king's 'friends', the body of royal officials and the army, all of them foreigners, or in the position of foreigners, in a conquered land. The Greeks came to recognise this. In the second century BC Greeks stopped identifying themselves by the name of their *polis* and began to call themselves and be called 'the Hellenes', a race of men really at home nowhere.

And the kings were dynasts. They wanted their successors to rule for ever. The old Greek confidence that tyranny was only a moment in the life of a *polis* was gone. Tyranny was not just something to live through till better days. Territorially huge states, ruled from their capitals by kings, had a great future. *Polis* had given way to *cosmopolis*. Henceforward, men were going to have to stop asking themselves what it meant to be a citizen of a city, and begin to ask themselves what it meant to be a citizen of the world.

TOWARDS THE LONELINESS OF STOICISM

It is easy to see the world-view of Stoicism as a grim view of a joyless world. Great Pan was really dead. The Stoics virtually replaced the old Pantheon with a god of reason and nature whose commands applied to all living creatures. Only men were likely to disobey, but the Stoic god was in some sense a punishing god, so that the wicked should not count themselves too lucky if they escaped the punishment of men. Like all ancient philosophies Stoicism promised to show the way to happiness, but the Stoics had first to work out a consistent view of the relationship between individual men and the rest of the world in which they lived their lives. Stoicism was only one of several possible responses to the problems of living in a world coming increasingly to be dominated by great empires. One of the problems which empires posed was the simple one of deciding what was the proper status of that which the Greeks had always thought of as 'politics', attending to the affairs of the *polis*. Nobody could be entirely immune from the perception that, with the rise of Macedon, might was everywhere triumphing over right. Political philosophy as the Greeks had thought of it had been about the right way of doing politics, and one of the plain implications of Macedonian success was that Greek politics had failed. Perhaps the idea that reason and law could contain the ambitious passions of men had always been a pipedream. Might had been right all along. Cities had always been ruled by their strongest parties, so that the question of how cities should be ruled had always been academic in the worst sense. Empires based on the right of conquest and very little else taught men the real nature of things.

What was to be the place of the rational and inquisitive man in the imperial scheme of things? He could no longer pretend with any conviction that he was an active participant in the process by which decisions which radically affected his life were made. Those decisions were now made in distant capitals where he had never even been. Alexander's conquests began the process by which men were encouraged to believe that they were only consumers of government, not producers, and in Alexander's time governing decisions were being made from lands so distant that most men had never even heard of them. From now on, men were going to have to make a career out of imperial politics and to pursue it they were going to have to leave their native cities for foreign capitals. Politics was no longer part of the immediately given world of experience. The response of the Cynics and the Epicureans to this state of affairs is sometimes regarded as a withdrawal from politics, but that is partly to misunderstand the political situation in the imperial world. It was not so much that men left politics; it was more that politics left them. *Polis* politics became truly local politics, parish pump stuff, hardly worth a rational man's attention, and certainly not worth the devotion of a whole life.

The Cynics' response was to snarl at the world's attempt to impose sets of rules which were so empty of all meaning (the word Cynic derives from the ordinary ancient Greek word for dog, Diogenes' nickname. Everything which the world admired was purely arbitrary, and this principle extended to all forms of law, human, moral or divine, and it extended beyond that to everything which the world called good. The Cynics saw everything which had been part of the Aristotelian good life – wealth, wisdom, beauty, truth and virtue – as worthless in the particular social, moral and political circumstances of the altered world of empire. Perhaps the *polis* had always been worthless, its rules and values shams, but what had been the insight of a few in the past was now plain for all those to see who were not self-deluded. What is a man to do in a world all of whose rules were arbitrary? Be wise, where wisdom meant pointing endlessly to these unpalatable truths, and, above all, bear witness to the world's untruthfulness by living in defiance of the world's conventions in so far as that was compatible with human survival. Expose what we would now call hypocrisy and cant, and wait, like Diogenes, for the big moment when you could tell the ruler of the whole world that the only thing he could do for you was to get out of your light.

There may be something admirable about the isolated integrity of the wise men of Cynicism, but a life spent denying the reality of what most people called goodness could not appeal to many as a recipe for human happiness. The Epicureans went in an altogether different direction. Why not call good only those things which are pleasurable in themselves or which lead to pleasure? Aristotle himself had praised hospitality for bringing friendship to the state. Why should conviviality not provide a refuge from the world, a kind of artificial re-creation of all that was best in the life of the *polis*, without its attendant responsibilities and risks? This did not mean gluttony. Only a child or a barbarian would opt for a life of self-indulgence, and the garden of the Epicureans was not supposed to be an extension of the chocolate factory or the whorehouse. Epicureanism was a way of relaxing in a world whose political pressures were remote but sinister and whose social pressures were near and nasty. A certain acceptance of the world as it was went with a distaste for the ways it obtruded on private existence. This had important political implications in Rome, where family life had long been thought of as the life of the republic in minuscule. The household held up a mirror to the *res publica*. Public life was supposed to be a reflection of all that was best in private life, and both were the schools of Roman 'virtue'. Some of the most virtue-inspiring moments of Rome's history were moments at which a choice had to be made between the family and the state, and the heroes always put the state first. The Romans, perhaps oddly, would have put this down as much to good family training as to good state influences. The authority of Roman fathers was as stern as the authority of the public magistrates, and Roman wives and mothers were supposed to fear nothing so much as dishonour as they waited, virtuously spinning, for their men to return victorious from the wars. Contrast this with the Epicurean idea of the household as an aesthetic fortress. Roman law had always allowed the household considerable autonomy because it could be sure that what went on inside was not harmful to the republic, and Roman law could not change quickly enough to be able to intrude into private circles of aesthetic subversives. Aestheticism got itself an even worse name when the poet, actor and musician Nero became emperor, one of the few artists in history to destroy art for art's sake.

The life of aesthetic pleasure was not well suited to a city which was a world power. Rome's policy had always been martial, and Rome's constant wars with her neighbours were recognised by Roman historians as a source of Rome's internal strength. A people who were so often victorious abroad were never going to take easily to being bullied by their rulers at home, so Rome developed a system of republican government which allowed the Roman people their just share in their own government. The constitution of the Roman republic survived long enough to be a miracle of longevity, and the standard explanation for that longevity came to be that Roman government was a fortunate mixture of the three basic types of government: monarchy, aristocracy and democracy. The Roman consuls were its kings, the Senate its aristocracy, and its people and their tribunes its democracy. It was standard doctrine in the ancient world that 'pure' forms of government were not likely to last. Even the best of monarchies eventually became corrupted, self-disciplined aristocracies degenerated into oligarchies admiring only wealth, and democracies always ended up in mob rule. Rome was lucky, because in the government of the republic each part of the state tended to cancel out the vices of the other parts, leaving only their virtues. The people tempered the natural arrogance of aristocrats, the senators tempered the natural turbulence of the people, while consulship for a year was a constant reminder to the consuls that they were only temporary kings. It was left to a later age to explain exactly why the Roman republic ended up having the good, mixed government it did. It was enough for most Romans to believe that the gods favoured their city with good government because of the virtues of the Romans themselves.

Roman politics, then, was never 'theoretical' in the Greek sense. Romulus and Numa Pompilius gave the Roman people the rudiments of their laws, and the Roman character did the rest. The Romans knew long before their government was 'theorised' that good laws make good men and good men make good laws. The good laws which were Rome's internal security, and the good arms which made her neighbours fear her, were the Roman character writ large. The Greeks might be very good at talking about the connection between good character and good government, but the Romans did not have to bother much about talking about it because they were its living proof.

Not everything changed when Rome became an empire. The Roman obsession with character did not disappear the moment it became difficult to think of the government of the Roman world as an extrapolation from that character. The Romans had pretended for as long as they could that the government of Rome was the government of a city which just happened to be getting bigger, and they shared the ancient commonplace that in the government of cities individual character really counted for something. Roman law was still thought of as the law of an Italian city-state as it applied to the whole world. It can never be said often enough that Rome conquered most of the world as a city-republic which was profoundly conservative about its political institutions and processes. All the cultural pressures were on the Romans *not* to re-think their government in the way that the Greeks had always been too ready to re-think theirs. This, no doubt, allowed considerable latitude in practice for innovation in the processes of government, and it also allowed *ad hoc* solutions to the problems of governing conquered peoples to solidify themselves into institutional arrangements, but the Romans stopped being the citizens of a free republic, and became the subjects of an emperor, with their fixed political ideas largely intact.

What Stoicism did was to connect the idea of individual character to the idea of *cosmos*. Hegel calls Stoicism 'the unhappy consciousness', a cast of mind which could never feel at home in the world. For those who still see Stoicism through Hegel's eyes, the Stoics will always appear to be essentially passive in the face of the world's demands. Being 'philosophical' in ordinary language still means being Stoical, a less than open-hearted acceptance of a contingent and sometimes brutal world outside the self. Stoicism, in this view of it, is something like what we would call resignation, the recognition that 'that is the way things are'. Only the Stoic sense of duty enables the Stoic to act in the world at all. For there is a Stoic god. He does not exactly rule the universe, and he may not take much interest in the world's day-to-day affairs, but he is there to call men to their duty. Scholars have often detected a strong flavour of eastern mysticism in the god of the Stoics. (Zeno, the founder of Stoicism, is supposed to have been a Phoenician.) 'Mystical' here simply means 'other-worldly'. The Stoic god calls men to do their duty in a world where duty might otherwise be meaningless. The Stoic world is meaningless without god, but god is not in the world in any very obvious sense. Unlike the gods of the ancient pantheon, the Stoic god does not make sport with human lives, and he is not like the providential god of the Christians, who concerns himself about the fall of a sparrow.

Nor does he talk to everyone, or if he does, not everyone can hear him, because the world's voices drown him out. We would say that living in the world is to become increasingly attuned to the world's wavelengths while the airwaves become increasingly crowded. The world's noise can only be silenced by a continuous effort of will, a lifelong training of the internal ear which the Stoics called the soul. Cut off every other voice, and the remaining voice is the voice of god. The world's voices can be shrill and raucous (*vox populi*), and refusing to listen to them often involves penalties. One of the ways in which a Stoic can cut himself off from the world's voices is to cultivate an indifference to the penalties attached to the refusal to comply with what the world ordinarily tells him to do. The Stoic knows he lives in a hard-edged world, and he expects to be cut and bruised. This indifference does not come easily, and it doesn't come once and for all. The

85

Stoics, like all ancient moralists, took the idea of a moral training seriously. Keeping in moral shape meant persistently trying to do one's duty in a world which did not take it easy. The world's rewards went to the trimmers, and the trimmers could always look upon the Stoics as prigs. Being a Stoic could come very close to Plato's picture in the *Republic* of the just man living in the unjust society. The unjust man always does the good and always receives society's obloquy for his pains. Retreat from the world by suicide is always an option for the Stoic, but it is not an easy option. There are no doubt times when doing one's duty by the state is horrendous. The Stoic always knows that there are fates worse than death, and becoming evil's pawn is one of them, but the god of the Stoics frequently orders a man to stay at his post in dangerous and disgusting circumstances. Desertion by suicide may be no more than running away from the battlefield because one is appalled by the sight of blood. The Stoic has to be very certain that his suicide is not the result of weakness, that he has stuck it out for as long as he can, that it is really god who is speaking to him and not his desire for the comfort of death as an escape from the discomforts of life.

The Stoic seeks above all else to control his own life in a world in which there is no very obvious controlling moral context. In so far as the world is controlled, it is controlled by power. Apart from god, the state is the only given of human existence. As the Roman state turned itself from republic into empire, it became increasingly unclear what the state was offering in return for obedience. In the republic's best days it had been possible for the Roman people to think of its victories as their victories and its laws as their laws. Being a Roman was supposed to mean something. The people of Rome had as much right as the senate to think of the city as their city. Expansion and empire changed that. Being Roman came to mean nothing very personal. Being a Roman citizen was still a useful thing to be, but the sense of privilege was diluted when so many could claim to be citizens. When the apostle Paul claimed to be the citizen of no mean city, he was probably only thinking of his right to civil treatment under Roman law. He certainly did not mean that his primary loyalty was to the Roman state. Obedience to law was one thing, but there were other obediences which took precedence.

Law-abidingness is the most passive of virtues, hardly a virtue at all in the old Aristotelian sense. Even Roman law felt the need to clothe the nakedness of state power with a universalising moral theory. The god of the Stoics was perfectly placed to be the author of a universal moral law of which the state's law was the positive earthly expression. The Stoic god was either nature's creator or its guardian; in either case, god must mean there to be a certain universality in nature. Nature's law must be the same everywhere and apply equally to all men. The doctrine that each man has his spark of divine fire proclaimed that the differences between men could not be as important as what united them. What men had in common could be extrapolated into natural law. This could happen at the level of ordinary life as well as at the level of philosophy. The universal empire had to find room for different local systems of manners and morals. Roman law was itself unchallengeable, but the more reflective of the Roman lawyers began to notice very quickly that there seemed to be the makings of a consensus about what was just and unjust which reached to the very edges of the Roman world. A fair deal meant much the same thing in a British market as it did in the markets of the Levant. Setting aside different languages, different weights and measures, and different market customs, a kind of universal equity shone through. Perhaps this was the divine fire revealing itself in the practices of everyday life.

The doctrine of natural law fits in well with what the Stoics thought about the human world in general. In the Stoic view of it, the voice of god speaks loudest when the world's voices are silent. This is not so very different from believing that god's voice also speaks when you have thought away from manners and morals everything that they owe to particular times and local circumstances. Think away everything that is *British* about British manners and morals, and think away everything that is *Levantine* about eastern manners and morals, and what remains is common to both and is nature's and god's law. Listening to god requires at least some idea of what you are listening *for*. The Stoic assumes that the voice of god always tells us the same thing, while the world speaks with many voices. Goodness is always the same; evil is the absence of goodness, not-goodness, and, being irrational, the guises which evil will assume are not predictable. Evil is really something like formlessness in Plato's sense. Trying to conceive of an 'idea' of evil is to attribute to evil a form and a coherence which it cannot possess.

This presents Stoic philosophy with a problem which it avoids rather than solves. How is the Stoic sage, or the ordinary man trying to do his duty, to distinguish between evil and those things which are neither good nor evil, but indifferent? The remoteness of the Stoic god makes it unlikely that he will go into much detail in his inner conversations with men. Stoics are therefore urged to keep on the safe side by sticking rigidly to the good and thereby avoiding things indifferent on the off-chance that they are in fact evil. What is certain is that only the good can cause itself. Indifferent things cannot either be good in themselves or be a means to goodness. It has often been pointed out how negative a doctrine this is. The sum of evil things and things indifferent could easily add up to most of the context of human life, or perhaps even all of it. The dry, negative goodness of the Stoics appears to exclude all of the things which have been called 'good' without meaning that they are part of moral goodness. The ancient sense of the goodness of 'the good things of life' formed no part of Stoic sensibility, and this would extend to what the ancients had always thought of as the just rewards of virtue. Physical strength and beauty (the results of ancestral good breeding), riches and fame were supposed to come within the category of indifferent things. Yet we know perfectly well that the class of rich and noble Romans among whom Stoicism flourished were not in fact indifferent to the good things of the world. Seneca was a usurer who built many palaces, Marcus sired the monster Commodus, and everybody knows that the more Cato shunned fame the more famous he became. Facts like these may be taken as evidence either that the Stoic ideas were very hard to live up to, or that the Stoic was supposed to take a particular attitude to the good things that came his way. Rich, noble and famous Stoics were not necessarily hypocrites, though they seem to have been pretty successful at avoiding the condition of slavery which they all agreed was in itself no obstacle to the virtuous life. Perhaps the proof that the Stoics were indifferent to the good things which surrounded them was the equanimity with which they could face their own deaths.

Some commentators prefer to call Stoicism a world religion rather than a philosophy, noting that, like all religions, it changed over time. Not everybody changes their minds at the same rate, if at all, when belief systems change, so that at any one time you would expect to find lots of different beliefs and opinions calling themselves Stoic. Stoicism lasted as a major belief system in one form or another for six or seven hundred years, from Aristotle's day to the days of St Augustine and beyond, so that anything one says of a general kind about Stoicism must be very general indeed and subject to many particular qualifications and exceptions. The picture is made more difficult to draw by the fact that the works of the founders of Stoicism exist only in fragments or in later compilations whose accuracy we have no particular reason to trust (or to mistrust). It does not matter much whether we call Stoicism a religion or a philosophy, because the distinction only becomes important with Christianity's insistence on the difference between itself and the learning of the pagans. If the distinction between religion and philosophy meant anything before Christianity, it meant the difference between how the vulgarly credulous majority and the learnedly discriminating majority thought about the attainment of the ends of life. Christianity differed from ancient philosophy because the simplicity of vulgarly credulous minds saved them from the sin of intellectual pride, so that their hearts could open easily to the simple truth of the gospels. Ancient philosophy and religion (and Christianity itself, for that matter) were at one in agreeing that the purpose of both was happiness (*eudaemonia*). Ancient superstition tried to propitiate the present by meticulous sacrifices and tried to see the future in the entrails of goats, but superstitition agreed with philosophy that the successful pursuit of happiness depended on having a particular kind of knowledge. Stoicism agreed, but insisted that only the good could lead to happiness. Virtue ceased to be a component of the good life but became the good life itself. Virtue still meant the practice of virtue, and virtue could only be practised in the world of other men. It was this determination to do his duty which anchored the Stoic in the present.

The Stoic philosophy had other consolations besides the knowledge that one was trying to do what god wanted, and chief among these was the knowledge that one had other company besides god. Ever since Zeno, Stoics had thought of themselves as belonging to an invisible city of the wise. This secret society was universal. Place and numbers did not matter to it. The city of the wise did not have to be a face-to-face society because membership was spiritual and not political. It was the thought which counted, not the deed. Membership of the invisible church of the Stoics required no outward signs, no ritual, and no prescribed patterns of behaviour. You just knew, and god knew, that you were part of the city. The extent of the city encompassed the whole world and beyond. Unlike the ancient city-state, the members of the city of the wise might be scattered to the ends of the earth, but a city it would still be. The invisible church of the Stoics was a true city within an empire, but it would be quite wrong to see anything subversive in this. The city of the wise and the Roman Empire were in no sense rivals. How could they be when they existed in different worlds? The Stoics almost, but not quite, managed to achieve what is usually attributed to Machiavelli – the separation of morality from politics. The Stoic lived in two worlds simultaneously: in the city presided over by the one true god of nature and reason, and in the Empire containing many gods, one of whom might be Caesar. There was no reason in principle why god and the idols should not each be content with their own particular spheres. Their cities existed on different levels of experience, so there was no reason to suppose that they would ever declare war on each other. There was none of that contiguity which made Jove, the lord of the land, sometimes fight Neptune, the lord of the sea, which made Athens fight Sparta, and which made Rome fight her neigbours. The only possible way for the two cities to come into conflict is in the minds of Stoics. The Stoic, being a member of two cities, must live his own inner life on two levels. The Stoic state of mind is in a state of vertical contiguity. When god commands the Stoic to do his duty to the Empire, the Stoic is effectively being asked to move down a level in his own mind and become a true citizen of the earthly city for a time.

Suppose that on a particular occasion he cannot make the descent. The imperial city can look very uninviting, and sometimes it resembles a theatre of horror. A Stoic might refuse even to come to the play, let alone play a part in it. His solution to his difficulty (I say 'his', but there were some notable women Stoics at Rome) is internal emigration by suicide. Suicide is the Stoic's way of taking up permanent quarters in the city of the wise. The city of the wise fights no battles, so it can never be put to the sword; containing only the wise it can never be divided against itself, because those who enter it already possess and love the wisdom which alone can create equality and therefore unity.

Perhaps calling the Stoic the city of the wise and 'invisible church' is to see Stoicism too much through the eyes of Christianity. However, there has to be something which explains the extraordinary success of Christian proselytising among the Roman upper classes at the end of the ancient world, and perhaps this is it. It is something of a commonplace in the history of ideas to say that one doctrine prepares the way for another, but it might be true for the Stoic doctrine of the city of the wise and the Christian doctrine of the true and invisible church. What Stoicism lacked was any sense of the visible church. The basic assumptions of the Stoics made it very difficult for them to champion any earthly institution with enthusiasm. A universal empire ruled according to law and presided over by a good Stoic emperor was about as much as a Stoic could hope for, and he would expect all kinds of fallings-off in the details of political life. Not the least of St Augustine's later achievements was to be able to give an account of the Church as an institution which was anchored in the fallen condition of man but which was also set fair on its course to the divine.

Augustinianism made better sense of Stoicism than the Stoics ever did. Augustine's clever mind managed to weave together the visible and invisible churches, and the state, into a single theory which justified all three, and he did this by ranking them in a value-order which put the earthly state at the bottom but with its authority completely intact. Augustine diminishes the significance of the Roman Empire, or any other earthly city, but does not diminish the legitimacy of its power by so much as a drop. Of course, the Stoics accepted the Empire, but that acceptance was always grudging, and, as far as the Stoics could see, the state was so provisional that its workings in everyday life would test the patience of a saint. The state as it actually existed was hard to fit into any divine plan, and that in itself justified the Stoic retreat into a quiet and manly despair. Augustine was quick to point out that all paganism lacked a convincing account of the connection between god-in-the-world and god as existing externally. Stoicism could only make that connection into an intensely private affair of inner voices in intermittent conversation. This effectively wrote off a good deal of human experience as meaningless. The Stoic world was riddled with godless interstices which were not theorisable at all. What Christianity in its Augustinian version did was both to extend and to particularise god so that there were no gaps left. Augustine's god filled out the eternal and the particular. He lived outside time while living every second of it. Perhaps one can see in this how dependent Stoicism was on the Roman Empire. For the Stoics, a world without the Empire would be almost completely unintelligible. What structure would it have? What could god mean by telling you to do your duty if that duty fitted into no recognisable pattern of duties as they existed in the universal empire? Stoicism did in fact need the Empire to make sense of the world at all. Augustine was able to see beyond the Empire: Christianity could still make sense of a world without emperors.

NOTES ON SOURCES

Alexander's star-quality shines just as brightly today as it did on his contemporaries. The historians seem unable to keep away, not to mention the poets, the dramatists and the novelists. Much of it is hagiography (and much of it is fun). A starting point might be Arrian's *Life of Alexander the Great*, trans. de Seligncourt (1962). W.W. Tarn, *Alexander the Great* (1948, 2 vols; reprint 1979), is for paddling about in. R. Lane Fox, *Alexander the Great* (1975), manages to be racy and scholarly at the same time. Some useful snippets of documents are to be found in Ernest Barker, *From Alexander to Constantine* (1956).

My treatment of Stoicism is scandalously brief for a world religion which lasted for six centuries. A.A. Long, *Hellenistic Philosophy* (1974), which follows his *Problems in Stoicism* (1971), is still the best introduction to its subject. E.V. Arnold, *Roman Stoicism* (1958), retains its share of Horatian gold. A recently published Stoic text is *Cicero, On Duties*, eds M.T. Griffin and E.M. Atkins (1991).

6

CHRISTIAN COSMOPOLITANISM
St Augustine's *City of God*

ST AUGUSTINE

Augustine wrote a celebrated apology of part of his life, the *Confessions*. The man protests too much. Augustine does not appear to have been a pleasant man, unless you have a taste for people like St Paul or Rousseau, who believe that confession of past sins is proof of present virtue. None of that can affect Augustine's standing as one of the most influential thinkers who ever lived. If anyone ever constructed a world-view which made a world, then Augustine did.

He was born in North Africa (then a Roman province) in AD 354 of a pagan father and a Christian mother (who eventually became St Monica), and his family was just able to provide him at Carthage with the education necessary to slip young men of modest origins into the imperial service. Augustine claims to have spent a sinful youth, but it wasn't *that* sinful. All it really amounted to was the theatre, a mistress and a touch of the Manichaean heresy.

Augustine began as a teacher of rhetoric (the 'classical' education of the day), and moved to Milan in 384 to further his career. It was there that he encountered neo-Platonism for the first time; heard the celebrated bishop of Milan, Ambrose, preach; and began to read St Paul. From the neo-Platonists he learned just how difficult it was going to be to persuade educated men that the word was made flesh; from Ambrose he learned that Scripture could be read symbolically (some would say 'twisted') to mean things beyond the literal meaning of the text; and from Paul he took those views about sexuality and sin which ever since have been damaging people's lives in the Catholic world.

Having been baptised by Ambrose in 387, Augustine went into monastic retirement at Thagaste in Africa, and it was only reluctantly, by his own account, that he gave in to local demands that he become first a priest and then Bishop of Hippo in 395. It was there that he defended the Catholic Church against heresy, especially Donatism, and after 410 wrote *The City of God*. Augustine managed all this while busy at his other episcopal duties. He remained at Hippo for the rest of his life, dying there in 430 while Hippo was under siege by the Vandals.

THE MAN, THE MIND AND THE PROBLEMS

Commentators sympathetic to Augustine praise his intellectual and spiritual honesty; hostile critics can only see intellectual and moral ruthlessness. Everyone agrees that Augustine's was a remarkable mind, and that it was remarkable because it never stood still. It comes as no surprise to us that Augustine saw human life as a pilgrimage, an odyssey of many twists and turns of a mind of many devices and many sufferings. Augustine was not modest, despite endless protestations about his Christian humility. Augustine's *Confessions* are meant to be more than the account of one man's spiritual journey. The story of Augustine's soul's progress from profanity towards grace is supposed in some sense to be everyman's own journey. As in Rousseau's *Confessions*, the story of one man's life stands for all humanity's loss of its sense of direction. The hero, by now as ungodly as Odysseus was god-like, confronts a moral world which is as hostile as it is meaningless. Rational men are increasingly at a loss about what to believe. Augustine's world is a world of competing loyalties. Study of the pagan authors could still elevate the mind and lead to official positions of considerable emolument, but four centuries' worth of Christianity had offered other things which a rational man might find equally attractive, a joy notably absent from Stoicism, for instance, or love for one's neighbour or resurrection.

Paganism and Christianity were no longer the stark alternatives they once were. Since Constantine, the Roman Empire had won its victories under the sign of the cross. Christianity had gone through its stages of being an intermittently persecuted religion, a tolerated religion, an officially encouraged religion, and then the official religion. Being a Christian had originally been risky; now there was a Christian bandwagon. The Church had become part of the nature of human things: where Rome was, there would the Church be. The problems of an official Church were far more complex than the problems of the persecuted Church. The heroic days of semi-clandestine evangelism and public submission to the sufferings imposed by persecutors gave way to a time when the Church could afford the luxury of quarrelling with itself. Questions about what the Church was and was supposed to be were now not so easily answered as they had been in the early days. And like other institutions, the Church had to settle questions about property and place. Who should be a bishop had become an important question, and who should be the senior bishop would become a very important question indeed. Bishops did not always see eye to eye with each other, and in disputes they were not always scrupulous about the weapons they used. Disputes about jurisdiction could easily shade over into quarrels about ecclesiastical organisation and into dog-fights between the orthodoxy and heresy. Matters which we can easily divide with hindsight into the separate matters of discipline, ecclesiology and theology did not always appear to be so clearly separate to the protagonists.

The Church in the late fourth and early fifth centuries was faced with one large question which manifested itself in any number of particular disputes: What was to be the relationship between the Church and the Empire? Earlier Christians had not exactly enjoyed being persecuted (though Augustine himself had to get quite sharp about the unhealthy cult of martyrdom), but being persecuted could only strengthen the Church's sense of itself as a body whose chief concerns were other-worldly. Other-worldliness did not imply that the

Church necessarily had to live as the world's victim, but the persecutions did mean that the question of what the relationship should be between the world and its powers could not rise in any doctrinally very important way. Once the problem of what the proper Christian attitude was to persecution had been settled, the Church could settle into a posture of charitable submission and would try its best to love its enemies. A Christian Empire, on the other hand, raised questions which it was impossible to ignore.

Not all Christians had been equally staunch during the bad times. Many had foresworn the faith and had crept back into the Church when the danger was over. Some traitors (*traditores*) had even handed over the sacred texts to the imperial authorities, and they too had crawled back asking forgiveness. Could the backsliders ever be considered as true members of the Church? Could the Church which readmitted them itself be called 'true'? This was a special problem in Augustine's own province, Africa, which already had a long tradition of ecclesiological purism. African Christians had long held that the Church, or at least the priesthood, should hold itself apart from the world's corruptions, constituting the state within the state which the old persecutors had feared. For the purists, 'Catholic' meant 'whole' in the sense of pure. The Catholic Church was whole in our biblical sense of making whole, of casting out devils and other impurities injurious to health. The Donatists hated fair-weather Christians and would insist on re-baptism as the least that the wandering sheep should be required to undergo before they were allowed back into the fold, and even then the welcome would be restrained.

Donatism appeared to be on strong ground when it came to the question of what the Church's relationship to its erstwhile persecutors should be. What enraged the Donatists, who had suffered for the faith or had been willing to suffer for it, was that some parts of the Church found jumping on the imperial bandwagon so easy. It was even more shameless than pretending that the persecutions had never happened. Certain bishops, who should have known better, were actually hailing the Empire as the divinely inspired agent of the eventual triumph of Christianity. Since Constantine, they argued, the imperial and ecclesiastical missions were all but indistinguishable. Imperial propaganda had not been slow to see the advantages which came from elevating the emperor so high that he appeared to be nearer to Christ than to other men, and the cult of Constantinople as the Virgin's specially protected city came close to implying that Christ and the emperor were brothers. What kind of times were we living in, the Donatists asked, where reversals like these could happen overnight?

The question of time was trickier than one might at once suppose. Christians had always had a sense of history which was fundamentally different from the pagan sense. It was not so much that sacred history attached overwhelming importance to events like the crucifixion which figured not at all in profane history, though that was different enough. Rather, sacred history was the history of specially privileged men and women, some of whom had looked God in the face, had been directly commanded by him, and some had even seen Christ die and had talked to him afterwards. The Gospel emphasis on the truth of Old Testament prophesy as revealed in the New meant that there was an unbroken chain of divine causation reaching back from the present life of Christ's Church to events which had truly happened 'In the beginning'. A special place was reserved in the story of God's providence for the martyrs of those times when sacred and profane history met in blood. The attribution to the Empire of a divine mission abolished for the future distinction between sacred and profane history. African Christianity, with its tradition of keeping the Church at arm's length from the world and its ruling institutions, was never going to take kindly to the new dispensation, even when the Empire's future looked very secure. The shock of the sack of Rome by Alaric and his Goths in 410 threw the question of the relationship between Church and state back into the melting pot. Christians had long been taught that the kingdoms of this world, unlike God's kingdom, were subject to corruption and death, but that was Sunday talk. In everyday life, nothing was easier to assume than that Rome would last for ever, perhaps even till the Second Coming. Rome's longevity, perhaps even Rome's increasing greatness, was a fundamental assumption with those who were keenest that the Church should throw in its lot with the Empire. Rome in 410 gave them pause. Rome had been sacked before, sometimes even by her own armies, but this was different. It began to dawn on acute spirits that Rome had a 'western' problem, and the political events of the fifth century were to bear this out. Three-quarters of the way through that century the Roman Empire had ceased to exist in the West. Gibbon's *Decline and Fall of the Roman Empire* had finally begun.

Historians no longer look at the Empire through Gibbon's eyes as declining over a thousand years, but we can still agree with Gibbon that in the fifth century the Empire in the West was a shaky investment. Augustine's *The City of God* shows how big an investment Christianity already had in the Empire. Christ's Church was the path to a kingdom which was in many ways the Roman Empire turned upside down. The Christian heaven was a utopia, and, like all utopias, it bears an upside-down, mirror-inverted relationship to its own contemporary world. Like the Roman Empire, the Church was universal and its heaven offered the immorality which the Romans had thought came only from fame or deification. God ruled in heaven in a way which could be glimpsed in the rule of an ideal prince. Paganism had always thought of the ideal prince's rule as being like the rule of the head over the body, of the intelligence over the desires, a co-operation so natural that it ruled out disobedience and the use of force to compel obedience. Contrast the earthly empire, barely able at times to contain the tumults of unruly desire or to satisfy the monstrous lusts of its tyrants. Heaven, where everybody triumphs and everybody is deified, makes every saved soul an emperor. The equality of souls in eternal bliss makes the earthly happiness of emperors pitiful by comparison. And if the good fortune of emperors is not the way to happiness, then what is to be said of the laborious lives of ordinary men? Most of them had no hopes at all of terrestrial happiness, while in heaven even erstwhile slaves could be happier than kings.

In *The City of God*, Augustine tried to imagine what difference a world without Roman dominion would make to the Christian view of things. This is by no means to attribute to Augustine the view that Rome was about to collapse. Rome would no doubt recover, but it was as well to remind the faithful that God was a taker-away of kingdoms, and that Rome, like the empires of the Scriptures, would also pass away. The Church was to be in an important sense the Empire's successor state, and, compared with God's kingdom, what did the sack of Rome matter? The Church's history was guaranteed because it was founded by the expressly declared intention of Christ. Rome had as her foundation the carnal lust of dominion. Augustine turns the catastrophe of the sack of Rome neatly round by asking: Why did Rome last so long? rather than: What has Rome done now to deserve her fate? Christians had believed since Paul that the powers that be are ordained by God. Nobody could deny that Rome had lasted a very long time. Augustine's explanation is very classical. He compares the present state of the Empire to Rome as she once was. Cicero defined a true commonwealth as a body of men united in their love of virtue. Rome was once a true commonwealth: witness the patriotism of the republican heroes. Augustine lays his flattery on the old heroes so thick that they begin to look like Christian martyrs. But nothing lasts in this world, and antique virtue was corrupted into the Rome of the Caesars.

It takes some effort of the imagination for us to understand what the sack of the city must have meant to Romans in late antiquity, but it is only after we have made that effort that we can possibly begin to realise the intellectual audacity it took for St Augustine to say that the most important event conceivable did not matter all that much. Augustine was going to have to take a very long view of the matter if the importance of the sack of Rome was going to be minimised, and that could only be *sub specie aeternitatis*. Rome was corrupt anyway, and Rome's gods had not helped her in her hour of need. Those pagans who went around saying that Rome's misfortunes had been caused by the desertion of the old gods in favour of Christianity simply failed to understand Rome's own history. It was the virtues of the old Romans which had found favour with the one true God and which had caused Rome's prosperity. The Romans may have thought that they were praying to gods, but in fact they were either praying to devils or to themselves masquerading as gods. Whichever it was, those whom the Romans called gods could not do in Rome's adversity what they had not been able to do in her prosperity. Early Roman history had its instruction for Christians. The self-sacrifice of the heroes of Roman patriotism could serve as an example to the Christians. If Rome was worth such sacrifices, then how much more does the city of God deserve them. No doubt, Rome was allowed to prosper partly because of the example her fortunate days could give to later generations, and, no doubt, Rome's present troubles were meant by God as a terrible warning of what would eventually happen to the wicked.

Rome was as much a cultural as a political fact. Paganism was still alive. Augustine's own father had been a Christian convert from paganism. Paganism was more than just a religion (and even to call it *a* religion is misleading, when paganism comprehended so many disparate beliefs and cults). Paganism was a whole culture, and to attack it was to try to re-shape the structure of men's minds, to change their minds in the broadest and most literal sense of the term. Augustine set out to do that from the heart of pagan culture. He had received the standard literary education of the day and could have expected to rise in the imperial service. He was a teacher of rhetoric, classical education at its most classical. Classical education, then as now, could be blamed for narrowness, but what it lost in narrowness it gained in thoroughness. Augustine knew his pagan authors (though he knew his Greek authors second-hand), so that when he confronts the bias and half-truths of the pagan philosophy with the truths of scriptures, he is not so much attacking paganism from the outside as filling the empty heart of paganism with the Bible. It is doubtful whether a change such as this is even possible. One man cannot change a world of ideas by himself, though he can signal that a world of ideas is coming to its end.

One of the ways in which Augustine softens the blow caused by the proclamation that a world of ideas is over is to preserve as much of the passing world as he can. He is ruthless in his insistence that paganism as a philosophical creed has manifestly failed to deliver on its promise to show men the way to happiness. Even paganism at its best, by which Augustine means Platonism as expounded by Plotinus, can neither show that the wise are truly happy nor that the supposed happiness of the wise is permanent. No pagan doctrine of happiness can possibly succeed where Platonism has failed. None the less, Augustine's own moral and political doctrine is saturated with Platonism and is unthinkable without it. This is not, perhaps, how Augustine himself saw the matter. Augustine scholars have distinguished between an earlier Augustine who saw Christianity as the fulfilment of all that was best in paganism, and a later Augustine who saw Christianity as a denial of everything which paganism stood for. The earlier Augustine saw the mind's engagement with the Platonic Form of the Good as a higher reflection of a late but still intermediate stage of the soul's longing for God. Conversion to Christianity was the last stage of human enlightenment, the nearest a human soul could come to God this side of the grave. The Augustine who thought like this could see no contradiction between Platonism and Christianity, and it was even possible to begin to see Platonism as a necessary stage on the philosophical path towards seeing the light. (I say a necessary stage on the *philosophical* path towards Christianity because there were paths to it which had nothing to do with philosophy.) Under the influence of his reading of Paul's Epistles, Augustine later came to see paganism as being so impregnated with the carnality of a world that had denied Christ, that he dropped the idea that there was a connection between the Platonic and the Christian views of the soul. But how far Augustine succeeded in ridding himself of his Platonism is another matter. What is not in dispute is the adroitness of his use in *The City of God* of an existing philosophical language to undermine the most cherished positions which that language had originally been developed to expound. Even then, there are still glimmers in *The City of God* of his earlier position with regard to Platonism, as for instance in his admission that the Platonists had at least some idea of the problems associated with the idea of the soul's immortality, however confused their thinking about the solutions to those problems might have been.

And it must always be said in Augustine's favour that he is prepared to take paganism on where paganism is at its philosophically most coherent. Much of Augustine's attack on Roman religion rarely rises above the level of smear journalism and the scoring of cheap debating points. Here his attitude is hard to distinguish from the ancient aristocratic (and Gibbonian) opinion that only fools and plebeians could believe such rubbish. But Augustine's erstwhile Platonism never betrays him into the exclusive intellectual elitism of Plato. Augustine is a radical because he never doubts that there is a form of knowledge superior to the Platonic Idea of the Good which is accessible by God's grace to those same fools and plebeians which Platonism excluded. This must have been a very startling claim. The stupidest Christian was wiser than the wisest of those who had either never known Christ or refused to recognise him. There was one way through Christ to God. Christianity is above all a *revealed* religion, and not an intellectual construction on propositions about the world. To put this another way, Augustine's Christianity as it is expressed in *The City of God* is a religion for those who are already of a religious disposition and who are dissatisfied in ways they cannot always explain with the religion which they already profess. Augustine's sense of audience is very acute. In *The City of God* he is addressing men who have been forced to think about their religion by events in the world. These are men who already know what religion is *for* but who are beginning to feel that their own religion is no longer adequate to the purposes for which all religion exists.

Augustine is walking several tightropes at the same time. The African problem meant that any view of the Church which he took had to be pure enough to satisfy African sensibilities but not so pure as to exclude too readily those who had abjured the faith and asked to be forgiven. He had to take a view of the state which downgraded Rome's vulnerability in the face of its barbarian enemies without writing the state off as having no importance at all in men's affairs. Augustine had to take a long view of human experience without diminishing the importance of that experience to the point where nothing in this life mattered. Augustine's Christianity was not a matter of giving up on life but of seeing life as it truly was, and that meant seeing it in every possible perspective. A Christian life viewed *sub specie aeternitatis* was a life lived with the special intensity which came from the possession of a knowledge which was very special and at the same time promised to everyone.

Above all, Augustine was keen to make men know what it meant to live life in a society. The problem for Christians was not what city to want to belong to, or whether not to belong to any city at all. Augustine was always classical enough to believe that, at bottom, all human problems centred round questions about what membership of human groups entailed. Like Aristotle, he believed that a failure to do one's duty was really a failure fully to understand the implications of membership of a society. In the modern idiom, human failure was always more or less a failure to play a role properly. But the days of Aristotelian citizenship, with its harmony of the roles of father, manager of a household, and a citizen, were over. It had never been clear in what sense the universal empire of Rome could be a proper city in the ancient sense. Calling a whole empire by the name of a single city could not hide the fact that Rome could not be a society in the ancient and hallowed sense because there were no terms of association except obedience to Roman law. The Empire was no association of free men who agreed what the virtues were and how they ought to be practised. Aristotle had pointed out long ago that obedience to the law was not enough to make a man a good citizen, any more than avoidance of offences against military law made a man a good soldier.

The men of late antiquity were men of divided loyalties, and loyalties to family, city, province and empire did not always sit easily together. Christians added loyalty to the Church, which was itself often divided, and to the eternal city, the Christian Rome, which all Christians hoped to enter in triumph. Augustine's political theory tries to sort out what membership of all of these different cities means. This is a difficult thing to do while living in a world where all the cities exist on top of each other. For Augustine, the secular world is complicated precisely because it is not given to men to know exactly where the boundaries between the different cities lie. Christians were constrained to believe that the city of God and the city of the damned will only be completely distinguishable from each other after the last judgement, but the details of eschatology are only partially revealed to men. Certain it is that saved and damned souls live together in human societies where even the good must still live partially blinkered lives. The scriptures tell us enough to be certain that the heavenly city is the city to strive for, but God's method of election to it is ultimately mysterious.

This had profound implications for the visible Church. It too would have to be a community of the good and the wicked, because to decide who was which according to some final standard of judgement was to usurp the judgement of God. What was true of the Church was *a fortiori* true of the state. The state could not simply be identified with the city of the devil because the state too contained its share of the good. The state can no more be completely identified with the devilish city than the Church with the heavenly city. There was, of course, a difference between the Church and the Empire, but that difference was never going to be simple. What was desperately needed was an account of how membership of the different cities affected each other. Church and Empire, heavenly and devilish city added up to four societies of which men could be members, with each man being a member of at least two. Christians were members of three, Church, Empire and one of the cities which were to last for ever. Nothing could remotely compare in importance with the question of which a Christian was going to spend eternity in. No Christian could ever say anything except that he wanted to spend eternity with God, but this did not necessarily make clear what his relations to the ecclesiastical and secular powers on this earth should be. Augustine's *City of God* was written with this problem at the forefront of his mind.

THE HEAVENLY CITY

For Augustine, what we call human history is only a moment in the divine scheme of things. God's reason for creating what we call space and time is not all that clear. What is certain is that there was a time, so to speak, when time itself did not exist, and it is equally certain that there will come a time when time itself comes to its end. Like the ancient philosophers, Augustine cannot think about time without associating it with change. God himself never changes. Time, therefore, is meaningless to him, but he did create time, and he must have done it for a purpose. Something must have happened which made the Creation necessary. The trouble probably began with the revolt of the fallen angels against God. Augustine is very evasive about the motive for the fallen angels' rebellion, but that was the moment when the city divided between the good and the bad. Again, Augustine is not very clear exactly why God made the Creation. Any attempt to know God's mind is attended by the possibility of impiety, because to know God's mind in its entirety is probably a blasphemous attempt to be like God. However, it is probable that God created man and told him to multiply in order to recruit enough saved souls to repair the original damage done to the heavenly kingdom by the fallen angels' revolt.

The original condition of man's soul was innocence. By nature, therefore, the soul is good. Augustine is adamant that good precedes bad. Bad has no independent existence; it is simply a falling away from God. Goodness, doing what God wants you to do, is always the same, whereas evil takes on as many forms as perverted human ingenuity will allow. The soul longs for its natural home, the heavenly city, and the heavenly city will be complete after the last judgement, when the last saved soul enters the city in triumph. There is, properly speaking, no 'after' after the last judgement, because nothing ever changes any more. In the language of the old pagans, the heavenly city is a city of being, not becoming. Eternity is now and for ever. So the burning question is: How do we tell who is saved and who is damned? Some human beings are destined for the heavenly city and some for the sinful earthly city which will exist for all eternity. The form of the Gospels committed Augustine to a rigid determinism. The Gospels emphasise the coming of Christ as the fulfilment of prophecy: God and certain privileged persons called prophets knew all along that one day God would make himself flesh and dwell among men. If God knew all that beforehand, then he surely knows the identity of all the eventual members of the heavenly city. God's foreknowledge creates notorious difficulties for Augustine's doctrine of the freedom of the will. How can the will be free, if God knows beforehand who is going to choose the thorny path to the heavenly city and who will go the easy way to the everlasting bonfire? Evil must be the result of human will, otherwise Augustine would be trapped into saying that God can create evil, or that evil is co-eternal with good, the heresy of the Manichees. Perhaps the faith requires us to believe in both God's fore-knowledge *and* free will. That is asking a lot, but then Augustine never says that dwelling in the faith is going to be easy.

God knows who is saved and who is damned, but men do not. The good and the bad live together higgledy-piggledy in the world. What strikes the observer first about the world is its sinfulness. Nobody can escape the consequences of Adam's fall. We come into the world in slimy and disgusting circumstances (*inter urinam et faeces nascemur*), and we arrive already equipped with a will capable of evil. The sinful world caters to all tastes. The original sin was to entertain a forbidden desire. Augustine makes sexual lust stand for all the lusts of the flesh. (Speculative commentators have always remarked how 'Freudian' Augustine is about sex, without recognising how 'ancient' about sex Freud knew himself to be.) Like the best of the pagans, Augustine recognises the hopeless self-destructiveness of a private life lived only to satisfy desires, and no-one believed more than he did in the ancient commonplace about the public blood-letting required by a tyrant's master passion. (Book IX of Plato's *Republic* was required reading in Nero's Rome.) Even a Christian fool could see that a Christian-persecuting monster of an emperor was not a very likely candidate for the heavenly city (though the example of Paul means that you can never be entirely sure), so why does God allow him to decide the fate of nations?

Augustine's answer is complex because his whole view of the state as it actually exists depends on the answer. Augustine asks us to imagine what life would be like without the coercive power of the magistrate. What would the Roman Empire be like without Roman law? No matter where we look, in the street or in the Scriptures, the answer is the same: life without the state would be unbearable. Augustine's social pessimism is complete: what is to be done with a world in which even the saved souls are sinful? We sometimes forget that the New Testament's emphasis on forgiveness is paid for by re-emphasising the sinful-ness which makes it necessary that God's forgiveness should be so widely available. If the good cannot be trusted, then what of the wicked? Augustine shares with the ancient Greeks an awareness of the possible extent of the anti-social effects of the pride and lust of even one or a few individuals. The ancient sense of the disruptiveness of pride is usually attributed to the cheek-by-jowl nature of the social life of the ancient cities. The wicked-ness of one or a few really could cause a lot of trouble in cities where everybody lived in everybody else's pocket: there just wasn't the social space available to absorb the shock-waves of *hubris*. Augustine extends the ancient obsession of the *polis* with neighbourliness to the whole world. Understanding the social state of fallen man is simply a matter of extrapolation from the fact of the universal pervasiveness of sin. The only man who never sinned was Christ. The difference between the most sinful man and the saint is as nothing when compared with the difference between Christ's perfection and the goodness of the best of men.

What applies to subjects must apply equally to sovereigns. The difference between the best and the worst of the earthly powers is as nothing when compared with the difference between God's rule over the heavenly city and the rule of the best prince over the best of the earthly states. And again, the rule of the worst prince over the worst earthly state is nothing compared to the hell of the devil's rule over his own. The search for a perfect prince to rule over the perfect city on earth is bound to be fruitless, but this is far from saying that Christianity has nothing to say to the lords of the earth. Part of Christianity's radicalism consisted in the insistence that emperors could expect only the same rewards in the afterlife as their subjects, and, more humbling, they were to be subject to the same punishments. Augustine echoes Plato's refusal to believe that princes must be the happiest of men, as the poets claim, because they can have 'everything they want'. Princes are undoubtedly different from other men, but only because they have greater scope for doing good and evil. The pre-Christian Roman emperors thought themselves happy if they reigned long, gained military victories, overcame rivals and passed their empires on undiminished to their sons, but Christianity has a very different story to tell about happiness. The happiness of a true Christian emperor consists of reigning justly, not being puffed up by flattery, being slow to vengeance and quick to forgive, successful in control-ling his lusts and regular in his public prayers for forgiveness. Such a prince will reign with charity, not pride, in his heart, and will rule in the hope of entering the eternal kingdom. Augustine knows perfectly well that the head that wears a crown often lies uneasily. It is only in the truly eternal city that the Christian emperor can afford to stop worrying about rivals.

Even such a prince, being only a man, will rule imperfectly, and Augustine's warning to us not to expect too much even of good princes sets the scene for his treatment of the monstrous prince. We must never forget that, laudable as the difference is between the good and the wicked prince, it is still as nothing when compared with the goodness of God's own rule over the heavenly city. God seems to give rule indifferently to good and bad princes. That distinction is certainly not to be taken as a distinction between Christian and non-Christian emperors. Christianity is not meant to 'soften' secular rule. The hangman of the good and the bad prince is the same hangman (and Augustine means a real hangman, with hangman's hands, not the nondescript public official of modern English times who used to appear on television talk-shows wearing a dinner-jacket). The evil prince employs the hangman against the innocent and the guilty alike, but Augustine comes close to saying that man's sinfulness makes even the innocent not all that innocent. Accusations of crime in the reigns of bad princes may be legally groundless, but nobody who falls into the hangman's hands is likely to be entirely innocent. Tyrants are fond of glossing their enormities with the forms of law, and Augustine asks us to see legal proceedings in a double light, as a means in good times of keeping a fallen social order together and in bad times as an Old Testament scourge of God. Only Christians can summon up the necessary humility to accept the justice of God's use of a wicked prince as the instrument of his divine will. The rule of an irrational monster can make sense to a Christian in a way that it could never make sense to a pagan. Stoicism, for instance, might equip a man for living through the bad times which universal reason told him would not last for ever, but Stoicism could not make sense of the bad times themselves.

Augustine, like St Paul, wants obedience to the powers both ways. Gone is the ancient doctrine of virtuous tyrannicide, and in its place we find the doctrine of passive resistance. Obey the state until the state requires you to do something which is directly against God's law. Then, and only then, may you refuse obedience, but you are still obliged to submit to judgement and punishment in a spirit of Christian humility. Even the consolation of wishing your tormentors in hell is denied you. This is grim doctrine, and not the least of its grimness comes from the lack of any ultimately positive value being attributed to the obligation to obey. The humility of the state's submissive victim may be pleasing in God's sight, but the state itself is such a provisional institution that it can have no value in the scale of values which really matters. The state is no school of the virtues as it was for the best of the Greeks, and its law is not a positive instance of the universal law of reason as it was for the best of the Romans. For Augustine, the state is essentially a fourth-rate institution. The state is certainly inferior to the heavenly city and to the Church, probably inferior to the best possible earthly state ruled by a prince inspired by the Gospels, and almost certainly closer to the city of the damned than is generally supposed. The state as a merely human institution would be downgraded further in the light of the experience of the great monastic communities united in their love of God.

The state is tawdry in virtue of its function. It can never be much more than a thief-taker, a bent policeman in pursuit of robbers and murderers who do not differ in kind from the pursuer, evil against the greater evil of social chaos. What the state calls justice is really honour among thieves, and justice is all that can be expected in the world as it is. Augustine executes an intellectually deft pincer movement in his theory of the state: the more the state is an inferior institution, the more we need it. The state's cause and the cause of our need for the state are the same. Augustine knows that the legitimacy of any political order is unlikely to survive a minute's close examination of its own origins. Rome's beginning in the murder of his brother Remus by Romulus can stand for the beginning of all early earthly dominion. The state begins in blood and human life begins in slime; each needs the other, and each deserves the other. All the state can ever do is to make it in the interests of thieves to act like honest men. Certain it is that the state cannot *make* thieves into honest men, and it would be ridiculous for the state even to try. The state is irrelevant to the inner life because it has literally nothing to say about redemption, and it is only relevant to human behaviour in so far as it can batten down some of the more disruptive effects of original sin. The proper stance of the state to human dispositions in general is therefore a stance of savage neutrality, unconcerned with the cause of wrongdoing but merciless to the deed.

This makes Augustine an odd kind of sociologist. For Augustine the search for the causes of society's ills is only in the remotest sense a diagnosis before a cure. We have become so accustomed, perhaps wrongly, to thinking that the search for social causes is halfway to the discovery of social remedies, that we can't help thinking of it as odd that the surer Augustine's grasp of the wickedness of social reality becomes, the further he takes us away from the possibility of remedies for society's problems. This is not the way Augustine looked at the matter. Human society's problem had never really changed: How were men to achieve happiness? All social thinking had been a more or less explicit answer to that question. Pagan culture was the theory and practice of one set of answers. Now that Christianity was the publicly enforced religion of the Roman Empire, it was easy for Christians to fall into the trap of believing that the Christian state could deliver more happiness, or a better kind of happiness, than the pagan state ever could. To think in this way is to fail to understand the reasons for paganism's own necessary failure. Paganism failed because most pagan thinkers encouraged men to believe that something like true human happiness was possible in this life. Augustine calls the Platonists the best of the pagans because they alone saw that the body frustrated the soul's longing for God by chaining it to the gross world of the senses. Socrates, on Plato's account of him, was the first to see that life and happiness were contradictory terms. The soul would always be alienated from its surrounding world.

The ancients had feared exile as a social death. Nobody knew what to expect from a stranger who called nowhere home, and Aristotle recommends treating such a man as a wild beast. Having been expelled from home amounted almost to the same thing (though there were notable exceptions). Banishment was a terrible punishment, and most ancient law codes recognised this by providing for exile for a term of years only. This sense of exile was reinforced for Christians by the story of the Old Testament wandering. The children of Israel had to struggle long and hard before they entered the promised land, and even then a worthy like Moses was only allowed to see the land but not to enter it. Nothing was easier, once the need to *interpret* the Scriptures was recognised, than to see the Jews' longing to come home as a metaphor for the Christian's soul's journey through life to its own Jerusalem. Christians were never to forget that life was meant to be difficult, a pilgrimage through a hostile country in which casualties were bound to be high. The best of the pagans had recognised that life for a good man was going to be tough, and they had always been highly suspicious of even the best things the world had to offer. The best was the fame which noble lives and actions won for good men in the eyes of other good men, but even this was unsatisfactory: inscriptions on the hardest marble eventually faded. The ancients were right to associate happiness with immortality but had never even come close to showing how that immortality could be found. All ancient paganism was a search for the way, and it was here that Platonism showed itself to be the most seriously misleading of all the pagan cults. Platonism put the world of the unchanging forms so far out of the reach of almost everybody (even Socrates) that finding a way of bridging the gap between the world of Becoming and the world of Being was impossible: by definition, the word could not be made flesh.

Christ was the way to heaven. He lived in this world of duly constituted powers. Therefore Christ's own attitude to the public authorities serves as a uniquely authoritative source for deciding what the Christian attitude to the earthly powers should be. Christ's life was law-abiding in the full Jewish and Roman senses. Submission almost without protest to the powers that be is to imitate Christ. Of course, this is only appropriate doctrine for extreme cases. It is extremely unlikely, now that the Empire is Christian, that the magistrate will ever again require those lesser Calvarys which were frequent during the times of persecution, but you never knew. The pagan emperor Julian's attempt to turn back the Christian tide in favour of the old gods was living memory when Augustine wrote *The City of God*. No doubt part of Augustine's purpose in writing it was to pin down the nature of the earthly state's relationship to salvation in such a negative way that a state-led attack on any religion would seem like foolishness. All that could be expected of the earthly state was a minimum of social peace, a convenient condition for the soul's pilgrimage through this world to God, but by no means essential to it.

THE QUESTION OF RELIGIOUS COERCION

So far, Augustine is consistent. The state is established by God to make life bearable in the human condition, which is the condition of sinfulness. The state is provisional; will, like time itself, not last for ever; and its proper function can never be to prescribe the ends of human life. No institution on earth, neither state nor Church, can decide what the ends of human life should be after the gospels have spoken. All the Church can do is speak with authority about the means of salvation. Christ plainly intended his Church to be more than a place to go to if it rained. Membership of the Church could not guarantee salvation, but outside the Church there was no salvation. In this sense, the Church was both a uniquely temporal and a uniquely eternal institution. Augustine did not doubt that the visible Church, the Church of bishops, priests and congregations, of councils and decrees, of authoritative pronouncement about liturgy and dogma, was a pale copy of the true Church, just as he did not doubt that in some ultimate mystical end the Church was identifiable with the city of God. What was certain was that the earthly state, however virtuous its ruler, could never hope to be much more than a devilish parody of the kingdom of God. No matter how hard it tried, the state had the taint of lust upon it. The state could never be 'good' enough to wipe out its stain and the Church could never be 'bad' enough to annul its promise of eternal life.

In practice, this scheme of things gave both Church and state very wide powers. This has to be emphasised because otherwise it would be tempting to see a kind of ethical pluralism in Augustine's view of the earthly state. The state, it might be said, exists only to provide the basis for a social order while leaving untouched the question of what ends men are to pursue within that order. The most the state could do would be to keep the peace between rival groups which became noisier about what the ends of life should be than was strictly compatible with public peace. In the modern idiom, it might seem to be the case that Augustine argues that the state should concern itself with behaviour, not action, with outward conformity rather than inward conviction. This would be a sustainable view were it not for the very awkward fact that Augustine favours religious coercion by the civil powers.

This matters a great deal. Augustine has not written the state off, but neither has he written the state up. The state exists to do the messy job of making social order at least possible in the world of sinful men. Every state, including the Roman Empire, is only a sin-policeman, hopelessly under-resourced for the job in hand. States, including the Roman Empire, come and go. God will see to it that there is always a state of some kind, but it is a great mistake to suppose that the temporary life of the state is connected in any way, except tangentially, with the things that really matter. God does not expect earthly life to be absolutely disorderly, and the peace which the state can provide is a godly though provisional end. Civil authority is deeply embedded in the flesh. Political motives, even the motives which lead magistrates to do their duties conscientiously, are suspect. A proconsul surveying a quiet, well-run province is likely to commit the sin of pride. And this is the state which Augustine expected to bring back erring Donatists into the Catholic fold.

We should remember that Augustine had once believed in the divine mission of the Roman Empire as an agency for bringing in the truly 'Christian times'. Belief in that agency is perfectly consistent with the belief that the Empire should use all the powers available to it in order to accomplish the divinely inspired task. If the state had been given the job by God of bringing pagans and heretics within the fold, then why should the state not do that by the state's ordinary means: punishment and fear of punishment? The ancients had never seen any clear difference between the laws of religion and the civil laws, and they had certainly not recognised any right of conscience to interpose itself between the citizen and his lawfully required religious observances. The idea that there was something especially problematical about religious coercion had yet to be invented. All ancient states were prepared to coerce for religious reasons. And perhaps especially for religious reasons. The *hubris* which drove a man to defy the gods was always a sign that he was going to be troublesome to his fellow men. Augustine's early agreement with most of his fellow churchmen that the state had a duty to enforce Christian religious practice could easily come within a received tradition with the only and welcome difference that Christianity was now on a different side. The difficulty with Augustine is that he came to deny the divine-mission orthodoxy of the Theodosian religious establishment. This meant a downgrading of the Empire's function, and, by implication, a downgrading of the function of all secular authority. The state had nothing to do with the 'In the beginning' and nothing to do with those four last things which Christians were supposed to look forward to as if nothing else mattered. If these things could be anybody else's business, except the individual Christian's, then it was surely the Church's business. Augustine could have argued perfectly consistently for the non-interference of the magistrate in religious affairs where religious contentions did not threaten the civil peace. Yet Augustine chose not to argue against traditional practice. Augustine separated the two cities, the heavenly and the earthly, only to connect them again in religious coercion.

Nobody was more aware than Augustine that he faced a charge of inconsistency, and his Donatist enemies were not slow to press it. How could a Christianity of the spirit be served by the secular power? To 'Compel them to come in' to the Catholic Church was really an admission of failure on orthodoxy's part. Augustine's only answer to these most obvious objections is banal: we coerce them for their own good. Once it is accepted, nothing is easier to cobble together than an *ex post facto* justification for coercion. The image of fatherhood is the simplest. Fathers correct their children in a spirit of love. God himself chastised the children of Israel *because* they were his chosen people, therefore his chastisement is further proof of his love. What is more lovingly done than keeping a people to the paths of righteousness? For fathers, read 'bishops and priests', assisted by the civil authorities, and religious coercion becomes part of ordinary pastoral duty. Bishops and priests, like all good fathers, and like God himself, will only use force as a last resort: example and argument first, then *ultima ratio regis*. Augustine still has the argument from fatherhood to cope with the abuse of coercion. Coercion used as a first argument is no doubt wrongly used, but that only amounts to a single case of the abuse of authority. The fact that one father abuses his children no more makes out a case for abolishing all fatherhood than the fact that one ruler abuses his subjects makes out a case for the abolition of all rulership.

There is good biographical evidence that Augustine came to his position on coercion with some reluctance. What is particularly chilling about the final doctrine is that Augustine adopted it because of coercion's evident effectiveness. If Augustine himself is to be believed, Africa was full of half-hearted Donatists and quasi-Christians who would be grateful to the magistrate's threat for giving them the final nudge into the Church. A classical liberal like John Stuart Mill could agree with Augustine that the only thing necessary for the success of religious persecutions is persistence.

It has to be said that Augustine spoke about coercion with the consensus of his age. Part of the reason why religious coercion sends a shiver down our spines is that we have become accustomed either to some kind of separation between Church and state, or, at the very least, to the idea that Church and state do, and ought to, use different methods to make sure of the loyalty and good behaviour of their members. In this, we are all the children of Max Weber's doctrine that the state should have a monopoly of violence to defend itself and uphold the law. Other social institutions, like churches, must conduct themselves 'within the law', and that, by definition, means that they may only conduct their business through persuasion. We sometimes forget that the modern view of the state's monopolistic right to use violence is only possible if we also take a specifically liberal view of the distinction between society and the state. Most political theory is not liberal, and most political theory denies that the liberal distinction between state and society is a valid one. The distinction between state and society once denied, then there is no reason in principle why other social institutions besides the state should not use violence to police their members.

And why should a church not be state-like in the other sense of enforcing membership?

Men have seldom actually chosen to be members of the states to which they belong, and conscious choice would be well down any list we were to make of the causes of why particular people become members of particular states. States try to universalise themselves within their own frontiers, so why should a church not try to do the same? Augustine's church could, after all, promise the certain hope of resurrection, which was more than the state could promise. What was a precarious earthly peace compared to peace eternal?

It is in the matter of religious coercion that Augustine just fails to be radical as a thinker about politics. He leads us to expect that his differentiation between the two cities, the city of God and the city of the devil, is going to lead to a similar differentiation between Church and state. Defenders of Augustine will say that it is anachronistic to expect Augustine to come out for the 'separation of church and state'. More serious is the contention that Augustine could not have separated Church and state because his basic thinking about the two cities would not allow him to. Augustine's most basic social insight is that the groups of which men are members occupy the same social space. They are superimposed upon each other and they overlap each other to such a degree that it is never possible properly to separate these different groups. All we can really know is that we are different subjects of different jurisdictions, so the only questions about politics which may properly be asked are about how being subject to one jurisdiction affects being subject to another. But there is no earthly answer to the question: Am I a member of the eternal city, the city of God? In this sense, human life is lived without ever knowing the most important thing about it. Election to the city of God remains and must remain mysterious. How could it be otherwise? Certainly, this knowledge would be a disaster for ordinary social living. If everybody knew who was elected and who not, then there would be no point in the elect living virtuous lives, because they were saved anyway, and it would be rational for the damned to live even worse lives than they do on the principle that it was better to be hanged for a sheep than for a lamb. Tolerable social living depends upon final ignorance, and perhaps it is part of God's goodness that he keeps the final things shrouded in mystery. The purpose of all authority, paternal, secular and ecclesiastical, is to try to get men to live in a human world of imperfect information as if they were saved.

That is a very tall order. No very convincing set of reasons emerges for obedience to either the state's law or to society norms. All binding norms and values come to the world by God's command. It can be the case that human social institutions also command what God commands, and this is good in God's sight, but human institutions do not thereby lose their entirely provisional status. Institutions, like the pagan state, which once puffed themselves up far enough to claim to be the source of the values necessary for living the good life have to be cut down to size. In its account of the reasons for obedience, Augustinianism comes up against the problem which Hobbes was much later to tackle head on: Why should *I* obey the law? I can, no doubt, think of a good reason why my neighbour should obey the law, but as a rational being I can see that it would be best for me if all my neighbours obeyed the law while I did not myself obey. Augustine's view of the earthly state would seem to lead to just such a position. The earthly state imposes a minimum and precarious peace on selfish men. The state is, in fact, telling me that I and others like me are selfish, and in telling me that, the state is only confirming what the Scriptures already say. A non-Christian would certainly be justified in getting away with as much illegal and anti-social behaviour as he could, and for a damned or a saved soul it could make no difference either way. The best of us is tainted with sin, and so, therefore, is the state. This must make the moral authority of the state's commands at least doubtful where they are not dubious. All Augustine can do is to fall back on a quotation from St Paul: the powers that be are ordained of God.

Augustinianism signals the definitive end of the ancient idea that the state is the school of the virtues and the stage on which those virtues are to be seen to their best advantage. Much of his perspective had long since been part of Stoicism and Epicureanism, but these were so much philosophies of the bad times that they always left open the possibility that the life of public duty could still be the best and most satisfying life. Augustinianism makes the ancient political idea impossible in any form at all, because there could no longer conceivably be 'good times' in anything like the old pagan sense. Henceforward, good men who have thought the matter out properly (and have prayed enough) will avoid the state if they can, or if they cannot then they would be wise to temper earthly rule with the occupation of a convenient bishopric.

NOTES ON SOURCES

St Augustine's *Confessions* exists in various English editions. His *City of God Against the Pagans*, to give it its full title, must be read in Healey's great seventeenth-century translation (2 vols, Everyman's Library, 1945, reprinted 1962). J.N. Figgis's *The Political Aspects of St. Augustine's 'City of God'* (1921), and H.A. Deane's, *The Political and Social Ideas of St Augustine* (1963), have been superseded by Peter Brown's superb *Augustine of Hippo: A Biography* (1967), and R.A. Markus's excellent *Saeculum: History and Society in the Theology of St Augustine* (revised edn, 1988).

7

CHRISTENDOM AND ITS LAW
St Thomas Aquinas

ST THOMAS AQUINAS

With Thomas, the work is the life, and there is a huge amount of it for a man who was barely fifty when he died in 1274. He was born an aristocrat in Aquino in southern Italy in 1224(?) and was early bound for a religious life. There is a story that as a youth he was kidnapped and held for a year by his brothers, and the story exists in two versions. The saintlier of Thomas's biographers attribute the kidnapping to a desire on the part of his family that Thomas should become a Benedictine rather than the Dominican he eventually became, because the high road to ecclesiastical preferment began at Monte Cassino. Other biographers say that Thomas's family wanted to put a stop to his religious vocation in order to marry him off to a rich heiress.

After a spell at the University of Naples, he was sent to Paris by his order to study under Albert the Great, whom he accompanied to Cologne in 1248. In 1252 Thomas was licensed to teach. He became regent of the Dominican school in Paris on the recommendation of Albert. Thomas had to give his inaugural lecture under the protection of a royal guard on account of some nasty piece of academic politics going on at the time.

He was back in Paris in 1269 after a longish sojourn at the papal court and began to play his crucial part in the struggle for the mind of Christendom as the Aristotelians and Augustinians slugged it out toe-to-toe. Thomas had no real taste for polemics. Perhaps he was a synthesiser by nature, but his was not a mind which could satisfy itself with facile compromises. No philosopher ever reasoned more rigorously than Thomas, and he has not many equals in erudition. It would also be a mistake to think of Thomas as a man of the cloister only. The closeness of his friendship with the king of France who became St Louis may have been exaggerated, and the story that Thomas was murdered on the orders of the arch-villain of his day, Charles of Anjou, is certainly a fabrication, but there is plenty of evidence in his works to more than suggest that Thomas had a shrewd idea of what actually went on in the world.

Thomas's outlook took in the whole of Christendom and the whole of philosophy. Thomas's political theory only occupies a corner of a vast philosophical enterprise, the aim of which was to make all right in theory those things which were already all right in practice.

Aristotle's *Politics* reached the West by a long and circuitous route. Other works by Aristotle were already deeply embedded in the world of Western learning, so that his *Politics* could hardly be ignored when it eventually made its appearance in the thirteenth century. The matter was complicated by the fact that Aristotle's works, including the *Politics*, had been part of the common currency of high culture in the Muslim world for several centuries, so that the *Politics* arrived in western Christendom well-encrusted with the learned commentary of a non-Christian and sometimes anti-Christian civilisation. And the *Politics* eventually found its way into a Christian world which had already had the politics of Paul and Augustine, and this politics was very different from the Aristotelian teaching about the state.

Augustine had very little good to say about the state, and hardly anything that was positive. Augustine came to his view of the state through Plato and Paul, and Plato's contempt for almost every state as it actually existed in the world informs everything that Augustine has to say about the earthly city. God wants law, even the law without justice which the earthly city offers. The Pauline doctrine of sinfulness showed Augustine why God wants the earthly city to continue its miserable existence. A carnal world is going to be vicious, so God in his mercy gives men the state to batten down some of the social consequences of man's original sin. The state's law may bear a relationship to God's law in some purely formal sense because everything is related to God, but in practice the law and its enforcement can be as ungodly as it pleases and still be law. There are even senses in which law which has fallen low is appropriate to the condition of sinful men. The law's purpose is always punishment, and sometimes God punishes a people as a whole by visiting thoroughly nasty law-givers and law-enforcers on them. The nineteenth-century French Catholic reactionary de Maistre got the spirit of Augustine's view of law exactly right when he said that God allows the executioner into the temple and permits him to pray just after he has broken a man on the wheel.

Augustine nails men to the state. Man's tragedy is that the state might never have been necessary. Man in his natural condition before the Fall lived without political order in Augustine's sense. Like the Jews before they demanded kings, Adam and Eve lived according to God's law in their state of grace. Augustine hammers home the theme of the state's unnaturalness; only a deformed human institution can begin to cope with the effects of a deformed human nature. A glance at Aristotle's *Politics* is enough to show that Augustine's view of the state is not just different from Aristotle's but its polar opposite. Aristotle is so insistent on the naturalness of the *polis* that most of the difficulties we have with his political thought arise out of that insistence. Aristotle's god approves of a well-ordered *polis* and he always wanted men to live in one. There is nothing provisional or second-rate about Aristotle's city. God, the great unmoved mover, willed political life as the true end of man. God willed the highest possible life for the Greeks alone; barbarians would live in disordered tribes and empires, and would be grateful to serve in their natural places as slaves in the well-run households of the Greeks. These Greeks were the chosen people of nature's god; they could do wrong, but only they could do right. And right was to be done publicly in the *polis*. Ancient Hellas was what anthropologists would now call a 'shame' culture. Doing the right thing, practising the virtues, was done in public. Ancient Greek showing-off grates on us now, but the other side of the coin was that citizens in the ancient *polis* were not subject to the moral agony of choosing between the ends of private life and the ends of political life.

This would only be true, of course, if the *polis* was well-constituted, and in practice there was always likely to be conflict between the *polis* and personal ambition and family loyalty. Alcibiades and Antigone are not great names for nothing. None the less, the Greeks assumed that the state could be taken back to the drawing-board; there was always going to be a sage hanging about in a marketplace somewhere who could design a better *polis*. Some remarks in the *Politics* itself can be taken to mean that Aristotle believed that over time the *polis* had an organic tendency to develop into its natural, that is perfect, form. He assumes that men can learn from their mistakes and profit from what they see other men do. Spartan institutions, for instance, were probably an improved version of the constitutions of the timarchic cities of Crete; even the Spartans were neither too proud nor too stupid to learn from others.

Thomas's problem was to try to reconcile the *polis* of the Greeks with Augustine's city of fallen men. Again, it has to be emphasised that ignoring the *Politics* of Aristotle was out of the question. The reputation of Aristotle was so much a part of the intellectual landscape of Thomas's time that Aristotle did not even have to be mentioned by name in philosophical treatises. When Thomas's contemporaries wrote 'as the Philosopher says', or even 'as He says', everybody knew it meant Aristotle. The Philosopher's views about politics would have to be reconciled with Augustinianism somehow. It was partly a matter of tone. Reading Thomas after reading Augustine is like returning to familiar ground. It is the Aristotelian world of beautiful formal definitions qualified in detail. Aristotelian classifications of types of state and definitions of types of law make their reappearance with their meanings glossed and teased out with references to the Scriptures and to the Fathers of the Church. The difference between Aristotle and Thomas is the difference between the idea of Hellas and the idea of Christendom. Aristotle had assumed that political thought applied only to that small portion of mankind which inhabited the Greek world. Political thought had nothing to say to the barbarian world, which was nearly everybody, and it had nothing very encouraging to say about how Greeks should treat any barbarians they came across. The barbarian question was relegated by Aristotle to minor technical questions about slavery, and his treatment of barbarians amounts to very little more than pragmatic advice to slave raiders and traders: make sure that those whom you make slaves really are good slave material, otherwise you might burden yourselves with very troublesome slaves. Stoicism and Augustinianism intervene between Aristotle and Thomas, so that Thomas thinks the whole world is worth a theory.

Thomas assumes that Christendom is minimally stable. Its disputes are essentially internal disputes, family affairs in which the disputants implicitly recognise that the survival of the family puts limits on how a dispute may be conducted and how far it can be allowed to go. Christendom is held together by the love of God and by a desire to do His will. Thomas's God is a rational God. Like Aristotle's Nature, God does nothing without a purpose. He has created a rational universe and a rational world for human beings to live in. God must therefore have had it in His mind at the Creation to make the physical and moral worlds obedient to his law. Indeed, the distinction between the physical and moral worlds which men inhabit is a distinction made only for the convenience of philosophers. Ordinary men live in a single law-bound world, because the God who made the heavens also made the earth and all its inhabitants.

Law is the coherence of the mind of God, and that coherence is reflected in the world of ordinary law, the law of *this* kingdom, *that* duchy, and *these* courts. Human law reflects the intense orderliness of God's mind but human law is very far from being a copy of God's law. If human law were to be a copy of God's law, then human living would be approaching that condition of perfection which the Scriptures and the Fathers tell us cannot exist in this world. The reality of the world of human law is in fact bound to be as it is, a confused and confusing patchwork of different and overlapping legal systems. A vertical dimension of human law adds to the difficulties. When legal systems overlap there is always a dispute about the priority between them, and this often takes the form of claims for the superiority of one system of law over another. One system of law is claimed to be 'higher' than another, or it is claimed that a higher law exists by which the priority of the claims of two 'lower' forms of law can be decided.

Time also makes its own claims for the lawfulness of law. Much human law, and nearly all of feudal law, arises out of custom. Most of what we call 'legislation' has happened through the expedient of making permanent lists of already well-established customs. Somebody somewhere, acting from motives which we can easily guess at, has always had the idea of carving the law in tablets of stone. Law becomes fixed, knowable and known. The great law-givers of history are really misnamed if we think of them as law-inventors. Rather, they are law-declarers, legislating in conditions in which it has become imperative to be able to answer the question: What exactly is the law? Like all legal theorists, Thomas had a healthy respect for law as codified custom. If God takes an interest in everything, then he surely must spend some of his time overseeing how law is actually made and enforced in particular societies at different times. Like Aristotle, Aquinas believes the finger of reason writes the law in different societies and then moves on. Aristotle's *Ethics* and *Politics* are proof enough of this for Thomas. There is nothing like Aristotle's range of empirical knowledge in Thomas's political writings. He just assumes that what was true for the Greek states in Aristotle's day is also true for Christian Europe: law is nearly always rational in some sense.

How can this be? Aristotle's own arguments take Thomas part of the way. Human law-givers make and change the laws for a variety of human motives, some good, some indifferent, and some downright wicked, but Aristotle appears to believe that there is something about law-making itself which is inherently rational. Nature has implanted a certain end in the human constitution – 'the good life' – and has also given men the capacity to perceive, more or less consciously, what the good life is. Two things would seem to follow from this. The first is that men who have an idea of what the good life is would have enough sense to be able to work out for themselves whether or not the laws of their city were compatible with the good life for whose realisation the city existed. It would be perceptions like this which would lead rational men to want to have their laws codified in the first place. Rational men know that nature is primarily a set of 'ends' and only secondarily the accomplishment of those ends, and, if men were wise, they would want to fix as much as they could in law in a world in which nature's purposes were often frustrated. Aristotle's second assumption about the rationality of law comes from the undoubted fact that some cities, and therefore some legal systems, last longer than others. For Aristotle, the longevity of a thing is bound up with the achievement of its end. Processes which do not get close to their ends fritter themselves away back into nature. Nature is endlessly patient, beginning and beginning again as long as time lasts. A world without partially achieved ends would be chaotic; even the most rational mind could make no sense of it beyond observing that everywhere chaos reigns. (And without the idea of ends, it would be hard to see in what sense the world *was* chaotic. Take away ends, and our very idea of chaos is chaotic.) Partial achievement of ends explains what stability there is in the world of politics, and one of the ways men learn to save and cherish their discoveries of what partial means to the good life is through a developing system of law. The law is a repository of the sensible decisions made in the past about how the good life· is to be achieved. Like Aristotle, Thomas is very reluctant to believe that human reason always gets things wrong, and he takes it for granted that there will be a greater or lesser degree of rationality in human legal systems, which only *appear* to have developed haphazardly. How otherwise was one to explain the persistence of legal systems except by saying that they must have served at least some of the purposes of human life?

Thomas never wavers from the ancient belief that all human activities presuppose a form of knowledge. All life is either learning or putting knowledge into practice, and in practice the two are often inseparable. (Only Plato believes that the just man's knowledge must be absolutely complete before he can be let loose on the world.) It follows that, whether we realise it or not, we spend all our lives in search of knowledge. Rational men look for guides when their own knowledge is incomplete. What is true of the world in general must also be true about law. The law guides men's actions, so that it is crucially important that the law itself should be well guided. Thomas begins from the Aristotelian presumption in favour of law, and, like Aristotle, he knows that human law cannot stand morally by itself. As in other matters, so in this, the greatest help is to be found in God who, as a law-maker himself, has a certain sympathy with human legislators.

The Thomist God is nothing if not rational. The orderliness of the Creation resembles God's own mind. The divine mind contains other purposes besides those which are implicit in the Creation. The Creation itself cannot be said to have exhausted God's mind, because that would be to say that God's mind is in some sense limited. This is another way of saying that man as God's inferior creation cannot expect to know everything that God knows. Knowing God's mind and being God amount to the same thing; therefore wishing to know more than God wants us to know is blasphemous. We can know in a very general sense that God wants us to live law-abiding lives because there is a divine law which governed even before time began. The universe which we inhabit is temporal and temporary. God's mind can create time but cannot be confined to it. Therefore, it must follow that there are parts of the divine law which men can never know except by direct communication from God, and it also seems to follow that such communications will be immensely privileged and hard for ordinary men to understand. All that men may reasonably hope to understand is their own historical world as it relates to God. Messages about what God intends for a timeless eternity are likely to mean very little, because they ask men enmeshed in the world of changing appearances to imagine a world in which nothing changes, a world which just *is*.

Like all Christian thinkers, Thomas believes that our temporal world was made by God for a purpose. How can we know what that purpose is? Like the ancients, and especially Aristotle, Thomas has a very sure grasp of the principle that, at bottom, intellectual problems are problems about procedures. Questions about how we go about finding something out have to be answered before we can actually begin the business of finding out. God must mean us to find something out, and, like Aristotle, Thomas finds the basic evidence for this in the fact that God singled out man as the creature which he would endow with the divine gift of reason. It would make no sense to believe that God gave men reason for irrational ends, and so the question immediately arises: what does God want us to find out, or, more precisely, what are the most important things which God wants us to find out? God's purpose for us is, by definition, the most important thing for us to know. God's gift of reason must therefore be an invitation to the human mind to share at least some of the eternal truths. This is what the Scriptures mean when they say that God created man in God's own image. The relationship between men and God is a special relationship. Again like Aristotle, Thomas takes a generous view of what constitutes human reason. Reason includes what we would call the formal reasoning of the philosophers but goes far beyond it. Reason's job is to find useful knowledge and, again like Aristotle, Thomas recognises that most men find things out by the ordinary processes of living in the world. The depth of suspicion about what the world can teach, common to the Stoics and Augustine, is lacking in Thomas. He is far from saying 'trust the world', but he does not think that all the world's lessons are likely to be lessons in iniquity.

Thomas's reluctance to write off the world of human experience even leads him into describing the state as the 'perfect' community, and this can puzzle readers who come to Thomas straight after Augustine, until we realise that Thomas is using 'perfect' in the strictly Aristotelian sense of 'most complete'. The state is the human community which is most fully formed. It must follow from this that God wills the state to exist. There may appear to be nothing very startling about Thomas's conclusion until one takes the Augustinian theory of the state into account. We have seen how Augustine's political theory is always bound to have the effect of denigrating the state. The Church was always going to identify itself with the heavenly city, despite Augustine's caveats, and in their disputes with secular rulers the princes of the Church were always going to make the most out of identifying secular lordship with the city of the devil. Secular communities were always going to be made to feel second-rate. And it is important to remember that lots of medieval kingdoms and dukedoms *were* second-rate when compared to very ancient and very modern states. Feudal societies were bewilderingly complex, interlocking and overlapping networks of competing jurisdictions when compared to ancient and modern states. Nothing in them existed which was the equivalent of the ancient *res publica* or modern sovereignty. Feudal lawyers could sometimes make sense of the different claims to jurisdiction, and they could sometimes make sense of the different kinds of law operating in feudal societies, but this legal order probably only existed inside the minds of learned and ingenious jurists, and it was probably not much of a help in the ordinary processes of government. The time was still long in the future when thinkers as diverse as Machiavelli, Bodin and Hobbes would work out a theory of state sovereignty in something like the modern sense. It would be in the middle of the seventeenth century at the very earliest that it would come to be recognised that political communities definitionally had to have sovereign centres which commanded whole societies through sovereign-made law.

The modern state arose in societies which were already awash with law. Sovereign-made law had to push its way into societies already well covered with legal systems. It had to find legal spaces to work from which were not already covered, or in which different systems of law conflicted, so that the state's law could intervene as adjudicator. What the world lacked in Thomas's day was not so much law as sovereignty. Looking back at the middle ages, we can now see that the development of a modern idea of sovereignty came out of monarchy. The story of government in Europe during the Renaissance and after is the story of the victories of state-centralising monarchies over the centrifugal tendencies of all the medieval realms. The Church was always one of the most centrifugal of forces because it was ruled from Rome and not from home. A thirteenth-century thinker like Thomas could not be expected to have guessed what the future was going to be like.

Thomas was writing for a time when the only state-like sovereign legislator was God. Most secular rulers were the reverse of god-like. Thomas's emphasis on the state and its law gave the state a much needed boost. The more an earthly king took God's rule over the creation as his model, the closer earthly justice would approach to heavenly justice. No matter that earthly justice was never going to get very close to divine justice. Human justice could still be more than the ghastly parody of divine justice that Augustine had thought it must always be. It has to be stressed that the shift from Augustine to Thomas is a shift of emphasis only. Thomas never doubts the fundamental carnality of the world. Like Augustine, he also accepts that human living is suffused with a mysterious quality, which means that men are cut off from the kind of ultimate knowledge which alone would enable them to make real sense of their lives. None the less, Thomas's reading of Aristotle enabled him to begin to unpick at least some of Augustine's closely argued political pessimism. Like Aristotle, Thomas began to think of justice as being in some sense natural to man, and this in its turn enabled him to begin to see the fundamental fact of the fall of man in a slightly different light.

Thomas argues that there must have been political life before the Fall. Some form of rulership must have existed in the garden of Eden. Thomas accepts Aristotle's opinion that men are naturally superior to women, so he infers that God must have wanted Eve to be guided by Adam; only then would life in the garden have been complete. A good deal hangs on this apparently innocuous inference. By getting political life in before the Fall, Thomas frees himself from the obligation to erect a great Augustinian barrier between the perfect life of paradise and essentially flawed political life. Augustine takes a stark view of the contrast between the life of the garden and political life, and everything he has to say about politics follows from that contrast. The life of fallen men is going to be tough. Men are going to get their bread in the sweat of their faces. The good things of life are going to be scarce, partly because nature outside the garden is hostile, and partly because men have discovered the will to want things which God would rather they did not want. The desires will multiply as the people multiply, so that there would still not be enough of the world's goods to go round even if men were eventually able to get as much out of nature as is humanly possible. Hence the perpetual carnal squabbling of men. Even in paradise Adam and Eve could not be trusted when God's back was turned; how much truer this is going to be in the sinful world when the magistrate's back is turned. The wise ruler would not take his eyes of God's children for a second. Hence the need for the repressive state, negative to the core. But if Thomas is to be believed, then there is something more to be said for earthly rule. If Adam ruled Eve before the Fall, then God must have planned all along for the state to exist, so Thomas is free to say, with Aristotle, that the rule of human superior over human inferior is natural after all.

Thomas is on sure ground once he has shown that rule is natural because it was willed by God before the Fall. Differences between good rule and bad rule now really begin to matter. The only difference which really mattered for Augustine is the difference between the state's justice and God's. The difference between the worst- and the best-run state pales into insignificance in the light of that fundamental difference. Not so for Thomas. If God intended rule to be natural in something like the Aristotelian sense, then it must matter a great deal to God whether government is well or ill conducted. Like Aristotle's nature, God wants men to live in well-constituted states, which must mean that He wants them to be subject to good law. There is more to our nature than Augustine allows for. Life in a good state is one of the things which God intends for us. We come programmed with more than our sinfulness. There is a light in the darkness.

Thomist Aristotelianism gives the state a boost, but this is very far from saying that it can give the state the kind of moral primacy that Aristotle appears to give it right at the beginning of the *Politics*. Aristotle says that the state must have the supreme end because it is the supreme association. This statement has always worried commentators keen to see a 'liberalism' in Aristotle to counterpose to the authoritarianism (and even 'totalitarianism') of Plato. Aristotle seems to be saying not only that the state has an end peculiar to itself, but also that the state has an end which is superior to and has priority over the ends of families and villages. For liberals, all talk of the state's own ends smacks of *raison d'état* or worse; it means at least Machiavelli, and it might also mean the allegedly totalitarian Rousseau of *The Social Contract* and the Polish Constitution. Liberals need not have worried about Aristotle's account of the end of the state, because he probably wants us to understand that the end of the state emerges from the ends of its subordinate communities. The end of the state can never be an end over and against the ends implicit in family and social life; the end of the *polis*, 'the good life', can only complete the sum of other human ends and can therefore never negate them. However, Aristotle does mean that the state is teleologically autonomous: the *polis* has no ends outside itself. A *polis* ought to be self-sufficiently rule-bound for it to need no law except its own.

Aristotle's account of the moral self-sufficiency of the *polis* creates problems for Thomas, some of which are easy to deal with, and some of which are not so easy. Thomas has no difficulty in subsuming Aristotle's doctrine of natural ends into God's law. All Thomas has to do is to say that God wills that men should will certain ends which Aristotle has already given an account of. Thomas's God then becomes Aristotle's nature in addition to what the Scriptures and the Fathers of the Church say He is. Patristic doctrine is thus not so much mistaken as incomplete; it will have to move over, but will not have to be changed much. Christians must have ends which are prior to the state's ends, but this does not create the theoretical problems that one might expect. All Thomas has to do is to add Christian ends to Aristotelian ends. The form Aristotle's own doctrine takes makes this addition relatively easy. Aristotelian ends follow each other in a progressive sequence, and he holds that it is the final end which gives coherence and meaning to the subordinate ends. Christianity is nothing if not a doctrine of the primacy of final causes: what happens after death completes the meaning of life and life's beginning is only fully comprehensible in the end.

However, there is no Aristotelian analogue for the position of the Catholic Church in medieval societies. Thomas is bound as a Christian to believe that a wholly secular society can never be autonomous in the fullest sense. The Church is the essential connecting link between men and the ultimate ends of life, ends which must by definition be 'higher'. Human ends can be seen as ends that God wills, or they can be seen as a step on the way to the realisation of higher ends, but there is no getting away from the fact that the Christian is obliged to believe in ends which could not be part of Aristotle's own knowable universe. Thomas does not even question the old Gelasian doctrine of two swords in a single scabbard. Ecclesiastical and secular authority occupy the same social space, and ecclesiastical authority is always going to be superior to secular authority while the ends of the religious life are thought of as superior to the ends of secular life.

The question is therefore about what this 'superiority' actually means in the world. Thomas is understandably reluctant to reduce this important question to a squabble about the exact limits of the jurisdiction of priests and lords, kings and bishops, and popes and emperors. Too much good ink had already been spilt on jurisdictional bickering, and much more was to be spilt in the future. Thomas faces the problem not as one of obedience but of disobedience; not 'When must I obey one power or the other?' but rather 'When am I entitled or bound to disobey the secular prince?'. There is a nuance here which is easily missed. Like Aristotle and Augustine, Thomas always makes a presumption in favour of obedience. Good government carries its own rationale with it, and this is definitely strengthened by the Aristotelian ends which Thomas embeds in secular authority. The effects of good government are certainly pleasing to God. Thomas assumes that there will be a substantial natural law content in nearly all positive law (and even in the positive law of Muslim kingdoms ruling over Christian subjects). Obedience to positive law is therefore to an extent obedience to God's law. Thomas is perfectly well aware that in fact men obey law out of a variety of motives, only one of which is a consciousness of law's goodness. This voluntary obedience is the best of all obedience, and is what God really wants, but obedience to secular law through fear of punishment is as acceptable to God as obedience to His commandments through fear of hell-fire.

Thomas ends up by claiming that most secular law is binding on Christian conscience, including most of what might appear at first sight to be the doubtful cases. No Christian had ever doubted that unjust law – that is, law which flies in the face of the direct commands of the Scriptures – is invalid law; and law that is obviously in keeping with God's commands is good law by definition. But what about law that is somehow 'in between', law which is neither very good nor very bad? Thomas's Aristotelianism enables him to establish a presumption in favour of obedience in conscience to this 'in between' kind of law. The question of obedience to a particular command of the positive law cannot be divorced from consideration of the ends for which positive law is in general established, and one of these ends is the secular peace on which the realisation of all other strictly human ends depends. A rational conscience is therefore obliged to consider the question of obedience to an 'in between' command very carefully. Disobedience is only justified if two criteria can be met. First, the law must be bad in itself, though not necessarily very wicked, and second, disobedience must not threaten the earthly peace to the extent that the ends for which earthly peace is in general established become more difficult to realise. The second criterion is obviously more difficult to meet than the first. It is not a blanket cover for obedience in conscience to every nasty law, but it comes close. The implication is that law bad enough to satisfy both criteria is only going to appear very infrequently, because no case is easier to make out than the case which argues that disobedience in *this* case of bad law is unjustified because disobedience might either cause social disturbance or indirectly encourage other kinds of law-breaking.

Thomas's argument that considerations of future peace and good order can bind the conscience to obedience of a bad law is only possible because peace and good order are necessary for the realisation of ends which are more than provisional. It is Thomas's Aristotelianism which enables him to offer more than a straightforwardly Pauline and Augustinian case for obedience in nearly all cases. There are even two cases, the Jews, and the Christian subjects of Muslim princes, in which the Pauline/Augustinian doctrine of willy-nilly obedience does not really hold in a direct way. Jewish obligation to their God-given law is contractual. The Jews made a deal with God and must stick to it. Consent freely given, and for ever, may not be revoked because God could never fail to keep his side of any bargain. This also applies to membership of God's Church. According to Thomas, the faith is only embraced in the right spirit when free will actively consents, and this also is an agreement for ever. Heresy is damnable precisely because it assumes that God will fail to keep the promises he makes in return for the Christian's commitment to the Word. Agreements with God must be definitionally binding for ever. The only circumstance in which a human being is justified in contractual non-performance occurs when the other party to a contract fails to perform. Human denial of a promise to God therefore implies that God is a cheat, something which by definition he cannot be. Heresy is therefore blasphemy. The case of Christian subjects of civilised Muslim rulers, as in Spain, does not present Thomas with any real problems. Thomas expects positive law to conform substantially with natural law. Natural law consists of those rules, conformity to which either leads to the realisation of truly human ends, or provides the framework of peace upon which the realisation of those ends depends. Muslim princes acting through law are therefore to be obeyed in all things short of an order to abjure the faith.

Thomas is no heresy hunter, but the doctrines of divine and natural law can leave him in no doubt that heresy is a crime. Natural law's modern defenders sometimes forget that the natural law case for the criminalisation of heresy is in its own terms unanswerable.

119

Morality either *is* natural law or lies at the back of it, and behind both lies God's law. Natural law is one of the ordinary means by which human beings can keep in touch with the divine, but Christians also have a more direct route to God through the Scriptures. Scripture confirms natural law, so that disobedience to what the Scriptures command ought to be considered as just as much of a crime as disobedience to natural law. Scriptural commandment, like the commands of the natural law, requires a legislator to translate general principles into positive laws. Christians had recognised this since Augustine learned from Ambrose that Holy Writ often contained instruction at a deeper level than the written word.

Scriptural instruction is law in the fullest sense because it commands right belief as well as right action, though Thomas sticks to his conviction that right belief must be voluntary. So the Church as scriptural legislator is in the same position with regard to scripture as the secular ruler is with regard to natural and positive law. The secular ruler insists that right action is performed by his subjects. He forbids theft, and this he does for two reasons. First, he punishes theft because theft is wrong, and he also punishes thieves as a warning to other potential malefactors. A wise Church would imitate the wise prince. The Church would insist on the outward forms of religion in the same way that the secular law makes the thief act as if he were an honest man. The Church would find it as difficult to distinguish between the true believers and the false, as the prince would to distinguish between the truly honest men and those who only choose to act honestly out of fear of punishment. But the Church would be likely to come down very hard on the open purveyors of heresy, because of the evil effects which their teaching might have on others. The heretic is not very different from the thief whose wrongdoing corrupts others. The worst thing about being enticed into theft by the example of others is not that theft is a crime only, but that it is a sin. The thief who encourages others plays dice with men's souls, and so, in his way, does the prince who fails to put down crime. The heretic does something worse. His dice are loaded when he plays for men's souls. Heretics always believe that others should believe as they do. Heresy spreads by contagion, and so it follows that a Church which failed to put down heresy would be as remiss in its own way as a secular prince who failed to put down crime.

Thomas's target is not so much heresy as heretics. He is not a great searcher into men's souls. Heretics are bad because heresy is bad, but the ruler should confine himself to the effects of heresy and leave the fact of heresy safely tucked up in the private life of conscience. This reticence about heresy should not be taken to mean that virtue is a matter of privacy. Thomas's idea of rulership is still more than tinged with the ancient conflation of the ruler and the educator. Like Plato and Aristotle, Thomas believes that it is the ruler's job to make subjects better men than they would otherwise be. The bedrock of ancient theories of rule was always the special kind of ruling knowledge which rulers were supposed to possess and which political thinkers might even be able to teach. The rule of a teacher over a pupil is almost as old a model of political rule as the rule of a father over wife, children and servants. From the Christian point of view, the carnal world can never be over-instructed, and all rulership can be seen as educative. Why should there be a difference in kind between learning the rules of grammar and the rules of life? The difference is not in what is being taught but in the agent who does the teaching. Most political thinkers agree with Aristotle that there are advantages to be gained by dividing up the work of education between different agencies. In Thomas's world, the ecclesiastical and secular authorities are the most obvious agents of instruction, and both are obviously limited because neither has direct access to men's souls, so neither can be sure of the true motives of human obedience.

It is the division of the work of education between the ecclesiastical and secular authorities which reconciles them to each other. Aristotle himself had said that several agencies would share the work of education in a well-ordered *polis*. Family, village, *gymnasia*, deliberation in an assembly, and war would all contribute to the development of the talents of those men capable of leading the good life. Socialisation agencies only compete with each other where there is disagreement about ends. Aristotle takes it for granted that the citizens of a good *polis* would agree about the ends of life. Agreement about ends is the most important qualification for citizenship in the first place. Thomas can count on a similar agreement about ends in a Christian society. It would be unthinkable for a Christian society to allow un- or anti-Christian groups or institutions to emerge which might challenge that society's own founding values. The ancient world's definition of a community as a group of men united in the objects of their love survives in Thomas, and enables him to see the whole of Christendom as a single society, a Greek city seen through the eyes of Roman imperial universalism and bound together by the love of Christ.

Quarrels within Christendom have therefore something of civil war about them. The kings of Christendom were notoriously fractious, and the days when everybody could pretend that the barbarian kingdoms were mere *regna* united within the Roman *imperium* were long gone. The medieval papacy and the Holy Roman Empire (which would effectively become a Habsburg fief) disputed the claim to be the heir to the universality of the Roman Empire, but they did at least agree that there was a heritage of universality worth squabbling over. Much more dangerous were the kingdoms. More than the re-discovery of Aristotle was going on in the thirteenth century. Experts in Roman law were everywhere pointing out to secular princes that much might be gained if they took the great law-giving Roman emperors for their models – Theodosius for instance, or Justinian. The kingdoms might come to see themselves as empires in miniature, each separate king having the right to *imperium* formerly exercised by the Caesars and a version of which still hung on at Byzantium. Aristotle himself might have much to teach these kings straining within the bonds of that natural law which claimed to be the common law of Christendom. As a churchman, Thomas has to walk a tightrope. Aristotle's *Politics* has to be woven into a recognisably Christian doctrine of the human community before Aristotle falls into the wrong hands. The *Politics* had already been assimilated to the Koran in the Arab world, and this was enough warning that the *Politics* was a mine of ideas useful to non-Christian princes. What might secular Christian princes not make of the *Politics* after that? Thomas's real problem was to hold the field against the Augustinian denigrators of the secular order while not letting in those who would see arguments in Aristotle to support the view that the secular order took a natural, that is God-given, priority over all other kinds of order, ecclesiastical order included. Thomas is best seen as a flexible conservative,

121

changing with the philosophical times, giving the state its due, but falling short of granting the state autonomy and falling a very long way short of celebrating the idea of state sovereignty.

The secular and ecclesiastical orders would have to find ways of co-existing for as long as God was thought of as the only true law-maker. The distinction between 'law-maker' and 'law-giver' is much more than a matter of words. Thinkers like Thomas were always going to be a little uncertain about the status of all law except God's law. Thomas never doubted that God intended that men should lay down the law to each other regarding those things about which God's commands were not detailed enough. The commandment not to bear false witness, for example, tells us plainly that perjury is wrong, but the commandment has to be fleshed out with the rules of natural justice before it becomes the basis for a rational set of legal procedures in a court of law. Hence the importance of natural mediating discourse between human and divine law.

Like Aristotle, Thomas asks us to look everywhere for the signs of natural law. The doctrine of natural law has frequently been criticised on the grounds that it is law of so generalised a kind that it is difficult to find a specific content for it. This kind of criticism would not have made much sense to Thomas, because, like Aristotle, he has the whole of created nature in which to look for the content of natural law.

Those who criticise natural law on content grounds have never taken natural law's claim to 'naturalness' seriously enough. Both Aristotle and Thomas are conservatives in a modern sense because they both believe that it is unlikely that men in the past have made no discoveries about how they ought to live. This is worth emphasising because it is easy to get the impression from reading Thomas that the given world of political experience does not figure very largely in his political theory, whereas the whole of Thomas's political theory is a reflection on that experience. The content of natural law is, so to speak, already *there*.

This would be true no matter whether one was to take a 'minimalist' or a 'maximalist' view of natural law. The difference between the two is very simple. The minimalist view of natural law holds that it is enough that positive law does not directly contravene natural law. We would take that to mean that natural law is a set of monitoring principles for government, useful no doubt, but essentially negative. In practice, the minimalist view of natural law would tend to place most of the routines and policies of government within the category of acceptability (or in a neutral category of things about which natural law has nothing to say either way). Government would continue to do the things which it had always done until somebody made a fuss, and it is easy to see that government's attempting to do something it had not done before would be the most likely occasion for a fuss to be made. Not, perhaps, a recipe for very good government, certainly not a recipe for very adventurous government, but rather a recipe for the decent government the orderly realm was always supposed to have had. The maximalist view of natural law holds that the only acceptable maxims of government must be deduced directly from the natural law itself. Governments may only act in ways, and in the pursuit of ends, which natural law explicitly demands. This much stricter view of the connection between natural law and government could imply either very conservative or very radical government. On the one hand one can imagine governments so afraid of putting a foot wrong that they would never try out anything new, and on the other hand one can imagine governments full of moral fervour dragging hitherto unnoticed maxims of government out of natural law, and eager to do God's reforming work. Each of these views of natural law is entirely consistent with the idea that at least some, and probably a good deal, of natural law is already implicit in the customs, laws and practices of mankind.

Christians are also in the fortunate position of having the help of scripture, and of the authoritative pronouncements of holy men, popes and bishops to guide them in their search for the content of natural law. Thomas adds Aristotle to the list of authorities. The *problem* of natural law can therefore be seen as being the reverse of what the 'lack of content' critics of natural law say it is. The criteria for judging whether something is or is not part of natural law have to be so strict because there are always so many would-be maxims of natural law clamouring for admission. It is worth spelling out again what those criteria are. For a maxim of morality or a maxim of good government to be part of natural law, it has to be consistent with scripture, with the writings of the Fathers of the Church, with papal pronouncement, with what the philosophers say, and it must also be consistent with the common practices of mankind, both Christian and non-Christian. This is a tall order. The only way the strictness of the judgemental criteria for natural law can be satisfactorily explained is by concluding that there is a very large amount of moral and political precept to be judged by natural law standards, and this would be the case no matter whether the view taken of natural law was the maximalist or the minimalist view.

It is sometimes suggested that the whole concept of natural law falls because it is so difficult to find specific maxims of morals or government to which universal assent could be given. That might, in the end, be true, even though on Thomas's account of the matter the end might be the end of a very long day. It is certainly true that the idea of natural law is vulnerable to the objection that, if its content can change, then the sense in which it *is* natural law is no longer clear. Natural law is meant to be the unchanging structure of the moral universe. How, then, can that moral structure change and at the same time still be unchanging? The only way out of the difficulty would seem to be the familiar one of making the precepts of natural law so general ('we ought on the whole not to kill each other') that only a lunatic or a monster would dissent from them. Setting aside the fact that large numbers of governments would in fact fail to meet this general standard (even if war were discounted), there might still be a case to be made out for saying that the true precepts of natural law have yet to be fully made plain. The roots of this view go right back beyond Thomas to Aristotle. Aristotle does not expect the perfect *polis* to spring fully armed from the head of Zeus; rather, the *polis* improves as its spirit develops in the accumulated political experience of its citizens. This is nature's intention, but nature's intentions are not always fully realised. Nature is tough, survival uncertain, so a *polis* that lasts is an achievement, and a halfway decent *polis* is a matter for celebration. A combination of nature's patience and the tireless ingenuity of the Greeks would eventually produce a *polis* as it was meant to be. Aristotle's view of the development of the *polis* sits well with the Thomist view of the development of natural law. There is no reason why natural law should be discovered all at once and there is every reason for thinking that its discovery could be a matter of accumulation and experience.

Even men of good will may be mistaken. Every form of human knowledge is an approximation. Thomas is no Jansenist. He does not stress the provisional nature of all human knowledge, but the hesitancy is there. The divine objects of true knowledge certainly exist. The Word once even existed in the flesh and the relics of the saints are precious because God has visited them in a special sense. Some forms of knowledge are closer to the divine than others, better thought out and more conscious of the diverse sources of knowledge available to rational men, but natural law as Thomas conceives it must be available at the level of ordinary life and widely available at the level of lay and ecclesiastical rulership. Thomas's is a mind classical enough to believe that conflict happens because somebody somewhere has got something wrong. Conflict at the princely level is more than a matter of ill-will between men. Princes, like other men, are supposed to be rational. Unlike animals, men think before they act. They have an idea of what they want to do. That idea may only be a fragment of a knowledge system, and it may be a fragment of a very incomplete version of the best system of knowledge available, but it is the presence of the idea which marks the difference between human action and the behaviour of other physical and animal bodies. Being a prince involves taking seriously the obligation to make decisions for the whole community, and it goes without saying that those decisions must be rational decisions. Part of that rationality means not making decisions hastily. A wise prince will not rush into war at the first opportunity. He will make himself as certain as he can that his cause is just (which probably means self-defence), that he has explored all the alternatives to war as a way of maintaining his cause, and that the probable good effects of the projected war will far outweigh the horrors which war entails even when conducted by a moderate prince.

These conditions will weigh most heavily on the prince who is considering war against another Christian prince. Both princes are under an obligation to be as certain as they can that their causes are just. No problem arises in cases where one of the warring princes is in the wrong, but the causes of war are not always that simple. The world did not have to wait for Machiavelli to tell it that good reasons to justify wicked actions are never lacking to princes. We do well to remember that the political world of the Middle Ages was juridically very complex, so that any conqueror who had a mind to it could cobble together a case to show that he acted with right and conscience. The most difficult cases of all would be those in which two belligerent princes both genuinely thought they were acting in good faith. How could this be? The only conceivable answer would be that at least one of the princes was acting out of a mistaken belief sincerely held. In these terms, it is hard to see how war within Christendom could ever really be lawful except in cases of self-defence against those self-aggrandising monsters whom Machiavelli was later accused of taking as his models for princes.

Thomist ideas about war could only live very uneasily in a world where the profession of arms was one of the very few honourable callings available outside the priesthood. Every man of gentle birth was encouraged to think of himself as a knight. Chivalry provided the knightly class with the agreeable fiction that knights existed only to defend the chastity of women, the nakedness of the poor and the unworldliness of holy church. The devil was always going to find work for idle knights; local skirmishes would have to do when the charms of the tournament began to fade and there was no war immediately in prospect. This presented Thomist political thought with a problem which it could not solve. War between Christian princes was entirely predictable, but it was still deeply worrying from the standpoint of those who saw Christian Europe as a single society subject to the common law of Christendom. If war there must be, then ideally it would be war with all the swords of Christendom on the same side. A war like this could only be a crusade to defend the cross against the crescent. It did not matter that the crusading princes of the West would quarrel in the East over exactly the same things they had quarrelled about before – lands and precedences – because the idea of the unity of Christendom was bound to survive while there was still a Christian army in the Holy Land engaged with the Saracen. If God's law could not ensure peace among the faithful, at least it could occasionally unite them in a godly cause.

Nothing could obscure the fact that Christ's cause was peace, not war. Thomism may have done something to mitigate the horrors of war by trying to hedge it in with codicils and provisos, but it did not try to conceal from itself the fact that war within Christendom should not be. War continued to be the most puzzling aspect of the political order. Thomas cannot allow himself the easy way out of the puzzle by emphasising man's sinful nature. He will not say with Augustine that the political order is, if anything, more corrupt than any other part of nature; nor can he say, with Aristotle, that there is nothing odd about the fact that part of citizenship, and not the least part, consists of the duty to bear arms against neighbouring cities. For Thomas, war is neither the occasion for magnification of the human vices, as it is for Augustine, nor the occasion for showing off the citizenly virtue of courage, as it is for Aristotle. It is this lack of any feeling for patriotism which makes Thomism so *medieval* despite its respect for ancient learning. The ancients just took it for granted that, in any battle, there would be good men on different sides who knew exactly what they were doing. Being a good Spartan meant fighting the Athenians, just as being a good Roman meant turning up when the consuls called out the levy; failure to appear in arms was shameful, like running away. War, as Machiavelli was to point out later, was normal, an ordinary part of political experience, unpleasant at times no doubt, especially on the losing side, but there was nothing puzzling about it. The arbitration of arms was a judgement of might, not right; good men were as likely to fall on the losing side as evil men were to live to triumph with the winners. Hobbes was later to compare war to bad weather, and he was right: the rain falls equally on the just and unjust.

Thomas's natural law doctrine proceeds from his theology and from his Aristotelianism; it is confirmed in the natural world but it does not rely on those natural confirmations for its validity. Natural law is willed by God, and men have the option of taking God's will for their own. Men sometimes take the godly option without consciously realising it, as when non-Christians lead good lives and non-Christian princes rule justly. At other times, men of good will are led into error for the want of good example and instruction, but they can almost always be led back into the fold. None the less, the truths of natural law would still be truths if nobody had ever heard of them and nobody had ever followed them. The natural law universe of the Thomists is not the self-regulating machine of the eighteenth-century Enlightenment. Thomas does not think that, if left alone, mankind would somehow find its way to natural moral life. Thomas's God is not the logically necessary first cause of eighteenth-century deism, the God who made the machine, ordained that it should work according to fixed mechanical laws, gave it a start, and then left it to itself. For Thomas, natural law is a force in the world because God actively continues to will it. Nor is God indifferent to the instruments through which men come to learn his will. Chief among these are priests and rulers; Thomas never doubts that the Church is mankind's divinely inspired teacher, or that princes exist to keep men to their duties by example and punishment. Much has always been made of fatherhood as the original image of princely power; Thomas reminds us how powerful the image of the teacher is.

Like the ancients, Thomas bases rulership claims on knowledge claims. Those who are in a position to know, either by birth or training, have both the right and the duty to keep others less fortunate to the paths of righteousness. Ordinary men can know the natural law in their own way. They are not ignorant but limited.

NOTES ON SOURCES

Thomas's political theory lies buried in his theology, and has not attracted much in English by way of learned commentary. E. Gilson, *The Christian Philosophy of St Thomas Aquinas* (1957), is a safe general introduction to Thomism. There are good accounts of Thomas's political thought in A.P. D'Entreves, *The Medieval Contribution to Political Thought* (1939), and in D. Knowles, *The Evolution of Medieval Thought*, (1962). D'Entreves's *Natural Law* (2nd revised edn), relates Thomism to the broader natural law tradition. *Thomas Aquinas*, ed. D'Entreves (1965), contains just about enough of Thomas on politics.

Part III

ROMANS AND HUMANISTS: THE REINVENTION OF SOVEREIGNTY

8

THE REINVENTION OF SOVEREIGNTY
Marsilius of Padua

MARSILIUS OF PADUA

Marsilius was probably born in Padua in 1275. He lived close to interesting events, but we know almost nothing about the part he played in them. We do know that he studied medicine in his native city, that he was rector of the University of Paris in 1313, and that he met his collaborator, the Aristotelian John of Jandun, there. The *Defender of Peace* was complete by 1324. It did not meet with papal approval, and both Marsilius and John were condemned as heretics in 1327. (The book was re-condemned in 1378.)

Unsurprisingly, Marsilius found a protector in Louis of Bavaria, who became the Holy Roman Emperor, Louis IV. The *Defender of Peace* served as philosophically up-to-date imperial propaganda in the seemingly endless quarrel between emperors and popes about who should dominate Italy and the world. Marsilius went to Italy with Louis, saw him crowned emperor in Milan, and entered Rome with him in 1328. The existing pope, John XXII, refused to confirm Louis as emperor, so Louis deposed him and put the anti-pope Nicholas V on the papal throne. Nicholas made Marsilius imperial vicar of Rome. Louis's sojourn at Rome depended almost entirely on the approval of the Roman notables who had acclaimed him. They soon fell out, and Louis, accompanied by Marsilius, returned to Germany. Marsilius died in Bavaria some time before 1348.

The Defender of Peace enjoyed something of an underground life after Marsilius's death. Wycliffe and Luther knew the work, which was first printed during the Reformation. Ominously enough, Thomas Cromwell is said to have had a hand in publishing it in England.

The history of political thought is full of the reinvention of ideas in new contexts. Political thinkers read other political thinkers, so that the history of political thought can often look as if it is self-contained and self-moved; but this, of course, is an illusion. Political thinkers re-contextualise their predecessors. Marsilius read his Aristotle as a Paduan, that is to say with an eye to independent or would-be independent Italian city-states in a Europe in which both the Holy Roman Empire and the papacy still had serious claims to put forward to a kind of universal hegemony. Machiavelli was later to read the ancient historians in the same re-contextualising spirit, though by then what we call the Renaissance had intervened between the Florentine and the Paduan.

One of the most boring intellectual activities known to man is re-reading the vast literature produced by the controversy between the Holy Roman Empire and the papacy. It is much less interesting, for instance, than the polemical literature engendered by the controversies between popes and kings over papal supremacy. None the less, the contest for the leadership of Christendom between popes and emperors was about something which everybody at the time thought was important. And it was. Medieval thinkers are sometimes thought of as too other-worldly to have a sure grasp of what we moderns call the 'realities of power', but nothing could be further from the truth. Part of the reality of power is always bound up with authority and prestige – slippery concepts but none the less real for that. We should never forget the lesson taught to the ancients by the comparative poverty of the *polis*. No properly constituted state wants to spend too much of its economic surplus on ruling itself. Good government has always been cheap government. The secular state has always had to pay a large price for disassociating itself from the constraining effects of established religions, because what religion once did the state then had to do for itself. No sensible medieval ruler ever dreamt of dispensing with the ruling functions of the Church, no matter how much he might hate the pope. The prestige of the priestly calling was too valuable a tool of social control for it ever to be lightly thrown over. Competitions between popes and emperors, or between popes and kings, were competitions about prestige in an age when prestige was probably, along with money, the most valuable ruling asset. Both sides always knew what game they were playing even when they were trying to change the rules.

That is why it is misleading to call the conflict between popes and emperors a contest 'between Church and state'. No state ever thought it could do without the Church; it would never have occurred to a pope that the Church could do without states (and the pope was himself a 'secular' ruler). Everybody agreed that, in some sense, about which definitions differed, both the Church and the secular princes had rights of rulership to men's bodies and souls. Even to speak of the 'state' in this context can be misleading. We speak of feudal 'societies' rather than 'states' because the idea of the state has come to be closely associated with the idea of sovereignty, and it is by no means clear that medieval rulers were sovereign in anything like the ancient or modern senses. Conflict over juris-diction was not the *problem* but the *condition* of medieval politics. Very complicated 'flow-charts' of authority and allegiance were drawn by medieval lawyers to show who was supposed to be obligated to whom, with kings and emperors at the top and serfs at the bottom, but it is safe to assume that things were much messier on the ground, especially

131

at a time when being high up the authority scale was no guarantee of literacy, clerks in holy orders excepted.

It is often suggested that the ecclesiastical hierarchy complicated the exercise of power in medieval societies, and so it did, but it should never be forgotten that secular authority was already messy. Kings were 'sovereign' because they were at the top of the feudal pile, but they were usually so hemmed in by feudal law and the customs of the realm that they were free agents in only a very limited sense. All kings tried to centralise governing functions when they could, and the kings of France were good enough at it to receive praise from Machiavelli in *The Prince*, a work not often fulsome in its congratulations of princes. Part of centralisation consisted of 'controlling' the Church in one's realm, which usually meant controlling the appointments of bishops and archbishops (or at the very least exercising an informal power of veto). This should not, however, be mistaken for an attempt to 'separate Church and state'. All secular rulers, like all the princes of the Church, freely accepted their rivals for jurisdiction into partnership in the business of ruling, and both saw their authority as coming more or less directly from God.

It has long been a commonplace among medieval historians that the sometimes bitter contests between popes and emperors for the leadership of Christendom was a contest between two churches or two empires. Emperors, like kings, based their cases against papal interference on biblical and theological grounds. They saw themselves as arguing from the same premises as the pope even when they weren't. We would now say that popes and emperors were different voices in the same world of discourse, and we would attribute the reluctance of Church and state to go their separate ways as a reflection of the fact that they shared a common discourse.

The common discourse was heavily weighted in the Church's favour. Augustine set the tone. Augustinianism clearly implied that there was a hierarchy of human communities ranked according to the objects of their love. The city of God came at the top, to be followed by religious houses, churches, and finally the secular state. God's own city loved only God, while the secular state was made up of all the varieties of sinful loves, with only the imperfect secular justice of the rack and the gibbet to hold it together. Nothing was easier to draw out from Augustinianism than the message that the more ecclesiastical a community was, the closer it was to God. The pope as head of the Church was, through St Peter, manifestly closer to God than emperors and kings, therefore it seemed to follow naturally that the papacy must be superior to all secular states. From there it was a short step to claiming that the pope was really the God-given ruler of the whole of Christendom and that the secular princes were his deputies. Not much of this kind of argument could make sense to those who attended closely to what Augustine actually said in *The City of God*, but that could not matter much to papal apologists who would take their ammunition from anywhere, anyhow. There was even a tendency to equate the Church with the city of God and the secular state with the city of the Devil, a doctrine which Augustine specifically denies he holds.

The relationship between ecclesiastical and secular power was often described in the terms of the doctrine of the two swords in the same scabbard attributed to pope Gelasius. The scabbard was the human Christian community and the two swords ecclesiastical and

132

secular authority. It was difficult to see how secular authority could prevail over the ecclesiastical as long as the community of the Church was seen as serving 'higher' ends than the secular community. If, as St Paul had said, all power comes from God, then it was hard to argue that the less 'godly' power should not be in some sense subordinate to the more 'godly' power. Thomism itself could be seen as just another way of reaffirming the two-swords thesis. Aristotle's Nature might will what God also wills, so that men are doubly encouraged to form human communities aiming to serve the highest possible human ends, but Aristotle was taken by Thomas simply to be reaffirming what Christians already knew. The practice of 'secular' virtue in a well-constituted human community was pleasing in God's sight, and God would look favourably on the prince who presided over it, but that was still subordinate to the really important thing about human living, which was the question of where one would spend eternity. This was the Church's business, not the state's. The state could help by creating conditions in which living virtuously was made that much easier, but there was no getting away from the fact that salvation was through the Church alone. That implied superiority over other forms of human community, though Thomas hedged about what this superiority meant in practice.

The papal claim to rule everywhere, with secular rulers effectively being papal vicars, was bound to be intellectually strong as long as all law was thought of as in some sense a reflection of or a derivation from God's law. The medieval world of thought was as messy about what law meant as medieval societies were messy about sovereignty. What there could be no disagreement about was that God's law was above all other kinds of law – feudal and customary law, municipal law, imperial law, laws made by courts and king-doms, all had to do more than bow in the direction of God's law. There was no getting away from the fact that law was 'good', that is to say 'lawful', to the extent that it either copied God's law or at the very least was compatible with it. All lawful law in this sense 'came from God'. It seemed to follow that all lawful authority came from God. Authority came down to earth from heaven. It followed that no purely human law-giver, individual or community, could in the true sense 'make law', because no human agency possessed a law-making authority which was not a delegation from the supreme authority which ruled the universe.

To think otherwise, that human beings really could make law, was to take a position with potentially very radical implications. Law either came from the top down or the bottom up. (The world would have to wait until liberalism for a really clear restatement that the world's 'natural law-givers' were 'in the middle'.) 'From the bottom up' meant from 'the people', however defined. This carried with it the rather startling implication that all 'higher' authority was dependent on the 'lower', a delegation from the sovereign people. This just could not commonsensically be true in medieval societies which thought instinc-tively in hierarchical terms, which meant that the lower was necessarily dependent on the higher. This was the case in religious, intellectual, social and political terms. No wonder the heresy-hunters smelled a rat in the ascending theory of authority when it was put so starkly. At its most unthinkable, the ascending theory taken to its logical conclusion implied that the highest authority of all, God's authority, must somehow be derived from popular consent. It would be a very long time indeed before anybody would go that far, perhaps not until the Enlightenment or even later. Radicals usually contented themselves by excepting God's authority from the ascending theory of authority by arguing that His authority was of so different a kind that it lay too far outside, or too far above, all human authority for it to be included in the ascending scheme at all.

As with everything in the medieval world, things were never quite that simple. Kings, for instance, were often careful to hedge their bets by incorporating elements of both the ascending and descending theories of authority into their rulership claims. Sensible kings claimed to be both God's and the people's choice, and were careful to cultivate the consent and friendship of great barons. Feudal societies ruled themselves through complex networks of contractual obedience based on oaths of fealty. Consent, real or enforced, lay at the heart of the feudal idea of service to superiors. Only consent, more or less freely given, could confer the rights of rulership, and it was perfectly possible, almost ordinary, for particular members of the knightly class to owe different allegiances to different superiors for different purposes on different occasions. This could lead to ticklish conflicts of loyalty when one's superiors were quarrelling with each other, and this in turn led to a very 'legalistic' view of the rights of rulership. Your lord was your lord, no matter what; if dying in his company was what honour demanded, then that was what you did unless you wanted to befoul your escutcheon. Utility did not come into it; that which was lawful was entirely a question of right.

Medieval apologists for papal power were always on strong ground while lawful obedience was discussed purely in terms of right in a society in which rights of rulership were claimed on the same basis at every feudal level. Everybody agreed that all human actions of whatever kind should be governed by some kind of law at a time when the difference between, say, the laws of ethics and the law of a particular prince was less important than the fact that both shared a lawful character. Because God made everything, all law in some sense or other contained its share of the divine. Where there was dispute about the lawfulness of law, the winner was always going to be that law which appeared to be more 'right' than its competitor. Justice was law's only saving characteristic.

Law and order were different sides of the same coin. The emphasis on the necessary 'rightness' of law tended to divert attention from the serious possibility that law might in certain circumstances be the reverse of order. In principle, medieval lawyers could always find the superior among two competing legal claims to an individual's or a whole community's obedience. In this sense, conflict of laws was part of the ordinary condition of the political life of medieval feudal societies. For the system to work properly there had to be some willingness on the part of one of the parties to the dispute to give way, and, of course, there were plenty of cases of disputed jurisdiction in which both parties stubbornly refused to budge. Cases could last for decades, and there was always the arbitrament of the sword, when God would defend the right, but this did not pose fundamental problems in societies which were always going to be rendered more or less disorderly by the inheritance of the sin of Adam.

What could cause real problems was the persistence of rival law-declaring agencies neither of which could ever give way. In Marsilius's time (*c.* 1275–*c.* 1350) this meant the Holy Roman Empire and the papacy, and later it would mean the papacy and any secular state feeling its way uncertainly towards the modern concept of sovereignty. Political communities could be seriously disrupted if competition between Church and state reached the point of enmity, because the papacy and secular rulers both had strong if negative weapons at their disposal. Oaths of fealty, for instance, being oaths sworn in God's name, could be claimed as a special concern of the Church's. Popes claimed the power of 'binding and unloosing', which meant that they could declare oaths of allegiance invalid. In principle, a king could lose the allegiance of the discontented half of his vassals overnight. Also, clerical jurisdiction over such ordinary things as christening, marriage, burial and inheritance could make its power felt right to the bottom of the social hierarchy. (Everybody remembers Chaucer's Wife of Bath who had had five husbands at the church door because England was under a papal interdict at the time which prevented 'proper' marriages inside churches.) In their own lands secular rulers could always make life difficult for the Church. Emperors and princes were often the feudal overlords of clerical vassals. Vast amounts of monastic and Church lands were held as feudal tenures, and kings could cause a good deal of trouble for the Church by refusing to appoint successors. Kings and emperors also had rights of consultation or appointment to purely religious offices. In addition, there was always the use of force against a Church which was technically defence-less without the support of secular government. Secular authority on the spot might not get away with murder, as in the murder in the cathedral at Canterbury, but it could get away with a lot in an age in which it took a long time for complaints to reach the holy father in Rome. Cases against legally well-advised kings were always going to be long drawn-out affairs, with all the opportunities for muddying the waters which that implied. And there were the crusades, impossible without the active and enthusiastic support of secular princes, and therefore giving secular rulers a certain leverage in other matters. It was not to be left to the twentieth century to invent 'linkage politics'.

Marsilius of Padua's *Defensor Pacis* ('The Defender of Peace') (1324) is only the best-known book in a huge literature devoted to the question of the rightful spheres of secular and ecclesiastical princes. What makes it remarkable is its firm overall grasp of the problems involved and the clarity with which Marsilius sets out his anti-papal arguments in favour of the power of secular authority. Marsilius never doubts for a moment that Christian revelation is true, just as he also never doubts that Aristotle's political arguments are decisive. The thrust of Marsilius's argument for the superiority of secular over ecclesiastical power in lay matters can be seen as an attempt to rescue Aristotle from the Thomists. Marsilius is 'un-Aristotelian' about Aristotle in a way that Thomas is not. We do well to recall that aspect of Aristotle's own method of enquiry which seeks for agreement first, and then goes on from there to discuss matters about which there is no general agreement. Thomas approaches Aristotle in Aristotle's own spirit of intellectual reconciliation. What is important for Thomas in Aristotle is the extent to which Aristotelian teleology can be seen to be compatible with, or at least not to contradict, the message of the New Testament. The God of the Christians turns out to be the Aristotelian unmoved mover, the great First Cause, Nature itself. Any differences between Christian and Aristotelian teaching are secondary when compared to this basic agreement, and any disagreements about politics are simply details.

Marsilius uses Aristotle in a very different spirit. He *begins* with Aristotelian politics, so that any political differences between the political teaching of the Christian Church and Aristotle become matters of primary concern. Marsilius finds plenty of these differences, and he uses them subtly to turn the flank of Thomism. Thomism tells us that the teachings of Aristotle and Christ are fundamentally reconcilable. It therefore follows, says Marsilius, that if Aristotle's political teachings are found to be at variance with Christian teaching, then it must be that somebody has got the Christian teaching wrong. And who else could that be except a whole string of popes? Marsilius uses Aristotle as a source of anti-papal arguments, with the important implied Thomist proviso that where Aristotle gets it right the Church's teaching must have got it wrong. Marsilius is also good at watching his back. He can play the game of biblical quotation better than the next man. In *The Defender of Peace* he is very careful to back up every anti-papal Aristotelian argument with impeccable Christian argument based on the Scriptures. We can easily imagine how galling that must have been to popes and their apologists, because the plain implication is that the papal side has misunderstood the Scriptures themselves.

MARSILIAN POLITICS

Marsilius is above all else interested in statehood. This is not the banality it sounds. We have had occasion to remark before that the idea of the state somehow got lost after the end of the ancient world, and the history of modern political thought could be written as the story of so many forms of the state's reinvention. Truly modern political theorising looks back to the ancient world and forward to a time when the modern state will be perfectly achieved. The ancient world was pagan and most of the modern world has been Christian. It is easy, though, to see the modern state as aiming for secularity, and to see the deists and the sceptics of the Enlightenment as the first typically modern political thinkers because they saw the state as being able to stand on its own two feet without clerical crutches. That is certainly one aspect of modernity, but it is far from being the whole story. Most enlightened thinkers were in principle egalitarians, but in practice most were elitists. Most would have agreed with Edward Gibbon in dividing the world up into the enlightened Few and the vulgar and credulous Many. This meant in political terms that the Few could understand their political obligations through reason alone, while the Many would continue to be able only to understand their duty to obey law in the superstitious terms of Christianity. The philosophical Few of mankind were capable of universal bene-volence, but the vulgar Many would continue for the foreseeable future to need God's command to love their neighbours. Perhaps the real breakthrough came with Hegel, who seemed to his contemporaries to be an odd kind of Christian because of his unambiguous assertion that on earth God marches through the state, so that for the first time the state could be genuinely autonomous in a Christian society.

Marsilius could not go that far. His arguments are so modern-sounding that we keep having to remind ourselves that this is a medieval thinker speaking to us out of a profoundly different context. The furthest Marsilius will go – and we have no reason to suppose that he wanted to go any further – is to argue that God works through Nature and that part of that Nature is human nature as it works itself out in politics. The difference between Marsilius and Thomas is that Marsilius is always on the lookout for instances in which God working through Nature seems to contradict what the papacy says God is in the process of achieving through the Church. Both can't be true where there is a contradiction, so what testimony are we to trust, the testimony of God's work laid out in Nature for all to see, or the testimony of one man temporarily occupying the chair of St Peter? There are no prizes for guessing that Marsilius opts for Nature.

Marsilius's strategy in *The Defender of Peace* is itself highly provocative from the papal point of view. The work is divided into three parts. The first part is a general treatment of secular authority and organisation from the Aristotelian point of view. This we can take to be Marsilius's account of what political normality is or should be, the ordinary course of events in a well-constituted and well-run political community. Part of describing normality consists of the impeccably Aristotelian procedure of comparing the causes of civil peace with the causes of civil strife. Marsilius does all this strictly within the Aristotelian perspective, thus making explicit the claim that political science can stand on its own without needing to be based on or filled out with scriptual reference. Part two of *The Defender of Peace* deals with the 'abnormal' case of the papacy as a cause of civil strife in political communities as they actually exist in the medieval world. In this part of the work Marsilius is careful to back up anything he says with biblical references, intending to show that God's own words contradict the papal claim to universal hegemony over Christian rulers. The order of the arguments used is deliberate. Aristotle and human reason first, Holy Writ second. Aristotelian arguments are confirmed by the New Testament, not the other way round. (Part three of *The Defender of Peace* is a summary of the first two parts.) The general causes of civil peace and strife can be known simply by the use of human reason guided by Aristotle's *Politics*. The particular pathological case of papal interference with the rightful powers of secular authority is treated in specifically Christian as well as in Aristotelian terms because ostensibly the history of Christianity partly explains how the papal interference problem arose in the first place. However, it is clearly Marsilius's intention to show that the case for papal hegemony is flawed on the only two possible grounds which count, Aristotelian *and* Christian. Take these grounds away, and there were simply no other grounds upon which the papacy could plead its case.

Marsilius's world is still none the less a medieval world in which the priesthood has a central role to play. All Marsilius is doing is to define that role in such a way that the priestly function is central to human living but at the same time restricted to the curing of souls. The Church would still be a great international institution, and Christians would still be expected to regard their membership of the Church as more important in a general scale of values than their membership of secular communities. I insist on this because it is easy to read *The Defender of Peace* from a modern secular angle and to imagine that in Marsilius's own day truly sovereign states in the modern sense actually existed. Marsilius's own direct transposition of key political terms from the ancient to the medieval world compounds the likelihood of an anachronistically modern reading of the work. Marsilius talks as if he is surrounded with political communities like the ancient *polis*, when in fact he lived in a

137

world of medieval empires and kingdoms. Even that is not quite the whole truth. Marsilius came from Padua, one of those north Italian city-states which tried to retain what independence they could by playing off the Holy Roman Empire against the papacy. He was Rector of the University of Paris, the seat of government of the successfully centralising Capetian monarchy of France, and he ended his life a refugee from the papacy at the court of Louis of Bavaria, one of the staunchist resisters against papal claims to interfere in secular government. So it could be argued that Marsilius spent most of his life in political communities which were among the most state-like of their day. Again, it has to be emphasised that in the fourteenth century this tendency towards statehood was a tendency and nothing more.

Marsilius's *The Defender of Peace* may 'look to the future', but it probably does so by the accident of his transposition of the Aristotelian vocabulary directly into the political theory of the high Middle Ages.

Like Aristotle, Marsilius treats the state as a natural organism, and it exists so that men can live the sufficient life. Like all natural organisms, the state is made up of different parts making different contributions to the life of the whole. The parts of the state are functionally identified as contributors to the sufficient life. Like all organic political thinkers, Marsilius is especially concerned with the pathological possibility that the whole might begin to malfuction if the parts try to do things for which they are by nature unsuited. (Trouble will be on the way if the lungs try to think or the brain to breathe.) Marsilius calls 'peace' the condition in which all the parts of the state contribute properly to the functioning of the whole. The other possibility of disturbance of the true balance of things comes about through conflict arising either between the parts or within one (or all) of them. It is the specific function of the ruling part of the state to nip this kind of trouble in the bud, before it has time and scope to endanger social peace in general. Any inter-ference in the dispute-settling ruling part of the state is therefore especially to be avoided, and that would include interference from outside the state itself. Government must be able to speak with a single and unambiguous voice, because confusion about jurisdiction would be a cause of discord, the thing the state wishes above all to avoid.

Marsilius's list of the parts of the state contains no surprises. The sufficient life requires farmers, artisans, priests, soldiers and merchants with a ruling part to supervise the whole and to prevent quarrels. Government is 'well-tempered' when ruling decisions are taken with the good of the whole state in mind, and government is 'bad' or 'diseased' when ruling decisions are made with the good of one of the parts only in mind. So, following Aristotle closely, monarchy, aristocracy or polity (Aristotle's government by the many where they are not the many-too-many) may be good or bad depending on the basis on which ruling decisions are taken. The state is made up of a variety of parts, but it is an error to suppose that the parts are of equal value. The 'vulgar' parts of the state – artisans, farmers and merchants – are not as valuable as the 'honourable' parts – rulers, priests and soldiers – and so should not be given the same weight in political matters. So government by the 'vulgar' would correspond to ancient democracy in the pejorative sense, and would be an unjust form of government. Again following Aristotle, good government is govern-ment through law and not by force and fear. Laws are general provisions which make the sufficient life possible, and, being general, much will be left to the rulers to decide in particular cases. This makes it important that the magistracy should be prudent, just and fair, because without these qualities law can become a dead letter.

The 'sufficient' life is a natural desire of all rational men, and so reason also tells us to declare what makes the sufficient life possible, which is a well-run state. We would say that most of what constitutes the sufficient life for Marsilius is economic. By the sufficient life he does not mean all that Aristotle meant by the 'good' life, or Thomas by the 'virtuous' life. The sufficient life is essentially about the *preconditions* of a good and virtuous life. As a Christian and a priest, Marsilius knows that there are human ends which are higher than sufficient life ends, but he does not appear to think of these higher ends as one of the concerns of political science. In his way, Marsilius is closer to Augustine here than he is to Thomas. What the state does is to provide some kind of basic framework within which men can pursue other, 'higher' ends. Marsilius is much more optimistic than Augustine about how secure that framework can be, but he shares with Augustine a very clear perception of what can be expected of the state and the limitations of those expectations.

Marsilius, like Aristotle, recognises that the first principle of political, that is to say social, life is that ordinary rational men share with the rest of the animal kingdom the desire to satisfy what we would now call 'basic needs'. States will be judged good or bad to the extent that they provide for these needs. The standard by which states will be judged is no longer even the Aristotelian 'good life'; nor is it the natural law of the Stoics, or the natural and divine law as it is with Thomas. The standard is really economic efficiency. The provision of peace and order is what government is for, so that men find themselves in a position to take advantage of the good things which God provides through nature. It can be said without anachronism that there is more than a touch of Hobbes about Marsilius here. Hobbes will later say that it is the state's job to keep men out of what he calls the State of Nature, that insecure condition of life in which there is no future, so that it is not worth men's while even to cultivate the earth because there is no guarantee that they will reap the harvest.

Properly speaking, Marsilius is only half an Aristotelian because the ends of the Marsilian state are not really Aristotelian ends at all, but means, and in this sense Marsilius is also only half a Thomist. For Aristotle, the *polis* exists to serve the highest ends, and, for Thomas, the virtue of a Christian state has its part to play in the process by which souls are ultimately reconciled to God. Marsilius, of course, does not deny that these ends are good and godly, but he thinks that they cannot intrinsically be the state's ends. What makes Marsilius different from Augustine is that he does not cry politics down just because political ends are far inferior to the real salvationist ends of life. Marsilius draws the opposite conclusion from the inferiority of political ends: it is precisely the inferiority of political ends which makes them achievable by the state. In this sense the state has 'ends of its own'.

MARSILIUS ON POWER

To say that the state 'has ends of its own' is another way of saying that political power is exercised for a purpose. Marsilius is under no illusions that the kingdoms he is speaking for are inhabited by self-commanded Aristotelian citizens who see their lives' work as the practice of the virtues. Marsilius is Augustinian to the extent that he believes that, like children, human beings can't be left alone for a minute. Power is the earthly antidote for sin. Government, therefore, is a full-time job, and its efficiency depends a good deal on governors having a precise idea of what exactly it is that they are trying to achieve. This is as true of means as it is of ends. Like Aristotle (and like nearly everybody else) Marsilius believes that good government is government by law. Government by law not force has a particular claim on the obedience of rational men. Part of being a rational man, therefore, is the desire that the law should be clear, knowable and known, and another part of being a rational man is the desire to know on what basis law is law. The commands of legal superiors are not always 'lawful', and it is sometimes the case that it is not always clear who actually is one's legal superior. This is especially true if two sources of supposedly legal command tell us simultaneously to do two different and opposite things. A rational man, as Hobbes would later say, wants above all to know who his sovereign is.

Marsilius's emphasis on law means that he cannot duck the question of what it is that makes law law. This may sound a straightforward enough question until we remind ourselves again of the messiness of law as it actually operated in medieval societies. A moment's acquaintance with any medieval society is enough to make one see how many sets of rules they contained which claimed for themselves the status of law. And the very fact that there were so many overlapping and competing bodies of law shows how many bodies there must have been claiming the right to make or declare law. What this meant was that no matter how Marsilius chose to define law and no matter whom he designated as a true law-giver, he was bound to tread on a lot of toes. And he would even have to be very circumspect about what he meant by 'law-giver'. We shall have occasion to remark again that it is not clear when men in the West began to believe that they could truly make new law. The distinction between 'law-declarer' and 'law-maker' was still alive and well at the end of the eighteenth century (and it is still fundamental in today's Islamic world). Medieval men were so accustomed to the idea that the only true law-maker was God (who made everything that was made) that those whom we call legislators thought of themselves only as declaring what God willed. Any crying up of earthly legislators was an invitation to the heresy-hunters to sniff out the attribution of god-like power to a human agency.

Marsilius begins to tread warily by distinguishing between two different meanings of the word 'law' which correspond roughly to the distinction we might make between 'natural' and 'positive' law. Law is first defined in deliberately generalised terms as the 'universal science' of justice for the common benefit of mankind, a definition so innocuous that only a medieval lunatic could take exception to it. (We might say that this is a definition of such a general kind as to be meaningless, but this kind of general definition of law was still being offered well into the eighteenth century. We will still find it, for instance, in Montesquieu's *The Spirit of the Laws* (1748).) However, there is, says Marsilius, another way of defining law, and that is through punishment. A law is a command whose disobedience leads to punishment. This is a view of law apparently innocuous enough in itself, but which has enormous ramifications (probably not all of which Marsilius saw). The natural law view of law emphasises the crime not the punishment. A crime is that which ought to be punished, and you can always find a bit of law lying around somewhere which tells you that it is a crime, so that, if no particular punishment is laid down for it, then you are perfectly justified in inventing one. In this view, the greatest 'crime' is that a crime should go unpunished. The second of Marsilius's definitions of law points to a way of looking at the connection between crime and punishment the other way round. Crime is defined as that act for which there is a specific punishment laid down in the law. Punishment, it might be said, defines crime.

Put in simple terms, the natural law view of law puts justice before any other consideration. If natural law says that something is a crime, then it is a crime, even though no human law-giver has yet got round to making it a crime in a law code. God the sovereign law-giver has already made violations of natural law crimes, and it is up to the human law-giver eventually to declare as law what God has already decided. Law can exist independently of a human law-giver, which in modern terms means that there can be law without a sovereign. Marsilius cannot, of course, deny that there is a connection between human law and divine justice, but he sees that connection in terms which begin to look very like the basis of the modern idea that law is always the command of a sovereign. God is the universe's sovereign, so the earthly law-maker must be sovereign in his own state. Law's 'lawness' lies in the fact of command. Law-making and law-enforcement are what characterise law, whether it is God's law or the law of one of God's vice-regents in an earthly kingdom. It was not for nothing that Hobbes was later to emphasise that kings are called gods (in the book of Exodus) by God himself.

This does raise the possibility that law can exist without justice. Effective earthly law-makers are perfectly capable of commanding those things which are unlawful in the natural law sense. Perhaps law on earth is often like that. Marsilius does not duck the plain implication that therefore true law can exist where justice is absent. The ruler or legislator is no longer to be seen as someone well enough qualified to understand the nature of justice. The legislator (we would say the sovereign) is now defined as that man or group of men who possess the authority to make laws and the power to make them effective.

This was anathema to the whole system of papal politics. The papacy's case for universal hegemony, that kings were the pope's vice-regents, rested on the claim that popes had privileged access to knowledge of divine law. The pope was always the first to know the latest news from God and had the unique duty of passing it on to the faithful. News direct from God was always, like the good news of the Gospels, news about justice, which the rulers of the earth were then supposed to put into law under papal tutelage. Now that law was defined as legislation and punishment, special knowledge of the divine will no longer constitute a valid claim for papal interference in the law-making and law-enforcing of secular states. These were, in the most precise sense possible, none of the pope's business. Peace, the end of law, was still, of course, a good and godly end, but it was now possible to see senses in which papal pretensions to interfere in the mechanisms of peace-keeping were actually pernicious. For Marsilius, the efficient cause of peace was law as the command of the law-giver, with the stress on the word 'command'. It is the merest commonplace that for orders to be effective they have to be unambiguous: order, counter-order, disorder is the oldest military maxim. Anything which interferes with the clarity of

141

commands is to be avoided at all costs. Nothing could be worse than two commanders giving different and contradictory orders. This would reduce any army to a shambles in no time at all. This is how Marsilius sees papal claims to hegemony. If the papal claims were to be upheld, there would always be two commanders in every state. People would always be uncertain which commander to obey and the result might well be chaos, the opposite of that earthly peace which it is the state's job to provide.

MARSILIUS AND THE IDEA OF POPULAR SOVEREIGNTY

If earthly sovereignty did not come from God via the pope, then where did it come from? Marsilius's answer will be 'from the people'. Marsilius knows that getting rid of papal interference in the internal affairs of states is only half the battle. After all, the papacy is not the only danger to peace in a secular state. Marsilius understands his Aristotle well enough to know that secular rulers do not always wish their fellow citizens well, and it might be said that Marsilius's own view of law as effective coercion could be construed as an invitation to the worst of all political regimes, which is tyranny masquerading under the forms of law. For his master, Aristotle, law is always a sign of moderation. Government by law for Aristotle comes close to what we mean by 'government by consent' (though Aristotle has never heard of the associated idea of 'natural rights'). Like many political theorists after him, Aristotle believes that the public reasonableness of law has a particular claim on the loyalty of rational men. Law claims obedience by its good sense, and its good sense comes from law's openness to public scrutiny. There is no secretiveness about government through law, nothing shameful. Aristotle takes the sensible view that the opposite to rule by law is rule by force, which is expensive and crass. And rule by force is insulting to rational men because it treats them no differently from brutes who need a whipping from time to time to 'teach them a lesson'.

Marsilius worries about the possibility of the rule of force under the forms of law. A tyrant could easily rule through the law as Marsilius defines it, and in such a way that 'the sufficient life' itself began to be threatened. Marsilius is still enough of an Augustinian to know what the effects of original sin are likely to be when they begin to affect a whole society through the whims of a tyrant. Marsilius is certainly enough of an Aristotelian to recognise that government by the democratic many can be just as tyrannical in its own way as government by one immoderate man. So Marsilius's solution to the problem of who should be the law-maker is classically Aristotelian: the many should make law, where the many are not the many-too-many. Marsilius locates the right to make law in the 'weightier part' (*valentior pars*) of the citizen body. It is the people, through the best citizens, who have the right to make laws, and so law for Marsilius turns out in the end to be more than simple coerciveness. Or, to put it another way, coerciveness is not only a matter of the effectiveness of power, but is bound up with the question of who has the right to coerce.

Marsilius's famous *valentior pars*, with its right to make and enforce law, is an attempt to give the state a measure of Aristotelian balance. Like all the ancients, Marsilius knows that it is always dangerous to leave the law-making and law-enforcing power in one section of the community, but, equally, he knows that this power has to be located somewhere. Like Aristotle, he thinks that the safest place is in the middle. The will of the whole people is the only way of securing the common benefit, but that will has to be filtered through the 'weightier part'. The Aristotelian 'collective wisdom of the multitude' could not be more different from the whim of the moment (and it is a pity that we are stuck with that word 'multitude' in the conventional English translation with its unhappy populist associations). That Aristotelian 'multitude' really means 'the few, over a long period of time'. Marsilius does not expect Rome to be built in a day, any more than Aristotle thought that the system of law in a *polis* would be the product of a single morning's legislation. A body of good law is the product of many legislative enactments at many different times. Law is the creation of many different 'weightier parts' on many occasions. In short, Marsilius is an oligarch in a sense that would have been recognisable in ancient Thebes.

Or would it? In strictly Aristotelian terms, Marsilius is obviously on the side of government by the few but not-too-few, but the problem of Marsilius's political thought lies in the question of how his definitions and arguments derived from Aristotle actually translate into the terms of the politics of his own day. Put simply, where in medieval societies were the few but not-too-few to be found? What contemporary social group is Marsilius pointing to as the 'weightier part' of the state? The problem is easier to solve in the towns than in the country. Self-governing cities, like the Padua Marsilius came from, contained merchant oligarchies which could, at a pinch, stand as substitutes for ancient oligarchies. (It was cities like Padua that Machiavelli was later to take as his models for a regenerated version of ancient republican life.) What is not so certain is how Marsilius's political thought relates to the feudal kingdoms which covered most of medieval Europe. We know what his political intentions were to keep the Church from meddling in civil affairs, but this was a problem of which the ancient pagans could have had no inkling. Perhaps all that Marsilius got from Aristotle was a series of arguments in favour of the political autonomy of the secular state which did not have much purchase on the real conditions of most contemporary politics. It did Marsilius's anti-papal arguments no harm that in Aristotle priests are only a part of the state and not the ruling part, the priesthood being particularly suitable for old men past the age when they could do the state any service as warriors or decision-makers, but it is a distinct possibility that Aristotle was for Marsilius what Marx was to be for Lenin – a source of convenient quotations to back up positions already taken on other grounds.

The question of the political relevance of Marsilius's political thought to the politics of his own day is part of the larger problem of how we are to read Marsilius now. So much of Marsilius on the state is 'modern-sounding' that there exists the constant temptation to regard him as an extremely prescient forerunner of the idea of the sovereign nation-state. This is obviously asking a lot of a fourteenth-century priest. We can probably never know how much Marsilius expected the political world to change; nor can we ever be certain in what directions he expected change to go. All we can know is that there was competition between secular rulers and the princes of the Church, that Marsilius was on the side of the secular rulers, and that, by and large, victory was to go to the secular princes. However,

143

being on the side of the eventual winners is not the same as prediction. And we do well to remember that it would be two centuries before a secular prince would dare to declare himself head of the Church in his own realm. What is certain is that Marsilius's *The Defender of Peace* provided marvellously effective ammunition for the anti-papal forces at a time when all learned men were obliged to take Aristotle seriously.

Marsilius was using Aristotelian arguments against papal supremacy at a time when others were ransacking the ancient traditions for similar arguments. Besides Greece there was always Rome. Popes had always pretended to be in some sense the true successors to the universal sway of the Caesars. The dispute between Holy Roman emperors and popes for the leadership of Christendom was an unseemly squabble about who would have the jackal's share of the Roman *imperium*. Papal propaganda had always made much of the Emperor Constantine's having been a faithful son of the Church, and the coronation of the Emperor Charlemagne in Rome on Christmas Day 800 by the pope was as good a reason as any for claiming that the crowner must be greater than the crowned. And busy papal forgers could produce imperial donation after donation to show that emperors themselves had recognised some kind of papal supremacy. While Marsilius was using his impeccably Greek arguments, astute Roman lawyers (there had been a revival of Roman law since the twelfth century) were encouraging emperors and kings to take as their models the great law-giving emperors Theodosius and Justinian. *Imperium* was the direction secular rulers were being asked to head in, where *imperium* meant supreme power including the power to make law. The fact that both Theodosius and Justinian were 'eastern' emperors was not without its own argumentative force. Constantinople was a long way from papal Rome, and the Byzantine emperors never tolerated from the patriarchs of their city what Holy Roman emperors had in the West to put up with from pushy popes. There was a Byzantine Roman emperor on the throne at Constantinople until 1453, which makes a truly sovereign independent secular ruler part of the furniture of the Middle Ages.

With the revival of Roman law and its obvious attractions for centralising secular princes came the revival of the most basic of all the maxims of Roman law: *salus populi suprema lex* (the people's well-being is the highest law). This is not the utilitarian commonplace it might at first look like. After all, where does history show us examples – Caligula, Nero and one or two others excepted – of rulers who did not claim to rule in the people's best interests? No ruler one has heard of ever said to his people that his prime object was to decrease their happiness. *Salus populi suprema lex* is not really concerned with happiness in this sense. Rather, it supposes a 'higher' law which makes actions lawful in emergencies which would be unlawful in ordinary circumstances. The modern notion it comes closest to is *raison d'état* ('reasons of state', in German *Staatsraison*), the idea that states are justified in doing what seems to them to be necessary for their own survival even if what they do is wicked. The Roman law maxim differs from *raison d'état* in holding that what has to be done in emergencies to save the people is still in some sense lawful. As interpreted by Christians, *salus populi suprema lex* means that princes take upon themselves the dreadful responsibility of deciding when something ordinarily deemed to be sinful must be done in order to serve the good of the whole kingdom. If they get it wrong, or if they invoke the principle lightly and frivolously, then princes will pay a dreadful price for their levity in the world to come.

God will judge. Examples might be the murder of Thomas à Becket in his own cathedral at Canterbury to stop divisions appearing in the realm, or the murder of the two little princes in the Tower to prevent the civil wars which always seemed to break out during the reign of child-kings as contending parties battled for the regency. Even the Church seemed at least implicitly to recognise *salus populi* by prescribing certain penitential exercises for kings in doubtful cases. Henry II of England went through his penances for the murder of Thomas but has not otherwise gone down in history as a 'bad' king.

Of course, *salus populi* was open to terrible abuses, but then what principle is not? It is easy to exaggerate the potential for abuse of such a principle in the Middle Ages. Princes, like everybody else, were expected to, and probably did, believe that the most important question in their lives was where they were going to spend eternity. We may find it difficult to take seriously what they took seriously, but if we don't, then we are in danger of misunderstanding how these people's minds worked. We find no difficulty in offering explanations of why they thought like that, but in compiling those sets of reasons we can lose sight of the crucial fact that that *is* what they thought. In the end, we have to say: They just *did* think that. And we have to remember that *salus populi* was a *Roman* maxim and not a maxim of barbarian kingship. The kind of ruthlessness and cruelty which the maxim sanctions in special conditions was always meant to be an expedient, not a turn-on. If Nero had burnt Rome to stop it falling intact into the hands of Rome's enemies, then he could have been forgiven. But Nero's was no scorched earth policy in a national emergency. What was unforgivable was that he did it for fun. Even Hannibal's terrible cruelty was not called sadism in the ancient world because it was a necessary part of policy. Contrast Alexander's burning of the palace at Persepolis to provide the fireworks at a drunken party.

With the argument from expediency we are already on the way to Machiavelli, though he would use it in a different moral context in which Christianity could be privatised and in which expediency could come to be seen as a part of 'normality'. *Salus populi* was in no danger of becoming part of the everyday business of ruling in a political world which was thought of as being fundamentally stable. Emergencies lose their edge if they are seen to be happening too often. Secular rulers could safely use the principle of *salus populi* against papal interference in the running of secular empires and kingdoms while papal interference was the only occasion for invoking the principle. *Salus populi* would come to have a more disturbing meaning in a world of perpetual emergency, because then it would have a bearing on the conduct of secular as well as ecclesiastical politics. In Marsilius's day all *salus populi* meant was that the ruler shall decide. There is no hint in *The Defender of Peace* that the principle could ever threaten rulers themselves.

Marsilius's political thought is meant to strengthen secular princes, not to weaken them. This has to be emphasised because there has been a tendency in modern commentaries on Marsilius to suggest that his doctrine of an ultimately popular sovereignty somehow has 'radical' implications. 'Popular sovereignty' can always be made to sound radical, but whether it really is radical or not depends almost entirely on circumstances. In Marsilius the concept of popular sovereignty is meant only to strengthen secular rulers at the expense of the temporal jurisdiction of the princes of the Church. Even this is to overstate the case a little, because, according to Marsilian doctrine, there is no reason in principle why the princes of the Church should not continue to exercise their jurisdictions under the ultimate supervision of the secular princes. We should never forget that the origin of the quarrels between the papacy and the princes lay in such matters as the right of appointment to great ecclesiastical benefices. There was no quarrel about the absolute necessity of government as such. Quite the reverse. Those who supported positions like Marsilius's did so because they wanted to strengthen government, not weaken it. It is one thing to say that the people, or the 'weightier part thereof' is the ultimate *source* of sovereignty, but it is quite another to say that the people should actually *exercise* that sovereignty. In the modern world the idea of popular sovereignty has come to be associated with the people actually exercising it themselves or through their own elected representatives, but it would be wildly anachronistic to read anything like that into Marsilius. The words 'popular sovereignty' remain the same in the medieval and modern worlds, but the different contexts give them very different meanings.

Why is it, then, that modern sensibility wishes to attach such a different meaning to an ancient term like sovereignty? The reason is probably that, at a time of widely shared 'democratic' feeling, it is almost obligatory to say that the only kind of government that a rational man or woman would give his or her consent to is some form of representative democracy. In the democratic age, any form of government which does not involve the widespread exercise of democratic rights like the right to vote is publicly unthinkable. (Even modern communist and fascist regimes have felt obliged to maintain some kind of electoral façade.) This, of course, is only a public assumption. It is what people feel obliged to say, and may not be what they really think. Perhaps another clue lies in the fact that in the modern world the idea of 'the people' has come to mean 'everybody'.

We can easily forget how recent anything like a general acceptance of the people as 'everybody' actually is. Indeed, the history of politics in the West since the Reformation could be written on the theme of the expansion of the idea of the people eventually to include every man and woman. This history shows a shift from what might be called a 'negative' to a 'positive' view of what constitutes the people. Negatively, the people means 'not the king' and 'not the aristocracy'. This was its early modern meaning, and it presupposes the existence of an organically conceived society of three great 'estates' of the realm – something like king, lords and commons. This is the people as the Third Estate which was to figure so prominently during the French Revolution. The theory of estates of the realm holds that each of the estates is a single body with a single interest, so that the representatives of the Third Estate speak for everybody who is not a noble or a king. The prominence of the idea that 'the people' have not one but many and sometimes conflicting interests dates only from the end of the eighteenth century, and it was left to the modern world to argue that voting rights should be widely spread because 'the people' consist of many groups with many interests. The final, 'positive' meaning of 'the people' only comes with the acceptance of the idea that each individual is the best judge of what his own interest is, so that each individual ought to have a vote in order to have a say in deciding who can represent his interest best. Acceptance of that position would take a very long time indeed – until well into the twentieth century.

There is another way in which the essential political conservatism of Marsilius (and of

146

the political thinkers of the early Reformation) can be understood. Marsilius had no doubt that he lived in a world in which sinful men needed a lot of ruling. The force of the old Augustinian *inter faeces et urinam nascemur* could not be entirely effaced by Thomas's plea that God's grace does not deny our own nature but perfects it. In attacking the temporal jurisdiction of the Church, Marsilius could have had no doubt that he was helping to under-mine one of the great institutions which controlled men's lives. It was left to Martin Luther, two centuries later, to spell out exactly what this meant for the state, but it is hard to believe that the thought did not occur to Marsilius too. Take away one of the controlling institutions of men's lives, and even more of a duty of repression remains with the governing institutions left intact. The secular princes would have to be more vigilant, not less, in a world in which the Church confined itself only to the cure of souls. The people's good might well require of them an even stricter obedience to secular law, which would itself have to stretch further now that the Church's coercive power was denied.

This emphasis on Marsilius's statism does not mean that in certain circumstances secular rulers could not find his political thought potentially subversive. When the government of Henry VIII, for instance, was looking round for propaganda arguments against papal jurisdiction in England during the Reformation, Marsilius's *The Defender of Peace* was a natural choice. It would have to be translated into English. However, Marsilius on popular sovereignty caused Henry's advisers to pause for thought. The English Reformation was going to be forced through by Acts of Parliament, and it occurred to Henry's advisers that the House of Commons might begin to get ideas about popular sovereignty from Marsilius which did not sit well with Henry VIII's far from modest views about the extent of royal power. And so it happened that when Marsilius hit the Tudor bookstalls, most of the bits about popular sovereignty had already been edited out.

NOTES ON SOURCES

The importance of Marsilius (who sometimes appears in library catalogues as Menandrinus, Marsilius) has not been reflected in extensive commentary in English. A. Gewirth's two-volume edition of *The Defender of Peace* (1956), contains extensive commentary. D'Entréves, *The Medieval Contribution to Political Thought* (1939), contains a workmanlike section on Marsilius.

9

MACHIAVELLI
The Prince and the Virtuous Republic

NICCOLO MACHIAVELLI

Scholars have gone through the life of the great Florentine with a toothcomb, hoping to find clues to the meaning of his books in the character of the man. Many accounts of Machiavelli's life are character assassinations to serve particular religious or political purposes. Machiavelli might be said to have had an 'interesting' life for a political theorist, and he certainly had the misfortune to live through interesting times for his native city.

The Machiavellis were an ancient Florentine family, of sound republican principles, who were a bit down on their luck when Niccolo was born in 1469. Machiavelli's lawyer father was able to provide his son with the education in the classics, then much in vogue both as a humanist training and as a preparation for public office. Machiavelli entered the service of the Florentine republic in 1498, and busied himself about its military and diplomatic business until his *annus horribilis* in 1513. During these years Machiavelli attempted to refound Florence's hopes of military glory on a citizen militia, and he met the rising stars of Italian politics, popes and princes, and especially the brightest of the shooting-stars, Cesare Borgia. Machiavelli also visited the courts of the French king, Louis XII, and the Holy Roman Emperor, Maximilian, and these experiences may have provided him with something like an outsider's view of Italian politics as petty, vacillating and mildly contemptible. Machiavelli moved in circles high enough to observe the highest fliers at very close quarters, and he was already shrewdly weighing up their actions and characters in his diplomatic reports to his masters in Florence.

In 1512, the Medici princes, backed by the pope and the Spaniards, returned to Florence, and the world began to fall in on the successful servant of the former republic. Machiavelli lost his job, and in 1513 he was tortured, imprisoned and fined for suspected complicity in a republican conspiracy against the Medici. Machiavelli still had important friends who he thought would be able and willing to lobby the great on his behalf, and his most famous work, *The Prince* (completed by the end of 1513), was intended to show Florence's new masters that its author was a man whom it would be foolish to overlook in the matter of public employment. None of this ever quite came off, and it is probable that after 1513 Machiavelli began reluctantly to see himself as a man of letters rather than a man of affairs.

The Medicis' loss was the world's gain. In his new poverty Machiavelli wrote the masterpieces for which he has become so justly famous, though, outside the academy, nobody will ever be able to detach his name from the obloquy poured upon it for the supposed wickedness of his little book about princes. The *Discourses on Livy*, the *Art of War*, the *Florentine History* and the brilliant comedy *Mandragola* can never hope to erase the adjective 'Machiavellian' from the popular mind. So much the worse for the masses, some of whom at least Machiavelli hoped would one day again play a real part, and share a real part of the glory, of their native lands.

The problem of Machiavelli's political thought can be stated very simply: anyone with the energy to trawl through the vast secondary literature on the great Florentine would have no trouble in finding fifty-seven varieties of Machiavelli. There is a Machiavelli for everyone. Machiavelli commentary from the sixteenth century to the present ranges across such a wide field that Machiavelli has been accused by his enemies of wanting to lead mankind to perdition, and praised by his friends for wanting to lead mankind to salvation.

How can this be? Machiavelli writes as a Renaissance humanist in beautiful Italian. There are no real problems with the Machiavelli texts. We have *The Prince* (1513), *The Discourses on the First Ten Books of Titus Livy* (1513–17), *The Art of War* (1521) and the *Florentine History* (1525) as Machiavelli wrote them, as well as other political writings, and we have the poetry, a famous play, *Mandragola* (which is still worth performing), and his correspondence, particularly with the historian Guiccardini. Machiavelli exists whole on the page; there are no prizes for restoring corrupt Machiavelli texts. There are none of those deeply buried contradictions in Machiavelli that we find in some of Rousseau's political writings. And Machiavelli is not Hegel, with his notoriously 'difficult' political writings and his German tendency to sacrifice clarity for profundity. Yet the battle for Machiavelli goes on, some wishing at all costs to show that they are anti-Machiavels while others are keen to show that Machiavelli is on their side. (Among these latter is the twentieth-century Italian Communist Party.)

The sheer volume of Machiavelli commentary testifies to the continuous importance of what he wrote about politics. There has always been something about Machiavelli's political writings which his readers have found attractive or repulsive, but it is far from easy to pin down exactly what it is. There seem to be, broadly speaking, five distinct possibilities for explaining the perennial interest in Machiavelli's political thought, though to say that there *are* five is, in a sense, simply to restate that there *is* a Machiavelli problem.

The first possibility is that what Machiavelli wrote about politics is profoundly shocking. This is the stock Machiavelli of the Elizabethan dramatists, the Machiavelli of 'Machiavellianism'. In this view, Machiavelli is the teacher of Iago in *Othello* or Edmund in *King Lear*, the advocate of utterly ruthless and devious methods for the acquisition of power or the doing down of one's enemies. This can even be made into a game played for its own sake, the game of power politics and intrigue played for enjoyment like games of chess, with no other object than to keep playing the Great Game. The Machiavelli of Machiavellianism certainly exists. His hands are not bloodless. *The Prince* is full of hard and calculated advice about how a new prince should act to establish himself in a recently conquered princedom, and a good deal of the advice is about the use of violence and deceit. So much is clear, but what is not so clear is why the advice should be considered to be especially shocking. Machiavelli is always careful to cite modern and ancient precedents for what he advises, not to *excuse* what he has to say but to convince us that his advice would work. His advice to new princes is an extrapolation from the actions of already successful princes, so it is hard to see what was so 'shocking' at least in the sense of being 'shock news'. Machiavelli seems to be saying to princes: 'do what others have already done', only choose your precedents carefully to make sure that you imitate the right prince in the right circumstances. And the notion that princes might have to do some pretty nasty things now and again to save their states had been a commonplace since ancient times. The ancient Romans, so much admired by the Renaissance humanists, had thought nothing of massacring whole peoples, would put their own surrendered armies to the sword to encourage the others, and would decimate a legion before breakfast. (It is only by accident that the word 'humanist' is cognate with our word 'humane'.) Aristotle himself had said that it was a part of political science to advise a tyrant how to survive, and Aristotle's own advice is straightforwardly Machiavellian: he tells the tyrant to 'act like a king' – that is, to deceive.

It is, then, hard to see who exactly it is that would find *The Prince* so shocking. Not princes, because the successful ones at least are already doing what Machiavelli advises. It is, of course, possible that Machiavelli's intended audience for *The Prince* was not princes at all but the people upon whom princely wiles are practised, but why the people should be 'shocked' to find princes doing what the people are already supposed to be looking out for is not clear.

It is possible that Machiavelli's *Prince* is so shocking not so much for what it says but for the way it says it. Machiavelli's realism, it is sometimes said, must have been devastating to contemporary Christians whose minds were still clouded by the bewitching speculations of medieval metaphysics. Here was a thinker who did not try to refute the intellectual assumptions upon which medieval political thought was based, but simply treated those assumptions as if they were not there. So in Machiavelli we find no natural law and very little original sin; nothing about the duty of princes to assist the preaching of the true gospel, and no scriptural reference (beyond admiration for Moses as a leader) and nothing from Augustine and the other Fathers of the Church. On this view of him, Machiavelli was able to throw over the whole intellectual baggage of his age, consigning it all to history's dustbin. To this can be added the element of parody in *The Prince*. The writing of 'Mirrors for Princes' was one of the stock features of medieval political writing. No sooner had a king's eldest son learnt to read than the court chaplain would write him a 'mirror for princes', setting out the Christian virtues which the prince would be expected to practice when he eventually succeeded to his father's throne. Mercy and liberality could always be relied on to come high on the list. By contrast, ruthlessness and stinginess head Machiavelli's list of the princely virtues. This deliberately parodic flying in the face of all decent convention could only compound the shock that Machiavelli's *Prince* caused to Christian sensibilities. Here was a man who not only defied the intellectual assumptions of Christian Europe but actually flaunted that defiance.

There is something in that view of Machiavelli, but not much. There *is* a sense in which Machiavelli's political thought is un-Christian, and it might be in some important ways anti-Christian (though Machiavelli never denies the truths of Christianity and seems himself to have been conventionally if erractically pious). But the problem with the 'shocking to Christian sensibilities' thesis is that it depends on comparing what Machiavelli has to say in *The Prince* to Christian political and moral theory at their most elevated, and not to Christian political practice. It is easy to forget that Christianity is a religion of forgiveness because there is always going to be a lot in human conduct that requires to be forgiven. Medieval political thinkers and good Christian princes had no illusions about human conduct in general and political conduct in particular. Medieval political thought suffers from the reverse of a lack of 'realism', if by realism we mean a jaundiced view of humankind. Even Thomas's appeal for a gentler view of human nature must have fallen on some deaf ears. And as we have seen in the case of Marsilius, *salus populi suprema lex* could cover a multitude of sins.

Part of the 'shocking to Christian sensibilities' view of Machiavelli is the contention that he is forward-looking in a sense that minds still intent on living in the Middle Ages would have found deeply disturbing. Machiavelli, it is sometimes claimed, looked forward to modernity, and he is supposed to have done this not by challenging the intellectual assumptions of his age but simply by ignoring them. But it is far from clear in what senses Machiavelli's political thought is forward-looking at all. Machiavelli is, after all, a humanist, which in part means he believes the 'rediscovered' classical past has important things to teach him and his contemporaries. In this sense, Machiavelli's political thought is just as 'backward-looking' as the Christian political thought to which it is compared. A case could easily be made for saying that Machiavelli's reliance on his classical sources, particularly Cicero and Livy, is more slavish than the reliance of Christian political thinkers on the Scriptures and the Church Fathers. Machiavelli seems to be saying to princes: 'imitate' the ancients rather than follow them. The lessons ancient history has to teach are not for Machiavelli *general* lessons but, on the contrary, very particular lessons which are supposed to be useful to princes confronted with particular problems in particular situations. The classical past teaches by specific examples and not by maxims so general that they provide no real help in particular cases. The 'Machiavelli versus the Christians' thesis boils down to this: both are essentially backward-looking but they look backwards to different pasts. Even this will not quite do because it ignores the enormous amount of ancient learning preserved and incorporated in medieval thought. Where would Augustine be without Cicero, or Thomas and Marsilius without Aristotle?

And besides, there was nothing necessarily anti-Christian about the Renaissance humanism of which Machiavelli was such a star. Modern historians have long amused themselves by discovering pre-Renaissance renaissances right in the heart of medieval Christian Europe. There is now a Carolingian renaissance and a renaissance of the twelfth century. There is a Byzantine renaissance (though why it had to be a *re*-naissance is not altogether clear), and no doubt there will be others. Secularism, anti-Christian cosmology and the puffing-up of man's pride were all directions which humanism could easily take, but that still left plenty of Christian alternatives. The Reformation itself can be partly explained as the outcome of humanist thought, and whatever else might be said about the Reformation, it cannot be accused of not taking Christianity seriously.

There is another way of looking at the extraordinary fuss that has always been made about Machiavelli's political thought, and it arises as much from the details of Machiavelli's own life as from what he actually wrote. Machiavelli came from a Florentine family of impeccable republican credentials and he held high office in Florence before the Medici family returned to extinguish for ever the city's republican institutions. Machiavelli wrote his *Discourses* to praise republican government, and he was even tortured on suspicion of being involved in an anti-government plot after the Medici had returned. Yet we find him writing *The Prince* shortly after, a work which appears to explain step by step how a new prince can subdue a newly conquered people. The book opens with a cringing dedication to a Medici prince which contains a thinly veiled plea for employment in Florence's new anti-republican government. History, it is said, hardly contains another such blatant example of public coat-turning. Machiavelli must have been an exceptionally wicked and cynical man to commit such a barefaced treason to his long-held moral and political beliefs. Other facts are then adduced from Machiavelli's life to add to the portrait of wickedness. *Mandragola* is an obscene play; Machiavelli wrote some scandalous letters and verses; he was not a model of husbandly fidelity. He was, in short, a libertine, just the kind of man whom one might expect to betray his political principles with the same levity that he betrayed the principles of ordinary decency. Machiavelli must have been a bad lot, through and through; woe betide the prince who got his statecraft out of *The Prince*, and God help his people.

It need hardly be said that this view of Machiavelli is sustainable only if we confine our reading of Machiavelli to *The Prince*, or if we choose to see a stark contradiction between *The Prince* and both the *Discourses on Livy* and the *Florentine History*. There can be no doubt that we would conclude that Machiavelli was one of the greatest republicans who ever lived if we were to do what nobody ever does, which is to confine our reading of Machiavelli to the *Discourses on Livy*. So the question seems to boil down to this: are *The Prince* and the *Discourses* reconcilable?, and the answer is a resounding 'yes!' Not only that, but the *Discourses* themselves provide us with a complete political theory into which Machiavelli's treatment of princely government in *The Prince* can easily be fitted. Far from there being a contradiction between *The Prince* and the *Discourses*, it might be said that *The Prince* is simply one part of the *Discourses* writ large. It may even be that, on a simple level, the fact that *The Prince* is called 'the prince' has misled many readers into thinking that it is specifically and solely intended for the princes of the Renaissance and the restored Medici princes in particular. This is far from being the case. By 'princely government' Machiavelli means any government by one man. 'One Man Rule', though an ugly phrase, would be a much less misleading title for *The Prince*. (It might conceivably be that very simple readers of *The Prince* have unconsciously paraphrased the title to mean 'the son of a king', as if Machiavelli were advising sons to turn against fathers, and to replace traditional Christian kingship with self-aggrandising tyranny. This, for instance, seems to have been a stock Elizabethan view of Machiavelli; it often turns up in Shakespeare, not to mention Webster.) Machiavelli does advise new princes to be ruthless and devious, but this does not mean that all rule has to be ruthless and devious. And even the most cursory reading of the *Discourses* will show that Machiavelli by no means thinks that rule by one man has to be the typical form of government under which men are destined to live. In the *Discourses* Machiavelli makes it perfectly clear that the ruthless rule of a new prince is only one of the forms of government which men must live through, and it won't necessarily last very long. Properly considered, princely government in Machiavelli's sense in *The Prince* need only be an episode in the necessary cycle of development in a state from one form of government to another.

If none of the views of Machiavelli that we have considered will explain the extraordinary effect this man's political thought has had since the sixteenth century, then what does explain it? The effect can be partly explained by the undoubted fact that many anti-Machiavels have only read *The Prince* and have treated some of its classical and Renaissance commonplaces about the occasional necessity for princely ruthlessness as evidence for Machiavelli's extreme wickedness as a political thinker. But this simple view does not account for the fact that very serious and learned commentary on Machiavelli has often found Machiavelli's political thought equally disturbing.

There has always been a feeling that Machiavelli is hard to pin down in that shadowy ground that lies between politics and ethics. It may even be that it was Machiavelli himself who made that ground shadowy by questioning the place that moral certainties occupy in political life. It is even suggested that Machiavelli did something called 'divorcing politics from ethics' (whatever that means). Perhaps the key to the whole puzzle of Machiavelli is really very simple. Machiavelli's politics is an attempt to derive a set of political axioms from a set of assumptions about human beings which will always *work*. It is sometimes said that Machiavelli has a very grim view of 'human nature', but statements like this can be very misleading. Machiavelli knows that human beings are sometimes very bad, sometimes very good, and sometimes in between. Machiavelli also recognises that a description of human nature like that is hopeless for a political thinker in search of certainties in political life. Building a political theory on the variability of human behaviour would be like building a fortress on quicksand. So Machiavelli begins to ask rather different sorts of questions from the 'What are men in general like?' kind of questions. He asks: 'What is there about human nature which is absolutely consistent?', or, better still, 'What assumptions can a prince make about human beings which are absolutely safe and reliable?' In political terms, this boils down to questions about what will always work.

To answer questions of the last kind, Machiavelli has to take a deliberately truncated view of human nature. He is not really interested in everything about human beings, but only in either what is consistent about them or what the prince may safely take to be consistent. This leads Machiavelli into some grim territory. Take the business of loving and fearing rulers, or, for that matter, loving and fearing anybody. Machiavelli knows that princes and ordinary people feel good about being loved. This is a fact of life and needs no further explanation. Naturally, it follows that a prince who is loved is more secure than one who is hated, just as an ordinary marriage is more secure if the partners love each other. A prince who is loved by his people will no doubt be tempted to love them in return. As Aristotle remarked long ago, even vicious tyrants cannot help loving their people at least some of the time. But love is a very insecure *basis* for princely rule because human beings often betray the objects of their love. We don't have to go as far as Oscar Wilde ('each man kills the thing he loves') to realise that the history of the world is the history of love's unreliability. (Rome herself was founded through Aeneas' betrayal of his love for widow Dido.) It is the unreliability of love which leads the poet Auden to speak of 'anarchic Aphrodite'.

In Machiavelli's terms, love does not always work because the behaviour of those in love relationships is usually but not always predictable. Fear, by contrast, never fails: 'If you have them by the balls, their hearts and minds will follow.' Therefore it is an axiom in politics that it is better for a prince to be hated and feared than to be loved only. Hence the motto of that monster of an emperor, Caligula: *Oderint dum metuant* (let them hate me provided they fear me). This is very far from saying that his people's love is of no use to a prince.

155

Of course it is, but a prince would be a fool to take seriously the Christian idea of a good prince basking securely in the warmth of the love of his good people. This would put the prince off his guard. A moment's reflection would tell a prudent prince that he can't actually be loved by everybody. (Christianity itself tells us that it is part of wickedness to hate the good.) There will always be a malcontent out there somewhere, and the world did not have to wait for Hobbes to teach it that any man may, in the right circumstances, kill another. Hatred can sometimes get the better even of fear. There are some men, though they are very rare indeed, whose hatred of a prince can overcome their fear of him, so that they are prepared to 'swing for' princes.

From this unlikely but always possible eventuality comes another of Machiavelli's political axioms for a prudent prince: treat everybody as a potential assassin. It can't matter to the prince that he has to operate on the basis of an assumption about human beings which is not true. Machiavelli is perfectly aware of the fact that assassins prepared to risk horrible deaths to kill princes are very rare. The point is rather that the only safe assumption a prince can make is that he is surrounded by assassins. From this follows a third Machiavellian axiom: dissemble affability. Princes are expected to be friendly to their subjects (within limits), and all princes have to live in courts among friends, family and advisers. The prince must wear the mask while unmasking others, concealing his inner malevolence while seeing through his familiars to the inner malevolence which the prince must always assume is there if he is going to survive. Not, you might say, a very pleasant prospect for princes, but again that does not matter greatly. Part of Machiavelli's message is that those who wish above all things for a quiet life have no business going into the prince business in the first place.

What does matter a great deal is the way the prince has to think, or the way an adviser to princes has to think on the prince's behalf. If there is a general message in *The Prince*, it is that the prudent prince will always think the worst of those by whom he is surrounded. It follows from this that *thinking* about politics and *thinking* about ethics involve profoundly different ways of looking at the world. Thinking about ethics at all requires that we think of our fellow men as neither very good nor very wicked. If men were very good by nature, then thinking about ethics would be superfluous because men could always be relied upon to act well. If men were very bad, then thinking about ethics would be redundant because men could always be relied upon to act badly. Thinking about ethics is thinking about the 'in between' the very good and very bad, on the assumption that saintliness and devilishness are both very rare. Machiavelli seems to be saying that useful thinking about politics can only proceed on the basis of the assumption that men are always very bad. If the prince acts on the assumption of the universality of human wickedness, it is a case of heads he wins and tails he doesn't lose. It must be stressed that this is a special kind of thinking which applies to politics only. Ordinary family life, or ordinary human life in general, would become impossibly miserable and diminished if it were to be conducted on the basis of the political axioms of Machiavelli. People living their ordinary lives have a choice about what assumptions to act upon as the occasion demands. Sometimes they will assume the best, sometimes the worst, and mostly they will make assumptions which fall somewhere in between.

Princes cannot allow themselves the moral luxury of choice available to their subjects. Thinking the worst the whole time is not something which comes naturally to most men.

It has to be learned. Suppose a prince refuses to learn his trade properly. Suppose he insists on conducting himself on the basis of Christian ethics, assuming that men are seldom very good or very bad. Suppose he even goes as far as thinking about his enemies like that. Machiavelli does not say that this is an improper way of conducting princely business in a moral sense; he simply says that it is unsafe. Love your enemies if you will; believe they will keep faith; turn the other cheek if you like, Machiavelli seems to be saying, but don't come complaining to me if you lose your state. Besides, men of sense, if they think at all about so obvious a matter, will naturally want to live in a state well-governed by its prince and feared by its neighbours. Nobody wants to live in a state which is weak and vulnerable to military takeover.

One of the annoying things about Machiavelli is that he refuses to argue that Christian ethics as conventionally conceived are not ethics at all. We would not have the problems we do have with reading Machiavelli if he would just say with an insider's wink that we all really know that the Christian virtues of the Sermon on the Mount aren't really virtues at all, or that they are pseudo-virtues for popular consumption, useful for keeping the plebs in their place but of no use at all to thinking men. But Machiavelli refuses to be Gibbon or Voltaire. The Christian virtues *are* virtues, and we are to take seriously Machiavelli's famous assertion that he was quite looking forward to going to hell because there he could enjoy for eternity the conversation of the ancient sages. Behind the moral bravado lies a real belief in hell's existence and a real sense of his own sin.

It won't do to move Machiavelli on a couple of centuries and put him in with the Enlightenment. Machiavelli is probably a Christian about everything important *except* politics. Commentators have not always emphasised enough just how *political* Machiavelli's political thought actually is. Thinking about politics is different from thinking about anything else. When we say that Machiavelli separates thinking about politics from thinking about ethics, we should add that thinking about politics is different from thinking about lots of other things as well as thinking about ethics. There may be a Machiavellian 'world-view' because nothing is easier to attribute to a great thinker than a view of everything. (It is as if having a world-view is part and parcel of *being* a great thinker.) But what should not be assumed is that whatever Machiavelli thinks about things in general is necessarily 'Machiavellian'. His view of politics is, but it simply does not follow that his view of everything is 'Machiavellian'. Commentators on Machiavelli have always been impressed by his intellectual range. Machiavelli might be Renaissance man writ very large indeed, but that does not mean that he has to be Machiavellian over the whole range; nor does it even mean that his thoughts about everything have to be particularly original. It may even be that Machiavelli is a rather conventional kind of Renaissance humanist in everything except politics.

THE ADVICE TO PRINCES IN *THE PRINCE*

The Prince is above all else what we would now call a work of political psychology. Machiavelli is always interested in what goes on inside people's heads. He always asks what political actors are likely to be thinking in specific political situations, and then goes on to ask whether they are wise to be thinking as they are. This applies particularly, as one might expect, to princes. Princes, no less than other men, are apt to react to situations in perfectly understandable and natural ways, but these ways are not always advantageous to princes. Part of being a prince is learning to react in ways which might seem unnatural, but the one thing Machiavelli never pretends is that the life of a successful prince is going to be easy.

The 'natural' reactions of men are likely to be especially automatic at moments of elation. This is why Machiavelli is particularly concerned with advising new princes, that is to say princes who have been successful in conquering new territories and are faced with the problem of what to do next. A prince in the first flush of victory is likely to make perfectly understandable human mistakes. Victory might make him feel warm and generous, qualities which Machiavelli thinks might lead to carelessness. Above all, the new prince must not think his problems are over just because he has won the battle and the defeated prince has been killed or has fled, because it is only then that his problems as a ruler begin. Machiavelli's advice to the new prince in these circumstances is based on a shrewd estimate of what his new subjects are likely to be thinking.

They can be divided into three distinct groups. The first group consists of those who remain loyal to the family of the old prince. Perhaps they are already dreaming of a government in exile which will one day return to claim its own. The new prince's problem is not so much the existence of such a group, which is entirely predictable, but the existence of members of the old prince's family around whom this dangerous opposition will eventually coalesce. The new prince cannot even identify the malcontents, who do not advertise their hostility and are content to bide their time. However, the prince can identify the likely members of the old prince's family who might become the focuses for resistance. Therefore the new prince must exterminate the ousted dynasty if he can. Leaving men alive to whom one has done injuries is always dangerous, and so the prince must not be generous to his conquered enemies. He should kill them to prevent future troubles.

The second group consists of a kind of fifth column which supported the new prince in the days of the old. Machiavelli praises the ancient Romans highly for never entering a new territory without receiving an invitation first. The invitation shows that the state to be invaded is internally divided, and therefore weak, and it gives the invader a show of legitimacy if he can pretend to be not so much a conqueror as a guest invited in to help sort out a problem. The people who invited him in present a new prince with a serious difficulty. They are likely to regard themselves as kingmakers, and they have not been kingmakers for nothing. They are likely to regard the princedom as being in their gift, and they will expect rewards commensurate with what they have given. The best thing a new prince can do is to ignore them. This will no doubt make them discontented, but this does not matter very much because they have no-one to turn to as a rallying point for that discontent. The rest of the native population will regard them as traitors, and so will the family of the ousted prince. Their only hope is the new prince. They have in fact been very foolish, because they are in the new prince's hands rather than he being in theirs. Besides, how could a new prince reward them sufficiently when their expectations are so high? He could either despoil his new subjects to reward people they regard as traitors, or he could reward them with resources from his old state. The first would make him even more enemies in his new state and the second would make him unpopular at home because he would have to increase domestic taxes to reward foreigners. He could reward his allies out of his own resources in a moment of grateful generosity, but that would be to forget why he bothered to conquer new territory in the first place. Princes do nothing except for gain, so what would be the point of a new prince beggaring himself to acquire what is his by right of conquest?

The third group in his new principality that the prince has to deal with are those who watch his entry into their country with sullen acquiescence. These might be minor oligarchs or gentry, people with something to lose. They have good reason to be frightened. They are not of the party which invited the new prince in, and they know perfectly well what to expect after a defeat because to the victor belong the spoils. They cannot even be certain of their own lives and they expect trouble. Machiavelli warns the new prince to be very careful in dealing with them. The prince must never forget that one day he wants them to feel that they are *his* subjects, and, as always, Machiavelli thinks they can be brought round if the prince does the opposite of what they expect. It is a Machiavellian axiom that doing good to those who expect injuries magnifies the gift. Real kings are supposed to be generous, and rewarding those who expect injuries gives the new prince the opportunity to act like a king at very little cost to himself. The greatest reward you can give a man is his own life, and the gift is increased in value if you give a man his life when others are losing theirs. The new prince will have to do some killing, and this makes all men fearful. The way to reward fearful men with their own lives is to make a clear signal that at a particular moment the killing has stopped. Get the killing over quickly, and preferably do it through a deputy who can be blamed later for 'over-zealousness' or 'exceeding his orders'. Better still, kill the killer, for there is no better way of showing that executions are over than hanging the hangman.

It does not especially matter that not everybody will be convinced of the prince's good intentions straight away, though Machiavelli appears to think that human gullibility is at its most exploitable in a conquered people, and it is easy to see why. Many Renaissance princes were monsters and many were new princes. The history of Renaissance politics is the history of gaining and losing states, the politics of the public massacre, not to mention the discreet poignarding or the hidden poisoning (even the *possession* of poison was a capital offence in some states). Conquered peoples often had very good reason to expect the worst. Very anxious faces would be watching the triumphal entry of a new prince at the head of his army, and it is not likely that there would be much cheering. Anxious eyes would be looking for *any* sign of humanity in the new prince to tell them that their situation was not entirely hopeless. Men wish to believe in their prince's good will almost despite themselves, because the opposite is unthinkable. This is what makes them willing to be deceived. (The victim looks for signs of humanity in the torturer in much the same spirit, and the fact that he *is* a torturer makes the victim even keener to see kindness in his face; not *despite* the torturer's profession but *because* of it.) The manipulability of the psychology of the conquered makes them clay in the hands of a skilful prince. He leaves them their lives and this has all the effect of a pardon on a condemned man. It does not occur to the prisoner in his gratitude that those who pardon him and those who put his life in jeopardy in the first place are the same people. Quite the reverse. The fact that the pardon comes from those about to execute him is what convinces the condemned man that the pardon is genuine. And it is.

A skilful prince can do much to make psychologically vulnerable men potential allies by always doing the opposite of what they expect. This will at least have the effect of confusing them and therefore they would be less likely to combine against him. Machiavelli makes much of the apparently minor question of whether a prince should reside in an acquired territory, and there are strong practical reasons for the prince's being on the spot where trouble is likely to occur. But there is also a psychological bonus which is by no means negligible. The conquered are likely to expect their new prince to be haughty. By being on the spot the new prince makes himself approachable to his new subjects, thus fulfilling one of the traditional expectations of a legitimate king, which is to listen to his people's grievances. Petitioning the monarch is the most ancient of all the rights of subjects.

It cannot be stressed too often that Machiavelli's new prince is wise to use any resources cheaply available to him to create the legitimacy which by dint of his newness he does not in fact possess. It is very hard for him to avoid being generous because kings, like fathers of families, are expected to be munificent from time to time, and negative rewards do not last for ever. You can buy just so much by giving men their lives. The memory of the gift fades because gratitude never lasts. The prince's problem over the giving of positive rewards is simple: he wants to get as good value for his money as he can. Machiavelli's solution to the problem would work over the medium term. Giving men their lives will work for a bit. What the prince must then do is to reward slowly, piece by counted piece, so that everyone may live in the expectation of reward. The new prince's motto should therefore be: kill quickly and reward gradually. This will convert sullen acquiescence to the new prince's rule into something more positive as his new subjects begin to look to him as the source of possible advantages. It goes without saying that a prudent prince would not beggar himself to reward everyone, and in the long term this will dawn on his subjects. Machiavelli's command of the principles of the psychology of a conquered people can easily accommodate the fact that eventually the prince's new subjects will catch on to what he is doing, because he thinks that by the time his new subjects do catch on, they will already have other reasons to thank him. In the long term those who have not been rewarded will come to realise that it is greatly to their advantage to live under a rather miserly prince because the prince's financial prudence means that he does not have to raise taxes in his new principality overmuch. Even the unrewarded will see themselves as the recipients of negative rewards. They retain their lives and fortunes more or less intact, and not being altogether stupid, the prince's subjects begin to think that the new prince is not after all going to change everything.

If the new prince doesn't increase taxes much and if he also has the sense to leave as much of the ancient laws in place as he can, then even initially frightened and discontented subjects can begin to relax, and some will become the new prince's supporters. Conquered peoples cannot avoid asking themselves questions about why the old regime was defeated, and part of the answer is always corruption in its moral or political senses. Either the ancient princes were too lazy to attend properly to affairs of state and so lost their thrones, or the ancient systems of rule were so putrified that they were dying a natural death, or both. It might well occur to people beginning to think like that that there is much to be said for being ruled by a prince who, though not of their choosing, none the less knows the business of statecraft. And so the new prince's subjects, or some of them, gradually begin to come round, perhaps only a few at a time, but each one is a potential assassin less.

The third group the new prince has to deal with is the people at large. They constitute the prince's real long-term problem. At first they are leaderless, a mere crowd; they have lost their old ruling family, and they observe the measures the new prince takes against nobles and leading citizens to neutralise them as possible leaders of resistance. But where does that leave the people? And why should the prince care? Machiavelli argues that a prudent prince will regard his new people as a long-term investment because one day he will have to ask them to fight for him. Machiavelli's love affair with his citizen militias is legendary. If the Romans could conquer the world with farmers conscripted into the legions, then why should the same not be true of a modern state? (Machiavelli ignores the objection that the art of war has improved so much since Roman times, when battles were simply a matter of pushing and shoving, that the day of the citizen-soldier has long gone.) The causes of Rome's greatness can be reproduced in modern conditions by a prince who has enough knowledge of the ancient world and enough foresight to put the ancient wisdom into practice. What might prevent a prince from seeing the truth of the ancient wisdom is rashness. A new prince entering a conquered and hostile territory might easily come to the conclusion that the best way to deal with his new people is to enslave them. Not literally, perhaps, but in the sense of screwing them down so efficiently with threats and taxes that it is unlikely that they will ever rebel. This is certainly an option open to a new prince, but it is fatally short-sighted.

The new prince must never forget that he acquired his new state by war, that in the future he will want to acquire additional territories by war and that other princes on the lookout for conquests of their own are bound to be casting an eye on his territories. War is not an option but a necessity for princes, so a prudent prince will not waste his time asking himself *whether* he should go to war, but *when*? and *how*?, and of the two questions the 'how' question is the most important. Machiavelli deals with this question with his customary clarity. There are three ways of going to war: with forces of one's own, with allies, or with mercenaries, and there are special problems with allies and mercenaries both during the war and after it. (Always assuming one is successful, that is; if you lose, your problems are over because by that time you will probably be dead.) Allies are always more or less reliable, because they are commanded by another and you can never be quite sure of them. However, the real problems of making successful war with allies come after the war, because what you win through the arms of others you hold by the arms of others. All kinds of jealousies can arise over the division of the spoils, and allies might even begin to think that what they have taken from others they can just as easily take from you. There is little enough security in a world in which kingdoms are being won and lost by the hazard of battle without having to worry about the predatoriness of allies. This is not to say that allies are useless, but the implication seems to be that an alliance in which a single ally predominates is dangerous for a prince.

Mercenaries are a menace both in peace and in war. Machiavelli is hard on mercenaries, and it seems probable that he makes them appear less reliable than they actually were in order to boost his case for citizen militias. Mercenaries serve only for pay, and they are naturally reluctant to fight because death is no more attractive to them than it is to any other man who practises a risky trade. Every mercenary captain will put off war as long as he can, because being paid while not actually having to fight is every mercenary's dream. Professional soldiers love to look warlike, partly out of professional pride and partly because employers are unlikely to hire pacific-looking weedy types, but they are just as shy of the battlefield as civilians. Mercenaries do not come cheap, and from their employer's point of view they are likely to appear as if they are eating him out of house and home while not actually doing very much for their money. On the other hand, their reluctance to fight makes their employer doubt whether mercenaries are likely to be much good in a real battle. Part of this doubt arises from a certain chuminess in the world of mercenaries as a whole. Mercenaries no more hate those they fight than they love those whom they fight for. They know perfectly well that in any war between mercenary armies they might well have been on the other side, and it is perfectly possible that in previous wars they have been the comrades-in-arms of today's enemies. It is hard to work up any genuine ferocity against others just doing a job as you are, unless the rewards are very high indeed. The last thing you would want would be a high butcher's bill after the battle, and so you would expect there to be all kinds of official and unofficial deals between opposing mercenary armies about quarter and ransom; you would expect battles of manœuvre with few casualties, and you would expect a fair number of honourable draws.

These would be expectations only. Nobody actually knows what is going to happen in a battle, and much that is unexpected can happen in the heat of the moment. None the less, these are reasonable expectations for an employer of mercenaries, and he would be a fool if he were to cast them entirely from his mind. And suppose mercenaries do all that is expected of them: they rout and slaughter the enemy. Where does that leave their employer? Could they not easily turn on him in the moment of victory? Every mercenary captain dreams of retiring one day to a little state of his own. Why not yours? This may not happen, but it is always something to think about. What the employer of mercenaries can be certain of is that the captain of a mercenary band will raise his fees after a successful war. This puts the prince in a ticklish position. To refuse a pay-rise to a successful merce- nary captain looks like ingratitude and meanness, and a prince has his reputation in the world to consider. On the other hand, war is expensive and all princes wage war for gain, so a winning prince who has to pay out his gains to keep his mercenaries happy can end up on the losing side after all. Besides, mercenaries are bound to have found out on the mercenaries' grapevine whether a prince is generous or not, so that, if their employer is mean, they are likely to take in plunder what they are uncertain of receiving in pay. However, no prince wants to take possession of a ravaged land, because there is nothing in it for him. Whichever way you look at it, mercenaries are always bound to be a problem.

A wise prince would consider problems like these when he begins to consider how a newly conquered people should be treated. Allies are dangerous and mercenaries are dangerous and expensive, so the far-seeing prince should always see a future citizen militia even in a cowed and abject people. This will affect what arrangements the prince will make for securing his new territories in the short and medium term. He will resist the easy option of holding his new state by garrisons, because these will consist of expensive professional troops whose pay will have to be wrung out of his new subjects, thus giving them greater cause to hate the prince while grinding them down still further. The best way to secure one-self in a new state is by colonists: yeoman farmers from one's old state who are given land in return for military service. Their loyalty is guaranteed by the gift and by the fact they are, like their prince, strangers in a foreign country. Each knows that the other depends on him. Colonists are planted neither too thickly nor too thinly: too thickly and the dispossessed are concentrated enough to resist; too thinly and the colonists cannot concentrate quickly enough for effective defensive action. This is a matter of fine judgement, and the prince had better get it right. What he is ultimately aiming for is intermarriage. The colonists are meant to become a kind of breeding cadre for a future militia and not a uselessly closed expatriate community longing for the old country while living off the fat of the new. Social integration will be that much easier if the conquered people is of the same religion, manners and language as the prince's own people. If not, then considerable care must be taken with the cultural sensibilities of new subjects. (Napoleon hit the right note when he said that if he were governing Jews he would rebuild the temple of Solomon.)

Machiavelli wants the new prince to regard his conquered people as a potential future asset. He wants them eventually to be able to regard the prince as *their* prince and so be able to think once again of the country as *their* country. These originally resentful and recalcitrant subjects must be seen as future patriots willing to die for king and country. This is a tall order. How can a conquered people ever really believe that the conqueror really is their king when they can still remember their real king and can probably still remember their real king's murder at the hands of the man who is now illicitly occupying the throne? And this is just as much a problem for the notables as it is for the people in general, and, what makes it worse, the prince knows that it is a problem. Every time a courtier bends his knee the prince sees a man for whom the act of obedience is something of a charade. He must be thinking that *he*, the courtier, could have been king if things had turned out differently. Luck (*fortuna*) always plays her part in the game of winning and losing kingdoms. Often, being the right man in the right place at the right time secures a princedom. It could have been *me*; it just happened to be *you*. The prince is forced to see that the courtier on his knees sees in the new prince a man not very different from himself who just happens to have been luckier. How different from a hereditary prince of the legitimate line, secure in his right to succeed to the throne of his fathers. All the new prince's 'acting like a king' cannot obscure the fact of the illegitimacy of his own origins.

The new prince is therefore faced with the most intractable of all problems, which is how to create his own legitimacy when the creation of one's own legitimacy is by definition impossible. Legitimacy is created by succeeding those who have gone before and is not created by oneself. Machiavelli's treatment of this problem is a brilliant *tour de force*. He turns the prince's luck into a legitimacy-creating agency, so that in the end the courtier on bended knee – and the people at large – begin to think that the prince's luck is of such a kind that he really is a creature apart, in his own way as different from ordinary men as an annointed king.

The successful new prince is a man who is *consistently* lucky. Machiavelli invokes the ancient Roman goddess of luck, Fortuna, as the successful prince's guiding spirit. Fortuna is a woman, so she likes her votaries to be young, handsome and masterly, combining the warlike quality of Achilles with the cunning persistence of Odysseus. Fortuna is a bit of a bitch, flighty and treacherous; she needs constant wooing, and sometimes she needs to be roughed up, but keep her sweet and there is nothing she won't do for you. Rough trade about sums it up, and this makes her the ideal mate for a prince on the make in the rough business of state-making. Fortuna can take the chance element out of luck, at least for a time – and perhaps for a long time as she did with her ancient Roman favourites. Some princes are so consistently lucky that their luck begins to appear to be uncanny. Observers begin to think that there is something not quite human, or at least quite out of the ordinary, about the prince whose luck holds through all the vicissitudes of high politics. It also does the prince no harm to spread the word that more than human agency is at work in his career. By degrees, Fortuna begins to show that her favourites are men apart. They become like the ancient heroes in whose fate the gods took an immediate and constant interest. Indeed, that is what made them heroes and created the distance between them and ordinary men. Who except another hero would dare to tangle with Hector? Only a fool would stand up to Achilles without some kind of divine protection. Successful princes are a bit like that. Taking them on is to take more on than a mere human being, and you would yourself have to be very sure of your own exceptional abilities before you even tried.

Fortuna does for new princes what God's annointment did for legitimate Christian kings. Traditional hereditary legitimacy was a way of setting kings apart from even the mightiest of their subjects. The courtier on bended knee to a legitimate king keeps his self-respect by saying to himself that *he* could never have been king. The courtier might be a better man than the king. The courtier might easily be the man who really does the king's business for him, rules his realm or conquers his enemies. None the less, the courtier cannot think of himself as the king's rival because, no matter what happens, the king is still king. This works from the king's side too. The legitimate king may see a better man on his knees than he is, but the king has no reason to be jealous because he sees in front of him a man who could be what the king is.

That sense of distance is what creates legitimacy in traditional kingship. What Machiavelli has done through the notion of Fortuna is to re-create that legitimate distance in a non-Christian way. The new prince's courtiers – and his subjects at large – are supposed to think that the prince is a man who has been touched by the divine. Yes, he has been lucky, but his luck is not entirely fortuitous, and his luck would probably enable him to survive any plot that a malcontent might get up against him. Something very like awe in the face of majesty begins to form in the minds of those who surround the prince, and this awe is by no means uncongenial to them. They begin to discover a new sense of self-respect in themselves. They now feel that there is nothing in the least demeaning in bending their knee to their prince. The sense that they and the prince are on the same level begins to fade as they begin to think that only a fool would try to compete with a prince whose luck never seems to run out, and men are generally content with the thought that they themselves are not fools.

Machiavelli was a playwright and there is plainly an element of play-acting in all this. The prince is on stage, and if he plays his part well enough then the other actors and the audience will begin to suspend their disbelief. They gradually come to believe that the actor in borrowed robes really is a prince. The stage setting helps. Renaissance drama was often set in princely courts, and the prince usually gets the best costume, the best place on stage and the best lines. The court drama is really a play within the play. In the Machiavellian drama of *The Prince*, the prince's subjects at large stand for the audience and the prince's closest associates stand in for the actors. Ordinary folk see the prince's friends treat him like a real king and so insensibly the ordinary folk come to believe that the prince is himself the real thing.

The prudent prince does not have to be reminded that you can't fool all of the people all of the time. The prince is a deceiver who must never allow himself to be self-deceived. These things take time, and they are never definitively complete. There can never come a moment when the new prince can say to himself that he has been completely successful. And besides, the suspension of disbelief can itself be suspended; any regular theatre-goer will tell you that any brilliantly successful actor in a long-running play has a dreadful night from time to time.

Machiavelli deals with this problem with his usual realism. The new prince really has to deliver, and that means success in war. Machiavelli has a very shrewd idea of the connection between the internal politics of a state and foreign policy. War is the trade of princes and it is in war that Fortune smiles or frowns. The prince might as well retire to a monastery if he can't cut the mustard on the battlefield. War is sexy where sex is about power, and it is in war that the prince really needs to have good fortune. The prince's *virtu* is put to the test, and each time he is not found wanting he adds to his prestige. If he has had the good sense to go to war with his own citizen militia, his subjects begin to feel the glow which comes from being part of a winning team. They begin to feel that they can't lose under their new prince, and any lingering affection for the old princely line becomes less as they begin to reflect what it was like to be ruled by losers. There are strong practical advantages to add to the psychology of winning. Machiavelli advises princes always to go on the offensive as the old Romans did. Attacking means that you go to war when you are ready and your opponent may not be, and in addition to the element of surprise there is the considerable advantage that the attackers fight on another's territory and not on their own. This advantage will not be lost on the prince's soldiers. Somebody else's house gets burned, somebody else's wife gets raped and somebody else's farm gets laid waste. The prince can easily allow his own soldiers a little plunder, because what he loses by plunder he makes up negatively by not having to pay wages to his own citizens.

The word 'citizens' is used deliberately here as a substitute for 'subjects' because it is a feature of good princely rule that there should be a transition from the one to the other. Subjects in original subjection are supposed to feel the prince's yoke less and less, until they begin to feel like citizens of a state which is truly theirs. This is, of course, highly advantageous to the prince. He gets soldiers free who feel that their country is worth fighting for. The prince begins to thank God he took Machiavelli's advice and did not enslave his people.

A citizen army returning victorious from its country's wars will not put up with being bossed about at home. Tyranny of a petty-minded and rapacious kind would be the least appropriate form of government for men conscious of their own strength and who had arms in their hands. The fact that a prince can trust his people enough to arm them shows that they have become partners. Partners regulate their relations with each other on the basis of consent. Machiavelli knows his ancient authors well enough to know that government by consent means government by law in the interests of all, and not government by force in the interest of the tyrant only. Good arms and good laws entail and imply each other, and a wise prince would be well pleased when his people began to think of the laws as *their* laws. That is one of the reasons why Machiavelli thinks a prudent new prince should alter the existing laws as little as possible. There is nothing people find more irksome than having laws imposed on them by foreigners. A prince should *add* to existing law whenever possible, and should be glad to acquiesce in the continuance of those local customs which over time have acquired the force of law.

Properly considered, princely government consists of the union of the interests of prince and people. Machiavelli anticipates Hobbes in believing that the glory of a prince can consist of nothing but the prosperity and contentment of his people. Subjects like these will follow the prince anywhere. Simple common sense might dictate that it is men with nothing to lose who will cheerfully put their lives at risk on the battlefield, but this is just another case where Machiavelli thinks that common sense is wrong. It is citizens with a good deal to lose that you can lead to war with confidence, and even losing cannot alter the fact that a citizen army still has a good deal left which is worth defending. Citizen armies cannot simply melt away after a defeat. Quite the reverse. They re-form with renewed determination to defend what is theirs, and the chances are that, if their prince has not been cowardly or incompetent, the citizen army will re-form around him. And the nearer they get to home the more determined they will become.

Machiavelli thinks that there is no reason in principle why a prince well-versed in statecraft and with luck on his side should not be able to unite the warring principalities of Italy. The kings of the French have managed to unite the various French provinces into a single kingdom, so why not Italy? The short answer is, of course, the papacy, which Machiavelli regards as the real Italian problem. The papacy enjoys a prestige so enormous that even Borgia popes have failed to destroy it. (Machiavelli has no inkling of the Reformation shortly to come.) On the other hand, the papacy has no real forces of its own. Even Cesare Borgia ultimately failed to produce a militia out of the peasantry of the Papal States. Popes, as secular princes, have their wars to fight. The only way they can do this is to invite allies to invade Italy, and the papal allies are no less dangerous than the allies of other princes. The French, the Spanish, the Swiss and the Germans do nothing but follow Machiavelli's own advice to princes when they descend upon Italy: they come by plausible invitation and they fight on another's land. In Machiavelli's own terms the foreigners would be fools *not* to come. What Italy needs is a prince who can knock some sense into Italy as a whole, perhaps forming an alliance strong enough to expel all the barbarians. No wonder that Machiavelli was to be a hero of Italian national unification in the nineteenth century. The history of the eventual unification of Italy could be written on the Machiavellian theme: When will the prince come and who will it be? Garibaldi? Cavour? Even Mussolini claiming to complete the Risorgimento?

NOTES ON SOURCES

People are still trying to puzzle out the meaning of Machiavelli's *Prince*, so, as you would expect, there is a huge Machiavelli literature. It can't be emphasised enough, though, that *all* study of Machiavelli must begin with *The Prince* and the *Discourses*, both of which exist in various English editions. For the life, R. Ridolfi, *The Life of Niccolo Machiavelli* (1963), is still essential. Q. Skinner, *Machiavelli* (1981), is a workmanlike introduction; S. Anglo, *Machiavelli: A Dissection* (1969), is brilliant and eccentric. Herbert Butterfield, *The Statecraft of Machiavelli* (1955), and Felix Raab, *The English Face of Machiavelli* (1964), have still got a lot to teach us, as has the characteristically careful account of Machiavelli in J. Plamenatz, *Man and Society*, vol. 1, (1963). Anybody who is going to take Machiavelli seriously has eventually to make the acquaintance of *Machiavelli – the Chief Works and Others*, trans. and ed. A. Gilbert (2 vols, 1965).

Part IV

THE THEORY OF THE SOCIAL CONTRACT

10

THE RISE AND EXTRAORDINARY PERSISTENCE OF THE THEORY OF THE SOCIAL CONTRACT

From the time of the radical Reformation until well into the second half of the eighteenth century political thinking was dominated by the idea of social contract. This is very far from saying that all important political theory was social contract theory, but it does mean that all political theorising, when it was not social contract theory itself, had to take account of social contract or to attack it. It used to be thought that social contract died after it had been definitively ridiculed by Hume and Bentham, but that was to ignore its persistence in the United States, where a version of it continued to be argued by the apologists of the right of secession in the South before the Civil War, and it continued well into the twentieth century as part of the argument for states' rights. Another version of social contract, this time appearing as a guide to the proper understanding of public policy, exists in the works of the contemporary American political philosopher John Rawls (*A Theory of Justice*). Social contract has been argued to support any number of political positions. It has been argued as a justification for executing a king, as it was in seventeenth-century England by the Commonwealth's leaders; it has been argued as a justification of limited government, as it was by Locke; it has been argued as a justification for some kind of revolution, as it was by Rousseau. It was argued by Southerners in the United States to justify breaking up the Union and it was argued by them later as a justification for being beastly to blacks, while John Rawls argues a social contract case for treating blacks decently.

Social contract can be used to argue anything, and the fundamental plausibility of social contract theorising is sometimes given as the reason for its remarkable persistence. Everybody, it is said, understands what a contract is. Social contract theory is typically used to explain why men should obey the state, or the law, or the sovereign. What could be more natural than to say that men are obliged to obey the state, or the law, or the sovereign, because they promised to obey? In ordinary life, everyone knows that promises create obligations (Why should I do that? Because I promised I would), so why should we not say that our political obligations arise in the same way? Of course, to say that political obligations arise in the same way as obligations in everyday life is not the same thing as saying that there are not going to be problems about political obligation. What exactly I agree to, and what the conditions are on which obligations to obey depend, would still be matters for urgent debate. It is certainly easy enough to find contract-sounding notions in the political thought of Europe before the Reformation. Socrates himself is supposed to have said that the reason why he did not use the opportunity to escape from the rigour of the Athenian justice which had condemned him was that he had always lived in the city and so had implicitly agreed to abide by its laws. The coronation rituals of medieval kings were shot through with contract notions. Kings received the blessing of Holy Church in return for promising to protect true religion and the Church as its earthly embodiment, received the homage of the barons in return for confirming them in their privileges, and were acclaimed by the people who expected kings to protect them from the wilder vagaries of men and nature. And all oaths of allegiance are to some extent contractual. In this sense feudalism was riddled with contract, but feudal contracts were not free in any real sense because sons always claimed the right to make contracts with feudal superiors on the same terms as their fathers. (One of the things which made churchmen a good prospect for feudal superiors with fiefs to dispose of was that, priests not being allowed officially to have sons, the fief was again at the free disposal of the lord when the priestly vassal died.) Of course, there is no end to the business of finding contract notions in political thought before the Reformation, but the fact remains that before then contract was never given as the *basis* for political society (with the great exception of the Jews, of which more later).

It might also be said that before the Reformation there was never a serious case to be made out for disobedience. This does not mean that everyone before then was always satisfied with the political authority which required their obedience, but it might mean that before the rise of social contract there was always a presumption in favour of obedience. The common law of Christendom was supposed to be binding on all men, rulers and ruled, and being God's Law, there could never be a case for disobedience. Matters became slightly more complicated, but not much, at the level of political practice. Suppose that the laws which require my obedience imperfectly express God's Law. How does that affect my duty to obey? At first sight, it might appear that it affects my duty to obey a great deal. I might be tempted to say that human law which imperfectly embodies God's Law is no law at all. That would be to say that I would obey no ruler except God himself, and that would turn me into a millenarian, obedient to no-one on earth until Christ and his Saints return to rule for a thousand years. A refusal to obey any earthly law would effectively make me into an anarchist. Besides, what I would be forgetting is that earthly law is, *by definition*, an imperfect embodiment of God's Law. No matter how well-intentioned earthly rulers are, no matter how mindful of the Church's teaching, no matter how saintly the king, all law made or declared by earthly law-givers is going to be, *sub specie aeternitatis*, bad law. Some laws will be better than others, and medieval thinkers had in fact disagreed about how good law which was not God's Law could be, but none could be wholly good. In these circumstances, the purist would always be in the position of saying that at best he was almost, but not quite, bound by law, so he would be almost, but not quite, bound to obey. Either you obey or you don't (you can't almost, but not quite, obey) so you would either be always bound to obey, in which case political obligation would not be a problem, or you would never obey, in which case political obligation is not a problem either. Neither complete acceptance, nor complete rejection is really an attempt to deal with political obligation: either you would always obey or you would never obey, and that would be that.

Political obligation, then, only becomes a problem – something worth thinking seriously about – when there is a serious case for disobedience in the minds of men who are prepared to obey law, even though law is imperfect, but not *that* law, or not that law made by *him*. Law becomes in some sense a matter for negotiation between rulers and subjects; in short, a matter of agreement or contract. This involves an important shift of emphasis in thinking about law. In the future, the question of law's 'goodness' was going to have to share the centre of theoretical concern with questions about law's legitimacy. Much more legalistic, procedural questions were going to be asked about law. Questions about who had the right to make law, and questions about whether the law was made (and executed) in the proper way, were going to be just as important as questions about whether law was 'good', and a time would come when all that law had to do was to be legitimate, when procedural considerations alone would determine what was good law and what was not. By the time that happened, the modern state, with its typical claim to sovereignty, was well on the way to becoming an accomplished fact.

It is important not to exaggerate either the speed or the extent of this transformation. Reformation means taking God very seriously, and Counter-Reformation means taking the Church very seriously indeed. Reformed political theory, which effectively means Protestant political theory, still thought that law served good and godly ends. The social peace, which only obedience to duly constituted authority could provide, was always going to be pleasing in God's sight. What was no longer so clear was that God intended us to obey *that* prince and *those* laws. How could God be saying anything very clear about political obligation when Christendom was split into two warring halves, one Catholic and one Protestant? In these circumstances it is no surprise that thoughtful men began to wonder whether it really was true that the laws under which they lived were instances of a universal law as it applies to particulars. That very general unease was sharpened by the very particular problem of what was to be done if you remained a Catholic when your prince became a Protestant, or if you became a Protestant and your prince remained a Catholic. The implied covenant of the coronation stated clearly that the prince agreed to preserve true religion, and, in an age when men felt obliged to believe that any religion other than their own was false, the fact that your prince's religion was not your own showed *prima facie* that the original contract to preserve true religion had been broken. It followed that a new contract could be made, perhaps with a new prince, to preserve true religion, as in the case of John Knox and the Scottish Covenanter movement to oust the Catholic Mary Queen of Scots in favour of a Protestant king.

The growth of literacy which came about as a consequence of the spread of printing meant that for the first time men could read the source book of their own religion in the vernacular. The Book of Genesis contains the first account, and the only account which Christians were obliged to believe, of the founding of a people, and that foundation was by agreement. The Children of Israel negotiated with God and agreed to keep the Law in return for the promise that they would eventually possess the Land. A people, a law and a land was the perfect image of the nation-state. The Covenant was not easy to keep, and the Book of Genesis is the story of the struggles of Moses to keep his people to the terms of the contract. Mosaic leadership is a perfect image of a prince keeping his unruly people to their faith in return for a promise of future benefits. Moses is both the people's agent and God's. The implications of the Genesis story are what its interpreters chose to make them, but one striking implication stood out clearly for those who were on the lookout for ideological ammunition to fire at the more extreme claims of kingly pretensions: if God himself had bargained with His chosen people, then the refusal of an earthly king to bargain with his people was to make a stronger claim for earthly authority than God himself had ever made for His own omnipotence. Of course, this was only one of the possible readings of the Moses story, and perhaps that is why it does not figure very largely in the formal accounts of social contract. It could so easily be argued that the Jews were a special case, that they were God's chosen people precisely because God had chosen to bargain with them: all other peoples were simply commanded to keep the Law. And besides, the fact that God was sole and omnipotent ruler of the Creation was itself so powerful an argument for monarchy (and even for universal imperial monarchy) that social contract theorists of the libertarian kind were probably wise to leave the Moses story well alone. None the less, ideas of a new covenant with God litter the political thinking of post-Reformation Europe, especially where that political thinking refers to the government of the Church.

The one thing God did not bargain about at the beginning was the content of the Law. The Ten Commandments were fixed for ever, and it was the easiest thing in the world to argue that the Catholic Church had failed to keep God's people to those commandments. It was also easy to argue that the Church's own hierarchy, from the lowliest village priest right up to the pope in Rome, lived lives which daily violated those commandments. A new covenant was simply a re-affirmation of the acceptance of the Law in the hope of receiving those rewards which obedience to the Law had originally promised. This had huge implications for Church government. The Church's hierarchy came to be seen as a bar to the salvation of God's people, holding them against their true will in sinful Babylonian captivity. Only a new Ark of the Covenant could promise eventual release, and only ministers who truly preached the Word could show God's people the way. Where were these ministers to be found? Not, surely, among those calling themselves priests, or at least not among priests who held fast to the old rotting establishment. Who, then, was to decide who was fit to minister to God's people? If not the Church, then only the congregations. From now on, churches were to be self-governing in the sense that they would choose (and dismiss) their pastors. And those pastors' title to their offices would henceforward rest on their competence as readers and interpreters of the Word.

These radically new (though in fact very old) proposals for the running of churches could only have radical effects on men's attitudes to the running of the state. On a very simple level, it could be argued that what applied to Church government should apply straight-forwardly to the state's government on the principle of *a fortiori* (the greater should contain the lesser). If the government of the community which means most to Christian people should be governed according to the reflection and choice of its members, then why should the government of the state, an inferior institution by comparison, not be governed in the same way too? The salvation of souls, which the membership of a properly constituted Church makes more likely, plainly takes precedence over that minimal earthly peace which membership of a state might provide, so it seems to follow as plainly as the night the day, that what the Church should concede the state should also concede.

Or should it? Perhaps a loosening of the bonds of authority in churches implied a strengthening of the bonds of authority in the state. The Reformation attacked the hierarchy of the Church in the full knowledge that the Church was not the least of the insti-tutions which controlled men's lives. In that sense, the Church's authority was profoundly of this world. The Reformers' objection to the hierarchy was not that it controlled men's lives in the secular world, but rather that the Church had itself become wordly. Taking away the Church's authority in the world could seem to leave a gap in power. Reformation did not mean that sinful men were to be left to do as they pleased. How could it, when Reformation itself came about because of the perception that sinfulness was so pervasive that it had even corrupted Christ's Church? One way out of the difficulty of imposing order on a sinful world without the Catholic Church was to place an even greater burden of repression on secular authority, as with Luther, and another was to place an even greater burden on the reformed Church, as with Calvin. (The English solution was to keep the hierarchy and call it Protestant, a manoeuvre which satisfied the orthodox Calvinist James VI of Scotland when he became king of England in 1603.) And it *was* God that men were making new covenants with, and there was no guarantee that He would not drive a very hard bargain.

The original of all contracts between God and the Jews had said nothing about changes in the content of the laws; God's Law was God's Law. Only the penalties for disobedience and the rewards for compliance were negotiable. What could never have been in dispute was that God was a lawful sovereign, and therefore the law which he made was good law. That was to be the ideal formula for law-making. The theory of the social contract was to insist on the equal importance of both conditions, lawful law-maker and lawful law, and it is easy to see why in an age when rulers were to change with alarming frequency. Suppose that quite suddenly men began to think that their prince was a wicked man because his religion differed from their own, and suppose them to begin a process to try to change their old prince for another more to their liking. Suppose that they were to succeed. What was then to be done about the law which a superseded prince and his ancestors had made and enforced? Was it suddenly to be considered bad law and therefore incapable of sustaining the allegiance of rational men? Of course not, but for it to remain capable of requiring the obedience of thinking men, a distinction had to be drawn between the law itself and those who made it. At least in principle, bad princes could make good law, and, at least in principle, good law could outlast the rule of wicked princes. Considerations like these accompanied a shift of emphasis onto the procedural constraints which made law lawful, and this concern for procedures fitted well with the strong legalistic current in social contract theory. How the law came to be made would be just as important a question as how good that law was. Very ancient ideas about what made law lawful could now co-exist with rather more novel questions about who was in fact entitled to make law. The old Natural Law tradition had always held that the positive law of states had to conform to the general law of Christendom which was itself part of God's Law, and, as we saw above, there had always been a tendency to see obligation to obey the law as part of the wider question of the goodness of the substantive content of the positive law. The procedural emphasis in social contract thinking altered the way men thought about political obligation in one crucial way: men no longer felt themselves bound by law, however good, if it had not been made by the proper sovereign and in the proper form. Social contract theory was in fact less concerned with the content of law than with correctly identifying the person who was entitled to legislate, and most social contract thinkers were in fact quite conservative about the content of law. They continued to think about positive law as being derived from Natural Law, though they sometimes reworked and extended the idea of Natural Law itself, and there could be no denying that Natural Law was morally binding on all Christian men (and on all men who were rational if they were not Christian). What became crucial was deciding who was entitled to make authoritative decisions about how Natural Law was to be embodied in the positive laws of particular polities, and how those authoritative decisions were to be made. Some, like Hobbes, argued an absolutist case for undivided

sovereignty in the hands of one man or a body of men; others, like Locke, argued a recognisably parliamentary case; and yet others, like Rousseau, argued a case for an absolutely
sovereign people as law-givers to themselves. But in all the cases the question of who was
entitled to make law took precedence over the now secondary, though still important,
question about what kinds of laws could actually be made. Indeed, what makes Rousseau's
Social Contract (1762) so remarkable is his frank insistence that a sovereign people which
knew beforehand what kinds of laws it should make would not be absolutely free and
sovereign; any pre-existing standard which told them what laws they could make would
effectively tie the hands of the sovereign people behind its back. Not every social contract
thinker is as clear as Hobbes that men cannot make law by contract but can only choose a
law-giver by agreement, but Hobbes speaks for nearly all social contract theory in the
emphasis he places on the fundamental importance of the legislator.

This shift of emphasis, from the content of the laws to the law-giver, had an effect on
the way men were being asked to look at the question of the content of the positive law.
With the increased emphasis on the right law-giver, men could afford to be a little less
choosy about the laws the law-giver made. Questions about the goodness of law shade
imperceptibly into questions about the legitimacy of law, and questions about the legitimacy of law shade imperceptibly into questions about the procedure by which laws are in
fact made. Law becomes good because it was made by the right people in the right way.
This is not the licence to make bad law that it might appear to be at first sight; nor is it a
recipe for requiring people to obey just any law. Procedures for making law can have a huge
effect, if only a negative effect, on what kinds of legislative decisions can in fact be made.
One of the ways of putting procedural constraints on law-making is to enshrine those
constraints in a constitution which is supposed to change only slowly, as in the case of
England, or in a constitution which itself lays down very strict procedures for altering the
constitution so that changing it is very difficult, as in the case of the United States. Emphasis
on procedures makes the case for disobedience more, not less, clear. It is much easier to
see that a law is unconstitutional because it was made wrongly, or made by the wrong
people, than it is to see, and convince enough people who really matter, that a law is in
some fundamental sense morally wrong. The trouble with the old Natural Law goodness
criterion for the lawfulness of law was, as we have seen, that a law had to be so fundamentally bad – say a law requiring the worship of false gods – that most positive law would
be of the more-or-less good, more-or-less bad kind, about which there could be endless
well-intentioned disagreement about whether it should be obeyed or not. Constitutional
constraints, on the other hand, are conditions about which more precise things can be said,
and about whose violation much more precise judgements can be made.

Not all social contract theory is constitutional theory in the sense of theory about the
constraints which can be put on government. The most brilliantly argued and sustained
contract theory, Hobbes's *Leviathan*, is designed to show that it is logical nonsense to believe
that formal constraints can ever be put on the sovereign. Hobbes in fact knew very well
that, in the England which was engaged in its Civil War, the Parliamentary side thought of
itself as defending an ancient constitution which limited kingship by insisting on certain
fundamental rights and liberties which Englishmen just happened to have, no matter who

was king or what that king's own view of kingship was. Hobbes set all later contract theorists the problem of how a people could make law, as distinct from choosing a law-giver and agreeing to abide by his laws. The Hobbesian argument is very powerful: men living without law, in some imagined State of Nature, would be men with every good reason for not trusting each other. They could not make ordinary contracts with each other because of the fear of non-performance in a lawless world. The State of Nature differs from Civil Society because in Civil Society (society with regular law-enforcement) any contract, provided only that it is lawful, will be upheld by the courts. Of course, only a tiny proportion of the contracts made in Civil Society will ever attract the attention of the courts, but the fact that the courts are there creates the confidence in the performance of the terms of contracts, without which no rational man would enter into a contract at all. It is the existence of an effective law of contracts which causes men to have confidence in the performance of contract, not the other way round; it is not men's confidence in the performance of the terms of contract which makes the law of contract work. Plainly, no such confidence in the performance of the terms of contract is possible in the State of Nature. It is not that men living in a State of Nature would not want to make contracts with each other, say contracts of buying and selling; it is just that, without the confidence in performance, it would never make sense to make an ordinary contract in the State of Nature. Hobbes then goes on to draw out an implication from the non-performance of contracts in the State of Nature which appears to be unanswerable: if men in the State of Nature cannot trust one another enough to make an ordinary, everyday contract, how could they ever come to trust one another enough to sit down together and construct a whole system of law by voluntary agreement? Hobbes's way out of the difficulty of explaining the origin of Civil Society and its law is simple: men got themselves out of the lawless State of Nature by agreeing to choose one man (or a body of men) as a law-giver, and by agreeing to abide by the laws he made as commands of a sovereign, provided only that those laws were effectively enforced. Sovereignty, the right to make law and enforce it, must have been thrust upon someone in the beginning, because anything was better than the lawless State of Nature.

The cunning part of Hobbes's masterly conjecture is the procedure which he thinks must have been followed in this original creation of sovereignty. Men in the State of Nature pointed to one man (or a body of men) and agreed among themselves to make him sovereign. *The Sovereign is therefore not party to the original contract.* Therefore there can have been no constraints put on the exercise of the sovereign power by contract; therefore sovereignty in its original form must by definition be both absolute and indivisible (for a more detailed account of Hobbes's arguments, see below, Chapter 11). There was nothing very startling about making claims like these for sovereignty in the middle of the seventeenth century. Kings had been making these claims for at least a century. What is very remarkable is that such absolutist claims should be argued in the terms of social contract, when social contract had practically been invented to deny absolutist claims. The absolutist argument in social contract's own terms offered by Hobbes (State of Nature, contract, Civil Society) put all later social contract theory on its mettle to make up the ground which a more libertarian version of social contract had apparently lost to him.

One of the ways in which later social contract thinking tried to sharpen its blunted libertarian thrust was to emphasise its latent constitutionalism. Nothing was easier than to regard a constitution either as some kind of agreement between rulers and ruled, or as an agreement of a whole people about how it should be governed. In England, William and Mary accepted the Bill of Rights in return for the crown in 1689, and in the United States a majority of the whole people accepted the new Constitution through the state ratifying conventions before 1789. Constitutionalism is the ideal solution to the problem set by Hobbes, a middle ground between questions about the detail of positive laws and high moral discourse about the rightness of obedience. Of course, nobody since the demise of the ancient republic had ever taken really seriously the idea that a whole people could settle the details of legislation, so that anti-contract argument seemed to be on strong ground when it harped on the impossibiity of making law by agreement. Constitutionalist argument attempted to get round that difficulty by insisting that a people, through its representatives, could agree to give itself laws of a very general kind, laws about how laws should be made. This also got round the difficulty about the goodness content of law, because there was no reason in principle, and good reasons in practice, why a constitution should not outlaw certain kinds of law from the outset.

In England, 1688 was the real turning point for libertarian social contract theory in its battle against Hobbes. When the Catholic James II left England for France he threw the Great Seal of England into the Thames. That was the supremely Hobbesian moment, because without the Great Seal there could be no legal government in England, and James's fit of pique was supposed to return England to the State of Nature, where every man's hand was against every other man's hand. Nothing remotely like that happened, and the people of England, through their representatives, negotiated an agreement with new sovereigns, William and Mary. What 1688 proved was that a political community could survive the temporary absence of a sovereign. That was the real answer to Hobbes. If a political community could remain in being without a sovereign, there was no reason why it should not negotiate a restriction on sovereignty with its rulers before appointing them. A social contract thinker like Locke would have no doubt that ordinary, recognisable human living is possible, though inconvenient, without a central law-making and law-enforcing agency.

That difference, between thinking that the temporary absence of a sovereign immediately leads to a chaotic, atomistic anarchy, and thinking that the social order would hold, at least for a time, is so fundamental (and continues to be fundamental) that it is worth asking what made the transition from the one point of view to the other possible in the thirty years between Hobbes's *Leviathan* and Locke's *Two Treatises of Civil Government*. It cannot simply be a matter of the temperament of authors, because everything that we know about Hobbes suggests that he was a cheerful man despite the gloom which infects his political writings, whereas everything we know about Locke suggests he was none too sanguine about humanity, despite the qualified optimism of his *Second Treatise*. It is important to be clear about what is at issue here, because it is basic to the distinction between state and society upon which the doctrine which was later to be called liberalism was to be based. Hobbes seems to be saying that society, in the sense of ordinary social living, is impossible without the state as a law-and-order mechanism. Social living, in his view of it, is fragile and has no independent force of its own; the life of society is parasitical on the state. All social engineering has to begin with political engineering, so that rational men will give their first attention to the business of setting up the state properly. Locke says something rather different: the life of society is much tougher than has hitherto been supposed; in that sense society is natural, arises more or less spontaneously, and has a life which is independent of the law-and-order mechanism which men create to cope with the inconveniencies which arise out of the incompleteness of society's own self-regulating mechanisms. Locke thinks that, at least in principle, and probably in practice, a society could survive the collapse of its formal structure of law and order, and by that he means that society's natural will would still be intact enough for it to be able to make a choice about how it wanted to be governed in the future. Hobbes seems to think that society has no will of its own, and Locke seems to think that the state need have no will of its own. Of course, neither need be true, but the question still has to be answered as to how such a startling difference of opinion about something so fundamental could arise in so short a time, especially as it won't do to say that Hobbes was temperamentally inclined to panic about law and order while Locke was not.

The easiest explanation of this increase in confidence in the future of social living would be to say that it reflected some kind of general improvement in the nature and quality of social life. The end of the Thirty Years War in Germany (1648), the consolidation of the monarchy in France, and the fact that England did not degenerate into anything like a Hobbesian State of Nature during its Civil War, may all have contributed to a feeling that stable patterns of human living were going to be the future norm. Of course, these were political factors just as much as they were social, and it could just as easily be argued that expectations about social stability were able to arise because state stability came first, but that is not necessarily how contemporaries like Locke saw it. He could easily have been struck by the fact that societies could survive the shocks which their politics had given them. Even German society could begin to reconstitute itself after the Thirty Years War. Perhaps it was one aspect of European society in the second half of the seventeenth century which above all others explains this new awareness of society's capacity to flourish independently of the state: capitalism.

Much has been made of the connection between social contract theory and the rise of capitalism, and on the face of it the connection is clear enough. What could be more natural than that a society which came increasingly to arrange its economic affairs on the basis of free contracts of buying and selling would become increasingly likely to come to see its relationships to the state in the terms of equally free contract? The way in which ordinary contracts of buying and selling actually work in the real world lends a certain plausibility to social contract. One of the standard objections which has always been made to social contract is that there is never any record of an original social contract which can be consulted. Of course, there had been attempts to cry up one document or another as an original contract between prince and people (in England Magna Carta was always a favourite choice), but social contract theory still remained vulnerable, at least in its opponents' eyes, because it could never produce the exact terms of the original contract which princes were obliged to keep, and which they could be cashiered for breaking. An objection to social contract thinking like that in fact fails to understand how the ordinary law of contract works. Most ordinary cases of contract occur when the idea of making a formal contract could not be further from the minds of the contracting parties. (Nobody goes into a shop and says 'I want to make a contract of sale with fixed terms' to the sales assistant.) What the law does is to infer a contract of sale from the behaviour of the parties to that sale. In the normal course of events, the law has nothing to say about the contracts which we make. Our ordinary behaviour shows that most of the time we are satisfied with the performance of the contracts we make because we go to law only infrequently, and buyers and sellers rarely give the matter a second thought. Social contract can also be seen in the same light. Men whose ordinary business is buying and selling can easily come to see their relationship to the state as contractual, and they can also come to see themselves as satisfied in the normal course of events with the state's performance on the other side of the bargain. They might be inclined to look to their bond only when there is good reason to do so, which would effectively mean when things were beginning to go wrong. And a legally minded observer would not find it difficult to infer a contract between rulers and ruled on the simple grounds that both act *as if* they had made an agreement, and on the even simpler grounds that both rulers and ruled would act no differently *if* they had made such an agreement.

This is a scheme of things which can accommodate political change quite easily. Social contract's later enemies, the Utilitarians for example, always spoke about the social contract as if it had to be an original contract valid for ever. As reformers of ancient ways, the Utilitarians ridiculed original contract, and as radicals, the Utilitarians denied that a contract in the past could bind present and future generations. In fact, there is no reason to suppose that an original contract cannot be renegotiated as circumstances change; nor is there any reason why an original contract should not be repudiated and negotiated from scratch as occasion demands. The ordinary law of contract does not allow contracts for ever. I cannot make a contract which binds my descendants till the end of time. When the Utilitarians ridiculed social contract, they were in fact ridiculing a particularly English, Whiggish version of it, which held that what happened in 1688 was binding for ever. What social contract theory was not always very clear about was what the conditions exactly were in which a renegotiation of the terms of the social contract was either necessary or justified. In particular, social contract theory, concerned as it was with the question of who was entitled to make laws, had to concern itself with the question: Who is entitled to begin the process by which the old contract is dissolved and a new contract negotiated? Hobbes gave the clearest answer: the old contract is dissolved when each man feels in his own guts that he is back in the State of Nature. He will know this when law enforcement has broken down to the extent that he fears his neighbours more than he fears his sovereign. Looking around for a new sovereign is not so much a matter of entitlement as of fact: you will know when the circumstances force you into finding a way out of the State of Nature again because your adrenalin will tell you. Other social contract thinkers are less clear on this vital question of the circumstances in which the contract must be renewed. Locke seems to say that a moment will come in the history of a society when it will be obvious to enough people, or to enough of the people that matter, that government has betrayed its trust and has to go. This may seem to be rather an all-or-nothing position for Locke to hold, but something like it seems to have been the position Jefferson and his friends had come to when they signed the American Declaration of Independence. Men would be unlikely to give up their political allegiance for 'light and transient causes'. Jefferson hit exactly the right note when he said that, on the whole, men were more prepared to put up with the deficiencies of their government than to begin again and construct a new one, but times did come when men were pushed into rebellion. What was remarkable about the beginning of the American Revolution was how *public* the events leading up to the Declaration of Independence were. This was no hole-in-the-corner conspiracy; the signers were not malcontents; they were doing nothing of which they had to be ashamed. This was one of those occasions when the public had to take back its trust from a government which had obviously betrayed it. It hardly matters that in fact only about a third of all Americans (by the conventional reckoning) thought that the break with the mother country was an urgent necessity. Time would show which side had the right of it.

Perhaps the whole experience of North American colonisation helped the idea of social contract. When Europeans first began to make contact with the North American Indians, they were struck not so much by the evident superiority of European civilisation as by the idea that the Indians were living the life that Europeans had themselves once lived. The simplicity of Indian manners and morals might have important lessons for Europeans because, as Locke was to put it, once upon a time all the world was America. What struck observers in particular was the equality of the warriors in the Indian tribe under the authority of a chief. How had it come about that braves roughly equal in strength obeyed a chief who was not very obviously stronger than any individual brave, and who was certainly weaker than any two of them? The puzzle was easily answered: the tribe obeyed its chief because it had agreed to. This may have been a simple answer, but it was in its way quite startling. The North American Indians had never heard of God; therefore it could not be true that they obeyed their rulers at God's command. It began to dawn very early on a few daring spirits that perhaps the original of all government was to be found in the simplicity of Indian contract, and that other justifications for government, the famous Divine Right of Kings, for example, were later inventions, designed to hoodwink men for the self-interested motives of a dynasty. This was not a very sophisticated anthropology (though it was to be remarkably long-lived), but in fact it was extremely double-edged. Nobody really thought that it would be a good idea to imitate savage Indian tribes, and there was a lively debate which lasted until the end of the eighteenth century about whether the discovery of the New World was the best or the worst thing that had ever happened to mankind. (Some cited the simple nobility of savage manners, while others dwelt upon the savages' blood-lust, their (by European standards) treachery, and their tendency to torture people, and it was not really until well into the eighteenth century that the noble savage found his way into political theory.) None the less, the postulate of rough natural equality in a State of Nature, which could actually be observed in America, did constitute a challenge to accepted ideas of natural hierarchy. This certainly did not mean that henceforth all inequalities were to be thought of as unnatural and therefore unjustifiable, but it did mean that in the future inequality would have to be explained and justified. In fact, social contract theorists proved themselves to be very adept at justifying inequality. Hobbes put it down to the buying and selling by contract which a properly constituted polity made possible, while Locke argued that men could agree to respect the value of money even in the State of Nature, so that inequalities of fortune would arise naturally, but that assertion of natural equality was a time-bomb which was later to explode in the writings of Rousseau. Rousseau refused to believe that rational men could ever have agreed to associate on conditions which could lead to vast inequalities of wealth and power, and this led him to believe that, granted that the state of the world was riddled with inequality, the transition from the State of Nature to Civil Society could not have come about by contract at all. A true social contract lay some time in the future, and this time its main feature would be to guarantee a measure of liberty and equality which the ordinary world so manifestly lacked.

The process of English colonisation in North America may itself have contributed to the acceptance of social contract theory in another way. Not only did the colonists agree to go to America to begin a new life, but they also frequently arranged their affairs on the basis of the charters of joint-stock companies. The colony of Massachusetts, for instance, used the charter of the Massachusetts Bay Company as its constitution from the beginning, and that charter continued to be the basis of the future constitution of the Commonwealth of Massachusetts after American independence. A joint-stock company was the ideal image of a community based on voluntary contract. The members of a joint-stock company agreed to hold property in accordance with agreed rules. There was a real sense in which the members were asking for the protection of the company and could leave it at pleasure simply by selling their stock. Agreement about property rights lay right at the heart of a joint-stock enterprise, and there was to be no nonsense about equality. The holders of stock in a joint-stock company usually hold unequal shares, and it follows naturally that those who hold the most stock should have the largest share in the running of the company. This in no way vitiates the more fundamental equality of equal rights to unequal shares. Of course, the large proprietors will tend in these circumstances to be the most powerful men in the community, but their concern for their property will reinforce property right in general, so that all proprietors, great and small, will benefit. The joint-stock idea was particularly appropriate to a political community which was expected to expand both territorially and in population. Immigrants to the already established states in America, and those who settled new territories not yet ready for statehood, could be seen as voluntarily joining an ongoing community as soon as they began to cultivate land and asked the law to establish their title to it. When a state joined the Union, it did so on the Union's terms and agreed to respect the Constitution of the United States as the fundamental law of the land. That way of looking at the matter was to cause a great deal of trouble in the era leading up to the American Civil War, when the southern states began to argue, to all appearances quite reasonably, that the Union was a voluntary contract between sovereign states on conditions which were now being violated. This forced northern spokesmen to argue the very dubious proposition that the Union was Union for ever, something which social contract theory had never held. (The tragedy of the South was that it was right about the Constitution but wrong about slavery.)

What has still to be explained about social contract theory is its intensely individualistic thrust. (I say individualistic 'thrust' because the word 'individualism' had to wait until the middle of the nineteenth century to gain currency as a neologism.) The autonomous individual capable of making a voluntary contract with his fellows to uphold certain publicly made and acknowledged laws did not spring from nowhere, and various attempts have been made to trace his origins. Social contract has been famously called the 'political theory of possessive individualism', and there can be no doubt that market relations of free contract of buyers and sellers contributed enormously to the plausibility of social contract theory. However, there are other places besides the market to look for the origins of the autonomous individual. Some commentators have looked to the new spirit of self-reliance implicit in Renaissance humanism; others point to the atomism of seventeenth-century science which so influenced Hobbes, but perhaps the best place to look for the origins of individualism is in the nature of the European state system itself. The nationalist historians of the nineteenth and twentieth centuries would have us believe that the nation-state, though long in the making, was always going to be the outcome of European political development, and this tends to make us forget just how fluid the boundaries of early modern European states were, and how likely those states were to collapse into civil war. Britain, which is usually given as a paradigm of successful early nation-state building, could have gone Jacobite, with all that implied about Catholic absolutism for British government, as late as 1745. A stable, long-established polity was very far from being part of the given political and moral landscape everywhere. It is still a matter of dispute which was the first truly modern state and when it was invented, but there is no modern equivalent of the apparent timelessness of the medieval feudal order. Of course, it is easy to see with hindsight that the feudal order was not timeless at all, but if you lived in it everything conspired to make you believe that, if God himself had not established feudalism, he certainly smiled upon it. The story of how the lay and clerical subjects of the feudal order became the citizens of the modern state is long and complex (and in many places that story is not yet over), but the fact that the same structural changes happened at some time almost everywhere in Western Europe must have encouraged the idea that, at least to an extent, the nature of the polities men lived in was a matter of choice where it was not a matter of chance.

The attack on the idea that the political and social order was part of the providential scheme of things was also an attack on the Roman Catholic religion which was its ideological prop. The secular hierarchy had the ecclesiastical hierarchy as its mirror image, and secular society was always bound to be considered second-rate while the clergy were thought of as a special race apart. Secular authority could do nothing much more than batten down on some of the more outlandish and detectable outcomes of ordinary men's sinful nature. The priests, on the other hand, really could help through the confessional, and the Virgin and the saints could probably intercede between men's sins and a judging but forgiving God. This amounted to saying no less than that even a man's sins were not entirely his own business and God's, and it was that idea which Protestantism attacked in the name of a man's purely personal responsibility for his sins. The idea of a priesthood of all believers, implicit in some forms of Protestantism, got men off their knees to face their God, and men capable of that were unlikely to bend easily to secular authority without good reason. These would be men who would be tempted to ask some very searching questions about what the state was and what it was for. If ecclesiastical authority was not a given, then secular authority was not a given either (despite St Paul's claim that the powers that be are ordained of God). In particular, men like these would eventually be bound to ask the really fundamental question: What is the state *for*? The old attitude of suspicion of the state as a peculiarly earthly and flawed institution did not die. Quite the reverse; but, now that the state's function was being discussed in secular terms, that suspicion of the state turned itself into a search for arguments for a limitation of the state's functions. If the state had been set up to do a particular job, then in principle at least it should be easy to define exactly what that job was and to determine exactly what powers the state needed to do that job. The state came to be seen as a mechanism, a machine invented, like other machines, by men with very specific ends in view, and from there it was a very small step to establishing failure criteria for the state. Like all other machines, the state could go wrong; it could be improved as circumstances change, and occasionally it could be scrapped altogether and men would have to go back to the drawing-board and redesign the state from scratch.

What has to be noticed particularly about the mechanical theory of the state is how straightforward it is. Absolute monarchs, or their ideologues, were fond of claiming that there was something mysterious about government. Kings were specially chosen by God to deal with the mysteries of state in ways that were beyond the comprehension of ordinary men. Kings might of course seek advice from time to time to assist them in the onerous business of governing, but it was up to them to choose where to look for that advice (the curse of absolute monarchy being the royal favourite or the royal mistress). Kings were not obliged to take advice from anybody because they were responsible to God, and to God alone, for the exercise of kingly power. Sometimes kings chose to gather representatives of their subjects in parliament-like assemblies, ostensibly to ask for their advice but in fact usually to ask them for money, but the king typically set the agenda, and was certainly not obliged to take any advice these assemblies cared to offer. The parliaments were the creatures of the kings; kings called them and dismissed them at pleasure. Pomp and circumstance, 'the divinity that doth hedge a king', touching for the King's Evil, and the fact that even the bloodiest of tyrants went unassassinated, all testify to fact that kingship was very big magic. The mechanical theory of the state was an attempt to de-mystify kingship and all other possible forms of government. An English Leveller summed up the matter exactly when he said that in commonwealths somebody was chosen to be king in much the same way as in well-regulated families somebody was appointed to buy the meat. As soon as the ruling function was narrowly defined, it was an obvious step from there to begin to look round for an institution which could in fact put limits on the exercise of executive power, and the obvious candidate everywhere was the representative assembly. From being a king's creature, representative assemblies became institutions in their own right, charged with a watching brief over executive pretension. Of course, this did not happen overnight; nor did it happen everywhere, but it remained the goal of political reformers until well into the twentieth century. By the end of the eighteenth century, the further step had been taken in Britain and America of coming to regard the legislature as the supreme sovereign body in the land. Publicly declared law, made after all the arguments for and against were made known, which was then 'faithfully executed' by the executive power – the presidency in the United States, His Majesty's Government in Britain – became the ideal in constitutional polities, though in practice the relationship between executive and legislature was subject to constant vicissitudes.

It is tempting to say that the idea of a constitutional, law-bound polity, based upon a wide representation of the people, was the inevitable outcome of the idea of social contract, but that is to jump ahead too quickly. It is certainly the case that since the middle of the seventeenth century, in England and America, advanced political thinkers had argued that a representative, constitutional polity was the only kind of state that autonomous rational men who loved their liberty would ever voluntarily join, but that was an argument which took a very long time to gain anything like a widespread acceptance on either side of the Atlantic. Much depended upon how literally the idea of the autonomy of the individual was to be taken. Common sense cried out that not all men (let alone women) were equally autonomous. If autonomy implied liberty, then the idea of the autonomy of all men came up against the obvious social fact that some men, landless labourers for instance, were so dependent on others for their means of subsistence that it made no sense to call them autonomous at all. Autonomy meant having made one's mark in the world, and the obvious way to make one's imprint on the world was to own part of it, either in the literal sense of land ownership, or in the sense of owning capital which could be converted into land. It must never be forgotten that the idea of social contract had to make its way in intensely, if not rigidly, stratified societies. Deference to employers and social superiors has perhaps been the norm in most human societies at most times and places, and it was especially likely to be the case in societies with a feudal past which took a very long time to die. Much is often made of the connection between the idea of social contract and a rising bourgeoisie who, being buyers and sellers, took easily to the idea of social contract, but that should not obscure the equally obvious fact that a rising bourgeois was just as likely to expect the social deference after he had risen which had hitherto been reserved for aristocrats. The bourgeois scramble after titles of nobility and gentility is testimony enough to that. (James I is said to have remarked about one candidate for knighthood that he could certainly make him a knight but God himself couldn't make him a gentleman.) Later defenders of the idea of the democratic and parliamentary republic were to argue for the autonomy of everyman (and even later of every woman), but by that time there already existed a genuine theory of individualism (though it was not called that yet) in the form of economic liberalism.

The theory of social contract never stood still. It is probably true to say it began as a mildly subversive doctrine in the eyes of its more conservatively minded opponents, and ended up in Rousseau's *Social Contract* as something like a charter for social and political revolution. How could this be? It has already been remarked that the contrast between the versions of social contract in Hobbes and Locke might be the consequence of an increased optimism about the permanence of settled social living. Hobbes seems to doubt whether men are naturally sociable. Men certainly want those things which only social living makes possible, mainly wealth and prestige, but their nature is such that only a very drastic version of social contract will ever get them into the social condition upon which the acquisition of all other human goods depends. Locke, on the other hand, seems to think that men are naturally sociable, though he hedges on the question of exactly how sociable they are. Over a century separates Hobbes's *Leviathan* (1651) from Rousseau's *Social Contract* (1762). By that time Rousseau can take settled patterns of social living so much for granted that he can make the social contract a way of explaining not how societies can be made stable but how societies can be made just. Social contract becomes a vehicle for the remodelling of all social and political institutions, something it could not possibly have been for a thinker like Hobbes who had been fearful of any social tinkering a century before. What had occurred in the meantime was the invention of economic liberalism, though it was not to be called liberalism until well on into the nineteenth century.

As it interested political theorists, economic liberalism was a theory of the natural sociability of humankind which did not depend on an altruistic, other-regarding view of human nature. Theories of human unsociability had always boiled down to a view of men as being essentially egotistical, therefore selfish, therefore potentially aggressive to their fellow men whom they would seek to dominate and exploit for self-seeking ends. If everybody tried to act like that, then it was not clear how settled human living was going to be possible at all, unless really coercive mechanisms existed to curb these anti-social instincts in the cause of a minimal social peace. The hectoring, moralising priest, and the hangman with bloody hands were socially essential; without them *homo homini lupus*. That way of looking at the world was very ancient, and it encouraged the view than men were very difficult to rule. Like children, they could not be left alone for a second. (The old story about the mother who shouts to the child in the other room whom she cannot see: Stop what you are doing immediately! captures the spirit of this perspective exactly.) Common sense suggested that these unruly, child-like people would be thieves as individuals and rioters in groups. The essential unruliness of human beings meant that rule had to be very strict. The theory of economic liberalism made considerable inroads into that vision of human living, and what made it so persuasive was that it was able to come up with a theory of the natural sociability of man without denying that human beings were essentially self-seeking and self-promoting. The great secret of social living was that private vices could be public benefits (the phrase is Mandeville's). Men pursuing their self-chosen ends within a minimum framework of law naturally create networks of interdependence based on the need for economic specialisation. As Adam Smith was to say famously in *The Wealth of Nations* (1776), it is not from the benevolence of the baker and the brewer that we expect to get our sustenance, but from their self-interest. Let men be free to buy and sell, set up laws to make sure that they don't cheat or steal, and the celebrated 'invisible hand' of Adam Smith would spontaneously create societies which were miracles of differentiated social co-operation if everyone pursued his own self-interest within the bounds of laws which were there to deal with the exceptions to the rules, on the assumption that those exceptions, which we call crimes, would be infrequent. Human societies arose naturally *because* men were naturally selfish.

Natural mechanisms would create natural harmonies. Hobbes was not true. Harmonious social living was not dependent on the prior existence of the state. The state could even be seen as interfering with the spontaneous emergence of natural harmonies. The visible and heavy hand of the state could frustrate the workings of the invisible hand; hence the suspicion of the state which was to be so prominent a feature of all liberalism. Economic liberalism was the great antidote to Hobbesian pessimism about the permanence of social life. Social stability could now become one of the givens of human experience. In simpler terms, societies came to be seen as being much tougher than had hitherto been supposed, and, in a way which is heavy with irony, it was this perception which made a potentially revolutionary theory of social contract like Rousseau's possible by the middle of the eighteenth century. If societies were naturally self-constituting, then it was possible to begin to think about schemes of fundamental political and social reform without running the risk of returning reasonably stable societies to the horrors of a Hobbesian State of Nature in which every man's hand would be at every other man's throat.

The formula: social stability makes revolution possible, is not of course to be taken too literally. There was no reason in principle why thinkers should not find the spontaneously arising kind of society perfectly satisfactory, and this was in fact to become the dominant theme of liberalism for as long as liberalism lasted. Not everybody had to be Rousseau, dreaming in his eccentric, Spartan way of a future society which would not only be stable but also just. But Rousseau did see one thing more clearly than any other social contract theorist, and that was that the idea of a spontaneously arising social life made the idea of social contract unnecessary as a theory of the *origins* of society and the state, because if societies arose naturally, then there was no need for a theory of origins at all. Rousseau himself believed that the origins of civil society were to be attributed to fraud and force, and he kept the idea of social contract for the voluntary agreement of men to form a just society at some time in the future.

There is a notable irony here. It was remarked above that the whole idea of social contract rested on a view of individuals as being in some sense autonomous, and it was also noted that it took a very long time for the idea of the autonomy of the individual to gain a modestly wide acceptance even in principle because of the obvious facts of social dependence and deference. Economic liberalism supplied the genuine theory of individualism which social contract had always lacked, only to find that the idea of a spontaneous social harmony arising out of the competition of selfish individuals made the idea of social contract redundant as a theory of origins. As soon as the idea became current that men formed societies whether they liked it or not, social contract's traditional function of explaining how men came to live peacefully together was no longer required. The attack on social contract by Hume and the Utilitarians did in fact concentrate on social contract's attempt to explain the origins of society and the state. Perhaps that vulnerability was social contract's own fault, because it had tried to explain too much. Of course, Rousseau was right when he said that, if social contract could not explain the past, it could still be used to explain future social and political possibilities.

The idea of social contract in its older form lasted longest in the United States, where the admission of new states to the Union from time to time could still be seen as a voluntary contract to abide by the rules of the American Constitution, and where part of the qualification for statehood was the voluntary adoption of a state constitution by the people of the territory petitioning for statehood. Even this was not quite the same as social contract as traditionally conceived, because states joined the Union on the Union's own terms. New states were not invited to renegotiate the terms of the Constitution; they either accepted the Constitution or they didn't, and all of them did. Even the secession of the Confederate states in 1861 did not really change this. The Constitution which representatives of the Confederate states drafted in a month at Montgomery, Alabama, was practically a carbon copy of the Constitution of the Union which they had recently left.

Social contract theory in one form or another lasted from about the middle of the sixteenth century to the middle of the eighteenth century, which is a very good record for a style of political argument. Shorn of its grander pretensions, the theory has never died. The question: What would we do if we had to start society and the state all over again? has continued to be asked as a guide to the future actions of government.

NOTES ON SOURCES

Social contract theory cries out to be understood in the context of religion and the rise of capitalism in Max Weber's and Tawney's sense. The surest short-cut to this understanding is C.B. Macpherson's outstanding *The Political Theory of Possessive Individualism: From Hobbes to Locke* (1962).

11

SOCIAL CONTRACT I
The Hobbesian version

THOMAS HOBBES

Hobbes was born prematurely in 1588, his mother's labour, it is said, being brought on by news of the Armada ('Hobbes and Fear were born twins'), but he survived all the vicissitudes of seventeenth-century English politics to die in his bed at the age of ninety-one in 1679. Hobbes was an Oxford man (Magdalen Hall) who found the prevailing Aristotelian-Scholastic philosophy little to his taste. He was recommended as tutor to the Cavendish who became the second Duke of Devonshire. He spent most of his life in the houses of noblemen. He discovered the new science on the Grand Tour in 1610, and in the early 1620s he became the friend and amanuensis of Francis Bacon. Hobbes was a staunch Royalist. By 1641, when he fled to France to escape the coming Civil War, he had met Galileo and many of the most noted scientists and men of letters of his day.

Hobbes spent some of his time in exile in France (1641–51) as mathematics tutor to the future Charles II. He also worked on *Leviathan*, which was published in London on Hobbes's return to England to make his peace with the Commonwealth. There is some mystery about why he actually came back when he did, though the probability is a combination of homesickness and his growing reputation in *émigré* circles for religious unorthodoxy, if not downright atheism. Charles II, in his good-natured way, always retained a soft spot for Hobbes. He was invited back to Court after the Restoration and given a royal pension of £100 a year.

It is in a way unfortunate for the history of political thought that the first masterpiece of social contract theory, Thomas Hobbes's *Leviathan*, should be so untypical of social contract theorising. Social contract was invented to support the case for disobedience to authority. In *Leviathan* Hobbes makes out a social contract case for the absolute government which social contract had been invented to undermine. Hobbes is a masterly political arguer because he meets and beats his opponents on their own ground. He uses social contract's own language to drive a coach and four through all the libertarian conclusions which previous social contract thinkers had come to. Hobbes is also subtle. He wrote at the time of the English Civil War (*Leviathan* was published in 1651), and his more acute readers soon realised that his arguments are double-edged. What would have been an argument for the absolutist pretensions of Charles I before 1642 could just as easily be an argument for Cromwell's power in 1651, and again for Charles II in 1660. Hobbes pleased neither the Royalists nor the Parliamentarians, though Cromwell left him alone, and Charles II received him at court where he delighted in watching 'the Bear' being baited by the court wits and giving as good as he got.

The basis of Hobbes's argument can be stated simply, though the implications of that argument are far-reaching. Social contract almost always imagined what things must have been like at the beginning before Civil Society, that is society and the state, existed. Hobbes takes that imagined beginning seriously by trying to think away from human life all that it owes to the existence of government conceived of as a regular system of law-making and law-enforcement. The condition of men living without government Hobbes calls the State of Nature, and he paints a memorably bleak picture of it. Men without government, and without the settled social living which Hobbes thinks only the existence of government makes possible, would all be roughly and naturally equal. No man is so much stronger than another by nature that he could not be killed by him by stealth. This natural equality of human capacities leads men to be suspicious of one another. This wariness makes men very reluctant to take risks in their dealings with other men. Every other man would effectively be a stranger from whom one would not know what to expect. Much better, then, to avoid human contact as far as possible. Life in the Hobbesian State of Nature no doubt provided a good deal of time for solitary reflection, and it is easy to imagine what each man must have been thinking about. Security for his life would be the prime consideration, and each man would begin to ask himself what the conditions would be in which he would not be in constant fear for his life, and it would soon occur to him that the only way he could feel safe would be if he could dominate all other men and make them fear him more than they feared each other. Dominion over others would be the ambition of all men in the State of Nature, but of course that is a programme which, in the State of Nature, it would be impossible to fulfil. Granted the roughly equal natural capacity of men, everybody in the State of Nature would be capable of working out the programme of dominion for himself, and while every man dreamt of dominion over others, no man could ever achieve it because every man was roughly equal in physical strength and cunning. The plan of dominion which would provide for security of the person in the State of Nature would in fact give men an additional reason to fear each other, because each man would now have good reason for suspecting other men of having aggressive intentions towards him. This would lead to a stalemate, a position without a future because the future would be a dreary re-run of the past.

Human aggressiveness would be compounded by the fact that nobody in the State of Nature could predict what he would have to do to preserve his own life. Hobbes calls the preservation of life the Right of Nature. Unlike the situation in an ordinary society where human behaviour is reasonably predictable, nobody in the State of Nature would ever know what to expect of other men, so the Right of Nature must be unlimited by definition. It would only be possible to break the Right of Nature down into specific rights of nature if it was in fact predictable what a man would have to do to protect himself. In Civil Society this right of self-defence is defined by law, but in the lawless State of Nature there can be no possible definition. Each man is free to do what he pleases to preserve himself, but of course this unlimited Right of Nature does not really help him because everybody else has it too. The natural fear that men feel for one another in the State of Nature would therefore be increased by the fact that each man would know not only that common sense dictates that other men are likely to be aggressive, but also that they have a right to do anything to others if they feel that their lives are in danger. In a situation like this the only sensible way of living would be to run away as quickly as possible from other men because the outcome of any contest with another would be uncertain. A rational egotist would always hedge his bets, though occasional clashes would be inevitable. Hobbes calls the State of Nature a state of war, because it is in the nature of war that there will be intervals between the fighting. As Hobbes himself puts it (*Leviathan*, Part 1, Chapter 13):

> For WARRE, consisteth not in Battell only, or the act of fighting; but in a tract of time, wherein the Will to contend by Battel is sufficiently known: and therefore the notion of *Time* is to be considered in the nature of War; as it is in the nature of Weather. For as the nature of Foule weather, lyeth not in a showre or two of rain, but in an inclination thereto of many dayes together; So the nature of War, consisteth not in actual fighting; but in the known disposition thereto, during all the time there is no assurance to the contrary.

It is not difficult to guess what life must have been like in the State of Nature, and Hobbes tells us in the most famous passage in *Leviathan* (Part 1, Chapter 13):

> In such condition, there is no place for Industry; because the fruit thereof is uncertain: and consequently no Culture of the Earth, no Navigation, nor use of the commodities that may be imported by Sea; no commodious Building; no Instruments of moving, and removing such things as require much force; no Knowledge of the face of the Earth; no account of time; no Arts; no Letters; no Society; and which is worst of all, continual feare, and danger of violent death; And the life of man, solitary, poore, nasty, brutish and short.

The question then arises as to how men managed to get themselves out of the awfulness of the State of Nature into Civil Society with its law and its reasonable degree of social stability. To understand that we have to go back to Hobbes's rational egotists contemplating the miseries of the State of Nature. Each man wished that he could dominate other men to the extent that other men would be too frightened to touch him, but each man also knew that one man could never achieve that by himself. Something else was needed if men were ever to live in subjection, and that something else was law. If only a way could be found to subject men to laws, the fear of punishment for breaking which would be strong enough to secure obedience, then all might yet be well. But how would a rational egotist in fact be likely to think about law and the process of law-making? Undoubtedly he would think that the ideal position for a rational egotist to be in would be a situation in which everybody else except him would be bound by law, and that he himself would make and enforce that law. Of course, a rational egotist would also know that every other rational egotist in the State of Nature would be thinking exactly the same thing. The State of Nature would not just be miserable; it would be anguished as well, because everybody would know that if he, or anybody else, were to be invested with the kind of power which would enable him, or anybody else, to make law and enforce it, then the State of Nature would be brought to an end and the blessings of social peace might reasonably be expected to follow; certainly, nothing could be worse than the State of Nature.

Hobbesian men are odd creatures because the two sides of their nature seem to conflict with each other. Their competitiveness leads to what Hobbes calls 'diffidence', that apprehensiveness about each other's intentions and fear of losing out which is at its most acute form in the State of Nature. On the other hand, men want what Hobbes calls 'glory', the wealth, deference and high position which only living in a stable society with an effective state can provide. Part of man's nature is therefore anti-social, while the other part can only be satisfied through social living. The desire for glory and the desire to minimise the effects of diffidence provide the crucial additional motives for getting out of the State of Nature. The solution to the State of Nature problem is in fact very simple. Men need law and law enforcement to live the kinds of lives they want to lead. Men's natural diffidence in the State of Nature makes it impossible that they could ever come together to make law. Even if they could agree to make law, which is highly dubious, there would still be two insurmountable difficulties. First, who would be the first to obey? The man who first put himself under law would be at an immediate disadvantage in his relations with his fellow men because he would be in the position of refusing to do to them what they might possibly do to him. Second, who would enforce the law? Everybody can't do it, so who would protect the first man to obey law? He could try to enforce the law himself, but that would be the same as saying that everybody else was still in the State of Nature except him. That is obviously the worst position for anybody ever to be in; being the only person to obey the law when everybody else is ignoring it or breaking it is straightforwardly absurd. The way out of the difficulty is not to try to make law by agreement, but to choose a law-giver and law-enforcer by agreement. Choose one man (or a body of men), make him or them the Sovereign, and authorise all he or they do. This in effect means that every man, or a majority, must give up his right of protecting himself, in so far as he can, to another. The choice of a law-giver and law-enforcer is the moment of contract. It is nothing less than the creation of political power; as Hobbes puts it, the sword is placed in the Sovereign's hands.

So far there is nothing very remarkabe about Hobbes's argument. It sounds like any run-of-the-mill social contract argument, but there is one crucial difference: Hobbes argues that the social contract cannot put any limitation on sovereignty. The Sovereign is entirely unbound. In fact, the Sovereign is not a party to the social contract at all. Sovereignty is not created on terms; it must be absolute and undivided. The Sovereign is absolutely unaccountable to his subjects; his law is their command. It hardly needs to be stressed that this is a very remarkable conclusion for a social contract thinker to come to. Before Hobbes, the whole point about social contract theory was to argue that there was some kind of bargain between rulers and ruled which rulers could sometimes break and thus absolve their subjects from their obligation to obey. Hobbes argues the opposite: even if men could go back to the beginning and re-create the state, they would voluntarily do so in such a way that they would set up a Sovereign more absolutist than any contemporary king dared to be. A large part of the argument in *Leviathan* is designed to show why this must be so. The argument is fairly technical, because Hobbes is a meticulous thinker. The argument is carried on at a high level of abstraction, but it is marvellously clear. Later in this chapter we will have to stand back from Hobbes's argument and try to give it a historical context, because none of Hobbes's readers at the time could have doubted that a very thorough commentary on English political history lay not very far below the surface. First we must see what the argument for unlimited sovereignty is, and then try to make it historically specific.

SOVEREIGNTY NOT LIMITABLE BY CONTRACT

Hobbes's argument that sovereignty is not limited by contract rests on the sheer impossibility of a Sovereign making a contract with his future subjects in the State of Nature, and on the sheer unlikelihood that he would make a contract with them in Civil Society. There are only two possible conditions of life for Hobbes, life in the State of Nature, which is a state of war of everyman against everyman, and Civil Society, which is a state of peace. The question then arises as to which of these conditions offers the opportunity and possibility for a Sovereign to make a contract with his subjects. Take the State of Nature first. Its chief feature is a kind of atomistic chaos. Men being solitary in the State of Nature, the only way a would-be Sovereign could make a contract with his future subjects would be to chase around making an agreement with each man individually. Not only would this task be next to impossible (why should they trust him rather than trust anyone else?), but it would also be pointless, because contracts in the State of Nature are unlikely to be binding anyway. Nobody in the State of Nature would be foolish enough to abide by the terms of any agreement made with anyone else about anything, because of the fear of non-performance of the terms of the contract in the absence of a system of law-enforcement. A contract to limit sovereignty in the State of Nature would not be a valid contract at all, so that only leaves Civil Society in which the Sovereign could make a contract with his subjects to limit his sovereignty. Hobbes thinks that a Sovereign who would make such a contract would have to misunderstand his own nature and to misunderstand the nature of sovereignty itself.

To understand why a Hobbesian Sovereign would have no motive for making a contract with his subjects to limit sovereignty in Civil Society we have to go back to the position a rational egotist would find himself in in the State of Nature. There, thinking the matter out, a rational egotist would come to the conclusion that the best possible situation for him to be in would be where everyone else would be obliged to obey laws made and enforced by himself, while he was not obliged to obey. We saw that one of the things which makes the State of Nature so unbearable would be the realisation that everyone would be thinking the same way, and this would lead to the conclusion that, if only someone were in that enviable position, then the end of the State of Nature would be in sight. In its Hobbesian version, the social contract effectively puts one man in the position that all men coveted in the State of Nature. By choosing one man (or a body of men) to be Sovereign, men make the Sovereign a beneficiary of the contract, not a contracting party. The transfer of the Right of Nature from separate individuals to a Sovereign requires no formal act of consent on the Sovereign's part, let alone any kind of deal. Any rational egotist would be bound by his own nature to accept the job. In formal terms, the Hobbesian contract is an agreement between contracting parties to make one man (or group of men) Sovereign; it therefore follows that in the transition from the State of Nature to Civil Society, everyone except the Sovereign makes the transition. The Sovereign himself therefore remains in the State of Nature, because he has made no agreement with anyone. It follows that if the Sovereign is the one man who gets what everyone else wanted, he would be a fool to bargain away some of his absolute power when everyone except him was in Civil Society. He would simply have no motive. His own nature would tell him not to limit his sovereignty by contract, and the beauty of Hobbes's argument is that any rational man who was chosen to be Sovereign would think the same thing, and so would any group.

Now it is just conceivable that a Sovereign chosen by chance or by choice might take it into his head, in a moment of mistaken benevolence perhaps, to make a contract with his subjects to hold sovereign power on terms. He might say: This will I do, and if I don't, sack me. Hobbes believes that a Sovereign who did something like that would be failing to understand the very nature of sovereignty. Suppose a Sovereign who had not thought the matter out properly were to make such an agreement. Who would judge when the terms of the contract had been violated? Each man judging for himself would not help much, because who would be the first to rebel when the Sovereign was still powerful enough to kill him? Suppose that all of his subjects taken together, or a majority of them, had the right to decide when the Sovereign had broken the terms of his contract. What then? This is where Hobbes boxes very clever indeed. How could that dissent be made known and make itself felt? Hobbes's answer is that a collective dissent could only articulate itself through the election of another Sovereign, and, sovereigns being in the State of Nature, the two rival sovereigns would have to fight it out, which would mean the miserable condition of civil war which is a condition only just preferable to the State of Nature.

Hobbes's argument that attempting to judge the Sovereign's conduct would lead inevitably to civil war is an ingenious one, and again we have to go back to the condition of men in the State of Nature to understand its full force. The atomistic chaos of the State of Nature clearly means that men can have no collective will. All choices in the State of

Nature are individual choices. (This is even true of the social contract, which is made when every individual, or a majority of them, agrees to give up his Right of Nature to the Sovereign provided only that every other individual, or a majority of them, does the same.) The only way that scattered, solitary individuals can have some kind of collective will, or even identity, is by choosing a Sovereign to represent them by providing that measure of law and order which all men want. As Hobbes puts it, the unity of a thing consists not in the thing represented but in its representer. A Civil Society acts only as a unity through the Sovereign; it is only then that Civil Society, Leviathan, that artificial man and mortal god, can come into existence. Unity, then, does not arise spontaneously, but is the deliberate creation of disparate human wills. Being artificial, the unity of Civil Society is always to a degree precarious. It is important to remember that Hobbesian men do not come into Civil Society in order to change their natures. On the contrary, they enter Civil Society to fulfil their natures as rational egotists in so far as that is possible within the bounds of law, so that in Civil Society the only unity that can exist between essentially egotistical and competitive men is provided by the Sovereign who stands for them all. If the people in Civil Society were ever in a position to judge whether their Sovereign had broken the terms of a contract, they would have to find another man, or a body of men, to represent them and make that judgement. There would have to be some kind of collective will which was not the Sovereign's will, but if Hobbes is right then the only way that men in Civil Society could exercise a collective will which is not the Sovereign's will would be to elect another Sovereign, because only sovereigns, by definition, can create that artificial unity without which all collective action is impossible. There would, in effect, be two rival sovereigns in a single Civil Society. That, by definition, would be civil war, which is only a step away from the State of Nature which all rational men rightly dread.

There is yet another difficulty about judging the Sovereign in Civil Society which in Hobbes's terms is the really killing argument against it. In Civil Society there would only be two possibilities for judging the Sovereign. Either the Sovereign would judge himself, or he would be judged by what would effectively be another Sovereign. Men being rational egotists, and both parties to the dispute about breaking a contract being single individuals (or small groups of individuals), each party would, given the opportunity, judge in his own favour. The Sovereign would always deny that he had broken the contract, while the rival Sovereign would always say that the Sovereign for the time being had broken the contract, because that would be the only way for the rival Sovereign to press his own egotistical claims. (We should never forget that according to Hobbes any man, or body of men, would be Sovereign if he could.) Each Sovereign would be judge in his own cause, which is a very odd principle of jurisprudence. There would only be one way of judging whether the rival Sovereign had judged the Sovereign for the time being correctly, and that would be to set up some other kind of mechanism for judging the judgement. This would be possible, at least in principle, but it would be a foolish thing to do because, in effect, it would amount to creating yet another Sovereign. All the arguments about creating unity out of diversity would apply to this third judging mechanism. The third judge would have to be one man, or a body of men, representing a considerable body of men in Civil Society, and so he would effectively be a third Sovereign. The civil war would now be worse, because there would now be three rival sovereigns. And why stop at three? This third Sovereign would act egotistically in exactly the same way as the already existing Sovereigns would act. He would always put in a judgement against both other Sovereigns to advance his own claims to sovereignty, and, since he is judge in his own cause, it would be necessary to create a fourth Sovereign to make sure that the third Sovereign had judged correctly. Of course, the same arguments would apply against the fourth Sovereign as applied to the previous three. The fourth Sovereign judging in his own cause would always find in his own favour, which would make it necessary to create a fifth Sovereign to judge him, and so it would go on, regressively, until there were as many rival Sovereigns as there were men living in Civil Society, and every man his own judge is the State of Nature by another name. The outcome of Hobbes's argument is clear: either you stick with a single Sovereign who makes no contracts with his subjects, or you begin to fall back down the slippery slope into the State of Nature, which no rational man wants.

SOVEREIGNTY CREATED BY INSTITUTION AND SOVEREIGNTY CREATED BY ACQUISITION

The account which Hobbes gives of the original contract is the paradigm case of social contract. It is what must have happened at the imagined beginning of Civil Society, and Hobbes thinks that it is what would have to happen again if a Civil Society were to be unfortunate enough to find itself back in the miserable condition of the State of Nature. It is always important when reading Hobbes to remember what he is arguing *against*. In particular, Hobbes has in mind the libertarian and egalitarian aspects of other social contract theory. Other social contract thinkers had always gone back to the postulate of an original, rough natural equality between men, in order to argue that some of that natural equality should be reflected in the arrangements of Civil Society. If men were originally free and equal, then surely they would be unwilling to give it all up when they entered Civil Society by voluntary contract. Hobbes argues the opposite. The original Right of Nature, by which a man may do *anything* which to him seems good to protect his own life, is for Hobbes not a blessing but a curse. If everyone has that same equal and unlimited liberty to do as he pleases in pursuit of the literally selfish end of self-preservation, then without law every man is a menace to every other man. Far from being an original endowment for which men should be grateful, the unlimited liberty of the Right of Nature is a millstone round men's necks, of which they would be wise to unburden themselves at the first opportunity. Of course, it is not in fact possible for men entirely to give up their Right of Nature to a Sovereign. In Civil Society men would retain the right of self-defence. A man would go armed on a journey, and at night he would lock up his chests even against his own children, and on these matters the positive law of a commonwealth might be silent. Again, no man is obliged to go unbound to the scaffold, because it would be unreasonable to expect a man who was in imminent danger of violent death at the Sovereign's hands to submit gracefully. With these exceptions, which are either everyday exceptions or exceptions of last resort, any rational man would rid himself of his Right of Nature if he could.

Hobbes has neatly turned the tables on his opponents. He says: Allow the maximum amount of natural liberty conceivable in the State of Nature and you end up with absolute Sovereignty if you think the matter out properly. The results would be the same even if an existing Civil Society were to dissolve itself into its component individual parts and begin again from scratch. So why bother even trying? Much better to put up with the system of government as it presently exists, no matter how absolutist its pretensions, than to go through the whole process of a return to the horrific State of Nature only to set up another absolutist form of government. (It may well be that if a Civil Society were to return to the State of Nature it would have to set up a Sovereign who was even more absolutist than the Sovereign who previously ruled in that society.)

Hobbes is of course aware that the states which existed in his own contemporary world did not have their origins in contract, or if they did all record of the original transactions has been lost. Voluntary contract-making, may never, or very seldom, have happened. This does not alter the fact that the creation of sovereignty by Institution is what men would have to do to get themselves out of a State of Nature at some time in the future; Hobbes knows very well that states do not exist in isolation, and he knows that most states were acquired by conquest. This creation of sovereignty by Acquisition is the ordinary historical case. What Hobbes is very clever at is applying the lessons to be learned from the case of sovereignty by Institution to the case of the creation of sovereignty by Acquisition.

On the face of it, the two cases could not be more different. The creation of sovereignty by Institution is voluntary, whereas the Acquisition of sovereignty is by conquest. According to Hobbes, however, the difference between the two cases is only superficial. What actually happens when a new sovereignty is acquired by a conqueror? Hobbes thinks the matter is very simple. Two Sovereigns lead their armies out to battle, and one Sovereign loses, flies the field, or is killed. Where does that leave his defeated subjects? Plainly, in Hobbes's terms, they are sovereignless, that is to say back in the State of Nature. Being back in the State of Nature, they fear violent death, but this time they fear it at the hands of the victorious Sovereign who may kill them if he chooses. Instead, the victorious Sovereign might say to the defeated army: I will kill you all if you do not agree among yourselves to recognise me in the future as your lawful Sovereign. It is quite unnecessary for the victorious Sovereign to put any conditions on his newly acquired sovereignty beyond sparing the lives of his new subjects, or at least of some of them. He may kill whom he chooses. As a rational egotist intent on the extension of the absolute sovereignty which he already possesses, the victorious Sovereign has no more a motive for making a contract with his new subjects than he had for making a contract with his old subjects in Civil Society, and it is equally obvious that the defeated and demoralised army is in no condition to force the victorious Sovereign to come to terms with them. They must be grateful for their lives, and that is all.

Hobbes says that the making of sovereignty by Acquisition is not in fact very different from the making of sovereignty by Institution. The main objection against saying that the agreement among themselves of a defeated army to recognise a new Sovereign is a valid contract is that it was made through fear. Hobbes thinks that this is no objection to the validity of the battlefield contract because, properly considered, all contracts are made through fear. Take the case of men in the original State of Nature. It was fear of each other which led them voluntarily to give up their Right of Nature to the Sovereign. Even in an ordinary Civil Society, men insist on spelling out the terms of contracts when they fear non-performance from the other contracting parties. If fear does not invalidate the original social contract by Institution, and if fear does not invalidate contracts in Civil Society, then why should fear of the victorious Sovereign invalidate the contract on the battlefield? We might still say that the battlefield contract was invalid because the defeated army had no option but to agree to recognise the new Sovereign. Not so says Hobbes. The human will cannot be coerced. Just as men could have chosen originally to remain in the State of Nature and take their chances, so could the defeated men on the battlefield. They could try to run away, for instance, or try to preserve their lives in any other way, and the Right of Nature would allow them to do it. Of course, Hobbes thinks that it would be foolish for these defeated and sovereignless men not to agree among themselves to recognise the new Sovereign because of the risk to their lives consequent on their refusal, but the choice is still theirs. The men in the original State of Nature would have been foolish to remain there, but they still had the choice. And besides, what we ordinarily call coercion of a man's will is really nothing of the kind. Take the case of a man on board a ship in a storm with his goods stored below. He very willingly throws his goods overboard to lighten the ship and increase the chances of preserving his own life if he thinks the ship might sink. Coercion through fear makes a man act very willingly indeed where he still has alternatives. The man on board the ship could choose to preserve his goods at the cost of risking his own life, but in fact he would very willingly sacrifice his goods. (The doctrine of the uncoercibility of the will is in fact at least as old as Aristotle's *Politics*, where he uses the same example of the man on a sinking ship.)

Hobbes thinks that a Sovereign can be one man, a few, or many men. He knows his ancient political theory well enough (he made a famous translation of Thucydides) to know that states are either monarchies, aristocracies or democracies. Although Hobbes developed a profound contempt at Oxford for the scholastic philosophy which was the legacy of Aristotle, he none the less has a remarkably Aristotelian view about possible forms of government. In particular, he thinks that the sovereignty which is exercised by a Sovereign is the same sovereignty, no matter how that sovereignty is in fact constituted. The sovereignty which is exercised by a Sovereign people, as at ancient Athens or republican Rome, does not change its nature as sovereignty just because it is democratic. Democratic sovereignty properly understood would have the same attributes as the sovereignty of an absolute monarch. Hobbes is remarkably far-sighted in seeing this. Ever since the theory of the democratic republic made its appearance in Western political thought in the middle of the seventeenth century, democratic theorists have been divided about what the democratic theory of sovereignty actually means. Some thinkers, notably in the United States, have tended to argue that democratic sovereignty (or republican sovereignty as it was originally called) is somehow less sovereign than the sovereignty exercised by kings, and hunting the Sovereign in the American Constitution, let alone in the American political system, is still an endless game. In democratic polities there has sometimes been a tendency, notably absent in France because of the Rousseauist tradition, to think that sovereignty will not bite so hard because it is democratically exercised, and this in its turn has sometimes led liberal democrats to be surprised that democratic states can on occasion act just as viciously as the monarchies they were meant to replace (or to modify into constitutional polities with universal suffrage). Hobbes could have saved them the trouble: sovereignty is sovereignty no matter who exercises it. Although Hobbes could not know it, the political science of the late nineteenth and twentieth centuries was to concern itself centrally with just this problem, and the conclusion most of that political science would come to is implicitly Hobbesian. A distinction would come to be made between how sovereignty is *exercised* and how sovereignty is *legitimised*. Mass democracy came to be seen as a way of making the exercise of sovereignty acceptable to citizens whose hands would be very far from the levers of power, and whose representatives in parliamentary assemblies would for ever complain how difficult it was in practice to control the exercise of the supreme powers of law-making and law-enforcement. It could even be argued that mass democracy makes the exercise of a Hobbesian type of sovereignty easier, not more difficult, because if everybody is involved in the process of law-making through the ballot box, then nobody can ever have a legitimate cause for complaint about what laws are made, provided only that those laws are made by the right people and in proper form. As Sam Adams, the erstwhile radical of the American Revolution, was to say after the revolution was over, any man who opposes the laws of a republic ought to suffer death. Hobbes would have liked that.

SOVEREIGNS AND WAR

Hobbes's argument that sovereigns remain in the State of Nature because they cannot make contracts with their subjects has very definite implications for international relations, and in particular for war. Like Machiavelli, Hobbes knows that most of the sovereignties as they actually exist in the world were acquired through conquest. Hobbesian sovereigns, remaining as they do in the State of Nature, are perfectly entitled to go to war with each other if they feel threatened. This would include the right of attacking first, because a pre-emptive strike might be one of the ways in which a Sovereign might increase his own sense of security. It might appear that this is a recipe for international anarchy. Would not sovereigns, who are in a State of Nature in relationship with each other, be inclined to fight each other the whole time? The answer is probably no. The idea that sovereigns in the State of Nature with regard to each other would always be fighting is based on a mis-understanding of the original State of Nature as it is described by Hobbes. It is easy to forget that men in the original State of Nature would be inclined to live solitary lives because trials of strength with other men would simply not be worth the risk where all were roughly and naturally equal. The same thought would occur to a prudent Sovereign. The doctrine of the legitimate creation of sovereignty by Acquisition would mean that every time a Sovereign went to war he would risk losing his sovereignty to another Sovereign, and we must never forget that, granted Hobbes's view of men as rational egotists, sovereignty is what all men want above everything else. A Sovereign would therefore be a fool to risk his own sovereignty in the uncertain trial by combat. Prudent sovereigns would certainly prepare for war in a world where nothing is certain, but going blithely into a war would be a different matter. Large and powerful states would probably tend to gobble up small and weak neighbours, but a time would come when a more or less stable international system of more or less equally powerful states emerged, or, if not more or less equally powerful, then states powerful enough in alliance with others to make rival states think twice about attacking them.

But even rationally calculating sovereigns sometimes make mistakes, and a risk-taking Sovereign always remains a possibility, so we should not be surprised if some sovereignties sometimes change hands. Much more likely, though, would be some kind of limited war for limited ends in which sovereigns would find ways of fighting with each other without ever risking their sovereignties. Limited wars followed by minor territorial adjustments would be conflicts in which sovereignties would not be put at risk. Even major wars could happen, as they did throughout the eighteenth century in Europe, because by later standards all eighteenth-century wars were limited wars. (It might even be that the implicit Hobbesian vision of international relations is a recipe for imperialism. *Leviathan* is, after all, an image of sea power.)

Hobbes's *Leviathan* is certainly not the blueprint for universal monarchy that it is sometimes taken to be. Quite the reverse. *Leviathan* contains a very clear explanation of why supra-national organisations like the League of Nations or the UN are bound to fail in their avowed purpose of keeping the international peace, or even in their intention to provide some measure of international co-operation which is different from traditional alliances between states for traditional foreign policy ends. For Hobbes, there is no peace without law, and there can be no law without a Sovereign whose command law is. Hobbes is absolutely insistent that individuals in the State of Nature cannot make law by agreement; all they can do by contract is to choose a Sovereign. What applies to individuals in the State of Nature also applies to sovereigns in their State of Nature in relation to each other. The only way there could be a guarantee of international peace would be if all the sovereigns of the earth, or an overwhelming majority of them, were voluntarily to give up the right of national self-defence to some kind of super-sovereign whose word would be law to all the nations of the earth. This the various nations of the earth have been notoriously reluctant to do. They have tried to make international law by agreement, but that has never stopped war. Hobbes could have told them why: covenants without the sword are but breath, without any power to bind a man at all. No all-powerful international Sovereign, then no international peace.

HOBBES ON THE ATTRIBUTES OF SOVEREIGNTY

Sovereignty's attributes are what one would expect from a thinker who believes that the creation of sovereignty is an all-or-nothing act. Either you choose to live under a Sovereign or you don't, and there is no point in quibbling about the Sovereign's powers: either he has them all, or men will find themselves back in the State of Nature almost before they know it. It should again be noticed that Hobbes derives all the attributes of sovereignty from the original case of the making of sovereignty by Institution. The eleven attributes of sovereignty which Hobbes lists would be the attributes of Sovereignty which rational men in the State of Nature would voluntarily give to their Sovereign, and in any case they would be attributes which any absolute Sovereign would take for himself if he were ever in a position to do so. Hobbes describes the attributes of sovereignty by Institution and then goes on to say that, the attributes of sovereignty being what they are, the Sovereign by acquisition would naturally have them too. Hobbes knows that the attributes of Sovereignty claimed by contemporary kings were capable of arousing furious resentments in their more liberty-loving subjects. Hobbes rubs salt into their wounds by arguing that, if these liberty-loving subjects thought about the matter clearly, they would set up a Sovereign by their own free will whose attributes would be much more absolutist than the claims of even the most absolute of contemporary kings. Of course, Hobbes's argument about the attributes of sovereignty works just as well, or even better, for the case of a Civil Society which has dissolved into chaos and is looking for ways to build itself up again. The gall for the liberty-lovers who would put constraints on the exercise of sovereignty is to be found in Hobbes's argument that either the constrainers would have to change their minds and admit that sovereignty by its very nature was absolute, or they would have to admit that they were being muddle-headed.

1 The first attribute of sovereignty is that the contract which sets it up repudiates all previous contracts. This must obviously be true of the original contract by which men got themselves out of the State of Nature. Contracts made in the State of Nature would have been invalid anyway, because a large part of what made the State of Nature so unbearable was that men would be unlikely to trust each other enough in the absence of a law-enforcing agency to make contracts in the first place. The case of a Civil Society breaking down and looking for ways to reconstitute itself is slightly different because there is always the possibility that men, or groups of men, might think that they had made a prior agreement with God, or they might be inclined to think that they could still make agreements with God after sovereignty had been re-created. Contracts like these could be very troublesome to a Sovereign, because contracts with God Himself would naturally take precedence over contracts men made with their fellows to create earthly sovereignty. Hobbes obviously has in mind here those post-Reformation covenants which peoples made with God by promising to live in good and godly commonwealths in the future. Hobbes is scathing about contracts with God which implicitly or explicitly put limits on the Sovereign's power. Contracts like these are really useless, because they have no force unless there is some power on earth to judge when they have been broken. That judge could only be the Sovereign because, as we have seen, to set up another judge in a Civil Society to judge the Sovereign's actions would be tantamount to setting up another Sovereign. When that happens a Civil Society is already on the way to civil war, the first stage on the slippery slope back down to the State of Nature which nobody in his right mind wants. Besides, any covenants with God, supposing there to be any, would have to be made by the Sovereign himself, not by his subjects. A people only has a will through its representative, and that representative by definition is the Sovereign. In the

social contract, the contracting parties agree among themselves to transfer their troublesome Right of Nature to the Sovereign, and it is this which creates the sovereign authority. The contracting people authorise all that the Sovereign does. That would include any contracts made by the Sovereign with God, and the Sovereign would not even be obliged to tell his subjects what the terms of that contract with God actually were. Any mediation with God's person must therefore be through the Sovereign, so what good would that do for the liberty-lovers keen to put restraints on the sovereign power? Besides, there is always the possibility that those who claim to have made covenants with God are simply lying. We only have their word for it that God agreed to keep his side of the bargain. And how do we know that God even listened?

2 The second attribute of sovereignty is that the Sovereign can never forfeit his right to it. This follows from the terms of social contract itself, and is therefore true by definition. By transferring their Right of Nature to a Sovereign who is not party to the contract, men make the Sovereign their agent-at-large in the world. They authorise what the Sovereign does. It is the nature of agency that what my agent does, I do. What my agent does, he does in my name. Because he acts with my authority, I and not he am responsible for his actions. Not only can the Sovereign not be said to have forfeited his sovereignty by breaking the terms of an original contract to which he was not party, but also he can never be accused of acting wilfully against my own will because he acts with my authority. *His* will *is* my will. To challenge him is to challenge myself, a self-accusation which has no more force than if I were to accuse myself of breaking an agreement with myself to keep a New Year's resolution. Judging one's own commands to oneself is a nonsense, or at best a metaphor. One can only punish oneself by agreeing with oneself to be punished. The same would be the case with a Sovereign. Because the Sovereign's will is my will, I would in effect be accusing myself, and because I have transferred that will, in so far as I am able, to the Sovereign, that would require the Sovereign to accuse himself, and of course he would always let himself off lightly. Being a rational egotist, the Sovereign would always judge in his own favour in his own cause. Of course, there is still the possibility of setting up a mechanism for judging the Sovereign, but Hobbes has already hammered home the obvious point that if the right to judgement is disputed 'it returns therefore to the sword again, and every man recovereth the right of Protecting himself by his own strength'. Multiplying judges is the same as multiplying sovereigns. The consequence is civil war and eventually a return to the State of Nature.

3 Hobbes thinks that it is sufficient that a majority should agree to the transfer of the Right of Nature to the Sovereign for the social contract to be valid. His reasons for thinking this are simple (and surprisingly Lockian). Hobbes has in mind the possibility that when the original contract was made by Institution to get out of the State of Nature, some men might have found its terms too hard to swallow and so they dissented. Hobbes thinks that that would not matter provided only that a majority agreed. He argues that by coming together to consider making a social contract, potential dissenters tacitly consented to be bound by the majority. But suppose they refused to recognise that. The dissenters, not being party to the contract, would remain

in the State of Nature. The chosen Sovereign, who is also not party to the contract, remains in the State of Nature too. He may therefore exercise his Right of Nature on the dissenters, and we already know that the Right of Nature is unlimited. The Sovereign could therefore compel the dissenters to come into Civil Society by agreeing among themselves to recognise him as Sovereign and authorise all he does, or he could kill them if they made him feel insecure. It is worth noting here that the condition of the State of Nature is not always the same. In the original State of Nature, men only had their roughly equal fellow men to contend with, but those who choose to remain in the State of Nature while others choose to enter Civil Society with a Sovereign find themselves in an even more perilous position than the original State of Nature where no sovereigns existed. A Sovereign with the sword in his hand would be a much more dangerous adversary than one of those roughly equal men likely to be encountered in the original State of Nature. A single individual in the State of Nature would have no chance at all of winning a trial of strength with a Sovereign. That individual would have to lie very low, living furtively and fearfully to such a degree that it would always make sense for him to come into Civil Society, and this would apply to everyone else who was in the same position. Straightforward prudence is a more than sufficient motive for original non-joiners to come into Civil Society on the same all-or-nothing terms which the other joiners originally agreed to.

4 Hobbes knows very well that, human nature being what he thinks it is, it is a certainty that men will be dissatisfied from time to time with the government which their Sovereign provides. Being the rational egotists that Hobbes thinks they are, men will be especially prone to complain about government as it affects them as individuals. Having a certain *amour propre*, men will be inclined to believe that they suffer injuries at the Sovereign's hands. These injuries could be real or imagined, but injuries they would certainly appear to be. Hobbes argues that the Sovereign, despite appearances, is incapable of injuring anybody. How can this be? Hobbes makes a crucial distinction between what he calls Iniquity and what he calls Injury. Iniquity is ordinary human wickedness and it is the same in Civil Society as it is in the State of Nature. Hobbes says that the State of Nature has a Law of Nature to govern it, and that Law of Nature is also God's command. Coming into Civil Society cannot abrogate God's commands, which never alter, so the Sovereign, being in himself a man like any other, can certainly act wickedly towards at least some of his subjects on the ages-old principle *ira principis mors est* (the prince's wrath is death). (There would in fact be strict self-limitations on the wicked acts of a rational prince.) Hobbes insists that to call acts of sovereign wickedness 'injuries' is to make a conceptual mistake. Injuries are literally actions which are not lawful. The Latin root of the word tells us that. Injuries are therefore defined by the positive law of a Civil Society, and are punished through the ordinary machinery of justice which is a Civil Society's distinguishing characteristic. But who can judge the Sovereign? The law is his command, so how can he be self-commanded? Of course, he has the Law of Nature to guide him in his actions, and of course a prudent and pious Sovereign would be foolish not to listen to God, but earthly judgement is another matter. The idea of justice and injustice can have its place only in a Civil Society where the Sovereign is both

law-giver and law-enforcer. To say that the Sovereign can do injustice is open to all the objections against judging a Sovereign which have been discussed. Besides, the social contract authorises everything that the Sovereign does, so that the Sovereign's actions are each man's actions, the Sovereign being his agent. It therefore follows that when it appears to me that the Sovereign has done me an injury, the supposed injury is something which I have done to myself, and nobody else can be responsible for a self-inflicted wound. The Sovereign may have acted wickedly towards me, but it is logical nonsense to say that he has done me an injury.

5 It follows from this that a Sovereign may never justly be put to death by his subjects because they would be punishing the Sovereign for their own act, and no principle of jurisprudence could ever conceivably justify punishing another for what one did oneself.

6 The Sovereign obviously determines all measures for internal peace. One of the great disturbers of the peace is diversity of opinion, particularly political and religious opinions. Therefore the Sovereign has the right to censor both. In political terms, this boils down to a sovereign right to decide the meaning of words, especially the words 'just' and 'unjust' about which so much controversy is possible. The Sovereign cannot decide the meaning of 'right' and 'wrong' because God has already decided that, but justice being the product of the Sovereign's own law, it is obviously up to him to decide what it means.

7 One of the Sovereign's main jobs would be to censor religious opinions and decide on forms of worship. A religious settlement rigorously enforced is an obvious necessity at a time when men took where they were going to spend eternity very seriously and were prepared to kill each other if they disagreed about the right path to heaven. Religious controversy had been tearing Europe apart for over a century when Hobbes wrote *Leviathan*. Hobbes probably knew that you could not change men's inner convictions by force, but the Sovereign could certainly decide what the public forms of worship should be. Beyond that, what men thought in their heart of hearts probably did not matter very much. (In his own heart of hearts Hobbes himself was probably an atheist.)

8 Decisions in the ordinary courts of the realm must be the Sovereign's. All courts will be his courts, just as all law will be his law. Different kinds of courts which might make different kinds of judgements would lead to confusion. Uncertainty about how the law actually worked would lead to a sense of insecurity, and it was for some measure of security that men quitted the State of Nature for Civil Society in the first place. The State of Nature was insecure because it was lawless. There was no machinery of justice in the State of Nature so it would be foolish to incorporate uncertainty and therefore insecurity into the machinery of justice in Civil Society.

9 The sword of Justice is also the sword of war. When the contracting parties to the social contract put the sword into the Sovereign's hand, they meant the Sovereign to protect them from each other and also from external enemies. Most sovereignties are acquired through conquest, and war is a nasty business whether it is the war of all against all in the State of Nature or foreign invasion. Disagreement over the question of war or peace would plainly be divisive. A state is most a state when it goes to war. War-making is

the ultimate act of sovereignty (*ultima ratio regis* – the king's final argument), so to deny the right of the Sovereign to decide matters of war and peace would be to deny him the very heart of sovereignty.

10 A Sovereign cannot do all the work of government by himself. All government will be government in the Sovereign's name (open in the name of the King!), but in fact the Sovereign will be obliged to work through agents. Sovereigns will naturally seek advice. They might even seek advice from parliamentary assemblies, or they might confine their advice-seeking to a few cronies, or even to a single royal favourite, but no matter where that advice comes from it is advice in the ordinary sense of the term, which the Sovereign may take or leave as he sees fit. Nobody could conceivably have a *right* to give the Sovereign advice, and that the Sovereign could ever be *obliged* to take advice from anybody is unthinkable. The choice of royal servants is therefore the Sovereign's alone and he may appoint and dismiss them at will.

11 Sovereigns will want to reward their servants from time to time. The Sovereign therefore has the right, and the sole right, to grant titles of nobility. He may even have the right of demotion, and he is certainly not accountable to anyone else for the way in which he exercises the ennobling power. Aristocracy is to be the Sovereign's creation in so far as that is possible in societies where aristocracies are used to thinking of themselves as hereditary.

Hobbes's account of sovereignty is sovereignty on the grand scale. It is worth repeating that Hobbes infers all the attributes of sovereignty from the original case of voluntary contract by Institution, and only then does he say that conquest sovereignty by Acquisition would enjoy the same rights. In *Leviathan*, the argument is carried on at a fairly abstract level, and it may not be obvious at first sight that *Leviathan* can be read as a philosophical commentary on recent European and English history, but this is in fact the case. What follows is an attempt to historicise Hobbes by showing how each of the attributes of sovereignty can be related to matters of contemporary political dispute. In itself, this should come as no surprise, because Hobbes is above all concerned with laying the ideological groundwork for an undisputatious and therefore stable commonwealth.

THE ATTRIBUTES OF SOVEREIGNTY AS CONTEMPORARY POLITICAL COMMENTARY

Nothing could be easier for the modern reader than to read Hobbes's *Leviathan* and miss the implicit references to seventeenth-century politics. What is required is not a detailed knowledge of political developments in the seventeenth century, but rather an awareness of certain typical political themes out of which Hobbes was quick to draw important theoretical lessons. The predominant theme in Hobbes's political theory is fear for one's life and possessions. (Fear gave rise to the picturesque legend that Hobbes's mother went into premature labour on hearing the guns of the Spanish Armada in 1588; being at Malmesbury at the time, she must have had remarkable hearing.) Hobbes and terror were born twins, and the theory of the awful State of Nature might have been the result, though we have to balance against this the fact that Hobbes himself seems to have been a notably cheerful man.

What, exactly, was it that Hobbes is supposed to have been fearful of? The simple answer is that Hobbes thought that England during her Civil War was returning to the State of Nature which Hobbes dreaded, but historians of the English Civil War have been pointing out ever since the Civil War was over that England during that war was nothing like a State of Nature as described by Hobbes. On the whole, the fabric of English society was strong enough to remain substantially intact, so Hobbes cannot be right about the State of Nature, or at best he exaggerates. This is to ignore the continental influences on Hobbes (he was in exile in France for the ten years after 1641). Hobbes scholars have always pointed to the influence of continental science and philosophy on Hobbes (Hobbes had met Descartes and Galileo during a continental visit in the 1630s) but they have been surprisingly mute about the possible influences of continental politics on *Leviathan*, and especially the influence of the Thirty Years War in Germany (1618–48). At times *Leviathan* reads like a philosophical commentary on Grimmelshausen's *Simplicissimus*, the standard account of Germany's descent into so chaotic a state, with so many sovereigns competing for mastery, that it begins to look very like the Hobbesian State of Nature. Hobbes probably thought that when the English Civil War broke out between the two competing sovereigns, king and Parliament, England was about to tread the terrible path that Germany had already trodden. Hobbes's explanation of why that did not happen in England would be that the English had the good sense to get themselves a new Sovereign, Cromwell, after the Stuart sovereigns had, temporarily as it turned out, disappeared from the scene.

Hobbes's assertion that a majority is enough to make the social contract valid and that the Sovereign may compel the rest to enter Civil Society means that Sovereignty can be legitimately exercised in a society where the consensus about government is incomplete. Perhaps consensus about government is always incomplete, but it matters particularly when the government of the day opposes itself to those institutions which are there to register consensus, which in the English case means Parliament. Social contract relies for its validity on the consent of the governed, either active or passive, and it begins to look bad for governments if consensus-registering institutions begin to dissent. This might not matter very much to kings like James I and Charles I who thought they ruled by Divine Right, but it would matter a great deal if an increasing number of their subjects were beginning to think about political obligation in social contract terms. These subjects could easily make common cause with other discontented subjects who were beginning to think that the Stuart kings were violating an ancient English constitution which put definite constraints upon sovereignty. By 1642 English Parliaments had been quarrelling with their sovereigns at least as far back as Elizabeth's reign, though historians still disagree about how serious those quarrels were. However, nobody seems to disagree that these quarrels became worse under the Stuarts, when they became so bad that Charles I managed to rule without Parliament for a decade (the Eleven Years' Tyranny, 1629–40). Most of us probably no longer think that the House of Commons 'won the initiative' by 1642. It used to be thought that continuous parliamentary opposition from the beginning of James I's reign built up to such a climax that the Commons felt strong and independent enough to enter into a contest with the king for sovereignty, but things could easily appear like that to a Royalist like Hobbes. A contested sovereignty is a divided sovereignty, and a divided sovereignty means civil war.

King and Parliament would soon meet on different sides of a battlefield, and what could be more divided that that? Hobbes therefore insists that sovereignty is indivisible and is for ever. English kings originally acquired their sovereignty by conquest (*1066 And All That*). In Hobbes's terms, the creation of sovereignty by Acquisition is a valid contract, so it cannot matter that late in the day some subjects, or even a majority, begin to argue erroneously that the king has no right to govern except on the advice of Parliament. By authorising all that the Sovereign does, his people gave up their Right of Nature, and it is not for them unilaterally to take some of it back by trying to put constraints on sovereignty. This would amount to no less than an attempt to renegotiate the original contract but, if Hobbes is right, that would be a fruitless exercise. Not only would Civil Society have to return to the State of Nature at least for a time, but also, if they thought about it properly, men would voluntarily set up a new Sovereign with absolute powers anyway. This effectively happened during Cromwell's Lord Protectorship after two civil wars. Hobbes could have saved Englishmen all that trouble.

Charles I was put on trial for his life and executed in 1649. Charles refused to recognise the court which tried him, and Hobbes obviously thinks that he was right. Hobbes is adamant that it is nonsense to say that the king can break any law. Kings may act wickedly, but in Hobbes's special sense they can do no man an injury, because an injury is specifically an offence against law. Law is the Sovereign's command and he cannot, except in the metaphorical sense of making good resolutions, be self-commanded. Being still in the State of Nature, the Sovereign can judge but cannot be judged. Least of all can he be judged by his own subjects, or by a body of them, because to set up a court to judge the Sovereign would effectively be to set up another Sovereign. As soon as this happened, both the king and his parliamentary accusers would be back in the State of Nature as rival sovereigns. The king was in Parliament's power in 1649, but the fact that he had fought two civil wars against Parliament was no reason to try him and to execute him, because sovereigns in the State of Nature have the Right of Nature to fight each other. Hobbes's argument is slightly ambiguous here. Sovereigns in the State of Nature have the right to fight each other, and killing in war in no crime. Presumably that means that Parliament had the right to kill the king, but not to try him. The trial may have been a farce, and so the judicial execution of the king was a farce too, but it would have been small comfort to kings to know that the only option open to their rebellious subjects would be to kill them straight away without any legal proceedings at all.

It was the radical Reformation which led Hobbes to argue that the Sovereign may censor opinions, particularly religious opinions, and that he may lay down lawful rules for public worship. This had been a contentious issue in England ever since the Reformation itself in the 1530s, and as parts of Protestantism began to radicalise themselves in the last quarter of the sixteenth and in the first half of the seventeenth century, the state had to begin to take notice of them in ways which had not been necessary before. In Protestant England, anti-Catholicism was no longer enough. All kinds of plucky little dissenting Protestant sects began to spring up, and these were of the kind which would follow the example of the Puritans at the Hampton Court Conference in 1604 who would not doff their hats to King James. Soon they would be arguing that the state should be run on the same voluntary basis as their churches, which in Hobbes's eyes would be just another attempt to constrain and divide sovereignty. Granted the Sovereign's duty to keep the internal peace, these dissenting sects would have to be stamped on. The best way to do this would probably be to regulate public worship. The Anglican *Book of Common Prayer* had been a matter for bitter controversy in its day, but the book of *common* prayer it was. English monarchs, with the exception of Bloody Mary, had been Heads of the Church since the reign of Henry VIII, and a decent public observance of its established rites by everyone in the realm would contribute substantially to social peace.

The Sovereign's right through his judges to make all decisions in courts of law is an attack by Hobbes on a particular view of the history of the Common Law of England. An important part of the anti-Royalist argument in England had always been that the Common Law existed independent of the royal prerogative. The Common Law, which was supposed to embody the liberties of the subject from time immemorial, was certainly not the king's creation, let alone his creature. Common Law courts and the king's courts had always engaged in an intermittent rivalry for jurisdiction (largely on account of the fees which litigation produced). Common Law was judge-made law, neither statute law made by king-in-parliament, nor the lawful command of a king issued through royal proclamations. In the seventeenth century, the Common Law, and especially common lawyers, came increasingly to be seen as the repository of the ancient rights and liberties of Englishmen. It must be emphasised that, at least in the beginning, there was nothing remotely republican about this stance. King James I got off to a bad start in England because on his way down from Scotland he hanged a thief. Nobody in the least minded the thief being hanged, but it had to be explained to James that in England thieves had to go through the ordinary process of law before they were strung up. Sir Edward Coke was later famously to argue before the king that the Common Law of England existed independently of the king, but Coke was on his knees when he did it. To argue that the royal prerogative – the powers the king had just because he was king – was limited in some way was not to argue against the principle of monarchy itself. Quite the contrary. The king *was* king. He had certain prerogative powers, and these powers were very wide; much better not to ask questions about *exactly* how wide those powers were. One of James I's faults was that he is the only king of England ever to be interested in political theory. As the wisest fool in Christendom, he would insist on trying to define how far the royal prerogative went. This in its turn led common lawyers, and eventually parliamentarians, to begin to ask how far the powers of Common Law courts went, and what exactly the powers of Parliament were.

Charles I began where James had left off, and that three-sided dispute about the division of sovereignty between king, Common Law and Parliament in England was the immediate intellectual context of the English Civil War. The immediate political cause of the outbreak of the war in 1642 was an issue of exactly this kind. Some English parliamentarians had always feared what a royal army might do to English liberties if it returned victorious over the endemically rebellious Irish. There was a Scottish rebellion, possibly egged on by English malcontents, in 1641. Charles I, who had just about been holding his own financially for the past ten years without calling a Parliament to raise new taxation, decided to call Parliament in the hope of getting the money to finance an army to put down the Scots. The parliamentary opposition was immediately suspicious. Parliament constitutionally provided extra taxation, but the king, while being obliged to give reasons why he needed the money, was more or less free to spend it how he liked afterwards, because in those days there was nothing like the Public Accounts Committee of the House of Commons. Suppose the king had in mind the putting down of others besides the Scots, parliamentary malcontents included? The crucial question was therefore about who was going to command the army the king intended to raise. Officers held the King's Commission (they still do). Appointment to military commands had been part of the royal prerogative for as long as anyone could remember, and that was the rub. Parliamentarians, or a large enough party of them, were not going to let the king pack an army financed through Parliament with royalist officers who, on the king's command, would be perfectly willing to put down a difficult House of Commons. And so to civil war. Nothing could demonstrate more clearly the dangers of a divided sovereignty to a thinker like Hobbes. If division of sovereignty leads to that halfway house to the State of nature, civil war, then what could be more sensible than to argue that sovereignty should be entirely invested in one man or a single body of men? Let the Sovereign make and execute the laws, and let him choose his own servants, and civil war would be far away. (It would come as no surprise to Hobbes that Cromwell was later to do to Parliament what the parliamentary party feared might happen in 1642.)

The question of who should decide who should serve the king went deeper than the immediate crisis of 1641–2. Parliamentarians knew that when they claimed the right to advise the king on who to choose as officers for the army, they were encroaching on the royal prerogative. What made them do it then was that some parliamentarians could look back to nearly forty years' worth of worthless or dangerous royal servants and favourites. Parliament had been trying to get at obnoxious royal servants through the rather drastic and cumbersome processes of impeachment and attainder almost ever since the Stuarts came to the throne in 1603. Cranfield, Buckingham and Strafford had all suffered in this way, and Strafford paid with his life. From an oppositionist point of view, the only way of getting kings with absolutist pretensions to listen to them when they disagreed about government policy (especially foreign or financial policy) was to attack royal servants with the only constitutional and legal means available. Attacks on the king's servants reduced the effectiveness of royal government. Small wonder that Hobbes, with his concern for a strong and effective sovereign centre to the state, should insist absolutely that the Sovereign had the right to choose and dismiss his own servants at will.

War is the business of kings, so it should come as no surprise that Hobbes puts the war-making power exclusively in the Sovereign's hands. The Sovereign decides when to make war, against whom, and where. This question of war had been contentious in England since the beginning of James I's reign. In ordinary times, the king was expected 'to live of his own', which meant that rents from royal lands and certain traditional forms of royal taxation (wardship, the customs) were supposed to be enough to keep the king in the style to which he was accustomed and to defray the ordinary expenses of government (and in those venal days probably about half the royal revenues came indirectly to the king in the form of 'gifts' to royal officials). It was accepted constitutional practice that in emergencies the king could ask Parliament, which effectively meant the House of Commons, for extra taxation, and war was one of these accepted emergencies. From the first of James's parliaments, discontented members of the House of Commons had begun to ask some very searching questions about royal requests for extra revenue for military and naval purposes. Parliamentary and popular memory could never rid itself of the thought that England had never prospered so much as in the old days of Elizabeth, when the foreign policy had been war with Spain and peace with all the world. That meant war at sea, not a land war in Europe. The cost of war was rising in the seventeenth century (as was the price of everything else), and land wars were generally recognised to be the most expensive of all. James I was an orthodox Calvinist, and Protestant Englishmen had always felt proud that England had become the leader of the European Protestant cause during Elizabeth's reign. James I's daughter, Elizabeth, was married to Frederick, Protestant Elector Palatine, and she became the Winter Queen when Frederick laid his claim to the Kingdom of Bohemia to begin the Thirty Years War in Europe. James was a meddler, and from 1618 onwards the parliamentary opposition was always afraid that he might meddle in the land war in central Europe. James never did, but it remained a possibility until the end of his reign. James's successor Charles did get himself involved in foreign wars under his favourite Buckingham's promptings, but his interventions achieved nothing tangible, and they were horribly expensive. Disputes between kings and the House of Commons about foreign policy were never far below the surface of seventeenth-century English politics, and these disputes were one of the contributing causes of the Civil War. Hobbes naturally puts the war-making power entirely into the Sovereign's hands to prevent this possible cause of discord and division.

Historians are still squabbling about what the lines were that England divided on in the Civil War. Marxist historians call the English Civil War and the Interregnum a 'bourgeois revolution', but the bourgeois revolution thesis has always had to live with the uncomfortable fact that the Civil War divided the English aristocracy. What could have induced English aristocrats to side with Parliament against their king? Perhaps Hobbes's assertion that it is part of the Sovereign's prerogative to choose whom for what rank gives us an important clue: both James I and Charles I sold honours. There appears to have been something like a regular tariff, and there is nothing which annoys a real aristocrat more than an upstart who has bought his nobility. Ancient service to the state is supposed to be the basis of rank, not moneymaking. Hume may be right when he says that aristocracy is merely 'reputation of ancient fortune', but that is not how aristocrats see it. The trade in honours became notorious under James, and continued under Charles. It appeared to debase the idea of kingship as well as debasing the idea of nobility, but more was at stake. Kings were not obliged to call Parliaments regularly in the seventeenth century, and there was still some doubt as to whether the constitution obliged them to call Parliaments at all. (Regular Parliaments was to be one of the consequences of the Revolution of 1688.) The king's motive for calling Parliaments was nearly always money. A universal European price rise helped the cause of parliamentarians because the king was always going to need more money for his own expenses and for the ordinary expenses of government. This desperation for money would be increased by the fact that much of the king's revenue came from rents from royal lands, and it is well-established that when prices rise, rents from land rise less quickly than the price of most other things. As long as kings were broke Parliaments would be called.[1] The converse was also true: if kings could really find enough cash to 'live of their own', then there was no reason in principle why they should ever call a Parliament again. Parliamentarians were playing a double game. They argued endlessly that James was spending as much in peacetime as Elizabeth spent at war, but on the other hand they were bound to look on with suspicion when kings found new ways of raising non-parliamentary revenue, because that could make the king independent of Parliament, a true separation of powers and the possible annihilation of one of them. Some aristocrats were Parliament men, and all could sneer at the jumped-up aristocrats who kept appearing in their midst by royal command. Small wonder, then, that some aristocrats were to side with Parliament in the Civil War, and small wonder that Hobbes, concerned as he is for the unity of the state, should argue that aristocracy should be the Sovereign's creature, if not his creation, in so far as that is possible.[2]

The English Civil War was fought for many things, but there can be no doubt that contemporaries thought that one of the things they were fighting for was religion. (Not everybody was as honest as the parliamentarian who said that we fight for religion because everyone has religion; if all men possessed land, we would say we fought for land.) We have already remarked that Englishmen had been quarrelling, sometimes bloodily, over religious questions since the Reformation of the 1530s. To remember how important religion was, all we have to do is to remind ourselves that the Civil War and its aftermath, the Interregnum, is sometimes called the Puritan Revolution. Hobbes, with his implicitly European perspective, could not help but have in mind the example of what the Thirty Years War, as a religious war, was doing to Germany. His argument that the Sovereign has the right to settle religious questions, including questions about official doctrine as well as ceremony, is the least surprising of all.

THE LAWS OF NATURE: SOME OF THE CONTROVERSIES WHICH SURROUND HOBBES'S DOCTRINE

Hobbes writes a classic English prose. All the commentators on Hobbes recognise that he writes with more than ordinary clarity and pungency, so how can it be that so much learned controversy surrounds Hobbes's *Leviathan*? In particular, how can it be that controversy surrounds the central theme of *Leviathan*, the theory of political obligation as it is derived from the Laws of Nature and social contract? Some commentators even go as far as to claim that Hobbes hasn't got a genuine theory of political obligation at all.

So what is the controversy *about*? The basis of it can be stated very simply: it is sometimes argued that Hobbes fails to provide any moral basis for political obligation, no reason for supposing that men would ever feel internally obliged to obey the Sovereign. Men would obey the Sovereign out of fear of violent death at his hands, but they would never feel that they *ought* to obey him. The old Natural Law doctrine always held that in most circumstances men ought to obey the supreme authority in the state. A moral basis for political obligation was essential in polities where law-enforcing agencies were not all that efficient. The internalised feeling that one ought to obey the law was a kind of inner policeman before policemen had been invented. Where, it is said, does one find in Hobbes an argument which would lead one to suppose that a Sovereign's subjects would ever feel that they *ought* to obey him? Hobbes appears to be misusing and debasing the language of Natural Law for purely prudential ends which, as it was traditionally conceived, Natural Law had never been used to serve.

Why does this matter? It matters on two levels, one philosophical and one practical, though the two are obviously connected. On the philosophical level, to say that Hobbes does not make out a convincing case for political obligation is to say that *Leviathan* fails in its main intention. Whatever else *Leviathan* may be about, it is certainly about why men ought to obey the Sovereign. On the practical level, if there is no moral argument for political obligation which would convince rational egotists, then these rational egotists would only obey the Sovereign when they were really compelled to by fear. That has huge implications for the practice of government as Hobbes conceives it. Fear would have to be real, adrenalin-pumping fear. Pretend fear would not be enough, and real fear would recede almost with the physical distance which men could put between themselves and the Sovereign in societies where law-enforcement was inefficient anyway. For the Hobbesian prudential scheme of political obligation to work, there would have to be literally armies of policemen and hundreds of law-enforcing agencies, because men would never obey unless they were actually confronted with the physical embodiment of the law's threat of punishment. This would be enormously expensive. A society like this would have to spend an unduly high proportion of its gross national product just to police itself. We have remarked before that the feeling of political obligation provides power on the cheap. If I feel I ought to obey, then no politically scarce resources have to be used up to secure my obedience. And if it were really true that rational egotists would only obey in the presence or the threatened presence of authority, then it is difficult to see, on this account of Hobbes's account of the matter, how the state could ever be really efficient. Having the Sovereign present through his agents everywhere would not only be ruinously expensive, but it probably wouldn't work because of the sheer impossibility of policing everybody the whole time. If *Leviathan* is about nothing else, it is about efficient government, so the argument in *Leviathan* would fail in this important practical sense.

Hobbes's argument about the Law of Nature is apparently simple. We have emphasised how lawless Hobbes's State of Nature is because there is no Sovereign, and therefore no positive law. Without a law-making and law-enforcing agency, men in the State of Nature would not be foolish enough to make contracts with each other for fear of non-performance in the absence of a law-enforcing mechanism. Hobbes does of course think that, but he also says that there is a law, but a very different kind of law, in the State of Nature, and this he calls the Laws of Nature. His definition of a Law of Nature is, again, apparently simple:

215

A LAW OF NATURE, (*Lex Naturalis*) is a precept, or general Rule found out by Reason, by which a man is forbidden to do, that, which is destructive of his life, or taketh away the means of preserving the same; and to omit, that, by which he thinketh it may be best preserved.

Nature's Law commands a man to preserve his own life, and Hobbes goes as far as saying that if a man were to make a contract in the State of Nature by which he promised something for fear of his life, the contract would be binding, because, by preserving his life, he would be getting something in return. All of the Laws of Nature are of this life-preserving kind. In the State of Nature the Right of Nature means that everyone has a right to everything because, as we saw above, the Right of Nature must be limitless in the State of Nature because there is no way of predicting what a man might think he has to do to keep himself alive. The Right of Nature is a permission while the Law of Nature is a command. Taken together they add up to a very pretty formula for lawlessness in the State of Nature. Therefore, the fundamental Law of Nature must be 'to seek *Peace* and follow it', which means that everyone has to give up their right to everything else and begin to respect the rights of others. This amounts to no more than the Gospels' injunction to do unto others what you would have them do unto you. This second Law of Nature follows naturally from the command to seek peace. In Hobbes's words:

> That a man be willing, when others are so too, as farre-forth, as for Peace, and defence of himself he shall think it necessary, to lay down his right to all things; and be contented with so much liberty against other men, as he would allow other men against himself. (Hobbes's italics.)

The question then arises in what sense the Laws of Nature are to be thought of as laws, because Hobbes usually insists that a law is the command of a lawful Sovereign, whereas he originally speaks of Laws of Nature as general rules found out by reason, not as laws commanded by a law-giver. After Hobbes has enumerated all of the peace-providing Laws of Nature, he adds what appears almost to be an afterthought:

> These dictates of Reason, men use to call by the name of Lawes; but improperly: for they are but Conclusions, or Theoremes concerning the defence of themselves; whereas Law, properly is the word of him, that by right hath command over others. But yet if we consider the same Theoremes, as delivered in the word of God, that by right commandeth all things; then are they properly called Lawes.

The problem is that 'if we consider', because it seems to imply that we are under no obligation to insist that the Laws of Nature are God's Laws, and Hobbes does in fact say that a man of even the meanest intelligence could at least work out the gist of the Laws of Nature for himself. Are these Laws of Nature, then, simply dictates of prudence, or does Hobbes *really* believe they are God's Law? He says that they are the equivalent of God's Laws, but that is not quite the same thing.

A good deal hangs on this question. Suppose the Laws of Nature really are God's Laws.

Hobbes says that in the State of Nature the Laws of Nature bind internally (*in foro interno*) but not externally (*in foro externo*). By this he means that in the State of Nature men know in their heart of hearts that they ought to treat other men as they would have them treat them, but nobody would be the first to follow this way to peace because that would put him at a disadvantage in relation to other men who might still be in a state of war. We know that Hobbes thinks that the way to get from the State of Nature to Civil Society, from a state of war to a state of peace, is by making the social contract as he describes it, which means creating a Sovereign. If the Laws of Nature really are God's commands, and therefore binding on all Christian people (and even on those who are not Christians), then it could be argued that there is in the State of Nature a prior moral obligation to make the social contract, and to obey the Sovereign afterwards, on the grounds that only in this way can social peace and stability ever be achieved. On this account of it, there is genuine moral obligation in the State of Nature and in Civil Society, so that there could be a genuinely moral basis for political obligation in Civil Society.

But begin to think of Hobbes's Laws of Nature simply as dictates of prudence, and very different consequences follow. If honesty, for instance, is the best *policy*, then at least in principle there might be occasions when honesty would *not* be the best policy because the idea of 'the best policy' depends upon circumstances. You would be in the position of saying: Honesty is usually the best policy, but I will wait and see. Hobbes's Law of Nature as dictates of prudence only would work something like that. In Civil Society, it might be wisest to tell the truth, keep bargains with others, and obey the law only when the Sovereign or his agents are watching. Out of their gaze, it might make perfect sense to break the law as often as you liked, if the possibility of being found out was remote. The Sovereign's commands would have no internal force as commands, because everyone would be able to think of circumstances in which it would be wise to disobey them. Rational egotists would only feel obliged to obey when they were actually forced to through fear, and we have already seen what an expensive and cumbersome business that would be.

Is there a way out of this difficulty when Hobbes scholars are still arguing about it (and about much else in Hobbes)? One way out of the difficulty might be to say that in fact there is nothing inconsistent between Hobbes's view of the Laws of Nature and the view of Natural Law as God's Law as traditionally conceived. We have seen that in the old conception of it, Natural Law had three separate sources for God's Law: revelation in Scripture, human reason, and ordinary social experience. The hand of God writes Natural Law in these three different ways: directly by Scripture, indirectly through philosophy and again indirectly on men's hearts through social experience (Paul to the Romans, II, 14). Hobbes's doctrine of the Laws of Nature certainly fits the two indirect criteria for Natural Law, and he is also careful to say that his own doctrine is nothing but the message of the Gospels writ large. 'Careful' is the key word. The seekers after religious heterodoxy had always sniffed around Hobbes, and the heresy-hunters were after him till the end of his life. It always comes back to trying to read Hobbes's own mind across the centuries. Perhaps Hobbes expected us to read a genuinely atheistic and materialistic theory of moral and political obligation between the lines of *Leviathan*, and it has to be said that such a reading is not difficult to make. (My own view is that all the elements of such a theory are there ready and waiting to be picked up out of *Leviathan*, and that Hobbes intended that this should be so.)

Another way out of the moral/prudential conundrum about obligation in Hobbes is to say that in *Leviathan* Hobbes is giving an account of how the substantive content of morality *arises*, not an account of how morality *originates*. The fact that Hobbes has a view of how men come to fill moral categories with a particular content does not thereby make morality less 'moral'. Filling moral categories with a moral content, it might be said, is a characteristically moral enterprise. And besides, the end of Hobbes's theory is social and perhaps international peace, and who is there who would deny that this is a godly end?

The controversy continues, and perhaps a way out of it might be found if we were to ask ourselves why the controversy, which has lasted since the middle of the seventeenth century, arose in the first place. The answer to that question is obvious: Hobbes, like Machiavelli, can give his readers sleepless nights. As Shakespeare says, 'Unaccommodated man is but a poor, bare, forked creature'; take a man out of his position in an ordinary society with law-enforcement, and he is a very unlovely sight. In *Leviathan* Hobbes certainly does not flatter humankind. Man in his natural state is an egotistical brute; much better, then, to bind him to a Sovereign. Hobbes's critics have been saying implicitly that there *must* be something wrong with the argument in *Leviathan* ever since his seventeenth-century enemies tried to discredit him with the taint of atheism. No doubt there is something wrong with the argument in *Leviathan*, but it might not occur where Hobbes's critics have always looked for it in the groundings of obligation in Natural Law.

HOBBES'S ACCOUNT OF SOCIAL CONTRACT PERHAPS NOT AN ACCOUNT OF CONTRACT AT ALL

In the normal legal idea of a contract there has to be what lawyers call a 'consideration'. By that lawyers mean that each of the two parties (or more than two parties) to a contract has to give something in return for something else. In a contract of sale, for instance, one of the parties pays the other, and that transfers the right of ownership from the seller to the buyer. No consideration, no contract, and therefore no transfer of right from one to another. On first sight, Hobbes's account of social contract appears to conform to the formal–legal criteria of contract: men by agreement with each other give up their Right of Nature to the Sovereign in return for social peace. Everybody gives up something and receives something in return. We could quibble, and say that there might be something wrong with Hobbes's idea of contract because what men receive they do not receive directly from the other contracting parties, but only indirectly through the Sovereign. It is the Sovereign law-giver and law-enforcer who is the provider of social peace, and he is not party to the social contract in Hobbes's theory. This is a technical niggle. Much more serious would be the objection that, in Hobbes's account of social contract, no consideration at all changes hands, and, as we have seen, it follows that if there is no consideration, no valid contract can be made.

In Hobbes, the consideration at social contract time is the Right of Nature. Hobbes is quite explicit about the transfer of the Right of Nature. Men transfer the Right of Nature, in so far as they are able, to the Sovereign, and a good part of *Leviathan*'s argument is designed to show that men in the State of Nature would have very strong motives for giving up their Right of Nature. It is a liability to them, whereas giving it up to the Sovereign would make it an asset, because the Sovereign could use the transferred Right of Nature to provide for social peace. Men would then really receive the defence against others which in the State of Nature the Right of Nature so notoriously failed to give except in a very restricted sense. But it can be argued that the whole business of the transfer of the Right of Nature, the consideration without which the contract is no contract, might be redundant in Hobbes, that Hobbes is playing an elaborate trick with alleged transfer of the Right of Nature and that *Leviathan* contains an equally elaborately constructed screen to prevent the audience from seeing how the trick works.

The argument is this. Ask Hobbes: What is the Right of Nature actually *for*? In particular, ask what the Right of Nature does for men that the Laws of Nature do not do? The chief characteristic of the Law of Nature is that men are 'forbidden' (Hobbes's word) to do anything which might put their lives at risk, or to neglect any precautions which make their survival more likely. This is a Natural Law, whether Natural Law is God's command or a simple dictate of prudence. If men are thus commanded, then they have no option but to obey, so why do they need the Right of Nature to give them permission to obey what is already a command? Law for Hobbes is the command of a Sovereign, and men do not ask their commanders 'Is it all right if I do what you tell me?' That is an absurdity. In real life the opposite would be much more likely to happen: petitioners would ask on occasions, and for good reason, if it would be all right to disobey, or modify, commands given to them by superiors. So why, of all things, do we need permission to obey what Hobbes does after all say is God's Law? Why the Right of Nature? The answer is obvious. Hobbes gives men the Right of Nature, which is not only useless but unnecessary as well, so that, at the moment of social contract, men have actually got something they can give up as a consideration in order to make the social contract conform to the formal–legal criteria of ordinary contract-making. If this argument about considerations is right, then Hobbesian men have done what they did by command, and not by contract, because how could they have made a valid contract without a consideration at all? The Right of Nature is something in the nature of a red herring. It is unnecessary; Hobbes knows this, and he only gives men the Right of Nature to save the appearance of the social contract as a valid contract.

Hobbes puts up a smokescreen to disguise this. He knows perfectly well that most readers of *Leviathan* (then as now) wishing to take issue with him on his account of social contract will immediately fasten on to the element of compulsion, especially as it occurs in the account of Acquisition of Sovereignty by conquest. Hobbes uses some long (by his standards) and meticulous arguments to show that compulsion by fear is never an argument against contracts in general. All formal contracts are insisted upon for fear of non-performance. In Civil Society, the only difference will be that the positive law will deny the validity of certain specific kinds of contract. Judges and juries in courts of law in Civil Society will be unlikely to hear sympathetically the plea of a bank-robber that he made

219

a perfectly fair contract with the bank manager by giving him the option: Your money or your life! A contract like that would be valid in the State of Nature (though it couldn't be made for money because there would be no Sovereign to coin sovereigns in the State of Nature), but not in Civil Society, because a prudent Sovereign would always make sure it was against the law. (Compare the American phrase 'taking out a contract on someone', which means hiring an assassin.) The argument about the compulsory nature of all valid contracts is one of the most ingenious in *Leviathan*, and we can now see that it is ingenious in two separate senses: first, it is ingenious in its own terms as an argument, but second, and perhaps more importantly, by arguing elaborately against the invalidity of social contract through fear and compulsion, Hobbes very cleverly tries to lull his readers into thinking that the only possible argument against his account of the social contract is the fear-and-compulsion argument. But we have seen that the real argument against him might be that the social contract as Hobbes sees it is not a valid contract because no consideration is really given up to another. The contract argument in Hobbes fails by the test of the formal requirements of ordinary contracts.

HOBBES AND THE LIMITATIONS ON SOVEREIGNTY: THE EFFICIENCY CONSTRAINT

Men being the egotists they are, and the Sovereign being the supreme egotist that everyone wants to be, what is to stop the Sovereign running amok in Civil Society? Hobbes may think he has set an eagle above the vultures, but what he may have done is to set a cat among the doves (I say 'doves' because doves are in fact quite aggressive creatures). If Hobbes ever uses inflated language, it is in speaking about Sovereigns and Commonwealths. Kings are themselves called gods by God himself (in the Old Testament), and Hobbes calls the state, that artificial creation of man, Leviathan, a 'mortal God'. Hobbes's reason for this hyperbole is partly witty; he is taunting his opponents who believed that formal constraints would be put on the Sovereignty by contract, but many a reader has come away from Hobbes with the impression that Hobbes's Sovereign could and would do anything he pleases. *Leviathan*, on this view of it, is a formula for the rehabilitation of Caligula, and some commentators have even seen in *Leviathan* a blueprint for the modern world's only contribution to possible forms of government, the totalitarian state.

The truth of the matter is more sober. It must be remembered that in *Leviathan* Hobbes is always attacking the possibility of formal–legal, contract-type constraints on sovereignty, and it is easy to forget that in the real world of politics non-legal constraints on sovereignty arise which do in fact limit sovereign power. What is at issue here is the tricky distinction (of which a great deal will be made when we come to discuss eighteenth-century political thought, especially in America) between 'powers' and 'power'. The 'powers' of a Sovereign refer to those things the Sovereign may do *by right*; what in the case of kingship is called the royal prerogative. Hobbes's argument is that the powers of the Sovereign are virtually unlimited and unlimitable. But it is often the case that sovereigns have rights to do things which it would in fact be impolitic to do, and this is especially true of a Hobbesian

Sovereign who, remaining as he does in the State of Nature, has the right to do virtually anything he likes to or for his subjects. But unlimited right does not imply unlimited 'power', where power means the capacity to enforce one's will on others, or, more simply, doing and getting done anything one pleases.

So what constraints are there on this Hobbesian Sovereign with virtually unlimited powers but limited power (on the commonplace assumption that all power is to a degree limited)? The answer probably is: efficiency of law-enforcement. We have to ask the question: What would induce a Sovereign's subjects actually to obey the law? Some subjects might think they ought to obey, and that would be a great bonus for the Sovereign because subjects like these would not have to be coerced into obedience. Other subjects might obey because they feared a return to the State of Nature, and they would be another bonus for the Sovereign because they too would obey voluntarily.

But there is still a catch. Hobbesian men do not come into Civil Society in order to change their natures but *because* of their natures. Each subject of a Sovereign might still be dreaming of being in the optimum position for a rational egotist, which is to be in circumstances in which everybody *except himself* was obliged and willing to obey laws. This might give the Sovereign in that commonwealth more than one sleepless night. The head that wears the crown might lie uneasily because the Sovereign would know that 'out there' there would be subjects dreaming of themselves becoming Sovereign. Not all of them, perhaps, but enough. These potential rivals for the Sovereignty would be thinking this: of course we don't want a return to the State of Nature, and of course that means that the Sovereign must be obeyed, but it would still suit me very well if everybody else *except me* obeyed the Sovereign and kept within the law. A rational egotist would want his neighbours to be law-abiding while he got away with murder.

How could a Hobbesian Sovereign cope with that? The only way he could keep these rationally egotistically would-be sovereigns within the law would be the fear of punishment. Men feared violent death at the hands of another in the State of Nature, and they must still be made to feel that fear in Civil Society. (And by 'violent' death Hobbes really means what he says: cruel and unusual punishments might be the required norm.) What this amounts to is that in Civil Society subjects must fear the Sovereign more than they fear anyone else.

It is out of this necessity to fear the Sovereign more than one's neighbour that the efficiency constraint arises. Men must somehow be made to feel that they are more frightened of the Sovereign than they are of their neighbours stealing a march on them by going outside the law while they remain within it. That must mean efficiency of law enforcement, which in its turn implies regular (and fair) administration of justice. I have to feel that my neighbour feels that law-breaking just isn't worth it because the risk of getting caught is too high for them to risk disobedience to the Sovereign's lawful commands.

Another way of looking at this question would be to ask: What does fear really mean for Hobbes? We can readily see why men would be fearful of each other in the State of Nature, but what changes when these fearful creatures come into Civil Society? The answer is obvious: in Civil Society men exchange a very generalised fear of violent death at everybody else's hands for a very particular fear of violent death from the Sovereign's sword of justice. It is not that men stop fearing those who have now become their neighbours. Quite the reverse. Men will always be afraid of their neighbours stealing a march on them, by going outside of the law, but Hobbes's point is that in Civil Society this fear of neighbours will be overshadowed by fear of the Sovereign. A very generalised fear is exchanged for an overriding fear of the Sovereign, and that is what makes social life possible. There is a useful analogy here with psychiatric medicine. Sometimes psychiatrists are confronted with patients in such a generalised phobic condition that they are frightened of everyone and everything, and this can lead to such generalised paralysis of the will that the patient is too afraid to do anything and is even afraid to leave the at least familiar surroundings of his own room. This is a sad parody of the solitariness of the Hobbesian State of Nature. The beginnings of a cure start to happen when the psychiatrist can get the phobic patient to say what *exactly* he is afraid of. If he can get the patient to convert his very generalised fear into, say, fear of large red buses, then it begins to become possible that the patient can begin to live a 'normal' life by avoiding large red buses (by moving to another town, say, where the buses are blue). When fear acquires a definite shape and direction, then you know where you stand, and a regular, socialised life becomes possible. Hobbesian men in Civil Society are in the position of the patient who swaps his fear of everything for the fear of large red buses; he can now get on with something like a normal life.

Hobbes's position therefore seems to be that Civil Society will remain intact provided only that subjects fear the Sovereign more than they fear anyone else. This means that the machinery of justice really has to work and to keep working. The Sovereign, being a rational egotist, wants to hold on to his sovereignty, and it would be a very stupid, and therefore irrational, Sovereign who did not realise that he could only keep the sovereignty by keeping the machinery of law-enforcement in good running order.

Under what conditions might the efficiency constraint upon Sovereignty fail? Plainly, you would begin to realise that it was beginning to fail when your fear of your neighbours began to increase and your fear of the Sovereign began to diminish. There need be no high-sounding proclamation in Hobbes, as there is in Locke, about the natural *right* of rebellion, because Hobbes implies the natural *fact* of rebellion. We will see that in Locke it requires some fairly sophisticated reasoning about the right to rebel before you can tell whether in your present circumstance you may exercise that right. Not so in Hobbes: any sane fool knows what he fears most. When a man begins to feel in his guts the fear of his neighbours more than the fear of his Sovereign, then the rebellion has already happened internally, and he is back in the State of Nature. This could happen by degrees, or it could happen very quickly, as circumstances demanded (war would be a slightly different case: the internal rebellion would be over as soon as a soldier began to fear the opposing Sovereign and his army more than his own commanding Sovereign; then it would be rational behaviour to desert, change sides, or surrender). Allegiance only lasts for as long as it makes sense. Clarendon (who wrote a famous history of the English Civil War and became a Minister under Charles II after the Restoration) got the matter exactly right when he said that Hobbes was such a fellow that he will have his Sovereign for better, but not for worse. In any social, political or military emergency, fear is a man's best guide. An analogy in the spirit of Hobbes might be what happens when people begin to man the lifeboats on a sinking ship. It appears that the ship is about to go down, say, in twenty minutes. Orderly queues form at lifeboat stations, women and children first, marshalled by ship's officers armed at the captain's command to make sure there is no queue-jumping or panic. In these circumstances, it makes sense for an individual passenger to obey commands on the assumption that *he* will get off in the remaining twenty minutes of the ship's life. Suddenly, word goes round that the ship will go down in five minutes. True or not, this change of circumstances alters what is happening in every passenger's own mind. His adrenalin tells him he must do something more to save himself than just queuing up for the lifeboat. He eyes up the officer with the gun, and he begins to sense that others are going to rush the lifeboats. That is his moment of truth. He realises that he has more fear of his neighbours jumping the queue than of the ship's officer acting as the captain's agent. Everybody else now becomes his enemy, he is back in the State of Nature, and knowing no duty of obedience to anyone, he fights his way towards the lifeboats like everybody else, and the final recognition that sovereignty has collapsed occurs when the Sovereign–captain himself recognises it and shouts 'Every man for himself'.[3]

THE SOURCES OF HOBBESIAN INDIVIDUALISM

We saw in the introductory section on the rise of social contract that social contract theory depends on a view of individuals as being in some important sense autonomous. We also saw that it is a vexed question where the idea of individual autonomy 'comes from'. In Hobbes's case, this difficulty does not arise. It has often been remarked how susceptible Hobbes was to the influence of the scientific and philosophical currents of his day, both English and continental. He had been Bacon's amanuensis, and he met Descartes and Galileo. Hobbes was also impressed by Harvey's discovery that the blood circulated, and by current ideas of motion and gravity. When Hobbes looked out of his window and saw the world, he didn't see it, as Aristotle and the scholastic philosophy did, as full of objects and creatures naturally at rest and having to be set in motion. What Hobbes saw was a world full of objects and creatures naturally in motion until they were arrested by some equal and opposite force. Motion, internal and external, is what constitutes human happiness. Unrestricted pursuit of human goods is what all men want, and moral rules and the positive law are ways found out by reason (and perhaps commanded by God) to ensure the maximum liberty to do that, combined with the minimum harm caused to others. Hobbes is an eminently physical, if not physiological, thinker. If the blood flows quickly and easily, unrestricted by hard arteries, and if men can go about their business in the world without bumping too hard against their fellow men, then a measure of human happiness and fulfilment is possible.

Long ago, Professor C. B. MacPherson (*The Political Theory of Passive Individualism: Hobbes to Locke*, 1962) taught us to look for aggressive, self-seeking, marketmen in Hobbes's political theory. Hobbes's men were possessive individualists, always in danger of coming into sharp and potentially damaging contact with others of their kind, unless regulated to an extent by law. The rush to acquire in a society rapidly becoming a market society in which the typical economic activity was buying and selling, including the buying and selling of labour, was always going to cause problems of disruption in the social and political orders as traditionally conceived. Hobbes offers one kind of answer to the self-seeking of market-men continually on the move, and that answer is the absolute Sovereign.

Self-moving, self-seeking marketmen are the rising bourgeoisie by another name, and historians have come to associate the bourgeoisie with a certain set of political institutions and practices: Parliaments; government limited by a constitution; political representation and the bourgeois freedoms of thought and expression. In short the rise of liberalism is often thought of as the necessary accompaniment of bourgeois domination of economy and society. Not by Hobbes: a rising bourgeoisie requires an absolutist state.

We once thought of this as an objection to Hobbes's argument in *Leviathan*. Hobbes appeared to be saying: Enrich yourselves as much as you like within the law, but don't expect a share in the exercise of sovereignty. Hobbes seemed to be denying what was soon to become the commonplace in theory which it had always been in fact: the connections between wealth and political power. Where was *class*, it used to be asked, in Hobbes? Large differences of wealth were there, no doubt, but a society in which there were great concentrations of wealth but in which political power was entirely invested in a very sovereign Sovereign didn't appear to make sense. Capitalism without bourgeois power in the state, factories without parliaments and vice versa appeared to be impossible. As we have seen, Hobbes has an answer to that: no matter how sovereignty is exercised, it doesn't change its nature as sovereignty. And besides, political experience since Hobbes's day teems with examples of national bourgeoisies which have been perfectly content implicitly to bargain away their claims to political power in return for political influence. Any tin-pot military dictatorship keeping down the reds in a society with a bourgeoisie intent on making money shows this. (Look at South America.)

HOBBES AN ORIGINAL, AND THEREFORE NOT A PARTY MAN

Hobbes could never please a party because his arguments cut across all the current political positions of his day in England (and in continental Europe). In England, three current types of political argument stand out: the Divine Right of Kings, a version of social contract theory, and arguments from the idea of an ancient and inviolable constitution. If Hobbes's arguments in *Leviathan* hold, then none of these other arguments holds water.

The Divine Right of Kings so beloved by the early Stuarts (and by continental monarchies, particularly the French) will not stand a moment in the face of *Leviathan*. The Divine Right of Kings holds among other things that, in some mysterious way, God wants the eldest son of a previous king (or failing that, the next in succession) always and really to be king no matter who actually rules the state. Charles II always dated his reign from 1649, when his father, Charles I, was executed. The Divine Right of Kings owes whatever strength it has to sentimental loyalty to a dynasty. 'The King over the water' was to become the Jacobite toast in the eighteenth century. This kind of sentimentality is completely lacking in Hobbes. Your Sovereign really is the man (or group of men) who is actually, now, keeping the peace: Charles I in 1642, Cromwell afterwards, and Charles II after the Restoration in 1660. The charge of atheism levelled against Hobbes by Royalists was a thinly disguised accusation of treason: if you don't believe in God, then you can't possibly believe that God wants *that* specific king to be king.

Social contract argument really bit in 1649 when Charles Stuart was indicted on the grounds that he was 'an elected king' who had betrayed his trust by making war on his people. This implied the novel idea that the king could be guilty of treason, a contradiction in terms to believers in Divine Right. Hobbes's argument in *Leviathan*, as we have seen, treats the idea that a Sovereign can be put on trial as logical nonsense.

An ancient and inviolable constitution is probably logical nonsense too. Hobbes foreshadows Hume in insisting that the real constitution, like the real Sovereign, is the constitution for the time being, what Hume was later famously to call 'the present established practice of the age'. Particularly galling to a certain kind of Parliament man, and later to a certain kind of Whig, would have been Hobbes's argument about the creation of legitimate sovereignty by Acquisition – that is, by conquest. The upholders of the ancient constitution, which kings violate at their peril, made great play with the idea of 'the Norman Yoke'. The story of the Norman Yoke was usually told like this: Once upon a time, there existed in England an Anglo-Saxon polity of free men. For long periods there was no single king – there were once seven – and obedience to kings was the half-voluntary, half-customary obedience of warriors to a chief. The Bastard William did not really alter all this at the Conquest. It could be said that William conquered England, not the English, who kept the love of the ancient free constitution in their hearts and struck back in its favour when they could. The great moments came slowly, but they did come: Magna Carta, Simon de Montfort and parliaments, some Puritan opposition to Elizabeth, and now parliamentary opposition to the absolutist pretensions of Stuart absolutism. This view, which was later to be elaborated into the Whig view of English history, needed an institution which it could focus on as embodying the desire of Englishmen to rid themselves of the Yoke of a too weighty royal prerogative, and this institution it found in Parliament, and increasingly in the House of Commons. Parliament men came to see themselves as the special guardians of the ancient and fundamental rights and liberties of Englishmen against the royal encroachment on them which had begun in 1066.

The Whig view of English history was to have a great future. It was alive and well in America at the time of the Revolution, and it received much subsequent embroidery from eighteenth- and nineteenth-century Whig historians. (Tory history held that the essential continuity of English history was provided by a more-or-less unbroken history of royal administration.) To Hobbes, such a view of politics is simply laughable. Protection from others provided by a sitting Sovereign is what legitimises a political order. We can now see how Hobbes's account of the creation of sovereignty by Acquisition, that is conquest, must have stuck in the craw of the Parliamentarians. Hobbes's whole account of Sovereignty, and especially his account of the creation of Sovereignty by conquest, is a thinly veiled argument that William the Conqueror was a true Sovereign by the free consent of the defeated English at and after the Battle of Hastings. According to the argument implicit in *Leviathan*,

Englishmen had been free to accept or reject William in 1066. Instead, of their own free will they made William king, and, because it is one of the attributes of Sovereignty that it abolishes all previous contracts, whatever happened in the Anglo-Saxon polity of free, consenting men before the Conquest was irrelevant afterwards. Englishmen accepted William the Conqueror on his terms, not theirs, and so they owe allegiance to him and his successors provided they keep the peace. By all accounts, William was an efficient and ruthless Sovereign, and on Hobbes's reckoning he was right to be.

THE HOBBESIAN LEGACY

Hobbes would not expect to make himself popular by attacking, implicitly or explicitly, the three great current styles of political argument in England, Divine Right, social contract in its libertarian form, and the Ancient Constitution. And so it proved. All of the contending parties were wary of Hobbes, and they were probably wise, for *Leviathan* contains little comfort for any of them. What, then, remains of Hobbism? Hobbes obviously contains much instruction for those who are worried about the social and political stability of their own society, though that instruction is not of a very reassuring kind. Civil Society is artificial, man-made, and was probably not made to last. Better, then, to stick with and support the government you've got than to start meddling with it, because before you get another you've got to go through the dreadful State of Nature again first. A profound, gloomy and fearful conservatism is the message which comes directly out of *Leviathan*.

There is a particular message which comes out of this very generalised disenchantment, and it is that any man without a Sovereign is really an outlaw who can be killed at will. Never be a stateless person is a doctrine as old as Aristotle (and even Homer), and Hobbes reinforces it powerfully. However, that might not be the worst position for a man to be in. Perhaps the worst position to be in would be one in which you were trying to be uninvolved while two sides disputed the sovereignty. Both sides might be making you offers which you couldn't refuse, which would put you in a position of wanting a Sovereign's protection but not knowing who your Sovereign was. This is by no means fanciful. Living in a no-go area of a city could be like this, or living in a society in which there was endemic guerrilla war, which means a lot of societies. Guerrillas move by night, government security forces by day. Someone living in a village might well find himself in the very uncomfortable position of having one Sovereign by day and another by night, neither of whom would be very pleased with his divided allegiance.

If the pessimism of these messages is hard to stomach, then the best thing to do is to deny that men are like Hobbes says they are. Hobbes is very rigorous, even geometrical (he discovered Euclid by accident in a gentleman's library and never forgot it), as a political thinker. The axioms are his view of man as a rational egotist, and the theorems deduced from those axioms are the *Laws of Nature*, the Social Contract, and the creation of absolute Sovereignty. There is more at issue here than a take-it-or-leave-it attitude to Hobbes's view of our natures. Rather, we might begin to ask how plausible Hobbes's idea is that men can pop in and out of the State of Nature at will. Hobbes appears to be saying that men have no settled *social* character, because if they had the State of Nature would not be the terrifying, looming presence that it is. We might be inclined to take a much more sanguine view of the social character of humankind, as Locke does, and then we would no longer be obliged to fear that the fabric of our society is thin. Then, if we do not support the absolutist pretensions of the Sovereign of the day, it is not necessarily the case that the Hobbesian State of Nature is just round the corner.

NOTES ON SOURCES

Aubrey's *Brief Life* of Hobbes is a must. The Penguin edition of *Leviathan*, ed. C.B. Macpherson (1968), is easily available. R.S. Peters, *Hobbes* (1956), holds its ground well, as does the clever and eccentric F.C. Hood, *The Divine Politics of Thomas Hobbes* (1964). Hobbes's *Leviathan*, ed. Oakeshott (1946), contains Oakeshott's remarkable introductory essay on Hobbes, which is reprinted in M. Oakeshott, *Hobbes on Civil Association* (1975). R. Tuck, *Hobbes* (1986), covers the ground. Anti-Hobbism may be followed in S.I. Mintz, *The Hunting of Leviathan* (1962), and J. Bowle, *Hobbes and his Critics* (new imp. with corrections, 1969). Hobbes wrote a lot more besides *Leviathan*, and he often wrote in Latin. The standard edition of Hobbes's work in English is still Molesworth's.

12

SOCIAL CONTRACT II
The Lockian version

JOHN LOCKE

Locke was born in 1632 and grew up with the seventeenth-century scientific revolution. He came from an upwardly mobile Somersetshire family who made it into the gentry class. Though not particularly forward at his books, Locke decided early on an academic career. He became a don at Christ Church College, Oxford, until he was illegally ejected for his allegedly subversive opinions in 1684. (The Tory university had burned banned books the previous year.) Locke was outwardly not much concerned with philosophy and political theory during his Oxford years, teaching some law and a lot of medicine. The young Locke even seems to have been a bit of a Tory, believing that non-resistance to established authority was the just price of political and social stability.

His friendship with the first Earl of Shaftesbury, whose life he saved with a miraculous operation on the liver, changed Locke from a mildly subversive Oxford don into a meddler in high politics as adviser and confidant to highly placed plotters against the Divine Right monarchy of the Stuarts. Locke no doubt provided Shaftesbury with arguments to use in the everyday political battle of the Exclusionist Whigs (who wished to exclude James II when he was still only the Duke of York from the succession to the throne on the grounds that he was a Roman Catholic) against their Tory opponents in the last years of the reign of Charles II. It was probably inevitable either that Shaftesbury would eventually ask Locke's opinions on the most important political question of all, the question of the grounds for legitimate resistance to government, or that Locke's own position in Shaftesbury's circle would eventually lead him without prodding to consider that question. It was in these circumstances that Locke wrote his famous *Two Treatises of Government* (the exact date of the works is still not certain, but a good guess would be 1679–80). It was while enjoying the patronage of Shaftesbury that Locke worked on the ideas which would see the light of day as *An Essay Concerning Human Understanding*. It was also about this time that Locke turned his attention to economics, education and questions of colonial government.

Locke's *Two Treatises* were published (though not written) to justify the Glorious Revolution of 1688, in which Locke was involved as the friend and adviser to a leading Whig, Lord Somers. Locke's own attitude to his famous political treatises appears to have been decidedly odd, not to say shifty. He never acknowledged his authorship of the treatises, but was very keen that they should be available in a true text. Editions were mangled by printers, and it may also be that Locke was worried that opinions more radical than his own would be attributed to him. On the other hand, it may simply be that there was an impenetrably secretive side to Locke's character which will always hide his true reasons for publicly denying his authorship of such famous books.

HOBBES, FILMER AND LOCKE

A political thinker can influence another in a number of different ways. One thinker can influence another's substantive political conclusions, as with Plato and Aristotle, or one thinker can come to his political conclusions by thinking through another's political thought and attempting to go beyond it, as with Marx and Hegel. Hobbes and Filmer influenced Locke in neither of these ways. Hobbes bequeathed to Locke a particular language of social contract and a particular view of the structure of social conduct itself, while Filmer influenced Locke in a purely negative sense: by attacking Filmer, Locke's own political theory turns out to be everything that Filmer's is not. We used to think that Locke's political thought was very different from Hobbes's, at least in its conclusions, but recent work on both Hobbes and Locke has made us re-think exactly what those differences are. No-one claims that there are no differences, but there is at least some disagreement about how deep those differences go.

It is easy to read Locke's *Second Treatise of Civil Government* (1681–3) as a straight attack on Hobbes, and perhaps it is, but there can be no doubt that Locke's *First Treatise of Civil Government* is a direct attack on Filmer. Sir Robert Filmer's *Patriarchia or the Natural Power of Kings* (1680) was probably the most systematic exposition to date in English of what has come to be known as the theory of the Divine Right of Kings. Across the Channel, the Sun King Louis XIV was making absolute monarchy shine brighter than ever before and was implicitly inviting other kings in Europe to imitate him. English kings might dare to follow his example, not Charles II perhaps, but certainly his brother who eventually became James II in 1685. Locke may have thought that absolute monarchy was becoming the prevailing political style, and that Divine Right theory was becoming the prevailing way of explaining political obligation. Locke makes fairly easy meat of Filmer in the *First Treatise*, but behind Filmer there was always Hobbes, with his much tougher arguments for absolute sovereignty.

The theory of Divine Right scores very high marks for intelligibility. Also one tends to forget how comparatively modern it is. Medieval kingship, like any other, had wrapped itself round with a certain mystique, but its grounds for the theory of sovereignty were not nearly as clear as in the later theory of Divine Right. Ideas of God's anointing, feudal contract, popular election and hereditary succession jostled one another about in what was an essentially messy theory of sovereignty. It was not a theory of *sovereignty* in the modern sense at all. Feudal societies lacked the sovereign centres of ancient republics and modern states. Medieval societies were patchworks of overlapping and competing jurisdictions, so that nothing like modern sovereignty was being exercised. Of course, kings tried to be as powerful as they could, but they knew that they were just one of a whole series of law-makers and law-enforcers, not least of which was the Church. And it was not even clear that kings could actually make new laws, as distinct from interpreting and declaring an older and higher law. The theory of the Divine Right of Kings was to change all that because it was very clear about sovereignty. Kings were appointed by God to rule Christian people, therefore they were responsible to God alone for the exercise of their stewardship of what God had given. The right of succession inhered in the heirs of the king's body, or in the collateral branch of his family if issue failed. Because hereditary right was indefeasible, it followed that any challenge to it was a sin (and some Divine Right apologists went so far as to argue that resistance to the commands of the Lord's Anointed was the greatest of all sins). Of course, kings were very special men, but men they still were, and therefore liable themselves to sin. So what were subjects to do if a sinful king were to command them to break God's Laws? The powers that be being ordained by God, the furthest a subject might go was passive resistance, a mute refusal to obey, with the crown of martyrdom as the eventual reward for true Christian humility and fortitude.

The theory of Divine Right was not without little subtleties of its own. There was obviously some kind of parallel between the way God ruled the universe and the way that a good king was expected to rule his people. The image of God the Father ruling in a universe full of his recalcitrant children was mirrored in the image of the king as father of his people. The king had the duties of fatherhood: to feed his people (in emergencies), to defend them, to educate them (in the Faith, a job a wise king left to Mother Church), and justice in the settling of disputes between them. Of course, not all kings, like all fathers, fulfilled these responsibilities equally well, but kings were no less kings if they failed in their duties, any more than natural fathers ceased to be fathers when they failed in theirs. A bad king was still king.

If it was God's intention that king's should rule by Divine Right then he was bound to have mentioned it somewhere. The Old Testament, containing as it does an account of the beginning of the world since the Creation, was the likely place to find the origins of Divine Right, and there the origins were duly found. God must have given the world to Adam, and to the heirs of Adam's body, to rule for ever. Adam was the first king, he ruled by God's choice, so to resist Adam or Adam's posterity was to resist God. (The Old Testament's obsession with genealogy reinforced the claim that Adam's successors had the same rights of kingship as Adam himself.)

Locke's *First Treatise of Civil Government* unravelled the argument for Divine Right from Holy Writ. Locke points out reasonably enough that the book of Genesis does not actually say that God gave the world to Adam to rule; Adam is never referred to as king. Locke then goes on to say: suppose we concede, for which there is no biblical evidence, that Adam really was king by God's appointment. That still leaves the awkward fact that Genesis makes no mention of the kingly rights of the sons of Adam; there is simply no reference to the right of hereditary succession. Locke then goes on to say: suppose we concede both Adam's title to kingship and the title of the sons of Adam, for neither of which there is biblical evidence, how does that help kings *now* to establish their titles by Divine Right? Despite the biblical concern with genealogy, the line of Adam's posterity has become hopelessly scrambled. How can *any* king at the present time seriously claim that he is in the line of direct descent from Adam? Like Hobbes, Locke meets and beats his opposition on their own ground by showing that the Divine Right argument as presented by Filmer is double-edged as far as kings are concerned. Because the genealogy since Adam is scrambled, it is perfectly possible that all the present kings are usurpers, or all the kings except one. Perhaps somewhere the real, direct descendent of Adam is alive and living in obscurity, cheated of his birthright to universal monarchy by those pretending to call themselves kings in the present world. Having, as he thinks, disposed of the title to government based on the direct gift of kingship to Adam and to succeeding kings, Locke is then faced with a problem: if God's gift is not the basis of legitimate government, then what is? Locke's answer, like Hobbes's, is the free consent of the governed, and this is the position argued in the *Second Treatise*.

Locke wants to argue in the *Second Treatise* that everyone, including the Sovereign, comes into Civil Society, so that all, the Sovereign included, are obliged to obey the law. In arguing this, Locke has to keep in mind the Hobbesian argument that it is impossible for the Sovereign, the law-maker and law-enforcer, to come into Civil Society because he cannot be a party to the social contract. Locke wants to limit government. It seems to him common-sensically absurd that all men but one would come into Civil Society, and leave one of their number still in the State of Nature with the right to terrorise the others if he saw fit. The problem, then, is to invent a new version of social contract by which the Sovereign too can be constrained by contract, something Hobbes thought was logically impossible.

LOCKE'S VERSION OF THE STATE OF NATURE

The most famous sentence in the *Second Treatise* is that 'though this (the State of Nature) be a state of liberty, yet it is not a state of licence'. Like Hobbes, Locke begins with a hypo-thetical State of Nature, gives an account of it, and then proceeds to show how men got themselves out of it. Locke's State of Nature is very unlike Hobbes's, because life there is recognisably social in a sense Hobbes would never allow, hence Locke's very firm statement that the State of Nature is a state of liberty, not licence. By this Locke means that men in the State of Nature, bound by Natural Law, would be able, on the whole, to recognise and respect the Natural Rights of others. Locke's whole argument in the *Second Treatise* depends upon this first postulate, so it is worth examining it in some detail.

By Natural Right Locke means an entitlement under Natural Law, which is God's Law. God did not create the world and people it for nothing. He certainly wanted men to get their sustenance, which means that He intended men to live, and to live as long as it pleased Him. In His original natural state, the Garden of Eden, Adam and Eve did not have to labour for their sustenance. God intended them to live off the land as contented vegetarians, but they rebelled against God, ate of the tree of the knowledge of good and evil, invented sex, were expelled from the Garden, and then all the trouble started. The irruption of desire meant that from thenceforth men would have to get their bread in the sweat of their faces – they would be obliged to plough, sow and reap the land. Although God was extremely angry at the Fall of Man, he none the less, as a merciful God, offered man an opportunity to get bread through useful labour (and he offered woman the chance to bear children through labour pains). Therefore it followed that men had a Natural Right to labour and a Natural Right to the land they tilled and to its produce.

From this alluringly persuasive account of origins, based securely on God's own word, Holy Scripture, Locke derives a fairly sophisticated theory of Natural rights, particularly the Natural Right to property. Like all law, God's Law, as revealed in the Ten Commandments, or found out by human reason, implies a corresponding set of rights. These Natural Rights Locke thinks are of three substantive kinds: the right to life, liberty and property. God means us to live at his pleasure, not another's, therefore no-one may kill me (except in self-defence, which includes war); God commands me to labour in order to sustain and live my life, therefore I have the right to the liberty to do so; and God must mean what I take out of mere nature to be mine, therefore a natural right to property originates in the command to labour: the land I plough, and its fruits are mine. Men, being made in God's image and therefore endowed with natural reason, could easily work out that this was so, and they have Holy Writ to help them.

Men's natural reason also tells them two other very important things. First, it tells each man that all other men have the same rights as he has. All rights have duties attached to them (a right without a corresponding duty, or set of duties, is a privilege, not a right, a sinecure for instance, which carries with it the right to a salary without the duty to work for it). Rational men are capable of working this out for themselves, and they easily recognise that claiming Natural Rights requires that they respect the exercise of those same rights in others, and it is this reciprocity which makes the State of Nature social. If everybody recognises naturally that Natural Rights are universal or they cease to be natural, then plainly this implies that men could live together without government. That is what Locke really means when he says that the State of Nature is a state of liberty, not licence.

However, the State of Nature is still the state of fallen man. Sinful men, alas, will sometimes invade the Natural Rights of others. From this it follows that men have another Natural Right, the right of judgement (and punishment) when they think their Natural Rights have been violated by others. This right is not a substantive right, a right to *something*; rather it is an energising right, or a right which gives life to the other Natural Rights. Rights are useless unless there is a right to judge when rights have been violated, and so the right to judgement completes the package of Natural Rights.

Therefore, for Locke, the State of Nature could be social, even if it was not completely harmonious because there would be occasional violations of Natural Rights. In particular, men in the Lockian State of Nature would be able to make contracts with each other, even contracts of buying and selling. God's command to tell the truth, and not to bear false witness implies that a man has a right to expect another man to keep his word, and to expect others to bear witness as to what that promise was. Looking around for evidence in the real world that men can come to make very generalised agreements with each other, Locke fastens on to two things: language and gold. Language is an agreement that certain sounds mean certain things, and the invention of language pre-dates the invention of the state (and survives after states collapse). Similarly, men agreed to put a value on intrinsically worthless gold which actually goes up in value when states begin to totter. Locke uses these as paradigmatic examples of what kinds of agreement are possible between men without government. Agreement to put a value on gold makes buying and selling possible, perhaps even the buying and selling of labour, and it certainly makes inequalities of property likely in the State of Nature. Men's slight inequality of natural capacity, which Hobbes had thought valueless in the State of Nature, is important for Locke precisely because it would lead to inequalities of fortune. Not all men are equally enterprising or industrious, and to the winner go the spoils of competition.

Agreement to put a value on gold alters the original State of Nature by removing the natural constraints on the accumulation of property. Originally, no man was entitled to more land than he could actually cultivate, the land he had actually 'mixed his labour' with. Laying claim to uncultivated land was an infringement of the Natural Right of others to take property out of nature by their own labour. Tracts of uncultivated land in ownership, or even land half-cultivated or occasionally cultivated, was waste, and in the absence of a currency, and therefore a market, it would be impossible for a man to get rid of any agriculture surplus profitably, and that surplus would spoil. The circulation of a currency in the form of gold changed this. Men could now buy, sell and make profits to their hearts' content. Gold does not spoil, or go to waste, so there can be no natural limits to its accumulation. Gold therefore effectively abolishes the natural limitations set on property accumulation, hence inequality of property in the State of Nature.

For Locke, then, life in the State of Nature is naturally sociable, because the State of Nature contains what we can easily recognise as the beginnings of economic interdependence and social stratification between rich and poor. And all this happens, thinks Locke, before the invention of the state, and it would continue to happen if all law-making and law-enforcement were to disappear. Therefore, a return to the State of Nature is not the terrifying possibility which Hobbes had thought it was.

THE STATE OF NATURE AND GOVERNMENT

Locke's picture of a social State of Nature profoundly affects the way he invites us to think about government in five different but related ways.

1 Locke seems to be saying that man should not be over-grateful for government. A return to the State of Nature would no doubt be attended by its inconveniences in the matter of law-making and law-enforcement because men would have to begin again to do these for themselves, but it is not unthinkable. *Any* state is certainly not better than no state at all, so Locke is not asking us, as Hobbes is, to put up with the government we've got because the alternative State of Nature would be horrific.
2 States, unlike societies, are not part of the given order of things. Societies (economics and social systems) arise spontaneously and naturally, but states do not. Unlike society, the state is not God-given. It follows that rational men may discuss what kind of states they would be prepared to live in, and under what conditions. States are useful, invented mechanisms, and like all invented mechanisms they can be improved or scrapped at will. Men will not, of course, scrap them 'for light and transient causes', but the possibility is always there.
3 As a mechanism, the state, like any other mechanism, is there for a purpose, and the position of men in the State of Nature can easily tell us what that purpose is. Men in the State of Nature expect to enjoy the exercise of their Natural Rights, and men come into Civil Society to enjoy them more securely. It is part of God's purpose for men that they should enjoy these rights, and so no Natural Right can be permanently alienated. Government exists to protect Natural Rights and should confine itself to that function.

It follows that any government which threatens the Natural Rights to life, liberty and estate (Locke's word for property) is a government in the process of forfeiting its title to govern.

4 Men enjoying Natural Rights in the State of Nature would plainly have to consent to the setting up of government, and Natural Rights being God's permission to act in the world, there must be a natural limit to what men may consent to. Just as the right to life rules out suicide and murder, the right to liberty means that men cannot consent to slavery. Even if they wanted to, it is obvious that Locke thinks that men do not have the right to set up the kind of absolutist Sovereign which Hobbes thinks men would invent if they thought about it properly. Natural Rights, being inalienable, could only be 'lent' to government on conditions. No rational man would surrender his right to life, liberty and property to government. What a rational man almost certainly would do, would be to entrust his right of judgement to the state on certain clearly understood terms. He could undoubtedly do this only by his own free will. Consent to government therefore confers title to govern, what we have come to call legitimacy.

5 Locke plainly thinks that society is natural while the state is artificial. Human nature being composed as it is of certain Natural Rights which rational men recognise that they and others possess, society arises spontaneously. It follows that, because society is prior to the state, both logically and as a matter of history, it is up to society to decide what the state shall be like, and not the state which shall decide what society shall be like. This insistence of the separation of society from the state, and a society's priority over the state, was to become the bedrock of the doctrine which came to be known as liberalism. Put another way, Locke thinks that what the state is like is a matter (within limits) of rational reflection and choice, but society is a given about which men have no choice. Society is what God meant it to be, capitalist and naturally harmonious, except that in the real world societies tend to become a bit ragged at the edges. Offences against Natural and positive law, murder, theft, fraud and riot for instance, happen from time to time, and men need the special agency of the state to cope with them.

What this amounts to is a reiteration of the Hobbesian claim, under very different conditions, that men do not come into Civil Society to change their nature but to fulfil it. For Locke, men are recognisably social before they become political, therefore very little of the social nature of men is owed to the existence of the state. An ongoing practical morality exists independent of government, so that legitimate government exists to protect and defend that morality.

LOCKE'S VERSION OF SOCIAL CONTRACT

Because morality existed in the State of Nature and was capable of being enforced there, perhaps imperfectly, by the voluntary actions of men, it follows that social contract is an extension of that pre-existing morality. Locke tends to lay stress on God's permissions rather than on God's prohibitions: Natural Rights before Natural Law. The distinction is still Hobbesian, but Natural Rights now being definable as rights rather than Right, they become an asset rather than a liability, something men desire to keep rather than to give up. Restricting the Hobbesian Natural Right to a given number of Natural Rights makes Natural Right much more manageable, and, being manageable, Natural Rights can be retained within the framework of Civil Society.

Perhaps the best way of looking at the Lockian doctrine of Natural Rights is to see them as a kind of moral cash, pocket money given to God's children to make their way easier in the world. Naturally enough, children often being very intelligent consumers, men will want to spend as little of their moral cash for as many goods as possible. The good which they buy at the moment of social (it should really be called 'political') contract is an increased protection by government of the Natural Rights of life, liberty and estate. To enjoy more of their moral capital in security, men give up to the state their right to judgement when their Natural Rights have been violated. Of course, a Natural Right being God's gift, part of defining what it is to be a human being, it is impossible to alienate it completely. At the moment of contract, Locke's men give up the absolute minimum for the maximum gain: they entrust the state with their right to judgement on the condition that the state uses the right to judge when Natural Rights have been violated in order to allow men to enjoy their other Natural Rights, to life, liberty and property, more abundantly.

Social contract is really a double process in Locke. An implied contract of society operates before the contract to form government is made. *Pace* Hobbes, the society which exists before government ever existed, and the society which would survive government's collapse, is capable of expressing a will before the state exists. Therefore, again *pace* Hobbes, men are capable of making a collective agreement with their rulers in the State of Nature, either in the very beginning or in some future, imaginable emergency when government has collapsed. And in Locke's account of the matter it is easy to see when and why government would in fact collapse: when it violates, or is seen to violate, enough men's Natural Rights for them justifiably to rebel by taking back to themselves the right of judgement because government has betrayed its trust and misused it. Men therefore have a right of rebellion, and perhaps even a moral duty to rebel, if government begins to frustrate God's purpose for the world. The moment for rebellion happens when enough men are prepared to repudiate their contract with their rulers and fall back on the original contract of society. In all events, the Lockian Sovereign is a party to the contract to set up government. The king is king on terms.

It follows that only my own, explicit consent can make me a member of a common-wealth, though Locke notoriously waters this down later with his doctrine of 'tacit consent' – just by walking on the king's highway I tacitly invite the protection of the law, so tacitly consent to obey that law myself. So what happens to the non-joiners? Locke is as ruthless as Hobbes on this point. In the beginning non-joiners, like dissenters later, may be killed if they appear to threaten Civil Society. A man who denies God's Law by invading other men's Natural Rights is at war with God and men, and killing in war is no crime. Locke is one of the first political thinkers to think that capital punishment is a special case of punishment and needs a special justification in a way that ordinary punishment – fines and imprisonment – does not. A man who violates another's Natural Rights by taking his life, or threatening to, is irrational, hardly a man at all, because his natural reason doesn't function well enough to tell him that his own enjoyment of rights implies the duty of respecting those same rights in others. This argument is the basis of all right to punish, either in the State of Nature or in Civil Society. If a man breaks God's Law in Civil Society, he is no better than a wild beast and may be killed.

What happens if, in Civil Society, I withdraw my consent? Locke thinks that that would not alter my obligation to obey the law, because I would then become as a stranger or visitor in my own country, and nobody ever argues that foreigners are not obliged to obey the laws of the particular country they happen to find themselves in. Strangers implicitly invite the protection of the laws in a foreign country, and they are subject to Natural Law punishments anyway. (The exception would be a group of men coming into another country bringing their own law with them, and therefore not implicitly asking for the protection of that country's laws. A group of men like that would be called an invading army, or a group of English football supporters.) Locke also uses the analogy of visiting another family. Guests are obliged to follow the habits and customs of that family where they differ from the habits and customs of their own.

LOCKE ON FORMS OF GOVERNMENT

What good, then, does it do a man to consent to become a member of a commonwealth if he is obliged to obey the law in whatever commonwealth he happens to find himself in? If the law does not differentiate between natives and strangers, then the only advantage which membership of a political community could bring would be some kind of exercise of political rights, including the right of rebellion. The commonwealth is *my* commonwealth, and the law would be in some sense my law. Locke holds the Whiggish doctrine of the supremacy of the legislature: that which gives legitimate commands to others must itself be supreme. What we have come to call the 'executive' and judicial powers must be secondary, because, being unmoved until they enforce the decisions of the legislature, they must be subordinate to it. For legislation to be *my* legislation, the laws a polity gives itself, I must be in some way represented in the process by which law is made. There is nothing especially radical about this proposal. It certainly does not necessarily imply democracy with universal suffrage: I might well be 'virtually' represented by my betters with no direct or indirect role in the matter of legislation at all. Nor is it intended to be anti-king. Locke is perfectly content that the legislature in England should be king-in-Parliament, and for the king to be head of the executive (but the judiciary presents special problems). A plural legislature is safer, and Locke can see no reason, a few special privileges like parliamentary immunity apart, why all the members of that plural legislature should not be bound like anybody else by the law it makes. The king in England might reasonably be called supreme because, as a branch of the legislature and head of the executive, he is called upon to exercise more power than anyone else, but this can be made perfectly clear without reference to a high-flown theory like Divine Right.

Locke thinks that there are even moments of national emergency in which the king may act without law, or even against law, in order to preserve the realm: *salus populi suprema lex* (public safety comes before everything else). This is a residual power, inherent in all government and best exercised by the head of the executive, because he, being one man, can make the quick decisions which are necessary at times of national disaster, say a flood, or foreign invasion. (This inherent or residual power of executive government was to be much invoked by President Lincoln at the time of the American Civil War, when he argued that to save the Union, the president had to make executive decisions which were probably illegal and almost certainly unconstitutional.)

The executive and the legislative powers are distinct in theory but, in the English case, they are clearly so close to each other that to read a separation-of-powers, checks-and-balances argument in Locke is to find something which isn't really there. Locke's theory is much more like the old idea of mixed government in which all the estates of the realm have a legitimate share. A theory of the separation of powers was later read into Locke, but that is a different matter. The exception is Locke's insistence of the independence of the judges. English common lawyers had been worried about the judicial power of monarchy ever since Sir Edward Coke had to explain to James I why he could not sit as a judge, and judges sitting by royal appointment and, more importantly, subject to royal dismissal instead of serving during 'good behaviour' (*quam diu se bene gesserint*), sent a shiver down the spines of right-thinking Englishmen. A judiciary dependent on the king was dangerous, and a judiciary dependent on kings who believed they ruled by Divine Right was really frightening. Hence Locke's insistence on the judges' independence.

In Locke's theory, any form of government which protected Natural Rights, and especially property, would be a legitimate government, but that leaves entirely open the question: Which form of government is most likely in practice to protect Natural Rights? A day would come in America when men would think that a democratic republic with a wide exercise of political rights, including the right to vote, was the only practicable solution to the protection of Natural Rights, but that was long in the future, and probably later than the new American Constitution ratified by 1789. But Locke is nothing if not a constitutionalist. Even though he fails to distinguish clearly between the executive and legislative functions of government, he is wary enough of power to want to put clear constitutional limits on its exercise. This had always been implicit in the mechanical theory of the state. If political power was originally created for a specific purpose, then power itself must be limited to that purpose.

The theory of *limited* government must never be mistaken for a theory of *weak* government. Government is still government, even if it is restricted government. In this sense Hobbes makes his presence felt in Locke's *Second Treatise*. We have become used to the idea that political power is quantifiable: we speak of institutions as being 'more or less' powerful. To concentrate state power for a few restricted ends, like the protection of life, liberty and estate, is to make government more powerful, not less. If power is a quantity, perhaps even a fixed quantity, then to try to do less with it is something like a guarantee that what government is set to do, it will do thoroughly and well. Locke himself makes the distinction between restricted and weak government with a graphic example drawn from war: a general may order a soldier to certain death, but cannot touch a penny-piece out of the soldier's pocket because the power of taxation lies elsewhere. This is constitutional government, but it is hardly weak government as far as the soldier is concerned.

MEN AND THE STATE:
THE PROBLEM OF LIBERTY UNDER LAW

Locke obviously thinks of men as natural bargainers, and he also thinks that men's automatic reaction to the world outside themselves is not to try to dominate it but to protect themselves from it. Natural Rights create a kind of moral space for the individuals who possess them, and that moral space may not be intruded upon except by explicit consent. Natural Rights in this sense create a proper moral distance between men, a claim to a certain individual autonomy. Men's natural liberty is their chief moral resource, and they will be inclined to spend that resource wisely. Giving up some natural liberty in order to enjoy the rest more securely immediately presents a problem: suppose too much has been given up for too little? There is a market in security, so security has its price, and that price would depend on the amount of security available and the demand for it. In the ordinary course of events, men might think they have paid too much for security under law, and that would always be a source of potential discontent. This Locke would approve of: perpetual suspicion of the state is healthy for liberty. Men in the State of Nature made the contract to form political society because they feared the power of others over them, the Law of Nature notwithstanding. By creating the state, men save themselves from the power of others, but in so doing they create in government a power which is much greater than the power of any individual or group of individuals in the State of Nature. What could be more natural, then, than to want protection from the state? The assertion of the Natural Rights of life, liberty and estate is therefore just as important in a commonwealth as outside it. Perpetually discontented men in Civil Society, grumbling that they've paid out too much of their liberty for security, are healthy for liberty.

But this might not always be the case. The price of anything, security included, depends on supply as well as demand. If there is not much security available in the world as it is, then its price might become unreasonably high. Take the cases of terrorism, or of a steeply increasing incidence of violent crime. Security is then at a premium as an ever-increasing number of people begin to feel insecure. The only way out of their difficulty would be to give the state larger powers to cope with the new situation. This is not the same case as national emergency, when the executive has to act quickly. Terrorism and crime are longer-term problems, about which the legislature might be asked to act. Men would be in the position of bargaining away more and more liberty in the hope of getting more and more security and it is conceivable that a point would be reached at which, security being very scarce, a huge amount of liberty would have to be spent on a very small, and therefore very valuable, amount of security, and in the end the bargain might not be worth it. What this amounts to is that the Lockian scheme of things would only work in societies which were already fairly stable and law-abiding.

CONSENT AND THE TITLE TO GOVERN

Nothing could seem to be clearer than Locke's assertion that only consent can make me a member of a commonwealth, and even when Locke qualified positive consent into tacit consent, the doctrine still seems clear: when I walk on the highway I consent to those laws whose protection I implicitly ask for. Consent confers title. Government is legitimised by consent. I obey because I actually or tacitly promised that I would, provided certain conditions are met.

The question immediately arises: Can promises, by themselves, create genuine obligations?, and the simple answer is: No. What I promise to do must be in some prior sense 'right' (or at least not wrong). (If I am caught in adultery *in flagrante delicto*, it would not console my wife if I told her I was committing adultery because I made an agreement with my partner to do it.) Promises are a way of explaining how I came to *think* I was under an obligation, but promises alone do not tell me enough to know that I really am obliged.

The further question then arises: If I know that there are some things I may or may not do, then am I not obliged to do the one set of things and abstain from doing the other set, with or without promises? Am I not obliged to do the 'good' and not do the 'bad' in any case? What differences, then, can promises make? Locke's answer to this problem is straightforward: it is not enough that law is good. It must also be made in the proper form and in the proper way. In Locke, the consent of the governed identifies the persons of those entitled to make law. It is not enough that law should be good law. It should also be made by the right people in the right form, otherwise any conqueror or usurper who left the laws of his acquired state unchanged (a tactic highly recommended by Machiavelli) would be a legitimate ruler.

Consent entitles specific people to rule under specific conditions. As a lawyer, Locke has a very juridical view of what it is to enter into political association. Like the ordinary law, Locke is less concerned with the question of whether it is *good* that certain persons should possess the law-making power, than with questions about their title. (The law doesn't ask whether it is *good* that I own my house but asks whether I really own it in law.) Giving up my right of judgement to the state cannot be permanent, because I may not permanently alienate Natural Right. Locke, again thinking juridically, sees government as a trust: trustees are entrusted with my right of judgement of when my Natural Rights have been violated, and if they betray that trust I may resume the exercise of the right of judgement myself, and even feel free to begin again and reform political society by a new contract. This is not as radical as it may appear at first sight. Things would only turn out like that in a political crisis caused by a government stupid enough to offend enough property owners for the return to the State of Nature to be attractive as an alternative to rational men. Something like that might have happened in England in the 1680s, and again in America in the 1770s, but it is a rare occurrence.

Consent always implies some sort of consensus. Locke insists on the priority of society over the state, and that profoundly affects how men should view government and how government should treat its citizens. What we ordinarily call 'opinion', or public opinion, arises in what Locke would call society, so it is thinking in society which decides what form the state should take. The state is the sum of opinion already formed, and it follows that it is certainly not the state's job to try to change men's opinions. Locke believed in the toleration of heterodox opinions (within limits) and the one thing he did not want was for the state itself to be an opinion-former. There has always been something English, even Anglican in the broad sense, about Locke as a political thinker. He himself seems to speak for a body of opinion already formed rather than trying to change anybody's mind.

Locke speaks for those who have had enough of the Stuarts for the second time round. The theory of the Divine Right of Kings had not made much of a splash in England before the Civil War. It was there, an irritant among other royal irritants, but it was not central. The execution of the king in 1649 after two Civil Wars and the virtual usurpation of the sovereignty by Cromwell changed all that. When the movement to exclude Charles II's brother James from the throne because he was a Catholic gathered momentum, the possibility of another Civil War on a grand scale, not to mention Monmouth's ill-starred rebellion, gained many supporters for Divine Right's contention that, no matter what happened, there was always a lawful, hereditary Sovereign in England. Locke speaks for the others. His patron was the Earl of Shaftesbury, leader of the exclusion party (in his other role as medical man Locke had performed a successful operation on Shaftesbury for the stone), and it seems that Locke began writing the *Second Treatise* early in the 1680s when exclusion was in the air, and he had probably finished it by 1683. It was published to support the Glorious Revolution of 1688 because it fitted that case so perfectly, not least because, *pace* Hobbes and James II, the State of Nature which England returned to after the departure of its Sovereign, James II, turned out to be Lockian, not Hobbesian, after all.

LOCKE AND THE FOUNDATIONS OF LIBERALISM

Liberals have always shown a certain fondness for Locke, and it is easy to see why. Certain assumptions which Locke makes, certain attitudes which he held, and certain arguments which he uses, fit in well with the doctrine which at the beginning of the nineteenth century came to be called liberalism. Some commentators go further, and say that Locke invented liberalism practically single-handedly, but that is to exaggerate. Too much of at least English liberalism came out of utilitarianism, a doctrine antithetical to Natural Rights, for this claim on Locke's behalf to be sustained. None the less, if you look hard enough in Locke, it is possible to find a thumbnail sketch of something which is at least beginning to look like liberalism.

The first liberal-looking assertion in Locke is the naturalness of property and the inviolability of property right except by free and voluntary consent: what we have come to call consent to taxation. Nine points of positive law will be about who rightfully owns what. What makes something mine is either that I have inherited it or, better still, that I have worked for it. Mixing one's labour with something is the surest title to possession of all. Locke is certainly not hostile to aristocracy, and he looks with favour on self-made men, the traditional alliance between Whig aristocracy and industrial wealth which was to form the basis of the English Liberal Party after 1859.

Locke wrote a famous *Letter Concerning Toleration* which still strikes a liberal chord. Locke's plea for toleration is an appeal for the privacy of the individual's own mind. The law should never be used to proceed against a man for what he thinks, but only for what he does or might be about to do. The exceptions are Catholics, a potential fifth column in the service of the nation's Catholic enemies, and atheists because, having no fear of hell-fire, they cannot be expected to tell the truth on oath in courts of law. Locke's appeal for toleration is, then, a plea for toleration of every kind of Protestant and dissenting sect, a view of toleration which seems unduly restricted in the light of the classic liberal statement on toleration, J.S. Mill's essay *On Liberty* (1859), but on the way there. What the state must never do is try to change men's opinions on the rack. The man may be coerced, but not the conscience, which is by its nature free, a doctrine surprisingly reminiscent of Hobbes's dictum that the will cannot be coerced.

Liberals like to think of themselves as putting a high value on human rationality, and this is an attitude they share with Locke. In the *Second Treatise* Locke is careful to argue against the naturalness of patriarchy in Filmer. Children only owe a duty of obedience to natural fathers who keep their children's Natural Rights in trust for them until they reach the age of consent. As soon as children know what they are doing, they become adults as fully endowed with Natural Rights as anybody else. Locke is very sensible here. The existence of a moral sense, which plainly exists even in very small children, is not enough to put a child in full possession of his Natural Rights. Rationality is still crucial; children have got to be able to understand that rights imply duties, especially the duty to recognise the same rights in others. (Little children are very good at remembering that they are entitled to their pocket money but often have to be reminded that they have to set the table for it.) Living with others means accepting mutual obligations, and failure to recognise this is a failure of understanding, either through incapacity or wilful obtuseness. Some such plea underlies the Lockian theory of punishment: a thief who denies the Natural Rights of others has failed to act as a rational man, and so must be corrected (some prisons in America are still called Houses of Correction). A useful analogy would be with membership of a club. We would say that a member of a club who said that its rules did not apply to them would simply be failing to understand what being a member of a club entails. Rationality also extends to the public reasonableness of positive laws: everything is to be out in the open (and Locke was saying this at a time when even the publication of parliamentary debate was over half a century in the future). Marxist commentators on social contract theory have always detected a bourgeois flavour in the liberal conception of law as being fixed, knowable and known, because these are exactly the conditions in which commercial judgements about the future can be made. If law is vague, or can change arbitrarily and quickly – say changes of the place where customs duties are to be collected, or constant variations in the rate of taxation – then the conditions for commerce worsen.

The Lockian model of society is a competitive, capitalist model. Men are free to acquire, and are encouraged by God to do so. There will be winners and losers, rich and poor. Strange, therefore, that Locke fails to mention class, which, on Locke's own account, would exist even in the State of Nature where there is buying and selling. What all individualistic theorists of society tend to forget is that there may be an important difference between acquisition and the defence of what has been acquired. Men may acquire as individuals, either through luck, effort or inheritance, but they tend to defend what they have as a group, which is class by any other name. Is Locke's state a class state in the way that his society is a class society? Locke never tells us in the *Second Treatise*, but there are broad hints elsewhere in his works, especially in his draft *Constitution for the Carolinas* (in whose pretend-aristocracy Locke was a margrave), where he refers to his American polity as 'a democracy of God's proprietors, ten thousand a year, debts paid'. It is still a matter for scholarly controversy exactly how literally men were then capable of taking the idea of democracy as implying universal suffrage, but there does not seem to be much doubt in Locke's case.

The idea of government as a trust which can be betrayed reeks of the liberal distrust of political power a century and a half before Lord Acton: 'All power corrupts, and absolute power corrupts absolutely.' Plato apart, political theorists before Locke are notoriously reluctant to tackle the question of why it is that men want power. Most would agree with Machiavelli that power aggrandisement is a fact of human nature as it applies to princes, or with Hobbes when he intimates that any man would agree to be Sovereign if the chance came his way. Locke at least has some feeling for what love of power can do to a man, hence his constitutionalism, and hence his emphasis on government as a trust. Perhaps Locke wishes us to think that, like the best trustees, the best governors would be those who get very little out of governing beyond the satisfaction of doing it well. The characteristic trait of men acting politically is not the desire for dominion over others but protection from them, and that obviously includes government. The worst rulers would be the grabbers for power, a view Locke does share with Plato.

Locke plainly thinks that there is a tendency, if it is no more, to harmony in human social life. This harmony is not perfect, otherwise political society would not be necessary. The state is therefore society's regulating mechanism, essentially extra-society, not its vital spring. Free activity will be the norm, coercion the exception in the cases of thieves and vagabonds. As a Christian, Locke believes that God's intentions for his Creation are benevolent: He did not put men in the world so that they would continually be at one another's throats. Government is 'outside' society in the same way as the governor of an engine is not part of the engine, but extraneous to it. The governor of an engine is there to stop the engine overheating, and only starts working when there is a danger of that. Government regulates but does not initiate. (The perfect image of Lockian sovereignty would be the stamping of a Sovereign's head on a pre-existing gold coinage, thus creating sovereigns.)

Locke's famous *Essay Concerning Human Understanding* shows him to be cautious, and to a degree sceptical as an epistemologist. Locke believes that the only form of knowledge we can properly trust is the knowledge gained through the perception of the senses. This denial of the truths of metaphysics (but not of religion because Locke believed in 'natural religion', the belief that the reasonableness of Christianity could be demonstrated) passes over into Locke's political theory in the form of a reluctance on Locke's part to attribute to the state any high, transcendent purpose beyond the peace and security of its citizens. Locke is no Rousseau, let alone Hegel. A certain becoming modesty informs Locke's view of politics. We must not expect too much of it: restricted political means for restricted social ends has a classically liberal ring to it. The only place in which Locke even approaches a higher *raison d'état* is in his discussion of the residual power which inheres in all government, but his treatment of it is characteristically low-key. Everyone could agree that government has to act swiftly in emergencies from time to time, and everyone could agree to that, provided only that 'national security' is not invoked too often or on trivial occasions. Otherwise people will begin to smell a rat. Besides, good government would always be prepared to justify its emergency actions *ex post facto*.

Allied to the sceptical epistemology, and in part deriving from it, is a certain reasonableness about Locke's political theory. There is no urgency about it, nothing raucous or shrill. Locke does not ask us to believe anything which a reasonable (Protestant English-) man might not already be prepared to think. Locke is writing for an audience in a society which is fast becoming commercial, and which is already involved in colonisation in America. Even Locke's legalistic tone would have helped, because ownership in the seventeenth century, especially ownership of land, often brought litigation with it, and the fact that making money is second nature to busy men in commercial society needs no emphasis.

What really dates Locke is his account of the social contract itself, which liberalism later sloughed off in favour of the natural sociability of man and therefore his natural tendency to construct political communities. Under the influence of the thinkers of the Scottish Enlightenment, and especially of Adam Smith, liberalism found that it did not need a theory of origins at all. The justification for social and political arrangements shifted from Natural Rights to the principle of utility, which cut across a notion of rights at many crucial points. Locke's plea that free men should keep their government under constant scrutiny to make sure that it does not overstep the mark finds its echo in the utilitarian idea that a government is more or less legitimate, depending on whether it increases or decreases the greatest happiness of the greatest number. Checking up on this should be almost a daily task for free men, but what utilitarians like Bentham lack is the suspicion of power itself, as distinct from a concern that power should be used for socially useful ends.

The other thing which dates Locke, though it doesn't disqualify him from being one of the main inspirers of liberalism, is the idea that we really could disobey the state by refusing to be bound by its laws. Perhaps in Locke's day it was possible to disobey the state without social chaos, because states did not in fact ask much of most of their citizens most of the time. Occasional service on a jury, occasional taxation, the odd turning out to parade in the militia was all that government demanded of those who were not its servants. By comparison, modern states are miracles of complication, because many of them provide a myriad of services of which seventeenth-century defenders of wide scope for government never dreamt. Perhaps in the modern state disobedience is impossible in a much more technical sense. Disobedience to laws at least implies some kind of rough knowledge of what those laws are. The modern world is an age of intense legal specialisation among lawyers, and it is technically impossible to disobey the laws because it is perfectly possible that I might *think* I was disobeying the laws while I was in fact continuing to obey some laws whose existence I did not even suspect. States in Locke's day didn't manage economies (though mercantilism was a try), and they did not even know the names, or even the number, or their own citizens. In circumstances like these, disobedience would not mean so much in social terms, and certainly not social chaos. This is part of what Locke means when he says that the State of Nature is a state of liberty, not licence. Rebellion and revolution are very different things, and the day was far distant when men would make a rebellion to remodel society, though there had been hints of that during the Interregnum.

This is not to say that Locke on disobedience is completely irrelevant to the modern world. Civil disobedience, to make government take notice, is at least in the spirit of Locke. Civil disobedience relies for its moral force on being the very opposite of a return to any kind of State of Nature. It relies on very law-abiding people disobeying *that* law on *that* occasion. Locke might have liked that.

THE STATE OF NATURE COMPARED IN HOBBES AND LOCKE, AND AN AFTERWORD ABOUT FILMER

The political theories of Hobbes and Locke both depend for their plausibility on the different pictures which they paint of the State of Nature. It might be said that Hobbes tells us too little about the State of Nature, and Locke too much. By that I mean that Hobbes tells us too little about the State of Nature for us ever to suppose that men could get out of it, and Locke tells us too much about the social nature of the State of Nature that we begin to wonder why men would ever have wanted to get out of it in the first place.

We are bound to say of Hobbes that, granted his view of life in the State of Nature as partly solitary and partly violent, it is not very clear how men would ever come to the meeting to transfer their Right of Nature to the Sovereign and so come into Civil Society. This matters for Hobbes, because either men had some kind of collective will in the State of Nature which enabled them to make the social contract, in which case the State of Nature could not have been as insecure and solitary as Hobbes depicts it, or there must have been some kind of miraculous occurrence which made men make their original agreement, and neither of these possibilities fits well with Hobbes's own argument. It also matters because if an original contract of the kind Hobbes proposes is an impossibility, then the original attributes of sovereignty which Hobbes deduces from the original contract might not be those which men would voluntarily give to a Sovereign in the State of Nature. This in its turn would take the polemical edge off Hobbes's implied argument that, *pace* the liberty-lovers and the dividers of sovereignty, if men had the chance to begin again and construct a polity from scratch, they would voluntarily set up a Sovereign with powers in the face of which any contemporary absolutism would pale by comparison.

The case of Locke's State of Nature is different. It is so naturally social that the absence of a state is by Locke's own admission only 'inconvenient'. Granted Lockian men's fear of government as being immeasurably more powerful and therefore immeasurably more threatening than any individual or group of individuals in the State of Nature, one begins to wonder whether rational Lockian men in the State of Nature would ever take the risk of setting up a state in the first place. What are the inconveniences of the State of Nature, it might be asked, compared with the possible invasions of Natural Rights of which a state is capable?

It has been fashionable for a long time to wonder how sane men could ever have been capable of believing in the theory of the Divine Right of Kings while forgetting that Lockian Natural Rights are equally divinely inspired. Filmer's special contribution to Divine Right theory, which had been long in the making, was to add to the usual compilation of biblical texts the idea that Divine Right monarchy conforms to the natural order of things. Nature is patriarchally ordered (even animals obey the authority of dominant males), God is the author of nature, therefore what is in accordance with the order of nature must be divinely intended. Just as God wants the father of a family to be its ruler, so he wants kings to be the fathers of their peoples. The Divine Right of Kings was the only natural right that Filmer was prepared to allow after the pattern of nature, but he took the crucial step away from arguing theologically to arguing naturalistically. All it took was for Locke to argue from the nature which God had created that all men are endowed with Natural Rights for an important shift to occur in the nature of political theorising. From Filmer on, political theorising could begin to cease to be a minor branch of theology and become a subject of enquiry in its own right. When the doctrine of Natural Rights in its Lockian version came under attack from others who were kindly disposed to human liberty and improvement, rights would come to be seen, as they were by the utilitarians, as just another means to human happiness, with no independent philosophical or political status of their own.

Of course, this did not happen everywhere or at the same time. The United States of America is the place where a notion of Natural Rights has survived as a kind of trumps which supersedes any other moral claim. To say in America that I have a right to something is to put forward a claim which, prima facie, overrides any other kind of moral claim. Jefferson's Declaration of Independence is the classic statement of the claim that men have a multitude of rights independent of government. Some of those rights are enshrined in the Declaration, and some in the first amendments to the Constitution, but only *some*. There is a clear implication that there are lots of other Natural Rights which from time to time Americans will ask government to recognise and guarantee, which has left the citizens of the United States with the paradox that government is expected both to increase liberty and to curtail it at the same time. As Bentham was to recognise, and as Locke would concur, government and liberty are two jealous antagonists, and it is making two contradictory demands on government that it should be asked to increase liberty by recognising more and more pre-existing Natural Rights while recognising that governments exist to stop men doing what they sometimes want to do. The whole history of American government could be written on that theme.

Theories of Natural Rights have never really progressed beyond their Lockian origins as rights granted to men by God. People are always bound to ask: Where do Natural Rights 'come from'?, and the only remotely satisfactory answer has always been: From God. No matter how much a Natural Rights thinker may have his doubts about what God's attributes are and what he does, he always does wisely when he keeps God up his sleeve with the job of giving men their Natural Rights.

NOTES ON SOURCES

The standard edition of Locke is *John Locke: Two Treaties of Government*, ed. P. Laslett (2nd edn 1967), and the standard life is still Maurice Cranston, *John Locke: A Biography* (1957; 2nd edn 1985). Recent studies of Locke include J. Dunn, *The Political Thought of John Locke* (1969), in which Dunn argues that Locke could only mean what his contemporaries could have taken him to mean, and Geraint Parry, *John Locke* (1978). Willmore Kendall, *John Locke and the Doctrine of Majority Rule* (1965), is wayward and brilliant. M. Seliger's *The Liberal Politics of John Locke* (1968), has never received the critical attention it deserves. J.W. Yolton, ed., *John Locke: A Collection of New Essays*, (1969), is useful. Like Hobbes, Locke wrote a good deal about other things. His *Essay Concerning Human Understanding* is the classic text of British empirical philosophy, and his essay *On Education* was probably the most widely read of Locke's books during his lifetime.

13

SOCIAL CONTRACT III
The Rousseauist version

JEAN-JACQUES ROUSSEAU

Rousseau was the first political thinker to make a text of his own life. His *Confessions* and *Rousseau Judge of Jean-Jacques* are apologies for a life which went wrong. Some readers of the *Confessions* find them embarrassingly frank; others point to how limited even honest introspection was in a world of pre-Freudian innocence. Rousseau always seems to have been able to arouse strong passions in others, not least in bluestocking upper-class women (about whom he could make appallingly ungallant remarks). The affection which Rousseau inspired in others sometimes turned into distaste, and even hatred. His was a trusting and suspicious nature by turns; his character contained a wide streak of paranoia, and, as is frequently the case with paranoiacs, his paranoia was self-fulfilling because it sometimes made enemies out of erstwhile friends. Rousseau's capacity for dividing people into sides for and against him by no means ended with his unhappy death. On one day you can find yourself detesting Rousseau, and the next day you can find yourself defending Jean-Jacques to the death. What is certain is that no-one who came into contact with Rousseau for long was likely to come out of it unscathed.

Born in Calvinist Geneva, the young Rousseau was destined for the life of an artisan, but, at the age of sixteen in 1728, he left Switzerland under a cloud, wandered into France, and at Annecy was befriended by Mme de Warens, who made him her lover to protect him from the corruptions of the world. Rousseau then began to climb the greasy pole in a France where noble patronage was the only hope for a man of the people who was also a foreigner. By 1743 Rousseau had settled in Paris, and formed his nearly lifelong relationship with his 'child of nature', Thérèse Lavasseur, by whom he had five children, all deposited in the Foundling Hospital by the man who wrote *Emile*. In 1751, Rousseau broke into the philosophic world with an essay on the arts and sciences, and in the next decade he wrote the works which we still read, including the second *Discourse*, the *Nouvelle Heloïse* and *The Social Contract*. These were the years when he tried to give up his social climbing and his posh friends, some of whom were to blacken his name all over Europe.

Rousseau returned to Paris in 1767 from a visit to England. He was already what we would now call a 'seriously disturbed' person, and his last ten years were far from happy. He tried to justify himself to the world, but the more he excused himself, the more he accused himself. In the end, he thought that even God had deserted him, and stories long circulated that he died in 1778 mad and a suicide.

THE ROUSSEAU PROBLEM

Rousseau has spawned a hugh body of commentary on his political thought, and it is easy to see what all these often differing commentaries have in common: they all agree that Rousseau himself is different. Rousseau (with the partial exception of Machiavelli) is the first political theorist to be blamed for a great political event, the French Revolution, and some of Rousseau's critics have argued as if Rousseau caused the Revolution almost single-handed. Perhaps the best way of approaching the rich but difficult (and perhaps contradictory) political thought of Rousseau is through some of his critics, because it is only then that one can get some idea of the trouble which this man has caused.

The business of blaming Rousseau for the Revolution began very early with Burke's *Reflections on the Revolution in France* (1790). As an intellectual, Burke assumed that the French Revolution had been caused by books and so could only be undone by other books. Critics of Burke, and of this kind of approach to the Revolution, have tended to underrate the seriousness of Burke's arguments, or arguments which follow Burke. When Burke singled out Rousseau as the chief culprit for the Revolution, he did so to point out what has become a very obvious truth since 1789, but which was not so obvious at the time, which is that the French Revolution was made in the name of an ideology, and, therefore, the counter-revolutionary position was incomplete without an ideology which was in its way as comprehensive as the revolutionary ideology which it was designed to oppose. 'Comprehensive' is the key word. The Revolution was made in the name of a view of the world whose origins lay in Rousseau's political thought and whose credo was the Rights of Man and Citizen.

Burke was extremely acute as a futurologist. He realised almost before anyone else that because the French Revolution was made in the name of a new view of the world it could not be contained within French national boundaries. Being new, this view of the world would appeal to the new men, looking round as they would be for a handbook of politics to supply their own lack of political experience when the Revolution brought them to the fore as revolutionary leaders. The works of Rousseau, in Burke's view of it, were the ideal source for revolutionary politicians in a hurry. Having been excluded from the old ruling class by definition, and needing to learn about politics much more quickly than long schooling in a ruling class would provide, the new men began to think like Rousseau, *a priori*, from a small number of fixed principles which they called the 'principles of human nature'. Men who have to learn quickly do not have the time to begin to think historically, because to think historically in politics requires a sophisticated political education gained in the only school of politics capable of giving it, which is a confident and politically skilful ruling class. Rousseau's great fault is that he convinced the new men that they only had to read him to be able to construct a political community from scratch and rule it. Find out what human nature in general is like and it is a matter of a moment to be able to construct a world of social, political and religious institutions to fit that nature.

For Burke, therefore, Rousseau is the most typical of the thinkers of the arch-rational Enlightenment, encouraging his disciples to reason deductively from political axioms. Others of Rousseau's critics, like the great historian of the French Revolution Hippolyte

Taine, were not so sure, or rather they point to a contradiction in Rousseau which leads them to wonder whether there might not be one Rousseau but two: Rousseau the arch-rationalist, and another, much more sinister Rousseau. The first volume of Taine's *Origins of Contemporary France*, which contains his critique of Rousseau, appeared in 1875 after the great French national disasters of the Franco-Prussian War and the Paris *Commune*. *La gloire militaire* was temporarily out of fashion, and this affected the views of the French Revolution which it was possible to take, and with it went a view of the political thought which was supposed to have been the Revolution's inspiration. Laudatory accounts of the Revolution before Taine had emphasised the heroism of the revolutionary wars of liberation, but after the fiasco of the war against Prussia and the débâcle of the *Commune*, attention began to shift onto the less savoury episodes of the Revolution like the lynchings by revolutionary mobs, the Terror and the September Massacres. With the irrational mob and institutionalised terror at the centre of the revolutionary stage, Taine began to look for their origins, and he found them in Rousseau. There was another, lunatic side to Rousseau's own character, the mad, paranoid dreamer of revenge upon his real and imagined enemies, as well as the supremely rationalist political thinker who could calculate arithmetically in *The Social Contract* the exact amount of state sovereignty possessed by each individual citizen.

Taine characterised the whole political thought of the Enlightenment as being dangerously infected by what he called the 'classical spirit'. By this Taine meant something like what Burke had meant when he said that the character of the enlightened mind was always inclined to reason *a priori*, from first principles. Eighteenth-century political theorising had always looked behind the appearances of human societies past and present to see the constant which lay behind them all, the just and immutable principles of human nature. This was one aspect of Rousseau's thought, the search for universal man, rational, innocent and benevolent. Eighteenth-century political and social thought tried to think away from men everything that they acquired as the result of living in a given moral, political and social order. What was left was natural man, man as he was intended to be. The political thought of the Enlightenment, therefore, lacked the authority of a real social science which seeks out the facts of social existence in order to show the differences between different national existences at particular moments of those lives' unfolding.

This is a view of enlightened political thought which enlightened political thinkers, with their adulation of the Science of Man, would not have recognised. Taine thinks that the Enlightenment misunderstood what science really was. In effect, the political thinkers of the Enlightenment mistook geometry for science, affecting a kind of perverted Newtonianism and expecting to understand the human world from a small number of fixed principles analogous to Newton's laws of motion. Their method was deductive from axioms, not inductive from the real facts of social experience. The real facts of social experience, which had made man the ignoble creature he was, could safely be written off to reveal the noble savage underneath. From this flimsy theoretical basis enlightened thinkers jumped much too readily to the theory of necessary and inevitable progress. In a world in which human institutions bore the imprint of human reason and worked on a rational humanity, then, for the first time in human history, the ordinary relationship between men and their institutions would be reversed. The past had been the story of wicked institutions for wicked men. The future was to be the story of rational institutions for rational men, and just as wicked institutions made men more wicked, so rational institutions would make men more rational.

What worried Taine was that the rationalist, Rousseauist account of human nature did not square very well with what happened in the French Revolution, and by extension in any revolution, when the restraints of supposedly wicked institutions were removed. Taine is aware of the obvious defence of revolutionary violence, that the downtrodden have learned their lessons in violence from the social and political order which they seek to overthrow, but for him the argument about human barbarism and animalism goes deeper. While not being an orthodox Darwinian, Taine accepts the depressing message of evolutionism that man has a past which is unimaginably longer than conservatives like Burke could conceive of a century before. Nineteenth-century science has taught men used to thinking of themselves as civilised the humiliating lesson that they have an anthropological and a biological past compared with which the span of civilised life is like the flicker of an eyelid. What a conservative (though a liberal conservative) like Taine cannot get out of the past is any of that comfort and reassurance that was available to Burke in the pre-Darwinian age. When eighteenth-century conservatives looked at the past, they could see the comforting story of the development of socialising institutions which kept men in their place. A late nineteenth-century conservative like Taine saw something very different in the past. He saw an anthropological and animal inheritance which men, or large numbers of them, could not hope to overcome. The thrust of the barbarous and animal past was what human institutions are there to frustrate. Rousseauist natural man will come to the surface in revolutions but he shows a very ignoble face. Taine invites us to see in the sane aspect of Rousseau's personality the absurdly over-optimistic rationalism of the political and social thought of the Enlightenment, and in the less sane aspect of Rousseau's personality the insane regression to a state of nature which is red in tooth and claw.

Taine's critique of Rousseau is ambiguous. On the one hand he wants to see in Rousseau the classical spirit at its most typical, but on the other hand he wants to see in Rousseau something new and disturbing. Rousseau is at one and the same time what all the thinkers of the Enlightenment would have been if they could, and something entirely new. In a famous essay of 1922, *Romanticism and Revolution*, Charles Maurras argued that Taine, for all his merits as a historian of the French Revolution, had simply failed to see that what was new in Rousseau was romantic egotism. Maurrasian conservatism based itself upon classical ideals of order, the order of a society, of classical architecture, of everything which affected the life of man, and so he had to deny Taine's thesis that there was something classical about Rousseau. All Maurras could see in Rousseau was a kind of pretend classicism in which a fantasised Sparta was made into Rousseau's own spiritual home. Rousseau's cast of mind was not classical at all, but romantic. Romanticism for Maurras consisted of judging the rest of the world according to one's own private values, finding the world wanting, and wanting to remake that world in the image of one's own inner image of oneself. Rousseau's is an unquiet spirit, and his values are intensely personal in contrast to the serenity of classical civilisation with its publicly made and publicly held values. The ideal of harmony in the soul of which classical philosophers speak, and that social harmony which was the ideal of classical political thought find no equivalent in Rousseau. Rousseau brought with him an alien spirit of turmoil when he came into Roman Catholic France from Protestant Geneva, a spirit reminiscent of the turbulence of the ancient Jewish prophets, in from the desert and daring to denounce the higher civilisation of the cities. The France in which he caused so much trouble did not need Rousseau's pretend classicism because it was already classical through its Church, which was the true means by which the classical values had been preserved in France ever since aristocratic Roman prelates had lain in wait to civilise the barbarian kings who were the political heirs to the Roman *imperium*.

Another important line of commentary on Rousseau is exemplified by Alfred Cobban's *Rousseau and the Modern State* (1934). Here, Rousseau is regarded as the progenitor of the modern nation-state characterised by homogeneity of culture and language, by a certain territorial integrity, and by a state which at least in principle treats all its citizens the same way by giving them all equal rights and duties. The modern nation-state is something like the Republic One and Indivisible, which is itself more than an echo of Rousseau's characterisation of the political community in *The Social Contract* as a 'new moral person' which, like a natural person, itself has rights and duties. The modern state is a jealous state. It will tend to be intolerant of other loyalties, especially when those other loyalties come between the individual and the supreme individual, the state. Loyalties to caste and class, to bosses and priests, to supra-national movements, especially when they involve a commitment to pacifism instead of patriotism, will all be suspect, and secret societies will be anathema. The only two legal persons which exist are the individual citizen and the state. What this effectively means is that the modern state will look askance at legally established corporations or estates as they existed under the *ancien régime*, those mediating institutions which come between individuals and the state. Legally incorporated estates of nobility, clergy, and the third estate are, from the strictly modern point of view, states within the state because they have an independent legal existence. The modern state's authority will rest on a very uncomplicated patriotism and a fairly complex notion of citizenship which itself is more than reminiscent of the idea of patriotism which was supposed to have existed in the ancient city republics (modern republicanism could never resist dressing up in the toga). Citizens will have a comprehensive list of rights and duties drawn up for them by the state. This requires everybody to have a proper name, a fixed and known address, and it will be necessary for the state to know both of these. That implies lists, and lists have to be kept up to date by someone, which in its turn implies bureaucracy. Bureaucracy has become something of a pejorative term, but modern bureaucracy has its origins in the perfectly laudable intention of the state to treat everybody the same. The characteristic practice of the modern state will be something like compulsory military service, when everybody will be called upon, and would willingly go, to sacrifice their lives, provided others are willing also, for the nation-state from which they acquire such benefits. *Ubi patria, ibi bene.* How much of this is traceable to the Rousseau of *The Social Contract* and the proposed constitutions for Corsica and Poland is debatable, but certain it is that at least the outlines of the idea of the modern nation-state can be found in Rousseau.

The totalitarian state has also been attributed to Rousseau, in particular in J.L. Talmon's *The Origins of Totalitarian Democracy* (1953). Talmon's argument is basically very simple, though it has very complex ramifications. Talmon thinks that the totalitarian state can demand unquestioning obedience and the right to interfere with what it pleases (so that the distinction between public and private practically disappears), because it does so in the name of a particular kind of legitimising ideology. Talmon thinks that ideology is a typically modern form of belief system, beginning towards the end of the eighteenth century, which answers the maximum number of questions with the minimum amount of answers. What characterises ideology, therefore, is not so much its particular content as its particular style, and the audience to which its persuasiveness is directed. Ideological thought will think in simple images and it will readily be reducible still further into slogans ('Enemies of the People', 'the traitors within'). Ideologies also work at a historical level. Ideologists typically find the world unattractive, and they find reasons, usually very simplistic ones, for why the world has got into such a mess, but they usually also promise to find ways in which the world can get out of the mess. To do this, ideologists point to groups as the agents of the world's degeneration and to a group which is going to act as the agent of the world's regeneration, and all this must be couched in a language comprehensible to the meanest human understanding. Above all, ideologies are circular; they contain sets of reasons, again simple, which explain why particular groups seem to be unable to grasp the truth of the ideology. The idea of 'false consciousness' arising out of a position of social dominance is never far below the surface of ideologies. *They* can't see the truth because they are *them*, the agents of the world's degeneration, by definition incapable of seeing what they are doing and certainly incapable of seeing that they are what separates the rest of humanity from the bright future implicit in the dismal present. Rousseau's insistence that the history of all hitherto existing societies is the history of force and fraud is an ideological statement. What he seems to be saying is that there is not much point in looking into different national histories because they will all tell the same sad story of the death of natural liberty. 'Man was born free and is everywhere in chains' sums up in nine words the entire history of the human race. It must be somebody's fault, and it can only be the fault of the lords of the earth. According to Rousseau the ideologist, only a complete fool, or a member of the ruling class, could fail to understand that. Rousseau is the first of the 'terrifying simplifiers', the model and forerunner of all those modern ideologues who think that understanding the world is easy, and who think that all that has to happen for the world to be made perfect is the implementation of an ideology.

These four kinds of Rousseau commentary show that Rousseau has been blamed for a lot of things. All the commentators on Rousseau scent out something peculiar about him, though there seems to be considerable disagreement about what it is. Perhaps Rousseau's critics divide over the question of the *theoretical* relationship between Rousseau's famous *Confessions* and his social and political theory. Rousseau is a man of the people. For the first time social and political theory is being written from the bottom up, not from the top down. Rousseau's *Confessions* is an account of what it is like to try to rise from the bottom in a highly stratified society dominated by an *ancien régime* aristocracy. In the *Confessions* Rousseau movingly describes the humiliations which are visited upon the parvenu, often quite unintentionally. Rousseau's own history of himself is also meant to be the story of how a naive son of the people becomes wordly, and he does that by losing sight of the simple virtues. Simplicity, honesty, goodness of heart, straightforward religious faith even, turn out to be among life's disadvantages. Nobody who set out to live his life according to the 'official' Christian values of his society would last ten minutes in the real world. *The Confessions* is an account of the realisation that nobody takes the values he has been brought up in seriously. Society as it is currently constituted is a tissue of hypocrisy because its operating values are very different from its nominal values. Rousseau generalises from his own experiences to a whole theory of society. He assumes that everyone living in a society as it then existed, and perhaps as it has always existed, is forced to divide his individual personality against itself. Ordinary social existence is a constant battle between what one knows to be right and one's own self-interest. My self-interest tells me to lie, cheat, gouge, connive and steal, whereas if I consult my simple and affectionate heart it tells me to do the opposite. Rousseau thinks that everyone living in society suffers from the same self-division; principle drives them in one direction, and self-interest drives them in the opposite direction. Christianity says 'love your neighbour', but ordinary social living soon tells you that the man who loves his neighbour as himself is a fool. Even survival in a society which is nominally Christian would be a problem if anybody was actually fool enough to take Christianity literally and try to live a truly Christian life.

Rousseau's account in *The Confessions* of what it is like to try to live justly in an unjust society reminds us forcibly of the account of that same problem in Plato's *Republic*. Rousseau does not go quite as far as Plato, who argues that the perfectly just man living in the perfectly unjust society would soon meet his death at the hands of unjust men, but he is plainly heading in that direction. What makes any given society so rotten is that one's own self-respect is corrupted into self-interest. Rousseau is rather biblical about self-interest, where biblical means Old Testament. Rousseau seems to think that even if there were to be enough of the good things of life to satisfy every reasonable human desire there would still not be enough. The Old Testament doctrine of the irruption of desire is never very far below the surface of *The Confessions*. The brute fact of human scarcity is compounded by the fact that the desires themselves are not fixed. Human desires multiply as human societies become more sophisticated. This puts Rousseau outside the bounds of Enlightenment. One of Enlightenment's central claims was that enlightened society, however governed, was differentiated in a way that barbarous society was not. This perception took many forms and came from a variety of different impulses, but all enlightened thinkers were liberals to the extent that they thought the increasing social division of labour argued well for human freedom. In the modern idiom, it came to be recognised that a free and progressive society was one in which there were a great number of social roles available to the members of that society. Rousseau sets his face against this kind of enlightened optimism. The more socially differentiated, the more sophisticated a society becomes, the more likely it is that the members of that society will lose sight of the simpler values which alone make a life worth living. What we choose to call progress is nothing more than getting stuck more deeply in the mire of unsatisfied desire.

Here Rousseau speaks the clear language of modernity, the language of alienated existence, where alienation means realising that even if you could have everything your society has to offer, you would still be unsatisfied. Rousseau's political thought is largely concerned with how we got ourselves into this mess and how we can get out of it.

THE *DISCOURSE ON THE ORIGINS OF INEQUALITY* (1755)

The *Discourse on the Origins of Inequality* contains Rousseau's explanation of how the world got into its mess, and he is very careful not to say that the world came to be as it is through social contract. Rousseau's State of Nature is very different from the State of Nature in Hobbes and in Locke. Nothing much happens in Rousseau's imagined picture of what life must have been like before the state and society arose. Human contact would have been fitful, and certainly not enough for men even to develop a language. Men would have been unequal in strength and cunning in the State of Nature, but that would not have led some men to dominate others because the motive for that domination would have been lacking. Naturally unequal men in the State of Nature would simply be unequal men with nothing much to quarrel about. It is only in society that inequality matters. How, then did society arise? Rousseau confesses in *The Social Contract* that he does not really know, but in the *Discourse* he makes a guess. The first man to claim a piece of land as his and to find others foolish enough to believe him was the true founder of civil society, because with the invention of property men suddenly found something worth associating and competing for. With property, everything changes, simply because inequality of property matters in a way that natural inequality does not. Naturally unequal men in the State of Nature become the rich and poor of civil society. Whatever the rich are, they are not stupid. They recognise that the cupidity of other men poses problems for their retention of their property. At first, each man protects his own with his own, but the wealthy soon realise that this is an extremely expensive way of doing something which can in fact be done on the cheap. Law is the next fraud perpetrated against the human race. The state and its law, it is said, is in everybody's interest, not just the interest of a few. The force of the whole community is used to protect what are in fact the ill-gotten gains of the few. By persuading everybody that the law applies equally to all, and by getting everybody to contribute their widow's mite to the upkeep of the state, the rich get others to pay for what only really concerns them.

What is remarkable about Rousseau's account of the origins of human society is that, although he is a social contract thinker, he does not use the idea of social contract itself to explain the origins of human societies. It was suggested in the introductory chapter on social contract thinking that an important shift of emphasis happens in the hundred years which separate Hobbes's *Leviathan* from Rousseau's *Social Contract*. In that time a growing confidence in man's naturally social nature led to a certain absence of panic in the face of the question of whether human societies were likely to survive or not. Hobbes's fear-ridden message that we ought to put up with almost any government because of the horror of the possibility of returning to the State of Nature gives way to a rather sanguine appreciation of the toughness of human societies. Because human societies arise of their own accord, so to speak, there is no need for an elaborately formal account of their origins of the kind that social contract theorists had typically given. What use, then, was social contract theory if it did not explain the origins of civil society? Rousseau has the perfect answer. Social contract as a theory of the origins of civil society is in fact an account of the origins of a legitimate society because men agree to construct that society out of their own freely given consent. This is a laughable account of the origins of any actual society, because it is obvious to the most casual glance that no actual human society is originally so constituted that a majority of its members would consent to its legitimacy. Therefore, to attribute the origins of any contemporary society to social contract is to invest that society with a legitimacy which it does not possess. Nevertheless, most societies in Rousseau's own day look pretty solid. It therefore follows that legitimacy is not necessary for the survival of civil society, which is just another way of saying that societies have such an in-built capacity to survive that they can keep going in defiance of the most elementary rules of justice.

That perception of Rousseau's had enormous implications for the political theorising of the future. It could be said that it is the central insight of the next two hundred years because it quite literally makes a theory of revolution both necessary and possible. Paradoxical as it may seem, the fact of social stability is fundamentally important to any theory of revolution. The central argument against all revolutions is Hobbes's argument (which was surprisingly to become Burke's argument against the French Revolution) that tinkering with government leads to chaos, and chaos of the most general kind, not just political chaos but every other kind of chaos as well. Hobbes invites us to look upon the political and social orders as fragile and imperilled. Being a revolutionary means having enough confidence in the social fabric to believe that to repudiate how a society is governed does not mean the end of that society as a society. Obviously, such a new perception about the nature of societies can be seen to be beginning in Locke, and it is there in Rousseau with a vengeance. That is the final message of Rousseau's dismissive denial that he knows how societies came to be as they are in *The Social Contract*, and of his rather perfunctory sketch of universal human history in the *Discourse*. The fervid search for the origins of stable societies is only worth it for antiquarian reasons or for reasons of fear for the continued existence of society itself. Not for Rousseau, who simply asks us to accept that stable human societies are a given part of the human landscape. Therefore, the question for the political theorist is not: How can we account for the existence of human societies as such? but: How can they be made much better in the future? Perhaps there is even the possibility that in the future human societies could be made perfect, or as good as they could possibly be. No society having been founded on social contract, the social contract moment can be saved up for the future, when men will make a society which is not merely reasonably stable, as with Hobbes, or legitimate, as with Locke, but just.

THE SOCIAL CONTRACT

The problem which *The Social Contract* sets out to solve is therefore posed by the *Confessions* and by the *Discourse on the Origins of Inequality*, and concerns how to get out of the mess that these actually existing societies are in. The key to the whole matter is liberty, but not the kind of liberty which men enjoyed in the now-for-ever-lost State of Nature. Going back to the State of Nature would mean having to unlearn everything, including language, which is impossible. Men living in social bonds still hanker after that lost innocence, that freedom from all sense of sin, that life lived according to nature, or as nature, but that life is gone for ever for those who have experienced life in one of the world's more sophisticated societies. Small pockets of natural existence might still be holding out somewhere, in high mountain valleys for instance, but for most of us that natural life, or anything approaching it, is out of the question. Therefore, the question for the political theorist becomes one of trying to devise a form of communal life which gives men something equivalent to that complete freedom which they must have once enjoyed in the State of Nature. This Rousseau also calls liberty, and it resembles the lost liberty of the State of Nature because it is complete. As Rousseau says right at the beginning of *The Social Contract*, the problem is to find a form of human association in which the members are as free 'as before'. We know that Rousseau does not think that we can return to the 'before', to the State of Nature, so he must mean that there is a form of human association in which there exists something as good as the liberty once enjoyed in the State of Nature.

How is this kind of liberty to be found? Obviously, we look for clues in the evil condition of our own societies, and in particular we ask what it is that makes them so unsatisfactory. We already know from the *Confessions* what it is that makes the divided self unhappy. The division between the self's sense of right and its sense of its own interest sets the problem right at the beginning of *The Social Contract*, Book 1:

> I mean to inquire if, in the civil order, there can be any sure and legitimate rule of administration, men being taken as they are and laws as they might be. In this inquiry I shall endeavour always to unite what right sanctions with what is prescribed by interest, in order that justice and utility may in no case be divided.

Rousseau seems to be saying that we have got so used to thinking that in our own societies those who do well are those who have violated elementary canons of right, that the separation of right from utility can be taken for granted. By 'taking men as they are', Rousseau means that however much we might want to control human self-interest, we simply have to accept it as a fact. Rousseau also asks us to accept as a fact that men following their self-interest at the expense of their sense of justice are unhappy men. Any new community formed through social contract will have to find ways of coping with the fact that in ordinary societies it is human self-interest, or the self-interestedness of groups, which separates men from each other. The problem of the new society, then, is to find a way for men to pursue their self-interest without dividing themselves off from their fellow men, and that is a very difficult proposition indeed. Rousseau is ruthlessly honest about our own natures: any altruism of which we are capable must not be bought at the expense of our self-interest.

LIBERTY AND THE GENERAL WILL

Rousseau's solution to the problem of the division between justice and self-interest lies in the notoriously tricky idea of the General Will. Ordinary societies, Rousseau thinks, are incapable of acting with a single will: that is one of the reasons that they have to be ruled by force or by the fraudulent claims of a ruling class. Ordinary societies are not free in another and equally important sense: the choices which we make in them are never free because we always end up following our self-interest, either individually or as a group. It is of the essence of Rousseau's concept of liberty that a choice which I make which is predictable in the terms of my own self-interest cannot be a free choice. (How could it be, when an observer can easily tell what I'm going to do, and when I myself have got so used to following my own interest that I probably don't even have to think about it any more?) Pursuit of one's own self-interest is simply another name for inequality. When everybody pursues his own self-interest, then they are bound to end up unequal because not everybody is equally good at pursuing self-interest, or equally lucky. The harmless inequality of the State of Nature has been exchanged for inequality of condition in civil society which really matters. So something really has to change if men are to get themselves into a social condition where they begin to want to rid themselves of that which prevents them living in that condition which Rousseau calls 'political right' (which is the sub-title of *The Social Contract*).

Rousseau knows perfectly well that some people who live in an ordinary society are less free in a straightforward sense than others. If I'm rich, there is a simple sense in which I can do more of what I might happen to want than if I am poor. The rich are less dependent on others, and one of the things Rousseau the rising man of letters hated more than anything else was personal dependence on aristocratic patrons. Rousseau thinks that in an ordinary society, before making a social contract to get out of what is frankly an unsocial state (because every man's hand is directed against every other man), liberty is always going to be a 'more-or-less' condition. Nobody will be completely free (everyone is dependent to some extent on others), and there will in fact be large variations in the amount of freedom enjoyed by particular individuals or groups of individuals. This is recognisably what we have come to call the Individualist idea of freedom, where men freely accept that some diminution of their freedom is necessary in order that they can live a social life at all. Individualist political theorists like Hobbes and Locke frankly accept that living a recognisably social life entails the giving up of some natural liberty in order to enjoy security of life and property, though they disagree about how much natural liberty must be given up and on what terms.

Not Rousseau. For his new state of the social contract, liberty is not going to be 'more-or-less' but 'either-or'; either men are going to be completely free, or they are not going to be free at all. The clue to Rousseau's solution to the problem of liberty within a political community lies in his assertion that the natural liberty of the State of Nature has gone for ever; we now live in a social condition from which there is no turning back. The only way lies forward, so that all this hankering after a so-called 'natural' liberty has to stop. Rousseau has already promised that man in his new state of the social contract will be as free 'as before', and this must mean that the new liberty of the state of the social contract will be as complete as liberty in the now lost State of Nature, but it will be liberty of a different kind. Rousseau's citizens in his new state are not going to be in the position of always wondering whether they have given up too much of their natural liberty for the benefits which living in civil society brings. They are going to be completely free. Rousseau even reverses the Individualist way of looking at liberty in an ordinary society. The most natural way of looking at liberty in an ordinary society is to say that the rich enjoy more of it than the poor. As a moralist, this sticks in Rousseau's craw. If ordinary societies are all corruptions of the original State of Nature, perpetrated by force and fraud, then must not those who do best out of these perverted societies be the most corrupt of all? Rousseau's famous sentence 'Man was born free; and everywhere he is in chains' is as much a moral statement as it is a political statement. The moralism comes out in the next sentence: 'One thinks himself the master of others, and still remains a greater slave than they.' Rousseau invites us to believe that those who do best in a corrupt world are more that world's slaves than those at the bottom of the pile. Freedom in an ordinary society is for Rousseau equivalent to the distance we have travelled from the original state of innocence of the State of Nature, and he seems to be saying that those who have done most of the corrupting, or those who have benefited most from it, have travelled farthest from the original State of Nature, and are therefore the least free. Rousseau loves paradox, and nowhere more so than in his treatment here of freedom in ordinary civil society.

Rousseau is also paradoxical in his solution to the problem of freedom and civility. If men are to be cured of their longing for a long lost natural liberty, and if they are not to put up with the restricted liberty provided by an ordinary society, then the only way forward is a complete submission to a voluntarily self-prescribed law. Rousseau formulated the problem very succinctly:

> The problem is to find a form of association which will defend and protect with the whole common force the person and goods of each associate, and which each, while uniting himself with all, may still obey himself alone, and remain as free as before.

For this to be possible, says Rousseau

> Each of us puts his person and all his power in common under the supreme direction of the general will, and, in our corporate capacity, we receive each member as an indivisible part of the whole.

This is the moment of social contract. It creates a new moral entity, a 'public person' which is called 'state' when passive, 'sovereign' when active, and 'power' when compared to others like itself. By this Rousseau really means that the moment of social contract, when the General Will comes into being for the first time, is a moment of imagined equality. Everyone gives himself and all his power (the power that proceeds from self-interest) up to the General Will provided others do the same. The General Will then decides what the arrangements, including the property arrangements, of the new society should be. This is what Rousseau means when he says that the state is called 'sovereign' when active: the

General Will acts as the decision of the whole sovereign people to decide those things which are important to it. Rousseau then adds one of his famously challenging statements: the Sovereign, merely by virtue of what it is, is always what it should be. Acts of the Sovereign, decisions of the General Will, Rousseau seems to be saying, can never be wrong, even though the General Will is decided by counting votes and so there is always the possibility of a dissenting minority. The majority is always right. How can that be?

Rousseau's answer is that the moment of equality when the Sovereign people assembles, either for the first time or thereafter, means that there can be no prior way of deciding what the General Will ought to decide. Rousseau means us to take this literally, and to understand why it should necessarily be so we have to go back to his analysis of what always goes wrong in an ordinary society. The lack of freedom in an ordinary society comes from the fact that our ordinary life-choices are made predictable by our differently perceived self-interest, either as individuals or as groups. Posit a moment of equality, then each man, when consulting his own interest, will be consulting exactly the same self-interest as everybody else because he will no longer have unequal self-interest to tell him which way to vote. Decisions of the General Will are therefore *by definition* unpredictable, and therefore free. Of course not everybody will make the same choice, because there is nothing prior which tells individuals what choice to make. There could obviously be minorities and majorities on all important questions and this lack of unanimity should not surprise us. Free choice is hard to make by definition, and it will be especially hard to make in the beginning in a human group which is used to having its decisions made for it by divisive self-interest. Such a group might even require a special figure, the Legislator, to bring wills into conformity with reason, the perfect outsider who could persuade a sovereign people what it really wanted because it is so difficult for them to make a choice now their conflicting self interested wills no longer make the business of choice easy for them. One of the things which a sovereign people ought to decide upon is the system of public values under which they should live, a system of civic morality. There is nothing very strange about this. Rousseau seems to be saying that all political communities end up with systems of public values which all the members of the community are expected to follow. Political communities as they exist in the world typically receive their systems of public values by accident or fraud, or a combination of both. Rousseau is saying that for the first time the social contract gives a people the opportunity to *choose* the system of values (including religion) under which it should live. Hence the need for the Legislator, because a people brought up under one system of social values will find it very difficult to choose another. Bewilderment might be the immediate reaction of people called upon in a moment of equality to choose the values under which they should live.

What about the coercion of minorities? Rousseau does not say that going along with the majority is the price the minority has to pay for living in a new kind of society. On the contrary, the minority is forced to go along with the majority decision, and Rousseau says that forcing them to do so is forcing them to be free, the most famous of all his paradoxes. What can that possibly mean? On the face of it, Rousseau appears to be making a difficulty for himself by not simply saying that minorities are always coerced in political communities, and that that's just the way things are. On the contrary, Rousseau seems to be saying that the minority really wanted to be coerced all along. The minority apparently suffers the double indignity of being coerced, and of being told that they are being coerced in the name of their own real freedom. Rousseau certainly accepts that all states coerce in the sense that in political communities everybody is expected to pay more than lip service to the prevailing system of public values, but he thinks that coercion under the General Will is so different that it is a mistake to call it coercion at all. Rousseau thinks that there are at least six main arguments which show that coercion of minorities is not coercion as traditionally conceived.

1 Decisions of the General Will are not predictable, for the reasons outlined above. If you find yourself in the minority, then you can be certain that the decision wasn't fixed beforehand. Those who find themselves in the majority could be just as 'surprised' as those who find themselves in the minority, so you are unlikely always to be in the minority.

2 Dissenters can be persuaded to go along with the rest. Force is not a first resort but a last resort.

3 If persuasion does not work on a specific matter on which the General Will has decided, then there still is persuasion available of a much more general kind. Dissenters could be reminded of why they left the old society to join the new. In the old society, it was divisiveness which made it such an uncomfortable place to live. The reason for joining the new state of the Social Contract in the first place was that here for the first time there was the possibility of acting *with* others, not against them. Standing out against the majority of one's fellow men is to replicate the conditions of the old society, something which those who have joined the new society show that they do not really want simply by being here.

4 If this does not work, then there is the further argument that agreeing with the others will get easier as you go along. You will get a taste for it until wanting what the others want becomes as automatic as following your own self-interest and spiting the rest in the old society.

5 Being in the minority in the state of the Social Contract is not the same as being ruled by the majority by force. Majority rule, rule by the superior weight of others, typically takes the form of exploitation. As in all forms of rule based on force, majority rule would be used to distance the majority from the minority and to make the minority different from the majority. The minority might, for instance, be forced by the superior weight of the majority to perform those menial tasks in a society for which the majority has no taste. The decisions of the General Will could never be of the kind which chose the street-sweepers, because the majority is asking the minority to do nothing which the majority is not itself prepared to do. It is not like saying '*You* do that' but '*we're* prepared to do this and you must too'.

6 If none of those arguments work, then coercion follows. Rousseau would say that all states from time to time require some of their members to do things against their declared wills. What makes the state of the Social Contract different is that those who have been coerced have been treated as rational, adult human beings capable of understanding why they should do what they should do. There is a world of difference between

just being told to do something and being given the reason why you should do it. (One of the standard reasons usually given for hitting children is that it will 'teach them a lesson' which they can learn in no other way.)

ROUSSEAU ON LIBERTY

These may be excellent and even convincing reasons for coercion, but Rousseau will not stop there because he wants to argue that his form of coercion is not coercion at all but liberty. In what senses could this be called freedom? It could be freedom in a very straight-forward and ancient sense. Rousseau himself came from the free city of Geneva which was a Calvinist theocracy. He may have thought that any city which gave itself its own law was free, and that included ancient Sparta and modern Geneva, both of which were in fact highly regimented societies. The speech which Herodotus puts into the mouth of Queen Artemisia when she addresses the Persian king sums up the matter exactly. The king had asked the queen whether the Greeks, being so outnumbered, would dare to fight him, and the queen especially singled out the Spartans as bound to fight whatever happened because their laws commanded them to conquer or die, and the Spartans feared their laws more than the subjects of the oriental despot feared him. It may never have occurred to Rousseau that a people who gave itself laws was not free. Rousseau was a great reader of Plutarch's *Lives*, and he must have been aware that it was in this sense that the Romans became free after the expulsion of their kings. Sparta, republican Rome and Calvinist Geneva were all free cities, where 'free' means anything but 'free and easy'. This was a lesson which was not lost on eighteenth-century thinkers. What seemed especially pernicious to rising stars like Rousseau and Voltaire was the system of personal dependence which an aristocratic society necessarily implied. Rousseau's *Confessions*, for instance, are full of the humiliations which are forced on a man trying to get on in a society where getting on is impossible without aristocratic patronage. Equal dependence on the laws, rather than personal dependence on patrons, could easily seem attractive, even though those laws, as at Sparta, allowed very little of what we would call 'personal' freedom. Hume, for instance, makes a distinction between governments of men and governments of laws, and he recommends the government of Venice as a government of laws even though it was a tightly controlled merchant oligarchy. Laws were fixed, knowable and known, so that dependence on laws which fell equally on all men could seem like liberty to those who lived in systems of absolute monarchy where the king was above the law, so that '*Si veut le Roi, si veut la Loi*' (what the King wants the Law also wants).

There can be no doubt that Rousseau's concept of liberty is a 'positive' concept of liberty in the classic sense outlined by Sir Isaiah Berlin in his celebrated essay *Two Concepts of Liberty*. In that essay Berlin distinguishes between what he calls 'positive' and 'negative' liberty. Negative liberty is what we mean in ordinary speech by liberty – that is, absence of restraint: I am free to the extent that there are no external hindrances to my pursuit of my own self-chosen ends. These external hindrances can be physical or legal, moral or religious. This is an 'end of the day' kind of liberty: you look around the world and you judge yourself free to the extent that physical, legal, moral or religious obstacles prevent you from doing what you happen to want to do. This view of liberty, which we have already called 'Individualist', frankly accepts that liberty will in fact be restricted: living in a world with other men guarantees that. Law, the positively enacted laws of a state, will itself be negative in this view of things. Law will typically forbid certain forms of human behaviour (cheating, assaulting, murdering, for instance) and human beings will therefore consider themselves at liberty to do all those things which the law does not forbid. (This would also be true of other kinds of law, like the moral law: a man would believe himself to be fully entitled to do that which the moral law did not specifically forbid.) 'Positive' liberty, on the other hand, is a 'beginning of the day' kind of liberty because it would actually tell you what to do. Positive liberty consists of the pursuit of behaviour laid down by a self-chosen rational principle. It emphasises the arbitrary and empty quality of negative liberty: what good is liberty if I don't know what to do with it? Positive liberty is a form of self-coercion which sees the attainment of liberty in the terms of self-fulfilment: I wish to become the kind of person that I know I have it in myself to be. Sometimes, self-coercion, like a New Year's resolution, fails. I do not really want it to fail, so I may welcome any outside constraints which keep me to my own resolution.

Rousseau regards acts of the General Will as coming within the category of outside constraints which help me to keep my own resolutions. Negative liberty is deeply personal: others can only threaten it, and above all so does the state: it is the kind of liberty which can only be preserved by eternal vigilance. Not so positive liberty, which is more easily attainable in a group than individually, because others can help to keep one to the path which one has chosen, and if the majority keeps everybody to the path that each has chosen then it is easy to see what a free people would be in Rousseau's sense. The pursuit of freedom becomes a collective venture, something *we* do, not something *I* do. Of course, very strong-minded individuals might be able to pursue positive liberty by themselves, the kinds of self-disciplined characters who never break their own resolutions, but most of us are not like that. (It is in this sense that deeply religious people will say 'Love God and do what you will'.) We have our better and our worse selves, and our better selves need a helping hand from others to keep us on the straight and narrow path of rational liberty. And there is no contradiction in speaking of the 'straight and narrow path' of liberty, because positive liberty is not doing just what you happen to want to do; rather, it is doing what you really want to do, or doing what you would do if you really thought about it. And in this view of liberty Rousseau is remarkably forward-looking as well as looking backwards to the ancient city-states. From the time of Rousseau's *Social Contract* onwards, negative liberty was to be only one of the ways that liberty could be conceived. Once the notion of liberty was posited as a central political value, then the political debate could centre round the question of the *unit* of freedom. If an individual could be free, then so could a whole community, or a nation, or eventually a class. Things would become very complicated indeed once negative, individual liberty and positive, collective liberty came to be seen as alternatives, or even opposites. The whole modern debate about totalitarianism centres round that question: how much negative liberty has to be given up, or how far does the chance of having negative liberty have to be given up, for the achievement of collective goals?

The idea of being forced to be free will always stick in the craw of those for whom liberty must always be unremedially negative. Liberals, for instance, have always been suspicious of any doctrine of liberty which is not negative liberty, freedom *from*. Liberals do not deny that groups can have certain collective goals, but they deny that the achievement of these goals themselves constitutes liberty. Most liberals would argue that liberty has to be given up for the collective achievement of even such modest social goals as security of life and property. What liberals always insist on is calling things, as they see them, by their right names: liberty is one thing, giving up liberty to enjoy something else like security is something else. Liberals regard as very fishy indeed the tendency to call anything else liberty, because there is no end to calling other things liberty once you have begun. Liberals will not even accept the rather commonsensical suggestion that one part of the self can coerce the other. Rousseau makes a distinction between citizens and subjects. We are citizens in the active sense, when we take part in the process by which law is made, and subjects in the passive sense, when we obey the laws which we have made in our collective capacity. Why should the citizen in each of us not coerce the subject? Some commentators on Rousseau have even read into his doctrine the Platonic idea of the soul ruling the body. As an active part of the General Will my better self legislates for my worse self, that self which would act selfishly.

The main question about the General Will which has still to be answered is: Where is its content to come from? Rousseau himself confuses the issue because he sometimes talks as if the General Will is something like what the utilitarians were later to mean by the general happiness, and it is easy to see why what the general happiness is could be ascertained by counting heads. At other times, Rousseau speaks of the General Will as if it were something like Kant's 'good will', our will not when it is directed to our particular and immediate interest, but when we are asking ourselves what everybody including myself should do in the circumstances. It seems clear that Rousseau does not mean that the General Will is what a majority just happens to want, because one of the things a majority could just happen to want would be the permanent subjugation of a minority. The problem of the content of the General Will is that Rousseau will not allow any kind of pre-existing moral law to give the General Will something to go by. (Rousseau in fact suppressed a chapter on Natural Law which he included in the first draft of *The Social Contract* because he realised that the pre-existence of a transcendental moral law would limit the freedom of choice of the sovereign people when it made laws for itself.) The only other possibility is that the content of the General Will would be supplied out of what we have come to call a national culture. Here we may trace the influence of Montesquieu's *The Spirit of the Laws* on Rousseau, especially on the *Project for a Constitution for Corsica* and the *Considerations on the Government of Poland*. In these works Rousseau shows his nationalist side, playing the outside legislator who can see so far into a people's spirit that he can give them laws. Perhaps he thought that every particular people had its own particular spirit, and that that spirit ought to be embodied in its laws, that is its constitution. It would follow from this that no two peoples should have the same set of laws, and that would explain the suppression of the Natural Law chapter in *The Social Contract*: nothing ought to inhibit a free people from choosing *its* own laws.

The idea that it is a particular national culture which furnishes the content of the General Will might explain the figure of the Legislator in *The Social Contract*. Rousseau says that ideally he should be a foreigner who has no personal or family or party interest in the constitution which he helps the sovereign people to form for themselves. Perhaps Rousseau thought that the ideal person to give a people laws would be the ideal outside observer who, because he *is* an outsider, can see the main lines of a nation's culture more clearly than those who are themselves steeped in that culture (and in the way that the best books about particular countries are often written by foreigners who often notice significant things about a national culture which natives miss). Rousseau certainly admired the great, god-like law-givers like Lycurgus and Solon, and his admiration for Calvin, the founder of Rousseau's own native city's laws, is as much based on what the foreigner Calvin did for Genevan government as on what he did for its religion. Of course, if we take this view of Rousseau's *Social Contract*, then views of it like Burke's or Taine's or Talmon's will not hold water, because they want to see in *The Social Contract* a blueprint for a future society, which it cannot be if each people is to choose different laws for itself.

In *The Social Contract* Rousseau has remarkably little to say about government, as distinct from what he calls legislation, and it is important to understand the difference. Legislation is what the General Will enacts when the sovereign people meet. Meetings of the sovereign people are not a legislature in the ordinary sense of the term, because the sovereign people can only make decisions of a very general kind which affect everybody equally. A meeting of the sovereign people is much more like a constitutional convention than a parliament. Its laws are much more like constitutional principles than what we mean by 'the details of legislation'. Rousseau calls what we would call 'government' a 'delegation' from the General Will, and he is careful to distinguish between acts of the General Will and what he calls 'acts of magistracy'. What magistracy – that is, government – is to be like is largely an open question. A government of the gods would no doubt be a democracy, but the actual government of men is a different case. Perhaps the best form of government would be a virtuous aristocracy, as in the best period of the Roman republic, or even government by a single respected family. Whatever form government is to take, and Rousseau seems quite timid as a political thinker here, Rousseau is clear that its acts are not to have the same moral prestige as acts of the sovereign people, and being a delegation from the General Will, government automatically ceases to exist when the sovereign people assembles in its own right. Rousseau's sovereign people, therefore, is best conceived as a constitutional convention with the permanent right of assembly. In a well-regulated state it is safe to assume that such meetings will be infrequent, but governors are supposed to have the possibility always in mind, and this in its turn is supposed to make governors moderate and reasonable in exercising the function of rule.

THE PROBLEM OF LIBERTY REVISITED

The rather lurid things which Rousseau's enemies have said about the potentially despotic or even totalitarian thrust of his political thought still sit rather oddly with Rousseau's reputation as a romantic individualist. There is no doubt that the doctrine of the General Will is in some sense a collectivist doctrine, and this has worried Rousseau's libertarian critics ever since *The Social Contract* saw the light of day. This problem in Rousseau's political thought has led some commentators to see in *The Social Contract* not one Rousseau but two, the romantic voluptuous solitary, and the possessor of a Calvinist conscience longing for the discipline of ancient Sparta. This line of criticism is of course the ages-old method of Rousseau's enemies who go from the supposed character of the man to read the works, and then read the works to discover the character of the man. But perhaps these enemies of Rousseau were right. Perhaps there is this conflict in the man and in the political theory. It is certainly the case that there is a personal-liberty sounding strand in *The Social Contract*. Book II, Chapter IV of *The Social Contract*, entitled 'The Limits of Sovereign Power', looks promising as a defence of individual rights against the collectivity:

> But, besides the public person, we have to consider the private persons composing it, whose life and liberty are naturally independent of it. We are bound then to distinguish clearly between the respective rights of the citizens and the Sovereign, and between the duties the former have to fulfil as subjects, and the natural rights they should enjoy as men.

These natural rights that citizens enjoy as men should protect men from the state, but Rousseau adds an ominous caveat:

> Each man alienates, I admit, by the social contract, only such part of his powers, goods, and liberty as it is important for the community control; but it must also be granted that the Sovereign is sole judge of what is important.

These two quotations show that Rousseau is well aware that there is such a thing as negative liberty, freedom *from* the state, but what he gives with one hand he appears to take back with the other. At the end of that chapter Rousseau again does what is most maddening about his political theory by redefining liberty as something else, this time as equality. Equal dependence on the acts of the General Will turns out to be liberty after all.

Of course, it is perfectly possible to argue that there is nothing particularly sinister about Rousseau's assertion that in the end the state decides what rights its citizens have. As equal members of the sovereign, no man can be expected to do more than another. Sovereignty treats all men equally, but where does that leave government? Acts of government are by definition acts which treat men differently. Each executive act implies that some men do one thing and others another, even if it is only that some command and others obey. If each man as subject were to claim the same rights as he had as citizen, as equal member of the sovereign, then government itself would be literally impossible because the only acts of government which were legitimate would be those of the same kind of generality as acts of the General Will and would become indistinguishable from them. All that Rousseau's assertion that we cannot have rights against the state may mean is that as subjects we have no right to refuse obedience to acts of magistracy as delegated acts of the General Will, with the safeguard that when the sovereign people assembles, all magistracy is dissolved. Rights against government are, for Rousseau, in the strictest sense impossible. His is one of those brilliantly paradoxical arguments: because men are equal as members of the sovereign, they can have no rights against government. Men do have rights, but only to be treated as equal members of the sovereign.

THE THEME OF POLITICAL CORRUPTION

When looking at the forms which actual states take, Rousseau takes a very long view indeed, or, to put it another way, he can talk of Athens and Sparta as if they were yesterday. It may be that Rousseau saw the whole history of politics since Sparta as the history of the degeneration of the General Will either into some kind of 'will of all', or into a fragmented chaos of particular wills. Rousseau goes against the grain of enlightened political thinking in France by denying that England is free, because, being governed by representatives chosen only once every seven years, the will of the people is effectively frustrated because their representatives in Parliament become prey to the corruption of executive patronage. France is an even worse case. Absolute monarchy, based as it is on force, is by its very nature lawless. French aristocracy, unlike its ancient counterpart, enjoys its privileges individually, not collectively. Each aristocrat enjoys seigneurial privileges, particular wills on which other individual wills are dependent. Contrast ancient aristocracy, government by the best where the best are few, which ruled out of a sense of duty and whose reward was the fame which came from rendering the state some service. The French aristocracy is feudal in the worst sense of the term. Aristocracy is a privileged, legally recognised corporation, virtually a state within the state. A society divided into different orders of men is not even a class society, but is something much worse. Each order hides behind its own legal identity, so that a state divided into estates cannot be a state with a General Will at all. Its institutions seem to be specifically designed to prevent any sense of a General Will ever emerging.

Of course, with the General Will there is always the problem of size. Rousseau's suspicion of social and moral sophistication always leads him to prefer the life of simpler, agricultural societies over the more complex life of towns. His is a theory of Sparta *versus* Athens, rural simplicity against urban sophistication. On this Rousseau can become lyrical:

> Men who are upright and simple are difficult to deceive because of their simplicity; lures and ingenious pretexts fail to impose upon them, and they are not even subtle enough to be dupes. When, among the happiest people in the world, bands of peasants are seen regulating affairs of State under an oak, and always acting wisely, can we help scorning the ingenious methods of other nations, which make themselves illustrious and wretched with so much art and mystery?

We find Rousseau writing in the same vein in *Emile*:

> Men were not designed to live in ant-heaps . . . The closer you pack them the more they spoil . . . Towns are the sink of the human species.

The course of political corruption in large societies is easy to plot. When numbers increase sovereignty declines because the amount of sovereignty each man exercises is the sum of one over the number of men living in that society. This is not as naively arithmetical as it sounds. What Rousseau is pointing to is the obvious fact that sovereignty matters less to the individuals who exercise it the more it is diluted. As the number of the citizens becomes greater, so political vigilance decreases, and it is this which enables governments to usurp the people's sovereignty. The exercise of sovereign liberty comes to mean less as men seek their satisfaction elsewhere – in the pursuit of wealth, for instance, or in the 'progress' of the arts and sciences, or in any other form of privatised existence. What came to be called 'progress' in the Enlightenment is no more than losing sight of the simple verities. That gilded Parisian society, where the *philosophes* shone so brilliantly and which Rousseau believed rejected him, should take a long hard look at itself and then it would realise how far it had gone down the road of moral corruption.

The question then arises as to what people is capable of receiving laws in Rousseau's sense. Not, surely, one of those large, ant-heap states which seem to abound in the modern world. Perhaps only those societies like Corsica, which are backward by the standards of Enlightenment, could ever produce anything like a General Will under the guidance of a wise Legislator; or Poland, which has managed to keep its sense of national identity through all its political vicissitudes. Rousseau is hard to pin down here, but he seems to be saying that some peoples have gone down the road of moral corruption so far that they have actually come to enjoy living in the societies they do in fact live in. Men fit to be part of a sovereign people again are really people of a very special type. They may not know why, but their consciences nag away at them because of the divided life they live in their own sophisticated societies, their sense of self-interest pushing them in one direction and their sense of justice pulling them in another. Men like these may not even know what the content of the moral law is that they should follow, but their sense of unease does show that they have not been so corrupted that they have forgotten that there is a difference between right and wrong. Anyone doing well out of a society is unlikely to be troubled by this unease. Rousseau's political thought is doubly radical. It comes close to writing off the rich and well-born, as well as writing off all those who have managed to still the voice of their consciences inside themselves. That can only leave those who really feel the pinch of what living in a society means.

ROUSSEAU AND DEMOCRACY

There is plainly some kind of democratic thrust in Rousseau's political thought, though whether it is the thrust of totalitarian democracy that Talmon would have us believe is another question. What is democratic about Rousseau's *Social Contract* is that massive consent is required before a state can be made legitimate. The social contract being at some time in the future (though it is possible that some ancient states were effectively legitimised in this way), it follows that all existing states are illegitimate. But the legitimacy of a political order, and how that political order actually functions in its daily practice, are two very different kinds of concern. The modern democratic state partly legitimises itself through periodic elections which are the palest of all the pale reflections of Rousseau's General Will, but it also partly legitimises itself by doing its duty by its citizens by providing them equally with those services which make the idea of citizenship worthwhile. Where Rousseau really does look to the future is in his recognition that the democratically legitimised state is the state which it is most difficult to deny legitimacy to. The history of political thought can be seen as the history of different legitimising arguments for the state, and it may be that the democratic argument for legitimacy is the most powerful of all. Who, it might be asked, has the right to oppose what all have agreed to? Of course, this argument only applies to the state *in general*, and it has very little to say about *government* and nothing at all to say about the day-to-day running of government. Early democratic theory in modern Europe hardly distinguished between democratic legitimacy and democratic government, and after the American Revolution almost everybody regarded electoral representation as the buckle which fastened democratic legitimacy to democratic government. However, Rousseau himself plainly regards representation as a sham. It can't really be *me* that my representative represents. At best, it can only be his idea of me that he represents, and, much more likely, his own interest will interpose itself between him and those whom he only appears to represent. Ancient democracies never had this problem because, being small, the sovereign people could represent itself. It is only in modern democracies that the *form* of government is an issue, and Rousseau leaves the question of what kind of government could be a delegation from the General Will dangerously vague. We do know that it is unnecessary for the General Will to speak and decide frequently, meetings of the sovereign people being much more like a constitutional convention than a legislature, and we do know that it may decide anything it likes about anything. In principle at least, nothing is outside the legitimate concern of the sovereign people as legislators. What Rousseau leaves out of the account is the possibility that the General Will could be manipulated by government. Rousseau tends to take a very passive view of government, assuming with the ancients that a government dependent on the General Will of its citizens will not be stupid enough to do anything detrimental to the interests of the whole because, the whole once assembled, government as a delegated power from the whole will cease to exist, and those who exercised executive authority on the people's behalf will return to the condition of private citizens.

But a government acting as a delegation from the General Will in a large democratic republic would be in a very different position. Granted that constitutional conventions cannot meet very often, and granted that there would have to be meetings of delegates, and granted Rousseau's reservations about delegates following an interest of their own, and granted Rousseau's suspicion that government can always corrupt delegates through patronage, then it is hard to see what Rousseau's scheme of things has to offer modern states, and very easy to see how Rousseau's own political theory could be used by a ruthless governing elite to manipulate 'public opinion' to agree, or at least not to disagree, with anything. That is the sense in which Talmon regards Rousseau as a totalitarian democrat: a manipulated General Will could be used to justify anything. One can only repeat that such a manipulation of the idea of the General Will is about as far from the original spirit of Rousseau as it is possible to be. Of course, it is possible that Rousseau himself is the cause of all the trouble. For all his insistence that the state of the social contract lies in the future, Rousseau is really extremely backward-looking as a political thinker. Ancient Sparta haunts everything he has to say about politics, and it may be that, in raising hopes for the future of European states, he raises them only to be dashed. Rousseau may not be so much mistaken as dangerous.

ROUSSEAU COMPARED WITH HOBBES AND LOCKE AS A SOCIAL CONTRACT THEORIST

Rousseau is obviously a very different kind of social contract theorist from Hobbes and Locke. Despite his timidity about forms of government, there are revolutionary implications in Rousseau's political theory which are notoriously absent from Hobbes and only faintly traceable in Locke. What these revolutionary implications are is often hard to pin down, but all of Rousseau's commentators, for and against, seem to agree that there is something dangerous about Rousseau. Perhaps the dangerous aspects of Rousseau's political thought have very little to do with the formal political theory as it is set out in the *Discourse on the Origins of Inequality* and in *The Social Contract*, and have more to do with the kinds of assumptions about man and society which make works like these possible. The key is that Rousseau does not find it necessary to use the theoretical device of the social contract to explain how men got themselves out of the State of Nature and into civil society in the first place. Right at the beginning of this section on the social contract it was pointed out that one of the explanations for the existence of a political theory like Hobbes's is an absolute conviction about the fragility of ordinary social living. Take away the Sovereign as law-giver and law-enforcer and the result will be a return to a law-of-the-jungle-like State of Nature. Locke is not so sure. Wishing to restrict the scope, if not the power, of government, Locke allows that the State of Nature may be more sociable than Hobbes would have us believe, but his conviction that men would always choose to set up government, albeit government on terms, still shows a certain reluctance to believe fully in the natural sociability of man. Locke's message seems to be the message of the English Revolution of 1688: a society can survive the loss of its sovereign, but it is best not to wait too long before finding another sovereign, because life without a sovereign is risky. With Rousseau the whole position about natural sociability changes completely. Human societies are so tough that they can themselves be jungles and still not fall apart.

It is Rousseau's idea that societies are already divided against themselves while still standing which makes the state of the social contract an attractive proposition. Rousseau does not in fact offer any real explanation of what makes this possible. He simply accepts it as an accomplished fact, but it is this accomplished fact which makes revolution possible. The standard argument against revolution, and especially social revolution, is that once you begin to change anything important, everything changes and the social and political orders degenerate into some kind of primal chaos. Conservative thinkers usually concentrate on how complex and minutely interrelated societies are, because they wish us to think that, because everything is connected to everything else, once you change one aspect of a society drastically you will begin to unravel the whole fabric of that society. (Burke is a notable example of this kind of conservative.) Anybody who thinks like that would be crazy to have anything to do with revolution, and would only change anything out of dire necessity. But if the social fabric of unreconstructed societies is much tougher than their conservative defenders would have us believe, then it follows that revolutionary action is not necessarily a prelude to anarchy. It is this underlying sense of social stability which makes revolution both a feasible and, in the opinion of revolutionaries, a necessary option. A contrast with medieval millenarianism may make this point clearer. Medieval millenarians looked forward to a time when Christ and the saints would return to earth to rule for a thousand years after they had defeated the ungodly in a great battle, Armageddon, which would not leave many people alive because the legions of the ungodly were so numerous. Implicit in this was a sociology of the damned in which the damned are in the vast majority. Therefore an ameliorated world can only be created at the cost of most of that world's destruction. This is not revolutionary in the modern sense at all. No revolutionary, except perhaps the most extreme, wants to destroy most of the world in order to recreate it.

The idea of the essential toughness of the social world adds a new dimension to the idea of political revolution. If the social world is as tough as modern social theory says that it is, then something equally tough, the modern state, is required to remodel that social world. The difference between pre-modern revolutions and modern revolutions is the difference between the American and the French Revolutions. In the American Revolution, the social revolution had already happened and the political revolution merely ratified it. By 1776, there already existed in America a political class socially and politically advanced enough to make a revolution when its own position appeared to be threatened by the encroachment on their rights by the government of George III. The last thing the American revolutionaries wanted in 1776 was to remodel society through the government which it created. The proof of this is that when the American Revolution threatened to take on a social dimension that same political class made and caused to be ratified in 1789 a new Constitution which was specifically designed to make the world safe for existing property relations. Contrast the French Revolution in its radical, Jacobin phase, when state power began to be used to remodel social institutions. That process is at least implicit in Rousseauism. How else could an entrenched social order be remodelled except by the use of the Terror?

When Rousseau's influence on the French Revolution has been discussed there has been a tendency on the part of Rousseau's defenders to go in for the 'of course Rousseau would have been horrified by what the Jacobins did in his name' apology for their hero, but it is difficult to see what the justification for that apology is. Either Rousseau meant to be taken seriously as a political thinker or he did not. If he did, then his is a recipe for the remodelling of both social and political institutions, and that is certainly how his revolutionary admirers read him, and that is certainly how critics hostile to the French Revolution read him in the nineteenth and twentieth centuries. It won't do to keep saying that Rousseau has been misunderstood, that all he really longed for was a Sparta of the imagination, or that his political thought could only be put into action in very small communities, because alongside Corsica there is Poland. Nor is it even necessary to argue that the Jacobins followed Rousseau's political theory word for word, because Rousseau was only the greatest of a whole host of critics of the *ancien régime*, and Rousseau-like ideas could have come from any number of other sources. Nevertheless, if we are right that what makes the French Revolution the first of the modern revolutions is that it was made in the name of an ideology, then Burke was right to see the main inspiration for that ideology in the author of the *Discourse on the Origins of Inequality* and *The Social Contract*.

NOTES ON SOURCES

It has so often been claimed that Rousseau's life is the 'text', that it is perhaps wise to begin the study of Rousseau with his *Confessions*. The political works begin with *The Discourse on the Origins of Inequality* and *The Social Contract*. All three exist in several English editions (though G.D.H. Cole's translation of *The Social Contract* famously mistranslates the resounding 'Man *was* born free and everywhere he is in chains', as 'Man *is* born free . . . ', which is a different thing altogether). Rousseau has found many commentators, some best described as enemies and some as dubious allies. J. McDonald, *Rousseau and the French Revolution* (1965), is a good introduction to this controversial connection, and A. Cobban's *Rousseau and the Modern State* (1961), can still hold up its head. J.N. Shklar, *Men and Citizens: A Study of Rousseau's Social Theory* (1969), is a brilliant re-reading of Rousseau. Rousseau, *Political Writings* (2 vols, ed. Vaughan, 1962), is useful. Serious students of Rousseau will have to tackle the formidable *Oeuvres complètes* in the Pléiade edition.

Part V

ENLIGHTENMENT AND THE DEVELOPMENT OF THE MODERN STATE

14

THE MODERNITY OF THE MODERN STATE

The modern state emerged from the feudal order. Beyond that nothing is certain. There is no agreement about how it happened or when it happened beyond saying that it happened at different times in different places. Serious thinkers were still debating well on into the twentieth century whether the state of the tsars had been a modern state or whether it had been some kind of left-over, half-oriental despotism got up in Prussian uniform. Happily, the case of the history of political thought is different, because there things often happen with greater clarity than they happen in the real world of politics. It is often the case that a particular political development in a particular place will catch a thinker's eye, and he will see in it the wave of the future. Changes in ideas do signal shifts of political practice, and the world of political practice is so varied at any particular time that it might well be a matter of luck if a thinker does spot in the present what the future is going to be like. The chances are that, if that thinker is at all historically minded, he will then look around for ancient precedents so as not to make what he has got to say too startling, and therefore inaccessible, to the audience he thinks he is addressing. This is certainly true in Machiavelli's case. We found him searching out ancient precedents for almost everything he had to say about the state, but what he had to say was equally certainly very new in the context in which he said it.

Seen from the perspective of contemporary states, medieval forms of rule look essentially amateurish and messy. Rule by kings, lords, bishops, priests and town oligarchies was a competition for rights of jurisdiction over the lower orders, and a member of those lower orders could be forgiven for not knowing who his real ruler was. Lords had rights in the labour of serfs and also rights of jurisdiction through manorial courts. The Church decided whom they might marry and how and to whom they could leave their property. The Church had rights of taxation and so did the lord if the labour services of serfs were commuted to a money payment. Different courts could try them for different offences, lay and ecclesiastical, and the king might call upon everybody's services in times of national emergency like foreign invasion. In feudal societies rights of jurisdiction were jealously defended. The Church kept secular authority out of its own lands if it could; towns governed by their own charters resisted kings, and part of being a king consisted of being beastly to barons. To speak of a state in these circumstances, let alone a centralised state, is absurd. The only thing in societies like these which remotely resembled ancient or modern states was monarchy, but the king was just a greater lord among great lords who owed him fealty, certain military services, and the duty to give advice if asked. The king was to his own tenants what other great lords were to theirs. The only time the realm was a single unit was in time of war. Then every subject and every knight had a specific duty to defend the realm, but even this duty was limited to a period of days, and armies often had to be paid to stay together when the period of agreed conscription was over.

Every medieval society was a patchwork of different forms of rule. It was common to deny jurisdiction to get oneself out of trouble. Benefit of clergy was the most obvious example: clerks in holy orders would be tried by other clerks who would understand. Kings competed for jurisdiction like every other power-wielder, and made monarchy hereditary where they could. The state, meaning the state of the realm, was really family business, though other estates of the realm had a legitimate interest in it. Kings were responsible to the Church for helping to maintain true religion, to lords and people for maintaining their rights and privileges, and to God for keeping the realm safe and passing it on unencumbered to their posterity. In these circumstances, rule, the equivalent of the state function, could not be anything but amateurish and unspecialised. Lots of different orders of men took part in the business of ruling and being ruled, and there could be no pretence that rule was somehow neutral while it was the business of a particular family, and while the fortunes of the realm were effectively family fortunes. Just as each king was supposed to bequeath an unchanged realm to his eldest son, so at every rung in the hierarchy sons were supposed to inherit their fathers' rights and duties.

Hence what might be called the Gulliver effect. Each man was tied down by any number of ties, no one of which was enough to keep him in his place, but the effect of them all taken together kept him in his place well enough. And it is important to remember that a man would be unlikely to distinguish between different kinds of tie. What the priest told him to do would be unlikely to appear to be different in kind from what his feudal superior told him to do, and his lord's economic function would not appear very different from his function as legal or military superior. When his lord presided over a manorial court, or raised his tenantry in time of war, or in a dispute with a neighbouring lord, it would not be very obvious to a medieval serf that different functions were being exercised. Lords would simply appear to be the lords of the earth. That is why medieval peasant revolts always seem to have a bull-in-a-china-shop quality to them. Peasants in revolt have always appeared to be indiscriminate. They burn manorial records (the government files of their day); they attack the ecclesiastical hierarchy; they profane the symbols of authority wherever they find them; they attack moneylenders, and so on. Peasant revolts in contemporary and later historians' accounts of them seem to have all the characteristics of irrational outbursts, but if the Gulliver image of medieval rule is the right one, then what revolting peasants did had a kind of sense. What was the good of attacking one of Gulliver's ties if the others remained in place? Demands could not be programmatic; they could not be economic, or political, or religious, when men could hardly be expected to distinguish between the different kinds of tie which kept them in their places. Disturbing one tie meant disturbing all the rest; in these circumstances a revolt was all, or it was nothing.

Another way of putting that would be to say that all pre-modern popular revolts were bound to fail because there was no public place which could be taken over, either symbolically or actually, no Bastille or Winter Palace. (Medieval kings were not stupid and moved about their realms from palace to palace.) In societies with widely diffused centres of authority and with no very exact borders, it might be difficult to decide when a revolt *had* succeeded. That is why in continental European countries in the Middle Ages, leaders of popular revolts often claimed to be the *real* emperor or the *real* pope. Claims to universal monarchy were made because the counter-claims on them were of such a universal kind that rebels had to make universal claims in return. So many different kinds of authority made their claims to jurisdiction that only imperial or papal counter-claims of vast pretension could override them.

Two other things made medieval societies remarkably resilient in the face of popular revolts: the ecclesiastical poverty of the Church and the monopoly of honourable arms by the knightly class. This meant that the people could not appear as a *populus* with plebeian demands in the ancient sense. The class wars of ancient republics usually took the same form. The people, victorious in war, came home to demand a redistribution of goods, usually the cultivated land. This they claimed in the name of their poverty and in the name of the arms in their hands. They had saved the republic and they should reap the benefits. Armed valiant poverty has a very strong moral claim, and had been a worry to conservative thinkers ever since Plato's account in the *Republic* of how oligarchy changes into democracy. The demand for an agrarian law was also the theme of the history of the Roman republic up to the time of the great civil wars. (There was still a hint of this in the victorious armies of 1918 and 1945.) In the medieval period, the class of knights monopolised honourable violence and the priests and monks monopolised the moral claims of poverty. Any popular violence was then by definition the violence of the insolent rabble, and any attack on the worldliness of Christ's Church must at best be delusion and at worst heresy. This left the real poor morally and physically naked, and it is a wonder that there were popular revolts at all, let alone so many.

The modern state came out of the feudal order. Of course it is a long story, but we can trace its progress from about 1500 to about 1800 in the works of Machiavelli, Bodin, Hobbes and Adam Smith.

In Machiavelli there is no trace of the idea that the political order is part of the god-given order of things. Machiavelli thinks that a state is a radically created order, not a differentiated social whole entrusted to and presided over by a king. The Machiavellian prince is a creator, an artist who designs and builds the state which he is to govern, and the artistic gift is not given to all men. A king of ordinary abilities who is not too lazy to deal with problems as they arise and who has no spectacular vices might do very well in keeping up his state in a hereditary realm whose subjects have become accustomed to being ruled by their princely family, but the creation of new kingdoms is the task of the specially gifted. There is nothing feudal about Machiavelli's account of the princely state, no mediating institutions between prince and people. Rivals in the feudal sense are simply killed off, for there must be no notable figures around which resistance to a new prince might consolidate itself. The prince gathers up all the reins of power into his own hands, and Machiavelli has lots of advice for princes who want to keep power out of the hands of others. Authority in Machiavelli's scheme of things must have a spatial as well as a personal centre. Princely government represents the victory of the city over the countryside. A prudent prince would do well to build solid walls round his capital, and to build a solid citadel for himself within the walls. There is to be none of the local self-government which is a characteristic of feudal societies. All decisions are to be the prince's decisions, and they have to be the right decisions, otherwise the prince might lose his state, because what can be won can always be lost again. What this means in the modern idiom is that policy has to be right, and that includes foreign policy. War is the trade of princes with armies of their own making, not the affair of a knightly class. Mercenaries are one possibility, but a prince who knows his business would do well to imitate the ancient Romans and go to war with his own citizen militia who feel that the prince is their prince and the state their state. There is no question of the prince being *primus inter pares* like a medieval king effectively having to negotiate with the mightier of his subjects. The true prince *commands*, and the subjects of a successful prince must come to feel that the prince's glory is their glory.

For all the rigour of Machiavelli's advice to princes, there is still something *ad hoc* about his political theory, which is really a tissue of expedients for princes to use in emergencies. Princely life for Machiavelli is a series of such emergencies. The last thing a prince should do is to dream of retiring to a little kingdom by the sea. Machiavelli does in fact admire the great law-givers as well as the great improvisers, but he talks of the great law-givers as if they were the successful devisers of expedients which lasted. The rules of necessity do not operate at those stages of history in which there is such great need for law-givers. Law-givers, like Moses or Lycurgus, are the founders of peoples which survive for centuries as viable political units, but Machiavelli can give no coherent set of reasons why such law-givers should appear, beyond saying that in the case of Moses we can see the hand of God. Law for Machiavelli is only one of the ways, though the best way, that a people should be made to feel that it is being ruled, but, the reiteration of ancient pieties apart, it is obvious that for Machiavelli law is only one arm in the armouries of princes, and it is certainly not the means by which a prince in a newly acquired state should begin to make his new people feel the force of his rule. When Machiavelli speaks of law-giving, what he really means is not legislation, where legislation means generally accepted laws according to some generally recognised standard, but the whipping-in of a lawless people, as with the Roman people under Romulus and Numa Pompilius.

Yet what makes Machiavelli modern, or what makes Machiavelli's political thought speak to a world which is no longer medieval, is his recognition that a particular kind of people, living at a particular time and subject to particular circumstances, needs a particular form of rule. (This was, of course, a truth well-known to the ancients.) Machiavelli's political thought is cast in generalisations about the universal character of human nature, but it does not take much of an effort of hindsight to see that princely government is being offered as the proper form of government for Renaissance men who are particularly hard to rule. The men that Machiavelli's prince has to confront are self-assertive, egotistical and opportunist, but they also have the obverse qualities of diffidence, gullibility and indolence. They are recognisably the democratic characters of Plato's *Republic*, notoriously fickle and at the same time self-confident. Such men may have a natural longing for democratic, that is republican, government; they are naturally citizens rather than subjects, but when men like these get themselves into a political mess, then princely government is the only answer. Despite his admiration for the ancient law-givers, Machiavelli in fact thinks that law and princely force are alternatives in the world in which he thinks he is living.

Something like that perception that the form of government must fit the circumstances of the day informs Bodin's *Six Books on the Republic* (1576), though the theoretical path which Bodin does in fact follow almost seems designed to obscure what is his most important principle. Bodin thinks he is the follower of Aristotle, but if he is, he is the follower of the wrong Aristotle, the Aristotle who offers a picture of the world as a series of formal definitions. Bodin is probably the first important political thinker to offer what is recognisably a modern theory of sovereignty, and in essence that theory is very simple: a well-ordered state needs an absolute and legitimate sovereign centre. Bodin's motives for saying that are much more intelligible than his arguments. We can see that the France of the sixteenth-century civil wars, those wars being based on differences of religious opinion, needed a strengthening of the monarchy if France was to survive as a political community. By harking back to Aristotelian precedents, Bodin took the theory of sovereignty out of Divine Right theology and tied it to a view of what a political community needed in its own best interest. Bodin is impeccably classical in his recognition that states are typically destroyed by faction, and the fact that these factions are religious factions does not alter this truth at all. (And it is in this sense that the rider on Machiavelli's political thought, that he doesn't understand the part that religion is going to play in the politics of the Reformation, is misplaced. Factions are factions, no matter how they arise.) Bodin's defence of sovereignty is really a defence of rule against faction. He accepts the division of Christendom's individual kingdoms into Protestant and Catholic as an accomplished fact. The problem is then how it can ever be that a realm divided into contending religious factions, each of which would coerce the other if it could, could possibly live at peace with itself and prosper.

Unfortunately for us, Bodin does not approach his subject in this 'modern' way. He might have, but he didn't. Instead, he approached politics from what he thought was a correctly generalised Aristotelian perspective. Far from confining himself to the task in hand, which was to explain how sixteenth-century France could be made to stick together, his *Republic* was meant to be an account of how any state could be given a solid basis. What we would now call political stability had to be approached from ancient and very generalised categories, and, Aristotle-like, Bodin decided that the two central categories of political theorising were the family and the state. The family, according to Bodin, was the natural community, and like Aristotle he included in the family both servants (though in Bodin's day they were not slaves) and private property. Bodin's idea of the family was Roman rather than Greek, since he believed that the state's authority stops at the threshold of the household. The family was a *res publica* in miniature, but there were important differences between the family and the state. As in ancient Rome, heads of families became citizens as soon as they stepped outside their own front doors. What made them citizens was that they all recognised the same sovereign, monarchical authority. No doubt the fact that private property inheres in the family and is inviolable puts a kind of limit on sovereignty, but property apart, the sovereign is supreme in the public realm, and the sovereign typically commands through law.

Bodin has in mind here the Aristotelian classification of states into lawful and unlawful. The tyrant rules through force in his own interest only, while the king rules through law in the interests of all. Yet behind this formal distinction between tyranny and kinship lies a very firm grasp of the condition of a kingdom which has yet to free itself from medieval and feudal notions of what law is. It was mentioned above that medieval societies were complex patchworks of competing jurisdictions. It may have been the case that law-givers in medieval societies did not think that they could really *make* law, only that they could declare it, but that could not make a difference to anyone who was trying to make sense in an Aristotelian way of the meaning of law. What law could make sense in a patchwork of different legal systems except the supreme law of a sovereign? Of course, law is not the only bond which can bind men together. Bodin is enough of an Aristotelian to realise what common sense also dictates, that language, culture, religion and locally made law can create human bonds, and he calls the naturally arising community of this kind a *cité* to distinguish it from the republic which we call a state. For all his Aristotelianism, Bodin recognises that the ancient city-state cannot be identified with the sixteenth-century realm of France. That is why the state's law must be supreme over other potentially competing systems of law, whether law means manners, morals, customs, or the law which defines minority or local privilege.

Bodin's commentators have often said that there is a contradiction between his avowed Aristotelianism and the fact that he cannot find an Aristotelian 'end' for a realm of millions of subjects, but this is just another example of the notorious difficulty of fitting ancient categories to modern problems. Rather, we should say that Bodin's Aristotelianism, quaint though it can seem, points to the real truth that for political stability to exist there needs to be some notion of the supreme community of which other naturally arising communities are the vital but subordinate parts. Bodin defines sovereignty as the 'supreme power over citizens and subjects, unrestrained by law', and by 'supreme' he means something very like the modern idea of sovereignty. Sovereignty is perpetual; it can only be delegated to magistrates as the absolute sovereignty that it is; it is unrestrained by law because sovereignty is itself the source of supreme law; the sovereign cannot bind himself or his successors; the sovereign has the power of making war and peace, appointing ministers, acting as a court of last resort, granting dispensations, coining money and taxing. Sovereignty is absolute and undivided. All surviving law-bound corporations – religious bodies, municipalities, commercial companies and guilds – owe their rights and privileges to the sovereign. It follows, therefore, that estates and parliaments exist only to advise the sovereign, and it also follows that the sovereign cannot be bound to take their advice.

Bodin's assertion, and it is only an assertion, that sovereignty really is sovereign, does not sit easily with his constitutionalism, which makes him want to preserve an ancient constitution of the realm which the king may not alter. Perhaps too much has been made of this contradiction. It is a very recent version of constitutionalism which has insisted that if a constitution is at the mercy of a sovereign then it is not really a constitution at all. In Bodin's day, a constitution meant that in *this* realm we have a particular way of doing things, and that customs and institutions which do not compete directly with royal power ought to be allowed to function as they always have. Only when such institutions come into conflict with the sovereign centre must there be adjudication in favour of the centre. It won't do to say that there are two sovereigns in Bodin's scheme of things: the family and the king. Why should they by rivals? An imprudent king might be tempted to interfere with family life, but this could mean nothing more than the assertion of the right to arbitrary taxation, and any king who was not altogether a fool would be bound to realise that arbitrary taxation without the consent of estates or parliaments was a trouble-making, and therefore politically destabilising, way to raise a revenue. This did not prevent the idea that absolutism was really slavery from lasting a very long time. It became a commonplace of British 'vulgar Whiggism' to say that, because the French king was absolute, no man's property was safe. Of course, that was bound to be true in some kind of straightforward sense, because the king was more powerful than anybody else and so anybody who became a special target for his spite was bound to be in trouble, but that would be true in any state which had a sovereign centre. As Bodin tellingly points out, the most absolute monarchy can rule popularly by delegating its authority widely, while the most popular democracy can, as in the ancient world, act despotically.

It has become fashionable to call Bodin's political thought inadequate or muddled, and it is easy to see why. His Aristotelianism led him into paths which were simply definitional. Sovereignty in his sense of the absolute rule of the law of an unlimited sovereign authority was a definition suspended over a state. Perhaps it existed or perhaps it did not, which vitiated his own 'historical' method, which was an attempt to show why it was the case that a well-ordered state could not continue to exist without sovereignty as he conceived it. Bodin was never very clear about the differences between the various systems of laws under which men live, and he had a backward-looking tendency to derive all systems of law from Natural Law; he was also unreflective about what Natural Law actually was. Perhaps he thought, like many another political thinker, that Natural Law was just obvious, and that it was obvious that kings would feel themselves bound by God's Law in the same way that everybody else was supposed to feel bound by it. Natural Law for Bodin is really a fall-back position, a formal bow in the direction of a body of thought which was becoming increasingly incompetent at explaining exactly why the government of a realm should be as it was. Above all, Bodin was anti-feudal where competing jurisdictions got in the way of the exercise of sovereignty. Far from thinking that the king's position was at the head of a hierarchy whose justification was the hierarchy itself, Bodin looked at the matter from the top down, and attempted to show that all subordinate authorities derived from the supreme sovereign.

It is in this sense that Hobbes on sovereignty can be considered as the successor to Bodin. That Bodin describes the guts of the modern state there can be no doubt, but whether he has a theory of the sovereign state is another matter. Bodin's theory of sovereignty is a theory waiting for an equivalent view of man and an equivalent sociology. As we noted above, the motives for Bodin's theory of sovereignty are clear enough, but the arguments are merely formal. What Hobbes did was to root Bodin's definition of sovereignty in arguments which owed nothing to Aristotle and everything to a well-worked-out view of man and society. Hobbes's Sovereign, like Bodin's, speaks to his subjects authoritiatively through law as command, but Hobbes talks as if it really were true that the only law which exists in a modern realm is sovereign-made law. Bodin had hoped that the sovereign's law would find a way of living with other types of law; sovereign-made law for Bodin was supreme, but that supremacy did not annihilate other kinds of law, including constitutional law. Hobbes's *Leviathan* speaks to a particular political problem, the English Civil War, but there is nothing makeshift about its construction. Significantly, *Leviathan* begins with a whole section 'Of Man', spelling out systematically why it is that particular kinds of men need a particular kind of state if they are to live together at all and to achieve any of the purposes which their nature prods them into. Every political theory implies a sociology, though you sometimes have to dig for it. Fortunately, you don't have to dig very deep in Hobbes. His social model is easily recognisable as an atomistic, market model of human relationships between ambitious but fearful men. Men like that would never live together at all were it not for the existence of an all-powerful Sovereign who makes and enforces law.

What is remarkable about Hobbes's account of the state in *Leviathan* is that the political order is natural only in a very extended sense because on Hobbes's account of the matter men would be very reluctant to give another power over themselves. The state is an artificial creation which is not *derivable* from human nature but which is *made necessary* by human nature. The political order is a radically created order, and Hobbes thinks that even if we could go back to the beginning, rational men would create absolute sovereignty because their own self-knowledge would prompt them to it. There is something miraculous about the existence of the Hobbesian state, but it is not miraculous in the sense of supernatural. There is nothing mysterious about Hobbes's political theory at all. It has no place for sentimental loyalty to a dynasty or for the reverence due to the Lord's anointed. The Sovereign may command loyalty and he may command obedience to himself as the Lord's anointed, but loyalty and reverence are the result of command, and not the other way round. Hobbes is careful to say that what reason dictates God also commands, but it is clear that unaided reason could work out the principles of constructing an absolute state whether God commanded it or not.

It is sometimes said that Hobbes's sociology and his political theory do not go well together because competitive, striving men intent on increasing their market value would be unlikely to put up with the absolute state which Hobbes constructs for them. Hobbes seems to be inviting men to enrich themselves but not to expect a share of the human good which we call political power. The plausibility of this critique of Hobbes is increased when we remember how innately aggressive Hobbes thinks men are. In the State of Nature, that imagined state of men without government, diffident men realise that their only hope of safety would lie in their being able to dominate all other men. Of course, they cannot do that in the State of Nature, because men are roughly and naturally equal, and it is this perception which Hobbes thinks would induce rational men to give to one man, the Sovereign, that power over others which all men would have, but recognise that only one man can have. Hobbesian men do not change their nature when they come into Civil Society, and so it is reasonable to assume that they will be jealous of their Sovereign because he is the one man who got what all the others would have had if they could. (Hobbes just assumes that any man, if chosen to be Sovereign, would grab at the sword with both hands.) A rising bourgeoisie, it is said, would want that share of the sovereignty which they would feel their wealth would entitle them to. However, this is to misunderstand the full force of the Hobbesian theory of sovereignty. The Sovereign does not necessarily have to be one man. It could be a body of men, an aristocracy or even a democracy. What is startling about the Hobbesian theory of sovereignty is that its nature as sovereignty does not alter with the manner of its exercise. A state could be the purest democracy but its sovereignty would still be absolute sovereignty.

The anti-feudal thrust of Hobbes's argument is unmistakable. Sovereignty, being indivisible, does not have to be shared with hereditary estates or parliaments. We some-times forget just how much feudal societies were riddled with ideas and practices of representation, and how much modern theories and practices of representation derive from them. From the Hobbesian point of view, political representation as a form of power-sharing could easily seem to be some kind of feudal remnant getting in the way of the exercise of pure sovereignty. When feudal ideas of representation were converted in the modern world into ideas of democratic representation, the political legitimacy they produced in its turn produced an idea of sovereignty which nobody could challenge because each has a part, however remote, in that sovereignty's exercise. Hobbes and Rousseau may be worlds apart about everything else, but they are in close agreement about what sovereignty means. The main difference between Hobbes and Rousseau as theorists of the state becoming modern is that Rousseau's version of the state requires it to be the vehicle of a collective moral enterprise. Hobbes sees the state as the expression of civil, not social, association. Men's relations with each other are juridically conceived, and the bond of law is neutral. Treat all other men as you would have them treat you and you will not fall foul of the law. The end of obedience to the Sovereign is social peace, which makes it possible for men to pursue their own self-chosen ends within a framework of law. Consideration of the end for which law as the Sovereign's command exists is not enough to make men obey, for the very simple reason that each man would think that it was in his own best interest for everybody else to obey except himself. Of course, men want their neighbours to be law-abiding, but that does not necessarily provide each man with a motive to be law-abiding himself. Each man's motive for obedience according to Hobbes is fear of the Sovereign, and fear of the Sovereign is directly related to the Sovereign's efficiency in seeking out and punishing malefactors. Nothing must get in the way of that, no local immunity or privilege, and not even the privilege of rank.

It is easy to see how difficult it would be for Hobbesian men to come together for any common social purpose if they cannot even be induced to obey the law except by fear of punishment. Social peace is no doubt a 'good' end, but our natures are so constituted that only the absolute Sovereign can guarantee it, and then only if he is efficient. The social peace is fragile because we are like we are, and it is really a miracle of human contrivance that there is any social peace at all. We noted above that a change takes place in social theory after Hobbes as men become less chary about human sociability, and Hobbes's obsession about the constant possibility of a return to a State of Nature very quickly begins to look dated. None the less, he goes a considerable way beyond Bodin towards modernity by firmly rooting his theory of the state in a coherent view of human nature as it expresses itself in social life. Hobbes has a firm *theoretical* grasp of the problem which all modern political thinkers have to face, which is that only a particular form of the political order will suit a particular form of social order. In effect, Hobbes separates the two long before the world had heard of liberalism, the political doctrine which, *par excellence*, rests on the fundamental distinction between state and society.

Hobbes puts his finger inadvertently on the problems which are going to concern political thinkers in the future when the theory of the natural sociability of essentially egotistical men was to become the commonplace it was already in Rousseau's day. What Hobbes does not spell out is what the mechanisms of modern government are going to have to be like. It is enough for him simply to say that the Sovereign's writ runs unimpeded throughout the realm. Hobbes seems to assume that the Sovereign's unimpeded writ and efficient government are the same thing. Hobbes's own sociology is only implicit (and Hobbes might not even have known that he *had* a sociology). It is still cast in the very generalised form of a theory of 'human nature'. By the end of the eighteenth century, much more self-consciously sociological theories of modern society had appeared, so that the problem of defining what kind of state suited what kind of society at what stage of that society's development became much more explicit. By the time Adam Smith came to write his *Wealth of Nations* (the first volume appeared in 1776), a particular view of the state is tied to a specific economic and social analysis of 'commercial' and 'opulent', that is to say capitalist, society.

Smith has no doubt that the important changes which occur in human life happen first in society, where society means the economy and the social structure, and only later affect the state. The priority of society over the state is a sociological fact for Smith, rather than an ethical position as it is in Locke. Commercial society is above all else efficient society. The social division of labour means increasing job specialisation and expertise, while the division of labour in industrial enterprises makes modern production miraculously more efficient than its pre-industrial counterparts. The question then arises as to what form the state should take in a society like that, and in particular, how government is actually supposed to work. More particularly still, the question arises as to what type of people ought to be government functionaries. Smith's answer to these questions are what one would expect. A state staffed with aristocratic amateurs owing their offices to patronage would be entirely unsuitable. A modern state has to be as business-like as the society in which it is required to operate. For the first time in human history, the social science exists which can offer a true understanding of social life, and while it is unlikely that those who end up governing us will themselves be social scientists, it is none the less true that rulers should be business-like men who at least understand the new society. The business of governance should be entrusted to those who are prepared to make it a profession. This enables Smith to take a view of the state which is instrumental in a sense not available to his predecessors. A genuine understanding of how a society works enables government to understand its own tasks in an increasingly precise way, and it will certainly enable government to identify those tasks which it has undertaken in the past which it is fundamentally incapable of performing properly. Commercial society has as its object the creation of wealth, and commercial society is so successful at wealth creation that the state had better stop trying to interfere with the serious business of making money. Smith's is the first project for the dismantling of state mechanisms. Mercantilism, or what was left of it, came to be seen as a drag on the creation of wealth. Society had better be left to invent its own wealth-creating devices. This separation of the state from society enabled the question: What does the state do best and what does society do best? to be asked seriously for the first time, and Smith's political theory in the second volume of *The Wealth of Nations* is largely an attempt to answer this question.

Readers who come to *The Wealth of Nations* expecting it to contain a blanket *laissez-faire* attitude to everything are often suprised by how much Adam Smith does in fact leave to the state, and there has long been a lively debate about exactly how much of a *laissez-faire* liberal

Smith actually was. None the less, Smith is clear enough in his general account of state action. Government should wait to see what problems arise from an increasingly commercial and opulent society, and then ask itself whether government is the best agency for coping with them. Smith even has a sense of how more sophisticated technology, especially military technology, should affect modern governments. Increasingly sophisticated weaponry means that the old amateurish militia can have no place on the modern battlefield. Professional armies (his model is Frederick the Great's Prussia) must replace older makeshift military forces. Liberals who take the trouble to read volume two of *The Wealth of Nations* are sometimes surprised that a supposedly *laissez-faire* thinker like Adam Smith should admire Prussia of all places, but it is not really surprising because in the future efficiency and instrumentality are going to be the hallmarks of government. It is not taking Smith too far to say that for the first time it becomes possible to sketch out failure criteria for government. Of course, it is arguable that all political theories contain implicit failure criteria, but it is only in the late eighteenth century that the idea gains ground that a government can completely fail the society in which that government operates. It is only then that it becomes possible to map out a minimum programme for government, a set of functions which government has to perform without which it cannot properly be called government at all.

As one might expect, the perception that government could fail completely first became a generalised perception in America. By 1776 enough Americans had learned from their own experience what Smith was to work out in a theoretically coherent way – that a whole system of government could fail. Englishmen living in America had long felt themselves entitled to be ruled by the same kind of constitutional government as Englishmen at home. Constitutional government of the English kind was supposed to be balanced government, where balanced government meant that the decisions of government should be shared between different agencies of state, most importantly the House of Commons and the king's ministers. Representative institutions were supposed to keep a watch over executive actions, and in particular to act as an implicit curb on the more destructive manifestations of the royal will. What was puzzling to thoughtful Americans before 1776 was that all the more outrageous things which British government set out to do in America were done through Acts of Parliament. Something must have altered the balance between the House of Commons and the king, and it was easy to see that what had altered the balance was what was politely known as 'influence' and less politely known as corruption. Skilful and systematic use of royal patronage meant that there were enough placemen in the Commons in receipt of salaries from the executive for the king's ministers to have a bought and servile majority in that house of the legislature which Englishmen had always seen as the mainstay of their rights and liberties in the face of executive pretensions. Americans began to see a parallel between what was happening in England and what was happening in America. Royal governors were beginning to act towards colonial legislatures in exactly the same way that George III's government was acting in relation to the House of Commons. Americans' own understanding of the circumstances which forced them into rebellion was therefore the perception that a system of government which had once served their interests well enough was no longer doing so. Constitutional government in America had failed but that was not to be the end of it. The American Revolution began with the construction of a new constitution for the United States, the Articles of Confederation, and with the conversion of the old colonial constitutions into state constitutions. Political experience in America after the War of Independence was over again convinced enough Americans that government under the Articles of Confederation did not come up to scratch, and so the new Constitution of the United States followed in 1787, to be ratified by 1789.

The history of the emergence of the theory of the modern state is also the history of the state's emerging claim to neutrality. For the state to be neutral it has in some important sense to be able to separate itself from society. Medieval monarchy could never be in any sense neutral because, in the modern idiom, the king and his family were just one special interest group among others. The king was probably the largest landlord, and it would have meant much more to be the king's tenant than to be his subject. In the medieval quarrels about jurisdiction, the king was simply the most important protagonist among other protagonists. The state's claim to neutrality was never plausible before a theory of sovereignty was worked out in the modern sense. Sovereignty made possible the idea that in any state there was one law which applied to everybody. For the first time, human relations could be conceived in a genuinely public and juridical way. Of course, it is extremely difficult to date such a shift in the way men saw their relationship with each other, and it would be a very long time indeed before the idea of the formal equality of all citizens would emerge, but a kind of juridical equality was always implicit in political theories which emphasised the need for a sovereign law-giver whose laws over-rode every other kind of law. This is not to say that a rudimentary idea of the rule of law could not exist in intensely hierarchical societies, but the rule of law in, say, the Hobbesian version, can be seen as an attempt to create sovereignty out of conditions which were by no means ideal for its exercise. Hobbes's own solution to the problem is drastic. Sovereigns will use titles of nobility to reward subjects without allowing them a corporate share of political power, just as men will be allowed to enrich themselves without allowing wealth to be a claim on the Sovereign's attention. How far such untrammelled sovereignty is possible is a moot point, because we have become so accustomed to seeing a close connection between wealth and political influence that wealth without political influence is almost inconceivable. None the less, Hobbes does put his finger on what was always going to be one of the central problems of the modern state. How can it appear to be neutral in a society in which men and groups of men are profoundly unequal? What is to stop the state becoming the cat's-paw of a class or party?

Hobbes and Bodin have no real answer beyond saying that sovereignty ought to be as sovereign as it is possible for it to be. Locke is no help either, because he seems to think that vigilant property owners, and probably large property owners, will always make sure that sovereignty will be confined within limits acceptable to the rich. This implies undue influence by a particular class. There is an argument from class politics which attempts to show that large inequalities of wealth are good for the state's neutrality. With his usual ingenuity, Hume is able to combine the selfishness of large wealth and the good of the commonwealth. Large wealth seeks to protect itself, and it does this through the political influence which wealth always brings with it. That is simply a fact of human nature as it applies to the rich. The rich are lucky enough to have surplus wealth, some of which can be laid out to protect the rest. The easiest way for this to be done is through law, and so in free polities some surplus wealth is always used to influence the legislature in favour of the protection of property. Law, of course, applies to everybody, not just the rich, so that the rich really do everybody else a service by using a part of *their* wealth to protect the goods of everybody. If wealth were evenly distributed then it could all be easily consumed, and if that were to happen, then the surplus which the rich used to protect everybody's property would simply disappear and nobody's property would be safe.

Perhaps it was not till Hegel that the implications of the separation of the state from society were systematically worked out. By that time the French Revolution had happened and had ushered in what Marxists were later to call bourgeois society. Of course, bourgeois society did not happen overnight, but the French Revolution meant that bourgeois society was here to stay, which meant that it would occupy the centre of theoretical concern for the foreseeable future. Indeed, it was the very rapidity with which bourgeois society happened which made the future foreseeable at all. Genuine social science, and certainly social science which speaks to the future, is only possible in a rapidly changing present. Social science is typically about social change, and so it is made that much easier if social change appears to be happening almost before one's very eyes. (Imagine what it would be like to try to do social science if one only had experience of a society where changes took centuries to happen.) Bourgeois society changes in complete independence from the state. All the state can do, so to speak, is to stand and watch and, if it has any sense, adapt to changing circumstances. Hence the instrumental view of the state as the solver of problems which arise in society.

There is, of course, no reason in principle why the problems which arise from a particular state of a society, at a particular moment in that society's development, should not seem so intractable that nothing short of a radical redesigning of that society would make the problems go away. In the slightly technical language of political theory, it is possible that civil association is not enough, and that the state may have to be rearranged on the basis of social association. That distinction between civil and social association can be a tricky one to grasp. Civil association is association based on the rule of law, where law regulates only men's external relations with each other. Each man is regarded as sovereign over his own concerns, and the only duty he owes to others is the legally conceived duty of obeying the law in his dealings with them. Individual sovereignty means that the ends of life must be self-chosen, and it is in defence of those self-chosen ends, or of the right to choose, that men negotiate, so to speak, with each other and with the state. The result of those negotiations would be something like a constitution, preferably containing a bill of rights, and that constitution would not be static because, like sovereign states in relation to each other, individuals would retain the right of renegotiating at least parts of the treaty of association from time to time. Breaking the ordinary law of the land, which rests upon the constitution, would be the equivalent in international relations of unilateral repudiation of a treaty freely made. The idea of sovereign individuals negotiating with each other and with the state does not have to be taken too literally. All it means is that there is bound to be a certain uneasiness about the relations between sovereign individuals, and about the relations between sovereign individuals and the state, and it is that uneasiness which the idea of negotiation tries to capture. The idea of civil associations sounds liberal, but it is not necessarily so, because the idea of civil association does not of itself tell us anything about the kind of society in which civil association is the political bond which gathers men together into a state. Civil association is compatible with profoundly illiberal *societies*. There is no reason in principle why men should not be associated civilly in intensely hierarchical societies, or even in corporate societies, provided only that the relations between individuals are regulated by law which applies to everybody. Civil association does not even necessarily carry with it the idea of political rights, as the case of Hobbes shows. None the less, civil association suits liberal society best, because it is only in liberal society that, according to its defenders, a fully fledged economic individualism exists as the necessary analogue to the individualism explicit in the theory of civil association itself.

Social association, on the other hand, is association for a common purpose which can only be collectively achieved, and so it can only exist in a society which is capable of acting with a single will to choose the end or ends for which that society can be said to exist. The ancient Greek *polis* had something like social association about it because the *polis* existed in order that certain freely chosen ends could be pursued, and it never occurred to the ancients that 'the good life' could be lived in anything except a properly constituted community, though they did in fact disagree about how that community should be constituted. The most obvious example of a theory of social association in the modern world is of course the political theory of Rousseau, where the General Will exists precisely to make choices about how men should live – the voice of a whole community choosing public values for itself. Problems arise when civil and social associations come to be seen as alternatives, especially when the problems arising out of civil association seem to be of so intractable a kind that the only reasonable alternative seems to be a remodelling of civil society by the state in the name of a social association out of which the problems of the old civil society will not arise. Rousseau's *Social Contract* is only the most famous of the projects which invite us to see civil and social associations as alternatives. Social association implies that we are all in the same business, and that is the business of promoting human happiness on the assumption that human happiness is not worth having unless it is shared equally. This in its turn implies that there is some kind of 'natural' group, a nation or a class for instance, which really is capable of that kind of shared enterprise. Hence the rise of the collectivist ideologies in the modern world, all of them alternatives to civil association and to the liberal society from which civil association does not in fact seem to be separable.

Part of the claim of the state which is the guarantor of civil association is that it is neutral. A state acting through a law which applies equally to everybody, and in which that law is impartially administered and enforced, must by definition be neutral as to persons and groups. Blind justice is the symbol of a neutrally binding civil association. This was clearly enough seen in eighteenth-century liberal thought. The thinkers who ushered in the French Revolution thought that the neutrality of the state meant an impartial defence of individual property rights against those remnants of feudal privilege which gave aristocrats rights in the property and labour of others. That was, of course, a great reforming programme in a France in which ingrained aristocratic privilege was bound to be stubbornly defended, and it had nothing necessarily to say about what form the state should take to perform such a task.

One possibility was always enlightened despotism. Despotism now seems to be so much of the past that it is hard for us to think about it in the terms of the modern state, but that is not how certain enlightened thinkers saw the matter. It is easy to forget that aristocrats are the natural enemies of kings in the political sense, just as aristocrats and kings are natural allies in the social sense. The fact that the king is typically the head of a hierarchy of carefully differentiated noble ranks can easily obscure the fact that kings and aristocrats are natural rivals when it comes to the exercise of political power. In France, kings had gone a long way by the end of the eighteenth century in neutralising the political power of the French aristocracy by turning it into the gilded ornament of a state which it embellished but did not rule. Centralisation of the ruling function in the monarchy, which effectively mean government by the king's chosen servants, provided the basis for enlightened despotism. What better than the centralised sovereign state for doing the work of destroying the remnant of feudalism and the clerical obscurantism which seemed to go with it? The concentration of power in a sovereign centre was, by definition, anti-feudal in a society in which aristocracy still enjoyed the exercise of that social power which comes from entrenched corporate privilege. A vigorous and enlightened despot could easily appear to be the ideal instrument to reform a society whose chief social problem was the existence of a seigneurial class possessing privileges to which no corresponding duties were attached.

Enlightened thinkers were fond of the illusion that they could succeed where Plato failed and turn kings into philosophers, but, like Plato's, their success was limited. Some enlightened thinkers looked beyond enlightened despotism and began to ask what would have to come after if enlightened despotism failed. Enlightened thinkers were clear enough that state power was *for* something. It was not enough that state power simply existed; it was also meant to be *used* in the cause of human progress, no matter how that human progress was conceived. The idea of time was the essence of Enlightenment. Things had to happen, and happen reasonably quickly, perhaps within a single generation. Part of enlightened despotism's failure was its failure to reform its own society quickly enough, and one way of looking at the causes of the French Revolution is to say that it happened because enlightened despotism failed. But enlightened despotism failed at the very moment when the idea had become commonplace that political power was there to be used to guide or push a society in a particular direction. If that power was not to be feudal or despotic then it could only be exercised in the name of the people. In this sense, the theory of enlightened despotism led to the theory of popular sovereignty.

The theory of popular sovereignty was not, of course, new. It had been one of the false ideas which Plato had combated in the *Republic*; it was a commonplace at Rome; Marsilius had revived it and so had Machiavelli. Even Hobbes thought a people created sovereignty, and Locke derived a right of rebellion from the idea that because a people could bestow sovereignty on government it could also withdraw its consent if government betrayed its trust. What made the enlightened idea of popular sovereignty different was the degree of literalness attached to it. Other theories of popular sovereignty had typically regarded the people as *ultimately* sovereign while arguing that the people should not be allowed to get their dirty hands anywhere near the exercise of political power. We do well to remind ourselves that in the ancient world election to office was an oligarchic, not a democratic, idea, because it implied that some were fitter to serve the public than others; since that time all ideas of election, where election simply means choice, carried with them the idea that choice of rulers implied choosing from an already favoured group. Kings were often thought of as being elected by the people through acclamation, but to the modern eye these were very odd elections because there was only ever one candidate. Holy Roman emperors were elected by imperial electors, and popes were elected by cardinals, but these were elections in which the choice of candidates and the electorate were very restricted indeed. Enlightenment led to a very different idea of election, to the idea that elections should have some effect on how political power was actually exercised.

It has to be stressed that this was not a *necessary* consequence of Enlightenment. Most enlightened thinkers were not democrats in anything like the modern sense of the term. Most of them continued to think of democracy as the ancients did, as direct rule by the mob, the very antithesis of Reason, but Enlightenment did the job of ridiculing aristocratic claims to rule so well that when enlightened despotism failed there was no other direction for the theory of sovereignty to go than further down the road to a truly popularly exercised sovereignty. Out of this came the theory of the democratic republic.

It is important to distinguish between the modern theory of the democratic republic and its predecessors. No political idea is ever entirely new. What is new is the emphasis given to an existing political vocabulary. The modern democratic republic was to be a polity which was democratic in a double sense. Not only was the people's will to be the basis of its legitimacy, but the people's will was to have an effect on how the government of that republic was actually to operate. Elections were to be both a test of the legitimacy of the system of government and, in the modern idiom, an input into how that system of government worked in practice. The people's wishes were to have an effect on *policy*. With that idea we are already in the modern world, almost in the world of modern political science with its concern for how far it is in fact possible for electorates to control, or even influence, what governments do. Democratic government had to wait a very long time before it could call itself democratic without blushing, so strong was the ancient idea that democracy was rule by the ignorant many. The enlightened compromise was government by representation. The Rousseauist idea of a people giving itself laws by assembling as the Sovereign was simply not practical unless states were to dismantle themselves into federations of small provinces. From the Enlightenment onwards, much of the political thinking of those friendly towards progress was to concern itself about who or what was to be represented by whom. It was far from obvious that representation implied universal suffrage; property had at least as good a claim to representation as individuals, and corporate communities had just as good a claim as property. The representation of individuals won in the end, but that took two centuries of wrangling over what the principle of political representation truly meant.

NOTES ON SOURCES

The question of the modernity of the modern state is vexed, especially if one assumes, as I do, that the question of modernity is closely allied to the liberal idea of the state. All I mean to suggest is that the modern state is either liberal, or that, in the modern world, the liberal state is the state. I say this to avoid committing myself on the difficult question of whether the 'totalitarian' state is a genuine alternative to the liberal state, as distinct from being a pathological distortion of it. My thoughts on these matters, in so far as they do not derive from great works of political theory, are heavily influenced by Marc Bloch, *Feudal Society* (1961), for what the modern state is not; Max Weber's various writings on bureaucracy; and on a particular reading of the section 'Of the expenses of the sovereign' in Adam Smith's *The Wealth of Nations*, vol. 2. I am aware of a tendency to make Adam Smith sound a bit like a mixture of Max Weber and Herbert Spencer, but perhaps I might be forgiven this piece of teleology.

15

THE POLITICS OF ENLIGHTENMENT

Enlightenment as an intellectual movement eventually covered the whole of Europe and America, but it really began in the more liberal political climate in France after the death of Louis XIV. His successors quickly lost his reputation for grandeur and piety. The Divine Right monarchy in France still had the same theoretical pretensions to absolute sovereignty, but with the state increasingly in debt to its subjects and decreasingly successful in foreign affairs the pretensions of the monarchy began to distance themselves from the realities of French government. That, and a genuinely secular and materialist philosophy, began the process by which all authority – intellectual, religious and secular – came under a concerted attack on a pan-European scale. This is not to say that all enlightened thinkers were political radicals, but they were radicals in the sense that they tried to get to the root of things. At first, they had to tread gingerly in a world still subject to royal and ecclesiastical censorship. The political and social message of the materialist philosophy which Enlightenment took and developed from the seventeenth-century science of Descartes and Newton was deeply coded, but, for those with eyes to see it, it had a profoundly radical message. Eighteenth-century materialism accepted the idea of the naturalness of motion, and built on it a view of the social and political worlds which effectively banished God from his own creation. It had long been regarded as convincing proof of God's existence (the idea is as old as Aristotle) that bodies were naturally at rest and therefore needed a First Cause to set them in motion, and that First Cause was called God. If, however, physical bodies were naturally in motion, as seventeenth-century physics taught, then the whole of the natural world (including the biological and botanical worlds) could be adequately understood without any references to the miraculous intervention of the Deity.

No theory of special creation was necessary to explain the origins of nature's crowning glory, man. It became fashionable in advanced intellectual circles in France to refer to the human body as a 'machine' to show that its workings could be explained by the same mechanical principles according to which the rest of nature operated. The springs of human behaviour (the phrase is Bentham's) were the passions, or, as in the primmer language of utilitarianism, the desires to seek pleasure and avoid pain. The passions were implanted by nature. They were what gave human life its vital motion, and the operation of the passions could ultimately be explained in physical, that is, physiological, terms. The faculty of reason which nature had implanted in the minds of men had as its function the direction of the human passions towards the accomplishment of desirable ends, though there was in fact no agreement in the Enlightenment about what the relationship between reason and the passions exactly was. Some thought, like Rousseau, that all natural desires were naturally virtuous, and that only living in a corrupt society implanted 'unnatural', that is wicked, desires. Others, like Hume, thought that reason was the slave of the passions, by which he meant that the ends of human conduct were provided by the desires, and all that reason could do was to show given desires how to accomplish their ends. The consensus of Enlightenment opinion seems to have been that reason could in some sense control and direct the passions towards ends which were ethically desirable. The passions were by their nature blind, even part of brute nature, and they were certainly shared by the other animals. Natural reason must therefore have been given to man to counterpose itself to the passions, either because the passions themselves could not know how to satisfy themselves without guidance, or because the passions themselves became fixed on ends which were undesirable on a rational view of the matter.

In the field of moral philosophy, Enlightenment's goal was a rational system of ethics which would at the very least modify, and perhaps completely replace, the existing systems of ethics derived from religion, custom, and accident. Some forms of human conduct, and some of the ends of human conduct it was hoped, could be rationally demonstrated to be preferable to others. Reason must have been implanted by nature to point these differences out. There must be a way of showing that true human happiness was attainable only through the attainment of virtuous human ends. The culminating point of moral philosophy would be reached when reason could demonstrate that the truest form of human happiness consisted of the encouragement and spectacle of the happiness of others. It is notorious in the history of ethics that the Enlightenment project failed to show that it was in fact possible to derive from reason a set of ethical principles capable of sustaining the loyalty of all rational men, and there is a notable irony in the fact that it was Hume, at the very heart of Enlightenment, who showed why the enlightened project in ethics was bound to fail.

Enlightenment only sought after the rational *principles* of ethical conduct, and was prepared to concede that there was a wide variety of admissible ethical conduct in practice. This sense of effective ethical relativism came naturally out of the Enlightenment's steps towards materialism. Just as the actions of physical bodies in the universe depend on the circumstances in which they move, so the conduct of human beings is bound to vary with the conditions of the social and political world in which they find themselves. The fact that human beings conduct themselves in different ways in different circumstances no more invalidates the general laws of human nature than the fact that physical matter works in different ways in different circumstances vitiates Newton's Laws of Motion. The rational principles of human conduct could be very generalised indeed, and, *pace* Hume, Enlightenment never stopped looking for them.

Implicit in that view of things was a certain spirit of broad-mindedness and toleration which characterised Enlightenment at its best. Physical matter in identical circumstances would always behave in the same way: all stones dropped from a great height fall to the ground. What applied to the physical world applied to the human world too. All human beings in human circumstances other than their own would act in very different ways. How human beings conducted themselves was not accidental, but the accident of birth into particular societies at particular moments in those societies' development determined what kinds of people they would eventually turn out to be. The implications of that view were clear: if you were born in Persia, instead of France, you would have been a Muslim, not a Catholic; if you had been born poor and brought up in bad company you would probably end up a thief; if you had been born a Protestant in northern Europe, rather than a Catholic in southern Europe, then you would be tolerant and love liberty, whereas southerners tended to be intolerant and to put up with autocratic government. If what human beings were like was the necessary effect of the circumstances they were born to, then nobody had a right to be too censorious about anybody else. A certain toleration of other ways of doing things, and a certain moderation in the criticism of social and political habits, customs and institutions, seemed the natural corollary of the materialistic view of humankind.

297

Enlightenment attempted to expand the principles of toleration and moderation into general principles of individual life and the life of society and politics, and it is no exaggeration to say that all that is best in the Western liberal tradition comes from Enlightenment. Enlightenment, it might be said, disappears as a separate identity into what came to be known as civilisation in nineteenth-century Europe. Enlightenment believed in institutionalism and in civil liberties; in the abolition of slavery; in gradualism and moderation; in the reform of manners, morals and politics; in peace and internationalism; in social and economic progress with due respect for national and local tradition; in justice and the rule of law; in freedom of opinion and association; in the balancing of the powers of government and the division of political authority between different agencies of government as a weapon against despotic rule by individuals, groups or majorities; in social equality but not to the extent that it threatened liberty, and above all Enlightenment believed in liberty under an enlightened system of law so that liberty would not disturb the orderly processes of government. This list is Isaiah Berlin's, and he points out that, by the middle of the nineteenth century, most of these ideals were, at least in theory, shared by the civilised governments and peoples of Europe.

Of course, not all of these values were emphasised equally by all the thinkers of the Enlightenment, and there were always individual thinkers, of which the most obvious is Rousseau, who struck discordant notes, but there is none the less an implicit appeal to moderation in the very plurality of enlightened values. No one value dominated all the rest, not even liberty. This implied that, in concrete social and political circumstances, values would have to be traded off against each other, because it is only in an ideal world that all values are ultimately reconcilable.

In his famous essay *What is Enlightenment?* of 1784, Kant offered a celebrated definition of what it was to be enlightened: to be enlightened was to 'dare to know'. Kant chose to regard the whole of eighteenth-century thought as a revolt against ignorance and superstition. Knowing was to know the basis of things, how things really worked. Kant's is a very tempting definition of Enlightenment. It readily brings to mind some of the great intellectual battles of the age. Biblical criticism, for example, began to ask seriously what kind of record of the past the Old and New Testaments actually provided (the measurements of Noah's ark described a vessel much too small to contain all the animals mentioned in Genesis). In France, there was a battle over the superstitious influence of the Jesuits, especially in education. Voltaire attempted to popularise and spread the teachings of Newtonian physics as the true constitution of the universe (and called his mistress Madame Venus-Newton). One thinks of the tremendous growth of interest in accounts of other, non-Christian, civilisations like Ancient Egypt, Persia and China, from which the Christian West perhaps had something to learn. Coupled with this concern with other civilisations went a genuine attempt to write 'philosophical' history, what we would now call comparative cultural sociology. This was a vast intellectual enterprise designed to show that all societies left to themselves were necessarily bound to go through the same processes of growth, maturity and decline. I say 'left to themselves' because an important part of Enlightenment consisted of devising ways in which that apparently ineluctable process of development could in fact be changed into necessary and inevitable progress, and all this without a word from God.

Enlightenment also meant an enquiry into the means of knowing itself: what we call epistemology. The great harbinger was Locke's *Essay Concerning Human Understanding* (1690), which showed that there was nothing particularly mysterious about how the human mind came to know what it did in fact know. Sensory perception was a full and sufficient cause of the mind's understanding of the world outside itself, and the senses really did understand the world about which they relayed information to the mind. The world was really there, and what the senses grasped about it was all that there was to know. There was to be none of that medieval mysticism which regarded the world as we see it as some kind of complicated metaphor of a deeper reality behind the appearance, accessible only to the theologically learned. Not that theology was to disappear, though it is still a matter of dispute how many enlightened thinkers were in fact atheists. Knowledge of God, and God's purpose for the world, was to be found in the world. That was why God made man in his own image by giving him natural reason. God was a rational God who meant men to understand at least part of His purpose for mankind. Locke's own claims for his epistemology and his natural religion were characteristically modest. Much of the work remained to be done, but it was plain in which direction Locke was leading. Lockian epistemology took literally the injunction to 'know thyself'. Knowing oneself implied understanding how what the human mind contains actually got there. Only then could minds be sure that they understood the world in which minds lived. Epistemology was the royal road to political science and to sociology.

Kant did not, of course, mean that the Age of Enlightenment was an enlightened age. Enlightenment's progressive discoveries had yet to make their way properly in the world. An enlightened age would come about when Enlightenment's rays had illuminated the last dark corner of the world. None the less, the implications of Kant's 'dare to know' are clear enough. A better world would be created if all the discoveries of Enlightenment to date were to be spread far enough. Enlightenment had become a reforming programme at least by 1784. Kant seems to be saying that all now agree about what Enlightenment is, and that from now on we had better get on with the propagandist job of increasing the number of the enlightened. Of course, Enlightenment could know no frontiers, though there was a tendency for the language of Enlightenment to be French. The *lumières* of Paris, the *philosophes*, would speak the same clear language as *Aufklärer* in Germany, *illuministi* in Italy and what Gibbon called the enlightened or philosophical part of mankind in Britain. The 'party of humanity', as they liked to be called, was a European fellowship in civilisation waiting for that civilisation to be fully realised in practice.

Yet Kant's essay, *What is Enlightenment?*, should give us pause. Kant assumes that the question: What is Enlightenment? is worth asking, and perhaps he assumes that it needs to be asked urgently. But Kant's own answer is suspiciously formulaic, automatic even. What Kant is doing is summing up for his age what that age already thinks about itself. He is inviting enlightened Europe to admire itself in its own gilded mirror. The essay is not smug. Enlightenment still has a long way to go before it penetrates its own world completely, but the tone of the essay is confident, and it is also intimate. *We* know what *we* are talking about. It is almost like a chairman's report about the progress of an enterprise or about the present condition of a club. In this sense, the essay may not be a public essay at all, or it may be public only in the sense that chairmen's reports are often published. This alone should be enough to make us slightly suspicious of the essay. There is something too self-conscious about the essay, too deliberate and too generalised. What Kant is asking us to do is to take the Age of Enlightenment at its own estimate of itself, something which we should do only with the greatest caution.

Perhaps Kant's definition of Enlightenment is not really a definition at all, but a translation or a synonym. The age is characterised as being in revolt against 'ignorance and super-stition', but that formula is very wide-meshed indeed, and it is meant to be. It is an umbrella opened so wide that as many thinkers as possible can shelter under it. After all, it creates a fine feeling inside to be told that you have disassociated yourself from ignorance and super-stition, and it creates an even finer feeling to be told that you are actually in revolt against them. Thinkers from Edinburgh and Stockholm to Madrid and Naples could share in the dare-devilry of being in the forefront of human knowledge. But perhaps the very generalised formula may be explained as a call to party unity. To change the metaphor, Kant might be casting the net of Enlightenment so wide because differences between the members of the party of humanity had become so great by 1784 that the net had to be cast very wide indeed to include them all. If all that enlightened thinkers could find to agree about was that they were against ignorance and superstition, then they could not have been agreeing about very much beyond clichés. (And who ever claimed to be on the side of ignorance and superstition anyway?) And it might very well be that the things enlightened thinkers disagreed about are more interesting than the things they agreed about.

One of the things enlightened thinkers disagreed about was politics. The date of Kant's essay, 1784, may in itself be revealing. It comes eight years after the American Declaration of Independence and five years before the French Revolution, yet on the face of it Kant's essay is very unpolitical, and what politics it does contain is extremely conservative. Kant was a citizen of a Prussia ruled by Voltaire's favourite enlightened despot, Frederick the Great. Kant draws a very odd moral for intellectual liberty from enlightened despotism. He says that only an enlightened despot with an efficient army at his back would ever dare to allow freedom of thought and discussion to his subjects, because his possession of physical force means that at the end of the day he can be sure of his subjects' obedience. Kant's own political position can be generalised. The traditional reason given for the un-political, or supinely political, position of German *Aufklärer* is that they, and the German bourgeoisie from which they came, were politically scared, or bought off, by the princes of Germany, or that they were politically without ambition or even hope. The assumption is that because Kant came from that class, he too was unpolitical, unlike enlightened men elsewhere in Europe.

There may be something very wrong about that kind of argument. Everything it has to say about the German bourgeoisie might be true, and everything it has to say about Kant may be true, but what has to be questioned is the existence of a bourgeoisie elsewhere in Europe which was as intensely political, perhaps even as revolutionary, as the German bourgeoisie was supinely passive. In the Enlightenment it was the French *philosophes* who made the most noise. That the enlightened party in France wanted changes is not in question. They wanted a rationalisation of the legal system, the abolition of legal torture and an end to barbarous punishments; they wanted an overhaul of the system of taxation, notably the abolition of the tax farmers; they wanted an end to the backstairs influence of the Jesuits, the abolition of outmoded forms of seigneurial privilege, and so on. None the less, Kant's distinction between the Age of Enlightenment and an enlightened age might be telling us something about the politics of the French *philosophes* which might not be obvious at first sight. Kant may be hinting that all is not as it might be in France, despite the fact that it was France which produced the real stars of Enlightenment and provided its universal language. Where, it might be asked, are the equivalents in France of the reforms of the enlightened Frederick the Great? France is behind. Voltaire may have corresponded with Frederick, but Kant lives in his kingdom and enjoys the benefits of his rule. Where, now, is the contrast between a muted German bourgeoisie and that confident enlightened French bourgeoisie out to change the world?

There is also something *dated* about Kant's essay. The distinction between the Age of Enlightenment and an enlightened age is meant to tell us that the Age of Enlightenment is complete, that Enlightenment has come of age, that it has really discovered all or nearly all that has to be known. No doubt there were details still to be filled in, but the intellectual programme of Enlightenment is substantially complete. For the enlightened party, the possibilities of its own given intellectual world are already fixed in 1784, eight years after the American and five years before the French Revolution. Enlightenment from then on is simply an exercise in propaganda, spreading the word in a more or less recalcitrant world. Revolution came as a bit of a shock to Enlightenment, especially when revolution took on a popular tone, and it is easy to see why. The Enlightenment was proud to call itself the Age of Reason (though there was no consistency about what reason meant), but a fundamental belief in the power of reason to change men's lives was perfectly compatible with an effective contempt for the ignorant and irrational multitude. Believing that all men at birth received the gift of reason sat easily with the counter-belief that the world's circumstances prevented most men's reason from working properly. Natural reason might work automatically in a world which was itself perfectly natural, but an important part of Enlightenment consisted of pointing out just how unnatural most of the world's institutions and practices were. Irrational institutions and practices perverted natural reason, the habits of deference to aristocratic superiors and adherence to Catholic superstition being the chief culprits. There was therefore no contradiction in saying that most men would have to be taught to use their natural reason all over again, and, granted the actual state of the world, that was a programme which stretched well into the future.

The improvement of the world's institutions and the improvement of its inhabitants would have to proceed together. Locke had said that at birth the mind was a blank sheet (*tabula rasa*) waiting to receive the impressions of the outside world, but this was a very double-edged psychological doctrine for believers in human progress. On one level the doctrine of the *tabula rasa* could give rise to considerable optimism. If the mind received the right impressions from a benevolent world then the mind itself would be benevolent. There were no innate ideas to complicate things, and certainly no trace of that original sinfulness upon which the repressive institutions of the social world relied so much for their basic justification. On the other hand, the *tabula rasa* theory of mind was a disturbingly passive theory. Minds were almost infinitely receptive, sensitive and perhaps even over-sensitive to the impressions of a world which, according to the doctrine of Enlightenment, was just the sort of place to pick up bad ideas. Everything depended on what got into the mind first, and, in a world in which Enlightenment was at best an affair of a philosophic and political elite, there could be little doubt that the world's irrational impressions would beat philosophy in the race to fill most men's minds. Much better, then, to trust a wise legislator to reorganise state and society, which would in its turn change men, but only in the long term.

Enlightenment's view of human nature was thus optimistic and pessimistic at the same time. In substance, it did not differ very much from the old Christian view that human life was lived between the polarities of good and evil, except that Enlightenment offered a very different explanation of how good and evil 'got there'. There was always a tendency to think that what was good about men came from themselves and what was bad about them came from society, a conclusion which does not seem to follow very easily from Lockian premises. It was left to Hume to point out in the second volume of his *Treatise of Human Nature* (1740) that there was no reason in principle, and every reason in practice, to believe that our impressions of good and evil both come from the society which surrounds us. Hume's argument was deadly, because it meant that ideas of goodness which come to us from the socialising agencies of contemporary society cannot then be used as a lever against that society, but Hume's was a lone voice amid a generalised belief that right reason could be used to find out what it was about justice that was independent of the special circumstances of a particular society at a particular time and place.

A true view of human nature was supposed to yield up a true view of what the human institutions should be like within which human nature could reach its fulfilment. The question then was: How do we find out what human nature in its natural state is really like? All enlightened thinkers could agree that 'mankind are so much the same, in all times and places, that history informs us of nothing new in this particular' (the expression is Hume's), but the problem was that human nature wrote very different histories in the different human and geographical landscapes in which it happened to find itself. The differences between those histories was the clue to unravelling the mystery of the real nature of man. The idea was in essence very simple. Collect as many accurate accounts as possible of contemporary societies as unlike European societies as it is possible to be, and collect as many accounts as possible of societies in the past as different from the present as it is possible to be. Then, by comparison, cancel out what seems peculiar to men living in any particular society, and what you are left with is human nature as it universally is. This was a vast intellectual enterprise carried on with great seriousness by enlightened thinkers. Eighteenth-century social science has often been accused of superficiality, but there was nothing superficial about its comparative cultural sociology or about its comparative history. Of course, travellers' tales from the Pacific islands and North America, or accounts of the harems of Persia and the burial customs of the ancient Egyptians, fed a certain superficial curiosity and a childish desire for novelty, but behind the taste for exotic detail lay a perfectly serious search for natural man. Perhaps he should be called Natural Man, because he was probably to be found nowhere but in the assumptions of the thinkers who went looking for him, and it was certain that he would not be found at the centre of one of the sophisticated European societies where most enlightened thinkers lived.

There does not even seem to have been any agreement about what the term 'natural man' actually meant. Sometimes, but only sometimes, natural meant primitive. Travellers brought back stories, some of them tall, about noble savages living lives of uncomplicated virtue without ever having heard the name of Christ or knowing anything like the institution which Europeans called the state. Perhaps European men might revert to the simple state of rustic virtue if their complex social, political and ecclesiastical institutions were to be dismantled. Rousseau thought something very close to that, though his was certainly never a majority view. None the less, primitive societies did have something to teach the more advanced. The thinkers of the eighteenth century did not make the automatic assumption of superiority over non-European societies which was later to become commonplace. On the contrary, societies at an earlier stage of development might well have important lessons for societies at later stages of development, by showing those more sophisticated societies where they might have taken the wrong turnings which made life in them less than satisfactory. And contemplation of the differences between 'rude' and 'polished' societies could provide insights into the political and social mechanisms which made progress from rudeness to civility possible in the first place. Comparative sociology made a theory of history possible.

Natural man more often meant man as he was meant to be. In one sense it was impossible to know what man was meant to be, because the way the world was organised had never allowed man to reach his full potential. Nevertheless, if it was possible to distil out the basic constitution of man from the multifarious manifestations of his nature in the world, then in principle it should be possible to infer from human nature what the social and political institutions of humanity ought to be like. Critics of Enlightenment have always had a field day with this aspect of its social science. Enlightened thinkers, the critics have always said, knew what they were looking for all along. Enlightenment had no feeling for the uniqueness of given examples of social experience; men do not exist for Enlightenment, only Man. For all its erudition, Enlightenment was not really interested in the facts of human experience (the exception is Montesquieu), but only in a supposed uniformity of human nature that lay behind them. Given an accurate account of the constitution of man, the construction of the political constitution was a straightforward matter of simple deduction. Enlightened political thinking loved nothing so much as a few simple axioms from which to build up architectonic social and political systems of considerable formal elegance but which had very little purchase on the real world.

These axioms could be of various kinds, but in the main they were what we would now call psychological: all men had the same sensory equipment for dealing with the world, or all men possessed a kind of natural reason or common sense, or all men possessed certain elementary rights by nature, or all men sought pleasure and avoided pain, or simply that all men would react to the same physical and social environment in the same way. Whatever the fundamental axioms of human nature were, they served the same purpose of bringing some kind of intellectual order into those human phenomena which there had always been a tendency to attribute either to the obscure workings of divine providence, or to pure chance. It is easy to see that the inspiration for this enterprise was Newtonian and Cartesian, and the rationalism of seventeenth-century science in general. What Newton and Descartes did in their different ways was to judge all human knowledge claims in the court of mathematics. As with the Plato of old, mathematical truths were thought to correspond to the nature of things. (In the Enlightenment there was only the Neapolitan recluse Vico to argue that mathematics was a radically created human invention, but almost nobody read him.) Mathematical truths were ideal truths, and any other branch of knowledge with pretensions to scientific rigour would do well to imitate mathematical procedures. Mathematical arguments were ideal arguments because they were either demonstrably true or demonstrably false; they also began somewhere and ended somewhere: mathematics was the one science in which it could truly be said that an argument was either true or false, and therefore over.

The mathematical method of deduction from axioms had a decisive effect on the social sciences of the Enlightenment. Newtonian physics reduced the apparently chaotic behaviour of matter in the universe to one simple principle, gravity, and a few simply and mathematically stated laws of motion. In the Enlightenment, everybody wanted to be the Newton of the social sciences. Find the axioms of human nature, deduce from them in the approved Newtonian manner, and a complete science of man became a possibility.

Enlightenment's enemies had no doubt about what such a view of the world would do to revealed religion. There had always been a strand in Christian theology which emphasised that God was a rational God, and Newtonian physics showed rational men what God's rationality actually meant. God was a transcendent watchmaker who had created a mechanical universe whose laws were God's Laws. That universe worked automatically; bodies were naturally in motion until their motion was regulated by the motion of other bodies. What this meant was that God had no real motive for interfering with his own creation. Why should God break the laws which He Himself had made? Why should He not be satisfied with what He had made? God must have meant rational men to find out how He had ordered His universe, and He can't have meant to deceive them. God breaking the physical rules of His own universe is what Christians call a miracle. That the miraculous happens from time to time is proof, for those who believe in miracles, that God continues to reveal Himself bit by bit and from time to time. The God of miracles moves in a mysterious way, so that miracles have to be interpreted by those specially qualified to do so. Men do not have direct access to divine knowledge, which they can never know completely anyway, so a special institution, the Church, must exist in order to explain continuing revelation to the faithful. The Church is therefore uniquely capable of telling men truths about God's creation. Hence, anybody who claims to be telling truths about God's creation which are at variance with what the Church has to say must at best be mistaken or at worst telling deliberate lies; hence the case for censorship. Newtonian physics and the social theories which modelled themselves on it were dynamite for the Roman Catholic Church as an institution claiming a share of the control over men's lives, and especially for the censorship of books, which the Church always supported. If God never broke His rules, or if, as Dr Johnson sensibly said, God *used* to do miracles, then there was no need at all for a special agency to interpret God's purpose for the world. This did not, of course, mean that there could be no churches, simply that those churches could advance no claims to a special knowledge denied to ordinary reasonable men. Natural religion was a deism stripped of all its supernatural trimmings. All there was to know about God could be found out by examining His creation. The God of the deists was not in fact very interesting, being little more than a formal first cause of the universe, a cause so rationally pure that Voltaire could say he did not believe in God but agreed with Him.

If God had established laws for the physical universe, it seemed reasonable to suppose that he established similar laws for the human universe too. There seemed no reason in principle why moral causes should not work in ways which were more than analogous to Newton's Laws of Motion. Newton's Laws were sometimes called the Constitution of the Universe, so surely there also existed a constitution which was its moral equivalent. The Lockian version of Natural Rights became something of a cliché as the fundamental structure of the moral universe because it fitted the Newtonian model so well. The natural passions of men made them actively seek human ends, like Newtonian bodies naturally on the move. These bodies have their own moral space protected by their natural rights which invite human beings to live closely together, but not too close. Rational men were perfectly capable of understanding that the enjoyment of their natural rights implied the duty of respecting the exercise of those same natural rights by others, and for as long as that was true – and why should it not be true for ever? – then harmony would reign on earth as it did in the heavens. Of course, the theory of natural rights was a programme rather than an accomplished fact. Certain beliefs and customs in the social world as it actually was got in the way of the understanding of natural rights. Human rationality was incomplete, and a good deal would have to be done before an understanding of natural rights was available to the meanest of human intelligences, but that did not matter a great deal because the temper of Enlightenment was reformist rather than revolutionary. Of course things took time, though there was every reason for optimism. Knowledge of other cultures really helped, because the natural rights to life, liberty and property were respected in those of them which had yet to be corrupted by despotism and superstition.

The theory of natural rights made political theory easy. One only had to ask which form of government best protects natural rights for political theorising properly to begin. There was not, in fact, a single answer to this question in the Enlightenment. Natural rights could, for example, be protected by an ancient constitution, as French *parlements* and English Whigs thought, or natural rights could be secured by a civilised monarchy acting through law on the Aristotelian pattern. There was considerable enthusiasm for constitutional contrivance as a way of guaranteeing natural rights from undue interference from government. Following Montesqueiu's eccentric view of the English constitution, and from a 'scientific' view of the operations of human nature, came a taste for the constitutional engineering of 'checks and balances' as a means of ensuring that executive power would be kept in its proper sphere by the natural operation of other powerful institutions against it in the appropriate Newtonian manner. What there does not seem to have been until very late is much enthusiasm for republican government with wide exercise of political rights (Rousseau is again the exception), and this might at first sight appear surprising in an age which was fascinated by everything the ancient Greeks and Romans did, a fascination which even extended to the publication of ancient Roman cookery books and (frequently disgusting) experiments with ancient recipes.

That there was much admiration for ancient republics in the abstract is well known. There was probably general agreement that something like the early constitution of the Roman republic had been the ideal form of government. Its balance between consuls, senate and people was universally admired, and so was the political virtue which was supposed to be the result of that balance. Rousseau extended this admiration to the virtues of the Spartan constitution as described in Plutarch's *Life of Lycurgus*. But the problem with the ancient republics was that they had been both agrarian and poor, whereas the states of modern Europe were becoming increasingly commercial and opulent, and the ancient republics had been tiny by the standards of the population (and population increase) of modern states. Ancient institutions, especially direct democracy, just would not fit modern conditions unless, like Rousseau, you were prepared to consider the possibility of dismantling modern states, or to agree with him that, almost without exception, modern states were not really improvable as they were, so that ancient precedents were not much help. Nor were the republics of recent political experience. Venice, Genoa and the united provinces were widely regarded as corrupt merchant oligarchies, a view which could also be applied, with some justice, to Hanoverian England.

It was the exhaustion of the alternatives to republican government in the light of bitter political experience which turned men's attention again to the ancient republics, and which led them to revolution at the end of the eighteenth century. American disillusionment with the supposedly constitutional government of Britain, and French disillusionment with the failure of enlightened reform in France, seemed to leave no alternative to the republic where the widespread enjoyment of political rights was the surest guarantee that natural rights would be respected by government. Enlightenment learned its eventual politics the hard way.

Enlightenment was nothing if not historical in its view of politics. Enlightened historical thinking was meant to highlight the theme of progress, and to do this it rooted the theme of progress in a genuinely universal history, and it felt obliged to make its history universal because the views of history which it attacked were themselves universal. The alternative theories of history which Enlightenment implicitly or explicitly championed came in two versions: pagan and Christian, where Christian really meant Augustinian. The pagan view of history, as it was taken out of thinkers like Aristotle and Polybius, was the circular view of history familiar to Machiavelli. What attracted enlightened historians like Montesquieu and Hume to Polybius in particular was his 'philosophic' quality. Polybius appeared to be the most reflective of the ancient historians because he was principally interested in how forms of government came to change. As we have already seen in the chapter on Machiavelli, Polybius followed Aristotle in his distinction between 'pure' and 'corrupt' forms of government, but, unlike Aristotle, Polybius had in the history of Rome an example of a state which had gone through all of the possibilities, pure and corrupt. In this sense, Polybius was more 'historical' than Aristotle, because the single case of Rome enabled him to connect together all the possible forms of government in a single historical narrative. What did not suit the enlightened temper was the ancient idea that the possible forms of government were reduced to six, because that made political history a closed system in which political change was the playing of endless variations on the same themes. There could be progress in the Polybian scheme, from anarchy to princely government, for instance, or from tyranny to aristocracy, but it was inevitably followed (though the time could be put off) by regression, as princely government degenerated into tyranny and aristocratic government into oligarchy. For the Enlightenment belief in progress to be sustainable, there had to be something which enabled political societies to break out of the cycle of Polybius.

Ancient historical theory was more than a historical curiosity in the Enlightenment, but it could hardly be said to impinge on men's daily lives. The case of the remnants of Augustinian theory was different because, at least in an attenuated form, it continued as the basis of the Church's historical teaching. Augustine, you will remember, hardly took human history seriously at all; nor was the state all that important. For Augustine, all the really important events which affect human life have either happened in the past or will happen in the future: the Creation, the Fall of Man, the life of Christ in the past, and the Second Coming of Christ to judge the nations at some time in the future. Compared to events like these, what importance can be attached to the paltry events of human life where those events are unconnected to the saving of souls? Unlike the ancient theory of history, Augustine's theory is linear, but he still thinks that the course of history is predetermined and so his theory is, in its way, just as closed as the circular theory of Polybius. In the Augustinian view, nothing significant could change very much in the human time-scale. History for him was literally one damned thing after another. Good princes and bad princes came and went and political rule was essentially carnal, corrupt and perishable, with no positive value at all. Thomism had made certain inroads into Augustinian pessimism, but the burden of sin which Adam caused to be placed on the backs of the human race set very definite limits on the amelioration of human life through political means.

It was this view of human history which the Enlightenment set out to disentangle, and it did it by devising a view of human history from the beginning from which the hand of God was notably absent. That was very far from saying that religion had no part to play in human history, but it did mean that the history of Christianity was to be treated in exactly the same way as any other aspect of history. Sacred history had no specially privileged status; it could be treated as sceptically as profane history, its sources critically examined, and extant versions of it challenged. Looked at as part of history in general, the history of organised religion in the West was not an encouraging tale. Eras of clerical domination showed themselves to be ages of darkness and superstition. Civilisation in the past had reached its height in the ancient Greek city-states and at Rome before it was corrupted by its emperors. A period of darkness followed on from the conquest of the Roman Empire in the West with the foundation of the barbarian kingdoms, which were eventually to become Christian. That part of the Roman Empire which survived at Byzantium fell an easier prey to the impudent fanaticism of monks than it did later to the armies of the Turk. The Renaissance's rediscovery and revitalisation of what was best in the ancient world was a step in the right direction, the beginning of that progress which was to be continued by the great discoveries of seventeenth-century science. Reason was on the move, and it was left to the eighteenth-century Enlightenment to spread the gospel of science into all areas of human enquiry and activity.

Enlightenment, then, represented a state of human civilisation at least as advanced as the ancient world at its best. What happened in between had at best been patchy and at worst disastrous. This may not be the most sophisticated of historical schemes, though it was probably the most sophisticated to date, but what it importantly did was genuinely to historicise the human condition. Human history was not just one damned thing after another. The way human beings lived their lives was subject to real historical conditions, and differences in those conditions really mattered. The word 'alienation' had not yet entered the vocabulary of social and political theory, but the idea was already available that alienation in the Christian sense was not, so to speak, a fixed quality or condition which would permanently disfigure the life of the human race. The Augustinian view of the Fall of Man was predicated on the permanent alienation of man from God literally till the end of time, and in the Augustinian scheme of things it simply could not make sense to describe one age as 'more' or 'less' alienated than another. Some ages might be more wicked than others, but that difference was as nothing when compared to the stark fact of original sin which gave every age its fundamental character. Enlightenment eroded that view. History was a series of ups and downs, no doubt, but the past really was over. Periodisation was definitive. There was no more chance of a return to the Middle Ages than there was of reconstituting ancient Sparta. Battles of the books, in which the virtues of ancient authors were judged superior or inferior to the moderns, continued to be fought, but, Rousseau apart, no one seemed to doubt that the Age of Enlightenment was about to surpass all other previous civilisations, and all other civilisations in its own contemporary world.

The question was: How? And how in particular were those conditions to be brought into being which would make possible a dismantling of a repressive social and political order? The old Augustinian view that human nature was fundamentally anti-social because of original sin had received a notable boost in the seventeenth century from the political theory of Hobbes. Hobbesianism was the old Augustinian theory dressed up in the very latest concepts of seventeenth-century rationalism. God did not get a look-in with Hobbes except as an afterthought; his was an Augustinianism expressed in the clear language of reason, the language of Enlightenment itself. Eighteenth-century enlightened thinkers had to dig very deep into the Augustinian and Hobbesian view of the human condition to come up with an answer to the assertion of the natural unsociability of man. Why is it, enlightened thinkers began to ask, that human beings have this tendency to prey on one another which makes social and political repression so apparently necessary? They found the answer in economics. Original sinfulness was really a theological gloss on a scarcity economy. The first thing God did after the Fall was to proclaim the brute fact that man was always going to find it hard to get his sustenance out of a barely yielding nature. Work was a curse laid on mankind. Bread was going to be earned in the sweat of men's faces. There was always going to be barely enough to go round, and human covetousness was going to extend beyond neighbours' wives to neighbours' goods. Therefore, a repressive social order was required to make men labour, and a repressive state order was required to batten down the effects of human envy.

The antidote to this appeared to be straightforward. Technology, the application of reason as science to nature, could show that scarcity was not a brute fact at all but the product of particular human circumstances. Economic change lay at the bottom of political change. The merest glance at Diderot's *Encyclopedia*, the great intellectual compendium of the age, shows how much Enlightenment wanted to spread the latest technical accomplishments in agriculture and industry. The thrust was profoundly political. Control of industry and trade by the state, and of agriculture by the servants of the aristocracy, was a bar to those improvements without which the creation of vastly increased national wealth was made immeasurably more difficult. Britain took the lead largely by ignoring in practice the superstructure of laws which was meant to regulate economic life, though it was the attempt to put them rigorously into practice again which was to cause the trouble with her American colonies. There seemed to be a growing consensus among advanced thinkers that the way to wealth lay with the freeing of trade and the gradual emancipation of economic life from state encumbrances, so that when Adam Smith published the first volume of *The Wealth of Nations* in 1776 he was speaking with something like the voice of the whole Enlightenment. (Again, the dissenter was Rousseau, who argued that increased wealth, even if widely spread, was not the road to human happiness.)

The enquiry into the causes of what we would now call economic growth was part of a wider inquiry into the causes of the development of all human societies from 'rudeness' to 'civility', and economic development was a fundamental part of economic progress. Human societies painfully dragged themselves in their different ways through the necessary stages of development from hunting and gathering through the agricultural stage and then on to the more developed stages of arts and crafts and so on to the modern stage of modern commerce and opulence. At each stage of the process societies developed the appropriate social and political institutions. By the second half of the eighteenth century the progress of the human race could be taken so much for granted, though that progress was very uneven, that attention shifted to the causes of what prevented further progress. Hence the extremely critical temper of Enlightenment and its suspicion of existing institutions.

In political terms, the story of human progress was not all that straightforward. The standard Enlightenment terms for characterising governments were 'free' and 'unfree', but it was far from being the case that the terms 'rude' and 'polished' meshed easily with the terms 'free' and 'unfree'. The ancient Greek cities had been polished and free, whereas the early Roman republic had been rude and free. The Roman Empire had been polished and unfree, and the barbarian successor kingdoms had been rude and free at least to begin with, and so on. In the modern world, civilised monarchy, that is monarchy ruling according to law, was unfree but polished, whereas constitutional monarchy of the British type was widely considered to be a successful hybrid balancing monarchical with republican institutions. The question, then, of what form of government was natural to man at what particular stage of his development offered no very easy answer. Probably the only way of telling would be to replant people from a polished society in a virgin physical and moral landscape and wait and see what happened. Of course, Englishmen and Frenchmen replanted in North America took their native institutions with them, but scientific curiosity interested itself in how those institutions would develop far away from their native soil, and in whether transplanted Europeans would develop a different character from their brothers left behind in the homeland.

Perhaps the American Revolution, despite the parochialism of its immediate causes, was proof that such a transformation had taken place. By the 1780s the quest for the 'American character' was already far advanced. In his *Letters from an American Farmer* (1782) Crèvecoeur thought he had an answer to the question 'What is an American?' Crèvecoeur in fact cast his net fairly wide, identifying not one but several American characters depending, Montesquieu-like, on the climate and soil of the region in which they lived; but there was no mistaking the general themes of liberty and opportunity which ran like a thread through the whole of American life (though slavery was a blight on the South). Europeans in America seemed to slough off the habits of cringing deference and the sense of their own limitations which characterised the Old World, and there was no reason to suppose that the process would not continue into the future.

The question of whether an American character existed was a deeply political question. Montesquieu had made it a commonplace that 'laws', by which he meant a constitution, or what we would call a political system, were characterised by a particular animating 'spirit' and that spirit comes very close to meaning what was later to be called 'national character'. Without a 'spirit of the laws' a constitution was at best an empty shell; without a distinctive national character a country could not properly be said to have its own constitution at all. From the enlightened point of view, it was literally impossible for a people to give itself laws unless that people had a settled character out of which those laws could come and which would give those laws their energising principles afterwards. In 1789, the Americans gave themselves a new constitution, and that constitution was republican. Human nature, partially corrupted at least by the manners and morals of Old Europe, had begun to write a new story in the very different circumstances of America, and in political terms that story was to be a republican story. Perhaps, after all, men were republicans by nature.

ENLIGHTENMENT'S CRITICS

Enlightenment's critics seem to be unanimous that the Enlightenment was deeply subversive. Burke was already saying that in the early 1790s, and it became the commonplace nineteenth-century view. Enlightenment came to be a byword for shallow and pretentious over-intellectualism, naively deductive, geometrical in spirit, indifferent to anything about men except their natural rights. It was this superficiality which led enlightened thinkers to attack, or at least ridicule, all existing forms of authority in the name of the individualism which the idea of Natural Rights implied, without having anything very definite to put in the place of the institutions of authority it so roundly condemned. Yet we have seen that the temper of Enlightenment was reformist rather than revolutionary, and even Rousseau, in a sense the most radical of enlightened thinkers, was really rather timid when it came to matters of practical reform. Revolution came to Enlightenment by surprise, and, while there can be no doubt that the slogans of revolution were slogans derived from

Enlightenment, it still seems surprising that Enlightenment's nineteenth-century critics should have been so insistent that revolution was Enlightenment's fault.

Various accounts of the connection between Enlightenment and revolution are on offer. The least convincing of all is the idea that there is some kind of direct connection between Enlightenment and revolution. What strikes one most about the case of the American Revolution is the extreme reluctance of the Americans to begin the revolution at all. On their own view of it, the Americans were forced into declaring independence by the intransigence of the British government in the face of demands which the Americans thought could be met within the existing constitutional structure of the British Empire. Again, what strikes one about the French Revolution is the surprise with which it caught almost everyone. These were not revolutions like subsequent revolutions in the nineteenth and twentieth centuries, many of which were long in the theoretical making and which were made by self-consciously revolutionary groups who had long prepared for the revolutionary moment. Rousseau may have made revolutionary noises, but we look in vain for a revolutionary programme in his writings, let alone revolutionary tactics.

What was it, then, which made Enlightenment the source of subversion? Partly, the answer lies in Enlightenment's ubiquity, and in its audience. Enlightenment was not populist. Its audience was the literate bourgeoisie and aristocracy, neither of which could be called naturally revolutionary classes. None the less, a century's worth of Enlightened propaganda must have had some effect on them. Rousseauist ideas about the natural goodness of the people, the idea of natural rights, the idea that most established religion was superstition and that no authority was altogether to be trusted, may have made the enlightened public at least the accomplices of subversion. There was certainly nothing in Enlightened social and political thought to prepare its eventual victims for the form the French Revolution would actually take. Whatever the Revolution was, it was hardly a feast of Lockian natural reason. Perhaps the basic mistake of Enlightenment (with important exceptions like Hume) was a psychological mistake in believing that reason could control the passions, and that out of this would come a rational system of ethics capable of sustaining the loyalty of all rational men. The idea of reason controlling the passions is at least as old as Plato, but Plato had confined it to an over-trained elite who would not be let loose to rule the world until at an advanced age when most passion was spent anyway. Enlightenment had much more sanguine hopes of reason. Only a fool could fail to reason syllogistically, and only a complete fool could fail to see the truths of ordinary common sense. What Enlightenment concentrated on were the unnatural, institutionally imposed barriers which prevented natural reason from getting out. When those barriers were eventually down, as they were in the Revolution, the result was not exactly what enlightened thinkers had foreseen. The peasant uprisings, the lynchings and the Terror were not the rational idyll which Enlightenment at its most simple-minded seemed to have promised would be the result of the liberation of the human race. Instead, man seemed to show himself to be a very ignoble savage indeed. It had been the much-ridiculed institutions of society which had kept the baser human passions in check all along. Let most men loose and they would gambol over the ruins of the civilisation they were in the process of destroying. Much of the work of undoing Enlightenment in the future would consist of an attack on the rationalist assumptions of enlightened psychology.

Enlightenment's critics were correct when they homed in on its belief in this universality of human nature. This line of criticism was already alive and well by the middle of the eighteenth century, but it took its full force from the events which followed on from 1789, in particular the revolutionary wars. Enlightened political theory (Vico and Montesquieu always excepted) dealt in very broad categories, and the broadest of all was 'human nature'. If it was true that the French Revolution was made in the name of the rights of man, then it was impossible that the Revolution could be contained within national boundaries. The rights of man existed everywhere, and it was the revolutionaries' duty to make sure that they were respected everywhere. A new kind of war was invented, the war of liberation, in which the object was not conquest of territory but the export of liberty. A universal human nature had a universal message through the French Revolution. All human beings everywhere deserved to live under the same rationally thought-out institutions which just happened to have come into being in France first. States and societies in the rest of Europe needed to be remodelled, and it was the attempt to do that which made the powers of Old Europe see Napoleon as some kind of Jacobin-at-large. The ubiquity of Enlightenment, and the revolutionary wars, taught a whole generation of European statesmen, the most characteristic of whom was the Austrian chancellor, Metternich, that from then on the political dangers facing European governments were all going to be the same. The French Revolution showed that political problems in the future were going to be pan-European problems, a view which was triumphantly vindicated in the European revolutions of 1848.

From Burke onwards, the French Revolution's enemies never had any doubt that the Revolution had been caused by, or made in the name of, a new view of the world. It was the first modern revolution because it was made in the name of an ideology, and there was no doubt that that ideology's roots lay in Enlightenment. What became increasingly obvious was that Old Europe had nothing like an equivalent ideology with which to play the revolutionaries at their own game. The *ancien régime* had never bothered to cover itself with much theory, beyond saying that the world was organised in the way God wanted it to be, a view bolstered by selective scriptural quotation. Enlightenment's alleged godlessness soon put a stop to that, though in most states atheists were thought of by the authorities as potential subversives until well on into the nineteenth century. Those who did not recognise the authority of divine law were unlikely to have much respect for the man-made laws of states. (This was, in fact, a very ancient idea: he who has no respect for the gods is unlikely to be reliable in his relations with his fellow men and with the *polis*.) Post-revolutionary conservative political theory was largely concerned with the construction of a counter-revolutionary ideology which was as complete in its own way as the ideology which was supposed to have been the Revolution's inspiration.

Counter-revolutionary thinkers insisted that Enlightenment must have been democratic because the revolutions which followed on from Enlightenment clothed themselves with democratic legitimacy. That this was a consequence of political events rather than political theory could not matter to the Enlightenment's critics, who perhaps understood where Enlightenment was heading better than enlightened thinkers knew themselves. Enlightenment's critique of authority of all kinds, biblical, ecclesiastical, social and political, in the name of the implicit individualism of the rights of man, was bound to have its effect when revolutionary action had destroyed duly constituted authority. Then Rousseau came into his own. If political authority was not to be royal or aristocratic, then it could only be popular because there was nothing else it could be. In the American case, democracy was tempered by complicated constitutional arrangements so that the people's hands were kept as far from the levers of political power as was decently possible in a popular republic. American democracy was to be pluralist from the beginning, because the Founding Fathers of the Constitution of the United States were as afraid of the 'tyranny of the majority', where that majority was poor, as they had been of the tyranny of George III. The American Constitution was designed to produce a political system in which any number of 'factions' (we would call them 'interest groups') would compete with each other so that no single group would be able to dominate the political system the whole time. This was, in its turn, designed to produce 'moderate' governing decisions, because those decisions would be the result of bargaining between various interest groups and between various governing institutions. Revolutionary democracy in France was very different. There, the Revolution was made *against* the special interest groups, the aristocracies of the sword, the robe and the Church. Rousseau-like, French republicanism was to be profoundly suspicious of special interest groups, especially when loyalty to those groups could get in the way of the moral unanimity of the Republic One and Indivisible. The Republic was there to be the expression of the popular will; unlike those of America, the Republic's institutions were not there to blunt or refine the popular will, but to make possible that liberty in action which was the mark of a truly popular republic.

It was this version of the tyranny of the majority which Enlightenment's and the Revolution's critics feared most. To let in the people was to let in the mob. The mob had been a semi-official part of English politics in the eighteenth century (Henry Fielding had called it the Fourth Estate), and Montesquieu had even said that popular unrest was one of the things which helped to preserve English liberty. The mob had also been raised in America, particularly in Boston and New York, during the period of the run-up to the Declaration of Independence. These were semi-permitted mobs, raised by leaders inside formal politics to defend a cause: Wilkes and the rights of the freeholders of Middlesex, Sam Adams and the Constitution of Massachusetts. There were signs during the American Revolution that the mob was beginning to find leaders and a programme of its own, and this is certainly what the critics of the French Revolution thought happened in France from 1789 onwards. The semi-tolerated mob was turning itself into what became known as the 'revolutionary crowd' with Rousseau for their sleeping king. The French Revolution had shown what could happen if riots got out of hand, and that was the fear that all nineteenth-century conservatives and liberals would have to live with.

The distance between the spirit of Enlightenment and the mob spirit, irrational, fickle, brutal and destructive, hardly needs to be emphasised, but Enlightenment critics hammered home the point that the spirit of the mob was bound to infect the politics of any country in which authority had come under such intellectual attack that it would begin to lose its nerve, and it was the easiest thing in the world to conflate mob politics with democratic politics. In the nineteenth century, the cause of democracy was to be forced to make its way inch by inch against the slur that democracy's cause was also the cause of the mob.

NOTES ON SOURCES

There is a huge body of commentary on the Enlightenment to supplement the Enlightenment's own vast output. In view of Enlightenment's self-declared propagandist aims, this was only to be expected. It is all too easy to get a distorted idea of what Enlightenment is by reading one of any number of volumes of 'selections' from the great enlightened stars, because these selections tend to concentrate on the politics and philosophy of Enlightenment at the expense of Enlightenment's concern with 'progress' across the whole spectrum of human life. Much better, then, to start by flicking through the *Encyclopedia* in order to find out just how far-reaching Enlightenment actually was. Isaiah Berlin, *The Age of Enlightenment* (1956), Peter Gay, *The Enlightenment* (2 vols, 1967–70), N. Hampson, *The Enlightenment* (1976), and Roy Porter *The Enlightenment* (1990), are good introductions.

16

ENLIGHTENMENT AND GOVERNMENT THROUGH LAW

Montesquieu

MONTESQUIEU

Charles Louis de Secondat, baron de la Brède et de Montesquieu, whom all the world knows simply as Montesquieu, was a delightful man whom everyone he met seems to have liked. He was born into the ancient *noblesse de la robe* (legal aristocracy) at la Brède near Bordeaux in 1689. Following the almost universal aristocratic custom of the time, he was put out to nurse with a countrywoman, but he never bothered to correct the distinctive local accent of the Bordelais which he acquired as a child. Nor is there any reason to doubt the story that, at Montesquieu's birth, a beggar, who happened to be calling at the chateau of la Brède at the time, was made one of Montesquieu's godparents to emphasise that both rich and poor were equally God's creatures. This is not to say that Montesquieu was indifferent to his seigneurial privileges or to the legal office he held (and sold) as *président à mortier* in the *parlement* of Bordeaux. Rather it is to suggest that he lacked hauteur and had that sense of *noblesse oblige* which is less common among aristocrats than defenders of aristocracy like to think. Certain it is that Montesquieu enjoyed being called 'the president' long after he had quit his office.

Montesquieu's father intended him for the magistracy and encouraged the boy's natural taste for study. The real delight of Montesquieu's life was reading, particularly the classics. Hence his advice to himself in his commonplace book: read much and note little (still good advice for scholars). Montesquieu became a member of the *parlement* of Bordeaux (an important provincial lawcourt, not a 'parliament' in the English sense) in 1714, and a *président à mortier* two years later. Montesquieu also became a member of the recently formed Academy of Bordeaux with the intention of turning it into a truly scientific society in the generous enlightened sense of the word 'science'.

In his middle thirties, Montesquieu settled down at la Brède as a full-time man of letters. The mildly scandalous *Persian Letters* (1721) had already made him famous and opened up for him the aristocratic salons of *ancien régime* Paris. He gave himself a generous allowance of time for what modern politicians would call 'fact-finding' tours, including the two years (until 1731) he spent in England forming his famous ideas about how the British constitution did not work. His *Considerations on the Causes of the Greatness of the Romans and Their Decline* appeared in 1734, and his masterpiece, *The Spirit of the Laws*, in 1748. He was a member of both the Académie française and the Royal Society.

Montesquieu died in 1755, probably from the influenza, which was still a killer in the eighteenth century. He is said to have 'returned' to the Catholic faith on his deathbed, but the matter is problematical. Some say that the deathbed religious orthodoxy was only a story spread about by the Jesuits; others doubt whether he could have 'returned' to the faith when it is not clear in what sense he ever 'left' it.

Nothing illustrates the internationalism of Enlightenment better than the fact that Montesquieu was a member of the Academies of Bordeaux, Cortona (in Tuscany) and Berlin, and of the Académie française in Paris and the Royal Society in London. The breadth of Montesquieu's interests shows Enlightenment at its best. The time was still far distant when the sciences were to be divided up into jealously guarded fiefdoms, and Montesquieu's curiosity ranged over what we would now call natural science, biology, botany, history ancient and modern, moral philosophy, psychology, comparative religion, demography, climatology, law, sociology and political science. His erudition was one of the wonders of the age. There was nothing that had ever happened in the world that he did not know something about, and he seemed to have read everything, much of it more than once and often in the original language and in translation as well. Even the more than two thousand references in *The Spirit of the Laws* (1748) do not do justice to Montesquieu's learning; as Montesquieu himself said, the secret of intellectual work is to read much and to note little.

Montesquieu himself is an engaging figure. The family came from the provincial legal nobility of Guyenne. Montesquieu was held at the font by a local beggar to remind him throughout his life that the poor are our brothers. He was put out to nurse at the local mill at la Brède, so he spent his first three years living with peasants and acquiring a strong provincial accent which he was never to lose even in the aristocratic and literary salons of Paris. He began his working life as a lawyer as *président à mortier* (so called because of a particular mortar-board hat worn by the incumbents of that office) in the provincial *parlement* of Bordeaux. The office was hereditary in Montesquieu's family, and it was saleable (Montesquieu was eventually to sell it), a typical example of the feudal privileges of the nobility which Montesquieu was later to defend as necessary if monarchy was not to degenerate into tyranny. Montesquieu was never to be all that serious a lawyer, and it is probable that early on in his adult life he intended to give up the law and live on his rents as an independent man of letters. Montesquieu, who was known as 'the president' long after he had vacated his office, travelled widely, including visits to Italy where he showed a great interest in the quality of the air at Rome, a prefiguring of his later concern in *The Spirit of the Laws* with the influence of climate, and to England where his connections with the opposition to the oligarchy of the Walpole Whigs stimulated his famous interest in the distribution of powers in constitutional government as a means to the preservation of liberty.

Montesquieu was fond of saying that *The Spirit of the Laws* was the fruit of a lifetime's labour. Up to the time of the publication of *The Spirit of the Laws* (prudently published abroad) Montesquieu was chiefly known as the writer of a witty and mildly salacious satire, the best-selling *Persian Letters* (1721), of a history of Rome, *Considerations on the Causes of the Greatness of the Romans and Their Decline* (1734), which, while bristling with original reflections (Gibbon admired it), was lightweight by the standards of the latest historical methods of its day. *The Spirit of the Laws* changed Montesquieu's reputation overnight. He was no longer regarded simply as a more than usually learned frequenter of fashionable and mildly subversive intellectual and social circles, but as the wisest and most learned man of his day. The reception of *The Spirit of the Laws* was not universally enthusiastic, and it was later to be put on the Roman Catholic Church's index of forbidden books because of some of the things it had to say about religion. None the less, it came to be seen as one of the foundation books of Enlightenment, as powerful an influence in its way as Locke's *Essay Concerning Human Understanding* and the *Two Treatises of Civil Government* were in theirs.

How is this to be explained about a work which commentators from 1748 to the present day seem to agree has no very obvious structure? And especially about a work about laws whose definition of the central concept of law is notoriously hard to pin down? Many reasons have been advanced for thinking of *The Spirit of the Laws* as the book for which the whole of enlightened Europe had been waiting. Some commend it for being a compendium of knowledge of other societies, both societies in the past and other societies in the book's own contemporary world. Others have regarded it as another work of Montesquieu the satirist, seeing in *The Spirit of the Laws* a covert attack on all forms of government except the republican, and this despite the obvious fact that, with a single possible exception, Montesquieu does not regard republicanism as a possible political option in the modern world. Others, concentrating on Montesquieu's treatment of religion, have seen in *The Spirit of the Laws* a barely coded materialist account of human institutions and behaviour, an account which, far from regarding the world as God's creation, regards religion as caused by psychological needs which ultimately derive from human physiology. Yet others regard the book as demonstrating that liberty and virtue are natural to men if they are properly governed, without realising that this statement is close to being self-contradictory.

It is perhaps not surprising that so many different reasons have been advanced for the greatness of *The Spirit of the Laws*, granted the enormous size of the book and the enormous variety of its subject matter. There is a real sense in which there is a Montesquieu for everyone (including the young Mao Tse-tung), and it is not necessarily the case that what impressed contemporaries is what should impress us now; nor is it necessarily the case that the book has always been used to support causes of which Montesquieu would have approved. *The Spirit of the Laws* has become famous for two of its doctrines – the separation of powers and the influence of climate on manners, morals, and forms of government – but the work contains a good deal more than that.

Perhaps the easiest thing to decide about *The Spirit of the Laws* is what would have tended to impress contemporaries. Enlightenment was an attempt to understand the world, and to understand the world in a particular way. Knowledge had to be scientific knowledge in the sense of bringing a wide range of naturally occurring phenomena within the understanding of a few fixed scientific laws, and the wider the range of phenomena and the fewer the laws, the better that understanding was. The bedrock of all respectable scientific explanation was physics, either Cartesian or Newtonian. Physics yielded up the true natural laws of the physical universe in the purely mechanical terms of cause and effect. For some enlightened thinkers, the materialistic explanations of science could be extended to the human world in a way which excluded God altogether. Human behaviour, it could be argued, was just as much determined by its causes as the behaviour of the physical world. Therefore, there was no free will because there was no choosing to act in a particular way because how one acted was just as predictable as the way physical bodies behaved. Without free will, there could be no morality and no justice as they had traditionally been conceived in the Christian tradition. It was not clear, in the materialist view of the world, how men could sin. A predetermined human action, say theft or murder, could no more be called the perpetrator's 'fault' than a tidal wave could be called sinful if it destroyed life and property. The idea that God commanded men to do some things and avoid others, and gave men the free will to choose between them, was not so much wrong as unnecessary: everything about human life, including religion, could be explained in the no doubt highly complex terms of moral (that is to say non-physical) cause and effect.

This was an extreme position, and more properly characterises the later Enlightenment than the early. Montesquieu comes somewhere in the middle. In *The Spirit of the Laws* Montesquieu still tries to keep God in the frame, while insisting that the human world can be explained in the terms of physical and moral cause and effect. There was really no contradiction in this. It was perfectly rational to argue that just as God had created a physical universe which worked according to rationally intelligible laws, so he must have created a human universe which was similarly intelligible. This led to initial puzzlement among Montesquieu's immediate audience. Montesquieu's celebrated definition of laws in general at the beginning of *The Spirit of the Laws* as 'the necessary relations deriving from the nature of things' is worth quoting:

> in this sense, all beings have their laws: the divinity has its laws, the material world has its laws, the intelligences superior to man have their laws, the beasts have their laws, man has his laws.

Contemporaries were confused by the generality of Montesquieu's definition, including as it did physical laws, the laws governing the behaviour of the animal kingdom, the moral law which defined justice and injustice, and the human positive law; but this sense of confusion was really unnecessary. Of course, it was not the case that physical laws and moral laws were laws in exactly the same sense, and human positive law was like neither, because human positive laws can change (and indeed *The Spirit of the Laws* is centrally concerned with changes in human laws). Critics might agree that laws were the relations deriving from the nature of things in the physical and animal worlds, but the mutability of human affairs and the wide variety of human experience seemed to be powerful evidence that what was true of the rest of nature could not possibly be true of the world of human social and political experience. The fact that human law could and did change was proof that human affairs were not subject to the same unchanging laws as the rest of nature. Perhaps Montesquieu's critics were misled by Montesquieu's legal background, when he was engaged in applying an existing legal system, and forgot the importance which Montesquieu attached to the legislator.

Legislators are human, and they can make mistakes. The fundamental determining factor which decides what a society is like, at least in the beginning, is climate. Montesquieu later adds the nature of the soil and of landscape, and later still he adds moral causes: religion, laws, government, tradition, manners and morals. It is the interaction of these causes acting on human behaviour which forms the famous *esprit général*, the (moral, social and political) culture of a given society. Montesquieu probably wants us to think of these causes as working in something like chronological order. At the beginnings of a society, its cultural configuration is largely determined by physical causes, but as a society develops the moral causes acquire an increasing purchase on a society's *esprit général*. The *esprit général* of a society, whether it is simple or sophisticated, is the legislator's raw material, so to speak. He legislates against it at his peril, and at the peril of the whole of that society. At best, laws enacted against the *esprit général* will simply fail to work; at worst, if vigorously enforced, they could destroy the society which the laws are meant to preserve. Laws, by which Montesquieu here means constitutional law and the laws governing manners and morals as well as the legal system as ordinarily understood, should almost always be made within the bounds of the culture which originally came out of the physical causes of nature. That is what Montesquieu means when he says that human laws are the 'necessary relations deriving from the nature of things'. There is a proper relationship between the man-made laws of a society and the nature of that society itself.

Of course, it is possible for an erring human legislator *in fact* to legislate against the *esprit général* of his own society, and it is even sometimes necessary. Montesquieu notoriously connects hot climates with large populations and idleness, and this raises the problem, for instance in India and most of China, of producing enough food to keep the population alive. A wise legislator there will therefore actually legislate *against* climate and social customs, though it is a battle which he can never finally win. *The esprit général* of ancient civilisations like India and China is in fact highly complex, and in legislating against only two particular aspects of it, the wise legislator would not be devising laws which went against the grain of the whole of a society's life. Sometimes a legislator might be tempted to legislate against the grain of the whole of a society's life, and Montesquieu believes that in cases like that time will tell. The legislation will fail, and the system of government which produced the legislation might well fall with it. It should be obvious by now that Montesquieu is far from fatalistic as far as human laws are concerned. The very complexity of the *esprit général* gives the wise legislator plenty of room for manoeuvre within it, and there is plenty of opportunity for reform within it.

In his view of how the wise legislator will act Montesquieu is in fact dealing with two distinct problems. The first is the question of how legislators *ought* to act, and the second is an enquiry into what nature really intends for man. It became a central philosophical problem after Hume's *Treatise of Human Nature* to decide where human 'oughts' in general came from. Hume argued that no given set of facts could, of themselves, produce a moral imperative through reason. There is nothing in the fact that I see a group of starving people which tells me I 'ought' to feed them. I may feel I ought to feed them, but that feeling does not come from seeing the starving but from a moral sense previously acquired from all the formative moral influences which derive from living in a particular society, part of which is a particular form of moral education. Montesquieu's account of the legislator seems to go against Hume's argument. What is there about the legislator's view of his own society which tells him what he 'ought' to do? Why does a legislator not just look at his own society, see that it is in a bit of a mess, and say to himself that there is nothing about the observed set of facts about his own society which could possibly tell him what he ought to do? Montesquieu does in fact think that that is what some governments do, especially in the East where things are notoriously slow to change. But in societies which do change, and Montesquieu typically means Western societies, ancient and modern, legislation is necessary to cope with problems unless those societies are to begin to fall apart. What he urges on the wise legislator is the acquisition of a prudent knowledge of the *esprit général* of his own society, otherwise his legislation will prove to be shots in the dark, and if the legislator insists on laws which contradict the *esprit général*, then he is at best banging his head against a brick wall and at worst endangering his own position as ruler, and only a fool would want either of those.

Montesquieu's doctrine of nature will not allow him entirely to be a moral relativist. Despite the huge amount of detail about differences in manners and morals between different societies which *The Spirit of the Laws* contains, Montesquieu continued to believe in the existence of pre-social laws of nature as they applied to human existence. He was no Hobbesian as Hobbes was understood in his day to be the thinker who denied that right and wrong existed until the human legislator defined them. (This is not in fact Hobbes's own position, but that does not matter here.) What confused Montesquieu's original readership was that Montesquieu appeared to derive his laws of nature from the world itself, and not from reason or from the commands of God. The things which Montesquieu regarded as natural laws were derived from how human beings actually lived. These laws were: peace; feeding oneself; sexual attraction; life in society; reproduction at a certain age; the attainment of mental maturity at a certain age; freedom and independence by birth; reasonableness; equality; fear of death; self-preservation. What worried critics still loyal to older natural law notions was that, on the face of it, these laws of nature contained no prescriptions, no commands from a moral superior for their obedience. Many of them men shared with the animals, and it had always been part of the doctrine of natural law that there was one part of the law of nature which applied to animals, and which could not be broken, and another part of the law of nature which applied to men with free will and so could be broken. Montesquieu seemed to be saying that all that was needed to establish a code of natural law was to examine the regularities which occurred in the patterns of human living. No reference was needed to a divine, let alone to a human, legislator. Quite the reverse: human legislators ignored these laws of nature at their own and others' peril.

Montesquieu never gave up the idea that nature, properly understood, prompts men to virtue, where by virtue one means benevolence and altruism, and he thought that the experience of living in a human society proved this. This seems to be a view he held as early as the publication of the *Persian Letters*, which contain the neat little anti-Hobbesian parable of the Troglodytes. The Troglodytes were a small society living somewhere in Arabia who one day decided to return to the State of Nature by throwing out their king. The State of Nature they lived in was Hobbesian. Each person pursued his own self-interest as far as his own strength and talents allowed him, and no one had a care for the interests of others. Returning to nature conceived on Hobbesian principles quickly leads to the disintegration of Troglodyte society. The strong naturally bully the weak, stealing their wives and their land. Other misfortunes follow as the country suffers two outbreaks of the plague. In the first plague, a doctor from outside cured them, but after they were cured the Troglodytes could see no rationally self-interested reason for paying him, so that when the plague returned they were refused all outside help and Troglodyte society nearly became extinct.

Only two families survived, and they decided that in the future they would live not selfishly but virtuously. They were frugal, they paid the gods their due, and they regarded their neighbours' interests as at least as important as their own. Troglodyte society grew and prospered, and so powerful was their example of virtuous living that their war-like neighbours no longer attacked them. As the society expanded, the Troglodytes decided that it would be sensible to elect a king to regularise the practice of virtue into a system of law. The legislator they chose was an old man, famous for his virtue, who accepted the office unwillingly, and who wept at the thought that the virtue of the Troglodytes was no longer enough to regulate their common life so that now they needed the discipline of laws.

The anti-Hobbesian implications of the fable are obvious. Human social living is impossible if nature intended men to be simply selfishly motivated acquisitive machines. Nature plainly intends men to live together, and if this is to be possible at all men have to act virtuously, either because they are virtuous, or because the law makes them act as if they were. Therefore, the practice of virtue is natural. This is very far from saying that all men in a society are in fact equally virtuous, or that there is an equal tendency towards virtue in all societies, but what it does mean is that there has to be some virtue in a society for that society to function at all. Montesquieu does put his finger on a possible weakness in Hobbes's own argument. If men are as fundamentally anti-social in the state of nature as Hobbes says, then it is stretching the imagination too far to ask us to account for the fact that human beings do live in society for most of the time. Hobbes's logically impeccable, but in fact logically contrived, arguments about an original social contract just are not enough to explain how the aggressively selfish creature man could be able to come to live peacefully with his fellows. Of course, Montesquieu *has* to argue that men are naturally capable enough of virtue to be able to live together peaceably because, if men were naturally anti-social, then the legislator would find himself in the position of having to legislate against nature the whole time and not just occasionally.

THE THEORY OF CLIMATE

Montesquieu says that climate is the first of all empires as it effects a nation's *esprit général*. He means us to take the idea of climate broadly as a physical cause of other physical causes, or as a physical cause which interacts with other physical causes. Climate interacts with landscape – mountains give shelter from winds – and with the nature of the soil – some good soil is well watered and some is not. Montesquieu also believes that climate affects human fertility, though he is not very precise about what the connection is. It would not be doing an injustice to Montesquieu's doctrine of climate to call it a theory of nature as it affects human living, though the basic idea in the doctrine is the way temperature affects the human body and its passions.

In this, Montesquieu is impeccably materialist. He thought that the whole of living nature could be explained as the actions of fluids working through pipes. This applied to plants and animals, and it also applied to human beings, which he saw as bundles of pipes and strainers (the phrase is Addison's). These 'fibres' of the body are highly sensitive to heat and cold. Cold makes the fibres of the body contract, so that in northern climates the constant exposure of the body to natural cold and artificial heat causes the body fibres to keep contracting and expanding, and this constant exercise means that the body fibres become more flexible. This in its turn means that the blood circulates more freely, strengthens the heart, and strengthens the body in general. Northerners, therefore, feel the strength of their own bodies, and this makes them courageous, confident of themselves, and therefore open and frank in their manners and morals. By contrast, the constant heat of southern and eastern climates leads to a certain rigidity in the body fibres because they do not receive the exercise which they get in the North. The blood flows less easily, and blood being a mixture of corpuscles and water, there is always the danger of the blood coagulating through sweating. This makes the southern and eastern people sluggish and disinclined to work hard, and this is compounded by the effects of climate on the soil. Sustenance is often easy to procure in hot climates with good soil, and it is only the effect of hot climates pushing up human fertility which prevents idleness in hot countries.

The case of the nervous system is different. Nerves exist in clusters near the skin, and so are also subject to the effects of heat and cold. In cold climates, the skin contracts, so that the nerves are to an extent protected from outside stimuli. In hot countries, where the skin is naturally more relaxed, the nerves are more exposed to external stimuli, so that those who live in the South and the East respond more readily to sensations from the outside. This gives them more imagination, taste, sensitivity and vivacity. The pleasures that men seek in cold climates are of the hearty kind, involving much hunting and drinking, whereas the taste for pleasure in hot climates is more sophisticated and more decadent. Northerners have therefore fewer vices by nature, and southerners fewer virtues. In Turkey, the ultimate in human felicity is the sultan's harem. Pain is felt less in cold countries: you have to flay a Muscovite alive to make him feel anything at all. Heat leads above all to indolence and a taste for the more exotic and wicked pleasures. Allied to that is a tendency in intellectual life towards abstruse speculation rather than attendance to the useful arts. Solitary contemplation is natural in hot climates, where the life of action is less attractive. Hence the tendency in the East to the anti-social practice of monasticism.

Climate, being the first of all empires, and leading to undesirable effects at its extremes of hot and cold, must be legislated against, and Montesquieu means legislation in its broadest sense, which includes the laws of religion and manners and morals as well as positive legislation by rulers. The *esprit général* of a nation is a matter of the balancing of physical and moral causes, and moral causes are, within limits, subject to human manipulation, though the possible speed of that manipulation varies from society to society. The natural indolence of the East makes its peoples slow to change their ways, or even to bestir themselves enough to get more than a bare subsistence from the soil. For such peoples, the force of religion, manners and morals and legislation combined are needed just for a society to remain at the stage of development which it has reached. In China, and to a lesser extent in Islamic countries, there is very little perceived difference between moral, social, religious and political laws: in China and Japan, disrespect for social superiors is punishable by death. With all laws tending in the same direction, it is very difficult to change anything, especially by legislation. Manners and morals can only be changed by the example of superiors and not by despotic edicts. All the despot can really do is to reinforce existing custom and practice.

Climate is one of the key factors in foreign relations. The worst position for a society to be in is one where there is no temperate zone between it and its neighbours. This is especially true in the East, where changes of climate between north and south are abrupt, so that civilised and indolent peoples living in hot climates are geographically very close to the active and warrior peoples of the North. This accounts for the number of times China has been successfully invaded. Europe, by contrast, enjoys a series of gradations in climate from south to north; hard and soft peoples do not live cheek by jowl, and that makes Europe harder to conquer: Rome fell in the West because all her northern enemies attacked her at the same time, which was also a time when Rome herself had been weakened by internal causes. By contrast, the effect on China of her conquerors has not been as great as one might be led to suppose. The very immobility of Chinese society has led to the gradual assimilation of native Chinese manners, morals and maxims of government by the conquerors themselves. Climate for Montesquieu is not invariable, especially the micro-climates of cities. One of the reasons Montesquieu gives for the difference between the Romans of his own day and those of the days of Rome's greatness is that the city's air must have been changed by centuries of human habitation, an early example of the politics of pollution.

Climate, of course, affects forms of government, especially in the early stages. Physical causes have their empire early; it is only with the advancement of societies that moral causes come into their own, but when they do they still interact with physical causes. In England, the climate still produces a disrelish for life (the English disease is suicide), and the consequent ill-temper caused by the east wind makes the English ever ready to find fault with their government. England is therefore fortunate to be governed by laws and not by men, otherwise a government by one man unlimited by laws would cause such mayhem that the government could not last. Even as it is, English politics is constantly agitated by riot and sedition.

Climate being the most obviously 'natural' cause as it affects the life of man, and granted its continuing dominance over the lives of animals, the question arises of how any other law can possibly go against nature. How can physical nature possibly be legislated against? How can the empire of physical causes be reduced, because in the end Montesquieu thinks it is 'opinion' conceived in the widest possible sense that determines what the nature of a society and a polity are going to be? Perhaps that is a false problem, because in a sense all causes are physical for Montesquieu. By and large, he accepted the Lockian epistemology's insistence that individual minds were made up of the sensations which they received from the outside world. These sensations of sight, touch, hearing, smell and taste were physical sensations producing physiological or chemical responses within the human brain. Montesquieu distinguished between two kinds of education, individual and collective. Individual education is what is ordinarily meant by education, and it forms what we call the individual character — *you* rather than *me*. This is the first of all educations simply because it begins first. But there is another, collective, education which comes from the wider society in which we live, and this second education (which we would call 'socialisation') proceeds as children come to know more of the world, and it continues until the individual becomes a perfectly socialised member of the society in which he lives, and it is this which accounts for why you are *like* me. There can be nothing 'unnatural' about this process because it happens in every society of which anything is known, past or present. Every society has its *esprit général*, and so this must be part of nature.

Not all societies work equally well, and not all aspects of all societies are equally admirable, but Montesquieu appears to think that most of the troubles which occur in the world come about as the result of a lack of understanding of these natural processes on the part of rulers. The nature of a society at any given time is determined by the interaction of many causes, and some of these causes at least are susceptible to human improvement. The end of government in different societies will be different – in England it is liberty, in China tranquillity – and the best government is the one which achieves its objective with the min-imum of effort and cost. Bad government is government which appears by its actions to ignore its own principle, and by ignoring its own principle government becomes the cause of discontent when it should really be a solver of problems. Montesquieu's benevolence means that he always considers government from the point of view of the governed, and in this he follows impeccable ancient precedents: men are not just producers of government, they are consumers of government too. In fact, Montesquieu means many things by good government, but in the end good government always means for him the feeling of security of the person and of property on the part of subjects. Tranquillity without fear is about all that subjects can hope for in general, though there are exceptions. What Montesquieu is intent on hammering home is that when we look around the world, and when we look into the past, it is surprising how few governments have been able to provide for even that minimum of human security without which life comes close to being not worth living.

TYPES OF GOVERNMENT AND THEIR PRINCIPLES

Montesquieu again follows ancient precedent in his classification of types of government, and his reflections on these matters are worth attending to, not for the classification itself but for his view of the vital spring of those governments. Each form of government – republic, monarchy and despotism – has its nature, its principle and its object. By principle Montesquieu means the 'spirit' of that government, what causes it to act in a particular way. By 'nature' he means the constitutional or formal structure of government, and by object he means the 'end' of government conceived in an Aristotelian way. A republic is a state in which the people, or part of the people, are sovereign, so his definition includes both democracy and aristocracy ancient style; monarchy is government by a single person according to established laws which include especially constitutional laws; despotism is the rule of one man without the restraining force of laws – despots can make and break rules as they please, so despotism is government by caprice and whim. What Montesquieu is interested in is not the formal structures of power (England is an exception) but the way power is exercised in different types of polity. Montesquieu is in fact interested in what we would now call government *policy* and how that policy is implemented over time. Hence the unique importance of Roman history. Like Machiavelli, Montesquieu regards Roman

325

history as the history of a state which has run its course. Rome had experienced every kind of government, even a variant of the separation of powers, so Rome is a kind of over-arching example to the political scientist of sometimes wise and sometimes foolish government. Of course, the policy of the various forms of government at Rome affected the Roman constitution but did not always lead to a change of constitutional forms. Like Machiavelli, Montesquieu is acutely aware that constitutional forms may remain unchanged after the spirit which originally created and animated them has long departed.

Montesquieu thinks that each form of government has its own activating principle – virtue in a republic, honour in a monarchy and fear in a despotism. Some of Montesquieu's contemporaries found this classification puzzling, because they took Montesquieu to be saying that you *only* find virtue in republics, honour in monarchies and fear in despotisms, whereas Montesquieu's definitions are really negative: he is saying that *without* virtue republics cannot survive, just as monarchies and despotisms cannot survive without honour and fear. And we must never forget the legislator. Very often it will be the task of the wise legislator to return decayed government to its first principle, and it is on the legislator's capacity to do this that the survival of a system of government largely depends. Thus *The Spirit of the Laws* contains advice to rulers on long-term policy goals, an idea which Montesquieu probably took and extended from Machiavelli's own reading of Roman history in his *Discourses on Livy*. Like Machiavelli, Montesquieu believed that a combination of good fortune and good policy enabled republican institutions to survive for so long at Rome. Rome had a self-correcting constitution while the republic lasted. Montesquieu's own *Considerations on the Causes of the Greatness of the Romans and Their Decline* (1734) follows Machiavelli very closely in regarding the endemic class war at Rome between the patricians and the plebs as the secret of the longevity of the republic. The agitations of the plebeians kept patrician arrogance under control, while the wisdom of the patricians moderated the rashness of the people. Each part of the state cancelled out the faults of the other, and so Rome had moderate and balanced government.

The form of government Montesquieu dislikes most is despotism. Despotism is not legitimate government in a literal sense because it does not work according to any fixed principles of law, and it does not always work very well anyway. Despotism probably has its origins in a corrupted kingship, and Montesquieu certainly thought that all monarchies needed careful watching if they were not to degenerate into despotism: Richelieu may have had despotic intentions for the monarchy of Louis XIV. (Despotism begins with sleep.) There is no virtue, where virtue means self-sacrificing love of country, in a despotism; nor does the passion for honour enable the despot to gather round him a loyal aristocratic class eager to fight his wars. To be a truly honourable estate aristocracy needs a certain independence from the sovereign; kings may make aristocrats, but they are not supposed to break them. Ambition in a despotism does not take the form of a desire for glory but a desire to become despot oneself. This makes despotisms chronically unstable because despots are feared rather than loved. They are capable of inducing an abject submission but not of inspiring loyalty. Despotisms are particularly subject to *coups d'état* through palace intrigues or to foreign invasions. Corruption of subordinate officials, violence and the spectacular shedding of blood, and a religion based on ignorance or superstition are always typically found in despotisms. Though simple, despotisms are not notably efficient in their modest aim of securing domestic tranquillity so that the prince is secure in his enjoyment of the pleasures of the harem. Constant fear of death through the wrath of the prince is eventually counter-productive. Men become so used to it that it ceases to have the desired effect of obedience after a time, despite the horrific nature of punishments in despotisms. That is why religion is so important: fear of the gods may make up for a declining fear of the despot and keep men to their duties.

In a despotism, everybody is potentially a dead man. What public tranquillity despotisms enjoy is nothing like the concord of a well-constituted republic or monarchy; it is the silence of the subjugated. Most of the world has been and is, or is threatened with being, ruled by despots, despite the hatefulness of despotism. How can this be? Montesquieu has to find a specific reason, otherwise the examples of Persia, Turkey, Japan, Russia and China might conspire against him and prove that despotism is natural. Of course, in one sense it is, because the causes of the rise of despotism are everywhere more or less the same, but despotism cannot really be natural because it does not easily secure even its own modest end of tranquillity and because natural reason tells men who have thought about it not to entrust all the powers of government to one man's fancy; that had been a commonplace since Plato. In fact, Montesquieu thinks that, natural causes apart, despotism is so general because it is so simple. Do what you are told and the rest is easy. What Montesquieu seems to be saying is that, despite appearances, despots do not really rule in any extended sense of the term. One-man rule in an extensive empire is impossible in practice, and Montesquieu knows perfectly well that, even if the princes's vices did not keep him from the concerns of his state, delegation of political authority is necessary. Delegated authority will be just as tyrannical as the supposed authority at the centre. Governors of provinces will be petty tyrants with what are effectively their own power bases, so that the centre will always have good reasons for fearing the periphery. The case of the petty despot will be no different from the case of the real despot: he will not really rule either because fear has its limits. What caused despotism in the first place, slowness of change owing to climate, will be the real ruler. Manners rule the East because they change at a pace not much slower than geology. This in its turn limits anything a benevolent despot might try to do in the way of change. Despotic heads wearing crowns must lie very uneasily indeed.

In Montesquieu's language, all other forms of government apart from despotism are 'moderate'. Again, Montesquieu's usage is remarkably close to Aristotle's. Republican government is government by the few or many according to law, while monarchy is government by one man according to law. Montesquieu assumes with Aristotle and Marsilius that government by law – that is, by what we would call constitutional law and the orderly processes of the ordinary law of the land – is legitimate in the literal sense and in the sense that it will be widely seen to be legitimate by its citizens. The animating spirit of republics is virtue, and Montesquieu's idea of virtue would have been recognisable to the great heroes of the Roman republic. Virtue is love of one's country, a self-sacrificing passion for equality and frugality for which the republic stands. That is what makes a democratic republic like ancient Athens or Rome survive. A good test of the soundness of republican government is private property and public affluence: when the public treasury is full and private purses empty, then that private wealth which can be used to corrupt the citizens when they vote is lacking (Montesquieu skips over the stickiness of Greek fingers when handling public funds). Virtue extends to jealous defence of political rights. Like Machiavelli, Montesquieu realises that political rights are empty husks without the will to exercise them, and again like Machiavelli, Montesquieu recognises that a certain necessary turbulence must always accompany the assertion of plebeian rights. Republican politics at Rome had been nothing if not robust, and, like Machiavelli, Montesquieu sees a source of Rome's strength, not weakness, in the class divisions within the city. Neither party could go too far without coming up against the institutionalised check of the power of the other, tribunes of the people against consuls and senators. The agitations of the people were a kind of political callisthenics for the senators, keeping them fit in the arts of government. The class war was a condition of Roman society, not its problem. Rome rose to greatness through the military virtues of its citizen army, and as Montesquieu shrewdly points out, men who were victorious abroad could not be expected to be supine and mute subjects at home. The city was their city because they had fought for it, and while poverty remained a public virtue at Rome, the claims of armed poverty were always strong. Since the commons at Rome had always to be managed and reconciled, the Roman patricians had no alternative but to develop the political skills necessary for handling a people who were always going to be troublesome to rule.

Montesquieu's treatment of government in the Roman republic is in part an answer to the question of why so much of the world is ruled by despotism, just as his treatment of despotism is in part an answer to the Hobbesian view of sovereignty. Good fortune, good laws and a certain level of political understanding are necessary if a system of liberty is to survive. The stark simplicity of despotism's 'fear me and obey me' can have no place among free and virtuous men. Despotism does not have to rely for its working on political skills at all. Fear is something which the meanest understanding can understand. A man would have to be very dull indeed not to know when he felt threatened, hence the connection between despotism and ignorance. Perhaps Montesquieu intends a double refutation of Hobbes. Not only does despotism not work very well because despotisms are seldom tranquil for long, but also they are unlikely to survive among a self-assertive people. Hobbes's argument that despotic sovereignty working through fear is the kind of government rational men would set up of their own free will if they thought about the matter properly begins to look a little shaky in the face of Montesquieu's account of despotism, and Hobbes's argument that fundamentally self-assertive men need despotic government begins to look a bit shaky in the face of Montesquieu's account of Roman liberty.

We do well to remember that it is not liberty but virtue which was the true 'end' of republican government at Rome. (Only the English constitution has liberty as its end.) Virtue leads to moderation in government not because those who are virtuous are necessarily moderate characters themselves but because they are forced into moderation by an equal and opposite power – that is, the power of the patricians. Indeed, it could be argued that the reverse is true: there would have been no moderating influence of one part of the Roman state on the other if the commons had not occasionally been over-assertive in their demands and if the patricians had not sometimes been haughty. This led to the codification of moderate maxims of government into constitutional and ordinary law, and a respect for the laws once established it was easy for Roman legislation to embody what was virtuous in Roman manners and morals and for special magistrates to be appointed to oversee what we would call the private lives of citizens. Why, then, did Rome fall? In particular, what changed her form of government from a virtuous democracy into a despotism? Montesquieu adduces many particular causes, but the chief one was Rome's success as a conquering power. Rome became too large for it to do more than pretend that it was an extended municipality. Most of the commons lived too far from the city for them to be able to see the city as *their* city, and virtue declined. With the decline of virtue went an increasing private opulence, which allowed ambitious citizens to buy the support of parties, and so the clash of the factions, so healthy while Rome was smaller, led in the end to civil war. Out of the civil wars came the emperors, and eventually the tyrants. In his account of the decline of Rome in the *Considerations*, Montesquieu makes a celebrated distinction, though it was not original to him, between historical 'causes' and historical 'occasions'. Causes are long-term, and probably irreversible, while occasions serve the purpose of causes and are accidental. It would have fallen to another Caesar and another Pompey to accomplish the ruin of the republic by their ambition, and neither Caesar nor Pompey aimed at empire. Accidental occasions are the product of human will and direction, but historical causes are what we would now call 'systemic', founded on the nature of things in Montesquieu's own language.

In an aristocratic republic, in which there is no institutionalised check on the insolence of rank, moderation itself should be the aim of the laws, otherwise the government will degenerate into what the ancients called oligarchy, government by the rich few, in their own interest, by force rather than by law. Hence the wisdom of the laws given to the Spartans by Lycurgus. The only reward available to the warrior-citizens of Sparta was honour gained from prowess displayed on the battlefield. Honour is inferior to virtue because, being essentially military, it leads to war and foreign conquest. (Montesquieu conveniently forgets that Rome conquered her 'empire' under the republic, and that Sparta was famously difficult to provoke into war.) A people who admire success in war will come to applaud other warrior virtues like stealth and cunning which in the ordinary sense are not part of virtue at all. Hence the legislation of theft at Sparta, where youths were deliberately kept on short commons to make them into successful food thieves and so into stealthy and cunning warriors. But much better a thousand times that honour should be ambition's goal rather than wealth, which is the case with the modern republics which Montesquieu observed at first hand during his travels in Italy and Holland. Venice, Genoa and the United Provinces were corrupt merchant oligarchies.

Montesquieu plainly admires the ancient republics at their best, but equally plainly he regards virtuous republics as a thing of the past. On one level, Montesquieu's explanation for the passing of a genuine republicanism may be very simple. Perhaps he just thought that the ancients at their best were better men than the moderns, nobler, more patriotic, with a much more solid sense of the public values of the cities in which they lived. There was not much of the 'man versus the state' feeling in the ancient republics, no sense of the disjunction between private and public goals which was to become something of a commonplace afterwards. On the practical level, Montesquieu seems to have thought that, with certain exceptions, among whom he included the Swiss, the sheer size of modern states mitigated against republican forms of government. The ancient republics were essentially what we would now call 'face to face' societies, where the sense of public virtue was so strong that each man acted as an automatic censor of the manners and morals of his neighbours. (And we do well to remember that in those states prosecutions were nearly always brought by private persons, and part of virtue was having the civic courage to bring actions against malefactors perhaps richer and more influential than oneself.) The chances of a state being either a despotism or a monarchy were proportional to its size. Montesquieu himself lived in an age when the idea of 'universal monarchy' in Europe was eagerly discussed: perhaps the Bourbons or the Habsburgs, by conquest or marriage, would establish a monarchy which was truly European in extent. This, of course, did not happen, but it is no coincidence that the European wars of the eighteenth century have come to be called wars of succession.

The fact that monarchy was the typical form of government in modern Europe did not in the least mean that the examples of the ancient republics had nothing to teach the moderns. Far from it. At their best, they were shining examples of moderate, free and balanced government. They were also examples of what came to be called 'mixed government' because at Sparta, Athens and Rome government was a mixture of the principles of monarchy, aristocracy and democracy, with the people ultimately sovereign. At Rome, the annually elected consuls were the kingly part (they led the armies), the Senate was the aristocratic part, and the people through their tribunes were the democratic part. This idea of the balancing of parts of government against each other was to have a great future as part of the modern liberal theory of constitutionalism. Montesquieu also makes one exception to the rule that republics have to be small, and that exception was also to be pregnant with the future. The exception was the Greek federated republic, an alliance of independent and sovereign republics created typically to defend the independence of cities against foreign aggressors, either Macedon or Rome. The idea of the federated republic looked back to the great days when all Greece united to defend herself against the Persian invasions, and more distantly still to the legendary time when the Greeks banded together to rescue Helen from Troy. The crucial argument in the American *Federalist Papers*, written to sell the new Constitution of the United States to the American people after 1787, was that a *federal* republic composed of the separate sovereignties of the individual states meant that the United States could both be extensive in territory and enjoy the good fortune of republican institutions as well. The United States of America is Homer's revenge on the kings whose fortunes he sings in *The Iliad*. Montesquieu's *Spirit of the Laws* was the channel by which the ancient idea of a federated republic reached the most famous federal republic of all.

The spirit of monarchy is honour. In the French case, the principle of honour has its origins in the customary law of the Middle Ages, which placed great importance on challenges and duelling, and the rules governing these were based on a fundamental idea of honour. What was honourable and what was not became the subject of minute discriminations in the knightly code. In a monarchy, the king is the fount of honours typically for military services rendered to the state. The spirit of honour is closely connected to the essentially martial virtue of courage, so that you would expect monarchy to interest itself greatly in war and in foreign conquest. Monarchy therefore imparts a certain hyped-up quality to the virtues appropriate to it, especially when these virtues are compared to the virtues appropriate to a republic. In a monarchy, the actions of men are judged fine, not good; great, not just; extraordinary and prodigious, not reasonable. The adulation of the doers of great deeds replaces a decent republican sobriety in the celebration of those who have done their duty by the republic (triumphs were rare at Rome while the republic remained virtuous).

Montesquieu's belief that monarchy is here to stay leads him to pay a good deal of attention to the details of its political life. Monarchy is a good form of government because it is moderate. There may always be a tendency for monarchy to degenerate into despotism, and a good test of whether this is happening or not is the extent to which monarchs recognise that there exists in their realms an unalterable body of what we would call constitutional law, or at the very least law which the monarchy cannot choose to ignore. In a monarchy, the natural guardians of that law are subordinate magistrates drawn from the nobility, a *noblesse de la robe* (Montesquieu was a member himself) exercising local jurisdiction and guarding the ancient constitution. The function of this legal aristocracy in a monarchy is to modify the authoritarianism latent in the royal power by seeing that that power flows through the proper channels. It is a power which is in no sense a rival power to that of monarchy; rather it mediates between the king's will and his subjects. Montesquieu broadens the concept of the mediation of power in a monarchy to include all kinds of legal and incorporated privileges which might be indefensible in themselves but which serve a useful mediating function in monarchies: local seigneurial privileges of jurisdiction and tax collection (as a lord himself, Montesquieu was a bit of a stickler for his feudal rights), corporate privileges of chartered towns, even the jurisdictional privileges of the Church, could be defended as those *pouvoirs intermédiaires* (mediating powers) which came between the king's subjects and the royal will. In a monarchy, kings exercise the legislative and executive power, and it is essential that the judicial power should be exercised by others. Otherwise, all of the three powers of government will be placed in the same hands, and that is despotism. This led Montesquieu to lay particular stress on the French *parlements*, provincial courts of law with a supervisory brief over the jurisdiction of the often different systems of law in the various provinces of France. The old *président à mortier* of the *parlements* of Guyenne at Bordeaux took especially seriously the right of the *parlement*, with the prestigious *parlement* of Paris at their head, to exercise a kind of judicial review of royal edicts before they really became law. As one might have expected, the *parlements* had been rather muted during the reign of Louis XIV, but they remained ancient institutions of vast prestige which quickly began to reassert themselves after the Sun King's death.

It might at first seem rather odd that an enlightened thinker like Montesquieu should be such an ardent defender of what were, after all, feudal privileges, or at least privileges which were feudal in their origin, but it is not really surprising granted Montesquieu's fundamental idea of the corruptibility of monarchy. Only an ancient constitution which held the king to the letter of its law, and only a legal system operating independently of the king's own will could moderate autocratic pretension and secure to persons and property that feeling of security within the law which Montesquieu calls liberty. Any mediating institutions, any claims for quasi-independent jurisdiction by legally privileged minorities were useful as a counterweight to royal power. Montesquieu knew his Tacitus, and he must have known Tacitus' own contempt for the Roman Senate's failure to keep a watching brief over the emperors, a failure which eventually allowed the principate to be exercised by monsters like Caligula and Nero. The French aristocracy was to succeed where the Roman aristocracy had failed. Of course, it was Montesquieu's *pouvoirs intermédiaires* which the French Revolution was to attack as it was to attack all remnants of the feudal past in the name of legal equality; henceforward there was to be no legal obstacle to separate citizen from citizen. Montesquieu knew perfectly well from his study of the politics of the ancient world that despotic government did not necessarily have to be the government of a single man. Any government, whatever its formal constitution, could act despotically if there were no institutional counterweights to moderate its force in practice. The One and Indivisible Republic of the Jacobins would have appeared to be just such a collective despotism to Montesquieu, for there was no effective independent power to balance against the republic's will exercised by a few in its name. It was to be left to the genius of the Founding Fathers of the Constitution of the United States to solve the problem of the tyranny of the majority being exercised in its name by its representatives, and when they came to do that they made much of the most celebrated of Montesquieu's doctrines, the doctrine of the separation of powers.

THE SEPARATION OF POWERS:
THE UNIQUE CASE OF ENGLAND

Montesquieu travelled in England in the years 1729–31, and as the famous author of the *Lettres persanes* he seems to have met everybody, including leading figures in the opposition to the Walpolean oligarchy which monopolised the state. We know that Montesquieu wrote the famous account of the English constitution (*The Spirit of the Laws*, Book XIX) almost immediately he returned from England to France, and we also know that this was the period in which Montesquieu was preparing his *Considerations on the Greatness of the Romans and Their Decline*. The two are not entirely unconnected. While he was in England, Montesquieu was struck by how easily the English party battles between Whigs and Tories, Ins and Outs, could be viewed by the protagonists themselves in terms of the party battles between plebeians and patricians in republican Rome. Rome at her best had been the most free of all the ancient republics, and Montesquieu could not help wondering if there might not be important similarities between the system of Roman government under the republic and the system of government of Hanoverian England. The Roman case fitted the English case quite well. Just as at Rome the principles of monarchy, aristocracy and democracy were expressed in consuls, Senate and people, so in England king, lords and commons each had a share in government. There, of course, the similarity ended, because there was nothing in the commercial and opulent kingdom of England to compare with the equality and frugality of the ancient Roman republic.

What, then, was it that kept the spirit of English liberty going? England is a unique case because, unlike Rome, its animating spirit is liberty and the '*end*' of its government is also liberty. The spirit of liberty is partly a matter of climate and its effect on the famous ill-temper of the English which works against government by a tyrant, and partly due to the fact that the English have become accustomed to their free institutions. Part of that freedom is freedom of trade. Since the English are lacking the virtue of the ancients, the institutional arrangements themselves play a vital part in the preservation of English liberty. Montesquieu's view of liberty in general is that it is secured where not all of the powers of government are exercised by the same hands. Liberty in a monarchy, for instance, is preserved by the independence of the judiciary from executive control. In England, this division of sovereignty has been carried a stage further, because there not only is the judiciary independent but there are no permanent judges in the sense that there are in continental countries. Trial by jury divides the judicial power within itself: juries are *ad hoc* bodies selected for one trial only (and the accused even has the right to object to particular jurors). Juries and judges divide the work between them, juries deciding on guilt or innocence and judges on sentencing. And Montesquieu notes with approval that the supreme judicial tribunal is the House of Lords, again independent of the executive. Judges are the king's judges, but they serve during good behaviour, not according to the king's pleasure.

Montesquieu also notes a certain division of sovereignty between Parliament (by which he typically means the House of Commons) and the king. Parliament is the supreme legislative body in the land, and the king and his government may not do anything unless it is sanctioned by law, or at least does not violate existing law. Parliament legislates and the executive is only supposed to see that the laws are correctly executed. Of course, as a matter of fact, the executive and the legislative were not entirely separate in Hanoverian England, because the king's ministers and many of the placemen (what we would now call, roughly, civil servants and army and naval officers) were also members of the House of Commons or the House of Lords. English governments in the eighteenth century had to secure parliamentary majorities, otherwise the ministry would collapse. Majorities were not permanent in an age when party discipline was either loose or non-existent, and the king's government had to work hard at securing those majorities. The system was oiled by patronage, giving members of the Commons government jobs, some of them sinecures, in return for supporting the ministry. Patronage, or corruption, made the system work. Montesquieu is often accused of naiveté because he could not, or would not, see that the English system worked because powers were not entirely separate. The king was part of the legislative, both through his right to veto parliamentary bills, and through the control of the legislature through the disbursement of government patronage by his ministers and party managers, supreme in which arts were Sir Robert Walpole and the Duke of Newcastle.

How could as shrewd an observer as Montesquieu not have noticed what was the inner scheme of English government? Montesquieu may simply have chosen not to. He chose instead to see English government through the eyes of the opposition to the Walpolean oligarchy. The theory of the complete separation of powers had been an old radical cry since the seventeenth century. What this meant in practice was the passing of a place bill which would exclude government employees from Parliament. Failed place bills had been commonplace, and none was ever to succeed. Opposition to the ministry always argued that true separation of powers was the 'real' English constitution, because only a legislative independent of the executive could guarantee the preservation of liberty. The more power was divided against itself, the less power became a threat. When Montesquieu says that the true separation of powers is permitted by the laws of England, what he probably means is that there is nothing in principle to stop Parliament passing a bill to exclude the placemen, though he must have realised that parliamentary management through patronage by the king's ministers made such an event extremely unlikely. And we do well to remember that, while Montesquieu may in fact have thought that a true separation of judicial, executive and legislative powers was the *best* guarantee of liberty, he by no means thinks that liberty is always and necessarily absent from a political system which is not based on the complete separation of powers. Liberty can exist, as in France, in a monarchy acting through law, provided the judiciary is independent and there exist those mediating powers which soothe monarchy's natural sting. Montesquieu's whole treatment of the separation of powers in relation to English government is meant both to emphasise the high degree to which power is actually diffused through different political institutions and to point out that the complete separation of powers is at least theoretically possible at some time in the future.

What is it then exactly, that *preserves* English liberty, if it cannot be the pure separation of power? We must remember that one of the essential aspects of a political system for Montesquieu is its capacity to return itself to its original principles from time to time. Montesquieu was acutely aware that political systems are subject to degeneration, which for him always means the loss of liberty. His admiration for republican Rome rested partly on that republic's uncanny ability to preserve its republican institutions for so long against so many threats that Rome might turn into a despotism or an oligarchy of the rich. Montesquieu's explanation of what kept Roman politics republican may be the clue to what he thinks keeps English government free. Montesquieu followed Machiavelli in thinking that one of the essential things which kept the Roman constitution republican and free was the spirit of turbulence in the common people of Rome. Machiavelli points out time after time in his commentary on Livy's Roman history how the turbulence of the people acted as a brake on the oligarchic pretensions of the Senate, demanding abolition of debts and a redistribution of the land. Popular clamours are the constant factor which restores the balance between the Roman aristocracy and the people. It is obvious in Machiavelli's mind, and in Montesquieu's, that the turbulence of the people was, to use a current phrase, a kind of 'permitted riot', not exactly legal but not exactly illegal either. This is what Machiavelli means when he says that Rome was fortunate that its constitution could be corrected by its own laws. (We would say without any permanent change in or damage to Rome's political system.)

We can now see what the true influence on Montesquieu was of the Roman analogues which he found so common in England to explain the workings of English politics and the preservation of English liberty. Like Rome, England was widely supposed to enjoy what is usually called 'mixed government' – that is, a mixture of the monarchical, aristocratic and democratic principles. The idea of mixed government was itself of great antiquity; Plato's *Laws* contains an account of it, and so does Aristotle's famous *Constitution of Athens*. The theory of 'mixed government' is frank about class and frank about sovereignty. The various orders in the state have a legitimate claim to share the exercise of sovereignty through the proper balance and co-operation between their different institutions, at Rome the consulate, Senate and people in their popular assemblies, and in England king, lords and commons. Mixed government is a theory both of the *legitimacy* of governing decisions and of the *efficient* exercise of sovereignty: decisions, especially when they take the form of legislation, will be legitimate because each estate of the realm had its share in making them, and those decisions will be good and acceptable decisions because they will be 'balanced decisions', decisions made through a process in which no one interest predominated. Decisions taken in this way are likely to be decisions which offend no single part of the state very much, and which do not very obviously work in favour of any single part. Being acceptable to all, these decisions can be easily legislated for and easily implemented.

So much for the theory of mixed government. In practice, mixed government suffers from the defect that aristocracy, by which is meant the well-to-do in general, will always tend to have their hands much closer to the real levers of power in the system, either directly through their own institutions (Senate, House of Lords) and through their engrossment of executive positions, or indirectly as the power which always tends to follow from large wealth. Something has to be done from time to time outside the formal structures of politics to keep the monarchical and aristocratic parts of the mixed government system from over-reaching themselves to the point where the popular input into government becomes nugatory. At Rome, that meant riots of the people, and in eighteenth-century England it meant the temporary rule of King Mob. Ever since the *Persian Letters* Montesquieu had been interested in the way that English liberty emerged revitalised from riot and sedition. The mob was a half-tolerated Fourth Estate which could always be called out by the opposition to government as a kind of informal supplement to parliamentary opposition to the ministry when it seemed that the king's ministers were getting their own way too much of the time. The English mob was to English politics what the Roman mob had been to republican politics at Rome.

It is now plain what Montesquieu thought preserved the liberties of Englishmen: the mob acting from time to time against mixed government's tendency to degenerate into oligarchic tyranny, or into tyranny itself. Montesquieu may have thought that in England, or anywhere else for that matter, liberty would be better preserved by a true separation of powers, but it is clear that what he actually thought preserved English liberty was the corrective actions of the mob to keep English mixed government true to its own basic principles of fair shares for king, lords and people in the government of England. Sometimes, popular representation through their own elected (on a very limited franchise) representatives in the House of Commons was not enough to preserve Englishmen's liberty from executive aggrandisement, and it was in these circumstances that the Fourth Estate, King Mob, was permitted to play its hand direct in English politics.

THE IMPLICATIONS FOR THE FUTURE OF THE DISTINCTION BETWEEN THE SEPARATION OF POWERS AND MIXED GOVERNMENT

Montesquieu was always careful not to generalise from the English experience. Analogies between English politics and the old Roman politics were just that, analogies. The English system was unique. It might even be vulnerable. Montesquieu says in *The Spirit of the Laws* that were England ever to lose her liberty (he does not suggest how), it would be very difficult for her to regain it, because in her enthusiasm for getting rid of her feudal past, England has rid herself of all those feudal *pouvoirs intermédiaires* which are so useful in France for taking the sting out of executive power. The English constitution, while it has demo-cratic features, can be no true republic of the ancient kind. For one thing, she is too big, and for another, England is a class-ridden society of great inequalities of wealth. England can only be a faint shadow of the equal, frugal and small republics of the ancient past.

But suppose a people becomes intent on recreating more than a parody of an ancient republic in a modern country of vast extent and large population, as was to happen in America after 1776. And suppose that people were to look round for precedents for their republican form of government, and suppose they were to find them in English and Roman politics as seen through eyes seeing much as Montesquieu's own eyes saw. And suppose that the purpose of that new government was to be the preservation of a high degree of liberty. Then it would matter a great deal exactly what Montesquieu thought preserved liberty in political circumstances which were again not the ideal ones for republican government after the ancient model. The Constitution of the United States was written by men whose minds thought about constitutional government like Montesquieu even when they did not come under his direct influence. But which Montesquieu? The Montesquieu of the separation of powers, or the Montesquieu of mixed government? This double Montesquieu is no fable. The Montesquieu of the separation of powers is a Montesquieu who wants to make government difficult, and the Montesquieu of mixed government is a Montesquieu who wants to make government easy. When it is put like that, one begins to wonder exactly what kind of government the Founding Fathers of the United States thought they were founding when they wrote the Constitution. Difficult government shades very easily into minimal government, and easy government shades very easily into strong government, and it was in these terms that the battle of the Constitution was fought during the two years' struggle it took to ratify it, and these were still the terms of debate on the nature of American government after the Constitution was ratified. The dialectic between what has come to be called Jeffersonianism and Hamiltonianism, between minimal and strong central government, is essentially a debate between the two Montesquieus.

These are matters which must wait for detailed treatment in the subsequent chapter on the American Enlightenment. What needs to be emphasised here is just how rich a thinker Montesquieu could be for future generations which concerned themselves with exactly the same kinds of problems that Montesquieu himself dealt with. Of course, this is not to say that future generations dealt with the problem of liberty in a large state in ways of which Montesquieu himself would have approved. For him, Rome was over, and England a special case; neither was in his view generalisable into a system of liberty for the modern world. Tocqueville was to come to believe that providence took a special interest in the destiny of the United States, a view which was to become commonplace as the conviction among Americans of America's 'exceptionalism'. Somehow, in a way hard to define but deeply felt, things were going to be different in America – that is, different from the ways of Old Europe. American independence was always going to be more than political independence. There was certainly something more than fortuitous in the fact that Americans who had originally come from the monarchies of Old Europe were to find themselves in what, with a little stretch of the imagination, could be called a virgin moral and physical landscape, and also in a position after the War of Independence to give themselves laws in something like Montesquieu's sense of the term. Montesquieu had taught that climate was the first of all empires, and we have seen that he extends the notion of climate to take into account almost the whole of nature. What fascinated observers of the American scene after independence was the question of what kind of men the interaction between them and nature in America would produce. The question was more than academic. If men and nature did not interact in such a way as to produce a new American character, then the chances of America's being able to produce a genuinely new system of laws informed by a new *esprit général* were slim. But if the interaction between men and nature in America had produced a new *esprit général*, if there really was a 'spirit of Americanness' which was significantly different from the configurations of national identity elsewhere in the world, then a new system of laws was not only desirable in America but necessary as well, because the necessities of physical and moral cause and effect could no more be suspended in America than they could be anywhere else.

And, most exciting of all, perhaps the interaction in America of men from Old Europe and the new landscape could produce a reversal of some of the worst human results of the less desirable aspects of contemporary European society. Montesquieu himself had spoken of the possibility, albeit limited, of legislators legislating against the climate. Perhaps, in America, climate in Montesquieu's sense could 'legislate' against laws, where laws mean manners and morals. Perhaps it was uniquely possible in America for the effects of new circumstances to cleanse the human soul, perhaps even to put it within reach of the pure agrarian virtue which had been the vital principle of the Roman republic. The Jeffersonian dream of a free, frugal and virtuous republic of yeoman farmers, plainly Roman in some of its antecedents, would have been impossible without Montesquieu. Again, it is worth stressing that Montesquieu himself did not predict Jeffersonianism, which only became a force a quarter of a century after Montesquieu's death, but it is equally worth emphasising that the Jeffersonian dream could only be dreamt in a head which had begun to think in Montesquieu's own way.

NOTES ON SOURCES

Montesquieu's *Persian Letters* are available in various English editions. His *Considerations on the Greatness of the Romans and Their Decline* has been translated and edited by D. Lowenthal (1965). *The*

Spirit of the Laws exists in two good English editions, Neuman (1949) and Cohler, Miller and Stone (1989). R. Shackleton's *Montesquieu: A Critical Biography* (1961), is magisterial. J.N. Shklar, *Montesquieu* (1987), in the Past Masters series is an excellent introduction.

17

THE AMERICAN ENLIGHTENMENT
Jefferson, Crèvecoeur, Hamilton, Jay, Madison, Paine

THOMAS JEFFERSON

Thomas Jefferson was born on the western frontier of Virginia in 1743. It was his father, a surveyor and land speculator, who made it into the 'aristocracy' (really the *nouveaux riches*) of colonial Virginia. Young Thomas graduated from the College of William and Mary in 1762 with a taste for the classics, a curiosity about the latest scientific discoveries, and voracious reading habits. He began very early to doubt the Bible as a source of religious truth and was well on the way to a Deism which remained the basis for an ethics not easily distinguishable from conventional Christian morality. He was trained for the law, the usual education for a Virginian land- and slave-owner.

Jefferson married a beautiful widow in 1772 and immediately settled at 'Monticello', then more of a building site than the national shrine it now is, and involved himself in Virginian politics as a member of its House of Burgesses. Though not eloquent, he was an excellent committee-man and a superb drafter of reports. From the beginning he took a strong anti-British line in the escalating quarrel between Britain and her American colonies. His *A Summary View of the Rights of British America* (1774) was a notable contribution to the ferocious war of the pamphlets which preceded the War of Independence, and, as the whole world knows, as a Virginian delegate to the Continental Congress in 1776, he wrote the Declaration of Independence and became one of the immortals.

Virginia's aristocracy of plantation-owners made its domestic politics the most 'conservative' of the new United States of America, and Jefferson took the lead in trying to make its state constitution conform to republican principles. He became governor of Virginia, but did not have a good War of Independence, and long afterwards his enemies dug up stories about Jefferson's alleged wartime cowardice. Perhaps Jefferson always intended to retire into private life when the war was over, but the death of his wife was probably the cause of his re-entry into politics after 1782. By this time he had completed his famous *Notes on Virginia*. He quickly became a diplomat, member of Congress, and, from 1784 till 1789, an American minister in Paris where he developed a taste for Château Lafitte and a sympathy for the aims of the French Revolution.

On his return to the United States (apparently his slaves were pleased to see him again) he became Washington's Secretary of State, the first under the new Constitution, which in general he admired. His initially cordial relations with the moving spirit of the administration, Alexander Hamilton, did not last long after Jefferson began to realise what powers the national government might engross if the new Constitution was to be 'loosely' constructed. The personal and ideological differences between Jefferson and Hamilton, which even Washington was unable to reconcile, formed the basis of the first American party system (Republicans versus Federalists). Jefferson served twice as president (1800 to 1808) (he was the first to be inaugurated in the new national capital at Washington), and displayed an authoritarianism (as in the Louisiana Purchase of 1802) as chief magistrate of which there had already been disturbing signs when he was governor of Virginia. For Jefferson, limited government did not mean supine government.

Jefferson was instrumental in the foundation and design of the exquisitely neo-classical University of Virginia. He is recognised as a pioneer in the American study of geography, palaeontology, ethnology, botany and pedagogy as well as political science and philosophy, not bad for a man who was also a planter, a lawyer, the drafter of the Declaration of Independence, governor of Virginia, Vice-President and President of the United States. Many contemporaries had come to think of him as the most perfectly enlightened man of the Enlightenment by the time he died in 1826.

MICHEL-GUILLAUME JEAN DE CRÈVECOEUR

Inheritor of a noble name when he was born in Normandy in 1735, Crèvecoeur also seems to have been born to wander. Facts about his life are therefore not all that easy to track down. As a young man he visited England (and may have received some of his education there) and emigrated to Canada where he served under Montcalm towards the end of what Europeans call the Seven Years War and Americans the French and Indian Wars. Crèvecoeur may have wandered extensively in the American wilderness in this period of his life. He turned up in New York in 1759, travelled extensively in the American colonies, became a naturalised American citizen, married (in 1769) Miss Mehitable Tippet of Yonkers and tried his hand at the settled life of a farmer. The details are sketchy, but it seems probable that he wrote his famous collections of essays (*Letters from an American Farmer*; *Sketches of Eighteenth Century America*) between the time of his marriage and his return to France in 1780. Crèvecoeur was a Loyalist, and it is his Loyalism that gives his picture of American life its authenticity: Crèvecoeur's is not the romanticised view of a natural republican in love with the simple rural virtue of Jefferson's agrarian dream.

Crèvecoeur met his own nightmare when he returned to America after the War of Independence: his wife had been killed and his farm burned in an Indian raid. He proved to be remarkably resilient, supporting himself as a journalist (under the by-line of 'Agricola') while acting as French consul in New York. He corrresponded with Washington, got to know Franklin, and Jefferson was a guest at Crèvecoeur's daughter's wedding. He returned to France in 1790, and died there in 1813.

ALEXANDER HAMILTON

As the illegitimate son of a far from prosperous Scottish family in the British West Indies, Hamilton was the real risen star of the American Revolution and the early republic. The lack of a proper early education could not keep this precociously brilliant and ambitious boy away from the academy, and he got into King's College (now Columbia University) in 1772. He became an enthusiast for the anti-British patriot cause (though there were persistent rumours about an expedient conversion from an earlier royalism) and contributed notably to the pamphlet war between patriots and Tories in New York.

Perhaps on account of his ignoble birth, Hamilton always dreamed of military honour and glory, and he had a very good War of Independence. Hamilton was what military men call 'a fine natural soldier'. His skill as a trainer of troops brought him to the attention of General Nathaniel Greene, who in turn introduced him to the C-in-C, General Washington, and Washington invited Hamilton to join his staff as aide-de-camp with the rank of lieutenant-colonel. Hamilton saw action in the war, and received his share of the glory at the siege of Yorktown, while at the same time showing himself to be a gifted military administrator. No doubt his experience of the dilatoriness of the government of the United States by committees of the Continental Congress under the Articles of Confederation did much to strengthen Hamilton's conviction that a strong central government was a necessity if representative government was ever going to work properly.

Hamilton married into the merchant oligarchy of New York and set up a law practice while keeping up a political correspondence with his old chief. Hamilton made a name for himself in the New York state legislature as a man who knew a great deal about the state of the republic's affairs in general, and he was a natural choice as a New York delegate to what became known as the Constitutional Convention, which wrote the new Constitution of the United States at Philadelphia in 1787. It was during this period that he wrote the *Federalist Papers* with Jay and Madison. If Madison was the mind behind the Constitution, Hamilton was the brain that saw how it might actually work and for whom.

As the first Secretary of the Treasury in American history, Hamilton quickly mastered the principles and details of government finance, coming out in favour of deficit finance through borrowing on the credit of a sound national bank whose own credit depended on the credibility of an effective national government. This policy tasted too much of the old fiscal policy of eighteenth-century British governments for many American stomachs. It made him many enemies, including Jefferson, and for the rest of his life Hamilton was tarred with the British brush despite his undoubted services in the revolutionary war. (Those with long memories remembered his alleged support for an American monarchy at Philadelphia in 1787, and those with even longer memories dragged up the charge of youthful royalism before 1776.)

Hamilton retired from his Secretaryship in 1795 to return to his law practice, federal salaries being stingy in the virtuous young republic. He was never again to hold high office, though there is every reason for believing that he meant eventually to return to public life. However, his bastard's prickly sense of honour led him into a duel in 1804 with Aaron Burr, who killed him.

JOHN JAY

Born in New York in 1745 with a silver spoon in his mouth, he became a bookish and serious, not to say priggish, young man who graduated from King's College in 1764 and trained for the law. By no means a democrat either by upbringing or temperament, he appears to have had what the ancients called *gravitas*, that quality which makes other men defer to the judgement and accept the leadership of those who possess it. Like the ideal Roman patriot, he occupied most of the higher positions in the republic without ever seeming to run for office.

Jay was a New York delegate to the Continental Congress. At first against independence because he feared mob rule as a consequence, he threw in his lot unreservedly with the independent United States, was for a time president of the Continental Congress and served his country well as a diplomat (though he failed to persuade Spain to ally itself with the Americans against the British). The definitive treaty of peace with Great Britain in 1794 has always been called the Jay Treaty.

Like a Roman, he tried to return to private life after the War of Independence, but he was persuaded by the Continental Congress to become its foreign secretary, and his experience in that office convinced him that the American national government was hardly worth the name in its relations with foreign powers. A Federalist before the fact, he contributed five essays to *The Federalist Papers* on the implications for foreign policy of the new Constitution of 1787. (He might have contributed more, but at the time his health was not good.)

Jay became the first chief justice of the United States (the post of secretary of state having been earmarked for Jefferson on his return from his stint as American minister in Paris), and his legal decisions were almost invariably of the 'nationalist' as against the 'states' rights' kind. He also served twice as governor of the state of New York, and his gubernatorial tenure was notable for its probity. A life-long and deeply committed, though far from bigoted, Episcopalian, he emancipated his own slaves and as governor signed the bill for the abolition of slavery in his own state. Jay's contribution to the American revolution and to the foundation of the republic was the combination in his character of administrative competence and political virtue. Not an amiable man, perhaps, but certainly admirable.

JAMES MADISON

A Virginian born in 1751 into comfortable but not rich circumstances, 'little Jemmy Madison' has a good claim to being the man who contributed most to the second foundation of the American republic under the new Constitution of the United States of 1787. Though melancholy, even romantic, as a youth, he was universally recognised as one of the best-natured men of his age, just as his wife, Dolly, with whom he was besotted, was the most amiable of women. Young Madison was turned into a good Whig at President Witherspoon's Princeton (then the College of New Jersey), and it seems likely that Madison was aroused from a melancholic torpor tinged with religiosity by the quarrel between Britain and her American colonies. He became a member of the Virginia Convention in 1776, held a variety of state offices and was chosen in 1780 as a delegate to the Continental Congress where he remained until 1783.

On his return to Virginia, he read law, became a leading light in the Virginia Assembly, and became a convinced Federalist because he saw very early that only a strong central government of a really united United States could possibly regulate successfully either inter-state commerce or American commerce with other countries. He was therefore a natural choice as a delegate to the Constitutional Convention of 1787. The original Virginia Plan, a proposed new constitution for the union, some of whose proposals were written into the final draft of the Constitution itself, bear all the marks of Madison's own mind though he did not actually write it, and it is no exaggeration to say that Madison's was the guiding mind behind the Constitution as it was finally adopted. That was the view of contemporaries who knew him and his contributions at Philadelphia well, though it is also possible that this is a view over-strengthened by the fact that it was Madison who made the most complete record of the proceedings of the Constitutional Convention. Nobody was keener than Madison to sell the Constitution to the state ratifying conventions, hence his contributions to *The Federalist Papers*.

As a congressman in the new government, Madison, the life-long friend of Jefferson, began to move away from his enthusiastic Federalism towards the opposition Republican Party beginning to form against Hamiltonian finance. He became Jefferson's Secretary of State in 1800, and was Jefferson's natural successor as president, serving two terms after 1808. The inglorious war against Britain in 1812, with its famous American victory right at the end at the battle of New Orleans, entered American national mythology as 'Mr Madison's War'.

Madison survived his presidencies for another twenty years, being eighty-five when he died at 'Montpelier' in 1836. He was one of the last of the survivors of the heroic generation of the Founding Fathers. His curiosity about the future of American government never waned; many sought his political advice, and everybody visited the sage of the early American republic.

THOMAS PAINE

Tom Paine was born the son of a Quaker corsetmaker in Thetford, Norfolk, in 1737. His life in the ladies' underwear trade, as a seaman, a schoolteacher, an exciseman and a shopkeeper (to say nothing of his record as a husband) was not a success until he emigrated to America in 1774 with a letter of introduction from Benjamin Franklin as his only asset. Two years later, in 1776, his pamphlet *Common Sense*, which urged the Americans to delare independence at once, immediately put him in the forefront of the American Revolution. The book was a bestseller, but Paine, always a model of financial rectitude, refused to make a penny out of it. By the time he had published Part I of *The Rights of Man* (1791) as a reply to Burke's *Reflections on the Revolution in France*, Paine was the best-known revolutionary of his day. He was charged with sedition in England in 1792 when Part II of the *Rights of Man* was published, and he was outlawed the following year. By that time he had escaped to revolutionary France. He represented Calais in the French Convention, where he sided with the moderate party of the Revolution, the Girondins. Paine is one of the few men of whom it may truly be said that his rise to fame was meteoric.

Paine was a professional revolutionary a century before Lenin, but he was not served all that well by the revolutions he took part in, being a victim of the American Revolution in its conservative phase and of the French Revolution in its Jacobin phase. Paine could number Americans like Washington and Jefferson among his friends, and he smelt powder in the American War of Independence, but Paine's radicalism and lowly origins (he drank rum, not brandy, and plenty of it) were not well-suited to the conservative temper of those who sought to consolidate the gains of the Revolution by founding a strong central government which gentleman of property (and especially slave property) could trust. By contrast, the Jacobin radicals in the French Convention began to see in Paine a candidate for the guillotine because of his opposition to the death penalty for Louis XVI. Paine was imprisoned in the Luxembourg and in all likelihood survived by accident to be released after the fall of Robespierre.

In 1802, Paine returned to the United States (whose name he invented) already notorious as the author of the allegedly atheistic (but in fact Deist) work *The Age of Reason* (1793–4). By this time, the political nation in America had decided that the God in whom the United States trusted was a Christian (and Protestant) God after all, conservatism in religion having come in with conservatism in politics. America had already begun to distance herself from her revolutionary origins, and Paine had to live quietly and in a condition approaching poverty until his death in New York in 1809.

Enlightened political thought had always toyed with the idea of forming a system of government from the beginning but, with the odd exception, had never actually expected to be given the opportunity to do it. Enlightened political thought was generally reformist in spirit because the state system of Europe seemed well enough set in the political firmament. Hence Enlightenment's search for reforming agencies in established states and its love affair with enlightened despots whose centralisation of state power seemed to offer the most obvious means of reforming existing institutions. Whenever the question of the origins of government was raised, it was a hypothetical question to guide present reforming practice. Imagining what rational men would write on a political *tabula rasa* could provide insights about what future direction political change might profitably take, but before the American Revolution it would be premature to attribute any degree of literalness to Enlightenment's concern for the origins of government.

The Americans of the revolutionary era found themselves in the position of having to take ideas about the origins of government very literally indeed, and we do well to remind ourselves that they had not chosen to put themselves in that position. Americans had not been obviously contented with the political systems under which they lived in colonial times, but by 1776 the old colonial governments had come to be covered with a haze of benevolence when compared to the altered nature of British government in America after the end of the French and Indian Wars in 1763. The Americans chose to see themselves as very reluctant rebels being forced to take revolutionary steps by the intransigence of an English government which appeared to be deaf to the reasonableness of the American plea that their government should be left standing where anciently it stood. In this the Americans showed themselves to be good English Whigs, taking their stand on the basis of an ancestral constitution which was being altered unilaterally by government. There was something ideologically safe about basing a case on traditional grounds, and this inherently Whiggish conservatism was to continue to obscure (and sometimes to obfuscate) the radical nature of some of the American experiments with new forms of government in the revolutionary age. Burke was one of the first to realise that if the Americans were goaded by the British government beyond a certain point, then it was likely that fundamental questions would begin to be asked about the origin and purpose of government in general. What would be radically new was that in America these questions could provide answers in a political context where the ordinary processes of government were beginning to break down and where it might be possible to begin to reconstruct a government from those first principles which Burke rightly identified as a threat to all existing political systems.

COMMON SENSE (1776)

What was needed in America was a statement of the case for independence which combined a firm grasp of the first principles of government with a critique of the existing governmental system, and both of these had to be firmly rooted in an appreciation of the situation in America in 1776. Open hostilities between the British and the colonies were over a year old when America declared her independence, and the British had already dissolved the colonial legislatures, suspended normal administration, and had begun to try to coerce the colonies by force. The Continental Congress had already been sitting for two years before the Declaration of Independence, and as the dispute with Britain escalated beyond the point even of armed conflict, the Congress gradually became the focus of the united sentiments of the resisters in the separate colonies. The effect of British policy in America was to create in the Continental Congress the first all-American political institution which, as it turned out, was to be the prototype of the first national government of the United States. For the first time there existed in America a truly national forum for the debate of, and eventually for the resolution of, the great issues of the day. (In the colonial period, the natural centre of American politics had been London, for only there could binding decisions be made which affected more than one colony.) Tom Paine's *Common Sense* was an eloquent plea for turning the Continental Congress into something like a constitutional convention which would frame a government for an independent United States. According to the testimony of contemporaries, Paine's pamphlet had a remarkable effect on the minds of Americans in the year 1776 when even the most rebellious Americans were still wavering about the crucial step of declaring independence. George Washington himself is supposed to have been finally converted to independence by reading Paine.

What makes Paine's *Common Sense* such a perfect example of enlightened political thinking is that it assumes that the fundamentals of enlightened political theory are true. Paine thinks that it is obvious that men have certain fundamental rights which, being antecedent to government, government may not violate. Ever since the early battles between the British and the colonies in 1775, the Americans have been engaged in a war of legitimate self-defence against their government. The British have declared war against the natural rights of all mankind by laying waste the country with fire and sword. This action of a government making war on its own people so violates the common sense of the basic purpose of government that Americans are forced to consider what exactly that purpose is. Paine had been struck by the fact that American society had not collapsed as a result of the suspension of the ordinary processes of government. No Hobbesian state of nature had followed upon the demise of law. This convinced Paine that society was natural and government artificial. Society, by which Paine means ordinary social living, provides for our happiness *positively*, 'by uniting our affections', whereas government provides for our happiness only *negatively*, by restraining our vices, hence Paine's famous dictum that 'Society is produced by our wants and government by our wickedness.' Paine regards government as a badge of lost innocence, something of a necessary curse laid on mankind as a consequence of his sinfulness. Society is always a blessing, but government's origins in human sinfulness should alert us to the fact that it is not an unmixed blessing. Even in its best condition government is a necessary evil because it is coercive. In its worst condition it is intolerable, and recent events in America furnish ample evidence for what intolerable government is like: men suffer at government's hands miseries similar to those which they would suffer if there was no government at all. The fact that government is artificial, that is man-made, adds to the burden, because men suffer from what they themselves have made. Men provide for government because they recognise that government alone can provide a minimum amount of safety over and above what each man can provide for himself. Government affects everybody, not just malefactors and potential malefactors, because the expenses of government fall equally on the just and unjust. Just men realise that they have to give up part of their property in the form of taxation in order to enjoy secure possession of the rest. Government is therefore the lesser of two evils, and its purpose is very clear. Given that security is the true end of government, then it follows that whatever form of government provides for security best is the best form of government, and by the best form of government Paine means the most efficient and the cheapest.

Having established the purpose of government Paine then proceeds in a typically enlightened way to describe how government must have originated. Paine's conjectural history focuses on the necessary simplicity of the origins of all government because later he will contrast the simple original with the unnecessarily complicated nature of governments as they actually exist in the world. A meeting, under some convenient tree which served as the first State-House, to discuss 'regulations' (Paine does not yet call them 'laws') for their common life was the first move towards government. Every man had a right to a seat, and the decisions of the meeting could have been little more than recommendations about respect for life and property, and the only sanction available to a community in its infancy would have been public disesteem. As society became larger and more complex, it became convenient to elect legislators rather than for each man to attend legislative meetings, and being the rational men Enlightenment assumes they must have been, they stipulated frequent elections so that the legislators did not get out of touch with the electorate. This frequent interchange between electors and elected would naturally tend to establish a sense of common interest in all sections of the community; government and the governed would therefore naturally support each other, and it is on this mutual support, and not on the 'unmeaning' name of king, that the strength of a government depends. The voice of nature and reason tells us that government is a human contrivance for a specific human end, though this has always been obscured by existing governments which always have a vested interest in concealing the fact that the original governments of mankind were simple, free and democratic.

Paine draws out of his account of the origin of government the 'necessary principle in nature' that 'the more simple any thing is, the less liable it is to be disordered', and this is the maxim he intends to bear in mind when he goes on to discuss the constitution of British government. He is prepared to admit that the British constitution was admirable in its day, because any constitution was better than none when the world was overrun by tyranny, but he also thinks that the current claims made for that constitution are hugely exaggerated. Paine undertakes to show that the British constitution is imperfect, that it is 'subject to convulsions', and that it is incapable of providing what its eulogists say it can provide.

The first thing Paine notices about British government is how complicated it is. The government of an absolute monarch, though a 'disgrace to human nature', is at least simple in the sense that the people know who their oppressor is. Not so in English government, where the various parts combine in ways which are so difficult to determine that the nation may suffer for years without its becoming obvious which part of government is causing the trouble. But if we get to the bottom of the matter, we find in English government the remains of two ancient tyrannies compounded with some new republican materials. Monarchy remains as a reminder of how tyrannically kings once ruled in England, the House of Lords reminds us how insolent rank once was, while the Commons represents that 'virtue' in the nation upon which its hopes of freedom depend. The original of all governments shows us that a constitution of government is the creation of a people, so that in a strictly constitutional sense neither monarchy nor aristocracy, being founded on usurpation, contributes anything to constitutional freedom. Only the Commons, the truly 'constitutional' part of British government, can make any contribution to English liberty, and it is supposed to do that by checking the usurped powers of the other parts of government. What this boils down to is that the Commons have the crucial constitutional function of checking the power of the king and his government. Paine takes issue with this standard view of British government. Monarchy is plainly the most powerful part of British government, both formally and in terms of the resources available to it. As part of the legislative process the king has the considerable power of veto, and as head of the executive he has at his disposal all those government jobs which can be used to corrupt members of the House of Commons, not to mention a civil list income of nearly a million sterling a year which can be laid out in pensions to further his political interest in that very House of Commons which is so often cried up as the guardian of the rights and liberties of Englishmen. The corruption of English government means that the constitution cannot work in the way it is supposed to work. Far from checking the power of monarchy, English constitutional practice in fact strengthens monarchy's hand. The will of the king is just as much law in England as it is in France and Spain, perhaps even more so because in England the king's will is handed down 'under the most formidable shape' of an Act of Parliament. The will of English kings has therefore the spurious additional legitimacy of the people's will.

In rejecting the traditional 'balance of the constitution' argument for the preservation of English liberty, Paine was in fact following a line of constitutional criticism which went back well into the seventeenth century and which included Montesquieu's own version of the oppositionist argument against the Walpolean oligarchy of self and place. The English Whig opposition deplored the increase of the influence of the crown in the House of Commons as the reign of George III proceeded. A bought and automatically servile ministerial majority in the Commons effectively meant that there was nothing the king and his ministers could not do. This was initially puzzling to the American Whigs, who were used to thinking of legislatures, whether in America or in England, as the guarantors of whatever liberty it was that Englishmen possessed. Paine certainly struck a powerful chord when he pointed to the complex nature of public policy-making under the British constitution. Americans found it difficult to know who to blame for what seemed to them to be a disastrous North American policy pursued by the government in Britain. Was it the king, or was it the ministry, or was it Parliament? Whiggery had taught Englishmen every-where to beware of kings, but what was to be made of a situation in which every measure which seemed to be designed to outrage American sensibilities came over to America stamped with the parliamentary seal of approval? And Americans were not slow to connect the corruption of the imperial legislature with the possible fates of their own colonial legislatures. With a tame legislature in London it could only be a matter of time before the colonial assemblies would disappear into the pockets of the colonial governors.

As a radical, Paine carried his argument right to the root of British government in monarchy. What, he asked, was the origin of this monarchical power which needed to be checked? The royal power could not have originated in the people's gift, because no people would make such a rod for its own back, and it cannot come from God (the Old Testament shows that God does not approve of monarchy), so the royal power must be a usurpation. English history makes that clear anyway, because English monarchy was founded on force by William the Conqueror. An original act of coercion can create no right, and even if it could the right of hereditary succession still has to be justified. The ordinary justification for the right of hereditary succession is that it prevents civil strife because everybody is supposed to accept the next in line to the throne as the true and legitimate king. Paine thinks this is nonsense, as a glance at the history of English politics since the Norman Conquest easily shows: there have been thirty-two kings since the Conquest and eight civil wars and nineteen rebellions, more than one for each reign. Monarchy is no guarantee of the peace of the realm, and is arrogant abroad. The English king gets his £800,000 a year to make war and give away government places, and this has 'eaten out the virtue of the Commons'. English monarchy is therefore unconstitutional by origin (for only a whole people can give itself a constitution) and has the effect of undermining the only institution in the land which is in any way capable of maintaining what constitutional virtue and liberty there is in England.

The inherent danger in royal power is nowhere more obvious than in the conduct of the British in America. There, monarchy has shown its true hand, which is violence. Monarchy under the British constitutional system is so far unchecked that the British king can make war with impunity on three million of his own subjects. Since the battle of Lexington in April 1775, force has met force in America, and since then everything has changed. The possibility of an amicable settlement of the affairs of America has gone for ever. It is now a question of a negotiated settlement rather than a friendly reconciliation. The only alternative is independence, which for Paine means 'continental government'. It is sometimes said that America has prospered under British rule because of the protection America has received as part of the British empire, but Paine thinks that whatever protection America has received was simply an expression of British self-interest. Again, it is often said that Britain and America together can face the world, but all that means is that when the British monarchy next chooses to embroil itself in foreign wars America will be swept into hostilities on the king's coat-tails. The interest of America is not war but trade – 'Our plan is commerce' – and every time Britain is involved in a European war American trade is threatened. The true interest of America is to act as a free port for all and trade with the whole of Europe will secure the friendship of all the nations of Europe. A special connection with Britain, which is only a small part of Europe anyway, is in fact harmful to American interests. America has outgrown the British connection. ''TIS TIME TO PART' (Paine's capitals). Interest and nature ('the blood of the slain') both urge America in the same direction. America has already grown up, and what kind of Mother Country is it anyway which would make war on her own children? 1776 is the great year of opportunity. America already has the basis of a national government in the Continental Congress, and America is united in its national sentiment. Independence is only a very short step. Independence has to come some day, and the present time is the best, not least because America has the breathing space to form a government for itself on natural and rational principles. There are only three ways America can become independent, by military force, through the action of the mob, or through the 'legal voice' of the people in Congress. If the Americans take the third course of action, they will seize the opportunity of forming 'the noblest, purest constitution on the face of the earth', an opportunity unparalleled since the days of Noah.

The uniqueness of the opportunity is what makes the case of the Americans the case of all mankind. Most nations have never had, or have let slip, the chance of making a government for themselves; they have all had governments forced upon them by some 'fortunate ruffian' like William the Conqueror.

> The sun never shined on a cause of greater worth. 'Tis not the affair of a city, a country, a province, or a kingdom, but of a continent – of at least one eight part of the habitable globe. 'Tis not the concern of a day, a year, or an age, posterity are vitally involved in the contest, and will be more or less affected, even to the end of time, by the proceedings now.

Paine's peroration strikes the universalist note of Enlightenment; and what is remarkable about his political thought is not its originality, of which there is little, but the fact that it bounces back the truths of Enlightenment from the edge of the inhabited world to its centre. Paine's Philadelphia was famous in eighteenth-century Europe as the home of Benjamin Franklin, who was the best-known American of his day, but it was also on the edge of the American wilderness. (Not quite on the edge, perhaps, but near enough for Europeans.) Paine's *Common Sense* addresses not only Americans, but the whole world. Political positions which were only implicit in enlightened political thought were acquiring a real cutting edge in America. That is what makes Paine, by birth an Englishman, an American political thinker. He is the first to make available to a general audience the fundamental American idea that what happens in America will affect the future everywhere. Paine's *Rights of Man* was sixteen years in the future when he wrote *Common Sense*, but the idea that enlightened Europe will be called by America to abolish monarchy and all its works is already there.

THOMAS JEFFERSON'S
DECLARATION OF INDEPENDENCE (1776)

Jefferson's *Declaration of Independence* is the foundation document of Americanness, just as the Constitution of 1787 is the foundation document of the United States. A good deal of what Jefferson has to say in the *Declaration* looks as if it might have come out of Paine's

Common Sense, but it would be a mistake to make the connection between the two too close. Rather, we should see both *Common Sense* and the *Declaration* as coming out of the political theory of Enlightenment in the most general sense. The significance of both pieces rests on their timeliness. Jefferson's *Declaration* does not argue a case from fundamentals; even more than *Common Sense*, the *Declaration* accepts the truths of enlightened political thought at their face value, in particular the ideas of natural rights and of the essentially instrumental nature of government. The importance of the *Declaration* lies in the fact that it was composed and signed by men of affairs, men about to form a government and fight a war. This was no fanciful declaration of rights emanating from the calm of the study; the *Declaration* was fighting talk, political theory alive and well and dwelling among men.

The *Declaration* comprises three parts: a declaration of rights, a list of grievances and the declaration of independence proper. The declaration of rights has come to be justly celebrated for its eloquence, and this has tended to distract attention from the form of the *Declaration* as a whole. The *Declaration* is written in the style of a petition for the redress of grievances, with the difference that the *Declaration* also says that the time for petitioning is now over. The *Declaration* sets out the basis for these grievances, and then goes on to list them. The list is not arbitrary. It took the Continental Congress a long time to come up with a list of grievances specific enough to be represented as infractions of law and general enough to be of concern to the representatives of all the thirteen separate colonies. The grievances fall into two categories: grievances about the violation of ancient rights and grievances about acts of war committed by the British against the colonists. The embattled farmers' shots had rung round the world more than a year before independence was declared; colonial government had been virtually suspended, and America was already ungovernable except by force. Tom Paine was there ready to remind Americans that Englishmen had been governed once before by force. The Norman yoke had lain long and heavily on the shoulders of Englishmen, and it had been the glory of English political development, or the Whig view of it, that constitutional rights and liberties had been asserted and preserved in the face of the power of kings. Backward-looking Americans could not see why they should not enjoy the fundamental rights and liberties of Englishmen. They saw themselves as Englishmen living in America, and the experience of American colonial government had accustomed them to a share in political decision-making, through the colonial legislatures, which was more than analogous to the share in government which the people of England enjoyed through the House of Commons.

The Continental Congress was no meeting of political radicals. The delegates to the Congress at Philadelphia represented the colonial elite, those who had been excluded from colonial government by the British resort to force. A governing class is unlikely to be radical even when it has been excluded from its natural place, and nothing could be more predictable than that its representatives should defend their place in the scheme of things by an appeal to ancient custom and practice. The inherent conservatism of the Congress is nowhere better seen than in the petition form which the *Declaration* takes. The right to petition the crown for redress of grievances was an ancient constitutional right, and there was a long and respectable tradition of petitioning the crown for reaffirmation of Englishmen's rights; the House of Commons itself had done this from time to time. In basing its case on ancient rights the Congress was acting in an impeccably Burkean way. Men of a conservative temper only feel safe when defending rights which they regard as part of the *status quo*, or of the *status quo ante*.

What had changed in America was that government, or a part of it, was making war on American society. There was no disguising the fact that the troops which were trying to coerce the Americans into submission were the king's troops. The king stood in the same relation to the colonial legislatures as he did to the English Parliament, and to make war on the people whose representatives the colonial legislatures were was really the equivalent of repeating the follies of the English Civil War of the seventeenth century when king and Parliament eventually faced each other from different sides of a battlefield. Of course, the difference in the case of America was that initially there was no real equivalent in the thirteen colonies of the single Parliament which existed in England. If the king was to be resisted in America then America would have to produce the equivalent of the English Parliament, and that could only be the Continental Congress. Englishmen in England had long been accustomed to thinking of Parliament, and especially the House of Commons, as the institutional basis from which rights and liberties could be defended (though this attitude had taken a blow in the reign of George III because the arts of parliamentary management of the Commons by the ministry seemed to guarantee the king a parliamentary majority). Historical memories were long in America in 1776, and it took no stretch of the imagination to begin to think of the Continental Congress playing the role in the 1770s which the English Parliament had played in the events of the English Civil War in the 1640s. Then, Parliament was forced by the circumstances of civil war to turn itself into a government, and as events unfolded in America it began to look increasingly likely that the Continental Congress would be forced to do the same. The *Declaration* makes a good deal of the war atrocity aspect of British policy in America because the implicit argument in the *Declaration* is that the British are already treating America as a foreign country by making war against her. There is more to this than a kind of school playground 'You started it, not us.' Rather, what is at issue is the status of America as a combatant power among the other 'powers of the earth'. The 'powers of the earth', that is separate states, are nominally equal, and each is entitled to treat with its equals as seems best to it. The act of war of George III's government against the United States is, in the *Declaration*'s view of the matter, an invitation to the United States to pursue an independent foreign policy. This fits in well with what we do in fact know about the immediate circumstances of the writing and signing of the *Declaration*. All the evidence points to the fact that the Continental Congress eventually declared independence after so long because by July 1776 it appeared to be certain that America would receive vital French help against the British if America formally declared herself to be a separate country. Then the government of France would find itself in the position of alliance with another state and not just interfering in the internal affairs of another state by helping a bunch of rebellious subjects.

With British violence, and the consequent Declaration of Independence on the assumption that foreign help would be forthcoming, all the precedents suddenly came to a stop. The English Civil War of the previous century had almost exclusively been an English affair, a dispute over national sovereignty which none doubted existed; the only question raised was the mode of its exercise. In America the *Declaration* went well beyond that. The war is not a civil war at all, much less a rebellion. The War of Independence is going to be a war between two different states. In one sense, this represents a radical break with the past because it had never happened before, but in another sense it was deeply conservative. The American rebels were very careful never to appear technically, that is to say legally, as rebels. For as long as it could, the Continental Congress kept up the fiction that it was a meeting of concerned and loyal citizens dutifully petitioning their good king for redress of grievances arising from the actions of his misguided ministers. Events in America after 1775, in which the British made all the running, turned America into a separate state at war with the state of which it had once been a part. Jefferson's implied argument is subtle: Americans were the loyal subjects of King George until King George's government turned them into a separate state – therefore they literally had no time to be rebels. At one moment they were British and at another American, and all this through no wish or fault of their own: Englishmen or Americans, there could be no question about their loyalty. How, then, could they ever have been rebels?

By what right did America declare its independence? This has been a matter of some controversy. It is plain enough from the text of the *Declaration* that its emphasis on British aggression makes the right of self-defence one of the bases of the right to declare independence. This is plainly a right which exists 'in nature'; animals have it, and it is to be presumed that human beings at the very least have the same rights as the brute creation. But the right of self-defence is not quite the same thing as the right to re-establish a government on different lines. The justification of the right to dissolve a system of government and to begin to erect a new one in its place is based on the typically enlightened concern for the ends of government. The whole process of the de-mystification of government which Enlightenment initiated and completed meant that for the first time the question: Has government achieved what government ought to set out to do? could be answered in the negative with distinctly radical implications. Part of the purpose of the list of grievances in the *Declaration* is to show that British government in America has failed according to the most elementary criteria of good government. Enlightenment's implied radicalism shines through the *Declaration*'s assertion that men are entitled to 'pursue happiness'. One of the most important things Enlightenment did was to make ordinary human happiness part of the business of government. This was not, of course, to say that it was government's business to regulate the details of people's lives to make sure that they were cheerful, but it did mean that a very exact sense emerged of government's duty to provide those conditions in which rational men could pursue happiness, that is further their own interests, without being hindered unnecessarily either by government or by their fellow men. This was more radical than it sounds, because in eighteenth-century political thought it meant that government's capacity to promote the happiness of its subjects, however negatively, was connected with the vital question of the legitimacy of government. No political theory ever invented, and no actual government since the Flood, had ever had as its proclaimed intention the idea of making men miserable. All governments more or less claim that they have their subjects' happiness at heart, but most governments have not based their claims to be entitled to rule directly on their happiness-creating function. The reason why governments do not typically base their claim to rule on their capacity to increase human happiness is obvious enough, because to do so would be to invite their subjects to judge whether their governments are competent or not. Indeed, it could be argued that most of the justifications for forms of rule which have been on offer since Plato are all careful to distinguish between questions about legitimacy and questions about happiness. In fact, most political theories want things both ways. They want the credit if the form of government which they recommend does in fact increase the sum of human happiness, but they also want to claim that their claims to legitimacy do not rest on the creation of human happiness in case things begin to go wrong. Connecting the legitimacy of government directly to the pursuit of human happiness was at the very least to put government on its guard against causing its subjects misery, and at the very best it went a long way towards making governments accountable to the people they governed. Elections, in this view of things, could easily come to be seen as ways of registering voter satisfaction or dissatisfaction about government's success rate in the business of providing for the increase of human happiness.

The *Declaration* speaks of life, liberty and the pursuit of happiness as rights for the protection of which governments were originally instituted, and there has been some controversy about what kind of rights these are that are being claimed. On one view of them, they are the rights of Englishmen which the Americans thought were being denied to them by the conduct of the government of George III. The Americans, it is said, simply claimed their traditional rights on a new basis; what was denied to them as Englishmen they reclaimed as men. Far from intending something new, the *Declaration* reaffirmed a very old idea of rights on the only basis now available for them. Nor was that basis all that new. There was a strain in the Whig tradition going as far back as the English republicans of the seventeenth century which had always couched its political theory in very general terms. The Whig tradition may always in fact have been speaking to specifically English political concerns, but there had always been a tendency to talk about political matters in the terms of a general political right. The arch-Whig John Locke himself had cast his *Second Treatise of Civil Government* in terms of very generalisable rights which all men had. Indeed, there is an important parallel between Locke's *Second Treatise* and the *Declaration* which is not often remarked upon, and it is that on the occasion both of the *Second Treatise* and of the *Declaration*, Englishmen of a Whiggish turn of mind saw themselves being denied rights which they thought they had under England's traditional frame of government, and both occasions called forth reaffirmation of existing rights couched in the terms of rights in general. All men were considered to have certain natural rights, and Englishmen were thought of as being only a specific case of a much more generalised truth about rights.

Another view of the rights claimed in the *Declaration* would have us believe that something more than traditional rights was being asserted. The *Declaration*'s language can be read as direct and unambiguous: all men are created equal in rights by God, and this is regarded as a self-evident truth. These are rights which God wants us to have. In the *Declaration* Jefferson neatly sidesteps the difficult business of making a complete list of natural rights by saying that there is common agreement that *among* these rights are the rights to life, liberty, and the pursuit of happiness. Clearly, the *Declaration* means us to think that we have all kinds of other natural rights, and perhaps Jefferson singled out the rights to life, liberty and the pursuit of happiness because these were the rights which most obviously affected and were affected by government. A government which threatens those rights is plainly a bad government, and it is just as plain that a government which guarantees the exercise of those rights is a good government. The problem is to decide in what sense these rights are meant to be 'self-evident'. 'Self-evident' cannot mean 'everybody agrees', because not everybody in the world is likely to have heard of natural rights, and even if they had, it is by no means likely that everybody would agree with the natural rights doctrine. Natural rights may be self-evident in the sense that anybody who has ever thought seriously about human rights would agree that as a minimal programme there would be a consensus that rights to life, liberty and the pursuit of happiness did in fact exist. This could be whittled down to a very exclusive notion of natural rights. Jefferson may be saying in the *Declaration* that those who do not agree with this minimum programme of natural rights – American Tories who would remain loyal subjects to King George, for instance – have no business to remain in America pretending to be Americans. It may be that to *be* American means accepting the doctrine of natural rights (and perhaps accepting the existence of the Creator who endowed men with them). The self-evident truth may simply be that it is now time for the Tories to leave. Of course, at a later date the *Declaration* could be read in the opposite direction: America is the place to come to if you accept the doctrine of natural rights and want to live in a country where those natural rights can be enjoyed in peace. Jefferson agreed with Paine that there is something inherently aggressive about monarchy, and he accepted with Paine that a republican form of government which took as its task the protection of natural rights would itself be a naturally pacific form of government, gentle with its citizens and benevolent towards its neighbours.

So far we have said nothing about the rights claimed in the *Declaration* which suggest that Jefferson's idea of natural rights differs in any way from the idea of natural rights as it is found in Locke's *Second Treatise*. However, that is a very different thing from claiming that Jefferson got his idea of rights directly from Locke's work, for that is to suppose that the political works of Locke had a canonical status in the America of the 1770s which they probably did not acquire until later. Garry Wills has argued convincingly (in *Jefferson's Declaration of Independence*) that Jefferson's direct source for the self-evidence of natural rights, or natural anything for that matter, was in fact the 'common sense' school of philosophy of the Scottish Enlightenment of which Hume is the most famous member. On this view of the philosophy underlying the *Declaration*, the 'common sense' of inalienable rights would be the emerging consensus of a community coming to be more conscious of the obligations of one man to another, and of the obligation of the state to respect the exercise of those rights by individuals which those individuals are already obliged to respect in each other. The basis of these rights is not reason in the Lockian sense. Locke seems to think that if we thought about God's purpose for the world before government even began we would come to the conclusion that by nature God intended that we should be equal in natural rights. The conclusion which emerges from that style of reasoning is that rights are natural and government artificial. The Scottish school denied that there was something 'artificial' about the fact that men live in societies with government. It was stretching ordinary language just a bit too far to say that what everybody always did was in some sense 'unnatural'. Civil society was the 'natural' condition of men, and so it must have been out of the experience of that common living that the 'moral sense' developed which apprehends that men have rights. The Scottish philosophy, while undoubtedly Whiggish, is couched in suitably general terms – all developing societies, if they are candid about the matter, will come to see that men have inalienable rights – while at the same time being sensitive to the obvious sociological fact that an idea of inalienable rights can only develop if there is a society coherent enough for the idea to develop *in*.

The Scottish philosophy would have no truck with the enlightened idea of pre-social, natural man wandering around in a hypothetical state of nature, with his mind busily working out for himself that he had natural rights, and coming to the purely rational conclusion that his own claim to natural rights entailed on him the duty to respect the exercise of those same natural rights by other men. The Scottish Enlightenment brought a degree of what they would have called a 'historical' (we would say 'sociological') realism to the whole business of natural and inalienable rights. That sociological realism may also account for the curious fact that Jefferson does not name the right to property as one of the inalienable rights which men have. This omission has always been an embarrassment to those who wish to read a straightforwardly Lockian doctrine of natural rights into the *Declaration*. Locke mentions the rights to life, liberty and estate (that is, property in the ordinary sense), so why does Jefferson not mention the right to property in the *Declaration*? One explanation is, of course, that to say that the American War of Independence, which had effectively already started, was to be a war to defend property right could be interpreted by ill-disposed persons as a proclamation of a war to defend inequality of property distribution. Much better, then, to say that the war was to be fought to defend every man's right to pursue happiness, because every man could aspire to increase his own happiness in a way that perhaps not all men could realistically aspire to increase their own personal or real estate, and the last thing that the declarers of independence wanted was to create the impression that the War of Independence was going to be a rich man's war. Alternatively, we could simply assume that the right to pursue happiness *includes* the right to property, because the form most men's pursuit of happiness takes is the pursuit of wealth, or, at the very least, it could be said that the way each man's pursuit of his happiness affects his relations with other men is through each man's desire to increase his wealth in an economic and social world in which others are trying to do the same in competition with him.

Garry Wills will have none of this. He wants to make a distinction between a Lockian and a later, more truly liberal, idea of property right, though the difference is really only a difference of emphasis. Locke's own defence of property right is a 'what I have I hold' defence which stresses the right of retention. Of course, Locke is not altogether indifferent to the question of how I come to have what I wish to hold on to, but the thrust of Locke's argument is literally a defence of existing property relations as they might be threatened by the state. That is why Locke is so keen to establish property relations in the state of nature, before the political state even existed. Wills points to a different idea of property right which emphasises the right to alienate property on the part of the property owner. In principle, Locke's own account of property right could just as easily apply to feudal property as to personal property.

There is nothing in the Lockian account which contradicts the remnants of feudal ideas about property like primogeniture (the right of the first-born to inherit all the family land) and entail (the denial of the right to break up an estate). The case could even be made out that a Lockian system of property relations would be the better preserved the more the state did in fact put restrictions upon the free alienation of property, especially property in land. A more truly liberal, that is to say free capitalist, idea of property relations would tend to lay its stress in the opposite direction, holding out for the absolute alienability of all property, personal and real. Jefferson may have left out the 'right to property' from the *Declaration* precisely because it had come to be too closely associated with the non-alienability of land. This fits well with the Jeffersonian programme for the new state of Virginia which, through his prompting, abolished primogeniture and entail, and it also fits well with Jefferson's later programme for the United States of a very free market in land as the basis for a truly agrarian democracy. The original promise of American life was that the poor of a Europe whose system of land tenure had not completely passed out of the feudal age would be able to acquire the real estate which was still out of their reach in the old country.

It has to be said again that these differences are differences of emphasis only. Of course it is true that the Lockian doctrine of property right allows for and encourages a wide right to the exchange of property by free contract and in that sense recognises and celebrates the realities of a commercial economy, and of course the Jeffersonian doctrine of free property acquisition and exchange allows for and encourages a retentive attitude on the part of free citizens towards state depredations through taxation on private property. (Jefferson would not have to be reminded that the origins of the American Revolution lay in a dispute with the British government about taxation.) In one sense the history of taxation in America since the beginning has been paradoxical. One might have expected that the typical form taxation would take there would be a tax on retained property, that is real estate, whereas the history of American taxation could easily be written as the history of the taxation of the free exchange of property – that is, taxation in its indirect form as a tax on sales. If the Jeffersonian idea of property has had any resonance at all in the history of American government then one might have expected a reluctance to tax, that is to say discourage, the free exchange of goods and services. However, to think like that is to forget that Jefferson's was not the only influence on the way Americans would come to think about property. In particular, we should remind ourselves that the Jeffersonian dream of America was a dream of a virtuous and frugal republic of yeoman farmers, republican Roman in modern dress. If these modern republicans were to practise an almost self-sufficient agriculture, sending only a modest surplus to market to feed the towns, then the system of free exchange would not be the typical economic activity anyway, and that activity would have to be encouraged if it was to work at all efficiently. The economic history of the United States in the nineteenth century was the history of the supercession of the Jeffersonian dream of virtuous agrarian frugality by the more immediately accessible vision of unlimited economic opportunity and growth. In America, the expansion of a modern capitalist market economy proceeded at a pace which was truly miraculous by almost any previous standards. The sheer volume of free economic exchange meant that government could tax exchange at rates so remarkably low that they could in no sense be seen as threatening to the system of exchange while easily raising enough revenue to defray the ordinary expenses of government.

It is sometimes said that the *Declaration* is oddly silent about the form which the government of the independent United States ought to take, and this has led to the suggestion that the form the government eventually took under the new Constitution of 1787 was somehow a betrayal of the ideals set out in the *Declaration* ten years before. This sense of betrayal has sometimes been formulated into the antithesis that the *Declaration* is a defence of liberty and the Constitution is a defence of property. The history of politics in the United States since its foundation has sometimes been written as the story of a dialectical clash of individual rights versus property rights, now the one and now the other gaining the upper hand. Is this a sustainable view?

The argument that it is sustainable goes something like this: the unequivocal assertion of rights in the *Declaration* entails a form of government which is the most likely in practice to protect those rights. These rights being popular rights, enjoyed by everybody (except slaves), it would seem to follow that that form of government would be best in which there was the largest possible amount of popular participation in government. There is nothing like being in a position to protect one's rights oneself. Trusting others to protect one's rights is always risky; much better, then, to have the closest possible relationship between individuals who wish their rights to be protected and the government whose job it is to protect them. On this view of the matter, both the executive and the legislative branches of government want careful watching, and all political experience teaches that it is the executive branch of government, which in the United States means the presidency, which has to be the most closely watched. English political experience taught that there had to be some kind of institutional basis, like the House of Commons, from which rights could best be protected, and so it was natural that in America the Congress would come to be seen as the champion of the rights of the people, with the Supreme Court as a court of last resort if rights were blatantly violated by government. Therefore, it would seem to follow that popular electoral controls should be put on both the presidency and the legislature. At the very least, the legislature ought to be frequently subject to electoral pressure so that it takes seriously its role as guardian of the people's rights as well as its role as the expresser of the people's legislative will.

The eventual Constitution of the United States fails to live up to these criteria. Not only does it make no provision for direct popular participation in government (a provision perhaps impossible in view of the sheer size of the population of the republic), but the electoral arrangements of the Constitution are designed effectively to distance the processes of the executive, legislature and supreme judiciary from the force of popular wills. The original, unamended Constitution provided for direct popular representation in the House of Representatives only; both the Senate and the president were to be elected by indirect franchise. A third of the Senate only was to be elected every two years by the individual state legislatures and the president was to be elected by the electoral college, the number of which was to be equal to the number of members of the House of Representatives coming from each state plus two (the two senators). These very fancy franchises meant that, with the exception of the House of Representatives, the whole of which was to be re-elected every two years, Americans would have to trust the protection of their rights to persons who were not to be popularly elected, or to the justices of the Supreme Court who were not to be elected at all and who were effectively to serve for life.

The nature of the original Constitution meant that the battle for a democratic constitution had still to be fought in America. The original Constitution was oligarchical while throwing a few scraps in the direction of the popular will, where 'oligarchical' means giving protection to the property and rights of the rich at the expense of the generality of men. Nobody had any doubt in 1787 when the Constitution was written that the indirect franchises for the presidency and the Senate were designed to produce presidents and senators who were 'sound' on issues like the redistribution of goods or the abolition of slavery. The subsequent constitutional history of the United States can be seen as a running battle to democratise what was originally an oligarchic Constitution, and the reason given for the only partial success of the democratic forces is that the Constitution being originally set up to protect an oligarchy makes that Constitution difficult to democratise without a root and branch reform. Too many powerful groups have a vested interest in keeping things the way they are, and this largely accounts for the essentially conservative thrust of American politics since the beginning.

The case that the Constitution betrays the *Declaration* has a certain plausibility, but the case against this is very damaging. First, there was no reason in principle and plenty in practice why the *Declaration* should be silent about desirable forms of government. The *Declaration* is about how bad British government in America has become, provoking reasonable men beyond endurance. The carefully drawn up list of charges against the British government is meant to show how uniquely malevolent the conduct of the British has become. The *Declaration* makes it clear that the generality of men are usually willing to put up with abuses of power rather than revolt. Put in the terms of the natural right argument, this means that most governments most of the time, or at least most European govern-ments, do not make such a bad job of protecting men's natural rights. Most governments, and this includes monarchy, are content most of the time to act within the law. The *Declaration* certainly does not assume that the protection of natural rights is confined to one type of government only. Of course, Jefferson has an eye to France, and the last thing he could afford to do was to proclaim to the world that all other kinds of government except participatory democracy were illegitimate because they failed to protect natural rights adequately. France (and Spain) were absolutist monarchies, and it would be an odd way to ask them for help by accompanying the request with the observation that their governments were an affront to the sensibilities of mankind.

However, it would be a mistake to emphasise the French connection too much and to read into the *Declaration* a deliberate avoidance of the question of forms of government simply because the Americans were out to curry favour with monarchical government in France. Enlightened political thinking had never in fact denied that natural rights could be safe under a king. Civilised monarchy of the kind which Montesquieu praised was civilised precisely because it guaranteed the orderly exercise of natural rights. It may have been the case that enlightened political thinkers had praised the ancient republics, but most of them recognised that in the real contemporary world monarchy was the norm and likely to remain so. It was still possible to regard uncivilised monarchy, that is, tyranny or despotism, as the worst condition for the exercise of human rights, but there was no reason in principle why even despotism should not become enlightened through philosophic tuition. What made America different was the chance to recast its institutions in a republican form, but we sometimes forget that the Americans of the revolutionary period were just as concerned about the individual state governments as they were about national government. Indeed, very early on many influential Americans began to see state governments and a national government as rivals, and this is completely understandable in men whose primary loyalty was to what they called their own 'country'. During the War of Independence, the individual states busily reformed their own governments on republican lines, and for many Americans it was the governments of the states which were there to protect rights. From there it was a very short step to thinking that any form of strong national government, in an America which had never had national government of any kind before, could easily begin to pose the same threats to natural rights in the future which Americans were presently suffering at the hands of the government of George III. (And some of the delegates at the Continental Congress had even been specifically mandated by their states *not* to discuss the form of a possible future government of the United States, so great was the animus in some quarters against national government itself.)

Everybody in America knew in 1776 that some kind of national government (even if it was not called that) was going to be necessary to fight the war and negotiate with potential allies, but it could be argued that the first form of national government under the original Articles of Confederation lacked both the force and the mechanisms to be an effective guarantor of individual rights. It is easy to forget that only forceful government can protect rights. Strong government and natural rights are not necessarily antitheses; a government so weak that it could never be in a position to threaten natural rights would never be in a position to protect them. In this sense, the strong national government which eventually came to be founded on the basis of the Constitution of the United States may have been the government, in the particular circumstances, which provided best for the necessary minimum of national power and the necessary maximum of the protection of rights.

CRÈVECOEUR'S *LETTERS FROM AN AMERICAN FARMER* (1782) AND THE IDEA OF THE AMERICAN CHARACTER

Crèvecoeur's *Letters From an American Farmer* is the first work to attempt to define the American character, a concern which was subsequently to become something of a national obsession in the United States. On the face of it, Crèvecoeur's *Letters* is the least 'theoretical' book imaginable. It consists of a series of letters to an English friend about the conditions, manners and morals of American life. The scenes painted are, with the exception of Southern slavery, highly enticing. On Crèvecoeur's account of American agricultural life, anybody would be mad not to want to be a farmer in America. However, the Introductory Letter (and the Dedication) contains a number of clues pointing to the theoretical positions upon which Crèvecoeur's treatment of American life is based. The book is dedicated to the Abbé Raynal, the French *philosophe* (who was later to write a famous book on the American Revolution), and this in itself shows us that Crèvecoeur's own mind is about to run on philosophic, that is to say Enlightenment, lines. Crèvecoeur's is an enlightened mind addressing an enlightened audience. In the Introductory letter, James the Pennsylvanian farmer discusses with his local minister what he is going to write in his letters to FB, a gentleman in England, and the minister persuades James that he really has something to say which would be interesting to a civilised Englishman. An account of the pleasing scenes of American life, says the minister, would be just as interesting as what historians have got to say about ancient Rome. Tales of American life would be 'more philosophical' than anything that can be said about the musty ruins of Rome: 'There the half-ruined amphitheatres and putrid fevers of Campania [the area around Naples] must fill the mind with the most melancholy reflections.'

What is it, then, about the reflections which arise from a contemplation of ancient Rome that would make them 'melancholy', and why would the reflections which are likely to arise from a contemplation of American rural life be more cheerful? Contemplation of Rome's decay might be depressing enough, but what would induce genuine melancholy is the reflection that the rest of the world is not in a much better condition than the ruins of Rome. The world in general is a dismal place. America is different; it's healthy in more than a physical sense. The rest of the world is depressed by a 'misguided religion', tyranny, and unjust laws (by which Crèvecoeur means rotten political systems). In a few lines, Crèvecoeur paints a picture of the Old World as decaying and decayed. It is a world which has lost its way; it is now very old, played out and moribund. Nowhere in the Old World can one still find traces of a healthy state of society, whereas in America one 'might contemplate the very beginnings and outlines of human society'. America is the only textbook example available of a society coming into being. Only Americans can safely say that they have not lost their way in the myriad institutions and practices of Old World corruption. Europeans have therefore a good deal to learn from the race of cultivators in America whose laws are 'simple and just', and who live close to nature. 'Nature' is a key word. It is what, in the Enlightenment, was the object of scientific curiosity. Crèvecoeur seemed to be saying that in America things are clearer, more easily recognisable, and that includes the necessary facts of social living. A life closer to nature is not to be understood as a romantic slogan, but as a life as it was meant to be lived by nature itself. Only in America can scientific scrutiny still trace the patterns of a natural life. Contrast old and over-complicated Europe, where so many late and perverted accretions have overlaid the ordinary business of living as nature intended it that it can no longer easily be studied as the place where the clues are to be found which will indicate what a rationally determined life ought to be like.

That, of course, was an enormous claim, and it was a claim which was to keep on being made on behalf of American life. Pennsylvania was, after all, on the edge of the known world in eighteenth-century terms. Paris was the centre of European culture, the place where things happened first. Paris was supposed to be the beacon which was supposed to light the rest of the intellectual world, yet here was Crèvecoeur staking a claim for the priority of the Pennsylvania countryside. No doubt, there is something mannered in Crèvecoeur, something which obviously derives from the Rousseau who was attracted by the simplicities of country life and who reacted badly to the sophistication of the Parisian salons. For Rousseau, the countryside was a different society from the society of towns, and something of his anti-urban bias creeps into Crèvecoeur as it was to find its way into romanticism.

Crèvecoeur obviously thinks that interest in America will have to compete with other interests, especially with an interest in ancient Rome. Why would that battle have to be fought? One answer is that Rome amounted almost to an obsession in the eighteenth century. Rousseau used to read Plutarch's *Parallel Lives* as well as the Bible every night before going to sleep; Swift compared the party battles of Queen Anne's reign to the faction fighting between the plebs and patricians in the Roman republic; Pope and the other poets liked to think of themselves as living in a new Age of Augustus; Hume wrote essays full of references to Roman politics and a famous essay on the population level of the Roman Empire; Voltaire called his mistress after the Roman goddess of love; most decent poets tried their hand at translating Vergil; Montesquieu wrote a book famous in its day and still read called *Considerations on the Causes of the Greatness of the Romans and Their Decline*; Addison wrote a play about the life of the great Roman patriot Cato which was George Washington's favourite (the officers of the American army staged a performance of it at the end of the War of Independence as a tribute to him); Washington himself was known as Cincinnatus after the old Roman hero who saved Rome from Carthage in the First Punic War, and there is a town called Cincinnatus in New York, and there is a Cincinnati in Ohio and another in Iowa; there is a Rome in Georgia, New York, Oregon, Pennsylvania and Tennessee; American public architecture is Roman – the original Capitol is in Rome; the United States has a Latin motto, *E Pluribus Unum*; when Jefferson was American minister in Paris he wrote to his daughter nagging her to learn her Roman history in Livy, and Jefferson got very excited about a rumour (it turned out to be false) that Livy's history of Rome had been translated into Arabic; in the year of the Declaration of Independence the first volume of Gibbon's *Decline and Fall of the Roman Empire* was published and it sold out in a week; the American army fighting the British saw themselves as a citizen army, embattled farmers like the army of the Roman republic, fighting the mercenary army of George III; the iconography of eighteenth-century republicanism was Roman – republican heroes appeared in paintings or as statues dressed in the toga, and the famous cap of liberty of the French Revolution was a copy of the Roman Phrygian cap given to freed slaves; and so on.

Why, then, this obsession with Rome? The short answer, though it can be made a very long answer indeed, is that eighteenth-century thinkers were deeply interested in historical change, but the French Revolution had yet to happen. For most nineteenth-century (and many twentieth-century) political theorists, the French Revolution is the great turning-point. The French Revolution marks the division between two worlds, the world of the *ancien régime* and the world of modernity. Most modern political and social theory is an attempt to explain and cope with the nature of this change. In other words, most modern social and political theories are at bottom philosophies of history however much some theories may deny it, and modern social and political theory has been made that much easier to construct because the French Revolution signalled that profound social and political change was going on. It soon became a commonplace that ten years' change in the world after the French Revolution was the equivalent of a century's worth of change during the *ancien régime*. Eighteenth-century thinkers before the French Revolution were interested in change, but they had nothing like the spectacle of the French Revolution before their eyes. They naturally looked into the past for an example of profound social and political change, and the most obvious change occurred when Rome fell in the West in the fifth century and allowed the development of the separate barbarian kingdoms of Christian Europe. Rome was an example, and for long the only available example, of a civilisation which had gone through the long processes of gestation, maturation and decline. Rome really was over; everything that could have happened at Rome *had* happened; in that sense Rome really was a complete example of a civilisation. As a complete example, Rome had important lessons for eighteenth-century theorists. We have seen that eighteenth-century social science was deeply concerned with the comparative study of cultures. Rome was the most important example of a culture different enough from contemporary cultures for the comparison to be worth making.

The comparison between different cultures was meant to enable theorists to separate out the basic constitution of human nature. What men owed to particular cultures could be cancelled out and what was left was the distilled essence of man. New systems of ethics and politics could therefore be constructed on a view of human nature which was itself the product of the latest social scientific thinking and methodology.

In Crèvecoeur's view, America offered a new angle to the problem. America provided an example of human nature as it has been corrupted by the Old World being given a second chance. Perhaps fallen Adam could do something to redeem himself in the virgin landscape of America. This is a programme that has to be taken seriously. The philosophic view of the world was that a uniform human nature adapted itself, and therefore changed, according to circumstances. Crèvecoeur is saying that what can be ravelled up can be un-ravelled. America would be the place where the corruption of man would be uncorrupted. Beginning again would literally mean *going back* to the beginning and beginning again from that beginning. America was supposed to work both ways on the people who went there to live; it would first purify them and then build them up into the kinds of people nature had always wanted them to be. Crèvecoeur follows and goes beyond Montesquieu here. Montesquieu had known perfectly well that climate and soil had an important influence on the characters of men and societies, and in the *Letters* Crèvecoeur takes what appears to be Montesquieu's line, emphasising how a close-to-nature agriculture forms the main outlines of the American's character. But there is an important difference. Montesquieu had thought that climate was the 'first' of all empires, by which he meant that it was only in primitive states of society that climate was the determining cause of the society's character. In more sophisticated societies other, non-physical influences tended to predominate, though the influence of physical causes is never entirely lost. In the case of America, on the other hand, we find men from the highly sophisticated societies of Europe confronting the physical causes of nature head on in the business of farming virgin lands. What a textbook case that would have made for Montesquieu!

Crèvecoeur does for America what Montesquieu would have done had he ever been in a position to do it. In the *Letters* Crèvecoeur makes it plain that he thinks he is in a position to observe the formation of a national character from scratch. It does not matter much that Crèvecoeur does in fact discover several American characters; what does matter is that Crèvecoeur began to put some flesh on the bones of the American character. Of course, there had been a good deal of talk about what Americanness meant when the Revolution first began, but most of that talk had been political talk. The Americans of the thirteen colonies had common interests, but these were common *political* interests (which happened at the time to outweigh their political differences). If America was founded as a nation by the Declaration of Independence in 1776, then it was founded by a political act. In this sense, America was founded the wrong way round when compared to almost all other nationalisms. The programme of all European nationalisms was to identify the nation in linguistic, cultural, religious and geographical terms, and then to claim its right to be a separate state on the basis of that separate identity. Not America. America was founded on the basis of an agreement to do politics in a particular way, the politics of the rights of man. Those who failed to agree about this had no business even staying in America. But an agreement about the moral basis of political authority is not enough to make a nation. Everyone who had even heard of Montesquieu in the second half of the eighteenth century knew that a national character was necessary if a community was to prosper as a separate state. The famous 'spirit of the laws' was the sustaining culture of a political system and was also to an extent the creation of that political system, because how a country is governed is one of the factors which influences its own general spirit. Crèvecoeur hints at this when he remarks that the touch of government is light in America, and that everyone can hope eventually to enjoy political rights.

This is only a hint. On one level, Crèvecoeur's *Letters* are remarkable because, on the surface at least, they are very unpolitical. The implication seems to be that in America men are not much bothered by government. This must be read as saying that in America man-made causes like political institutions have far less purchase on the lives and characters of men than they do in the Old World. Nature therefore counts for more. But there is another level, on which Crèvecoeur would have contradicted his own basic enlightened premises if he had pointed up American government and politics too much. He may have thought that in America it was really too soon to tell with any certainty what American government should eventually be like. After all, America was unique; no comparable case existed anywhere, not even at ancient Rome. All that could be said with certainty is that American political life, like American life in general, was going to be very different. Crèvecoeur has not the experience of American politics that Tocqueville was to have when he made his celebrated remark that in America men were to shape the institutions in which they lived, whereas in Europe men were shaped by their institutions.

The experience of the War of Independence may or may not have brought a truly American character to the fore. Some argue it did and some argue it did not. The political experience of the victorious United States between the end of the war and the making of the new Constitution in 1787 seems to suggest that, if national character means national unity, then the process of the formation of a uniform national character was far from complete. Perhaps there had always been some necessary pretence about the existence of the American character. It is certainly true that those who made the running in the period leading to the Declaration of Independence themselves exaggerated (as Tom Paine does) the extent to which Americans were of one mind over the great issues of the day. The question of Americanness was to rise again very quickly during the time when the ratification of the new Constitution was being discussed. It was by no means obvious that the new, federal Constitution was going to be ratified by the states. Arguments of an anti-Crèvecoeur kind were being used to support the creation of several republics, not just one. The northern, central and southern states were so different, it was argued, that each group ought to form a separate republic of its own. This was, in fact, an argument about how enlightened political thinking ought to apply in America. An age which learnt its politics from Montesquieu knew that a political system without the requisite general spirit to sustain and animate it would be an empty shell. The history of the world abounded with examples of constitutions from which the sustaining spirit had departed. Plainly, the more the idea of an American character could be sustained, the more plausible the case was for a single federal republic, and that is the case which ultimately prevailed.

That the Constitution was ratified does not prove one way or the other that the American character actually existed, and the subsequent history of the United States does not admit of a definitive answer either. What is clear, however, is that as the immigrants came to America in their millions, it became increasingly necessary to stress that there was an American character which they could acquire. Otherwise, in what sense could it be true that the peoples of the world could become American at all? That character had to be easy to assume to accommodate the extremely diffuse national characters which the immigrants already possessed as the legacy of the countries from which they came. There is more than an echo of Crèvecoeur in this idea of a character accessible to everyman. Crèvecoeur's own description of the American is nothing if not an account of a character which has been formed by influences which are much less complex than the influences which shape character in over-complex and corrupt old Europe. Perhaps it has always been the case that the American character has had to be simple (foreigners are apt to describe Americans as 'superficial'); otherwise the whole process of becoming American would itself be over-complex.

THE FEDERALIST PAPERS AND THE CONSTITUTION

The Federalist Papers are the one undoubted masterpiece of political thinking written by men who were themselves active and successful politicians. The Papers are quoted everywhere, though perhaps, like many classics, they are more often quoted than read. There seem to be three broad views of the Papers, at least two of which are contradictory. These views might be called The Thesis of Timeless Wisdom, the Thesis of Particular Wisdom, and The Conspiracy Thesis.

The Thesis of Timeless Wisdom

The Thesis of Timeless Wisdom attributes almost superhuman mental powers both to the Founding Fathers who made the Constitution of the United States and to the authors of the *Papers*. They made and explained a Constitution which has worked in something like its original state for over two centuries, and it has worked in places for which it was not originally designed. America was very near the eastern seaboard in 1787, whereas since then the Constitution has worked in the thirty-seven states which have come into the Union. The Constitution (and its amendments) is a remarkably short document, and it is this fact which gives *The Federalist Papers* its overwhelming theoretical status. The wisdom which the Founding Fathers compressed into the bare bones of a government in the Constitution has to be fleshed out by the *Papers*. The Constitution, it is said, makes very little sense unless it is accompanied by the *Papers* as its essential gloss. In particular, the Constitution does not tell us what constitutional government and politics in the United States was going to be like. The Founding Fathers, and Hamilton, Jay and Madison especially, had a very good idea about what kinds of government and politics the new Constitution was designed to make possible. No doubt some of the delegates to the Constitutional Convention which met at Philadelphia in 1787 had come to discuss such constitutional niceties as the separation of powers, but most were just as likely to be inter-ested in what the real power relations were going to be in the political system which was going to develop after the Constitution had been ratified by the states. On this view of it, the Founding Fathers designed a political system as well as designing a Constitution, and it is sometimes suggested that the political system has lasted as long as the Constitution. Not that nothing has changed; rather, what is remarkable about the political system of the United States is its continuity. So little has fundamentally changed that modern American politics would be easily recognisable to the constitution-making generation. No doubt American politics is more democratic than it was, and it might come as a shock to some present-day Americans that the Founding Fathers did not on the whole like democracy very much at all, but none the less we still see the same institutions at state and federal level performing their constitutionally allotted functions, and we still see the interplay of interest groups around those institutions.

The Thesis of Timeless Wisdom is really a thesis about the future social basis of American politics, and that thesis is best expressed in Madison's famous *10th Federalist*. In that paper, Madison is discussing what in the eighteenth century was called 'faction' and what we should call 'interest groups' or 'special interests'. 'Faction' had a pejorative sound to it in Madison's day. It meant any special interest which was opposed to, or at least different from, the common weal or interest. In a republic, everybody was supposed to put love of country above love of self; so much had been clear since Montesquieu had so defined the animating spirit of a republic. It had been equally clear since Aristotle that the particular danger in a republic was faction, the spontaneous appearance of particular groups, typically groups of the rich and the poor, patricians and plebs, which saw their own interests as opposed to each other. Each would try to capture state power to use it for its own ends, hence the endemic class war in republics noted by all ancient and by many modern political thinkers. Madison recognises that in an ideal world a republic like the United States would rely for its future well-being on disinterested love for the public weal, but he also is a realist who does not expect the American republic to be faction free. Why should this be the case when every other republic of which history has taken any note has been faction ridden? The United States, then, like every other republic, is stuck with faction.

What is to be done? Faction arises because different groups of men have different interests. The only way of getting rid of factions entirely would be to get rid of the cause of faction, which would mean that a way would have to be found to make all men the same, a governmental programme clearly out of the question in a free society. An alternative would be to allow the cause of faction to remain but to eliminate the effects of faction – that is, to stop men of similar interests from banding together to further their interest – and that is equally plainly not a possibility in a free country. The only alternative that Madison can see is to found a republic so extensive and diverse that the number of factions is as large as it can possibly be so that it is impossible for one faction to dominate all the rest.

The problem of the ancient republics had been that there were really only two factions that counted, rich and poor, each striving to gain mastery of the state. What made ancient faction-fighting so bitter was that each side thought that it could win all the spoils of political victory. The very diversity of the sorts and conditions of men in America should ensure that no single faction can come to dominate government. Madison's is therefore an argument for a large federal republic, and it can obviously be easily made to accommodate the admission of other states into the Union at some future date. The more the diversity of the United States is encouraged, the less likely it is that any one faction will gain the upper hand. The federal system in the new Constitution also helps prevent single-faction domination. The separation between the functions of federal and state governments will mean that for many purposes factions will operate at state level. Each state's politics will be interest group politics, and these state interest groups will see no reason why they should attempt to operate at national level at all. Many factions, therefore, will not even begin to try to become national factions. On this view of it, Madison's *10th Federalist* is obviously a blueprint for pluralist, interest group politics, and it needs no stressing that the American political system has long been the classic case for the practice and study of interest group politics.

The other great leavener of factional politics is the principle of representation. Madison regards representation as a kind of filter which will take some of the edge out of factional politics. The United States must be a representative democracy because direct democracy in the style of the ancients is not a practical possibility even in the individual states of the Union on account of their size, and it would be a simple absurdity to try to institute direct democracy on a national scale. Representation will take the edge off faction even at state level, either because the plurality of factions will mean that each representative will have to tread carefully between the factions if he is to be elected to state government, or because so many factions will be represented in the state legislatures that no one faction will predominate and each faction will come to realise that it will have to bargain and compromise with the rest. And even if the states come to be the scene of some pretty nasty faction politics, there is no reason to suppose that nasty state politics will disturb the general councils of the nation. All the chances are that the nastiness will be confined to individual states, and besides, the Constitution itself sets limits to what can happen in state government. The Constitution guarantees a republican form of government to each state, and a state governor can always call on federal assistance if the proprieties of republican government go unobserved. At national level, Madison lays great stress on the effects of distance, both physical and mental: representatives from the individual states serving in the national legislatures are unlikely to come as mandated delegates no matter how factional the election was which elected them. Most factions, being local, will not necessarily have views on national issues, and what the national issues are going to be are not necessarily predictable anyway. The only national institution which could conceivably be colonised by faction is the House of Representatives, because it alone is elected directly by popular vote, but the Constitution wisely provides for the re-election of the whole House every two years. That means that if the unthinkable happened, and the House was dominated by a majority faction, it would not last for long. Besides, there is the cooler wisdom of the Senate, whose members are to be elected by the state legislatures, to oppose any too obviously factional measures passed by the House. And beyond that, there is the presidential veto. Perhaps, above all, what really counts is that the national representatives will learn their trade at a national level. They will become a different kind of political animal from the politicians at the state and lower town and county levels. Being a United States Senator is going to be a fine thing to be, and, while the representative system ensures that national representatives will never get completely out of touch with their constituents, there will nevertheless be a sense in which national concerns will appear to be distinct from local concerns and national politicians will differentiate themselves from local.

The explanation of why the Constitution and its political system has lasted usually homes in on the idea of balance, especially a self-regulating balance. Speculation about what makes a constitution or a political system survive in a world which eventually brings corruption and death to everything had been taking place ever since political theory was invented. There seem to have been two broad general views. Some thinkers, of whom the Plato of the *Republic* is the obvious example, thought that the only way to make sure of a political system's survival was to make it perfect to begin with and then make sure it never changed by writing a proviso against change into its constitution. Other thinkers, like Aristotle and Machiavelli, looked for ways in which a political system could be made to be self-regulating. The political system outlined in Plato's *Laws, The Constitution of Athens* as famously described by Aristotle, and the Spartan constitution were all supposed to be examples of what has come to be called 'mixed government'. Mixed government was government composed of the different and contradictory principles of monarchy, aristocracy or oligarchy, and democracy – or of any two of these, typically oligarchy and democracy. The ancients were so aware of the mutability of human affairs that they realised that a pure monarchy, aristocracy or democracy was bound to decay: monarchy into tyranny, aristocracy into oligarchy (rule by the rich), and democracy into ochlocracy (rule by the mob). Mixed government, on the other hand, had the virtue that its opposing principles cancelled out the worst tendencies of each. Machiavelli, for instance, analyses the constitution of the

Roman republic in those terms: diffidence in the face of the people curbed the arrogance of the patricians while the short-sightedness of the roused multitude was tempered by the wise caution of the senatorial class. Each order in the state reacted naturally to the faults of the other, creating a balanced system of government which was self-correcting.

Something like that balance is supposed to characterise the Constitution of the United States and the political system which followed from it. American politics is supposed to be a balancing act of considerable formal and informal complexity. Institutions are balanced against each other, legislature against executive, and judiciary against both; the Senate is balanced against the House; the original electoral systems for the Senate and the presidency balanced the claims to representation of political influence against numbers; the jurisdiction of state government is balanced against the jurisdiction of the federal government, and at the state level the state capitals were typically kept away from the larger cities as a symbol of the balance between wealth and virtue, town and country; every interest group calls forth its opposite; capital and labour; farmers and industrialists (and small farmers against large, small business against corporate wealth); north and south, east and west; anti-polluters against polluters, and so on in a never-ending list. Even ethnicity has its place. It does not much matter whether America really is the melting-pot of national differences because there is a perfectly good *10th Federalist* argument to the effect that the ethnic variety of America, including as it does all the nations of the earth, is just another example of interest group politics at work because each ethnic group is free to and actually does constitute itself as an interest group playing pluralist politics with other groups.

That the idea of balanced government was not new in 1787 is obvious. The Founding Fathers immediate source for it was probably their reading of recent English constitutional experience. English government in the eighteenth century was supposed to be mixed government *par excellence*. All the authorities seemed to agree that English politics was in its day a unique blend of monarchy, aristocracy and popular government. What needs to be emphasised is that the idea of balanced government is not one idea but two. The idea of balanced government is both a constitutional principle and a functional test of the proper working of constitutional government. Mixed government is supposed to be balanced government in the sense that no one part of government is expected to predominate over the others. What this effectively means is that governing decisions will be shared decisions, legitimate because they have been arrived at in a particular way. Decisions are legitimate because the proper procedure has been followed, and the most obvious example, though by no means the only one, is legislation by king-in-parliament, when the shared decision-making process is attended by considerable formality (and not a little mummery). The theory of mixed government is frank about class. All sorts and conditions of men have a right to participate in decision-making, either directly, as in the case of the king and members of the House of Lords, or indirectly through their representatives in the House of Commons. All can be seen to have a share, however tangential, in the process of decision-making, and so all can be said to be justly bound by the decisions made. What works for the most solemn acts of state legislation will, by extension, work for other areas and levels of government. Provided no one class pretended to a monopoly of decision-making power, it could be argued plausibly that all governing decisions were legitimate.

Balanced government is also a test of the functioning of constitutional government. Shared decisions are supposed to be good and efficient decisions. We can easily forget how easily the categories of 'legitimate' and 'good-as-efficient' decisions melt into each other. Legitimate decisions are supposed to be acceptable decisions, decisions which do not have to be put into practice by the threat or use of force, both of which eat up scarce government resources. An easily acceptable decision is an efficient decision because it is easily implemented. Decisions which meet with resistance on the part of citizens are, prima facie, bad decisions, and people begin to wonder how they could have been made in the first place. How easy it is in a system of mixed government to explain how a bad decision came to be made by blaming it on unbalanced government, government in which the mixture is not quite right. In the theory of mixed government, each of the parts is supposed to contribute something valuable to the decision-making process. In the English case, this had become standardised in the formula that the king was supposed to contribute decisiveness, the Lords wisdom, and the Commons virtue. We do not have to attend to the meanings of these terms too closely to be able to see how easily a wrong decision could be attributed to the fact that one or other of the parts had contributed too much or too little to it. The decisions taken by the British government after 1763 which eventually led to the alienation of the American colonies were seen in America (and by some in England) to be flawed decisions of this kind. There seemed to be too much of the temper of a wilful executive steamrolling bad governing decisions through a controlled House of Commons. British government had become unbalanced; in the phrase of the day, the 'balance of the constitution' had been disturbed because the king and his ministers could always get what they wanted.

The government of America under its new Constitution was never going to be like that. Careful constitutional engineering was going to make sure that supreme governing decisions, acts of Congress, were going to be shared decisions no matter how formally the parts of government were to be separated. The world of federal government in Washington was always going to be a small and, to an extent, isolated world. Everybody was going to be able to get to know everybody else and to know what everybody else was thinking about public policy matters. Each part of the system, House, Senate, president and Supreme Court would have a very shrewd idea of what the other parts would stomach by way of governing decisions. Either the parts co-operated and compromised, or the system of government would not work at all. At best there would be a repeat of the rather inactive government of the Continental Congress under the Articles of Confederation, hardly national government at all, and it must never be forgotten that, in the beginning at least, most of the government which was going to happen in America was to happen at state level and lower. This suited the spirit of mixed government very well. All sorts and conditions of men would thereby find themselves directly and indirectly involved in the process of political decision-making. Roughly speaking, each state was to have a system of internal government analogous to the system of national government, and state governments (thirteen of which were in place when the new Constitution was ratified) were to be just as mixed as the national government.

Balanced government in America was meant to work with the human material already available. In *The Federalist Papers* Hamilton, Jay and Madison take no high-minded view of the majority of humankind. It is not that they think that men are incapable of disinterested patriotism, of putting country before self, caste or party. Rather, what they seem to be saying is that you can never *rely* on men to be disinterested patriots concerned only for their country's good. Self-interest, especially the self-interest of groups, both is predictable and can be relied upon to work over time, whereas patriotism is a bonus. Political institutions work because groups pursuing their own group interests make them work. American institutions at all levels were going to be the scenes of the conflicts between groups through their representatives. The game had to be worth the candle. It really had to be the case that interest groups at every level of government would come to think that playing the interest group game was worth it in the sense that they could in fact get something, if not every-thing, of what they wanted. For this to happen, American politics was going to have to be very open politics, with in-groups prepared to make room in the system for out-groups to be tolerated in, if not exactly welcomed into, the game. (Poker is the quintessentially American card-game because the number of players is not fixed, and players can enter and leave the game while the game itself goes on.) This group interest feeling was also going to operate at the level of governing institutions themselves. Members of the House of Representatives, members of the Senate, the president and those close to him, and members of the Supreme Court of the United States were all supposed to develop an *esprit de corps* which would make them jealous of their own rights and privileges under the Constitution. Indeed, the Constitution is largely taken up with spelling out what those rights and privileges are. A certain institutional prissiness about the limits of the powers of other institutions is supposed to characterise the various branches of government in their relations with each other. The branches will co-operate, but at the same time there is to be no invasion of one branch's territory by another. This is not, of course, supposed to lead to an institutional stand-off, though it could. The pursuit of group interests means above all else that government is supposed to work, and that means that government is not supposed to find itself in institutional deadlock.

All the fashionable talk about checks and balances, fashionable in the eighteenth century as now in the textbooks of American government, tends to lay a false trail about the nature of American national government as it was originally intended to be. Endless harping on the separation of powers/checks-and-balances theme can easily lead to the mistaken impression that American government was supposed to be in some kind of static equilibrium. We do well to remind ourselves that in *The Spirit of the Laws* Montesquieu himself had said that a perfect system of separation of powers would lead to a system of government 'in repose', that is to say doing nothing very much. *The Federalist Papers* can leave us in no doubt that the Founding Fathers intended to construct a much stronger frame of government than the Articles of Confederation ever did. American government was supposed to bite, at home and abroad, and besides, we have already seen that only strong government can defend basic rights. A moment's simple reflection about the new Congress under the Constitution is enough to put all thoughts of a government in America 'in repose' right out of our minds. The future Congress was going to have to legislate the basic legal structure of American government, and it was going to have to do it quickly. (The

Constitution itself, being only six thousand words long, is barely a skeleton.) How could that possibly happen if the American system of government was intended to be naturally in repose? Partial separation of powers is really no separation of powers at all, or at least has no particularly American meaning. Partial separation of powers means that the institutions of government take part in each other's functions: the executive will have some judicial functions, the legislative will have some executive functions, and so on. In these circumstances it may in fact be difficult to distinguish at all clearly between the three functions. The problem is that, an imaginary and super-efficient despotism apart, it is hard to think of a system of government which is *not* a partial separation of powers/checks-and-balances government in some important sense. Madison hints at this at various moments in *The Federalist Papers*, as, for example, when he says that 'checks' are in the nature of things, or when he says that while it is easy to distinguish between the three functions of government in principle, it is often very difficult in practice. Partial separation of powers, where it is difficult to distinguish between the personnel who are to carry out these different functions, is mixed government by another name, government where the lines are, and necessarily are, blurred.

It is a measure of the persuasiveness of the Thesis of Timeless Wisdom that one is always tempted to make the foresight of the Founding Fathers and of *The Federalist Papers* more acute than it actually was. Perhaps the account given above of the premonition of pluralist politics in *10th Federalist* is a little overdrawn. It might be said that Madison did not really predict how the American political system would develop in its pluralist direction to the extent that it has, but the temptation to argue as if he had is testimony enough to the power of his own more modest predictions. Again, the view that American government was going to be balanced government could be a view that substantially post-dates the making of the Constitution and the writing of *The Federalist Papers*. The standard form that eulogies of American politics have taken in the twentieth century has always been that American politics is uniquely pluralist and balanced. America, it is always said, has reason to be proud of its pluralist politics and has no reason to be afraid of its balanced government. Arguments without end have been advanced to show that American politics is not pluralist at all (and we will consider some of them later) and there is certainly no shortage of arguments designed to show that American government can from time to time become very unbalanced. No doubt these can be very plausible arguments, but the point is that the Madisonian arguments can be put forward with equal plausibility in the modern world. It may be that Madison has so colonised the political mind of America that from 1787 Americans, with notable exceptions, have been unable to understand their own politics in any but Madisonian terms. It is even conceivable that Madison invented the American political system and also invented the world of concepts in which that politics was always to be understood. If this is true, or even partly true, then Madison's is an extraordinary achievement, unique for a political theorist.

Enough has been said about the Timeless Wisdom of *The Federalist Papers* for it to be obvious where this interpretation of them leads. The thesis is perhaps over-enthusiastic, but it is serious. *The Federalist Papers* are the first and the definitive commentary on the American Constitution and on the American political system. After *The Federalist Papers*, commentary on American politics is simply a matter of dotting a few i's and crossing a few t's; any serious commentator on American politics cannot help but stand on the shoulders of Hamilton, Jay and Madison. Above all, perhaps, we should be *grateful* for the *Papers*; they come, so to speak, straight from the horse's mouth; it is not every day that we are privileged to see right into the minds of those who actually made a Constitution and designed a political system which were to last two centuries.

The Thesis of Particular Wisdom

No-one would deny that *The Federalist Papers* let us into the minds of Hamilton, Jay and Madison, and by extension into the minds at least of some of those who were at the Philadelphia Convention in 1787, but what kind of minds these were can be a matter of considerable dispute. It might be that the political mind we are given access to in the *Papers* is a characteristic mind of the late Enlightenment, a mind so closely attuned to its own time that it cannot speak directly to us. It may well be that the world of concepts inhabited by the generation that made the Constitution, and made it work, is a world that we have lost. If this is the case, then it has very serious implications for the interpretation of *The Federalist Papers* and of the Constitution. Accept for a moment that *The Federalist Papers* is the definitive commentary on the Constitution, and accept that the *Papers* themselves need a commentary because they do not speak directly to us. If the definitive commentary on the Constitution needs a commentary, then where does that leave the Constitution of the United States in American political life? American politics is supposed to be profoundly constitutional politics. The American Constitution is supposed to be alive and well and living among ordinary Americans. This is true at a very ordinary level of discourse about American politics. Discussion about American politics, either in the street or in the classroom, always sooner or later ends up with a discussion about the meaning of this or that part of the Constitution. Not only that, but agreement about what the Constitution means as it bears on any issue is usually taken to be a clinching point. Arguing against what the Constitution is agreed to mean comes close to blasphemy. Constitutional discourse is a very particular kind of discourse. It comes midway between discourse about ethics and discourse about positive law. Outside constitutional discourse there are only two questions which can seriously be asked about governing decisions: Are they really lawful? Are they ethically correct? The first question is a question about legal fact: was the decision made by the agency legally entitled to make it and was it made in the legally correct way? The second question is a question about judging whether the decisions of government conform to a fundamental code of ethics. The problem about the first question is that horrendous governing decisions can be made in the correct form, and the problem about the second question is that in any given society, and especially in America, there is likely to be a plurality of different ethical codes. Discourse about constitutionality fits neatly between the two. Constitutionality is about both the form and the content of governing decisions. To say a government decision is 'constitutional' is to say more than that it was made by the appropriate agency in the proper way, and it is to say something less than that everybody could say that it is strictly ethically correct. Constitutionalism is a source of values itself, and these are supposed to be values capable of being shared by a whole political society. Argument in America about what the Constitution means presupposes an agreement to do politics within the Constitution and an agreement that it is in fact possible to settle political questions which are value-loaded by reference to the Constitution.

It would be possible to write the whole history of American politics as a history of disputes about constitutional interpretation. For this to mean anything at all, it has at the very least got to be true that understanding the Constitution is available to everyman. (You have to show some rudimentary knowledge of the Constitution of the United States before you can become an American citizen, and even getting into the United States as a visitor requires a declaration that you intend the Constitution no harm.) Now suppose that the definitive commentary on the Constitution, *The Federalist Papers*, itself needs a commentary, then where does that leave the Constitution? It must mean at the very least that the Constitution cannot be speaking directly to ordinary Americans and perhaps it means that the Constitution speaks directly to hardly any Americans at all. Understanding the Constitution becomes a very specialised job; perhaps only a few academics and the Justices of the Supreme Court really understand it. None of these is elected, while the elected officials and politicians of the United States may be trying to make a Constitution work which they do not begin to understand. The most holy moment in American politics, when the president of the United States at the ceremony of inauguration promises to preserve, protect and defend the Constitution of the United States, becomes hollow farce because neither the president nor the millions watching on television are likely to have a clue about what it is that is being promised the special protection of the republic's chief magistrate.

It will not do to say: but the Constitution has changed since 1787, and that present under-standing is adequate to the Constitution as it works now, because that is to ignore the central claim always made for the Constitution, which is that it is still identifiably itself despite the changes. Most of these changes have gone in the direction of democracy. Presidents and senators are now elected by popular vote, and political rights are now available to everyone, but these are a graft on an original stock which continues to determine how democratic politics will in fact work. Indeed, one of the standard contemporary arguments about the American political system is that it can never be truly reformed because America is stuck with a Constitution which is itself very difficult to change. If it's difficult to change in the present, then it must have been difficult to change in the past, which is just another way of saying that the original Constitution has substantially survived.

So what was the mind of Whiggish America like in the 1780s? What were the fundamental concepts which were used to understand the world in general and the world of politics in particular? By a fortunate coincidence, an ingrained Whiggish attitude to power fitted neatly together with the picture of the Newtonian universe which Enlightenment had made available to the world. Whigs had always thought that unchecked power had the tendency to grow indefinitely, and it was easy to find a confirmation of that view in the very latest scientific thinking. The Newtonian view of the universe held that all the heavenly bodies were kept in their proper spheres by the force of gravity acting from one body to the other. Everything in the universe was kept in its place by the action of everything else. A body like the earth, without the force of gravity of the other heavenly bodies acting on it, would probably begin to do some very bizarre things. Control in motion was the watchword of the Newtonian universe. This vast, self-regulating system of co-operation could serve as the perfect model for a society, for a political system, or for a constitution. Set power against power and nothing would ever leave its allocated place. The beauty of the Newtonian scheme was that it could be designed and set in motion once and for all. The Newtonian universe was plainly the creation of a very rational God. God was the original of all legislators, giving the laws of their motion to the bodies in the heavens, and this was the fundamental law of the constitution of the universe. This view in its turn sat well with a particular kind of enlightened Protestantism or Deism (what came to be called 'natural religion'). God's work was over after the Creation. Man he created so that one of his creatures would be able to understand the inner workings of the created universe. God was the perfect constitutional monarch because he would never break the laws of his own making. There was, therefore, no need for continued revelation, and certainly no need for miracles. Miracles happen when the ordinary scientific laws of the universe are broken, as when people rise from the dead, or statues of saints bleed, or a sprinkling of holy water allows the halt and the lame to pick up their beds and walk. If God allowed miracles to happen, he would be acting like an arbitrary despot riding roughshod over law. Implicit here was an attack on some of the more outlandish beliefs and practices of Roman Catholicism. It was the Roman Church which emphasised both continued revelation and miracles, and enlightened thinkers were not slow to point out the close connection between the Church of Rome (itself an absolute monarchy) and doctrines of the sinfulness of disobedience to those kings, however bad, whom the apostle Paul says are ordained of God. Catholicism and arbitrary and absolute monarchy seemed to go hand in hand, so that it was not clear in what senses Catholic kings could be constitutional monarchs like God.

The political implications of both Whiggism and Newtonian 'natural religion' were clear enough. Arbitrary, uncontrolled power was unnatural. God himself wanted government to be constitutional government. This, again, fitted in well with the history of the separate governments of the American colonies before independence. American government had always been constitutional government. Of course, the original governments of the American colonies were not founded on any self-consciously Newtonian principles. Yet men do seek to find ways to make their governments make sense. Newtonian physics was an ideal way to do that. It fitted exactly into the way that the governing class in America had already come to think about government. Regular government which observed the forms of law and which kept everything in its proper place was good government. Bad government was government in which one of the parts got above itself and began to dominate the other parts in an arbitrary way. Something like that was supposed to have happened in England in 1688 (and 1688 had its equivalents in America) when a bad king, James II, arrogated to himself the right to suspend the law in favour of his Catholic friends. Power which had emancipated itself from the controlling context of other powers – in the case of James II from Parliament and the law – was power which was going to increase without limit. The turning point for America came in 1771 when, under the promptings of Tom Paine's *Common Sense*, Americans began to realise just how far a British government which had a more or less secure parliamentary majority could go without formally breaking the law of its own constitution. In that case, it was not altogether clear in what sense Britain had a constitution, if a constitution was there to put a check on government. (And to this day Americans still puzzle over the nature of a constitution like the British which can be changed by a simple parliamentary majority.) Any constitution that America was going to have would have to be of the kind which bound the parts of government together so tightly, and which was absolutely clear that constitutional law was fundamental and binding law, so that no single power-centre could ever escape the control of the others.

It is obvious that the generation which made the Constitution thought in terms derived from seventeenth-century physics and mechanics. That is how they explained the world in general to themselves. This is very far from saying that everybody was likely to agree about everything, but they did agree about that. What this meant in political terms was that, whatever kind of government America was going to have, at whatever level, it was going to be constitutional government. That was what enabled the Constitution of the United States to be so short. There was no need to explain what constitutional government was because everybody thought they already knew, and America was fortunate in 1776 to have a class of political leaders who had already learned the arts of constitutional government in their native colonies before independence. When the supposed crisis of American government came at the end of the 1780s, with the United States rapidly becoming the disunited states, those who made the running for the new form of government eventually provided for in the Constitution of 1787 never doubted for an instant that the new government was going to be constitutional government in the sense currently understood. (And it is a remarkable testimony to the strength of constitutionalist tradition in America that when the Confederate States seceded from the Union in 1861 the first thing they did was to write a constitution for themselves which was almost a carbon-copy of the Constitution of the Union which they had just left.)

If that analysis has any merit then it follows that the Founding Fathers saddled America with a constitution finely tuned to the intellectual attitudes of the time of its making. There was no guarantee, of course, that the machine was going to work, or that it was going to work in the way that was intended. In this sense the Constitution can actually be misleading. *The Federalist Papers* invite us to take a particular view of how constitutional politics is going to work, and it may be that that particular mechanical model fits eighteenth-century American government only. Continuing to try to understand all American politics in the terms of the original model may be not to understand American politics at all. Take, for instance, the commonplace view that democratic politics in America has been notoriously corrupt politics. How is this to be explained in the terms of the original model? There can be no doubt that the Founding Fathers were aware of the dangers of political corruption. The whole of the American case against the British rested on a view of the British political system as having been corrupted by the wealth available to monarchy in the form of places and pensions to buy a majority in the House of Commons. Republican politics was going to be cleaner politics because America was going to have balanced government. It had been the accepted view of balanced government at least since Machiavelli that the balancing of parts tended to lessen the effects of their faults and tended to bring out the effects of their virtues. The Roman plebs softened the arrogance of the patricians and the Roman patricians curbed the tumultuousness of the people; that left only the patricians' wisdom and the people's virtue, both of which could only serve the republic well. It may well be that the Founding Fathers thought something like that dressed up in the concepts of Newtonianism. If each of the parts of government, at whatever level, is supposed to keep a watching brief over the other parts so that none of the parts goes wrong, then how can political corruption be explained? Of course political corruption *can* be explained, and America even had a political movement, the Progressive movement, which spent all its time explaining it, but the real point is that the original model of American government *cannot* explain it. Quite the reverse. The original model is meant to explain why corruption can't happen.

None of this would matter if it were not the case that *The Federalist Papers* have been extremely influential on the ways American government and politics have in fact been explained. The concepts and the language used to explain eighteenth-century constitutional engineering serve very well to explain modern pluralist democracy: groups pushing and shoving and being limited by the pushing and shoving of other groups until some kind of systemic equilibrium comes out of the apparent chaos. But again, a model like this cannot explain why some pressure groups are spectacularly more successful than others. Some pressure groups are so deeply locked into government at both state and federal level that it is often hard to tell where government ends and pressure groups begin. Of course, this *can* be explained, but there is nothing in the mechanical model to explain it. What applies to pressure groups can easily be applied to institutions. How are we to explain the extraordinary success, in the twentieth century, of the presidency as an institution? Some have even spoken of an 'imperial' presidency, a presidency so self-moved that it can take on all of the other institutions of state and still not lose. Of course, the imperial presidency *can* be explained, or even explained away, but it cannot be explained in the terms of the original mechanical model because that original model is in part an explanation of why the presidency cannot become imperial.

So there are really two ways of looking at the Thesis of Particular Wisdom. Either we say that *The Federalist Papers* are so closely attuned to their own time that they have nothing to say directly to us, or we say that they are actually misleading when their understanding of American politics is applied to any American politics outside their own time, and that they are especially misleading about modern democratic politics in America. The legacy of *The Federalist Papers* may be an intellectual disaster in another sense. It cannot be a coincidence that enthusiasm for the modern science of politics has always been warmer in the United States than elsewhere, and it cannot also be a coincidence that the world of concepts which that science of politics inhabits is essentially the world of physics and mechanics. The term 'pressure' groups itself tells us that. A more serious claim is that power is somehow quantifiable, or even that power is a fixed quantity which can be seen to be distributed among various groups and institutions, the assumption being that what one group or institution gains, another loses. The study of American politics, and by extension all politics, becomes the business of assigning power quantities to particular power centres and of monitoring the changes in those power quantities. In so far as this is true of the science of politics, it continues to be true that politics is being explained in the terms of seventeenth-century physics and mechanics. Of course, there are other models, biological, statistical and even cybernetic, but my hunch is that, by and large, the seventeenth-century model still dominates the field. If this is so, then all cannot be well with a science which has failed to outgrow its own origins.

The Conspiracy Thesis

The notion of 'consipiracy' is not to be taken too literally when applied to the making of the Constitution and to the writing of *The Federalist Papers*. After all, the Founding Fathers did not attempt to solve the supposed crisis of American government after the War of Independence by proposing a *coup d'état*; there may have been some loose talk at Philadelphia about the restoration of monarchy in America but there can be no doubt that if monarchy had been restored it would have been impeccably constitutional monarchy. Besides, the idea of monarchy would not necessarily have spread panic among late eighteenth-century republicans because it had long been a commonplace that the 'monarchical' element was an essential part of well-constituted republics: Spartan kings, Roman consuls, Venetian doges and Dutch stadtholders (one of whom, William of Orange, became king of Great Britain) all held office in republics with mixed forms of government. Absolute monarchy was not an option for America since the pretended absolutism of George III had been denounced in the Declaration of Independence, but there was every reason in principle (and perhaps every reason in practice) that, granted the way the Founding Fathers thought about mixed and balanced government, a strong monarchical element should be written into the Constitution. The president was to be a species of temporary king, exercising the traditional royal powers of commanding armies and attending to foreign affairs in general, and having a watching brief over the efficiency of executive government and the 'state of the nation'. (There was an eighteenth-century precedent for this in the election of the kings of Poland, though the kings of Poland served for life.)

None the less, the Founding Fathers knew perfectly well that they were founding a national government which was intended to be much more powerful than the national government by committees of Congress which is all that the Articles of Government allowed. And they meant *government*. *The Federalist Papers* show us just how clearly it was possible to think about the realities of government at the end of the eighteenth century. The three great powers of government were national defence, law and order, and the power to raise a revenue; without this last, the other powers were meaningless. The national government under the Articles of Confederation did not have the revenue-raising power. When it wanted money, all that the first government of the United States could do was to go cap in hand to the individual states and ask them to raise the money for them. This system of national taxation had not even worked very well during the emergencies of the War of Independence; everybody knew that Washington was forced to pay the troops at Valley Forge out of his own fortune to prevent them dispersing that winter. *The Federalist*

Papers were largely written to convince the citizens of the United States, or the citizens who mattered, that America in 1787 needed a national government with all the powers normally associated with government and therefore without which national government could hardly be said to exist at all. America was to have a government like other governments and take her rightful place among the powers of the earth.

The *Papers* make much of the problems of American government under the Articles of Confederation as a preliminary to arguing that the government to be provided under the new Constitution will be able to cope with these problems. The list of those problems could be made to look formidable, and even a glance at the list can give the impression that the problems were of such a kind that by 1787 America was crying out for strong government. Most of the problems stemmed from the conflicts of interest between the individual states. Part of the problem was that co-operation between states was often made difficult because they had different systems of government. States quarrelled between themselves about western land claims, disputed their borders with each other, haggled over their commercial systems (tariffs) and over what the various states' treaties with the Indians meant. The disputes could be bitter and long-lasting, and it was easy to think, when the temporary unity of the War of Independence was fading, that there was a tendency towards disintegration. That list of inter-state bickering could be made very long indeed, but we have to ask ourselves the question: What's new about it? The colonies before 1776 had always quarrelled about much the same things, and some of the particular quarrels were of long standing. What *had* changed was that, after the Americans had set up their own national government under the Articles of Confederation, for the first time a national forum existed in America for the settling of inter-state disputes. Up to independence, the colonies had London agents instructed to press one colony's claim over another on the Privy Council or on other agencies of British government. It is hard, therefore, to give full credit to the case that since independence it had become more, not less, difficult to solve these disputes, and it is equally hard to believe that they can have been so pressing when they, or something very like them, had lasted for as long as anyone could remember.

If we are to stick to the 'crisis of American government' thesis, and we may have to in order to provide a motive at all for the calling of the Philadelphia meeting which wrote the new Constitution, then we have to find a problem facing American government in the late 1780s which American government had not had to face before, and the most obvious new problem was the democratisation of politics in the states. Democratisation meant a good deal more than getting rid of the American Tories and extending the franchise. During the War of Independence a kind of democratisation took place in the states; there was a certain amount of Tory-harrying, and some states found it convenient to sell up the estates of departed Tories (often at knock-down prices), to help pay for the war. When the war was over, it was very difficult to deny political rights to those who had fought (and the larger number who claimed to have fought) in the war. In fact, before independence there were wide differences in the extent to which political rights were distributed in the various states, but after the war it seems to have been the case that political rights were there for the taking in any of the states (women and blacks always excepted). This was, no doubt, something which had to be accepted even by those who disapproved of it, but what did not have to be accepted was the use to which the widespread exercise of political rights was being put. Rag-money was the rage almost everywhere; popular clamour in the states was about to authorise the issue of paper money and to urge the state legislatures to pass legal tender acts to make rag-money compulsorily acceptable for the payment of all debts, public and private.

Why did this matter so much? Part of the reason was that America had been awash with funny money ever since the Continental Congress had begun to print its own dollars to help pay for the war. These quickly became discounted (sometimes by as much as 100%) and the phrase 'not worth a Continental' entered the language. Real money in America was still British currency or any other form of gold and silver. Before independence, there had always been a shortage of cash in the colonies; everybody lived on credit, and discounting bills of exchange (roughly, dubious cheques) became a special art in American economic life. These circumstances, and the fact that many borrowed the passage-money to America and to pay for the stock of a trade, or a farm, meant that debt had a very special place in American life. One man's wealth was another man's debt; staying wealthy, or even solvent, could easily depend on being confident that the value of the debts owed to oneself stayed constant. Wealth, then, could be very unstable in uncertain times, which were likely to be times of inflation: 'real' money becomes more valuable when things get tough. (This was also true of that other unstable form of wealth in eighteenth-century America: claims to land 'in the west'. Credit could only be raised on those claims if the claims themselves were credible.) In the twentieth century we have become so thoroughly colonised by the idea that inflation is a bad thing that we tend to forget that it is a very good thing indeed for people in debt whose debt is expressed in money terms. Imagine a situation in America in the late 1780s in which all the states got out the printing-press and began to pump paper money into their economies and passed legal tender acts to make acceptance of rag-money compulsory. Inflation would soar (by eighteenth-century standards), and the value of debts would begin to go down spectacularly.

Abolition of debt was seventeenth-century Commonwealth social levelling by any other name. A time could even be foreseen when the distinction between creditor and debtor, rich and poor, would disappear for ever. Not very likely to happen in practice, perhaps, but a likely enough nightmare for the nervous rich. And they would certainly be aware that monetarism in reverse is the natural economics of the poor. The taste for levelling might not stop at the printing-press. Most of the Founding Fathers had had a sound classical education, and most of them would have read their Roman history. They would remember from their Livy the story of the scabby debtor in the Forum getting everybody's sympathy, and those who remembered their Livy well could not help but recall Livy's account of the rhythm of the class war at republican Rome. The consuls would call out the levy; the Roman people would arm themselves, go out to defeat Rome's enemies, and on their return they would demand an agrarian law to redistribute the cultivated land. Why not? The people had defended the republic, they were poor, and they had arms in their hands to enforce the moral claims of poverty. The cry for the redistribution of wealth seemed to be the natural voice of a citizen army home victorious from its country's wars. The idea of a free and equal citizen army had been central to American propaganda during the War of Independence. Embattled farmers withstood the professional army of George III, heroic virtue against mercenary greed. The problem with successful heroic virtue is that it is never its own reward (and America was America, where nothing is for nothing). There were murmurings in America about redistribution of land. Shays's Rebellion in Massachusetts in 1786 brought all of these fears to a head. In truth, Shays's Rebellion wasn't much of a rebellion (though it was rumoured that he had more men under his command than Washington ever had in the War of Independence). None the less, the rebels' demand for levelling measures could easily appear to be the very thick end of a wedge into the principle of private property right itself.

Another way of looking at this problem would be to ask what the American revolutionary experience had been about. It can never by emphasised enough that the American Revolution began as a protest by aggrieved taxpayers. An aggrieved taxpayer is somebody who owns property and is damned if he is going to give up a fraction of it to government without his own consent freely given. (One of the enduring attitudes in America was to be that every cent in taxation was paid unwillingly.) The American Revolution had been made in the name of the inviolability of property right. All the slogan 'No taxation without representation' means is that nobody takes anything from me without my permission. There was no secret about the defence of property right in the period leading up to the outbreak of hostilities with the British. Nor was there much of a theoretical difference between property right and other kinds of rights. All rights are 'my' rights, something which I own and whose loss will be a real loss to me. That is how Locke had thought about natural rights: I own a right to own my possessions in exactly the same way that I possess a right to enjoy my own life, which another may not rightfully take from me. Not all rights at issue in the dispute between the colonies were natural rights. Some of those rights, the rights which Americans thought they possessed under their original charters of colonial government, were incorporated rights, rights written down in the same way that the rights of Englishmen were supposed to be written down in Magna Carta. These chartered rights, deriving from the original constitutions of American government, came to be seen as the prized possessions of the Americans, to be defended at all costs, because these were the rights to self-government attacked by the British policy of direct rule after 1774. The eighteenth-century political context, in Britain and America, is to be seen as a thicket of all kinds of different and interlocking systems of rights. (Sam Adams, the great Boston radical, could 'pass from Magna Carta to the rum trade in the twinkling of an argument'.) It was easy, in the first rush of American blood, just to assume that all the different kinds of rights – religious, natural, chartered or whatever – were consistent with each other, and it was politically and militarily expedient to believe that all American defenders of rights of whatever kind were on the same side. Washington did not cross the Delaware to score a point in a rights debate.

Things may have changed after the peace, when the old distinction made at Putney between rights inhering in property and rights inhering in persons again began to surface. As in seventeenth-century English Levelling, so in post-war America it began to be said that the spoils of war, and that included the political spoils, belonged to all the victors. It could not matter that in the meantime Locke had pointed out that all rights were at bottom property rights. It began to be thought that the meanest that was in America had the same rights as the greatest; Dan Shays had the same rights as George Washington. That was very hard to deny as far as political rights were concerned, but the question remained open as to what the Dan Shayses of the world would do with their political rights. A distinct possibility was that those who sided with Dan Shays would fail to see that an attack on George Washington's property rights, or if not on George Washington's rights then on the property rights of George Washington's friends, was an attack on all rights, including the rights of Dan Shays and his friends. (The world had to wait for Burke's *Reflections* to point this out clearly.) Demands for the redistribution of property through the free exercise of democratic rights (perhaps even through the exercise of the right of rebellion enshrined in the Declaration of Independence) were to drive a coach and four through the notion of the consistency of all types of rights with each other. That was a real problem, because it was very difficult to explain to the newly enfranchised that their political rights could be used for some purposes but not for others, to defend property and not to attack it. Voting for wicked and immoral purposes could not simply be declared invalid, for who, exactly, was to decide what was wicked and what was not? And besides, that was a recipe for a permanently divided republic (or for thirteen permanently divided republics). That was 'faction' written in capital letters, the bane of all republics since the world began.

The solution to the problem was to devise a system of government which would blunt popular wills and outlaw tumults of the people, and this the new Constitution duly did. The system of representative government explicated in *The Federalist Papers* would have the effect of 'refining' the rude passions of the multitude. Government everywhere was to be indirect. There was to be no repetition of the direct democracy of ancient republics, and the very fancy franchises to elect the president and the Senate were meant to create a social and moral distance between the people and their government. Physical distance would also help a great deal. National government was to be removed from Philadelphia and planted in a swamp on the Potomac. Memories were long, and nobody was likely to forget the part played by the mob of artisans and mechanics in persuading the Pennsylvania assembly into voting for independence in 1776. Useful at the time, no doubt, but those times were over and America now needed quiet and orderly government. Washington, DC, wasn't even a town yet and it was unlikely to acquire a town mob in the foreseeable future. There was still the possibility of mobbish, levelling politics in the states. State legislatures might be subject to the same mob pressure as the legislature in Philadelphia in 1776 (and to the same pressure as the House of Commons was famously subjected to during the Gordon Riots of 1780 when Parliament was mobbed), but that was easily taken care of by writing a clause into the Constitution allowing state governors to call in the federal militia (commanded by the president) if ever there was a mob surrounding a state capital which needed dispersing. Tumults of the people were ruled out of national government and safely banished to the states. This was not to say that the Constitution was unalterable. The presumption was not that the people of America were always going to be satisfied with their frame of government for all time. Rather, a ponderous system of constitutional amendment was written into the Constitution itself, so that the widespread exercise of political rights was supplemented with the right to alter the basic frame of government in a constitutional, that is to say orderly, way. Who could want more? As the erstwhile 'Jacobin' governor of Massachusetts, Sam Adams, was later to say, a man who takes arms against a republic ought to suffer death.

A 'refined' system of politics working through the principle of representation was unlikely ever to produce a congressional majority for the redistribution of property, and there was still the presidential veto as a last resort. The later invention of a full-blooded doctrine of judicial review brought the Supreme Court into the balance. When the Federalists (roughly those who approved of the new Constitution from the beginning and who thought it ought to work in a thoroughly 'conservative' way) saw the tide running against them in the era of the Jeffersonian presidency they made straight for the judiciary, and allowed John Marshall to develop the view that the Supreme Court was there to strike down law (federal or state) which threatened to eat away at the fundamentals of American life, conceived as the inviolability of property right and freedom of contract.

The Thesis of Timeless Wisdom credits the Founding Fathers with inventing a political system as well as writing a constitution. Nobody would bother to design a political system unless they had a pretty shrewd idea of how that political system was going to develop. The conventional view of that political system is that it was going to be pluralist, never dominated or dominated for long by any particular group, and it was going to be a system of open pluralism which was going to be easy for out-groups to join. Critics of *The Federalist Papers* have sometimes noticed a contradiction between the proclamation of pluralist politics in *10th Federalist* and the partial separation of powers in the constitutional arrangements. The partial separation of powers in the Constitution is there partly to ensure that the parts work with each other, and partly to enable them to check each other if things start to go wrong. By dividing the legislature into the House of Representatives and the Senate, the Founding Fathers effectively put a senatorial veto on House legislation: all bills have to pass both houses. But if Madison's account of what America's politics is going to be like is anything to go by, then it is hard to see why that internal check in the legislature is necessary. *10th Federalist* is quite explicit when it says that, in the extended republic planned by the Constitution, it is going to be impossible for there to be *national* majorities for the kinds of wicked and immoral purposes that were being discussed and implemented in the states around the time of Shays's Rebellion. Yet here we are faced with a Constitution which installs an internal check within the legislature, for all the world *as if* wicked and immoral bills are going to be passed by the democratically elected House, a possibility which on a reading of *10th Federalist* cannot be (and if this cannot be, then why the presidential veto behind the senatorial veto, and the supreme judicial veto behind that?). Something else must be going on.

That 'something else' is not that easy to dig out, but a beginning can be made by re-reading *10th Federalist* in a slightly different way. Everybody agrees that *10th Federalist* is about faction, and everybody agrees that Madison's chief anxiety is that there should one day be in the United States a majority faction which could permanently dominate all the others for wicked, that is to say levelling, purposes. This dominant faction could only be a faction of the poor and many, and its victim would be the faction of the few and rich. Therefore, let there be as many factions as possible and pluralism will be the inevitable consequence; therefore let America rejoice in its diversity, because its diversity will secure its liberty now and in the years to come. The conventional view says: good for you, Madison, you've got it right. The poor will be divided into many factions (and the rich into at least two: the holders of real estate and the holders of mercantile wealth). What this picture of cosy pluralism ignores is the possibility of a faction of all the wealthy against the multiplicity of the factions of the poor. Of course it is going to be difficult for a Massachusetts fisherman to make common cause with an artisan from Philadelphia, and both are going to find it difficult to make common cause with a frontier farmer. But could the same be true of the rich? Much easier for a northern nabob to get together with a southern planter, especially when nabobs and planters are beginning to wonder together what the world is coming to, what with democracy, rag-money, rebellion and all that.

Plurality of *other* factions is the natural condition in which the faction of the rich would survive and prosper. Perhaps that is what the Founding Fathers had in mind (and it was certainly never far from the mind of Alexander Hamilton). This is the key to unravelling the mystery of the internal check in the legislature between House and Senate. The House was meant to speak with several voices. Being popularly elected, it could do no other because, being elected through a wide franchise in thirteen different states, it would be a miracle if it could come to speak with one voice on anything very radical. With any luck, the bills which the future House of Representatives would send up to the Senate would already have been subject to that process of 'refinement' which the principle of representation was originally designed for. But if the unthinkable happened, the Senate would speak with one voice and put in its veto.

A straightforward reading of *10th Federalist* explains exactly why the Senate would be able to speak with a single voice. The origin of faction is interest, where interest means economic self-interest. (There is a literature which suggests that Madison is not *entirely* an economic determinist, but he is economic determinist enough for this argument.) The only thing (apart from disinterested patriotism) which can make men speak as one is interest, and the only conceivable interest which the Senate could have over and against the House is the interest of wealth. Elections to the Senate, according to the original Constitution, are doubly 'refined'. Senators are to be elected by the states' legislatures, election by the already elected. They are to have long tenure (six years as opposed to two in the House) to ensure that the Senate is not to be a body which easily changes its mind. And there are not to be many of them, so that being a United States senator was going to be membership of a very superior club. One is tempted to use 'aristocracy' to describe the Senate. And why not? Of course, the Senate was not going to be an aristocracy in the sense which that term had in England. In the Old World, aristocracy had come to mean hereditary aristocracy, but those aristocracies had had to come from somewhere. One remembers Hume's celebrated definition of aristocracy as 'reputation of ancient fortune'. At Rome, the aristocracy had come out of the law-giving of Romulus. Fathers of families would constitute a special class and have the Roman Senate as its special institution. It could be said that, over time, it was the institution of the Senate which created the senatorial class. We have become so used to thinking of political institutions as deriving their nature from the social groups composing a society that we are in danger of forgetting the force which political institutions can have in determining social classes. If at Rome, why not in America? Why should the Senate not become the focus of the political aspirations of the rich, the basis for the formation of a senatorial class? We have already seen how easy it is to identify what those aspirations, albeit negative, would be. The rich are not, after all, stupid. They have good reasons to fear democracy; what better for them than to have their own special institution, the Senate, right in the middle of the legislative process, and with an effective veto on any levelling legislation?

It must be stressed that I do not use the word 'veto' loosely in place of the more anodyne 'checks and balances'. 'Veto' is the prohibition of a single voice, and we have become accustomed to thinking that the only veto possible in the American political system is the veto of the president because he is one man. I argue that, originally at least, there could have been a genuine senatorial veto against the kinds of popular legislation which were being mooted all over the United States. On this view of it, *The Federalist Papers* are the cover-up for a conspiracy of the rich to make the world safe for themselves. The word 'conspiracy' is not to be taken too literally, because this reading of *The Federalist Papers* and the Constitution is readily available from a reading of the *Papers* themselves. Charles Beard was busy reading the papers in this spirit before the First World War, and, looking back on the furore that Beard's reading caused, it is hard to understand what all the fuss was about. Nobody now expects the Founding Fathers to have been disinterested patriots concerned only for their country's good. And if they identified their country's good with their own good, who is to blame them? History provides us with examples without number of the purest patriotism allied to the purest self-interest. And besides, the country they were founding was America, and what's un-American about holding on to a buck?

Holding on to what you already have is one thing, but planning to make more is another. We can readily see how the Constitution incorporates features which would be likely to still the nerves of the rich and well-born, but how, exactly, could one make money out of it? Making money out of government was not much of a secret in eighteenth-century Europe, and in England it was a very open secret indeed. It was Sir Robert Walpole who discovered how to make government work in an oligarchic age. Rich people, on the whole, do not much like being taxed by government, but government cannot work without a revenue. The simple solution is to borrow from the rich at a guaranteed rate of interest (set by Act of Parliament). This binds the wealthy to government by giving them an immediate interest in political stability above and beyond the interest of the average citizen who has no money invested in the funds. The national debt so created is the bond between those who really matter and their government. It is so easy to assume that the rich have a natural interest in political stability that we sometimes forget that the rich were the natural targets for governments on the lookout for easy money in times when the system of taxation was a good deal less efficient and permanent than it is now. The lessons of both the English Revolution of 1688 and the American Revolution show how easy it was for government to alienate a large enough section of the rich and powerful for that government to fall. The leaders of the American Revolution came from the natural political class in America; the rag, tag and bobtail got a look in from time to time, and they were useful to fill the ranks of the continental armies, but that was about all. If the American Revolution taught any general lesson it was that the most foolish of all paths for a government to take was the one which would lead to the alienation of its natural supporters.

The problem of binding the rich to national government did not disappear after the War of Independence was over. For many, their own state governments were the natural focuses of their affections and attentions. It was easy to think of the national government after the war as being far away and not being in a position to decide much of any importance anyway. Alexander Hamilton saw very clearly what would bind the rich and powerful to national government. That national government had to be strong enough to attract the attention of powerful men. A strong government was one with strong credit. That meant effective government, government capable of defending the currency and the commerce of the United States, and government able and willing to pay or at least to guarantee its own debts. Men holding fistfuls of Continental paper could be relied on to support a government ready to pay out a hundred cents of sound money on the dollar; men with doubtful land claims in the west would pay more than lip-service to a government which policed those claims. Everybody since Tom Paine's *Common Sense* had known that the policy of the United States was going to be commerce, not war, but, equally, everybody had always known that the United States would have to live in a world with other states. Britain, France and Spain still had vital interests to defend in America, and Hamilton saw clearly enough that America was going to have to be a state like other states if she was going to protect her interests. No doubt, the American state was going to have different political forms from other states, but the outside face of government was going to have to be the same as the outside face of any other government. Hamilton was very impressed with British government, a combination of oligarchy at home and commercial empire abroad, and there can be no doubt that he wished American government under its new Constitution to develop along British lines. It is easy to see, reading Hamilton's essays in *The Federalist Papers*, that there was going to be trouble in the future over a national bank to manage government's deficit financing. No bank, no national debt, no fundholders, no natural class of government on the Walpolean model.

Hence the split between what has come to be called Hamiltonianism and Jeffersonianism. It is the difference, in eighteenth-century terms, between opulence and empire on the one hand, and agrarian virtue and frugality on the other. The first requires strong central government with strong federal credit and a stable currency, while the second is satisfied with that government which governs least. What need, after all, have yeomen farmers of the complex structures of government which Hamiltonianism envisages? Beneath the question of the structures of government lay a much more fundamental question. Independence had always meant more than just political independence. The *Declaration of Independence* is a moralising tract for the times. British government has been corrupted so thoroughly that it has been able to provide Americans with that long list of grievances (and the list could have been longer). Whatever American politics was going to be like in the future, it was certainly not supposed to be like Britain politics. Yet here was a constitution designed to enable the rich to survive and prosper, and designed to produce a political system whose difference from the British system was not going to be easily visible to the naked eye. What had happened to the idea that America was going to be *different*?

If the Hamiltonian scheme were to succeed, what would happen to the American claim to *moral* independence? The claim to American exceptionalism, already being made at the very beginning of the republic's existence, was going to be tarnished. In retrospect, we know that in fact the terms of the claim to exceptionalism changed and changed very quickly. The original promise of American life as we find it in Tom Paine, Crèvecoeur and the Declaration of Independence – a life of virtue – was converted into the promise of unlimited economic opportunity. Wealth was going to grow at such a pace, and be so widely distributed, that its corruptions were going to be a matter of mere detail. Some wealth was always going to slop over into politics when there was so much wealth sloshing around, but the confidence in the future that wealth creation was going to provide meant that there were going to be no problems which were insoluble in principle, the problem of political corruption included.

The Federalist Papers: a summing up

It should be obvious by now how difficult a text *The Federalist Papers* actually is. It should be equally obvious that the reading of the *Papers* that one chooses to make is to an extent determined by what one expects to find there and which of the individual essays one chooses to concentrate on. Each of the three readings offered here (and there are others) is a good reading. That the Founding Fathers got so much right for so long is remarkable, and that they thought within the available concepts of their own time is very unremarkable indeed. If the Constitution was a conspiracy and the *Papers* its cover-up, then it was a remarkably lawful conspiracy and a remarkably open cover-up.

Perhaps the best way of looking at the *Papers* from this distance in time is to try to answer the unfair question: What did the authors of the *Papers* get *wrong*? This question, fortunately, admits of a fairly specific answer. The Founding Fathers may have forgotten just how momentous their work in writing the Constitution was destined to be. How could they have expected the new Constitution not to have divided the American nation on national lines for and against? The process of ratification took a long time and was never a foregone conclusion. The argument that in America there would be no national factions was no sooner off the press than America divided nationally on the question of whether to accept a constitution which would make national factions impossible. The question of whether to accept the Constitution was just the kind of question to promote what the Constitution was designed to prevent. The Federalists won, the Constitution was ratified, and immediately two national parties divided on the issue of what the Constitution actually meant. And then there was the question of the presidency. Little did the Founding Fathers know when they designed what to them must have seemed like a very modest presidential office, that the country would find it worthwhile to divide on the question of who should occupy it. Presidential politics became national faction politics within a decade of the ratification of the Constitution. Defenders of the Timeless Wisdom Thesis would argue that none of this matters much. Parties emerged on great issues – constitutional ratification, strict versus loose construction of the Constitution, who should be president – but these were parties in a sense that was different from the old idea of faction. The parties themselves were coalitions of factions, not factions as such, and certainly not factions of the rich against the poor. In *10th Federalist*, Madison may not have had national political parties exactly in mind but, by a process which he might well have foreseen, the parties as they eventually developed in no way contradicted the plurality of factions thesis. A plurality of factions on each side of the electoral divide was still a plurality of factions. Conspiracy theorists might still point to the oligarchical sources of party finance after the electoral systems for the presidency and the Senate had been democratised, but the Madisonians could still point out that party finance came from many sources.

And perhaps the most enduring tribute to Madison has been the politics of ethnicity in the United States since the Civil War. It has become a commonplace that the United States has never quite worked as the great melting pot of the immigrant nations, and a good case could be made out for saying that a lot of American politics for a lot of the time could be understood as ethnic politics. But, again, a Tocquevillian Providence seems to have intervened in the life of the United States. American ethnic politics has been the pluralist politics of many ethnic groups. The crude divide of black against white cannot account for the sheer multiplicity of ethnic politics in the United States. All immigrant groups have played the pluralist game either at national or state, and especially at city, level. When Americans talk about politics they talk as easily about race as Europeans talk about class. That may be the final triumph of Madisonianism. The original factions which Madison feared were class factions, the many poor against the few rich. Americans, with exceptions of course, have never found the language of class or class conflict very satisfactory as a way of explaining their politics to themselves. Disadvantaged groups have tended to target other specific groups as the cause of their disadvantage – farmers against bankers and railroad tycoons, migrant labour against agri-corporation managers, out-groups against the 'special interests', the Mid-West against the 'eastern Establishment', workers against particular companies, and so on. This has had its effects on national politics in an impeccably Madisonian way. What it means is that presidential elections in particular are essentially exercises in group coalition management. Counting up the different constituencies which a particular presidential candidate can hope to capture is the beginning of how presidential politics is played, and the second stage is always a delicately Madisonian balancing act of not being seen to stand too firmly on policy positions which might favour one constituency and so alienate another. There may be some things which James Madison would find bewildering about contemporary American politics, but he would certainly feel at home with that.

TOM PAINE, *THE RIGHTS OF MAN* (1791–2)

We have remarked before that Paine is not the most original of enlightened thinkers, but he has the knack of seeing very clearly what the implications of enlightened political theory are for particular times and situations. *Common Sense* hit a nerve, and so did *The Rights of Man*. Paine had the good fortune as an author to give the world two books it had been waiting for. Paine's *Rights of Man* does not examine the idea of rights in any novel way. The rights of man had been launched on a highly successful career in the world by the American Declaration of Independence. Paine seems to be saying that the doctrine of rights no longer needs defending (which is far from saying that everybody agrees with it). America had already fought a war and instituted a government on the basis of the rights of man (and was shortly to amend its Constitution to include a Bill of Rights to put the matter beyond all doubt). When Burke wrote his *Reflections on the Revolution in France* (1790) to argue that it was foolish to base a whole system of government on the rights of man, he conveniently forgot about America. There, the supposedly 'metaphysical' rights of man were alive and well and living down to earth. Paine takes that for granted. His attack on Burke's *Reflections* is really a survey and a condemnation of all political systems, not just the British, which are not founded on the basis of natural rights, and he does this from the perspective of the American experience from declaring independence to founding a workable national government. It is an early example of judging all political experience from an American point of view. In essence, Paine's argument is very simple: if the rights of man are justified and work as the basis for government in America, then why not everywhere?

We already know Burke's argument against the rights of man. The rights of man are philosophically dubious and are in practice destructive. Burke does not in fact deny that men have something called 'natural rights'. Of course God meant men to have natural rights, but he also meant men to exchange those natural rights for the real rights which could actually be enjoyed by living in a particular natural community. Natural rights could only be relevant to a pre-social, 'natural' community, but happily men have progressed far beyond natural communities and have developed highly sophisticated states and societies. What have the rights of man to tell men who live in the societies they do in fact live in? Next to nothing. And how, then, could the rights of man be a basis for *government*? What have the rights of man to tell a government, involved as a government must be in the day-to-day business of routine administration and problem-solving? Is government to be continually asking itself whether what it seems necessary to do offends one of these vague things called a right of man? Clearly not. Government is, of course, obliged to take the real system of rights in a society very seriously indeed. These are obstacles in government's path. The exercise of power has to find ways round them, so that the obstacles do in fact determine the directions and ways in which the governing power may properly be exercised. But how could the exercise of power avoid 'metaphysical' obstacles? Burke thinks that the rights of man are so vague and generalised that you could never really be sure if the exercise of governing power was likely to bump into one of them. The rights of man would effectively paralyse government.

Not so, says Paine. The example of America shows us what the rights of man are (and there are still a few which he could name and does). There is nothing at all mysterious about the rights of man. Of course it is possible that different people would make different lists of human rights, but in practice there is likely to be considerable agreement. The mistake which Burke makes, and of course it is a mistake which he makes deliberately, is to caricature the grounds upon which natural rights are claimed. According to Paine, there is nothing really new, and certainly nothing 'metaphysical', in the way demands for the

390

rights of man arise. Far from being the result of grandiose metaphysical speculation, the demand for the rights of man arises out of the experience of living in a particular society, and in particular of living at its sharp end. Ask the poor, and they will tell you quickly enough what the rights of man are. Put another way, all that the rights of man ever really amount to is the demand that everybody in a society should enjoy as a right what some only enjoy as a privilege. In this sense the rights of man are eminently practical. Paine has caught Burke out here. Burke argues that it is the vagueness of the rights of man which makes them dangerous. Surely it follows that, on Burke's own terms, the way to draw the sting out of the rights of man is to convert them into real rights in a society, the kind of rights which Burke himself says may be defended with safety. Or has Paine found out in Burke a tendency to believe that the rights which are actually being enjoyed in a particular society at a particular time are the sum total of the rights which could possibly be enjoyed in that particular society at that particular time? In that case, how can Burke possibly know? Simply to assert that, as for now, the possible number of enjoyable rights is fixed, either is to go in for a pretty piece of metaphysics involving a complex philosophy of history which would be a kind of pre-figuring of Hegel, or there must be a positive explanation of why the possible number of enjoyable rights cannot be radically extended. Burke never gives us such an explanation, so we have to work it out for ourselves. It is not difficult: who else but Burke's own admired ruling class could possibly prevent the people of England from enjoying what Paine calls the rights of man? The explanation of why they would do this is equally obvious: the ruling class wants to continue to enjoy as privileges what should be extended to all men as rights.

It is only considerations such as these which enable us to realise how rhetorical Burke's distinction between 'real' rights and the 'rights of man' actually is. Burke wants us to see the contrast as a contrast between the old and safe and the new and unsafe. Reliance on the former is what makes a man a conservative and support for the latter is what characterises a radical. To put it crudely, the conservative has history on his side whereas all the radical has to go on is a metaphysical doctrine invented out of his own head. This presupposes that demands for political change, and especially radical change, come as bolts from the blue. The whole American experience shows how untrue this is, and, by extension, how untrue it can be everywhere. The matter can be put another way. There is a perfectly good Burkean argument to be made for the validity of a radical *tradition*. Burke talks as if all tradition is somehow on the side of the *status quo*. But could it not equally be the case that a cumulative, slowly evolving tradition of grievance could arise in a society, grievances handed down from generation to generation, altering no doubt, but wasting very little, until the point came at which those grievances could no longer be contained by existing social and political arrangements? That is certainly a possible view of the American and the French Revolutions, and it is the view of those historians who emphasise the continuities of history. Some historians of revolution contend that nothing really new happens when revolutions break out (apart from the fact that they do). Revolutions are just as much a product of their past as any other event or series of events. The causes of revolutions can be as deep-seated as one cares to make them, hence the 'it's been downhill all the way since Runnymede' school of history.

Of course, we *know* why Burke has to argue this way. To admit that a revolution could come, so to speak, through the system would be to admit that the inherited system is itself rotten, and this Burke will not have in the case of France because he will not have it in the case of England. Burke has the problem that all political thinkers have who argue by analogy from a living thing to a political community, and that is that living things die. Organic thinkers celebrate the health and wealth of the communities they defend (though they admit that the health of a community can sometimes be precarious). How, then, do communities come to perish? The organic answer is almost never 'natural causes', because that might encourage radical spirits to think that a community about to die might as well be given a helping hand to die more quickly and painlessly. (We do, after all, need some help to get into this world, so why should we not need help to get out of it?) Organic theorists, and Burke is no exception when he argues like this, are therefore constrained to argue that political communities collapse when something nasty is introduced into them from the outside. Political communities are by their nature healthy, just as the body is meant to be healthy; pathological states of an organism must be caused by influence from the outside, something unnatural slipped into the body when its natural guardians are not looking. Hence Burke's attack on Rousseau as the thinker who introduced alien ideas into a French civilisation which, whatever its faults, was still a going concern in 1789.

Burke's concern to defend the *status quo* against its detractors rests on a view of the efficiency of political institutions. It is no secret that Burke is an admirer of the English ruling class, and he admires them for being able to make the governing institutions of England work. Institutions, in Burke's view of them, are problem-solvers. A ruling class ought to be able to stand on its record, and the English ruling class can take particular pride in its record since a time which is almost immemorial. Not so, says Paine. Buried in Burke's defence of English institutions is an assumption which simply is not true. Far from being problem-solvers, the English ruling class have been at the very most connivers in the continuance of English problems, or at worst the cause of those problems. What, Paine asks, have really been the problems of English government in recent years? Plainly, American problems. What, then, has enabled the British government to make war on the Americans? Paine was a failed businessman and an indifferent tax-collector, so his answer could only be: money. What the king of England does, or what his government does for him, is to collect a tax. The sums collected are enormous, and the king uses them to bribe Members of Parliament and make war. War, in Paine's view, is the typical activity of monarchy and aristocracy. Monarchy needs the support of aristocracy. They might bicker a bit when nothing very interesting is going on, but a wise monarchy allows its aristocracy the amusement of war from time to time to keep them from further mischief. The patronage of parliamentary corruption and of war is the business of kings. The case of America makes this obvious to anyone who ever had any doubts about the matter. What kind of a government is it which has money enough to make war with mercenary armies on a substantial section of its subjects? And armies officered, unlike the American citizen army, by aristocratic idlers, consumers not producers.

Paine's analysis of the function of English institutions is the opposite of Burke's. Institutions – monarchy, Lords and Commons – do not solve problems, they *create* them.

What Paine does here is to continue the argument about the uselessness of aristocracy begun in the year of the French Revolution. The French revolutionaries attacked aristocracy on the grounds that it was useless when it was not dangerous. Burke had replied, saying that, in England at least, aristocracy was functional in the sense that it had managed the affairs of England tolerably well as long as anyone could remember. Paine's view of English institutions could not be more different from Burke's, because there cannot be any greater difference than that between problem solver and problem creator.

The attack on existing English institutions enables Paine to draw very different conclusions from Burke about the course of English history. Burke's celebration of English history on the grounds that it has produced such an efficacious set of governing institutions begins to look distinctly hollow beside Paine's trenchant critique: if the institutions are defective, then why celebrate the history which produced them? Paine probes into the very heart of the Burkean view of the continuity of society as it is based on inheritance. Paine says: why not repudiate an inheritance when it is a *damnosa haereditas*? Heredity is a claim for the dead to legislate beyond the grave. We are no more obliged to accept our political arrangements from our ancestors than we are obliged to accept the inconvenience of a dreaded heirloom. Paine realises here how far Burke's rhetoric merges political metaphor with the language of legal fact. Burke says that the common people of England receive their rights from their ancestors in much the same way that the eldest son of a duke inherits the ducal lands intact. The eldest son of a duke would be a fool to refuse to inherit the family's broad acres (and the eldest son of the king would be crazy to refuse the crown); therefore, the poor but free-born son of an Englishman would be mad not to accept the inheritance of his English rights. These English rights do, of course, imply the duty to respect the exercises of their rights by other Englishmen, including the rights of the king's son and the son of the duke. But suppose I choose to look at English history in a very different way. Suppose I choose to say that I reject what the past has chosen to give *me*. *Your* share from the past may satisfy *you*, but my own share is not enough, and certainly not enough for me to give my approval to the way shares are distributed in general in this society. I might even begin to wonder how it was that the share-out was arranged in the first place. Who, exactly, was it who decided who should have what, and why? Burke, of course, would say that looking into the past for origins is a fruitless and dangerous business. Paine argues that Burke's own argument must lead us back into the mists of English history, or as far back as we can go without encountering the mist, and that must mean going back to the fact about English history that everybody knows, the Conquest of 1066. Burke celebrates the continuity of English political history, and that must mean continuity as far back as ordinary historical memory goes. At the Conquest, rights in England were distributed by force, king and aristocracy to one side and the common people of England to the other. The development of English history to the present is the story of variations on that same simple theme.

This account of English history is not the Burkean account. Paine acutely spots a flaw in Burke. For all his pretended veneration for the past, Burke tells us remarkably little about it in the *Reflections*. The only serious history that Burke gives us is an account of the Revolution of 1688. In his enthusiasm for the Revolution settlement of the Crown in the Protestant succession in 1688, Burke rather incautiously concentrated on the Act of Settlement's claim

393

to settle the question of the succession of the Crown *for ever*. Of course, we know why Burke chooses to emphasise the succession question and the answer to it given in 1688. Burke wants to argue that all 1688 did was to affirm the traditional principles of English government, one of which is monarchy. By settling the Crown for ever in the Protestant line, the makers of the Revolution settlement showed how firmly they were attached to the ancient constitutional principle of monarchy. Paine does not deny the right of each generation to settle the outstanding questions of government. Quite the reverse. What he does deny is that any generation, or its representatives, has the right to entail its own solutions on posterity. By what right did a minority of Englishmen in 1688 decide the future course of English government for all time? Burke may indeed have been right when he said that that was the intention of the makers of 1688, but by what right did they foist their own idea about what government should be like on the whole nation for ever?

Shall the dead or the living decide? That is Tom Paine's most serious question. And not just the dead, but a tiny minority of them. Burke's insistence on praising the generation of 1688 really works against his veneration for the English constitution. Constitutional fetishism works best when the question: Who made the constitution? is least easily answered. (The ancients understood this best: *our* constitution was given to us by a god-like law-giver, a legislator who, if not a god himself, had access to the wisdom of the gods, and the wisdom of the gods is not to be called into question. Gods are, of course, immortal, and we may assume that they continue to watch over the constitutions which they have created.) A constitution must at least claim to be politically neutral if it has any chance of being generally accepted, or at the very least it must not make it too obvious that power has been distributed too favourably to certain individuals (like kings) or groups (like aristocracies). Knowing who actually made a constitution makes matters worse, because then fingers can be pointed at a particular group of constitution-makers and it can be said that they stacked things up in their own interest and in the interests of those like them. (Compare the Conspiracy Thesis of American constitution-making.) Paine particularly attacks Burke's view of the Revolution of 1688 because Burke's account of 1688 in the *Reflections* inadvertently points to a truth about the British constitution which he ought to have allowed to remain hidden – namely, that the English constitution, as it has come down to Englishmen of Paine's generation, is the product of the past actions of deeply self-interested parties at moments of political crisis. Of course, Burke does not conceal his admiration for the role of the ruling class in English constitutional politics, but it is one thing to argue in general that the English ruling class has in the past done rather well in the business of managing the nation's affairs, and quite another to see them actually doing it at a particular moment like 1688. Then the ordinary question of *cui bono* (in whose interest?) cries out to be asked and is very easily answered 'in their own interest and in the interest of others like them'.

Burke might choose to brazen the matter out. He might say, 'Of course it has been the ruling class, or a section of it, which has made the constitutional decisions in the past which have determined what the present is like, but that's the way that things have turned out for the best in England.' Whether that kind of reply is enough to satisfy someone with Paine's doubts must be open to question. Paine's own position is that no constitution is valid unless it is the product of a decision by a whole people through their representatives. The Constitutions of the United States and the new French Constitution meet that criterion. The English constitution, on Burke's reading of it, does not. Paine says that the American and French Constitutions have a particular, democratic legitimacy. A people makes a constitution for itself and is therefore bound to obey the decisions of the government which that constitution makes possible. Burke, on the other hand, wants us to believe something quite different. He wishes us to believe that we are bound by the decisions of a government whose legitimacy rests on an inherited constitution in whose making living men had very little part, and in whose making the vast majority of living men's ancestors had no part at all. On Burke's own account of the English constitution, both of these comments must be true, so what Burke is asking the vast majority of Englishmen to believe amounts to this: a constitution which was the product of the past decisions of *other people's* ancestors is right for you. If *my* ancestors provided me with a set of political arrangements it might just be possible that I could be persuaded to love and cherish them, but asking me to love and cherish a set of political arrangements which *somebody else's* ancestors have handed down is asking too much. Ancestorship only works if everybody's ancestors are venerable. Asking people to accept a state of things because somebody else's ancestors are venerable is asking them to stretch their credulity in the age of Enlightenment too far.

Inherited institutions, in Paine's view of them, are not acceptable just because they are inherited. Again, he puts his finger on a weakness in Burke's own argument. Burke is very careful to say that institutions and practices are old because they are good, not good because they are old. Burke does in fact use a thoroughly enlightened argument: institutions last because they are good at doing what institutions are supposed to do. Burke may take pains to disguise the fact, but his is a utilitarian argument. After all, the utilitarians believed that the only reliable course of future action was to follow the course of action from the past which had produced the greatest happiness of the greatest number. Burke seems to be urging this course of action on Englishmen: do what you have always done and on the whole the outcome will be a happy one. What Burke does tend to dodge is the question of where and when one chooses to make the calculation of utility. Calculations of utility in the past are difficult to make. To ask the question: Have English governing institutions and practices since the Norman Conquest produced the greatest happiness of the greatest number? is to ask a question which admits of no sensible answer. But, on Burke's own terms, *some* kind of calculation of utility has to be made, otherwise he will be caught in the conservative trap, which he is at pains to avoid, of saying that institutions are good because they are old. So what kind of calculation of utility can a conservative like Burke accept? Not, assuredly, a simple calculation of *present* utility, because that way radicalism lies. Nothing is simpler than demonstrating that the governing institutions and practices of the present do not in fact provide the *greatest* happiness of the *greatest* number; any set of institutions could be arraigned on the charge that they are not providing happiness to the greatest imaginable extent. So what, then, is Burke's own calculation of the utility of English governing institutions? If it cannot be a real calculation of utility back to the Conquest because that calculation is impossible to make, and if it cannot be simply a calculation of present utility, then the only calculation left to make is a calculation of longevity. Burke says: Look how long these institutions have lasted and see how they have improved over time. Burke ends up saying that, in effect, institutions are good because they are old, a claim which he does in fact deny that he is making. If a calculation of past utility is impossible and a calculation of present utility unwise, then that only leaves longevity. 'Useful' for Burke simply means long-lasting, and can only mean long-lasting.

Hence the strength of Tom Paine's argument about inheritance, which can now be seen as a double-edged argument. Not only has Paine shown that the question of the inheritance of institutions and practices is itself doubtful (why should I accept a set of political arrangements handed down by *somebody else's* ancestors?) but he has also shown that there is no good reason even to think that we should be grateful for the inheritance itself, because we have no way of knowing, on Burke's own account of the matter, that the inheritance is worth having. Of course, it must be said that Burke is not a utilitarian in the technical sense, and the spirit of Burke's political theory is as far as it could possibly be from the spirit of Benthamism. None the less, being the kind of rational conservative he is, Burke is confident that the record of English government is a record capable of a reasoned defence. In the *Reflections* Burke talks openly about the happiness of the English under their government as it has long been constituted, so it is reasonable to regard the *Reflections* as an attempt to explicate and defend the happiness-producing effects of English government. In fact, Burke does very little defending of the past beyond admiring the wisdom of the makers of the 1688 settlement. It is as if Burke feels himself being dragged the whole time towards a defence of existing institutions on the basis of present utility, and he knows the dangers of that too well to allow it to happen. The result is that Burke is caught in a historical no-man's land. He is perfectly prepared to defend yesterday, but not yesteryear, and he is not prepared to defend today except as the product of yesterday.

Paine sees this flaw in Burke and ruthlessly drags the question of the utility of government into the present, and in doing so he shows how unwise Burke was to tamper with the idea of utility in the first place. Paine is also more 'historical' than Burke despite Burke's invocations of the past, because Paine really is prepared to examine the record of English government since the Conquest. Of course, Paine cannot literally examine the whole record of English government since the Conquest, any more than Burke could. Rather, the Conquest serves Paine as a convenient bludgeon with which to beat down Burke's house-of-cards view of English history. If English government, as Burke defends it, is the product of its history, then we are entitled to look into that history. The Conquest stands out as the great founding moment in the history of English politics. Those who, like Burke, defend English government on historical grounds have to be made to face up to the fact that English government was founded on force, not right. This might not have mattered much in a world in which it could be said that all systems of government could trace their origins to an original act of conquest, but in the modern world the United States and now France provide examples of people freely giving themselves new constitutions of government. The old argument, which is also Hume's, that the common opinion of mankind has always acknowledged the right of conquest with the passage of time, will no longer work. We now begin to see how prudent Burke's tactic is of not going too far back into history. Burke recognises that the origins of *all* states are probably shameful (Cain and Abel; Romulus and Remus) so that it is wise to cover those origins with the decent veil of ignorance. However, that tactic could only be defended in a world where it was in fact the case that all origins *were* shameful. America and France changed that for ever. Constitutions of government could be refounded and legitimised by a whole people; men could see right replacing might before their very eyes.

Where does that leave Burke? Presumably in the position (which he would never acknowledge) of saying that only constitutions of government with a shameful past are legitimate, whereas all attempts to redesign constitutions are impious and bound to fail. That comes close to being a caricature of Burke's arguments in the *Reflections*, but then it has to be pointed out that this is precisely the light in which Paine invites us to read Burke. Paine wants us to see that, after the American and French Revolutions, Burke's *Reflections* is really a period piece which has been written out of its own time, dated before it left the press. It would have been impossible for Paine to say that convincingly had it not been for the American Revolution. Put quite simply, the American experiments with constitution-making at state and national level since 1776 have made all *European* governments out of date, because Tom Paine has come a long way since 1776 and *Common Sense*, and so has America. It needs no stressing that in 1789, the year the French Revolution began, the Americans ratified their *second* written constitution, so that there were already no less than fifteen new constitutions in America if we include the state constitutions. The American contribution to the art of politics was the art of constitution-making, and of making constitutional politics of the new kind work. In *The Rights of Man* Paine is confident enough about the new politics to address not just England but the whole world (or at least the whole European world). The American experience has gone beyond *Common Sense* and the Declaration of Independence with their rather circumscribed attacks specifically on the government of George III. By 1791, when the first volume of *The Rights of Man* appeared, the American experiment has got beyond the experimental stage. America works. Why should *all* mankind, then, not do what America has already successfully done and the French are presently doing, and refound their politics on the basis of the rights of man?

In *The Rights of Man* Paine does what Jefferson did not dare to do in the Declaration of Independence, but at the same time it could be said that just as Paine invites his readers to view every country's politics in the light of the American experience, so, by implication, he invites us to view the Declaration of Independence in a new way. The Declaration was addressed to the whole of mankind, but it was addressed to mankind as a witness to the justice of a particular cause, the cause of the American colonists in their quarrel with George III. Far from asking the peoples of the world to copy America, the Declaration assumes that the powers of the earth are stable enough and durable enough to be able to help the Americans against the British without a moment's unease about the possibility that the American Revolution might spread to them. All that has changed by 1791. *The Rights of Man* served a warning on the governments of the earth that their days were numbered. In the future only the democratic republic would be able to engage the loyalties of men who bothered to think about politics at all.

Much has been said about the principle of present utility in dealing with Burke and Paine, yet it has also been pointed out that neither Burke nor Paine is in a technical sense utilitarian. This needs some explaining. The system of ideas which we call 'utilitarianism' was made coherent towards the end of the eighteenth century and at the beginning of the nineteenth century and it arose partly as a response to the supposed inadequacies of the fashionable 'rights' or 'natural rights' theory. In this sense utilitarianism was a critique of both Burke's rights of Englishmen and Paine's rights of man. All utilitarian thinkers argued under the banner of the greatest happiness principle: that government was best which produced the greatest happiness of the greatest number. Utilitarianism has been well-described as 'moral arithmetic' because it asks us to take numbers seriously. A calculus of felicity was taken very seriously; most utilitarians believed that the rightness and wrongness of government could be arithmetically demonstrated in terms of measurable amounts of happiness or misery. This was a new departure in the history of political thought, and it must be clearly understood that the new departure consisted of the *measurability* of pleasure and pain. Utilitarianism was an attempt to be scientific in the sense that for the first time in the history of the human race pleasure and pain, the things which matter most to most human beings most of the time, were, like the rest of nature, to be subject to accurate quantification. The matter of accurate quantification of pleasure and pain has to be stressed because otherwise it might appear that all political theorists had always been utilitarians. No political thinker had ever tried to support his own theory by saying that it would contribute to the sum of human misery. (Plato, after all, thought it was possible to demonstrate mathematically that the just man was always happier than the unjust man, appearances notwithstanding.)

Just as obviously, both Burke and Paine, in their different ways, believe that mankind will be happier when enjoying the good fortune to live under governments which respect and guarantee rights for everybody. Utilitarianism will have very little of this. For utilitarians, the enjoyment of rights is only one of the roads to human happiness. If it could be shown that men under government would really be happier if they forgot all about the idea of rights, then the idea of rights would have to be forgotten. This would be true whether rights were regarded as the rights of Englishmen with Burke or the rights of man with Paine. Burke and Paine agree that rights ought to be enjoyed by everybody in a political community. For them, rights are part of the given moral and political landscape, whereas for utilitarians rights can get in the way of good government. This is especially true of entrenched rights, the kind of rights which Burke admires. Burkean rights could be any kind of rights. There is no telling what kind of rights might become encrusted on a body politic. It might even be the case that feudal rights could survive and prosper and still be accounted prescriptive rights in Burke's own sense. These might easily be rights the defence of which would prevent the exercise of governmental powers in pursuit of the general happiness. If it meant anything, Enlightenment meant an attack on privilege as entrenched feudal or seigneurial right. What Enlightenment never realised was that it opened a can of worms when it proclaimed the idea of the rights of man. Of course, enlightened thinkers thought that enjoyment of natural rights would make men happier, but what they never really faced was the idea that natural rights could stand in the way of good government. Enlightened government was supposed to be positive government, government whose centralisation would be able to overcome inherited obstacles defended as rights. But suppose a very different scene, in which men who had been liberated from their ancient shackles would continue to think of their rights as obstacles to government. And suppose something else, that men being the incompletely benevolent creatures they are, they might put the exercise of their rights to uses which the natural reason of man, on which the notion of natural rights depends, might well consider inappropriate.

Rights and utility could plainly be incompatible, and both came out of Enlightenment. Their potential incompatibility remained concealed for a considerable time. After all, both the rights-of-man philosophy and the utilitarian philosophy argued in the direction of reform if not revolution. It was to be the working-out of the philosophies of rights and utility which was to expose clearly the differences between them.

NOTES ON SOURCES

An older style of commentary on the Declaration, and one which is still resilient, is Carl Becker, *The Declaration of Independence* (1964). Nothing recent compares with Garry Wills, *Inventing America: Jefferson's Declaration of Independence* (1980), which sparkles on every page and is full of surprises. Tom Paine's *The Rights of Man* is available in a Penguin edition, introduced by Eric Foner. D. Powell, *Tom Paine* (1965), is spirited, and A.J. Ayer, *Thomas Paine* (1988), is a good introduction to Paine's thinking in general. There is a Penguin edition of Crèvecoeur's *Letters*. American constitution-making has produced a huge secondary literature. The best basic introduction is probably the relevant chapters of Hugh Brogan's *The Longman History of the United States*, which now exists in a Penguin edition. Invaluable are B. Bailyn, *The Ideological Origins of the American Revolution* (1992), and G.S. Wood, *The Creation of the American Republic* (1972). R. Hofstadter, *The American Political Tradition* (1948, and various reprints), is still worth reading. *The Federalist Papers* can be found in various paperback editions.

18

THE LIMITATIONS OF ENLIGHTENMENT
Hume and Burke

EDMUND BURKE

Edmund Burke was born to modest Irish parents (Protestant father, Catholic mother) in 1729. He made his way in life by his brains and his pen, no small achievement in the aristocratically dominated politics of eighteenth-century Britain. Burke was a Whig whom even the arch-Tory Dr Johnson could admire unreservedly: 'Burke, Sir, is such a man that if you met him for the first time in the street, where you were stopped by a drove of oxen, and you and he stepped aside to take shelter but for five minutes, he'd talk to you in such a manner that when you parted you would say, "This is an extraordinary man."' Burke's performance in the impeachment of Warren Hastings for misgovernment in India made the novelist Fanny Burney positively swoony.

After graduating from Trinity College, Dublin, Burke came to the Middle Temple in London in 1750 to train for his father's profession, but he soon quit the law to follow a highly successful literary and philosophical career which gave him access to the aristocratic Whig patronage which opened his way into politics. Burke became secretary to Lord Rockingham when he became Prime Minister in 1765. Burke entered the Commons as MP for Wendover, and subsequently was Member for Bristol from 1774 to 1780, when he lost his seat because of his support for the repeal of the penal laws against Roman Catholics, which effectively meant his fellow Irishmen. Burke's relationship with the electors of Bristol has since come to be seen as a case study in the difference between seeing an MP as a delegate who does only what his electors tell him, and a representative who, while he always listens with attention to what his electors say, always keeps his own judgement free when it comes to deciding questions which affect the whole nation. (Tory MPs, it is said, still quote Burke when they are in trouble with their constituency parties.) Thereafter Burke sat for Malton in Yorkshire. He was Paymaster of the Forces (and a Privy Councillor) in Rockingham's second administration in 1782, but he never held cabinet rank; nor did he hold ministerial office after 1783. He did well enough for money though, buying a country seat near Beaconsfield, Butler's Court, in 1769.

Burke made his political name as a supporter of the cause of the American colonists, as the scourge of misgovernment by the British in India, and as the implacable enemy of the French Revolution and of revolutionary ideas in general. George III is supposed to have thought of rewarding Burke with a peerage, but the scheme fell through. Burke was so affected by the death of his only son that he died a broken man only three years later in 1797.

DAVID HUME

Hume wrote an account of 'My Own Life' which is just about as unconfessional as such an account could be. It is Hume as others saw him, philosopher and man of the world, exuding common sense, good manners and that moderation which lay at the heart of Enlightenment. However sceptical Hume may have been as a philosopher, it does not appear from his little autobiography that he had any doubts at all about how an enlightened man should live.

Hume was born in 1711 into a Lowland Scottish gentry family fond of claiming noble descent from the ancient house of Home. Young David Hume was a youth of 'acumen and parts', as they used to say, fond of his books (especially Virgil and Cicero), and was ambitious for 'literary', that is to say intellectual and philosophical, fame from a very early age.

After a gentleman's education – he was a student at Edinburgh – Hume was pushed by his family in the direction of the law, which he had no taste for, and of business, for which he had neither taste nor aptitude. He had a small private fortune which he thought could keep him if he went abroad, and he spent two years in France, returning in 1737 with part of his *Treatise of Human Nature* ready for publication in London. Like most of the books Hume was to publish, it was not well or widely received. His two volumes of *Essays* (1741, 1742) did better, and by this time Hume was on the lookout for a university chair in Edinburgh, but Hume's religious scepticism did not go down well in that northern capital of Calvinism, and he was unsuccessful. Like Hobbes, he tried his hand at tutoring noblemen, but this was not a success, and for a time he served as secretary to a general ('I wore the red coat of an officer') whom he accompanied to Vienna and Turin.

It was during the early 1750s that Hume's works were coming to be known abroad, especially in France, but this did not help Hume in his attempt to succeed his friend Adam Smith in the chair of Logic at the University of Glasgow. Instead, he was invited to become keeper of their library by the Faculty of Advocates in Edinburgh, and although the pay (never a matter of indifference to Hume) was not good, the leisure and facilities available were. He produced the first volume of his *History of England* ('Tory as to persons and Whig as to things') in 1754, and, despite a slow start, it began to make money, so that by 1760 Hume was not only independent but opulently so.

Hume was the convivial clubman about Edinburgh and knew all the luminaries of British intellectual life – the Johnsons, the Boswells, the Burkes and the Adam Smiths. He was also a great success in Paris. The great Parisian hostesses all loved him, broad Scots accent and all. Hume tried to be decent to Rousseau in his English exile, but the meeting between reasoned moderation and paranoid romanticism ended in disaster.

Hume was briefly an under-secretary and George III gave him a pension (as the king was wont to do to anti-Jacobite Scotsmen). George III also offered Hume the chance to consult royal archives, not knowing that Hume was not that kind of historian. As he got old, Hume became corpulent. He became ill in 1775 of a 'disorder of the bowels', and, momentarily deserting his scepticism for stoicism, died a truly philosophical death in 1776.

It is important to distinguish right at the beginning between what we might call the 'loyal' and the 'disloyal' critics of Enlightenment, or between what has come to be called an 'internal' and 'external' critique. Hume and Burke are critics from the inside of Enlightenment itself, loyal critics who would accept much of what Enlightenment came to stand for but who see themselves as putting a healthy break on some of the wilder claims that the Age of Reason made for itself. Both were political conservatives (though Hume's Tory sympathies have probably been exaggerated, and Burke was a Whig), taking their stand on the established system of constitutional politics as it developed in eighteenth-century Britain after the Glorious Revolution of 1688. (It is important to say Britain, because Hume was a Scot and Burke was Irish. Neither was a natural 'insider' in purely English politics, and it may be that each in his own way was able to bring to English politics that outsider's sharpness of eye which has been so fruitful in the history of political observation and analysis.) Both Hume and Burke are to be sharply distinguished from the 'disloyal' or 'external' attack on the Enlightenment which occurred after the French Revolution and which makes up so much of the story of the development of European political thought in the nineteenth and twentieth centuries. This does not, of course, mean that Hume's and Burke's were not names to be conjured with in the later root-and-branch attack on the values and attitudes of Enlightenment, but it would be quite mistaken to include their names in the roll call of anti-Enlightenment's heroes. Both Hume and Burke came to doubt whether Reason was all that it was cracked up to be by the sloganeers of Enlightenment. Both came to think that the role Enlightenment gave to reason in human affairs had been exaggerated. Reason had been overloaded by Enlightenment, asked to do too many things, and asked to do things which reason itself could not do.

In their explorations of the limitations of reason, whether in moral philosophy or psychology or in political theory and political life, neither Hume nor Burke can be said, even remotely, to be attacking reason. It could be said of all the really great thinkers of the Enlightenment – Hume, Rousseau, Kant and Vico – that they tried in their different ways to give to reason as wide a scope in philosophy and in life as it was possible to give it, but that none the less Enlightenment had simply asked too much of it. It must never be forgotten that Enlightenment was a movement of ideas with a strong sense of its own identity. As with all intellectual movements, there was a tendency to exaggerate what made Enlightenment different from the opinions of its enemies, and this made Enlightenment march into every battle under the banner of Reason without always being clear about what reason actually meant. The list of things which reason was against could be written easily enough, and there was a tendency on at least the propagandist side of Enlightenment to neglect the fact that reason itself might have its own, essentially self-imposed limits. With so many easy targets around, it was easy to forget that reason might not always be able to build up again on a new footing what had already been rationally destroyed.

This was especially true in two of the fields which Enlightenment had made its own – ethics and politics – and it had given pride of place to a new theory of human nature which placed increasing emphasis on the function of reason as a fundamental and therefore overriding constituent in that nature. This seemed so obvious, and it seemed to be confirmed from so many philosophical quarters and by so much of human experience if properly understood, that a crucial part of Enlightenment's job came to be seen as the revelation of those moral, social and political causes which had prevented reason from coming into its own as the rightful sovereign of the world (the phrase is Hegel's). The thrust of Enlightenment was thus negative in two related ways. Enlightenment was extremely adept at showing up the absurdities of the moral, social and political worlds; no outmoded belief of practice seemed to be able to stand up against the sheer intelligence and bravura of Enlightenment's attacks against it. Enlightenment was also negative in the sense that it concentrated on the causes of why reason had hitherto failed to acquire that dominion over the affairs of men which was undoubtedly its own after reason had shown men just how many of their beliefs and practices were so feebly grounded from a rational point of view. What Enlightenment tended to assume in its bolder moments was that the given world of human experience having been shown to be riddled with error and super-stition, it was only a short step to the rational deduction of moral and political systems which would be capable of commanding the loyalty of all rational men.

Both Hume and Burke in their different ways began to doubt whether this was a feasible project. What they did in a sense returned Enlightenment back to its own sceptical origins. In being sceptical of all rivals and established systems of morals and politics, Enlightenment had forgotten to be sceptical of its own claims in reason's name. What Hume especially did was to carry a philosophical scepticism right into the heart of Enlightenment. What was then called the basis of the 'science of man', and what we would call psychology, was subjected to such a keen philosophical glance that doubt began to be cast on what it really meant to call man a 'rational' creature. We have already seen what a store Enlightenment put on the soundness of its own view of human nature. A new view of human nature was the bedrock constitution of the human universe, upon which could be constructed new systems of morals and politics. Everywhere you looked in Enlightenment you saw human reason being cried up. Plato was back, but a Plato in modern dress with the elitism of the Platonic view of reason severely toned down. Perhaps the enlightened view of reason was little more than common sense and the ability to think clearly which we have come to associate with Plato's teacher Socrates. Reason was now, at least in principle, for everyman, and not just for the highly gifted and trained few. New systems of morals and politics would be constructed on a rational basis in the double sense that reason would be the source of new value systems, and those new value systems would find increasing support as humanity began to emancipate itself from the irrationalism of the past and found itself capable of a true understanding of the rational basis of the new moral systems.

HUME ON REASON AND THE PASSIONS

Hume had no doubt that reason could go a very long way towards understanding the world in which it found itself, and one of the things which reason could certainly do was to construct the basis of a true science of man. This meant carrying on where Locke had left off, and coming to a wider understanding of what was then called 'human understanding', what we would now call human cognitive psychology. Enlightenment had tended to forget just how modest Locke's own claims for his theory of knowledge were. Locke had warned that his own epistemological doctrines were intended to clear the ground a little, and that much remained to be done. Locke had shown how the human understanding worked through receiving the sense impressions of sight, touch, hearing, smell and taste from the outside world which were then organised by the mind into coherent patterns until the world outside the mind began to make sense. This formed the basis of our ordinary understanding of the world, and it formed the basis of the whole scientific enterprise when the understanding became conscious enough of itself to formulate the rules of scientific procedure. Locke did not, of course, *invent* science, but he did something which in its own way was just as important: he showed that there was no difference in principle between how the ordinary understanding came to understand the world and how the scientific understanding came to understand the world. There was nothing arcane, esoteric, alchemical or mysterious about 'true' knowledge. True knowledge, whether of the ordinary of scientific kind, was at least in principle available to everybody.

This had profound implications for the whole programme of Enlightenment. Since Plato's day, knowledge claims had also been claims to moral and political power. Knowing, really knowing, had always in the past been the privilege of the Few, and the claim that the true knowledge of the Few was superior to the ordinary opinions of the Many had been the most important part of the Few's claims to rule the Many. No matter what that knowledge claim had in fact consisted of – Platonic wisdom; Aristotelian teleology; an understanding of God's providence (or even ability to read the Scriptures); the divine right of kings to understand the mysteries of state; papal infallibility in its early versions – it had always been used to set a distance between *them*, those needing to be ruled because they are ignorant, and *us*, the high-minded keepers of the wisdom necessary for ruling. Enlightenment's reading of Lockian epistemology's denial of the essential difference between ordinary and true (that is scientific) understanding was profoundly liberating. For the first time in the history of the human race it became possible to believe that the time was not far distant when all men could really understand themselves and the world in which they lived. The idea of science in the Enlightenment shaded easily, as it had in the ancient world, into technology. Science was *for* something. Enlightenment's scientific understanding of the world was meant to bring the world under rational control. This applied just as much to the internal world of the mind as it did to the world outside the mind. Just as science as technology would enable men to control nature and transform it into a world subordinate to human needs, so the internal world of the mind could be brought under the control of reason. When men looked inside themselves they could see the simmering passions waiting to be brought to boiling point with all that meant for established patterns of peaceful social living. Let the passions loose and, in a sense which was more than metaphorical, all hell would break loose. But a true understanding of human nature meant that the dangers of the passions could be controlled by the exercise of enlightened reason. Morality had not, in fact, changed much since Plato's day. Reason would control the passions by directing their force towards the accomplishment of rationally demonstrable ethical ends.

The problem with Enlightenment's search for a rationally based system of ethics was that it rested on the fundamental assumption that the human mind did in fact have the hierarchical structure which Plato had insisted it had all those years ago. What Hume did was to look into minds 'experimentally', that is to say into minds as they actually worked in the real world, and he could discover no such rational hierarchy. There was nothing in introspection, and nothing about human behaviour, which suggested that reason was superior to the passions, or that reason could even control the passions in ways which had hitherto been supposed. The passions simply *are*, and if we look into ourselves, or if we look at the behaviour of our fellow men, all we can see is our reason aiding the passions to get what the passions want. Hence Hume's famous statement that reason is the slave of the passions, and can do nothing else but to obey and serve them. By reason, Hume means the human 'understanding' as it discovers matters of fact and the relations between facts. Human understanding for Hume is essentially passive in the sense that the understanding is not set in motion until a desire sets it on its way to find something out which is useful to desire's own satisfaction.

By the 'passions' Hume means something very like the ordinary desires of life, desires for food and shelter, sexuality, love of family and friends, desire for a good reputation and in general the desire to live well and to enjoy life. Most of the passions are not necessarily anti-social, but the passion of self-interest is. Self-interest knows no natural limits. All the passions are self-interested in the sense that they cry out to be satisfied, but the passion of self-interest is peculiar because it is not in principle satisfiable. This is especially true in well-advanced societies where there is no limit to the amount of riches a man may strive to possess. The passion of self-interest in its natural state knows no 'mine' and 'thine', would never hold a man to a contract when it was in his interest to cheat, and would not hesitate to bear false witness. What, then, can check the anti-social nature of the passion of self-interest? Not reason, for reason only serves to show a man where his best interest lies. Only a passion, being active, can check a passion, and Hume thinks that it is only by dividing the passion of self-interest against itself that its fundamentally anti-social character can be curbed. At the very beginning of human societies it must have been obvious to men that human living was going to be very uncomfortable if they did not respect one another's property. Each man must have begun to realise that the unruliness of the passion of self-interest worked against him when he saw that his own desire to possess what belonged to another was duplicated in the desires of all other men to possess what belonged to him. Self-interest uncontrolled by rules leads at the very least to a feeling of insecurity, and at the worst to the loss of life and goods. Therefore, says Hume, there must have arisen gradually a kind of 'convention', whereby men began to respect the property of others in return for others respecting what was theirs.

Hume is very careful not to describe this as a contract based on a promise. He speaks of the rules of justice arising slowly and stumblingly, a process, not an all-or-nothing social contract. Hume knows very well that the weakness of social contract theory lies in its historical implausibility. It would, in fact, only be sophisticated men living in a society which already had a grasp of what 'making a promise' meant who would be capable of making an original contract to respect the rules of justice. Hume's own account of the origins of justice is just as conjectural as the social contract account, but at the same time it is more 'historical' because he sees the sense of justice, which is at bottom no more than a respect for property, arising out of social development and not just being invented out of men's heads. Hume has another reason for wanting to emphasise how slowly the sense of justice came into being. If there was no one moment at which the rules of justice were invented, then there is no moment in the history of the human race to look back to with particular veneration, let alone an 'original contract' which is eternally binding. The rules of justice of past ages have no special claim to our attention. Quite the reverse. Primitive justice is appropriate to an undeveloped society but has very little to tell us about how we should live now. 'Respect one another's goods' is no doubt a maxim of justice at all times and places but it has very little to tell us about how justice is actually to be organised at any particular stage in human development.

The original convention to respect property does owe a great deal to the development of human understanding. Reason is not absent from the process of original convention-making, but the original convention is not reason's bolt from the blue. Men came gradually to realise the usefulness of justice, and they came eventually to see that justice is in everybody's interest. This was originally a very rough and ready notion of justice. At the very beginning, there was probably nobody special whose job it was to enforce the rules of justice, and this may in part account for the slowness of justice to catch on. Once the idea of justice in its primitive form had emerged it was probably not very difficult for justice to work because there could not have been much worth quarrelling about anyway. In a static and primitive agricultural society everybody was bound to know what belonged to everybody else. Perhaps the rules of justice did not have to be formalised, and an agent to enforce it appointed, until there really was a source of trouble to make them necessary. The most likely new pressure on a primitive society would be war. The necessity of common action, and the need afterwards to ensure a fair distribution of the booty if the war was successful, would naturally lead men to put themselves under the authority of a chief. Primitive monarchy was therefore the most likely form of government to begin with, and we can readily see how it would become hereditary. Men who expected to pass their possessions on to their own loved ones would see nothing unusual when their chief wanted to pass on his authority to his son.

Of course, as *history*, Hume's account of the 'in the beginning' is conjectural, but he takes it seriously in the sense that he thinks his account is much more plausible than the rival social contract theory account. All accounts of the origins of morality and government are bound to be conjectural, and Hume knows this. His purpose in offering his own conjectural history is to show that there is no reason in principle why accounts of origins, however plausible, should carry any special weight with us when we discuss our own moral and political concerns. The idea that there is an original constitution of government which can tell us where we have gone wrong, and to which we would do well to return, is a nonsense. How can there be, when those origins are obscure and when more than one account of them can be given? As far as the origins of government are concerned, Hume is a 'lots of water under the bridge' theorist. Questions about origins are intellectually interesting, but so much has happened since those beginnings that we would do well to attend to our own affairs when we dispute about government, and not to go looking for an ideal model to follow in the mists of time.

Hume's conservatism consists of an attachment to the present, not to the past. In the context of British politics in the middle and later eighteenth century, there could be no doubt about how Hume's very abstract arguments in the *Treatise of Human Nature* applied to the politics of the moment. Both Whigs and Tories tended to argue from principles which were bolstered by historical accounts of the origins of government. Whigs argued either for an ultimately popular sovereignty because there must have been an original contract of government, or that there was an ancient and free constitution in England which the king might not alter. Theirs was an essentially libertarian position, suspicious of strong government in principle however much the Whigs dominated government in practice. The Tories, still tainted with the Jacobite inheritance until almost the end of the century, insisted on the wide extent of the royal prerogative and of its indefeasible residence in the House of Stuart. The ideological stance of both Whigs and Tories was essentially backward-looking. Hume knows that the past is an inexhaustible source of political arguments for and against anything. His *History of England* was written partly to dismantle the myth that there had been a single, original free constitution in England since the beginning, a constitution which had developed but which at the same time still bore the outlines of its original foundation. Hume's history demonstrates that there has been no such thing. We look in vain for any settled pattern of liberty in English political history before the seventeenth century. What we do find is a series of different political systems according to the age, and the only connecting link between them seems to be monarchy. Hume's analysis of the development of English governing institutions is remarkable because he has a very modern-looking idea of the nature of the exercise of political power. His is almost a 'political science' approach, concerned as it is with how power in the realm has actually been exercised at different times. Hume comes to the commonsensical conclusion that there is no particular reason for emphasising the continuity of a political system. Why should there not be sharp breaks in its development? The fact that one political system follows another as the centuries roll by does not mean that the political system remains essentially the same. Besides, and this would be galling to the Whigs, historical investigation confirms what ordinary observation finds: whatever continuity there has been in English government since the beginning is obviously to be located in the development of the supreme British institution, the monarchy. Resistance to monarchy has had at best an episodic character, and it was not until the seventeenth century that the myth was developed that Englishmen had been resisting the royal prerogative since the Norman Conquest, and that the story of that resistance was the story of the development of the British constitution which preserved the rights and liberties of Englishmen.

Hume's two kinds of history, conjectural and English, can both be seen as attempts to de-mythologise the past. He seems to be saying that the past is a minefield for those who go seeking there for legitimations of political authority. Hume looks forward to the utilitarian position that the origins of government in the past have nothing to do with the legitimacy of government in the present. What, then, for Hume, makes a system of government legitimate? Hume speaks with the general voice of Enlightenment when he puts his emphasis on justice, which for him is simply rule by law. He is, however, careful to distinguish between questions about how justice developed (the anthropology of law) and questions about what law is actually like (the business of political theorising). However law originated it will be obvious that, in the present state of society, law is what makes an ordered life possible. The limited benevolence of humankind means that our care for the interests of others does not easily extend much beyond our immediate circle of family and friends. Our immediate relationships are therefore readily ordered by the natural promptings of the human heart, but our relations with those outside the circle need to be managed 'artificially' by the rules of justice. Justice is certainly a human invention, and is to that extent unnatural, but justice is also natural in the sense that human reason every-where has seen the need for justice if human living is ever to advance beyond a very primitive state. Man is by nature an inventive species, and it is no accident that one of the things he always seems to invent is justice. The discovery of justice may be halting and accidental, but once justice, however primitive, is established, human reason has no difficulty in seeing its advantages. Of course, it is likely that the law will be surrounded by all kinds of mumbo-jumbo in the early stages of its development, but in a rational age law has no reason to dress up in anything except its own obvious utility. Even in an age of reason there will be people who never think about law at all, and for them it is enough that they have become used to living under the laws and law-makers of their particular country. The human mind is a great associator of ideas. It naturally associates the long possession of a piece of property with the idea of a right to ownership, and this principle extends to the right of rulership: long possession of rulership by a particular family, or by a particular group of men, easily associates itself with the right to rule. Long possession does not have to mean 'from time immemorial'. A few generations is often enough, and that is why humankind in general is content, and wise to be content, with the 'present established practice of the age' in matters of morals and politics.

Like all enlightened thinkers following Montesquieu, Hume thinks of government through law as moderate government. Unlike many of his contemporaries, Hume refuses to believe that government in an absolute monarchy like France is lawless. It was a common-place in eighteenth-century Britain to contrast British 'liberty' with French 'slavery'. British insularity insisted that only the mixed government system of polity was a guarantee of liberty because it put the British people in the enviable position of not being able to be taxed or punished without their consent freely given through their representatives in Parliament. The king was no doubt the most important man in the kingdom, but the lives and fortunes of the British were not at his mercy because, while the king was the fountain of executive power, the legislature was the supreme law-making body in the land, and the royal assent to parliamentary bills was only part of the process of law-making. Contrast an absolute monarchy, where the king's word was law. Hume could see that this was a contrast amounting to caricature. The actual facts of the case were that in Britain the influence of the king in the process of legislation went far beyond the mere formal right to accept or reject parliamentary bills. The linchpin of the British system of politics was the influence of the king's ministry over the House of Commons, where all the force of royal patronage could be used to secure a majority for the ministry in important matters. The king was 'in' Parliament in a much more real sense than the theory of the 'king-in-parliament' seemed to suggest. Unlike the fervent anti-ministerialists, Hume can see nothing wrong with 'influence' in principle, though it can be taken too far in practice. Hume saw more clearly than most that British government needed influence if it was to work at all. With the example of the English Civil War always in mind, a series of events which he put down to the fanaticism of party, Hume realised that the primary problem of the British system of government was not how to separate powers but how to unite them. The king and his party, and Parliament with its party, on different sides of a battlefield, was the separation of powers gone mad. The problem of English government after the Civil War, and again after 1688, was to find a means by which king and Parliament could live together, if not happily, then at least through necessity. Influence was the essential link between government and legislature because it meant that the king's ministers did not often find themselves faced with an implacably hostile lower house. The noisy faction fights between Whigs and Tories, 'ins' and 'outs', tended to obscure this obvious truth about British politics. The ministry's enemies shouted the cry of 'corruption' for all it was worth, and the ministry defended itself as best it could. Neither took Hume's detached view that what its opponents called corruption was systematically necessary. Indeed, it was the raucousness of faction fighting which threatened the moderate system of politics by its lack of moderation, promising a return to the fanaticism of party which had caused the Civil War in the previous century.

It is sometimes said that Hume is not quite in the first rank as a political theorist because his thought is essentially negative. Hume, on this view of him, is remarkable because he is able to see the glaring faults of the social contract theory, and because he is able to see how the natural law thinkers necessarily exaggerated natural law's claim to be founded in the facts of nature. Hume's famous distinction between 'is' and 'ought' in the *Treatise of Human Nature* is only one example (and a much overplayed example) of his suspicion that almost all natural law theorising is fallacious. Natural law thinkers had typically reasoned that because something *is*, therefore something *ought* to be. Traditionally, natural law thinkers had argued that what is, is right, because God had wished it to be so. Of course, not every-thing that actually happened had God's approval, because the free will that God had given to man meant that men frequently did things which caused God pain, but, properly considered, the good things which happened in God's creation pointed the way towards a way of life of which God would approve. Hume began to wonder. It was not that the world as it was actually organised could not teach important moral lessons. Far from it. The world as it actually was, was the only moral teacher. The problem with the moralists in Hume's own contemporary world was that they were too quick to move from 'is' to 'ought', too ready to move from descriptions of the world as it actually was to prescriptions for the world as it should be. In short, all of the thinkers whom Hume implicitly condemned had really failed to understand how the world as it *is* had actually changed. For Hume, a view of the world which in any sense leads to a view of the world as it ought to be is a view of the world as it really, historically, is. Very generalised views of the world as it must have been since the beginning simply will not do. The world changes, and prescriptions for what the world should be like should change with it.

Hume plainly thinks that what the world should be like is implicit in the world as it is. This perception he shares with all conservatives. A proper understanding of one's own contemporary world is the route to what that world should be like. That meant taking contemporary history seriously, where contemporary history meant social development. For Hume, the question: What is the world actually like? is not the same question as asking: What has human nature always been like? Rather, the question for Hume always is: Where has human nature got to now, as it writes its story in its own human landscape? Critics of Hume have congratulated themselves on finding that Hume is an ideologue of the Hanoverian succession, or, even more wickedly, that Hume is an ideologue of the kind of developing capitalism which characterised the reign of the first three Georges. They could have saved themselves the trouble. There is nothing secret about the fact that Hume was the defender of the established practices, political and economic, of his own age. His emphasis on the rules of justice, which at bottom are the rules of possession, buying and selling, is obviously an extrapolation from the commercial practices of his own contemporary world. Living as he did in eighteenth-century Edinburgh, and with friends like Adam Smith in Glasgow, Hume could not have failed to notice the development of a commercial and opulent society in his native land. The whole of the Scottish Enlightenment had taken its cue from Montesquieu in interesting itself in the progress of society, and Scotland was as good a place as any in the eighteenth century to contrast a 'rude' state of society with a 'polished'. The Highland Line was very close to Glasgow throughout the eighteenth century, and it was easy to see the Jacobite rising of 1745 as the assault of the barbarous highland clans against the more advanced civilisations of the Scottish Lowlands and of England.

There is nothing much that is exciting about Hume's political thought, but then there never is about conservatism which is not reactionary. What has to be emphasised about Hume's conservatism is that it is entirely free of any misty-eyed romanticism about the past. He saw more clearly, or he saw earlier, than anybody else in eighteenth-century Scotland, and perhaps more clearly than anybody else in eighteenth-century Britain, that what was needed was a defence of the *status quo*. It is easy, with hindsight, to think of a defence of the *status quo* as the hallmark of conservatism. What is difficult is to imagine a time when all the main political arguments were arguments derived from a particular view of the past, and only incidentally from an attachment to the present. Hume was very conscious that he was applying the 'experimental' method, that is the scientific method, to moral and political subjects, and the reasonableness of Hume's moral and political theory comes out of the very commonsensical truth that we have more reason to be confident about our experience of the present than of the past. Argument about what the present ought to be like from alleged sets of facts about the past is always bound to get bogged down in bickering about what the past was actually like, and it is a truism that the record of the past can be stretched to render up any tale which the teller wants to be told. Hume is on strong ground when he uses the greater certainties of present experience as a basis for moral and political theorising.

BURKE ON THE CONNECTION BETWEEN ENLIGHTENMENT AND REVOLUTION

As a conservative thinker writing in 1790, Burke has the great advantage of being able to blame Enlightenment for the specific series of events which made up the early history of the French Revolution. Burke has as good a claim as any to being the first to spot that the politics of the modern world was at bottom going to consist of a clash of opposing ideologies. Burke's *Reflections on the Revolution in France* (1790) is an attempt to clothe pre-revolutionary social and political institutions with an ideological justification which is in its way just as comprehensive as the revolutionary ideology in whose name those institutions were being attacked. Burke is very quick to point out that the French Revolution is not just another event in the political history of the world. It is definitely not like the English Revolution of 1688, and it is probably only a bit like the American Revolution which preceded it. The French Revolution, in Burke's view of it, was made in the name of a new view of the world, a view so new that it threatened the existing world root and branch. Old Europe showed itself to be in urgent need of defending itself with its own view of the world, and the structure of that view would have to be copied from the structure of the Enlightenment view, able to meet it point for point. The traditional defences of the existing state of things were inadequate. Old Europe had its own theoretical defences, divine right monarchy, for instance, or natural law justifications for the existence of the social and political orders, but there was nothing of comparable modernity to match the sheer diversity of Enlightenment's critique of the intellectual and moral bankruptcy of Europe's ageing institutions, beliefs and practices.

Burke's own critique of Enlightenment, where it does not amount to a critique of a caricature, goes right to the heart of the matter. Unerringly, Burke focuses on the enlightened claim to have invented a science of politics capable of rendering up finished truths about the moral and political worlds. In particular, Burke homes in on the claim that the truths of the moral and political worlds will be simple truths. How can this be, he asks, when the moral and political worlds are in fact so complex? Burke is on strong ground when he emphasises the complication of social and political systems. Human societies, comprised as they are of interlocking moral, economic and political orders, are really wonders of nature. Burke is careful to keep to Enlightenment's claim that society is natural, but what he chooses to do is to see the natural creation as the work of the mind of a very complex God. God made human societies through a largely unknowing human agency, and what actually holds a human society together is no easy thing to understand. Burke hints at mysteriously working *latent* causes, aspects of a society's inner functioning which are by no means obvious at first sight and which, when seen, may seem to be trivial, but which, when interfered with, may cause a society's disintegration. (Burke very prudently neglects to give a list of latent causes, so as not to fall into the trap of saying that he can spot causes which are in fact very difficult to identify.) Human societies display all the delicacy of finely wrought things. That delicacy is particularly vulnerable to well-meaning schemes of improvement, which may sound fine in the abstract but which can easily have the effect in practice of upsetting a society's own natural balances. Burke sometimes, though not always, speaks of a society as if it were a living thing, with a past, and with a future which is going to be different from that past, but which is determined by it, just as the future of any living thing comes out of its own past but is in all kinds of ways different from it. The conserva-tive implications of this line of thought are obvious. Only God can make living things, but human beings can easily destroy them. The ultimate human folly is to kill off a living society and to attempt to make another one to put in its place. That is the kind of thing a child would do, because children are often impatient with the complexity of the problems which confront them and usually go for a cutting of the Gordian knot kind of solution. How can human beings be expected to create a society from scratch, when an existing society is hard enough to understand? Would *you* trust someone who doesn't even understand how existing clocks work to design an entirely new kind of clock which he claimed was going to be better than any clock which ever existed before in the world?

To say that societies are complex is not to claim that they are perfect. Burke is no reactionary. He recognises that the world changes, and he can see that some changes are for the better. This seems to be particularly true of the course of English history because, as a good Whig, Burke thinks that the glory of English history is the development of what has come to be called the English constitution. The English constitution certainly had not always existed in its developed eighteenth-century form. Therefore it must have come into being as the result of change. The question for Burke is: What was the role of deliberate human agency in that development? Burke is faced with the sight of the French National Assembly making a whole new constitution for France and claiming that they are doing nothing very different from what the English themselves did in 1688. Burke is therefore obliged to give the French and their English sympathisers a lesson in English constitutional history. In his eyes, the English Revolution of 1688 was glorious because it established no new principles of government. Far from it. Burke thinks that it is part of the wisdom of the ruling class in England that it does not go looking for trouble; rather, it deals with each case as it comes up, and acts only when it feels it has to. Over the centuries, the English ruling class has become adept at constitutional management by limiting damage during crises. One such crisis came in 1688. James II was a bad king with a good title to rule. The last straw was his claim that he could suspend the law in favour of his Catholic friends. This made political action against him necessary, otherwise James, by claiming the right to put aside the ordinary processes of law when he saw fit, threatened the whole idea of the rule of law in England. This would effectively reduce England to the level of a continental despotism, where the king would ride roughshod over legal niceties any time he felt like it. What was to be done? The answer was to make as little change as possible in order to preserve as much of the existing constitution as possible. James would have to go; there was no disputing that. The best way to limit the damage to the continuity of the constitution would be to invite his daughter, Mary, and her husband, William of Orange, to occupy the vacant throne. The hereditary principle would be preserved, in so far as that was possible, and in return the new monarchs would agree not to repeat the unconstitutional errors of their predecessor. In 1688, a prudent ruling class, or their representatives, were able to act quickly before there was time for fundamental questions to be raised about how England *ought* to be governed. The question in the abstract was never considered, least of all by those who made the revolution. What they intended was that as much of the constitutional *status quo ante* as possible, in the circumstances, was preserved. Otherwise, fundamental questions about English government might have been raised, and that would have been to repeat all the constitutional troubles which agitated England in the middle of the seventeenth century and which had caused the Civil War.

Burke seems to think that the effect of these exercises in crisis management is cumulative. Over time, constitutional readjustments produce new, emerging, constitutional principles whose efficacy is confirmed by the fact that they continue to work. In the course of this process a constitution will in fact change, but it is never entirely redesigned at any particular time by any particular group or generation of the ruling class. The whole point about a tradition of constitutionalism is that such a radical re-thinking of it in its entirety is unnecessary. The last thing one should do is to be forever asking whether a constitution is at bottom alive and well. This would be the equivalent in politics of what children tend to do in gardening: continually digging up the roots of a plant to see whether it is growing properly. Burke is not exactly an ancestor-worshipper, but he does think that to reject an ancestral constitution is to claim superiority over those who have gone before us. To attempt to rewrite a constitution is effectively to say that the work of ancestors is useless, if not actually pernicious; it is to claim that no important discoveries about what a political system should be like were ever made in the past. The revolutionary thus adds the crime of arrogance to the crime of patricide by claiming that only he, *now*, understands the true business of government.

The revolutionary is not just a parricide and arrogant; he is also a wastrel. He is like the inheritor of a fortune who is prepared to squander it all in a single generation. No concern for those who laboriously accumulated that fortune disturbs him, nor has he any thought for his posterity. The root cause of this arrogant wastefulness is not difficult to find. Burke does not in fact think that our ancestors were supremely wise, and there is no reason in principle for thinking that men of the present generation are not cleverer than those of past generations. The point is that ordinary experience teaches us that men of inferior ability can frequently see faults in, and improve, schemes devised by men of far superior ability, particularly when they have had time for reflection. Why should this not have been true of the development of the constitution in the past? Burke's argument is more subtle than it is often given credit for. He is not claiming some kind of elevated wisdom for ancestors, but we can at least concede that some of them must have been men of sense, and we can surely concede that they had a long time for reflection in past generations. This the revolutionary refuses to acknowledge. He thinks that his own present cleverness is all that he needs to go on. The revolutionary makes the mistake that the whole Enlightenment made by thinking that all of the important discoveries have been recently made, and that therefore the wisdom of the past, which he thinks of as no wisdom at all, can safely be set aside.

Two questions then arise which Burke must answer: Where does this ancestral wisdom *come from*, and how do we actually know that it is wisdom and not foolishness? The question about where ancestral wisdom comes from is really another question about the nature of constitutional changes, and about who decides what constitutional changes should occur. The constitution, in Burke's view of it, is a record of decisions made about what government should be like. Legitimate changers of a constitution are always aware that specific changes should be made in order to make the constitution more coherent. The impulse towards constitutional change always arises out of a sense that some governmental practice does not fit well with all the other practices. But that still leaves open the question about the agency of change. Who is it, exactly, who makes those changes? Burke's answer is unequivocal: a wise ruling class. This aspect of Burke's political thought has come in for a good deal of criticism. Can it really be that the English ruling class has always been unfailingly wise? Is there not something obfuscating in Burke's political thought here? Can he be really serious?

The answer is that Burke is being serious, though his arguments have been frequently misunderstood to mean that almost anybody born into the ruling class is a fit guardian of the English constitution. Burke definitely does not think that. What he does think is that there must have been at least a section of the British ruling class, with a care for the constitution, which must have existed almost from time out of mind to provide the continuity of constitutional development which is so remarkable a feature of English political life. In Burke's view of the matter, no continuous ruling class must equal no continuous constitution.

Burke's assertion that there has been a ruling class in England with claims to continuity need cause no surprises. What might cause a surprise is that Burke thinks that this ruling class has always had a care for the constitution. Surely, one might say, ruling classes since the world began have been keen to break out of the constitutional constraints on their own self-aggrandising behaviour. That has been a commonplace view of ruling classes since Plato's *Republic*. Burke thinks that the case of England is different. England has been fortunate in having a ruling class which has been divided in its political attitudes. For extremely complicated political reasons, part of the English ruling class has always seen its own future advantage in supporting the royal prerogative, while the other part of the ruling class has always seen its own future advantage in supporting Parliament. This split (and Burke can hardly do more than hint at it at a moment when all ruling classes must appear to stand united against the French Revolution) got out of hand in the seventeenth century and in part caused the Civil War, but in general it has been healthy for the English constitution. The dialectical clash between king and Parliament, executive and legislature, has provided the continuous dynamic of English constitutional politics, and such a dynamic cannot fade away while there exist in England devoted defenders of the king's power and robust defenders of the rights of Parliament. Burke by no means thinks that the events of the Revolution of 1688 have settled the question of the relationship between king and Parliament for ever. Nothing can.

This camouflaged internecine quarrel can only be productive of good. In ordinary times it preserves a balance between the authority of government and the liberties of the subject, and in times of crisis the ruling class has to make a decision about where the balance ought to be struck. The motive for the striking of those balances is always obvious. In England, the survival of the constitution, and with it the survival of the ruling class, depends on the ruling class, or a section of it, getting the balance right. A decision on a matter of constitutional importance by no means decides the nature of the constitution for ever. The great moments of constitutional decision are moments at which great questions of government have to be *decided*. Such a moment has occurred when a matter of passionate debate and great political import has been settled one way or the other; after really *is* after. To try to undo such a decision is to be obscurantist. This wilful perversity can occur in English politics; Jacobitism is an obvious example. The course of English history is supposed to show that Jacobitism has had its day, but of course there will always be those who fail to learn the lessons of English constitutional history properly.

Burke's constitutionalism comes out of what is really a rather grand view of the continuity of English politics. The Whig view of the continuity of English politics was far from parochial, if by parochial one means narrow-minded. It holds that, since the Norman Conquest, English history has been one continuous constitutional history lesson taught by freedom-loving Englishmen to their foreign kings who have typically had too elevated an idea of the royal power. In England, the king is expected to share power with the other estates of the realm, nobility and commons, and the king is also expected to acknowledge that there is an English way of doing things which he may not alter at will. The royal prerogative, the power which the king has simply because he is king, is supposed to be extensive but at the same time limited by the powers and privileges of the other orders. In the ordinary course of government the various powers are supposed to act in partnership. Occasionally they come to be seen as rivals, and that is an indicator that things have begun to go wrong, a signal that one of those cases has arisen in which adjustments have to be made so that each of the powers can be returned to run in its proper track. As Montesquieu pointed out, keeping a political system like this in its proper condition requires a certain level of political intuition and a certain body of political skills (despotism is much simpler). A wise ruling class is the vehicle by which those skills are transmitted from one generation to the next. There is nothing mysterious about this, no aristocratic cult of noble blood. Aristocracy, according to Burke, is, in the modern idiom, a socialising agency, teaching the manners, morals and skills to each new generation of its members which will enable constitutional politics of the English kind to work. Such an aristocracy must never become a caste. It must keep at least a half-open door to outside talent (Burke himself) and to new wealth. It would be both wasteful and dangerous if the spirit of caste were to exclude all the outsiders with a claim to joining the ruling class, and Burke knows perfectly well, though he doesn't mention it, that the history of aristocracy in England is not all that smooth, and that new ennoblement over the centuries has become a commonplace. It won't do to enquire too closely into the origins of titles. Ennoblement also has the advantage of civilising new wealth. New wealth must be welcomed into the charmed circle, but the process must not be too quick. The first generation must not feel too comfortable in its elevated condition, and this tames the arrogance of wealth; later generations will feel much more at home in their position of privilege.

Inheritance is the key to Burke's politics. Everyone in England, from the king downwards, has something valuable to hand on to his children. The king inherits his crown, the nobility its privileges, and the common people their rights and liberties. Each of these three instances of inheritance is consistent with, and indeed bolsters up, the others. Every estate of the realm claims what is valuable to it by the same title, and so no estate can have a good reason for quarrelling with another. Each part of the realm is supposed to realise that, in denying its privileges to any other order, it begins to undermine its title to its own privileges.

Burke stresses the rights and liberties of all Englishmen as an antidote to the new-fangled doctrine of the rights of man which threatens to cause so much trouble in the world. Burke boxes very cleverly with the whole idea of rights. He recognises that the two questions which have to be answered above all others about rights are: What are they? and Where do they come from? Natural rights are vulnerable to those questions. One of the real problems of natural rights theory is always knowing where to draw the line. Most lists of natural rights would include the rights to life, liberty and property, but why stop there? Why not natural rights to a whole host of other things, until the list gets very long? A list of natural rights which included everything that anybody had ever thought of as a natural right would be very long indeed. The problem would then be to decide which was a natural right and which was not. This problem simply will not go away whenever natural rights are under discussion, and it is the problem which enables thinkers like Burke to regard natural rights as a rather airy-fairy concept, meaningless when it is not actually dangerous. The motive for making a list of natural rights is nearly always to contrast the rights which men have in principle with the rights which they are being denied in practice, a contrast in which the existing political order always comes out very badly. What Burke cannot stomach is the idea that an existing and successful political and social order should be threatened by belief in a concept of natural rights which is not itself solidly based.

The problem of what natural rights are pales when compared to the problem of where natural rights *come from*. The usual answer is: from God; but this does not really help much, because it is not clear on what occasion God actually made the gift. Holy Writ no more helps the believer in natural rights than it helps the believer in the divine right of kings. As far as one can tell, God gave neither the right to rule for ever nor natural rights to Adam and his posterity. Arguments of some sophistication may be adduced to show that God really means us to have natural rights (Locke's argument is one such example), but the fact remains that, in the absence of positive scriptural proof, these are only arguments. Burke himself has a certain sympathy with the idea of God the giver of natural rights, and as a Whig he cannot altogether ignore Locke, but he defuses the idea of natural rights by saying that they would apply only to men in their primitive, pre-civil state, a condition which men long ago exchanged for living in civil society. The idea that men ought to base their present conduct on what was the case in the mists of time is an absurdity. Of course, men living in settled societies do have rights, but they are rights which are relative to the condition of the society in which they presently live.

Rights, for Burke, are rooted firmly in the processes of a society at a particular moment of that society's development. It is only by looking at rights like that, that Burke thinks a reasonable answer to the two vital questions about rights can be answered: What are they and where do they come from? Established practice tells us what our rights are, and we know where they come from because we have received them as an inheritance from our ancestors. To say this does not mean that Burke is complacent about rights. Rights are not self-sustaining; they have to be defended. Burke's Whiggishness gave him a very keen sense of the vulnerability of rights in the face of executive encroachment. The rights of Englishmen, he thought, were rights of the type which can be easily and safely defended – easily because what they were (and Englishmen's title to them) was so clear, and safely because to defend inherited rights was to reinforce the *status quo*, not to threaten it. Burke also seems to think that there is something about the straightforwardness of the rights of Englishmen which is wonderfully in keeping with the English temper. That temper is phlegmatic and untheoretical as a general rule, naturally resistant to the wilder flights of metaphysical fancy which a belief in natural rights involves. At the same time, English history displays a generous and manly disposition to defend rights won and preserved through the ages. The Englishman in defence of his rights is a patient man whose anger is therefore to be feared, and it is in defence of these real rights, not metaphysical rights, that he is willing to risk his fortune and his life.

BURKE'S DEFENCE OF THE ARISTOCRATIC ORDER

The basis of Burke's defence of aristocracy is a belief in the complication of the social and political order. Burke knows perfectly well that the argument against aristocracy is that it is both expensive and useless. That argument was already commonplace in revolutionary France, and it was to be restated in Tom Paine's celebrated reply to Burke, *The Rights of Man*. The French Revolution is accounted a bourgeois revolution because it attacked aristocracy as an unproductive estate foreign to the body politic. Aristocracy was a consumer, not a producer; the best that could be said for it was that it was decorative. Aristocracy, then, needlessly complicates the social order, and part of the purpose of revolution was to create a social order which would consist of the productive classes only. All early nineteenth-century radicalism was to take up the same cry. The societies of the future were to be simplified societies, societies of the producers only. Societies of the producers, which mean societies of the buyers and sellers of labour, were going to be naturally harmonious societies because everybody was going to work for their living. Cut out the aristocratic drones and there would be more to go round anyway, and cut out the aristocratic influence on the state and the state would be more in keeping with the productive spirit of the age. It was this expected simplification of societies which made the first half of the nineteenth century the great seedbed of social theory, because it seemed to be the case that, as societies simplified themselves, their inner nature could be more easily understood.

Burke understood the connection between social science and political radicalism as well as anyone, because on the face of if there was no denying that the simpler societies were the easier they were to understand, and from there it was only a short step to claiming that what was easily understood could just as easily be reconstructed from the beginning. Hence Burke's insistence on the complex nature of societies. In Burke's political thought, complication was just another way of saying that existing societies were miracles of social integration. Societies consisted of different parts which all seemed to work together to produce what we call the life of a society. All the parts are functional, and that is why Burke places so much emphasis on the *function* of aristocracy. If aristocracy has its part to play in the functioning of the whole, then it cannot be true, as aristocracy's radical enemies claim, that aristocracy is redundant because it does nothing. In England, aristocracy's function is the preservation of the constitution of English government and the preservation of the constitution of English society. Admittedly, aristocracy does not exactly earn its own living directly, but its function of keeping English society and politics in working order means that in practice it more than earns its keep.

Of course, Burke's argument is not altogether new. Livy's history of the early Roman republic contains just such an argument as Burke's in the parable of the belly and the limbs. The Roman commons had seceded to the Sacred Mound because they seemed to do all the work while the Roman patricians seemed to do nothing but glut themselves on the labour of the poor. Menenius Agrippa persuaded the commons to rejoin the city by pointing out that the patricians were like the belly which, by digesting the food, sent out strength to the working limbs of the body; therefore the belly-patricians were not idle at all but performed a vital function for the good of the whole. Menenius's argument is subtler than it may seem to be. He does not claim any kind of intellectual or moral superiority for the patricians; they are not the head or the brains but perform just another physical function like the limbs. Burke is claiming more than that for his ruling class. They exercise an overall ruling function very like what Aristotle meant when he said that the intelligence naturally rules the rest of the body, both in the individual man and in the body politic. Burke seems to be saying that his ruling class performs the most vital function of all.

Behind Burke's defence of the ruling class lies an extremely functional view of political and social institutions. It is not enough for Burke that political institutions simply exist, or that social stratification simply continues to be. Political and social institutions exist to solve the problems which arise naturally out of the common life of men in society. Burke is remarkably forward-looking in pointing to the essentially efficient nature of institutions. Its institutions are all that a society has going for it when problems do arise. This the French have fundamentally failed to understand in their own present troubles. Instead of using their inherited institutions and practices to solve their problems they have chosen to regard their ancient institutions as themselves constituting part of the problem. Being radical means digging up the roots and starting again, and that includes digging up the roots of old institutions and discarding them, thereby discarding the only means available for coping with national problems. In doing this the French fail to realise that they are compounding the problem in the worst possible way. Government's policies may come and go, but the implementation of those policies relies on tried and trusted institutional procedures. If Burke is right, then it is the construction of institutional procedures, and of the legitimacy for those procedures, which is the most difficult of all political tasks. If the construction from scratch of new political institutions is so difficult, then what chance is there that new institutions will in the near future live up to the expectations placed upon them? Institutions are only legitimate if they can deliver, and institutions with teething troubles can hardly be expected to do that. Burke does not say so, but one of the implications of his view of what the revolutionaries in France are up to is that there is going to be a good deal of bickering in the future about the nature of France's institutional forms, and a political system bedevilled by endless questions about the legitimacy of its own institutional forms is not going to be a political system which is likely to produce good governing decisions.

Burke has in fact got a very sure grasp of what happens when a polity changes its institutions. He knows that the political institutions of a society are in a sense the property of, or in the keeping of, a particular power group. Pleas for changing a society's institutions are therefore open or disguised attempts to change one power group for another. Burke's argument against ever doing that is straightforward. How does one know that a new power group will do as well by its society as the old power group did? All the indications go in the other direction. The chances are that the new, would-be power group consists of exactly those people who erroneously think that it is easy to reconstruct a state from scratch, and they will by definition be a group from outside the old power system. Men from nowhere have their work cut out. Not only are they likely to be politically inexperienced, but they have set themselves the most difficult of all political tasks, the construction of new political institutions. Even the most experienced statesman would baulk at that, but France offers us the spectacle of entirely inexperienced politicians setting themselves a task which Burke thinks even the most skilful politicians would avoid if they could. To ask an out-group both to invent a new set of political institutions and then to make them work is nothing short of a recipe for political disaster.

BURKE'S WHIGGERY

Burke is notoriously hard to categorise politically because he began his political life as a Whig and continued to regard himself as a Whig to the end of his life. Whiggism was what we would call 'on the left', however vaguely, in the eighteenth century, yet Burke has been identified with conservatism ever since and we are used to thinking that conservatism is 'on the right'. The difficulty partly arises from Burke's use of arguments from history to bolster up his own political positions. We have become accustomed to thinking that political positions which look to history for their legitimations must somehow always be right-wing positions, but that was not necessarily the case in late eighteenth-century England. It needs to be emphasised that, in eighteenth-century England, it was the liberty-loving Whigs who typically used arguments from history. It was the Whigs who 'invented' the idea of the ancient English constitution which the king could not alter at will. Toryism was connected with the idea of the divine right of kings and therefore with Jacobitism. That meant an obsession with who was *really* king at the moment, and that in its turn meant he whose father had been king before him. We have become so used to the kind of Burkean argument for monarchy, which emphasises the long possession of the Crown in a particular family as the legitimising factor in monarchy, that we have tended to forget the stress put on the presentness of kingship by eighteenth-century Jacobites. What Burke did was to provide Whig arguments for Tory things. Of course, the Tories had always defended the ancient institutions of Church and King, and of course one of the reasons for loving Church and King was that they were ancient, but Tory arguments had always rested on present legitimacy. Burke's arguments were instantly available to defend historically the established institutions of England, and that is in fact how Burke's arguments were used by those calling themselves Tory in the nineteenth century. The defence of unreformed England became an invitation to love the ivy which covered the walls of institutions which stood their ground against the Whiggish and radical clamour for innovation.

In his own day, Burke the Whig was often accused of inconsistency. Burke led the Whig charge against the policies of George III's government which eventually alienated the American colonists into their Declaration of Independence. As MP for Bristol, whose commercial prosperity depended on its trade with America, Burke could hardly avoid some involvement in American affairs, but that does not explain the completeness of his commitment to the Americans' cause. How, then, could such a consistent defender of American liberties turn almost overnight into the scourge of the liberties of the French? Was not the French Revolution a continuation of the democratic revolution which had already taken place in America? Some of Burke's friends on the Whig side insisted that Burke had turned his coat. The accusation always rankled with Burke, and he always insisted that there was no inconsistency between his position on America and his position on France.

Perhaps we should look into how the Americans saw their own cause against the British government to understand how deeply Whiggish Burke's own position on America was. For as long as they could, the Americans confined their struggle with the British government to matters internal to the British constitution. The American case long remained the case of Englishmen living abroad asking to be treated exactly as Englishmen at home were treated. Crossing the sea to America could no more vitiate the rights and liberties of Englishmen than could the crossing of a county border in England. All the Americans said they wanted was for their government to be left in the condition it had been in before the beginning of the Seven Years War (what in America were called the French and Indian Wars) in 1757. The British government's determination to raise new taxes to pay for American defence after 1763 seemed to the American colonies to be the thin end of a very thick wedge. The war had come close to bankrupting Britain, so who could tell whether or not Britain was going to tighten the fiscal screw on America to get the British Treasury out of its difficulties. Americans had a very exact sense of the open-endedness of taxation once it has begun, and so they sat back on their ancient prescriptive right not to be taxed much at all. Seen from the British point of view, taxing America for its own defence could only seem to be reasonable. Americans were not even being asked to pay for the whole of the cost of defending the thirteen colonies, and, besides, nothing is for nothing in the world of politics, so why should Englishmen living in America get for nothing what Englishmen living at home had to pay for?

So far, the debate about American taxation had taken the course of an ordinary dispute about finance, a dispute of the kind with which English political history was littered. What threatened to take the dispute out of the ordinary political arena into the more dangerous area of political principle was a hardening of the theoretical positions of the protagonists. Each side felt itself forced by the other to couch its position in the terms of fundamental right. The British government insisted on the absolute right, by parliamentary sovereignty, to tax America, however much that right might be attenuated in practice, while the Americans insisted on the principle that they could not be subject to any new taxation without the right of representation in the imperial Parliament. What was particularly galling to a thinker of Burke's temperament was that the British government probably had no more intention of taxing America to the hilt than the Americans had of wanting to put themselves to the trouble and expense of sending representatives to Westminster. As the dispute dragged on, Burke could see both sides finally taking up positions of right from which no retreat was possible, and, as Hegel was later to say, between equal rights force decides. Burke always said that the language of abstract right applied without a care for the circumstances in which that language is used is bound to lead to fatal consequences. The statesman looks to what is reasonable in the circumstances and leaves the dispute about the exact boundaries of rights to the schools, for there only may they be debated with safety.

There is an exact parallel between Burke's view of the rights question in the American and French cases. In both, it was the assertion of abstract right which caused the trouble. In the case of America, it was the assertion of the essentially abstract right of the British government to tax America by the principle of parliamentary sovereignty which led the Americans into their assertion of the equally abstract right of no taxation without representation. The forms which these two opposed assertions of right took were abstract in the sense that they were new, thought out in the protagonists' heads in defiance of established practice. Each, in its way, was an assertion of right which would upset the present state of things, and the tragedy of America for sympathetic observers like Burke was that he could see both sides in the dispute slowly but inevitably backing themselves into theoretical corners from which there was no escape without losing face. As a good Whig, Burke could see that the end result of denying the Americans the rights they thought they should enjoy as Englishmen would be that they would claim their rights not as Englishmen but as *men*. That was the most abstract form which the assertion of human rights could take, because the rights of man, coming as they did from no specific political and social order, threatened every existing social and political order. And so on to the French Revolution, where the whole of the existing social and political fabric of old Europe was threatened by the assertion of rights of so abstract a kind that a whole new set of social and political institutions would have to be created in which these new-fangled rights could be embodied.

Burke's claim to consistency over America and France is therefore a good claim. The cases of the American and French Revolutions both showed what could happen if political problems were not to be resolved within the existing framework of government. Both, in Burke's eyes, represented failures to exercise adequate political skills (and one of the reasons why Burke does not mention America in the *Reflections on the Revolution in France* is that he knows in his heart of hearts that the American case is one of those occasions, no doubt infrequent, in which the ruling class in England failed to exercise those political skills which comprised so large a part of its *raison d'être*). Again, Burke cannot lay much emphasis on the French nobility's failure to make its constitution work by reforming it, because he realises that old Europe is going to need all the allies it can get to combat the French Revolution, the French aristocracy included. Therefore he cannot say too openly that the French aristocracy has failed its own constitution, and therefore its own nation. Any example of ruling class failure is damaging to Burke's own case for government by a wise ruling class, and so it should come as no surprise that he plays the whole theme down. In his account of the causes of the French Revolution Burke is therefore obliged to concentrate on the part played by abstract and alien ideas, taking it for granted that the primary cause of the revolution is ideology of the Rousseauist kind. The only difference between the French and American cases is that the French Revolution began in the name of an ideology, while the Americans were eventually forced into ideology which made them revolutionaries.

423

Burke writes about the French Revolution in a classically rhetorical prose which can sometimes be irritating and sometimes bewitching, and it is important not to be swayed by Burke's eloquence into missing the finer points of what is really a massively commensensical political theory. There can be no doubt that there are weaknesses in Burke's arguments, and nobody had a surer eye for them than Tom Paine in *The Rights of Man*, but Burke's account of what kind of politics a tradition of constitutionalism makes possible and requires has never been equalled. The limitations of Burke's political thought are in fact the limitations of a system of politics so conceived. It was to remain a moot point whether a political theory as inward-looking as Burke's could continue to survive long in the age of outward-looking radicalism which Burke's own theory was designed to stifle at birth.

NOTES ON SOURCES

Hume's *Treatise of Human Nature*, Book III, 'Of Morals', is forbidding for non-philosophers. Hume's *Essays* (various editions) are a much easier route to Hume's political thinking, but Hume's political thinking does not quite make sense without his philosophy. Hume's *History of England*, 6 vols, is hard going but is worth it for the appendices. Duncan Forbes, *Hume's Philosophical Politics* (1975, and various reprints), is the best thing in print on Hume. Burke's *Reflections* is thoughtfully introduced by C.C. O'Brien in the Penguin edition. F. O'Gorman, *Edmund Burke: His Political Philosophy* (1973), is a good introduction. Also valuable are A. Cobban, *Edmund Burke and the Revolt Against the Eighteenth Century* (1960), and C. Parkin, *The Moral Basis of Burke's Political Thought* (1968).

Part VI

THE RISE OF LIBERALISM

19

THE RISE OF LIBERALISM

LIBERALISM AND ENLIGHTENMENT

There is an idea of liberalism which would have us believe that at a given date liberalism was complete. Certain dates, 1789 for example, or 1848, or 1859 (the date of the publication of J.S. Mill's *On Liberty*) have been strongly canvassed as the moments when the doctrine of liberalism became recognisably itself. Some even go as far back as John Locke's *Second Treatise of Civil Government* and see the bare bones of liberalism there. (And 1789 is at least two dates, the date of the French Revolution and the date of the ratification of the Constitution of the United States.) What does not seem to be in doubt is that liberalism as a set of ideas, and as a first, tentative approach to the treatment of political and social problems, began in the Enlightenment. So much is obvious. What is not so obvious is the connection, mentioned before, between the advance of Enlightenment and the development of the modern state. Liberals, it is commonly said, are suspicious of the state, yet the period of liberalism's triumph is also the period of the triumph of the modern state. Chaste liberals choose to look upon this connection as a paradox: how odd, they say, that liberalism, and liberalism's chief enemy, should emerge into full view together. The paradox can be pointed up more sharply. Both liberalism and the modern state are commonly regarded as benchmarks of modernity, yet there seems to be some kind of tension between the two. Are liberalism and the modern state reconcilable?

The problem is partly a problem of history. It is often said that liberalism takes a 'negative' view of the state in contrast to some ancient and modern political theories which ascribe a morally 'positive' and heavily interventionist role to the state. What must be emphasised is that the liberal state could only be negative in an ideally liberal society, with an ideally liberal economy, and with a citizen body which actively chose to act in the ways which liberals expected. All the emphasis on liberalism's supposedly negative view of the state – the 'nightwatchman state', for example – tends to obscure the very obvious fact that, as a reform programme, liberalism was always going to have to come to terms with state power as the agent of liberalism's own plans for economic, social and political transformation. (We should never forget Enlightenment's long love affair with the enlightened despots.) Any reforming programme with any realistic hopes of success must have the strengthening of the state very near the top of its political agenda: state power equals the capacity to change the world.

One of the things which reconciled liberals to state power was that they thought that the worlds of society and economy were going in liberalism's direction anyway. The power of the state would therefore be used more sparingly than would otherwise have been the case. The reforming programme consisted largely in allowing societies to advance according to their own autonomous laws of development in so far as that was compatible with the state's need to raise a revenue to provide for law and order and for national defence. In practice, this meant dismantling all of those now dated legal mechanisms of economic and social control which modern societies had inherited from the past. These inherited structures were partly medieval and partly mercantilist, laws about how industrial production should be organised and laws about how international trade should be carried on. This was a vast reforming programme, because every European country was cluttered with legally entrenched vested interests, many of them local. Liberals had to find an agency which could roll back centuries' worth of deeply embedded social and economic controls, and that agency could only be the state.

Nationalism helped. In some of its versions nationalism was the natural ally of liberalism, as was an efficient system of railways, posts and telegraphs, and uniformity of weights, measures and currency. Anything which emphasised centrality as opposed to locality, the nation-state as opposed to local and provincial loyalties, helped the new against the old. In economic terms this meant the creation of truly national markets, which suited the state very well. Land had always been difficult to tax, while trade, and especially international trade, was easy by comparison. What the centralising modern state did was to create a tax base for itself (though all thought of an income tax was well in the future). Centralisation and taxation reinforced each other, and this had the effect of putting liberals on the side of centralising governments because without them economic life would have been confined to production for markets which were effectively local markets. Tom Paine, for instance, a liberal in economics, argued for the new federal Constitution of the United States on the grounds that, if left to themselves to regulate commerce, the individual states would develop the system of putting up tariff barriers against one another to such an extent that there would be no national economy in the United States at all. The Revolution did the same thing for France. Before the Revolution there were said to be fourteen different customs posts on the road from Calais to Paris, so that when the fish arrived it was too expensive to buy and too stinking to eat.

This often piecemeal dismantling of the ancient structures of authority was made possible only by a shift in the way men looked at authority itself. Using the state's power to dismantle inherited structures of authority may seem in retrospect to have been an extremely optimistic, not to say hazardous, thing for liberals to do, but liberals had good reason to feel confident about a deregulated future. The new moral and social sciences of the Enlightenment all seemed to speak with the same voice when they said that human life was over-regulated. What Adam Smith called the 'hidden hand' was really only shorthand for the enlightened and liberal belief in a series of naturally interlocking harmonies in the human world. This was the great intellectual revolution which had been brewing since Newton. The old commonsensical idea that if left to themselves men will get up to mischief was on the point of being scrapped in favour of the idea that, on the whole, human life could get on pretty well if left to itself. Crucial in this shift was the discovery that social science might be true. Montesquieu pointed the way forward with his suggestion that the human law-giver was just one source of law, and not the most important, among a whole series of law-givers, the first of which was climate. For the first time the inherent ambiguities in traditional ideas of law began to be explicated in a sociologically systematic way.

The nature of this change must be understood very clearly if liberalism in general is going to make sense. The idea that law, in the sense of norms which determine behaviour, arises spontaneously in a society was not new. Part of the ancient idea of natural law had always been that God's Law could be written in the hearts of men by social experience. Men could come to know God's Law simply by living an ordinary life in an orderly society. (It was in this way that medieval Christians could regard communities of Jews and even Muslims as being not altogether ungodly.) The problem arose when you took God out of the scenario. In what senses could spontaneously arising social norms still be called laws? And in what senses could these laws have any binding moral force? The answer to the second question was implicit in the first. Spontaneously arising social norms could be said to be law-like in two impeccably enlightened senses. First, they did actually arise independently of human will or reflection, just as the Newtonian laws of the universe did; and second, the fact that social behaviour was law-like implied that there was a natural harmony in the social world in the same way that there was a natural harmony in the physical world. Not only that; social harmony, for those who chose to continue to see the hand of God in these matters, was plainly a godly end. In his eccentric way, Hobbes was probably the first to catch a glimpse of the idea that an 'artificial', that is to say entirely man-made, community could still serve the godly end of social peace. (Hobbes is dated in the sense that he gave the human legislator too great a hand in the creation of the conditions which make orderly human living possible.)

Imagine the relief of liberals when they rediscovered that God meant men to live harmoniously with each other after all. In the complete theory of liberalism, notoriously difficult to date accurately, though it was certainly complete by the second half of the nineteenth century, this idea of harmony had been theorised into a system of considerable formal beauty and sophistication.

LIBERALISM AND THE THREE ECONOMIES

Liberalism at its most intellectually coherent moment can best be seen as a structure of three interlocking and dependent economies. I use the word 'economy' here in a slightly old-fashioned sense to mean any system which is well-organised, or tightly organised, so that nothing is wasted. In an 'economy', as in the concept of the 'economy of nature' (the phrase is Darwin's), there are ideally supposed to be no loose ends, everything is meant to fit together without awkward spaces in between. An economy is also supposed to be self-regulating. Economies are supposed to behave in predictable ways and one of those predictable ways consists of the parts of an economy reacting to changes in other parts in such a way that the whole economy keeps its equilibrium; an economy is ideally self-moved and self-correcting. Liberalism, sometimes called 'classic liberalism', is an account of the 'moral' economy, the 'political' economy and the 'international' economy. Again, I use words like 'moral', 'political' and 'international' in a mild way. By 'moral' economy I mean men's relationship with each other in eccentric day-to-day life, which includes at least a part of what we normally understand as a particular national economy (the 'British economy' for instance) and also how government affects that particular national economy (what is ordinarily understood by the phrase 'political economy'). By 'international' economy I mean both what is ordinarily understood – the phrases like 'international trade' or the 'terms of trade' – and also most of what is intended by a phrase like 'international relations'.

The moral economy of liberalism is complex because it has more than a single intellectual source. The complication is further complicated by the fact that those two sources, the natural rights tradition and utilitarianism, are, as we have already seen, potentially contradictory. At their margins at least, utilitarianism and natural rights do not sit easily together, but there is none the less an agreement in the two doctrines about the possibility that individually chosen paths to human happiness can be harmonised with each other. If we take Locke as an exemplar of the natural rights tradition, then we can easily see how his belief in the capacity of human reason to work out unaided that rights imply duties means that most men will exercise their natural rights in the pursuit of happiness with a regard for the duty to respect the rights of others. The utilitarian version of this argument holds that the pursuit of rational self-interest by individuals will, by and large, result in social harmony. Neither Locke nor the utilitarians believe that human beings can achieve social harmony unaided. Both stress the need for *rational* conduct, and this idea of rational conduct is to be understood on at least two levels, one of which is rather grander than the other. On the grander level, human beings are actually expected to work out for themselves what their social duties, that is their duties to other men, are. In the utilitarian case, all that had to happen was that human beings had to recognise that 'pleasure' was alone 'good' for its own sake and pain 'bad'. This was a truth so easily accessible to the meanest intelligence that anybody could be converted to utilitarianism overnight.

Alas, both Locke and the utilitarians had to recognise that men do not always act rationally in the special senses which they attach to the word 'reason'. Locke knows that in their pursuit of happiness men do have a tendency sometimes to treat the rights of others cavalierly, and Bentham in his own way recognises the same thing: human beings sometimes minimise the happiness of others when seeking to maximise their own. These perhaps infrequent cases of irrational behaviour have to be dealt with specially, and, to make this easier, they are given the special name of 'crimes'. A 'crime' can be regarded as a special case of 'pain' deliberately inflicted on somebody who has chosen to pursue his own happiness in a direction forbidden by law. Punishment is also supposed to be a deterrent. Even the criminally inclined, those who by definition are likely to consider acting irrationally, can work out for themselves that criminal behaviour is irrational because, all other things being equal, it will call down upon them the special pains which the law reserves for these cases. The state, which in this context means the formal structure of law-making and law enforcement, exists to repair the natural harmonies when they become a little ragged at the edges.

The state could only do this on the assumption that the cases of raggedness would be exceptional cases. In the liberal view of the matter, the state was to have a watching brief over society but was not to be society's own vital spring. What was it, then, which would enable a society to become essentially self-moved? Liberals, like the ancients, thought that a society was kept in motion by the passions, but the passions in modern dress with most of their anciently pejorative connotations removed. Political theory always had had a down on the passions. It had always been recognised that sexual passion and the desire for more than one's fair share of the world's goods were socially and politically disruptive: a tyrant was somebody who wanted and got more than his fair share of everything. Political theory had learned to distrust the passions very early, and it created a generally unspoken consensus that a world given over to passionate self-indulgence would be an anarchic world. This was a view which seemed to be confirmed by social experience. Ancient and medieval societies allowed themselves bacchanalian holidays from the ordinary processes of social and moral repression; the people were allowed to run riot from time to time on the very clear understanding that when the party was over it really was over. It was easy to see the times of permitted riot as paradigms of what a society would be like if the constraints on the passions were permanently removed. The letting-off-steam effect of carnival showed exactly what lay just below the surface of a society. The passions were fundamentally anti-social: sexual self-indulgence had to be tamed by the friendship of marriage, and all other tendencies to debauch had to be tamed by the twin disciplines of hunger and work. God did a service to social order when he commanded that men get their bread in the sweat of their faces.

In this view of the world, it made perfect sense to back up social taboo and economic custom with the force of the positive law. All sources and systems of authority, formal and informal, social, political and religious, could be seen as being on the same side and as having the same end in view – the repression of the unsociability of the human passions. Of course, it was perfectly possible for sources of authority to see themselves as rivals from time to time, but they would all speak with the same voice in the face of the central problem of ruling the turbulent spirit of man. Except when there were quarrels about jurisdiction, there would not be any good reason to make sharp distinctions between the various forms of social control (and quarrels about jurisdiction would tend to take place at a very high level anyway, between emperors and popes, kings and archbishops). Priest and squire, master and magistrate would all easily see themselves as exercising part of the same function of rulership.

Liberalism changed all that, and an important part of that change was caused by changes in the way men thought about wealth. The state had always been expected to regulate possession through the administration of a legal system. Possession had always been nine-tenths of the law. Before the modern era, political authority had also typically involved itself in the business of getting and spending. Again, there was no good reason why the state should not do that. The state is one of the great economic actors as a buyer of goods and services, and it has an interest in the economic prosperity of its taxable subjects. Beyond that, the state as a regulator of human behaviour could not ignore the fact that cupidity was among the most disruptive of the human passions. Cupidity took the very public form of what we would call economic life, and a wise political authority would do well to keep a very close eye on men who were intent, where they could, to earn much more than an honest living. Liberals like Adam Smith thought of this version of things as decidedly primitive, and as distinctly self-serving. The idea of men prepared to jump on each other's backs every minute of the day for a piece of raw fish might suit the inhabitants of a Hobbesian State of Nature, but it hardly made sense in commercial and opulent societies. These societies, of which Britain was the leading example, seemed to be miracles of voluntary social co-operation through the division of labour. Smith's famous example of the pin-maker in *The Wealth of Nations* was the beginning of a hymn to spontaneously arising social and economic differentiation within a harmonious social whole. Societies appeared to divide themselves naturally into different economic and social functions, and the remarkable thing was that these divided functions supplemented each other. That, as we have had cause to remark before, was the remarkable fact. Different kinds of different human beings appeared to be able to live harmoniously with each other. Indeed, it became possible to *define* a society as the harmonious interplay of very different kinds of human beings living very different kinds of lives without the social whole dissolving into chaos.

It takes something like a leap of the imagination to grasp the difference between the old view and the new. The new view meant that differences between men were socially integrative. The old view that a society was better the more its members were the same was simply overturned. Even Aristotle, to liberals the most attractive of the ancient philosophers, could only tolerate a *polis* containing six different categories of people. Smith was now saying that a perfectly tolerable society, indeed a progressive and opulent society, ought to be constituted of so many types and conditions of men that the old typologies, with their restricted number of classes, could be consigned to the past. The future would be characterised by lots of different sorts and conditions of men living a socially harmonious life together.

As a progressive, Smith could not help asking himself questions about why the progress of society was not happening at a quicker rate. Obviously, the question of progress was connected with the question of the rate of the creation of wealth. We have seen above how enlightened thinking in general had made a connection between the necessary repression of the institutions of rule and the brute fact of economic scarcity. Enlightened thinkers had always thought that the only justification for repression was economic scarcity. Make plenty, and the rationale for social repression would collapse. Thinkers like Adam Smith began to wonder about the reasons why economies appeared to produce too few goods and services to go round. The classic Enlightenment answer to the question of scarcity had been that the new technology had not spread far enough or had not gone deep enough. Reason as science and as technology, in industry and agriculture, would so increase the rate of production that in the not-too-distant future brute necessity would not impinge on men's behaviour in the way that it had in the past. Smith pointed the way ahead by forwarding the claims of another science: political economy. He was the first to point to a truth which has become something of a commonplace in the twentieth century – that it is often the inadequacy of human organisation which causes the trouble, and not just the inadequacy of physical plant used in the processes of production. (A factory with wonderful machines but hopeless management would soon go out of business.) The wonder of Smith's observations on the division of labour in modern industry was that division of labour happened without central direction.

If the division of labour happened without central regulation, then questions had to be raised about the state's economic role. Interference in getting and spending was in some way or other interference in the world of divided labour. What might the effects of that be? Smith's answer was straightforward. Suppose that state regulation of the economy (what we would call the 'political economy') did in fact slow up the business of wealth creation. Smith's analysis of why this should be so works on two levels, one very general and one very particular. On the general level, we can all now see that the attempt by the

433

state to regulate the minutiae of industry and trade is constricting. On the particular level, Smith argued a straight *ad hominem* case. The states of Smith's day were run by aristocratic cliques, just the sort of people who would be unable to see the truths of the new economics if those truths stared them in the face. (And those truths were probably not fully knowable before Smith himself published *The Wealth of Nations*.) These were just the sort of people who were likely to have been educated at places like Balliol College, Oxford (Smith himself was there for a time), where there was no regular plan of study and no study at all of modern subjects like political economy. (What made Lord Palmerston unusual in England was that he was an aristocratic Whig educated at Edinburgh.)

A species of frenetic *laissez-faire* has become so attached to Smith's name that it is worth emphasising that, as far as *laissez-faire* is concerned, Smith thought of economic life as a special case. States as they were in fact constituted in Smith's own day were simply not competent to run economies. Smith himself probably doubted whether states ever would acquire that competence, and he certainly did not think they would acquire it in the foreseeable future. There was nothing specially immoral about state regulation for trade. It just happened to be the case that, from the point of view of wealth creation, regulating trade was a stupid thing to try to do. (Witness the fact that the great 'black' economy of the eighteenth century was smuggling.) Undue state interference in the economy did, however, have one immoral consequence: it meant that more wealth than was fair went to aristocracy – consumers, not producers. The regulation of trade and the taxes on trade created jobs and pensions for the aristocratic parasites on government. Smith had no doubt at all that it was capitalists and labourers who actually created the wealth which all men desired (though hymns to entrepreneurship are notably absent from *The Wealth of Nations*), and he never doubted for an instant that those who did the work deserved the reward. As against this, Smith recognised perfectly well that there were other socially desirable ends besides the creation of wealth which could not be achieved in a society which made wealth creation its only end. Education (Smith was after all a Scot) would not simply appear as if by magic. These would have to be provided by the state, and to do this efficiently the state itself would have to change. The aristocratic sneerers at the vulgarity of trade who tried to get their hands on as much as possible of the indirect profits of trade would have to go. Smith thought that this would probably happen anyway. Political power tended to follow wealth, and he hoped that the decently rich would replace the indecently wealthy at the centre of affairs.

For liberals like Smith, aristocracy reeked of incompetence and corruption. In this we can perhaps see the natural view of a Protestant Lowland Scot who saw, in the failure of the Jacobite Rebellion of 1745, the failure of a system of society and polity inherited from the past. This notion of political *failure*, as we have remarked before, has to be taken seriously. Smith has no doubt that there is a possibility of political failure which is just as real as the possibility of economic failure. It is probably not saying too much to say that the idea of political failure, of the failure of a whole system of politics, *comes from* the idea of economic failure as we find it in Smith. If an economy can underperform, so can a polity. Smith's reaction to economic underperformance is the typically modern reaction of calling for a radically new economic policy. Smith is also modern in another, quite specific, way. He sees that questions of economic policy are inseparable from questions about how a polity is fundamentally constituted. Economic policy is often so deeply woven into the texture of a polity (and into the thinking processes of that polity's ruling group) that to call for radical economic policy changes is the same thing as calling for radical change in the nature of the polity itself.

The question therefore remained: what kind of state were rational men, fully equipped at least in principle with Enlightenment's new learning, likely to give their free consent to? The social contract model of explaining consent now seemed to be very old. The origin of states and societies no longer had to be explained; they just *were*. Gone, therefore, was any idea of original legitimacy of society and the state as it affected the present. This had one theoretical advantage over all the others. It meant that the either/or view of the legitimacy of the state could be discarded. An old-fashioned thinker like Locke spoke as if the state, by which he meant the whole political order, was either legitimate or it was not. There were no halfway houses, no shades of grey. The political order either served the ends for which it was originally created, in which case it was to be supported or tolerated, or it subverted those ends, in which case subjects had the right and perhaps the duty to rebel. It does not take much imagination to realise that these were genuine alternatives only in extreme cases. As the American Declaration of Independence pointed out, most men, most of the time, would put up with defective systems of government rather than pull them down and risk setting up a new system. Things must have come to a pretty pass before rebellion becomes a rational alternative to established authority. Locke has, in fact, very little to say about government in the ordinary course of its getting better or getting worse. He speaks as if most government is legitimate most of the time. The theoretically interesting times may be those in which rebellion is justified – but who wants to live in interesting times?

The fact that, in the future, the question of the origin of society and the state could safely be left to anthropology and history did not rule out the different question of how the present state of things came to be, and how it could best be changed. Origins were one thing, the causes of the present quite another. All liberals were anti-Hobbesians to the extent that they believed that the basis of government was opinion, not force. They were by no means consistent, or even clear, about what they meant by 'opinion', but it was a concept always used as the opposite to force. It seemed a commonsensical enough truth that it could not be armies, militias and such police as there were which kept men to their allegiance, because the ruling part of any state was minuscule when compared to the ruled. In Britain, the occasional but very real panics caused by the urban mob were testimony enough to the frailty of force in the face of even a tiny fraction of the population which temporarily repudiated its ordinary obligation to respect the law. (And we sometimes forget that the Jacobite Rebellion of 1745 was a very close-run thing.) Granted, then, that opinion and not force was the basis of government, then it must surely follow that the nature of government itself was deeply influenced by the prevailing opinions of a society, 'Opinion' here means anything that goes on inside people's heads: religion, morality, culture, tradition and 'public opinion'. Liberalism's sure sociological feel made liberal thinkers very wary of concluding that all of these instances of opinion pulled in the same direction or worked in the same way. There was always likely to be a difference between how 'public opinion' worked and how other aspects of opinion worked. Religion, morality, culture and tradition were part of the social and political landscape in a way that public opinion was not. Other forms of opinion were likely to be static where they were not actually backward-looking, whereas public opinion, and especially enlightened public opinion, could question the present and look to the future.

As reformers, liberals had a vested interest in what enlightened public opinion could achieve in the real world. More was at stake than the success of liberal propaganda, important though that was. Liberals were always committed to the idea that the state did not exist to form men's opinions for them. The long alliance between an intolerant Roman Catholicism and unenlightened despotism, between the king and the rack (Hume put Philip II in the Nero class), warned liberals of the pitfalls to liberty lying in wait if the state concerned itself too much with what went on inside its subjects' heads. Yet liberals were also committed to the view that the legitimacy of government, not to mention its stability, actually depended on what went on in the heads of subjects. How could these two apparently disparate views be reconciled? The liberal answer was simple: government ought to reflect the sum of opinion *already formed*. Government ought certainly to keep out of the business of opinion *forming*. Government certainly ought to *take account of opinion*, but, all other things being equal, government should not meddle with opinion.

How, then, could things ever change? Only in one or two ways. Either the state could actually try to determine what went on in people's minds, either directly or through some specially authorised agency, or opinion could change independently of the state through mechanisms of its own. Liberalism ruled out the first, and so came to rely heavily on the second. Enlightened public opinion would gradually work its way through the other forms of opinion which existed in a society, and, the state being in some sense the emanation if not the creature of opinion, then it followed that the state's own institutions would them-selves change. In liberalism there were to be no 'revolutions from above'. Liberal changes, and especially changes in government institutions, were to come about when liberal society was ready for them. In practice, this meant that political change had to wait for a formed body of influential enough public opinion actually wanting a particular change to happen, and being able to see clearly enough what the benefits of that change would be. The battle for the public mind would be long and arduous, but it was worth it because nothing could be worse than forcing political changes on a public which did not actually want them. This accounts for the apparent 'conservatism' of liberalism, its apparent willingness to allow institutions and practices to wear thin. Governments calling themselves liberal, or governments seeing themselves as part of the liberal tradition, will always be careful to 'carry opinion with them' when they set out to change aspects of the given world. This attitude is of a piece with liberalism's general attitude to the use of force. The more that can be done through opinion, the less that has to be done through force. The more a state has opinion on its side, or a large section of opinion, or the more advanced part of public opinion, then the more a state and a society can be changed through that society's own consent.

Of course, that scheme of things is attended by great dangers from liberalism's own point of view. Minimal though the liberal state is meant to be, it is none the less one of the most powerful social actors – perhaps the most powerful. How can a great social actor not influence the formation of opinion? This would be a special problem in states with liberal governments implementing programmes of liberal reforms. Reforming programmes tend to develop a momentum of their own, from which the idea comes that more of the same is always good. The further a government goes down the reforming path, the more it carries opinion with it, the stronger the general conviction will become that more reform is good. Government can also form opinion in a more indirect way. Reforms have social consequences, otherwise there would be no point in them. Liberals, committed as they are to the view that the proper place for opinion to arise is in society, not the state, are bound therefore to believe that reform, and especially social reform, will in fact change opinion.

In practice, this may not be quite the dilemma that it appears to be. Liberals do not, after all, believe that all opinions are as good as each other (though they would deny the right to exist of almost no opinions at all). How, then, is one to tell which opinions are good and which not so good? Here liberals believe fearlessly in the winnowing effect of public debate. 'Debate' means more than formal debate in public meetings and political assemblies. Rather, formal debate comes about as the result of the prior formation in society of different bodies of opinion. Liberals have no doubt about why this happens. Different interests in a society produce different opinions. That had been a commonplace of political thought since time out of mind, and its consequences for modern societies had been definitively explicated in *The Federalist Papers*. Liberals had come to expect that in free political systems, that is to say political systems allowing political representation, political opinion would divide into parties of movement and parties of order roughly corresponding to the divide between liberalism and its right-wing opponents. This divide is no more than the difference between two umbrellas under which lots of different opinions seek shelter. This plurality of different opinion comes about as the result of society's own plurality of many different social groups. Of course, not every group opinion is opposed to every other group opinion, but it is hard to find a group opinion which hasn't got its opposite somewhere. Liberalism sets great store by this competing plurality of opinion. If the liberal temper is optimistic, it is in the conviction that good opinion will drive out bad: Gresham's Law in reverse. Exposure to the light of day will often be enough to drive out bad opinion, especially where that opinion is based on blatant self-interest. The classic case is the repeal of the English Corn Laws which, to the great advantage of the landed interest, forbade the import of corn into England until the domestic price had almost reached starvation level.

In the interest of national harmony, liberalism did not expect all of its victories to come overnight. Liberalism expected to be able to live with its opponents at least for a time by conceding that those opponents were entitled to political representation. The politics of representation was to be, above all, politics carried on through enlightened public debate on the great issues of the day. One of those issues was to be the nature and extent of political representation itself. The American Revolution had put political representation at the head of the list of possibilities for the creation of political legitimacy in post-absolutist politics. The French Revolution complicated matters by adding a distinctly democratic thrust to the idea of political representation in a world which was still capable of thinking that the principle of representation and the democratic principle were different principles.

437

The modern world has become so used to the elision of democracy and representation that it is easy to forget that at one time they were thought of as alternatives. The pre-modern world was full of the idea of political representation, but it was left to the modern world to discover that the unit which ought to be represented was the individual human being. Pre-modern ideas about representation were clear that what had to be represented in a nation's councils was what really counted for something in the nation's ordinary life. Property, therefore, was entitled to representation, and so were rank and all kinds of incorporated privilege. Communities like boroughs in England were represented in their corporate capacities in parliamentary assemblies, and they naturally chose as their representatives those who really mattered in the corporate life of the town. Much of the feeling that representation ought to be corporate representation was still alive in America when the government of the states and the federal government was being remodelled. There was sharp debate even in a very 'democratic' state like Massachusetts about whether the unit of representation ought to be the individual grouped into constituencies, or the chartered towns and ancient counties. The matter was resolved in favour of representing individuals, grouped at national level into congressional districts, but this was as much a consequence of the circumstances prevailing in America after the War of Independence, when it was difficult to prevent the right to vote from becoming widespread among a successful revolutionary people.

Even in America (perhaps one should say especially in America), the granting of widespread democratic rights was attended by considerable, if unofficial, lack of enthusiasm. *The Federalist Papers* make it clear only just between the lines that, for those with eyes to see it, there were to be important corporate-looking representational presences within the new federal political system. Not only were the individual states to be represented in the Senate in their capacity as states (senators being originally elected by the state legislatures), but it is also possible to see a corporation-like representation in the complex system of interest representation which the *Papers* predicted would obtain in the politics of the United States after the new Constitution was ratified. And it needs no stressing that these corporation-like elements were built into the political system to act as a counterweight to any dangerously radical and levelling tendencies which might be inherent in the thorough-going democratic principle of one man, one vote.[1] The unofficial corporatism of the American system of representation worked remarkably well as a substitute for and as an antidote to the allegedly levelling tendencies of all democracy, but it was difficult to copy the American experience in the France of the French Revolution for the very simple reason that the French Revolution was made to put an end to the power of corporations themselves. When the Estates General met to consider the nation's difficulties in 1789, the first great issue was whether the Estates should deliberate and vote as the separate estates of Church, nobility and people, or whether they should all meet together. The Third Estate's insistence that the Estates General should meet as one was the first revolutionary act, the prelude to the time when corporate distinctions between Frenchmen would be abolished and every Frenchman would become an equal citizen before the law. It was in these circumstances that the civil egalitarianism of Rousseau's *Social Contract* was to exert its greatest appeal, and it was as a consequence of this moment of democratic levelling that conservative Europe after 1815 looked with such horror upon democracy. Representation might be one thing, but democracy was quite another.

Liberalism was neither radically democratic nor conservative. What kind of representation was liberalism to go in for, corporate or individual? Liberalism's own origins in Enlightenment individualism meant to point to individual representation, but liberalism's stress on the connection between freedom and rationality was enough to give liberalism second thoughts about democracy. Democracy, in those early days, did not just mean choosing between different parties canvassing different policy options; it also meant making important choices about what the system of government men lived under should be like. Liberalism was nothing if not progressive, and the reform of governing institutions, in Church and state, was the first item on its political agenda. Choosing between electoral alternatives was considered to be a highly rational activity, but questions about national policy were as nothing in difficulty when compared with questions of national policy. It is one thing to choose what government should do, but quite another to choose what government should *be like*. Learned men had been discussing this last question since Plato and were not yet all agreed. How foolish, then, to pretend that everyman could reasonably be called upon to make his own decisions in such a high and complex matter, especially in an age where everyman was not even likely to be literate.

Caution was therefore to be the liberal watchword where extension of the franchise was concerned. Liberals should never forget that theirs was a reforming programme, not an accomplished fact, in a world which was still largely unregenerate. A too hasty extension of the franchise could only benefit liberalism's own enemies to the left and to the right. Liberals did not take a dewy-eyed view of humanity in general. Their sense of history taught them that when aristocracy had been in control of the state it had always used that control to enrich itself, and there was no reason to suppose that a mass working-class electorate would not see its control of the state, if it ever got it, in its own interest as a class. That, of course, implied a working-class consciousness of a kind which socialist thinkers like Marx and Engels were predicting would only develop in the future. In the meantime, universal suffrage, or something like it, could only benefit aristocratic and conservative forces in societies which were still on the whole deeply deferential. A working class consistently voting for its aristocratic superiors would confine liberalism to the middle class who were its original adherents, making it a sectional interest unlikely ever to come to political power by democratic means. This mattered to liberals, because liberalism's own origins in Enlightenment meant that liberals never gave up the enlightened hope that there was a system of political belief which could engage the loyalty of all thinking men. Extension of the franchise would have to keep pace with the extension of popular education, so that the newly enfranchised would be able to judge fairly liberalism's claims to be a belief system capable of commanding respect through all sections of society.

This caution in the face of democracy fitted well with Enlightenment's own cautious optimism about politics. Liberalism's reformist but not revolutionary temper emerged easily from the enlightened view of human reason. At first, reason was bound to be the privilege of the few, and in this sense it could be looked upon as essentially an inherited privilege in circumstances of very restricted access to the means of education. The spread of education meant converting a privilege into a right for everybody, part of liberalism's programme of ridding society of all the vestiges of inherited privilege and so opening the career to the talents. This was going to take a long time, and in the meantime it was well to keep in place those elements of corporate representation, like the British House of Lords, which might be useful in the near future if the craze for democratisation produced universal suffrage too quickly.

Liberals could claim that this was a scheme of government by consent in a very special sense. Reform meant reform of the institutions of government, and in an age of increasing democratisation that meant that more and more people in liberalising societies were to be given the opportunity to make their voice heard in the debate about how a society ought to be governed. This was real, ongoing consent, not the pretend or watered-down implied consent of social contract theory. It has been pointed out before that one of the weaknesses of social contract theory, at least in its traditional Lockian form, was its 'all-or-nothing' quality: either a system of government was legitimate or you rebelled. Consent could therefore be assumed if citizens were not actually gathering in the streets to string up their governors. Liberalism took a much more realistic view of consent. Ideally it might be true that a rational man would only consent to a rationally organised system of government designed by himself, but that was an impossibility. The next-best thing, and it was a very good thing indeed, was that from time to time the governed were to be given the opportunity of registering their satisfaction or dissatisfaction with the way their system of government was being improved. The assumption was that the better things became, the greater would be the degree of rational consent available to a system of government. In effect, liberals saw the consent of the governed and the idea of rational progress as entailing and implying each other.

A risk-free scheme of politics was no part of the liberal view of the world. The scheme of institutional improvement meant that there had to exist in every society a sovereign power capable of over-ruling the practices of centuries and of remodelling institutions from a past which in most countries was very long indeed. Constitutional reform, for that is always what it amounted always to, implied in most cases a government which could constitution-ally, that is legitimately, overthrow existing constitutions. Constitution-making became one of the great spectator sports of the nineteenth century. There were obviously dangers here, especially when one begins to look at constitution-making from the perspective of Anglo-Saxon, that is to say British and American, constitutionalism, or even from the constitutional point of view which is as old as Aristotle. Constitutions are supposed by many to put a check on government, setting limits to the exercise of governing power and prescribing the channels in which that power may legitimately flow. There was no having it both ways. Either a constitution was alterable by political will or it was not; the government of the day either had the right to change the constitution or it had no such right at all. There were, of course, ways available of clouding the issue, the favourite being the English Whiggish device of pretending always to be *improving* the constitution of England without at the same time altering its 'fundamental character', whatever that meant. Nobody, and certainly not liberals, could reasonably oppose improvement, because improvement was progress by another name. Sensitive as they always had been to the idea of limitation of the power of government, liberals were aware that they were in a quandary as constitution designers. Suppose that, one day – and that day might come soon in an age which had learned quickly how quickly things could change – the exercise of legitimate governing power would come to be used for fundamental constitutional changes which pointed in a different direction, and perhaps in the opposite direction, to the way liberals hoped polity and society would develop. Suppose, for instance, that the constitutional power which governments had to alter the constitution were to be used, in a future era of working-class suffrage, in the pursuit of socialist ends. Liberals were entitled to dread that possibility, and part of that dread came from the honest perception that constitutionally they would have no cause for complaint, provided only that some future socialist government stuck closely to the constitutional rules. Liberals, like Machiavelli and Montesquieu before them, knew perfectly well that constitutional rules could continue to be respected long after the spirit of a constitution has departed. And besides, if constitutionalism was to consist solely in the observation of constitutional forms, then Philip II of Spain, famously a stickler for the rules, would become the ideal constitutional monarch.

The risk was there, but it could be minimised. In England, the minimisation took the form of the importation from America of the virtue of constitutional delay. Half-consciously no doubt, Englishmen began to look at their own very different constitution through something very like the eyes of American constitutionalism. The American Founding Fathers had deliberately written a constitution which could only be altered through a ponderous and difficult procedure (and if they had had the world entirely to themselves they would probably have written a constitution which could not have been amended at all). Even ordinary congressional legislation was so hedged around with constitutional procedures that pressures for delay and for obstruction could be brought to bear at any stage of the cumbersome legislative process. In England, the legislative process had always been supposed to be simple by comparison, but under democratic pressures a virtue came to be detected in procedural complexity. Those same democratic pressures which had caused the Founding Fathers to write the politics of involved procedure into the American Constitution caused eyes wary of the full implications of democracy to seek out an analogous delaying politics in English legislative procedures. It must again be stressed that this was only supposed to be a holding operation until the progress of rational reform had had time to work its cautious way through English society and its governing institutions. When the English House of Lords took it upon itself to extend its considerable delaying and nullifying powers beyond their proper time, a Liberal government took it upon itself to curb those powers drastically.

The individualism which is the basis of liberalism has often led to the charge against liberalism that it has a genuine theory of community. Liberal economics (based as it is on the free choice of individuals) and liberal political theory (based as it also is on the free choice of individuals) are often said to fail to provide a coherent set of reasons why a liberal society should continue to exist in equilibrium with itself. Much is made, for instance, of the 'hidden hand' of Adam Smith, the supposedly mysterious intervention of a deity miraculously bringing social order out of a seemingly chaotic, because unplanned, social universe. This criticism shows how much of a more ancient view of human nature actually survives into the modern period. The old, commonsensical view that, if left to themselves, the choices which individuals will make will be anti-social choices has never died. Liberalism's critics have always maintained that, as the first political and social theory actively to celebrate the freedom of individual choice, liberalism can only encourage the already anti-social behaviour of human beings. Liberalism seems to its political enemies to celebrate the fact of human selfishness.

This criticism is superficial because it fails to take into account the historical context of the rise of liberalism, and it also fails to take into account the historical dimension of liberal thought itself. It is easy to forget what the aristocratic world was like which liberalism set out to change. Worlds dominated by aristocracies usually make very few claims for themselves as being worlds which suit everybody. (That is what makes Burke's *Reflections* so peculiar.) A world divided between aristocracy and the rest is an 'us' and 'them' world. Neither society nor the polity could be 'ours' in any general sense. The exclusive nature of the world of aristocracy is neatly caught by the use of the term 'society' to mean what Americans call 'high society'. The only 'society' which matters is that part of what we would ordinarily call society which dominates the rest. The same would be roughly true of the economy where the economy was still dominated by agriculture, especially agriculture which was typically dominated either by share-cropping or by tenant farming. That aristocracy should try to engross the great and minor offices of state goes without saying. In circumstances like these, it is easy to see how the great bulk of the people would think, and would be encouraged to think, that social, political and economic affairs had nothing really to do with them.

Liberalism meant to change all that. Liberals intended that the creators of wealth should get almost all of the benefits, and they wanted the state to be responsive to what people felt it should be. No doubt in practice liberals turned out to be keener that capitalists should get their fair share of wealth than workers, and, no doubt, when liberals spoke of the state being responsive to opinion they typically meant enlightened bourgeois opinion. None the less, there was always in liberalism the good intention of breaking down the 'us/them' divide and of creating in its place a society and a polity which would increasingly come to be thought of as 'ours'. What this amounted to was a scheme of material and moral progress. As more and more people were able to drag themselves out of the gutter as a consequence of the advance of modern industry, and as, therefore, it became safe to grant voting rights to ever-increasing numbers of people, a society and a polity would emerge which a larger and larger number of people could genuinely say was theirs because they had a part and a stake in it. A progressive consensus would be created which an increasingly high proportion of a nation's citizens would have good cause to join. The prospect of an even better future was supposed to reconcile people to temporary setbacks in the flow of progress, and would serve to take the really radical edge off demands for social and political change by claiming that changes which were justified in principle could not be expected to happen overnight. Liberalism looked forward to a future when everybody in a particular country would be able to think of themselves as being within the pale, full members of society and polity. A bonus would be the satisfaction obtainable from the reflection that society and polity were good places to be because they were progressive.

Both society and polity would come to be seen as well-run operations, conforming increasingly to the very latest standards of efficiency and order which characterised the best industrial organisation of the day.

For liberals, this meant that for the first time in human history societies would develop in which the rationality of individual human beings would correspond to the rationality of social and political organisation. Rational men would inhabit a rationally organised world, and in that sense the world would become everybody's world. That sense of satisfaction about progress, and confidence in future progress, was supposed to go far to create a spirit of human community. This was to be a world in which authority did not need to clothe itself in fig leaves. Those fit to govern would naturally rise to the top in the competitive economy and in the representative state. Captains of industry would come increasingly to find their counterparts (or their friends) in the offices of government as competence took over from family as the criterion for judging who was capable of running the governing enterprise.

The other great boost to national harmony was undoubtedly a sense of nationalism itself. The twentieth century has seen nationalism turn nasty so often that it can come as a surprise that most nineteenth-century liberals were also nationalists. In the nineteenth century, the connection between liberalism and nationalism was almost always taken as a given, and it is not difficult to see why. If government was going to become truly 'our' government, then being ruled by foreigners made no sense at all. Getting rid of foreign rule was the first step towards getting a government that men could call their own. In fact, this could be a pretty nasty business (even the enthusiastic philhellene Lord Byron found some of the things Greeks did to Turks in the wars of Greek liberation hard to stomach), but if the foreign rulers would not leave of their own accord then the only alternative was war. Most Europeans before 1848 lived under foreign rule: Greeks ruled by Turks, Poles ruled by Russians, Italians ruled by Austrians and Spaniards, Slavs ruled by Germans in the Habsburg lands, and the Irish ruled by the English. The nation-state hardly existed: most Germans were ruled by Germans, but where was the single state of the German nation which a pure nationalist theory demanded? Rule by foreigner, or the division of a nation among many rulers, created resentments without number in the different political units in which men found themselves.

The world in general would become a quieter place, and different political communities would find it easier to live in harmony with themselves, if the world were to be re-divided into genuine nation-states. Then each would live with his own under a native government, so that all the troubles associated with ethnicity would be things of the past. This, like the liberal plans for economies and polities, was a vast reforming programme, implying as it did that almost all national boundaries would have to be redrawn. Liberals tended to assume that, when the boundaries had been redrawn, ideally by agreement though usually by war, the various peoples now living in what were really their own countries would choose to be governed by liberal institutions.

This was a fair enough assumption at the time. Foreign rule was typically unrepresentative where it was not downright brutal, so that all nationalist movements were also movements to reform government as well as movements which intended to form governments of their own. The only viable models for new governments were the democratic republic of the American kind, or constitutional monarchy with parliamentary government (and opposition) of the English kind. There were theoretical alternatives without number to the established governments of the European empires, but there was something reassuring about copying governing systems which appeared to work well in practice. And these new governments were expected to be peaceable. Again, we have become so used in the twentieth century to the connection between nationalism and war that we sometimes forget the vision of world (or at least European) harmony which most nineteenth-century nationalists accepted almost without question. There might have had to be some violence and unpleasantness at the moment when nationalist forces felt themselves strong enough (typically with aid from elsewhere) to challenge what to them looked like an occupying power, but after that all was to be sweetness and light. Successful nationalisms were meant to take the heat out of international relations – if not all of the heat, then the heat which arose out of xenophobia. What reasons would men who all lived in their own countries find for hating foreigners? (All foreigners in one's country would now become tourists, and countries do not fight wars because tourists can be disagreeable.)

The peaceful international economy of peace was to receive a strong reinforcement from liberal economies and liberal politics. Liberal economics begins in Adam Smith with a theory of international trade. Gone was the old mercantilist assumption that, when two partners traded, one was always bound to lose. Mercantilism held that the inequality of trading advantage could be maintained by throwing in the state's power on the winner's side. This is one of the things which soured economic relations between Britain and her American colonies: if one side had to lose in the trade with America it certainly wasn't going to be the mother country. The liberal answer to mercantilism was that it artificially maintained an improper trading advantage and that it retarded domestic economic growth in both the parties. Free trade would change all that. A world economy would develop in which each nation-state would be a vital interlocking part. Adam Smith had spoken about the wealth of *nations*, of different national economies as if they were separate, like more or less autonomous individuals. Mercantilism had taught that individual national competitors were competing individuals in a game in which somebody had to lose. That was the world as Smith found it, but he looked forward to a time when international trade would bring nations closer together in a spontaneously arising co-operative harmony which was more than analogous to the spontaneously arising co-operative harmony arising in domestic economies through the division of labour.

There was nothing idealistic about that vision. All a nation had to do was to consider where its best interests in the future lay. Every national economy was bound to benefit from being able to buy freely in the cheapest markets and sell freely in the dearest. Liberalism, unlike mercantilism, did not see national wealth in terms of hoarded gold. Liberals saw the level of economic activity a the true index of a nation's wealth, especially the level of industrialisation, division of labour, and the accumulation of capital. Nations existing in the new world economy would have plenty of competitive incentive to increase their levels of economic activity and liberals looked forward (like Marxists, though for different reasons) to a time when domestic industrial development would create the appropriate economic conditions for the emergence of just that kind of enlightened bourgeois opinion which was already changing the world in more advanced countries like America and Britain. International free trade meant that the nations would come to see how dependent the prosperity of each was on the prosperity of all the rest. Trading relations would become the new diplomacy in the liberal world order; nations would come to the world market with their wits about them, no doubt, but they did not have to be armed to the teeth.

Ever since Tom Paine's *Common Sense*, there seems to have been some kind of liberal consensus about the inner connection between the nature of a government and its probable foreign policy. Monarchy was always bent on war, and the more absolute the monarchy the more likely it would be to disturb the peace. War was an aristocratic game invented for aristocracies by kings who wanted to keep them occupied and out of mischief. Since Montesquieu, everybody who didn't realise it before knew that the principles which animated aristocracies, honour and glory, were essentially military virtues, and kings and pretenders still frequented battlefields until well on into the eighteenth century. Everybody knew that even the symbols of monarchy included the sword. Kings everywhere liked to have their portraits painted in uniform, and in this the first president of the United States, George Washington, followed the example of the kings. Trading republics and trading constitutional monarchies, on the other hand, had a straightforward interest in good relations with all mankind. No doubt it was always tempting for newly industrialising countries to protect their domestic markets with tariff barriers, but that was essentially a short-sighted view. Instead, nations would come at first to making bi-lateral trade treaties, and the process would continue until the world realised that, in effect, the multitude of trade treaties amounted to one vast common market. More than an analogy prevailed between what was supposed to happen in the national and in the international market. The first step towards national prosperity was the creation of a truly national market, and it seemed to be obvious that the first step towards a prosperous world order was the creation of a truly international market.

Liberals were optimists, but they were not fools. Theirs was a recipe for international harmony on the day after tomorrow, and they no more thought that international harmony would be created overnight than they thought that the creation of a stable and prosperous domestic order was the work of a day. Wars there would still be, but now even the nature of war was to change. The causes of war would at last be easy to determine in a world increasingly organised according to the principles of enlightened self-interest. Wars would now have very specific war *aims*, which the people of the various combatant countries could at least understand even if they did not actively support them. Limited war for limited ends would be the wave of the future. Pan-European wars of the French revolutionary and Napoleonic type would be a thing of the past. After all, historians were still arguing (and are still arguing) about what the revolutionary and Napoleonic Wars were *for*. What made them *worth it*? On what calculations of utility could the human and material costs of the wars be justified? These were hard questions to answer, proof that the revolutionary and Napoleonic wars were not worth fighting at all. Modern war was going to be different (though the American Civil War was a difficult case). Not only was the business of being a soldier about to be thoroughly professionalised on a national basis, but war itself was to be put on a proper business footing. The game had to be worth the candle; war was no longer going to be fun. The civilising mission of colonial wars apart, war was going to be the result of a rational decision to pursue a vital national interest at an acceptable cost. The picturesque aristocratic blundering responsible for the Charge of the Light Brigade would no longer do. War was to be the business of hard-faced measurers of cost-effectiveness and much too important to be left to the generals.

It must again be stressed that, although liberalism sought out natural harmonies in the human world, it expected the world to improve gradually rather than to become perfect. The three economies of liberalism, individual, national and international, displayed only tendencies towards harmony. In practice, liberals expected a good deal of mess. What gave liberals their optimism was that they saw themselves engaged in an effort to push the world in the direction that the world appeared to be heading in naturally. The basis of the liberal faith in the future was undoubtedly economic. In what we have come to call the Industrial Revolution, something had happened which could not be stopped until it had worked its way through every national economy in the world. This became such an obvious truth that even Marxists came to believe it. Capitalism (which as a word had not yet become a term of abuse) and the division of labour did not allow other forms of economic organisation to survive alongside them for long. The better would drive out the worse, the more efficient would drive out the less. There was a very close analogy between the liberal view of the future in economics and the liberal view of the future in ideas. Obscurantist and reactionary opinion would not survive for long alongside the new opinion, based as that new opinion was on reason and evidence. Free trade in the economy found its counterpart in the free trade of ideas. All the new ideas needed was a chance to show what they could do. Liberalism needed a certain level of toleration of opinion to get going; after that liberals could safely argue for a thorough-going toleration of opinion of almost all kinds because they felt convinced that they would always be on the winning side. Liberal opinions could make their way in the world without the rack and the thumbscrew; quite the reverse: given half a chance, those opinions would prevail against the rack and the thumbscrew as rationally organised politics came into being everywhere. The rule of law, by which liberals set great store, would come to replace almost completely the latent violence which in the past had always underpinned the social and political orders.

By the time the nineteenth century was reaching its close, liberalism and violence came to be seen almost as antithetical terms. This was as true at the level of practice as it was at the level of theory. Liberals looked forward to a time when violence as a means of ordering political and social relationships would be a thing of the past. This was to be the case in the relations of individuals with each other, in the workplace, and in the state. Liberals always saw pre-modern societies as inherently violent, dominated as they typically were by aristocracies whose only honest trade was war. This gives a bad example to social inferiors, who would thereby be encouraged to imitate their superiors, albeit on a minor scale. A society ruled by steel-encased ruffians could not expect to be a peaceful society, and if it is true that the relationship between rulers and ruled always tends to invite imitation of that relationship lower down the social scale — between fathers and wives and children, for instance, or between squire and labourer, teacher and pupil, master and man

– then you would expect to find a good deal of unofficial but tolerated violence through-out the social order. In societies in which the hangman and the torturers mediated between subjects and the state and in which public executions were the most spectacular form of public entertainment, it was hardly surprising that there would be a high degree of toleration of violence in private as well as in public life. Liberals were Aristotelian enough to believe that all human action is directed towards some good, or at something which men call good. The use of violence must therefore be directed towards some individual or collective end mistaken for the good, and it was easy for liberals to see how that mistake had arisen. It arose from the ages-old assumption that violence, or the threat of violence, was the only way to bring some kind of order to the affairs of sinful men. Any order among sinful men was bound to be precarious anyway, so violence as a first resort seemed to be the only way to teach sinful man a lesson. It was a lesson which even the most brutish would understand, hence notions like the one which held that the only way to rule Russia was with the knout, an especially devilish kind of whip.

Liberalism, as we have already seen, was intended largely to untangle assumptions like this. Properly considered, violence was disorderly rather than orderly; let the mechanisms of progress take over from the artificially created mechanisms of rules backed by force and it would in time become clear that a form of society and polity would develop which created more happiness all round. Liberals knew perfectly well that liberalism would have to make its way in a largely hostile world, at least to begin with. Violence could not be ruled out overnight from the domestic and international orders. The fact that liberals thought most forms of violence were irrational did not mean that they discounted the possibility of situations arising in which violence, or at least counter-violence, would have to be used. Liberals were therefore keen to limit and control violence, in so far as that was possible, by giving the state a monopoly on violence, as if it were like salt or tobacco. In the ideal liberal society, the only legitimate form of violence would be violence used by the state, under the forms of law, for the detention and punishment of malefactors. All other forms of violence, perhaps even including cruelty to animals, would be outlawed. Something similar was supposed to prevail in the international order. War was to be the last resort after every other means of solving international disputes really had been exhausted, and war had to be fought for specific and limited ends which in the end were worth the means of their accomplishment.

Liberalism was to pay dearly for giving the state a legitimate monopoly on violence. Monopolies tend to make their holders over-possessive, but here was a case in which it was thought to be progressive and civilised to create a monopoly on violence under modern economic and political conditions. The means of violence were becoming more deadly as they came to be mass-produced (though just how deadly only the First World War would show) at a time when doubts about the use of force by the state could only be the monopoly of cranks. Now that the state had become 'all of us', an over-nice conscience could interpose itself between the citizen and his duty to do his bit to save his country. The mass democracy which came out of liberalism manufactured mass armies just as surely as the factories of the liberal economy mass-produced the weapons to arm them. The First World War turned out to be a horror for liberals everywhere. It was not just a question of

447

war's awfulness; anybody could feel that. What was particularly galling for liberals was that the First World War turned out to be one of those wars for which it was very difficult to find a set of rational causes. Not only was it difficult to explain the war in terms of rational calculation, but it was also difficult to conceive, even in principle, of a set of war aims which could justify the scale of the war's slaughter. (It was left to American liberal optimism in the form of President Wilson's Fourteen Points to provide aims grand enough to begin to justify the war's cost.) General war, which Europe had seen a century before, was exactly the kind of thing which liberalism was invented to prevent, but it happened. Different political forces would learn very different lessons from the war when it was over, just as different political forces learned very different lessons while the war was on. Liberalism came out of the war with shell-shock and looked round for ways to repair the damage and stop it happening again; liberalism in the 1920s and 1930s meant more of the same. Not so the awakening forces of European fascism. The solution to problems by violence was again put on the political agenda, and a cult of violence arose to challenge everything that liberalism has ever thought about the world.

NOTES ON SOURCES

Of the general books on liberalism, A. Arblaster, *The Rise and Decline of Western Liberalism* (1984), is probably the best since H. Laski, *The Rise of European Liberalism* (1936).

20

LIBERALISM COMES OF AGE
Bentham and John Stuart Mill

JEREMY BENTHAM

Bentham was born in 1748 into a Tory family at a time when Tories and Jacobites were indistinguishable in the eyes of their Whig opponents. These were not auspicious circumstances for the infant prodigy who was to become one of the great radical thinkers of the late eighteenth and early nineteenth centuries. Bentham went through the ordinary course of education of the comfortable bourgeoisie, first at home, then at Westminster School, and then at Queen's College, Oxford, which he left at the age of fifteen. The very young Bentham was evidently something of a prig, suffering pangs of conscience at the age of twelve at having to sign the Act of Thirty-nine Articles to get into Oxford, and taking Fénélon's *Télémaque* as his role model.

Like other fathers, Jeremiah Bentham wanted his son bred up in his own profession of the law, and so young Jeremy was entered into Lincoln's Inn in 1763, but as things turned out, Bentham was less interested in laws than in legal science. Very early on Bentham conceived a plan of legal science on a vast scale, to which he devoted the whole of the rest of his long life.

Bentham was a radical in the literal sense of going to the root. He thought that all law which had not been thought out from coherent first principles was in fact likely to be founded on nothing. Most law was therefore fraudulent. Law, to adapt an anachronism, was all superstructure with no basis. This was especially true of English law, in which the Daemon of Chicane was as obviously present as any organising principle was absent. English law was a lawyers' racket which needed root and branch reform. Law science was to be understood in the widest sense to include criminology and penology. This last was to connect Bentham's name for ever to the Panopticon, the famous design for a prison in which a single sharp-eyed gaoler could, as the spider at the centre of the web, keep all the prisoners under constant supervision. Parliament shillied and shallied over the Panopticon, eventually buying Bentham off with the considerable sum for those days of £23,000, and the only Panopticon ever built was at Joliet for the use of the citizens of the progressive state of Illinois.

The older Bentham became convinced that a new science of law was impossible to construct using language inherited from unregenerated legal systems. Bentham's later writings are therefore much concerned with the invention of a new legal babble whose superiority to the old is by no means obvious. This did not affect his worldwide reputation as a legal reformer, and when Bentham died in 1832 he was one of the most famous Englishmen of his age.

JOHN STUART MILL

Opinions differ about whether John Stuart Mill was fortunate to be born the son of the Scottish historian, philosopher and administrator James Mill. John Mill was barely out of the cradle (he was born in London in 1806) when his most famous of educations began at James's hands. By the romantic standards then in fashion, young Mill can hardly be said to have had a childhood at all. James Mill appears to have thought that lack of years was no bar to difficult learning of any kind. John Mill first read Bentham (in a French translation) when he was fifteen, having been admitted to the great man's conversation at an even earlier age. Mill never played cricket; instead he had to spend his adolescence being precociously clever at utilitarian ethics, classical economics and lots and lots of history. By the age of twenty Mill probably had more book-learning than most men acquire in their whole lives. This has led some to suppose that Mill's was a 'made mind', or, at the very least, that Mill's education made his mind overly susceptible to outside influences. Mill's writings do show that he had an unusually open mind (the influence of Auguste Comte is the most obvious example), and Mill himself unintentionally emphasises this, partly by his own honesty in acknowledging his sources and partly by wishing the world to think that the work we read under Mill's name is in fact the product of a partnership with his wife, Harriet Taylor. All this is very far from showing that Mill's mind was so open that his brains escaped. What is over-influence in one man is receptiveness in another; besides, an overblown romantic idea of the untutored solitary genius lies behind judgements of Mill's thought as derivative and therefore second-rate.

When he was twenty, Mill experienced the most famous burst of tears in the history of ideas. It is still hard to be unmoved by his account of it in the *Autobiography*. Whether Mill wept for his lost youth or for the loss of his youthful utilitarianism has never been entirely clear, but after the emotional crisis Mill put the education and cultivation of the feelings on the agenda of Philosophical Radicalism in a heroic attempt to disassociate utilitarianism from the unfeeling rationalism which the public mind tended to associate with the treadmill and the workhouse.

At the age of twenty-three, Mill followed his father into the service of the East India Company, and stayed there until he retired in 1858. His was one of the very few voices raised in England against the treatment of the prisoners after the Indian Mutiny was put down. Mill's intellectual energy alone is enough to make him an eminent Victorian. All the cross-currents of the age – romanticism, positivism, political economy, the suffrage question (including votes for women), birth control, socialism (Mill had generous things to say about the Communards) – met in Mill's mind. He was MP for Westminster from 1865 to 1868. Harriet Taylor died the year before *On Liberty* came out in 1859, by which time Mill had established himself as one of the leading social scientific thinkers of the day, and, in a happy phrase, he became the schoolmaster of liberalism. He died and was buried in Avignon in 1873.

Benthamism had a lethal cutting-edge. Its deadlines can best be explained by the political and ideological context in which Bentham originally sharpened his wits. Bentham's fundamental postulate was that those actions, private and public, moral and political, which produce the greatest happiness of the greatest number are good actions. That may sound innocuous enough, but it had profoundly radical implications in its day (and it probably still has almost everywhere in the contemporary world). It implied, for instance, that government should get into the happiness-producing business as quickly as possible, and it also implied that government should have been in the happiness-producing business ever since government had existed. Bentham's 'greatest happiness principle' also implied that, as a matter of fact, most governments since the world began had been in the misery-creating business. Any happiness which government had ever produced was probably produced by accident. Bentham was happy to concede that different forms of government, and their different theorists, had always intended to promote human happiness. After all, Plato had argued in *The Republic* that the just man was always happier than the unjust man, and Plato realised that he would have to demonstrate this if his political philosophy was to win the loyalty of rational men.

So what made the Benthamite version of the happiness philosophy so different? It was partly a matter of Bentham's awareness of the *cost* of human happiness. Bentham's treatment of happiness proceeded along a frank cost–benefit path. What this meant in practice, and especially in political practice, was that somebody would have to pay for the happiness of the others. Political theorists had always tended to neglect this aspect of human living, either because they took the existence of slaves for granted like the ancients, or because they looked forward to a time when human living would be so consensual and harmonious that nobody would really be called upon to pay for the happiness of others. Bentham faced this problem squarely. Benthamism is 'moral arithmetic'. It is about being able to calculate as accurately as one can the total amount of human happiness caused by a particular action, and that calculation has to include the amount of pain which that action also causes. Bentham just accepts as obvious the fact that actions are seldom 'pure', that is produce happiness or pain only. All public actions in a crowded world are bound to work to the advantage of some and the disadvantage of others. Benthamism holds that an action is good if, overall, it produces more pleasure than it produces pain. And actions are very good if the pleasure they produce preponderates over the pain.

The formal Benthamite assumption that there would be losers as well as gainers could not help striking a chord in late eighteenth-century societies. Benthamism did not point its finger at a particular group as gainers and another group as losers. From the Benthamite point of view, it was a matter of indifference who gained and who lost, provided only that the sums came out right and happiness outweighed unhappiness. Societies as they were actually constituted in eighteenth-century Europe certainly tended to benefit social superiors and the rich over the lower orders and the poor. That some had to pay for the convenience of others would have been a truth which nobody needed to be taught. Now here was Bentham reiterating that same truth at the level of moral and political theory, but with the important proviso that moral and political theorising was necessarily indifferent to the question of *whose* happiness was actually being increased. That would have given pause for thought. In the eighteenth-century present, it looked as if society and the state were organised in such a way that a small, superior group seemed to get most of the benefits and rewards, while the much larger group of the lower orders seemed always to come off worse. Yet Benthamism insisted that each and every human being should only count as one in the sum of happiness and misery. Societies as they actually were seemed to be constituted on the very opposite principle to the greatest happiness: a small group's happiness was attended to the whole time, whereas the happiness of the vast majority was consistently neglected.

It was this consistent neglect of the happiness of the vast majority of their subjects which made Benthamism the enemy of all established governments. Established governments and established societies were manipulated by 'sinister interests' (a favourite phrase of Bentham's), closet powers operating behind the façade of seemingly respectable institutions. Bentham was no stranger to the idea of human selfishness. The Benthamite assertion that human beings have no option but to seek pleasure and avoid pain enshrines a version of self-ishness at the heart of utilitarian doctrine. What Bentham could not stomach was the fact that societies were organised so that the selfishness of a small group permanently thwarted the equally legitimate happiness-seeking of the vast majority of their fellow men. If the pursuit of happiness was selfish, and if human selfishness was a universal principle of human conduct, then everybody ought to be given a chance to achieve what seemed to be happiness to them. At the very least, a coherent set of reasons would have to be given which showed convincingly that happiness achievement ought only to be the privilege of a few. And, of course, such a set of reasons is very difficult to find.

Benthamite utilitarianism was, then, no respecter of persons. In principle, George III's happiness was no more important than the happiness of the meanest of his subjects. This was not a thought which was likely to appeal to George III; nor was it likely to appeal to those who happened, through the accidents of birth and wealth, to have collared positions of influence, prestige or power in the existing order of things. These would in the future be called upon to give a rational account of themselves and of the social and political system which allowed them to be what they were. Occupying the positions of social power, the entrenched ruling class was in a strong defensive position. It was never going to be easy to bring those positions out into the open to be subject to the light of critical reason. Of all the thinkers of the Enlightenment, Bentham had the clearest grasp of the problems confronting the new social science as it made its way in a recalcitrant world. Church and state would not give way easily before the greatest happiness principle.

The Church was going to be just as formidable an enemy to the spread of utilitarianism as the state. Benthamism offered a challenge to established religion, Protestant or Catholic, both at the level of theory and at the level of practice. In theoretical terms, Benthamism demystified religion. All religions were for Bentham not much more than systems of moral precept. Religion, at bottom, taught men the difference between good and evil. The trouble was that most religions made a great song and dance about morality and about the origins of morality. Mysterious and miraculous tales were told about gods and saints, and the faithful were called upon to believe all kinds of ridiculous things in order to see the truth of the moral precepts which each religion attempted to din into its adherents. In

Benthamite eyes, most religion was not so much wrong as redundant. It was perfectly obvious to the Benthamites that the basis of morality was the injunction to cause happiness and to avoid causing misery. Men had always, so to speak, been secret Benthamites, because the actions which they had called good had always been of the type which produced the greatest happiness of the greatest number possible in the circumstances. The Christian message to love one's neighbour amounted to no more than that one should seek to cause him pleasure and not pain. All the rest of religion was mumbo-jumbo, so much window-dressing, so that there was even a danger that the basic happiness-creating truth of all morality would be lost sight of. The basis of Benthamite morality was so simple, and so deeply engrained in the religious tradition anyway, that it hardly needed to be taught, and it certainly did not require cumbersome and complex ecclesiastical hierarchies to teach it. Everyman, with a moment's thought, could work it out for himself.

That this threatened to put the established Churches out of a job is obvious, but the threat went deeper than that. Since the beginning, the Christian Churches had claimed a special place for themselves in the business of the achievement of human happiness, and the Churches had also claimed to speak with a special authority about what human happiness truly meant. Ultimately happiness meant happiness in heaven, but a happy human life was still a life of preparation for the final bliss, and Churches everywhere took it upon themselves to teach the special wisdom about how best to prepare oneself for the final, awful judgement. The world as Christians saw it was full of snares for the unwary; therefore the Churches, with varying degrees of conviction, urged men to self-denial: what was the world's sinful trash compared to the reward of heaven? In simple terms, Churches everywhere preached selflessness as the motif of a Christian life; the ultimate aim, eternal bliss, could be as selfish as you like, but the proper course of a Christian life was to deny the gratifications of the self in order to achieve the final and eternal gratification. Besides, God commanded men to live that kind of life, and to do what God commanded was obviously right. Benthamism cut into that perspective. Living in the happy expectation of eternal bliss was only one way of increasing the sum of human happiness in this world. It was not exactly irrational to want to be happy for ever and ever, but, from the utilitarian point of view, it might not be sensible. How could you *measure* the uncertain future gift of eternal happiness against the ordinary human happiness which Christianity said would have to be forborne as a condition for the attainment of the ultimate happiness? Much better, then, to stick to what was knowable and measurable, and try to stock up on the happinesses which the world had to offer. Avoiding what was ordinarily called human happiness in the unsure and uncertain hope of eternal bliss was probably a mistake, a miscalculation of the amount of happiness actually available. Leading the Christian life of self-denial, which might even entail a good deal of suffering, was to take too big a risk on what was likely to happen after death. If there was no heaven, then there was nothing on the plus side of the ledger to put against the unhappiness actually incurred in the virtuous life, and going hell on earth to get to the real hell was the biggest mistake of all.

Christianity, from the Benthamite point of view, preached a doctrine which was particularly unsuited to rational men in pursuit of happiness, but the Benthamite greatest happiness principle bit deeper than that. It was difficult to defend Christianity, or any other moral position, from Benthamism because the Benthamite knife was double-edged. On the one hand, the Benthamites argued that all other moral positions either were mistaken or obscured the real issue, and on the other hand they argued that, if their rivals examined their own moral positions candidly, they would soon find out that they had really been utilitarians all along. All moral codes were in fact recipes for the increase of the greatest happiness of the greatest number. What else could the Christian message to love one's neighbour possibly mean? The fashionable natural rights philosophy, which Bentham ridiculed, added up to no more than the assertion that men would be happier if they were able to enjoy natural rights. But natural rights themselves needed no high-flown theological and philosophical justification because they were not moral ends but simply one of the conceivable means towards the greatest happiness of the greatest number. As a happiness-producing means, natural rights had in principle no claim to superiority over the claims of eating a series of good dinners. The natural rights philosophy was only one of the ways in which the natural desire for human happiness could be articulated, and as such it had to be judged according to utility's own rigorous standard. The question had to be asked: was it really true that the recognition of natural rights was the surest path to the greatest happiness of the greatest number? If it was, fair enough; if it wasn't, then natural rights would have to go.

The Benthamite assertion that all other moralities were utilitarian at bottom was more than just an intellectual strategy. Like other moral systems, utilitarianism had to find for itself the basic building-blocks of a theory, and this it found in the fact of morality itself. Nothing was more obvious than that men had always devised moral codes for themselves. In this Humean sense, morality was natural. It might be interesting to speculate about the origins of morality, but there was no disputing the fact of its universal existence. Men already knew what it was to be good, or to seek the good, or to try to act well. This was very far from saying that all men were good men, and it was obvious, from the punishments attached to moral codes, that all systems of morality expected to have to live with the fact of human wrongdoing. The moral impulse could, by and large, be taken as given. It was not something which had to be explained. What had to be explained was why all previous moral systems had singularly failed to produce the greatest happiness of the greatest number. That was easy. In previous epochs, in which the truths of utilitarianism had not been clearly seen, men of good will had always found themselves on different sides of moral and political arguments because the basic moral positions from which they agreed were either different, or at best unclear. Lack of clarity about what is at issue is the great mystifier of any dispute about questions of right, whether moral or political. The Benthamites argued that all men of good will would end up on the same side if they recognised clearly that it was always the measurable happiness-creating or unhappiness-preventing characteristics of possible lines of moral or political conduct which were at issue. And a world of obfuscated and obfuscating moral and political argument, where no agreement was possible about what right conduct was, was the ideal stalking ground for men of no good will at all. The defenders of vested and sinister interests could have a field-day when men of good will could not even agree about the basic building-blocks of counter-argument.

Benthamism is a moral system for men who are already moral but who find themselves in the position of being unable to convince other men of good will of the truth of their arguments. Benthamism is a kind of language of translation for all other moral systems besides its own. It is possible to argue in the utilitarian manner from any moral position. Utilitarianism does not promise that there will always be agreement in arguments in which the arguers begin from different moral positions. Different moralities differ over the question of what is a legitimate source of human happiness and what is not, but utilitarianism is on strong ground when it urges arguers at least to talk the same language of the greatest happiness principle. Of course, Benthamites looked forward to a time when all men would accept the greatest happiness principle as an unvarnished truth, but that was bound to be some way into the future. Getting people to realise what they were really talking about when they engaged in moral or political argument was a start.

What applied to individuals applied equally well to institutions. Institutions, in the Benthamite view, are just as much actors in the world as individuals, the only difference being that the way institutions act affects the happiness possibilities of much larger numbers of people. In that sense it is probably more important that institutions act for the greatest happiness of the greatest number than that individuals do. Bentham was fond of medical analogies, and he compares the legislator to a doctor curing millions at a time. Benthamite utilitarianism is only interested in institutions as efficient happiness creators. It is important to remember that utilitarian theory was substantially complete before the French Revolution. It is undoubtedly true that utilitarianism, in the political form of Philosophical Radicalism, had to wait until the nineteenth century effectively to influence the course of politics and government, but the doctrine itself was the product of the mature Enlightenment. We also do well to remember that enlightened thinkers were often enthusiasts for sovereignty, wishing state power to be concentrated in a state centre which would then be capable of strong and effective reforming action. The liberal 'fear of the state' theme and the theme of the fear of the tyranny of prevailing social opinion in a democratic age were still in the future (America alone excepted). The Benthamites were frank in their acceptance of the realities of state power. They were not interested in constitutional theory of the kind which was so widespread, especially in Britain and America, at the end of the eighteenth century. All that mechanical juggling with Newtonian analogies seemed to them to be so much sophisticated cant. Either governing institutions had enough power to act to achieve the greatest happiness of the greatest number, or they hadn't, in which case they had better find some from somewhere.

The Benthamite suspicion of constitutional engineering arose out of a very shrewd estimate of the real power of government even in impeccably constitutional polities. Paper constitutions designed to protect the rights and liberties of citizens were really not worth very much. They might even be pernicious. The endless eulogies on the British constitution, of which Sir William Blackstone's *Commentaries on the Law of England* was only one example, stuck in Bentham's craw. Unlike his French liberal contemporaries, who tended to envy British constitutional liberty, Bentham could not help wondering what British constitutional cant was meant to conceal. He soon found the answer: British government under its constitution was as powerful as it chose to be. Like Tom Paine, Bentham saw

British governing institutions as the repository of an almost limitless power to delay reform. British governments could, if they chose, close down the future. This would be especially true in the period of the American and French Revolutions, and would continue until well into the nineteenth century. It was very easy to mistake do-nothing-new government for government which weighed lightly on the backs of the citizens, and it was very easy indeed to mistake that lightness for liberty. This liberty was always being cried up in British constitutional eulogy: other nations may be very good at prating about liberty, but British politics as organised under its unique constitution actually allows the British people to enjoy liberty.

A certain kind of theory of political legitimacy underlay the prevailing idea of British (and American) constitutional liberty. This was the familiar theory that the legitimacy of the state was an all-or-nothing affair. Either a political order was legitimate or it was not. There were no halfway houses, because in this view of things it made no sense to ask a people to support the existing political order half-heartedly, and it made no sense at all to ask a people to obey the instructions of the governing authorities in a half-hearted way. Bentham saw the implications of this kind of view of political obligation very clearly: in effect, it meant that only armed rebellion could challenge the legitimacy of the existing order. If there was no rebellion, then the political order was legitimate, and that assertion of a fundamental and generalised legitimacy could easily be made to slip into the assertion that there was nothing wrong with things as they stood, and especially that there was nothing wrong with existing governing institutions. When the young Bentham, in the *Fragment on Government* (1776), ridiculed Blackstone's account of the British constitution, he was setting Philosophical Radicalism's face against the smug presumption, which was to become increasingly common to both Whigs and Tories, that the English had an inborn and unmatched capacity for good government.

For what constituted good government? To call 'legitimate' government 'good' government was simply to evade the question. What could the fact that government was considered legitimate tell you about what government was actually like *today*? What was needed was a standard by which the acts of government could be judged on a day-to-day, or at least a year-by-year, basis. That standard could only be the greatest happiness of the greatest number. It is only when it is applied to government that the fully radical implications of the utility principle become clear. If it was the function of government to act in such a way as to produce the greatest happiness of the greatest number, then government could not stand still. Government misunderstood its own function if all it did was to keep things ticking over (which is more or less what English governments tried to do after the revolutionary shocks which Europe had experienced in the period of the French revolutionary wars and Napoleon). Government was meant to increase the sum of human happiness, and that was a task which had no end even in principle, because it would always make sense for the citizens of a particular government to want to be happier than they actually were. The Benthamite theory rested on the assumption that happiness was the only human good which was desirable for its own sake, which was another way of saying that happiness was the only thing under the sun which it always made sense to want more of. (Only the Romantics were beginning to suggest that there was something about what was ordinarily meant by human happiness which did not quite fit the bill.) People in their ordinary lives showed clearly enough that happiness acquisition, or pain avoidance, was not the business of a day but of a whole life. Human beings sought pleasure and avoided pain from their births to their deaths. It followed that their governments ought to do the same. It made no more sense for a government to say that things were all right as they were, than it made sense for an individual to say, at a moment halfway through his life, that he wasn't in the business of happiness acquisition any more.

Governments, like individuals, would have to keep going. Governments as they were actually constituted were prone to the self-interest which takes the form of institutional laziness. Why try to do anything, and especially why change anything, when things seem to be going on quite nicely? What this attitude (which is sometimes called 'conservative') meant in practice was that those who were in control of the institutions of state, and people like them, were doing quite nicely out of the existing state of things. Lazy institutions were always the locus of the entrenched interests of a ruling group and their friends. Of course, there was nothing wrong in principle with self-interest. What was wrong was a self-interest which could only be self-serving. The Benthamites had to find a way of making the self-interest of ruling groups serve the interests of the whole of society, or at least of its greater part. An entrenched ruling group failed on both counts: either it served the interests of themselves only or it served the interests of the class from which it came. How, then, could the perfectly understandable desire of rulers to increase their own happiness, or to continue it by continuing to enjoy the perks of office, be made also to lead to the increase of the general happiness of the society over which they ruled? The answer could only be democracy. Let the people choose their rulers and dismiss them at the next election if they failed to increase the greatest happiness of the greatest number. This would form a perfect happiness-creating pact. If rulers wanted to continue in their offices then they would *have* to satisfy the desire for increased happiness on the part of the ruled. To govern otherwise would be to risk electoral failure, a possibility too awful for the successful politician to contemplate. Therefore an elected ruler has a vested interest in increasing the happiness of its own electorate.

It is sometimes said that the Philosophical Radicals were reluctant democrats and this is probably true if by enthusiastic democrats you mean adherents of the Tom Paine, rights-of-man type of democratic radicalism. No man ever stormed a barricade with the name of Bentham written on his heart. Utilitarianism's hesitations in the face of democracy come partly from utilitarianism's own origins in the Enlightenment and partly from the fact that in principle any form of enlightened, centralised government could put a reforming utilitarian programme into practice. Enlightened despotism seemed for a long time to be the best option for eighteenth-century reformers, and it is probably fair to say that the democratising aspects of the American and French revolutions, with help from Paine and Rousseau, caught most enlightened thinkers unawares. After the American Revolution, some form of extended representative democracy became one of the real political options for reformers, but the exact political direction of representative democracy was not all that clear. The circumstances in which the American Revolution happened were certainly not favourable to strong centralised authority. George III's American policy ended up in an attempt to govern the American colonies by coercion: direct rule from London through the king's generals in America. The colonies lost their separate systems of government as, for the first time, an attempt was made to govern America from a single source of power. Americans did not forget that experience when they came to write their Constitution. Account had to be taken of that fear of centralised government, and it was written into the Constitution by formally dividing the sovereignty among the branches of government. *The Federalist Papers* made no secret of the fact that this was meant to make it very difficult indeed for the Congress of the United States to pass really radical reform legislation, and they also made no secret of the fact that the presidential veto on legislation was there to block radical legislation if, by some miracle, it got through the Congress. Utilitarianism's dependence on strong and active government for the implementation of its political programme did not square easily with the constitutional suspicion of power which seemed to lie behind representative government in America.

The case of England was different. Bentham believed that there were adequate provisions for the forceful exercise of state sovereignty in British theory and practice. The problem there was that the great institutions of state, including Parliament, used their considerable formal powers in the entirely negative cause of keeping reform at bay. What was needed in England was a way of making the institutions of state work properly to produce the greatest happiness of the greatest number. That could only mean extending the right to vote in order to bring as many happiness-seeking wills as possible to bear on the processes of government. A popular will to legislate was what was needed to break the deadlock in British governing institutions. At first, it would not even be necessary to give votes to everybody. It would be wise to enfranchise enlightened middle-class opinion first. Enlightened opinion would blow a wind of change right through the established order of things. Later, it might be expedient to widen the franchise further as society itself began to feel the improving effects of utilitarian legislation. There might even come a time when the general level of social improvement justified the democratic principle of universal suffrage, but that was probably a long time in the future.

It must be stressed again that democracy was not a matter of principle for Benthamites. Democracy was a means, not an end. Of course, democratic thinkers like Paine always thought that democracy would have a beneficial influence on the practice of government, but democracy meant more to them than better government. There was a very strong feeling among late eighteenth- and early nineteenth-century democrats that to deny a man the exercise of political rights was to deny half of his humanity. It was the old Rousseauist idea that a man who had no part to play in the exercise of the sovereignty of his country was no better than a slave, and this, in its turn, echoed the very ancient idea that the good life could not be lived unless political and constitutional decision-making was widely shared. Part of being a fully developed human being entailed having a say in the making of decisions which could seriously affect your life. To deny that to adults was the same thing as keeping children in nappies long after they had learned to control themselves. In the modern world, adults were expected to be able to make decisions which radically affected what their own lives would be like, so it seemed to be inconsistent to deny them the same opportunity in the public life of the state. (Anti-democrats insisted that 'the people' were

459

'like children', or better, 'like sheep', or better still, 'like wolves', in order to counter this kind of argument.) The idea of the free exercise of political rights was dressed up in the fashionable natural rights theory of the day: to deny a man his right to vote was to deny him something which was by nature his.

Benthamism carefully avoided this kind of rhetoric. Its own argument for the extension of the franchise was less spectacular, but it was tighter as an argument because it rested on much more modest foundations. All that one had to concede, for the Benthamite argument for democracy to work, was that electors have a legitimate interest in their own happiness being increased by government and that those who govern want, on the whole, to stay in power. That was not much of a concession to make, and it was certainly not in the elevated league of the natural rights school who had to argue that God had given men political rights by nature. As it turned out, the modest nature of the democratic argument of the Philosophical Radicals was polemically very useful indeed. Conservative Europe had heard enough about the rights of man by 1815. Prussia, Russia and Austria formed a Holy Alliance against them, and, while Britain kept its distance from the alliance, British governments could not be expected to look kindly on the rights of man while they still appeared to be overshadowed by the guillotine. British government has probably never been as reactionary as it was between the fall of Napoleon and the first Reform Act. All talk of the rights of man appeared to nervous authority to be a prelude to a French-style revolution of the lower orders. On the other hand, it was difficult to see the Benthamite argument in the same lurid light. Its very modesty seemed to suggest that it would never have a mass appeal. It was more likely to appeal to thoughtful bourgeois minds used in their everyday working lives to paying careful attention to profit and loss. Utilitarianism was based upon a kind of social cost accountancy. Every benefit had a cost. Happiness was not to be got for nothing, and every legislative attempt to increase the general happiness was attended by risk. After all, there was no absolute guarantee that any particular piece of reforming legislation would have its expected beneficial effects. Costs would also include non-money costs. Any piece of reforming legislation was bound to cause a measure of unhappiness in a society where reform was typically directed against vested interests, and those vested interests could be expected to fight the most effective delaying action of which they were capable. This would make the process expensive in terms of human energy, and it was possible that in certain cases the expenditure of energy was simply not worth the gains. A society could afford to expend only a certain amount of its best human resources on reforming itself, and the benefit had to be so much greater than the cost if people were to be persuaded that reform was worth it. One can easily see how attractive that way of looking at the world would have been to the hard-headed, no-nonsense school of bourgeois thinking. It was a businessman's language in which to talk about morals and politics: pleasure and pain, cost and benefit, profit and loss. It was also a language which did not sound revolutionary because it was so naturally at home in the world of capitalist enterprise. Capitalists knew and were proud of the fact that they were changing the world of everyday work. Why should they not think about the world of politics in exactly the same accounting terms which they thought in when they set about changing the world of economics?

The Benthamite 'felicific calculus', which was to be used to determine whether the amount of happiness produced by a piece of legislation exceeded the amount of pain, was something of a blunt instrument. Its bluntness came not as a result of the difficulties of calculation but as a result of what it was that was being calculated. What exactly was this thing called happiness which the felicific calculus was supposed to measure? Benthamism appeared to give a straightforward answer: happiness was what everybody said it was and something which everybody wanted. Put another way, happiness was something which people did not have to be persuaded to want, they just did. Bentham put this more formally: human beings have been put under two sovereign masters, pleasure and pain, and have no option but to obey them. Pleasure and pain were susceptible to arithmetical calculation. All that had to be done was to count the number of people affected, calculate the intensity and duration of the pleasure, make a sum, and then do the same thing for pain. Subtract the pain number from the pleasure number, and if the remainder is a high plus number, then the piece of legislation is undoubtedly good; a minus number result means that the piece of legislation is bad. The felicific calculus, as Bentham develops it, is much more sophisticated than that, but Bentham is not at all sophisticated in his view of the happiness which is being measured. It does not matter to him what the source of human happiness is, provided only that it is the kind of happiness which is socially useful, and 'socially useful' is defined tautologically as that which produces the greatest happiness of the greatest number. That definition does in fact exclude all human behaviour of the lying, gouging, conniving, stealing, murdering, cheating and raping kind, but beyond that Bentham makes no judgement about the superiority of one kind of happiness over another. Yet Bentham must have known that not all legitimate forms of human happiness are the same, and his critics have never stopped pointing out that not all forms of human happiness are of equal value.

So why does Bentham insist on treating all legitimate forms of human happiness as if they were the same and therefore of equal value? It is partly a question of the felicific calculus itself. The calculus is only useful to the law-maker if it actually works. Introducing a qualitative element into the calculation would be to add yet another layer of complication to an already complicated business. Different kinds of happiness would have to be either discounted or given a premium. That would not only make the business of calculation more difficult, but it would also lead to endless arguments about which forms of happiness should be up-graded and which down-graded. And who was to decide? Besides, in principle utilitarianism was committed to a programme of social, political and legal reform which could know no boundaries because it was always going to make sense to go on trying to increase human happiness. Therefore, no form of human happiness (except illegitimate forms) could be excluded *a priori* from utilitarian concern. Everything which men called happiness was on the utilitarian agenda from the beginning. Of course, as a political movement Philosophical Radicalism had to decide on its priorities because everything could not be done at once, but that was easy. Simply do the most obvious things first. Nobody would deny, say, that to remove sources of drinking water from the vicinity of cesspits in order to cut down the risk of cholera epidemics was likely to improve public health and so remove a cause of human misery and create the possibility of increased happiness for a large number of people living in cities. Health was so obviously a human good in utilitarian terms that it was an obvious candidate for early attention, and the large number of people who would benefit from improved public health would also be a compelling reason for putting public health high on the political agenda. Number would always be the clinching argument as far as reform priorities went, for the very simple reason that numbers would always add to the reliability of the felicific calculus. It is often very hard to tell whether single amounts of happiness are greater or less than each other: we might argue endlessly whether the amount of happiness which I enjoy is greater than the amount of happiness that you enjoy. What is not a matter of dispute is that $x + y$ is greater than x or y alone. The utilitarians were men in a hurry to reform their own societies, and they could not afford to waste precious human resources like time and energy on footling debates about single amounts of human happiness. Much better, then, to go for those reforms which would affect a large number of people because the larger the number of people affected by a reform, the more certain it was that human happiness was in fact being increased. The legislator is supposed to be a medical man operating on a large scale, and the greater the scale, the greater the effectiveness of the social cure. And it must not be forgotten that it was utilitarianism's concern with the greatest number which was supposed to turn it into an effective political creed and which pushed the doctrine in the direction of democracy. The 'greatest number' element in the utilitarian formula was meant to pack the people onto utilitarianism's bandwagon.

There may also be something insistently liberal about Bentham's assertion that the legislator must treat all legitimate forms of human happiness as if they were the same. Accepting that which people happen to call happiness means accepting the values which individuals living in a society already have. There can be no question of imposing ideas about what is good or desirable onto individuals who compose society. The utilitarians were always prepared to work with the human material which they found. A certain amount of rationality was no doubt necessary in a society if utilitarian reforms were going to be acceptable, but the amount of rationality required did not amount to very much. People had to be able to distinguish between pleasure and pain, and be able to identify the source of those pleasures and pains which come from good or bad government, but that was all. Trying to get people to see that they ought to want something which it had not occurred to them to want before was both extremely difficult and politically dangerous. It would be tantamount to introducing a set of values into a society from the outside, the sort of thing Rousseauism tried to do. Much better to continue to call good what was ordinarily called good, and to concentrate on providing as much of it as possible for the greatest number of people in the circumstances.

Benthamism's emphasis on the role of government as a happiness-producing agency has caused some of its critics to begin to wonder just how deep Benthamism's liberalism goes. Liberals have always found the pain-removing function of Benthamite government more to their taste than the positive side of happiness-creation, for the very simple reason that it is easier to agree about what causes pain than it is to agree about what really produces pleasure. The negative side of a reforming programme is always easier to draw up than the positive. It was always going to take some considerable time for the utilitarian principle to work its way through the reorganisation of English governing institutions themselves.

Institutional reform, including especially reform of the antiquated legal system, was the essential prelude to positive social reform. Cutting out abuses was one thing, but positive provision was quite another. At the beginning, the Benthamites thought that English life was over-governed and governed in the wrong way, and the enterprise of dismantling outmoded governing structures could easily appear to rise from a distrust of *all* government; but this was a mistaken view. The Philosophical Radicals wanted to reform government to use it.

Only two things qualified the utilitarian enthusiasm for active government, Smithian economics and Malthusian demography. Classical economics warned the utilitarians off government interference with trade, and made them queasy about government measures to relieve the distress of the labouring poor. This reluctance was increased by the gloomy predictions of Malthus's famous *Essay of Population* (1798) which was intended as a refutation of all the most radical hopes of Enlightenment. Aiming directly at William Godwin's *Enquiry Concerning Political Justice* (1793), a lunatic compendium of all that was most radical in the Age of Reason, Malthus argued the simple proposition that, sooner rather than later, population growth would far outstrip the available food supply, and that the only ways of keeping the population within the bounds of its available sustenance were vice and misery. On the Malthusian view of things, human beings were in for a hard time. Malthusianism seemed to argue that human misery was natural, against the enlightened view that un-happiness was unnatural. The utilitarians could not fail to take Malthus to their hearts. Malthusianism came decked out in numbers (and established demography in England as the first real social science). In one way, Malthusianism fitted in well with the greatest happiness principle. After all, the greatest happiness principle did not *guarantee* happiness but simply legitimised its pursuit, and the Malthusian prediction of increased future misery reinforced the utilitarian belief that the business of happiness creation, governmental and private, was going to have to go on for ever. But if Malthus was right, the business of happiness creation by governments was going to be even tougher than the Philosophical Radicals had originally thought, because government would have to work against increasingly tough human circumstances. Malthusianism cast a long shadow over the reforming enterprise wherever it was taken seriously. The effect was to tone down considerably the hopes for a future in which happiness would be widely shared, and to infuse utilitarianism with a certain hardness in the face of the misery which it was utilitarianism's declared intention of alleviating. Utilitarianism had never been sentimental (it's easy to see why Dickens hated it), and Malthusianism made a very hard shell for the utilitarian doctrine. It may be that utilitarian-ism thought for a time that it was fighting a losing battle against human unhappiness; in the war against misery, misery might win. Hard-headed Malthusian pessimism tended sometimes to overshadow the optimistic side of utilitarianism, and it accounts for the reforming legislation like the new English Poor Laws of the 1830s. The poor who could not support themselves by their own labour were to be corralled into workhouses (commonly called 'Bastilles' by the poor) where the conditions were so unpleasant that the rational poor would soon realise that their chances of avoiding misery were probably greater in the hostile world beyond the workhouse door. And they were *work*houses, sending out a clear message to the labouring poor that they could never expect life to be agreeable. In effect, Malthusianism sentenced the poor to hard labour for life.

Benthamism's emphasis on active government, its tough-mindedness about the treatment of social problems, and its straightforwardly instrumental attitude to liberty worried later liberals like John Stuart Mill. What had begun as a philosophy of human happiness, and the liberty to pursue it, seemed to be in imminent danger of becoming a tight-fisted, Scrooge-like caricature of itself, with the state doling out pitiful little amounts of human happiness, and being subject to the law of diminishing returns in an increasingly tough happiness market. Happiness just had to become more expensive as the natural tendency of human life to misery worked itself through a society, and so the happiness dividend on the state's investments in the happiness market were bound to diminish. What the Benthamites had never worried about was that, if there was to be no end to human unhappiness, then there could be no end to active government. Democracy and political theory in general were for the utilitarians simply the means by which governments could be made to set themselves up in the happiness enterprise. This meant a more efficient state apparatus, and the Benthamites never concealed the fact that state power was essential for reform in societies where the reactionaries were themselves so powerful. Utilitarians had no qualms about creating what is recognisable to us as the modern state encumbered with the duty of social reform. But the modern state could do much more than reform society on utilitarian lines and it might turn out to be more powerful than the utilitarians expected. What only a few disgruntled conservatives perceived early was the effect which democracy was going to have on the state. Early democrats looked upon democracy as a system of government. Since ancient times democracy had been thought of primarily as a way of making governing decisions, what the moderns call 'direct' democracy. Direct democracy was not an option in populous modern states, so what came to be called 'representative' democracy seemed to be the only viable democratic option.

What democrats tended to forget, the utilitarians excepted, was the tremendously legitimising effect that democracy would have on the state. Some democrats looked at democracy as a way of bringing the state under some kind of popular control by confining state actions within limits unrecognised by the dynastic absolutisms of the eighteenth-century, and all democrats saw democracy as a way of pushing state action in some directions and of preventing it going in others. But as democracy began to gain ground, modestly enough in Europe to begin with, another process was set in motion by which it became more and more difficult to devise state-limiting arguments because acts of state came increasingly to be seen as acts of all-of-us through our own chosen representatives, whose acts were the electorate's acts because they had authorised them. It was difficult in the age of coming democracy to devise genuinely principled arguments against state intervention when all arguments against the scope of democratic government could be pilloried as the special pleading of individuals or groups with special interests and privileges to defend. There was an even greater danger. Suppose representative democracy were to work in a literal sense. Suppose that representatives really did see it as their job either to share or to pretend to share the opinions and interests of the people who elected them. What then? There was the very distinct possibility that unenlightened opinion would come to outweigh enlightened opinion in the highest councils of the nation. 'Public opinion' was in danger of changing its nature. In the liberal mind, public opinion had always been associated with enlightened and reforming opinion, active opinion directed at the public good and opposed to passive, reactionary opinion which put up with or defended the existing state of things. Public opinion had no sooner won the battle against reaction when it threatened to turn itself into common, everyday opinion. That was bad enough. What made it worse was the possibility that that common opinion would be able through democratic mechanisms to give itself the force of law. If the democratic slogan that 'the will of the people shall have the force of law' meant anything, it meant that ordinary opinion should be government's guiding light.

This was a perspective which caught the Philosophical Radicals off their guard. They had been arguing for the best part of half a century that government ought to be responsive to opinion, but what they had really meant was *their* opinions. Opinion seemed about to triumph over government at the very moment 'public opinion' was ceasing to mean enlightened opinion and was coming to mean anybody's opinion, provided only that there are enough of them. It was in relation to considerations like these that the pessimistic streak which utilitarians took from Malthusianism really mattered. The utilitarians, like all enlightened thinkers, did not doubt that most men derived their bigoted, stupid or super-stitious opinions from the illiterate misery in which they were compelled to live. It was always going to take a long time to bring most people out of grinding poverty, and the Malthusian perspective cast a doubt upon the enlightened hope that one day the ordinary human condition would be such that people's opinions would not be dictated to them by their own awful circumstances. In the meantime, ordinary opinion would have to be care-fully watched, because with the advent of democracy the old, reactionary and deferential opinions of the poor might take over that active public opinion which Philosophical Radicalism had once dominated. A dominant and bigoted public opinion could exercise a double tyranny. It could give itself the force of law, and, perhaps more sinister, it could so dominate a society that the dissenting voice could only be heard, if at all, at the risk of the dissenter's being cast out from society to lead a pariah's life. Behind this lay the more generalised fear that the people would come to feel the state's power as *their* power. There was then no telling what might happen. Hence later liberalism's concern, seen most clearly in John Stuart Mill and Herbert Spencer, with the limits of collective action.

It is part of the austere charm of Benthamism that it wears its faults on its sleeve. Its enemies saw its faults from the very beginning: its view of human nature as an adding and subtracting machine; its circumscribed view of human happiness; its failure to propose a set of ends for human life which could engage the finer feelings; and perhaps above all its rather bland assumption that, if they thought about it properly, people in general would come to associate the increase of their happiness with the cost-accounting reforms which made up the political programme of the political wing of Benthamism, the Philosophical Radicals. How much these were actually *faults* of Benthamism rather than things Benthamism deliberately chose to ignore, is another question. Perhaps Benthamism's great strength as a political theory, and as a polemical weapon, lies in the fact that Benthamite theory did not try to do too much. In sticking to what it knew, and to what it thought it could measure, Benthamism gained more in clarity than it lost in profundity. Its persua-siveness consisted of not asking its potential adherents to believe too much. In the place of

465

trying to answer questions about the ultimate ends of human life, Bentham contented himself with asking much more modest questions about how human beings typically acted when they pursued their own self-chosen ends. The pursuit of happiness was the only programme which made sense in the long run. (Even masochists understand this: if they were consistently to seek pain they would soon be dead.)

Benthamism is nothing if not systematic, but there has probably been no political theory before or since (the possible exception is Machiavellianism) which required so few assumptions for it to work. Bentham had a very exact insight into what made political theories vulnerable. Political theories, like any other theories, rest on fundamental assumptions. Some assumptions are more reasonable than others, but all assumptions are what they are, assumptions, not provable truths. The best kind of theory is therefore the one which asks us to assume the least and builds on that. You can't *prove* that happiness is alone good or desirable for its own sake; perhaps other things are; or one might settle for contentment, rather than happiness, and who says what happiness truly consists of? And is happiness *really* measurable? Bentham simply asks us to believe, on the evidence of human life, that it is a safe bet that human beings will seek pleasure and avoid pain, now and in the future, and that when people use words like 'happier' and 'less happy' the words have some sensible quantitative meaning. Reject this, or even modify it, and Benthamism is not for you.

There would, however, be no inconsistency in rejecting Benthamism as a personal ethic while still wishing the public authorities to act upon Benthamite principles. The more one agonised over one's personal ethic the more one might want governing decisions to embody the clarity of the Benthamite scheme. Individuals can allow themselves the luxury of self-doubt about ethical fundamentals and can allow themselves a lot of time to decide how those fundamentals apply in particular cases, but this is not how one would necessarily want the public authorities to act. Public policy decisions have to be made, and often made quickly, if they are to cope effectively with pressing problems, and what easier principle to operate on in these circumstances than Benthamite principles? Making public policy decisions is usually such a complicated business, and nowhere more so than in a representative democracy, that it would be foolish to complicate matters by adding to them disputes about fundamental principles. The famous Benthamite felicific calculus of pleasures and pains might not work as accurately as Bentham hoped, but it would always do as a rule of thumb for legislators in a hurry. (And one might begin to reflect that all individuals are likely to be utilitarians in an emergency. Anybody after an accident involving many people would concentrate rescue resources where they would 'do the most good' – that is, save the largest number of people.) In this sense Benthamism was marvellously attuned to its own time. Reform had been put off for so long in England, and the new world of industrial capitalism put so many new problems on the political agenda, that it is possible to regard English government as being faced with an emergency for the best part of the nineteenth century. Problems 'cried out' so loudly for governmental action that only the wilfully obtuse could turn a deaf ear. This is just another way of saying that Benthamism works best when the problems are obvious. It might be that the decline of classical Benthamism coincided, at least in England, with the breathing space provided for English society by the relative prosperity of the high Victorian age. Beginning to think about what happiness really means is a luxury only available in a reasonably stable society with a reasonably stable political order, when the sense of emergency has begun to recede. The relative decline of classic Benthamism was a sign for liberals to move on to the consideration of problems not easily accommodated within the original utilitarian scheme of things.

JOHN STUART MILL AND THE CRISIS OF AUTHORITY IN NINETEENTH-CENTURY POLITICAL THOUGHT

Like many another nineteenth-century thinker, John Stuart Mill had to face the crisis of authority which had been implicit in Europe since the French Revolution and which became pressing after the Revolution of 1848. The question can be put very simply: Who was going to speak with authority in the modern world? Where was a centre of moral authority to be found which could do for the modern world what the medieval Church had done for its time, and where was the centre of political authority to be found which could convincingly occupy with conviction the place once held by kings and aristocracies? No nineteenth-century thinker doubted that modern society was heading in a radically different direction from the societies of the past, but the question of what was the most appropriate form of political authority for the new society was still open. The political experience of the French in their revolution did not really help to answer this question, though French experiments with different types of regime after 1789 did at least point to what some of the political alternatives were. Between 1789 and 1815 France was governed first by a kind of constitutional monarchy, then by a democratic republic, then by a Robespierreist dictatorship of virtue, then by an oligarchic Directory, then by Napoleon as First Consul, then by Napoleon as a particularly modern kind of emperor, and finally the old monarchy was restored in 1815. French history since 1815 did not help much either. France went round the same possibilities again, without seeming to be able to fix on one of the particular political forms, and when Mill wrote his famous essay *On Liberty* France was going through a phase of one-man Napoleonic rule for the second time.

This crisis of regimes was a crisis of authority, and this crisis became both more open and acute after the European Revolution of 1848. The powers of Old Europe managed a precarious holding operation during the thirty or so years after Waterloo. Everything revolutionary and Napoleonic which had been released into the world during the turbulent revolutionary years had to be extirpated. The insularly English view of Napoleon as the Corsican Ogre, rolling up the map of Europe by his own domination of it, should not obscure the fact that the ruling dynasties of Europe saw Napoleon as a dangerous radical, a Jacobin at large intent on forming a dynasty of his own. The Austrian Chancellor, Metternich, the most notable casualty of 1848, was the chief protagonist of this view, and the revolutions of that year against the continental kings and emperors announced that dynastic absolutism, founded on the grace of God, had had its day. From now on, the Holy Alliance's insistence on viewing all atheists, free-thinkers and religious doubters as dangerous revolutionaries, because they could not believe that God told them to obey their appointed rulers, would look not so much mistaken as foolish. God's will was simply not adequate as a basis for political authority in the modern world. Of course, this latter view had been explicit in advanced political theory ever since the beginning of the Enlightenment (and it was explicit, though hedged in, in Machiavelli), but it was the liberal Revolutions of 1848 which eventually told everybody in Europe who could read that a new basis for political authority had quickly to be found in the real world of politics.

Nineteenth-century political thought in general can be seen as so many different answers to the question: Who should rule in the modern world? Adam Smith gave one sort of answer, and Hegel another; in France Comte, who influenced Mill a great deal, pleaded the case for rule by an elite of sociologists because they alone were capable of understanding the new society of the nineteenth century; Marxism advanced the claim of the working class by arguing that only the proletariat or its spokesmen could *really* understand the true nature of modern and industrial society. Anarchists would argue that all state authority would have to go, and most of industrial society with it, if truly natural forms of human association were ever to emerge out of the ruins of the old society. The elite theorists of the second half of the century argued that all this talk about political forms was probably so much wasted breath, because elites always took over the reins of government in any society at any stage of history, though this did still leave open the question as to what kind of elite was best suited to the realities of power in the modern state.

Whatever the argument for whatever form of political authority, each argument directed its energy, implicitly or explicitly, against the more radical implications of the idea of popular sovereignty. The people had been making its claims to be sovereign heard since the moment in 1789 when it had stormed the Bastille. If the modern age was to be the age of democracy, as democracy's champions hoped and its opponents feared, then prima facie the people now had the right to speak with the authority once exercised by kings and priests (*vox populi, vox Dei*). Of course, many different things could be meant by the phrase 'the people', but behind the many different usages there lurked the single fear that the people as crowd or mob could take over a society if government was not careful. Nineteenth-century political thought was to spend much of its energy in devising coherent sets of reasons why the people's voice was not to be taken quite literally. The people's voice needed to be interpreted, or toned down, or modified, or merely represented, and some of the most original thinking of the latter part of the nineteenth century spent most of its energy explaining why the voice of the people should not be heard at all.

Why was this so? It was partly a matter of realistic political calculation and partly a matter of profound ignorance. Political calculation is always based on the experience of the past, and past experience of aristocratic government taught those who thought about it that any class worth its salt was bound to use every available lever to further its own interests as a class. Extension of the franchise to the middle class, and eventually to the working class (and in continental Europe to the peasantry), would bring contending classes into the political frame. The middle class could be tolerated, welcomed even, because bourgeoisies always ape their social betters and they are always committed to the sacred character of inequalities of property distribution. The working class was another matter. They could not be trusted to leave existing property relations and property distribution where they are.

Enfranchisement of the toilers could leave the system of property distribution in tatters: witness what had happened, at least for a time, during the French Revolution.

But a profound ignorance about what the toiling masses were actually like compounded the fear of social levelling. When Disraeli wrote about 'Two Nations' in England, he was not only pointing to a class divide between the working men of England and the upper classes. More importantly he was pointing to the ignorance of the one about the other. Who *were* the working men of England? And more particularly, what would the people be like who became their spokesmen, their leaders, and eventually their representatives in parliamentary institutions? There had been distinct traces of this fear of the unknown since the American Founding Fathers had wondered anxiously who would turn up at the first session of the democratically elected popular house in the new government, the House of Representatives. They had a pretty shrewd idea who the new senators would be, because Senate elections were based on sound oligarchic principles, but any leveller, demagogue or Jacobin might turn up in the House. What the political classes thought they knew about the lower orders was not encouraging, because those lower orders typically forced their attentions on their social superiors only in times of upheaval. It was easy, then, to see the lower orders as profoundly disorderly, natural mutineers, or strikers, or machine-breakers, or incendiaries, and, the lower classes being practically indistinguishable from the criminal classes, deeply anti-social at heart. The political message was clear to those who looked at the French Revolution, and by extension all revolutions, as a bread riot which was allowed to get out of hand by a government which had lost its nerve. The people had to be kept down. They were the natural target for government. Government existed to keep them down, but here was the new-fangled democratic idea that the people should have a hand in government through the ballot-box, a contradiction in terms.

John Stuart Mill was writing at a time when the democratic tide was on the flow, but also at a time when the traditional doubts about what democracy might mean had by no means entirely been put to rest. Democracy was still going to be a 'leap in the dark'. Mill's own problem, as he faced it in *On Liberty* (1859) was that, as a progressive, he was in favour of the extension of the franchise as widely as it was practicable (including votes for women), but he was in the dark as much as anybody about what the exact consequences of democracy would be. What Mill already thought he knew about democracy was not altogether reassuring. The only up-to-date and reliable guide to democratic practice, and to the effects of democracy on society in general, was Alexis de Tocqueville's *Democracy in America*. Tocqueville's reservations about American democracy did not stem from the ages-old gibe that democratic government would not work very well. Quite the contrary. Representative democracy worked very well in America, and it worked in ways which had hitherto been unsuspected. Tocqueville was the first to spell out the obvious truth that American democracy was not just a political system but a 'way of life'. The democratic spirit affected everything in America, not just its politics. Equality in the democratic process meant equality in everything else. Americans called equality of political rights 'liberty', but American liberty seemed to mean only the liberty for everyman to be as like his neighbours as possible in his life and opinions. There were, of course, strong counter-currents to this cultural levelling, but Tocqueville certainly put his finger on the contradiction in American culture which was going to fascinate foreign observers of America down to our own day. A 'culture of democracy' was developing in America which would eventually penetrate most of American society and American culture in general. Tocqueville saw the beginnings of what some Europeans contemptuously call 'Coca-Cola culture' today.

This worried Mill. Mill had Scottish origins, and as an observer of England he had some of the foreigner's eye for developments in English culture which might not have been so obvious to a native. Mill saw, perhaps through Tocqueville's eyes, a contradiction in English society between the desire for political liberty and an increasing desire for social tyranny. Extension of political rights was making England a freer political society while at the same time there seemed to be an increasing taste for social convention, and even for bigotry. The age of Queen Victoria was turning itself into the Victorian Age. Mrs Grundy and Dr Bowdler were coming into their own. A tyranny of accepted opinion was on the lookout for eccentricity and dissent. In the nineteenth century, political reform had rocked the English establishment but only for established opinion to set up a regime which made the eighteenth century look like a golden age of dissent.

This mattered much more in England than it did in Tocqueville's America. The American federal system, and the complex machinery of legislation designed by the Founding Fathers, made it very difficult for commonplace bigoted opinion to turn itself into law. It was possible for bigotry to get on the statute book in a particular state, and if enough bigots clubbed together at the national level they could usually prevent enlightened law being passed through the Congress, but the American system was designed to make it very difficult even for majority opinion easily to acquire the force of law at national level. Besides, the amendments known as the Bill of Rights formally enshrined the right to dissent in the Constitution. The case of England, and perhaps the case of the whole of Europe, was different. England had a unitary system of government. In contrast to the American Constitution, the British constitution prided itself on the free exercise of parliamentary sovereignty, untrammelled by the constitutional hedges so carefully cultivated by the makers of the Constitution of the United States. In England, a parliamentary majority in both Houses of Parliament, plus the royal assent, was enough to make anything law, and the king-in-parliament could even make new constitutional rules if it so wished. Ease of legislation, which had once been a great boon to the reformers, now looked dangerous to later liberals like Mill. Democracy in England could mean that a bigoted people could give their own prejudices the force of law through the ballot-box.

In a democracy, which Mill in 1859 was sure that England was about to become, commonplace opinion could have a universal legitimacy simply because the polity was democratic. Why should the people's opinions not rule in a country which was becoming increasingly dedicated to the principle that the will of the people should have the force of law? The tyranny of everyman's opinion was not as spectacular as the tyranny of a Nero or a Heliogabalus, but it was more powerful in the long run because it worked consistently. It worked everywhere that people gathered, and it worked through every human group. Mill had a very shrewd grasp of the realities of opinion forming and especially of opinion reinforcement. If all the effective socialising agencies in a society, families, churches, schools, classes and private associations, spoke with one voice about what the basic social values ought to be, and if all the great opinion-forming institutions, newspapers, universities, parliamentary assemblies, pastors and masters, spoke with the same voice, then dissenting opinion would remain the possession of a few increasingly isolated cranks. Mill's essay *On Liberty* is sometimes seen only as a plea for the wilder shores of individuality, but that would be a mistake. His is not just a plea for the toleration of the eccentrics of Hyde Park Corner; rather, Mill wants heterodox opinion to be tolerated, and even encouraged, where opinion really matters. Mill's *On Liberty* can be read as a call for the foundation of a debating society on every street corner, but even that would not be enough. If dissenting opinion is really to bite, then it has to be effective in those institutions whose opinions and actions really can have an effect on society at large.

Committed as he was to the extension of the suffrage, Mill could not quite bring himself to say that the voice of the people could be the voice of the devil, but he comes close. Mill certainly thinks that the voice of popular opinion seldom, if ever, speaks with the voice of true authority. No doubt, in a society where political rights are widely shared, there are good reasons for listening to what the people say they want, but there is no reason, *a priori*, for supposing that the people ought always to get what they say they want. Mill was on dangerous ground in doubting the people's will, because in utilitarian terms this was tantamount to saying that the people were not the best judges of their own happiness. Mill tried very hard all his life to keep within the bounds of the Benthamite orthodoxy he inherited from Bentham and his father James Mill, but by denying that the people are the best judges of their own happiness he was sailing very close to the wind. If Benthamism had a democratic thrust, then that democratic thrust went in the direction of assuming that each man was the best judge of his own interest. This did not mean that every man was equally expert in the pursuit of happiness, and we can all make mistakes, but at bottom orthodox utilitarianism had to assume that each man knew what was best for himself, otherwise the gate was open for one man's idea of happiness to be forced on another. The Benthamites were right always to be suspicious when one man, or a group of men, claimed to know the public's interest better than the public knew itself.

Mill always insisted that the ultimate test of his own doctrine was utility, but for him the idea of the greatest happiness of the greatest number included qualitative judgements about different levels or kinds of human happiness. Pushpin was not as good as poetry; only Pushkin was. Mill had taken on board some of the Romantic, and especially German, idea (his immediate source was Wilhelm von Humboldt) that the higher reaches of both freedom and happiness consisted of self-development, of a human being's being able to become the best that he had it in him to be. So much the Romantic philosophy owed to Fichte and Hegel, and ultimately to Kant and Rousseau. Cultivation of one's own individuality should be the goal of human existence. Mill did not doubt, any more than the earlier utilitarians, that material conditions would have to improve out of all recognition before mankind would find itself even on the verge of happiness, but what Mill did was to propose a happiness-creating programme beyond that. By all means carry out the social reform programme urged by the Philosophical Radicals in the first half of the nineteenth century, and God knew how far that programme was from full realisation, but the realisation

471

of that programme would by no means exhaust the utilitarian agenda as Mill understood it. There were mountains beyond the foothills, and peaks beyond the mountains. Who knew how high human beings could rise if they put their hearts and minds properly to it? Mill did assume that men would turn out to be very different from each other if each strenuously cultivated his individuality in his own way, but this was a boon to society, not a threat. Men were useful to their fellow men in proportion as they differed from them, so that a society of individuals in Mill's sense would gain in useful progress anything it might lose through the passing of a mediocre consensus.

Mill knew perfectly well that his additions to the utilitarian agenda were not amenable to the arithmetical rigours of the Benthamite felicific calculus, and it has long been standard practice to maintain that Mill effectively deserted the spirit of orthodox utilitarianism while sticking to the letter as far as he could by always maintaining that his ultimate standard was the greatest happiness of the greatest number. There is something in this, but not as much as has often been supposed. Of course, Mill went beyond what he called an 'uninstructed view of happiness', by which he meant the idea that people would be happy simply by getting what they just happened to want. What constituted full human happiness had to be thought about, and it would not be obvious at once to everybody, and the difference between 'ordinary' happiness and ultimate happiness was not quantifiable. None the less, it must never be forgotten that Mill always took most of the earlier Benthamite reforming programme as a given. Of course all of the measurable happiness-creating reforms had to be put into effect before there was even a remote chance that the majority of men could begin the process of self-cultivation which was the royal road to true felicity. Mill's idea of self-cultivation is perhaps better seen as an addition to orthodox utilitarianism rather than as a departure from it, and it is certainly not an attempt to replace orthodox utilitarianism with something else.

There were certain uncomfortably elitist implications in Mill's additions to the utilitarian canon which were not there before. How could one tell that the 'higher' human happiness was better than the 'lower' if that difference was not measurable? There was a further complication. While there was scarcely a human being miserable enough not to have experienced some small share of ordinary human happiness, so that everybody knew what ordinary human happiness was, the same was not true of the higher happiness. Only those who had experienced both kinds of happiness were in a position to pronounce on the question of the superiority of the one over the other. Only those who enjoyed a high degree of material comfort and a high degree of mental cultivation could possibly have an opinion in the matter. And besides, one of the things which made the higher happiness higher was that, in the world as it was, the higher happiness was (perhaps only temporarily) out of the reach of most ordinary men. Surely, then, these superior minds had the right and the duty to instruct the rest. Nobody except reactionaries now denied the fundamental utilitarian postulate that life was a happiness-acquiring business; so it seemed to follow that those who knew how true happiness was to be found would be able to speak with a special authority to their fellow men.

How was the instruction to proceed and what were the likely obstacles to it? Instruction could obviously not come directly from the state, partly because the state was likely, in the

472

contemporary climate of opinion, to get things wrong, and partly because an important part of individuality was individual initiative, and initiative does not sit easily with dogma emanating from the centre. Instruction backed by force was ruled out *a priori*, and that only left persuasion: rational argument would carry the day. Mill has sometimes been criticised for his faith in rational persuasion, and this on two grounds. First, it has been said that his belief in the power of persuasion is dangerous to his own doctrine of freedom of opinion, because Mill lays much emphasis on the capacity of enlightened minds to bring their fellows round. The modern eye catches a glimpse of brainwashing here, the possessors of a higher truth drumming their opinions into the rest. The second criticism of Mill tends to contradict the first when it begins to doubt whether rational argument can do what Mill says it can. Neither criticism is really sustainable. Mill's faith in persuasion is simply a way of turning a bigoted age's weapons against itself. Bigotry must have spread itself by persuasion in the first place, so what was wrong with using the mechanisms by which bigotry had spread to eradicate bigotry itself? That people were willing to accept and sustain bigoted opinion showed that they were already easily led. That wasn't Mill's fault. He had to take human material as he found it. If the alternatives were bigoted and irrational opinion, or enlightened and rational opinion, then progress plainly lay with the latter. Mill's faith in the eventual victory of rational over irrational opinion is not perhaps as optimistic as it may sound. One of the contradictions of the age was that it was at the same time a bigoted age and the age of science. Mill had absorbed enough of continental Positivism to believe that, in the long run, the moral and social doctrines of the modern age would have to be grounded in something like scientific proof. Like the French positivist Comte, Mill thought that the world's belief systems could be divided chronologically into three types: theological, metaphysical, and positive or scientific. Theological belief is the belief that all kinds of supernatural agencies – gods, demons, spirits, magical powers – are there to teach us our duties, in their various, sometimes contradictory, ways and keep us to the paths of right. Metaphysical belief is belief in monotheism, the idea of one god who instructs us in our duties through various agencies all speaking with the same voice. In the West, the historical form of monotheism, Christianity, had long been under attack by advanced and enlightened thinkers for its failure, not through want of trying, to ground its truths in reason and evidence. The moral truths of Christianity might still be moral truths, but Enlightenment's objection to them was that Christianity itself offered no convincingly rational basis for believing either that they were truths or that they comprised the whole of moral truth. As the age of science, the modern age would increasingly come to demand the re-foundation and refinement of traditional truths on grounds acceptable to the scientific spirit. As technology, that scientific spirit was already spread wide in all progressive societies. All that remained to be done was for the same spirit to inform opinion in the way that it already informed the everyday world of work.

Christianity worried Mill because of its tendency to close down other moral options. It was a fragment of truth claiming to be truth itself. In its less tolerant forms, Christianity set out to repress that part of human nature, the human passions, of which it disapproved. In the past, Christianity had been only too successful in its repression of the passionate and spirited sides of human nature, and its legacy to the present was a dull conformity of moral

473

belief and practice. The vital energy of the doctrine had long gone (though there were disquieting signs of revival among some of the more Calvinistic sects). The final victory of Christian moralism came at the very time when its rational basis was being widely challenged. Mill thought that it was time again for the human passions to be given their chance. The balance between passionate spontaneity and moral order had been tilted much too far on the side of order. Mill was prepared to concede that in some states of society – the Greek *polis* for instance, or really barbarous societies – the argument went the other way. The ancient Greeks were so superbly self-assertive, and savages so naturally averse to moral and legal rules, that it was only sensible to come down on the side of social and political authority if they were to enjoy any kind of stable collective life. The modern world was different. Spontaneity had to make its way in a resistant world of congealed moral order. Individuality, both intellectual and emotional, was at a discount.

This had important political implications. There could be no doubt at all that the chief characteristic of the modern state was its claim to general sovereignty within its own borders. The state would always be naturally hostile to other claims to sovereignty and it was bound to be suspicious of informal sovereignty, provided always that it was exercised through law; but later liberals often were wary of the sovereignty which they had helped to create. Mill chose to see politics and society as a world in which three different claimants to sovereignty, individual, political and social, each contended for mastery. The state acted through law and society through prevailing opinion. The only way open to individual sovereignty to defend itself was through eternal vigilance over the state and through self-assertion over prevailing opinion. In Mill's view, state and society were secure in their formal and informal sovereignties, so it was no time for the balance to be tilted back in favour of the sovereignty of individuals. This could only be a matter for individual initiative. Mill had no illusions about what it would cost individuals to stand out against the grain. Initially, it would be up to a few heroic individuals to stand up and be counted. Mill was fond of comparing these heroes of opinion to the Hebrew prophets. He thought that the glory of Jewish history was that the prophets always gained a hearing. They were the enlightened public opinion of their day, and their opposition to the kings of Israel created a fruitful tension in the midst of Judaism which meant that Jewry never stagnated; hence the remarkable survival of the Jewish people and their culture. Mill hoped that something like that prophet-led public opinion would develop in his own day, and if it could penetrate the great public institutions so much the better.

Individual sovereignty delineated

Mill knew that the fundamental theoretical problem was to draw the borderlines between individual sovereignty and the competing sovereignties of state and society. After all, there was not much point in distinguishing between different sovereignties if the lines of demarcation could not be drawn in practical life. The fundamental distinction Mill draws is between self-regarding and other-regarding actions. The individual ought to be sovereign over his actions which only affect himself. Other people only have legitimate cause to interfere with a fellow human being's actions if their happiness is likely to be affected by them. Mill thinks that collective interference with the actions of another can take two forms: political, that is to say legal, and social, and these forms of interference should be directed at different kinds of behaviour as it affects others. Some forms of human anti-social behaviour violate the legal rights of others, the ordinary catalogue of crimes, and the appropriate action in these cases is legal punishment by the state. There exists a whole range of anti-social behaviour which is not of the rights-invading kind, and Mill thinks that purely social sanctions are the appropriate method for censoring it. Public drunkenness, a favourite example of Mill's, is one of the obvious cases of anti-social behaviour best rebuked by public opinion. All other forms of behaviour, and the opinions which go with them, are a matter of purely individual concern.

Mill scholars have had a field-day showing that Mill's distinction between self-regarding and other-regarding actions is not sustainable. One might regard masturbation as the ideally self-regarding act and rape as the ideally other-regarding act, but what about all the cases in between? (And even masturbation could conceivably affect somebody else, a spouse for instance.) What Mill's distinction does not provide is a clear-cut list of actions which are always self-regarding and a list of actions which, with a very few exceptions, are clearly always other-regarding. What it in fact produces is a sliding scale which would have rape at the top, masturbation at the bottom, and seduction and marriage somewhere in the middle, with a presumption in favour of non-interference. The distinction between self-regarding and other-regarding actions is not meant to close down public debate about the proper scope and limits of state action by solving the problem once and for all. *On Liberty* is a contribution to that debate and suggests in what direction the debate ought to go. The presumption of non-interference, except in the obvious cases of violation of rights, means that where there is a doubt the arguments for interference have to be both very good in themselves and very pressing.

It is also important to remember the position which Mill was arguing against. At its most extreme, the position Mill was attacking held that it was wrong not to attempt to try to put down opinions or actions which were wicked in the eyes of the beholder. The most obvious form this position took was religious: God will punish us for not punishing heresy. Heresy is not only an affront to true believers but an affront to God; it must therefore be God's will that heresy be put down. We are in this world to do God's will; therefore we must put down heresy, because we have no choice about what concerns the will of God. In nineteenth-century terms, a position like this meant inviting the state, or public opinion, or both, to censure any heterodox opinions or actions which happened to appear to be wicked in the eyes of public opinion, or of the majority of opinion, or of the opinions of whatever group in society had its hands closest to the levers of political power at any particular moment. Mill is especially keen to destroy the idea that the fact that something is wrong is not a good prima facie reason for the state to move against it. Mill thinks this partly because he thinks that there is no end to the road of state interference with its citizens' behaviour once that road has been taken.

It is easy to see in Mill's attitude to state interference how far utilitarianism had travelled since Bentham and since enlightened political thought's alliance with enlightened despotism. The righting of wrongs, even social wrongs, is no longer enough on its own to justify state action. The benevolent wish to increase human happiness, or to take away from the sum of human misery, is only one of the considerations relevant to the question of what constitutes proper governmental action. Of course, Mill would say that *ultimately* his argument is utilitarian: too much state interference will, in the long run, actually diminish the sum of available human happiness. As we have seen, an important part of happiness for Mill lies in active human self-development. The political and social conditions which produce despotism and which are produced by despotism (Mill follows Montesquieu here) are those which are the most antipathetic to self-development as Mill understands it. Wicked and slothful despotism produces nothing but fatalistic acquiescence (Montesquieu's concord of dead men), and benevolent and active despotism can at best only produce a dull contentment. In *On Representative Government* (1861) Mill makes an important addition to the traditional utilitarian definition of good government. Now it is no longer enough that government should perform the happiness-creating tasks of government efficiently. Government must also act in a way that will encourage the greatest possible degree of mental cultivation in its citizens. This is, in fact, a very ancient part of the definition of good government. Plato and Aristotle are as full of it as they are of the distinction between contentment and true happiness. Happiness as activity can only be provided by representative government in the modern world. The days of direct mass participation in government were over when the ancient republics declined. The vast majority of modern men will have to settle for the more modest participatory actions of voting for representatives and holding very minor public offices (on juries and in local government), but the more of this the better. The alternative is that men will never think of government as *their* government, something we can do ourselves and not something that is done to us.

Participation in the political process, however watered down, does bring other benefits besides mental cultivation. The interests of groups left out of a constitution by being denied the vote always tend to be forgotten. There is nothing like attending to your own interests in the company of others like yourself. At the very least, exclusion from participation in the political process will mean that your own interests will always be seen through the eyes of others. It is not necessary to assume that the middle-class parliamentary representatives of the middle class are naturally hostile to the condition of working men in order to realise that they see the problems of working men entirely from the bourgeois point of view. With the best will in the world, bourgeois representatives will never be able to see the problems of the working poor as the poor themselves see them. Participation in the political process does of course involve far more than voting. Mill believes that want of mental cultivation arises just as much from lack of motivation as it does from lack of education. Most men are not naturally stupid, but they have an incentive to be politically passive when there is no chance of their thinking about public matters having the least effect. Only a few intellectuals get any pleasure out of thinking for thinking's sake. Most men take the view that the game has to be worth the candle. They are prepared to think intelligently and creatively about the management of their private affairs because this has a beneficial effect on their lives. The same has to be true of politics. However remote it may be, bothering to think about public issues must have some end in practical action, otherwise it is simply not worth it.

All of Mill's central concerns meet in what he calls 'progress'. Mill does not share the most sanguine hopes for the inevitability of progress which had been commonplace among enlightened spirits around the time of the French Revolution. Both *On Liberty* and *On Representative Government* are informed by the realisation that societies can go backwards as well as forwards. Mill is not an economic determinist. He does not think that the progress of industry will necessarily bring with it any progress in social and political life. Even further material progress is not guaranteed. The spirit of individual energy and enterprise could as easily be crushed as encouraged by the prevailing state of feeling in a society, and Mill is just as concerned with the future of industrial enterprise as he is with the future of liberty and self-development. Mill affects to see no difference between the party of order and the party of progress as they currently manifest themselves in European and in English politics. The party of order is dedicated to the preservation of the results of progress in the past, while the party of progress looks to progress in the future. The one is the necessary condition of the other, because there can be no future progress without the preservation of the present progressive state of society. Besides the debater's point of daring the conservatives to admit that they want to preserve non-progressive features of the past, there is a real concern here that a generalised social smugness about the progressive nature of the present age could in fact conceal social regression.

If Mill is any kind of determinist he is an ideological determinist. Opinion really counts, and leading opinion most of all. What impressed Mill about enlightened opinion in the eighteenth century was the ease with which it penetrated the upper ranks of society. The middle class and the aristocracy welcomed the discoveries of the Age of Reason, and kings and their ministers were not immune to reason's charms. Even Naples, a byword for reactionary tyranny in the nineteenth century before Italian unification, had been ruled by an enlightened despot. Things seem to have changed since then. No doubt as a result of the French Revolution and the European reaction to it, an unholy alliance seems to have developed between the middle and upper classes, designed either to stop heterodox opinion in its tracks or to maintain that there has been enough progress for the present. And Mill has no illusions about the connection between opinion and social and political interest, especially in a society which is beginning to enjoy free political institutions. Special interests can easily clog up the processes of free politics and frustrate reforming initiatives. The English ruling class was an adept at the game of using representative institutions to further its own narrow interest. Mill tends to think the opinion which arises out of selfish interest will be lazy opinion, no match for radical opinion if radical opinion is vigorous enough. In the coming age of mass democracy it will no longer be enough simply to take the leading classes in society into account. Some way must be found to interest the generality of men in the great political questions of the age. Mill hopes that the extension of the suffrage will have this energising effect. Democracy for Mill is not just about electing leaders. Democratic politics itself is supposed to have an educative effect upon the electors. Asking the people to choose representatives means that the public opinion which interests itself in political questions will extend itself right through the nation. There will be a ferment of clashing ideas which cannot but have the effect of energising government.

Mill thinks that democratic politics is good in itself as well as having a good effect on government. Like Aristotle and Tom Paine, he believes that involvement in the political process is good for people. The potential messiness of democratic politics for Mill is a benefit, not a cost. Democratic politics is expensive in social energy. Democracy's critics have always been quick to point to the social costs of democracy, arguing that the resources a society uses in the business of elections could be spent more profitably on other things, and even democracy's friends have sometimes doubted whether its benefits are worth its costs. Not Mill. Bringing the people within the constitution by giving them votes will actually improve them. This will take time, but it is the best hope for future progress.

Democratic politics in a system of political representation is the ideal ground for the practice of liberty. All of those freedoms which Mill thought were under threat through the social disincentives to practise them would be given a free rein. Democracy was an invitation and an incentive to practise liberty. Free thought and free speech could be the means by which things really could be made to happen. Democracy would also make political institutions more stable. Conservative Europe had lived in fear of revolution since 1789, and the European revolutions of 1848 were a living memory when Mill wrote *On Liberty* and *On Representative Government*. All the revolutions since the first taught the same lessons: political institutions were unlikely to survive in the modern world unless they could be defended by rational argument and had widespread popular legitimacy. The only way to contain rational argument was by institutionalising it within the political system. Democracy was the only system of politics which actually invited and encouraged argument while being at the same time the most obvious way to provide a governing system with popular legitimacy. Far from being the unstable system which its critics since Plato had alleged, democracy in its representative form was the most obviously stable of all forms of government. Above all, the effects of democratic practice on a political community would be cumulative. Democracy was popular education in the widest sense. One must never forget Mill's addition to the utilitarian criteria of good government. Government must not only transact the public business efficiently but it must also seek the improvement of its citizens. Representative democracy seemed the ideal recipe for both these ends. The voters' sense of their own interest in efficient government would keep government up to the mark while active participation in politics and government would expand the citizens' concerns from the merely private into the public sphere. A community of citizens like these was never likely to stagnate.

An afterthought about J.S. Mill

No one can read Mill, and especially Mill's *On Liberty*, without being struck by the sincerity and candour of the man. Mill is only ever genuinely eloquent when he defends liberty and the eloquence can easily conceal weaknesses in his arguments. Does he regard liberty as an end good in itself, or is liberty only a means to other, less clearly specified ends? Some have argued that Mill wants to advance the cause of freedom of thought and speech as the only means by which the principles of utility could make further progress in England. Others have added that Mill saw the chief obstacle to further progress in Christianity, and they see *On Liberty* as a kind of free-thinkers' bible. The proper sphere of individual sovereignty is notoriously hard to define: surely the whole of our lives, inner and outer, is necessarily affected by the circumstances in which we live, so that the essential preliminary to liberty would be a de-programming of our own conscious and subconscious minds (to say nothing of the unconscious). There is nothing in Mill which comes remotely near an explanation of how this could be brought about. These are all well-known criticisms of Mill. Perhaps the most telling criticism of Mill's argument in *On Liberty* is that he tends to argue as if liberty is the good upon which all other human goods depend. Mill insists that all human progress, except in the very early stages of social development, comes about as a result of liberty, and he certainly assumes that all future progress depends on liberty. This position rests on a very selective view of history. Nothing is easier than to choose counter-examples, instances in which particular societies were unfree but progressive in their own time. Mill's idea of progress is very close to what we would call creativity and it is easy to find periods in human history of extraordinary intellectual and artistic creativity in societies which were not free in Mill's sense. (Think, for instance, of the Age of Enlightenment in the bosom of French and German absolutism, or the fact that the only original American art-form is jazz, originally the music of slaves.)

Mill sometimes writes as if he is aware of this line of possible criticism, and his awareness leads him into a sleight of hand. Mill sometimes writes as if liberty and progress were the same thing. The strong self-development component of Mill's idea of liberty enables him to imply that where there is self-development, that is to say originality, then there must also be liberty. This is the merest tautology: show me creativity and I will show you liberty; therefore liberty and creativity are inseparable. Of course they are, but only by defining each in terms of the other. This might not have mattered much if Mill had not extended the principle to the creation of wealth. He could easily be forgiven for getting some art and literary history wrong, but getting the conditions necessary for the creation of wealth wrong is less forgivable in a political thinker. Mill does write as if liberty is the only, as well as the ideal, condition for the creation of wealth and for economic progress in general. It might have been true that liberty was the ideal condition for the British economy to expand and advance during what we call the Industrial Revolution, but it certainly does not follow that economic advance can only happen where liberty exists as Mill defines it. Economists still disagree among themselves about the necessary conditions for industrial take-off, and there are lots of examples of remarkable industrial progress in countries with repressive social and political systems. Free market economists will argue that these are the wrong circumstances in which to go for maximum economic growth, and they will contrast the rate of growth in 'free' societies with the inferior rate in less free societies with centrally controlled economies. (And the partial dismantling of centralised economic controls in erstwhile Soviet bloc countries sends free market economists into ecstasy.) The buried argument in neo-liberalism, though it is not buried very deep, is really an argument about liberty which is the reverse of Mill's own argument. Some free-marketeers argue that the free exchanges of the market *are* liberty, not just the condition which makes liberty possible. Mill thinks that liberty is the precondition for economic growth, but he also thinks that liberty is something additional to the system of free market exchange which makes economic growth possible.

We noticed above that Mill is not an economic determinist because he sees no necessary connection between industrial progress and the growth of political and social liberty. Liberty has still to be struggled for in the age of industrial capitalism. And Mill is one of those defenders of the free market who feels obliged to apologise for the free market's tendency to create losers as well as winners. In this Mill follows the tradition of Hegel (and of the Scottish Enlightenment). The free market, it was said, is not exactly the ideal way of organising economic power relations between men, but it is the best way available *and* it brings other benefits, the chief among which is liberty. Mill is less optimistic about the liberty which the free market brings, and his agreement shades over into the problem of trying to decide what kinds of trade-offs are to be made between the direct and indirect benefits of a free market, liberty included, and the social disadvantages which the free market bestows on its society's less fortunate members. This problem has been either explicit or latent in free market political economy since the beginning. Mill's attempt to solve it is to make liberty something different from the operation of the free market itself by arguing that liberty is only one of the possible consequences of a free market economy. This enables Mill to be sceptical about the chances for liberty unless there exists in a society the thrust of embattled free opinion against the prevailing tendency of the age towards conformity in its general ideas.

Neo-liberals simply talk as if this problem does not exist. By defining liberty as the system of free exchange, and regarding free politics in Mill's sense as the froth on top of free market exchange, desirable, no doubt, but not essential to liberty, the neo-liberals have made themselves into reductionists and economic determinists, something Mill never was. This would not matter very much if the central value of all liberalism was not liberty. But liberty being central to liberalism, it has to be pointed out that neither reductionism nor economic determinism sits very easily with the very notion of liberty. If liberty is reduced to being a function of the prevailing system of free market relations, then liberty no longer has to be striven for in Mill's sense. Politics being reduced to economics, freedom being equated with the freedom of the market, then you are either free or not, depending on the economic circumstances. This is the kind of reductionism and economic determinism traditionally associated by liberals with Marxism. Marxism, it is said, denies liberty precisely because it reduces politics to a variable dependent upon economics and denies even the possibility of human freedom in the superstructure which capitalism inevitably erects on its economic base. It may be that what has come to be called neo-liberalism has forsaken any notion of liberty as being in any sense related to that liberty of human will and cognition which liberalism has hitherto always clutched to its heart.

NOTES ON SOURCES

W. Harrison's edition of Bentham's *A Fragment on Government* and *An Introduction to the Principles of Morals and Legislation* in the Blackwell's Political Texts series is still standard. L. Stephen, *The English Utilitarians*, 3 vols (1950), is still useful. M.P. Mack, *Jeremy Bentham* (1962), is an odd but brilliant study. Mill's *On Liberty* and *On Representative Government* exist in easily available student editions. Mill is probably the easiest to read of the famous political theorists, and *On Liberty* is genuinely eloquent. Commentary on Mill is vast. For critiques of Mill, see J. Fitzjames Stephen, *Liberty, Equality, Fraternity* (1960), for the nineteenth century, and M. Cowling, *Mill and Liberalism* (1990), for the twentieth.

21

LIBERALISM IN MATURITY AND DECLINE
Spencer, Sumner and Green

HERBERT SPENCER

Despite ending up among the bishops as a member of the Athenaeum, Herbert Spencer was a child of provincial religious dissent. The Derby of Spencer's boyhood (he was born in 1820) bubbled with radical politics and religion (Spencer himself was a Methodist). This was long before England's political and cultural life had been all but swallowed up by London, and while the beginnings of the Industrial Revolution in the Derwent Valley were still a living memory. 'Provincial' in Spencer's day does not mean second-rate. In Spencer's lifetime, Derby was fast becoming the great English railway town (rivalled only by Swindon). There is a notable irony here, because the coming of the railways was meant to sap the moral fibre of the nation (think of Dickens or Mrs Proudie) but, as things turned out, the railways united England enough for London to become its centre in almost every important sense.

Spencer's father was a Derby schoolteacher who once tried his luck but failed in the lace trade in Nottingham. Spencer spent the later part of his boyhood with his uncle, a country parson with radical views, and it was he who provided the boy with a sound education of the no-nonsense kind. Spencer spent ten years (1837–46) as a railway engineer, 'participating in', as his biographer puts it, 'the last great battle of the Industrial Revolution'. He was always restless in his profession, and during the 1840s he was drawn into the radical journalism which, together with his output as a writer, was to support him for the rest of his life.

There was a moment in the early 1850s when it looked as if Spencer might marry Marian Evans (who later became George Eliot), but her ugliness seems to have put him off in the end. Spencer became a leading English positivist in the broad sense of that word, and by 1857 he had settled down to write those huge books of social science which were to be his monument. By the late 1860s Spencer had begun to acquire an international reputation. He toured America in 1882.

It is hard to date the beginning of the decline of Spencer and Spencerism. He had never been especially healthy, suffering bouts of mental incapacity (probably depression) throughout most of his adult life. Spencer's own optimism about the necessity of evolutionary progress seems to have begun to wane at about the same time as Spencer's reputation as a social scientist and prophet. There was already something quaint about Spencerism when he died in 1903. Still, it was reading Spencer that put the young Mao Tse-tung on the road to Marxism.

WILLIAM GRAHAM SUMNER

Sumner was born in 1840 in New Jersey, the son of a Lancashireman of the artisan class who had emigrated to America and who was a carbon-copy of those autodidactic working men who were devouring the works of Herbert Spencer in mechanics' institutes all over England. The Sumner family tried a spell in the West before Sumner's father settled down in Hartford, Connecticut, as an employee of the old Hartford and New Haven Railroad Company. Sumner might therefore be said to have been brought up at the bottom end of modernity.

Always forward at his books, Sumner made it to Yale in 1859, where he proved to be a brilliant scholar. He also made friends with some of the sons of the American elite, and it was with their help that Sumner was able to do graduate work, mainly in theology, at Geneva, Göttingen and Oxford. He was a tutor at Yale, 1866–69, and in 1867 entered the ministry of the Protestant Episcopal Church. Back at Yale, Sumner began to turn his attention to social and political affairs (though he was always a vigorous preacher and conscientious pastor), and he was given the new chair of political and social science in 1872. It was as a professor of social science that Sumner became famous, the first (and nearly the last) to do so.

Sumner's lectures at Yale were packed out. He was a notable modernising influence at the university, and won a celebrated battle to make Herbert Spencer's *The Study of Sociology* a course textbook. Sumner's intellectual range and energy were vast. He read a dozen languages, and his work was by no means confined to the social sciences, in each one of which he was a master.

Sumner's name has become a byword for anti-statist *laissez-faire* liberalism, and socialists still cut their teeth on his anti-socialist arguments, especially as expressed in the classic *What Social Classes Owe to Each Other* (1883). Sumner also invented the Forgotten Man, the law-abiding citizen who quietly gets on with his life, pays his way, and who is always the taxman's target when government has schemes of social improvement in mind. Sumner was always heavily engaged in hugely ambitious schemes of research. The famous *Folkways* came out in 1907, three years before his death, and his *Science of Society* was published posthumously in 1927.

THOMAS HILL GREEN

T.H. Green was an 'eminent Victorian' in the post-Lytton-Strachey sense of the term. Jowett's Balliol, that powerhouse of Victorian moral energy, could equally well be called Jowett's and Green's Balliol, so much did T.H. Green contribute to it. At times Green practically ran the place, and his was the great moral influence on its teaching of anything remotely modern in the humanities. Green was not himself a particularly promising pupil at Rugby (where he went at fourteen in 1850). He was always a good Latinist, though, which is mildly surprising in a man who was never quite able to shake off a certain reputation for indolence.

It was as a shy and awkward young man that Green went up to Balliol as a pupil of Jowett's in 1855. He took a second in Mods, a first in Greats and a third in Law and Modern History. He became a fellow of his college in 1860, signing the Thirty-nine Articles of the Church of England only after some hesitation.

Green was always a liberal in politics, and was in many ways a typical bourgeois radical of the age, interesting himself in franchise reform (he spoke from public platforms in favour of the great Reform Bill of 1867) and the reform of education. From 1872 he was deeply involved in the temperance movement, believing with many of his contemporaries that, if the English working classes were going to vote, it would be better if they voted sober.

Green came into his own when Jowett became Master of Balliol in 1870. He taught modern philosophy as well as ancient, Kant and Hegel as well as Plato and Aristotle, and he was much involved with the exposition and critique of the works of J.S. Mill, at that time the subject of much discussion at Oxford. By all accounts, Green began as a rather reserved teacher, but he softened with time; he took his students on the famous Oxford 'reading parties' during vacations, and none of Green's students had any doubt that they were the pupils of a serious man. Green was not considered particularly well-read even by the standards of nineteenth-century Oxford, but his grasp of the fundamentals of the systems of philosophy he taught more than made up for it.

In politics, Green found himself in the rather curious position of agreeing with almost everything utilitarian radicals like J.S. Mill stood for, while rejecting the utilitarian philosophy upon which the opinions of the philosophical radicals appeared to be based. Green's philosophical idealism led him to refound the basis upon which advanced opinion could stand.

Green was always the soul of courtesy in learned and political debate, and, as the good and rational citizen which his political theory urged others to be, he was always much involved with local politics in Oxford. From about 1878 onwards he began to show the symptoms of a hereditary heart disease which killed him at an early age in 1882. He lives on as 'Mr Gray' in Mrs Humphrey Ward's novel *Robert Elsmere*.

HERBERT SPENCER: THE VICTORIAN AGE IN THEORY

Histories of political thought conspire to forget that the Victorian Age was the age of Spencer. Spencer is an honoured figure in the history of sociological theory, but nobody reads him now. He is one of those thinkers whose theories come so naturally out of the world which those theories explain and celebrate that the validity of the body of thought seems to end with the age itself. Spencerism was intellectually dead by the beginning of the twentieth century. Spencer's immensely elaborate attempt to explain the working of everything in the world, including the world of society and politics, through the single principle of evolution was already breaking up. This was partly due to the fact that the world of the natural and biological sciences was travelling in directions either unfamiliar or hostile to Spencerism, and partly due to the fact that Spencer had made predictions about the future development of industrial society and its politics which did not square very easily with the developments which actually occurred. Spencerism wears its faults on its sleeve. The old utilitarian impatience with obscurity and muddle are nowhere seen to more effect than in Spencer's writings. This clarity led to Spencerism's eventual demise in intellectual circles. Spencer took pride in the capacity of his social and political theory to accommodate the facts about the natural and social worlds which science was busily turning up in his own lifetime, but it was some of those facts which put paid to Spencerism's claim to be a true over-arching theory of the nature and development of human societies and of everything else in the world besides.

The great Spencerite idea was evolution. Charles Darwin wrote his signature so authoritatively on the idea of evolution with the publication of *The Origin of Species* in 1859 that it is difficult to recapture the extent to which the general idea of evolutionary development had colonised so many different areas of intellectual enquiry by the middle of the nineteenth century. The idea of evolution has so many intellectual origins that trying to catalogue them would involve a history of evolutionary ideas in itself. Let it be enough to say that the idea of evolutionary development, physical, biological, social and political, was a commonplace by the end of the Age of Enlightenment. What had Enlightenment been interested in, if not the evolutionary history of the human race? Enlightenment saw evolutionary development everywhere it looked. What Enlightenment lacked was any real grasp of a general cause which operated within the different fields, physical, biological, social and political, which were amenable to evolutionary explication. This was especially true of explanations of evolutionary progress in the social and political worlds. Some thinkers of the Enlightenment put human progress down to the march of reason and others to the growth of free trade; some saw the hand of God in special progress while others thought that human progress happened according to the operation of social laws of development which might have been commands of the deity and might not.

The other thing which the enlightened idea of evolution lacked was the antithesis between evolution and revolution which was to become a cliché in nineteenth-century social and political theory. The idea that evolution was 'natural' in some sense that revolution was not was to become the cornerstone of all nineteenth-century thinking from the moderate left to the reactionary right – of all thinking, in fact, which was not itself advocating revolution. We can see this partly as the result of an understandable reluctance on the part of the spokesmen of the upper and middle classes to see the horror of the French Revolution repeated, and partly from the realisation that the French Revolution signalled clearly that the world was changing very rapidly indeed. Evolutionary ideas, with their progressive overtones and their undertones which muttered that progress could not be expected to happen overnight, suited a cautiously progressive Victorian age very well. Pessimistic evolutionism, which came out of a realisation that the message of Darwinian evolution was not altogether a happy one for the future of the human race, itself evolved as a systematic body of social and political doctrine only very late in the century. For most people in the half-century before 1900, the years in which Spencer was intellectually active, believed that evolution meant progress, and that was that.

Darwinian evolutionism was only one of the ways in which evolutionary ideas could be applied to a particular field of study, biology, and the origin of *Origin of Species* itself lies not in biology but in Malthusian demography. The gloomy prediction of Malthus's *Essays on Population* that men would have to struggle harder and harder for the means of life was applied by Darwin to the evolution of biological life from a primitive simplicity to the very complex matrix of a large number of minutely differentiated species. Darwin took the ordinary evolutionary idea that life moves naturally from simplicity to complication, from homogeneity to heterogeneity, and discovered that biological evolution came about as the result of the survival of the fittest. Darwinism gave a tremendous boost to the validity of all evolutionary study, biological and non-biological. The increased influence of evolutionary ideas should not surprise us. Not only were evolutionary ideas commonplace in the middle of the nineteenth century, but the year of publication of *Origin* occurred in that still happy time when what men now call the sciences in the plural had still to distinguish themselves so definitively from each other. It was still possible to regard science, by which is meant the body of scientific ideas and the methods of science, as being essentially the same in all areas of human enquiry. What the mid-nineteenth century lacked was, oddly enough, any clear idea of the past and future evolution of the scientific enterprise itself, though specialisms did of course already exist. Science was just as susceptible to voluntary imperatives as any other area of human life; science too would develop from simplicity to complication, from homogeneity to heterogeneity. The Victorians had inklings of this, but it was unlikely to strike a thinker like Spencer, whose mind was formed by early nineteenth-century influences, one of the most important of which was the idea of the unity of science. It was axiomatic for Spencer that all the sciences spoke with the same voice. All scientific knowledge had the same essential character; therefore whatever any piece of scientific activity discovered must be compatible with what had already been discovered by every other piece of scientific activity. This compatibility could even serve as a criterion for what was scientific knowledge and what was not. It seemed to follow (though of course it doesn't) that all scientific enquiry is fundamentally finding out about different manifestations of the same thing. The thing was evolution in all its aspects, and what science was really after were those general laws of evolutionary development which worked themselves through every activity under the sun.

Looked at like that, the scientific enterprise easily welcomed grand theory, and the grander the better. 'Grander' meant simpler. Newtonian physics as popularised by Pope and Voltaire was never very far below the surface of mid-nineteenth century science, and nowhere more so than in Newton's own birthplace, England. The search was on for some kind of general law which would explain not just the physical universe this time, but everything else as well. There is a closer parallel between Newton and Spencer. Newton did not invent the idea of gravity. As is usual with great scientific discovery, the idea had wide currency in Newton's own day. What Newton did was to take ideas about gravity and fuse them into a single idea and then show how the single idea could be used to explain how a huge range of physical phenomena worked. Spencer's (and Darwin's) case is similar. What Spencer did was to fuse existing ideas about evolution into a single over-arching explanation of how everything worked.

The other impulse towards nineteenth-century grand theory was undoubtedly religious. The Enlightenment was always called the age of atheists by its clerical opponents, and it is true that most enlightened moral and political philosophy tried to owe as little as possible to the existence of the Deity. However, eighteenth-century philosophers, however hard they might wish things to be otherwise, always came up against the fact that most men received their moral sense from religion and that most men still regarded their religion as a guide to practical life. By the middle of the nineteenth century, science had made considerable inroads into most of the wilder and some of the more sensible tenets of Christianity. In particular, it became increasingly difficult even for believers to accept that a liberal interpretation of the Scriptures provided an adequate account of how the world came to be as it was. Guides to practical life must to an extent come out of practical life itself, or at least be consistent with it. Religious doubt, which affected many intellectuals in mid-century, often came from the realisation that it was now obligatory to believe that the world of human experience was chaotic, unless some kind of guiding hand or principle could be found to replace the idea of a God-directed universe which had been so consoling to ages of simpler faith. This desire to see Nature behind its appearances, to find general laws of development among the most disparate and bizarre manifestations of the spirit of humanity, could, if successful, provide a set of propositions about the world which were true, and that set of propositions could be the basis of a guide for life. This guide would be practical in the sense that it was rooted in practical life and would therefore stand a good chance of success as a guide to living in the practical world.

A practical guide for living in the modern world could not evade the job of finding out how the modern world worked. Science in general, and social science in particular, would explain that. In particular, social science was meant to expose the mechanisms of the social changes which were now so obvious a feature of a world turning increasingly to industrialism. If that social science could show that these mechanisms tended to work in the cause of social progress, and if it could be shown exactly what social progress was, then modern and rational men could find a moral guide to life by putting themselves and their work on progress's side against the forces of obscurantism and reaction.

It was not clear what part politics was to play in the future progress of mankind until Spencerism put politics firmly in its place as a nuisance and a hindrance. Some, indeed, have spoken of a latent anti-politics in liberalism which came into its own with Spencerism.

It is as well to remember the original political ambiguities of progressive thought at its Enlightenment origins. Enlightened political thought arose at a time when, by and large, the European state system had taken on the appearance of being a permanent feature in the political landscape. The state was therefore one of Enlightenment's central problems: how could unenlightened, that is unreformed, states help Enlightenment's own cause? Some enlightened thinkers were for tearing down existing states and replacing them with properly designed ones, while others wanted to concentrate power in a sovereign centre still further as the only way to create an engine for enlightened reform in the foreseeable future. This tension in enlightened thinking was the outward face of an even greater tension about the nature of society. The centralisers, and their descendants the utilitarians, had no doubts about the state's ability to reform society if only the political will was there. Implicit in the thinking of the replacers of existing states was a doubt whether the state could ever be said to reform society except in a very negative way. Thinkers like Paine, for instance, wanted new kinds of states in order to give spontaneous social development its head. Society was the school of virtue and the state was the school of vice. Society was where men lived a good and satisfying life through their own efforts. The necessary existence of some kind of state, but not the old state, was proof that human beings had not reached such a state of progress that they could do without the state and its law to curb what still remained of their wickedness. Dismantling inherited state mechanisms would leave society freer to develop progressively towards its own self-chosen end of near-perfection.

Enlightenment meant, first of all, the creation of as wide a body as possible of enlightened opinion. Enlightenment's state centralisers hoped that enlightened opinions would eventually be in a position to direct the state's energies towards progressive reforms, but the more radical spirits of Enlightenment, like Paine and Godwin, hoped that eventually enlightened opinion would do most of the state's job for it. Enlightened opinion would regulate the behaviour of mankind, so that the state's regulatory laws, backed up by force, would gradually wither away where they were not actually abolished by reform. In political practice, what was supposed to happen was that enlightened opinion would induce the state to dismantle itself and allow opinion to take its place. That is why the repeal of the Corn Laws in 1846 was such a triumph for liberalism and radicalism. The Anti-Corn Law League arose outside the mechanisms of formal politics. In this sense it was a genuinely *social* movement, and eventually it broke through into formal politics by persuading the state to stop regulating the trade in corn, and so stop regulating the price of bread, which affected the lives of nearly everybody. What was required was a convincing account of the development of social life to show that what was true in practice was also true in theory, that the state could wither away while society through opinion could adequately perform its own regulatory functions. This was provided by Spencerism.

The ground had been long prepared for Spencerism. Liberalism had been complaining about state interference since Locke, and by the end of the eighteenth century there already existed a body of advanced liberal opinion which held that societies, if left to themselves, would be essentially self-regulating. Adam Smith went a long way in this direction, and so did the utilitarians, and it might be said of eighteenth- and early nineteenth-century political thought that it was just as aware of the socially damaging potentialities of state power as it was of its potential to further the cause of social reform. So why did non-intervention need a brand new theory of the Spencerite kind? Why was the existing provision of liberal theory not enough?

The new theory was needed partly because of that tension in liberal thought which we have already remarked on. There was an unresolved and ultimately fatal contradiction in liberalism, especially in its Benthamite form. Liberal arguments could be used both for and against state intervention. You could argue that the sum of human happiness could best be increased by state intervention for social reform, or you could argue that the sum of human happiness could best be increased by taking the state out of society and allowing society to pursue its own self-chosen forms of happiness untrammelled by positive law. In fact, the Philosophical Radicals reached a compromise simply by deciding that it was economic management which they did not like, while promoting all kinds of other regulatory mechanisms in the name of the public good. Classical economics in the form of 'political economy' was the argument which kept early nineteenth-century liberals away from economic interventionism, but there was no reason *in principle* why, from a strictly utilitarian point of view, the state should not regulate the economy if it could be convincingly shown that economic management would lead to the greatest happiness of the greatest number. At some time between 1850, when Spencer's *Social Statics* was published, and 1885, when Spencer's *The Man versus the State* appeared, the balance within liberalism seemed to have tilted in favour of interventionism. What began to worry some liberals was that state interventionism had become principled interventionism, interventionism at the level of liberal *theory*. Benthamite interventionism in the first half of the nineteenth century could always be defended by the argument from emergency: certain social reforms needed doing *now*, otherwise popular misery would turn to sedition for its remedy. In the second half of the nineteenth century, British society and its government took on the aura of stability as prosperity increased and the political class in England regained its confidence in its capacity to reform existing institutions without changing their nature drastically. So what was the argument for increased state intervention now? Finishing the tasks already begun was one thing, but attributing extra tasks to the state was quite another. Even the arch-liberal J.S. Mill had begun to wonder whether the state might not properly be called upon to regulate the distribution side of the economy by determining how much of the social product each man should get. (In this Mill foreshadows the late twentieth-century liberal concern with what came to be called 'social rights' and 'social citizenship'.) T.H. Green and his school were already well on the way to constructing a version of liberalism which owed a great deal to German Idealist philosophy in general and Hegel in particular, and, as we would expect from such influences, the English Idealist philosophy was markedly collectivist both in its basic assumptions and in its conclusions about the role of the state. Spencer strongly felt the need to re-establish the individualistic liberal philosophy at a time when liberalism was turning towards a stronger role for the state both in practice and in theory.

The second great influence on Spencer was the half-century of experience of industrial society after 1800. I say 'after 1800' because by that date something like a coherent liberal philosophy already existed, and it was based upon assumptions about the future of industrial society which could not be convincingly defended half a century later. I have remarked before that one of the assumptions of European liberal thought in the Enlightenment was that modern society and politics would be far less complex than hitherto. Aristocracy had had its day in theory and would play a decreasing political and economic part in the society of the future. Aristocracy had everywhere complicated social and political affairs by adding an unproductive class to the social structure and by colonising positions of institutional power within the state. A complex social order and a complex political order were the result. The future society of those who worked for their living would be structurally less complex and, being composed entirely of those who earned their living as buyers and sellers of labour, the new social structure would not cause those class resentments which had been so marked a feature in societies dominated by their aristocracies. But by 1850 half-a-century's worth of experience of industrial society, and of societies in the process of industrialisation, had begun to make thinkers wonder whether their societies were in fact moving from complication to simplicity.

The idea of movement from complication to simplicity was directly challenged by the prevailing ideas of the evolutionists, of whom Spencer was to become the most vociferous. Evolutionary ideas looked at development the other way round – everything evolved from homogeneity towards heterogeneity, which was development from simplicity towards complication by any other name. It is true that all liberal thinkers believed in progress, though with very different degrees of conviction, but for them social and political progress often consisted of simplifying things as they presently stood. Feudal society, for instance, made such a muddle of sovereignty by diffusing it so thoroughly among the upper ranks of ecclesiastical and lay society that 'hunting the sovereign' in feudal societies became a very difficult game indeed. Feudal economic relations were similarly complex, and at bottom feudal relations between lords and kings, and between serfs and lords, were not even supposed to be economic at all, but military. Contrast that mess with a modern liberal society, in which economic relations were regulated by the transparent and rational process of free contract between buyers and sellers of commodities, the most important of which was labour. Enlightened progress was really intellectual progress, and this meant being able to see natural simplicities behind the superfluous, man-made complexities of human life. And, because the laws which governed the development of societies were supposed to be simple, like Newton's Laws of Motion, there was a tendency to believe that the societies whose functioning those laws explained would be simpler societies.

The experience of industrial society taught the opposite. Adam Smith's principle of the division of labour worked in complex ways that its originator could hardly have dreamt of. Industrial society seen through Spencer's eyes at mid-century was nothing if not complex. The spontaneous division of labour of which Smith was the spokesman had taken off with economic growth and had produced a myriad different sorts and conditions of men performing a myriad interlocking and interdependent social tasks. This minutely differentiated society cried out for a new society to explain the fact of complexity, and for a new political theory to accompany it. Evolutionism, and especially the analogy with evolutionary biology, was the obvious basis on which to build the new social and political theory. Evolutionism fitted the bill remarkably well, both as to content and to form.

Evolutionism told the same story of the movement from simplicity to complexity in whatever area of study it chose for itself, and this was especially true in biology. Social science also dealt with the life of man, and man was a biological creature, so that social science conceived in evolutionary terms was not so much analogous to the 'real' science of biology as a continuation of it. This even provided social science with a methodology: social science would deal with complex social phenomena like whole societies by breaking them down into their component parts and discovering how the complexity of the whole came out of the combination of the parts. That was exactly what a biologist did when dealing with complex forms of biological life. Any form of biological life was a particular combination of living cells which had evolved in a particular way. Why should this not also be true of a living society? A society was a complex combination of complex biological organisms, and so there seemed to be no reason in principle why social investigation should be any different. The principle of evolution also suited the prevailing idea of what a theory should look like. The unity of all science was taken so much for granted at the mid-century that a scientific principle was expected to cover many of the branches of science. The day was still far distant when the scientific community would tolerate different pieces of theory from different parts of the scientific enterprises which are not easily reconcilable with each other. The idea of a theory had not changed substantially since the Enlightenment eulogised Newtonianism as the simple key to the complex mysteries of the physical universe. A principle's adaptability to the service of a large number of what we would now call different scientific enterprises was considered in Spencer's day as convincing evidence of its truth and usefulness. It was only much later that science began to be suspicious of principles which explained too much.

It is easy to recognise most of the current radical ideas of the mid-century in Spencerism, especially radicalism's suspicion of the state. Liberals had always been suspicious enough of the state to want to reform it, but Spencer went much further by arguing that the state was a positive menace. We have already seen how the idea that the state could upset the economy had become current in the days of Adam Smith, but Smith had regarded the economy as a special case, peculiarly at risk through the bungling regulatory attempts of aristocratic governments impervious to the truths of political economy. Spencer extended the anti-state argument to society as a whole. Social mechanisms were as complex as biological mechanisms, and the more a society progressed up the evolutionary ladder, the more complex and therefore more delicate its mechanisms became. The balances of nature were always more or less precarious. The last thing that one wanted was for the state to go charging round a society, making alterations which might well, in the longer term, upset everything. Spencer's was a knee-bone-connected-to-the-thigh-bone social theory with a vengeance. A society was a complex organism which worked because spontaneous evolutionary processes caused that differentiation of social function which was more than analogous to the evolution of species in the biological world. The state, by contrast, still worked through the crude mechanisms of positive law, rules backed up by force or by the threat of force. For Spencerites, this amounted to allowing ignorant children to use a hammer and chisel to try to make a watch keep better time.

Something superficially similar to Spencer's organicism had been part of the English conservative tradition since Burke, but the difference between Spencer's radicalism and Burke's conservatism is very striking. Burke, no liberal in political matters despite his qualified support for free trade and parliamentary reform, was very careful not to distinguish between 'state' and 'society', the fundamental distinction made by all liberalism. Quite the reverse. Most of the plausibility of Burkean conservatism rests on the assumption that the governing mechanisms of a society are an organic part of that society itself. Cut the governing part of a society away from the rest of society and that society becomes something like a body without a head: dead or dying. Part of Burke's defence of government in England is that it is so well integrated with English society, and performs its integrating function so well, that at the level of theory it makes no sense to separate state and society, and on the level of practical politics even contemplating the possibility of cutting the ruling part away is a recipe for social and political disaster. Spencer turns the organic argument against English conservatism of the Burkean kind, and against all conservatism which lays its stress on the central authority of the state. Spencer, like any true liberal, does distinguish between state and society. Society, by which Spencer means social stratification and the economy, develops organically but the state does not, and when the state is in the hands of conservatives and reactionaries it changes either too slowly or not at all. And fundamentally, state mechanisms, all state mechanisms everywhere, are physical force mechanisms introduced into an organically developing society from the outside.

Spencer thinks he has put his finger on an important truth about political institutions in the modern world. Far from developing naturally as a society changes, political institutions can easily work against the way a society is going. Burke is wrong. The institutions of a society do not naturally change as the society, of which those institutions are an important part, changes. Implicit in Spencer's view of state institutions was a critique of the radicalism of the first half of the nineteenth century and of some aspects of the radicalism of the Enlightenment. Previous radicalism had tended to regard political change as easier to accomplish than social change, and all radicals thought that the first stage in a continuing process of reform was to reform the state. A reformed centralised state could then be used as the engine of progress in its own wider society. Earlier radicals did not deny that social change could and did occur independently of state mechanisms, but they typically thought that these changes did not go far enough, or that they went in the wrong direction. Enlightened thinkers understood very well that they were living in a changing world, and most of them thought of the reformed state as being in the forefront of those changes. Not Spencer. Ham-fisted bungling was about all that a Spencerite could expect from political action designed to make things better, and the likelihood was that social progress would be slowed down or even retarded. Spencer thought that in the long run the progressive evolutionary process taking place in industrial society would overcome all state-directed opposition, but misguided state action could make the long run very long indeed. And social organisms, like any other organisms, can be killed by inept human intervention, or simply by inadvertence. (Had he lived now Spencer might have regarded atmospheric pollution and the state support of lame ducks, which kills individual initiative, as different examples of the same lethal process.)

One of the clearest statements of the Spencerite case against state interference in social problems is to be found in the works of the American Social Darwinist William Graham Sumner, especially in *What Social Classes Owe to Each Other* and in the essay 'The Absurd Attempt to Make the World Over'. Sumner wrote at a time when the idea was current even in the United States that the national government ought to take steps to relieve poverty. Sumner always connected arguments for state intervention with socialism, and he is particularly clear about how the Spencerite view of industrial society differs from the socialist view. The Spencerite sees minute gradations of different sorts and conditions of men on an evolutionary ladder with many rungs, while the socialist sees only two human groups which really count, capitalists and proletarians. The Spencerite sees society in the future as increasingly and naturally more differentiated, while the socialist sees the future of industrial society in polarisation between bourgeoisie and proletariat with everybody being forced to choose a side. Sumner began to wonder what part the state might play in deciding what the future would be like, and he came to some clear and startling conclusions.

Sumner's first thought was for the delicacy of the natural scheme of social differentiation. The social ladder had many rungs so that the social top was very far from the social bottom. At the very bottom were the paupers and at the very top were the owners of super-capital. However, most people in America are making it while not being rich, and so they are graded in the middle. The top of the middle is far from the bottom of the middle because there are many grades of middle, but Sumner defends his calling the middle the 'middle class' on the grounds that all of its members are more like each other in income than they are like paupers or millionaires. It is these paupers, people who are not even breaking even, that a government welfare programme is supposed to help. Sumner asks the straightforward question: Who is to pay for welfare? Plainly not paupers, and he takes a very realistic view of the tax-paying propensities of the very rich: one way or another they will weasel out of their obligation to pay taxes, because the rich are very good at that. Only the middle, ordinary law-abiding citizens are really taxable. They are making it in America; therefore they have surplus income, and their law-abiding tendencies mean that they will actually pay up when asked to by the federal government.

What we have to remember is that government, being unproductive, has no money of its own. It takes citizens' money as taxation under the forms of law. How would this affect the middle? The middle will contain those who are just making it, with a very small surplus, as well as those who are doing well, with larger surplus. The first effect of taxation for welfare services will be to bring the lower middle near the pauper line. It will not put them under it, because they cannot be expected to pay tax to the point of destitution, but taxation will make the lower middle very vulnerable. They will probably no longer be able to save for a rainy day, which in effect means that small farmers, small businessmen and hired men will all become potential welfare clients at the next bad harvest or business recession. Taxation for welfare has the effect of increasing the clientage for welfare and narrowing the tax-base for raising the revenue for welfare spending.

The other question which has to be asked is: Is there in principle an amount which could be spent on welfare which could be considered *enough*? Sumner thinks not. Once you begin to go down the welfare-spending road there is no end to it. (And don't forget that welfare spending increases the number of clients for welfare anyway.) There may be no end in principle to the amount which could be spent on welfare, but there is a limit in fact. That limit would be reached when all of the surplus of the wealth of the middle class, in Sumner's sense, was to be collected in the form of taxation to spend on welfare. This would have the effect of making everybody in a society, except the very rich, an actual or a potential welfare client. The paupers would be welfare clients already, and the middle class, having no savable surplus, would all become potential welfare clients on the next rainy day. That would have the effect of making it in everybody's interest, except the very rich's, to press for generous state welfare provision, and, America being a democracy, this pressure would no doubt be successful. (Even the rich might not have any very good reasons for opposing welfare, because the rich never pay their fair share of taxation anyway.) The burden of Sumner's argument is clear: once you start welfarism all the pressures build up for increased welfare spending. This is not just a matter of ideology, as more and more people become convinced of the rightness of welfarism. On the contrary, welfarism itself creates its own constituency of actual or potential recipients.

Why does this particulary matter? It matters to a Social Darwinist (a name virtually interchangeable with that of Spencerian) for two main reasons. First, it creates an entirely false, man-made relationship between the members of a society. Sumner divides the members of a society into two groups, creditors and debtors. Creditors are Sumner's middle class and those above, people who are making it and who therefore have surplus wealth; debtors are all those who are not making it, those below the pauper line. As a Spencerian, Sumner regards this as the natural outcome of events. Human living, like biological life in general, is subject to the pressures of competition for survival, and economic survival is no different from other kinds of survival. This was supposed to be especially true of America. The promise of American life was an invitation to the immigrants from Europe to come and make it in America, to pursue happiness with a good chance of success but with no built-in guarantees. The man who made it in the tough conditions of American competition was the true American.

Welfarism could change all that. It must always be remembered that when people say that *government* should pay for welfare, they are always saying something which is misleading. Government has no money of its own, so that when people say that government should pay for welfare, what they really mean is that government should force those who can be taxed to transfer some of their property to paupers. The taxpayers are Sumner's creditors, those making it and who therefore have surplus, taxable property. The forms of law under which taxation is raised make those who are making it recognise an obligation to provide money for those who are not making it. This effectively means that creditors, those who are making it, now have to recognise that they owe a debt to paupers because the laws of taxation force those who are making it to make a contribution to the upkeep of those who are not. Welfarism means that paupers, the natural debtors, are owed something by those who are making it, the natural creditors. Debtors become creditors and creditors debtors. The natural outcomes of living in a competitive, Spencerite society, are reversed by the state. This matters everywhere, but it mattered particularly in America, because America promised the debtors of Europe a chance to become creditors in

America. Welfarism meant that anybody who made it in America no sooner became a creditor than the national government immediately made him into a debtor to the poor, insult being added to injury because the man he owed money to, the pauper, was himself a debtor by the laws of nature. The ultimate horror of a welfare programme would be to turn all Americans, except a very rich and tiny minority, into debtors by the state or by nature, which amounted to breaking the whole promise of American life. Why should a man who was in debt in Europe come all the way to America to get into debt again?

Sumner's second objection to welfarism and its social effects is that welfarism would tend to polarise a society and so do the Marxists' work for them. We have to remember that the poor pay no taxes and the rich always find ways of avoiding paying their fair share. The taxpayers are therefore Sumner's middle class, a middle class defined as all those who have surplus wealth on no matter how modest a scale. Suppose the welfare bandwagon started to roll in the direction Sumner fears it might, and suppose it to kept rolling until the very end, when all the surplus wealth of a society, except the wealth of the very rich, is going in taxes to government to pay for welfare. This effectively polarises a society: at the bottom clients of welfarism or potential clients of welfarism, then a huge empty gap because nobody is middle class in Sumner's sense any more, then the very few super-rich at the top. What is this but the pre-revolutionary condition of a society in which a Marxist revolution is about to break out? Marxists dream of a polarised society, of the over-whelmingly many poor confronting a tiny group of the super-rich. Marxists hope that this will come about as the result of the natural development of capitalism. Sumner, as a Spencerian, cannot believe this; the natural progress of a society is towards more complex differentiation, not polarisation. But the welfare state could easily do for society what Marxists think society will do for itself. The action of the state in going down the welfare road can polarise a society through excessive taxation for welfare by making everybody, except the very rich, potential or actual welfare clients.

Sumner's plea that the 'forgotten man', the man in the middle, should not be forgotten is a plea for a minutely graded system of social stratification of the Spencerian kind. Within the general Social Darwinian thrust of Sumner's tightly controlled argument is a specific argument against what might be called the 'conservative' argument for welfare, particularly the form that argument took in Europe, and especially in Bismarckian Germany. Germany was the home of Marxist theory and practice. The origins of Marxism were German, and it was in Bismarck's Germany that a well-organised Marxist mass party, the party of German Social Democracy, appeared for the first time in Europe. The party had revolu-tion as the first item on its agenda. What could Germany's capitalists, and their agents the German government, do about this threat? One answer was to buy the German working class off with a welfare programme which would blunt their revolutionary edge by weakening their taste for orthodox Marxist politics. A modest welfare programme organised by government would give working men a stake in that system of government's survival, and also in the survival of the society which paid for welfare and produced the government which organised welfare. These palliatives for revolution were no doubt expensive, but the game was worth the candle. Sumner could see that kind of conservative argument for welfare crossing the Atlantic at the same time as immigrant masses. Sumner's own argument against going down the welfare road was designed for circumstances in which the Bismarckian argument might become the orthodoxy in America. American organised labour might turn the screw on American capitalism to such an extent that employers would go cap in hand to the American government, begging them to set up a rudimentary welfare state in an attempt to placate working-class discontent. Sumner's argument was meant to show that there was more chance of the revolutionary polarisation of a society through state action than there was of revolutionary polarisation happening as the result of the normal operation of the laws of social development.

Social Darwinists like Sumner had to be very confident that Spencerism was right to be able to offer advice like this to governments. Spencerism was above all designed to make men confident about the future development of industrial society from homogeneity to heterogeneity. Beneath Spencerian interventionism lies the fundamental assumption that the intentions of most governmental interference, and of all governmental interference with the natural laws of social evolution, will be frustrated by Nature itself. Hence the Social Darwinists' extraordinarily negative attitude to state action. They had no doubt at all about the state's capacity to frustrate human progress in the short term. For them, the state is an agency which causes problems rather than a problem-solving agency. This always stemmed from a desire on the state's part, frequently, though by no means always, well-meaning, to do more than the state could possibly manage, let alone manage efficiently. Evolutionists like Spencer were struck by the fact, which could be observed in the whole of nature, that a single biological organ usually stuck to a single job and did it well. This 'biological division of labour' (the phrase was contemporary) was the secret of nature's efficiency, and so should apply to the state too. Spencerians expected little more from the state than enforcement of contracts freely entered into, and national defence.

How did the state survive to become a menace to social progress? Spencer's evolutionism provides a neat answer. He knows that the state, as part of nature, must have developed too. However, it is not the case in nature that everything evolves at the same speed. The state has typically failed to keep up with the rate of evolution in its own society. Political institutions differ from biological organisms only in their capacity to set conscious goals for themselves. The state's elite can, and typically does, form intentions for itself which are behind the times. The state continues to use force or the threat of force in its internal and external relations as if the military age had not been superseded by the age of spontaneous industrial co-operation. Aristocracy's traditional game had always been war, and so it was natural that the government which evolved with aristocratic society should be government which had a tendency to use force as a first resort, and it was equally obvious that it was in the interest of aristocracy to try to preserve the kind of society in which social relations were organised on the basis of a more or less naked exercise of social power. This was frankly reactionary, and social evolution would make sure it could not last, but it could cause a lot of unnecessary trouble in the meantime.

It was considerations such as these which made Spencerians such activists. Spencer is plainly an evolutionary determinist, but Spencerian determinism is not supposed to lead to passivity in the face of the inevitable. Spencerians have the confidence about how to act which comes from being sure which way the world is heading, and this confidence they share with other kinds of predestinarians, millenarians, for instance, or Puritans, or Marxists. You might expect a resigned life-stance from inevitablists because they are supposed to think that there is nothing worth doing but to wait for the unavoidable outcomes which their view of the future necessarily contains. This might be the 'logical' position for a determinist to hold, but the history of ideas turns up many instances in which determinists are anything but passive. Spencerism is a case of this kind. Knowing the future put a duty on Spencerians to bring that future in as quickly as possible, and Spencer himself looked forward to a long haul. Such progressive measures as votes for women, for instance, were not to be expected in his own lifetime. Spencer disliked and attacked Benthamism for its reliance on the state to increase human happiness, but he was an ethical utilitarian at heart. Nature was evolving towards a stage of human happiness barely conceivable at the present time. To put oneself on Nature's side and to support 'natural', that is anti-state, policies and reforms, was to put oneself on the side of the happiness creators. Spencerism was entirely lacking that Malthusian pessimism which we noticed hung long and heavily over utilitarianism. Spencerians were not worried about the brutalising effects which population pressure on the food supply was supposed to bring because they had a sound evolutionist argument for the inevitable decline of human fertility. Nature showed everywhere that there was an inverse correlation between fertility and intelligence: the more intelligent a species was, the lower its rate of reproduction. As evolution advances, the more intelligent the species, the greater its chances of survival. Why was this so? The answer lies in adaptability. The more intelligent the species, the higher its chances of adapting to changed circumstances. What is true between species is also true within species. Low fertility species are likely to survive, and low fertility individuals within species are likely to survive. Therefore population rise will slow down, perhaps stop, and population might even decline. Malthusian fears for the future could therefore be safely set aside.

Spencerians looked forward to universal suffrage and eventually to votes for women with none of the caveats of some other liberals. The Spencerian argument for democracy was partly psychological, that is to say natural, and partly political, which is really to say natural again because politics is part of evolving nature like everything else. Spencer's psychology was firmly based on the idea of human faculties. Nature implanted faculties in the human mind for them to be exercised, and the most necessary exercise of the faculties was to 'resist' the outside world. 'Resistance' is another word for adaptation. Beings who take the world as they find it, and who allow life simply to happen to them, are not likely to be good adapters. This interplay between self and the world is ideally the greatest degree of self-assertion compatible with a world which is not of the individual's own making. In political terms, this is potentially a radical's psychology because it encourages co-operative activism in the industrial age, and democracy is co-operative activism writ large. In the modern world, things get done by co-operation, not force; therefore it follows that political evolution must be heading in the direction of the greatest degree possible of human voluntary co-operation, which is a democratic political system. All this could easily be some time in the future, not now. Spencerism suited the reformist temper of the Victorian Age very well. Nature taught that evolution was a process bereft of cataclysms, so there was no need to go rushing into the future. Spencer had very little of that fear of the working

497

masses which characterised the thought of other reformers. This equanimous attitude was partly made possible by Spencer's general faith in human progress – the working class will 'improve' like everything else – and partly by the Spencerite belief that, in the future, state functions would naturally diminish. All nineteenth-century radicals, the early Benthamites excepted, expected government to diminish in the long run. J.S. Mill, for instance, took it as axiomatic that primitive states of society required more government than advanced states of society, because primitive men were supposed to be naturally lawless. It was a Victorian truism that the working class were more 'primitive' than the middle and upper classes. They lived closer to nature because they had to struggle physically for their bread, lived like brutes and displayed animal-like characteristics when they ran riot. Progress would change all that, though there was considerable disagreement about how long that would take. Spencerism hedged about the time-scale, but did say that it was inevitable. The scheme of progress explicit in the industrial age necessarily meant that rule by force through the state would be superseded by social regulation through voluntary co-operation. Therefore, the old fears about what the working class might do if they were to capture state power through the ballot-box could be seen to be increasingly groundless. Not only were the working class improving anyway, evolving into something less animal-like, but the state power which they might capture was being steadily emptied of its content anyway. The working class which might make state power its own was becoming increasingly less terrifying, while at the same time state power itself was diminishing in value as a prize.

Spencer's view of the state was essentially voluntaristic. He even revived the idea of natural rights and social contract. Spencer had never liked the utilitarian downgrading of rights to the position of being only one potential source of human happiness, and that not the most important. Spencerian natural rights were not Tom Paine's rights of man warmed up. Spencer is even shallower than Paine about natural rights. Natural rights simply follow from the fact that Nature intends men to exercise the faculties which she implants in their minds. All artificial hindrances to the exercise of the faculties are barriers to the free exercise of rights, and recognition of this is the beginning of political wisdom. The typical example of the exercise of a natural right in a politically organised society is the right to make free contracts. The state exists to protect that right, properly removes hindrances to it, and can have no other function save defence. Even membership of a state is optional, another matter of free contract. I may choose to opt in or I may choose to opt out. Membership of a state involves costs (duties) as well as benefits (protection of rights), and Spencer seems to think that, at some unspecified time in the future, social evolution will have come to a stage when it is really true that some men living in a society could choose to ignore the state without any danger to the existence of the state itself. Perhaps it is correct to see here the influence of provincial dissenting religion on Spencer. The English dissenters (Methodists and their like) chose to ignore the state religion in England and founded their own chapels. Theirs was not exactly a frontal assault on the state Church; rather they chose to go their own way despite the laws on the statute book which enjoined Anglican worship and the payment of Anglican tithes. The dissenters knew that solid enlightened opinion could make the law of the state unworkable as it affected religion, and they also knew that the state Church did not collapse just because a large minority chose to opt out. Perhaps something like that could happen in the future to the state. The state would, in effect, be like a joint-stock company to which you paid the necessary entrance fees and from which you received stated benefits, and like a joint-stock company, anybody could get out of it if he chose without threatening the existence of the company.

It has already been said that Spencerism was a response to a particular moment in the history of English society and politics at which the state interventionists (Dicey called them collectivists) seemed to be winning both in theory and in practice. Spencer restated the individualist and anti-statist position of English radicalism in the latest terms of Victorian science with a strong biological tinge. He was also celebrating the progress of English industrial society. Spencer's *Social Statics* should have been on show at the Great Exhibition the year after it was published. By the time Spencer published *The Man Versus the State* in 1885, liberalism itself had become interventionist in the theory of T.H. Green and in the practice of Gladstonian liberalism, and the theory of socialist interventionism was already complete enough to exist in several different forms. It was on the right wing of politics that the non-interventionist position was gaining new supporters everywhere. There is always a tendency to forget that the political right, for all its worship of (certain carefully selected aspects of) the past, has never been averse to singing its opponent's tunes. The non-interventionist argument suited a right-wing in power very well. Interventionism meant social interventionism, and social interventionism meant an alteration of the social structure from which the aristocratic right could only lose, and so could their natural allies the very rich. Entrenched right-wing forces were not slow to learn the advantages to be gained from an adaptation of a non-interventionist position like Spencer's. Politically reactionary elites in Prussia and Japan, for instance, began to see the possibility of marrying a Spencerite view of the inviolability of social agreements with a sure grasp of the huge gains the elite could make by selectively exploiting modernity. The efficiency of modern governing institutions, like bureaucracies and armies, and the exploitation of modern industry and the railways as the logistics of war could easily come together to produce a statist and militaristic politics of the kind that Spencer himself both hated and thought was a thing of the past.

Spencer, like many another nineteenth-century social and political thinker, made the mistake of supposing that there was really only one possible future for industrial society and its politics. Spencerism never seems to have spawned the latter-day justifiers of its predictions which, for instance, Marxism has. Marxism, since Marx's death in 1883, has never lacked supporters prepared to defend Marx to the last ditch by saying either that his predictions *have* come true, though most of us are too stupid to see it, or that Marx never made predictions at all, so that it couldn't be true that his predictions failed. Spencer's own clarity about the industrial future made Spencerism peculiarly vulnerable to being played false by history. The rise of militaristic politics in the middle of industrial or industrialising societies gave Spencerism the lie. Behind the failure of Spencerism from the 1890s onwards lies a fundamental assumption which in the nineteenth century was common to all advanced social and political institutions, which was that political institutions were going to count for less in the future, and social development for more. There was a tendency to see social and economic development as the primary cause, and to regard the development of political institutions as a secondary and dependent effect. Long before the end of the century, vulgar Marxists, and economic determinists in general, were already talking as if you could guess what the political institutions of a society would be like from an accurate description of its economic and social base. This way of thinking affected many who were by no means economic and social determinists. What the determinists tended to forget was that political institutions can play an active part in the social and economic game if elites are prepared to take their opponents' ideologies seriously. A bright Junker or samurai could easily come to think that the world might well go Spencer's way unless something was done about it. Of course, the elite itself would have to change some of the ways it thought about the world. That triumph of nineteenth-century political theory, the theory of elites, had plenty to teach traditional elites about what happened to them if they did not adapt to changing conditions. Spencerism forgot one of its own principles, that adaptation leads to survival. Traditional elites were traditional precisely because of their survival capacities. Spencerian evolutionism and the elite theory of Pareto, Mosca and Michels almost screamed 'adapt or die' to traditional elites. Up to the time of the Great War, traditional elites still clinging to some of their reactionary political and religious ideas ruthlessly modernised those aspects of their own societies which would fit them for war. The Great War was, above all else, a war of the powers made great by industrialisation, a war of the masses in the age of mass production. Spencer's predictions about the necessarily pacific conditions of industrial society lay in ruins. After 1914, the great political questions of the day would again be settled by force.

LIBERALISM BEGINS TO FEEL AT HOME WITH THE STATE: THE IDEALIST POLITICS OF T.H. GREEN

It is tempting to assume that the history of political thought develops serially, with bodies of theory appearing on stage only to make their exit when they are succeeded by opposing bodies of thought. We do well to remind ourselves that political theories are not like scientific theories, to be definitively junked when more intellectually satisfying theories come along. Almost nobody now believes in a flat earth, or phlogiston, or the theory of spontaneous generation, and we are probably right to regard these believers as cranks, best left to the psychiatrist's couch or to the sociology of knowledge. Political theories cannot, by their nature, be so compellingly satisfying to our curiosity as scientific theories, and the reason for this is obvious. One of the things political theories try to do is to locate politics on the map of experience. Political theorists have always asked how politics affects everything else and how everything else affects politics, and at the level of theory this has always taken the form of asking questions about how other kinds of enquiry, mathematical, theological, scientific, economic and sociological, ought to affect political enquiry. While science has increasingly come to satisfy its own curiosity by asking narrower questions in increasingly specialised fields, the curiosity of the political theorist has continued to ask very large questions about the relationship of politics to the whole of experience, biological experience not excluded.

Human experience changes; the experience of human beings living in the world is cumulative. As Hegel teaches us, nothing is ever entirely lost. If this is true, then the activity of being a political theorist becomes more difficult, not easier, as time advances, for the simple reason that more has to be taken into account. The pace of change in the modern world poses special problems. We have had occasion to notice before that by 1850 it had become something of a commonplace to say that a decade of change was now worth a century's worth of change in the Middle Ages, and that includes changes in ideas. No mistake is worse in the history of modern political thought than the fallacy of seriality, the idea that doctrines come and go in a straight line. In a world characterised by rapid change, ideas, and especially opposing ideas, develop side by side. This is especially true within traditions of political thought, and nowhere truer than in the history of liberalism. Thus Mill's political theory does not signal that Benthamism is over; nor does Spencerism mean that the world had seen the end of Mill; similarly, the appearance of T.H. Green's modifications of liberalism in the direction of German Idealism does not mean that Mill and Spencer dropped out of the practical canon of liberalism.

These considerations lead one to reflect about what it is, exactly, that keeps a tradition going. Liberalism provides one type of answer to this question. It is by its own internal dissensions that liberalism has survived as a creed for so long. In language dear to Hegel, traditions of thought have a dialectical quality, and as soon as those traditions lose the sense of internal tension, they begin to decline. In free soceties they can simply disappear. In societies where doctrines become official ideologies which will brook no ideological splits or deviations, the official ideology is subject to all those enervating causes which Mill outlines in *On Liberty*: a living faith becomes a dead dogma. Traditions of thought are also kept in being by their opposites. A tradition of thought is in a healthy condition when it is subject to two dialectics, internal and external. The external dialectic of liberalism's struggle with conservatism and later with socialism could have surprising effects both on liberalism itself and on its ideological competitors. If it is true, as Hegel said, that nothing is ever truly lost in the history of ideas, then we are encouraged to look for ideological survivals outside the traditions in which these ideas originally appeared.

So, if we bear Hegel in mind, we should not really be surprised if ideas swap traditions fairly regularly. Bits of socialism come into Mill, and we have already seen how bits of Spencerism got into conservatism. (And in America, Spencerism in the form of Sumnerism *became* conservatism.) As the nineteenth century progressed, older ideological alignments were superseded by new ones. At the beginning of the century, the chief alignment had been of liberals (there is a tendency to call them liberals if you approve of them and radicals if you don't) versus conservatives, with liberals generally on the side of less regulated human life and conservatives generally on the side of authoritarian regulation of life at all levels from the state to the family. (Benthamism, as we have seen, cut across this alignment.) By the end of the century things had changed. The argument was not so much for and against authority, because nearly everybody outside Marxism and anarchism accepted the peculiar legitimacy of the modern state founded on the people's will, however much that will was attenuated in practice. Political debate centred round the question of what that central and legitimate authority should be used *for*, which really amounted to the question of how much state regulation there should be of social life. 'Individualists', as they came to be called, said 'very little', and 'collectivists' said 'much more'.

Even this is too simple, because the collectivist/individualist, interventionist/non-interventionist split is not a split between two positions but a division among three positions. Non-interventionism meant nearest to what it appeared to mean. It was the spiritual descendant of *laissez-faire* (what was sometimes called Manchesterism), and clung to the belief, strongly reinforced by Spencerism, that, given time, all economic and social problems would solve themselves if they were in principle solvable. (But even non-interventionism was not quite as straightforward as it seems, because the non-interventionists divided into those who would tolerate those schemes of state intervention already in place and those who would attempt, as the recent phase has it, to 'roll back the state'.) The interventionist and collectivist position divided about what kind of state intervention was necessary, and the difference between them can be understood as the difference between those two typical figures of Victorianism, the inspector and the administrator.

Inspectors inspect afterwards, when the damage may already have been done. A factory inspector, or an inspector of schools, administers neither the factory nor the school. He visits when the factory or school is already a going concern, and what he does is to see that the concern lives up to certain standards (of safety, for instance, or training). The inspector awards rosettes or deducts penalty points. If a case of mismanagement is very serious he may recommend legal proceedings, but what he typically does is to make recommendations for improvements with the intention of re-inspecting the concern to make certain that recommendations are followed up. This kind of intervention can be called indirect, or negative, because it does not seek to take over the running of industrial or other collective enterprises. Its function is to monitor the performance of enterprises in accordance with certain publicly decided criteria. Intervention it certainly is, but it is far from the positive kind, which is itself a sub-system of the social system, say an education system or a system of nationalised factories, or a system of national administration which takes any effective control of local government out of the hands of the local authorities. The second half of the nineteenth century had two striking examples of administered government close at hand: France and colonial administration everywhere. Post-revolutionary France, along with Prussia, was held up in England as the classic European gamble of a centrally administered state. In the early nineteenth century, English radicals tended to admire the 'rationality' of post-revolutionary French government, though the Napoleonic state, run by what we would now call technocrats, was a little hot for their blood. The other great example was British rule in India (and the India House bureaucracy in London). There a system of rational administration could gradually be put in place which did not have to worry itself unduly about either popular legitimacy or the rights of man. Pope's 'Whate'er is best administered is best' was the hallmark of the British Empire, and there was an early and firm connection between imperial administration and utilitarianism: both J.S. Mill and his father were London officials of Indian government. It was the Indian Civil Service which was the first British example of anything like bureaucracy in the modern sense of Max Weber. India House officials, and Indian civil servants (British, of course, not Indian, though technically Indians could apply) were recruited by competition and were supposed to hold their offices

502

through their own competence and not by patronage. The British home Civil Service soon followed the pattern of Indian Civil Service recruitment, and a British bureaucracy of high-minded and competent officials emerged which developed a strong sense of *esprit de corps*.

Liberal thinkers at least as far back as Adam Smith had been arguing for something very like this, but the problem for late nineteenth-century liberals was that the essential organs of the modern state were being developed at a time when there was lively debate among liberals about what forms state interventionism should take, with some liberals like T.H. Green arguing that something more than the old negative, factory-inspector kind of intervention was now appropriate to the times. The factory inspectorate was itself a bureaucracy, and the tendency of the age was increasingly bureaucratic, so that a bureaucracy which could easily be converted into a state administration was already coming into place when positive interventionism was added to the liberal agenda. As a matter of bureaucratic practice, there was no reason in the world why a bureaucracy recruited to intervene negatively should not convert itself almost overnight into a bureaucracy which intervened positively.

It must again be emphasised that what is being discussed here are matters *internal* to the development of the liberal tradition. It was not only liberals who were considering positive state intervention in the late nineteenth century. The greatest of all interferers were the socialists, who were joined only twenty or so years later by the fascists. This had its effects on liberalism. Liberal interventionist arguments had to be careful to keep a distance from socialist arguments on the same theme, as later they had to keep their distance from fascist interventionist arguments. Also, many liberals sniffed the way the wind was generally blowing and found it increasingly difficult to distinguish the theoretical basis for liberal interventionism from the theoretical bases of non- and anti-liberal interventionism. This effectively split at least English liberalism by pushing old-style liberals further back towards their true ancestors, J.S. Mill and Spencer. It is, therefore, a historical mistake to suppose that there is a serial relationship between Mill and Spencer on the one hand, and the positive liberalism of T.H. Green on the other. These two positions are rather to be seen as strands in the same rope, and in political practice individual liberals and liberal politicians found themselves on the interventionist side on some political issues but not on others.

T.H. Green's *Lectures on the Principles of Political Obligation* and the Case for Liberal Interventionism

As an interventionist Green is a Benthamite who comes to his interventionist position by an intellectual route which could not be more different from Benthamism. Benthamism's oddity in the liberal tradition comes out of its potential statism. We have already noted that Benthamism was double-edged as far as the state was concerned. The classical economics which the Benthamites believed in, coupled with their Malthusianism, can easily combine to give the impression that all Benthamism was anti-interventionist. We tend to forget that trade and population were special cases for which special arguments for non-intervention had to be found. Government, as a happiness-producing agency, could work best in special cases by leaving well alone, but this was never a generalised principle of the Benthamites.

503

(Even free trade was not an absolute principle, as opposition to the slave trade shows.) There was still a huge potential range for government intervention of a kind which would positively produce happiness or the means towards happiness, and in practice the Philosophical Radicals proceeded on a case-by-case basis.

The Benthamite case for intervention was rooted firmly in the view of the natural and human worlds current in the Enlightenment. The enlightened view was that nature was there to be controlled. Nature, including human nature, worked according to fixed and knowable laws, and a knowledge of those laws was the essential preliminary to making nature, in the form of technology, work for man. Nature, and man himself, was really a complex machine which could be made to work to serve human ends. Bentham thought about human nature like that. The human machinery worked by feeling pleasure as the result of certain kinds of stimuli and pain as the result of the opposite kind of stimuli. Mind was a register of pluses and minuses, pleasures and pains. A happy and successful life was a life lived on the plus side of the ledger. In economic terms this meant increasing control over nature. Economic growth, without which the greatest happiness of the greatest number was impossible, was just as essential to the success of Benthamism as a programme of statutory reform. A reforming programme, if it was to work, had to work on the human calculating machinery. The way to get men to begin to live different lives was to wave the carrot and the stick. Sometimes government would threaten to inflict pain in the form of punishment in order to get human beings to behave in the way they should, and sometimes government would offer positive, pleasure-producing incentives to change human behaviour. The distinction corresponds roughly to the difference between a judicial system and a system of social services (though the phrase 'social services' when applied to Benthamism in its early stages is anachronistic).

Green's interventionism does not come out of a view of nature of the enlightened kind. If Green has a view of nature, it comes out of the German tradition of *Naturwissenschaft*, of nature not as a permanent fixture of the universe either subduing or to be subdued, but as a living thing in which certain tendencies are gradually coming to fulfilment. Nature is something to be worked with in a spirit of informed co-operation, not something to be competed with, and certainly not something which it is possible to look forward to the final victory over. The Benthamite view of nature, and especially human nature, was acutely vulnerable to objections like those of Herbert Spencer that nature's laws would always win out over human endeavour in the end. Struggle *with* nature in the enlightened sense was very different from the Spencerite 'survival of the fittest' (the phrase is Spencer's own) struggle *within* nature. The evolutionist conception of all nature as a struggle for survival could not easily fit with the Enlightenment's central claim that human reason as technology could overcome nature. Spencerism can be seen in this perspective as optimistic Malthusianism. Nature is evolving our way, not against us. We have, therefore, no quarrel with nature. The only human institution which perpetually quarrels with nature is the state in its attempts to force nature to go in directions in which nature itself refuses to go. Green himself shares with Spencer the idea of nature as something to be co-operated with but Green has also to cast around for an idea of nature which can easily accommodate the activist state.

This he finds in the oldest of all coherent accounts of nature, Aristotle's. Evolutionism tended to play down the differences between men and all other animals because it regarded all forms of life as only minutely different from the next form of life down in the evolutionary scale. Aristotelian biology, or the view of man which Aristotle partly derived from biology, stressed that some kinds of men, who just happened to be Greeks, were separated by speech and reason from all other men and from all other forms of biological life. Aristotelian theology holds that every living thing has an end to which it naturally develops. What makes men, or at least Greeks, different is that reason and language enable them to know what their end is and consciously to strive towards it. Dogs don't try to be fully developed dogs; they either end up as fully developed dogs or they don't. Men are different because they can consciously tell themselves what the proper ends of their own lives are. Green generalises from the Greek example to include all human communities. Human societies can set themselves collective goals, or, in the language of Rousseau, human communities typically exercise a 'general will'. All human communities as communities are informed by sets of public values. Only certain very particular kinds of community actually legislate for their public values or goals, the Greek *polis* at its best, for instance, or a perfect Rousseauist community. All historical communities develop sets of behaviour-governing norms which are often as rigid and frequently much more binding than their formal laws. (One is reminded of the old Stoic definition of a community as a body of persons united in the thing they love.)

Green follows Rousseau in thinking of the content of the general will as being ethical, where the word 'ethical' is used in the opposite sense to 'utilitarian'. Green uses the word utilitarian to mean the pursuit of anything which you just happen to want and which you think at that moment will bring you satisfaction. Perhaps utilitarianism was never the 'when-I-itches-I-scratches' theory that Green says it is, but he is on to something when he says that people are capable of setting collective ethical goals for themselves as well as setting individual hedonistic goals, and he is certainly on to something when he points out that collective ethical goals require some sacrifice of inclination. Men want both the immediate satisfactions which their desires ask for, and also to pursue goals which require deferring or relinquishing the satisfaction of immediate desire. All this means is that men are prepared to make sacrifices for a higher good provided only that others are prepared to do the same.

But in what sense could this curbing of desire be considered to be 'natural'? Green's answer is that it always happens in communities. (He is tautological here, because he defines community as a group capable of willing an ethical end.) Living in a community, any community, means that one has to sacrifice inclination, and this becomes clearer as communities develop and their values and goals become more explicit. The question then becomes one of reconciling individual hedonistic goals with collective ethical goals. Green believes, like Mill, that freedom is the condition upon which the accomplishment of all goals, human and collective, depend, but his idea of freedom, and of the relation between freedom and the state, differs markedly from Mill's, and it also differs more markedly still from the ideas of earlier liberal thinkers like Paine and Locke. Green wishes to re-found the idea of natural rights to set his theory apart from utilitarianism and also to make the difference clear between his own idea of natural rights and an earlier idea of natural rights deriving from Locke.

Green's fundamental doctrine of rights is based on the criterion of social recognition. How, he asks, could a notion of natural rights arise? The old answer was always that natural rights were God-given and could be discovered by reason. God meant men to have natural rights and he meant them to be able to understand that they had them and he also meant them to understand that natural rights did not depend on society or government. Hence the invention of the idea of the State of Nature, where men enjoyed natural rights before government had been thought of and in a social state so primitive that it could hardly even be called a society. Green, like the utilitarians, will have none of that version of natural rights. The idea that we all have rights proceeds from the existence of a society. Rights are nothing without social recognition, and the very fact of the social recognition of rights in a community means that that society is capable of forming for itself an idea of mutual recognition of rights as a common good. Any society, then, is capable of that collective will which Green calls the general will. If rights do not precede the existence of a society but on the contrary proceed from it, then it follows that the formation of political society cannot have been done by contract. The classic contract theory holds that men agree to set up the state to protect their natural rights, and it is the consent required in this contract which makes the state legitimate. Again, Green thinks that this must be historically and logically false. The idea of contract, like the idea of natural rights, proceeds from the social recognition of the idea of contract itself, and it is probably fair to say that the idea that men should stick to the agreements which they make could only come to be widely diffused in a society with a legal system. Social contract theorists typically put the cart before the horse, arguing that the legal system of which the law contract is a part derives its legitimacy from the original act of social contract. They think that all law, including contract law, is itself based on contract. Green thinks that it is much more reasonable to suppose that general ideas about keeping agreements, and indeed the idea of social contract itself, was much more likely to emerge as a real society develops. Political society is not based on contract, but all ideas of contract, including social contract, come *after* the formation of political society. Therefore it follows that political society cannot have its origins in contract, and, more importantly, it follows that men's obligations to the state cannot be explained in contract terms.

The burden of Green's argument seems to be that living in political society naturally and straightforwardly entails political obligation in some form or other. Somebody who lives in a community but who doesn't think the rules apply to him has simply failed to understand what it is to live in the company of other men. Hence the real question is never: Am I obliged to obey commands of superiors or the law?; instead it is: What kinds of instructions and laws am I obliged to obey and in what circumstances? Green thinks that everything that is known about human association, past and present, domestic and foreign, testifies to the rightness of the way he poses the question of political obligation. We begin with the fact of obligation and try to unravel its practical and ethical nature. Ethical matters are plainly matters to do with rights, and Green's political philosophy is importantly concerned with finding out what rights can be enjoyed in political society and, more importantly, what rights are really worth having.

Green knows perfectly well that the idea of natural rights which he attacks arose at least in part from the desire to show that men have rights which the state may not violate with propriety and that they also have rights which are enforceable against the state itself. Green approaches the problem of rights within political society by recognising that the idea of rights against the state must have arisen out of a sense of alienation from the state, the feeling that the state is not mine, its values are not my values and its goals are not my goals. The state can thus appear as an alien thing to its members, one which at best can only expect a surly acquiescence from them. Rights against a state which you felt hostile to yourself might well be the kinds of rights which you thought were worth having. The problem with rights against the state is that it is hard to find a basis for them which is not vulnerable to Green's own attack on natural rights as they have been traditionally conceived. And besides, the state is almost certainly always going to win in rights conflict cases between itself and its members, except in the very exceptional cases of rebellion. Green thinks that a better approach to the problem, of which rights against the state is the solution, would be to ask why the feeling of alienation from the state arises in the first place, and this he explains in an unmistakably Aristotelian doctrine of 'end'.

We already know that Green believes that individuals and communities are capable of setting, and typically do set, themselves ethical goals, and that these goals are ethical in the opposite sense to the way Green uses the word utilitarian. He also realises that history teems with examples of communities which have found it difficult to set up ethical goals for themselves and history also teems with examples of communities whose own general will in Green's sense is completely at variance with, or simply irrelevant to, the state's will as that will is exercised through law and government. All conquered peoples fall into this category. Green was writing in the heyday of European nationalism and national unification, which meant the dismemberment of European empires into national states. Hobbes was turning out not to be true. When the sovereignty of foreigners collapsed or was expelled, the liberated territories did not return to a Hobbesian State of Nature. On the contrary, they stayed intact as communities and formed new governments for themselves more in keeping with their own communal will. Newly liberated communities frequently had fairly precise ideas about what kinds of governments they would like to have. Green took this as evidence of a real general will operating independently of government and in opposition to it. Alienation from the state can be collective as well as individual, and successful national liberation movements were examples for Green of the state's political will coming into conformity with the general will of a national community at the moment when it forms a government of its own.

The other place that Green looks for examples of the harmony between the general will of a people and its state is the ancient *polis*. Green's view of the ancient city-state is a bit dewy-eyed. He thinks of the ancient Greeks' political culture as being fortunate because it recognised no difference between individual and collective goals. Following Aristotle, he thinks that the ancient Greeks were incapable of conceiving goals as anything but collective. The Aristotelian good life could only be lived in a properly constituted *polis*. A man who could do without a *polis* was either a beast (or a barbarian) or a god. What this meant was that the citizens of the ancient cities – though not the women, slaves and foreigners – were capable of willing the city's good as their own good, the clearest example in history of the voluntary harmonisation of individual and collective will. Like Hegel, Green thinks that things went badly wrong after the Greeks, but that the modern world offers the conditions and the possibility for doing something about making individual wills conform to the collective will and vice versa.

Green, like all nineteenth-century reformers, sees the way forward in the exclusively modern phenomenon of public opinion. The real change which the eighteenth century brought to the world was that for the first time a substantial and influential body of public opinion arose independently of Church and state and was critical of both. Hume had said that government always rests on opinion, but by opinion he meant settled opinion, opinion accepted simply because there was no counter-opinion to unsettle it. It became a commonplace of Enlightenment that opinion-makers were the unacknowledged legislators of the human race. Customary opinion held the East in thrall so that even powerful emperors were powerless against it. The rise of public opinion really meant the rise of informed and dissenting opinion in social classes which mattered. By the middle of the nineteenth century even reactionary forces in European politics knew that they would have to fight reaction's battles in public. Public opinion was articulate and programmatic and represented the best thinking of the age, something like a change for the better in the general will of a society in Green's sense. Green thought that there was a chance for opinion to make its way in established states. The spread of democracy he regarded as giving teeth to opinion which would henceforward be able to get those teeth into government. Progress for Green, as it did for his philosophical mentor, Hegel, consisted of sifting existing institutions and practices to find what was rationally defensible in them with a view to discarding the indefensible and putting new institutions and practices in their place.

Green does not so much explain why progress happens as describe how it actually does happen. Enlightenment's habit of being as precise as possible about the aims and values of the state finds strong echoes in Green's belief that in the modern world a society can consciously propose a whole ethical programme for itself, with public opinion and the free debate of democratic politics as its vehicle. Green calls this freedom. His idea of freedom is variously derived from the ancient Greeks and from modern German Idealist philosophy, and in coming to a view of freedom as self-realisation Green seems to have travelled an intellectual route already familiar to Mill. Freedom for Green, as for the ancients and for Kant and Hegel, consists of the opportunity to develop oneself in the best possible direction. Human beings are capable of setting themselves rational ethical goals, and so are human communities. By 'rational' Green means what Hegel in his less rarified moments means by rational, that is to say 'thought out'. Like Hegel, he sees a time coming when the rules which men live by will be the product of rational choice informed by public debate. Again like Hegel, Green does not specify in advance what the final ethical goal of the state should be. He rather expects a political community to move towards ethical goals step by step, with public opinion now urging certain changes and now responding to positive changes by moving ahead to reformulated public aims.

The theory of natural rights in Green also serves as a rudimentary sociology. A political and social order is the essential condition for the mutual recognition of rights and for the idea to be general that mutual recognition of rights serves the public good. 'Recognition' is the key word. Green, like Hegel, thinks that as societies advance, larger and larger numbers of people will come to see the rationality on which their obligations as citizens are founded, and, again like Hegel, Green expects a fuller understanding to emerge of what it is to be a citizen. This emergence of a more inclusive and fuller understanding of citizenship can alter the state drastically as the state begins to sift and codify custom into positive law which appeals to men's reason for its legitimacy and obedience. What both Hegel and Green have in mind is the change from a state ruling by force, or through force of habit, to a state which increasingly sets itself the task of pursuing rational collective ends. A state like this, dependent on the general will of a society, when that general will becomes more rational and explicit will increasingly be able to feel confident that its laws will acquire the voluntary obedience of rational men.

Green then has to face one of the central questions of political theory: Are men always obliged to obey the state? Green knows perfectly well that one of the things which made the traditional theory of natural rights attractive was that it appeared to be unequivocal about the question of principled disobedience. States had the duty to protect pre-existing, State-of-Nature natural rights, so that when the state either failed to protect the exercise of natural rights or violated them, then men had the right, and even the duty, to refuse their obedience – that is, to rebel. Green is a liberal, and liberalism could never be seen to be giving the state a blank cheque to draw on its citizens' obedience. Yet Green is stuck with the idea that moral persons, capable of exercising and recognising the right of others to the exercise of natural rights, are only to be found in the state. He seems to be caught in the trap of having to say that asking for rights against the state is like asking for rights against oneself because we are what we are by virtue of what the state is. Green's way out of the dilemma is to offer a sociology of dissent which owes more to Locke than Green is prepared to admit. Green's sociology of disobedience again centres round the idea of recognition. Suppose the idea arises that the state refuses to recognise the exercise of something which can be called a natural right. Green again asks the question: How could such an idea of a natural right unrecognised by the state arise? Surely by the same sociological mechanisms which allowed the idea of natural rights to arise in the first place – that is, by social recognition. Therefore it follows that, for an idea of a natural right unrecognised by government to arise in a society, it must also be true that this idea of an unrecognised right is in fact recognised by a large group of the members of society.

The doctrine of emergent recognition gives Green his answer to the central question of political obligation: Should I obey the state all the time and under any circumstances? Green's answer is that this is not a question for individuals but for groups. A random individual is clearly not entitled to opt out of the state, as Spencer argued. Rights being dependent on collective recognition, only groups can have a say in the matter. If a state were consistently to fail to recognise emerging natural rights, that is, if a state consistently acted against the declared general will of its citizens, then resistance would obviously be justified, and since Montesquieu it had been a commonplace that this would be likely to happen anyhow. Green buttresses his position further with a sociology of obedience which again carries strong echoes of Montesquieu. He asks the very simple question: What is rule like when it is not based on continuing rational consent? (This question elides imperceptibly with the other question: What is rule going to be like in a state which fails to improve itself?) Obedience in such a state can only be rule by custom or rule by force. Rule by custom is hardly rule at all, because rulers are just as much the slaves of custom as the ruled in customary societies. (Montesquieu had pointed out more than a century before that the one thing Chinese emperors could not do was change China's laws.) That only leaves force and the threat of force. Green is concerned to attack Hobbes here, and the current jurisprudential idea of Austin that law was typically a command of a superior backed up by force, an idea of law still commonly shared by the utilitarians. Green thinks that rule by force is really another characteristic of non-rule. If it were really true that people only obeyed through fear, then few would obey because the prince's arm is short. Rule by force is a last resort of decaying states and empires. It is a signal that the ordinary consensual mechanisms of rule are breaking down. What, then, holds autocratically ruled societies together when these societies, if Green is right, cannot actually be held together by force? Again, Green's answer is custom, the general will of a society as expressed in commonly recognised values and goals (the chief of which is probably, following Montesquieu, religion). Whichever way you look at the question of why people do in fact obey or stick to their obedience, it always comes down to the general identification of individual goals with communal goals, the identity of individual wills with the general will. Hence the tag from Green's *Lectures on the Principles of Political Obligation* which everybody knows: 'Will, not force, is the basis of the state.' (The counter-tag, 'If you have them by the balls their hearts and minds will follow', forgets that it is impossible for a ruler to take the law completely into his own hands.)

Green's sociologies of obedience and disobedience get him out of the difficulty of having to say that one is always obliged to obey by showing that no real obedience to the state is being asked for in societies ruled by custom or by force. However, Green is still faced with the problem of deciding what the state may actually and legitimately do. Like Locke, Green thinks that the state exists to uphold natural rights, but he makes the crucial addition, which puts him worlds away from Locke, that the state is there to guarantee that every-body does in fact exercise rights. For Locke, the exercise of rights is optional. Men may not permanently alienate their rights to another, but whether they do exercise them in a positive way is up to them. Nobody ever argued that a man with the right of free speech was forbidden to be silent. Failure to exercise rights may be a waste of rights, and may even be impious if you believe that natural rights are God-given, but that is a matter between you and God and not between you and the state. All you can expect from the Lockian state is that it will protect you when you choose to exercise a natural right. The exercise of natural rights, as Locke conceives them, may even be good for you in some sense, but that again is a matter for individual choice. Not for Green. If one thinks of natural rights as the means by which human self-improvement happens, then self-improvement can be a collective as well as an individual goal. Of course, it can't be collective in a psychological sense without its actually being the goal of individual minds as well, or the goal of a large enough number of individual minds for the goal itself to matter by incorporating itself into the general will of a society. In our language, the idea of self-improvement must become a widely held value in a society for that idea to affect a society's politics.

The state, in Green's view, at least has the duty to encourage self-development. We are already a long way from J.S. Mill's fear that the state, and opinion in general, might be a threat to individual self-development in the coming age of democracy. How does the state promote self-development? In a famous phrase of Green's Idealist successor, Bernard Bosanquet, the state exists to hinder the hindrances to freedom. What that amounts to in simple terms is making a list of those institutions, customs and practices which hinder individual self-development, and using state power to remove or reform them, hence liberal interventionism. (And, liberal critics of Green might add, there can be no end to state intervention because there is no end to human self-improvement.) The state must try to make sure that the social conditions for the exercise of rights actually obtain, in so far as that is possible, at any given stage of a society's development, and this process is supposed to be cumulative. Under this heading come such social measures as making sure that the living and working conditions of the poor are tolerable (which means interfering with pure freedom of contract), that children are adequately instructed in the 'basic arts', that public health becomes a political priority; all of those things which the new interventionist liberalism put high on its agenda.

The state can only provide the conditions for moral self-improvement, and for Green it is a mistake to suppose either that the state can be indifferent to morality or that the state can impose moral ends on its citizens. The aim of Green's Idealism in general is that individuals will make the state's end their own, that wishing to act in accordance with the common good should become each individual's ordinary motive for moral, that is to say freely chosen, action. Green is punctilious about human motive. The true motive of right action is a conception of the common good, the free exercise by everybody of natural rights in Green's sense. Protection of natural rights is always embodied in law in a civilised society, so the citizen's first duty is legal obedience. Green knows perfectly well that some people only obey the law because of fear of punishment, so that their obedience is not free. Others obey the law because they have a conception of the common good which they see partially embodied in law. But there is a third category of obedience: those who come to conceive an idea of the common good through fear or through fear of social disapproval. Green counts this third class of law-obeyers on the side of the angels, because a conception of the common good does eventually come to be their motive for obedience. Their motive for the motive, so to speak, their reason for adopting an idea of the common good in the first place, may not have been 'good', but it is good that they eventually come to will the common good as their own will.

There are very strong Rousseauist overtones in Green here. He comes as close as he ever does to the idea that men can be forced to be free. Green's third category, those who really do come to an idea of the common good through either fear of punishment or social disgrace, are a kind of bonus, citizens who come to think the right thing for the wrong reason. These wrong reasons can easily be seen as Hobbesian or Benthamite. Fear or utility are at the back of them, and Green shows here that he fully understands the force of both the Hobbesian and Benthamite arguments because, as a matter of social fact, some will obey the law through fear, and some will come to their conception of the common good for utilitarian motives because they find living in a society easier if they share its idea of the

511

common good. Green, like Hegel, does not so much refute arguments (though he also does that) as show how they are only partial, single-sided, expressing a half-truth but not the whole truth. Green incorporates Hobbes and Bentham into his own argument, as he also does with Mill's idea of self-development, in a typically Hegelian way. One could go further, and take a Hegelian view of the development of English political theory through Hobbes, Locke, Bentham and Mill to Green. Earlier political theories might well be made to stand for the whole of political society as it had developed up to the point when a particular political theory gained currency. It might well be that a Hobbesian view of political obligation was appropriate to England in the middle of the seventeenth century, a Lockian to 1688, a Benthamite to the England of the early and middle stages of the industrial and democratic revolutions, and that Mill was appropriate thereafter. As Hegel says, nothing is ever completely wasted in the history of philosophy. Everything shades dialectically into everything else, and nowhere is this truer, and more deliberately true, than in T.H. Green.

What about the workers? They are Green's real problem. In England, aristocracy is on the run (though it still has a long way to go) and the middle class has already adopted that moral earnestness about public issues which Professor Richter has called 'the politics of conscience'. For Hegelians like Green, the English word 'conscience', meaning an inner conviction of right, is never very far away from what in English is ordinarily meant by 'consciousness'. It is not enough that the law should make thieves act as honest men (which Hume saw as the secret of the constitution of Venice). Thieves should act as honest men because the idea of the common good demands that they should not interfere with the exercise of the rights of others, which is the basis for the common good. Hegel had pointed out long ago that the 'rabble of paupers' which market society always produced were living at such a basic, animal level that the idea of consciousness of freedom for self-development becoming their ideal was a nonsense. It was just not sociologically possible for the bottom of the social pile even to begin to think what freedom might be. This might not matter to a particular kind of early nineteenth-century *laissez-faire* liberal, who would say that the poor are free, whether they know it or not, because they possess the freedom of contract to buy and sell like everybody else. Hegel will not have this, any more than will Marx or T.H. Green. Part of freedom was consciousness of freedom, so that it was the state's job to see that its lowliest members could take part in the conscious enjoyment of freedom.

What was to be done? To begin with, the working class had to be got out of the pub and into the classroom, and if that meant fewer pubs and shorter licensing hours, so be it. It also meant massively improved publicly financed education. It also meant better housing. All of these proposals were politically loaded. The brewers were Tories (the Beerage) and everybody knows that publicans are Tories. Public education meant increased taxation, including taxation of the 'unearned increment' (rents on land). Better housing meant treading on the toes of landlords and finding ways of making the aristocracy part with more land for building. No wonder that, as we noted above, a certain kind of Tory turned himself fast into a Spencerian non-interventionist. Green's list of interventionist measures in the *Lectures on the Principles of Political Obligation* is not very long, nor can it be. Green's confidence in future progress was much too Hegelian to allow him to plot the future in detail. New ideas of reform would come out of the future progress of society. Much better to get on with urgent present tasks, but on the clear assumption that there would be tasks in the future which would have to be attended to with a future urgency.

However, there is in Green much more than a hint of what the politics of the future will be like; collectivist not individualist, the politics of organised groups. The political theory of Idealism from Hegel to Green and beyond is often accused of being of a building castles in the air type, but it is arguable that the Idealists had a much surer grasp of the political sociology of modernity. All the talk about individualism in English political thought since the Enlightenment can easily give the impression that thinkers like Bentham and Spencer expected individuals to count in the political processes of modernity, but individuals don't count, only aggregrates. One of the things which democrats had to learn, and the lesson could be painful, was that only voices shouting in unison could be heard in the noise of democratic politics. This is already implicit in Green's doctrine of social recognition. Emergent demands for the state to recognise and to provide for the exercise of new rights must be the demands of groups for these claims to be taken seriously as claims to rights. All demands for enfranchisement are demands for group enfranchisement. This again had been implicit in the development of rights theory ever since feudalism began to decline. The idea that rights were good because they were enjoyed by only a few as privileges gave way to the idea that rights were good because they ought to be enjoyed by everybody. All reformist politics, except enlightened despotism, had been group politics, what we would now call 'pressure group' politics. The ideas which underlay any political movement could be as individualist as you please, but the form that politics must take in a democratic world must be collective. Green has none of the misgivings about this which beset other liberal thinkers like Mill. Fear of the collective, the idea, for instance, that group opinion is probably bad opinion simply because it is group opinion, does not seem to have worried Green as it worried earlier liberals and as it was later to worry the theorists of the elite and the crowd. Thinkers as different as Montesquieu, the nationalist theorists, and Hegel had reinforced the old Aristotelian idea that intellectually there was safety in numbers. One still sees in Green the Hegelian idea that the historical process will sift out the good from the bad, the gold from the dross.

Some of Green's critics have seen something potentially sinister in Green's celebration of collectivities, and especially in his insistence that the state may meddle with ideas of the good. It does not matter to the critics that Green expressly states that the state may not meddle with morality direct but only with the conditions in which morality arises and strives to perfect itself. A certain kind of highly individualist critic reaches for his Mill *On Liberty* when he sees the words 'state' and 'moral goodness' in the same sentence. The origins of this impulse go right back to the methodological individualism of seventeenth-century science via the liberalism of the first half of the nineteenth century and the Enlightenment's emphasis on God-given rights, one of the natural enemies of which was the state. The great corrective to this view was undoubtedly Hegel and the extent to which Hegel follows Rousseau. Like it or not, the state will always at least try to clothe its own acts with the language of morality. Even Machiavelli believed that consistent action in the service of a system of values was essential for the very survival of the state. So the question to be put about the state is not: Ought the actions of the state to be informed by a particular morality?, but: What particular morality ought to inform the state's action? The state has always been a moral agent in another sense. States had always preached obedience as a good. States have been peddling moral truths ever since the state began, and all Rousseau, Hegel and Green do is to accept that as an inescapable fact and begin to wonder whether it might not be good idea for a real collective choice to be made about what morality the state does in fact embody or attend to.

And if T.H. Green is sinister, then so is Aristotle, which almost nobody ever argues. Green reiterates Aristotle's contention that obedience to the law alone does not make a good citizen. The state exists to promote 'the good life' by creating the conditions in which the good life may be lived. Some of those conditions will be essentially negative. Any good *polis* would outlaw lying, cheating, assault and murder as being so obviously inimical to any idea of the good life that they may safely be made into the prohibitions of positive law. But that is only a beginning. Aristotelian citizens are expected to use the social peace which law provides to become active citizens, taking part in ruling and being ruled, and as a body they are supposed to be able to agree among themselves what it is to be a good citizen and even a good man. Amiable competition in the exercise of the virtues completes the Aristotelian *polis* founded on law. Green shares that perspective. Why should the state not have an end and direct its affairs with a conception of the end in mind? Like Aristotle, Green thinks that men do in fact already do this in their capacities other than as citizens. Aristotle had taught long ago that all human action is directed towards the good, or towards something which men call good. Men already know how to be good husbands and fathers, and how to manage a household before they become citizens. Other collectivities are end-directed, so why should this not also be true of the state?

Green is not Aristotle. Nowhere is this more obvious than in the suspicion of great landowners which Green shares with all radicals from Tom Paine to Lloyd George. Landed aristocracy is a thing of the past. Aristocratic ownership was originally founded on force, not right, (the Norman) conquest, not law. The great landed estates are a reminder that the world was once ruled by force. Land is not like capital, because the stock of land is fixed. What one man owns excludes others from land ownership (Britain had a peasant problem in the nineteenth century in Wales and Scotland, and above all in Ireland). Ownership of capital, on the other hand, was not exclusive. Any man, even the worker with his savings bank or building society, could aspire to modest capital accumulation and, the growth of capital being unlimited in principle, one man's gain was not another's loss. Aristotle had taught men to view as suspect all mercantile wealth and had warned against treating slaves as tools for making wealth increase. Green believed with all liberals that economic growth had put a reasonable stake in the country within the reach of more men that any previous generation had thought possible. Capital ownership takes over from Aristotelian land ownership as a politically and socially cohesive force. (I leave unanswered, as being anachronistic, the question of whether Aristotle would have approved of the extent of landholding of some members of the British aristocracy in the nineteenth, or indeed in the twentieth century. I merely wish to allude to the fact that nineteenth-century liberalism deviates, probably for the first time, from the ancient connection between the ownership of land and political virtue.)

What Green does get right is that the distinction intervention/non-intervention is theoretically dubious and practically arbitrary. The state is an 'interferer' by its very nature, requiring men to do this and not to do that. We do well to remind ourselves that the original non-interventionist argument in Adam Smith was technical and not based on high principles of liberty. Smith is as certain as he can be that, whatever else might be true, it is certainly true that states as then constituted were not competent to manage economies. (And we do equally well to remind ourselves that Smith was just as sure that certain necessary social tasks like education and public works in general could not safely be left to the market.) The liberal consensus since Smith had been that free enterprise is the most efficient way to increase wealth, so that no liberal ever dreamt of favouring a state-managed economy. But there was a huge theoretical and practical difference between saying, on the one hand, that free enterprise was the most effective wealth creator and saying, on the other hand, that government should never do anything which can affect either the wealth-creating process itself or the results of that process. Mill had pointed the way forward by suggesting that the state might take an interest in how the wealth created was actually distributed. What liberalism had to do in the second half of the nineteenth century, Spencerism expected, was to try to untie the knot which Manchesterism had tied between classical economics and *laissez-faire*. To the chagrin of the *laissez-faire* liberals, it was not all that difficult. There were hundreds of ways that the state could intervene in a society whose wealth was created by private enterprise without actually taking over the running of enterprises itself.

And there now existed a state which had made great progress towards the acquisition of the expertise necessary to make social intervention work properly. Liberals of an earlier generation than Green sometimes forgot where their call for efficient government was leading them. The attack on aristocratic incompetence since the second half of the eighteenth century had by Green's day largely won its case. Civil Service was the Victorian ideal of government, and this meant the growth of a professionally competent administrative corps (though that was too French an expression actually to be used) which could do what they did efficiently and cost-effectively. Liberals, without knowing it at the time, had long been busy creating the means by which government could intervene in society without bungling. The real danger to the *laissez-faire* rump of liberalism was that some day a liberal economist would proclaim to the world that Adam Smith's original warning about governments running economies need no longer be heeded because there now existed a body of true economic doctrine which showed how government could manage economies better than those economies themselves. Looking back at Adam Smith's *Wealth of Nations* after Keynes is to realise what a hostage to liberal fortune the original non-interventionist theory actually was.

Nothing in the history of political ideas is ever wholly new, but it is surprising how quickly the new can become the old and then become the new again. What was Green's interventionism, and liberal collectivism in general, but the positive side of Benthamism back with a vengeance in the borrowed clothes of continental Idealism? The Idealist arguments themselves were not new – Hegel himself had died the year before the first great Reform Act of 1832. Hegelianism was in fact contemporaneous with Benthamism,

515

so that the Oxford Idealism (as it came to be called) of T.H. Green was the result of the combination of two older sets of ideas. This was sometimes confusing to Green's own contemporaries in England. Old surviving Benthamites could not understand the new arguments for state intervention, couched as these arguments were in an Idealist language utterly foreign to the native tradition of Benthamism; nor could those who accepted Mill's arguments for liberty easily accommodate the vocabulary which Green used to show what freedom really was. But what Green's liberalism lost, the native English tradition of liberalism gained, because, compared with Green, Bentham and Mill at least talked the same language.

NOTES ON SOURCES

Spencer's politics makes easier reading now than his large volumes on psychology and sociology. The latest edition of *The Man Versus the State* is Mack and Nock (1981). *Herbert Spencer on Evolution*, edited by J.D.Y. Peel, is a useful collection. Peel's *Herbert Spencer: The Evolution of a Sociologist* (1992), is an excellent intellectual biography.

For T.H. Green, see Harris and Morrow's edition of his *Lectures on the Principles of Political Obligation* (1986), and M. Richter, *The Politics of Conscience: T.H. Green and his Age* (1964).

Part VII
REACTIONS TO
LIBERALISM 1:
HEGEL – THE STATE
AND DIALECTIC

22
HEGEL AND THE HEGELIAN CONTEXT
OF MARXISM

GEORG WILHELM FRIEDRICH HEGEL

Hegel led a very unexciting life for a thinker who was such an inspiration to his contemporaries and successors. Nineteenth- and twentieth-century social and political thought are unthinkable without Hegel, yet Hegel's own life (1770–1831) did not come into much contact with the great events he lived through and commented on. The one exception is the famous occasion when Hegel saw Napoleon – the world soul on horseback – at Jena in 1806. Prussia's defeat at the battle of Jena established French hegemony in Germany. That hegemony only lasted a few years. Nevertheless, it was Jena and its aftermath that made Germany one of the key players in world history in Hegel's sense.

Nearly all of Hegel's life was spent as a teacher and a scholar. He was brought up a Protestant in the relatively liberal south German atmosphere of the Duchy of Wurttemberg, and he was a student at Tübingen (1788–93) when the Bastille fell. From then on, Hegel's own life can be seen as a paradigm of the responses and reactions to the French Revolution of liberals all over Europe: the initial enthusiasm for Reason and Liberty; the doubts beginning with the establishment of the French republic and then quickening with the execution of the king and queen; the hostility to the wars of conquest, and then the full nationalist reaction when Napoleon conquered nearly the whole of Europe.

While all this was going on, Hegel was quietly climbing the academic ladder. He spent some years as a tutor, then was appointed at the University of Jena (1801) where he completed *The Phenomenology of Mind* (1807), thus setting the agenda for the study of the history of culture for a very long time to come. After that he spent eight years as a rector of a *Gymnasium* (1808–16) at Nuremberg; he got married and finished his great work on logic. There followed a chair of philosophy at Heidelberg and later (1818–31) at Berlin. We are told that as a lecturer he mumbled, which is odd, considering that some of his works were put together posthumously from lecture notes taken by high-minded students who were members of the Prussian officer corps. His great work, *The Philosophy of Right*, appeared in 1821.

Hegel's Christianity was always eccentric, and it is hard to pin down. Some argue that Hegel's theology (in so far as he had one) is the way into his politics, while others argue the reverse. Hegel was taken in his own day (and especially by the radical Left Hegelians) to be a supporter of Hohenzollern rule in Prussia, and it is true that he was translated to his chair in Berlin University to combat dangerously liberal tendencies among its teachers and students. Hegel, however, is nothing if not a constitutionalist, and Prussia had not even become a constitutional monarchy when Hegel died in 1831.

Hegel has the reputation of being a 'difficult' thinker in the English-speaking world, and it is easy to see why. Hegel speaks the language of German Idealist philosophy, which is at the same time technical and slippery in translation. Nobody denies the influence of Hegelianism on the development of Marxism, though there are disputes about the extent to which Hegelianism can still be detected in Marxism as a finished product. This question of how influential Hegel was on Marx has had the unfortunate tendency, happily now beginning to be reversed, of making people think that Hegel is only interesting to the extent that he influenced Marxism. Hegel's political theory, it is sometimes said, was seen and seen through by Marx in his *Critique of Hegel's Philosophy of Right*, and this in its turn has led to the view that Hegel on his own isn't up to much. Hegel is in fact a much tougher thinker than this view would have us suppose. What follows in the next section is an overview of Hegel's political thought as a whole which bears in mind that Hegel leads to Marx, but which still tries to give Hegel his due as a thinker in his own right.

HEGEL'S VIEW OF HUMAN CONSCIOUSNESS

As a philosopher, Hegel is interested in how the thinking mind actually views the world. Philosophy is about mind, what Hegel calls 'the thinking view of things', and so he is interested in the history of human consciousness. The mind is there for understanding the world outside the self, while that self is still part of the world which the mind seeks to understand. Hegel thinks the mind really does *try* to grasp the world outside the self. Mind is active. It does not wait for sense impressions queuing up at the fingers' ends or at the eyeball to ask politely for admission to the mind. The mind reaches out to make the world coherent. And Hegel means the world as a Whole. Hegel is an Idealist; he thinks that an Idea of the world presents itself to mind, or is created by mind, *as a Whole*. Thinking minds are full of impressions from the outside, and the more a mind is a thinking mind the more it will go after those impressions, but mind's real job is to organise these impressions into a coherent whole. In a sense, we have a view of the whole *before* we have a view of the parts of the world because the mind which reaches out to understand the world is a whole mind already.

Hegel thinks it is a mistake to suppose that we build up a view of the world bit by bit, as if we were mapping a landscape. We may pretend we do that, but we do not. As a theorist of knowledge, Hegel is poles apart from the English empiricist tradition following Locke which holds that we build up a picture of the world gradually as the senses provide more and more sense experience, so that the more experienced adult, 'having seen more of the world', has a fuller picture of the world 'out there' than is possible for the relatively inexperienced child. Children can't know the world as adults know it, and advanced civil-isations know the world better than primitive peoples. The triumph of the Lockian scheme is science, which patiently builds up knowledge of the world and organises it into a body of tested and reliable theory. This science contains all the sciences as we know them: natural science, social science, the science of history and political and economic science. Hegel does not think that we look at the world like that. He thinks that the child has a view of the world as a complete view (children 'live in a world of their own'), and so does the adult. The moderns have a view of the world as a whole, and so did the ancients. These views of the world are internalised. There is no 'out there', with an existence independent of the observer, which these internalised views of the whole world can be compared to and judged true or false. Views of the world are simply different. The World as it is experienced by human consciousness is the picture of the world a man carries about with him in his own head. Cultures differ because members of a culture carry round in their minds a view of the world which is different from the view carried round by members of a different culture.

It follows that the World is Mind, if all we have is a self-made (or a culture-made) view of what goes on 'out there'. The 'out there' becomes a metaphor for the 'in there' which is Mind. It follows, therefore, that all understanding, philosophically conceived, is Self-Understanding. When we attempt to understand anything about the world, what we are in fact trying to do is to fit new experience into a view of the whole which already exists in our minds. Of course, this must mean that our minds change, and Hegel knows that the child's mind is not the adult's mind, nor is the mind of the ancient world the same mind as the mind of contemporary man. Mind develops, but does not develop in the way that, for example, a map of the sea-bed is developed: one moment we know what *this* bit is like, but not *that* bit. The development of mind is not 'taking away from ignorance', or shining a light where before there was darkness. Of course, taking away from ignorance happens, otherwise positive science would be impossible, but this Hegel thinks is not the same as a change of Mind. Mind does in fact change gradually (and Hegel will later give a set of cogent reasons why changes of Mind should never be hurried), and these changes are cumulative, but Mind changes as a landscape changes. A landscape changes gradually, so that we are hardly aware of each little change. We know it is altering, but at each moment of change the landscape is still a whole and therefore still recognisably itself. Cumulative change over a period ultimately becomes qualitative change, the moment at which we say: but it's *all* changed. Landscapes can even change overnight, but that is only a metaphor. What we really mean is that one last change has completed a transformation which has in fact been going on for some time. For us, a Whole can quite suddenly become a different Whole. Hegel thinks that a culture can change like that, or a constitution, or a political or social system. Even the world of learning can change overnight in this sense. Some books can change the intellectual landscape of a subject. They don't just 'add to the subject', as most books do – another electoral study, another commentary on Hobbes – but change the whole shape of an area of enquiry. When that happens, we know that we are confronted with a different Whole.

These Wholes, views of the world, Hegel calls 'real'. They are Ideas of the world, and that is why we call Hegel, and those who think like him, Idealists. Ideas of the world are real because they are the only things which we can be sure we really have. The only thing we can be really certain about is that we carry a picture of the world as a whole inside our own heads.

The question then arises: What do we do with these ideas of the world when we know we've got them? The answer is that ordinary men do not do very much with their ideas of the world (with the one possible exception of their religious observances). Hegel would say that the proper work for thinking men is trying to understand the world, which, as we have seen, means understanding what they carry around inside their own heads. What, then, does understanding these ideas of the world mean? We already know what it cannot mean. It cannot mean comparing a view of the world to the world outside the self, because no world exists beyond our idea of it. Ideas of the world are an internalisation of the 'out there'; they are not a photograph, or an approximation, and these ideas are literally all we've got, or all we can be sure we've got. What we can do with these ideas depends on what we *want* to do with them. Hegelian men are not passive creatures. Their minds reach out to grasp the world, and they have a will, and this will is a will to understand what it is to have a view of the world, and a will to understand particular views of the world, including one's own.

According to Hegel, one of the things men want is to feel at home in the world, to be easy with their view of it. Men feel uneasy when they do not feel at home in the world of which the self is a part. This feeling of not being at one with the world Hegel calls 'alienation' (*Entfremdung*). A feeling of being at one with the world is what Hegel thinks characterised the ancient world at its best, especially the world of the ancient Greeks. The best of the ancient Greeks were whole men. They lived without fear (except the fear of death). They embraced the world, and so were not narrow. Of course, that did not mean that they were always happy. Odysseus was a man of sorrows, but the world of Odysseus contained every requisite for human fulfilment. It would never have occurred to the ancients, at least before they invented philosophy, to want another world. They knew about other worlds, Rome in the West and Persia in the East, for instance, but they knew that 'the good life' could only be lived in a properly constituted *polis*. If the world of the Greeks was good enough for the gods to share, then it was good enough for men.

The ancient world was a whole world, and while that world was whole there was not any real point in thinking self-consciously about it. It was only when the wholeness of their world was challenged by the new experience forced upon it by Alexander's conquests in the East that philosophers like Plato and Aristotle began to ponder their own world's real meaning. Philosophy, the thinking view of things, is always a bad sign for a world, because it signals that a world has had its day. The weakening of Hellas caused by the Peloponnesian War in the days before Plato, and the threat that the *polis* would become a sideshow to Alexander's new-fangled multi-racial world empire, *caused* philosophy. The very existence of philosophy, and later of philosophical change, is always a sign that things in the world are changing, and philosophy, coming *after* change occurs in the human landscape, cannot put life back into a dying world. As Hegel famously says in the Preface to *The Philosophy of Right* (1821):

Philosophy comes too late to teach the world what it should be. When it paints its grey on grey, a form of life has already grown old, and in grey on grey it can never be made young again. The owl of Minerva takes its last flight when the shades of twilight have already fallen.

HEGEL ON THE FUNCTION OF PHILOSOPHY

If philosophy cannot breathe life into a dying world by making recipes for the future, then what is philosophy to *do*? Hegel answers the question of what philosophy can do through a critical commentary on what philosophy has tried to do in the past and failed to do. The process of the dissolution of the ancient world set men on the path of thought. As Nietzsche was later to say, Socrates taught men to question their desires. Men began a kind of uneasy introspection, the beginnings of that 'unhappy consciousness' which was to figure so prominently in Stoicism and later in Christianity. When they began to question themselves, men began to think that they had possibilities within themselves which living in the world could not satisfy even in principle. Alienation is not human unhappiness, though unhappiness of a particular kind can be a sign that alienation is happening. The alienating moment comes when men become aware that even if they could have everything the world has to offer, they would still not be satisfied. In the ancient world, not everybody had been satisfied, and one class, the slaves, had served as the means which made the good life possible for free citizens, but at least the possibility of human fulfilment was *there*. To fail to live the good life was to have been unlucky, or to have missed an opportunity, or to have accepted the second best, or to have been lazy. We only have to read a few pages of Aristotle to realise how strenuous the good life was. The ancient claim to virtue was literally to be good at being good. To keep on being fit for goodness required practice. Without the constant exercise of it, goodness can become rusty, but in the ancient world the possibility of living the good life was at least there.

What is a man to do in the world of the unhappy consciousness? In it, there is no life which is whole and good. Nothing which a man does will wholly satisfy him. There are always the consolations of religion, but the religion of an alienated world will always be an other-worldly religion. Man comes to separate his God from the world. From now on there is to be no happy sharing of the good things of life by both gods and men. God confronts a wicked world. He becomes a judging God, the terrible Jehovah of the Old Testament, a God outside life and who disapproves of it. (A perfect image of this is certain forms of devil-worship in the Middle Ages: the Creation has become so corrupted that the only way God can get back into his own is in the guise of the devil. Therefore you worship the devil on the chance he might be God himself.)

How, then, does philosophy cope with this alienated world? In the past thought has typically coped with an alienated world by utopian dreaming. Men have looked at the world and have used their thoughts to judge it: *this* is what the world is like, *that* is what it ought to be like. Philosophy has been doing something like that since Plato's day, confronting a hostile world and remaking it in the image of its own thoughts. Philosophers have been trying to teach the world what it should be. Hegel believes there is a certain truth in utopianism, but that it is not the truth which the dreamers suppose. The fact that philosophers have felt constrained to paint pretty pictures of an ideal world is proof that consciousness is dissatisfied with its own world. Utopianism's error is to mistake cause for effect. Alienation is philosophy's cause, but philosophy of the utopian kind cannot even begin to bring about the end of alienation. The critical philosopher looks at his own contemporary world and sighs for a better. Rousseau did this before the French Revolution, but what Rousseau failed to understand was that his sighs for a better world were a sign that his own world was in fact beginning to crumble. The very act of trying to understand a world, and then questioning it, is only possible when a world is complete, and to say that something is complete is to say that it is over: a life is only complete at the moment of death. This accounts for the form which utopias nearly always take: they are their authors' own worlds turned upside down. Thomas More's Utopians make their piss-pots out of gold, and the most gaudily dressed among them are the servants while the big-wigs are plainly dressed. A utopian dream is its own complete world turned on its head, but to be able to see his own world turned on its head, the creator of a utopia has to be in a position to see his own contemporary world as complete, and whole, and therefore about to pass away. Utopian dreams are dreams about the improvement of worlds at those worlds' last possible moments. Philosophy in this sense comes after; it is an effect and not a cause.

As a cause, philosophy is usually a disaster. Utopian philosophy tries to breathe life into a dying world. The French Revolution in its radical phase tried to bring a social order back to life by turning it on its head, and to do that the Jacobins had to use the Terror. Terror is the only weapon available to revolutionaries because only fear can lead men to think the right way up after they have been socialised by the world to think the wrong way up. It must never be forgotten that for Hegel the world is not just an *out there* in which an *I* operates. The world is already *my* world. I act in the world as it appears to me, and I literally cannot know how to act in a world which is not mine. (And that is another reason why utopias are worlds turned upside down: utopian worlds are meant to be recognisable in a topsy-turvy way.) Revolutionaries notoriously want to 'change the world', which clearly means changing what goes on inside my head. This cannot be done by reasoning, because what goes on inside my head *is* reason. My mind has been spending its life constructing the view of the world which I happen to have. Without reason, the only weapon is the Terror. All revolutions, Hegel seems to be saying, are excessive, and necessarily excessive. Utopian philosophy is not, however, wasted. It signals change, though it misunderstands its own function when it tries to direct change.

Not all philosophy is of this utopian, world-changing type. Some philosophy is frankly reactionary, and a reactionary philosophy was especially attractive after the excesses of the French Revolution. Utopian philosophy is at least rational, though it finally misunderstands the function of reason as philosophy. Utopian philosophy is philosophy making a mistake. Utopians condemn the world because it is not like the new world they have constructed in their own heads, therefore the world is not rational enough. Reactionaries, those German romantics for instance who longed for a return to the world before yesterday when nobody had heard of Rousseau or of Liberty, Equality and Fraternity, affirm and glory in the world because it *is* irrational. The reactionary accepts the world as it is, and the more senseless the world appears to be the more he loves it. Ancient customs, institutions developed by accident, chance historical survivals, throw-backs and missing links are cherished because they are ancient, are accidental, and have survived. That is what lends them enchantment. Any unbiased observer can see that what is being admired here are the surviving fragments of a vanished world. A world of accidental survivals cannot be a real world because it can no longer be made whole. The fragments have no coherence, and to try to construct a whole world out of them is not so much mistaken as ridiculous. What makes it irrational is not a mistake about the function of thinking so much as a wilful failure to understand that a world has passed away. To pretend that the French Revolution and Napoleon have not happened is an irrational closing of the mind to the world which presents itself to it.

So if philosophy is not to be utopian, and not to be reactionary, what can it do? What is the mind's job? Philosophy is the thinking view of things, so what is philosophy to think *about*? Hegel's answer is to say that the mind's job is to understand itself and the forms which it has taken in the past. The mind's job is to plot and understand the process of its own development from where it began to where it is now. This is a vast programme, because it amounts to no less than a whole history of philosophy.

THE HISTORY OF PHILOSOPHY AND THE PHILOSOPHY OF HISTORY

Hegel thinks about history on the grand scale. The history of philosophy is the account of the great world-historical changes of mind. It is the philosopher's special task, and so it is worth asking how the philosopher's mind differs from the minds of ordinary men. Hegel has a tendency to speak of all minds as if they were the same, but this cannot really be true. The World-as-Mind which presents itself to the mind of the philosopher and to the mind of the ordinary man is the same world, so what can the difference be between the mind of the philosopher of history and the mind of an ordinary man? It is easy to see what the difference is not. It is not that the philosopher of history knows more about the world and its past than others; that might be the difference between a learned man and an ignoramus, but it is not the difference Hegel is trying to pin down. Still less is it a difference in knowledge about how the natural processes in the world work, because that is what distinguishes the man of science from the layman. Rather, what distinguishes the philosopher from others is that the Philosopher has an *Idea* of the interconnectedness of things over long passages of time.

But how can the philosopher be sure that he has such an Idea when there are things about the world which the historian or the scientist knows that he does not? Plainly, there must be a criterion of importance which tells the philosopher what he must know and what he can safely leave to one side. Hegel thinks that the study of history, philosophically conceived, involves the development of a special skill which enables the philosopher of history to distinguish between what he calls 'Horatian gold' and 'mere externality'. 'Mere externality' is the dross of history, things which just happen or happen by chance. 'Horatian gold' is buried in the dross, and it is the philosopher's special job to sift through the dross, discard it, and what is left is the gold he had been looking for all along.

What could this high-sounding project entail and how could it be carried out? Hegel in fact thinks that the march of history itself makes the job easier because history does its own sifting of the dross. How, then, does the dross get washed away so that only the real stuff of history is left? Hegel thinks that the stuff of history is plain for the philosopher of history to see when an epoch has passed away. What a particular historical epoch has it in it to be only becomes apparent when everything about that epoch except its spirit has disappeared, in the same way that you can only see the bones of something after the external flesh has perished. What survives from one historical epoch into another is what was real about it. What was true about one epoch in history is most easily seen and identified when it appears later in an epoch which is not its own. For Hegel, what survives from one epoch to the next never dies, but it stands out most clearly in different surroundings, a plant if you like in a different garden, in different soil, surrounded by different plants, but still recognisably itself, even though effectively it has become something different in order to be recognisably itself in the same way that a plant transferred from one soil to another becomes in some senses a different plant.

These survivals from one epoch to the next are what give history its continuity and coherence, what keeps history moving. What, then, distinguishes one historical period from the next? As an Idealist philosopher Hegel has to say an Idea, and that Idea is always an idea of freedom. What constitutes a world-historical era is the prevailing idea of freedom which was possible in it, but not an idea of freedom narrowly conceived. Hegel thinks an epoch's idea of freedom informs and is informed by everything else of importance in that epoch, so for the idea of freedom we should read in the modern idiom a particular culture, including but not confined to a political culture. For Hegel, there are only really three great world-historical epochs: the world of the ancient despotisms; the world of the classical city-states, and the modern period which is Christian Europe leading to what he will call Constitutional Monarchy. In the ancient despotism, say Persia, only the despot was free, and Hegel thinks that his own time is about ripe for Constitutional Monarchy (which he sometimes refers to as 'Germanic') in which all men can be free. Epochs change when they have developed to their full potential, when they have become what they have it in them to be within their own limitations. Of course, men living in their own time, and even the philosophers among them, cannot see their own limitations, so each epoch presents a view of itself to itself as a finished and eternal truth. Aristotle's *Politics*, for instance, is the most complete account we have of what it was like to live in an ancient *polis* because it comes near the end. Perhaps Aristotle even knew this himself (though the city-state lasted as a caricature of itself for a lot longer), but he cannot know or acknowledge anything else. As Hegel says, you might as well ask a man to jump over the Colossus of Rhodes as ask him to jump over his own time.

The history of philosophy becomes the philosophy of history because a distinct pattern makes itself apparent in the process of historical change itself. History does not stand still, nor does it move at random. Hegel thinks that these great world-historical changes of mind are leading somewhere, and that something is guiding them. In the *Lectures on the Philosophy of World History* Hegel says that the Sovereign of history is Reason. He appears to be saying that reason is both the motor-force of history and the means by which history is to be understood. How can this be?

HISTORY AND DIALECTIC

The history which reason investigates is not ordinary history, which concerns itself with everything which happened in the past, but that special kind of history which deals with how one world-historical epoch shades into another. If Reason is to be the Sovereign of history that must mean that it is Reason which causes the great historical changes, and if Reason is to be both the force for change in history and the means by which history is understood, then it must be the case that history and the investigating mind of the philosopher work in the same way. Hegel calls the motor-force of history, and the way the philosophical mind works, dialectic. History's rules, and mind's rules are dialectical rules. The rules of historical change and the rules of intellectual method are the same. Dialectic operates in individual minds and in what minds set out to investigate. This may be massively tautologous, another way of saying what Hegel already thinks, that the world *is* Mind: two things which act in the same way must be the same thing, or two different ways of looking at the same thing. Dialectically operating minds can be perfectly attuned to the understanding of historical dialectic.

Everything we said above about Plato's dialectic applies to Hegel's idea of dialectic, and we would do well to remind ourselves just how complex the idea of dialectic is when it applies to what goes on in a single, finite mind, let alone when it is applied to the whole process of world history from the beginning. Dialectic in the investigation of something has the following six characteristics:

1 Dialectical investigation proceeds by stages, and at each stage of the argument a position is advanced which is presented as a finished truth.
2 Nothing is ever wholly true or wholly false. Nothing is wasted because a position needs its contradiction to move on to a higher stage of synthesis.
3 Because nothing is ever wasted, because everything is incorporated into the higher stages of argument, it follows that the nearer to truth dialectical argument gets, the more comprehensive the truth being offered becomes.
4 Truth comes from the process of argument itself and is not introduced from the outside.
5 Because truth comes out of the process of argument, it is not invented but discovered, not created but grasped.
6 There are no short-cuts to truth in dialectical argument, and for dialectical argument to work the participants have to recognise that each stage is necessary. Dialectical argument will not be hurried.

Hegel thinks that the historical dialectic works like that.

1 An idea of freedom arises in a society which is its prevailing idea of freedom until it is contradicted by a new idea of freedom. This new idea of freedom becomes a blend, a synthesis, of old and new ideas, and it too has its day until it in its turn is challenged and a new idea of freedom blending old and new emerges to take the world into another historical epoch. The process continues, Hegel thinks, until Absolute Freedom is

reached, corresponding to truth in ordinary dialectical argument. Like truth, Absolute Freedom both is internally consistent and exists without contradiction – no new idea of freedom emerges to challenge it.

2 Any idea of freedom incorporates all past ideas of freedom. We have no reason, therefore, for being scornful of the past, or even particularly superior, and certainly not smug. If we patronise the past, the future is likely to do the same thing to us.

3 But there is progress, because through dialectic freedom becomes both more comprehensive and more comprehensible, which means that more and more people are capable of understanding freedom and therefore of being free.

4 Freedom is at first dimly perceived, while at some time in the future it will have emerged clear, ready for all to see. But the process cannot be hurried. Freedom comes out of the historical process, so every stage in its development is necessary. Freedom, therefore, is an affirmation of the historical process, not a denial. Therefore, all revolutionary attempts, like the French Revolution, to abolish the past in favour of a completely new future are doomed.

5 Freedom comes out of the historical process, therefore it follows that it was really there the whole time. Rousseau, therefore, cannot be true; freedom is not invented out of someone's head.

6 There can be no short-cuts, so attempts to storm heaven are a waste of blood. A revolution is an attempt to see too far ahead, guesswork, and the French revolutionaries got it very badly wrong. Instead of Reason, Liberty and the Rights of Man, they got the Terror and Napoleonic despotism.

FREEDOM DEVELOPING TO ABSOLUTE FREEDOM

Hegel's theory of history is progressive: more and more people are coming to understand what freedom is and more and more people are actually coming to enjoy freedom as the form of the state changes. But Hegel still has to deal with the sceptic who might say: It is one thing to say that the world is freer today than it was yesterday, but how can we be sure that the world is going to be freer tomorrow than it is today? In particular, the sceptic might be tempted to ask *where to look* to find out whether there is this general improvement in mankind's lot. And in a philosophy of history like Hegel's there is a special problem. Hegel seems to be saying that we can never know the present, let alone the future, in the way we can know the past. We may be able to read the signs of the future in the present, but that is an enterprise fraught with the difficulties associated with utopianism, which Hegel criticises on precisely the grounds that utopianism always and necessarily reads the future wrongly. And suppose, further, that by commonsensical standards the present seems to be worse than the past, so what of the future? And how does this affect ordinary men? Philosophers of history may be temperamentally inclined to take the very long view, but what about the rest of us? Hegel hedges. We may take consolation in religion: the march of freedom is also the march of God.

Hegel calls God Reason in Process. By this he means that God is not outside the world judging the world. God is not an Old Testament god, turning up from time to time to judge a world of which he disapproves. In the words of the hymn, 'God is working his purpose out as year succeeds to year.' God is in the world and is the essence of the process by which the world progresses, but it is not just by living in God's world that we receive the grace of His approval. God puts us to the test from time to time (one of the things we pray for is that God will not put us to the test, lead us into temptation, too often). One of the ways God tests us is that from time to time He tests our faith in His ultimate purpose, and He does this by making a generally progressive world temporarily disagreeable to see if we can keep our faith in his Providence. That is what Hegel means by the famous phrase 'the Cunning of Reason': God tests us in ways at which we can only guess. In part, the idea of the Cunning of Reason comes from the older traditions of Jewish and Christian messianism. What we suffer now has a purpose in an end which we can now only dimly perceive. As the good book tells us, there will come a day when all will be made plain. The suffering of the Children of Israel will make sense on the day on which they enter the promised land; the suffering of Christians will make sense at the moment when they enter heaven. Hegel differs from these messianic visions because his is not a 'big bang' theory. Deliverance does not happen all at once; there is no 'moment' of entry into the promised land or heaven, no miraculous moment of revelation. God does not do it all at once, either in His own person at the Second Coming, or in its secular equivalent, the French Revolution. Hegel's God is eminently Protestant. He does His work thoroughly and steadily as the ages unfold.

FREEDOM AS MEMBERSHIP OF RATIONAL STATE

God may be testing the faith by temporarily obscuring some future good, but where do we look for that future good? Hegel's answer is unequivocal: the locus of man's present and future freedom is the state. It is here that Hegel's political thought can be tricky for those brought up in the Anglo-Saxon tradition to believe that the state is the locus of constraint and that society is the locus of freedom. In the Lockian tradition, men are members of society and of the state. As members of society men are spontaneously and naturally free to pursue their self-chosen ends, and as members of the state men are obliged to obey those laws which exist so that citizens do not pursue their ends by such illegal means as theft, assault or murder. Society is the locus of freedom and the state is the locus of constraint, and liberalism is a set of arguments about just how much constraint is necessary for men to pursue their self-chosen ends without causing actual harm to others. Freedom and law are two jealous antagonists, as Bentham said, and it is no good pretending otherwise. For the utilitarians, as for Locke, all the state may do is constrain, and liberals will watch the state as a constraining mechanism every inch of the way.

Hegel does not look at the state like that. Though he knows the liberal position and even has some sympathy with it, Hegel is one of the first thinkers to begin to think beyond liberalism almost before liberalism itself had become a recognised and complete political, social and economic doctrine. We have already seen that Hegel accepts that worlds change. He accepts that the French Revolution was what Marxists were later to call a bourgeois revolution, which means a revolution in the name of Lockian natural rights, and therefore a revolution in the name of liberal, free society coming out of the remnants of a seigneurial past. Hegel also accepts that the French Revolution has had an irreversible effect on Germany. Not to accept that would be to fly in the face of all reason; the dismantling of the *ancien régime* is now far advanced even in backward Germany. Men now live in what Hegel calls Civil Society, a form of society in which men may choose to live any life they please, provided only that they *can*. Civil Society is feudal society's opposite. In feudal societies, men are supposed to live the same lives their fathers led: serfs passed on their serfdom as an inheritance to their children. Hegel is too good a historian to believe that feudalism lasted unchanged till the storming of the Bastille and then disappeared in a moment, but he does think that the French Revolution signals that the old order is definitively over, and that the future belongs to bourgeois society, which means factories and parliaments.

The Lockian liberty of Civil Society is the liberty of buyers and sellers, and one of the commodities which will be on sale will be labour. It was his observations of what happens to sellers of labour (coupled with more than mere acquaintance with the political economy of the Scottish Enlightenment) that made Hegel look at Civil Society with a slightly jaundiced eye. Bourgeois society was the sphere of what Hegel calls rights, not Right. The freedom of bourgeois society he describes as 'unimpeded activity', and he claims that Civil Society is concentrated on the 'particular', not the Universal. In the unimpeded activity of buyers and sellers in bourgeois society, Hegel noticed that the sellers of labour often do particularly badly (he is not so concerned that the buyers of labour do particularly well). There is a tendency for a 'rabble of paupers', what was to become the famous 'industrial reserve army' of Chartists and Marxists, to accumulate at the bottom of Civil Society. What could the freedom of Civil Society mean to them? Hegel accepts that Civil Society is freer than the society of the *ancient régime*, but it is plain to him that Civil Society cannot universalise freedom. Membership of the rabble of paupers may change, as men go into and out of it as they find and lose buyers for their labour, but the group itself remains, what in the modern idiom could almost be called an underclass.

Why does that matter to Hegel? It matters because of the connection which Hegel insists upon between freedom and rationality. For Hegel, freedom is not a condition which you can be in whether you realise it or not. Part of the mind's progress since men began to think was the progress of the consciousness of freedom, which meant that more men were becoming free and could understand what being free meant. How could this mean anything to a class intensely concerned with where its next meal was coming from? Freedom moves from particularity to generality, until it stumbles over the Hegelian underclass. In the ancient despotisms, only the despot was free, so that the only way for a subject to dream of freedom would be to dream of becoming despot himself. Slaves in ancient cities might have dreamt of becoming free men and owning slaves themselves, but slaves there would always be. The modern world's claim to modernity, according to Hegel, is that it holds out the hope that all men can be free, but how can this be with a rabble of paupers at the bottom of the social heap?

Hegel's way out of the difficulty comes when he begins to ask himself what it was about previous epochs of world history which meant that in them freedom could not universalise itself. His answer always comes down to the fact that in previous epochs there was no separation between state and society. In the ancient cities, the citizens were the rulers, and part of rule was keeping down the slaves. To be on top in the ancient city was to be on top politically, and economically and socially. Freedom was the cause of an intense competition between slaves and free men which free men were meant always to win. The world of bourgeois society separates the state from society. There are no longer any stately constraints on what kind of life a citizen might live. All liberalism rests finally on that distinction. Hegel thought, though, that men at the bottom of the pile did badly out of the separation between state and society. What was to be done about them?

The answer was obvious: if Civil Society could not universalise freedom, then that only left the State. The State, then, must be the locus of true freedom in so far as true freedom can be realised at any particular time. Only the State is capable of concerning itself with the Universal, not the particular. The State has to rise above the selfish striving of Civil Society, and to be able to do that it must be as separate from Civil Society as it can possibly be because the State must be able to take a very high-minded view of Civil Society.

THE SEPARATION OF CIVIL SOCIETY FROM THE STATE

What does the rather grandiose phrase 'separation of the State from Civil Society' actually mean? It is really an attack on amateurism in government. Mixing society and the state means that rulers come out of society because of their position in it. Local government by JPs in England in Hegel's day is an obvious example. Those who were socially at the top of the pile were chosen to exercise the function of rule in that society. In this sense, all premodern forms of rule were amateur, especially rule in feudal societies where the functions of boss and ruler met in the feudal lord, so that it was impossible to distinguish between the two roles of economic and social, and political superiors. Adam Smith had argued some sixty years before Hegel's *Philosophy of Right* was published, that, in modern commercial society with its increasing divisions of labour and increasing business efficiency, rule too should be professionalised. The militia had had its day; from now on the very model of a modern state was to be the Prussia of Frederick the Great. That position is fully worked out in Hegel's *Philosophy of Right*, with its plea for rule by a scholarly and socially objective bureaucracy serving a constitutional monarch advised by estates of the realm. Being separate from society, the bureaucracy can take a very long view, and the king, being king by hereditary right and constitutional legitimacy, need fear no competitors for his crown, so that he too is above the selfish competition of Civil Society.

Hegel thinks that the present does not abolish the past but completes it. Modern constitutional monarchy is not the abolition of medieval or divine right monarchy, but its completion. What Hegel seems to be saying is that constitutional monarchy is monarchy thought out by rational men for whom hereditary succession alone is not enough to make a man king. Constitutional monarchy re-founds an old institution on a rational basis. The same is true for other social institutions and customs. These are not abolished but thought out again. Families do not cease to be families because men have thought out what family life actually means, and customs are not abolished when they are transformed into rationally thought-out law. The modern world in Hegel's language becomes more 'self-conscious'. Mind is its own age reflected in thought, but modern men have history to help them. By reflecting on what has gone before, the modern mind can become more conscious of itself by knowing what it is different from. Mind does not abolish the past but builds on it. In a sense, men had always known that: even Plato realised that the world of the Homeric poems was over, and that in the future the Homeric hierachy of kings, heroes, ordinary men and slaves would have to be re-argued from scratch.

In a more self-conscious age, law must share that self-consciousness. Hegel describes law as 'the World of Mind brought out by Itself', by which he means that it is no longer enough that the king should simply will something to turn it into law. Law must be rational, reasonable and thought out. Hegel's *Philosophy of Right* is not a law-code but an account of the grounds for a rational theory of law. Hegel thinks that the modern state is rational because constitutional monarchy invites our understanding. The modern state's claim to our loyalty is not simply dynastic, traditional, or sentimental, though Hegel does not despise these types of claim, and it might still be true that most men are only capable of seeing their loyalty to the state in these terms. Rational men, and especially philosophers, are different. They can look at the world and see that it is right.

THE STATE AND FREEDOM REVISITED

It can still be objected against Hegel that he has shown how the state is rational, but failed to convince us that, in being rational, it has universalised freedom. And in what does this freedom consist? It is a notorious problem in Hegel that he can say on the one hand that the state is rational to the extent that it realises freedom, and on the other hand that the state as an end has supreme right over the individual whose supreme duty is to be a member of the state. Whatever that sounds like, it does not sound to liberal ears like freedom at all. Hegel has been accused of being a 'cock crowing on the dunghill of servility', and it has to be said that on freedom he is hard to pin down.

Perhaps the best approach to Hegel on freedom is to regard his theory of freedom as a philosophical commentary on the epoch of the French Revolution and its aftermath, particularly in Germany. Before 1789, Germany was little more than a geographical expression. There were over three hundred German states, duchies, free towns, seigneuries, towns ruled by bishops, as well as the larger states like Prussia, Bavaria, Saxony and Austria (which was itself a patchwork of different jurisdictions). The effect of the French Revolution was to rationalise the German state system as the smaller states were incorporated into the larger. Hegel was enthusiastic about the French Revolution, which broke out when he was a student at Tübingen, but, as with many another intellectual, what began as enthusiasm ended in disillusionment. But Hegel never lost the initial inspiration that the Revolution was made in the name of reason and liberty. After the Restoration in 1815, Hegel found himself in a quandary, caught between the sentimental reactionaries, who wanted a return to what was left of Germany's feudal past, and the romantics who thought that the Revolution signalled the end of all restraint whatsoever. Hegel wants to steer a middle course between the two: on the one hand he wants to argue that there is a case for the state, but on the other hand he wants to argue that there is a case only for a certain kind of state. To do this, Hegel has to argue that there is some point to being part of the world. Hegel thinks that all revolutionaries reject the world in its entirety and want to begin again. He also thinks that this enterprise is as doomed as trying to regain virginity.

In the Introduction to *The Philosophy of Right*, Hegel takes up the problem of how we can be free while recognising restraints in his theory of the Moments of the Will. Hegel says that there are three moments of the will which desires to be free. The first moment Hegel calls 'pure abstraction', the moment when the will wants to free itself completely from the world's constraints. This, Hegel thinks, is only a single aspect of will, though it is easy to mistake it for the whole will. Examples of the will as 'pure abstraction' would be Hindu mystical asceticism, where the will truly seems independent of the world which surrounds it, or Jacobinism, in which the whole of previous history is discarded in favour of a virginal re-beginning. In the first moment of the will the Understanding is not, properly speaking, active in history, for it is by definition indeterminate, not tied down, 'pure mind'.

The second moment of the will is a moment of 'determinacy'. This represents the moment when the will recognises that pure abstraction is an absurdity because it prevents the man whose will it is from taking part in history by existing empirically as a fact, taking part in events, and institutions. Indeterminacy was a denial of the whole world of objects, of the world outside the self. Determinacy is the desire of the self-conscious individual to act *in the world*. So how does indeterminacy become determinacy? How does the thinking individual overcome his alienation from the world outside himself, what Hegel calls 'action in the service of reason'? The moment of determinacy consists of more than the desire for biological survival and more than just accepting the world as it is. The original negation of the world is replaced by a desire to be 'of the world', what Hegel calls the 'negation of the negation', or echoing Fichte, the 'finite or particularisation of the ego'. It implies that the original negation of the world by 'pure understanding' is itself negated by a desire to re-enter the world of human existence.

How is this to be done? Hegel says through 'singularity', the merging of the two moments of the will. Will, he says, makes itself 'objective' by seeking to repossess what had once seemed to be an alien world, which in simpler language means working to possess objects, or simpler still, property. Men seek to negate the separate existence of the world of objects by possession, and possession is coercive in the sense that possessors need the protection of the state's law to confirm them in the possession of that without which they would not be part of the world at all. Possessions bind us to the world of other men, and work allows us to make our impression on the world.

It is easy to see here what Hegel does *not* mean by freedom. He sets his face against any idea of freedom which means mere caprice. Of course, he seems to be saying, the world of objects impinges on human consciousness, the Hindu ascetic in his cave possibly excepted, but free will does not consist of being able to do uncaused or unpredictable actions. Freedom in the sense of unpredictability would be called madness or eccentricity or negation of the self ('he is not himself today'). Freedom is not the expression of that which is different in each of us, which is not that different anyway, but on the contrary the expression (echoes of Kant) of that which in us is universal. At best, freedom as eccentricity or caprice is to be found in Civil Society, not the State.

It is through the rationally pondered law of the State that men become free because they recognise in the State their own aspirations writ large. In this sense, the State is 'objective will', will freed of all selfishness and egocentricity. Law as compulsion is therefore freedom realised, as far from the hotch-potch of conflicting selfish wills which go to make up Civil Society as it could possibly be. Of course, this acceptance of the State entails an acceptance of the State's own limitations at any particular moment in the State's development. What the State is, is really the maximum amount of freedom which is possible at any given time, and to expect more is to expect the State to jump over the Colossus of Rhodes. Hence the Hegelian aphorism that 'freedom is the recognition of necessity'.

THE STATE DIFFERENT FROM ITS INSTITUTIONS

It is easy to mistake the State's institutions for the State itself. The State needs its institutions, the bureaucracy, estates and monarchy in order to function, but, properly speaking, the State is all-of-us, but all-of-us thinking about ourselves in a way which is different from the everyday way. Hegel makes a very useful distinction between everyday morality and Sunday morality. On Sundays, we put on our moral Sunday best, go to church, and pay allegiance to a morality which is higher and purer, but not substantially different from, the morality of the workaday world. Hegel wants us to think of all-of-us as the State like that. The ordinary world of Civil Society is a world of conflicting wills, controlled by law, no doubt, but none the less conflicting. The State is the moment when we stand back from our ordinary selves and think of ourselves as having a single will, all dressed up in our Sunday best.

THE HEGELIAN CONTEXT OF MARXISM

When Marxists talk about the history of socialism, they tend to give the deliberate impression that because socialism is really Marxism, it follows that the invention of socialism comes *after* Hegelianism. We therefore do well to remind ourselves that socialism was being invented in France and England while Hegelianism was being invented in Germany. It should not surprise us, then, if Hegelianism and early socialism addressed themselves to much the same problems (and indeed Hegelianism is sometimes called 'Prussian socialism'). Of course, it was not Hegel who made Marx a socialist, but it was Hegel who turned Marx into the kind of socialist thinker he eventually became. Marxism was to share with Hegelianism a concern for alienation, for the socially disruptive nature of capitalist individualism and for the nature of the modern state, and Marxism in its formative stages was largely a critique of Hegel's view of all three.

What Hegel hated about traditional religion, especially Catholicism, was its other-worldliness and consequently its affirmation of this-worldly alienation. The Catholic view of the human condition as it comes out of St Augustine (and is only modified by Thomism) accepts the alienation of man from his true nature as a given of human existence. The burden of sin is permanent until death or the Second Coming. Man's true nature lies in his union with God before the Fall, and in heaven after death. This alienated human nature also alienates men from their fellow men because sinful men live uneasily with their fellow sinners. Dents in this gloomy version of human living had been made by certain kinds of Protestantism. Living in a godly commonwealth, for instance, might make the salvation of souls more likely, but the alienating burden of sin was still there. Strictly speaking, in this view of things, there was not much to human history. All the great events were either in the past – Creation, Fall, Redemption through the life of Christ – or in the future – Christ's eventual return to judge the nations. Some human communities were better than others, and God had permitted them to survive and even to prosper, but on the whole human existence was conditioned by events over which men had no control. Hegel offered a way out of this trap by suggesting that the alienated condition of man had a genuinely historical dimension to it. Men had not always been equally alienated from their fellows, and the historical process, properly understood, showed a tendency to make those improvements in human living which would be pleasing in God's sight. In the ancient Athens of Pericles, the distinction I/We did not have the force it was later to have, and the march of freedom through the State as God's march meant that one day, perhaps even soon, men would come to live in a society whose level of self-consciousness and self-understanding was such that they could begin to enjoy some of the Absolute Freedom which Hegel always indentified with God. Hegel owes a good deal of his theory of history to Enlightenment theories of history as progress, but what was really new was that Hegel was able to tie God so centrally into his scheme.

Marx was an atheist, but he retains the Hegelian idea that alienation is a historical category, capable of a genuinely historical explanation, and therefore capable of changing, perhaps drastically, in the future. Marx's own explanation of Christianity owes to Hegel a contempt for its other-worldliness as an attempt to reconcile men to the inevitability of an alienated human existence, but Marx will look for the causes of that alienation in the processes of capitalist-industrial production in a way that Hegel never did. For Hegel the Idealist, alienation results from a wrong way of looking at the world and not from the material conditions in which men earn their daily bread. Reason is even more cunning in Marx than in Hegel. Hegelianism had always had the problem of explaining away an un-progressive present in the cause of its general contention that things are getting better, and this was done by arguing that God temporarily obscures future good in order to test the faith. Marx goes one better. He says: look into the present mess itself, and you will see the bright future in the dreadful now. Industrial capitalism in crisis is not a pretty sight, and it has horrifying effects on the working class, but, properly understood, industrialism's future lies with socialism, not capitalism.

The disruptive effects of capitalist individualism are plain to see in Hegel, especially in the famous paragraphs on Civil Society in *The Philosophy of Right*. Marx shares with Hegel the

536

view that the French Revolution signals the ushering in of a new kind of social and economic order whose chief characteristic was going to be economic and social individualism. The career would be open to the talents as men were invited to compete with each other. Marx was greatly encouraged by the young Engels' *Condition of the English Working Class in 1844* to look at the chaos of the Manchester cotton industry in slump to see where the future lay. It lay in Manchester, not London; in social and economic conditions, not politics; in Chartism properly understood, not in liberalism; in the reports of the factory inspectors, not Royal Commissions. Hegel's 'rabble of paupers' in Civil Society becomes in Marx the proletariat with the threat of unemployment hanging permanently over their heads. An increasingly divided society, with workers and employers shaking their fists at each other across the class divide, is what the future has to offer, a dialectical contradiction which cannot be mediated by the state for ever. Something has to give, and Marx thinks that the future belongs to the proletariat once it becomes conscious of itself and its historic task in a way which more than echoes the Hegelian idea that rational men will come to be self-conscious about their place in a properly constituted state.

It is over the question of the neutrality of the State that Marx really begins to part company with Hegel. Hegel thought that the State, if separated from bourgeois society, could really be a neutral umpire in the conflicts which would necessarily arise from bourgeois society's 'unimpeded activity', that is to say its uncompromising individualism. A State which provided good education for everybody, which fixed maximum prices and minimum wages, and which made provision for the deserving poor could keep the conflicts arising out of bourgeois society permanently on the back-burner, so that they were not dialectical contradictions at all. The very existence of the State was proof that a society recognised the alienating effects of capitalism and was responding to them in a positive spirit. Marx cannot think like that. For him, Hegel's solution to the problems of capitalism is nothing short of a farce. Marx makes Hegel's theory of the State stand for the modern state in general. In one sense the modern state is separate from society because it does not attempt to regulate economic life in detail, but in another sense the State is profoundly of its own time because it attempts to mediate dialectical contradictions in favour of those who run the present, which can only mean the bourgeoisie. The central insight which Marx shares with early socialists like Saint-Simon and Robert Owen is that in capitalist society the bourgeoisie only *appears* to be in control of the economy – otherwise why would there be booms and slumps? – while it really does control the State in the sense that it never occurs to the state to do anyone else's business. It was his *Critique of Hegel's Philosophy of Right* (1844) and his close observation of the British state during his long exile in England which enabled Marx to see that the claims to neutrality for the modern state were fraudulent. The modern state might possibly be separate, but it was certainly not neutral.

Marx's critique of Hegel begins from the end of Hegelianism, the theory of the State, and works backwards towards a fundamental critique of Hegelian Idealism. For Marx, Hegel's theory of the State does not solve the problem of class conflict but on the contrary institutionalises it. Hegel's constitutional monarch will have estates to advise him, and these estates will be based on social divisions: agricultural, industrial, and a third estate. What is that if not the institutionalisation of aristocracy, bourgeoisie and the rest? The problem of the bureaucracy is even more obvious. Where is that bureaucracy to be recruited from? Scholarly and high-minded bureaucrats will either represent the interests of the class from which they come, or, more likely, will come to think of themselves as a fourth estate with a class interest of their own. Far from mediating class conflicts arising out of Civil Society, Hegel further complicates the conflicts of Civil Society by adding extra class interest to it. Far from taking a detached and universal view of Civil Society and so overcoming the social aspects of alienation, the existence of the Hegelian state is the proof that alienation does in fact continue to exist. How could it be otherwise, when Hegel's state institutionalises class divisions and adds the bureaucracy as another particular, not universal, class to Civil Society?

HEGEL AND THE YOUNG HEGELIANS

Both Marx and Engels began as Young Hegelians, and it might be useful to ask what it was which attracted them to Hegel in the first place. In a very general sense, the Young Hegelians were attracted by Hegel's claim to have 'realised' philosophy and to have overcome the latent tension between thought and the world. This tension had taken many forms in the history of philosophy – as the tension between ideas and experience, for instance, or between thought and action, or between spirit and matter, or between philosophy and reality, or between God and the world. Plato thought that the world was a shadow and that only philosophy was real. Christians believe that the world is a tissue of vanities and only God is real. Rousseau thought that the world betrayed an idea of justice, and so on. What all these ways of looking at the problem of the relationship between philosophy and the world have in common is that they use thought to *judge* the world: what *is* is what *ought not to be*. Socrates failed to bring philosophy down from the heavens to be realised among men. All of these views posit an ideal world outside ordinary human sensuous experience and contrast the world of experience to it.

Not Hegel. God is 'Reason in Process'. God is in the world and marching with it, not outside judging it. Gradually and dialectically, ideality becomes reality. Part of what the world *ought to be* is realised in what *is*. Hegel had apparently solved the most tricky problem of all, the relationship between the world of philosophy and the world of experience, and that is what attracted the Young Hegelians and in particular Karl Marx. It was only later, under the influence of Ludwig Feuerbach's *Essence of Christianity* (1841), that Marx and Engels began to realise that Hegel had merely substituted one crucial problem for another. Hegel might have explained the relationship of ideas to reality, but he failed to offer any satisfactory answer as to which was primary – ideas or the world.

The question of primacy matters a great deal, because for Marxists everything else hangs on it. If Hegel is right, and thought conditions life, then solutions to the problems of human living are a matter for thought, or of looking at the world aright. The world is explained in terms of ideas, and in Hegel's case the ideas are ideas about freedom developing dialectically from the beginning. Human problems, then, can be substantially solved in consciousness. If, on the other hand, life conditions thought, then thoughts can only be changed by changing human circumstances, what Marxists call *praxis*. (A more sophisticated Marxism adds that the relationship of ideas to the world is itself dialectical.) The Idealist position leads to a certain political quietism in Hegel: the world has to wait for ideas to change, and it has to wait a very long time for these changes in ideas to penetrate the consciousness of ordinary men. Ideas of freedom are realised in the State, and because the process by which ideas change is slow, changes in the State must be slow too. There is a lot of waiting around implied in Hegelianism.

But suppose life conditions thought and suppose a life that is changing very quickly. Then both life and thought can change quickly, which means *everything* can change quickly. In this perspective Hegelianism denies its own premises, because it is at once a response to a rapidly changing world and a denial that the state can change very quickly with it, and perhaps Hegel came to think that because he over-concentrated on the political at the expense of the economic, or in Marxist language, on superstructure at the expense of basis. Perhaps Hegel was active as a political thinker just too soon to realise how quickly capitalism could change the world while at the same transforming itself. By 1850 it had become a commonplace that ten years' change in bourgeois society was worth a century's change in feudal society because feudal society could not change itself. Surprising things could happen to the state in a world where the pace of economic and social change was so rapid; at some time in the future the state might even disappear.

Another way of looking at the connection between Hegelianism and Marxism is to ask what it was that allowed such a revolutionary style of thinking as Hegel's dialectic to be used to come to such tame political conclusions. Hegel's Prussia was not even a constitutional monarchy in Hegel's own lifetime. Marx and Engels have no doubt that, properly considered, the Hegelian dialectic dissolves all dogmatism. Hegel's great service as a historian of philosophy was to show how closely thought is attuned to its own time. It is not necessary to refute all past systems of philosophy in order to argue a philosophical position in the present. After Hegel, all that had to be done with philosophical systems from the past was to show that they were so attuned to their own time that with the passage of time they became redundant. What is true of ways of looking at the world is also true of how the world is organised. Forms of the state, like forms of thought, have had their day. According to Marx and Engels, Hegel saw this but failed to have the intellectual courage to think the matter through to its end. If the Roman republic was 'real' in its day and so was the Roman Empire after it; if the French monarchy was 'real' before 1789 and so was the French republic after it, then what is the point of stopping at the Prussian monarchy and saying that it will be eternally 'real'? Surely the dissolution of all forms of dogmatism in philosophy through the dialectical method implies the dissolution of all forms of dogmatism about the State. There lay Hegel's great mistake, in founding a system of politics at all.

But if Hegel's philosophy, and the form of the State which it defends, is to end up on the scrap-heap of history, then where does history itself end? The clue lies in Hegel's philosophy itself, in the idea of a universal class. Hegel had vainly hoped that the universal class would be his bureaucracy of high-minded and scholarly officials whose title to rule would be Weberian expertise. Not so, says Marx, because the bureaucracy either represents the class interest of the class from which it was recruited, or constitutes itself as a class with an interest in its own right. Therefore the Hegelian bureaucracy cannot signal the changeover from the particularity of Civil Society to the Universality of freedom or, what comes nearest to it in a still imperfect world, the Hegelian state. Where, then, is the class to be found which can be truly universal? Where is the class which can universalise itself because it needs no eternal dialectical opposite to give itself consciousness of itself as a class? That class can only be the proletariat, because, while the proletariat needs conflict with the bourgeoisie to make it begin to feel its identity as a class, that identity once established, there is no reason why everyone should not eventually become a proletarian. In doing this, the proletariat would abolish itself as a class, there being no other class against which the proletariat would need to form its own consciousness. Divided humanity would become humanity again, and truly human history could properly begin.

NOTES ON SOURCES

Hegel's *Philosophy of Right*, ed. T.M. Knox (1942 and various reprintings), is essential reading, especially the Preface. Duncan Forbes's edition of the *Lectures on the Philosophy of World History* (1975) contains an excellent introduction. There is a useful collection of Hegel's *Political writings* (1964),by Knox and Pelczynski. H. Marcuse, *Reason and Revolution: Hegel and the Rise of Social Theory* (1963), and S. Avineri, *Hegel's Theory of the Modern State* (1972), are outstanding commentaries. C. Taylor, *Hegel* (1975), is also first-rate. R. Plant, *Hegel* (1973), is a very good introduction. Karl Popper, *The Open Society and its Enemies*, vol. 2, is good, knockabout stuff.

Part VIII

REACTIONS TO LIBERALISM 2: SOCIALISM

23

MARXISM AND OTHER SOCIALISMS

KARL MARX

Born in 1818, the son of an enlightened Jewish lawyer and convert to Christianity, at Trier in Rhenish Prussia, Marx grew up in a culture in which the rationalism of the Enlightenment met the Romanticism of nationalism to produce a welter of contradictory liberationisms, one of which was socialism. (Marx would eventually marry a Prussian baroness, Jenny von Westphalen.) The young Marx disgraced himself in his year at the University of Bonn. At the University of Berlin Marx took up the prevailing Hegelian philosophy with considerable enthusiasm, wrote his father some conspicuously mendacious letters about the amount of work he was doing, and decided to pursue an academic career. He had already been something of a red (of the utopian socialist kind) in his adolescent years, and at Berlin he became one of the left-leaning Young Hegelians. The reactionary politics of the 1840s effectively closed the door on the possibility of Marx's ever gaining a university post in Prussia, so Marx turned instead to radical journalism. The following year Marx decamped to the centre of radical Europe, Paris, where he met Engels for the first time and quickly became a communist.

The revolutionary peripatetic years followed before Marx moved to England in 1849, where he settled himself in Dean Street in London's Soho to earn a living (often subsidised by Engels) as a journalist. The years 1848–9 saw Marx heavily engaged in the German *émigré* working-class politics of the Communist League and it was as young revolutionary members of the League that Marx and Engels wrote *The Communist Manifesto* in that great year of the revolutions, 1848. There is every reason for supposing that at the time Marx regarded his stay in England as a temporary measure to escape the attentions of the European police, but he was to remain an English resident for the rest of his life: Marxism, like Aristotelianism, is therefore a metic's doctrine.

Marx's fortunes in England improved enough for him eventually to settle comfortably enough in Hampstead. He was back in revolutionary politics in the early 1860s with the foundation of the International Working Men's Association (the embryo of the First International), whose inaugural address and statutes Marx wrote. The publication of the first volume of *Capital* (in German) had to wait till 1867 (and it was not to appear in an English translation in Marx's own lifetime). It failed to make him famous, and most of the modest notoriety that the living Marx enjoyed came from his writings about the Paris *Commune* of 1871, and from the very late *Critique of the Gotha Programme* (1875). Marx spent the remaining years of his life working on further volumes of *Capital*, but it was left to Engels after Marx's death in 1883 to edit them into publishable form.

Marx was once asked what he hated most in all the world, and his answer was not capitalism but servility.

FRIEDRICH ENGELS

Engels was the original of all salon bolshevists. From the age of fifty until he died in 1895, he was able to live more than comfortably off his capital while subsidising Marx and writing impeccably Marxist books and tracts which were an inspiration to revolutionaries from Ireland to Siberia.

Engels was born in 1820 into a prosperous, pious and mildly philistine German family which claimed Huguenot descent. His great-grandfather had established the family textile business at Barmen in Rhenish Prussia, the most highly industrialised part of Germany. Young Friedrich preferred the Germany of the poets and dreamers, becoming a member of the literary and radical Young German Movement (Heine was a member) and writing himself while he pretended to attend to his business education as a clerk in Bremen. He began to turn away from literature to philosophy, and he frequented Young Hegelian circles, then considered rather advanced, while doing his military service in Berlin. On his way home in 1842, he met the editors of the communist *Rheinische Zeitung*, including Moses Hess and Marx, though the latter and he were cool towards one another.

In 1842 Engels escaped from the stifling atmosphere of Germany to Manchester, right in the heart of Chartist Lancashire, and the fruit of that first stay in England was the first Marxist classic, *The Condition of the Working Class in England*. Engels again met Marx (in Paris) in 1844 and found that they were both on the way from 'utopian' to 'scientific' socialism (though the terms themselves date from slightly later). The years from 1844 to 1850, when Engels settled in Manchester, were full of revolutionary propaganda and activity. Engels was prominent in anti-government demonstrations in Germany in 1848 and took part in the popular uprisings in south Germany in 1849 (where his opinions were a bit red for what were essentially peasant movements).

From 1854, when he established himself in the firm of Ermen and Engels in Manchester, Engels enjoyed himself in the time he did not have to devote to the business. He listened to the Hallé, rode to hounds, slept with factory girls, became something of a clubman, and drank his fill. Burning the candle at both ends led to some kind of breakdown in 1860, but his father's death in that year left Engels well-off. Ten years later he was clear enough of business to move to London to live the life of a gentleman of independent means who never lacked for doting women and devoted servants (sometimes they were the same thing).

Engels spent time in the 1870s mugging up his maths and science, a foretaste of his not altogether happy forays into the Marxist theory of science (and of everything else) in the *Anti-Dühring*. After Marx's death in 1883, Engels busied himself with editing volumes two and three of *Capital* (he was used to reading Marx's awful handwriting) while keeping an eye on the ideological purity of the German Social Democratic Party, whose Erfurt Programme of 1891 he helped to draw up.

Engels died in 1895. As was fitting, his body was cremated, cremation being at that time the socialist way of death.

It has become something of a cliché to say that the Left automatically fragments while the Right understands the value of solidarity, but there is enough truth in the cliché to make it stick. When the Left fragments, it typically does so for doctrinal rather than tactical reasons. 'Betrayal of socialist principles' is always the cry of splinter groups intent on keeping the faith, and it is often the case that one kind of socialist will say to another that he is not really a socialist at all. Those calling themselves Marxists are particularly liable to this kind of heresy hunting, and with Stalinists it became a full-time job. The easiest way of avoiding this kind of silliness is to remind ourselves that, like Hegelianism, socialism was an attempt to cope with and understand profound changes in the nature of European societies and polities at the end of the eighteenth century. Socialist theory stands or falls by the criterion of whether it can cope with the facts of its own contemporary world, and it would be surprising if socialist theory did not change as its own contemporary world changed. And it must never be forgotten that the world of which socialism is a critique, the capitalist world, is expected to transform, itself in ways which could not have been true of the worlds which capitalism superseded. One of the outstanding features of *The Communist Manifesto* of 1848 was Marx and Engels's insistence that capitalism devours its own favourite children, the capitalists. Not only had industrial capitalism brought into being, in barely a century, more productive forces than all of the forces of production of all previous forms of society combined, but also capitalism ruthlessly consumed its own productive forces in the drive towards monopoly capital. Feudal society, or ancient slave society, could not transform itself and remain feudal or slave-owning. Previous forms of society either remained themselves or changed into different forms. Not capitalism, which quickly transformed itself from its more primitive to its advanced stages.

As one of the possible reactions to capitalist industrialism, socialism can now look back to at least a century-and-a-half's worth of theoretical development. In other words, there is a socialist tradition, and it is one of the characteristics of a tradition that either it adapts or it perishes. Socialist theorists themselves have sometimes tried to obscure the fact that socialist theory changes. It might even be said that there is an in-built conservatism in the socialist tradition, or at least a reluctance to admit that theory needs to be brought up to date combined with reluctance to shed any of its intellectual baggage. Four broad reasons may be adduced to show why this is so.

1 Socialism as a political movement always begins outside the system. Socialism rarely begins from the inside, which means that at first it lacks institutional bases. Socialists expect existing institutions to be hostile. All socialism has got going for it in its early stages is a sense of moral outrage at industrial conditions and the socialist doctrine which is that outrage in a more or less systematic form. Socialism begins with no patronage; all it can hope to do is to persuade. The theory, it might be said, is what holds the Socialist movement together and the theory is what enables socialism to penetrate those few institutions which are not automatically hostile to it, like trade unions. If it is the doctrine which holds the movement together in its early stages, then it is important that the doctrine is right, and that it is clear, and that means doctrinal orthodoxy. The movement makes a considerable *investment* of its human resources in its doctrine, and there is

a perfectly natural human reluctance to write that investment off, and you would expect that in its early circumstances socialism would endow its thinkers with high prestige, the doctrine being the movement's main hope of survival, growth and eventual success.

2 But the world does not stand still, and it is its claim to understand the changing world of industrial capitalism which is socialism's main claim to attention. Socialist intellectuals, especially when they are also socialist leaders, are then faced with the problem: What do we change and how do we change it in such a way that we do not weaken the movement? Saying that doctrine has to be changed is risky when it was hard enough to establish it in the first place, and when it was hard enough to convince enough people of its truth for socialism to matter in the real world of politics. And don't forget that socialism is a doctrine for outsiders, people who have been disadvantaged by their society mentally as well as in their labour. Their minds are probably filled with the superstitions of priest-craft, and they have probably been excluded from even the most rudimentry kinds of education. Many of these may therefore become convinced adherents of socialism without understanding its theory very well, and socialist movements have always been keen to found their own educational institutions and practices in order to remedy this defect, but a defect it will continue to be. What are people like this going to say when it is announced that the doctrine has all got to change, or enough of it for it to matter? Much better, perhaps, to fill old bottles with new wine, to say that the old doctrine fits the new facts of its own contemporary world if the doctrine is *properly applied*. Of course, doctrine does in fact change when this happens, but it might change its essence much more quickly than its appearance. An old conceptual apparatus and an old language of politics will tend to survive, creaking a bit. It may be that socialists will find it increasingly difficult to say what they want to say in the available language, and at its worst this can lead to the corruptions of double-think and double-speak. The plough will be invented, but only at the cost of making it look like a hoe.

3 But things are never quite that simple. We have already noted that socialist theorists will tend to enjoy high prestige in socialist movements. The making and keeping of doctrinal orthodoxy can be a claim to leadership, so that even modest demands for doc-trinal change can come to be seen as rival claims to power within the movement. The movement has a high investment in its doctrine, and its leaders have an interest in its orthodoxy. Combine the two, and you have powerful institutional reasons for doctrinal conservatism.

4 Even that is too simple. From about the middle of the nineteenth century at least socialists have been claiming that socialism is an international movement. That means that in practice there will be movements calling themselves socialist in countries whose national economies are at very different stages of capitalist development, and there are likely to be movements calling themselves socialist in countries which have hardly begun the process of capital accumulation which makes industrial development possible in the first place. There might even be countries in which socialist movements have come to power and are using socialism as the ideology of primitive capital accumulation on the way to industrialisation, though they will not call it that. That means that 'earlier' versions of socialist doctrine developed to understand and cope with an early stage of

capitalist development will still apply to some backward countries in the contemporary world, while 'later' versions will apply elsewhere. (There might even be socialist theories of *post*-capitalism appropriate to some societies.) What holds for individual socialist movements developing in their own countries also holds for socialism as an international movement. Just as doctrine holds these individual socialist movements together in their developmental phase, so doctrine holds socialism together as an international movement. But which version of the doctrine? This again can be the disguised question of which individual socialist movement will lead the international movement. The 'senior' movement – German Social Democracy before 1914; or the most successful – the Bolsheviks after 1917? These are important questions for socialists who take socialist internationalism seriously, and it may account for socialist reluctance to shed any of its intellectual baggage. There is bound to be some country somewhere which is like Germany in 1848 when Marx and Engels wrote the *Manifesto*, just as there is bound to be some country somewhere that is like Russia in 1917 when the Bolsheviks seized power. Hence the banality of the statements of international socialist congresses: only a very generalised, rather anodyne version of socialist theory will not offend some movement calling itself socialist somewhere.

The fact does remain that there have been competing forms of socialist doctrine in given societies at given times. Real disagreement about socialist theory is nearly always disagreement about what the future will bring. There have been six great historical moments when that disagreement made itself felt among socialists: *c.* 1840, *c.* 1900, after 1917, *c.* 1930, *c.* 1948 and *c.* 1970, and all of these were moments of intense debate about the future.

Circa 1840

Some of the early socialists were not convinced that the past was really over. In the England of Luddism and Chartism it was not always clear that industrialisation was going to last. The English cotton industry was a miracle of modernity, but this was also the time of talk about national strikes and national lock-outs. Manufacturers were arguing that only a national lock-out to depress wages could save their profitability and keep the factories working, while workers were arguing that only a national strike could raise wages above the starvation level. As it happens neither was right, but the debate is testimony to a sense of unease about the future of industrial society. Some socialists, uncertain about the future, have wondered whether some aspect of the society of the past could be universalised in the present. Production was not always industrial, appropriation was not always individual, and the processes of production were not always alienating. Why not retain only agriculture labour, as with Fourier and Cabet, or production in small craft workshops, as with Proudhon. (Even American Jeffersonianism can have a socialist tinge to it in this light.) Some socialists even began to wonder whether it might not be possible to skip the stage of industrialisation altogether, the socialism of the agrarian commune as it shades into populism. Again, this concern about the de-humanising effects of large-scale industrial production is where socialism shades over into anarchism. What distinguishes Marxism right from the beginning from other kinds of socialism is the conviction that large-scale industrial production is here to stay. Backward-looking socialists have made the most elementary of errors by confusing capitalism with industrialism. The one must go, but the other must be organised in a socialist way in the future. This promises human liberation from its hardest master, scarcity. Only when there is enough to satisfy every reasonable human need can men begin to think of a society which is truly human, and that means the preservation of the productive capacity of modern industry to serve truly human ends.

Circa 1900

By the turn of the century, socialists in Europe had been waiting for some time for the collapse of capitalism under those internal contradictions which as good Marxists they had been taught to believe was inevitable. Perhaps the next economic crisis would see the whole capitalist edifice toppling down, or perhaps the next crisis but one. What was certain was that capitalism was a long time a-dying. The possibility began to dawn on some socialist thinkers that capitalism, and the bourgeois state which was its inseparable accompaniment, were capable of reforming themselves. Real wages were rising, monopoly capitalism was not becoming as monopolistic as socialists had been led to expect, and the bourgeois state had come to terms with trade unions, mass socialist parties, and had even made a modest start at economic management and the welfare state. Capitalism and the state could be reformed without revolution, and certainly without the violence which, in that progressive age, could be seen to be primitive, even atavistic. This was the socialist position which came to be known as Revisionism, and it divided many a European socialist party. It certainly annoyed Lenin, ever ready to brand fellow socialists in different countries as renegades.

Circa 1917

The social democratic failure to prevent war in 1914 (only the Serbian social democrats refused *en bloc* to vote for the war subsidies in Parliament), and the successful Bolshevik seizure of power in the October Revolution made the Russian socialist movement the most successful and prestigious socialist movement in the world. After 1921, the Communist International under Russian domination decided the conditions under which other socialist parties could join and so receive the Bolshevik seal of approval. This effectively split all of the Western socialist parties into communist and social democratic parties, and the consequences of that split were to be long and bitter. The split was not about the desirability of a socialist revolution in Russia, about which the whole left agreed, but about the rightness of the Bolshevik seizure of power in October as a minority party, and their treatment of opposition afterwards. Social democratic parties in the West began to wonder just how democratic the successors to the old Russian Social Democratic Labour Party actually were. The tradition 'no enemies on the Left' dies hard, and it caused particular problems during the fascist era in Europe and the rise of the Popular Front.

Circa 1936

The rise of European fascism and its consequence, the Spanish Civil War, again caused European socialism, communist and non-communist, to search its own heart. Comintern orthodoxy, which meant Russian communist orthodoxy, was that fascism was capitalism's last throw of the dice. Fascist brutality and the fascist attack on all forms of autonomous working-class organisations was a last and desperate attempt to shore up a failing capitalist system through thuggery. Lenin on the state had always taught that socialists were to expect that the capitalist state on its last legs was likely to be vicious in ways it had not been vicious in before, and the rule of fascist gangs seemed to fit Lenin's predictions. Fascism, therefore, ought to be allowed to run its nasty but short course, and communist parties with Soviet help could pick up the pieces afterwards. Socialist opposition to fascism, especially if allied to other, non-socialist 'progressive' forces like bourgeois liberalism, was simply to prolong capitalism's death agonies. Socialists who sought allies from the centre against the extreme right were labelled 'social fascists', objectively helping fascism to survive by opposing its early victory and therefore prolonging its inevitable collapse and with it the collapse of the capitalist order whose hirelings the fascist parties were. This important question of theory about whether fascism *had* a future gave way in the era of popular-frontism, the alliance of all progressive forces against fascism, when it was tacitly admitted that fascism *had* a future at least in some kind of longer term than had been official Comintern orthodoxy.

Circa 1948

The period of the Cold War was for Western socialists the equivalent of the period after 1917 intensified. Soviet takeovers in Eastern Europe spelt the end of socialist non-communist parties in every country occupied by the Red Army (except Austria which the Russians left). This put Western non-communist socialist parties on the spot. In national foreign policy and economic policy it meant that they had to begin to move towards capitalist America through NATO and the Marshall Plan. Revelations about the horrors of Stalinism in the 1930s made this shift easier to bear, but the idea that in the world which had got rid of fascism (at least for a time) the greatest enemy of social democracy was communism took a long time to die and is probably not yet dead while the question of whether the Eastern European people's democracies and the Soviet Union can reform themselves is still moot.

Circa 1970

The question of whether Eastern Europe could reform itself is tied in with the question of whether Western communist parties could reform themselves. Hungary in 1956, the

Prague Spring, and the destruction of a Marxist government in Chile all had the effect of making Western communist parties ask themselves where they were going, if they were not going the way of the old Stalinist Communist Party of the Soviet Union. If they were no longer to be old-style Bolshevik revolutionary parties waiting for a crisis of bourgeois hegemony in order to seize power, then what were they to be? Being anything other than Bolshevik parties meant accepting the rules of the bourgeois parliamentary game and accepting the bourgeois freedoms at face value and not decrying them as sham. Parliamentarism was no longer the façade behind which the money-power operated that a century-and-a-half's Marxism had led socialists to believe, and the bourgeois freedoms of press, association, ballot and combination were now to be proclaimed as real and as having a real future. And so to Euro-Communism, national loyalty, and an end of even the pretence that communist parties in the West were conspiracies against the state. (And hence, also, to 'red terrorism' in those countries where communism turned itself into Euro-Communism.)

MARXISM AS THE THEORY OF PROLETARIAN REVOLUTION

There was nothing particularly odd about being a revolutionary in nineteenth-century Europe. A lot of the *ancien régime* survived into the nineteenth (and some even into the twentieth) century, when there were literally thousands of revolutionaries. Nor were revolutions or failed revolutions all that unusual. The great French Revolution of 1789 continued to be the model of revolutions for governments and revolutionaries alike, and all the revolutions of the nineteenth century were, or were seen to be, more or less copies of the great original. The revolutions of 1830, 1848, and the Paris Commune may have differed from 1789 in both form and content, but those who took part in them, and those who put them down, could all agree that the French Revolution was the unique source of revolutionary inspiration and tactics. Not all revolutionaries learned the same lessons, but all could agree that something was going wrong with nineteenth-century revolutions. In 1848, for instance, there were revolutions, or what looked to the authorities like revolutions, in England (if we count Chartism), France, Ireland, Germany, Austria, Hungary and what was to become Romania. As revolutions, all failed (though some had beneficial consequences). How was it, men asked, that in the brave new world of the nineteenth century, a world of industrialisation and progress, reactionary governments like those of the Habsburgs and the Romanovs managed to survive?

One of many thinkers who put his mind to that problem was Karl Marx. Like Hegel, Marx concluded that the Revolution of 1789 had not ushered in an era of universal freedom because the time had not been ripe, though the Revolution had some solid gains to its credit. The *ancien régime* in France, based on an absurdly over-inflated idea of monarchy and a creaking system of seigneurial privilege, had been practically destroyed and in its place the bourgeoisie had begun its own career as the dominant class. The Revolution had half succeeded. The restored monarchy of Louis XVIII and Charles X could not last, and in

1830 France got herself bourgeois constitutional monarchy. The new king, Louis-Philippe, walked about Paris wearing a bowler hat while his government very obligingly called out the troops to put down strikes, and what could be more bourgeois than that?

So, for Marx, the bourgeois revolution was only a halfway stage between the remnants of feudalism and the socialism of the future. There had been intimations of socialism during the French Revolution and before, but they had come to nothing because the bourgeoisie was then becoming the dominant class. The socialist revolution to come would complete the work of 1789 and of the abortive revolutions of the nineteenth century. But Marx did not simply claim that the coming socialist revolution would be just another, even in a history whose future pattern was becoming clearer for all who had eyes to see. He claimed that the proletarian revolution which was to usher in the socialist millennium was not just another event in history. It was to be *the* event in history which would be the beginning of a new kind of history. Marx liked to call the events which had happened in the world up to now 'pre-history'; events beyond the revolution he called 'truly human history'. Fine words, but what do they mean? Up to the revolution, the history of man has been the history of man's exploitation of man, of class by class. Pre-history is the history of human alienation, the formation of human consciousness by a hostile world outside the self. The circumstances of the world have made men what they are, and men have failed to exercise their consciousness on the world in any rational or systematic way. Men are creatures to whom history happens, not creatures who make their own history.

The way this happens alters in capitalist, industrialising societies in one crucial way. In pre-industrial societies, men confronted nature directly with the plough. It made a kind of sense to speak of men's nature being formed by Nature in an agricultural world, but this is no longer the case in the world of the industrial town. The townscape which industrial workers inhabit is a man-made world. Human consciousness, shaped as it is by the world outside the self, is in fact being shaped by what men have created in the past and are continuing to create in the present. The capitalist world itself changes very quickly, so you would be a fool not to realise that human consciousness is being shaped by the results of human activity itself. Of course, the world the bourgeoisie have made is not in any extended sense a planned world, though town-planning is as old as the ancient Greeks. The bourgeois plans ahead, and needs a stable state and the existence of a stable system of law to enable him to do that, but he plans in competition with his fellow capitalists. Marx does in fact think that all capitalists will come to think about the future in the same way; larger and larger enterprises and greater and greater concentrations of capital will be the wave of the future, the inevitable built-in dynamic of capitalist development, but this will have no overall rational plan. The transition to truly human history happens when men come to realise that their consciousness, what they are and what they think themselves to be, is the product of one set of unplanned man-made circumstances and that, therefore, a rationally guided man-made future state of socialism can make men whatever men want to be. Truly human endeavour in a man-made landscape can for the first time since the ancient Greeks produce truly human beings.

Plenty is an important part of this plan. The efficiency of industrial production can provide the cornucopia which men have been searching for ever since the expulsion from the Garden of Eden. What seemed so stupid to Marx was that the productive capacity of modern industry was effectively being wasted. Industrial capitalism was subject to booms and slumps, which became institutionalised in bourgeois economics as the trade cycle. Crises of over-production were followed by periods of under-employment and capital concentration as capitalists failed to survive bad times and their capital was swallowed up by larger capital. The tendency of wages to remain at or near subsistence-level even when the factories were all running seemed to Marx the stupidest of all the aspects of capitalism. Modern technology was the triumph of reason-as-science over nature. Modern technology and methods of production should be freeing men from that brute scarcity which had been their burden since the Fall. Instead, the capitalist way of organising industrial production (and capitalist farming) created a false scarcity and hence the need for a repressive state.

The bourgeois state is not less repressive than its predecessors simply because it no longer tries to regulate trade. The argument for the hangman had always been that human cupidity in a world of scarcity would always lead men into sin, individual or collective. In previous epochs of human history there perhaps was unavoidable scarcity, but not in the modern world of efficient industrial and agricultural production. It must then be the capitalist way of organising the present which produces a false scarcity, and therefore the repressive state survives into the modern world. The bourgeois state is the guarantor of an enforced scarcity. It exists to protect the bourgeoisie in the possession of its ill-gotten gains wrung from workers in the competition of capitalist society. The bourgeoisie appropriates more than it needs, let alone more than it deserves, thus creating in the proletariat a deprived, and needlessly deprived, class which the bourgeoisie looks upon with very mixed feelings. On the one hand, the bourgeoisie needs the proletariat in order to keep the factories going and therefore keep the bourgeoisie going, but at the same time the have-nots represent a potential threat to bourgeois peace of mind individually as thieves and collectively as rioters. And it is as well for the bourgeoisie to remember that its own Revolution of 1789 began with a riot which was allowed to 'get out of hand'. Hence the continuing need for the whole machinery of law and police to protect individual property from theft with the army as a last resort in those conditions of collective threat to property which we call revolutions.

If the state is what Marx says it is, the organ of class repression, then it follows that there will be no need for it in the socialist future when the proletariat 'universalises' itself and there will only be one class left. A class without another class exploiting it is not a class at all, but is simply humanity. This does not, of course, mean that in the future all regulation will disappear, because there is a certain degree of regulation necessary to the organisation of large-scale production (a point over which Marxism was later to clash with the anarchists), but for the first time in human history regulation was to be kept to the absolute and necessary minimum. Certainly, the state as the agent of class domination disappears with class antagonisms.

HEGEL AND MARX ON HISTORY

It is important to ask: How does Marx's vision of the future differ from other visions of the socialist future, of which there was no shortage in the nineteenth century? The answer is that Marx's own idea of history, rooted as it was in Hegelianism, saw the future as implicit in a defective present. Marxists always claim that Marx's own socialism is the reverse of utopian, because utopian socialism paints a pretty picture of the future and invites people to make that future now. Marx knew his Hegel well enough to realise that more was required of a theory of history than simply to proclaim the possibility of a future state and to hope that the moral impulses of mankind would induce them to embrace that future. Hegel had always taught that the future is implicit in the present, but that the signs of the future were hard to read. The reason for this was that the past, the present, and the future belong to the Idea. As an Idealist, Hegel was bound to think that the motor force of history was the way in which human thoughts change. In the Hegelian twilight land, history is moving towards a full consciousness of freedom, but, by definition, at any given time men's idea of freedom will be restricted because freedom will not yet unite itself with the Absolute.

History moves dialectically. On this Hegel and Marx are agreed, but the question then is: Where are we to look for evidence that dialectic does in fact push freedom along? Hegel says, unequivocally, in the State, but that means in our ideas about the state. Not Marx. Marxists claim to be materialists, not in the sense of the materialism which Hegel had attacked in the *Phenomenology of Mind*, that bone produces brain, but in the sense that real human circumstances produce our consciousness of the world. This involves diverting our attention from the state to the real social world where most of us spend most of our time. The problem with Hegel according to his Young Hegelian critics was that he always saw the real world through Plato's eyes as a mere imperfect reflection of a perfect world of ideas. No doubt Hegel, unlike Plato, believed that these ideas change, but it was still in the world of a mysteriously changing consciousness that truths about the world were to be found. It is in this sense that Marx *materialised* Hegel's dialectic. Marx does not deny that the history of ideas is where the battles between different views of the world are fought out, but the dialectic of ideas is shadow-boxing, a reflection of real struggles in the real world. The word 'reflection' is not to be taken too literally here. Hegel had been keen to show that ideas follow developments in what we call the 'real' world. Philosophy always comes after, too late to teach the world what it should be. Marx's own idea about the relationship between ideas and reality is rather different, and he does not believe that the world of ideas is a simple mirror image of its own contemporary world. The ideological battle sometimes happens before the social forces which those ideas represent are fully aware of themselves in the real world, a kind of rehearsal for the real struggle to come. At other times, the relationship between ideas and the world is deeply problematic, we might almost say dialectical, when ideas seem to contradict the world, but whatever the relationship is between the world of ideas and the real world, Marx never doubts that it is the real world which makes sense of ideas about it, and not, as Hegel thought, the world of ideas which makes sense of the real world.

HEGEL, FEUERBACH AND MARX: THE ROAD TO DIALECTICAL MATERIALISM

Marx was an atheist and a materialist before he systematically criticised Hegel's *Philosophy of Right*, but it was probably his critique of Hegel through the ideas of Feuerbach which made him the kind of materialist he became.

According to a much later work by Engels, *Ludwig Feuerbach and the End of Classical German Philosophy* (1888), it was the 'transformative method' of Feuerbach's *Essence of Christianity* which enabled Marx and Engels to go beyond Hegel's contemplative Idealism to a thoroughgoing dialectical materialism (though the term 'dialectical materialism' is a later invention). Feuerbach again faced the old Hegelian problem of alienation as evidenced by an other-worldly religion. Hegel's own answer was to get God back into the world as Reason in Process, but Feuerbach continued to insist that most men would continue to feel that there was a perfect world beyond the real world, and that the real world would always suffer by comparison. And he meant 'suffer'. While there existed a perfect heaven, with a perfect holy family, then men would continue to be persuaded that the imperfections of their own world, and the imperfections of their own families, were inevitable this side of the grave. Feuerbach came to see the perfect world of God as a projection of human suffering and aspiration. The perfection of the heavens was a human invention to make human life more bearable. Man created God, God did not create man. Of course something very like that idea had been around ever since clever Greeks had begun to wonder why the gods were anthropomorphic, but the significance of Feuerbach was that his critique was an 'inside' critique, a critique from inside the Hegelian philosophy itself, and that is how Marx and Engels read him. The categories of the Hegelian dialectic had to be filled by a genuinely materialistic content, a content drawn from the real conditions of human existence, and for Marx and Engels that meant a content drawn from the process of men struggling with each other in history.

Where was this content actually to be found? Where was this specially privileged class of facts to be located? Marx was enough of a Hegelian even after reading Feuerbach to know that to look at the whole of human history was an absurd business for the political theorist. Some criterion of importance is necessary to dig out the materialist equivalent of the Hegelian 'Horatian gold' from the 'mere dross' of the endless availability of historical fact. The opening of *The Communist Manifesto* gives an answer to this problem: the history of all hitherto existing society is the history of class struggles. The class of specially privileged facts comes out of class struggle which is itself determined by what the prevailing means of production are in any given epoch of human history. It is important to be clear about what Marx and Engels mean here. They do not mean that the most obviously striking feature of a given historical epoch is the class struggle. Indeed, part of their purpose is to explain why it is that in previous epochs of world history it was extremely difficult to see class struggle going on, because each epoch's ideological configuration is designed to conceal the real struggles going on beneath that epoch's surface. By class struggle, Marx and Engels mean the real motor force of history, that which turns one epoch into another. It is the nature of the class struggle which is going to determine what the future will be like. One is irresistibly reminded of the Hegelian aphorism: the new is the freed truth of the old. Like Hegel in his view of freedom becoming more conscious of itself, and therefore becoming more easily recognisable, so too Marx thinks that, as human history develops, classes become more conscious of themselves and therefore the class struggle becomes more easily recognisable. Only a fool could fail to recognise the existence of two great historical classes, the bourgeoisie and the proletariat, in the era of industrial capitalism.

MARXISM AS A CRITIQUE OF CAPITALISM AND OF POLITICAL ECONOMY

We do well to remember that the subtitle of Marx's *Capital* is 'A Critique of Political Economy'. Like Hobbes, Marx likes to meet and beat his opponents on their own ground where they think their arguments are strongest. The theory of political economy (shorthand for the whole school of the 'classical' economists from Adam Smith onwards) has a certain relationship with the world of industrial capitalism which it explains and justifies. Marx carries the battle to the theories of political economy before industrial society is itself even universally realised and before its class struggles have come into sharp relief. His typical method is to seek out the assumptions of political economy and ask whether the conclusions drawn by political economists themselves from their own premises are really valid. Marx thinks that, if he can find contradictions within the theory of political economy, there are bound to be analogous contradictions in the society whose product political economy is.

Easily the most accessible of Marx's economic texts is an early tract, *Wage, Labour and Capital* (written in 1847 but not published until 1891). In this work, Marx sets out to show that, even on the most favourable assumptions of political economy, an expanding and innovative capitalism is fatal for capitalists and workers alike. He begins with what is a glaring contradiction at the very heart of capitalism and capitalist economics: their inability to explain the *raison d'être* of capitalism, profit. The implication is clear: a system of thought which cannot explain profit, the one thing which really matters to capitalists, must be covering something up. Marx points out that the labour theory of value espoused by capitalist economics simply fails to explain how profits arise. The labour theory of value, which is capitalist in origin, not socialist, holds that the value of a commodity is the amount of labour expended on its production. This explains, for instance, why a ton of iron ore and a ton of razor blades have very different values. A ton of iron ore is only worth the trouble of digging it out of the ground, while a ton of razor blades is worth far more because a lot has to be done to iron ore before it becomes razor blades. Now in capitalism, labour is a commodity. It sells on the labour market and its price is wages. What, then, is the value of labour? Labour's value must be the amount by which the value of raw materials increases in value in the process of manufacture. On the face of it, then, the value of labour is wages, the amount of value which the worker gets in return for his labour. But if manufactured articles contain only labour, and if the only way a commodity can have a market value is through the amount of 'congealed' labour it contains, then how can the capitalist make a profit and accumulate more capital? There must therefore be some *extra* value in a commodity, which the capitalist does not pay for, which accounts for his profit when the commodity reaches the market.

Marx concludes that the capitalist does not, properly speaking, buy the commodity labour, but *labour power*, and the difference between labour and labour power is crucial for Marxist economics. The capitalist buys labour power, which is measured in time, and which is defined as the bodily strength and presence of a worker in a factory. Labour power is the commodity which the worker sells to the capitalist in order to live. How is its price – wages – determined? Marx, again following classical economics, says that the price of the commodity labour power is determined like the price of any other commodity in a capitalist market economy. The price of commodities in a market is either above or below their cost of production, so that we may speak of the *average price* of commodities. This is a simple truism of political economy. It is a law of markets that commodities must be offered at competitive prices, and the price is fixed *as an average* of the costs of production, while in fact, because some manufacturers are more efficient than others, a portion of the same commodities will be offered at above their actual cost of production and some will be offered at below their cost of production. Producers offering products at a price above their cost of production will make profits, while producers offering products at below their actual cost of production will make a loss. Markets are supposed to be like that: to the more competitive, the spoils. The uncompetitive manufacturer either does something about it, or he goes out of business.

How does this analysis of the price of competition, based as it is on sound principles of political economy, apply to the commodity labour power? As a commodity, we may speak of the *average cost* of labour power. Labour sells for its price, wages, which, as is the case of the price of any other commodity, is at or near its own cost of production, and Marx defines the cost of production of the commodity labour power as 'the cost required for maintaining the worker as worker and of developing him into a worker'. The value of labour power and its price as wages is therefore the necessary means of subsistence, which enables the worker to turn up at the factory every day to do his work. (This also explains why a skilled worker is paid more than an unskilled worker, because the skilled worker costs more to train. It also explains why child labour is the cheapest of all: children eat less.) The labourer, then, is paid the cost of producing him.

As for other commodities, so with labour power we may speak of the average price of labour power. It is an axiom of markets that *average price equals average cost, but only as an average*. This is again a simple truism that Marx draws out of classical economics. It simply means that in markets, including the market for labour power, commodities tend to be priced competitively at their average cost of production. Now we know that this is only true as an average. In fact, for markets to work, some commodities must be offered at below their cost of production (the ones which make profits) and some offered at above their cost of production (the ones which make a loss). To put this another way, in order to sell a commodity whose cost of production is above the average, it must be sold at a price which is below what it cost to produce. If I manufacture plates at a cost above that of my competitors because I am less efficient than them, then to sell plates in the market at all I have to offer them at a loss. What is true of plates is also true of labour power: average price equals average cost, *but only as averages*. This effectively means that some men must be selling their labour power for less than it costs to produce it in order that others can sell their labour power for more than it costs to produce it. Put more simply, for some workers to live above the breadline, the cost of producing themselves, other workers must be living below the breadline, the cost of producing themselves. Workers, like any other producers of commodities, have to compete with each other in the market for labour power. If they are offering their labour power at below its cost of production, then they have to find ways of making themselves more efficient as producers of their commodity, labour power. They can tighten their belts and consume less, or they can work longer hours at the same hourly rate of wages. Of course, subsistence is at least partly conditional on the society in which one lives. Different peoples have different notions of where the level of subsistence should be put, and that can change in the same society. The Irish were always cheaper than the English because they expected less, and Englishmen who were content to live on bread and tea were always going to be cheaper than Englishmen who expected to live on beer and beef. Women would be cheaper than men, and children the cheapest of all.

This is a bleak enough picture of capitalism for workers, and Marx thought it would get even worse. It is important to remember that the assumptions Marx begins from are assumptions about capitalism taken from capitalism's own ideologues. His is a picture of a buoyant and innovative capitalism, competitive, and with plenty of capital accumulation through profits. Marx takes capitalism's own best assumptions and shows how there will always be a tendency for wages to be at or near subsistence level, not a very alluring picture for workers.

What is supposed to happen to capitalists while immiseration is happening to workers? In particular, what is supposed to happen to the inefficient manufacturer, offering commodities on the market below their actual cost of production, but not much. Really inefficient producers will go to the wall, but what about the manufacturer who is almost but not quite making it? Plainly, he must innovate. He must invent a new process of production, new machinery perhaps, and new ways of organising labour. Suppose he succeeds in this. It certainly helps him for a time, because he might now be producing so far below the old average cost of production that he would begin to make truly fabulous profits. But, says Marx, the old law that *average price equals average cost* must in the end re-assert itself. The original innovator is followed by other manufacturers who innovate too, though some may go to the wall, and eventually he finds himself no better off because a new average price asserts itself as a new average cost. Marx wants to show that the ideal conditions for capitalist development – the spirit of innovation and lots of capital to innovate with – are not in fact the ideal conditions in which capitalists are likely to survive. The capitalist who originally innovated now finds himself back where he started, in a changed market with a changed average cost of production, and hence a reduced average price. Of course, the original innovator will still have the option of innovating again, but by this time he is being rushed off his feet, re-innovating because of his own previous innovation.

Our original innovating capitalist is in deeper trouble than even he knows. He sees other capitalists failing to innovate, going out of business and perhaps joining the proletariat themselves, but he thinks that he is doing the right thing by being part of that innovating, buoyant capitalism which all capitalism's ideologues agree is the best condition of a modern industrial economy. But our innovating capitalist is puzzled by one thing: despite his doing everything which capitalism expects him to do, he finds his rate of capital accumulation falling. Technical innovation costs money. The innovating capitalist finds that he has less and less capital to spend on those innovations which his own duty as a good capitalist, and the imperatives of capitalism as a system, force upon him. Why, he asks, is this happening to me? The answer is very simple, and has to do with the process of innovation and the effect it has on capital. Marx divides capital into fixed and movable capital. Fixed capital is build-ings and machinery, while movable capital is capital for investment and the paying of wages (this simplifies the matter, but not much). At any stage of capitalist development there is a particular ratio of fixed to movable capital, and Marx thinks that as capitalism progresses the ratio of fixed to movable capital changes in favour of fixed capital. Technical innovation, more and more expensive and complex machinery, is clearly fixed capital, and we noted that in order to survive a good capitalist would in fact innovate, which means tying up more and more of his capital in expensive plant. Then the capitalist remembers his own classical economists' labour theory of value, and he solves the riddle of why it is that the rate of capital accumulation is falling. The matter is really very simple: the more the work is done by machines, the less labour is expended in the course of production, and labour is the source of value. Therefore, even allowing for the labour that has gone into the making of complex machinery, the less labour expended in the course of production, the less value created. Profits therefore fall, and so does the rate at which capital accumulates, which in its turn means that there is less capital available for those technical innovations which the good capitalist has been making all along, and which he knows he must continue with in the future.

And what about the bad capitalists, the ones who fail in the rush to innovate? They go to the wall. There is a vein of bitter irony in Marx here. Capitalism, he seems to be saying, is good for neither the good nor the bad capitalists. Competition gets them all in the end, the bad first and the good later. And what is happening to the workers while all this is happening to employers? Plainly, less and less labour is required as modern industry becomes more fixed-capital intensive, even allowing for the labour expended in the making of the machinery which the capitalist buys in order to innovate. Work also becomes less skilled and less arduous: skilled labour is replaced by unskilled labour, English labour by Irish labour, male labour by female labour, and female labour by child labour when labour literally becomes child's play. Each stage represents labour which costs less to produce, and knowing as we do that the commodity labour power, like all other commodities, tends to sell for its cost of production, wages are obviously falling because it costs far less to produce child labour than skilled adult labour. Capitalism, then, appears to be good for neither capitalists nor workers. It must therefore be a stupid way to organise industrial production.

Some of the arguments rehearsed above in fact come from Marx's masterpiece, *Capital*. There he uses the famous term 'surplus value' to denote the difference between labour and labour power. The most famous equation in the whole of Marx's work is: labour − labour power = surplus value. Capitalism gets surplus value for nothing, and it is the source both of profit and of capital accumulation. Surplus value is produced no matter how long the working day is: even if the factory only ran for an hour the capitalist would still extract his quota of surplus labour and therefore surplus value. Why, then, does the working day seem to get longer and longer? Again, the answer is simple: the longer the working day, the more surplus value extracted. Why do workers put up with that? Again, the answer is simple: as wages decline, the worker has to work longer hours to earn the means of subsistence. There is one difference among many between capitalists and workers which is crucial. The capitalist can always go out of business, take his losses (his liability will be limited anyway), try to build another life, and he might succeed in doing this without dropping into the ranks of the proletariat. The worker, on the other hand, has not got the option of 'going out of business', stopping producing labour power and selling it on the market, because that would be to take the option of either going to the workhouse (popularly known as the Bastille) or starving with his dignity intact. Neither is an attractive choice.

It is important always to remember that in *Wage Labour and Capital*, and to an extent in the first volume of *Capital*, Marx is not describing any particular national capitalist economy, though the model at the back of his mind is always England. Rather, what Marx does is to take capitalism's own best assumptions about itself and asks whether, on those assumptions, the future is going to be bright for buyers and sellers of labour. His answer is a resounding: No.

THE MYSTERY OF COMMODITY FETISHISM EXPLAINED

Volume I of *Capital* is witty in a heavy-handed, Germanic sort of way, and nowhere more so than in its treatment of the Mystery of the Fetishistic Character of Commodities. In a way this is unfortunate, because Marx's playing about in the Hegelian manner with commodities right at the beginning of *Capital* has put more people off reading the whole work than anything else. What Marx is trying to get at at the beginning of *Capital* is the tendency of bourgeois economics, not to mention bourgeois 'common sense', to regard a commodity as a 'thing'. Marx always insists that any economic category – commodity, capital, value and so on – must be regarded as part of a process. Marx is still a good enough Hegelian in *Capital* to see the world as a never-ending process and to look behind the appearance of things to find their true nature. A fetishist takes the thing at its face value. 'The heathen in his blindness bows down to wood and stone' because he takes the thing he bows down to as really being a god, and not just representing God. Fetishes are big magic, and Marx thinks that bourgeois economics has made big magic out of commodities by failing to see beyond them to what they actually mean.

For Marx, commodities are really contradictory because they contain two different forms of human relationship connected with the nature of commodities as use-values and exchange-values. In his Hegelian way, Marx chooses to regard use-values and exchange-values not just as different but as opposites. Use-value and exchange-value represent two different modes of social living, of which only the first is truly human. Production of use-values means exactly what it says: *I* produce something which *you* need. That is my reason for doing it. This presupposes a much simpler society than industrial capitalism, say a society in which economic life takes place through barter, where there is nothing resembling a market, and where money in the form of coinage does not exist. In these conditions *my* labour, the labour I put into an article of use-value, say a saddle, really is *my* labour because in the system of crude exchange the saddle is 'worth' the labour I put into it. It matters not at all that somewhere else there is somebody else making saddles in less time than it takes me, because that only means that where the other saddle-maker lives a saddle is 'worth' less than mine. This plainly implies a face-to-face society in which mutual exchange of use-values is the typical form of economic activity, hardly economic activity at all in the modern sense because the only way that anybody could make a 'profit' out of use-value exchange would be swindling.

In capitalist society, the position changes. The existence of a market reduces *my* labour to *abstract labour*, not mine at all because my labour is indistinguishable from anyone else's. The value of industrial goods, exchange-values for the market, is not determined by the amount of labour which actually went into the production of those goods, but, on the contrary, the value of industrial goods in the market is determined by the *socially* necessary labour time for their production. This is the simplest possible truism. If all the manufacturers of plates except one are producing them at the cost of x in labour time, and the odd manufacturer is producing plates at the cost of $2x$ in labour time, and if in markets *average price equals average cost as an average*, then the plates costing $2x$ to produce will still only sell for x in the market. In simpler terms, inefficient producers cannot charge more for their products in the market to cover up for their inefficiency. Commodities contain the human essence of man as worker in a 'congealed' form. When commodities come onto the market they command a price measured in money, so that, implicitly at least, when commodity encounters commodity in the market, what is really happening is an encounter between two lots of abstract human labour. Hence Marx's view that, in the system of industrial production for the market, men do not encounter each other face-to-face as human beings, but through the commodities they produce, *as things*.

Capitalist economies are clearly economies which produce exchange-values, and equally clearly Marx regards the production of exchange-values as de-humanising, as alienating. Why does this matter so much to him? It matters because Marx and Engels take a particular view of what it is to work. In the *Economic and Philosophical Manuscripts of 1844* Marx argues that work is the defining characteristic of man, his essence as a 'species being'. The best life is a life of creative labour, not a life of political action or contemplation as it was for the ancient Greeks, not a life of prayer and meditation as it was for the Christians, and certainly not a life of moneyed idleness which is the *rentier*'s dream of capitalists. (Engels even believed that an important part in the transition from ape to man was caused by the invention of primitive productive techniques.) The capitalist tries to appropriate as much of the world as property as he can, and this affects the way everybody looks at the world as the locus of possession and consumption. This can even affect some kinds of socialism, especially the 'fair day's wages for a fair day's work' variety. This kind of socialism shows just how far capitalist attitudes have colonised the minds of even the politically advanced socialist working class. The demand for the full product of labour means the redistribution of surplus value to the workers themselves. Marx calls this kind of socialism 'crude communism', because it represents the universalisation of bourgeois property right. Workers demand what is theirs by right, an attempt to universalise a particular aspect of the pre-socialist order and calling it socialism. At best, it represents a reform of the capitalist order and not its final overthrow. The economic system of crude communism would still be a system of the production of exchange-values, and it is only with the abolition of the market altogether and its replacement by a system of production in terms of ability, and a system of distribution in terms of needs, that the socialist future can begin. Crude communism may be a necessary stage on the road to socialism, but it can only be a stage. Marx is asking a lot of workers here. He is asking them to give up their claim to what is theirs almost before they have got it, the only class in history ever to be asked to do that.

MARXISM AND THE STATE

You will remember that Marx's critique of Hegel began with a critique of the Hegelian theory of the State and then began regressively to unravel the whole Hegelian philosophy. The burden of Marx's critique of the modern state in general was the falsity of its claim to neutrality. Marx recognises that the modern state of salaried officials does in fact separate itself from what Hegel had called Civil Society as state functionaries divide their labour off from other specialised callings. The state is obviously part of what Marxists call the 'super-structure', its nature depending as it does on the economic 'basis' upon which it rests. What is characteristically Marxist about Marx and Engels' view of the state is their insistence upon the state's historicity. Nothing could be easier than for working men to believe that the state as it exists, *their* state, not *ours*, has always existed in more or less recognisable form, hence the Marxist insistence that the state is historically conditioned and therefore historically limited. The ancient *polis*, the Roman republic and the Roman Empire, the feudal system, absolutisms and the modern state differ each from the other in important ways. If each other form of the state was historically limited, then why should the modern state's time not be historically limited also?

The modern state is the bourgeois, that is to say more or less liberal, state. Marx and Engels hedge about whether the personnel of the state, legislators, higher police functionaries, army commanders and high officials, must themselves be bourgeois before the state which they constitute can properly be called 'bourgeois'. For them, any state, no matter how constituted, which successfully manages the affairs of the bourgeoisie for them is a bourgeois state. Marx and Engels use some fairly slippery language about the bourgeois state, for instance referring to an 'alliance' between the bourgeois state and the stock exchange, but never committing themselves beyond that. Perhaps they thought, as liberals thought, that there would eventually be a bourgeois takeover of its 'own' state. The idea of the social division of labour, which enabled the business of government to be handled on the same scale of efficiency as private enterprises, has a bourgeois ring to it.

What this means is that in bourgeois society the bourgeoisie does not fight its own battles in the war of classes, but fights through its state agents. A rising class like the proletariat has to fight its own battles and so has to confront its class enemy indirectly through the police and the army. Plainly, 'smashing' the state in some extended sense is going to be very difficult because part of the theory of the modern state is that it legitimately monopolises violence, which means that, whatever happens, *they* have got the Maxim gun and we have not. Much better, then, to find ways of making the state change sides, for the state to become *ours*, and here the tendency of capital accumulation towards monopoly really helps. The ideal revolutionary preconditions would be those in which a small group of monopoly capitalists confront a politically conscious proletariat whose ranks have been swollen by failed small capitalists. The bourgeoisie almost dig their own grave. By concentrating capital by swallowing up pygmy capital, the bourgeoisie assemble the proletariat into larger and larger concentrations as the economies of scale enlarge the factories. Proletarians would have to be very stupid indeed if they did not realise that the only responsibility which their betters feel towards them is to pay their wages for that day. Equally, they would have to be very stupid indeed not to realise that the factories could practically run themselves because capitalists do no labour and therefore create no value. It was a very short step from there to regarding capitalists as parasites and therefore dispensable. The same thought is expected to occur to servants of the state. The old order does not disappear overnight, so there should be plenty of time for the state's servants to begin to wonder whether the capitalist rump is worth defending. Disaffection would no doubt occur piecemeal, and revolution would be as likely to divide the state as it would to divide society. The revolutionary proletariat's aim should be to make the state *their* state, prepared to do its task of extirpating the remnants of the old order.

POST-REVOLUTION AND THE STAGES OF SOCIALISM: TOWARDS LENINISM

It is sometimes claimed that the chief difference between Marxist 'scientific' socialism and other 'utopian' socialisms is that utopian socialisms predict what the future society is going to be like, whereas scientific socialism does not. Passages in the works of Marx and Engels on the future are not in fact all that infrequent, though it remains true that they have left no specific treatment of the future as a whole.

In the *Economic and Philosophical Manuscripts of 1844* Marx sees the future of communist society as a development in two stages, the first 'crude communism' and the second 'real communism', and Marx treats the difference between them as the equivalent of the theoretical distance between his own socialist theory and earlier communist theory (a distinction which he will repeat in *The Communist Manifesto* four years later). We have already seen that crude communism is the universalisation of a particular aspect of the old order. Its ideal is crude sharing on an egalitarian distributive basis. Everyone is to become a wage labourer, a part of a community which is itself a universal capitalist. This kind of communism is merely the extension of private property on a grand scale. 'General envy constituting itself as a power is the disguise in which avarice re-establishes itself, only in another way.' The really revolutionary content of the revolution is the process by which men become capable of looking at the world in a new way, and not just as the locus of crude possession. Crude communism is the parcelling out of objects for possession, not revolutionary at all. The problem is again about how human consciousness is formed. Marx seems to be saying that in capitalist society all we can think about is grabbing the world's good things for ourselves. We are alienated from that world and the only way we can get back into it, so to speak, is by possession.[1] What is at issue here is a Marxist humanism: in new economic, social and political conditions a new type of man will arise whose consciousness is formed by a world which is *his* world, so that he forms his own consciousness himself through the mediation of a world which is already his. This represents the 'negation of self-negation', the beginning of a process whose end is the abolition of alienation itself. To do this men have to give up the idea of the universalisation of bourgeois property right to their own surplus value. There are echoes here of the doctrine of freedom of the Rousseau of *The Social Contract*. There Rousseau had said that the freedom which men ought to want is a new kind of freedom which it has not occurred to men to want before. Marx is saying something analogous in the *Manuscripts*. It is 'man for himself', coming to regard the world outside the self not as a locus of possession but as a scope for action. This represents quite a remarkable change which is ultimately explicable in aesthetic terms: up till now, history has been the history of the *formation* of the senses; now the senses *grasp* the world.

This vision of the communist future as the emergence of a new human sensibility tells us nothing about the mechanisms of the change, and we noted above that Marxism's claim to be 'scientific' and not 'utopian' rests on its claim to be able to explain how the future will come out of the present. What is certain is that the change will not come about all at once. Some remarks, though rather terse, in his *Critique of the Gotha Programme* (of the German Social Democratic Party in 1875), show that Marx was in fact rather cautious about the road to socialism. In the *Manifesto* thirty years before, Marx had set out a ten-point programme for a socialist revolution in Germany and perhaps elsewhere, but that programme was an emergency programme for feeding towns during a revolutionary crisis, and it contains only very generalised advice about taxation, credit, education and the like, and it does not even contain any advice about what to do with the factories beyond recommending the extension of factories and means of production already owned by the state. (Commentators on Marx have long pointed out that the ten-point programme of the *Manifesto* is the manifesto of a social democratic party, not a revolutionary communist party.) The *Critique of the Gotha Programme* is a little more forthcoming, but not much. Marx insists that after the revolution society will still be fraught with the difficulties necessarily consequent upon the birth pangs of the new order, and these difficulties will affect proletarian labour. At first, it will not even be possible to pay all workers the same because, in the new order as in the old, the standard of wages will be determined by the amount of labour done. This will be an inequality imposed by economic circumstances of some complexity and chaos, and to attempt to go beyond what reality demands is utopian. The notion in the Gotha Programme itself that workers will receive the full and equal return for their labour is both bourgeois and utopian – bourgeois because it universalises property right and utopian because it will be impossible immediately to pay all workers the same because some are stronger than others and the only way of stopping them earning more would be to stop them working so hard. The truly revolutionary moment comes when the tyranny of the division of labour has been overcome. When the distinction between mental and physical labour has been abolished, 'after labour has become not only a means to life but life's prime want', the stage of true communism will be in sight.

All this tells us almost nothing about the political mechanisms of revolution, and especially it tells us nothing about the 'withering away of the state' which Engels promises in his *Anti-Dühring*. How is this to come about? Perhaps it would be useful here to recap on the Marxist view of the state in general as a prelude to a treatment of this most contentious question of Marxist theory. We already know that for Marx and Engels the state in capitalist society is the committee for organising the affairs of the whole bourgeoisie. The important thing to grasp is that Marx and Engels regard the state as separate from but absolutely susceptible to bourgeois influence. The offices of state could be filled with aristocrats and the state could still be a bourgeois state, and certain state policies like imperialism combine perfectly the aristocratic interest in armies and the bourgeois interest in expanding markets for trade. This view of the state is in line with the liberal view of the state as a mechanism which is apart from the naturally occurring harmonies of bourgeois society and which only interferes if that harmony begins to look a bit ragged. The state, in other words, operates through man-made law, while society works by spontaneously arising natural mechanisms.

What, then, causes the state to separate from society? Engels' answer in *The Origin of the Family, Private Property and the State* (1884) is class struggle. The ancient state, as in Greece and at Rome and among the ancient Germans, was literally the 'armed people'. The ancient republics were really aristocracies of free warriors, whereas in bourgeois society the state is a body of armed men and a bureaucracy standing apart from society claiming to monopolise legitimate violence. The bourgeois state is therefore capable of oppressing its own society or a majority in it when allied to a particular minority class. It is its separateness from society which makes the state vulnerable to revolutionary takeover. For that to happen, all bureaucrats have to do is to stay away from their offices for a time, and soldiers to refuse to leave their barracks. If class antagonisms cause the state, and if that is still true, perhaps especially true, of the bourgeois state, then it follows that as class antagonisms become more acute the necessity for the state becomes greater. Paradoxically, attempted but failed revolutions strengthen the state. That is the theoretical message which Marx drew out of the history of the state in France since the Revolution. In *The Eighteenth Brumaire of Louis Bonaparte* (1852) Marx explained why the French revolutions of 1789, 1830 and 1848 all strengthened the French state. All revolutions contain a component of class alliance. In its own revolutions, the bourgeoisie has always looked round for worker allies, but has always turned against those allies when the workers have tried to take the revolution beyond its bourgeois stage. The bourgeoisie has in fact made the possession or control of the state machinery the spoils of the bourgeois revolution itself. In times of really acute class struggle, the June days in Paris in 1848 for instance, strange things can happen to the state. Marx has to explain why it is that when the bourgeoisie and the working class are at one another's throats the result is the plebiscitary despotism of Napoleon III based on massive peasant support. How can this be when it is the bourgeoisie, and after them the proletariat, which is becoming the dominant class? This Marx explains by saying that there are times when class war is so acute that the state benefits by acquiring a kind of social independence when the social forces coming into dominance cancel each other out in their struggles with each other. And of course the bourgeoisie were eventually reconciled to Bonapartist imperialism when they realised that the French state was always going to be hostile to workers' demands.

If class war between bourgeoisie and proletariat becomes more acute as bourgeois society develops, then it follows that the period of the run-up to proletarian revolution will be a period of increasing nastiness on the state's part as agent of the bourgeoisie. There can, therefore, be no 'withering away' of the state in bourgeois society, no matter how beneficent a view of the modern state liberals invite us to take. The immediate aim of the revolutionary proletariat must be the conquest of state power as *theirs*, the act of making the state change sides which we have already seen constitutes a revolutionary takeover. This means that the bourgeois state is 'abolished' because the proletariat through its own state agents begins its own period of dictatorship in place of the old bourgeois hegemony. The 'dictatorship of the proletariat' simply means that the proletariat now uses the mechanisms of state violence to achieve its class aims in exactly the same way that aristocracy and bourgeoisie used the state during their own periods of hegemony to pursue their class ends. It is the state of the dictatorship of the proletariat which 'withers away', and it withers rather than abolishes itself because the old social order does not necessarily give up easily. (There is even the possibility of two 'states', one bourgeois and one proletarian, fighting it out in a Hobbesian State of Nature.) The dictatorship of the proletariat withers away gradually as the tasks of the working class are accomplished.

The question of the 'abolition' and the 'withering away' of the state was to become crucial in the debate among Marxists about Revisionism at the turn of the nineteenth century. One of Revisionism's strongest arguments was that the bourgeois state could 'wither away' without the necessity for a period of proletarian violence, and one of Lenin's strongest arguments was that to think this was to misunderstand the nature of Marxism itself.

NOTES ON SOURCES

The *Economic and Philosophic Manuscripts of 1844*, *The Communist Manifesto* and the first hundred pages or so of *Capital* ('The mystery of the fetishistic character of commodities') are essential reading. They all exist in various English editions. There is an excellent *Selected Works of Marx and Engels*, 2 vols, by Lawrence and Wishart, but the standard collected edition of Marx is now probably D. McLellan, *Karl Marx: Selected Writings* (1977, and various reprints). It has been hard to keep up with commentary on Marxism since the deluge of books which greeted the centenary of Marx's death in 1983. Isaiah Berlin, *Karl Marx* (1965), is still an excellent introduction, and S. Avineri, *The Social and Political Thought of Karl Marx* (1965), is still an outstanding commentary. D. McLellan's *Marx Before Marxism* (1970), and *Karl Marx: His Life and Thought* (1973), are also good student introductions. R.C. Tucker, *Philosophy and Myth in Karl Marx* (1961), is good but cold-warish. T.B. Bottomore, *Modern Interpretations of Marx* (1981), gives a good idea of what is on offer.

24

SOCIAL DEMOCRACY
Bernstein and Crosland

EDUARD BERNSTEIN

Bernstein was born in Berlin in 1850 into a Jewish family of modest circumstances. The family had emigrated from Danzig, so it was understandable that young Eduard should be an enthusiast for German national unification, because in those far off days a German national state was seen by radicals as a prelude to the establishment of democracy in Germany. Bernstein became a bank clerk at the age of sixteen. He seems to have been a youth of unusual truthfulness and good humour, so that his capitalist employers were not unduly troubled when in 1872 young Bernstein joined one of the socialist groups in Germany which were to merge to form the German Social Democratic Party in 1875. At this time, Bernstein's socialism was of the undogmatic and pacifist kind common in the early days of the Second International.

It was the great depression in Germany in the twenty years after 1870 that convinced Bernstein of the coming collapse of capitalism, but Bernstein was nothing if not a *political* socialist, and it was the anti-socialist laws of Bismarck which eventually drove him into the revolutionary left and into exile in Switzerland. In Zurich, Bernstein became the editor of the newspaper which served as a kind of rallying point for the clandestine wing of the German socialist movement. The Swiss police moved him on at Bismarck's request, and so in 1888 Bernstein made the almost obligatory journey of the wandering revolutionary to London. He continued editing his newspaper and became the intimate of Engels, who admired his talents as Marx himself had.

The new England of liberal democracy had its effects on Bernstein in the decade he stayed there. He was impressed by the social tolerance of Gladstonian liberalism, and he was especially impressed by the no-nonsense socialist progressivism of the British Fabian Society, though how great an influence his British experience had on the content of Bernstein's eventual 'revisionism' is a matter of some scholarly dispute. What is certain is that an English translation (entitled *Evolutionary Socialism*) of his German classic of 1899 (or 1900, depending on whether you go by the actual date of publication or the date of publication given in the book by the publisher) appeared relatively quickly in 1909.

Bernstein became the main protagonist of the Revisionist position in German social democracy after his return to Germany in 1901. There was nothing furtive about Bernstein's Revisionism. He used the word himself, and it is important to remember that, before 1917, Revisionism was a current *within* Marxism; it was only later that Revisionism came to mean an anti-Bolshevik masquerading as a Marxist and who therefore deserved to be shot. Bernstein was a member of the *Reichstag* from 1902, and he sat in the parliament of the Weimar Republic until 1928. He was a minister for a short time in 1919. He was instrumental in diverting German social democracy away from its Bolshevik fantasies after the end of the Great War, and he saw, with sadness, the German Communist Party become a tool of Moscow.

Bernstein never really understood that Nazism had a future, preferring to think of the Nazis as deranged toughs from out of town (Munich, not Berlin) causing a bit of trouble. Hitler came to power six weeks after Bernstein died in 1932.

ANTHONY CROSLAND

In Anthony Crosland's day, graduates of the University of Oxford were an important fief at the highest level in the Labour Party. The party led by Clement Attlee, Hugh Gaitskell and Harold Wilson was an alliance of trades unionists, activists at parliamentary constituency level, and middle-class socialist intellectuals, and it was to these latter that the Gaitskells, Crossmans and Croslands belonged. They moved easily between universities, journalism and politics, and nobody doubted that they became members of parliament because they expected to be elevated to ministerial or cabinet office whenever Labour won a general election. This was partly because of the high prestige which intellectuals have always enjoyed in European social democratic movements, and partly because these were the sort of people who got the top jobs in the governing institutions of British life anyway, so why should Labour governments be any different?

Crosland was born in 1918, the son of a civil servant and a university teacher. After Highgate School, he went up to read Classics at Trinity College, Oxford. His undergraduate days were interrupted by the war. Crosland went into the army (Royal Welch, the Parachute Regiment) a classicist and came out of it an economist. He taught economics at Trinity until 1950, when he became an MP.

Politically, Crosland had shared the Marxism common in the Oxford Labour Club before the war, but in 1940 he went with the breakaway Democratic Socialist Club. He gave this shift its theoretical expression in *The Future of Socialism* (1956). Crosland wanted Labour to dump its Marxist and quasi-Marxist baggage without falling back completely on its rather joyless Methodism and Fabianism. Labour was portrayed by its enemies in the 1950s as the party of rationing and austerity. Crosland had to point out that fun would be allowed in a democratic socialist society.

As a politician, Crosland only made it to the top a few months before his death from a brain haemorrhage in 1977. He had been foreign secretary in the Callaghan government for barely ten months. He had tried for the leadership of the Labour Party in 1976, and had finished fifth out of five candidates. For all his manifest talents, Crosland was never a House of Commons heavy, and he seemed to bring out the worst in a certain kind of Conservative heckler. But his constituents at Grimsby, whose MP Crosland was from 1959, liked him, despite, or perhaps because of, his dandyish braces.

ENGELS, BERNSTEIN AND THE PROGRESSIVE CONSENSUS

Marx died in 1883 and Engels dies in 1895; both had written the *Communist Manifesto* of 1848. Marxism has always prided itself on the fact that it can face the facts of its own contemporary world without flinching, and that includes the facts of its own contemporary intellectual world. Darwin's *Origin of Species* appeared ten years before the first volume of *Capital* saw the light of day, and what followed was the triumph of those evolutionary ideas about society and the state which had been quietly gaining ground since the Scottish Enlightenment. Under the influence of the scientific boost which Darwin's evolutionary biology gave to every other kind of evolutionary theory, liberalism itself began to change its nature. From being the rather simplistic theory it had been in its origins in Locke, liberalism began to acquire the authority of the very latest scientific-biological thought. Social theory rooted in Darwinian biology began to argue that there were scientifically demonstrable natural imperatives which moved human nature in a liberal direction.

The main inspiration was Herbert Spencer and the doctrine of Social Darwinism. Spencer argued that the natural balances and harmonies which characterised the world of animal biology also characterised the world of human societies. Just as biological evolution demonstrated the wonderful and minute differentiations between species, so a social science working along the same lines would demonstrate that a human society was also a miracle of minute and spontaneous differentiation. The social division of labour which arose spontaneously in complex societies was the social equivalent of the other miracle of evolution, the human body, in which an exponential number of different parts naturally co-operated to produce a human being capable of sustained life. What made Spencerian evolutionism especially convincing was that nature's balance came about through a struggle for life, and this suited the liberal temper in its individualist mode. Human beings who consciously competed with each other in fact ended up spontaneously co-operating with each other through the social division of labour. Each man following his own calling in competition with his fellows was in fact doing them a service. Natural harmonies, among men as in the rest of nature, are to an extent precarious, and nature itself is always dangerous. Spencer completed the long love–hate affair of liberalism with the state by proclaiming that society and the state are really enemies. *Man Versus the State* (1884), Spencer's most famous work, argued frankly that the state was the main danger to gradual social improvement on evolutionary lines.

Social Darwinism mattered a great deal in liberalism's own intellectual struggle with conservatism. Since Burke, conservatives had been arguing that societies are much more complex than progressive reformers and revolutionaries had hitherto supposed, so complicated in fact that Burke and thinkers like him doubted whether a social science which explained how societies worked was possible at all. Only God could make a human society, just as only God could create a living creature, and perhaps trying to understand how a human society works comes a little too close for orthodoxy to knowing God's own mind. In his own way, Burke believed in the spontaneous co-operation of the constituent parts of a society in an organic whole, but he argued this to defend aristocracy. Aristocracy, like any other order in a society, had its functions in the scheme of things, and was not, as its

570

detractors thought, a useless and expensive social embellishment. The case against aristocracy was always that they were unproductive, parasites neither toiling nor spinning, needlessly complicating the social order and dominating the state. That explains the connection always sniffed out by conservatives between social science and radicalism. Radicals want to simplify the social system by getting rid of its extraneous class, the aristocracy, and it plainly follows that a simpler society will be easier to understand, hence the possibility of a genuine social science.

Conservative and reactionary social theory therefore battened on to complication after the American and French Revolutions, because the more complex a society is and the more delicate its internal balances, the less attractive an option is tinkering with that society, let alone renovating it. The question for non-conservatives then becomes: What is a society which consists of producers, buyers and sellers of labour going to look like, and how is it going to work? It is easy to see that, put like that, the answer was always likely to be that society which lacked the consuming but not producing class of aristocracy was going to be a much simpler society than had hitherto existed. In its social explanations conservatism, then, went in for complication, and liberalism and radicalism went in for simplicity. Earlier liberalism, say the liberalism of a Locke or an Adam Smith, only had embryonic liberal societies to look at, and neither could really guess how complex liberal society would become. The idea that as societies progressed in a liberal direction, force would increasingly come to be replaced by spontaneous co-operation, law by mechanism, was certainly there, but early liberals could not even begin to see how minutely differentiated an advanced liberal society would become.

When it began to dawn on liberals in the second half of the nineteenth century just how complicated advanced societies were becoming, Spencerism came as a godsend. Here was a version of liberalism which was liberal about the state while acknowledging just the complexity of societies themselves. Indeed, it was that very complication which made state action backed up by the threat of legal violence look like a survival from more primitive times. When Herbert Spencer published his *Social Statics* in 1850, a new half-century of liberals could cheerfully admit that what conservatives had always said about the complexity of the social order was true and still remain liberals.

What did socialism and Marxism look like from the Spencerian perspective? The answer must be: very primitive indeed. If an immensely complex system of social division of labour is going to be the way of the future, then socialism's insistence on the importance of class begins to look like a survival from an earlier age. Polarisation of a society into bourgeoisie and proletariat simply ignored the differentiations within those classes themselves, and it also ignored the multitude of gradations between the proletariat and the bourgeoisie. Societies were not getting simpler to the point where two contending classes could meet on different sides of a barricade. Quite the reverse: societies were composed of thousands of different sorts and conditions of men from the bottom to the top and each sort and condition of men differed only minutely from the one above and the one below, just as in the Darwinian scheme each different species was only minutely different from the one which preceded it and the one which followed it.

And the barricade itself was worrying, implying as it did that in the future problems could be solved through violence. If liberalism was anything, it was committed to the eradication of both domestic and international violence. Free trade between the nations would, from a rational point of view, be sheer madness when nations that trade together should fade together: xenophobic nationalism had no place in a world in which nations traded together to their mutual benefit. Violence would increasingly become a thing of the past in the domestic order too. The modern idea that the state legitimately monopolises violence was meant to be taken literally. Violence in the relations of the workplace would disappear as brute strength became less necessary for work with the new technology. Husbands were expected to beat wives and children less, and there was even talk about kindness to animals. Of course, this was a programme of hope rather than present and settled fact, because it was always going to take time for liberalism to work its way against and through existing social institutions and prejudices, but liberalism was progressive rather than revolutionary and so could afford to wait.

Out of all this came a progressive consensus that violence was to be strictly controlled by the state and was only to be used as a weapon of last resort as men's relation with each other came to be regulated by naturally arising mechanisms and by the public reasonableness of law. In this perspective the Marxist concept of *class* struggle and *class* war could easily be seen as atavistic, as a primitive way of acting, savage even, a bit like asking a blacksmith to use a hammer to mend a watch.

Marxist theory could not keep itself aloof from the intellectual currents of its own time. Marxism, after all, claimed to be scientific, and Darwinism was science, so at the very least Marxism had to be compatible with Darwinism, but it had to be a different Darwinism from the Social Darwinism of Herbert Spencer. It is a matter of some dispute who began the process of incorporating the evolutionary consensus about social development into Marxism. Some say Marx himself, others say Engels, and yet others say the revisionist Eduard Bernstein.

MARXISM AND THE ENGELS PROBLEM

It is perfectly conceivable that a good deal of what we have come to call Marxism is really Engelsism. Engels survived Marx by a decade, and the fact that Marx never settled down to write the definitive tract about what Marxism means is notorious, and there is even a doubt about the moment when Marxism became coherent enough to be called a social and political doctrine with claims to universal applicability. Besides, Marx himself was a prolific correspondent, and it was easy enough for socialists to write to Marx and ask his advice about particular questions of theory and practice. It is equally notorious that the finished statements of Marxist theory are by Engels, and they all come very late. Works like *Socialism Utopian and Scientific* and *The Origins of the Family, Private Property and the State* were heavily influenced by evolutionist ideas, and these were the texts which gained canonical status in the German Social Democratic Party, which before 1914 was the largest, best organised, and most orthodoxly Marxist of all the European socialist parties.

Considerations such as these have led to the contention that Engels somehow doctored the legacy of Marx and sent Marxist theory in directions which Marx himself might not have taken. Engels, it is said, made Marxism into the kind of 'scientific' dogma which found favour in Stalin's Russia as the exposition of scientifically verifiable laws about the future of capitalist society, tying historical materialism to predictions which as things have turned out have given the lie to Marxism. On the other hand, it is perfectly conceivable that the old Marx really did think that he had found out the secret of the future, and there was always a dogmatic thrust to Marx's own thinking. Engels certainly thought that to disbelieve Marxism was the same as continuing to believe that the world was flat, and it is possible that Marx thought this too. However, what will not do is to think that Engels's contributions to Marxist theory were all 'late', because there is considerable evidence that Engels's inputs into Marxism began very early, and we have the authoritative judgement of Lenin that the Marxist theory of the state is to be found in its completed form in the works of Engels alone.

The question of Engels's early and continuing contribution to Marxism is partly a question of intellectual biography. Both Marx and Engels began as young Hegelians, and both reacted against Hegel's Idealism at about the same time and for the same reasons, and there is plenty of biographical evidence that from very early on there was deep argument between Marx and Engels about philosophical, economic and social questions. The thesis that Engels fiddles with the legacy of Marx fails to acknowledge the contributions which Engels made to Marxism right at the beginning, and his continuing contributions. It was Engels, after all, who wrote the first extended 'Marxist' account of how English capitalism affected the working class. *The Condition of the English Working Class in 1844* already contained the crucial insight that the evils of capitalism were not the result of the wickedness of capitalists but were systemic. Capitalists would be shocked to be told that in factories they were getting something for nothing – what later came to be called surplus value. Marx himself had done nothing comparable at the time, and we have Marx's own specific statement that when he and Engels met again in 1844 their common work together began.

It must also never be forgotten that not only did Engels collaborate with Marx in writing *The German Ideology* (1859), which contains the classic statement of the ideological nature of the Hegelian philosophy and a defence of historical materialism, but also the classic account of the *transition* from Hegelian Idealism to historical materialism via Feuerbach's transformative humanism is the work of Engels. Marx's own *Theses on Feuerbach* (1845), which Engels found among Marx's papers after his death, is always printed as an appendix to Engels's own *Ludwig Feuerbach and the End of Classical German Philosophy* (1888), which contains the classic account of how a dialectical view of the world conceived materialistically comes out of a Feuerbachian critique of the categories of the Hegelian philosophy. Positions which we have come to regard as classically Marxist: that Hegel's dialectic properly understood marked the end of all finality because everything that has existed deserves to perish including Hegel's 'system' of politics; the idea that every stage in history is justified for its own time, and the idea that the revolutions of 1848 everywhere began to kill off dynastic absolutism idealistically conceived, are all to be found in Hegel's *Ludwig Feuerbach*. We also have Engels's own explicit statement that in all their collaborative work over nearly half-a-century, Marx and Engels never once discussed Feuerbach, and so it might be that not only did Engels arrive at his critique of Hegel independently of Marx, but also it was in fact Engels who worked out the details of exactly how a Feuerbachian critique of Hegel affected the world-view that came to be called historical, and eventually dialectical, materialism. When we add to all this the fact that Engels spent the last ten years of his life putting together Volume III of *Capital*, and the fact that, as Lenin says in *State and Revolution*, the Marxist theory of the state, without which Marxism could not be considered anything like complete, was fully developed by Engels, then we may have to take a view of Engels not as Marx's loyal but subordinate colleague but rather as a thinker equal in his own right to Marx.

If this view of Engels' contribution to Marxism is taken seriously, then it follows that if Engels did any fiddling around with the terms of the Marxist legacy he was fiddling around with something which was half his anyhow. What is unquestionable is that Engels took 'scientific socialism' much further in the direction of 'real' science than had formerly been the case. Even the word 'science' was undergoing a change, from meaning any organised body of knowledge, to meaning specific sciences like biology. If it is really true that Engels thought that Marxism was a science which could explain everything, including how the natural world works – what we would call the 'real' sciences of physics, chemistry, and biology – then Engels's is the first Marxist theory to call itself 'scientific' in a recognisable modern sense. Whether the internal coherence of Marxism was completed or diminished by Engels is a moot point, but there can be no doubt that at around the turn of the century the 'Marxism as science' banner was the one that most Marxists preferred to march under.

FROM ENGELS TO BERNSTEIN:
'SCIENTISM' TO REVISIONISM

Not the least of the problems raised by scientific socialism was the problem of why one ought to be a socialist. If it was true that capitalism was 'scientificably' doomed by the necessary laws of the progression of capitalist societies discovered by Marxism, then it was not clear what part human will and volition was to play in the process. Presumably human will and volition could hasten the process a bit, or could delay it a bit, but that was about all. Of course, Marxism as a set of predictions about the future was vulnerable to the facts of its own contemporary world in a way it had not been vulnerable before. The Marxist idea of *praxis* of dialectically informed voluntarist action, which is the theoretical message of *The Communist Manifesto*, comes to be overtaken by the very different position of waiting for the inevitable to happen, if not at the next great crisis of capitalism then at least at the next but one.

But suppose the period of waiting becomes longer and longer, then Marxism as a science of everything becomes an apology for revolution *not* happening this time, a position which gets more apologetic with every passing year. And what is a Marxistically committed party like the party of German Social Democracy to do in the meantime? Waiting is tedious, so why not use the party's electoral strength to get some short-term gains out of the capitalist class and its state? Out of this practice came Revisionism, a genuine extrapolation from the practice of a Marxist socialist party waiting for the final collapse of capitalism which its own theory appeared so confidently to predict. And to predict as happening *soon*. It can still come as a surprise to us how quickly nineteenth- and early twentieth-century social theory expected its predictions to happen, but we should never forget that it was the speed of economic, social and political change after 1789 which made nineteenth-century social theory possible in the first place. Paradoxically, it was this perceived speed of change in the nineteenth century which could persuade people to wait; to live in daily expectation of change only makes sense if one daily expects it. However, there does come a time when it begins to make sense to ask whether the expected cataclysmic change really is going to happen soon, and if not, then what the implications are for the theory upon which the expectations for change are based. This is what Eduard Bernstein did in his famous work which in the English-speaking world is known by the title *Evolutionary Socialism* (1900). What follows is an account of what Bernstein actually said, and what follows that is an attempt to understand its importance in the socialist tradition.

EDUARD BERNSTEIN'S *EVOLUTIONARY SOCIALISM*

If Bernstein was a heretic inside the Marxist camp, then there are at least three major heresies in *Evolutionary Socialism* and eight minor heresies.

1 Bernstein was struck by the way in which the bourgeois state in Britain and Germany was willing to listen to workers' demands and was prepared to meet calls for working-class improvement half-way. How could this be? If the bourgeois state was listening sympathetically to working-class demands, then it must be because either the state was becoming less bourgeois, or the bourgeoisie was beginning to abandon its own doctrines of political economy as the ideology of bourgeois hegemony. Bernstein thought that both were happening, that modern economic development was freeing thought from its economic underpinning. Capitalists have even stopped using competition with other capitalists as an excuse for keeping wages low, the very bed-rock of political economy's own theory of wages. Co-operation now exists between capitalists, and co-operation now exists between workers, and employers' associations seem to be able to make deals with workers' associations. This is progress of a kind which an earlier form of capitalist economics and an earlier form of socialist economics would not have led one to suspect was possible, but we can see it happening before our very eyes, and it is progressive because each side is showing itself able to rid itself of theory inherited from the past as prejudice.

2 This progressive consensus is possible because modern industry is profitable in ways which were not conceivable to earlier generations of economic forecasters, bourgeois and socialist. This must mean that the rate of surplus value is increasing, and improvements in workers' wages must mean that more of that surplus is being redistributed to workers. This presents a special problem for Marxist theory, because it becomes unclear what surplus value is actually a measure of. There had always been a tendency in Marxism to

regard surplus value as a measure of the exploitation of workers by capitalists. Bernstein was struck by the fact that workers appeared to be better paid in those industries where profits, and therefore the rate of the extraction of surplus value, were highest and it was not obvious how on the classical Marxist account of surplus value this could be. Above all, as Bernstein looked at modern economies, it was not obvious exactly what surplus value could be if it was not to be a measure of exploitation. If it's not that, then what *is* surplus value?

3 Perhaps it followed that Marxists had been getting value theory all wrong from the beginning, just as the classical economists had been wrong about value theory before Marxism. Of course, the political and social thrust of the labour theory of value and of surplus value had always been clear from the Marxist point of view: all those who did no labour with their hands, capitalists say, or bankers, or middlemen, were parasites on the surplus value extracted from workers in factories. Bernstein began to wonder about that. Perhaps Marx had not taken his own theory of *exchange*-value seriously enough. Perhaps everyone who contributed to the price which commodities finally fetched on the market was a value-creator, and that could include capitalists, middlemen and even salesmen and advertisers; everyone who was involved in the process of production, distribution and exchange. These former parasites now became value-creators in their own right, not parasites at all but workers by brain.

These were all of them major heresies, or contained the seeds of major heresies. The minor heresies are only minor by comparison. These include:

1 Capital is not becoming concentrated in fewer hands: both absolutely and relatively, the number in the possessing class is increasing. This in its turn must mean that the class structure of contemporary societies is becoming more differentiated, not more polarised. The spread of shareholding means that not all those who own the means of production are capitalists in the old sense because they do not come into direct contact with labour. They are a *rentier* class, not directors of labour. These are much harder to dispossess than the few monopoly capitalists of the classic model of the ideal preconditions for revolution.

2 Increasing prosperity means that the possessors consume less than the non-possessors, so the image of the bloated capitalist has to go. The society of mass-production is changing into a society of mass-consumption so that expropriation of the expropriators would not help the living standards of the working class much. The increased productivity of modern industry is consumed by workers, so where does that leave the Marxist theory of the decline of wages and the tendency towards immiseration which features so largely in Marx's own account of the plight of the proletariat as capitalism develops?

3 The number of small businesses in Germany is increasing, not diminishing: there are over a million separate enterprises in Germany and the number is on the increase. The expropriation of a widely dispersed *rentier* class might be difficult enough, but the 'nationalisation' of a million separate enterprises is a daunting enterprise even for socialists. Taking the means of production into collective ownership would only be possible in an era of massive concentrations of capital, but this does not appear to be happening.

4 And what would a revolutionary takeover of the means of production in these unforeseen circumstances actually be like? The clue lies in the case of the Jacobin dictatorship in the French Revolution, which Saint-Simon famously called the 'government of men without means', enemies to all who have a stake in the *status quo*. Now that prosperity is increasing and the numbers of possessors of capital is increasing, the have-nots are becoming an even smaller group, so why would the 'dictatorship of the proletariat' not divide the working class, a large proportion of whom have a stake in the economy? Proletarian dictatorship would be a ganging-up of those who have nothing to lose (a diminishing number) against those who truly have something to lose (an increasing number). In these circumstances we only have a repetition of the Terror to look forward to.

5 Bernstein is far from denying that classes still exist, but he thinks that democracy based on universal suffrage will end the class nature of government without 'at first' abolishing class. Marx himself had been against universal suffrage in Prussia because it would legitimise the rule of Bismarck and Junkerdom but Bernstein thinks that Marx's own view was very short-sighted. Even Bismarck has recognised that things are changing. The anti-socialist laws have gone, a rudimentary welfare state has come into existence, and the day is not far distant when the representatives of the people will come to recognise that they are the people's servants, not their masters. Non-class government will gradually introduce measures which will gradually abolish class, though Bernstein is vague about the details.

6 This is not just happening in Germany: look at the 'moral progress' of English Liberalism under Gladstone. Liberalism is unlike the rule of, say, feudal barons, because it is 'flexible', and liberalism through democracy can reform itself by transforming the state into something like a social republic. Granted the nature of the modern state and its capacity to redistribute wealth, the resort to revolutionary violence would be 'political atavism', a return to political barbarism which the very concept of an evolutionary present and future condemns. To believe that domestic violence can solve the problems of the social and political order, is the equivalent of thinking that violence in the home can solve the problems of child-rearing.

7 *Pace* the Marx of *The Communist Manifesto*, so many workers now have a stake in country that they can now be said to have a Fatherland worth preserving: they have become citizens with their political rights and a modest economic prosperity to lose. Workers can now support imperialism, Hegel's old 'false universality' of bourgeois society, because imperialism is progressive and, besides, natives often have very doubtful titles to their land. Imperialism is not to be confused with a militantly expansionist nationalism whose aggressiveness could cause war. On the contrary, countries with strong social democratic movements would never go to war with each other: politics will prevent war (*pace* Clausewitz).

8 If capitalism is not on the verge of collapse, then why be a socialist at all? Socialism in the future will plainly not consist of waiting for the revolution: that is to believe in a chimera. Being a socialist in the future will make sense provided socialists can rid themselves of the idea of an apocalyptic goal. The end becomes nothing, the road to that end everything. Be a socialist, Bernstein seems to be saying, because to be a socialist is to be

progressive, and therefore to be right. Socialism becomes something like a Kantian categorical imperative: not to be a socialist is to deny the possibility of human progress.

THE IMPORTANCE OF BERNSTEIN

Like J.S. Mill's critique of Bentham, Bernstein's critique of classic Marxism is a critique from within. Bernstein was Engels's literary executor and was a leading figure in the German Social Democracy Party: he was flesh of their flesh and bone of their bone. This meant that, not wishing to cause more trouble than he had to, Bernstein's message has to an extent to be de-coded. Bernstein's *Evolutionary Socialism* is a much more radical critique of Marxist orthodoxy as it existed around 1900 than might appear at first sight. Take, for example, Bernstein's claim that the 'new' industrial revolution in Germany based on the steel, electrical, chemical and ship-building industries was introducing an era which freed thought, especially bourgeois thought, from its economic underpinnings. This sounds like anodyne progressivism – the bourgeoisie have become wiser and more tolerant – but it is more than that, because in classic Marxism there is no explanation of how this could be so. The theory of history which Marx took from Hegel and turned into historical materialism expected each stage of history, through its prevailing ideology, to present itself as a finished truth to a world which was not expected to alter in any significant way. The Marxist doctrine of 'false consciousness' relies for its plausibility on asserting that the bourgeoisie cannot be expected to think beyond its own time, and certainly not so far beyond as a social republic (though admittedly Bernstein thought that the social republic was a long way in the future). Asking and expecting the bourgeoisie to come to terms with a future socialist majority in a parliament which would eventually use the democratic mechanisms of the bourgeoisie's own state to redistribute wealth, was the equivalent of asking the bourgeoisie to become something other than itself before the revolution had even happened, something which on the classic Marxist account of class the bourgeoisie could never be. It is revolution which transforms class in bourgeois society by universalising the proletariat out of the ruins of the old order. Bernstein seemed to be saying that the bourgeoisie could transform itself without revolution, which in the classic Marxist conception was impossible.

Also, in the classic conception of class, the class war is supposed to hot up as capitalism develops, and this has important consequences for the nature of the bourgeois state in its last days. The bourgeoisie does not fight the class war direct but through its state agents. The bourgeois state can therefore appear to be strengthening itself, or at least becoming nastier, in capitalism's final stages, and it is the bourgeois state in its final form which has to be abolished as a class state by making it into the agent of the proletariat in its struggle to establish its own hegemony. Bernstein appeared to be saying something very different, that the class nature of the bourgeois state could change gradually. In effect it could begin to 'wither away' as a *bourgeois* state, and not as a proletarian state as the period of the 'dictatorship of the proletariat' gradually came to an end as the proletariat completed its historic task of universalising itself as a class and transforming itself into humanity. Carts were being put before horses by Bernstein in a big way.

Again, it is not clear how much of Marxist economics can survive Bernstein's treatment of surplus value and the tendency towards monopoly. To say that the total amount of surplus value in modern economies is increasing may sound innocuous enough, but Bernstein did not draw the orthodox conclusion that therefore the rate of capital accumulation was increasing. On the contrary, Bernstein came to the conclusion that more of the total 'social' surplus value was being redistributed as wages. Not only did that drive a coach and four through the theory of necessary immiseration but it also seriously undermined the classic Marxist analysis of labour as a commodity which would always sell at or about its cost of production. If there was so much surplus value sloshing around a capitalist economy that capitalists could begin to share it out among workers, then it was no longer clear in Marxist terms what the theory of surplus value was actually *for*. Bourgeois economics had already been shaken out of its own labour theory of value into the ultimate utility theory of value, which is price theory by any other name. Perhaps this happened just too late for Marx to cope with, because there could easily have been a moment of Marxist triumph as Marxism chased political economy out of one category of value and into another. *Capital* was, after all, a critique of political economy as well as an indictment of how capitalism actually worked, and therefore a new Marxist critique of the new value category of bourgeois value theory should have been possible. But what Bernstein did was effectively to take the bourgeois ultimate utility theory of value into Marxism as a finished truth, and it was this which enabled him to make the non-labourers into value-creators, not parasites, because anyone who contributed to the final price then became a creator of value.

Of course it could be argued in Bernstein's favour that what he was challenging was Marxist orthodoxy, not truth. His critique only made sense as a critique because an Engels-type Marxism had encouraged Marxists to nail their colours to the mast of prediction. All socialism stands or falls by its capacity to cope with the facts of its own world, and 'scientific' socialism made itself uniquely vulnerable to being given the lie by a future which was not quite turning out as the predictions suggested. The business of waiting for the inevitable revolution which refused to happen can be represented as the disunity of theory and practice: if theory tells you to wait for the revolution, then in what sense waiting can be revolutionary practice is not clear. The German Social Democratic Party did have a practice, but it was the practice of acting as one of the parties in a bourgeois parliamentary system whose rules it had perforce to accept. The plain truth of the matter was that German Social Democracy had become part of 'the system' and it had just enough of a past for that past to be worth defending. The party was one of the great institutions of German politics, and doctrinal orthodoxy was already part of the claim to party leadership. Bernstein's Revisionism was an extrapolation from twenty years of non-revolutionary practice, and all his Revisionism really amounted to was to ask the party to preach what it practised.

The problem of social democracy was part of the wider problem of democracy itself. In 1848, when *The Communist Manifesto* was written, it was easy for reactionaries and conservatives to think that the problem of democracy and the problem of socialism were the same problem. Universal suffrage was bound to mean that the working class would use their votes in their own interest *as a class* in exactly the same way that other classes had used their political resources in their own cause as classes. Even someone as friendly to the extension of the suffrage as J.S. Mill still thought that in 1861 (*On Representative Government*). This was especially true of countries where the struggle for socialism and the struggle for democratic rights were all but indistinguishable, and that meant most countries except the United States and perhaps Britain. By 1900 there was just about enough experience of mass politics to make it possible to see that there was no *necessary* connection between democracy and socialism. There was just enough experience of socialist and democratic politics – in Britain, France, Germany and Italy – to begin to convince observers who might be inclined to think otherwise, that there was something about bourgeois democracy which meant that working-class parties with socialist ideologies would begin to act in ways which were not dissimilar to the ways in which their rival bourgeois parties acted, or even rival bourgeois parties with strong aristocratic admixtures. The theory of elites and of *embourgeoisement* was in the air. This new way of looking at mass working-class socialist parties had many impulses and took many forms before it became one of the stock truisms, perhaps *the* truism, of modern political science. Some of the impulses are very obvious: the oligarchic tendencies of American democracy after the Civil War; the electoral success of Disraelian conservatism in Britain; the longevity of leaders in European socialist parties; the electoral success of centre parties, especially in Germany; plebiscitary despotism in France; aristo-populist politics in Italy in the attacks on Giolitti. It was in Italy that the Iron Law of Oligarchy was first worked out as a formal principle. It was there by 1884 and already a commonplace by 1900. The central idea in the works of the oligarchic theorists Pareto, Mosca and Michels is very simple: political parties, *just because they are political parties*, turn themselves into oligarchies, ruled by the few and not by the many. Parties are characterised by their structures, not by their ideologies. The leaders of socialist mass parties are leaders in the same senses that leaders of rival parties are leaders. They are forced to make the same kinds of choices and are subject to the same kinds of pressures and are forced into the same kinds of compromises. It follows that ideology is not a good predictor of how socialist parties will act, no matter how important the ideology is to the party. In socialist parties, as in other parties, ideology is only one of the pressures to which the leadership is subject. Whatever ideology does, it won't dictate policy, or if it does, it won't be a reliable guide to day-to-day party activity.

From there it is a short step to the realisation that ideology can become a nuisance, an embarrassing millstone round the necks of party leaders, especially in their dealings with other party leaders and with the electorate. That, or something very like it, was probably happening in German Social Democracy around 1900. Talk about the future revolution was just talk, and it was damaging talk for a party looking for electoral support from conservatively minded working-class voters, and it could always serve as an excuse for state repression. One of the reasons why Bismarck repealed the anti-socialist laws in Germany was that he, along with others who really mattered, had come to believe that, beneath it all, Social Democracy meant the state no harm, but that could change. Talk about the future revolution could also be damaging to the party faithful. A party working in a system with other parties and vying with them for electoral support has to deliver on its promises, but the one thing the German Social Democrats consistently failed to deliver was the revolution. What were the party faithful supposed to think while they waited? What was to be done in the meantime? Plainly, getting some concessions out of the bourgeoisie by using electoral and parliamentary muscle on the bourgeois state. Of course, there were good 'left' arguments against this policy. It smacked of opportunism, and suppose the parliamentary game became the thing? And what if the concessions won from the bourgeois state had the tendency to lull the working class into a sense of security? Could it not lead to a diminution of revolutionary energy, playing the parliamentary game to play into the hands of the state-opportunists and postponing even further a revolution which had already been postponed several times already?

Bernstein's way out of these difficulties had the virtue of honesty and directness. Why not make the parliamentary game itself ideologically respectable? Bernstein's evolutionary socialism was, after all, an extrapolation from a practice, so why not say that Revisionism was the re-unification of theory and practice? Bernstein's theory came at the moment when German Social Democracy had just enough of a track record to make the position 'continue to do what we have always done' a feasible option. Socialism in Germany had just enough of a past to make an extrapolation from that past a possible ideological option. Marxism, indeed all socialisms, is a doctrine of how the present came out of the past, and the account of how that happens is supposed to determine both the doctrine and future tactics and strategy, and there is not supposed to be a difference between the two. On the Marxist account of how consciousness comes to be formed, there is a perfectly orthodox case to be made out for saying that socialist practice should influence the course of socialist theory. If the actual course of German Social Democracy was going in the direction of making it one of the great unofficial estates of the German Empire, along with the industrialists and the Prussian bureaucracy and general staff, then Revisionism made perfect sense, though Bernstein could not expect his theory to be popular with those who were content to continue to repeat revolutionary platitudes while in their daily lives they continued to go down the revisionist road which Bernstein pointed out.

POSTSCRIPT. A LATTER-DAY BERNSTEIN: ANTHONY CROSLAND, *THE FUTURE OF SOCIALISM* (1956)

The extraordinary conservatism of the socialist tradition which was noted in the previous chapter operated nowhere more powerfully than in the reluctance of socialists to accept Revisionism. This was even true of the British Labour Party which did not have a revolutionary past to live down, unlike most continental socialist non-communist parties. The British Labour Party, like all socialist parties, has always found it difficult to get rid of intellectual furniture inherited from the past. Labour after 1945, and especially after 1951, found itself saddled with the famous Clause Four of its Constitution of 1919 which Labour's opponents claimed made the Labour Party the party which would, given the opportunity, nationalise everything in sight. In these circumstances Anthony Crosland had the kind of Bernstein courage to ask: What is socialism *now*? How much of what socialists have inherited from the past should be jettisoned and how much should be retained? And what should be emphasised?

Like Bernstein, Crosland began by asking what could be assumed about his own contemporary world, and he decided that there were three major assumptions about that world which could safely be made:

1 Capitalism was certainly not going to collapse under its own weight in the West, either because it wouldn't or, what amounted almost to the same thing, because governments would not allow it to collapse. Since the New Deal, Western governments had freely and openly admitted what had in fact been true for some time: that government was in the business of managing the economy. Governments had begun to listen to economists more seriously than hitherto, and in Keynesianism they had found the theoretical basis for demand management of the economy, and governments were getting better at it. The pressures coming from a democratic society would never again allow governments to preside over the kind of economic collapse which characterised Weimar Germany or the United States and Britain in the 1930s, partly because people with votes would never elect a party to government which would tolerate such a repetition of the mistakes of the past, and partly because an economic collapse comparable to pre-war economic conditions might let in the communists and as a good social democrat Crosland would not countenance that.

2 The capitalist economies of the West, including the British, were growing, and this growth would be accompanied by full employment. This growth and full employment has now become the policy of all Western governments no matter whether they call themselves socialist, conservative, or anything else.

3 It must follow that the capitalist cannot be said to be the working man's class enemy in anything like the old sense. Now that there is full employment, primary poverty has been abolished, a Health Service exists, trades unions are in a strong bargaining position and there is a strong nationalised sector in the economy, it could hardly be said that workers are 'at the mercy of employers', and they are certainly not at the mercy of the owners of capital who rarely manage enterprises anyway.

Crosland drew seven major conclusions from what he took to be an accurate description of what was going on in the Western world:

1 Now that the ownership of enterprises has been divorced from their management, the problem for socialists in the future is not going to be ownership but control. The social democratic way forward was worker participation in the running of enterprises, a kind of industrial democracy.

2 Britain is still in many ways a class-ridden society. The aim of a socialist movement should not be nationalisation of enterprises which provide full employment and a taxable surplus which can be creamed off into social provisions which will lead to greater equality.

3 Therefore a future socialist programme is not so much a matter of structural economic change as of the democratic political will to democratise British society. This is a matter of reform, including comprehensive education, opening up the public schools, and a measure of industrial democracy.

4 A social democratic movement must care as much for liberty as for equality. Equality is really the business of progressive taxation, while liberty is the business of legislative removal of restrictions. Rights for women, including abortion, rights for homosexuals, and an end to the sillier forms of censorship should all be part of a socialist programme. Socialism does not mean puritanism and austerity, and nor does it mean the boot-faced moral earnestness of the Webbs. Socialism must allow a place for dissent, eccentricity, fun, and even frivolity.

5 Socialism really becomes a form of moral and economic pluralism. Enterprises will be state-run, privately run, and run by co-operatives. There is no reason in principle why the state has to own things when it can occupy the commanding heights of the economy as an economic manager. The state can fix exchange rates, interest rates and the level of taxation, and the state as a consumer has enormous purchasing power in the market. The question which will in the future divide left and right will be over the relative shares of the public and private, and above all the question: Who is best able to run a mixed economy and the welfare state, Labour or the Conservatives?

6 A socialist programme will in the future be the fulfilment of a truly democratic programme. It's not the economy which naturally and automatically decides the degree of inequality in a society but the political will of its governments. Labour has a natural majority anyway, but Labour governments – even the radical and reforming Labour governments like Mr Attlee's after 1945 – tend to run scared. The democratic will of the people expressed through a future Labour majority in the House of Commons will demand not economic but social engineering achieved through impeccably democratic and parliamentary procedures.

7 The democratic programme, socialism as the fulfilment of democracy and not national-isation, must be the party's way of looking at the future. (Besides, nationalisation either bores the voters or puts them off, and so does the Labour Party's image as the party of Crippsian austerity.) The future is going to be good, prosperous, even fun, as the demo-cratic state redistributes the good things of life. This will not, of course, happen overnight, and perhaps it is better not to have any very fixed idea of an ideal future because there is so much to be done in the meantime that the future can be left to take care of itself.

We noted right at the beginning of this section on socialism that there seems to be some kind of in-built mechanism in socialist movements which disposes them to doctrinal conservatism. One way of explaining this is to say that in the case of non-communist democratic socialist movements there is always going to be the problem of living down a revolutionary past. The faithful have been brought up on revolutionary expectations and do not like to give these expectations up, and those revolutionary expectations become an electoral liability because rival parties can always play the 'reds under the bed' card at election time. Yet the British Labour Party has nothing remotely like a revolutionary past to live down, and it has always contained a good proportion of the most rabidly anti-communist British politicians who saw what communist takeover in the wake of the Red Army did to democratic socialist parties in Eastern Europe after the Second World War.

Yet even in the British Labour Party's case, Clause Four is still a bone of contention despite Crosland's *The Future of Socialism*. Its recent formal abolition is unlikely to efface it from the hearts of a certain kind of Labour activist, to say nothing of a certain kind of Labour voter.

NOTES ON SOURCES

Bernstein's *Evolutionary Socialism* (1961), is remarkable among the works of German socialists for its clarity. Bernstein's *Cromwell and Communism*, ed. Stenning (1938), testifies to his interest in England. Crosland's *The Future of Socialism* (1956), is another good example of how clear socialist writing can be when it is free from the more Hegelian aspects of Marxism. T. Labedz, ed., *Revisionism* (1962), covers the ground well. C.E. Shorske, *German Social Democracy, 1905–1917* (1983), is a brilliant study.

25

THE SYNTHESIS OF JACOBINISM AND MARXISM–BOLSHEVISM

Lenin, Trotsky and Stalin

VLADIMIR ILICH LENIN

Lenin's is not a life about which it is easy to be neutral. For the seventy years since the Bolshevik revolution until quite recently, adulation of Lenin was compulsory for the millions living in that part of the world which we used to call 'communist', while for many outside that world the idea of a Lenin Peace Prize was nothing short of obscene. There is no no-man's-land between the Lenin who was the saviour of mankind and the Lenin who begat Stalin. To take a view of Lenin's life as a professional revolutionary before and after the Bolshevik seizure of power in 1917 is therefore almost impossible without taking a political stance.

Lenin is an example of a revolutionary 'from above', one of those free-floating bourgeois intellectuals Marx talks about who split off from their class and ally themselves with the proletariat. Nobody seems to doubt that in Lenin's case the motivation was the execution of his brother for his part in a plot to assassinate the tsar (executions for revolutionary activity in tsarist Russia were relatively infrequent, the usual punishment being internal exile).

Vladimir Ilich Ulyanov (he only began to call himself Lenin in 1901) was born in Simbirsk in 1870, the son of a schoolmaster and inspector who eventually attained noble rank. He was a good scholar from an early age, and read voraciously in the Russian classics. The execution of his brother put the whole of Lenin's family in disgrace, so they moved to Kazan, where Lenin became a university student. He was soon embroiled in revolutionary student politics and was arrested for the first time in 1887. Lenin gained his degree from the law faculty of the University of St Petersburg as an external student. By 1893 Lenin was himself in St Petersburg, studying Marxism, and making a name for himself in Russian Marxist circles.

Until 1919, Lenin lived the underground and exile life common to Russian and other nineteenth-century revolutionaries. Much of that life centred on clandestine newspapers, with the attendant bickerings over who should decide editorial policy. This was partly because editorial policy questions were indistinguishable from leadership questions, and partly because in exile there was not much else to do. Lenin also did his time in Siberia. Much of his life afterwards was spent in Western Europe, and it took him the best part of a decade to establish himself as one of the leaders of the Russian Social Democratic Party and as one of its leading theoreticians. (This was the party which was to split into Lenin's Bolshevik Party and the Mensheviks. It was only after seizing power in Russia that the party began to call itself Communist.)

It was the Russian collapse on the Eastern Front in the First World War that gave Lenin and the Bolsheviks their chance. Lenin famously returned to the Finland Station in St Petersburg in a *sealed train* thoughtfully provided by the German General Staff. The rest everybody knows: the October Revolution, the Civil War, and Lenin's early death in 1924, to be succeeded by Stalin.

LEON TROTSKY

Trotsky was probably the only well-known Bolshevik leader who could genuinely be called charismatic, and Trotsky is certainly the only one whose life has been the subject of a great biography in English: Isaac Deutscher's *The Prophet Armed* (1954), *The Prophet Unarmed* (1959) and *The Prophet Outcast* (1963). Any view of Trotsky's life has to be written either for or against Deutscher, whose Trotsky has his warts but is the real hero of the Russian Revolution as well as being the only really heroic critic of Stalinism. It now takes an effort of the historical imagination to be able to picture what the loweringly eloquent presence of Trotsky in exile in Mexico meant for the infant communist state in Russia and for all Marxists outside the single communist state in a seemingly uniformly hostile capitalist world. That Trotsky, a powerless exile, could be thought of as being a threat to Stalin, or even as an alibi for Stalinism, tells us something about the prestige of the man.

Trotsky was born Lev Davidovich Bronstein in 1879, the son of a Jewish farmer in the Ukraine. He was a revolutionary in his student days at Odessa, was first arrested in 1898, exiled to Siberia in 1900, and escaped to London where he joined Lenin and the *Iskra* group in 1902. Trotsky had early doubts about the direction in which Lenin was trying to lead the Russian social democratic movement. He went with the Mensheviks against Lenin's Bolsheviks (a fact which was to cost him dear in the later struggle with Stalin), while at the same time working out the famous theory of 'permanent revolution'. He emerged as the true socialist hero from the Russian Revolution of 1905, after which there followed another spell of internal and external exile. Trotsky returned to Russia after the February Revolution, threw in his lot with Lenin. He became People's Commissar for Foreign Affairs responsible for negotiating the peace of Brest–Litovsk which took Russia out of the Great War.

In 1918, Trotsky began his great work of organising the Red Army, which was eventually to win the civil war, and in this he showed that imperious, intolerant streak which made his enemies think of him as a future Napoleon. Trotsky failed to stop Stalin's rise to power after Lenin's death partly because Trotsky, not Stalin, seemed to be more likely to make a bid for 'Stalinist' dictatorship.

Trotsky was banished to Alma Ata, and then expelled from the Soviet Union in 1929. Then followed the wandering – Turkey, France, Norway – before Trotsky was allowed to settle in Mexico in 1937. He was murdered in 1940.

RUSSIAN MARXISM AND THE RUSSIAN AUTOCRACY

It was a fundamental fact in the nineteenth century that all progressive groups in Western Europe hated the Russian autocracy. (One of the reasons for Marx's own hatred of English Liberalism in general and Gladstone in particular was the trend in Liberal foreign policy to make concessions to Russia at Turkey's expense in the Middle East, which made Marx the unlikely ally of English Tory foreign policy under Disraeli.) Marx, Engels and Western socialists in general looked forward to the downfall of tsardom, and they followed the wave of political assassinations in Russia with growing enthusiasm. But, for all its desirability, socialists in the West could only think of the downfall of the Romanovs as being marginal to the development of socialism, though it was central to the development of bourgeois democracy in Russia with all that meant for the development of those political and economic conditions without which a future socialist revolution in Russia was impossible. After about 1870, it began to be obvious that the end of autocracy in Russia would lead to the establishment of either a constitutional monarchy in the style of Bismarckian Germany or a French-style democratic republic. German Marxists were doubly willing to welcome a change of regime in Russia because the era of the Second International was also the era of the Franco-Russian military alliance, and it seemed that the future of Social Democracy might be jeopardised in a war in which Germany would have to fight for her national existence against the Russian menace, and against a conscript French army itself containing many socialists. Memories were long in 1870. Old men had been boys when the Russian armies in the fight against Napoleon had trampled their way through Germany on their way to Paris and gathered as they went a reputation for brutality towards their supposed allies that the official enemy the French has never gained. The Polish Rebellion of 1863 was fresh in the mind. It had failed as Polish rebellions always do, and the whole of Western Europe was filled with atrocity stories arising out of the suppression of the rebellion by the Russians. Any change in Russia would be a change for the better, and Western Marxists hoped it might even lead to a diminution of that Prussian militarism which was the reactionary pillar of Bismarck's *Reich*.

Revolutionary circles in Russia looked sympathetically to the works of Marx and Engels as an analysis of capitalist development, and looked forward to the days when that work would be relevant to Russian conditions: even the anarchist Bakunin thought that. But the way forward in Russia seemed to many revolutionaries to lie with populism, a revolution of the peasantry who might in the future be organised in rural communes for which a rudimentary organisation already existed. The tactics of revolutionary populism were anarchist and Blanquist, that is to say terroristic and political rather than emphasising 'objective' conditions and downgrading 'merely political' solutions which had become fashionable among revolutionary circles in the West. This latter attitude had been at the heart of Marx's own discouragement of the Paris *Commune* (as distinct from the posthumous eulogy of the Communards themselves). Political and violent attempts at socialist revolution where the objective conditions were not there, was a typical Jacobin and Blanquist fantasy, doomed to fail. This contempt for opportunism, for dialectically uninformed action, was what was supposed to distinguish Marxist socialism from the (typically French) utopian socialism from which Marx had learned to be a socialist but which was now supposed to have been superseded by the 'scientific' socialism so dear to Engels and his German contemporaries. This by no means meant that Western Marxists should actively discourage Marxist groups inside Russia, but they should certainly not be encouraged to think that a proletarian revolution was on the Russian political agenda. The orthodox Western position on Russian Marxism was that Russian Marxists should join with all other progressive groups – populist, anarchist, quasi-Marxist and bourgeois liberal – to form that alliance of revolutionary forces which would eventually accomplish the bourgeois revolution in Russia which was to be the Russian equivalent of the French Revolution of 1789. Beyond that, Marxists would have to wait and see. Certainly, there seemed to be not the slightest possibility that the centre of Marxist orthodoxy would shift eastwards from Germany to Russia.

The problem with Russian populism was that it wanted to save Russia from capitalism, and the populists took what was from the Marxist point of view an absurdly over-romanticised view of rural life. Western socialists could still vividly remember what happened to the revolutions of 1848, when peasants in Habsburg uniforms had declared open season on left-wing urban intellectuals and working men. Rural life's idiocy must be a universal fact of life in predominantly peasant Russia. But, at the same time, Russia *was* industrialising, and there might be something about the conditions of Russian industrialisation which would yield to a Marxist analysis of a rather different kind from the more scientifically orthodox analyses of capitalism which were then current in the West, and this became more imperative as scattered groups of social democratic intellectuals, the most important of which was Plekhanov's Russian Socialist group (which included Vera Zasulich and Axelrod), began to emerge from populism. These groups quickly made contact with workers' revolutionary circles in some of the leading Russian and Polish industrial centres (Petrograd, Moscow, Kiev and Vilna). What hope could be offered to them? If an orthodox Western Marxist were to say to the Russian groups: wait until the objective conditions obtain, wait until there exists a fully matured and politically conscious proletariat, then that would seem to the Russians to be the equivalent of being asked to wait forever, and it might conceivably drive them back into the populist camp in the meantime. But suppose an orthodox Western Marxist were to say to the Russian Marxist groups: make a revolution soon, then in Marxism's own terms that would be nothing short of asking for a repetition of the suicide of the Paris *Commune*. The way out of this dilemma was provided by the Russian Marxist Plekhanov.

Plekhanov rejected even the qualified encouragement which Marx and Engels had given to the Russian populists in the 1870s and 1880s. He thought that the populists would never achieve anything in Russia, or if they did it would be something very unlike the bourgeois democratic revolution which all progressive forces in the West looked forward to. A populist revolution in Russia could only be the revolution of a clique who would turn out to be latter-day Robespierres, not liberators but terroristic dictators. The populist project of distributing the land among a free peasantry would only serve to increase the legendary graspingness of peasants and would greatly strengthen the principle of private property, so that the future socialist revolution would be retarded without even the saving grace of a genuinely democratic revolution in the meantime. Plekhanov knew perfectly well that the proletariat by itself could not assault the autocracy; the proletariat would have to join with all the other progressive forces in the essentially bourgeois democratic revolution against the tsar.

Only ostriches could seriously doubt that the democratic revolution was coming in Russia. Plekhanov began to wonder what the relationship between the proletariat and other revolutionary groups would be. Like Marx in the *Manifesto*, Plekhanov began to think that a well-organised and dialectically informed proletariat could wield an influence in the revolutionary alliance far in excess of its own numerical strength. The proletariat was not likely to try like the populists to save Russia from capitalism, but it might be able to save Russia from a long period of bourgeois hegemony. If it conducted itself intelligently, the proletariat would emerge from the bourgeois revolution well-prepared for the next, socialist, revolution. However, there were problems which the revolutionary proletariat would have to face squarely. Bernsteinian Revisionism was in the air, and if the period of the bourgeoisie in Russia was not to be artificially curtailed by proletarian revolutionary action, then there was always the possibility that the proletariat would lose its revolutionary edge. If the Russian bourgeoisie was to live a short unhappy life between the tsarist hammer and the proletarian anvil, then some way had to be found of keeping the proletariat moving in a revolutionary direction.

Plekhanov's answer to the problem of the possibility of Revisionism in Russia lay in his conception of revolutionary leadership. The workers' movement in Russia was to be led by a revolutionary intelligentsia which was to be the special repository of revolutionary consciousness. In Russian Marxist circles the emphasis on proletarian self-education was to be replaced by an emphasis on the education of a revolutionary elite. After all, the example of German Revisionism showed what could happen if working-class education was the main thrust of an avowedly Marxist movement. Legal trade-unionism and harmless legal political parties which had no real quarrel with the existing order was the result if the working classes were left to educate themselves, and even the Russian autocracy recognised this. Indeed, Peter Struve and his section of Russian socialists were well on the way to what was coming to be called 'legal Marxism', plainly a perversion of proletarian revolutionary energy.

This attitude of Plekhanov's was to become central to Bolshevism (though Plekhanov himself was to end up a Menshevik). It had its roots in the conspiratorial methods of Russian populism, and it was perhaps natural that Plekhanov and his group, working in exile in Switzerland far from the day-to-day workers' struggle in Russia, should emphasise the role of dedicated revolutionary intellectuals and their leadership of the movement through correctness of theory. Besides, Plekhanov was the towering figure in Russian Marxism. Since the publication of his first specifically Marxist work in 1882, Plekhanov had stood head and shoulders above all other Russian Marxists as the thinker who had single-handedly made possible in the first place the application of Marxism to Russian conditions in a way which made revolutionary sense. Even Lenin was to defer to Plekhanov for a time, and when Lenin came to Switzerland after his release from exile, Plekhanov was the senior figure in Russian Marxist *émigré* circles. The ensuing debate about how that group of *émigrés* was organised itself was to produce something which began to resemble what has come to be called Leninism.

THE PROBLEM OF THE RUSSIAN SOCIAL DEMOCRATS, 1900–07

After 1900 splits began to appear in Russian Social Democracy (as Russian Marxists called themselves after the Western example). Originally, perhaps, the disputes were not so much doctrinal, or organisational, as generational. Plekhanov was personally dictatorial; he was the orthodox Russian Marxist, and he would decide, but he did none of the active work inside Russia and when he was joined by a younger generation – the Economist faction as they came to be called – who had been active in Russia, the trouble started. The 'youngsters' expected the day-to-day decisions of the Russian Social Democrats to be made by a majority, whereas Plekhanov expected things to be arranged as they always had been by himself in consultation with Vera Zasulich and Axelrod. While the youngsters were offended by Plekhanov's dictatorial manner, he was scandalised by what he called their 'ignorance' of Marxist theory, to which they replied that while he had been reading Marx in Switzerland they had actually been active in the revolutionary movement inside Russia. The growing tension between the generations was one of the reasons Plekhanov welcomed Lenin in Zurich in 1900, and he especially welcomed Lenin's new publication *Iskra* ('The Spark') which he regarded as the means to restore unity and orthodoxy in a movement which was fast approaching a crisis which perhaps Plekhanov was actively encouraging in order to precipitate a split as a preliminary to purging the movement.

In his attempts to regain control of the movement, Plekhanov had been forced to place increasing emphasis on the need for ideologically pure and tactically correct leadership in order to buttress his own position in the Russian Social Democratic Party, but despite his organisational claims, Plekhanov was primarily a theorist: he believed in the ultimate power of argument. Lenin's own view was very different. He regarded it as his special task to rebuild the Social Democratic Party inside and outside Russia brick by brick, using *Iskra* not just as a propaganda sheet but as a rallying point for all who agreed with him. Significantly enough, *Iskra* was published in Munich where Lenin and his associates could enjoy a degree of independence from Plekhanov. With Plekhanov the question of organisation had been only a potential cause of a split in the party. With Lenin the split became a certainty, and it was in that split, and in the arguments which it engendered, that the principles of Bolshevism were hammered out.

THE PROGRAMME OF THE RUSSIAN SOCIAL DEMOCRATIC PARTY IN 1902

The debates between Lenin and the Economist faction, whose principal spokesman was Vladimir Akimov, centres round the Programme of the Russian Social Democratic Party as adopted at its Second Congress (1902), Lenin's writings in *Iskra*, and his *What Is To Be Done?* (1902). The issues were three: the premises of socialism, the theory of pauperisation, and the dictatorship of the proletariat.

The premises of socialism

The question of the premises of socialism centres round the nature of the class struggle in Russia. The Party programme spoke of the development of the material conditions for proletarian revolt but said very little about the effects of this development on the consciousness of the proletariat. Its critics, speaking through Akimov, argued that the Party programme looked at the proletariat as a social category to which things happened and not as a class capable of making its own history:

> The proletarians are regarded here [in the Party programme] merely as the *instrumentum vocale*; these instruments became sufficient in number . . . Just as giant machines are made up of individual mute tools and implements which were formerly separate units in the artisan's workshop, so do modern plants and factories muster within themselves whole collectives of human instruments, once scattered through outlying districts . . . The draft [of the programme] also states that: 'the labouring and exploited masses become increasingly dissatisfied' and that the struggle between proletarians and their exploiters 'became even sharper'. But these were precisely the characteristics of the slaves of ancient Rome – mere 'speaking instruments'. However, this was merely a technical flaw in the instruments. The exploiters took account of this flaw just as we today take into account imperfections of machines. Neither the exploiters nor the exploited thought of abolishing the institution of slavery as such.

The alleged passivity of workers under their conditions of exploitation is mirrored in the Party programme's view of the proletariat as simply revolution fodder. Akimov's demand is that

> I want our programme to state that as the contradictions inherent in bourgeois society grow, there is also an increase in the conscious revolutionary class struggle, the rebellion of the proletariat. Instead, it speaks merely of their [the proletarians'] struggle with their exploiters. Such a struggle has been characteristic of all oppressed people, under all systems of productive relations in past eras.

What is at issue here is the highly important question of how workers do in fact acquire not class- but revolutionary class-consciousness. Akimov takes issue with Lenin's view that revolutionary class-consciousness, which in Marxist terms in the only class-consciousness which matters, is something which must be forced into the workers from the outside because it does not develop automatically as a product of the class struggle itself. According to his critics, Lenin has made the elementary mistake of confusing Marxism as a revolutionary doctrine, and therefore the product of intellectuals, with what Marxism is supposed to predict, the growth of working-class revolutionary consciousness which is the result of the capitalist mode of production. Did not *The Communist Manifesto* itself say that by bringing scattered workers into the socialised production of the factories, the bourgeoisie themselves were creating the ideal conditions for the development of that revolutionary class-consciousness? Lenin denies that the class-consciousness of Russian workers is the result of the propaganda and agitation of Marxist intellectuals. Lenin thinks that this is not only true of Russia but applies generally:

> The theory of socialism grew out of the philosophic, historical, and economic theories that were developed by the educated representatives of the propertied classes, the intellectuals. The founders of modern scientific socialism, Marx and Engels, were themselves, in social position, members of the bourgeois intelligentsia. Similarly, in Russia the theoretical doctrine of Social Democracy arose *entirely independently* [italics in original] of the spontaneous labour movement; it arose as a natural and inevitable outcome of the development of the thought of the revolutionary intelligentsia.
>
> (What Is To Be Done?)

Lenin then goes on to make the famous distinction between the trade union struggle and revolutionary activity. In the trade union struggle, the workers became conscious of the antagonism between themselves and the capitalists, but it is only through the work of the intellectuals that the worker becomes aware of the irreconcilable nature of this antagonism:

> They [the Economist faction and Lenin's opponents in general] imagine that a pure and simple labour movement can and will evolve its own independent ideology . . . But this is a profound mistake ... There can be no talk of an independent ideology, developed by the labouring masses in the process of their movement. [In creating an ideology] the workers take part not as workers, but as socialist theoreticians, as Weitlings and Proudhons. Spontaneous development of the labour movement leads precisely to its subordination to bourgeois ideology . . . The spontaneous labour movement is trade-unionism . . . and trade-unionism means the ideological enslavement of the workers by the bourgeoisie.
>
> (Ibid.)

In Lenin's view of it, the Russian labour movement, and any other labour movement, could not be revolutionary until doctrinally orthodox intellectuals had got to it. To leave a labour movement to its own devices was to postpone socialist revolution indefinitely.

The theory of pauperisation

The Economists believed, and not without good reason, that if the tendency of capitalism in Russia was an absolute decline in the living standards of the labouring poor, then there was little hope in proletarian revolt from the bottom. Then the Leninist faction would be correct in saying that the only hope was for revolution from above, because slaves rarely revolt, and if they do they do not make socialist revolutions. But if the reverse is true, and the Russian workers are allowed by Russian capitalism to raise themselves above the level of mere brutes, then there is the possibility that the workers will be able to re-make their own consciousness and so the anti-Leninist position is the correct one. Plainly, the reason why Lenin attacked Akimov on this question was Bernstein. If Lenin admitted that capitalism in Russia was capable of providing a higher standard of living for workers, then he was in danger of letting in Bernsteinian Revisionism. Akimov saw the solution to the problems of Russian Marxism along German Social Democratic, but not Revisionist, lines. His model was the Austrian Social Democrat Victor Adler, who welcomed the short-term gains of the proletariat through its trade unions and its party, while never committing himself to the overtly revisionist thesis that the day of the revolution could be postponed indefinitely. Adler denied that there was any contradiction between short-term democratic victories and the revolution in the future, and this became the orthodox position of the Austrian Social Democrats.

The real reason why Lenin rejected Akimov and the Economist faction had nothing to do with the apparent question about working-class living standards and everything to do with the Russian peasantry. Lenin realised above all that if a socialist revolution was to occur in Russia on his model, then the differences between the proletariat and the peasantry would have to be minimised. On the peasant question Plekhanov himself had hedged with vague formulae about the Social Democratic Party welcoming into its ranks all the poor and oppressed. This was unacceptable to Akimov and the Economist faction, because they saw the Party as an organic part of the working class, and the working class should keep its distance from the peasantry whose consciousness was by definition not proletarian. Besides, if the Party were to unleash the barbarous and property-loving instincts of the peasants, Russia would be thrown back into the Middle Ages for an indefinite time to come. Lenin differed with Plekhanov on the peasant question, but for different reasons. He thought the Party should keep its distance from the peasantry in a way which was similar to his view that the Party should not link itself organically to the proletariat, and his reason was that one day the Party would have to settle its accounts with the peasantry. Lenin was very clear-sighted about this: the peasantry was revolutionary when it demanded land but counter-revolutionary when it wanted to keep it. Hence Bolshevism's own rather shadowy formula about 'democratic dictatorship of proletariat and peasantry', which meant that, in some ill-defined sense, rule in Russia after the socialist revolution would be in the name of both, but with the problem of the peasantry's obsession with private property in land not far off the political agenda of the future.

The dictatorship of the proletariat

It was over the question of the 'dictatorship of the proletariat' that the Economists really differed from Lenin. It finds its parallel in the disputes between Plekhanov and the *émigrés* about the internal organisation of the Party, but with Lenin it becomes the crucial question about the future revolution in Russia. The term 'dictatorship of the proletariat' was publicly used for the first time by Lenin in *Iskra*. Marx himself had toyed with the idea in correspondence, had hinted at it in the *Manifesto*, and Engels had pointed to it in, for instance, his introduction to Marx's own work on the Paris *Commune*. Plekhanov himself had claimed he was going right back to the roots of Marxism by claiming that Russia from 1880 onwards was at a similar stage of development to the Germany of 1848 to which Marx and Engels addressed the *Manifesto*. Marx and Engels seemed to be saying that there was something in the peculiar German conditions of 1848 which made a communist revolution possible, though the struggle would be long and hard – much harder, for instance, than the struggle would be in more highly industrialised France. A similar programme was on the cards for Russia: a bourgeois revolution could occur, out of which the politically organised working class would emerge to begin its own struggle for socialism. No doubt much Marxist theory had passed under the bridge since 1848, but this return to the *Manifesto* had the stamp of Marxist orthodoxy on it. But again, Plekhanov hedged about what the crucial term 'dictatorship of the proletariat' meant. When asked, he answered with the lame formula that the 'dictatorship of the proletariat' meant the 'rule of the proletariat', but the Economist faction was not to be put off. Why, they asked through Akimov, use a word like 'dictatorship' if all you mean is 'rule'? Surely, the word 'dictatorship' means something more.

Akimov could not help asking in whose name the dictatorship of the proletariat was going to be exercised. It could not be made in the name of the peasantry, because Lenin was explicit, and so was the future Bolshevik Party, that the Party was in some sense a proletarian party. But the Party was to be a party of the proletariat with a difference. It was to be a party of the proletariat not in the sense that it had *sprung from* the proletariat; rather than being a part *of* the proletariat it would become a party *for* the proletariat. Lenin himself was quite explicit that any party which sprung from the proletariat spontaneously would only be capable of developing bourgeois trade-union consciousness, so the party could not be *of* the proletariat at all. Akimov was forced to the conclusion that, being of neither the peasantry nor the proletariat, Lenin's party only represented itself. Akimov's critique of Lenin's theory of the Party was that it would lack a real sociological base. Marxism had taught socialists that a party without a real sociological base must resemble the Jacobins during the Terror in the French Revolution, and Akimov could not resist the parallel. How can a party maintain itself in power without a true class base? The answer could only be a repetition of the Terror, in which friends and enemies of the revolution would alike perish in a bloodbath. That is the true danger of revolution from above. Akimov and his friends had worked out all that by 1904.

It is still important to keep some kind of perspective on these disputes, no matter how much they appear to predict the future of revolutionary Marxism in Russia. These were doctrinal squabbles overlaid by personal spites among a group of *émigrés* who had contacts with socialist groups inside Russia but who had no idea when the decisive revolutionary moment would come when the tsarist autocracy would come crashing down. These were disputes about what would happen after a bourgeois revolution in Russia, and nobody could even predict when that would happen. It could be argued that the Russian Social Democrats (they did not call themselves Communists until the early 1920s) were caught off their guard both in 1905 and again in 1917, both occasions on which discontent about a war produced massive and spontaneous political upheavals. There is absolutely no reason to suppose that because, by 1902, Lenin had already worked out the main principles of the Bolshevik organisation of the Party he therefore thought that these principles would be put into operation in the near future. Lenin's positions were for the strategy and tactics of the Party after the democratic-bourgeois revolution and before the workers' revolution after that. This was futurology, and not very optimistic futurology, because what the Party lacked was a future revolutionary calendar. This future revolutionary calendar was made possible by what came to be known as the theory of 'permanent revolution', and through the theory of imperialism. Taken together, these amounted to a compelling case for a Bolshevik seizure of power at some time in the not too distant future.

THE THEORY OF PERMANENT REVOLUTION: TROTSKY

Trotsky's early revolutionary life had been spent in activity inside Russia, and he did not join the *émigrés* until he caught up with Lenin in London in 1902, where he was greeted with the words 'Here is the Pen!' by Lenin's wife (who also had to pay his cab fare). This was the period of Lenin's dispute with the Economist faction and the period of the prelude to the split between the Bolsheviks and the Mensheviks over Lenin's intransigence over the matter of Party organisation. Trotsky eventually broke with Lenin and went with the Mensheviks because, like the Economists, he simply did not think that the Party could or should have an existence independent of the working class. It seemed to Trotsky that Lenin's position smacked of 'substitutism' – the Party substituted itself for the working class, the Central Committee substituted itself for the Party and a potential dictator would substitute himself for the Central Committee. (If not a prediction of Lenin's leadership, it was a remarkable prediction of Stalinism.) Trotsky was later to pay dearly for his early opposition to Lenin. Stalin was to harp on it in his successful struggle with Trotsky. Trotsky was later to break with the Mensheviks too because they seemed to be making no effort to heal the breach with the Bolsheviks. When the Mensheviks, largely through the help of Plekhanov, gained control of the editorial board of *Iskra*, they acted just as high-handedly as the Bolsheviks ever had. So until his reconciliation with Lenin in the October Revolution, Trotsky seemed to be a brilliant but apparently unreliable outsider in terms of party factions, though he remained within the ranks and gained for himself a huge reputation for his part in the Revolution of 1905 for his leadership of the Petrograd Soviet for the fifty days of its existence (Lenin was not in Russia in 1905). It was the events of 1905, and the influence of the Russian Marxist A.L. Helfand – known as Parvus – that led to Trotsky's formulation of the theory of 'permanent revolution'.

THE INFLUENCE OF PARVUS ON TROTSKY

Parvus was a Russian Jew who made his home in Germany and who had won a reputation as a Marxist theorist of the worldwide significance of Marxism. Lenin had reviewed one of Parvus's books with approval in 1899. Parvus contributed to Kautsky's *Neue Zeit* and ran his own periodical *Aus der Weltpolitik* where he was predicting the outbreak of the Russo-

Japanese War as early as 1895. He contributed to *Iskra*, where Lenin relegated his own articles to the inside to give Parvus the front page. In the German Social Democratic Party, Parvus stood on the extreme left, ridiculing the revisionist party's pious affirmations of its revolutionary intentions. Parvus was also a financier with a reputation for shady dealings (he was to end up as financial adviser to Ebert, the president of the Weimar Republic, when his revolutionary days were over). So Parvus was a brilliant if slightly suspicious interloper with a European reputation, and the young Trotsky was dazzled.

In 1904, Parvus began a series of articles in *Iskra* called 'War and Revolution' which for the first time linked the fortunes of the Russian proletariat to world revolution. Parvus's main idea was that the nation-state as it had developed under capitalism had had its day. Of course, Marx had said something of the kind in the *Manifesto* half-a-century ago, but by 1900 a nation- and empire-conscious Europe had relegated the disappearance of the nation-state to the sidelines, a point of Marxist doctrine (and liberal doctrine in some of its manifestations) to be reiterated on feast-days and quietly forgotten afterwards. Parvus saw the Russo-Japanese War as the beginning of a series of wars. Developments in the world economy made states retreat from free trade into protection, and it had been free trade which English political economy had predicted would turn the world into one big happy trading family. The result of protection, on the other hand, was to sharpen national antagonisms while strengthening national states. The weaker states, like Russia, were in a quandary, because a foreign policy success in the East was one way out of her domestic troubles with the reformers and revolutionaries, but expansion in the East would eventually mean war with Japan, a state which was stronger than Russia and getting stronger by the year. Besides, in the changed conditions of the modern world, only the strongest states could act independently because the capacity to fight wars depended on industrial potential. Russia's industry could not stand up to the pressures of war, heavily dependent as it was on foreign, mainly French, capital.

The immediate cause of the Russo-Japanese War of 1905 was a territorial dispute over Manchuria and Korea, but it was really a war for the political leadership of South-East Asia. Russia's inevitable defeat would involve not only Russia and Japan, but the whole balance of military–industrial power in the world. So Parvus's conclusion was that world capitalist development leads to political upheaval. Industrialisation develops the capacity for war and the world situation makes war more likely. The development of a proletarian revolutionary movement makes war an attractive option for a government looking round for some sort of success to bolster its flagging prestige, and success and failure in war will have a profound effect on other capitalist countries. As Parvus said, the Russian revolution which will come about as a result of defeat at the hands of Japan 'will shake the bourgeois world . . . And the Russian proletariat may well play the role of the vanguard of social revolution.' Parvus was not saying that the coming revolution in Russia caused by discontent over defeat in war would cause a *socialist* revolution in Russia, but Trotsky was to draw out of what Parvus was saying the theory of the 'permanent revolution', the idea that the socialist revolution must follow hard on the heels of the bourgeois revolution in Russia. Parvus did not only influence Trotsky on world problems but on problems of Russian political development too. The Russian state, according to Parvus, was a hybrid, a cross between an

Asian despotism and a European absolutism. What had always really frightened the tsars in the nineteenth century was the encroachment of West European ideas into Russia and their political effects, so that Russia had developed a Western-style army, police and bureaucracy to combat the West's own ideas. One only had to look at the string of frontier fortresses to see that it was the intention of the autocracy to insulate Russia from the rest of Europe. The new international situation and Social Democracy represented a breakdown of tsarist policy. Social Democracy was internationalist, and the Russian state would have to recognise that it lived in a world of other states and was subject to the same political and economic imperatives.

THE INFLUENCE OF THE RUSSIAN REVOLUTION OF 1905 ON TROTSKY

Parvus's prediction that political upheaval would occur as a result of defeat in war was triumphantly vindicated in 1905. What impressed Trotsky in 1905 was the sheer effectiveness of the working-class movement in Russia. Akimov appeared to be right. The Petrograd Soviet lasted fifty days and was largely a spontaneous growth. The local Bolsheviks at first regarded it as a rival, so effective had Lenin's attacks on the Economist faction been. Also, Trotsky became increasingly convinced that the Russian bourgeoisie would not live up to Marxist expectations of their becoming the 'national class' through their own revolution. 1905 was supposed to be the long-heralded equivalent in Russia of the bourgeois French Revolution of 1789, the revolution made by an alliance of all progressive forces which would be the beginning of bourgeois hegemony in Russia. The events of 1905 convinced Trotsky that the Russian bourgeoisie was not to be trusted, that it would fail to lead its own revolution, and that, forced to choose between the tsar and their worker allies, the bourgeoisie would choose the tsar every time. As soon as a politically conscious revolutionary proletariat appeared on the revolutionary scene, the bourgeoisie would go running to the tsar for protection. This posed a problem for the orthodox Marxist position on Russia. Essentially, 1905 was a failed bourgeois revolution, and it was the bourgeoisie's own fault. What would happen next time, when the same class alliance of bourgeoisie and proletariat would again try to make a bourgeois revolution? The lesson of 1905 was that the bourgeoisie could only be relied on to sell out their working-class allies. The working class and its organisations were faced with the choice either of not taking part in the revolution, which was unthinkable, or of participating in a revolution by class alliance only to see their erstwhile allies turn against them when they had gained control of the state.

THE THEORY OF PERMANENT REVOLUTION

To understand the originality of Trotsky's position in *The Balance and the Prospects: the Moving Forces of the Revolution* (written in prison in 1906 – the more famous *The Permanent Revolution* was not written until his exile from the Soviet Union) we have to recap a little and remind ourselves what the differences were between Economists, Bolsheviks and Mensheviks. Theirs was a dispute about the correct revolutionary tactics and organisation in the forth-coming bourgeois revolution in Russia. This revolution was to be the Russian equivalent of 1789. The Economist, Bolshevik and Menshevik positions were based on the perception that some way had to be found for the workers' party, however conceived, to maximise its effectiveness in the coming bourgeois revolution. Trotsky's theory of permanent revolution challenged that whole perspective. His main thesis was that the coming revolution in Russia could not be contained within its bourgeois phase, because the Russian bourgeoisie could not fulfil its own revolutionary role.

Why not? The answer lay in the peculiarities of Russian history which Trotsky had learned from Parvus. Influences from outside Russia had made the Russian state what it was. It had been military pressure from the European powers, chiefly Poland and Sweden, which had forced the tsars to construct a state which exacted an enormous amount of service and money from its subjects. Because in Russia the state consumed an inordinately large amount of social wealth, social differentiation – and especially the growth of a strong bourgeoisie – had been retarded and Russia entered the twentieth century as a country of peasants. This profoundly affected the nature of Russian capitalism, which could almost be seen as the state's creation, and the bourgeoisie which developed as a result of industriali-sation could be seen as the state's creation too. The state encouraged the investment of foreign capital in Russia, and this had the effect of strengthening the autocracy, not of weak-ening it. As a consequence, the Russian bourgeoisie did not get the political benefits which its counterparts had received in the West: none of the bourgeois freedoms which went with the development of the parliamentary republic or constitutional monarchies which were supposed to be the typical bourgeois forms of the state. In the past, the Russian towns were not centres of production but of consumption, the product not of economic development but of military and administrative necessity. Hence capitalism in nineteenth-century Russia did not find a class of small craftsmen in the towns, which had been the case in France in 1789, but four million small craftsmen scattered in the villages. In 1789, the small craftsmen concentrated in Paris had provided the rank and file of the bourgeois revolution, but an equivalent class simply did not exist in Russia.

Even the advance of modern industry did not significantly strengthen the bourgeoisie in Russia because Russian industry was in the main fostered by foreign capital. In their own countries, the bourgeoisie were supporters of free liberal governments, but the European bourgeoisie, like their Russian counterparts, were only interested in the future of their investments, which meant foreign support for the Russian state in its struggle with the reds. But, while the development of large-scale industry did not bring the bourgeoisie to the fore, it certainly brought the Russian proletariat to the centre of the stage. The period of concentration of capital and its productive forces had happened very quickly in Russia, telescoping several stages of capitalist development into a very short time. The Russian proletariat had thus been given the opportunity almost overnight to organise itself into a concentrated mass for political action.

So in Russia the classic revolutionary pattern was effectively being reversed. In previous revolutions the bourgeoisie had either taken the lead, as in 1789, or had ducked out of revolutionary leadership, as in 1848. On both these occasions the proletariat had been too weak and insufficiently self-aware to take over a revolution which nobody else would lead. Russia in 1905 was a different case: the bourgeoisie had shown themselves too feeble to lead their own revolution and the organised working class had managed to put themselves at the head of the revolution. This pointed the way forward, because, in the next revolutionary round with the tsar, the proletariat would have to try to seize power immediately, or at least very soon. Plekhanov had always said that in Russia the period of bourgeois hegemony would be much shorter than it needed to be in Western Europe. Trotsky was now saying that in Russia the bourgeois revolution would be stillborn. And what was really revolutionary about Trotsky's view was that he thought the Russian proletariat could seize power before its Western counterparts, while Lenin and Plekhanov were arguing about what the Russian revolution would be like in its bourgeois stage against the background of an almost daily expectation of revolution in the advanced capitalist West. Trotsky's perspective was very different. He was arguing about a situation in which proletarian seizure of power could take place in Russia before it happened anywhere else.

Trotsky could not ignore the peasantry. In Russia he certainly expected the peasantry to be at least neutral, if not actually on the side of the proletarian revolution, and it probably never occurred to him that revolution could succeed in Russia without the support of a majority of the population, which meant peasant support. The peasantry could never hope to lead the revolution because it had always been the fate of Russian peasant uprisings in the past to strengthen the state apparatus, and, besides, the Revolution of 1905 had convinced Trotsky that a thousand railwaymen on strike were worth a million scattered villagers. The organised strength of the proletariat would attract the peasantry to it. But Trotsky knew as well as Lenin that a proletarian Marxist revolution was bound to attract the hostility of the peasants in the end, both because of the revolution's ultimate aim of abolishing private property and because of its internationalism: peasants are nothing if not parochial. But it would be the internationalism of the Russian proletarian revolution which would be its saving grace. Like the French revolutionaries of 1793, the Russian revolutionaries would be forced to export their revolution. As Lenin had said, the peasants were revolutionary when they demanded land and reactionary when they wanted to keep it. Only support from other dictatorships of the proletariat in the West would prevent the dictatorship of the proletariat in Russia falling into the reactionary and barbarous hands of the Russian peasantry. If the Russian proletariat did not take the initiative and spread the revolution, then the reactionary bourgeois states of the West would gang up on the Russian revolution in exactly the same way that European reaction had ganged up on the Jacobins. In Russia, the period of the dictatorship of the proletariat will only be the breathing space within which the proletariat has the opportunity to break down the 'Chinese walls' which all along the tsars had hoped would insulate Russia from the subversive West.

With the Leninist theory of the Party, and the Trotskyite theory of the permanent revolution, Bolshevism was two-thirds complete. All that was needed was a theoretical account of the opportunity for the proletarian revolution in Russia, and that was provided by Lenin's theory of imperialism and his *State and Revolution*.

LENIN ON IMPERIALISM AND ON THE STATE
AND REVOLUTION

The strands of Lenin's theory of imperialism come from many sources, and unkind critics of Lenin's *Imperialism: The Highest Stage of Capitalism* (1916) have often remarked that in it Lenin is predicting the outbreak of the First World War two years after it had started. Lenin's argument is very simple, but the circumstances in which he composed it were not. By all accounts Lenin was deeply shocked by the failure of Western social democracy, and especially German Social Democracy, to oppose the war in 1914. Up to that time, Lenin had not taken much notice of what was going on in social democracy outside Russia, and he appears to have taken the pacifist declarations of social democrats at their face value. In *Imperialism: The Highest Stage of Capitalism* Lenin again took up the question of what Russia's position as a power among other belligerent powers meant for the future of socialism. He came to the conclusion that the war was an imperialist war, fought because each industrial nation wanted to expand its markets in a finite world. The extension of 'spheres of influence' and the international tension which that caused led to the war. Drawing on a whole series of writings on the peculiar nature of Russian industrial development, Lenin came to the unsurprising conclusion that Russia would be the first country to succumb to the internal pressures which discontent with the war was bound to cause. As the least industrialised of all the belligerent powers, Russia would be defeated again as she had been defeated by Japan in 1905, and this defeat was bound to have revolutionary consequences. This was to be the decisive moment for which the Revolution of 1905 had been a mere rehearsal, and it was out of this new revolution that a resolute and well-organised proletarian movement would emerge victorious.

What was the revolution caused by the war going to look like? In particular, what was going to be the relationship between the proletarian revolution and the state? In *The State and Revolution*, written just before the Bolshevik seizure of power in October 1917, Lenin lovingly quotes the teaching of Marx and Engels on the state and the dictatorship of the proletariat. Lenin reminds his readers that it is not enough simply to believe in the class struggle to be a Marxist. Marx did not invent the notion of class and class struggle; the bourgeoisie did. What distinguishes a Marxist from a bourgeois is a belief in the particular consequences which the struggle of classes must produce. Lenin makes the belief that the class struggle results in the dictatorship of the proletariat the touchstone of Marxism: 'A Marxist is solely someone who *extends* the recognition of the class struggle to the recognition of *the dictatorship of the proletariat*' (italics in original). Lenin points out that in the classic text Engels had said that it was the old bourgeois parasite state which would be abolished, and that was the state described by Marx in *The Eighteenth Brumaire of Louis Bonaparte*. This is not to be taken to mean, as the anarchists think, that all the organs of state power will automatically be smashed. The post-revolutionary state will be like the Paris *Commune*. To begin with, the bourgeois parliamentary state will be replaced by the fuller democracy of elected workers' councils (soviets) whose members will be subject to direct recall. The function of the soviets will be to smash the bourgeoisie and its institutions and to effect an alliance with the poor peasantry who stand in the same relation to the rich peasants as the proletariat stands to the bourgeoisie. This alliance of proletariat and peasantry breaks up the old state machine. There is no need for a specialised body of armed men – a standing army – to do this because the people in arms can do it themselves. It will not even be necessary to have a special mechanism to check the excesses of individuals, or of the new 'state', because the armed people will do this automatically.

Lenin's *The State and Revolution* is not just an apologia for the Bolshevik seizure of power in October 1917, though it plainly is that too. In that work, perhaps we should see Lenin walking a very thin line between Revisionism on the one hand and anarchism on the other, between those who deny that violence is necessary to socialist revolution and those who put too much faith in violence itself. By claiming that the bourgeois state can 'wither away' before revolution, the Revisionists show themselves to be ignoring the Marxist theory of the state in late bourgeois society. The Russian Social Revolutionaries and the Mensheviks were tending to go down the revisionist road when they argued that the bourgeois democracy of February 1917 could 'wither away' through reform. A class state is a class state, and if class war is becoming acute then the class state becomes at least more vicious, and can even, as Marx had explained in *The Eighteenth Brumaire of Louis Bonaparte*, constitute itself for a time as an independent power. Lenin points out that his opponents cannot have it both ways: either the class war is becoming more acute, which makes the proletarian revolution possible and which strengthens the state in its last moments, or the state is not strengthening itself, in which case the class war is not becoming more acute and therefore the proletariat revolutions is not on the agenda. What is not tenable, Marxistically, is that both the bourgeois state is 'withering away' and the class conditions are coming into existence which make a proletarian seizure of power possible. Again, Lenin is arguing, against the anarchists, not to expect too much from revolutionary violence: the remnants of the old order, both tsarist and bourgeois, will not give up easily. It takes the proletarian 'state' to extirpate the remnants of the old order, possibly involving a protracted period of revolutionary struggle.

The Leninist Party and the proletarian state are what Stalin was eventually to inherit with all that that meant for the history of the Soviet Union. In defence of Lenin, it could be said that the modern state as a repressive apparatus made the Leninist theory of the party necessary. Perhaps Marx, and even Engels, never really understood just how efficient a modern state could become as a repressive agency. Both Marx and Engels envisioned societies with liberal states and in which proletarians represented the vast majority of the population, and what chance had the liberal state against these? What they may have forgotten is their own lesson about the efficiency of the liberal state in a bourgeois society whose increasing social division of labour would increase the efficiency of the bourgeois state as it increased the efficiency of all other bourgeois institutions. Besides, Russia in 1917 was not a bourgeois society, though its state as repressive apparatus had learned Western lessons about efficiency well enough. Part of classic Marxism had always been that the bourgeoisie would fight the class war not directly but through its state agents. The Leninist Party came out of the perception that, at least in countries where the proletariat was not fully developed, the proletariat too would have to fight its class battles through the Party as its revolutionary agent, and to be able to do that the Party had to be as efficient, well-organised and dedicated in its own way as the modern state. Looked at in this way, the Leninist Party is the last form of socially divided labour which capitalism produces.

TROTSKY VERSUS STALIN

As with all doctrinal disputes between individuals in close proximity with each other, it is always difficult to distinguish between points of dispute which are doctrinal and points of dispute which are personal. (One view of Stalin's victory over Trotsky is that it represents the victory of the pipe-smoker who bides his time over the neurotically overactive cigarette smoker.) In another sense, the dispute between Trotsky and Stalin was not a debate about theory at all, because of all the great leaders of the Bolshevik Revolution Stalin was the least intellectual. Lenin, Trotsky, Zinoviev, Kamenev and Bukharin all personified Marx's eleventh thesis on Feuerbach that the philosophers had only *interpreted* the world differently, the point is to *change* it. This is not, of course, intended to denigrate the importance of correct theory, because, in another famous dictum of Marx's, it is in philosophy that the proletariat finds its spiritual weapons just as it is in the proletariat that philosophy finds its material weapons. This is a reiteration of the old dictum of Enlightenment that the way forward lies with the correctness of thought, which must always precede correctness of action. It is only in 'vulgar Marxism' that we find a pronounded anti-intellectual thrust, and there have been few Marxists more vulgar than Stalin.

The vulgar Marxist holds that to explain the class origin of any system of ideas is to give a full account of it. To the vulgar Marxist there seems to be a rejection of genuine intellectual discourse between opponents to be dug out of the Marxist notion of 'false consciousness'. The vulgar Marxist seems to be saying that, if we disagree, it must be because the class backgrounds of our ideas are different, because Marx teaches us that ultimately all differences are traceable back to class differences. If I disagree with you, I may, indeed typically will, be unaware of the real nature of the difference in a class difference, and the vulgar Marxist would go on to say that there is really no point in our discussing a matter of disagreement any further because I, being falsely conscious, literally do not know what I am saying. Some, like Professor Popper, have argued that Marx himself is the original vulgar Marxist, but it is hard to see how that could be true. Marx did not, of course, deny that there were relationships between property, class and belief, but he also believed that these relationships, being dialectical, were complex, and could only be explored through the skilled use of Marxist dialectics. What is famously absent from classic Marxism is the idea that bourgeois ideology or bourgeois institutions simply mirror the facts of bourgeois economic reality. Indeed, in *Capital* and elsewhere, Marx seems to go out of his way to show that it is infrequently the case that the Marxist is in the position of being able to guess what a society's superstructure is like from an account of its economic base. Such was the case, for instance, of late eighteenth- and early nineteenth-century England, where a state dominated by the aristocracy was able to co-exist with a bourgeoisie which was in the process of becoming the dominant class by pursuing an imperialist foreign policy which nicely balanced the aristocratic preoccupation with war with the bourgeois preoccupation with trade. The same case could be made out for late nineteenth-century Germany, where the rapid advancement of German industrialisation was able to happen in a state dominated by an aristocratic Junker military and bureaucratic elite. This would be a contradiction in vulgar Marxist terms, because the vulgar Marxist typically says something like: Show me what a country's economy is like and I will infer from that what everything else in that country is like.

This distinction, between classic Marxism and vulgar Marxism, shows how easily Marxist dialectics can be abused. Nowhere is this more obvious than in Stalin's struggle with the Trotskyist opposition. Stalin was fond of branding the opposition as 'petty bourgeois', and that was not just a smear. The Stalinist argument went something like this: Marx teaches us that all political differences are the reflections of class differences. All good Bolsheviks agree that the Party (and in the Party the Politburo) is the repository of the proletarian line – about anything. Stalin is the leading figure in the Politburo, therefore Stalin's line is the proletarian line. Trotsky disagrees with Stalin about important matters, and as Marxists we all agree that such differences ultimately reflect class differences. Stalin represents the proletarian line, therefore by definition Trotsky must represent a different class line because there can't be two opposing proletarian lines. What class interest does Trotskyism in fact represent? Leninism tells us that after the revolution the bourgeoisie has been abolished, and aristocracy has gone too. Lenin also teaches us that the period of the dictatorship of the proletariat will be the period of the class alliance of the surviving classes, petty bourgeoisie and proletariat. Stalin's line is the proletarian line, therefore Trotskyism must be a petty bourgeois deviation from Leninism – QED.

The question arises: How did Stalin convince undoubted Marxist intellectuals like Kamenev and Zinoviev with arguments like these? The answer might be that genuine Party intellectuals were not very impressed by Stalin's arguments, but Stalin's strength might have lain precisely in the crassness of his arguments. Stalin had always been an organiser and administrator, and it may be that other members of the Politburo were prepared at first to go along with Stalin's anti-Trotsky line because it never occurred to them that Stalin could succeed Lenin simply because they expected Lenin's successor to be both a practical politician and a theorist like Lenin himself. This description fitted Trotsky, Kamenev and Zinoviev much more closely than it fitted Stalin. That socialism could not be confined to one country, as Stalin argued in the pamphlet *Foundations of Leninism* (1924) and more fully in *Problems of Leninism* (1924), was axiomatic to most of those who had worked closely with Lenin. Like all the classic Bolshevik thinkers, Lenin regarded the revolution in the West as the next step in the building of socialism, and it was an essential step, not a matter of choice. Socialism in one country ran counter to the whole Marxist tradition, or so it seemed to Trotsky and a large section of the Party in 1924. The question was not simply one of how the Revolution in Russia could be best defended, a matter of revolutionary tactics, though this did count. (There was a perfectly good argument that the new Bolshevik state should use all of its resources at home to strengthen the only proletarian regime anywhere in the world rather than use precious energy in the West and invite further retaliation from the Western powers.) Rather, what was at stake between Trotsky and Stalin was the nature of Marxism as a political doctrine in the twentieth century, and closely linked to this very general question was the very specific question of how the Russian revolutionary experience since 1917 was to be understood.

The subject divides itself into three separate but related questions: What did the Bolsheviks think they were doing in October 1917?; What did the Bolsheviks think they were doing after the end of the civil war and the death of Lenin?; and third, what was the dispute between Trotsky and Stalin really about?

What did the Bolsheviks think they were doing in 1917?

The obvious answer to this question is 'making the revolution', but that will not quite do because Marxism had taught its adherents to distinguish carefully between different kinds of revolution. The question for Russian Marxists was therefore about whether the Revolution of 1917 was a bourgeois or a socialist revolution. We have already seen that the older generation of Russian Marxists thought, like Plekhanov, that the bourgeois revolution had to come first, with the 'dictatorship of the proletariat' to come at some unspecified time in the future, and they thought this at a time when it was Marxist orthodoxy every-where that the most that could be hoped for in Russia in the near future was a bourgeois revolution which would partially dismantle the feudal–religious state of the Romanovs and install a measure of genuine parliamentary democracy. The failure of the Russian revolution of 1905 convinced those who still needed convincing that the future revolution would have to be bourgeois. Orthodoxy, before Lenin and Trotsky, meant expecting a socialist revolution in the capitalistically more advanced West. It was a combination of Lenin's theory of the Party and Trotsky's theory of permanent revolution which enabled those Marxists willing to see it to perceive that that scheme of things could be reversed, or at least radically altered. It might be possible in Russia for the period of the dictatorship of the proletariat to precede, not follow, the period of democratisation. Democracy was no longer conceived as a stage of development which had to be endured under bourgeois hegemony until conditions were ripe for a proletarian revolution. This applied, of course, only to backward countries like Russia, and there was always what Lenin called 'the Jacobin strain in Marx's own thinking' in the *Manifesto* of 1848, which had spoken of the possibility of running into one of the democratic and proletarian revolutions in 1848's special circumstances.

The real question in Russia was what was to happen after the proletarian and democratic revolutions had been telescoped into each other. The revolutionary alliance between the proletariat and a discontented peasantry in a backward country leaves an unresolved contradiction after the seizure of power. The peasantry is categorised as petty bourgeois in the Marxist language, because it is still wedded to the idea of private property in land. Therefore the work of the socialist revolution proper begins after the seizure of power when inroads into private property, both industrial and agricultural, begin to be made. The question then arises: What is to be the relationship between the proletarian–peasant revolution in Russia and world revolution?, and it was over this question that Trotsky and Stalin began to diverge. For Trotsky, a revolution in a single country, and a backward country at that, could only be meaningless except in the context of the revolutionary potential of the well-developed proletariats of the advanced Western economies. In the classic Marxist conception of it, the socialist revolution is to be a revolution of plenty. In this, Marx was in the tradition of the *philosophes* of the Enlightenment who hoped that the spread of reason as science and technology would one day free the world from want. Classic Marxism shares this hope, adding that the era of want will not end until a mature capitalist economy is taken over by the revolutionary proletariat and organised on socialist lines. That is certainly what Trotsky thought. There could be no question of a completed socialist revolution in a backward peasant country, let alone a country recently ravaged by civil war. What Trotsky envisaged, or what he realised through hindsight (*The Permanent Revolution* was not written until 1928 and it was not published until 1930), was that the revolution in backward Russia could only hope to be a holding operation until the proletariats in the advanced countries of the West came to the rescue of their revolutionary brothers in the Soviet Union. For Trotsky it was inconceivable that Moscow could remain the capital of world revolution. It would have to be in Paris, or London, perhaps even in New York. Trotsky meant this literally. At the height of the succession crisis in the Soviet Union after Lenin's death, Trotsky offered to go to Germany because he thought that the objective conditions existed there for the proletarian revolution as classically conceived. The revolution was therefore permanent in two senses for Trotsky: in the Leninist sense of running together the democratic and proletarian revolutions in Russia, and in his own sense of a continuing fight on the international front which would usher in the true socialist revolution based on the takeover of economies which could provide the plenty which the Soviet economy could not. The permanent revolution, then, is a continuation of the Revolution of 1917, both internally and internationally.

What was Stalin's position? At first he appears to have been an orthodox about the international dimension of the socialist revolution. In the pamphlet *Foundations of Leninism* Stalin had asked the question:

> Can this task [the organisation of socialist production] be fulfilled, can the final victory of socialism be achieved in one country, without the joint efforts of the proletarians in several advanced countries? No, it cannot. To overthrow the bourgeoisie the efforts of one country are sufficient; this is proved by the history of our revolution. For the final victory of socialism, for the organisation of Socialist production, the efforts of one country, particularly of a peasant country like Russia, are insufficient; for that, the efforts of the proletarians of several advanced countries are required.

As time went on, and Stalin's need in the leadership struggle to brand Trotsky as an 'adventurer' became more acute, Stalin began to change his tune, suggesting that the efforts and resources of Russia alone might be sufficient to build a socialist economy. He cleverly put his opponents on the defensive by ascribing to them an un-Bolshevik degree of pessimism about revolution in Russia which he contrasted with his own 'creative' idea of the revolutionary future. Stalin continued to pay lip-service to the revolution in the West, but shifted the balance in favour of the Soviet Union.

One is tempted to ask: Is this all that was involved in the dispute over 'socialism in one country'? Was all this necessary just to be able to call Trotsky an adventurist in foreign policy, likely to bring down again the wrath of the bourgeois West upon the Soviet Union? The doctrinal difference between Trotsky and Stalin was not all that great. They shared the same Marxist and Leninist past, and they both accepted the desirability of revolutions in the West, and they both agreed that an attempt should be made to build a socialist economy and society in Russia, no matter how difficult that would be. The full force of Stalin's attack on Trotsky can only be understood in terms of the self-searching which went on inside the Bolshevik Party at the end of the civil war.

What did the Bolsheviks think they were doing after the end of the civil war and the death of Lenin?

That Russia at the end of the civil war was on the verge of collapse needs no stressing. The war ended in 1921. There was famine and it was said that in some areas there had been a return to cannibalism. The revolutionary struggles of the civil war had not so much transformed as destroyed Russian society. The question the surviving Bolsheviks were forced to ask themselves was: Whom do we represent? The proletariat hardly existed as a revolutionary force because so many of the politically active workers had been killed in the war, and first-generation workers were being reabsorbed into the countryside. In these circumstances it was very difficult to see what the Party represented except itself. The immediate problem which the government faced was how to feed the towns. During the civil war, the towns and the armies had been fed by what was euphemistically called 'war communism', which effectively meant the forced requisitioning of supplies from the peasantry, but the rebellion of the Kronstadt garrison in 1921 showed that the country was in no mood for a continuation of war communism. The only solution seemed to be backwards to what was called the New Economic Plan which was in effect a return to private enterprise in food production.

The NEP gave many Bolsheviks pause for thought, especially the more historically minded. They knew that revolutions could have their Thermidors, a repetition of the Bonapartist 'whiff of grapeshot' across the bows of the fine revolutionary ideals of 1789. The French Revolution itself had produced two opposing groups, the Girondin moderates and the Jacobin extremists. Bolsheviks began to ask themselves: Who are the Girondins and who the Jacobins? When can we expect the purges and the guillotine?, for it was a commonplace that the French Revolution had devoured its own children. And above all, who was going to play the part of Napoleon and turn the revolution back towards reaction? This searching after historical parallels should not surprise us. It was perfectly natural for the Bolsheviks to look for parallels to explain their own position, and the French Revolution was the most obvious. The failure of the German revolution of 1923 strengthened the Bolsheviks' feeling of isolation, a feeling analogous to the position of the French revolutionaries with the whole of Europe ranged against them. The hostile West seemed to threaten the existence of the Bolshevik Party itself.

It was in these very special circumstances that Stalin and his associates sought to expel Trotsky and the Left Opposition from the Party. When Stalin arraigned the leaders of the opposition before the Supreme Tribunal of the Party (a combination of the Central Committee and the Central Control Commission) the dialogue between accusers and accused was couched in the language of the French Revolution of 1789. There is something unreal about those proceedings in 1926–7. They read like a history lesson, and the implicit question is always: Has the Revolution failed? It is only in the terms of the Bolshevik sense of history that this literary-sounding debate makes any sense. History is about to play tricks with the Bolsheviks, and it frightens them.

Looking at the only historical perspective that made sense, the Bolsheviks not only had to look out for Thermidor and Napoleon, but they also had to watch for the growth of the equivalent of the Jacobin bureaucracy, the Revolution's real legacy in France. It was a Marxist cliché that the bureaucracy in France had been recruited from ex-Jacobins. At his trial, Trotsky made much of the French revolutionary parallel. He demanded to know whether the Left Opposition were being tried as revolutionaries or counter-revolutionaries:

> During the great French Revolution many were guillotined. We, too, brought many people before the firing squad. But there were two great chapters in the French Revolution: one went like this (*The speaker points upwards*); the other like that (*he points downwards*) ... In the first chapter, when the revolution moved upwards, Jacobins, the Bolsheviks of that time, guillotined the Royalists and the Girondists. We, too, have gone through a similar great chapter when we, the Oppositionists, together with you shot the White Guards and exiled our Girondists. But then another chapter opened in France when ... the Thermidorians and the Bonapartists, who had emerged from the right wing of the Jacobin party, began to exile and shoot the left Jacobins. [The prosecution should] ... think out this analogy to the end and answer ... this question: which chapter is it in which [the prosecution] ... is preparing to have us shot? This is no laughing matter; revolution is a serious business. None of us is scared of firing squads. We are all old revolutionaries. But we must know who it is that is to be shot and what chapter it is that we are in. When we did the shooting we knew firmly what chapter we were in. I fear ... that you are about (to shoot us in) ... the Thermidorean chapter.

Trotsky went on to draw the parallel even more closely:

> The odour of the 'second chapter' now assails our nostrils ... the party regime stifles everyone who struggles against Thermidor. The worker, the man of the mass, has been stifled in the party. The rank and file is silent. [Such had also been the condition of the Jacobin Clubs in their decay.] An anonymous reign of terror was instituted there; silence was compulsory; the 100 per cent vote and abstention from all criticisms were demanded; it was obligatory to think in accordance with orders received from above; men were compelled to stop thinking that the party was a living and independent organism, not a self-sufficient machine of power ... The Jacobin Clubs, the crucibles

608

of revolution, became the nurseries of Napoleon's future bureaucracy. We should learn from the French Revolution. But is it really necessary to repeat it?

(Quoted in Deutscher, *Trotsky*, vol. II, pp. 344–5)

What Trotsky is doing here is to use the French revolutionary analogy to predict the future history of the Party in the Soviet Union. The really frightening thing was the cry of Robespierre to Danton after he had been condemned to the guillotine: 'After me it will be your turn, Danton!' Why were the Left Opposition on trial at all in 1926? As a good Marxist, Trotsky's answer was that contradictions leading to different lines about the future of the revolution are bound to exist when revolution has occurred in a country insufficiently modernised, and when the revolution in that country remains isolated. The dictatorship of the proletariat and peasantry was a contradictory revolutionary alliance which only a revolution on an international scale could hope to resolve. Stalin's policy in the early and middle 1920s of cosseting the *kulak* (the rich peasant) in order to solve the problem of feeding the towns seemed to Trotsky and the Opposition to be leading in a counter-revolutionary direction. The middle and lower peasants seemed to be just as ground down as in the last days of the tsar. There was even a movement afoot to re-introduce private property in land. Stalin did not go that far, but he did go part of the way by allowing very long leases. Collectivisation was unthinkable to the Opposition without the superior technical resources of the West. What worried them was that Stalin seemed to be using the failure of revolution in the West as an excuse for not doing anything about the agricultural question at all.

Then Stalin's proclamation of Socialism in One Country effectively reversed his previous policy. All agreed that in economic terms the Revolution's real problem was the difficulty of organising socialist production in Russia. With the policy of Socialism in One Country, this could only be done by force, by government and by Party. This stuck in the craw of the more classically minded of the Russian Marxists as an attempt to remould the economic and social bases of society according to ideas emanating from its superstructure, something they had always been taught was the theoretical equivalent of putting the cart before the horse. Large-scale industrialisation, and the 'liquidation of the *kulaks* as a class' implied the use of force on a huge scale, and a consequent development and strengthening of state and party organs to carry out the task, in effect a blueprint for a police state.

What was the dispute between Trotsky and Stalin really about?

Even the aforementioned is not enough to explain completely the break between Trotsky and Stalin. It was not just a question of economic policy, crucial though that was, but rather a problem of culture and of Marxist humanism. The classic Marxist vision of the Revolution as a leap forward into 'truly human history' seemed, according to Trotsky, to come to nothing with Stalin; if Stalin appreciated this side of Marxism he never showed any signs of it. If one looks, for instance, at Trotsky's *Literature and Revolution* (1925), one finds a vision of what the revolution could be which simply had no equivalent in Stalinism. For Trotsky, socialism in one country meant, ultimately, the acceptance of Russian barbarism. Trotsky shares with all nineteenth-century socialists and liberals a real horror of the backwardness and brutality of Russia. The isolation from the West, which socialism in one country implied, meant that Russian culture would go backwards. The emigration of the intelligentsia in the face of *Proletkult* would create a genuine vacuum in Russian culture. What would emerge was not a Marxist culture but a proletarian culture in the worst sense of the term. Cultural emigration would leave the cultural life of Russia in the hands of ill-educated party cadres. The result of cultural decadence is finally the exhortation to Soviet intellectuals to 'write like Stalin'.

This cultural decadence is embodied in Stalin's own personality. Lenin had promoted Stalin because Stalin seemed to embody the efficient brutality without which a revolution of any kind in Russia was impossible. Stalin, in Lenin's own words, could be relied on to serve up 'peppery dishes', but for Lenin the rule of Stalin and Stalinist boneheads was inconceivable without the corrective of Trotsky. During his first illness, Lenin recommended Trotsky and Stalin to the Party as the ablest and most indispensable of the Bolsheviks. However, Lenin, like all Marxist intellectuals, was steeped in history, and he knew the historical commonplace that conquerors could be overcome by the superior or inferior cultures of conquered peoples, and Lenin came to realise before his death that the cultural inadequacy of the Bolshevik personnel made them vulnerable to the brutalising traditions of the old tsarist bureaucracy. The suppressed 'Testament of Lenin', the existence of which even Trotsky denied for the sake of Party unity, advised the Party to clip Stalin's wings.

We know how the story ends. By astute political manoeuvring, which had always been his strong point, Stalin won the battle for the succession and Trotsky ended up in exile and was eventually murdered on Stalin's orders in 1940. Socialism in one country implied the liquidation of the *kulaks* as a class, which in its turn meant brutal methods, which in its turn meant rule by men in the Stalinist mould. Opposition to this brutalisation of Soviet life could too easily be written off as petty bourgeois gentility in opposition to real proletarian values. Stalin was able to argue on the same grounds that the Party was serious, that it was not a 'debating society', and so criticism of Stalin's policies became anti-Party.

Whatever else could come out of Stalinism, the new socialist man dreamt of by Marxist humanism could not. There has been a temptation, therefore, to see Stalinism as a perversion of all that was best in Russian Marxism, to regard Trotsky as the true heir of Lenin, and to blame everything one does not like about the Soviet Union on Stalin. It may be that this is a travesty of the truth, that Stalin is being used as a scapegoat for the whole tenor of Russian Marxism in the twentieth century. Lenin was dead and Trotsky in exile by 1927, and it may simply be convenient to say that all that happened in the Soviet Union from 1927 to 1939 was all Stalin's fault.

But the question then arises: How did Trotsky, a superb propagandist with the Western press at his disposal, gather so little support around himself in the West? Why was it that most Western socialists and communists, while sometimes disassociating themselves from the Stalinist terror, followed the Stalinist line that socialism in one country was historically necessary for the Soviet Union at the time and that the future of world revolution could best be served by socialism in one country? This shades into the question so often debated:

Was Stalinism really necessary? The case for Stalinism at its strongest goes something like this: grant that there was no chance of a Bolshevik-type revolution anywhere in the West, and grant that it was not possible in China; grant also that the policy of the Comintern under Stalin's control did not retard revolution in Spain and China as Trotskyists claimed, and then turn again to the question of Soviet economic policy in the late 1920s.

The first thing which has to be said about Russian economic policy is that if, as all the Bolsheviks seemed to agree, some kind of attempt had to be made towards building a socialist economy in Russia, then it could never be done voluntarily. 'Socialism' became a code word for dealing with the peasantry; collectivisation of agriculture was always going to go against the grain of peasant life. Rapid industrialisation could not take place without a reduction of the living standards of industrial workers as the price to be paid for industrial investment, and such a policy could not be popular. Economic control implied political control, and opposition to collectivisation necessitated a strengthening of the state's police powers. Tough, coercive government was always going to be the order of the day. Given the material and moral state of the Soviet Union in the period immediately after the end of the civil war in 1921, and granted the raw material for the collectivisation of agriculture, then state 'excesses' of one kind or another were bound to occur. Granted also that Lenin and Trotsky and the rest of the Bolshevik leadership thought that they had to go some way down the socialist road, then it could be argued that at least some of the aspects of what came to be called Stalinism were 'objectively' necessary in the 1920s and 1930s. The 'moderate' policy of the Bukharinists, implying as it did the encouragement of the rich peasants as the only section of agriculture producing a surplus to feed the towns, was anathema to most Bolsheviks, so some form of collectivisation was probably inevitable, and many of the former opponents of Stalin did go over to him after 1929 when the liquidation of the *kulaks* began. Therefore, it is reasonable to suppose that had collectivisation occurred under Lenin or Trotsky, it would have to have been carried out in a 'Stalinist' way.

To say that solves no problems, because we are then forced back to the most difficult question of all: What were the specifically *Stalinist* aspects of Stalinism? These might for convenience be divided into two, mistakes in policy and the terror which resulted from the suspicious and vindictive character of Stalin himself. Among the mistakes must be included the speed of collectivisation among an illiterate peasantry deeply committed to ownership of the land. When the peasants began to be herded into collectives and their cattle requisitioned, many peasants forestalled the collectivisation by killing their beasts for hides and food, and some estimate that the livestock of the Soviet Union was cut by half. The industrial programme to produce tractors, for instance, merely filled the gap left by the slaughter of cattle, all the misery of primitive capital accumulation for no real gain. But the Stalinist purges are another matter; no defence of them is possible.

These were the Party battles of half-a-century ago, so perhaps we are entitled to take the very long view of them. There is a view of the Trotsky–Stalin confrontation which regards it as another round in the endless Russian self-questioning about whether Russia is European or Asiatic, whether Russia should survive on her own moral and material resources, or whether she should open her doors to the West. One can almost see Stalin's point of view here: while Western Marxist intellectuals just talked about revolution (and after his exile that included Trotsky), Russia and her peasants were getting on with it.

NOTES ON SOURCES

Lenin's *What Is To Be Done?* and *The State and Revolution* exist in various English editions. A. Ulam, *Lenin and the Bolsheviks* (1966), and L. Schapiro, *Lenin* (1967), are still standard. Neil Harding, *Lenin's Political Thought*, 2 vols (1983), breaks genuinely new ground. Among the collected editions of Trotsky in English are *The Essential Trotsky* (1962) and *Trotsky: The Basic Writings* (1962). I. Deutscher, *Trotsky*, 3 vols (1954–9), is magnificent but has also achieved cult status, and so must be approached with caution, as must Trotsky's own life of *Stalin* (1947). B. Knei-Paz, *The Social and Political Thought of Leon Trotsky* (1978), is a thorough treatment.

Part IX

REACTIONS TO LIBERALISM 3: IRRATIONALISM AND ANTI-RATIONALISM

26

THE MORAL EXCLUSIVENESS OF NATIONALISM
Herder

JOHANN GOTTFRIED VON HERDER

Herder tried hard to be a true son of the European Enlightenment but has since acquired a reputation as one of the Enlightenment's most devastating critics because he was a critic from the inside. How far Herder did in fact stray from the true path of Enlightenment does, of course, depend on what kinds of general judgements we are prepared to make about the mainstream of Enlightenment itself. We have all been taught by Herder's countryman, Kant, to think of Enlightenment as a single intellectual movement. Perhaps Enlightenment had a kind of intellectual unity when enlightened thinkers still thought they had to defend themselves against a largely hostile world, but it would be a mistake to think of German Enlightenment as only *really* Enlightenment when it slavishly imitated the French, and as being anti-Enlightenment when thinkers like Herder struck out on their own.

As a learned bourgeois in the service of German princes pretending not to be despots and masquerading as enlightened, Herder was always struck by the close connection between French Enlightenment and the enlightened despotism of Frederick the Great. Enlightened Prussia meant the intellectual despotism of the Academy of Berlin, Frenchified to the core. Hence Herder's striking out for his native Germany had a radical political as well as cultural message. The ecclesiastical civil servant to princes made no secret of his radicalism. His princes, no doubt, thought Herder's politics, like his unorthodox Christianity, was safe enough while tucked up in learned books. There is a tendency to think of Herder as one of history's great silver minds, hemmed in as he is by Goethe and by Kant, but if it can be said of any man that he 'turned a whole culture round', then it can be said of Herder.

Born in modest circumstances in East Prussia in 1744, patronage took him to the University of Königsberg. Originally a medical student, a distaste for the sight of blood sent him in the direction of theology. He taught as a schoolmaster at Riga, became *Konsistorialrat* to the Count zur Lippe in 1771, and moved to Weimar in 1776. He visited France and Italy. Neither visit was successful. Herder's travelling companion to Italy insisted on bringing his mistress along. Herder, though a minister of religion, was no prude, but the lady was tiresome, and Herder suffered some of the unease which often comes unawares to Protestants when it hits them forcibly that ancient Rome is also the centre of Catholic Christianity. Herder liked the good things money could buy, and was often in debt; he was a smooth dresser, was happily married, and greatly enjoyed domestic life.

The *Travel Diary* was written in 1769, the *Treatise on the Origin of Language* appeared in 1770, *Another Philosophy of History* in 1774, and the great *Ideas for the Philosophy of the History of Mankind*, in four parts, from 1784 to 1791. Herder spent the last years of his intellectual life locking horns with Kant over the freedom of the will. Herder died in 1803.

One of the ways that nationalist political theorists have made nationalist political theory difficult to understand is by pretending that nationalism did not have to be invented. Nationalists have always pretended that the feeling of nationalism is natural, that it happens automatically, and that it has existed for ever. The national spirit, it is said, is as natural to a people as its landscape, its language and its religion. A man without national feeling is a fragment broken from the whole. He will feel at home nowhere, and he will be a stranger to some of the deepest emotions available to human feelings. All peoples, according to this view, have been nationalists.

All peoples have not, of course, survived. Roman history, for instance, is full of the names of peoples who make their appearances in history and geography only to be wiped off the map by Rome. The disappearance of nations has always been something of an embarrassment for nationalist thinkers intent on emphasising nationalism's permanence, and nationalist political theory has always accommodated itself to this awkward fact by saying either that the longevity of a nation is dependent upon the extent to which its ideas of itself are strongly developed or that nations, naturally struggling for life with other nations, are sometimes bound to perish. Nations deserve to die, or die naturally.

The nationalist case that the nation has always existed can be made to sound very plausible. The ancient Greeks described barbarians as living in nations to contrast them to civilised Greeks who lived in a *polis*. The Romans spent their time subduing other nations. In fact, nothing was easier for nationalist theorists than to use the examples of any community in the past which looked vaguely like a modern nation to bolster their case. At bottom, any example of longing for home, Odysseus pining for Ithaca, could be regarded as an example of nationalism. Any case of a people's longevity added strength to the nationalist claim that nationalism had always existed. Certain peoples, especially those who survived the experience of the Roman Empire, like the Jews, or those who took part in the process which led to the Empire's downfall, like the Germans, were always good candidates for being the prime example of what a nation had always really been like.

The necessary theoretical insistence that the nation, and so nationalism, has always existed has had a certain effect on how nationalist political theorists argue, and on the kind of language they tend to use. Nationalists often address their own nation. Perhaps more than most political thinkers, nationalists must have a very precise sense of their audience, and they have an irritating tendency to assume that their audience already thinks in the way that they are being persuaded to think. The belief in the permanence of the idea of the nation entailed the idea of the 'latency' of the national idea, that it was somehow always there in the hearts of the nation's members even though it might not always be actively present in their minds. The national idea did not have to be invented so much as brought to consciousness of itself. The national idea had to be brought to life by bringing it in to active consciousness. This way of looking at national consciousness is very similar to the way the new idea of class-consciousness was conceived. You didn't have to see the working masses making a revolution in the street to believe that such a thing as class-consciousness exists. Quite the reverse. The most interesting thing about class-consciousness was that it quietly made its way in between the more overt forms which the struggle between classes could take. The same was true of national self-consciousness. Like class-consciousness, it never died, but made its way steadily underground until it was ready to surface into the world of political struggle by freeing the nation from its (external and internal) enemies. Like class-consciousness, national self-consciousness would make its revolution only when the time was ripe. Any apparent absence of the national spirit was simply evidence that it was at work beneath the surface of formal politics and government.

Nationalism can be distinguished from the generalised dislike of foreigners which we call xenophobia, but nationalist thinkers (and nationalist politics) often make the distinction very difficult to draw. It is a rare nationalism indeed which does not claim some kind of superiority for its own nation, even if it is only superiority over an immediate neighbour. The idea of the national struggle for self-realisation eventually became entangled, like all other political ideas, with the biologism of the second half of the nineteenth century. Spencerian, survival-of-the-fittest, Social Darwinism fitted the national idea only too comfortably. The struggle between nations came to be seen as a nature-red-in-tooth-and-claw struggle, with war as one of its natural outcomes. Nationalism became one of the weapons in the armouries of reactionary military elites, but it is important to remember that nationalism had not always had that violent edge. However, nationalist rhetoric, and especially the rhetoric of struggle even when the struggle was not thought of in Darwinian terms, had always appealed to heroic values like self-sacrifice in a cause, and not much had to be done to turn nationalist rhetoric into a rhetoric of war. Nationalism may have had its European origins in the struggle of different vital national cultures for cultural hegemony, but in a Darwinian world the idea of a culture had unmistakable biological overtones. Nationalist biologism was deeply infected by the teleology which was common to most forms of Social Darwinism. As in Spencerism, an 'end' was smuggled in to which the nationalist struggle was supposed to be leading. One day, the spirit of the nation would be fully realised in the nation-state, with natural frontiers (the Rhine was much disputed as a border), its own language, and culture.

It was no step at all from the idea of the struggle for national self-realisation to the idea that the nation was only really itself when it was struggling, and the struggle could easily come to be seen as an end in itself. In a way, Darwinian biology encouraged this view. The Darwinian struggle for life was essentially open-ended, or any end to which it was developing had to be put very far into the future. Nobody really knew whether the struggle for life which happened in the whole of nature was leading somewhere or not. The struggle might be directed towards an end as yet only dimly perceived, and nothing could be easier in these conditions than to convert the idea of struggle as a means to an end into an end in itself. Struggle became the form which even a realised national idea could take. I say 'realised' and not *fully* realised' because it was always possible for nationalists to argue that there were things still to be accomplished, some piece of national territory to be re-conquered, some scattered folk to be brought into the fold of the nation-state, some goal of national culture to be pursued, even revenges for slights on the nation's honour. There could also be periods when the national idea embodied in a nation-state might be nodding when it ought to be wide awake. Other nationalisms might be rising to challenge a nation's position in the world.

NATIONALISM AND ENLIGHTENMENT

Nationalist political theories began to appear right in the middle of Enlightenment, and so they accepted the fact of political and social change. The struggle for national self-realisation was going to be one of the forms, and nationalists claimed the most important form, that political and social changes were going to take. Enlightenment predicted a very busy world, a world where nothing ever stood still. It was easy for nationalist theorists, with the help of nineteenth-century biology, to turn the enlightened forecast of a changing world into a forecast of perpetual national struggle. From its beginning, nationalism had an uneasy relationship with Enlightenment, though it took quite a long time for forms of nationalism to emerge which set their faces against everything Enlightenment stood for.

We cannot help being reminded how many enlightenments there were when we begin to look at the relationship between Enlightenment and nationalism. On the one hand, Enlightenment looked to universal solutions to the world's social, intellectual, moral and political problems, solutions which would in principle be valid for all times and for all places. Enlightenment's solutions to the world's problems would take longer to work in some places than in others. There had to be some adaptation to particular circumstances, but that did not alter Enlightenment's claim to be legislating for human nature as such, and not for particular manifestations of it. Enlightenment stood for the rights of man, not for the rights of Englishmen or for the rights of any particular national group. Adaptation to circumstances was the Achilles' heel of Enlightenment. All those thinkers who either took Montesquieu seriously or followed him independently stressed the fact that human nature could write very different stories in different geographical and moral landscapes. All that was required was for this acknowledgement of difference to be given a new kind of theoretical explanation and the road to nationalist political theory lay wide open.

Nationalist theorists like Herder found their theoretical explanation of cultural differences by celebrating an idea of nature which owed a great deal to enlightened ideas about nature but which differed from them in a number of significant ways. Herder, and the nationalist thinkers who followed him, picked up and took seriously the idea that nature was somehow simple, but began to conceive that simplicity in organic and mechanical terms. Even Montesquieu, the most 'organic' of the really famous enlightened thinkers, thought that the workings of the whole of nature, human nature included, could ultimately be reduced to physics and mechanics. The mechanical universe was an invitation to human intervention. Newtonian science plainly implied a technology, and it was a technology which would be used to control nature. Learn nature's own few simple laws and nature itself could be tamed. Enlightenment's ideal piece of nature was a landscaped garden. The organic view of nature implied a severe modification of enlightened optimism. Enlightenment had looked forward to a time when a sophisticated society could be built on the basis of the sciences, including political and social science, which Newtonianism made possible. An organic thinker like Herder could not stomach Enlightenment's rather glib pretensions. Perhaps nature itself, as a force outside human control despite the illusions engendered by the technology of the day, would have something to say what the future would be like.

But where was the voice of nature to be heard? Herder takes the same side as Rousseau:

nature is to be heard in the voices of simple men as yet uncorrupted by the sophistries of Enlightenment. Herder did from the centre of the German Enlightenment what Rousseau did from the centre of the French. What language did nature speak? German, of course. French was the universal language of Enlightenment, spoken in salons and courts everywhere. It was the language of elegance and good taste, of the courtier and the man of the world, of the *savant* and those who kept abreast of enlightened learning as part of good breeding. Every enlightened man tried to sound like every other enlightened man. Herder, like Rousseau, thought he saw through Enlightenment, but added the all-important judgement that Enlightenment effectively meant the universal cultural hegemony of the French. The famous universalism of the Enlightenment was what we would now call the ideology of the cultural imperialism of the French language. Herder, like Rousseau, thought that the French had to pay dearly for their cultural exports. In part this was due to the formalisation of the French language by the French Academy which effectively made it a state language, the language of officialdom and the class from which officials were recruited, and in part it was due to the process of further formalisation which the universalisation of a language entailed. Foreigners could not be expected to learn idiomatic French very easily, and they could not be expected to learn dialect French at all. As a consequence, 'correct' French moved further and further away from the language spoken by the common people of France. The French language is therefore divisive in French society, another means of social stratification in a country already notorious for its class divisions.

Germany was supposed to be different. French has been purified but German has kept its original purity. German is not the language of class, but forms a deep cultural bond between all Germans. Language is how one is identified as a German and it's how Germans recognise their kinship with each other. German is therefore a natural language in a way French is not. The German language has developed organically from time out of mind. Its natural simplicities contrast vividly with the sophistication of French. This makes it easier to tell deep inner truths in German. No wonder that French is the language of diplomacy, the language of professional liars. We can already see in Herder how cultural nationalism easily slops over into politics. Language is a potential source of national unity, and the aim of that national unity will be to rescue national cultures from the cultural hegemony of foreigners.

It would be wrong to see nationalism in its original form as being implacably hostile to Enlightenment in general. Nationalism was not so much a reaction to Enlightenment as it was a doctrinal readjustment within it. The Enlightenment which spoke to eighteenth-century nationalism was the Enlightenment which admired Montesquieu's *Spirit of the Laws*. Montesquieu was convinced that it was a fact of nature that every civilisation is characterised by its own particular spirit. Montesquieu's own reading of Machiavelli had convinced him of the important truth that systems of government could formally outlive the spirit which animated them and which the system of government was supposed to reinforce. Machiavelli observed that Italian city-states were often ruled by princes and strongmen despite retaining republican constitutions. The spirit of republicanism must have departed and republican constitutions remained more for form's sake than for anything else. Montesquieu generalised this into a whole theory of comparative political culture. If there was no proper animating spirit then a country's formal system of government was an empty shell. Montesquieu's own emphasis was not especially nationalist. He thought in the broad terms of political vice and virtue which did not apply exclusively to any particular national group. Rather, what interested Montesquieu was how a national group at one moment had virtuous, that is republican, government, and at another moment had vicious, that is despotic, government.

It was the experience of the American Revolution and the War of Independence which showed how easily Montesquieu's idea of the spirit of a constitution could be put to the use of men who were striving to build a nation.

The founders of the United States knew better than anyone else in politics that a constitution and its system of politics were bound to fail, or to turn into caricatures of themselves, if the animating spirit was absent. America was founded on a political act, the Declaration of Independence, and being American came originally to mean agreement to do politics in a certain way, republican, free and representative. The Declaration implied that those who could not share in that agreement had no business even being in the United States and certainly had no business calling themselves Americans. America invented the usual national symbols for itself during the War of Independence – flag, anthem, national ballyhoo – to bind Americans to the original agreement. By the time that the Constitution of the United States was being written in 1787 there was already enough faith in the existence of a true national spirit that the whole American people were given the chance to 'give themselves laws' in Montesquieu's sense. The ratifying conventions set up in every state to decide whether to accept or reject the new Constitution could be trusted (though in fact it was a close-run thing) to realise that the Constitution on offer fitted well with the spirit Americans had been acquiring since the quarrel with Great Britain started. It just so happened that the spirit which the Americans had acquired was the liberty-loving, virtue-inculcating, natural-rights-oriented republicanism which Enlightenment in general so much admired. America took Enlightenment for its own in a literal sense.

The fact that American nationalism was originally enlightened nationalism meant that America was fortunate in a way that European nationalisms were not. As Tocqueville said, a special providence seemed to hover over the American republic. Beginning, as America did, as an experiment in enlightened politics, American nationalism was never in doubt about what its politics should be like. America was stuck from the beginning with an enlightened system of government (and an oath of loyalty to the Constitution of the United States is still the basis of citizenship in America). Other nationalisms had to decide for themselves what kinds of government they wanted. The nationalist movement in America is the wrong way round when compared to nationalist movements in Europe. Most European nationalisms were cultural nationalisms long before they were political in the sense of being in a position to form governments of their own. (Some had to wait till the end of the First World War, and some are still waiting.) America is different. The idea of Americanness was founded on a political act and not on the prior existence of a national culture. (It could even be argued that American culture in general has been made to fit, or to fit in with, the original political values which at the beginning all real Americans were supposed to share.) When European nationalist movements demanded their *own* government they still had to decide what their own government should be like. What exactly was the form which truly German or truly Italian government ought to take? Monarchy? A democratic republic? (If so, unitary or federal?) Government by a special group which embodied the national idea more fully than other groups? Government by one man who could be trusted to realise the national idea because that national idea was already uniquely realised in him? All were possibilities.

The problem of forms of government for national communities was compounded by the fact that there were so many different forms of government on offer and the number of possibilities increased as time went on. Some nationalists derived the principle of individual self-determination from the principle of national self-determination (and others the other way round) and struck out for a version of liberal democracy. It seemed to them contradictory that a nation should throw out its foreign rulers only to curb its own freedom by settling for less than the parliamentary republic or constitutional monarchy. Others, no less convinced, argued that there was no necessary connection between nationalism and liberalism, that nation-states were founded by heroes whom it was unwise to shackle with the rigmarole of liberal constitutionalism. The world was going to be a tough place for new nations to make their way in, so it was stupid to throw away the asset of dynamic national leadership for the nit-picking of the procedural politics which liberal constitutionalism entailed. Freedom had a fine ring to it when a people was struggling to free itself from the foreign yoke. Who had not thrilled to Byron's death in the cause of the Greeks against the Turks? The cry 'freedom' seemed to unite men of goodwill everywhere, and it seemed to be cavilling to point out that different cries for freedom meant very different things. Freedom for the nation did not necessarily mean freedom in the liberal sense within the liberated nation-state.

The generous assumption that all who valued freedom were on the same side concealed a potentially illiberal thrust in nationalism for a long time. After the general failure of liberal nationalism in the revolutions of 1848, the tensions between the two meanings of freedom became clearer, and they could even be seen as alternatives. The self-sacrifice demanded by nationalism in its early struggle with foreign powers could be considered equally valuable after the nation-state had been founded. The foundation of a nation-state was only half the battle. The formality of a nation-state's foundation gave that state a minor place among the minor powers of Europe, but it could not make it into a front-runner. Nation-states might become formally equal legal persons in international law, but diplomacy and war were games played by different rules. All emergent nations wished to assert their individual personalities in the society of nations. In this sense, the nationalist movement could never be over. A 'satisfied power' was a dangerous illusion. Powers might pretend to be satisfied with their borders in Europe, but that was merely the preliminary to carrying on the struggle for *real* international recognition by other means, international trade for instance, or the imperialist 'scramble for Africa'. In the twentieth century, it is arguable, the need to constitute oneself as a nation-state in order to take part in the international game has largely determined the forms in which emergent nation-states have cast themselves. The question of desirable political forms has been subordinated to the larger question of what form the new nation-state is to take if it is to survive in international competition.

It took nationalism about a century to expose the ambivalence of its relationship with Enlightenment, and the more raucous nationalism became the more it became obvious that the heart of the Enlightenment project had failed. Enlightenment had tried to found a scientific morality and a political science which would appeal to all rational men. A system of moral values and an attendant system of political values were supposed to gain a universal loyalty. Enlightenment spoke a universal language because it spoke to the whole of suffering humanity. Enlightenment might have paid more attention to Hume when he said that humanity was too large to love. Burke's 'small platoon' of family, friends, caste or party was the natural unit of affection. There was a biting irony in Hume's remark that there was nothing in reason to prevent me preferring the death of twenty Chinamen to the pricking of my finger. Enlightenment manifestly failed in its universalising mission. No set of universal values emerged which all men could even pay lip-service to.

Hence the character of much post-Enlightenment political thought as a moral sociology, the search for communities of men who were in fact capable of sharing the same assumptions and values. The two great candidates were nation and class. Some thinkers argued that a whole nation, and others a whole class, was the natural unit of common feeling and self-expression, and the history of the post-enlightened world could easily be written as the story of the struggle of nations and of classes. A good deal of that history, the history of fascism for instance, or of international relations, could be written as the struggle *between* the ideas of nation and class. Historians are fond of making a distinction between vertical and horizontal divisions in the world of states. Vertical divisions are the divisions between nation-states and horizontal divisions are divisions which pass over state frontiers. Ideas of nation and class are the great horizontal dividers. Nationalism claims that everyone who belongs to a nation is on the same side, no matter what state a member of the nation happens to live in. By implication, at least, that makes a man a foreigner in his native state, and it might even make him an enemy of his own state. All nationalists living under foreign rule are supposed to feel this. Members of a particular nation often live in a number of different states, and states are naturally cautious about, if not actively hostile to, these national aspirations that one day soon the world will be a pattern of perfect nation-states.

Class loyalty is the other great horizontal divider. Marxism, for instance, claims that the toilers have no fatherland; how could they feel affection for a social and political order which exploits them and in which they can only ever occupy a subordinate place? The natural loyalty of proletarians is with each other, no matter what country they happen to be living in. Both nationalism and international socialism cause trouble for existing states because they appeal direct to a section of a state's people over the heads of that state's government, and that state's government is often the object of attack. Socialists in one country sometimes appeal to their brothers in another state to overthrow their government and replace it with a socialist one. The consequence of this is that the modern state has often found itself in the position of having to deal with internal as well as external enemies.

You can have nation or class, but you can't have both except by sleight of hand. Either all members of a nation are naturally brothers or all members of a class are naturally brothers. Nationalists are usually more honest about this than socialists. Nationalists do not deny the existence of class, but they do deny that class loyalties can ever take precedence over national loyalties. Socialists sometimes try to weasel out of the difference between national and class struggle with phrases like 'the class struggle is in its nationalist phase', but these are only phrases. Perhaps the most successful attempts to ally the categories of nation and class have been made by the fascist and communist social engineers of the twentieth century. Communists take over the state apparatus in a particular country in order to use state power for revolutionary ends, and that means moving against the remnants (often considerable) of aristocracy and bourgeoisie in that country. Post-revolutionary social levelling by bulldozer is an attempt to make nation class and class nation. It has not been notoriously successful.

HERDER AND FICHTE AND THE IDEA OF THE NATION

There has been a certain consistency in the way nationalist political theories have been put together, despite the fact that there is potentially a different nationalist theory for each separate nation. Each nationalism, in its different way, tends to stress that there is a spirit of nation seeking cultural and political expression. The question always is one of finding where that idea does express itself, however faintly, and finding ways to encourage that expression. Herder began this by concentrating on language, but his route to that concentration was deeply political. What originally bothered Herder was the connection between Enlightenment and enlightened despotism. This led him to the conclusion that friendship with despots had shackled the implicit radicalism of enlightened thought. Herder began to wonder whether reform from above was possible. This took considerable courage on the part of a member of the politically impotent German bourgeoisie whose only means of having an effect on how the world was ruled was to become an adviser to one of the German princes. Herder's journey to France in 1769 was the turning point in Herder's own life and in much else besides. Herder began as a German spokesman for Enlightenment and he did what all enlightened thinkers had to do and learned French. Unkind critics of Herder have said that Herder's French was not good enough to be understood in France, and that turned him against all things French like an unsuccessful lover. It is certainly true that the French journey convinced Herder that French culture, by which he really meant European culture, was dying or dead. Like Rousseau, Herder despised, or affected to despise, the great figures of the glittering intellectual salons of Paris. The *Encyclopedia*, that wonder of the age, was for Herder simply a list of pieces of knowledge devoid of vitality, and this lifelessness is made to stand for the lifelessness of culture in general. The *philosophes* were either too timid or too lazy to think their politics through to political radicalism, and so they talked themselves into thinking that Catharine the Great, whose courtiers played cards for serfs, really could and would reform Russia.

If reform is not to come from above then it must come from below. Herder, the would-be cosmopolite, the citizen of the world, learned from his French experience that his own enlightenment had made him into a *déraciné* (the word is a later coinage of Barres's), one of those uprooted people who are at home nowhere. But where can home possibly be? Like Rousseau and Jefferson, Herder became very suspicious of the complex and sophisticated life of towns, and he began that ominous love affair between German urban intellectuals and

624

the simple peasantry rooted in the soil. (The best example in English is to be found in the opening pages of D.H. Lawrence's *The Rainbow*.) German peasants are supposed to have retained an organic purity in their language, and the purity of language becomes for Herder a measure of a nation's inner strength and quality. French, for instance, is a formal language only, good for expressing politeness, elegance and wit; it cares only for effects, to astound; what it cannot do is to cope with the waywardness of genius. And there are no exceptions: Rousseau is just as bad as Voltaire. For all his sincerity and sentimentality, Rousseau is really only concerned with the effects produced by the novelty of his ideas. The truth, reasonableness and applicability of his ideas concern him hardly at all; he is a modern Sophist. The nature of the French language accounts for the fact that the French have produced so few historians, political theorists and philosophers. These need to speak the language of truth. Truths can no longer be spoken in French at all, and where there is the will to truth it is sacrificed to a brainwave or to a turn of phrase.

The Germans are no better. The cultured classes ape French and classical models in everything, and this has blinded them to the truths of their own national history. Herder begins to unravel the enlightened view of history almost before the enlightened view is itself complete. What he dislikes is Enlightenment's universal history with its universal categories 'rude' and 'polished'. The history of the Roman Empire was bound to be 'polished' in enlightened terms, so that the victories of the German tribes which overcame the Empire in the West could only be seen as the victory of barbarism over civilisation. This view ignores the service to mankind performed by the German tribes, who brought a new vigour to the West with their feeling for liberty and their 'spirit of Nordic chivalry' which superseded the effeteness of the Romans. (This cultural enervation had already communicated itself to the French.) Enlightenment's admiration for the universalising values of classicism is an attempt to breathe life into a dead past:

> Poor, regimented Europe, devourer and sacrificer of your children, if heaven had not ordained that these barbarian times should precede you and had not maintained them for so long, against various kinds of attack and vicissitude, what would you have been with all your erudition and enlightenment? – a desert.
>
> How strange that anyone in the world should find it hard to understand that light does not nourish men, that order and opulence and so-called free thought can be neither the happiness nor the destiny of everyone.
>
> *Yet Another Philosophy of History* (1774)

The vigour of the Germans has been kept alive in their language. If only the Germans would realise what their language is. It is not just a means of communication, but a treasure-house of the national soul. Human happiness is not uniform, as Enlightenment maintains, nor is it the result of a high degree of reflection and refinement, and it is certainly not the result of a universally valid form of political and social organisation. The key to human happiness and fulfilment is language, which in its structure, symbolism and vocabulary really unites those who understand it. Language becomes a matter both of individual and group self-definition. Self-definition comes through living through a language, not by 'learning' it.

No language can be truly learned in the book-learning sense, and the sense of national identity is what is always lost in translation. Language is the defining mystery of what men are:

> What a treasure language is when kinship grows into tribes and nations! Even the smallest of nations in any part of the globe, no matter how underdeveloped it may be, cherishes in and through its language the history, the poetry and songs about the great deeds of its forefathers. The language is its collective treasure, the source of its social wisdom and communal self-respect.
>
> *Origin of Language* (1770)

It follows that the natural human group is the nation. How can it be otherwise when men divide themselves into different nations by language and by folk-memory? The natural political group must therefore be the nation too, identified with a particular language and with a particular landscape. It also follows from this that customs, laws and institutions are not to be judged 'good' according to some universal enlightened standard, but according to a local and particular standard. The question is not: Would a particular institution or custom suit humanity at large? but: Would it suit *us*?

A nation's strength depends upon whether it can in fact protect and develop its own culture. Implicit in this idea is a superficially similar but in fact very different view of the history of humanity from the view current in Enlightenment. Enlightened thinkers had looked forward to a time, no doubt far distant, when the whole of humanity would be united in a single community based on reason and on voluntary submission to laws which reason told them were good. If this were not possible, then Enlightenment would settle for a series of such communities which would never have good cause to quarrel with each other because each community was based on the same universally valid principles. There was room for local variation, of course, but the similiarities would far outweigh the differences. In this view, the incident of the Tower of Babel was a curse, not a blessing. Differences of language were just another sign that humanity was divided. Perhaps one day all mankind would speak the same language; in the meantime, French would do. Reason could create communities, either by social contract, the most rational of all models of community formation, or by the process of reforming existing communities on rational principles so that those communities could engage the loyalties of increasing numbers of rational men. Herder, and the many nationalist thinkers of many different nations who followed him, denied that reason could found true human communities at all. Natural communities were founded by a national mind or spirit, *Volksgeist*, embedded in language, and these national communities wax and wane to the extent that the national spirit becomes conscious of itself. It follows that the national mind both develops naturally and can be encouraged to bring itself out of itself in the way a human personality can be encouraged to develop while remaining essentially the same. Like human personalities, national personalities develop in a world of other personalities struggling to develop themselves. The final ideal of the national struggle for self-awareness and self-expression is a world which is characterised by a wealth of national minds freely competing with each other, and finding in that competition one of the chief sources of their own progress.

The emphasis on progress gives the nationalist programme an enlightened appearance, but it is progress conceived in a very different way. Nationalism looks forward to a competitive, not a co-operative world. Implicit in nationalism is the drive towards cultural hegemony by different nationalisms. At any given time, one nation will enjoy hegemony, but will eventually have to pass the torch on to the next. The eighteenth century is the French century, the nineteenth century will be the Germany century (and the twentieth century turned out, after all, not to be a German century but an American one). Nations cannot hope to outstrip all the others for long. Nations learn from each other, and all are valuable to each other because without international rivalry there would be no competition and no prize. There is a view of humanity in this vision, but it is a view of humanity which is very different from the enlightened view, and very different from the Stoic view of humanity from which the enlightened view is partly derived. The universalist tradition is based on the conviction that reason is a universal legislator. Reason can give laws to the whole of mankind, either directly, as in the universal sway of Roman law embodying Stoic principles, or indirectly, as positive law takes notice of universal justice, ignorance of whose demands invalidates the laws of particular communities. Now nationalists were beginning to argue that all thought and feeling should be judged 'good' in relation to standards which were not universal but national. Humanity would gain in the end, because cultural competition leads to cultural progress, but different national minds can be expected in practice to progress at very different rates, and some will probably never make it at all.

Herder's nationalism was invented right in the heart of Enlightenment and can be seen as a reaction to Enlightenment's universalist principles. However, there was more to Enlightenment than universalist principles. Some of the greatest minds of Enlightenment had in fact doubted whether the Enlightenment's claim for reason as the universal legislator was as sound as enlightened propaganda made it out to be. Some of the greatest minds of Enlightenment set themselves the task of confining reason to its own proper sphere, Hume and Kant in ethics, for example, and Vico and Montesquieu in social theory. What Herder saw in them all, however, was the generalising tendency. Even Montesquieu, who spoke of a spirit behind each separate example of moral and political culture, could only come up with a classification of cultures into three different types.

Herder's critique of Enlightenment anticipated and influenced what was to become the classic critique of Enlightenment in nineteenth-century positivism, and that was that the enlightened view of science was deeply confused. For all its parade of scientific pretension, Enlightenment could not make up its mind whether it wanted its social science to be inductive or deductive, and, trying to be both, it ended up by being neither. Enlightened social science collected facts about the world with great enthusiasm, but the intention was always to see behind those facts to the simple uniformities which lay just beyond them. Newton was a disaster for enlightened social science, because enlightened social scientists all wanted the glory of being the Newtons of their subject. Find a few easily verifiable laws which explained all of the disparate phenomena of social life and that social life would at least be adequately understood. What Enlightenment hardly understood, and what it certainly did not parade on its banners, was how complex the scientific enterprise was bound to become. Some thinkers even went so far as to believe that, except for crossing a few t's and dotting a few i's, the scientific enterprise was complete. There is something of that in Kant's essay *What is Enlightenment?* And witness Hume's essay *That Politics May be Reduced to a Science*: a few elegant pages and the matter is proved beyond all reasonable doubt.

Herder celebrated the particular against the general, the concrete historical fact against the sweeping theories of necessary historical progress which were all the rage in the eighteenth century. His disdain for the universalist thrust of Roman hegemony is the key to Herder's politics, or to the lack of it. Roman *imperium* was an act of state against nation. Political power was the nation's worst enemy because nations fall victims to power's expansion. Herder can see this happening in his own contemporary world. It's being done by the English, in Ireland and Scotland, and by Europeans to red, brown and black men everywhere. Nature makes nations, not states. Most states as they are in fact constituted are an affront to nature, a mechanical meddling with nature's own course of organic development. It is here that Herder really parts company with Enlightenment. Any attempt to impose the same political institutions and practices everywhere is an affront to the variety of human experience. Enlightenment's search for the constitution of human nature as a prelude to sketching out the political arrangements which would suit that nature everywhere was anathema to Herder. He is not much of an optimist, less so perhaps than Montesquieu, who at least thought that legislation against the spirit of a people is doomed from the start. Herder is not so sanguine. Lots of countries are ruled by foreigners, by mechanically imposed rules and regulations and not by organically developing laws.

There is nothing aggressive, nothing overtly political, nothing remotely Machiavellian about Herder's nationalism. It did not stop him sharing the enlightened view that all men were brothers under the skin and that war was fratricide (he specifically attacks Kant for believing that war sometimes leads to progress). Herder's nationalism leads to no particular political programme, and certainly not to the kind of political programme which has come to be associated with nationalism in the nineteenth and twentieth centuries. He loves Germany, but his Germany is the Germany of poets and scholars. Nobody could be further removed from the raucousness of German nationalism in its less agreeable manifestations. German culture could be a light to the other nations, but there was nothing sword-in-hand about it. If Herder was anything, he was, as Sir Isaiah Berlin has pointed out, a cultural pluralist. No national culture has a prima facie case for feeling superior to another. The values which men try to live by arise in the course of the development of a nation's life, and to try to divide fact from value, as Hume is supposed to have done, or body from mind, as Descartes did, is to make something like a historical mistake. Fact and value are different aspects of a nation's life process. The nation is like this and its values are like that; each is part of the other, and to try to build a wall between them is akin to cutting a nation in half. What is obviously absurd is the enlightened enterprise of trying to work out a system of morals and politics which rational men could believe in at all times and places. This sounds to Herder like an attempt to re-run Roman cultural imperialism. When the armies of the French Revolution over-ran Germany in the name of a universally valid mission of inter-national liberation under the banner of the rights of man, the Germans found that they had taken Herder's doctrines to heart. Herder's nationalism was far from being a call to national liberation on the battlefield, but German nationalists found in it the ideal cultural basis for an appeal to the Fatherland in danger.

FICHTE AND THE FRENCH REVOLUTION

The French Revolution and its wars abroad come between Herder and Fichte's *Addresses to the German Nation*, a series of lectures given in occupied Berlin in the winter of 1807–8. The Revolution was itself nationalist in its own way, despite the allegedly universalist nature of the rights of man. All Herder's fears were confirmed at the level of political action. A particular country with ambitions to civilise the whole of mankind was using the idea of liberation to establish its own universal hegemony. There were already ominous signs of French nationalism in 1789, in the great revolutionary pamphlet of the abbé Siéyès, *What is the Third Estate?* In 1789 Siéyès was on the lookout for arguments which would bolster the political claims of the people's representatives against the nobility and clergy. Siéyès took one side of an eighteenth-century debate about the nature of the French aristocracy and turned it into a propaganda weapon on behalf of the French bourgeoisie.

French historians in the eighteenth century had been interested in the origins and traditional rights of the aristocracy in France. One side argued that the French aristocracy, being of Frankish, that is Germanic, origins had originally elected their king in the manner of all the German tribes as the first warrior among equal warriors. Therefore it followed that the power of French nobles was prior to, and independent of, the power of the king. Others, defending the royal power, preferred to see the French aristocracy as the king's creation, the implication being that what the king had once made he could also break. This essentially harmless piece of political antiquarianism was harmless enough while it was confined to argument within the aristocratic elite of the country, but it was dynamite in the way Siéyès handled it. Suppose it was really true that the aristocracy were originally Franks, and therefore foreigners, who conquered the native Gauls when Rome fell and had ruled the conquered Gauls ever since? Might could not make right. French aristocracy was founded on an unjust right of conquest, and, properly speaking, had no business to be in France at all. Add to that the obvious fact that aristocracy was a consumer, not a producer, a national embellishment and a hugely expensive one, then the argument was set up that in France the aristocracy were a class of foreign parasites that France could well do without. The people, and their representatives, the bourgeoisie, were the true French people. The only hope for aristocracy was integration with the nation, and this they could only do by a voluntary renunciation of their legally incorporated privileges, and this they duly did on the famous revolutionary Night of August the Fourth, 1789. Now all Frenchmen, nobles included, really were equal members of the nation.

We can already see two central characteristics of later nationalism emerging in the first year of the French Revolution. 'Nation' was already a term of exclusion: not everybody who lived in France was a member of the nation in the true sense. Nobles' claim to be French rested on the ownership of land, but territoriality was no longer enough. The idea of the nation came to imply that the nation was a *people*, no doubt identified with a particular territory, but no longer identified purely in the terms of national frontiers. The integration of the nobility into the nation showed the nation to be its members and the common bonds between them, and special privileges came to be seen as an obstacle to the further strengthening of those bonds. Admission to the nation could only be bought at a price. This change was symbolised by a change in the French king's title; he was no longer Louis by the Grace of God King of France and Navarre, but Louis, by the Grace of God and the Constitutional Law of the Realm King of the French, *roi des Français*.

What, in Siéyès's eyes justified those changes in political institutions and processes which made up the French Revolution in its early stages? Why, the national will. The answer was, of course, the national will expressed through the will of representatives of the Third Estate expressed through the Assembly of the nation. The national will simply had to have the 'natural qualities of a will' for it to act. The whole nation could be conceived, Rousseau-like, as a new moral person having rights and duties like any natural person. Like Rousseau's General Will, the national will knew no moral or legal restraints. That something *was* the national will was a good enough reason why it ought to be.

The need the Third Estate felt for a self-justifying argument in 1789 was the immediate occasion on which Siéyès cobbled together his argument about the nation, but the argument outran the source of its immediate inspiration. Like the American Revolution, the French Revolution began with the intention of doing politics in a new way. The emergence of Lafayette, erstwhile comrade-in-arms of General Washington, as an early revolutionary hero served to point up the American precedent for 1789. Like the Americans, the French revolutionaries proclaimed their creed in very general terms. What they did in 1789, they did in the cause of suffering humanity everywhere. The Declaration of the Rights of Man and Citizen of 1789 was meant to apply to Frenchmen first, but there was no reason for the rights of man to stop at the French borders. Burke was among the first to spot that the enlightened logic which lay behind the idea of the rights of man meant that, if the French had the will, they would be obliged to export the Revolution. The Revolution's need to defend itself against a coalition of its reactionary enemies meant war anyway. What better way to fight that war than as a war of liberation? The war of liberation would not stop until the last king had been hanged in the entrails of the last priest.

The cause of national liberation and international liberation met in Jacobin patriotism. The Jacobins took the Rousseauist idea of the moral personality of the republic very seriously, perhaps even literally. The Jacobin republic wrote a catalogue of its citizens' duties which was much more austere than any absolute king's catalogue ever was. One of the state's rights was conscription. Those who enjoyed the privilege of living in the One and Indivisible Republic had a duty to defend it. The old idea that the king might, in some vague and unworkable way, call on all his subjects to help defend the realm in an emergency was converted back into the soldier-citizenship of the ancient republics (and of Machiavelli's ideal republic). Fighting for the nation's life, and for the ideals and institutions which gave the nation its political will, had to be worth it. Many might die abroad for European liberation. What better reason could there be for a death on a foreign field than remaking the whole of Europe, and perhaps the whole world, in the French Revolution's own image? Enlightened political theory had long toyed with the idea that the perfect form of government, or the best available, was republican government; America provided an example of a newly formed republic replete with martial and republican virtues; now the French were going to republicanise the rest of the world.

Jacobin nationalism, for which the term 'patriotism' ought perhaps to be preserved, was a very odd-looking nationalism when seen from the later vantage-point of other nationalisms, because it was exclusive and universalist at the same time. Jacobin nationalism was exclusive because by no means all men could be true members of the republic. 'Enemies of the people', the code-name for kings, aristocrats, fat priests and anyone else who was less than enthusiastic for Rousseauist and Robespierreist purity and virtue, were automatically exempt, both in France and in any potential republic abroad. On the other hand, Jacobin nationalism was a proselytising nationalism because it asked foreign peoples to embrace the same political principles which the Jacobins had already converted to political practice in the French republic. The Jacobin, and later Napoleonic, attempt to impose the same political institutions and practices in every conquered country, no matter what the customs and even religions of those countries were, appeared to the Revolution's enemies to prove that the Revolution's origins must be blamed on the Enlightenment itself. It could not matter to the Revolution's enemies that most enlightened thinkers had in fact been very cautious about politics, and none more so than Rousseau. Universalism meant Enlightenment, and universalism meant Jacobinism (and eventually Napoleonic Empire, the Continental System, and 'rolling up the map of Europe'). The French had tried this before under Louis XIV, and the Habsburgs had tried it in their day too, but attempts in the past to establish Universal Monarchy had at least been 'official'. There had been no attempts to get a people to rise against its lawful government, no attempt to create a 'horizontal' split between the peoples of Europe and their legitimate, *ancien régime* governments. The Jacobins were intent on creating just such a split by appealing to oppressed people everywhere because their governments were not founded on the correct principles. This had its effects on governments themselves, who were being invited to identify their internal as well as ther external enemies. After 1815 the Holy Alliance of Austria, Russia and Prussia, with Britain more or less benevolently neutral, would come together to agree that an enemy of one was the enemy of all, and the distinction between domestic and foreign politics was lost for ever.

The problem with wars of liberation is that they are not always distinguishable with the naked eye from wars of conquest. An invasion is an invasion, however pure the motives. French invasions, however motivated, were bound to evoke nationalist reactions in an age when the idea of nationalism was clearly enough understood to begin to affect political practice. Hatred of foreigners when they appeared as conquerors was easily given a nationalist gloss, and this happened wherever the French armies went from the early revolution to the final defeat of Napoleon in 1815. Italian, Spanish, Russian, and above all German nationalism, all began to take on something like their modern forms as a result of French liberation, thus ushering in that particularly modern phenomenon, later to become so familiar to imperialists, of the foreigners being expelled in the name of those same principles which the foreigners thought they had originally come to put into practice. Napoleon, for instance, appears to have been genuinely shocked when he realised how much he was hated outside the circle of the European aristocratic elite because, like all conquerors with a mission, he expected the conquered to be grateful.

The lessons to be learned from the French example of national mass-mobilisation were not lost on other European states. Nationalism appeared to be the best way of getting everybody in the nation on the same side. It worked better than religion, and it was a lot cheaper. The experience of the expansionism of the French Revolution, and the reaction to it, provided nationalism with the political dynamic which had been lacking in early nationalist thinking like Herder's. The Revolution put some nationalist flesh on the bones of the doctrine of liberty as self-determination.

The idea of self-determination had impeccably enlightened credentials. In a very general sense, the whole of Enlightenment had been about self-determination. Any style of moral and political theorising which regards rights as being more fundamental than duties must contain at least an element of the idea of self-determination, and any style of theory which emphasises liberty under law must offer encouragement to men to choose the ends of their own lives provided only that those ends are not positively illegal. The formal doctrine of the self-determination of the will is to be found embryonically in Rousseau and fully developed in Kant. Both Rousseau and Kant believed in what has come to be called 'positive' liberty, the doctrine that a man can only be said to be truly acting well if he wills what the moral law itself wills. The will is free when it makes a conscious choice to follow the moral law. It is clear that neither Rousseau nor Kant thought that obedience to the moral law was enough to make a man good. Fear of punishment can be the reason for obedience, but that is unfree obedience because it stems from moral coercion. Free obedience, if that is not a contradiction in terms, is only possible if my will and the law's will coincide, when I make the law's ends my own ends. Rousseau and Kant do not think that this is easy. Like T.H. Green later, they are well aware that men's motives for obedience are always mixed, but both Rousseau and Kant see the process by which men come to obey the law for the right motive as liberating. Obedience is self-determining because I go through a process in my own mind by which I come to obey the law for motives which are good. Rousseau was more sanguine than Kant that it was possible for the life of a properly constituted political community to be ordered according to the good will, so that Rousseau's General Will eventually becomes a collective moral will. Kant's solution to the problem of self-determination is strictly individual. Each good man determines in his own mind the course his own moral life will take. We are fortunate if we live in a state like Frederick the Great's Prussia where the army guarantees a certain degree of social and political order, because that leaves us free to pursue the moral life in stable conditions.

Kant was the means by which the doctrine of moral self-determination spread in Germany, and the doctrine escaped the strongly individual bonds within which Kant had confined it. Rousseau had recently shown in his *Social Contract* that there was no reason in principle why the doctrine of self-determination should not apply to collectivities as well as to individuals. Rousseau himself saw very clearly that the basis of the Greek *polis* was the identification of the ends of the state with individual ends, and he thought that there was every reason to try to recreate those conditions in order to overcome that feeling of alienation of the individual from the collectivity which was going to get worse as the individualism of Enlightenment made its way in the world. Herder had made the idea of organic community all the rage and Napoleon's defeat of the Prussians at Jena in 1806 made Germany a French dependency. Something was needed to rouse the Germans again against the national enemy. What better than to couple Herder's view of the nation with a Kantian doctrine of self-determination now applied to Herder's community, and to preach a crusade against the foreigner in the name of national self-determination?

That was how Fichte's *Addresses to the German Nation* began. Fichte's was fighting talk. Gone was the idea of the German nation as a nation of poets and scholars. In its place Fichte put the nation struggling to be free, with no vagueness about what freedom meant. The time for hunting for fragments of medieval German verse was over. The nation had to declare its intentions to be free in the most obvious way it could, and that meant on the battlefield. Private dreams were to become public realities as the individual will found its fulfilment in the nation's collective work. Everyone could help, because anything which tended to raise the national spirit would somehow be useful in the struggle.

Officially, Fichte's *Addresseses* were about education, but he turned his treatment of education into a treatment of what he thought had recently gone wrong with German life and had led to the national disaster. The great defect of German education was that it was geared to provide only material rewards for those who were successful in the education system. Education in Germany had failed to 'mould men'. What was required was a truly 'national' system of education which would make culture something 'inner' and vital, not something merely external and dead. Parents' ambitions for their children's worldly success were just as much to blame for this lamentable state of affairs as the schools. For national education to work, children had to be separated from the corrupting influence of their parents. The system would have to be directed by the state in the first generation so that the resistance of parents could be overcome, but state coercion would gradually wither away as the beneficial results of the new system made themselves felt. Fichte uses the very modern-sounding argument that investment in education is investment in the future, when the state will see the benefit.

On the face of it, Fichte might seem to be just another pedagogical theorist, but he did make one startling claim: only Germans were capable of receiving the new education because only Germans possessed the 'fundamental character' without which all true education was pointless, and the reasons he gives for this are reasons straight out of Herder: only the German kept his language pure after the fall of Rome in the West. The tribes which conquered France, Italy and Spain adopted other languages, and these superficial, neo-Latin languages cannot be a mother-tongue. The difference between the Germans and all others is that through their mother-tongue they are still alive; all the rest are culturally dead. Speaking a mother-tongue as he does, the German can easily enter into the superficial language of others, but others cannot enter into the German's language, and so will never be able to understand him. Only German culture remains true to its primitive roots; all other cultures have severed their connections with their origins and so can live only artificial lives.

> The genius of foreigners will be like the amiable hummingbird [or] the industrious and skilful bee which gathers in the honey . . . but the German spirit will be the eagle

who, on powerful wings, will lift his heavy body, and through a long and exciting flight, climbs ever higher and higher towards the sun, the sight of which enchants him.

(Addresses to the German Nation)

In Germany all Germans matter. Fichte is a populist in his own way. Germany is different from other nations because only in Germany is it possible for most of the people to take an active part in culture. The other conquering Germanic tribes took over a foreign, Latinising culture fit only for the aristocracy, just as the Romans Romanised the upper classes of the peoples they conquered. In Germany, the language cements the classes together, while in other countries the people are simply the tools which serve the pride and arrogance of the aristocracy. Finally, only the Germans are still capable of truly religious life. Germans preserved through Luther the inner, sacred religious life. Reformation saved Europe from a religion of outward observance only.

Unlike Luther, Fichte addressed himself to the whole German people, regardless of class. All Germans could unite in the love of the Fatherland. In fact, only Germans could truly be said to have a Fatherland, for the German alone, through his culture, is still in touch with the primitive origins of his race. German national vitality means that only the Germans can dominate the state and not be dominated by it. For Fichte, the state is no mechanical contrivance to guarantee the merely formal and external freedom which liberals make so much of. On the contrary, just as Lutherism provided the way to inner freedom against the external observance of Catholicism, the German state, through the education system, will guarantee inner freedom by encouraging the organic freedom of the national consciousness. My use of the phrase 'the organic freedom of the national consciousness' as if it meant something clear shows how easy it is to fall into the habit of talking about German nationalism in German nationalism's own language. Presumably a thinker like Fichte would say that a foreigner has no business using language like this (and particularly not in translation) because its full meaning must necessarily be inaccessible to him. Only Germans can be on Fichte's wavelength, and the reception of what he has to say must necessarily sound fuzzy to foreigners. That cannot matter to Fichte, because part of being German is already possessing the right internal receiving equipment for his broadcasts. If *you* can't receive the message clearly, then all that shows is that the message is not meant for you. All those incapable of receiving the message in the fullness of its clarity are foreigners by definition. If Fichte is right, the most important political messages in the future will not be addressed to the whole of mankind. Nationalists will assume that mankind is already divided into nations by nature, and the dissemination of nationalist doctrines will resemble calls to the faithful to prayer.

Something obviously happens to nationalism in Fichte's hands which cuts it off definitively from the spirit of Kant and Herder, and from the general spirit of Enlightenment. Nationalism becomes deliberately and self-consciously parochial. Herder was a genuine cultural pluralist who still stood by an idea of humanity as a whole. The human spirit realised itself in different national forms and he gloried in the fact, but he was still capable of seeing the different manifestations of human self-development as different aspects of the same thing. For Herder, the whole of human experience from the beginning had a kind of organic coherence. He never denied, for instance, that human cultures could learn from each other. Herder also had a Montesquieu-like feeling for the interplay of cause and effect in the development of separate cultures. Like Montesquieu, Herder saw the spirit of a culture partly as an effect of that culture and partly as a cause. A culture develops and sustains itself, and part of the process of sustaining itself can be self-conscious. Wise rulers will always legislate with a view to the preservation of the national spirit and will legislate against it at their peril. Fichte takes the idea of the national spirit a stage further and cuts it off from all Enlightenment. For him, the national spirit is a mysterious inbred quality, present in the breast of every member of a nation. It is a mysterious first cause, informing everything that a nation does. It is constant, has existed from a mysterious time immemorial, and can never change. It decides how a German speaks, thinks, writes a poem, makes love, wears his clothes; it decides what kind of a father he is, his attitude to his work (and what kinds of work he finds honourable and dishonourable), his duties as a citizen or a subject and his attitude to his God. This spirit indwelt at such a depth of feeling that it could only communicate with others like itself. That, and a self-obsessive introspection, was its mode of operation. Everything profound, everything worth knowing and feeling, arose from this mysterious inner essence, and it was this inner essence which took the form of a culture in the outside world.

Anything less enlightened would be hard to imagine. Profundity was cried up over clarity, feeling over reason, the primitive over the sophisticated, the rooted over the cosmopolitan. At bottom, Fichte's nationalism was self-assertion clothed in a Kantian language of self-realisation. Fichte himself had begun as a philosopher of individual self-assertion, of the famous Fichtean Ego, but in the *Addresses* he put all his previous arguments at the service of national self-assertion. And of course, Fichte exaggerates. One has to remember the circumstances of the composition of the *Addresses* and the audience to which it was addressed. A conquered country was not the place to pull ideological punches, and Fichte's audience was that over-educated German bourgeoisie, generally without political ambitions except as the servants of princes, who would expect their nationalism to be hot stuff if they were to come to any idea of collective national destiny. The German rulers were unlikely to be very sympathetic to the implicit political radicalism in Fichte, and the German peasantry were unlikely to understand it no matter how much they were praised as the nation's organic basis. That only left a bourgeoisie famously without a political identity to take Fichte seriously, and they were not likely to be in a position to do anything serious of their own about it. It would not be until 1848 that bourgeois nationalism in Germany would feel confident enough to assert itself, and it failed. Getting rid of the French from Germany after 1806 was always going to be a job for the reactionary German states, either Austria or Prussia, neither of which could stand the radicalism of nationalism because that would mean the dismembering of the multi-national Austrian empire and the absorption of Prussia into a Greater Germany. The failure of bourgeois, greater German nationalism in the revolution of 1848 forced German nationalism into a very hard choice. Either it backed reactionary Prussia as the probable unifier of the German state, which meant leaving out the Austrian Germans and strengthening the Prussian monarchy and the conservative Prussian Junker class which produced Bismarck, or it faced a future without a united Germany at all. Prussia won, hence the later attempt to argue that the Prussians had been the *real* Germans all along (and hence the perception of many foreigners that all Germans would be Prussians if they could).

Like Herder's nationalism, Fichte's was ominously silent about political forms. Fichte's call to the whole nation to throw the foreigners out had certain populist implications. If the whole nation was to be involved in the crusade of national liberation then it no doubt followed that they should in some undefined sense be involved in national politics when Germany was finally free. However, the circumstances of German liberation put the reactionary states Prussia and Austria firmly back in control of the destiny of Germany. The question for the future was still the German question as it had always been: Who was going to dominate Germany: Austria or Prussia? Neither was even a constitutional monarchy, and the principle of dynastic absolutism was not seriously challenged until 1848. Circumstances in Germany always seemed to push the question of political forms into the background. More urgent national tasks always seemed to occupy the present than deciding what the best political form was for the united German nation. National tasks took precedence over the job of constitution-making for the future. If Prussia was eventually to accommodate herself to German nationalism it was going to be on Prussia's terms and not on the terms of those impeccable constitutional liberals who tried to unite Germany at Frankfurt in 1848. Prussian terms were going to be military and dynastic terms, neither of which fitted well with the more liberal aspirations of those who called for German unification.

The question of political forms, as we have had occasion to remark before, is the really confusing question about nationalism. If you were a progressive in general, then you would expect newly formed nation-states to adopt progressive political institutions. Nationalism could easily appear to be the natural vehicle for those politically progressive aims. Foreign rule, or the rule of petty princes, was usually reactionary where it was not downright brutal. Therefore, the national revolution and the liberal revolution could be the same cause, but, intellectually, there was no necessary connection between the two. Nationalism could go hand in hand with Enlightenment, or they could go their separate ways. The history of German nationalism is one such story.

NOTES ON SOURCES

Herder may be read in English in F.M. Barnard, ed., *J.G. Herder on Social and Political Culture* (1969), and T.R. Clark, *Herder* (1955), must be one of the best intellectual biographies in the language, and deserves to be better known. H. Schultze, *The Course of German Nationalism* (1991), is a good account. Of the more general treatments of nationalism, H. Kohn, *The Idea of Nationalism* (various eds), is a classic (though it is easy to get the impression from the work that nationalism is the only important thing ever to happen in Europe). The same author's *The Age of Nationalism* (1976) is also highly recommended. C.J.H. Hayes, *The Historical Evolution of Modern Nationalism* (1968), is old but good. E. Gellner, *Nations and Nationalism* (1983), is excellent.

27

THE ELITIST CRITIQUE OF
DEMOCRACY
Pareto and Michels

VILFREDO PARETO

Pareto was born in exile from his native Italy, did most of his important work in Switzerland, and ended his life in intellectual exile far away from the optimistic, rationalist liberalism of the first half of his intellectual life. Pareto's father was exiled as a dangerous radical from Genoa by the ruling house of Savoy. Vilfredo was born in Paris in 1848, but the family were not allowed to return to Italy until 1858.

After a solid education in which he showed considerable aptitude for mathematics, Pareto studied engineering at the Polytechnic Institute in Turin. He was a practising engineer for over twenty years (1870–92), as well as being the director of two railway companies. These were the Giolitti years in Italian politics, when to be a positivist, that is to say a progressive liberal in the Spencerian tradition, meant wanting Italy to have a decent railway and telegraph network as the beginning of the process of real Italian unification and as a way of integrating south Italy into the more progressive life of the north. (Much might one day be made of the connections between modern political thought and the steam engine in Spencer, Sumner and Pareto.)

It might be said that Pareto became a social scientist by chance. He read widely, met some of the leading economists of his day, and particularly impressed Walras as somebody whose mind was sufficiently mathematical to see the way modern economic analysis was going to go. Thus it was that, at the age of forty-five, Pareto succeeded Walras in his chair of economics at the University of Lausanne in 1893. Five years later, Pareto became comfortably off as the result of an inheritance. He became something of a recluse in Switzerland, and it was in his years of semi-solitude that he produced the works for which he became famous. His massive general treatise on sociology was published in Italian in 1916 and in French from 1917–19. It is to the shame of the English-speaking world that the English translation, *The Mind and Society - A Treatise on General Sociology*, did not appear until 1963.

A change seems to have come over Pareto around the turn of the century. The earlier and ancestral liberalism dropped away, and a much less sanguine Pareto emerged to doubt whether the rationality so much emphasised by liberalism had much to do with how societies actually worked. 'Non-logical' ideas and influences were the true determinants of human behaviour; reason in the form of rationalisation came later, as an *ex post facto* justification for actions which people would have performed anyway. In basing his sociology on this fundamental insight, Pareto, despite his Swiss solitude, joined the irrationalist current of *fin-de-siècle* psychological, political and social theorising. What made Pareto different from, say, somebody like Sorel was that Pareto's irrationalism was based on massively respectable research in the social sciences. By comparison, Sorel is a rowdy shouting from the sidelines.

The temper of Pareto's irrationalism, like Sorel's emphasis on the energising power of myth and Le Bon's crowd psychology, fitted well enough with the fascism of Mussolini, who made Pareto a senator before he died in 1923.

The democratic republic happened to liberalism almost by accident. Liberalism as a specifically political doctrine came out of Enlightenment's disappointed love affair with the enlightened despots. If reform was not going to come from above then it could only come from below. Liberal political theory took two different directions at the end of the eighteenth century, some thinkers taking the natural rights road and others the utilitarian road, but all liberals could agree that the state existed to further the progress of mankind no matter whether it chose to protect natural rights or to increase the greatest happiness of the greatest number of its citizens under the banner of the utilitarian principle. It should be noted that neither the natural rights philosophy nor the utilitarian *necessarily* implied democracy. Democracy was only one of the options available to those who wanted the state to protect natural rights. In principle, any kind of civilised state, monarchy ruling according to law, or aristocracy, could protect the rights to life, liberty and property, and any civilised form of government could increase the greatest happiness of the greatest number if it tried. The point was that, democracy apart, there was no guarantee that government would be progressive. Participation in government by the many who wanted their natural rights protected or their happiness increased seemed to be the only way of making sure that those who governed had a care for the legitimate interests of the governed.

The principle of political representation was therefore accepted by all liberals in the nineteenth century. Liberals might argue about who should be represented and on what basis, and the history of European (and American) liberalism in the nineteenth century could easily be written as the story of the more or less reluctant conversion of all liberals to the principle of the democratic republic based on universal (male) suffrage. The reluctance is easy to understand. European liberals were used to aristocratic control of state power and they were accustomed to seeing that power used as an instrument of class domination. This was true even where representative institutions were alive and functioning, as in England. English radicals spoke of the 'class legislation' of their unreformed Parliament. Liberals did not like to think of themselves as a class. Rather, they preferred to see aristocracy on the one hand and the working class on the other as the true classes. Liberalism was, after all, the universal creed of rational men. Only aristocracy and proletariat would use state power selfishly, as class power. Liberals did not want to unclasp aristocratic hands from the levers of power only to see the proletariat grab those same levers through universal suffrage and manipulate them for its own selfish ends. Political reform had therefore to proceed slowly with liberal guidance every inch of the way. Liberals' faith in ultimate progress did much to reconcile them to the great political fact that it was impossible to stop the extension of the franchise once the process had begun.

It can be seen in hindsight that there was nothing inevitable about the victory of the idea of the democratic republic based on a wide exercise of political rights. When President Lincoln said at Gettysburg in 1863 that the Union dead had not died in vain because through their sacrifice free government would continue to exist, he was pointing to the sad truth that representative democracy was on the run. Free government in the American sense only existed in the United States north of the Mason–Dixon line, and nowhere else in the world. England had yet to extend the franchise to working men; France was ruled by a military dictatorship under Napoleon III; in continental Europe the powers had already reneged on the constitutional promises of 1848; Russia still had serfdom in all but name. After the American Civil War, and partly as a result of the Northern victory, the democratic idea took hold of the politics with a renewed vigour. The pessimism of the mid-century gave way as universal suffrage was put on the political agenda of every European country.

Friends and enemies of democracy could only guess at what the practice of democratic politics was going to be like. Democracy's enemies did not find what they thought they already knew about democratic politics to be very encouraging. Ancient Athenian democracy had killed Socrates; the people as the mob had frequently disrupted English politics in the eighteenth century and had had a hand in the loss of the American colonies; the people (so it was thought) had stormed the Bastille and cheered on the guillotine's grisly work; the mob had no doubt been at the back of 1848 and at the front of the Paris *Commune* of 1871; American politics, democratic in a sense since the beginning, was rabble-rousing and notoriously corrupt as well. People who thought like this could be forgiven for thinking that the unruliness of the people was government's problem. Making the people partners in government was nothing short of inviting criminals onto the bench. There was no shortage of anti-democratic ammunition, but very little of it derived from a critique of democratic practice. Tocqueville apart, the question still remained open: What would European democracy be *like*?

The only consensus was that the politics of the liberal democratic state was going to be different. The history of political thought is littered with failed predictions, and this is as true of liberalism as it is of any other body of social and political doctrine. Liberals expected their political ideas to gain general acceptance among rational men everywhere. This was not expected to happen without a struggle. The entrenched forces of ignorance and super-stition would not give up easily, and that is why liberals, despite their anti-state rhetoric, always kept state power up their sleeves as a means of dealing with the recalcitrance of the lords of the earth. Predictions about the liberal future came in two different versions, depending on whether the future was read with the liberalism associated with the name of Herbert Spencer. It has been noticed before that liberalism changed in the nineteenth century from a theory of the increasing simplicity of industrial society to a theory of its increasing complexity. Either societies simplified themselves as aristocracy and entrenched aristocratic privilege declined or they complicated themselves as a result of increasing social division of labour, but, oddly enough, both sociological positions were used as the basis of a political theory which, in broad outline at least, changed remarkably little. Whichever way a particular liberal chose to think about the future, the liberal belief that the world was becoming easier to understand never wavered. The connection which Burke made between radicalism and the possibility of a true social theory still operated. As public education increased literacy, and as rising living standards (*pace* Malthus) increased leisure for reflec-tion about the social condition, more and more men would come to see the social truths upon which liberalism was based. To think otherwise was to put oneself on the side of those who opposed the latest scientific thinking of the day – in other words, to be obscurantist or wilfully obtuse.

Liberal politics was supposed to be public affairs in a way affairs had not been public since the days of the ancient city-state. The great liberal weapon was public embarrassment. Certain things could be tolerated in the politics of the salon (and the boudoir), of the club and the country house which would be intolerable in the clear light of day. In England, liberals were fond of referring to the legislation of the unreformed Parliament as 'class legislation', thus signalling that they knew that what went on in Parliament was determined by the intrigues of a clique. Liberal politics would be very different. Leaders there would be, but they would be leaders of opinion arising out of society and not leaders emerging from a clique to foist measures for their own advantage on their grumbling fellow-countrymen. Aristocratic politics was what was later to become known as 'special interest politics', with the difference that aristocratic self-interest was the only special interest which got a look-in. Liberal politics was above all supposed to be a politics of publicly stated principle. Loyalty to principle, not loyalty to caste, was what distinguished liberal leaders from less enlightened political leaders who could be seen as the spokesmen of factions. Conservative parties and socialist political movements could be tarred with the same brush. Each represented a sectional interest and claimed it was the interest of the whole. Only liberalism was entitled to speak in the name of all rational men; therefore there must be something irrational as well about conservatism and socialism. This was not difficult to identify. All aristocrats were really warriors at heart, preferring to use violence to solve national and international problems. Socialist movements were irrational because they failed to see that modern societies were heading in the direction of Spencerian differentiation and not in the direction of Marxist polarisation, and there was always a dangerous Jacobin strain in Marxism which looked to revolutionary violence as a way of bringing in the socialist future. Conservatism, despite its perennial 'one-nation' rhetoric, and socialism, despite its dream of proletarian self-universalisation, were both essentially socially divisive. Liberals saw themselves as holding the vital centre of societies and politics, speaking to both right and left, and hoping to convert both or enough of both to make the centre of political life one of its permanent features.

And we should not underestimate liberalism's success in its universalising mission. Eighteenth-century Enlightenment made considerable headway among the aristocracy in Europe and especially in France, where conservatives never forgave the aristocratic patrons of Enlightenment for allowing the Revolution to happen and failing to protect their king and queen. In the nineteenth century liberals expected working men to use their new right to vote in the cause of those liberal parties who had campaigned for the extension of the right to vote in the first place. Many working men everywhere did in fact become adherents of liberalism. I stress this because there has been a tendency to emphasise the failure of liberalism in the face of its ideological enemies at the end of the nineteenth and the beginning of the twentieth centuries. Liberalism was a much tougher doctrine than the idea of its inevitable collapse in the face of nationalism and socialism would seem to suggest. Liberalism took much longer to die than is sometimes suggested. Again, it is important not to fall into the fallacy of seriality. Liberalism does not go away the moment doctrines appear which are critical of it. Indeed, it is perfectly possible to see liberalism and socialism as doctrines which developed simultaneously, though liberalism undoubtedly had a head start. It could also be said that liberalism set the tone for all other modern political doctrines.

Burke was only the first to realise that an effective doctrinal antidote to the enlightened doctrines which caused the French Revolution would have to be as complete in its way as the revolutionary doctrines were in theirs. Socialist doctrines, for instance, attempted to match liberal doctrine point for point. If liberalism had a view of the past, then socialism had one too; liberalism's and socialism's views of the future share the same general structure – each points to future harmonies and each points to a particular group as the bringers-in of that harmony. Early socialism is a critique of early liberalism, late socialism is a critique of early socialism, and late socialism incorporates late liberalism into itself.

This tendency of all important social doctrines, including even anarchism, towards the same typical structure meant that all social and political doctrines were wide open to an attack which aimed at the way that doctrines in general were constructed and at the assumptions common to them all. In the age of Positivism, all doctrines with serious knowledge claims had to assimilate themselves to the prevailing paradigm of scientific knowledge, and this they all duly did. Marxism claimed to be scientific socialism, and so did Revisionism. Liberalism prided itself on its origins in seventeenth-century scientific rationalism and on its championship of science in the face of clerical obscurantism. J.S. Mill attempted to conduct social enquiry in a way which was the same as the procedures of the natural sciences, and Spencer tried to do sociology in the same way as biology. Even conservatism made the leap into modernity by assimilating some of the ideas of Social Darwinism. Every important political ideology based its claims to attention on the grounds that what it said about the world was true. The difference between them was that they were asking people to believe very different things about the world. Perhaps liberalism was the most vulnerable doctrine because liberals believed that it was possible for *everybody* to believe that what it had to say about the world was true. Liberalism never deserted the enlightened project of trying to discover a morality and a politics which was acceptable to all rational men everywhere. (Socialism and conservatism were less sanguine; both would settle for a majority of believers.) Nineteenth-century moral sociology had made some inroads into enlightened universality, nationalists arguing that only national groups could share moral and political values, and socialists arguing that only classes could. Only liberalism stood out for the universal values of Enlightenment.

The political sociology of Pareto was only one line of attack on liberalism's claims for itself around 1900. Nietzsche had been saying that all political and social doctrines – Christianity, liberalism, socialism, Hegelianism, Marxism – were merely the outward and respectable surfaces of an inner Will to Power, with a truth content of zero. Sorel in the Marxist tradition had begun to urge socialists to regard Marxist theory as 'social poetry' which was energising but mythic. In Vienna Freud had already begun to see the reasons people gave for their behaviour, individual and collective, as rationalisations for erotic and murderous drives originating in the unconscious mind. Pareto's political sociology was devastating for those liberals who chose to believe it because his theory of 'residues' and 'derivations', and his elite theory, came out of the liberal tradition itself. Pareto began his political and intellectual life as an impeccable Italian liberal. Italy's future, he thought, lay with modernity, which meant parliamentary democracy with constitutional monarchy, sound finance, free trade, posts, telegraphs and railways, and the integration of 'African' south Italy into the more advanced life of Italy north of Rome. Spencer was a central influence on Italian social and political theory (and on criminology like Lombroso's) in the post-Risorgimento, and being a liberal and a positivist in Italy meant wanting Italy to be like England. Like Spencer, the young Pareto believed that the world in general was evolving in a liberal direction, and that it was only a matter of time before Italian liberalism worked its way through Italian institutions and practices, economic, social and political, and that Italy would catch up with its more advanced and socially integrated neighbours and become a modern society with a modern state. And beyond that, Italy would become what Italians had always (more or less secretly) wanted her to be, a Great Power.

Pareto's own participation in Italian politics, and his observation of European political life from Lausanne in Switzerland, convinced him that there was something very badly wrong with the way that nineteenth-century social theory and political theory dealt with the connection between political ideas and political practice. The scientific age was awash with social and political theories making scientific truth-claims for themselves, but these theories hardly stood up to a moment's rigorously scientific scrutiny. Besides, social and political theories with vast scientific pretensions contradicted each other on fundamentals, so they couldn't *all* be true. At the very least, all of them minus one must be false, and it was highly likely that they were all false. Pareto became convinced of the problematical nature of most of what passed for political, social and economic theory by the speed with which political actors could act contrary to theory when circumstances made repudiation of theory advantageous. He was particularly struck by the ease with which bourgeois-liberal parties persuaded themselves around 1900 that protective tariffs were justified to boost the competitiveness of domestic products on the home market. There had always been more to liberalism than free trade, but free trade had become a kind of litmus test for liberalism. You could think all kinds of other things and still claim to be a liberal, but you couldn't be a protectionist and a liberal. Protectionism, and policies associated with it like 'imperial preference', were based on mercantilist, not liberal, assumptions. In France, Sorel was similarly struck by the feebleness of the bourgeoisie in accepting collective bargaining as a way of settling wage disputes. The Iron Law of Wages, which employers of labour had been swearing for a century on their mothers' graves was true, was junked overnight. Also, socialists were becoming Revisionists as if they had never even heard of the scientific inevitability of Marxist revolution in capitalist countries. Pareto became more and more convinced that what political parties and movements called 'scientific theory' was really optional. As soon as theory became an embarrassment it could be dropped, and the more quietly dropped the better.

One might have expected a disillusioned liberal like Pareto to be driven to something like despair by the perception that most of what passed for political and social science was so much ideological junk. European liberalism had been committed since the Enlightenment to the idea that good arguments would drive out bad. It is no exaggeration to say that liberalism was dependent for its intellectual validity on its capacity to produce a social science which really could explain the world. Comte's dictum that the modern age was the positive age, that is to say the age of science, meant that modern men would only accept bodies of moral, social and political doctrine grounded in proof. The era of

Christian metaphysics was over, not because metaphysics was false but because metaphysics was not *falsifiable*. There simply was no way of showing scientifically whether the propositions of metaphysics were true *or* false. Modernity meant grounding belief-systems on assumptions about the world which were demonstrably true (or as demonstrably true as they could possibly be in the present state of knowledge). If no such body of assumptions lies ready to hand, then it follows that all political doctrines are equally true or equally false, and that nobody can tell the difference.

What made this particularly irritating for Pareto the erstwhile liberal is that he began to realise that political theories were junk at the same time that he realised that in the modern world political ideas had begun to count for more. It wouldn't have mattered so much if junky ideas didn't count for much in social and political life, but the reverse was true. Late nineteenth-century political sociology (and much else besides) was coming to the ghastly conclusion (ghastly for liberals, and for all those who believed in the scientific truth of their own doctrines) that the truth content of belief-systems had nothing to do with their effectiveness, and some were even beginning to argue that the effectiveness of ideas was in inverse proportion to their truth content. This amounted to no less than saying that in the battle between science and ignorance, ignorance won.

How did what Pareto had to say differ from Marxism, and in particular from the Marxist theory of ideology? There is a certain superficial similarity between Marx and Pareto, because both were intent on unmasking political parties and movements. Bodies of social and political doctrine were for both the outward and respectable faces of inward and self-seeking drives. Marx's attack on bourgeois political economy is that it is the (intellectually incoherent) ideology of the bourgeois drive for economic and political hegemony. Ideologies are merely the outward surface of group interests. Pareto would not disagree with that, though he would argue that the Marxist theory of ideology could be applied to Marxism itself. Marxism is also an example of an incoherent set of ideas which an interest group, the working class, uses to further its own drive for hegemony. But in his *Treatise on General Society* Pareto goes beyond even this. What really interests him is where political argument really comes from and why it is effective. Pareto regards all that passes for political and social theory as essentially secondary or derivative, so he calls these theories 'derivations'. They can be more or less sophisticated, and their modern varieties are very sophisticated indeed. Derivations in Pareto's language derive from what he calls 'residues'. Residues are to derivations what a root word is to its derivatives. The derivation always contains the residue, though to see this frequently demands something like the special skill which enables a philologist to see the root word in the derivation no matter how distorted the derivation is. These residues are very simple and generalised attitudes and beliefs (Pareto often calls them 'sentiments') very widely spread in a society and they only change very slowly over time. Residues do not add up to an ideology in a Marxist sense because in general they are not class-specific. Some residues, about attitudes to authority for instance, can function as ideologies in something like a Marxist sense, but residues are more general than that (Pareto sometimes calls them 'instincts', something which we all respond to automatically). Derivations, sets of political arguments intended to be persuasive, exploit residues, and in principle residues are politically neutral in the sense that they are available for exploitation from any political perspective. Marxists, liberals, conservatives, and later fascists, exploit the residues for their different ends. Their doctrines are simply different derivations from the same residues, and this would explain why modern political ideologies share the same vocabulary and assume the same typical shape. This should come as no surprise, because all derivations are the result of playing the same game of residue exploitation.

It follows that, because everybody is playing the same residue exploitation game, there is really no way of choosing between the players from a rational point of view. Residues are irrational. They are not thought out, they just are, and they are very hard to change and they certainly cannot be changed by rational argument in one generation. If residues are irrational, then derivations cannot help being irrational too. The ordinary political arena of liberal democratic politics is therefore a 'darkling plain where ignorant armies clash by night'. Most political behaviour, when that behaviour is ideology-based, is irrational, and one of the proofs of this is that ideology can simply be thrown overboard when it is no longer useful.

Pareto is very far from saying that all behaviour in society is irrational. Science itself is a social enterprise and it proceeds rationally (Pareto's word is 'logically') because it proceeds step by step, grounding its progress in proof every inch of the way. Science is logical because it apportions means to ends properly. Science knows what questions it wants answered, knows how to find these answers, and knows why what it calls answers really are answers. Much of economic life is like that. Individuals and groups will pursue economic ends which can be clearly stated and they intend to act rationally by pursuing those ends in as cost-effective a way as possible. Afterwards, if they have been successful, it will be obvious both to them and to an observer that their actions have been rational. Political groups sometimes pretend to be logical in the same sense by proposing goals like 'equality', or 'liberty' or 'revolution' or whatever, but these goals are so general that they are unattainable, or so vague that you couldn't possibly ever know whether you had attained them or not. Of course, some political behaviour can be rational, but it would only be rational to the extent that it could conform to the rationality model in economics. Limited policy objectives can be achieved cost-effectively, but this modest politics is not the kind that Pareto is really interested in. It is the great ideological systems which fight the political battle in the name of rationality which are Pareto's special target, and his aim includes all political and social thinking in the past which appears to lend its support to the rationalist fantasies of the thought of the present age. If we take Pareto's claims seriously, then Plato and most of Aristotle, Aquinas and Rousseau ('miserable drivel'), Natural Law and social contract, a lot of Social Darwinism, most of Marxism, all political thought which retains a trace of religion, Progress, humanitarianism and pacifist internationalism, liberty, equality and fraternity, has got to be thrown on the scrap-heap of the history of ideas. All are derivations from residues.

Political and social doctrines may look new in their own time, but that is easily accounted for. Some residues are 'innovative' (this is not Pareto's own terminology) while others are 'conservative'. What Pareto calls Class 1 residues, which can be given the general name of the Instinct of Combinations, can lead to derivations which rearrange the associations between facts and ideas. Nothing is easier than to associate all 'good' with 'progess' and all 'bad' with 'reaction', just as in times past all 'good' was associated with the 'spirit of the ancestors' and all 'bad' with innovation. And derivations themselves are infinitely variable. Just as there is no predicting the derivations of a root word, so there is no predicting what human ingenuity will come up with by way of derivations from residues. Indeed, one of the residues which Pareto lists under the general heading Instinct of Combinations is the 'Urge to seek logical explanations', by which Pareto means that men have been covering traditional behaviour with rationalising glosses ever since the world began. The only difference now is that rationalisations have to take a pseudo-scientific form because the modern world has embraced the idea of science as the only valid criterion for truth. If Pareto is right, however, there is no real difference between saying 'I believe I should do this because science shows me that it is the right thing to do' and saying 'I believe I should do this because God wants me to.' The modern world has simply chosen a different God, science, whom it is always rational to listen to and obey.

Pareto calls the deep-seated and largely unchanging urges, values and sentiments of mankind 'residues' because he believes that the residues are what we have left when we take reason and rationality out of the social frame. The only rational activities which Pareto will allow are science, strategy and the pursuit of economic self-interest, so that most of what we would call social life is left after reason has been removed. Only the forms of thought associated with science, strategy and economics are logical (in Pareto's sense of not being derived from residues), so when reason is removed from the frame most human thought is still left. This is Pareto's central and most startling claim, and its implications for liberalism are profound. Liberals look to a world which is supposed to become increasingly rational. To be liberal is to be modern in the specific enlightened sense that modernity means being free from the outmoded thought patterns of the past. Ever since the eighteenth century liberals had looked forward to the day when human behaviour and human institutions would be refounded or reformed on a rational basis. If Pareto was anything to go by, then this had always been a mirage. Residues are extremely persistent, persistent enough for Pareto sometimes to call them 'instincts'. Commentators have sometimes chided Pareto for not distinguishing instincts, eternal and immutable, from values and sentiments which, though slow to change, are not 'given' in the way instincts are given. Pareto does not distinguish between the two clearly enough, but the failure could easily be polemical. It may be that Pareto wants to point to the fact that residues are so persistent that there really isn't much point in distinguishing them from instincts. Besides, residues last so long that trying to find their origins is probably pointless. The way to a residue is through behaviour and derivation, and that is how you find out about instincts anyway. So what is the point of distinguishing between instincts and residues?

Liberals had tended to assume that the growth of rationality would be one of the things which bonded a society closer together. The belief in progress meant the elimination of those beliefs, and of the practice and institutions based upon those beliefs and reinforcing them, which had neither a tendency to divide society nor to retard its progress in some other way. Hence the liberal equation between the rational and the socially useful, and between the socially useful and the increase of human happiness. Pareto drove a coach and four through that cosy liberal scheme of things. He took great delight in showing that there was absolutely no connection between the rationality of beliefs and actions, and social utility. Residues and the behaviour which arose from residues were what kept societies in working order, and, far from having rational origins, the origins of residues were usually so obscure that residues themselves might as well be classed as instincts. It is not difficult to understand why political and social thinkers have been committing the rationalist fallacy ever since the ancient Greeks. Political theorists are logicians by trade, and they wish in their heart of hearts that all social action was the result of the exercise of reason. Some social behaviour always is the result of the exercise of reason, and political theorists have an in-built tendency to exaggerate this by claiming that most social behaviour is either rational or the result of irrationality in the sense of miscalculation. Rational behaviour is then to be seen as 'good' behaviour, and 'bad' behaviour is seen as irrational behaviour, sin becomes error, and error in its turn comes to be seen as being caused by institutions and beliefs which are irrational. It is irrational to think that crime pays, but criminals have been so let down by their societies that they have ended up too stupid to see that crime does not pay. There must, therefore, be something wrong, that is irrational, about the organisation of societies which can leave some of their members in the lurch like this, therefore more reason in society is needed to eradicate crime. What the easy syllogisms of the rationalists ignore are the deep-seated residual beliefs in a society which do in fact keep down crime. All that liberal rationalism can do is to pour scorn on these beliefs for their irrationality, and thereby possibly encourage crime.

It is very easy, but wrong, to get the impression that Pareto thinks that all social action is irrational, and that nothing much ever changes. Pareto plainly thinks that more social action is irrational than liberals are prepared to admit, and he equally plainly thinks that the mind of mankind changes much more slowly than rationalists are prepared to concede. Nonetheless, there is a large area of human life – the pursuit of interests – which is rational, and Pareto is not fool enough to deny the obvious fact that the world does change. Men do pursue ends which they call good, partly out of instincts like the instinct for food, clothing and shelter, and the sexual instinct. The pursuit of wealth comes into this category as the pursuit of what we generally call 'interest', and this can be done individually or collectively. Rationality in conduct is reserved by Pareto for means and not ends. Beyond what we would call the satisfaction of 'basic needs' there is no general criterion for calling one end of human conduct 'more rational' than another, and there is no reason why human individuals or groups should not pursue ends which are mutually contradictory. Pareto invites us to look at the real world and ask ourselves whether we can see in it an end, or a set of ends, which all rational men could agree to pursue, or actually do agree to pursue. The whole project of Enlightenment stands or falls on the question of whether it is possible to demonstrate that such a set of ends exists. Pareto obviously thinks that a set of universally valid ends is impossible to find, the pursuit of interests generally excepted, and Pareto equally obviously thinks that statements of the kind 'all men pursue their own interests' are either far too general to have any meaning, or are seriously misleading. What amazes Pareto is that men sincerely pursue individual and collective ends which are not 'self-interested' in any very precise sense of the term. The pursuit of economic self-interest, and that form of self-interest which translates itself into power-seeking, he will allow as rational but the extraordinary thing about human societies is the amount of end-directed behaviour which is not self-interested in either of these two senses. Men seem perfectly happy to pursue chimeras, and to expend precious human resources in the pursuit. They chase 'progress', or 'humanity's happiness', or liberty, equality and fraternity, or socialism, ends so vague that you could never even tell if you had ever achieved them.

This for Pareto is the ultimate irrationality of human conduct. Irrational ends are often pursued at the expense of rational ends, and this is true no matter what the particular moral or political opinions of the individual or group pursuing them. It applies just as much to socialists as it does to liberals, and it will apply just as much to communists as it will to fascists. Pareto's is a very intellectually ambitious claim because he thinks that he has seen through almost everybody. If what Pareto says is true, then most of liberalism is intellectual junk, and so is a lot of Marxism. Pareto never denies that there is much truth in the view of the world we have come to call historical materialism. Any fool can look at a modern society and see the development of capitalism. Like Marx, Pareto can see a logic in capitalist development, and, like Marx, Pareto thinks that any view of the world which does not give an important place to capitalism is wilfully obtuse. Again like Marx, Pareto is interested in the difference between what capitalists *say* they are doing and what it is that they are actually doing. Marx teaches us to be ever on the look-out for 'ideologies', belief-systems which are designed, consciously or not, to explain and justify self-interested conduct by claiming that the conduct in question is conducive to the happiness of the whole human race. What Marxists call 'bourgeois ideology' easily translates into a derivation in Pareto's language, but what Marxists call ideology is only one among hundreds of possible and actual Paretian derivations. Marxists sometimes talk as if all belief-systems were in their sense ideological; only Marxism itself can escape the damning ideological label. Pareto's theory of residues and derivations is designed to show that this is too narrow a view of systems of belief. Belief-systems may sometimes be derivations from interests, but it is Pareto's intention to show that most belief-systems are not interest-derived, that is, that most belief systems are not even rational enough to be ideologies in the Marxist sense. Interest-orientated human behaviour does at least make sense, so that there is some sense in ideology, but most of what Marxists call ideology are sets of non-logical arguments for the pursuit of non-logical ends.

Again, Pareto does not deny that it might be rational for the proletariat to pursue socialist ends, though he does in fact think that it is hopeless to try to think of socialism as a single end. In so far as the working class, or working-class parties, pursue ends specific enough to be formulated in the clear terms of economics, they act rationally, and the arguments they use to attain those ends, in so far as they are arguments about means, are rational. (And it may even be sensible to use non-logical arguments if these can play on the residues in a society in such a way as to provide active or even passive support.) Socialists get silly when they expend valuable energy on the pursuit of the woollier ends on the outer fringes of socialist doctrine. Doctrinaire socialism does in fact use its energy like that, which all goes to show what fools, and self-deluding fools, doctrinaire socialists are.

Pareto has an elegant and consistent theory of change. Change is such a commonplace of modern life and thought that Pareto realises that what has to be explained is not the fact of change but the rate. Included in the question of the rate of change is the interesting possibility that different parts of a single society will change at different rates and in different directions. Pareto takes liberal sociology at its word. Modern societies are heterogeneous societies, societies made up of many different parts. The ideal modern society, according to the liberal view, was a society in which the different parts worked together in an efficient and coherent way. All the parts were supposed to pull in the same direction. Political and social change no doubt happened in one part of the social organism first, but the other parts were expected to follow down the progressive path. Social integration required that the parts all kept up with each other. Otherwise, how could they work efficiently with each other? This perception formed the intellectual basis of the liberal reforming programme. Liberalism would not be fully realised until liberalism's progressive ideas had worked their reforming way through all the political, social and economic institutions of a society. Liberals in fact had a pretty shrewd idea that important changes would first occur in the economy. Economic modernisation, capitalism, would be followed by social and political modernisation. In practice, all three might proceed at the same time once the economy had started the ball rolling. Even liberalism's Marxist enemies thought along similar lines. Marxists expected the development of capitalism to affect everything which happened in a society, and in the whole world. Nothing could stop this process happening, though Marxists predicted a very different end for it from the end predicted by its liberal apologists.

Pareto denied that social equilibrium depended on all the parts of a society being able eventually to catch up with each other in the rush to modernise. Liberals knew as a matter of fact that progress within a society could be uneven, but they thought that social equilibrium depended upon being able to iron out the unevennesses, and liberals certainly thought that a society would come under considerable strain if there was great unevenness between the parts as regards modernity. Pareto invited his readers to look at societies in the modern world to see if this was actually the case. Pareto's own Italy was a case from which it was possible to argue in a direction which was contrary to liberalism. Progress in the liberal sense was spectacularly uneven in Italy, both in geographical and institutional terms. Economic, social and political modernity was concentrated in Italy in the few northern industrial towns. Italy south of Rome was 'Africa' to northerners, ruled by priests, landlords and bandits. The Italian political system was designed on the latest liberal lines, a constitutional monarchy with parliamentary democracy, and Italian administration modelled itself on the very latest Western European designs, but none of this could disguise the fact that by, say, English standards Italy was not an integrated society at all. Of course, Italian liberals like Giolitti recognised this, but they still made the mistake of supposing that parliamentary democracy, rational administration, industrialisation, railways and telegraphs would have the required integrating effect. To Giolitti's critics, this seemed to be putting carts before horses. Modern parliamentary political institutions and processes only worked in societies already enjoying a high degree of integration: witness the United States and Britain, and contrast Italy and France, and the South American republics with their impeccable copies of the Constitution of the United States. And, above all, Italy had the papacy right at her heart, an institution so reactionary that its social teaching would still take some time even to be reconciled to some of the less radical tenets of liberalism.

If the example of Italy was anything to go by, societies could keep themselves in being while different parts of them were at very different stages of social evolution. This opened up the intriguing possibility that some parts of a modern society could survive at stages of arrested development and some parts might even be going backwards. This posed two connected theoretical questions for political sociology: What was it which actually kept societies like Italy together in the modern world? and: Who was really running them? If Italy's brand-new, imported political and governmental institutions were not working properly, then something else must be running Italy and keeping it together. Pareto's celebrated theory of elites comes out of the answer to these questions.

ELITE THEORY

Pareto's elite theory comes out of the perception that it is hard to tell who is calling the shots if all we look at is the formal ruling arrangements of a state. Machiavelli lurks behind everything that Pareto has to say about politics. No-one understood better than Machiavelli that constitutional forms can be empty formulae which serve actually to conceal the realities of power. Constitutions frequently serve to legitimise power which is exercised in a way which is directly contrary to the spirit of the constitution. The Italian states of Machiavelli's own day were tyrannies masquerading as republics, and the tyrants, or the monsters among them, were actively working within republican constitutions to destroy republican liberty for ever. Pareto shares Machiavelli's concern with Italy as a special problem, even though Pareto's political thought is expressed in impressively general terms. A society which does not enjoy a high degree of integration is bound to be a society in which all kinds of different groups and individuals exercise social power. If we define 'power' as the capacity of one group or individual to affect radically the life chances of another group or individual, then we would naturally expect there to be more than one power centre in a society which was not well-integrated. In liberal terms, a heterogeneous society – that is, a society of many parts – can be expected to produce a set of power-exercisers for each of its constituent parts. This is what Pareto finds in all societies which are in some sense modern, and the chief difference between evolved and less-evolved societies is that in modern societies the elite is functionally much more varied. In ancient societies the priests and the warriors probably called the shots. It could hardly be other-wise in societies which were not highly differentiated and where warriors and priests would be the only really distinct groups. By contrast, in highly differentiated modern societies membership of the ruling elite would be spread wider among different social types. Pareto believes that every important social group produces an elite of its own, and the elite in general is the sum of those spontaneously emerging elites in society at large. The elite obviously includes parliamentarians and bureaucrats but extends far beyond them. Pareto therefore distinguishes between the elite in general and the *governing* elite, a distinction which it is not always easy to make. The governing elite is really the political elite, those who decide what political decisions will be made which will affect the future. Plainly, not all the decisions which are going to affect the future are political decisions, and all elite decisions can be said at least to have an effect on the governing elite's own range of possible choices. (It would become one of the main problems of modern political science to try to separate out 'political' decision-making from 'economic' and other kinds of decision-making, and the best way of doing that is still to follow Pareto and say that the difference lies in who makes the decisions rather than in the decisions themselves. From one point of view, all political decisions are economic and all economic decisions are political, for the exercise of power is involved in them all. It is much easier to distinguish between groups of politicians and businessmen than to distinguish between what they actually do.)

Elites come in different shapes and sizes. Some are 'closed', like castes, and some are 'open' as Pareto believes modern governing elites tend increasingly to be. Elites change. The 'real' elite in any society is the elite of talent and energy, but the 'real' elite does not always 'wear the label'. Old governing elites defend themselves against the up-and-coming elites, and the political battle in any society is largely a struggle between the two. Elites also operate in different ways. Some elites rely mainly on force and others on persuasion. Persuasion is really what we would call 'legitimacy', the creation of opinion favourable to elite rule. In the past, elites relied more on force: witness the class of knights in feudal society; in the present, persuasion seems to be the most cost-efficient way to further an elite's cause. Persuasion is aimed either at interests or residues, or at both. Pareto's anti-Marxism will not allow him to grant priority to (economic) interests over residues. Any political theory and any propaganda effort which ignores the importance of residues does so at its peril.

Pareto's distinction between force and persuasion is not to be read as another optimistic gloss on the liberal idea of progress. All liberals thought that in the modern world affairs of all kinds would come increasingly to be governed by opinion and not by force. So much had been common ground since the Enlightenment. But by 'opinion' liberals had meant enlightened opinion, advanced opinion, opinion like theirs. If Pareto is right, then one part of the liberal prediction was coming right only to be contradicted by the other part. Nineteenth-century social science spoke with one voice when it gave a crucial social role to ideas and theories about the world, but the social science of the end of the nineteenth century began to ask itself what the ideas were like which had such a social influence, and most social science spoke through Pareto when he said that the social influence and intellectual value of ideas were probably unconnected, and many social scientists began to see a negative connection between social influence and intellectual value: the worse the ideas were in the intellectual scale the better they seemed to suit social purpose. Pareto's elite operating by persuasion lacked even the barbarous honesty of the knights of old who ruled by the sword. The new governing elite were so many foxes taking over from the lions. Modern political belief-systems were all foxy legitimising derivations in Machiavelli's and Pareto's language. And there was no reason in principle why all modern elites should be open elites relying mainly on persuasion. Pareto is no progressive; the future, or parts of it, could easily be a re-run of the past. No modern would-be governing elite is going to be stupid enough to leave the propaganda weapon unsheathed, but there is no reason why it should not revert to force if its own sense of its own future requires it. The fascist twist to Pareto was to make propaganda *through* violence, a highly imaginative synthesis of force and persuasion. The fascist party became the perfect Machiavellian prince, fox and lion at the same time. (It could not matter as a matter of tactics that the anarchists had thought of 'propaganda by the deed (that is, by the bomb) first').

It is easy to miss how intellectually radical Pareto's political thought is, and how much re-casting it requires of the time-honoured world of concepts which political theorists inhabit. Political thinkers had been trying to classify forms of rule since before Plato's time. Aristotle's classification of the forms of rule into three 'pure' and three 'corrupt' forms is only the most famous of a whole host of such attempts, and it is remarkable how many later thinkers either followed Aristotle's classification or offered a variant of it. So much classification had been a waste of time if Pareto is to be taken seriously. No matter what the form of government was, government by the One, the Few or the Many, kingship, aristocracy or oligarchy, or democracy, government had always in fact been government by a governing elite. All the future efforts to discover a typically modern form of rule – the parliamentary republic, for instance, or totalitarianism – were bound to fail.

It is equally easy to regard Pareto's main contentions as commonplaces. One might be tempted to say that men had always known that the belief-systems which dominated societies were intellectually laughable, and it is equally tempting to say that men had always known that an elite ruled. One could cite any number of authorities from Plato onwards to show that what Pareto has to say about politics is an ancient commonplace. It will not even do to say that Pareto sets out to prove his contentions empirically. Pareto's political thinking forms part of a formal theory of sociology of considerable formal beauty, but there is nothing particularly empirical about the way he defends that theory (and critics of Pareto have never been slow to point out that, by recent standards, the evidence which Pareto adduces to support his theory is merely anecdotal, tales of the ancients and yesterday's headlines). What these criticisms fail to take into account is context. Almost all the world agreed that the past had been oligarchic. Hitherto, government had been the plaything of cliques buried deep in the woodwork. Liberals thought that modern government was going to be government by elected leaders responsible to elected assemblies and responsible through those assemblies to the people. The representatives of the people were supposed to put their qualifications for office on display at elections. Good qualifications would drive out bad, and there was at least some expectation of turnover in office. (In the same way, permanent officials were to be appointed on publicly announced criteria of excellence.) Modern political leaders were expected to be an elite in both of Pareto's senses of the term. They were supposed to be the real elite and also to wear the badges of office. They were to be agents of the people's will; were supposed, at least in principle, to come from the people; and they were supposed to stand frequently at the bar of electoral judgement. Not since Plato's *Republic* had such an effort been made to make sure that those who were supposed to be the rulers of the people really were their rulers. Publicness was all. Elite theory began to drive a thick wedge into liberal democracy's view of itself. Parliamentary leaders lasted an uncomfortably long time in politics for the thesis of elections as quality control processes to be altogether convincing. Modern elites did not consist exclusively of elected officials or officials appointed for their excellence, and the fact that elite theory had to go looking for its elites showed how little had changed since those bad old days when governing elites operated in secret behind the scenes. The fact of elections might make the modern elite more legitimate for those fool enough to be taken in by liberalism, but its character as an elite was not all that different from the elites which it had superseded.

For Pareto, all elites use persuasion. In Pareto's language, all elites exploit residues, and we know that residues change slowly enough to be classed with instincts. Residues can be exploited in any number of ways and combinations. All political change can therefore be seen as the result of different sets of residues being played on in different ways. Modernity, of which liberalism is the most important part for liberals, is just another in a long series of themes played on the same available set of notes. Pareto does not think the past can predict what tune is going to be played on a piano. None the less, the residues, conceived as different notes on the piano, determine to a very large extent what piano music is going to be like because the instrument does not change, or changes so slowly that the changes will never be very noticeable. What liberals choose to call modernity arises from causes which are in fact very ancient. Liberalism began in the Age of Reason with the belief that the determinants of behaviour in the future were going to be different. A reconstructed world was going to guide individuals along paths which led in new directions. The onward and upward paths were going to be open to all so that lives which had seemed impossibly privileged in the past were now to be lived by everyman. That was always going to take time to bring about, but modernity's future promised a life for the humblest member of a society which would have been the envy of most pre-modern men. The theory of the elite proclaimed against this a fact which novelists and socialists had known all along, that the gap between the elite and the mass was still the same where it was not actually getting wider.

Liberalism and the critiques of liberalism cover the whole range of political theories possible in the world of modernity. Most of the anti-liberal theories borrow their form from liberalism itself. This was true of the original of all anti-liberal theories, Burke's *Reflections on the Revolution in France*, which tried to make itself as far-reaching and coherent as the doctrine which it set out to attack. All attacks on liberalism, from the nationalist through the Hegelian to the socialist, have displayed the same tendency to rationalise in the double sense of reasoning and offering specious reasons. Like Nietzsche in his different way, Pareto wants us to cram all this theorising into the same category of the intellectually worthless. The only differentiating criterion he will show is scientific content, and by this standard there is something to be said, but not much, for Marxism and Spencerism. The difference between the most scientific political theory and the others is as nothing when compared to the difference between science proper and the pseudo-sciences of political and social theory. This is, of course, devastating to liberalism's own claim to ground itself in the scientific revolution of the seventeenth century, and it is also devastating to most of the claims of Marxism as scientific socialism. Pareto's is not an attack from the outside on the scientific pretensions of political theorising. He is no Nietzsche, hurling thunderbolts from the mountains. Pareto is best compared to Bernstein, an insider questioning the faith. The difference is that Pareto goes much further than Bernstein. Bernstein preserves the Marxist

653

decencies in much the same way as John Stuart Mill kept up the Benthamite decencies. Pareto does not even bother to keep up the liberal decencies. His insistence that strategy is rational, for instance, could not be mistaken by his contemporaries for anything but an attack on the liberal (and socialist) view that in a rational world there would be no war. In Pareto's terms, war was a perfectly rational option in the right circumstances, just as in certain circumstances it was perfectly rational for elites to use force. Liberalism had looked forward to the eradication of violence in national and international life, but Pareto seemed to be saying that the impulse towards social peace and international pacifism was just that, an impulse not very different from an instinct, not rational at all.

Pareto was not alone in formulating the theory of elites, and if there is a fault in Pareto it is the lack of any real empirical treatment of an actual elite or of an elite from the past. The question was how to prove that both Pareto and his compatriot Gaetano Mosca were right when they claimed that, all appearances to the contrary and even with the best will in the world, all organised human life was ordered by elites. It was Robert Michels, in the work known in the English-speaking world as *Political Parties*, who produced the convincing evidence with a most elegant piece of experimental design. Michels decided to look for evidence of elitism in the human organisation whose principles were specifically designed to attack all elitism. This human organisation was obviously the socialist mass party. All socialism is anti-elitist. Elites of all kinds, bourgeois, aristocratic and clerical, are socialism's natural enemies. Socialism will not be satisfied by the formal, bourgeois notion of equality as equality before the law and equality of political rights. For socialists, equality has to be real, everyday equality, with the distinctions which divided man from man abolished. Michels saw very clearly that, on the principle of *a fortiori* (the greater contains the lesser), if the socialist parties were themselves elite-ridden, then no other form of human organisation could possibly run itself without a ruling oligarchy. If a concealed ruling oligarchy is to be found right in the heart of a socialist movement dedicated to equality then we are entitled to conclude that oligarchy rules in any organisation simply because it is an organisation. Michels found what he was looking for in the German Social Democratic Party of his own day. The effective gap between leaders and led, between salaried officials and the rank and file members, was as wide as the gap that one might expect to find in other organisations which were not dedicated to human equality. That socialist leaders called themselves the servants of the Party, or that the permanent officials of the Party were referred to as the Party's employees, could not disguise the fact that leaders and officials acted more like masters and employers than like servants or hired hands. Of course, it was possible that political scientists might subsequently find organisations which were not run by oligarchies, but the chances were slight. Most modern political science has wallowed in the fact that all organisations contain elites.

Michels, like his intellectual progeny, always claimed that his theory of the Iron Law of Oligarchy was 'value-free'. Michels saw himself as setting the record straight by telling truths about socialist parties, and, by implication, about human organisations in general. But the truths of political science have a tendency to turn themselves into home truths. Just to say that something is 'value-free' is no guarantee that it will have no relevance to values. Political and moral values do not stand alone in a world by themselves. Values are parts of arguments which in turn go to make up political positions. The socialist aim of equality also presupposes that equality is in fact achievable. That something *ought to be* implies that it *can in fact be*. No *can in fact be*, then no *ought to be*. At the very least, Michels provided the political Right with some useful ammunition. If the parties of the Left could not even realise their aim within their own organisation, then how could they expect ever to create equality in the wider society? The Party was in principle controllable and manipulable. Society at large was likely, on the socialists' own account of it, to be made of sterner stuff. Society at large, containing as it did many individuals and groups who were not socialists, was likely to be less amenable to re-modelling along socialist lines than the Party faithful. If you couldn't even organise the Party faithful along socialist lines, then it was just silly to try to do it to society at large. Hence the charge of political innocence or hypocrisy levelled at the Left by the Right for most of the twentieth century. Despite their egalitarian rhetoric, socialist leaders were men on the make just like their own opponents whom they affected to despise for their frank defence of inequality; any socialist too stupid to see that socialist parties were oligarchies was certain to be too incompetent to be let anywhere near the levers of political power. Hence the claim of the Right to understand the 'real' world.

There were, perhaps, two unintended consequences of the elitist theory which are worth mentioning, both of which were favourable to parliamentary democracy. The Iron Law of Oligarchy, as it came to be known, could easily have the effect of reassuring people whose natural instincts were profoundly undemocratic. Mass democracy might not mean social levelling after all. All of democracy's critics, and many of its friends, assumed that universal suffrage meant that the future belonged to the class politics of the proletariat. The bourgeoisie used its political muscle to further its own ends, and so had the aristocracy before it. Why should the working class act differently when the right to vote gave them the leverage necessary to produce governing decisions favourable to themselves? If socialist parties turned out to be parties like any other, then socialist governments might turn out to be governments like any other. The person who saw this earlier and more clearly than anybody else was the maverick Marxist Georges Sorel, a thinker claimed by both the extreme Right and the extreme Left in twentieth-century politics. Sorel realised that the Iron Law of Oligarchy was only a step away from the complementary theory of *embourgeoisement*. The theory of *embourgeoisement* is alluringly simple, though some of its ramifications are not, and it is admirably empirical, based as it is on observations of how socialist mass parties actually conduct themselves. Socialist parties are ruled by elites like any other parties. The official doctrine of a socialist party may be revolutionary. The party may long for the revolution on its high days and holidays, but that does not tell it much about what its day-to-day practice ought to be like when the party is actually waiting for the revolution to happen. The constraints of a parliamentary or representative system of politics mean that the party has to attract votes from those who are not actually party members – that is, from those voters who may sympathise with its aims, or some of them, but who might not exactly share the revolutionary faith. This locks the socialist party into the political system of the country in which it is operating, and it is a system in which the ground rules for success or failure are laid down by others besides themselves. The danger in this, from the revolutionary point of view, is that socialist leaders will begin to act in the way that the leaders of other parties are already acting. Leaders of liberal and conservative parties are already adepts at securing the votes of electors who may or may not agree with their parties' generally stated ideological ends, and the leaders of these other parties are already familiar with the routine business of appearing to be all things to most men. (It was said of Disraeli that he was a protectionist in the counties and a free-trader in the boroughs.) Leaders of liberal and conservative parties already understood that the wilder shores of doctrinal purity could be electorally embarrassing, so that it came to be increasingly realised, by leaders and voters alike, that party ideology was not always to be taken as a reliable guide to the future conduct of the party, either in or out of office, and one of the spectator sports of parliamentary politics was to be reminding a party in office of what they said they were going to do before they came into government.

Why should this process not happen to socialist parties? Why should socialist leaders not begin to find the party's official revolutionary and egalitarian creed a bit of an embarrassment too? The last thing one wants in electoral politics is to put the voters off. The leaders of parties have a special interest here. They are typically professional politicians who do not want to spend their time in opposition. Opposition to the system may make the party faithful feel all warm and runny inside, like a soft-boiled egg, but not the leadership. Their sense of their own self-esteem impels them to the seats of real power, and, in the game of electoral politics, it is always expedient to be able to show the party and the voters that the party leadership have solid political gains behind them. Waiting for revolution is all very well, but it is always a good idea to give your supporters something on account, something to be going on with, something to keep their appetites keen. This means making deals with other political forces inside the system, especially if the party is outside government. What, then, have socialist party leaders got to offer to the other parties and to government that makes the party leaders worth bargaining with? The first thing is electoral support, which an outside party might put at the disposal of an inside party in the form of support in parliament or the assembly: coalition politics in fact. But Sorel and others like him saw something much deeper that socialist leaders had to bargain with, and that was the threat of revolution itself. The obvious tactic for the leader of a socialist party was to say to the leaders of other parties that dealing with him was better than revolution. The socialist leader would say to other political leaders, explicitly or implicitly, that he was the only person who could keep the revolutionary energy of his followers in check, and the only way he could do that was to be able to show his followers that they were getting something out of the system: hence the deals. The socialist leader would then say to his followers that only he could deal with the forces of reaction and bring solid gains to his supporters. Socialist leaders became power-brokers, channels of communication between the working class and their class enemies, and therefore putters-off of the revolution itself by making it easier for the working class to live with the forces of reaction and making it easier for the forces of reaction to live with ideologically revolutionary parties. Of course, socialist leaders have to pay a price for being power-brokers. They have to accept the rules of the pressure group politics game. Other groups must expect to gain out of the system too, otherwise the game is not worth playing. It has to be recognised that working-class demands are not the demands of the whole of humanity seeking to universalise and liberate itself. On the contrary, the working class comes to be seen as just another interest group playing the same political game with the same rules as every other group.

It cannot be helped that playing the political game has its effects on socialist leaders, even if they have come up through the party from the working class itself. They begin to sound like all other political leaders, and eventually they even come to look like them. It is not always obvious to the naked eye what the difference is between working-class and bourgeois leaders, and it might increasingly be the case that disaffected members of the bourgeoisie, especially if they are intellectuals, will begin to look covetously upon the career possibilities which leadership positions in mass socialist parties provide. The career and the charm of the parliamentary game will do the rest, and socialist leaders will find themselves so thoroughly socialised by bourgeois politics that they will have become bourgeois themselves, with a vested interest in the system remaining as it is. The beginning of this process is, obviously enough, the elitism process pointed to by Pareto and demonstrated by Michels. Not all elitism in socialist parties implies *embourgeoisement*: witness Lenin and the Bolsheviks, keeping their revolutionary energy pure by an effort of the will. But elitism plus too long an immersion in the parliamentary game of bourgeois politics does lead to *embourgeoisement*. Opponents of socialism, aristocratic and bourgeois, could not but find all this reassuring if they thought about it properly. The parliamentary system might be a lot tougher than had hitherto been supposed, and it might be the only way to domesticate the rude revolutionary forces of proletarian politics. As President Lyndon Johnson famously said on another occasion, much better to have them inside the tent pissing out than outside the tent pissing in.

The other aspect of the theories of elitism and *embourgeoisement* which was favourable to bourgeois democracy was their implicit recognition that there was a world of difference between representative and direct democracy. There had always been a tendency in radical circles to regard representative democracy as a second-best copy of the real thing, direct democracy. Witness all the excuses democrats since Tom Paine had given for opting for representative democracy and not the real thing: modern states were too large for direct democracy and so on. Ever since *The Federalist Papers* it had been possible to see representative democracy not as a version of direct democracy but as an alternative, with its own alternative rationale which was aimed directly at real democracy itself. *The Federalist Papers* make it quite clear that the main advantage of representative democracy is that it blunts popular wills because, properly engineered, representation through election will produce an elite whose values and expectations will be very different from the rude masses whom they are called upon to represent. Not everybody could even read the *Papers*, but everybody could see the processes of elite formation happening in European democratic politics before their very eyes. Parliamentary politics based on the representation of the people could now be defended precisely because it was an alternative to direct democracy. Socialist leaders were the vital link in the chain, because they were the necessary representative elite which would socialise socialism into the bourgeois system. Democracy's enemies no longer had to fear direct action by the people. Representation was the alternative to direct action, and therefore representation was a much better option for the enemies of democracy and socialism. Direct action by the people is only another name for the socialist revolution, and the representative principle came to be seen clearly for what it had really been all along: the true antidote to the possibility of a revolution of the working class. Representation now had a rationale in its own right.

NOTES ON SOURCES

Pareto can be read in English in *Sociological Writings*, ed. Finer (1966), and *The Other Pareto*, ed. Bucolo (1980). R. Michels, *Political Parties: A Sociological Study of the Oligarchical Tendencies of Modern Democracy* (1962), still shines with its original brilliance. Also available is *Pareto and Mosca*, ed. Meisel (1965).

28

LIBERALISM'S SPECIAL ENEMIES
The Crowd and its Theorists

GUSTAVE LE BON

It is not easy to find anything likeable in Le Bon except his *chutzpah*. He is a character out of a Maupassant novel, a provincial on the make, guzzling and sleeping his way to the top of the social and intellectual world in Paris. ('Maupassant' means not quite up to Proust.) Le Bon came from a bourgeois family to study medicine in Paris (he qualified in 1876), but he soon decided that he would make his career as a scientific populariser. The choice is not in itself odd, because medicine had yet to become the very closed specialism from which it is only now beginning to emerge. In Le Bon's day, the borderlines between medical science and the related sciences of criminology, anthropology and ethnography were yet to be drawn, and the shapes of all the sciences were being redrawn in the light of the great prestige given to evolutionary biology by the publication of Darwin's *The Origin of Species* in 1859. It is no exaggeration to say that evolutionism exerted an influence on almost everything that was thought or written in the second half of the nineteenth century, whether that influence came from Darwinism direct or through other evolutionary doctrines, like Comtian positivism or Spencerism, which did not originate in Darwinism but certainly fed off it.

Le Bon caught a moment when the literate public of Europe wanted an explanation of how the new science was going to affect the way they looked at the world and how the new world of science was going to impinge upon them. The age of Le Bon was also the age of imperialism, and his reading public wanted to know how the European nations stood in relation to the colonised peoples along the evolutionary scale. Le Bon was already a successful author before *The Crowd* began its extraordinary career as a bestseller in 1895. He lived in a fashionable house between the Opéra and the Madelaine, kept a gourmet's table, and held *déjeuners* to which he invited famous intellectuals, nobles and ladies of fashion.

Yet there was always something of the outsider about Le Bon. He yearned after the great scientific prizes, but he received a magisterial put-down from Einstein for claiming to have been the first to have conceived the theory of relativity. Yet he was not without his successes. He became a Grand Commander of the Legion of Honour in 1929, and two princesses (one of them a Bonaparte) were at his deathbed in 1931. And to this day *The Crowd* continues to be reprinted.

Liberalism had expected great things from human reason ever since John Locke had argued that men could work out God's purpose for the world themselves. Liberals were not always very clear about what they meant by reason, and liberals sometimes took different views about what reason was, but liberals cried reason up with one voice. At bottom, liberals believed that people could take responsibility for the decisions which radically affected their own lives, or, if they did not go that far, liberals believed that men could become competent judges of the decisions made for their lives by others. Liberalism certainly taught men to be suspicious of those who claimed to possess a special knowledge which enabled them to tell others what kinds of lives they should lead. This always smacked of priestcraft, or of the mumbo-jumbo of the theory of the divine right of kings. Claims to special knowledge came to be seen as the outward surfaces of vested interests, and it was always the liberal hope then that the rationales for vested interests would not stand up in informed and public debate. Liberalism stuck to the distinction between vested interests and rational self-interest. Vested interests were always selfish and minority interests which were an affront to the interests of others either potentially or actually. Rational men, if given the choice, would always opt for social, economic and political systems which allowed the free play of individual or group interests. A liberal society, in our modern language, was not supposed to be an 'end-state'. Human self-interest, expressed by either individuals or groups, was supposed to remain ever unsatisfied. In the language of eighteenth-century political thought, the passions, of which the passion of self-interest was politically the most important, would never be still. Human societies would therefore be continuously in motion, and it was in the interests of all except vested interests that this should continue to be the case.

As the nineteenth century progressed, there seemed to be a growing consensus, which would eventually take everybody in except extreme conservatives and anarchists, that the political form best suited to this kind of society was parliamentary democracy (with or without constitutional monarchy) of some kind. Such a consensus certainly did not prevail even among radicals at the end of the Napoleonic Wars in 1815. Commentators on the Left and on the Right realised that the French Revolution and what followed left a great political question unanswered: What was the appropriate political form for the modern society which the French Revolution showed had arrived? Nobody doubted that the French Revolution was the sign, plain for all to see, that feudal and seigneurial society was definitively over. What Marxists were later to call 'bourgeois' society was now an accomplished fact. This did not, of course, mean that bourgeois society prevailed everywhere in Europe, let alone the world in general, but it did mean that bourgeois society was the wave of the future. Market society, the society of free contract, of the buying and selling of labour, of capitalist farming and industrialised production, would eventually make its way everywhere, and those reactionary forces which set their faces against it either were wilfully obtuse or had failed to understand their own times. But the bewildering changes of forms of government in France between 1789 and 1815, from constitutional monarchy to republic to Jacobin dictatorship to oligarchic Directory to Consulate to Empire and back to the *ancien régime*, left the question unsettled as to what the political form of bourgeois society should be. Nineteenth-century political thought was largely an attempt to give a definitive answer to this most important of all questions, and the era of the bourgeoisie came to the conclusion that its own appropriate form was parliamentary democracy.

The societies where parliamentary democracy established itself were supposed to be societies in which the free play of interests and interest groups was the main source of social and political energy. A society like that virtually extended an invitation to everybody to play the group game, and a society like that was progressive to the extent that modernising groups did well and reactionary groups did badly. (Hence bourgeois hostility to socialism on the grounds that collective ownership of property was appropriate only to a more 'primitive' form of society. It was well known, for instance, that the primitive Church might have held goods in common.) Reactionary vested interest groups would quite simply not be able to stand the pace of modern social and political change. But there was one group, which could according to taste be called 'the crowd' or 'the mob', which did not fit in well in this progressive scheme. The crowd or the mob plainly came from the people, and during the French Revolution the people had made themselves effective as the 'revolutionary crowd'. One of the easiest ways of looking at the causes of the French Revolution, and of its great symbolic moment, the storming of the Bastille, was to see the Revolution as a series of great riots which eventually got out of hand. No matter that the Bastille did not require much storming. The crowd was in at the beginning of the Revolution which everybody agreed was itself the beginning of modernity. The crowd was therefore, from one point of view, part and parcel of modernity. The politics of the democratic age, a politics which was going to mean representative government in practice, was going to hear more from the crowd, and the extension of the franchise meant extending formal democratic rights to it.

But there was a problem. Crowd politics might be the coming democratic style, a politics of modernity, but there was also something ugly about the crowd which the term 'mob' had always pointed to. It had been a commonplace since the ancient world that the mob was backward, primitive, animal-like, anti-rational, fickle in making up whatever mind it had, anti-social, dangerous. The message was unmistakable for those who chose to see the people as a crowd when passive and as a mob when active. The crowd was an affront to modernity, where modernity meant the progressive elimination of everything which was rude and irrational from a nation's life. Mobs were above all else destructive. Violence or the threat of violence was the crowd's first argument, but modern life, on the liberal account of it, was supposed to be characterised by the decreased use of force in social and political life and by the increased effectiveness of the public rationality of law. Relations between individuals and groups arranged on violence or the threat of violence were supposed to be replaced by relations either of law or of voluntary co-operation based on the recognition of mutual self-interest. Either violence would be outlawed or it would come to be seen as an irrational way of doing business in the ordinary course of a nation's domestic or international life.

It was not clear how the crowd fitted into this scenario. On the one hand, democratic politics seemed to be an invitation to the crowd to make itself heard, but this was happening in societies in which the crowd introduced an inappropriately raucous note into the civilised conversation between interest groups and between interest groups and government. It was inevitable in the age of Darwinism that the supposed 'primitivism' of crowds should have been given a heavy evolutionist gloss. Le Bon's *The Crowd: A Study of the Popular Mind* (1895) put all the fears which the crowd aroused into a simple formula: the modern era was the era of crowds. Le Bon set out to write a bestseller, and he did. He did not miss a single trick when emphasising the crowd's primitivism in ripe evolutionary terms. Modern life was indeed progressive in an evolutionary sense, but this progress was threatened by the crowd. Evolution had passed the crowd by, and this despite the fact that the most advanced body of modern political thinking, democratic theory, was giving the crowd a central place in the democratic republic. The crowd was irrational, primitive and animal-like. It really had no place in a modern society at all. It belonged low on the evolutionary scale, with primitive peoples, for instance, or with animals. Of course, the crowd was only dangerous in its active form, as a mob. The crowd of modern society in its passive form was everybody. Everybody was potentially a member of a mob, so it followed that everybody was not one self but two, a normal 'civilised' self and an abnormal 'uncivilised' self. Everyday life might be orderly and peaceful, but that everyday life was continually threatened by the mob-self which each one of us contains bottled up inside.

Le Bon and others began to wonder if there might not be circumstances in the modern world itself which made the mob an increasingly likely occurrence.

The crowd's theorists saw a clear connection between Enlightenment and the crowd, and they saw a causal connection between Enlightenment and the great crowd scenes of the French Revolution. In its haste to abolish the incorporated privileges of the social orders of the *ancien régime*, Enlightenment had gone down the path of the assertion of the equality of individual rights. Modern society was to be free society in the sense that everybody was supposed to be equal before the law and everybody was to be able to choose, in so far as he could, his own way of life. Traditional society, in which a man followed in his father's footsteps in all the important things of life, was supposed to be superseded by a society in which the relations between man and man were legal relations, the relations of free contract under a law which applied equally to everybody. In the new society, men would still have duties, but these duties would be largely confined to respecting the rights of others or they would consist of the duty to perform what had been freely agreed to be done. In this sense Enlightenment was individualistic, no matter how this individualism was hedged in by the details of enlightened political and social theory. Sociologically this implied that the ancient social categories would become increasingly fragile as larger numbers of people would vacate their inherited social roles and acquire new ones in the new kind of society. This process was considered to be natural because people would for the first time be in a position to choose what their roles should be without legal interference. In practice this was always going to be easier for some than for others, but the kind of social theory expounded by Spencer and others showed how role-choice could be extended to cover a whole society. The social division of labour meant that in liberal society more and more social roles would become available, and the more the better, because the idea of a liberal society was closely associated with the idea that each man should choose what his life was going to be like.

The problem as crowd theorists saw it was the transfer of large numbers from traditional to new social roles. The old social categories had worked well enough as containers for rude social energy, but the same thing was unlikely to be so true of the new. Roles like town-dweller and factory-worker, landless wage-labourer, or voter expecting one's voice to be heard, might not be clearly enough defined or familiar enough to teach men their social duties. Rights were heard of frequently, but duties were another matter. Rights could easily come to be seen as antitheses to duties, rights to strike, for instance, as against the duty to labour for one's wages for bread, or rights to mass protest as against the citizens' duty to exercise whatever political rights they had through the peaceful mechanisms of elections. What was required of the masses was above all patience, the willingness to wait until the general scheme of human progress eventually caught up with them. But rights and equality were the thing. They existed or ought to exist over and above particular forms of role-playing, and in a sense willingness to play modern social roles was dependent on the consent of the role-players. There was no prior duty to play the role of factory worker; quite the reverse – workers had the right, if they could, to stop being factory workers – by changing their jobs for instance, or by striking, or even by rising into the ranks of the bourgeoisie. A society as mobile as this was always a worry to conservatives concerned for the stability of the social order, because behind the cry for rights they saw an individualism which was far more menacing even than the individualism of the rights of man, an individualism so abstract that it tended to obliterate the differences between men which made them individuals distinguishable from one another. The abstract individual invented by eighteenth-century political and social theory was the individual stripped of all his characteristics which he owed to living in a particular place in a particular social position in a particular society at a particular moment in that society's development, and it is hard to see how a definition of the individual could be more abstract than that. This was eighteenth-century Natural Man possessing natural rights which are pre-social and pre-civil, rights which just are.

The theorists of the crowd could not help being struck by the resemblance between natural man and crowds man. Men in crowds seemed to be able to slough off their ordinary social selves. The crowd's notorious unanimity lay precisely in the fact that it could be 'of one mind'. The plurality of social groups with different interests, and different opinions as a result of that difference of interest, seemed to disappear in the group. Human heterogeneity seemed to be swamped in homogeneity. This did not matter so much while it was still possible to think that the mob only came out of the lower orders. It was the easiest thing in the world to attribute a brutal sameness to the degraded lives of the poor so that it was only to be expected that they would riot from time to time. However, as the nineteenth century advanced, this view became less and less tenable. Crowds did not always consist of people from the same social group, yet they were still subject to the same unanimity. Theorists also began to ask themselves how this unanimity worked, and to explain this they began to concentrate their attention on the leaders of crowds.

The demagogue had received theoretical attention ever since Plato, but the difference between ancient and modern concern with demagogues was that modern thinkers came to believe that a scientifically valid body of theory was emerging which would once and for all establish what the basis of the demagogue arts actually was. This psychology can be called the psychology of hypnotism, or, more generally, the psychology of the unconscious.

Hypnotism enjoyed a great vogue in eighteenth- and nineteenth-century Europe. It was a popular parlour game and a successful music-hall stunt, full of mystery and associated with charlatanism as mysteries often are. Nobody really knew whether to take it seriously or not. Everybody had seen or heard about hypnotic phenomena, but what prevented hypnotism from receiving the imprimatur of scientific respectability was that no very convincing account of it could be given. Everybody knew that hypnotism had something to do with unconsciousness, but there were always those to say that the unconscious mind was a contradiction in terms. Either mind *was* consciousness, or it was nothing. From the 1880s onwards some of Europe's best scientific minds established that hypnotic phenomena were genuine and the search for a truly scientific explanation for hypnotism was really on. The political implications of the acceptance of hypnotism as a scientifically verifiable fact were very striking. Everybody knew that skilful hypnotists could hypnotise groups as well as individuals. Perhaps this explained the unanimity of the minds of crowds. The leader of the crowd was really what he had been always called, a spellbinder. Everybody in the crowd would be fascinated by the leader. Everybody would do what the crowd's leader wanted the crowd to do; everybody was of the same mind. The mental unity of the crowd was therefore a verifiable fact in the latest psychological theory's own terms. Hypnotic skills could be learned, though it was also true that some were more gifted hypnotists than others. (Freud, for one, was not much good at it.) Perhaps crowd leaders were naturally gifted hypnotists, hypnotists by instinct, so to speak, but hypnotism was a skill which could be learned or improved, and modern politics was always going to be in some sense mass politics. Therefore, Europe had a lot of hypnotic politics to look forward to as every aspiring political leader in the age of the masses was sure to equip himself with the necessary hypnotic equipment to make him a successful leader of crowds.

By the time Le Bon published his best-selling work on *The Crowd*, hypnotism was already something of a hackneyed subject. There seemed to be general scientific agreement that hypnotism was a very fundamental fact about human minds. Especially interesting was the hypnotist's ability to make hypnotised subjects re-live their childhood experiences. Hypnotism was therefore a way into experience buried deep in the unconscious minds of subjects. Subjects regressed during hypnotism, and psychologists began to wonder what the unconscious mind contained besides often painful childhood memories. Like all nineteenth-century science, psychology was deeply influenced by evolutionist ideas, and crowd theorists very quickly made the evolutionary connection between the painful childhood memories of the individual and the painful childhood memories of the human race. Late nineteenth-century biological and social theory was centrally concerned about the question of the transmission of values and attitudes from one generation to the next. Many late nineteenth-century thinkers were implicit or explicit Lamarckians, believing that characteristics acquired in one generation could be automatically transmitted to the next. Sometimes, what was inherited by the next generation was called 'instinct', and it was called instinct because it did not have to be consciously learned. Therefore, what one generation passed on to the next tended to be called 'unconscious' because it was not thought out: Paretian residues by any other name. The hard and fast distinction between the hereditary and social acquisition of characters was not always clearly made, and a social theory like Pareto's tells us why. Some of what we would now call 'socially acquired' human characteristics appeared to have been 'acquired' (if they were) so long ago that the difference between acquisition and instinct is a matter of small importance as far as social theory is concerned. If certain of the social characteristics of men were so old that it was all but impossible to trace their origins, then the really important question was not 'acquisition' or 'instinct', but the question of how these characteristics passed down the generations affected social and political life. The theory of hypnotism relied heavily on some such notion of inherited characters. During hypnotism, the childhood of the race could be re-lived as well as the childhood of the individual. Hence the theory of double regression in hypnotism. The hypnotised subject could re-live both his own early experience and the early experience of man in general. It was in this way that the time-scales of evolutionary theory became important for social and political theory as well as for biology.

Evolutionary theory revolutionised how people thought about time. Pre-modern men lived in a world which they thought of as a recent creation. God had created the world in Adam's time, and Adam was thought of as living not much before Abraham. Everybody was supposed to be waiting for the Second Coming, and there were always some who believed that Christ would come again to judge the nations very soon. This was a world which did not have much of a past and might not have much of a future. It was a world in which it made sense to think that what happened 'in the beginning' might well have a bearing on what happens now; hence the idea of social contract as the origin of all government and as a guide to contemporary practice. Evolutionary theory taught men to live in several different time-scales, each of which invited them to see the past as going so far back that the idea of time itself lost its ordinary meaning. Prehistoric time lay behind historical time; anthropological time lay behind prehistoric time; biological time lay behind anthropological time; botanical time lay behind biological time, and geological time lay behind botanical time. The question then was: How much of that past is preserved in the present? In what senses could the past be said to be over? If crowd behaviour was hypnotised behaviour, and if hypnotised subjects could be commanded by the hypnotist to re-live early experience, then did it not follow that the leader of a crowd could command the crowd to re-live the collective experience of the human race? That past was far from reassuring. In the crowd men could be made to recapitulate the stages of development in which everybody had been barbarians and savages (crowd theorists were always on the lookout for cannibalism) and animals. There were even fears that human nature in the raw meant raw vegetables. The demands of civilisation came to be seen as too exacting, as requiring too many consciously self-denying choices. Perhaps what men really longed for was the endless round of vegetative existence, a life lived not according to nature but *as* nature.

Some of the wilder panics of crowd theory may make us smile, but the very fact that these were serious speculations should alert us to the depth to which crowd theory could frighten serious men. Crowd theory could only mean that a very jaundiced view of the masses was the sensible view to take. It is important to see how the crowd theory view of the masses differed from traditional views of 'the people' as all potential trouble-makers. Conservatives since Plato had taught men to view the crowd with apprehension, but conservatives had always tended to look to the past for comfort. The great crowd-taming institutions of any society were the product of the past, and there was always a tendency, by no means yet dead, to think of the unruliness of crowd behaviour as a thing of the present which would not have been tolerated in better days. Not all anti-crowd sentiment had always been reactionary, but the reactionary strain had always been there. Modern crowd theory was different in two important ways. First, it invited men to see the past as a catalogue of horrors, and the further back you went the worse the horrors became. Second, crowd theory, far from being backward-looking as theory, was based on the very latest scientific thinking of the day. Reactionaries spent the second half of the nineteenth-century shouting evolutionary theory down. Evolutionary theory was therefore forward-looking in two separate but related senses. Not only did evolutionary theory regard itself as part of the great advance in science in general but it also looked forward to a future which was likely to be at least as long as the past, a future in which changes were going to occur which might be as momentous as the changes which had occurred in the evolutionary past.

But one particular part of evolutionary theory, crowd theory, began to erode the confident sense of future progress in the evolutionary scheme. The crowd's primitiveness was an affront and a threat to all progress, past, present and future. The crowd was a throw-back to earlier evolutionary stages in the life of man, not revolutionary, or even forward-looking, but deeply conservative. The crowd was proof that there was something in men which was not compatible with the modern world at all. This was obvious in the commonplace terms of liberal sociology as it derived from Spencer and more distantly from Adam Smith. Modern societies were supposed to become more heterogeneous. In sociological language, modern societies were supposed to be groups of sub-groups, a myriad conflicting but ultimately co-operating group wills. Ever since *The Federalist Papers* liberals had begun to doubt whether there was such a thing as society, if by society we mean a single group. From the liberal point of view, the mistake of political thinkers of the past had been to put too much emphasis on social uniformity as the basis for social solidarity. Plato is the arch-culprit because he wants the mass in his ideal society all to live the same kind of lives, in so far as that is possible, because that will make them easier to rule. Social conflict, on this view of it, is less likely to arise and cause trouble for rulers if the mass in any society is as homogeneous as it is possible for it to be. Liberals think the opposite: the greater the number of distinct groups in a society the better. What this effectively means is that in liberal society there will be a large number of social roles available to each individual, and liberal individualism relies sociologically on the possibility that the sum of the roles played by one man will be a sum of roles different from his neighbour's sum. Crowd theory challenged this view. The crowd's unanimity translated into sociological terms meant that the crowd was a group without sub-groups; the crowd was *sui generis*, unique, the only one of its kind. Everybody in the crowd acted and thought in the same way. In sociological terms, to act in the crowd was to play one role and one role only. Crowd men acted as if only one role was available to them, the absolute antithesis of liberal society. It is no exaggeration to say that men in crowds acted as if liberal society had never existed. The role 'crowd-man' abolished all other social roles. A crowd could form with frightening speed. All crowd thinkers agreed about that. What that meant was that the carefully and painfully developed heterogeneity of bourgeois liberal society could disappear in the twinkling of an eye.

This mattered fundamentally because everybody seemed to argue that the future of liberal society lay with democracy of some kind. There was a sense in which the democratic idea, loosely conceived, legitimised the crowd. Crowds, or the leaders of crowds, always claimed to be acting in the people's name when they did not actually claim to be the people, and democracy was supposed to mean that the will of the people shall have the force of law. When the crowd claimed to be the people, it was coming perilously close to claiming that it could do no wrong: *vox populi, vox dei*. If the will of the people was meant to have the force of law, then what the crowd did in the people's name might not even be considered illegal. This had been a possible view of the crowd in the French Revolution. The crowd storming the Bastille could be seen as the kind of legality peculiarly appropriate to the coming age of democracy. What some saw as lynch law was for others the beginning of a democratic exercise in popular sovereignty not seen since the demise of the ancient republics (and the modern republic, in America and in France, was quick to dress up in the toga).

The scientific interest in hypnotism from the 1880s onwards opened up further possibilities for the crowd. Hypnotism concentrated theoretical minds onto the problems associated with the leadership of crowds, but it did not stop there. From its inception, crowd theory had remarkable pretensions to theoretical generality. Crowd theorists very quickly began to wonder whether all leadership, not just the leadership of crowds, might not be hypnotic, and they also began to wonder if crowd psychology might not be the key to understanding how all human groups worked, not just crowds. All leaders might be hypnotists, all men might be crowd men, and all human groups crowds. This possibility came directly out of debates within the technical area of the theory of hypnotism. Psychologists were coming round to the view, which they accepted with varying degrees of willingness, that everybody was hypnotisable and everybody could learn the technique of hypnosis. Some kinds of people were more hypnotisable than others, and some people were natural hypnotists while others could learn the hypnotic art only with difficulty, but the distinction between hypnotisers and the hypnotisable on the one hand, and everybody else on the other hand no longer held. This had a potentially devastating effect on social and political theory. It meant, in short, that the ages-old elitist distinction between the crowd and *us*, between barbarism and civilisation, between the high-minded guardians of culture and the culture-hostile mass, no longer had the clear-cut validity it was once supposed to have.

Hypnotic phenomena were plainly unconscious in some important sense, and, if everybody was hypnotisable, it seemed to follow that unconscious forces might have a part to play in all forms of collective life. The lives of human groups might derive their binding power and their dynamism from unconscious sources of which social and political theory had hitherto been largely unaware. The unconscious was the antithesis of everything which reason stood for. In one sense, social and political theorists had always understood that there was a dark and irrational side to human nature. Nobody knew that better than Plato, and none feared it more than the thinkers of the Enlightenment. The forces of unreason had always been seen as the political theorist's and the wise statesman's particular enemy. Everything which was not thought out, everything which was 'instinctual', everything which was not directly subject to conscious control, was dangerous. Hence there had always been a very strong tendency to regard the irrational side of life as anti-social, anarchic, revolutionary even, where 'revolutionary' means a prelude to the return to a very nasty state of nature. Irrational psychological and social imperatives were what reason was there to control, and the history of political thought from its beginnings in ancient Greece to the second half of the nineteenth century had largely been the history of different arguments which supported the rational authority of the One, the Few or the Many over what Nietzsche called the Many-too-Many, the irrational mass of men, the crowd and the mob by any other name. Well-ordered social and political life was the product of reason. Hence the political theorists' perennial claim that they preached what a wise ruler would practise if only he would think the matter out properly.

Crowd theory flew right in the face of this fundamental assumption in the development of Western political thought. It now began to dawn on social and political theorists that those stable patterns of social and political living which had hitherto been thought of as the products of reason might themselves be the products of unconscious motivating forces. The unconscious came to be seen as the source of both social and anti-social forces; the unconscious gave and the unconscious took away. Social and political stability, and social and political instability were both the products of forces which were outside human control and which social and political theory had barely begun to understand. In this perspective, it was not clear that reason had any social or political function to perform at all. All reason could do was to look on while unconscious forces shaped and unshaped the world. Reason as psychological, social and political science might hope one day to understand all this irrational world through the construction of reliable theory, but what the *use* of this theory was was not altogether clear. This again shattered a dream which had been going since the ancients. Political thinkers had always assumed that political theory was useful, that it could form the basis of successful political practice. The idea of a political *technology* had been implicit in political science since Plato. Indeed, Aristotle is so confident that political science is useful to rulers that we translate as 'science' both his words for theoretical knowledge about politics and his word for the practice of wise government. What the technology of control was which could be extrapolated out of crowd theory was anybody's guess, though there were several distinct possibilities.

On the face of it, crowd theory would blow most of democratic theory sky-high. The identification of 'the people' with 'the crowd' meant that democracy could not be taken seriously as a form of *government*. Democracy since the Enlightenment had at least meant rational choice between electoral alternatives. Even democracy's friends admitted that. Democracy's enemies had always said that the mass of the people could not be expected to exercise the right of electoral choice rationally because their educational attainments were simply inadequate for the task. Some of democracy's friends agreed; hence the importance of the connection between the advance of public education and the extension of the franchise. But if all the implications of crowd theory were true, and the imperatives to human action, individual and collective, were all largely unconscious, then *nobody* was likely to be making rational choices when they voted, educated or not. Democratic politics was truly the darkling plain where ignorant armies clash by night. And what of those chosen as leaders and legislators by the democratic process? What reason was there for supposing that they were likely to be any more rational than their supporters? Was it not likely that the voters would choose leaders who appeared, to all intents and purposes, to be like them-selves? Plato had argued this against democracy in *The Republic*. Now the latest psychological science was belatedly finding out that the old anti-democrat had been right all along.

Or would the irrational electoral crowd choose leaders who took care to appear to be like the crowd only at election time? The crowd produced leaders, but not all leaders came from the crowd. One of Le Bon's main purposes in writing *The Crowd* was to explain, to those who were prepared to listen, what kinds of leaders the crowd was likely to accept from outside itself. Leaders who dreamt of leading the crowd while keeping their distance from the crowd could learn a great deal about leadership technique from the leaders which the crowd produced from inside itself. Le Bon is a latter-day Sophist. Like Plato, Le Bon believes that the arts of demagogy can be learned. And the arts of demagogy can and must be learned quickly. Le Bon, over-dramatically, calls crowds the last surviving power of modern times. Elites have conceded the field or have been driven from it. What princes say now counts for nothing. All is not lost, however. A breed of Machiavellian prince might still emerge to manipulate the crowd. The fact of crowds will remain, but it is still possible, though time is getting on, for members of society's elite themselves to become crowd leaders. Elite values and attitudes can be defended in the face of the crowd by elite leaders who only have to appear to share the crowd's values and attitudes. The crowd's atavism makes its values and attitudes atavistic: the barbarian crowd can't help thinking like barbarians, and in the crowd, as with children and savages, the wish is father to the deed. Crowds don't stop to think. No sooner have they decided to do something than they do it, like children impulsively at play, or barbarians risking everything in a single impulsive charge at the legions. A crowd leader who really knew how the mind of the crowd works might achieve much in the way of diverting the crowd's impulsive energy away from cherished cultural, political and social artifacts. Ideally, the engineer-ruler would so channel the crowd's barbarous energy that eventually the crowd would lose itself in the desert sands. For Le Bon, the politics of the future is going to be a contest between 'natural' and 'artificial' crowd leaders, between those who emerge from the crowd and share the crowd mind, and those who emerge from a society's elite to manipulate the crowd for the elite's own ends. At times, it is going to be difficult to distinguish between the two. There is always the cheering possibility that the crowd's own leaders will allow themselves to be socialised into society's existing elite, but there is also always the danger that an elite leader of the crowd will go native and take the crowd to his heart. Parliamentary systems are especially useful for the socialisation of outsiders into the elite, and even trade unions are not to be scorned. Unions are the schools for the little Caesars of this world: trade union leaders quickly learn to domineer over their followers in a way that their bosses might envy.

Le Bon is an adept at generalising from crowd theory, and all of Le Bon's critics since the 1890s have pointed out that Le Bon stretches the category 'crowd' so wide that eventually every recognisable social group becomes a crowd. Le Bon means us to take the universality of the crowd seriously. He thinks that we mistake the nature of the modern world if we confine the term 'crowd' to the physically proximate throng threatening mayhem in the street. For Le Bon, the crowd is essentially a mentality, a particular mental set. Le Bon makes great play with the idea of a 'group mind' which he thinks appears in the crowd. It does not matter whether we take the idea of a group mind literally or not. It may be hard to think of a mind which inhabits no particular brain, so that the group mind can never be anything more than a metaphor, but the reasoning which led Le Bon and others to the hypothesis of the group mind has to be taken very seriously indeed. What Le Bon and his followers wished to emphasise was that the workings of the group mind could not be explained as the workings of the mind of a particular member of the crowd writ large. The group mind was a law unto itself. What Le Bon rather portentously called The Law of the Mental Unity of Crowds worked in the crowd mind in ways which were not predictable in the terms of individual psychology. This is largely what thinkers like Le Bon mean when they say that crowd phenomena are 'unconscious', or are 'of a hypnotic order'. Individual minds can reason well enough. Individuals, often enough, think before they act, and they are capable of rationally following what they take to be rational social rules. Utilitarian calculations of individual utility, what we loosely call self-interest, can account for most individual action well enough, absolute fools and madmen always excepted. Crowd behaviour cannot be accounted for according to any version of the utilitarian calculus. Crowds think nothing is impossible. The notion of prudently adjusting means to ends means nothing to them. Individuals in crowds often desert their everyday self-serving prudence and perform acts of heroic self-sacrifice. People in crowds appear to be able to believe a thing and its opposite, as if they had never heard of the principle of contradiction which prevents us from believing that black is both black and white. And not only this, but crowd men are prepared to act immediately on the basis of belief so self-contradictory that a moment's reflection in ordinary life would be enough to convince them of that belief's absurdity. So, if Le Bon is right, then both versions of liberalism disappear in the crowd; utilitarianism and Spencerian social differentiation. If ordinary minds work according to Benthamite and Spencerian principles, then ordinary minds cannot be working in the crowd, hence the hypothesis of a new, group mind working according to principles of its own.

Looked at like that, there is no reason to suppose that the crowd, in the sense of the physically proximate group, is the only place where the workings of the group mind are to be found. Other kinds of groups, cabinets for instance, or colloquies of learned men, or juries, or widespread groups reading the same newspaper, might begin to think in crowd-like ways. All especially 'close' human groups, religious orders for instance, or armies, are likely to think like crowds, especially when these groups 'close ranks' in the mental sense. Le Bon no sooner extends the idea of the crowd beyond the crowd in the street than he begins to imply that all human groups are either crowds or are capable of thinking and acting like crowds. The theoretical problem is no longer one of distinguishing crowds from other, essentially different, human groups. Rather, what Le Bon does is to place all groups on a sliding scale, with some groups so high on it that they are reasonably safe from beginning to think and act like crowds, and some groups so low that their transforming themselves into crowds is a permanent danger. Le Bon wants us to see his sliding scale as an adjunct to the evolutionary ladder. 'Lower' means more primitive, savage, animal-like, regressive.

The breakthrough which Le Bon thinks he has made is to discover that all men are

671

potentially crowd men, no matter how this may be attenuated in particular political and social circumstances. Highly disciplined and hierarchical groups are, of course, less likely and perhaps in practice are never likely to become crowds, but Le Bon steadfastly refuses to divide human societies into 'the crowd' and 'the rest', barbarian men and civilised men, 'them' and 'us'. Le Bon realises that social categories are not fixed in the world after the Industrial and French Revolutions. Le Bon follows Tocqueville in seeing the modern world as 'individualistic', a world where rights are going to count much more than duties. Le Bon knows perfectly well that the exercise of individual rights renders all social categories fluid almost by definition. The passage of time is essential to Le Bon's way of looking at groups in a society. Society is not a collection of groups to be distinguished according to discrete types. Rather, what Le Bon does is to locate all groups on his sliding scale of crowd-likeliness with no group in principle excluded. The only real difference between groups is that some almost never become crowds, some are likely to become crowds only infrequently, and some are likely to act as crowds the whole time. Le Bon fits this view of human groups into a commonplace historical sociology of increasing individualism: as modern societies become more individualistic we can expect to see the crowd more frequently.

Le Bon rightly sees individualism and traditional social categories as antitheses. His crowd theory is a ghastly commentary on the French Revolutionary credo of Liberty, Equality and Fraternity. The Revolution's enemies from Burke onwards had always bewailed the possibility that social levelling could be taken so far that everyone would be reduced to an aesthetically dismal sameness. The beauty of social order would give way before the cry for equality; the angels would disappear back into the lump of marble. Spencerism rescued the world of individualism from the primitiveness of homogeneity by arguing that a world of free individualists would naturally differentiate itself. Liberal society would have its own spontaneously evolving natural order after all. Now along came Le Bon to spoil things for liberals by arguing that all social groups had a tendency, more or less strong, to become homogeneous crowds. All sense of individuality was lost in the crowd. It was in this sense that the crowd was 'primitive'. The crowd was a group with-out sub-groups, was 'of one mind', utterly lacking in differentiation. There was no social space between members of the crowd. The crowd closed ranks, its members touched each other, annihilating the ordinary distances which separated one man from another in every-day life, and annihilating the distance between the various social groups and classes which men were members of in their everyday, non-crowd selves. The future was bleak for those who didn't like the crowd and who believed with Le Bon that the modern era was the era of crowds.

Le Bon is obviously feeling his way towards something like a theory of crowd society, and we have come to be familiar with Le Bon's legacy as the 'theory of mass society'. Almost all the elements of the theory of mass society were there in Le Bon's *The Crowd* in 1895. Modern society had lost its way. Modern men no longer knew who they were and how they ought to live their lives. Whatever social order there was appeared to be fragile. Men no longer looked to their natural leaders and began to look round for leaders of their own whose claim to legitimacy would be very different from the claims of traditional elites.

The increasingly undifferentiated mass would look for the kinds of leaders which the masses had always been likely to find, Caesars popularly acclaimed by the crowd. The ancient categories of political thought once again became massively persuasive. All ancient oligarchs had feared the people, and, since Plato, oligarchs had been taught to watch out for the demagogue who would use crowd legitimacy as the means to a power so absolute that oligarchy would seem benign by comparison. Roman history gave the name of Caesarism to the crowd's leader. The Roman Empire came out of the Republic when the Republic had lost its way in the civil wars, Marius against Sulla, Pompey against Caesar, and out of that came Augustus, sole master of the known world. Caesarist leaders would come out of the atomism of modern societies. The crowd of individuals, all drearily the same, just could not wait to rid itself of its liberty by putting the sword into its sovereign's hands.

There is something heavily ironic in Le Bon's account of individualism, the individual and the crowd. The crowd achieves its equality literally in the sameness of the mentalities which go to make up the crowd. Individuals at the same time lose their individuality, everything which makes one man different from another. Individualistic society, properly understood, contains no individuals in the real sense at all. That this is a kind of Marxism in reverse needs no stressing. The Marxist idea of class society, as it applies to modern times, is also a denial of individuality. Class relations can never be relations between individuals because the laws which govern the development of bourgeois economies dictate that every buyer of labour has to deal with every seller of labour in the same way that every other buyer of labour has to deal with every other seller of labour. Capital is in this sense a *social* power, impersonal, and labour is a *social* product; every man's labour is worth the same, 'abstract' labour. The bourgeoisie's hymns to entrepreneurialism celebrate the supposed individualism of bourgeois society, but that is to miss bourgeois society's real nature. No doubt there are a few great 'captains of industry', but they lead great industrial armies, and armies are not notorious for encouraging individualism. Who knows the name of even one of Alexander's pike-men, or of a Napoleonic *soldat de première classe*? Factory production needs hands not bodies and souls, and one pair of hands is as good as another. The people that these hands are attached to are only distinguishable outside the factory. In the one thing that matters to them all, getting their living, they are the lowest common denominator of a class. Le Bon lived in fear of Marxism, and crowd theory added its own twist to Marxism's terrors for the bourgeoisie. The crowd was an agency for mass-producing barbarian robots outside the containing discipline of the factory system. The socialist crowd was likely to turn against the system which had produced it, returning society to that primitive communism which is appropriate only to a very early stage in the development of the human race.

The generaliser in Le Bon could not resist adding a final twist. If all human groups were potential crowds, then it followed that all men were potentially crowd men. Nobody, therefore, has any particular reason for feeling superior to his fellows. The idea that a society consists of the crowd and the elite cannot really survive Le Bon's argument. Ultimately, the perception that all men are crowd men derives from the theory of hypnotism. As soon as it was realised that everybody could be hypnotised, and that therefore hypnotisability was part of 'human nature', it began to dawn on social theorists that every-body was vulnerable to the leaders of crowds. There was an attempt to keep the ancient distinction between *us* and *them* alive by making a further distinction between those who could be 'deeply' hypnotised and those who could not. Being deeply hypnotised meant being put in such a state by the hypnotist that the hypnotic subject would follow the 'suggestions' absolutely and in all cases, no matter what the hypnotist suggested. Not being susceptible to deep hypnosis meant that the hypnotised subject retained an integral moral centre immune from hypnotic control. De-coded, what this meant was that some thinkers believed that the leader of the crowd could make the crowd do anything, literally anything, that he wanted the crowd to do, while other thinkers thought that there was some kind of psychological limit to the crowd's potential for depravity. It was possible that some members of the crowd, or some crowds, could not be pushed by leaders into the violation of deeply embedded ancestral taboos of which cannibalism was the archetype. Others were not so sure. Everybody could agree that eating people is wrong. Cannibalism was the last resort of human beings under stress so unbearable that everything that they owed to civilisation disappeared, a regression to a state of nature so basic that it was as if millenia of civilised life had never happened. All that was required to affirm the truth of this horrifying possibility was a single instance of crowd cannibalism to supplement widely believed tales (some of which turned out to be true) about shipwrecked sailors *in extremis* devouring cabin boys. There the matter rested, with no general agreement about the ultimate lengths to which the crowd could be made to go. The distinction between 'deep' hypnosis and other kinds of hypnosis was never much of a distinction when compared to what all crowd thinkers agreed about, which was that the crowd could descend the ladder of civilisation very rapidly. Perhaps the crowd would never actually hit rock bottom, but everybody seemed to agree that the crowd could get near enough rock bottom to put terror into everybody.

Crowds were also capable of collective acts of physical and moral heroism: People's Crusades, storming Bastilles, legendary cavalry charges, putting out fires, defending Paris against the Prussians, Garibaldi and his Thousand, and so on; but the fact that crowds performed these prodigies under the Le Bon Law of the Mental Unity of Crowds meant that these could not be acts of conscious virtue. Nothing had changed since Hobbes attributed the courage of the parliamentary armies in the Civil War to ignorance: the lower classes could be frightened by the sword and the pike, but they were too stupid to realise that musket-balls which they could not see could actually kill. (And perhaps nothing had changed since Plato argued that courage was a kind of knowledge because the true warrior knew what he was up against.) The moral qualities of crowds were not predictable. It was an article of faith among crowd theorists that the reasoning power of the crowd mind was negligible no matter what its moral qualities were. The standard of the crowd's intelligence was even lower than the intelligence of its stupidest member, and it was this stupidity which accounted for both the crowd's heroism and its barbarism. Which way the crowd went depended solely on its leaders. Crowds, like children and savages, were easily led, seeming to have no will of their own, and certainly no rational moral will.

Crowds came to be seen as being beyond good and evil in a Nietzschean sense. The crowd's good and evil were unconnected with rationality, and, by implication, good and evil were unconnected with rationality in a general sense because even supposedly rational men were potentially crowd men. Le Bon's own conviction that good and evil are a function of rationality adds a certain piquancy to what he has to say about the contingency of the moral qualities of the crowd and the mob. Rationality is what makes morality reliable, and rationality is now only possible in those minds which are sensible enough to keep their distance from the crowd and strong enough to walk with crowds and avoid the common touch. Rationality, in Le Bon's view of it, is like a doomed psychological Vendée, a holding operation against the future. Whichever way one looks at the future, politics is going to be demagogical in the Greek sense. Enervated, atomised crowd society cannot wait for its demagogues to appear from the outside; so it creates its own leaders. The crowd's deeply felt desire to turn itself into a mob is a standing invitation to mass hypnosis. The elite's only chance is to produce leaders of its own who can make the mob easier to live with. Being able permanently to control the mob, and to lead it in directions in which it does not itself want to go, is probably impossible, and it is silly to try. The mob's rude barbarian energy will win through in the end. Civilisation may therefore have to begin again.

There is no mistaking the apocalyptic flavour of crowd theory. Some political theorists called crowd theory 'imperialistic' because they could see it taking over the whole of the social sciences. Le Bon certainly had intellectually imperialistic ambitions when he spread the crowd category wide enough to include most human groups. There was, in fact, a publicly conducted debate between the crowd theorist Gabriel Tarde and the sociologist Emile Durkheim about the difference between crowd theory and sociology in general. The debate centred round Tarde's concept of 'imitation'. Crowd thinkers had always been interested in the massive uniformity of the crowd's behaviour. What was it at bottom, they asked, which accounted for the extraordinary unanimity and uniformity of the behaviour of crowds? Tarde said: imitation. Unanimity and uniformity must spread themselves through the crowd by imitation, a mechanism common to men and to animals. The tendency to mimesis was widely diffused throughout nature and it explained, for instance, how animals learned to behave from each other. Imitation required no intelligence at all, or, at the very least, it required no intelligence in the ordinary sense of the word. If mimesis required intelligence, and ants and wasps could do it, then it followed that what we call intelligence was so general in nature that it could not be used as the criterion for distinguishing men from animals. Biological science was making great strides in the understanding of the collective lives of animals and insects. 'Miracles' of nature, ants domesticating aphids, for instance, were no longer seen as miraculous but simply as other examples of intelligence working in nature. Human husbandry was in principle no different from insect husbandry. Most human intelligence probably worked in exactly the same way as an ant's intelligence worked when the ant domesticated his aphid. Human herdsman learned their trade by copying a dairy farmer and ants learned their trade by copying other ants.

Tarde was quick to generalise from examples of imitation to a general theory of imitation as the working principle of all social groups, including society itself. Tarde was a judge and criminologist by profession, and he was as struck as everybody else by 'copy-cat' crimes, epidemics of murder, for instance following wide newspaper reporting of famous or horrendous murder cases. Likewise, Durkheim's work on epidemics of suicide cried out for some kind of general explanation. Taking someone else's life, or taking one's own life, seemed to be the most serious acts that a human being could do, the most *individual*. Ordinary criminal law looked upon murder as the worst of crimes because the murderer was responsible for the worst thing he could do to a fellow-creature, and the greater the responsibility the greater the crime. Hence the law's concern with 'premeditation': murder was deliberate killing and therefore deserved the death penalty. But 'copy-cat' crimes and criminal statistics, which were beginning to be gathered in a systematic way, told a story which did not sit very easily with the idea of serious crime as premeditated and deliberate. The new idea of the crimewave seemed to suggest that some kind of imitation was at work, and everybody knew that imitation required no intelligence in the ordinary sense if insects could do it. In what sense, then, could those who committed crimes of imitation be held to be responsible for them in any rational way? Tarde was quick to point out that all collective crimes were probably the result of imitation in groups. Those born into a criminal milieu were likely to become criminals. Criminals working in criminal gangs were likely to commit grosser crimes than criminals working on their own, because of the regressive mechanisms at work in all human groups. The collective crimes of crowds were likely to be the worst of all, because regression to barbarism is likely to happen most quickly in the criminal mob. For 'criminal mob' substitute 'revolutionary crowd' and you end up with a neatly criminological version of conservative politics.

But not that conservative. Tarde added a perverse twist to his criminal crowd argument. Imitation worked elsewhere besides the criminal gang and the revolutionary mob. All social life can be explained in the terms of imitation.[1] If all group life, including the lives of whole societies, can be explained in the terms of imitation, then it follows that the principle upon which a society is based must also be the principle on which the crowd is based. Crowds are not really anti-social in the accepted sense at all. Tarde came to see the mob as a caricature of a society because in the mob all the ordinary social mechanisms of imitation are speeded up to a grotesque degree. The social bonds which may take centuries (or in the modern world years) to build up in a society appear as if by magic in the crowd. Tarde takes the crowd's unanimity and uniformity simply as a speeded-up case of ordinary group formation, not anti-social, but absurdly over-social. Tarde even had the temerity to extend the principle of over-sociality (though he doesn't call it that) to the criminal underworld and to crime in general. Far from being anti-social, criminals were *much too* social. They could not stop themselves imitating those immediately around them. Born criminals are those who are born into what we would now call a criminal sub-culture. Tarde pointed out that criminals take to lives of crime in much the same way that people take to any trade or profession. Everybody is, properly speaking, born into a sub-culture and is subject to its influences. People become judges in much the same way that they become criminals.

Tarde is the most relaxed of the crowd thinkers. Not for him the panic-stricken view that the crowd is everywhere and is about to gobble us all up. Crowds are simply special cases of what goes on in the process of the formation of social groups, and they are only so noticeable because what happens in a crowd happens so quickly. The antithesis mob/society is false. Tarde can even rescue a kind of pluralism out of crowd theory. All crowd thinkers were interested in the political effects of mass circulation newspapers because a leader speaking through a newspaper might be able to form a crowd off the streets. Mass circulation newspapers could make ordinary people part of a crowd in the comfort of their own homes. Tarde noticed the extraordinary growth of an explicitly political newspaper press in France towards the turn of the century. Every political group seemed to have a newspaper of its own. Tarde thought that this would create a plurality of crowds (he called them 'publics') rather than the single great crowd which all crowd theorists except him feared. Tarde argued that in modern society the crowd was *passé*; rival publics would emerge to confront each other through the solitary reading of newspapers. Newspapers domesticated the crowd by getting it off the streets. Only somebody close to social panic already could be frightened of the watered-down version of the crowd all quietly reading the papers at home.

CROWD THEORY AND THE FUTURE

Crowd theory as Le Bon summarised it made an impact on both the academic study of politics and the world of ordinary literacy. Le Bon's *The Crowd* seemed to probe an exposed cultural nerve in 1895. Plainly it was intended to be read as a very generalised attack on democracy and socialism. Le Bon exemplifies an explicitly modern kind of theorising through the microscope. What Le Bon does is to take at face value certain democratic and social democratic dogmas and then look carefully at a particular part of the world of politics to see whether what the microscope reveals to us is compatible with those dogmas. Democrats and socialists make certain assumptions about the world which are testable against the facts of political life. Le Bon looks at democracy in action, the people on the move in crowds, and generalises from this to a theory of all human groups.

Le Bon may be wrong, but the way he proceeds to build up his theory is easily recognisable as one of the cornerstone methods of the political science of the twentieth century. A good deal of modern political science begins with assumptions about how politics works and then tests those assumptions against the facts of political life. Le Bon does this with democracy. The ideas of 'the people' and 'popular sovereignty' had been cried up ever since the Fall of the Bastille. The modern age was always going to be the democratic age in some sense, but democracy was also always going to be a 'leap in the dark' because nobody really knew beforehand how it was going to work, though there were plenty of equally pessimistic and optimistic guesses. What Le Bon did, and the elite theorists who followed him, was to turn the microscope onto how the world of democratic politics actually functioned. If crowds were everywhere, then the crowds of voters in democratic elections (and the crowds of deputies in democratic assemblies) must be as irrational as crowds always were. In saying this Le Bon was trying to untie the ages-old connection democrats had made between the rights of man and reason. 'Let the people decide', let them exercise democratic rights, and rationality has a chance against vested interest and superstition. Institutions which had only the sanctity of centuries of languid self-seeking in the cave of high politics would never be able to withstand rational criticism in the daylight. Democracy was either going to be a feast of collective reason or it was going to be the political condition in which rational political argument thrived. From Tom Paine to J.S. Mill, thinkers in the least friendly towards democracy had looked at democratic politics as a civil education for the electorate, a modern echo of Aristotle's contention that politics was good for people. Now, Le Bon seemed to be saying that democratic politics in general was crowd politics, and that elections were 'psychological orgies', crowd-feasts of unreason, the demagogue's paradise and the ad-man's dream.

Le Bon thinks that in the long run there is probably no way out of the mess. Democracy is here to stay. Le Bon offers two kinds of qualified hope. The one is obvious: elite politicians can use Le Bon's own crash course in crowd psychology to divert the crowd from its de-civilising mission. No doubt this is a holding operation against an uncertain future, but *faute de mieux*. The other hope which Le Bon implicitly offers is the germ of a distinction, never fully worked out, between two different forms of crowd politics. The electoral crowd and the Tardean public are not, on the face of it, really the same as mobs in the street. 'Mob psychology' may be at work during elections, but for all that democratic elections are meant to be very orderly affairs and they frequently are. The perception then arises that peaceful electoral politics is really an alternative to the direct-action mob and not a version of it. Le Bon moves the anti-democratic focus away from democracy's formal arrangements like elections and away from its formal institutions like parties. What really interests him is the possibility that the peaceful, if irrational, electoral crowd might turn itself into a real mob. Le Bon has begun to realise that the rituals and paraphernalia of democratic politics actually make the crowd less dangerous. Irrational the electoral crowd certainly is, but democratic institutions and processes can effectively tame it. Democratic politics cannot make the crowd rational. All the pressures of democratic politics work in the opposite direction, the blind leading the blind. Le Bon looks beyond the democratic formalities to what has become known in the twentieth century as the 'politics of culture'. Like Nietzsche, Le Bon believes that the barbarians are on this side of the wall, inside trying to get out, not outside trying to get in. Societies in the future will have a democratic 'feel' to them. The possessors of high culture will come to feel increasingly threatened, and the game of democratic politics itself will be under continuous threat from the real, direct-action crowd. The maverick Georges Sorel read Le Bon with great attention, and he found there the perfect recipe for real class war, as distinct from the anodyne shadow-boxing of electoral politics. With this perception, that one of crowd democracy's targets should be the empty formalities of democratic politics, fascist politics finds its way onto the political agenda in liberal democratic states.

It is very tempting to read Le Bon's *The Crowd* as a prediction of fascism. Mussolini, for instance, professed to admire the work. What makes Le Bon forward-looking, despite his rather timid conservative political opinions, is his idea of a whole society as a crowd, and of the function of the mob in crowd society. Crowd society (the 'mass society' of twentieth-century political sociology) is passive; when it is activated it produces the mob. The crowd gets a good deal of contempt poured on it in the history of political thought, and it is poured from opposite directions. At first, the crowd and the mob are interchangeable terms. All crowds are really mobs, threatening social order and the civilisation which social order makes possible. That had been the conventional view of the crowd since Plato. The arrival of mass urban society, and with it modern individualism, began to make it possible to see a whole society as a faceless crowd (modern factory production needs hands, not faces, and in mass democracy faces are hidden in the polling booth). The crowd shifts from being active to being passive, not culture-hostile but culture-indifferent, not barbarians coming over the walls, but already inside the city. The faceless crowd is the mob's permanent incubatory culture. The politics of the mob, or the gang, or the hunting-pack becomes a distinct future possibility.

An attitude to democracy changes here. While democracy was once thought about as the crowd in action, psychic mobbery, there now came a new twist. Experience of democratic politics made a new assessment of democracy necessary around 1900. Mass electoral politics was certainly irrational, but it was also peaceful. The people might occasionally riot for the right to vote, but they seemed perfectly capable of exercising that right peacefully once they had it. In time, people would begin to wonder what all the fuss about the right to vote had once been about. The right to vote would come to be seen as a very minor, rather infrequently exercised right, civically modest because votes only counted in aggregates, not singly. Voting would become just another item on life's shopping list, and it would be unlikely to come very near the top. What was now worrying was that the facelessness of crowd society would join up with the faceless mass of democracy, so that the crowd and the mob could come to be seen as alternatives. Fascism's attack on the parliamentary republic in continental Europe was importantly based on a keen perception that the crowd and the mob were alternatives. The faceless electoral crowd produced governments without energy. There seemed to be a connection between the moral enervation of crowd society and the lack of drive and direction of democratically elected governments. The fascist parties were organised mobs, fond of childish display, uniforms, marching, secret signs, braggadocio, medals, holidays, all that is dear to the heart of the healthy schoolboy and the unhealthy adult. Youth was opposed to age, vitality to decadence, action to thought. Societies had to wake up from their habitual sloth, get moving again. The mob would take over the streets again, and, in the institutionalised form of the party, would do it permanently. The crowd would look on, and the party would give them a standing invitation: become one of us, and together we will storm the commanding heights of political power; today the streets, tomorrow the cabinet chamber.

This could be the prelude to some very nasty mob politics. The crowd of crowd society was here to stay. What, then, was to be the political position of those who, like Le Bon, disliked both the crowd and the mob? Those with any feeling at all for the liberal tradition would settle for crowd politics over mob politics every time. The electoral crowd was at least peaceful. Mass political parties of the left, whose leaders were likely to be smothered in the parliamentary embrace, were preferable to the johnny-come-lately leaders of organised extra-parliamentary mobs. Institutionalising the crowd through its democratic rights seemed the obvious way to bring it 'into the system'.

That was before the Great War and the Bolshevik Revolution. After, the mob parties could play a cleverer game. There had always been a tendency to regard crowd politics as a politics of the left, as insurrectionary and therefore potentially revolutionary. The French

Revolution had begun with a few riots in Paris, and look where that led. All crowd theory before the Great War implicitly assumes that crowd politics will be politics of the lower orders with socialistic or anarchistic tendencies. Hence Le Bon's Spencerian insistence on the undifferentiated primitiveness of communism. The crowd was pretty far down on the evolutionary scale and its political aims were too. For all his insistence that the crowd is everybody, Le Bon knew his bourgeois audience well enough to know what really frightened them. It was the great unwashed, them 'out there' somewhere, the people in Zola's *Germinal*, not *us*, who were the real threats to civilisation. After the war and the Bolshevik Revolution it became possible to revise the earlier picture. The imagined Bolshevik threat to every country west of Brest-Litovsk began to make people begin to look more closely at the newly forming fascist parties. Mob parties they might be, but anti-communist they undoubtedly were. The Bolsheviks were telling everybody that the class-conscious masses were everywhere waiting for the signal for revolution. The next great economic crisis would see the Bolsheviks taking over the whole of Europe. The red scare frightened enough people for them to see the rivalry between communists and fascists as alternative ways of getting at the crowd. Left-wing class-consciousness and right-wing hyped-up nationalism were simply two different bids for leadership of the crowd. There was now not one form of mob politics but two, and if these were the only alternatives on offer, then it was not very obvious which one to choose.

Whichever way you looked at it, the republic based on the widespread exercise of democratic rights came off rather badly, especially in continental Europe. The democratic republic could easily come to be seen as the ideal locus of mob politics. If a political choice had to be made which was to be neither left nor right, then the basis for that choice would be a lingering liberalism shorn of most of its optimistic assumptions. The democratic republic would come to be seen not as a solution to problems but as the only viable alternative to the class-war party or the fascist party. Out of this stoical and disenchanted liberalism came the idea of the democratic republic as a holding operation until better times. Enlightenment's confidence in liberalism would have to be massively toned down, to be replaced by a modest hope for the survival of the public decencies. Human equality was out. No one could doubt, after elite theory, that the democratic republic was oligarchical. All it had going for it was a plurality of possible leaders, and the hope that leadership would be shared. The fascist parties were already putting a very Le Bonish idea of political leadership into operation. The mob leader, with his party as an institutionalised mob whose first argument was violence, was the coming political style. Even Marxists began to wonder why the fascists should have all the good leadership tunes. One of the reasons for the cult of personality in the communist world was the realisation that big, up-front leaders had become the order of the day.

By 1900, crowd theory was enough of a publicly recognised genre for it to concern itself with the specialised problem of the leadership of crowds, where 'crowds' meant human groups in general. This would become a special concern in the 1920s for obvious reasons. The end of the Great War saw the end of several European dynasties. Romanovs, Habsburgs and Hohenzollerns disappeared from their thrones but did not necessarily disappear from the psychic lives of their peoples. It could be a shock suddenly to find oneself emperorless, even if that emperor had had no clothes. Who was going to fill the gaps left by the departing monarchs? It had been long recognised that there was an intimate psychological connection between monarchy and people, emperor and crowd. People always seemed to be willing to stand for hours on a crowded street to catch a glimpse of the back of a crowned head. Could all that psychic emotion be transferred to new kinds of leaders, fascist leaders for instance? Was there a general theory of the leadership of men in groups which would fit all the cases, old and new? What does not seem to have been doubted is that such a theory, if it was not to be Marxist, would have to be a theory derived from all the psychologising of politics which had gone on before 1914. Le Bon-type crowd theory was the obvious place to begin.

NOTES ON SOURCES

Crowd theory has been much neglected until recently. Le Bon's *The Crowd: A Study of the Popular Mind*, has recently been republished in English in Dunwoody, Georgia (n.d.), and so has his *The Psychology of Socialism*, ed. J.L. Stanley (1982). R.A. Nye, *The Origins of Crowd Psychology* (1975), and S. Barrows, *Distorting Mirrors: Images of the Crowd in Late Nineteenth Century France* (1981), are recommended. J.S. McClelland, *The Crowd and the Mob: from Plato to Canetti* (1989), is an extended historical treatment of crowd theory.

29

THE LEADER AND HIS CROWD

Sigmund Freud's *Group Psychology and the Analysis
of the Ego* (1921)

SIGMUND FREUD

Freud was born in 1856, in Freiberg, Moravia, into a large, bourgeois, Jewish family. The Freuds soon moved to Vienna, and it is with that city that Sigmund Freud's name has always been linked. His parents were ambitious for their children, and Freud, as his mother's favourite son, more than fulfilled her hopes. Freud was a promising boy, but, despite an early and well-developed desire for fame, he was no infant prodigy. Freud's early career as a doctor and man of science was a model of conventional scientific rectitude. When Freud began recognisably psychoanalytic work in the early 1890s he was already approaching middle age, and he had by that time established himself, in the Berggasse, in Vienna, as a family man building up a medical practice well within the accepted borders of contemporary medicine. The great founding text of psychoanalysis, *The Interpretation of Dreams*, was not published until 1900, and at first it sold depressingly slowly. None the less, Freud had already begun to gather around him those kindred spirits, chief among whom was Carl Gustav Jung, who were to help him to make his way in the medical and scientific worlds. Freud always thought that the initial resistances to psychoanalysis were attributable to anti-Semitism. This in part caused him to make the Christian Jung the Crown Prince of the psychoanalytic movement in order to facilitate the breakthrough of psychoanalysis into the hostile world of Christian culture. Jung's 'defection' therefore hit Freud particularly hard.

Fame came to Freud in the 1920s, nearly thirty years after he had begun his psychoanalytic work. However, fame came at the same time as Freud's cancer of the jaw was first diagnosed, and also at a time of further defections from the ranks of orthodox psychoanalysis. Life's troubles had no appreciable effect on the awesome intellectual output of this extraordinary old man in a hurry. These were the years in which Freud turned psychoanalysis into some-thing like a worldview, though, looking back, we can see how relatively modest his general claims for psychoanalysis actually were.

Freud's later years were lived out in physical pain, and, towards the end, in perilous political circumstances. Austrian Jews had always had good, if qualified, reasons for being grateful to the Habsburg monarchy, which had always tried to keep the lid on anti-Semitic nationalism, but the new Austrian republic might not prove to be so robust. At the very least, the Austrian republic was always going to be vulnerable to events in the Weimar republic across the border in Germany. *Anschluss*, and the Nazification of Austria, was the result. Freud and his immediate family escaped to London at the last minute. Freud died in Hampstead in 1939, in the house which was later to become the Freud Museum.

When Carlyle was establishing his reputation as Europe's premier grumbler he predicted that heroes were going to have a thin time in the modern age. Napoleon was the last of the would-be heroes, but there had always been something hollow and quackish about him. Industrialisation, urbanisation, utilitarianism, everything which made the modern age modern was stacked up against heroes. Carlyle liked his heroes to be strong, silent, and peasants by origin if possible, and these seemed to be unlikely to appear in the conditions which prevailed in the modern world. Such modern leaders as there were had got too close to the masses, loved the plaudits of the crowd too much, and always seemed to allow themselves to be brought down to the crowd's own level. Carlyle might have been right (and granted his own definitions he could hardly have been wrong), but that did not stop the political and social theory of the second half of the nineteenth century being interested in the exact psychological mechanisms of leadership.

There is nothing particularly surprising in this. It was partly due to Napoleon himself. By any standards, ancient or modern, he was a remarkable leader of men, and historians were to spend the whole of the nineteenth century (and much of the twentieth) wondering what the secret of his leadership was. Such was the interest in Napoleon's career that he eventually became a hero for everyone. The Europe of dynastic absolutism had always seen him as a Jacobin at large who founded an upstart dynasty, a dangerous parody of what they were. This made Napoleon a hero of the Revolution, the revolution made flesh and dwelling among men. To conservatives, endlessly grateful for the whiff of grapeshot, he was a hero of order. Napoleon's success in making France and then the whole of Europe feel the purchase of his single will made him a romantic hero, while those of a classical turn of mind could admire him for his attempt to re-establish universal empire in Europe and the East. The military hero could also masquerade as a kind of democratic hero when his reign began to be compared to the monarchical and oligarchic regimes in France after Waterloo, and out of this came the peculiar combination of military dictatorship and the plebiscite of the Second Empire. A liberal empire followed that, and there was even a tendency to convert Napoleon III into a socialist hero because of his Saint Simonian banker friends.

This was an extremely diffuse leadership legacy. What nobody denied (not even Carlyle) was that Napoleon was a new kind of leader, and Hegelian phrases about him, like 'the World-Soul on horseback', didn't really go very far towards explaining Napoleon's extraordinary career. The history of political thought did not really help. Plato had been interested in why tyrants want power, but his was a tale of steady degeneration associated with secret and monstrous lusts, whereas, as Nietzsche says, Napoleon, like Caesar, was the most self-controlled man of his day. Machiavelli had been interested in the truly outstanding man, part of whose character was wanting to rule a state and lead it on to greatness, but this seems to Machiavelli to be part of human nature as it applies to princes and so requires no special explanation (unless we count some fuzzy ideas about the man on whom Fortune smiles). Perhaps Hobbes spoke for a consensus of the famous political theorists in regarding political power as just another human good which anyone would be a fool not to grab if it came his way.

Napoleon's career rekindled the ancient interest in Caesarism. It had been one of the stock commonplaces in Greece and at Rome that what oligarchs had to fear most was a demagogic partnership between a successful aristocratic general and the people, whom he would lead against the rich and well-born. The interesting questions, about what made Caesars tick, and about what the secret of their success was, had since remained largely unanswered. It was all very well to call any leaders 'little Caesars', or the leaders of crowds 'kings for a day', but that was no explanation at all. Plainly, a special psychology was at work here, but it was a matter about which the world of official psychology was uniformly silent. This explains the almost universal enthusiasm for hypnotism as an explanation of the leader-led phenomenon in the cases of crowds. Questions about how generalisable the hypnotic model was to cases of leadership other than crowd leadership had been raised long before Le Bon's *The Crowd* proclaimed to the whole world that all human groups were crowds at heart. The idea began to dawn on political and social thinkers that the example of the crowd leader might be the paradigm example of all leadership. Ordinary leadership came to be seen as an institutionalised form of the leadership of crowds, more predictable and longer-lasting, no doubt, but not different in principle from leaders in the street.

That was just about the position that crowd theory had got to when Freud began to take an interest in it. Crowd leadership, operating according to the psychological mechanisms of hypnotism, was coming into its own as a very generalisable theory of leadership. The line between leadership and rule was not an easy one to draw. 'Leadership' had an 'on-the-move' ring to it, while 'rule' suggested institutionalised routine, but beyond that it was not very obvious what the difference was. Crowd theory could easily become the explanatory theory of those same institutions of established authority which the crowd seemed to have been threatening since the Bastille. Theoretically, the crowd had come a very long way since the French Revolution. The crowd was taking over every political and theoretical space. The crowd was everywhere, in society and in the sociological literature. Nowhere was safe. This was just what Le Bon had wanted. His intention had been nothing less than sensational: look anywhere you like, in social practice or social theory, and you will find the crowd.

PROBLEMS WITH HYPNOTISM

It is a measure of how accepted as a social and political theory crowd theory had become by 1921 that Freud, who was to become one of the intellectual giants of the twentieth century, should have been eager to do a little spadework in one of its specialised corners. Freud began with the special problem of the mechanisms which bound the led to their leaders, but he eventually came up with a set of answers to problems of crowd theory which turned that theory upside down. Freud's intellectual procedure was eccentric. He began at the end of crowd theory and then worked his way back to its explanatory beginnings.

Crowd theory thought it was founded on the solid base of hypnotic theory. Freud began from the bond which everybody agreed existed between leaders and led and began to ask questions about what that bond actually consisted of. Psychoanalysis, though still uncertain of itself in 1921, had long ago discovered love. Love binds everything together in the world, so why should this not be true of the closeness between leaders and followers? Freud adds a characteristic twist to this psychoanalytic banality. Why not begin with highly institu-tionalised groups, like churches and armies, rather than with crowds as they are usually thought of? Previous crowd theory had begun with the crowd in the street and generalised from there to other, less 'crowd-like', groups. Freud decides to try his theoretical fortunes the other way round. He begins with highly formal groups like churches and armies, and it is only when he thinks he has sorted out the theoretical problems of the formal groups that he turns to informal crowds, and the procedures produce some surprising results. Established institutional groups turn out for Freud to be 'perfectly formed' crowds, what all crowds would be if they could. By extension, established authority patterns are not to be seen as being the opposite of the spontaneous and temporary authority of the leaders of crowds. On the contrary, crowd leadership turns out to share all the characteristics of established political leadership except its permanence. The psychological mechanisms at work which bind the crowd to its leaders are exactly the same mechanisms which work to keep any society's established leadership patterns in being.

This way of looking at the psychological basis of authority did not square easily with the hypnotic model of crowd leadership as that model had traditionally been used. The hypnotic model's plausibility depended largely on the closeness of the leader to his followers. Hypnotism never quite outlived its associations with the music hall. Critics of the hypnotic model of crowd leadership never failed to point to a certain theatricality about hypnotism. Hypnotism had more to live down than its origins as a music hall act. It had always been easy to extend the relationship between the hypnotiser and the hypnotised subject on stage to include the audience. Either the hypnotist could in some sense be said to create a hypnotic relationship between himself and the entire audience in the theatre, or it could be said that any performer could 'electrify', or 'magnetise', or hypnotise an audience. Whichever way it was looked at, there seemed to be a necessity for physical proximity between hypnotiser and hypnotised, and this necessity transferred itself easily to the hypnotic model of crowd leadership. The leader haranguing the crowd was just another case of successful performance, street theatre in the most precise sense. The more that sense of direct communication between performer and audience was diluted, the less crowd-like the relationship between leaders and led became. So in the crowd theory tradition as Freud received it, authority became less crowd-like with the distance between that authority and those over whom that authority was exercised. The idea of 'distance' between rulers and ruled is no more than the idea of routine and habit. Authority is obeyed when authority is not present or visible, or is there only in the forms of its rules and its servants. Rulership is no longer big magic; being ruled becomes just another reflex in the automatic life of a society.

There is an implicit view in the received crowd theory tradition of what successful and acceptable authority should be like. Authority will be 'internalised'. Each citizen or subject will carry an internal policeman around with him in his own head. This internalised authority figure will do all the authority monitoring that is necessary, so that the person whose head the internal policeman inhabits will never really have to do any thinking about authority at all. Nineteenth-century sociology had discovered the idea of socialisation very early, and one of the reasons sociology went looking for the mechanisms of socialisation was a certain conservative distaste for the rationalist social theory of the Enlightenment, especially social contract theory. Ideas like social contract were supposed to have been responsible for the French Revolution because they encouraged the view that rational argument to join a society was the only way that a society could become really viable. Nineteenth-century sociology set out to teach that the socialising agencies of society worked perfectly well without much rational tinkering with them, and certainly without any rational choice on the part of those upon whom socialising agencies worked. Family, class and Church were enough to make men well-adjusted subjects of a state, and these agencies of socialisation even seemed to work best when the people paid no particular attention to them. In this sense, patterns of authority arose and were sustained un- consciously in a society. They were not the product of rational reflection, and their legitimacy arose from the fact that they worked and not from the fact that they had been chosen by those who lived under them. No doubt this was a very wide use of the idea of the unconscious because it could be stretched to include almost everything that went on in the day-to-day life of a society, but it was a perfectly justified riposte to those nineteenth- century followers of Enlightenment who kept on believing that there would always be something fundamentally wrong with social life until it was refounded on the basis of freely chosen rational principles.

The great thing about socialisation theory was that it showed that people were inducted automatically into a society. Very little direct ruling by policemen and courts was necessary. The state of course still needed the threat of legitimate violence as a last resort in trouble- some times, but the fundamental cause of social and political order was the set of unconsciously learned norms and values which every socialised member of a society carried around with him inside his own head, and the less he thought about them the better they worked.

It was this set of norms and values which seemed temporarily to disappear in the regressively barbarous life of crowds. Members of crowds were just as automatically obedient to crowd leaders as men ordinarily were to authority in everyday society, but the behaviour which resulted from the obedience of men in crowds appeared to be exactly the reverse of ordinary behaviour. The primitiveness of crowd behaviour provided the clue to what was really going on in the crowd. There must exist in everyman a psychological inheritance from ancestors much more ancient than their immediate social predecessors. This pointed unmistakably in the age of Darwinian evolutionism to savages and to animals. The battle between settled patterns of law and order, on the one hand, and violence and social upheaval, on the other, could easily be seen, therefore, as a battle between two uncon- scious minds. The civilised mind was the mind socialised by the world which immediately surrounded it, while the uncivilised mind derived its content from a time when living beings could hardly be said to have been socialised at all. It followed from this that there must be the greatest possible difference between the authority of the powers-that-be and the authority of the temporary kings who appeared from nowhere to command the crowd. The one was the guarantor of 'civilisation as we know it', while the other threatened a return to a state of things before civilisation had even been heard of.

When Freud began to write *Group Psychology and the Analysis of the Ego* (1921), he was able to treat crowd theory as an established body of knowledge with half a century's intellectual pedigree. Crowd theory was complete enough for Freud to see himself as working on one of its special problems, the theory of leadership. Despite previous crowd theorists' insistence that a crowd without a leader was a contradiction in terms, the theory of leadership had never advanced much beyond the hypnotic model. The susceptibility to be hypnotised seemed to be a fundamental fact about human mental life. Some people were easier to hypnotise than others, though no satisfactory explanation for this was ever produced, but hypnotisability was a universal fact or a theoretical dead-end.

Two things made the hypnotic model of crowd leadership unsatisfactory, both of them very general. The first had to do with the very general crying up of leaders. There was a good deal of rather loose talk about the iron will and eagle eyes of crowd leaders, who were the spellbinders of the people. These were plainly exceptional men, comparable either to the great hypnotists like Charcot or Bernheim, or to the great leaders of history like Caesar or Napoleon. The theoretical problem arose when crowd theorists tried to explain the other form of bonding which exists in the crowd, the bonding between members of the crowd. All crowd thinkers had remarked on the double tie which existed in the crowd. Members of crowds did what their leaders wanted them to do while at the same time they were also very susceptible to suggestions communicated to them by other members of the crowd. It was the combination of these two bonds which explained the often-observed unanimity of crowds. The quickness with which an idea could spread through the crowd was explained in the usual way by the suggestibility of people in crowds: they were suggestible to the commands of leaders and they were suggestible to the behaviour of other members of the crowd. Suggestion is really only another word for hypnotism, and that is where the theoretical problem lay. Members of crowds seemed to be just as susceptible to other members of the crowd as they were to crowd leaders. What, then, made the leaders of crowds so special? Why was it necessary to cry up the leaders of crowds when what the leader did to the crowd was not all that different from what the members of the crowd were able to do to each other? Everybody, leaders and led, more or less became hypnotisers. The hypnotic mechanism explained the bond between leaders and followers and between the followers themselves, but it did so at the price of appearing to diminish the significance of the leader-led relationship which all theorists thought was the most remarkable feature of crowds. The suggestibility of members of the crowd to each other really made leaders redundant, or reduced them to the status of the person who thought of something first but who was not responsible for the spread of the idea through the whole crowd. On this account of the matter, almost anybody could be a leader of crowds. All he would have to do was to communicate an idea to the man next to him and the renowned quickness and unanimity of the crowd would do the rest. A special theory of leadership was not really necessary, and this despite the fact that, since Le Bon at least, crowd theory had been moving inexorably towards the theory of leadership.

Hypnotism was plainly being used to explain too much, and it was also easy to forget that hypnotism itself had yet to be explained. Hypnotism obviously worked, but to say that susceptibility to hypnotic suggestion was simply a fact of human nature went no further than saying that hypnotism worked because people were hypnotisable, and that was the barest of tautologies and not an explanation at all. Freud may have suspected from the beginning that the real theoretical problem was hypnotism itself, but he did not tackle the problem of hypnotism direct. Rather, he chose to construct a theory of all group formation in the terms of the psychoanalytic theory of libido, and then almost as an afterthought he applied his group theory to explain hypnotism as just a special case of group formation, a group of two.

THE LIBIDINAL THEORY OF GROUPS

In general, psychoanalytic theory had one huge advantage over rival psychological theories when it came to explaining the nature of groups. Other thinkers in the crowd tradition had been instinctive utilitarians who believed that rational human self-interest was the basic psychological and moral fact about human individuals. This theoretical individualism made the phenomenon of psychological groups much more puzzling than it need have been because the unanimity of men in groups and their self-sacrificing heroism did not fit at all well with the egotistical hedonism of everyday life. The leap from selfishness to selflessness which crowd formation entailed could seem very long indeed for thinkers who began from the premise of individual autonomy and went on from there to try to explain the mystery of how individuals in a crowd came to be prepared to sacrifice that autonomy by merging it into some kind of group mind. As Freud points out in *Group Psychology*, the distinction between individual and group psychology is not a very real one from the psychoanalytic point of view. An old fashioned liberal himself, Freud does not seem to have shared nineteenth-century liberalism's illusions about individuality, and psychoanlysis, with its emphasis on the very early development of the Oedipus complex within the family, does not square easily with an original, atomistic individualism. Psychoanalysis does, of course, contain an account of the development of the personality in relation to parents and siblings, and later in relation to the other groups of which one is a member – race, class, religion, profession and so on. All psychoanalytic theory is in this sense social theory.

The particular force that psychoanalysis gives to the social determinants of personality and behaviour means that Freud can begin to see the problems of group psychology in a way which is radically different from the way they were traditionally conceived. Freud's individuals are social long before they can have an impact on the world outside the family. Socialised individuals confront the social world to be moulded by it, the very antithesis of Hobbesian individuals waiting for the world of other men to make them social in the first place. Freud shares with Hobbes the view that there is something both social and anti-social about all of us, but he does not have the problem, shared by all methodological individualists, of having to find a special explanation to bridge the gap between the two. Given Freud's view, there is no reason why social consciousness should not in some sense precede individual consciousness, and Freud does in fact end up by believing that group consciousness is the norm and that true psychological individualism is very rare and is in most cases highly undesirable.

Freud was originally attracted to crowd theory of the Le Bon type by its insistence on the part played in the group mind by the unconscious. References to the unconscious in work like Le Bon's tended to play up the mysteriousness of unconscious psychological forces. Hypnotism undoubtedly brought unconscious forces into play, but the unconscious was bound to be a matter of mystery while hypnotism itself remained unexplained. The unconscious before Freud was so mysterious because there was no real theoretical agreement about how the unconscious mind 'got there'. If there was an implicit theoretical consensus about the unconscious mind, it was that the unconscious was a permanent sub-stratum which existed in everybody. It probably consisted of instincts, or forgotten memories, things inherited from the past of a people, or a race, or from parents, or from animal ancestors. There was also a tendency to regard the unconscious as fixed, like dangers lurking under the sea, unknown, uncharted, and probably unknowable. By contrast, psychoanalysis had developed its own theory of the dynamic unconscious, the terms of which were fairly settled when Freud wrote his *Group Psychology*.

Freud's *dynamic* unconscious is not fixed. It is an unconscious which is more or less successfully repressed and which continually presses its almost always unwelcome attentions upon consciousness. Not everything which is unconscious is repressed, because there is such a thing as ordinary forgetting and remembering, but the unconscious repressed is the cornerstone of the Freudian theory of the unconscious. The basic component of the Freudian unconscious is the repressed drive or wish. These repressed wishes are denied access to consciousness by an inner censorship which develops through the famous Oedipus complex. These denied wishes or drives are mainly sexual for Freud, or they derive from sexuality. A very young child is indiscriminate in its sexuality. The strongest wish of the boy-child is the desire to possess his mother. The father's sexual possession of the mother makes him and his son deadly rivals in a struggle for the mother, a struggle which the father, in the nature of things, must win. Sons are forced to accept their hated fathers' ban on incest, but the enmity lives on. Sons also have that love for their fathers to which ordinary experience bears witness. The relationship of all children to parents is in this special sense ambivalent. The boy-child therefore feels guilt at the fact that he hated his father as well as loving him, and this feeling of ambivalence must be strongest at the time when the son is forced to accept the father's ban on incest, because this is the time when the son felt really murderous towards his rival in love. This internalised feeling of guilt therefore associates itself with the prohibition on incest, and so there begins the development of a conscience which thereafter denies the son's incestuous wishes access to consciousness.

This prohibition against incest is only the first of a whole series of prohibitions which individuals are obliged to internalise in the course of their socialisation into the world of adult social living, but it remains the prototype of all such internalisations. The prohibiting mechanisms of conscience are never entirely successful. Most individuals come to acquiesce in the sexual and other rules of the societies in which they live (though some individuals become neurotic casualties), but the repressed drives never 'go away'. They continue trying to shove their way past the internal censorship and to take ordinary consciousness by storm. Freud's metaphor is unremittingly dynamic. Drives, sexual energy, repression, libidinal pushing and shoving, are the stuff of the mechanical vocabulary of psychoanalysis. This 'economics of libido', of demand seeking supply, of market forces at work as gratification lies in wait for desire, lets a particularly nineteenth-century version of Newtonian mechanics into the unconscious to bring it under theoretical control. For Freud, the unconscious is no longer romantic, or even mysterious; it becomes as drearily predictable as any other mechanical system once the general laws of its functioning have been worked out. The unconscious repressed does try to make things difficult for its own internal censoring conscience (and for the dismal scientist whose job it is to understand its workings). The unconscious repressed is devious. As in dreams, it writes its messages to consciousness in codes which can reach considerable levels of sophistication; sometimes the unconscious repressed resorts to a kind of psychic invisible ink, but these are no more than childish tricks which in principle can always be found out. Unlike previous ideas of it, the Freudian unconscious is a *system*, and, like all systems, its workings can always be puzzled out.

As it works in the family group, the unconscious plays a particularly murderous game, and the game is complex. The family is not the simple building block out of which more complex social structures are made. In the Freudian picture of normal family life we find an erotic model which is already complicated enough to form more than just the basis of a theory of all groups. The family is a group held together by erotic bonds which are sometimes contradictory (ambivalence) yet at the same time strong enough to make the family 'almost indestructible'. Crowd theorists had always been struck by the strength of the ties which bound the leaders to the led, and the led to each other, but crowd theorists before Freud had never really been able to make up their minds whether the psychology of the crowd was simpler or more complex than the ordinary psychology of individuals. Freud avoids that difficulty because his individuals have already been through a tough family course in individual psychology before they get near those larger human groups which are the subject of social and political theory. Psychoanalysis shows above everything else that it is Eros which holds the family together, and the crowd, or, as Freud prefers to call it, the psychological group, is obviously held together by a power of some kind: 'to what power could this feat be better ascribed than to Eros, which holds everything together in the world?' If an individual chooses to give up his distinctness and desires to be in harmony with others, perhaps he does it '*ihnen zu Liebe*' (for love of them, for their sake). The Freudian theory of the family has already prepared us, though, for the now obvious expectation that a theory of psychological groups based on Eros will be far from simple. Eros is not clever, but he is devious.

The first groups on which Freud tries out his erotic hypothesis are churches and armies, 'artificial' groups, not natural groups like the crowd. (Freud thought of himself as breaking new ground here because, despite knowing the crowd literature, he always exaggerated the extent to which previous crowd theorists concerned themselves with 'natural' groups, chance crowds, and not with lasting, 'artificial', that is institutionalised, groups.) Formal constraints to prevent disintegration exist in churches and armies, but Freud thinks that these formalised constraints explain only very inadequately why it is that these groups are famous for their cohesion. He rather suspects that it is the illusion that a leader, Christ or a commander-in-chief, loves every member of the group equally which explains the cohesion of churches and armies. The commander of a subordinate group in an army functions as a kind of elder brother, a father-substitute for the commander-in-chief: every captain is supposed to love every soldier in his company equally, and the same is supposed to be true of every sergeant and his section. In the highly organised formal group, the members are bound by a double emotional tie: to leaders and to the other members of the group. These ties taken together easily explain the 'alteration and limitation' of individual personality which crowd theorists had always remarked on.

It is not until Freud begins to look into the question of which of these two ties is the stronger that we begin to realise how original the thrust of Freud's argument about groups is. Freud wants to argue that the 'artificial' group, with its highly formalised leadership structure, is more 'complete', in the sense of being more 'primitive', than the crowd which forms in the street and has a leader only for a day. The crowd in the ordinary sense of the word is a less complete formal group, and not the other way round. The highly structured group is the original of all groups, the group in its most primitive form. The highly structured group is not an 'evolved' group, therefore it is not more advanced and more civilised. Quite the reverse. Crowds in the ordinary sense of the word are simply pale copies of the most primitive of all groups, those with highly authoritarian and lasting leadership structures.

In fact, Freud takes two different but complementary routes to the problem of the nature of authority in groups: the first through the psychological development of individuals, and the second through a highly speculative evolutionary anthropology. Freud began his scientific career as a biologist, and this was a mind formed when every science had to do more than nod in the direction of Darwinism. It was a commonplace of evolutionary biology that phylogeny recapitulates ontogeny, which is jargon for saying that the history of the race goes though the same series of developmental stages as the history of the individual. At its crudest, it means that the collective life of the species *homo sapiens* was 'childish' in the beginning and only later became 'mature', just as the human individual begins in childhood and develops towards adult sophistication. Every human being in this sense recapitulates the life of the species, from the 'untrained dawn of the world' to the highly developed and civilised societies in which most of us now live. Freud takes both routes to the theory of groups by constructing a theory of individual psychology as it applies to group formation and a theory of the development of the psychic life of the human species. These two stories are not meant to be taken separately; rather, each version of the story is meant to confirm, and be confirmed by, the other. Both versions emphasise how 'primitive', that is to say early, events lie heavily on human individual and collective life.

THE INDIVIDUAL THEORY

Both the ontogenetic and the phylogenetic psychologists tell the story of the relationship of sons to fathers, and both stories largely consist of untangling the complex and devious ways of Eros. For psychoanalysis, everything that binds people together is either erotic or contains an erotic component, and psychoanalysis consists very largely of disentangling the different forms that erotic binding can take. A form of the erotic tie is more 'primitive' in psychoanalytic language if it is formed early in the psychic life of the individual or the

693

species. The earliest individual male erotic tie is father-identification, and this tie is far from simple. Eros is usually thought of as being directed towards sexual possession, towards having and holding, but Freud thinks that identification is an even earlier stage of erotic binding. The boy-child wants to be his father even before he wants to possess his mother. Identification fits in well with the boy's subsequent desire for his mother because part of being a father is possession of the mother, and, because Eros always has a tendency towards complication, there can be a double erotic tie between the boy and his father – the little boy can want his father as well as wanting to be him. The Oedipus complex develops out of these potentially anarchic erotic entanglements by imposing a kind of order on them. Identification itself is ambivalent from the outset because there is an obvious contradiction between the boy's choice of the father as *subject*, wanting to be him or to be like him, and the choice of the father as *object*, wanting to have him in the double sense of possessing him and killing him to gain access to the mother. This ambivalence of simultaneous love and hate causes feelings of guilt in the boy-child, and the introjection of the guilt feelings as a conscience is the first stage in the process by which some kind of institutionalised stability begins to impose itself on the erotic anarchy. The father's prohibition against incest, and the guilt which is the consequence of the boy's ambivalent feelings towards his father now become internalised as the little boy's own conscience which tells him that incestuous feelings towards his mother, and murderous feelings towards his father are wrong. The father now says 'love and respect me, and respect your mother' from inside the little boy's own head, and so normal family life can safely begin.

Freud goes to considerable lengths to support his thesis that identification is the most primitive form of love because his whole theory of the formation of psychological groups will depend upon it. Hence the psychoanalytic concept of 'regression', the idea that love even in adults can regress from sexual desire as normally understood, wanting someone, to identification, wanting to be someone else by wanting to want what they want. The most common form that regression takes is what Freud calls 'substitution', where the impossibility of ever possessing a loved object leads to the introjection of the loved object into the lover's own self. This happens in chivalrous and selfless love, in which the lover idealises the loved object and sets out to live his life as She would want it to be. The deviousness of Eros in its drive towards possession makes the loved object the lover's own 'I', the highest and purest part of himself, an 'ego-ideal' (Freud's first term for what was later to become the famous Freudian Super-ego), often hopelessly overvalued, and always capable of making fools of us all.

This tendency on the part of those in love to overvalue an idealisation of the objects of love provides Freud with the link between Eros, hypnosis and the leadership of crowds. Crowd theorists and theorists of hypnotism had always been struck by the mindless compliance of members of crowds and hypnotised subjects: they lack all initiative; they obey the suggestions of leaders or hypnotists in an automatic, dream-like way, and no part of their minds seems to test for reality. These are the qualities which are at their most spectacularly obvious in hypnosis, and they are what made hypnotic suggestion such an attractive model for the explanation of crowd behaviour. But Freud's sharp eye for the erotic even in its absence could not help noticing the extreme 'purity' of hypnotic phenomena. The very absence of potentially anarchic impulsions uninhibited in their sexual aims towards hypnotists must therefore come about because the hypnotic subject shows all the limitless devotion of someone in love, but with the possibility of sexual possession removed.

The selflessness of the romantic and sentimental lover, the selflessness of the hypnotised subject, and the selflessness of the member of the psychological crowd all have the same cause. In psychoanalytical terms, sexual energy, libido, has been temporarily thwarted in hypnotism and in the crowd. The love which aims at the possession of a loved object comes to recognise that the loved object cannot be possessed. Yet the dynamics of libido will not be denied. Narcissistic love has its part to play. The love of self-satisfaction takes a blow when it realises that the loved object outside the self is beyond possession, and with this goes a diminution of self-esteem because the self can no longer be considered as the centre of the erotic universe. Narcissistic love finds an underhand way to satisfy itself through introjection. The loved object, the hypnotist or the leader of a crowd, is introjected as part of ourselves. This ego-ideal can easily be a substitute for an unrealised ego-ideal of our own. We attribute the perfections which we have striven for in our own ego to the intro-jected ego-ideal, and so satisfy our own narcissism by becoming a better person than we were before.

Love's endless ingenuity in finding ways to satisfy itself led Freud to begin to wonder if it might be possible for identification to occur while the possibility of sexual possession remained intact. Perhaps a loved object could be both introjected into the ego-ideal and also not be so completely 'idealised' that it remained permanently beyond the reach of love's grosser clutches. In romantic and selfless love, the loved object takes over the whole of the ego. Occupying the whole of the self, the introjected love-object leaves no room for any part of the ego even to contemplate sexual possession. Therefore, if it is to be at all possible that a loved object can be introjected into the ego without the ego's complete surrender to it, then there must be what Freud called a 'differentiating grade' in the ego, what was to become the classic Super-ego of the later work *The Ego and the Id* (1923). Freud has already begun to suspect in *Group Psychology* (1921) that there must be a difference between what we ordinarily mean by 'I' and something else which, though part of the 'I', operates according to different rules.

What is at issue in the distinction between Ego and Super-ego is still the selflessness shown in being in love, in hypnosis, and in crowds. (It seems sensible, now that the Super-ego has made its appearance, to give Ego, Super-ego and Id the capitals which translations of Freud gave them after 1923.) Selflessness always implies a diminution of Ego. At first, Freud had believed that there were two different ways of being in love. The first, 'fascination and bondage', entailed the abject surrender of the Ego to another, the mooning and swooning kind of love, while the second, identification, involved an 'enrichment' of the Ego as the (real or imagined) ideal qualities were introjected into the lover's own Ego. However, common sense quickly showed Freud that there was no reason in principle why fascination and bondage, and identification could not happen together in the same Ego. You can easily love someone in the physical sense and also take their standards for your own. Now, 'being in love' could be understood, psychoanalytically, in an entirely new way. There were now three ways of being in love: 'fascination and bondage', identification, or a combination of the two. All three involve a diminution of Ego, exactly the condition found during hypnosis and in crowds.

In *Group Psychology* Freud very quickly realised that it was possible that the particular kind of 'being in love' characteristic of psychological groups could be understood in the terms of the psychoanalytic distinction between Ego and Super-ego. Perhaps in crowds Ego mechanisms and Super-ego mechanisms became entangled with different objects. All love involves some surrender of the self to another. This can in general be understood as a form of substitution, the replacement of what we want (or part of what we want) by what another wants. Freud's own theory of the formation of psychological groups depends on the possibility that substitution can take two different forms simultaneously. The member of a crowd substitutes the leader for his own Super-ego and substitutes the other members of the crowd for his own Ego.

Again, what is at issue is the selflessness of individuals in 'psychological groups'. All crowd theorists before Freud had pointed to the dualism of the psychological ties which bind men in crowds. Men in crowds were bound by ties to the leader and to each other. Thinkers before Freud had seen these two ties as reinforcing each other, because they thought of them as being essentially of the same type. Explanations of crowd behaviour which relied on hypnotic suggestion had never been able to make a distinction between these two types of bonding. Leaders, it was said, suggested certain kinds of behaviour to the crowd, some crowd members responded, and they in their turn suggested the same behaviour to other members of the crowd. When crowd theory turned to the specialised problem of leadership, and began to make a great fuss about leaders, then this idea of double-suggestion began to look rather feeble: the leader was simply one source of suggested behaviour among others. Freud's libido theory at last solves the mystery: '*A primary group of this kind is a number of individuals who have put one and the same object in the place of their ego ideal and have consequently identified themselves with another in their ego*' (Freud's italics). The erotic tie which binds the leader to the led is of a different type from the tie which binds fellow members of the crowd to each other; the former is an ego-ideal, that is Super-ego, tie, while the latter is an Ego tie. The leader-led tie is a case of introjection, the internalisation of the leader's own values and wishes as one's own, while the bond between followers is a case of the recognition that all crowd members are in the same position with regard to the leader.

The key word in Freud's definition of a psychological group is 'consequently'. Introjection and identification do not happen together by coincidence. Identification between members of the group happens *as a consequence* of introjection. Introjection, the internalisation of what another wants as what we want, is in adults a substitute for sexual object-choice. The basic aim of libido is sexual possession, and aim-inhibited libido always finds another object if it finds sexual possession beyond its grasp. Introjection is one of the ways in which aim-inhibited libido finds a substitute satisfaction, but introjection is even enough to satisfy libido as a whole. Libido is to be looked on as a quantity which either is fixed, or, when it is 'spent', renews itself to its former level. It is its capacity for self-replenishment which makes Eros so potentially unruly. The easiest and most prodigal way to spend libido is orgasm, but where ordinary sexual release is impossible, other ways of sexual spending must be found if the pressure of unspent libido is not to become burdensome and lead to neurosis. In the case of the replacement of the Super-ego by the leader of crowds, the intensity of feeling can be high while the amount of erotic spending can be low because the leader can never be sexually possessed. Lots of libido, therefore, is left over to be spent on other members of the crowd, hence the erotic binding of identification with other group members. Submission to the leader is therefore accompanied by feelings of love – selflessness, altruism, 'loving one's neighbour as oneself' – for other members of the crowd. The leader cannot be 'possessed' by each group member; each group member knows this, and the amount of aim-inhibited libido this leaves over finds its satisfaction in identification with fellow group members. In the language of Eros this is a 'cost', but it brings with it the benefit of the relief that one feels as a member of a psychological group. All the usual tensions which arise in ordinary life when we encounter strangers, of different classes, races and religions, disappear in the crowd. We begin to value others as we value ourselves, our differences are dissolved into the whole, and the group becomes one.

This analysis of the libidinal structure of groups has the great virtue of making plain what it is about group formation that is unconscious. Crowd theory before Freud made great play with the idea of mysterious unconscious forces operating in crowds without ever being very explicit about what the term 'unconscious' actually meant. At their least plausible, crowd theorists had talked as if being in a crowd was a kind of sleep-walking, as if the members of crowds did not really know what was happening to them; like hypnotic subjects, who did not know that they were in hypnosis, and would 'forget' about it afterwards. There is no such difficulty in Freud's account of the crowd in *Group Psychology*. For Freud, the mechanisms of group formation are ego-mechanisms; they concern an 'I' and not a 'me'; they concern a subject and not an object, something which I do, not something which happens to me. It is no doubt true that the particular I's which happen to be involved in particular examples of group formation do not understand exactly what is going on because not everybody understands psychoanalysis or has even heard of it, but I know that I am involved with a group; I know that I have internalised my leader's standards as my own, and I know that I feel altruistically about the other members of my group. I am neither hypnotised nor a somnambulist. Being a member of a psychological group entails a state of awareness at least as acute as in the state of 'being in love'.

Freud was in fact to change his opinion about the relationship of the Ego and consciousness while he was writing *Group Psychology*, and that change was complete when he wrote *The Ego and the Id* (1923). In *Group Psychology* Freud sometimes still talks as if all Ego functions, including Super-ego functions, are conscious in the same sense, but he came later to believe that Super-ego functions were unconscious. What this means for crowd theory is that after the internalisation of the leader's standards as our own, these standards work within ourselves automatically like the unconscious Super-ego, but there is nothing 'mysterious' about this in the old somnambulistic sense. The exchange of one set of internalised standards for another could happen, so to speak, behind consciousness's back, but only a particular kind of fool could fail to realise that it had happened.

Freud's later position that Super-ego functions are unconscious opens the way for an explanation of the more horrific manifestations of crowd behaviour which had not been available to his predecessors. Crowd theorists before Freud had been interested in crowds because the crowd could so easily become a mob howling for blood, but the crowd's potential bloodthirstiness had always been explained by very generalised references to instincts men shared with animals, or by the bloodthirstiness of the suggestions of leaders, or, more generally still, by reference to the collapse of social restraints which necessarily accompanies the temporary madness of the mob. This kind of explanation of the mob's awfulness almost invariably harked back to Darwinian evolutionism. The mob was simply a regression back down the Darwinian evolutionary scale: primitive, hence irrational and barbarous. These explanations all suffered from the very serious drawback that they failed to account for the differences between mob behaviour at different times and places. All crowd thinkers remarked on the different types of behaviour between different national crowds, and this the very generalised explanations of crowd behaviour simply could not explain. What, after all, had national differences to do with the Darwinian time-scale? National differences were obviously of incomparably more recent date than the biological time-scales which were the stuff of Darwinism. How could the regressiveness of crowd behaviour be 'national' unless nations themselves had actually existed for the first time along with apes and dinosaurs? Either national differences in the behaviour of crowds were not all that important, or the Darwinian heritage was not all that important, but it was extremely difficult to have it both ways. Freud's account of the Super-ego goes some way towards reconciling the idea of the regressive behaviour of crowds with the fact of national differences by suggesting that the Super-ego might in fact function differently in different cultures. To explain this we will have to look a little more deeply into the Freudian Super-ego.

The Super-ego is best thought of as a kind of primal critic. It is primal because it begins its development in individuals as identification, the first of all the libidinal bondings which occur in an individual's life. Little boys want to be their fathers before they want to possess their mothers; they identify with their fathers and take them as models for themselves. The desire for their mothers, and the consequent desire to kill their fathers, produces the first pangs of guilt in the boy-children, and this guilt becomes internalised and hardens as the taboo against incest. This internalisation of the taboo against incest does not kill incestuous wishes, and an internal struggle takes place between these wishes and the prohibitions of the Super-ego. The formation of the Super-ego begins within the family, but its development occurs in the wider context of the society in which an individual lives. Social living outside the family adds prohibitions of its own, until the individual becomes a properly socialised member of his society. The dynamic nature of the psychoanalytic view of human personality sets great store by the repressive functions of the Super-ego. It follows from Super-ego theory that, in societies which are repressive, the Super-ego will be given a very heavy workload, and this can lead to a high number of neurotic casualties because the internalised burdens of guilt can become too heavy for individuals to bear. Neurotics are over-socialised individuals who are too keen to do what they think their society expects of them, and they never feel that they have lived up to the standards which they have internalised from the outside world. The paradox of neurosis is that neurotics often end up not even being able to live the 'normal' life lived by those around them.

698

The neurotic is testimony to society's success, an exaggerated version of what all of us are. Neurotics are not dangerous madmen but parodies of ordinary, law-abiding citizens. But Freud's psychology tells us that there is something *dangerous* about neurotics, or that there is something dangerous about the societies which produce neurotics in large numbers. Neurotics possess overactive Super-egos in societies in which Super-egos in general will be working overtime. In psychological groups, the individual exchanges his Super-ego for the wishes and commands of leaders. This, in the Freudian view, is what enables leaders to take over the inner lives of followers. It follows from this that the effectiveness of the commands of a leader will depend on the strength of the Super-egos which he replaces *and will have nothing directly to do with what it is that the leader actually wants his followers to do*. Leaders of a traditional kind, like the Habsburg emperors who ruled Freud's own Austria until they were deposed after the First World War, would command easily because they were steeped in traditional Austrian values and sought only to reinforce them. That ease of command can easily mislead us into thinking that it is the nature of their commands, and not the unconscious supporting commands of the Super-ego, which is the root cause of the effectiveness of the commands of traditional authority. When a new kind of leader appears, of the kind predicted by crowd theory since the Paris *Commune*, it is easy to think that he will have a hard time of it because he will have strongly established Super-egos to contend with. However, in the Freudian view, this is in one respect seriously misleading, because established Super-egos can easily become victims of their own erstwhile success. When the members of an established 'psychological group' exchange their Super-egos for a new leader, that new leader will command with all the force of the Super-egos which traditional leaders did so much to build up. Super-ego exchange in very repressed societies will be explosive, because the degree of the release of pressure will be proportional to the success of past repression: the greater the burden, the greater the release. The process of Ego-exchange can be accompanied by the release of some very nasty repressed creepy-crawlies, hence the regressive, primal barbarism of the mob.

The Freudian theory of the Super-ego also elegantly solves one of the theoretical problems which had bedevilled crowd theory from the beginning. Ever since the French Revolution had been seen as a riot which 'got out of hand', crowd thinkers had been faced with the paradox that there was something both very modern and very primitive about the crowd. Freud's theory of Super-ego replacement in crowds solves this apparent problem. It is the very success of the modern state and of the rigidity of modern social norms which *causes* the explosive barbarism of the crowd. After Freud, we are no longer entitled to ask 'How could it happen here of all places?' if by 'here' we mean highly ordered states and successfully repressed societies. From the Freudian point of view, it is in those kinds of societies that one would expect crowd barbarism to occur, and with it violent crowd politics. Nor, after Freud, are we likely to fall into the simplifying error of supposing that crowd politics will be the same everywhere. The Super-ego is universal, but it is not everywhere the same.

FREUD'S COLLECTIVE PSYCHO-ANTHROPOLOGY

Freud's account of the crowd in the terms of the psychology of individuals could stand on its own, without the confirmation it receives from the Freudian version of evolutionary anthropology. However, Freud's was a mind formed in the late nineteenth century (the published date of his famous *Interpretation of Dreams* is 1900), when all of the sciences had to do more than nod in the direction of Darwinian evolutionism. Freud had introduced evolutionism into psychoanalysis in *Totem and Taboo* (1913), where he used the psychoanalytical idea of ambivalence to suggest 'some points of agreement' between the mental lives of savages (as they were then called) and neurotics. The minds of savages and neurotics (and also children) were especially prone to ambivalence because they could easily contain the opposed feelings of love and hate towards the same object without being in the least troubled by the contradiction, or even aware of it. Freud was struck by the very obvious contradiction in what the anthropologists had discovered about the primitive practice of totemism. In totemism, the most terrible of all crimes is to kill the totem animal, except that once a year the totem animal is ceremonially killed and eaten. Freud was also struck by the complexity of the social life of savages which seemed to be designed to make incest impossible. Freud goes on to consider whether the ambivalence of the savage mind and the ambivalence as discovered in the minds of children towards parents might not be attributable to a single source.

Freud begins his enquiry from the suggestion in Darwin's *The Descent of Man* (1871) that in their most primitive social state men lived in hordes dominated by a single powerful male, and from this conjecture follows Freud's celebrated account of the slaying of the primal father, the event which hangs heavily over the psychic history of the human race.

The story of the slaying of the primal father is simple enough (though it has far-reaching implications). The domineering primal father is supposed to have monopolised the women in the primal horde. The sexually frustrated brothers rebelled against their father's tyranny, killed him, and, being cannibal, they ate him. The period that followed was a time of fratricidal anarchy: each of the brothers had taken part in the primal crime because each one of them secretly wanted to take the father's place and monopolise the women. The original rebellion could not have come out of a feeling of injustice and a desire for fair shares for all, because before the primal crime no sense of justice existed. The primal horde was a society in which the rules were imposed externally by the father's domination, and, in a society like that, there would be no need for rules to be internalised. Brute strength, not conscience, kept the primal horde in being. The quarrels between the brothers, each one of whom wanted to monopolise the women, neutralised them as a social force, and may have led to a period of matriarchy. Anarchic competition between the brothers, like the competition of Hobbesian men in the State of Nature, had no future because, as long as it continued, nothing would ever change. Again, like Hobbes's men in the State of Nature, it would not take the brothers long to realise that they had much to gain by finding a way to end the war of all against all, and the way to do this was equally clear: the brothers would have to renounce all claims to the women of the horde and seek satisfaction elsewhere. (Monogamy as a solution appears not to have occurred to them.) What all wanted, none could have, because in those days libido was undifferentiated, which meant that it would always be possible for the war of the brothers to break out again while any of them had access to any of the women of the horde. There was no stopping anarchic libido: when each of the brothers saw the women of the horde he saw the possibility of endless sexual satisfaction, and this would inevitably lead to another outbreak of the fratricidal war.

The brothers realised that they had to renounce the women of the horde for social living to be at all possible, so the first social contract was effectively an agreement to forbid incest. In the future, male sexual satisfaction was to be sought outside the family, and of course it followed that female sexuality would have to be satisfied outside the family too. But a contract, rationalistically conceived, is not enough to turn a prohibition into a taboo. A taboo is an internalised prohibition which each man carries within himself, not a ban policed externally by force. Taboos are self-policing by guilt. Guilt feelings had no place in the primal horde because whatever morality and law it had were policed externally by the father by force. The original guilt feelings arose in the brothers during the fratricidal war of all against all. The brothers must have used their opportunities during that time for solitary reflection to realise the full force of what they had done. It occurred to each of the brothers that they had forgotten their love for their father in the anger of the primal murder. They began to repent. They wished they had not killed their father; they longed 'nostalgically' for his return, and this longing was compounded by the prudent reflection that the fruits of their victory over their father were bitter, because the women he had enjoyed none of the brothers could now enjoy. The contractual renunciation of the women became in effect the return of the father's authority in an internalised form because the brothers added to the ban on incest a reinforcing feeling of guilt. They felt they had *wronged* their father, that they had *betrayed* their love for him.

The brothers then cast about for a way of making the father return so that they could re-declare their betrayed love for him. They 'displaced' their love for their father onto a totem animal, and made it taboo to kill it. Totem and taboo, taken together, constitute as complete a return of the slain father's authority as is possible short of reincarnation. But the original ambivalence towards the father as an object of both love and hate would not die. When they set up the totem as a re-declaration of their love for their father, the brothers could not forget that they had hated him too, and the continuing pain caused by the ban on incest reminded them why. Nostalgia for the father's return mingled with a nostalgia for the original act of parricidal rebellion which they now knew they must never repeat. So the brothers institutionalised the memory of the primal revolt and procured a substitute satisfaction for it, in the yearly totem feast, in which the primal father is again killed and eaten, symbolically, as the totem animal.

Freud finds the origins of religion, morality and law in totem and taboo, and he also finds there the origins of individual human psychology. The ambivalence towards fathers is still clearly visible in the everyday Oedipus complex, and in *Group Psychology* Freud begins to wonder whether there might not still be other traces of the horrific primal events in psychological groups. Crowd theory had always insisted that the crowd was regressive and what put Freud onto the idea that ambivalence might be the clue to the regression mechanism was an observation of Le Bon's in *The Crowd* (1895) that the group mind could believe simultaneously in contradictory ideas with equal conviction, and that words seemed

701

to exercise some kind of 'magical power' over the crowd. In *Group Psychology* Freud compares Le Bon's description of the crowd mind with the account psychoanalysis gives of the mental lives of neurotics, and he is again struck by the fact that the crowd mind and the neurotic mind are guided by the (often linguistically coded) illusions of 'psychological reality' and not by ordinary reality. For instance, 'hysterics suffer mainly from reminiscences' in the form of compulsions to repeat remembered fantasies of experiences and not of real experiences; their repetitions are repetitions of unfulfilled wishes from the past. This comparison, combined with the regressive tie of identification between the led and the leader in the 'psychological group', is Freud's route to the rather startling thesis that the psychological group is nothing less than a repetition of the primal horde of *Totem and Taboo*. Freud is careful to say in *Totem and Taboo* that his account of the horrors of the primal horde is a Just-So story, or a 'hypothesis such as archaeologists use to lighten the darkness of prehistoric times', but he cannot help observing that the regressive quality of the mental life of groups is exactly the quality you would expect to find in a primal horde. Freud makes the spectacular leap from this observation to conclude that 'just as primitive man survives potentially in every individual, so the primal horde may arise once more out of any random collection of individuals'. Just as the oldest form of individual psychology is the father-identification out of which comes the Oedipus complex, so the psychology of the primal horde must be the oldest form of the collective psychology of the human species.

It is well to remember that the psychology of the primal horde had its own primitive complexities. The brothers of the horde dominated by the primal father were bound to each other by ties which arose necessarily out of the aim-inhibition of their libido. They loved the forbidden women but, being denied sexual satisfaction, the brothers had plenty of libido to spare to love each other, and they loved their father while hating him. Whichever way they looked, the brothers were tied by love, but 'the father of the primal horde was free'. His was the strong and independent mind and will, giving away no more than was 'strictly necessary', the Superman which Nietzsche expected only from the future. Before the Ur-slaying, the father was a sovereign individual, completely narcissistic, whose will needed no reinforcement from the outside, while the brothers were trapped in group psychology. The more the father dominated the horde, and the stricter the enforcement of the ban on sexual contact with the women, the more relentlessly the aim-inhibited libido of the brothers would find its substitute satisfaction by reinforcing the ties of group solidarity among them. The only way out of group psychology within the primal horde was through the act of love. The primal father was not immortal; he had to be replaced when he died or was killed, and his place would be taken by one of the brothers, perhaps the youngest, who would be likely to have been the secret favourite of the women. The primal father's successor would then give up his group ties as he satisfied his libido direct. He would lose interest in his brothers and would allow his narcissism 'to rise to its full height'. The primal father is loved by the brothers, but his own love is anti-social because, being directed towards sexual objects, or narcissistically towards himself, he has no love left for the brothers. The father in the primal horde is absolutely satisfied and self-satisfied; he is obeyed but acknowledges no obedience. The primal father is an erotic Hobbesian sovereign from the beginning. He exists not by the free choice of atomistic individuals, but by the strength of his own will. He is the original individual, trapping others in group psychology, and subjecting them to that rude, natural equality which Hobbes had thought could only exist in the absence of a sovereign. Unlike Hobbes, who saw the original sovereign as coming out of the frustrations of equality, Freud sees the frustrations of equality as arising out of the domination of a sovereign.

Freud's social theory and his theory of authority does not begin from the postulate of a generalised atomistic individualism, so he is not faced with the problem of having to explain how stable collectivities come out of a chaos of competing individual wills. Freudian social contract comes after the primal father as original sovereign has been deposed. The deposition of the original sovereign is to be seen as an attempt by the brothers to break out of group psychology into individual psychology, but the only way the brothers knew how to do that was for each of them to try to take the primal father's place. It was this which led to the frustrations of the fratricidal war, and out of those frustrations that the percep- tion came to the brothers that social living would only be possible again if they brought back the father's authority in the institutional forms of totem and taboo. So, for Freud, true individuality was only a moment in the mental history of the human race, and it was either a moment of sovereign domination or a period of fratricidal chaos. Group psychology in recognisably human history is simply a recapitulation of events in the primal horde.

It follows that, for Freud, the different forms which human living have taken and can take are the different forms available to the recapitulation of primal events. The illusion in churches and armies that the leader loves all followers equally is an 'idealistic' remodelling of the primal horde, a reversal of the position in the primal horde where all of the brothers were equally persecuted by the father. This 'recasting', 'upon which all social duties are built', is presupposed by the form of society which succeeds the primal horde, the totemic clan, in which everyone regards themselves as equals in the duties which totemism imposes. Taboo means that everyone must now seek sexual satisfaction outside the clan, and this in its turn leads to the patriarchal family as we know it, in which the father really can love all the members equally. It is in the family that those Oedipal prohibitions begin which are the prototypes of all the instinctual repressions, and they form the basis of what we call ordinary civilised life.

The human family as Freud knew it is the point at which his two accounts of group psychology meet. Oedipus meets his father, who is himself a remodelled primal father. Each man carries within himself, as a Super-ego, the scars of his early and unsuccessful attempts to supplant his own father. This Super-ego, reinforced and supplemented by the norms and values of the society in which he lives (or of the groups in that society of which he is a member), is what each man exchanges for the commands of a leader in a psychological group. It is because the love relationship with the mother must exclude the possibility of sexual satisfaction that the individual in the group has so much libido to spare for his fellows, and so he comes to love them too. The development of the Oedipus complex is itself a recapitulation of the much more ancient family struggle of the primal horde. Sons have been trying to oust fathers ever since the primal rebellion, and, as in the beginning, those rebellions continue to fail.

Apparently successful rebellions never really succeed because every rebellion – individual

703

within the family, or collective in a wider society – is a repetition of the rebellion against the primal father. These rebellions are always followed by a reinforcement of internalised guilt. This reinforcement happens no matter whether the rebellion is 'successful' or not. An 'unsuccessful' rebellion against an established leader like a king or emperor leads to a reinforcement of his authority when the rebellious sons come to realise the guilt-ridden nature of what they have tried to do. Just as in the primal crime, so in the unsuccessful rebellion the father's authority returns in an internalised form compounded by the guilt which the latest example of attempted psychic patricide entails. The rebelled-against king's or emperor's authority can even return in a doubly compounded sense. Suppose the failed rebellion to have had a leader, and suppose that leader to have been left to his fate as the rebellion failed. Guilt at joining the rebellion against an established ruler in the first place would lead to a Super-ego reinforcement which the rebellion's leader could exploit as a new father-figure. His authority would be greater than the authority of the rebelled-against ruler because the rebelling sons would internalise their guilt for their rebellion into their Superegos which would then exchange the defeated ruler's authority for the rebellious leader's commands. This compounded guilt would then be recompounded if the rebellion failed, because the rebels would feel they had betrayed their rebel leader-father, so that when they returned to their old allegiance the rebelled-against ruler would be able to take advantage of the recompounded guilt so that his authority would be even greater than it had been before. As in the primal horde, failed rebellions reinforce authority by increasing the burden of internalised guilt.

Much the same thing is also true of the 'successful' rebellions we sometimes call revolutions. Revolutions always have leaders, and successful revolutionaries always have the increased patricide guilt of their followers to exploit. If Freud is right, the guilt which the revolutionary rank-and-file feel at deposing and perhaps killing their former rulers reinforces Super-ego guilt, and that reinforced Super-ego guilt is the main leadership resource of successful revolutionary leaders. What this means in plainer language is that revolutions, unsuccessful or successful, always increase the authority of leaders, no matter what the stated aims of revolutions happens to be. Revolutions are typically made in the name of liberty, however defined, and Freud's message of libertarian revolutions is bleak: revolutions in liberty's name always produce regimes more authoritarian than the ones they replace.

Like all great thinkers, Freud solves a problem by showing that it is not really a problem at all. Since the French Revolution, everybody had been wondering how it was that a revolution conceived in the name of reason and liberty could end up by devouring its own children. The problem was in fact very ancient. Plato, for example, spends a good deal of time in the *Republic* showing how it is that democratic revolutions end up by producing regimes in comparison with which previous regimes look like golden ages of liberty. What had been a problem for other thinkers no longer is for Freud. No rebellion is ever really worth it in a world in which the capacity for feeling guilt is limitless and in which there is always lots of aim-inhibited libido pursuing substitute satisfactions. It is this human capacity for compounding guilt which in the long run makes Freud a conservative. All rebellions increase guilt, and increased guilt makes people more amenable to the forms of authority under which they live. This makes a successful rebellion in the name of liberty a Freudian contradiction in terms. Reform may be possible, but revolutions are always recapitulations of the primal rebellion. Freud thought that this compulsion to repeat the (real or imagined) events of the primal horde was a necessary constituent part of our psychological nature. There is certainly a grim Augustinian fatalism about Freud as a political thinker, and that fatalism makes him the kind of conservative who can find comfort neither in the past nor in the future. Freud is neither Burke nor Hegel. The evolutionary past cannot be seen through rose-tinted spectacles and the problematical future can only be looked forward to with stoical disenchantment.

GENERALITIES AND PARTICULARS

Freud's theory of the libidinal structure of psychological groups is pitched at a very high level of generality. Freud seems to mean it to apply to the hypnotic group of two, to the crowd, and to highly formalised groups like churches and armies. On the face of it at least, Freud's group psychology lacks the anti-popular thrust of nearly all the predecessors in the crowd theory tradition. Previous crowd thinkers had typically begun from a sense of horror about what the revolutionary or criminal crowd was capable of, and they typically pointed to the lower orders as the social milieu out of which the crowd and the mob could be expected to come. Some crowd theorists had been pessimistic enough to believe that anybody, regardless of social rank, could join the crowd or the mob, but most crowd thinkers tried to make a distinction between groups which were very unlikely ever to become crowd-like and groups which threatened to degenerate into crowds and mobs the whole time. Most crowd thinkers settled for a sliding scale of groups, with proletarian crowds in the street at the bottom of the scale, and with highly organised, corporation-like groups at the top.

Freud's highly original account of the psychology of groups turns the scale upside down. Previous crowd thinkers had regarded the crowd in the street bent on mischief as the paradigm, primitive case of the group, but Freud regards the highly organised group with a leader as the paradigm, primitive case of the group. What Freud's predecessors had called corporations, churches and armies are not for him variants and improvements on the crowd; rather, the crowd is a less complete variant of the corporation. In Freud's view of the matter, when a crowd in the ordinary sense of the word finds ways of institutionalising itself into some kind of permanent life, it does not jack itself up the rungs of the ladder of civilisation. Quite the reverse. Institutionalisation requires leadership, and it is in its relationship to its leaders that a group begins to regress towards a recapitulation of the events of the primal horde. For thinkers working in the evolutionary tradition, it was always the crowd's primitiveness which made it a group to be feared. The revolutionary mob howling for blood came out of the crowd, and the mob was seen as a throwback to evolutionary primitive times. In this perspective, the crowd and corporations like churches and armies were seen as opposites, agencies which a civilised society could look to as crowd controllers in the first and last resorts, guardians of civilisation as we know it. In crowd theory, corporations were as high up the evolutionary scale as groups could possibly be, and crowds featured right at the bottom in that same evolutionary scale. Not for Freud. Stable groups like armies and churches are the archetypes of the primitive group, and crowds in the ordinary sense are their pale reflection. What is the mob compared to the army which is called in to save us from it? Combine this view of organised groups with Freud's account of the primitive psychic struggles within the family and it completes a very dark picture of human social life.

The very general message which comes out of Freud's social theory is that all leaders are dangerous, but it would be a mistake to think that Freud thinks that all leaders are equally dangerous. Leaders are always after obedience, and Freud thinks that the cravenness of human obedience is practically limitless because there is in principle no limit to the amount of guilt human beings are capable of feeling, and a guiltless existence is for Freud a contradiction in terms. Rebellions, failed or successful, compound guilt. It follows, therefore, the more rebellions the more guilt, and the more guilt the greater the thirst for obedience. If we accept this, then it follows that a successful rebellion in the name of liberty is also a contradiction in terms. Those who in any sense value liberty, therefore, had better stick to old leaders rather than go looking for new ones. Freud's is an ingenious argument for conservatism in the name of liberty.

Freud's social and political theory has been criticised for being over-generalised. In one sense it is. It must never be forgotten that Freud's was a late nineteenth-century mind, formed at a time when social and political theories were judged useful or useless according to the wideness of the range of social and political phenomena those theories claimed to explain. Generality was in that sense a virtue and not a vice, and we do well to remember that the young Freud was the contemporary of Marx and Herbert Spencer.

The other sense in which Freud's social and political theory is said to be over-generalised is that it lacks contemporary social and political reference. Everything important about Freudian theory either seems to refer to events which happened far away in the mists of time (and Freud is not really certain that they *did* happen), or refers to very early events in an individual's family life. Real politics and real societies do not appear to come into the matter at all. This notion is, however, very quickly dispelled by even the most cursory glance at Freud's own life and letters. The one thing that stands out is a life-long concern with anti-Semitism in its nastier varieties.

'Democratic' anti-Semitism of the mobbish kind is Vienna's contribution to the art of modern politics. By the time Hitler had got round to writing *Mein Kampf* (1924–6), Austrian political anti-Semitism was already half a century old. Austrian political anti-Semites worked both the streets and the intelligentsia with its vicious Germanic nonsense, so that Freud lived all his life in the immanent and sometimes real presence of the anti-Semitic crowd. He was eventually to have to flee from Vienna to England after the Nazis had annexed the Austrian Republic into the Third Reich.

So what was a Jewish intellectual bourgeois like Freud to think about politics? Psychoanalysis does not sit easily with Marxist historical materialism because Freud saw all conflicts as basically sexual or relating to sexuality, whereas Marxism's emphasis on class conflict leaves room only for a few scattered remarks on the theme of sexuality. Besides, Marxism looks forward to a time of universal liberation, a leap into the future, whereas psychoanalysis emphasises the importance of the inescapable (and baleful) influence of early events in the individual and collective life of the human race. A populist politics of the Right, like that practised by the Christian Social party under Hitler's role model Karl Lueger, was out of the question because of its anti-Semitism. The only politics which made sense outside Marxism and populism was a certain preference for the Habsburgs and Franz Josef, coupled with a high-minded but disenchanted hope that the liberalism of the Enlightenment might one day come to govern the lives of men. The Habsburgs understood perfectly well that a multi-racial and multi-cultural empire like theirs could only stand if it was the unfaltering policy of government to contain the hegemonic impulses of the Empire's competing races and cultures. This aim had always conflicted with the usually unspoken assumption of effective German domination, but that domination had always been played down, and it did nothing for the Empire's stability if its German subjects were allowed to declare open season on the Empire's Jews. So it was that enlightened Jewish intellectuals like Freud came to see the emperor as a shield between Jews and an endemic German (and Slav) anti-Semitism. The Habsburgs had once been enlightened despots, and even an unenlightened anti-anti-Semitic despot was preferable to nearly all the alternatives available in the Austro-Hungarian Empire.

When his country entered the First World War, Freud remarked that all his libido was given to Austria-Hungary. This should cause us no surprise, even though the alliance between Freud and Franz Josef was always uneasy (Freud used to have bad dreams about him). Psychoanalysis is the only intellectually credible defence of the Habsburg monarchy. At almost all costs, avoid the Alladin's lamp view of politics: almost never exchange old rulers for new. If the choice is between Franz Josef and Karl Lueger, then it is Franz Josef every time. Freud's sound classical education would no doubt have persuaded him in favour of tyrannicide, but Freud stands with Hobbes in the belief that the government that you know is almost certain to be no better than the government you don't. Freud's social and political theory is correctly tuned to some of the nastier aspects of twentieth-century politics. On the whole men are not very good at learning lessons from history, but if the politics of the twentieth century has anything to teach us, then it surely is that we ought to be very wary of leaders, and very wary of leaders who promise to lead us into the land of human liberty. Freud's political theory is a timely warning against both; it precedes both Stalin and Hitler, but not by much.

The fact that Freud's Vienna also produced Adolf Hitler is very striking. It must surely be more than coincidence that the same city at the same time should produce both the theorist of total leadership and its most notorious practitioner. It seems to follow that Freud and Hitler must have been learning the same thing at different levels – Freud in the study and Hitler on the streets. Austria was Habsburgless after the First World War, just as Germany was bereft of the Hohenzollerns, and of course people were going to look round for new leaders to replace them in their psychic lives. War, revolution imposed by the victorious Entente powers and the accompanying guilt that Austrians and Germans felt at letting their leader-fathers down was bound to lead to obedience to new leaders of an intensity which had never been shown to the old.

The idea of Freud as the predictor of Hitler (and Stalin) must not be pushed too far. It must never be forgotten how generalised Freud's theory of the libidinal structure of groups is. There is, in principle, no reason why it should not be applied to any psychological group with a leader. Psychoanalysis was itself a movement with Freud as its leader, so there is no reason to suppose that Freud's theory of leadership should not apply even to himself. Freud's own life and letters show that he was remarkably unjittery until very late about the rise of European fascism, though the *Anschluss* could very easily have cost him his life (he died a refugee in England in 1939).

The poet Auden famously called Freud 'a whole climate of opinion', by which he meant that European and American culture in the twentieth century would be as unthinkable without Freud as it would be without Darwin or Marx. Freud's contribution to the way we think about the world is ambiguous. On the one hand, as a therapeutic technique psycho-analysis holds out the promise that the world's neurotic casualties will be sympathetically treated and perhaps even cured, but on the other hand there is the unmistakable message of the uncertainty and fragility of what we call civilisation. Group psychology as a return to the primitive is only a part of that message.

For Freud, as for so many others, the turning point was the Great War (see his essay of 1915, 'Thoughts for the Times on War and Death'). All idea of a 'fellowship in civilisa-tion' at once departed. The idea of progress which the nineteenth century inherited from the Enlightenment was now a thing of the past. There were two groups of instincts at work in the world, Eros and Thanatos, the one unruly and the other deadly, Thanatos the slayer of cities and anarchic Aphrodite. Freud is a Stoic without even the Stoics' qualified belief in human fellowship. Freud's message is that there is something inherently murderous about collectivities and something inherently parricidal about individuals. What we call civilised living requires such a degree of instinctual renunciation that it would not be surprising if huge numbers of people, perhaps whole societies, thought that it wasn't worth the effort required to construct a civilisation at all. The pain of the first instinctual renunciation of the brothers of the primal horde can never be completely assuaged. Freud's later meta-psychological essays, especially *Civilization and Its Discontents* (1929), hammer home the perception that the Aristotelian premise 'man is a political animal' contains an unresolved contradiction. Enlightenment had assumed that no effort would be spared in the cause of civilised life once men in general had learned what a civilised life was. Not Freud. He thought that neurotics were wet, most of mankind not much good, and leaders a menace. Non-civilisation, however defined, was no longer to be explained as civilisation's negative; rather, civilisation is to be seen as a moment in a vast time-scale, the exception, not the rule. Freud is a secular Manichee, but with the difference that he weights the odds heavily against the light. Oddly enough that is what makes him a modernist, for all his longing for the lost world of Enlightenment.

NOTES ON SOURCES

Freud's *Group Psychology and the Analysis of the Ego* can be read in various English editions, or in the great *The Standard Edition of the Complete Psychological Works of Sigmund Freud*, 24 vols (1955–74). Also essential are Freud's *The Ego and the Id*, *Civilization and its Discontents*, and *The Future of an Illusion*. Out of the vast pile of commentary on Freud, P. Rieff, *Freud: The Mind of the Moralist* (3rd edn, 1979), P. Roazen, *Freud: Political and Social Thought* (1968), and R. Wollheim, *Freud* (1971) are recommended. Freud commentary is a minefield, so tread warily.

30

FASCISM, OR BEING REVOLUTIONARY WITHOUT BEING MARXIST

ADOLF HITLER

Writing a short life of Adolf Hitler, let alone trying to relate that life to his work, is a crime against proportion. You cannot treat one of the world's monsters simply as a writer who had some important, though misguided, contributions to make to a debate about 'the Jewish Question' to which he thought he had found the Final Solution. The matter is further complicated by the fact that *Mein Kampf* itself contains a highly contentious autobiographical account of Hitler's life up to about 1924, and there is an important sense in which Hitler's political life consisted of living out that account of his own life, first on a local scale, then on a national scale, and finally on a global scale.

Everybody knows the macabre facts about Hitler. The plain facts are these: he was born an Austrian subject in 1889 at Braunau-on-the-Inn, the son of a minor official of the Habsburg state. Most of his childhood was spent at Linz to where his father had retired. Hitler wasn't much of a success at school, dreamt of being an artist, mooched around Vienna in self-imposed, marginalised exile from life and ended up in Munich when war broke out in 1914. Hitler joined up in the German, not the Austrian, army, in the List Regiment (named for its colonel). He saw the whole war out as a fighting soldier, rose to the rank of corporal, was wounded and gassed, and won the Iron Cross, First Class, a decoration for bravery rarely awarded to lowly corporals.

Hitler found himself at a loose end after the end of the Great War. He remained on the strength of his regiment until 1920, but he became involved very early in south German right-wing politics as an agitator for groups of disgruntled ex-soldiers who had enjoyed the war, were now without serious employment, and who could not abide the Weimar Republic as being un-German and as being the only German beneficiary of the so-called victory of the Entente powers. He joined the German Workers' Party, the ancestor of the Nazi Party, in 1919, took part in the botched Munich *Putsch* in 1923, was imprisoned (he only served nine months), wrote *Mein Kampf*, and came out of gaol to resume his party work.

The Nazi Party's history and Hitler's own history are the same. Up to about 1929 neither's fortunes were particularly spectacular, Nazism being a force in south German politics only, and a nuisance in the north. Nazism became a recognised part of German politics through the willingness of other right-wing parties to make alliances with it and to channel funds in its direction. The slump of 1929 helped, so that by 1930 the Nazi Party was polling six million. This meant that an alliance of Nazis and other right wingers could form a majority of the German *Reichstag* and therefore outvote the 'Weimar Coalition' of liberals and socialists.

Hitler was therefore brought into the respectable right-wing fold by highly placed intriguers, and he got his reward in 1933 when President Hindenburg invited him to become Chancellor of the Republic in what was to be a coalition government of the right. Office was meant to tame Hitler, but he used state (and any other available) power to establish a Nazi dictatorship in which the oath of loyalty was made to himself as Führer. And so to the re-militarisation of the Rhineland, the *Anschluß* with Austria, the occupation of the Sudetenland, the invasion of Poland, the Second World War, and the horrors. Hitler shot himself in Berlin in 1945.

The German army which invaded the Soviet Union in 1941 contained units (many of them Waffen-SS) from eight countries besides Germany. It could easily have appeared to the Russians that Operation Barbarossa began not just a German but a European fascist[1] war against the world's only communist country. The New Order in Europe after the German conquests of 1939–40 was no doubt intended to be German-dominated, but for all that it was meant to be a European and eventually a world order. Hitler's Nazi Party was always going to be the senior party in the fascist international, but the Nazi Party was meant to link up with indigenous fascist parties in other (temporarily occupied) European states to solidify the new anti-Bolshevik Europe which had been united by the Second World War. Fascist parties outside Germany were to be encouraged to develop social roots which would allow the fascist revolution to penetrate deep into their own societies, and so choke off the Marxism which thinkers like Mussolini thought decadent parliamentary liberalism had allowed to flourish.

Like 'socialism', 'fascism' can be a slippery term. We should learn to speak of 'fascisms' as we learned long ago to speak of 'socialisms', but the juxtaposition of the two words should give us pause. Fascists always tend to talk as if all socialisms were the same, and socialists always tend to talk as if all fascisms were the same. There appears to be something which socialists recognise as a fascist worldview just as there appears to be something which socialists recognise as a socialist worldview, and these are worldviews of a kind generalised enough to accommodate considerable local variations. Fascism, like socialism, is hard to pin down to a set of core ideas without those ideas being in danger of becoming so general as to become virtually meaningless. It can mean very little to say that fascists like 'order' (who, including the anarchists, doesn't?), or that there is an element of poetry and fantasy about their politics, or that they are fond of Caesar-type leaders. There is also the problem of the 'socialist' components of fascist ideologies. Mussolini thought of himself for a time as the only 'true' socialist in Italy, and the word Nazi is, after all, a shortened form of the term National Socialist. 'Socialist' types of fascism, that is fascisms carrying some kind of social programme on their banners, are frequently contrasted with the more 'militarist' or 'clerical' fascisms of, say, Spain and Poland, the implicit comparison being between a rabble-rousing, street-gang kind of fascism and a fascism firmly anchored in traditional institutions like armies and churches. (Try to imagine what the Germanising Neanderthal thugs of French fascism must have looked like to a thinker on the borderline between traditional monarchism and fascism like Charles Maurras.)

The difficulty of pinning fascism down is compounded by the lack of a really definitive text, which is why we are always driven back in the end to Adolf Hitler's *Mein Kampf* (1924–26), which is in many ways an unsatisfactory, though necessary, substitute. All fascists are nationalists, if only because fascists attack Marxism for being 'internationalist', and, as we would expect, fascisms are made to suit particular national traditions. Of course, fascisms share ideas, and even copy each other, and fascisms see themselves as being on the same side when faced with international socialism and other international conspiracies, but fascism's conviction that it is the fulfilment of a unique national destiny means that fascisms frequently differ a great deal. There would be no contradiction, for instance, in two fascist states shaping up to fight each other, though there are usually good practical reasons why they do this very rarely.

The slipperiness of the concept of fascism is reflected in the vast body of scholarly commentary on fascism, not to mention the commentary on the practice of fascist movements and governments. Some commentators have emphasised the unity of fascism and some have emphasised the diversity of fascisms. Yet everybody seems to agree that fascism was suddenly 'in the air' in the 1920s and 1930s, in much the same way that the divine right of kings was in the air in the seventeenth century or that Rousseau was in the air before the French Revolution.

How did this come about? Mussolini once famously said that fascism was against everything the French Revolution stood for. This piece of flash-harry journalistic rhetoric does contain two useful clues about fascism. First, we are still *arguing* about what the French Revolution stood for, which effectively means that there is a French Revolution for everyone. Reactionaries, conservatives, liberals, socialists, Marxists and anarchists can all take their stands for and against any or all of the answers offered during the Revolution to any or all of the questions the Revolution raised. What this means is that fascism is going to cover a lot of ground if we are going to take Mussolini at his word, and it would be surprising if every fascism were to cover exactly the same ground in the same way. Second, fascism puts forward serious claims to being revolutionary in the same sense that it claims to be a definitive critique of all the other systems of politics which we associate with the modern world. This does not mean that everything fascists have to say is new. Fascism, like any other political ideology, borrows from its rivals in the course of criticising them, but fascism is original in what it rejects and in the way it fits together what it borrows.

This borrowing which fascism does has enabled its many opponents to denigrate fascist political thinking as being intellectually second-hand, and therefore necessarily second-rate. This alleged lack of intellectual quality in fascism, together with the frequency of fascist attacks on 'intellectuals' (a codeword for Marxists and the intellectually decadent or effete) has given rise to the idea, much encouraged by the centre and the left, that fascist political theory is not to be taken seriously *as theory*. Fascists themselves even encourage this view by frequently saying things like 'Fascism is Action': others only talk; fascists act. We need not be taken in by any of this. Many a fascist intellectual, like many a conservative intellectual since Burke, has made a career out of 'anti-intellectualism'. Fascists throw sand in our eyes to obscure the very obvious fact that 'anti-intellectualism' is an intellectual position which has to be argued just as hard as the 'intellectual' positions it attacks. Fascists often write books attacking books, but this is just another episode in the political battle of the books which has been going on since Plato. Fascists sometimes even destroy books, showing that the greatest tribute you can pay to the written word is to burn it.

There is a danger in this tendency to underrate fascism as a political doctrine believable only to men still wearing short trousers. This is a view only sustainable if one's knowledge of fascist doctrine is confined to fascist slogans, or to some of the sillier things that fascists say about race. Liberals get justifiably angry if liberalism is reduced to 'Liberty, Equality, Fraternity' or is confined to the wilder shores of free market theory, and there is certainly more to Marxism than 'Workers of the World Unite!' and the labour theory of value. The view that there is nothing much more to fascism than a certain boy-scoutishness – the uniforms, the marching to fife and drum, the clean teeth and finger nails – leaves entirely out of account the fact that fascism was able to attract some of the clearest thinking minds in Europe when there appeared to be a straight choice between fascism and communism.

LIBERALISM AND FASCISM

Fascism has *caused* so much that it is easy to forget that fascism has causes of its own. The fact that the Second World War was a war 'against fascism' (among other things), and that the Cold War came quickly after and as a result of that war, can easily focus our attention entirely on fascism's post-history. Fascism can then be seen as a rabbit which popped out of the hat after the end of the First World War and was despatched in the Second. This neat tying-up of fascism not only is historically tidy, but also fulfils an important political and ideological function. It enables fascism to be seen as only an episode in the history of Europe, and an unexpected episode at that. Nothing is easier than to view fascism as appearing in the world of the 1920s almost without provenance. Nazism can then be seen as a ghastly nightmare from which Europe fortunately woke up.

Fascism, it is often implied, has no intellectual antecedents worth the name, or, if it has, those antecedents, Nietzsche for instance, or Le Bon, or Sorel, must have been so mis-understood or twisted by fascists as to become unrecognisable. Nazism was characterised by a particularly virulent and murderous anti-Semitism, and the horrors of Auschwitz to which it led have themselves led to a tendency to want to see Nazi racism as unique, a thing so horrible as to be unprecedented. Yet fascists like Mussolini and Hitler grew up in a *fin-de-siècle* Europe in which racism was commonplace, and in whose intellectual life 'race' was a perfectly respectable and almost universal category of historical, cultural and political explanation. No doubt, as an explanatory category 'race' was rough-hewn. We can look back on, say, the novels of the great Dreyfusard Emile Zola, and see perfectly clearly that by 'race' he often means what we would call 'culture'. Evolutionary biology and the transmission and development of a culture got themselves horribly mixed up in the intellectual life of the late nineteenth century, but this cannot take away from the fact that they were often thought of as being the same thing. Zola thought of culture as being in fundamental ways biologically determined. This was part of the fashionable Social Darwinism of the period, and it is important not to stress the 'Darwinism' too strongly. Social Darwinism was a very broad church, containing as it did thinkers whom we would now recognise as unreconstructed Lamarckians. 'Darwinism' was just a prestigious label to apply to a whole rag-bag of evolutionist concepts, some of which had absolutely no connection with each other, some of which flatly contradicted each other, and some of which were crazy. Nearly everybody, Freud for instance, believed that acquired ideas and attitudes could be inherited along a breeding line, and that the effect was cumulative: if the acquisitions were bad, then degeneration followed; if good, then progress.

Again, it is important to emphasise that the closer a nineteenth-century social science got to evolutionary biology, the better its scientific credentials were. Biology was 'real' science, and the social and cultural sciences imported biological ideas by the gross. What now seem implausible analogies to us did not appear to be analogies at the time to the historians, sociologists, anthropologists, psychologists, palaeontologists and political theorists who used them. The famous English constitutional commentator Walter Bagehot wrote a book called *Physics and Politics* as early as 1876. The book has almost nothing to do with what we would call physics because it is about evolutionary biology and politics, but the choice of the word 'physics' tells us a great deal. If all the sciences speak with the same evolutionary voice, then why not call every science 'physics' for short? It is also important to emphasise that it was the most progressive of the sciences, or the most progressive of the scientists, who used evolutionary-biological models and methods. Intellectual reactionaries stuck as close as they dared to the biblical account of how the world had come to be as it was, or wallowed in the twilight-land of Hegelian metaphysics. The 'favoured races' of Darwin's unfortunate sub-title to *The Origin of Species* became part of the ordinary discourse of civilised life. Racism came in all possible varieties, from imperialist to socialist, and it was an unfortunate national group indeed, or a group with a very unusual skin pigment, which could not think of itself as superior to somebody else.

Nazi racism added some particularly nasty twists of its own to the commonplace doctrines of race superiority, but it would be idle to pretend that Nazi racism was a million miles away from other racisms. Perhaps we should not even ask why it was that racism was so general in late nineteenth- and early twentieth-century European culture, but should rather interest ourselves in the different forms it took. This certainly applies to European anti-Semitism. A substantial gloss on the history of European culture might be written on the theme of the ingeniously different ways Europeans have found of hating Jews. We need go no further back than the Dreyfus Affair in France to find anti-Semitisms to suit all tastes and pockets, from the gutter Jew-baiting of an intellectual thug like Drumont, to the intellectually sophisticated anti-Semitic cultural musings of thinkers of the stature of Barrès and Maurras. Hitler came from Vienna, the greatest Jewish city in a world which had yet to hear of Tel Aviv. Anti-Semitic mob politics seems to have been Vienna's contribution to the art of modern politics, for it was its late nineteenth-century mayor, Hitler's one-time role-model Karl Lueger, who hit on political anti-Semitism's possibilities for the mobilisation of mass electoral opinion in Viennese elections. As with Social Darwinism, so with anti-Semitism we find anti-Semitisms which flatly contradict each other. Contrast the high enlightened anti-Semitism of a Gibbon or a Voltaire on the grounds of Jewish religious fanaticism and kabbalism with the anti-Enlightenment anti-Semitism of Barres and Maurras, who attack Jews on the grounds of their cosmopolitanism and their rationalism. And everybody knows of the anti-Semitism which hates all Jews because the ones who are not millionaires are Bolsheviks. All Nazism had to do was to go a step further, and push Jews so far down on the human scale that they fell off it, becoming not really human at all. Then the 'Jewish problem' could become a problem of public health or social hygiene; Jews were not disease-carriers but were themselves hostile bacilli in the social body.

Biologised social and political explanations were an important part of liberal Europe's own view of itself, and it is customary to see the third quarter of the nineteenth century as the high age of European confidence in the progressive future of its own culture. What Europe, or the best parts of it, was, the whole world might one day become. However, there were always dissenting spirits acute enough to see that explanations of European superiority based on evolutionism were ominously double-edged. They worked well enough when the going was good, but they could easily rebound when the going was bad. Spencerism can be taken to stand as the apogee of optimistic liberal progressivism. Spencerism marvelled at the intricate social differentiation of evolved societies in which the organic co-operation of the different parts was nothing short of miraculous. The problem was that these organic growths became more fragile as they became more complex, less like turnips and more like orchids. This vulnerability of highly differentiated liberal societies had been implicit in the liberal view of the state since Adam Smith. Part of liberalism's attempt to free societies from the never-ending attentions of the state had always consisted in emphasising the state's capacity to upset the natural order of things. In the fully fledged liberalism of the late nineteenth century, the state had come to be seen as a threat to the naturally evolving social complexity which was taken to be the hallmark of an advanced, civilised society, a view which found its most eloquent expressions in Spencer's *Man Versus the State* and William Graham Sumner's *What Social Classes Owe to Each Other*.

A human society worked, and worked best, when each of its individual parts was different from the others, just as in a human body each separate cell is minutely different from all the others. What optimistic evolutionists tended to forget is that organisms die and that a body dissolving into its component cells was a perfect image of social disintegration. Again, organic thinkers who equate evolution with progress forgot that in biological nature almost all mutations are fatal. Changes in nature typically herald the deaths of species. Why should this not also hold true of social change, if social life was seen as the natural extension of biological life?

On one level, liberalism coped with these possibilities perfectly well. The most obvious threat to highly differentiated social organisms was violence. Predatory violence was the unacceptable face of nature: most creatures spend most of their time trying to eat each other. Human life was supposed to be different, because that wonder of evolution, Man, was capable of reflection on the life that he lived, and reflection would enable him to realise that the perfectly natural ends of human survival and prosperity would be served best if men were to find ways of regularising their natural predatoriness a long way short of the awful primitiveness of the cannibalism which most Europeans probably thought was part of the normal digestive processes of 'savages' the world over: a missionary in every pot. For this liberals turned naturally to the market. Market mechanisms would civilise human competitiveness both within societies and between them. Thinkers as different as Tom Paine and Kant had long ago insisted on the essentially pacific nature of international free trade. Mercantilist regulation of trade was the natural policy of militaristic monarchies intent on putting gold in their war-chests. Commercial republics, what we would now call capitalist societies with representative government, were naturally peace-loving. So peace-loving, in fact, that George Washington could tell the nation in his Farewell Address that America, properly speaking, hardly needed a foreign policy in the ordinary sense at all. The watchword of commerce was universal friendship. Let the buyer still beware, but what he had to lose was his money, not his life.

Violence was supposed gradually to disappear from the domestic, national and inter-national lives of European peoples. The state was supposed to monopolise violence within its own borders, which meant that any act of violence which was not either the state's or sanctioned by the state, was illegal by definition. There was always the possibility of violence in the international order because not all state borders were definitively settled according to the liberal principle of national self-determination, but wars of national liberation could easily be seen as leading to peace in the end. A typical nineteenth-century argument ran along the lines that a universal and lasting peace among the nations would only be possible after all the border disputes had been settled along national lines to the mutual pacific progressive consensus that violence was 'of the past'. To be in favour of violence as a way of settling any kind of dispute, domestic, national or international, was to resort to something primitive, out of keeping with the spirit of the age.

It was this consensus which led Georges Sorel to begin his *Reflections on Violence* in 1906. Sorel was a Marxist who wanted to put the 'war' back into the by now formulaic 'class war' of the orthodox Marxists, but the significance of his *Reflections* goes wider than that. Sorel saw an age which had become squeamish about all violence, except the sneaking violence of lawyers institutionalised in the bourgeois state. Brute strength has all but vanished from the mechanised workplace, and with it the sometimes savage initiation rites which used to induct young workers, and in schools masters are no longer even allowed to beat Latin into their pupils. The bourgeoisie of early industrialism had been a class enemy worth fighting, but now they negotiate with 'respectable' working-class leaders so that both the great contending classes of capitalist society have gone soft. And all this has happened in the thirty-five years since the French working class and the army of Monsieur Thiers's bourgeois republic slugged it out toe-to-toe in the streets during the Paris *Commune* of 1871. Sorel instinctively grasped a dialectical contradiction in bourgeois liberal society, and, in particular, in that society's view of itself: the Europe of the turn of the century was fast writing violence out of its social programme while at the same time being peculiarly vulnerable to violence. The Marxist in Sorel realised that it probably would not take much actual violence to frighten liberal society to the root. The 'myth' of violence could go a very long way towards polarising liberal society between proletariat and bourgeoisie. One had only to consider all the fuss being made about anarchist bomb outrages to see what sporadic violence could do in a society which was prematurely congratulating itself on its necessarily pacific future.

Hence Europe's notorious theoretical unpreparedness for the Great War. There was nothing in liberal Europe's self-conception which even hinted at the possibility of the scale of the casualty figures from the Western Front. I say 'liberal Europe' because that was, in a sense, 'official' Europe. There was another Europe which was not liberal at all, the Europe of the conservative military elites and their bureaucratic allies. Liberals had always realised that it was going to take time for liberalism to work its way through the social and political institutions of even the most advanced European states. Liberalism in 1900 was still a programme rather than an accomplished fact; liberals always assumed that the future was going to be theirs, but liberalism had still some tenacious enemies in the field. Aristocratic elites which thought that war was the only fit trade for a gentleman always seemed to liberals to be throwbacks to an earlier stage of civilisation, likely to fade away as progressive ideas and attitudes penetrated more deeply and widely in the societies of Europe. A warrior aristocracy was so plainly an anachronism in the age of factories and parliaments that time would eventually see it off. Aristocrats still had a limited usefulness as the officer corps of armies which the modern state unfortunately could not yet do without, but the military function was supposed to be just another example of socially divided labour in societies which were composed of literally hundreds of differentiated social roles. Liberal society could even be pleased with itself for finding something useful for aristocrats to do. Aristocracies were expected to accept their 'professionalisation' with the high courtesy by which they set so great a store. Aristocracy would cease to think of itself as a caste apart, and would come to see soldiering as just one profession among many, with no possible claims to authority outside its own specialism.

However, liberalism had made two mistakes which only a futurologist or genius could have seen were already implicit in volume two of Adam Smith's *Wealth of Nations*. It was not only armies that were going to be professionalised in the liberal age but every aspect of government. Liberalism, as we say, was going to 'take the state out of society' by making the typical maker and enforcer of rules and laws a salaried official whose title to his job was his professional competence. Gone would be the days of the old aristocratic and gentry rulers, when most government was local government. The centralised state-machine required properly qualified personnel to run it; a centralised state-machine run by well-born amateurs would have been the same as taking good manners as the equivalent of having passed a driving test. In creating the modern bureaucratised state as a machine separate from society, liberalism created a state which was ripe for a takeover by militarism. And liberalism had also done something else. It had taken the idea of the citizen-soldier seriously enough to make compulsory military service part of the duty of a citizen. If the modern state was 'all of us', then none of us could reasonably refuse the duty of defending the state in which we enjoyed citizen rights. Take an aristocratic military elite as the training cadre of a conscript army, and imagine that elite and its civilian allies able to take over the domestic and foreign policy apparatus of a modern state, and you have a recipe for Germany's willingness to go to war in 1914.

Liberalism's theoretical error is easy to see looking back. Liberalism had accepted the formula: industrialisation equals peace, because that meant modernity. They assumed that the world was going their way and that traditional elites would supinely accept their replacement by bourgeois society's own elite. What liberalism always forgot was that liberalism's enemies could learn to play liberalism at liberalism's own game for ends of their own. Industrialisation could just as easily mean war as peace. The industry which liberals (and socialists) thought would mean a necessary bourgeois takeover of the state, which would then be run in the interests of international trade, could just as easily, in the right political conditions, be made to produce the armaments necessary for the mass slaughter of modern war. Traditional elites could buck the trend of modernity if only they had the will, and that will was a will to violence. National and international problems could be solved by violence, and the most successful of the modern states would be the ones which harnessed industrial power to the violent pursuit of national policy ends. And

719

so progressive liberals and the socialists of the Second International turned out to be wrong: modern war was not a contradiction in terms after all.

NAZISM AND THE GREAT WAR

It can be a hard fact to face that some people were not put off violence forever by the Great War. English culture has been so penetrated by what the war poets said about the war that Englishmen find it hard to think of it as anything other than futile heroism and pointless slaughter. With this goes a certain bitterness, the feeling that the young men of the war generation had been betrayed. As Kipling says: 'If any question why we died/Tell them, because our fathers lied.' Hitler's own account in *Mein Kampf* of his service in the German army in the war (he joined the Bavarian List Regiment) is very different. His account is not primarily military. For him the First World War was a political experience, the violent continuation of the political education he had been painfully acquiring as a down-and-out in pre-war Vienna. He makes it clear that in the army (German, not Austrian) he found his first real home since childhood, and his first Fatherland. This enables Hitler to see the war as *his* war, and the defeat of Germany as his own personal tragedy. By 1918 Hitler probably only felt at home in a trench or in barracks. He had no life to go back to – no real family, no home, no friends, no job – and so it was natural that he should home in on an army camp in Munich after the peace, and begin his career as a political agitator for a mildly disreputable political cause run by reactionary army and ex-army officers.

Hitler's account of the war is remarkable because of his identification of his own aims with the aims of the High Command. Whether this was 'true at the time', or a later embellishment, does not greatly matter. What does matter is the sheer impersonality, objectivity even, of the account, which is at the same time deeply felt. Perhaps without realising it, Hitler gives us an account of himself in the Great War which would have been instantly recognisable to a pre-war crowd theorist like Le Bon as the perfect crowd-man. Hitler's self-description is of a man who is a soldier pure and simple; a member of no other groups, familyless, therefore having no past of his own; jobless and penniless, therefore classless, and therefore having no identity outside the group he chooses to identify with. His real experience is his army experience, an experience he shares with millions. He has no intervening loyalties which mediate between that collective experience and his own. The very ordinariness of his service in the poor bloody infantry (*der arme Frontschwein*) means that he has shared the experience of the collectivity to the full. Nothing gets in the way. He has 'been through it all', so that the defeat and humiliation of 1918–19 is his own defeat and humiliation.

The crowd-man's experience of the defeat as *his* defeat leads Hitler to look round for somebody to blame for it, hence the idea of the 'stab in the back'. Somebody else must have failed to keep the faith which the army kept. This leads to a sense of betrayal which is worlds away from the sense of betrayal in the English-speaking world. Hitler's sense of it is not that the older generation betrayed the younger by allowing the war to happen in the first place. Rather, the 'stab in the back' view holds the opposite: there was nothing wrong with going to war – how could there be when its effect was to unite the Germans now that the Austrian Germans were at last united in arms with their brothers in the Reich? The national shame of having been on different sides of the internecine battles of the nineteenth century could now be forgotten. What was criminal was pulling the army of all the Germans out of the war when the victory against the Slavs in the East had already been won, and when the final victory in the West was within the army's grasp. What was *wrong* with the war was not the beginning of it but the end of it. The violence was something that had to be lived through, necessary, but secondary. The psychological origins of the myth of the stab in the back have no doubt got something to do with the usual contempt of the front-line soldier for everybody else, but Hitler's version of it leads him down a recognisably Nietzschean path – *theirs* was the failure of will, not ours.

The attitude to violence with which Hitler came out of the First World War could not have been more different from the attitude of the victorious liberal democratic powers. Either the war had been Germany's fault, or it had all been some kind of ghastly mistake. The Entente powers could only see their view of violence confirmed by the Great War. If anything showed that war was never worth it, no matter how the calculation was made, then the Great War did. (And the liberal democracies needed no reminding that Lenin and the Bolsheviks were one of the very few groups to do really well out of the war.) It had now been definitively shown that the pains of war could no longer be contained within reassuring obstetric analogies; nor could the international order any longer tolerate limited Cabinet wars of the nineteenth-century type, because the Great War had shown that war could not be contained by policy. The international order came to be seen as particularly vulnerable to violence, perhaps even more vulnerable than the domestic order.

Before 1914, liberalism had partly realised its own dream that recourse to violence in the ordinary life of a society would be the exception to the rule, only to find after 1918 that the problem had transferred itself to international society. Hence the hopes which liberal democracies placed or misplaced in the League of Nations. In the international order, states were expected at least to pretend that they had renounced violence except as a very last resort at the end of a very long day. They were now obliged to claim that they were the victims of violence, not its instigators; they could be expected to lie about the extent of their armaments, claim their war-plans were entirely defensive, and in general to cover up. Whether this could have any effect, other than to intensify the customary mendacity of diplomacy, only time would tell, but the League had the fundamentally decent intention of making it in the interest of the world's knaves to act, or at least to talk, like honest men.

We can easily see with hindsight that the hope placed in the League was an extension to the whole world of the squeamishness about violence which Sorel had complained about in *fin-de-siècle* Europe. Sorel had argued that violence had a future, that violence was worth it. After 1918 almost everybody appeared to disagree, but the revulsion from violence could mean nothing to a mind like Hitler's which blamed Germany's failure to achieve her war aims on a failure of civilian strength of will, and which thought that the casualties were a small enough price to pay for the sense of comradeship in the ranks which he extrapolated into a sense of national and racial identity. Hitler's own view of violence is a mixture of the two anti-liberal views of violence available in late nineteenth-century Europe: on the one hand, he espouses the Sorelian view of violence as the means to create a heroic group consciousness; on the other hand, he accepts the older, Bismarckian view, traceable to Clausewitz, that violence is a legitimate instrument of policy. What is remarkable is that Hitler could combine the two. Sorel had seen his own view of violence as being anti-state. His was to be the violence of a heroic working class against the legalised violence of the modern democratic republic. Hitler saw a very different possibility: combine the Sorelian and Bismarckian views of violence, the heroic and the instrumental, within one national state; then the Sorelian violence of a mass movement could be used to capture state power, whose legitimate violence could then be used in the pursuit of Nazi foreign policy ends: first the Party and the SA, and then the Wehrmacht.

NAZI SOCIOLOGY AND MASS MOBILISATION

That war comradeship which in *Mein Kampf* stands for national and racial unity (*Volksgemeinschaft*) was to be the model both for the spirit of the Party which was to capture power in the Reich and for the spirit of the Reich itself. The question remained of how this scheme was going to be put into operation. This meant that a technique of political mobilisation had to be worked out which would be effective in the circumstances that Germany found herself in after the war. By accident or design, Hitler's conception of the condition of post-war Germany is a description of a crowd society which would have realised the worst fears of a pre-war crowd theorist like Le Bon. Le Bon came very close to saying that the French Revolution had turned France into what in the twentieth-century would come to be known as a 'mass society'. Only political and social catastrophes like the French Revolution could create mass societies, and they did it by destroying the stable social categories and identities of a civilisation in the name of the new principles of a new social and political order. The French Revolution's tragedy for France was that its new principle, individualism, was essentially a principle of social disorder. Le Bon's highly exaggerated description of what the individualism of the French Revolution did to French society could easily come from *Mein Kampf*'s own account of the society of the Weimar Republic as a society of lost souls. Individualism, Le Bon says in *The Psychology of Socialism* (1899), isolated the Frenchman from his caste, from his family, from the social groups of which he was a unit, and left him delivered over to himself, and thus transformed society into a mass of individuals, without cohesion and without ties. This was the kind of society which Le Bon had predicted in 1895 would be taken over by the crowd and its Caesarist leader, and it was the Weimar variant of mass society that Hitler had his eye on.

However, Hitler adds a twist of his own to Le Bon's theory of the crowd as it appears in *The Crowd: A Study of the Popular Mind*. Le Bon had looked upon mass society as enervated and purposeless, as made up of a random heap of individuals who were no longer sure about how they ought to live their lives. The politically agitated crowd bawling for anything its leader wanted was a symptom of this social malaise. Serious popular politics and universal suffrage were harmless, and so was most trade unionism, because trade union leaders had their memberships well whipped-in. The insurrection of crowds temporarily roused out of their listless torpor by a demagogue was the real danger, and Le Bon tried to cope with the threat of popular insurrection by providing a crash course in crowd-leadership skills for existing elites, so that they too could manipulate the crowd by substituting themselves for the leaders which the crowd might itself produce. Le Bon's was essentially a theory of informal politics, what we would now call fringe politics, threatening to edge its way into the centre of the political arena. Crowd politics was also non-Marxist. As a sociological category, the crowd was the absolute antithesis of class. The crowd was what happened when people were shaken out of their class categories by the shock of great events or by the demagogic eloquence of a Caesar. Crowds appeared when ordinary social stratification broke down. This was what enabled Marxists and aristocrats to share a contempt for the crowd: the *Lumpenproletariat* of the one was the *canaille* of the other.

Hitler's solution to the problem of the mass society which he thought existed in the Weimar Republic was to make a formal separation between the idea of the crowd and the idea of the mass. Le Bon had used them interchangeably, or had seen the crowd as the symptom of the disease of mass society. In *Mein Kampf* Hitler gropes his way towards the idea that the crowd can be a cure for mass society's problems, and in so doing he puts his finger on what had always been wrong with crowd theory. In its Le Bon version, the social category 'crowd' had been stretched too wide. It included very tight-knit groups which displayed a 'crowd mentality' and it included huge, ill-disciplined mobs in the ordinary sense of the word 'crowd'. This reflected contemporary criminological usage of the term 'crowd'. Collective crime was what interested late nineteenth-century criminologists most, and the crimes of crowds included the pillaging of mobs at one end of the scale and organised criminal conspiracies like the Mafia at the other.[2] Using the crowd as a catch-all for every anti-social group was always an affront to common sense outside the specifically criminological concern with the malfeasances of groups, though its early association with collective crime lingered on to give the idea of the crowd its frightening edge. To a mind like Hitler's, there was obviously not one crowd but two, which we might for convenience call the 'crowd' and the 'mass'. The mob had always been the 'true' crowd, and Freud's *Group Psychology* (which Hitler had certainly never even heard of) had recently confirmed that the 'truest' crowds were churches and armies. Hitler instinctively understood the crowd in Freud's sense as a libidinally organised group under a leader-father. The Nazi Party, and eventually the Third Reich, was to be precisely that. The party as organised crowd was to come out of the mass society which the Great War had made out of Wilhelmine Germany.

Hitler had always hated the racially hybrid empire of the Habsburgs, with its pretend parliamentary system which served only to give a public voice to Slavs, socialists and Jews, and he might well have directed similar criticism at the pseudo-parliamentarism of Bismarckian Germany. Yet Hitler seems again to have grasped instinctively that the end of the Habsburgs in Austria and of the Hohenzollerns in Germany would leave profound psychic gaps in the psychological lives of the people. What would fill that gap? The obvious answer was a new father-leader, who this time would do what the old emperors had failed to do, which was to create a racial and national identity strong enough not to experience that failure of political will which had led to the defeat in 1918 and which was the cause of all the subsequent troubles of the Germans.

Part of the strategy for energising mass society was the use of violence and the symbols of violence. The Party and its military wings, the SA and the SS, were to be much more than a parody of an army. They were to be a substitute for the German army which had been all but banned by the Treaty of Versailles, and to show that they were a 'real' army they had to fight battles in the streets. Above all, the Nazi Party had to march. Nazism was above all else a *movement*. Its goal was the realisation of the original party programme of *Mein Kampf*, which Hitler would never alter, not even after the massacre of the Night of the Long Knives in 1934 had rid the Party of its quasi-socialist elements. The programme was left unaltered as a Sorelian 'myth', a future goal which the Party would always be moving towards. Street violence – 'Possession of the streets is the key to power in the state' was one of the favourite slogans of the SA – or the threat of violence, was part of the propaganda appeal of Nazism, and only indirectly a means to a political end. Sorel had been right as long ago as 1906: it would not take much actual violence to make a society which expected to be peaceful sit up and take notice, and it wouldn't take much more violence to begin to polarise that society. If mass society was a heap of directionless, atomised individuals, led by well-meaning politicians of the centre-left whose liberalism was reducing itself day-by-day to a set of pious clichés, then it was not going to be difficult to energise and polarise it.

Le Bon certainly exaggerated the extent to which France was a mass society before the Great War, and Hitler (and the academic sociology of 'mass society' after 1945) no doubt exaggerated the extent to which the Germany of the Weimar Republic was a mass society, but this does not matter over-much. After all, an age has only its own sociological concepts to understand itself in, and one of the prevailing explanatory paradigms available at the time was crowd theory of the Le Bon type. It was sufficient that enough people saw themselves as living in a mass society, knowing what kind of politics mass society could expect, for crowd theory of the Le Bon type to 'work'. Literate Europe had known long before the Great War that modern individualised societies could expect to see a lot of mass Caesarist politics, for which the adventurism of General Boulanger, the original man on the white horse, was the paradigm. What had changed by the 1920s was that liberalising societies had suffered the great trauma of the First World War, and had begun to look much more like the mass societies which acute spirits had seen beginning to develop before the war.

Two other things had changed which might help to explain a certain lack of jitteriness about the arrival of fascist movements and leaders in the 1920s. Crowd theory of the Le Bon type had always assumed that crowd politics would be a politics of the left, whereas the crowd politics of fascism was undoubtedly a politics of the right. It does not take much historical imagination to see why crowd politics was always previously thought of as being necessarily leftist. European conservatism and European reaction had defined itself as a way of coping with the French Revolution whose great symbolic moment had been the storming of the Bastille. Late eighteenth- and early nineteenth-century conservative political theory had never been very good at explaining anything like the long-term causes of revolution, because that would have been to imply that there was something wrong with the *ancient régime* whose passing they were determined either to minimise or to postpone indefinitely. So conservatives looked round for a *deus ex machina* ('rabbit out of the hat') explanation for the Revolution, and they found it in the revolutionary mob which came from nowhere. The whole French revolutionary experience could then be explained as the result of a riot which had got out of hand because of a critical failure of nerve on the part of France's rulers. Being a reactionary after the Revolution meant being determined never to let the mob 'get out of hand' again. Any form of popular disturbance was likely to turn itself into a re-run of the French Revolution if it was not nipped in the bud. Better a few broken heads and the odd hanging right away, than a repetition of the Reign of Terror in the near future. All nineteenth-century aristocrats (and would-be aristocrats) lived their lives in the shadow of the guillotine. That was the thread which bound the Duke of Wellington to Metternich, Metternich to Bismarck, and Bismarck to Lord Salisbury (who used to confront the revolutionary mob at Hatfield in his nightmares).

Those who did not find the French Revolution a matter for celebration were not likely to be very discriminating about the different kinds of radical political doctrines available in the nineteenth century, so it was inevitable that they should see socialism as a natural extension of the Rights of Man doctrine which had been the Revolution's original theoretical expression. European conservatism was always therefore likely to expect insurrectionary politics to come from the left. The whole Caesarist theme in pre-war crowd theory drew on the very ancient oligarchic fear that the crowd would put itself under the leadership of a demagogue to plunder the rich. It was natural that those on the look-out for dangerous crowd politics after the Great War would still be looking left, and they now had the example of the successful insurrection of the Bolsheviks to sharpen their eyesight. A crowd politics of the right was a theoretical novelty, something for which the world of the 1920s was theoretically unprepared. It must have come as something of a pleasant surprise to some of the crowd's natural enemies to see crowd politics take such an unexpected right turn. Of course, it was perfectly possible to take a position of high elitist disdain for any kind of mass politics, left or right, but if the question came to a choice between the two, then there could not be much doubt which one the elites of Europe would be likely to choose. The notion of 'our' crowd became a perfectly feasible theoretical and practical possibility. Fascist parties understood this perfectly well. They played on the Bolshevik menace, and the Comintern obliged by saying that the communist takeover in the West would come very soon. The Nazis always saved the legal, frock-coated side of their character for election time, to emphasise that they intended to come to power by con- stitutional means. The Party's revolutionary army, the SA, were kept out of sight, and it was this respectability as much as anything else that showed conservatives in Germany that Hitler was a man with whom they could eventually do business. The Nazis looked a bit rough at times, and Hitler had some funny friends, but what was that compared to the Lenin of the sealed train who the Prussian General Staff had so disastrously (as it turned out) returned to Petrograd in 1917?

The other great change in the attitude to crowd politics had been brought about by the violence of the Great War itself. It was unusual for the Great War to make people like violence more, but it probably did more than anything else ever did to raise the threshold of people's tolerance of violence. Millions had died in the war, but millions had also survived, and it is to be supposed that those millions included many who had come through relatively unscathed. The men of the left could easily think of the violence of the Great War as useless violence as the armies of European working men slaughtered each other at the behest of their common class enemy. Men such as these could not react with anything like horror to the violence of Lenin and the Bolsheviks against their class enemies in the Russian Revolution and Civil War, because Bolshevik violence was at least *for* something, and the casualty figures from Russia, in so far as any were available, were bound to seem puny when compared to those which had come from the Western Front. The same could be said of the right. What was a little direct action violence in domestic politics when compared to the international violence of the war? Besides, nobody of any political persuasion, with the exception of pacifists and anarchists, had come out of the war with much of their credit still good, and this could be seen to be especially true of the liberalism of the Entente powers. Observers in all the original belligerent countries had remarked on the war fever which seemed to have gripped the masses in 1914. The liberal states could no more keep themselves out of the war than the continental autocracies. Indeed, one liberal democracy, Italy, came into the war for no very good discernible reason a year after it had started, and another liberal democracy, America, came all the way across the Atlantic to join a war already nearly three years old. Men of every political persuasion appeared to be able to find good reasons for fighting the Great War, the Serbian Social Democrats always honourably excepted.

The world of the 1920s, then, was a world which had become inured to violence and it was a world in which almost nobody could convincingly take the moral high ground. It was above all a world in which it would always be easy to wink at the relatively harmless level of fascist violence when compared to the shared experience of the millions who came back from the war in 1918. How could men like these be shocked by the odd street-fight or two, or a few beatings-up in cellars, or by political parties which chose to dress up in uniform? Failure to be shocked by violence is, of course, a very different thing from actually approving of violence. So who did approve? Who wanted to march in the fascist army-parties? Those who missed the comradeship of the war, no doubt, and who could find no equivalent in civilian life. Also to be included are those who missed the war because of age, who felt the humiliation of the peace, and who held their manhood cheap when they compared themselves to the heroes who returned from the war. The Nazi Party gave the ones who had missed out a chance to prove themselves, and it is easy to see how old front-soldiers could enjoy the prestige of men who had already gone through the mill.

What must be added in the case of Germany is that there was no 'normal' political life to go back to. The victors had forced a republic on a people not all of whom accepted that they had actually been defeated, and many of whom thought that the victorious powers had not the shadow of a right to determine what their political arrangements should be. Acceptance of the legitimacy of the Weimar Republic was indistinguishable from admitting both the German defeat and German war guilt, because these were the only possible justifications for the right of the victors to impose a republic on Germany. This republic was invested with the hope that it would turn out to be a copy of the stable democracies of the Anglo-Saxon world. What tended to be forgotten in the liberal enthusiasm for the end of German and Austrian imperialism was the long tradition of continental criticism of liberal democracy, which was already in place in both France and Italy before 1914, and which was just waiting to be applied to the new liberal democracy in Germany. The failure of French and Italian liberalism to produce stable governments with strong political leadership was a byword before the First World War. Now liberal democracy was being forced on the Germans in the place of the only successful political leadership they had ever had in the modern world. Not only would the Weimar Republic have to establish itself in a political culture partly hostile to it, but it would have to do it quickly because the republican government in Germany was going to be called upon to solve economic and social problems which were common to most states in the 1920s and 1930s. This was always going to be a tall order, because even the states with well-established systems of democratic government were going to find the task difficult enough, and were to go through many twists and turns before they reached even the partial solutions which they stumbled upon.

German post-war democracy came into being when the political agendas of all the democracies were much fuller than they had ever been before 1914. The Third Republic in France before the Great War had been content if it could just survive. Its governments had been content simply to occupy power. This infuriated their right-wing enemies, but it seemed to have pleased republicans well enough if the republic continued to keep its enemies out. Things were to be very different after 1918, when European governments were to find themselves being pushed into the unfamiliar business of full-time economic management, while at the same time having to work out how economic management was actually to be done. There is an important sense in which all governments outside the Soviet Union were drifting in the 1920s, and this mattered particularly in the Germany of the Weimar Republic, whose system of government had both to establish itself and to deliver solutions to problems over which well-established governments elsewhere were themselves stumbling. All the old anti-democratic and anti-liberal arguments which Action Française had worked out before 1914 against a parliamentary republic in France which was not expected to do very much applied with renewed force to the new German republic which was required to do a great deal in a very short time.

The combination of the awareness of the coming of mass society and the critique of parliamentary democracy as failing to provide the dynamic political leadership which that society required was a powerful enough polemical weapon. Wedded to a technique of political mobilisation based on the latest collective psychology available, and to ruthless targeting of 'the Jews' as a convenient shorthand for the causes of all Germany's problems, the combination appeared to be well-nigh irresistible. That is, at least, what Hitler thought.

THE NAZI RACE DOCTRINE

Nazi race doctrine is as dreary as it is deadly. It was entirely unoriginal apart from some late genocidal twists of its own. It is important to emphasise this lack of originality for two reasons. First, we have come to think of the Final Solution to the Jewish Problem as a central twentieth-century event, so that it is easy to forget that its doctrinal origins are to be found in the evolutionary social biology of the nineteenth century. This means that Hitler addressed his race doctrine to a world which was already used to thinking in race terms. The fact that the race doctrine was not original was therefore a source of polemical strength, not weakness. All the Nazis did was to take the race doctrine's biologism a bit more literally than their nineteenth-century predecessors had done. We have already noticed the late nineteenth-century rush of all the human sciences to assimilate the models and methods of evolutionary biology, and we have also noticed the tendency to elide the concepts of culture transmission and biological heredity to which this led. Where *we* would see only analogies between biological and social development, late nineteenth-century social and political thinkers saw social development as a *continuation* of biological development. No matter that now this seems quaint, because at the time it was regarded as a perfectly respectable enterprise within genuine social science (and it could be argued that it is an enterprise which is not yet over). The Nazi race doctrine thrived for years on the literalising of this analogy. Blood was what counted for them, and by 'blood' they meant more than the stuff you see when you cut yourself. 'Good' blood was 'pure'. It could easily be 'corrupted' by the admixture of 'other' kinds of blood. Any kind of 'pure' blood was probably better than any kind of 'mixed' blood, except in the cases where part of the mixture was 'good' German blood. German blood was peculiar because, while being the best of all blood, it was also especially vulnerable to corruption by other kinds of blood, by Slav and gypsy blood, and especially by Jewish blood. Corruption of the original Teutonic blood supply explained why the Germans had not always been the top nation nature had intended them to be. Nazi race doctrine posited a view of human history as an extended blood-feud. The true struggle of nations was struggle for race purity, and all blood mixture led eventually to political and cultural decline. These processes were by no means irreversible, or at least not before a certain point had been reached. There might be bad blood between nations, but bad blood could be bred out as well as bred in. All that was required was a state which understood blood, and which had the moral courage to institute a race policy which outlawed breeding across alien blood-lines. Any state which recognised that its national bloodstock was its most precious asset was bound to get ahead of the rest, and any state which made appropriate arrangements to increase and purify that stock was sure to go on to greatness.

This was probably true even of the Jews. Nazi anti-Semitism was predicated on two assumptions about Jews which are not easily reconcilable. Jewish blood was at the bottom of the blood-scale on which German blood was at the top; Jewish blood was as bad as blood could be, but at the same time you do not have to read very deeply between the lines of *Mein Kampf* to detect a certain perverse admiration for the historical strength and tenacity of international Jewry. How otherwise would the success of the international Jewish conspiracy be explained? Jews have done better in the modern world than the Germans. God's chosen people has all but conquered nature's master race. It is unlikely that this has happened by accident. Jews, having no fatherland of their own, are determined that no other race should entirely possess its own fatherland, and what better way to achieve this than by deliberately setting out to corrupt the host nation's blood to the point where that nation is so weak that it lacks the racial will to expel those very Jews who are the cause of its weakness? Racially weak fatherlands are the natural spawning ground for Jews, and their natural political disguises are liberalism and socialism.

FASCISM AND CORPORATISM

Ever since the Enlightenment and the French Revolution had proclaimed the essential unity of humanity and had endowed even Jews with equal natural and civil rights, it had been said that liberal cosmopolitanism had sheltered the Jewish moneymakers. These were all doctrinal positions which had been worked out during the Dreyfus Affair in France by Action Française, and there too we find the apparent contradiction between the anti-Semite's association of Jews with international high finance on the one hand, and socialism on the other. This is not quite the blatant contradiction it is often made out to be. From the anti-Semite's point of view, international high finance and international socialism are two different sides of the same coin. Enlightened cosmopolitanism could go either way, and so you would expect Jews to be heavily involved in both. There is also a causal connection between the two. Part of the right-wing attack on the parliamentary republic had always been that it allowed far too much room for the development of mass socialist parties, and part of the right-wing critique of capitalist individualism had always been that the un-fettered development of modern industrial production created the economic and social conditions in which large numbers of working men and women would inevitably be attracted to socialism. This can be seen as part of a Europe-wide effort in the second half of the nineteenth century by conservatives to try to drive a wedge between the enfranchised or about-to-be enfranchised working classes and their liberal or socialist leaders. Disraeli was probably the first leading European politician to try to convince working men that it was the aristocracy and not the bourgeoisie who were their natural leaders, while it did not take much in France after the *Commune* to persuade some French working men that the bourgeois republic would never be theirs. Action Française had been quick to see an opening here for its own brand of corporatism, and Maurras himself never tired of pointing out the difference between how the republic of Monsieur Thiers had treated the Communards and how a king would have treated them. The government of the republic had slaughtered the Communard rank-and-file and had allowed the leaders who had misled them to escape; a king would have punished the leaders and let his good people off with a caution.

Fascist corporatism was to be a neat solution, to the problems of both liberalism and socialism, by providing an alternative means of political representation to the one, and an alternative method of working-class organisation to the other. Conservatism had always been uneasy about the abstractness of the liberal democratic idea of citizen representation, for the simple reason that it assumed an equality which was at variance with the ordinary facts of human experience. What it was that men had in common was a very elusive thing. Liberals had talked about equality of natural rights, or the essential sameness of men's natures as seekers after pleasure and avoiders of pain. Conservatives had always countered by saying that generalised formulae like these tell us nothing very interesting about men as they actually live in the world.

Liberal individualism existed at such a level of generality that it was an affront to the very idea of individuality. Surely, conservatives argued, what really mattered to human beings was their own actual identity, what made them different from other men, or at the very least what made them different from other kinds of men. To see human identity in conservative terms was impossible without the existence of a given society into which human beings fitted, and the most obvious way a man fitted into his society was through the work he did. Work was what mattered to most men because it was the fundamental shaping activity of their lives.

Yet liberalism's idea of representation expressly excluded the representation of a man's work as being a pre-modern form of guild representation, properly associated only with the government of medieval towns. The ideal citizen of a liberal state was supposed to be able to cast off his economic and social identity when he went into the polling booth, and vote as a rational individual solely on the basis of what he thought would increase the public good. Even assuming that such a remarkable transformation into rational man is possible, and even assuming that the notion of the public good is generally intelligible and accessible, this still leaves open the question of what the business of exercising the citizen's right to vote can actually mean to the real social and economic man who is voting. The answer must be: not very much. Add to that the fact that democracy is a matter not of individual votes but of aggregates of votes, and we can readily begin to see the force of the anti-liberal argument that the matter of voting is something of a charade in which an unreal man does something which to him must seem rather trivial if he thinks about the matter clearly or at all.

By 1900, critiques like this of parliamentary representation were ten a penny. Thinkers on the left and the right queued up to say what *really* happened in parliamentary elections. *Of course* people did not cast off their workaday selves when they went into polling booths. Quite the reverse. They knew perfectly well that they voted for candidates who openly supported separate interests and solicited the suffrages of the voters expressly on the grounds that the voters shared the interest which a particular candidate represented. How effectively that interest did in fact come to be represented was part of the luck of the game. It was necessarily chancy, but then that was what gave electoral politics its particular charm. As a matter of electoral fact, some interests were rather better at getting themselves represented than others, and some interests always found themselves more or less permanently excluded, either because of the nature of particular electoral systems, or because of the accidents of political geography. At the very least, some interests were likely to be over-represented and some under-represented.

The corporatist argument addressed itself directly to the chanciness of electoral representation. Why not just admit openly, says the corporatist, that liberal democratic electoral systems are systems of interest representation? Why not, then, systematise that interest representation into law? That would rule out the unfairness of under- and over-representation by guaranteeing that every group of any significance will have its collective voice heard in government. Organise a society into its economically functional groups, and make sure that the leadership of each group has the opportunity to state its case, with government acting as an honest broker between the groups. This, say its defenders, is an especially honest form of politics because everything is out in the open. Nobody can be in any doubt about what the system of representation is for. The system also has the considerable advantage that it cuts down on the customary mendacity of liberal electoral politics. Every candidate in a liberal democratic electoral system feels obliged to pretend that the interest which he represents really is the general interest and not a particular interest at all. So parliamentary elections degenerate into unseemly parades of special interests, each pretending that its own selfish interest is the interest of the whole nation. Somebody must be lying, and the chances are that everybody is lying.

The corporatist scenario leaves no room for any other kind of representation except functional representation through economic function. The corporatist would say not only that there was no need for further representation, but also that other kinds of representation, parliamentary say, or trade union, would merely confuse people about who was actually representing them. The idea that a particular person might feel more secure if he were to be represented in more than one way, or as a member of more than one group, simply does not feature in the corporatist view of functional representation. It might appear from the corporatist view of representation that corporatists are sociologically naive because they think that it is a simple matter to divide an industrial society into its constituent economic groups. In fact, corporatists think the reverse. Their theory of representation is a response to the social complication of industrial societies, and they think it will require a certain amount of finely tuned social engineering to make the economic divisions without which the corporatist theory of representation could not work. What corporatists do think is that it would be stupid to complicate the representation system still further after having engineered some sort of order out of the seeming chaos of modern industrialised states.

FASCISM AND POLITICAL LEADERSHIP

Corporatism puts a very high value on the visibility of political representatives, which effectively means the visibility of political leadership. It had again been Action Française which had led the way in the critique of political leadership in parliamentary republics. The Third Republic in France, along with the Italy of Giolitti, were the classic cases of parliamentary democracies which in the eyes of their right-wing critics failed to provide effective political leadership. This failure could be directly attributed to the system of parliamentary representation, which in both cases failed to produce parties with stable enough majorities in the legislatures to form long-lasting governments. Government after government would be defeated in the chamber. Governments were temporary coalitions of professional politicians, often with considerable continuity of personnel, so it seemed to right-wing critics that more or less the same political gang formed more or less the same kinds of governments, with not much to show for it beyond providing the sweets of office for politicians not noted for their political sincerity or for their financial probity. We can readily sympathise with the political viewpoint which finds its country being let down by its official political leaders, and perhaps we could sympathise with that viewpoint more when it was pointed out that the governments of the parliamentary regime were so weak that they couldn't possibly be 'running the country' anyway. If the official representatives of the people were not running the country, then who was? Faceless bureaucrats, people accountable to nobody because they had been elected by nobody. And no doubt other, more sinister, forces lurked behind the bureaucrats, the secret money-power, Jews, and Freemasons.

Fascism deals directly with the sense of political frustration which can come from not knowing who your leader really is. The corporatist theory of representation scores very high on the visibility of political leadership scale, and this is obviously connected with the huge fuss that fascists make of their leaders in general. This crying-up of the leader can seem childish to liberals who are ever-mindful of the dangers inherent in political power, and who are therefore reassured when they are led by modest leaders wearing ordinary clothes; but this is not how fascists see the matter. In their way, they take the concept of political responsibility much more seriously, or at least much more literally, than most of their political opponents. In a state with a big, up-front leader, nobody is ever supposed to be in any doubt about where the buck stops. The leader may not always be right, but he *is* the leader. This idea lies behind what might otherwise be taken to be some rather hysterical remarks that Hitler makes in *Mein Kampf* about truly Germanic democracy, in which a leader will answer with his life for the decisions he makes, which presumably means for his mistakes. This can easily be taken for a typical piece of fascist theatricality, but it is not just that. It reflects a long right-wing tradition of dissatisfaction with the quality of liberal-democratic leadership, and with the growing realisation that, in liberal systems of separated and developed power, nothing is easier for a wily politician than to pass the responsibility for some piece of political ineptitude onto someone else.

The leadership principle in fascism no doubt owes something to a sense of nostalgia for departed kings. The progressive English conservative Walter Bagehot had got this feeling exactly right in his account of monarchy in *The English Constitution* (1864). The British, he believed, would need the symbolic leadership of a monarchy for a long time after the real power of government had passed into other hands. Anglican mummery, and pomp and circumstance, seemed still to be necessary to a people who had yet to grow up politically. Bagehot was an evolutionist who believed with the consensus that some layers of a society, like some whole peoples, had failed to progress as quickly as others. These less advanced groups still had to be treated like children. A monarchical magic lantern show from time to time was just the thing, coupled with displays of armed force. A show of force with the king at the centre was the best way of reminding children where their duties lay. Fascist leaders, on the other hand, knew perfectly well that they were not kings (though some fascist leaders hedged their bets by keeping a king up their sleeves in case one day he might be useful), and fascist leaders knew equally well that the difference between themselves and kings was that everybody knew where kings *came from*. The same could be said of the presidents and prime ministers of the liberal democracies, who appeared by constitutional right as the result of electoral choice. In a sense which would have been familiar to Machiavelli, fascist leaders had to create for themselves the legitimacy which prima facie they so obviously lacked.

Each case had its special features, but it can roughly be said that fascist leaders went about the business of creating their own legitimacy in two different ways. Some fascist leaders sought legitimacy by casting round for the institutional support of armies, churches, bureaucracies, academies and even dynasties, hoping that some of the authority of these institutions would rub off onto them. Fascist leaders could run highly respectable-looking protection rackets, offering traditional institutions protection at a price against the common enemy, 'the reds' or 'the communists'. No doubt offers were made which were sometimes difficult to refuse, but in this rough trade everybody knew what they were getting. Armies and churches were always the best bet, because the use of violence is expected of soldiers, 'clean' violence as against the messy stuff of guerrillas or terrorists, and a display of orthodox piety was always useful as a signal to a nervous population that the established moral order, and so the social order, was not under threat. This was, with exceptions, the pattern of fascist leaders in the deeply Catholic countries of southern and eastern Europe.

The Hitler case and to an extent the Mussolini case are different because they both chose the 'popular' or crowd route to political legitimacy, and Hitler's *Mein Kampf* is chiefly remarkable because in it Hitler is able to identify his own struggle to become leader of the Reich with the whole German people's struggle to recover from the deeply unjust humiliation it suffered at the hands of the so-called victors after 1918. We should never forget that the crowd theory of nearly half a century before 1914 had been predicting crowd leaders of a type which fitted Hitler to a tee. Social science can create expectations when it passes into the world of general literacy, and there can be no doubt that that was what happened to crowd theory once Le Bon had got his hands on it. Le Bon's relentless message to existing elites was that, if leaders were not found for the crowd, then the crowd would find leaders of its own. Nobody quite knew what the leader who came out of the crowd was going to look like, though there were lots of guesses: perhaps a bit like Rousseau, half-genius, half-mad, or a brigand chief, or Atilla the Hun, or a hypnotiser on a grand scale. What everybody seemed to agree about was that the society which produced a crowd leader of the expected type was in for some rough politics. The fascist leaders who came from armies, and who attached themselves to the institutions of the existing social order, can be thought of as crowd leaders found for the crowd from outside, while leaders like Hitler and Mussolini can be thought of as leaders who came out of the crowd itself.

We do well to remind ourselves what the concept of the crowd had come to mean by the time the fascist leaders began to pick up followers in the mass societies which were supposed to have been created as a result of the multiple shocks passed through them by the First World War. A crowd had come to mean a heterogeneous group of people who replaced their various social identities by a common psychological identification with each other as followers of a particular leader. Mass societies were supposed to be societies of collapsing or worn-out social categories, large numbers of whose people were supposed no longer to know who they were, and who were just waiting for the first group to come along which offered them some kind of psychological home. The crowd was frightening precisely because it inhabited no properly mapped-out social space. The crowd's critics had never been slow to identify the crowd with 'the people' for polemical conservative reasons, but we can see that there is a real sense in which the crowd's conservative enemies got their sociology and their social psychology absolutely right. What was 'the people', after all, except what would be left if you took everybody's ordinary social categories away? The French republican historian Michelet and those following him in the republican tradition have come in for a lot of right-wing and Marxist criticism for saying that 'the people' stormed the Bastille and made the French Revolution. How, it has endlessly been asked, could 'the people' actually have done that? Surely, it must have been a special category of the people, ruffians for the right, workers for the left, who did the storming, just as it must have been particular categories of people who took part in all the great events of the Revolution. And so into the minutiae of retrospective political sociology. The tedious business of taking a questionnaire to people who should be spared that particular modern indignity in the quiet of their graves is completely unnecessary, because crowd theory solves the mystery of who stormed the Bastille. If it was the crowd, then it must also have been 'the people', because in crowd theory we can see that 'the crowd' and 'the people' are interchangeable terms. The lack of sociological precision of the term 'the people' turns out to be an analytical advantage after all. Classes, or any other social categories, are not the sub-groups which together make up the group 'the people', because crowd theory shows us that 'the people' is a group of an entirely different kind, not sociological at all, but psychological.

It cannot today matter very much whether it was a 'psychological' or a 'sociological' group which stormed the Bastille all those years ago, but it does matter if we are to understand what kind of leadership it was that a man like Hitler thought he was offering to his 'crowd' or to his 'people'. Remember Hitler's self-description in *Mein Kampf* as a man of intense ordinariness whose only real experience is the war experience he shares with millions. The German army of the First World War is the psychological crowd out of which Hitler came. Armies are the perfect crowds in the Le Bon sense. Hitler's own political career can be seen as an attempt to re-create that crowd out of the Nazi Party and then out of the whole German nation. And he takes the idea of the whole German nation literally. (It was going to include the Austrian Germans, and all the Germans who had been left to live in other states by the First World War treaties. This 'gathering-in' of the Germans outside the Reich had startling foreign policy implications, because it meant that Hitler would eventually take the Reich to them in the comfort of their own homes. This was a new departure for crowd theory, which in its nineteenth-century version had barely hinted at the redrawing of international borders.)

Hitler's ordinariness was therefore an advantage, not a disadvantage, because he could claim that his was a more authentic voice of the common man than any fascist general's. Hitler wants to be seen as the personification of the common man, and wants his own experience to be seen as the common man's experience in an intensified form. Hitler has already been through the experience of struggle which was and will be everyman's struggle, so that his own experience becomes the collective experience of the whole German people.

734

The political sociology implicit in Hitler's conception of himself is a crowd sociology. People like him, Hitler seems to be saying, were held back by the constraints of the old societies into which they had been born. Hitler had always hated the Habsburg Empire as a rotten hybrid state, over-stratified, with layer superimposed upon layer of social, racial and religious discrimination. Being born near the bottom of the Habsurg pile left a very long way to go even for men of more than ordinary talents like Hitler. Mob politics in mass society was to give men like him their chance. The advent of mass society loosened the hold of the old social distinctions, and the Party, and eventually the whole nation, as organised crowds would give the German people a chance to start again. A new system of power relations would come out of the leader's will. He could be relied upon to get these matters right, because the leader who came out of crowd politics understood the people in a way which was not available to legitimate leaders of the dynastic or liberal-democratic kind. The mass experience was *his* experience and the organised crowd was *his* crowd; their will was his will. There could be no valid contradiction between the will of the nation and the will of its leader. They were, in the strict sense of crowd theory, equivalents.

The basis of Nazi political thinking in crowd theory is worth emphasising because, without it, the Nazi theory of the Party and of the leadership principle in general can seem to be composed almost entirely of mystical eye-wash. It may still be eye-wash, but if it is, then the latest psychological theory on which it is based must also be eye-wash. Whether it was or not can be endlessly debated. What there can be no doubt about is that, at the time, the individual and group psychology upon which Nazi theory was based was state-of-the-art psychology. Much good scholarly ink has been wasted in trying to show that Hitler must have read a German translation of Le Bon from one of the lending libraries which he frequented when he was down on his luck in Vienna before the First World War. Certainly, the passages in *Mein Kampf* about the techniques of political propaganda look like a summary of Le Bon, though whether they came direct from Le Bon is still a moot point. None of this would matter very much, except that this determination to find a textual correlation between *Mein Kampf* and Le Bon's *The Crowd* seriously underestimates the ubiquity of the influences of social theory like Le Bon's before and after the First World War. You would no more have had to have read Le Bon to know about crowd theory around the time of the First World War than you would have had to have read Rousseau to be a revolutionary in 1789, or to have read Marx to have been a Bolshevik in 1917. To say that ideas are 'in the air' may seem a lazy way to do the history of ideas, but sometimes it just happens to be the case. This seems to be as likely to have been true of crowd theory as it is to be true of any other kind of political theory. If Freud could become 'a whole climate of opinion', then why not Le Bon?

Another reason for emphasising the crowd theory aspects of Nazism is that it helps to sustain the view that Nazism was genuinely revolutionary. Nazi ideology eventually incorporated so much antiquated Teutonic-Wagnerian junk that it is easy to see Nazism as essentially backward-looking, and this is a view encouraged by Nazism's many enemies who wish to see fascism in general and Nazism in particular as 'reactionary'. In fact, Nazism was based on the most modern political sociology and social psychology available at the time. This aspect of Nazism tended to get lost in the enormous historical and sociological literature which emerged from the ruins of the Third Reich to explain the whole European fascist experience. The theory of mass society has a central place in that explanatory literature. Mass society theory was invented to explain the rise of fascism. What should rather be said is that the theory of mass society was needlessly re-invented after 1945 to explain the rise of fascism, because the theory of mass society was already there in crowd theory in 1895 before Europe had even heard the word 'fascist'. Literate Europe knew it was about to live in a mass society by the time Le Bon had popularised crowd theory. Crowd theory wasn't called 'mass society' theory, but that was about the only difference. We can now see that it does not matter very much whether, say, Weimer Germany 'really' was a mass society in the sense understood by mass society theorists after 1945. What does matter is that mass society in all but name was available to European societies after the First World War as their own self-understanding. If enough people living in a society share a particular view about what kind of society it is that they are living in, then that particular view becomes part of that society's politics. It is worth repeating that a society has only got its own social theory to understand itself in. The social theory available will of course consist of several competing social theories, and the one that is likeliest to gain the most widespread acceptance is the one which seems to explain their perceived social situation to most people best. Suppose there are large numbers of people, for various reasons unwilling to accept Marxist explanations yet still feeling that their society is in need of explanations of its conditions that traditional conservatism no longer provides. And also suppose a fairly generalised disenchantment with bourgeois liberalism. Then where else would such a society go except to fascism? This would be especially likely if fascism could convincingly show that a good deal of how it did in fact explain the world was itself the product of systematic reflection on the nature of modernity. And where else would fascism be likely to go for such an explanation than to crowd theory, which set out to explain the modern world to itself in the terms of the modern world's own evolutionary psychology and sociology?

This chapter began with the warning that fascist political thinking is not to be under-estimated. Fascism's many political enemies[3] do themselves no good by keeping up the pretence that fascism is only for morons. Nor does the catch-all epithet 'reactionary' come near to describing adequately some of fascism's particular arguments – its attack on parlia-mentary democracy, for instance. Fascism makes perfectly good sense as an anti-Marxist but still revolutionary response to the apparent failures of liberal democracies in their troubled period after the First World War. Fascism can be seen as an attempt to reintegrate societies which were going through the painful process of becoming mass societies, or were seen to be going through such a process. No doubt fascists exaggerated the extent to which their societies were disintegrating into heaps of atomised, anomic individuals all but indistinguishable from each other, becoming formless crowds just waiting to be energised into mob politics by leaders of the kind that crowd theory had been predicting since the 1870s. It has, for instance, become something of a cliché to point out that many of those who supported fascism, either actively or passively, did so because they thought that fascist movements could protect their traditional social categories. Far from having to quit traditional social categories to become fascists, many supported fascism so as not to have to quit those categories at all. All of this is no doubt true, but the fact remains that fascism was a way of getting out of what appeared to be enervated liberal democracies with some form of social integration left intact. In a world which everybody agreed had changed quickly and could change quickly again in the future, it made perfectly good sense to millions to see fascism as the wave of the future. And who dares to blame them, any more than they would dare to blame anybody who ever espoused a doctrine without having the foresight to see what its real future was going to be?

NOTES ON SOURCES

It is perhaps surprising that the works of fascist thinkers are not that readily available in English, and there is room for much speculation on why this is the case. Hitler's *Mein Kampf*, trans. Manheim (new edn, 1974), is the standard edition. Also to be read are Jose Antonio Primo de Rivera, *Selected Writings*, ed. Hugh Thomas (1972), *Italian Fascisms*, ed. A. Lyttleton (1973), and *The French Right: From De Maistre to Maurras*, ed. J.S. McClelland (1971). For Hitler, see A. Bullock, *Hitler* (rev. edn, 1964), J.P. Stern, *The Führer and the People* (1984), I. Kershaw, *Hitler* (1991), and Dick Geary, *Hitler and Nazism* (1993). For a general treatment of fascism, see E. Nolte, *Three Faces of Fascism* (1965), which has been the source of much debate. For an idea of the range of commentary on fascism, see W. Lacqueur, *Fascism: A Reader's Guide* (1976).

31

CONSERVATISM
Maurras and Oakeshott

CHARLES MAURRAS

Charles Maurras lived three lives, as a Provençal, as a Frenchman and as a European. Maurras himself could never see any contradiction between them. Maurras lived long enough (1868–1952) and at just the right period of French history to be able to feel all of the great dramas of modern French political history, either personally or vicariously. He was proud of having learned his catechism from a veteran of Napoleon's Grand Army, which retreated from Moscow in 1812, and he lived well into the era of the atomic bomb and the Cold War. He took part in the Dreyfus Affair and lived on into the post-Auschwitz world which included the state of Israel. The France of his birth was a Napoleonic Empire; he lived through the whole of the Third Republic, saw Vichy come and go, saw de Gaulle in and out of politics after the Liberation in 1944, and saw out his days under the Fourth Republic. He was imprisoned under both the republican regimes he had the misfortune to live under. And he did all this without changing his mind once about anything really important.

How could this be? Surely this man must have had his head in the clouds. How could anyone see everything that Maurras saw in his long life and not change as the world changed? Yet most of the people who knew Maurras, either personally or through his work, speak of him as the supreme avoider of fantasies. A famous portrait of Maurras written by the critic Robert Brasillach in 1934 refers to Maurras's pursuit of the essential. In English, we would say that there was no flannel about Maurras. The France which he loved wasn't mystical – like Barrès's France it was concrete, the France of everyday life, a land, a people, and, Maurras would add, a dynasty. Maurras's politics was pragmatic: have a policy for everything, have an answer ready for every question.

Was Maurras, then, one of those extremely rare creatures (Machiavelli might be another): realists who create myths? Was his royalist France a figment of his imagination? On the one hand, a royalist country without a king is perfectly conceivable; but on the other hand, for how *long* is it conceivable? If Maurras was right, for a very long time indeed. Yet one still comes across perfectly sane people in provincial France who, with the recent decline in popularity of the house of Mountbatten–Windsor in mind, will say with perfect confidence that, at heart, France has always been more royalist than Britain.

MICHAEL OAKESHOTT

Born in 1901 the son of a prominent Fabian socialist, Joseph Oakeshott, and sent to a progressive school, Oakeshott's origins were not promising for a conservative political philosopher who would eventually be compared in importance to Burke. He went up to Gonville and Caius College, Cambridge (one of the better foundations in the University), and stayed there as a fellow in history for twenty years (and he was later to become an honorary fellow of Caius). His first book, *Experience and Its Modes* (1933), fell stillborn from the press, perhaps because it went against a certain philosophical grain, for Oakeshott's Cambridge was also the Cambridge of Russell and Wittgenstein. Oakeshott's next book, *Social and Political Doctrines of Contemporary Europe* was more than a skirmish in a war with the age. The war itself kept Oakeshott away from Caius for five years. Ernest Barker's old chair of Political Science at Cambridge having gone to an outsider from Oxford, Oakeshott was translated to Harold Laski's old chair of Political Science at the London School of Economics.

Laski was something of an intellectual hero of the left, and Laski's appointees at LSE were less than enchanted by Oakeshott's appointment to one of the intellectual capitals of British socialism, and they were not cheered up by Oakeshott's celebrated inaugural lecture which painted a picture of political studies which was just about as un-Laskiish as it could be. In time, Oakeshott won most of his new colleagues round, with his unfailing courtesy, his insistence that his conservatism was not Conservatism, by his failure to preach, and, not least, by administrative skills of a high order. He was also something of a bon viveur and he had a sense of fun.

Oakeshott never published very much (so he would not have lasted very long in a contemporary university) – a volume of essays under the title *Rationalism in Politics, On Human Conduct*, and *On History*, these last two being the products of his old age. No political thinker of his eminence is harder to pin an ideological label on. He was always acutely conscious that his was a voice which was always going to be difficult to hear in the din of ideological politics. He called himself a conservative and voted Tory as the least objectionable of electoral alternatives, but he can be called neither in any of the conventional senses of those words. Perhaps the comparison with Burke is the most apposite, for Burke was a Whig, some of whose arguments Tories (and later conservatives) found congenial. Like Burke, Oakeshott was an original, and, like all originals, invites imitators only at their peril. He died in 1990.

Democracy's enemies got one thing right: politics in the democratic age was going to be raucous. This raucousness was more than a matter of tone. Exasperation with opponents is the great indicator of ideological politics. Politics in Europe since the original French Revolution of 1789 has been emphatically ideological. Burke was the first important political thinker to realise that a counter-ideology was going to be an essential part of the armoury of counter-revolution. Burke's strategy was to provide a counter-revolutionary ideology part of whose claim was that revolutionary politics was ideological while conservative politics was not. Ideology got a bad name from the start. Ideological politics seemed to be especially intolerant of opposition, especially intellectual opposition. This was in part due to the fact that ideological politics tended to be politics in the name of a cause, and crusaders are not notorious for their tolerance, but it was also partly due to the nature of ideological thinking itself.

Ideological systems, of the left or the right, always tend to see themselves as universal in their appeal. On their surfaces, ideologies always appear to appeal to everyman, but ideologists are not altogether fools, and they recognise that in practice they cannot persuade everybody: Marx did not write to convince Lancashire mill-owners, nor Lenin to convince the tsar. However, the universalising nature of ideologies, the idea that in principle they contain truths capable of gaining the assent of all rational people, has led ideologists to incorporate into their ideologies sets of reasons why certain people, or certain groups of people, will always refuse to acknowledge the truths which ideologies claim to contain. Ideologies typically point to groups of people who, either wilfully or unwittingly, cannot see that the claims of a particular ideology are true. This accounts for the exasperation which ideologists display towards opponents. Ideologists are known for their resistance to the idea that ideologies are circular. Ideologies contain all kinds of truths about the world, and they also contain certain observations about the world which explain why some people will never acknowledge these truths. Hence it follows that an ideology's truths about the world are true whether people accept them as true or not. Indeed, part of the proof of an ideology's truth lies precisely in the fact that certain kinds of people will be unable to see that truth.

Ideological politics is, none the less, frequently accompanied by the kind of intellectual honesty associated with medieval inquisitors. Honest ideologists will do all they can to convince the unbelievers, just as medieval inquisitors were duty bound to do all they could to convince heretics of their errors. But, like inquisitors, ideologists often find that they come up against the devil. A level of invincible ignorance will often be encountered, a bedrock of unconvincible error which puts the possessor of it outside the pale. People with this fundamental recalcitrance are the enemies of truth, and therefore the enemies of humanity, for who would not prefer human living to be founded on truth, not error? Hence the tendency of the practitioners of ideological politics to exasperation and intolerance at the end of a long day when realisation comes that certain people will never grasp it.

The people who cannot or will not recognise ideological truths tend to fall into particular categories, and, of course, the categories will be different for different ideologies. Foreign conquerors will be found to be impervious to the truths of emergent nationalisms, capitalists will be unreceptive to the truths of socialism, absolute monarchs will be unmoved by the truths of liberalism, and so on. Ideologies, then, from the start identify groups as their enemies, and it is a very short step from there to saying that it is really a waste of ideological time trying to convert the unconvertible. Why bother to proselytise where there is no chance of conversion? And it is a very short step from there to saying that enemies really ought to be identified and dealt with right away, with no arguing. Ideological political thinking sometimes adds one further refinement, and that is that ideologists (theorists and practitioners) do not say that opposition to an ideology's truths is their opponents' fault, if by 'fault' we mean an act of will. Some men will oppose an ideology out of sheer self-interest or sheer cussedness, but these are not the really interesting cases. The really interesting cases are those in which the opponents cannot 'with the best will in the world' see an ideology's truth. Marxists call this 'false consciousness', a way of looking at the world so blinkered that the eyes which see so narrowly will never be able to see anything else. This is a condition which is beyond self-interested righteousness or cross-grainedness. No man blinkers himself; rather it is the rest of the world or the sum total of his life circumstances which puts the blinkers on, and after a bit he can run in no other way. In other words, the ideologist does not necessarily find fault with his opponent in the sense of attributing malice to him. Opposition can be seen as part of the given world of existence, almost as a part of nature, so that in principle there is no reason to feel more guilty about blowing one's opponents up than about blasting a natural obstacle out of the way of a road that is being built.

Conservatives since the French Revolution have usually claimed that their brand of conservatism is not ideological in the same sense that their opponents' political theories are ideological. I call 'civilised' those conservatisms that attack the ideological style of political theorising in general as well as attacking particular ideologies. We can easily see from reading Burke's *Reflections* how difficult it is to construct a counter-ideology without oneself falling into the ideologist's trap of making ideological arguments circular by maintaining that they are true both because people believe them and because they don't.

Civilised conservatism avoids the ideological trap by working and re-working a national tradition. Like Burke, twentieth-century conservatives like Maurras in France and Oakeshott in England think about tradition as the living hand of the past. Both think that a national tradition is at least notionally available to everyone who belongs to the nation, but both accept that it is probable individuals and groups will, from time to time, and for varying reasons, self-consciously put themselves in positions which are adverse to what they perceive their own national tradition to be. Like all conservatives, Maurras and Oakeshott think that it is a mistake to try to repudiate the past, and both doubt that it is in fact possible to do so, but neither thinks that there is something which objectively compels to belief those who choose to stand apart from their received national traditions. Another way of putting that would be to say that, while tradition works automatically in a society, it is wrong to suppose that it automatically evokes the same responses everywhere. What some members of a society find reassuring, others can easily find irksome. Maurras and Oakeshott both explain in their different ways why it is that tradition rejection happens, and both think that this rejection can at least be partly explained by the tradition rejectors' failure to understand fully what a tradition is, but this misunderstanding is a *genuine* misunderstanding. It does not stem in some sense 'objectively' from the life-circumstances of the rejectors.

It follows that modern conservatism is a conservatism which is above all else conscious of the need to explain and justify itself. Like other political credos, civilised conservatism tries to defend the exercise of political power by a particular group and in a particular way. Conservatives typically do this through a justification of certain kinds of authority. It could even be said that conservative arguments *begin* with justifications of authority. Opposing political credos begin from rights, or liberty, or equality, and try to reconcile the exercise of political power with them. This has often proved difficult because power is coercive by nature. Conservatives recognise that power is coercive, but they tend to think of power and authority as alternatives. Power is *exercised* but authority *speaks*. Speaking with authority always implies easy compliance, and an ideal conservative society would be one in which a hierarchy of authority figures, from fathers to kings, spoke authoritatively and easily to subordinates. Authority should not often have to raise its voice, and it should have to use the vulgar force of coercion only rarely. Such a society should have many sources of authority, and it is probably enough that these sources of authority should simply not contradict each other, though ideally they should co-operate and reinforce each other.

The problem which modern conservatism has, which its predecessors did not have to face, is that in the modern world authority is not self-justifying. This is the result of the French Revolution. After 1789, all institutions which exercised power were called upon to give an account of themselves whether they wanted to or not. In this sense duly constituted authority in Europe was right when it said in its different languages that the French Revolution challenged all authority, everywhere. Before the French Revolution, authority either *was*, or it was nothing. It spoke easily to its subordinates because it had never really been challenged, and so it had never urgently felt the need to arm itself with a theory. There were of course exceptions, especially in England and France, but duly constituted authority was right to feel intuitively that something about itself had changed the moment it felt it needed self-justification.

Conservatism could no longer be complacent now that it faced rival political doctrines which were remarkably confident of success. Perhaps I exaggerate the extent to which ruling dynasties and classes felt confident before the French Revolution, but at least they understood the need to appear confident. The insolence of rank is a constant radical theme from the Revolution onwards. Traditional elites were going to have to act much more modestly if they were going to survive in the modern world, but thereby hung a paradox, because a certain amount of swagger is always an important ingredient in a traditional ruling class's self-conception. It is by swaggering that members of a ruling class recognise each other and are recognised as such by the lower orders. A traditional ruling class with a king at its head needs no arguments to defend it as long as its airs and graces work. It is when somebody shouts that the emperor has no clothes that the trouble starts.

In France in particular the traditional ruling elite was vulnerable to the charge that the Revolution was its own fault. The Revolution was something which the aristocracy had allowed, and even encouraged, to happen. This accusation could be made against the French aristocracy at different levels of sophistication. It could be argued, for instance, that liberal ideas about equality and liberty had made considerable progress in aristocratic circles before the Revolution and, along with the cult of Rousseau and 'back to nature', made an important section of the ruling class tepid in its defence of the *ancien régime*. Part of the French nobility had embraced Enlightenment's suspicion of authority in Church and state and had laughed when Voltaire had made a mockery of both. On a less sophisticated level, the French Revolution had shown up the emptiness of the aristocratic ideal of chivalry. The ancient aristocracy of France took great pride in being a nobility of the sword which would leap from the scabbard to defend honour, women and the weak. Yet those swords were notoriously absent when the revolutionaries laid violent hands on the French king and, horror of horrors, on the French queen. What honour was there in skulking with the Duke of Brunswick's counter-revolutionary army at Koblenz when Marie Antoinette was being taken to the guillotine in Paris? The execution of the queen fouled the honour of every gentleman in Europe. The French aristocracy found itself in an odd position in nineteenth-century France. The French Revolution had effectively displaced aristocracy. It made something of a comeback in the period of the Restoration of the Bourbons (1815–30), but the history of French politics since the Revolution shows just how tenacious the anti-aristocratic and anti-royalist republican tradition of 1789 has proved to be. What this has meant in practical politics is that the French right has effectively been excluded from control of the great governing institutions of France. Maurras's political thought is a plea for letting the right back in.

The British right has never been ejected wholesale from the institutions of public power. Marxists in Britain complain that there has never even been a bourgeois revolution in Britain, by which they mean that the British aristocracy has never had to undergo anything like the emigration (and the guillotine) forced on the French aristocracy during the Revolution. It can therefore be argued that in the case of Britain conservative political thinkers have the advantage of being able to reflect upon and extrapolate from a virtually unbroken tradition of more or less conservative government. This is a contentious view of the history of British governing institutions, and it is dubious in the case of Ireland, but the alleged continuity of British government gives a thinker like Burke the great advantage of being able to say that British conservatism is rooted in the practice of government and therefore does not have to make grandiose abstract claims for itself. The same is true of Oakeshott's account of British liberty. Foreigners, he seems to be saying, have nearly always been constrained to see liberty in the abstract because they are unused to the practice of it (the great exception is Hegel). This is another way of saying that foreigners have usually made all-embracing ideological claims for liberty as a principle, a more sophisticated way of restating the British commonplace that foreigners have always been very good at talking about liberty but not very good at doing it.

Maurras hates everything German and so he is no Hegelian, but he does his best to do for French conservatism what Hegel had earlier done for German conservatism and what Oakeshott later did for British. Maurras argues that the break in the continuity of the French monarchy is not so much a break as an interval, and this interval is as nothing compared to the real continuity of the French monarchy, which goes right back from 1848 to Merovingian times. How can a mere decade or two of republican government be compared with that? For Maurras, the question is not merely rhetorical. The French monarchy has a record upon which it can run for office. Neo-monarchism of the

Maurrasian kind is the reverse of sentimental: the record of the kings of France can stand comparison any day with the record of the republicans and the Bonapartes.

THE CIVILISED CONSERVATISM OF CHARLES MAURRAS

Maurras's political theory seems to have shared Maurras's own political disgrace. Maurras was purged for collaboration with the Germans at the liberation of France at the end of the Second World War, deprived of his civil rights and imprisoned. The disgrace transferred itself to Maurras's works, many of which appeared even before the First World War. It is worth insisting on the date of Maurras's great *Enquête sur la monarchie* (1909) to emphasise that Maurras's was a mind formed in the early days of the Third French Republic, the republic of the aftermath of the Franco-Prussian War and the Paris *Commune*, the France of ardent revanchist feelings against the newly risen German Empire and, above all else, the France of the Dreyfus Affair during which Maurras made his name.

For Maurras, the history of France since 1789 had been a series of national disasters. Nobody had doubted that *ancien-régime* France had been the greatest of the European powers. Louis XIV's France had been a model for civilised monarchy everywhere; even the princelings of Germany made copies of the court at Versailles, proof that France dominated Germany culturally as well as politically. Since the Revolution, France had been the source of all the world's disorder, and France herself served as a warning of what the instability of the political regime could do to a country. Since 1815, France had never had strong government. France went absurdly under-prepared into the Franco-Prussian War, was given a terrible beating by Prussia, and it was Prussia's victory which enabled Bismarck to unite Germany and to create the German Empire which was bound to dominate Europe at France's expense.

Maurras understands very well that the French Revolution and its Napoleonic sequel failed to solve the problem of government. The revolutionaries all agreed that the old France of absolute monarchy had to go, but agreement among the revolutionaries stopped short of agreement about what kind of government ought to replace royal absolutism. French politics underwent a bewildering series of changes of regime between 1789 and 1815: absolute monarchy, constitutional monarchy, democratic republic, Jacobin Terror, oligarchic Directory, the Napoleonic Consulate and Empire, and finally back to the monarchy, restored by the victorious powers after the defeat of Napoleon. The legacy of the revolutionary experience to modern France was a very wide range of possibilities of forms of government. In a sense, nineteenth-century France had no political history of its own. Modern France seemed destined to recapitulate its own revolutionary origins; modern French politics was going to be a series of answers to the original revolutionary question: What is the appropriate governing form for France? France has the misfortune of being unable to give some kind of consensual answer to the most fundamental of all political questions: how should we be governed? Legitimists, Orleanists, Bonapartists, republicans and socialists all give different answers to the vital question. The inevitable result of every important political group's touting for a different kind of regime was that matters of ordinary political disagreement got mixed up with questions about forms of government. This was a standing invitation to different political groups to argue that they would never get what they wanted until the regime was changed. This in its turn meant that it was very difficult to do politics at all in France without challenging the legitimacy of the political order. With so many alternative regimes on offer, it was hard to think of any existing regime as anything other than provisional. Constitutional fetishism of the American and British kind was unthinkable in France. To attack the constitution, or to do something unconstitutional, was not very wicked and might be illegal only in the sense that public order disturbances were against the ordinary law of the land.

Maurras boxes very cleverly with the question of the instability of regimes, though, like everybody else, he failed to guess that the Third Republic would last from 1870 to 1940. Maurras wants to know how France as a nation-state can survive so many different regimes. Every regime is only a single alternative among many, and probably none of them is capable of engaging the loyalty of a bare majority of Frenchmen. How can it then be that France has not fallen apart? There must be some kind of continuity, and Maurras finds it in the Jacobin state. Regimes come and go, but the state goes on forever. By 'the state' Maurras means the centralised bureaucracy created in the Revolution and brought to a condition of near perfection by Napoleon. The succession of different regimes during the Revolution made certain that the state machinery would survive because their very longevity would give the governing institutions of the state a legitimacy which short-lived regimes could not have. The bureaucracy in France strengthened itself at every change in the form of government. The France of the *départements*, each of whose prefects was a little Caesar to his subjects, and the France of the *communes*, each of whose mayors was a miniature Caesar to his constituents, together with the great centralised bureaucracies in Paris, constituted a Procrustean bed into which Frenchmen would be forced to fit till the end of time. Regional, religious, linguistic, social and racial differences just did not matter. As far as the state was concerned, a Frenchman was a Frenchman, and that was that.

Where did this abstract idea of a Frenchman come from, so that he could be governed by an equally abstract state? Maurras points to the French Revolution, and, more particularly, to Rousseau as the Revolution's progenitor. Maurras thinks that *ancien-régime* France was a true community. True communities are not perfect, but they have a genuinely lived life in which each man and woman has an acknowledged place. Maurras believes that Rousseau, the interloper from Geneva, could never see that France was a viable community in the second half of the eighteenth century. When Rousseau crossed the French frontier he brought with him a disease which rapidly infected the French elite. Maurras has no doubt that, if Rousseau did not cause the French Revolution single-handed, Rousseauism made such headway among France's natural rulers that an important section of them were very slow to realise the lethal potential of the calling of the Estates General and the fall of the Bastille in 1789. Maurras understands very well that a state whose ruling class remains solid and keeps its nerve is likely to be able to weather any crisis which comes its way. This idea is not original, but Maurras is right to single out the France of the *ancien régime* as a classic case.

Maurras's attack on Rousseau works on both the personal and the theoretical level. Rousseau's *Confessions* have always been a godsend to his enemies. The *Confessions* set the tone for all subsequent confessional literature by giving all of us a taste for the really nasty bits. Rousseau may have thought that he was simply being honest, but his chronicle of his own nastiness and dishonesties made his readers doubt whether he could ever have been truly sincere in anything. What was particularly galling was Rousseau's claim to be a naturally virtuous person corrupted by the vanities and insincerities of the world, when it was easy to argue on the basis of the evidence provided in the *Confessions* that Rousseau was so easily corrupted that it was hard to see in what sense he could originally ever have been virtuous. What was worse was Rousseau's implicit claim that his case was the case of everyman. Like that later piece of autobiography, Hitler's *Mein Kampf*, the *Confessions* make a double claim: first that the author is special enough for his own doings to interest the reading public, and second that his own life is somehow typical of the life that he sees around him. The claims are not really contradictory because Rousseau, like Hitler later, seems to be saying that his own experience is ordinary experience in a form so intensified that the chief characteristics of that experience stand out clearly enough for all to see. It follows, therefore, that ordinary men can see the lineaments of their own experience more easily in the *Confessions* than they can in their own lives.

It is in this sense that Rousseau is inviting us to see his own life as a critique not just of French society and politics in the second half of the eighteenth century, but of most societies at most times and places (the exceptions are Sparta, republican Rome and possibly his native Geneva). Rousseau, like many another eighteenth-century political theorist, thinks that what human societies have and have had in common far outweighs the differences between them; these differences he dismisses as obfuscating and irrelevant detail. Maurras, in a famous essay of 1922, 'Romanticism and Revolution', goes in for the kill. The differences between different societies are what really matter. The things which societies have in common are either so general as to be meaningless or simply matters of definition: all societies are societies. When the wandering madman Rousseau arrived in France he found a society which had no natural place for him to call his own. Too bad: human societies are not obliged to find a place for just anybody who happens to turn up. Rousseau then goes on to say that what is true of himself must be true of everybody else, and that of course includes native-born Frenchmen. How, Maurras asks, could Rousseau possibly know? How can a man who has no fatherland of his own know what goes on in the hearts and minds of those who do?

The question is not just rhetorical. Every man needs somewhere to call home, Rousseau included. Rousseau's problem is that he is such an oddity that he cannot feel at home in any of the societies which exists in his own lifetime. He tried enough of them – Switzerland, Italy, France and England – but none of them seemed to be organised quite as Rousseau would have wished. Rousseau's own corrupted innocence is proof enough of that: look what the world has done to *me*. What Rousseau then does is to invent a fatherland for himself in his own head. Rousseau's *Social Contract* is therefore an outline of the kind of political community he thinks *he* might like to live in. The monstrousness of this romantic egotism nearly causes Maurras to explode. Rousseau is inviting every national political community to abolish itself, to begin from scratch to build a state which only exists in Rousseau's head, and all this on the off-chance that if Rousseau turned up he would enjoy living there.

Rousseau is not just mad and bad; he is also dangerous. Everybody had always known that there was something disquieting about him: Rousseau's effect on his own contemporaries is enough to tell us that. Maurras puts his finger on exactly what it is that makes Rousseau dangerous: Rousseau takes the self to be the measure of all things. Like all the romantics, Rousseau makes self-obsession into a public stance. What should be private, or shared among intimate friends, becomes a critique of the world. It is what some readers thought made the early Wordsworth and Byron dangerous, profoundly anti-social beings who apparently led dangerously attractive lives. That attractiveness is easily explained. Human nature and the nature of human societies fight out their battle in the individual soul. A romantic is someone in whose soul nature has already won, and this makes the romantic a kind of time-bomb. If there is a connection between romanticism and revolution, then the romantic is someone in whom the revolution has already happened. The romantic is a post-revolutionary living in a pre-revolutionary society, and so existing societies live with the constant danger that sometime, somehow, these post-revolutionaries will find enough imitators to cause a real revolution. There don't have to be many of them; it is enough that enough people have heard of them. Romantics' lives are their texts. Romantic political writing is important, of course, but what really matters is the life which defaces the story which a corrupted society has written on the romantic soul.

Something of that quality hung about all the romantics, and it made Rousseau their first hero. (And something of that frightening quality was to hang about the late nineteenth-century anarchists, men and women who had already utterly transformed themselves in defiance of existing social and political values.) It almost goes without saying that this attitude can be profoundly anti-historical, where historical means traditional. Traditions are specific to particular national cultures. 'International tradition' is a contradiction in terms. The Rousseauist attitude is 'international' in the sense that it writes off all specifically national cultures. The Rousseauist attitude discounts the differences between national traditions. How can different national histories matter when they all tell the same story of human corruption and hypocrisy? The description of a particular national tradition may dot a few i's and cross a few t's, but this cannot alter the fundamental fact, the only fact that matters, that every national culture tells broadly the same tale of man's unnatural inhumanity to man.[1]

Writing off a national tradition has a profound effect on the *form* that a political theory takes. Avoidance of the concrete means that political theory must be cast in abstract terms. Revolutionary Liberty, Equality, Fraternity will eventually set themselves up against any concrete liberty, equality and fraternity as it exists in the world. There will always be fools willing enough to exchange an imperfect present for an imagined future good, and the abstractness of that future good does not always make men suspicious of it. The problem as Maurras sees it is that, properly speaking, no thought is ever truly abstract. Theories never spring virgin from the imagination: all theories come covered with the finger-marks of the past. Every vision of the future is a re-hash of the past. The only difference between the visions is that different visionaries choose to dish up different versions of the past. And the choice itself is arbitrary because no part of the past has any particular claim to our attention, and no part of the past, one's own nation's perhaps excepted, has an *a priori* claim on our admiration. The imagined state of Rousseau's *Social Contract* is no more Rousseau's own invention than any other utopia. Men have always known that utopias are their own worlds turned upside down, or inverted images of their own reality. We can recognise the existence of Tudor England in More's *Utopia* simply by standing Utopia on its head, thereby standing Tudor England back on its feet. All Rousseau does in the *Social Contract* is to find in an idealised ancient Sparta and republican Rome a model for a state and a society so different from the present that he, Rousseau, would rather enjoy living there.

All those evenings Rousseau spent reading Plutarch show through. Rousseau himself is a kind of ancient hero, the kind of man Plutarch would recognise in the Spartan *agora* or Roman *forum*. Rousseau's political thought is really a way for him to get himself retrospectively into Plutarch's *Lives*. The enterprise is absurd in itself, and it is also superfluous. Rousseau admires classical values, but what he forgets is that classical values were transmitted to modern Europe through the Roman Catholic Church. Rousseau pretends that modern Europe needs an injection of classical values when those values are already there. Those aristocratic Roman prelates who lay in wait to civilise and convert the conquering barbarian kings laid the foundations of what was to become Christian European civilisation. Cultural and religious authority was added to the power of the sword, and out of this combination arose the realm of France. Maurras was probably not a *bon croyant* Roman Catholic himself. What attracts him to the Church is not religious dogma or even the Gospels (the work of obscure Jews), but a particular version of Roman moral authority. Rousseau is either too ignorant or too Protestant (and for Maurras there's probably not much difference between the two) to realise just how much of the ancient classical idea of order survives and prospers through the Church. Catholicism for Maurras is a Christian gloss on Roman *imperium*. The fundamental classical value is the value of order which pervaded every aspect of the life of the ancient world and was easily recognisable in a city plan, a line of verse, a statue, a constitution or a religious festival. All classical cultures are serene. This is far from saying that everybody was happy in the ancient world, or that everybody approved of, or even was aware of, imperial order. What Maurras wants to argue is that the world of classical order was a world which invited its citizens to feel themselves at home.

Classicism is the opposite of psychological, social and political turmoil. The model Maurras has in mind is obviously Rome threatened from the outside by restless Germanic barbarians and from the inside by disquieting religions like Judaism and Christianity in its early subversive form before it was allied to the empire by the Emperor Constantine: *in hoc signo vinces*. This spirit of turmoil manifested itself again in Europe in the Protestant Reformation of the sixteenth century, one of the great centres of which was Geneva, which was eventually to produce Rousseau. (Maurras conveniently forgets that Calvin was French.) The Rousseauist spirit is the romantic spirit of tumult dressed up in the toga, and the French Revolution was later to dress up in the same borrowed Roman clothes. The Revolution was notoriously to attack the Catholic Church in France, and at one of its more farcical moments was to try to invent a Rousseauist, pseudo-classical cult of the Supreme Being intended to replace Christianity.

Maurras invites us to think of the antithesis between monarchism and republicanism as the antithesis between two kinds of classicism. The first is firmly rooted in a native French tradition stretching back to the Merovingian kings, while the Rousseauist romanticised classicism of the French republicans is a tawdry and late foreign import which has never been properly assimilated.

It is fundamental to Maurras's perspective to believe that aliens, and alien ways of thinking, can never really be domesticated. Alien cultural imports are at best an irrelevance in a nation's life and at worst a menace. However, Maurras cannot push this point too hard because he knows very well that after the Revolution the republic is the form of government in France to which all the other possible forms are alternatives. French government is going to be republican or something else, and Maurras recognises that a return to monarchy is only one of the alternatives. All French oppositionists knew that republicanism was the form to beat. That being the case, did it not follow that the republican idea had been at least half-assimilated? Did it not follow that, no matter what had been the case in 1789, by 1900 there was in France a domestic tradition of republicanism with more than a century's worth of legitimising age? Surely by 1900 it was simply perverse of Maurras to deny that republicanism was part of the warp and weft of French politics? After all, the Third Republic was the *third* Republic, and it was to last for seventy years.

Maurras knows that he has to do some intellectual wriggling here. He has to argue that the republic is some kind of nationwide, if not international, consipiracy against the 'real' French nation. Maurras makes a distinction between the 'legal' France and the 'real' France. Legal France is, roughly speaking, the way France is governed under whichever non-monarchical system of constitutional law happens to be currently in operation. This was the republic for most of Maurras's own adult life, with only Vichy as an interlude. For Maurras, the republic is merely provisional, the regime imposed on a defeated France in 1870 by the only Frenchmen to do well out of the Franco-Prussian War. That republic was not even properly consolidated legally for the first five years of its existence, and the frequency with which republican politicians were afterwards to proclaim that 'the Republic is in danger' was to show how shallowly rooted even the republic's greatest defenders thought it was. Historians are still debating the question of how seriously we ought in retrospect to take the whole 'Republic in danger' theme, but it is probably still true to say that in 1870 almost nobody would have predicted that the Third Republic would last until 1940. This alone shows how wobbly the Republic was.

Maurras accepts, as everybody in French politics has accepted since the Revolution, that no regime is ever neutral. Every constitution in France is a minority constitution designed to exclude its enemies. The questions for him are: Which regime excludes the most and which regime excludes the least? Maurras plainly thinks that there is no natural republican majority in post-revolutionary France: the real France has remained monarchist at heart. How, then, is one to explain the persistence of the republican idea? Maurras's answer is engagingly frank: the democratic Republic is always going to be good at its own political game of democratic politics, and the more chaotic the game the longer it is likely to go on. The parties of the Third Republic were notoriously unable to produce parliamentary majorities for themselves. Effectively, this meant that all of its governments were going to be short-lived because they were based on more or less fragile parliamentary coalitions. A fragmented party system is the perfect instrument for producing weak governments and political stagnation. The only people who really have a stake in the political game are republican politicians chasing votes to get elected to the Assembly to give themselves a chance of enjoying the prestige and perks of ministerial office. This ties up the electoral system and allows very little opportunity for an outside force which is itself profoundly anti-democratic to make its way in official democratic politics.

A genuine reactionary force, like the Action Française which Maurras came to dominate and convert to his own brand of monarchism, like a genuine revolutionary force, is always bound to have to face the question of whether or not it should dabble in parliamentary politics. If it does, it risks the damaging charge that it seeks to undermine the very political system which gives it life, and if it doesn't, it is open to the charge that it will not play the game of official politics because it knows it can't win. This is the necessary condition of any anti-system political movement. (In this condition there are only two things an anti-system political movement can do: either it waits for a national catastrophe so great that the political system which caused the catastrophe, or allowed it to happen, finds itself generally execrated and therefore vulnerable to really radical change; or it can adopt the tactic of institutional infiltration. And, of course, it could do both, using infiltration as an immediate tactic while its long-term strategy is to wait for the crisis.) Not all of the institutions in a democratic republic are imbued with the democratic spirit, and in France the national Catholic Church stuck to its view that the republic was essentially anti-clerical if it was not actually atheist. The officer classes of armies are not noted for their support for democratic causes, and the same can be true of the upper echelons of judiciaries and bureaucracies, indeed of any institutions whatsoever.

This point of view is easily translatable into the terms of political sociology: it is perfectly possible for large sections of the power elite of an officially democratic society to be profoundly hostile to democracy. It is not necessarily the case, however, that all the various anti-democratic sections of a power elite are anti-democratic for the same reasons, but it is always eminently possible that the varied forms of anti-democracy can, over time, be shaped into a single coherent political doctrine. Maurras thought that this was a definite possibility in the France of the Third Republic. His feel for the plurality of institutional power actors in what was notionally a liberal democracy could easily induce a feeling in Maurras that the field of democratic politics could be left to his enemies because the real work of Action Française was to be done elsewhere.

Maurras on the state

The central problems which Maurras has to address can be stated very simply: if post-Revolutionary France is as politically fragmented as Maurras claims it is, then why has France survived as recognisably herself? Maurras's answer is that, while regimes come and go in France, the state always quietly strengthens itself. The story of the French state is remarkably consistent, if by 'the French state' we mean centralised, day-to-day adminis-tration, crudely 'the bureaucracy' or the army of permanent officials. This process began back in the mists of French history. In *The Prince* (1513) Machiavelli was already holding up the French monarchy as an example of a successfully centralised state, and by the middle of the eighteenth century the French monarchy was the standard example of centralised power both to those who admired and to those who feared it. There was in fact a debate among enlightened political thinkers in the eighteenth century about exactly how despotic the France of Louis XIV and his successors actually was. Some thinkers, like Montesquieu, argued that there was an ancient constitution in France, a kind of fundamental law embodied in the *parlements* (provincial legal assemblies looking to the *parlement* of Paris for political leadership) which monarchical power could threaten but not actually efface. Other thinkers, like Hume, made a distinction between 'arbitrary' and 'absolute' power, arguing that the former existed in Asiatic despotisms (Turkey and China) while the latter existed in the 'civilised' monarchy of France because the French monarchy operated through the forms of law. Despotism was government by the whim of the despot, while 'enlightened despotism' was supposed to be government by a king or emperor acting through law. Maurras defends the tradition of French monarchy as 'civilised monarchy' in the Humean sense (though Maurras himself does not actually use the term).

Maurras, for all his hostility to the democratic republic, is still a very modern political animal. He knows that an exiled monarchy cannot hope to return to the France of its ancestors on the basis of an outmoded theory like the divine right of kings. That might have worked in the days of Louis XIV, or even immediately after 1815, but it is not going to work in the twentieth century. Monarchy, and especially insurgent monarchy, has to be defended on its previous record, just as the opponents of monarchy have to be attacked on theirs. In this sense, the party of the monarchy has to conduct its campaigns in a way similar to any other party campaign in a modern democracy. The only difference is that the party of monarchy knows that in the democratic game it cannot win. Maurras's central claim for monarchy is that internally it was not over-centralised and that it was always successful in foreign policy terms. French kings ruled France with moderate dominion and royal France was respected and feared by its neighbours. Contrast the France of the Third Republic, politically divided, defeated by Prussia and so making possible the creation of the Bismarckian Reich, and subjected internally to the frustrations caused by the endless fussiness of the bureaucratic state.

The necessary connection between domestic government and foreign policy is always uppermost in Maurras's mind. The foreign policy of French kings before the Revolution had always been to keep Germany divided and weak. The last thing France had wanted was a strong, united Germany across the Rhine. A weak Germany had been an effective buffer between the French monarchy and the lands of Austrian Habsburgs, and, provided French diplomacy was successful enough in sowing the seeds of discord between Prussia and Austria and in playing the Russian card when it was necessary, then there was always a fair chance that France would be the dominant power in continental Europe. The internal condition of the French state was always going to be crucial if France was going to play the hegemonic game. What was needed was a monarchy powerful enough to rule and tax its own subjects effectively while being able to count on the support of the nobility and clergy: it was not for nothing that French kings prided themselves on being Their Most Christian

Majesties. Aristocratic support was essential for war. Aristocracies are in one sense the natural enemies of monarchy because every baron would be an over-mighty subject if he could. Kings have always come up against this problem, centralising kings in particular. The success of the French monarchy of the *ancien régime* depended on striking a lasting balance between aristocratic claims to exercise local power and the needs of the centralised state. The ideal way to match the two was war, the only fit trade for a gentleman outside the cloister, the study or the law. Tax the people to pay for the aristocratic game of war, and everybody (with the exception of taxpayers) gets what they want. Efficient taxation is strong government by any other name, which should keep the king happy, and the wars it pays for provide the nobility of the sword with the opportunity to achieve that military glory which all aristocrats are obliged to pursue.

One would not expect things to be that simple in practice, and neither were they. Allowing the French nobility as high a degree of local autonomy as was compatible with a strong centralised monarchy meant that in reality French government under the *ancien' régime* was messy; but this was a source of strength, not weakness, while the system continued to work. The patchwork of local and provincial jurisdiction which underlay royal government had the salutary effect of involving local notables in the business of government. This had to be watched, of course, just as royal encroachments on local rights and liberties had to be watched, but this again was a source of strength, not weakness, because it meant that the governing system in general was unlikely to become ossified. A certain fluidity in the relations between central and local government is always preferable to relations which are so rigidly fixed that the system allows for very little flexibility.

What the Revolution did, in Maurras's view, was to continue the process of bureaucratic centralisation while dealing a death-blow to the countervailing influence of local and provincial autonomies. The France of the roughly equal *départements*, each ruled by its prefect appointed by Paris, together with the great centralised bureaucracy in Paris, is the real governing legacy of the Revolution. It has become something of a cliché in the Anglo-Saxon world to say that the French minister of education knows exactly what is being taught in every state school in France every minute of the day. What is not pointed up so much is the nature of the education received, which was impeccably republican and unremittingly bookish. The higher reaches of the French civil service were recruited by competitive examination, and one can easily guess what kind of education enables a candidate to be successful in those examinations: republican and bookish. The system of state education in France is administered by bureaucrats to produce the bureaucrats of the future: the centralised state feeds itself. And so it was that an important part of the battle between left and right in France centred on (and still centres on) the question of lay versus clerical education. The Revolution's anti-clericalism survives in every French village in the running ideological battle between the mayor and the schoolmaster on the one hand and the *curé* on the other. Counter-revolution meant support for the Church and Church schools as the practical manifestation of anti-republicanism. State education and compulsory military service were the schools of republicanism, and they could only be challenged by Catholic education and the Catholicism of the French officer class.

What was true of French republican education was true of the state in general. Maurras shares with Marx the perception that every revolution in France since 1789 has strengthened the bureaucratic state. By that he means that the ideal condition for virtual bureaucratic autonomy is regime instability. Every revolutionary force in France dreams of capturing the state, but what every revolutionary force in France fails to recognise is that to threaten the regime means to strengthen the bureaucracy because the bureaucracy will still be there under the next regime and the next regime but one. How else is one to explain the continued existence of France as a political community? No matter what the regime is, the postman will still get through, though with regime changes he will have to change his official buttons from time to time. The permanent threat of revolution weakens any regime which France has, because it makes any regime a temporary expedient and every government a provisional government. What could be better for an entrenched bureaucracy? Unstable regimes and weak government mean that the business of running France is largely left to the occupants of permanent positions of bureaucratic power.

Bureaucracies are strong on permanence but weak on political leadership. Every bureaucrat wants to do tomorrow what he did yesterday. This is perfectly acceptable behaviour in a state which enjoys a wide consensual political legitimacy and which is lucky enough to live in a reasonably stable international state system. The problem of the modern world is the speed of domestic and international change. Maurras is a reactionary, but he is not a fool. His argument is that only a monarchy, and at first a royal dictatorship, can possibly cope with the implications of change for France's internal and external problems. The governments of the Third Republic were notoriously short-lived because they depended on unstable parliamentary coalitions, there being no natural party of the majority in a France which was split politically by the party system of the parliamentary republic. Weak political leadership equals weak defence and foreign policy. This mattered desperately before 1914 with the establishment of German hegemony in continental Europe, and it was to matter desperately again in the 1930s as Germany pulled herself up again under Hitler and the Third Reich. Maurras was also fairly consistently anti-British and anti-American, jealous of the success of the British Empire and alarmed by the rise of American super-capital. The only sensible policy was to re-establish monarchy in order to re-establish France as a great world power.

Maurras and Dreyfus

Part of the French problem before 1914, and perhaps the most important part, was military. The Franco-Prussian War was a psychological as well as a military defeat because it all but destroyed two ideas of military glory, republican and Napoleonic. The supposed invincibility of republican arms (France's army in 1870 was largely conscript) was no longer believable, and neither was the legend of invincible Napoleonic military leadership: Louis Napoleon, though personally brave, could not compare with his famous uncle, Napoleon Bonaparte. The shattering of these illusions led to a good deal of historical heart-searching, particularly about the French Revolution and the career of the great Bonaparte. Up to 1870 it had been perfectly possible to believe that the glory of the French Revolution was its wars against the kings and emperors of reactionary Europe. This view of it stressed the continuity between the Jacobin republic, the Directory, the Consulate and finally the Napoleonic Empire. No matter that Napoleon had ended up trying to found a dynasty, because rational administration and a career open to the talents would be available in any of the lands ruled by the Bonapartes. This might not have much to do with the liberty which was the French Revolution's original promise, but it had everything to do with rational progress in the face of European dynastic reaction. If Napoleon ended up as a dynast he was at least a modernising dynast.

The military shambles of 1870 was only very marginally redeemed by the heroism of the people during the long siege of Paris, and the credit of the Parisians was defaced in all eyes except the left's by the uprising of the Paris *Commune* in 1871. *La gloire* was at a discount in the Third Republic, and this made possible a view of the French Revolution, exemplified in Hippolyte Taine's massive *Origins of Contemporary France* (1875–96), which played down the libertarian messianism of the revolutionary wars and played up France's rather nasty internal politics from 1789 to 1815. Taine tried to get the French to look at their revolutionary past through the eyes of Dickens and the English in general (he wrote a *History of English Literature* and a famous travel book, *Notes on England*). Dicken's *Tale of Two Cities* taught the English to see the guillotine as the central revolutionary symbol, and the English had long ago learned to see Napoleon as the Corsican Ogre. Like Taine, whom he admired (though, as always with Maurras, with reservations), Maurras invites Frenchmen to see the Revolution's political legacy to modern France as a *damnosa haereditas*: Frenchmen still expect France to win wars with glory, but the revolutionary legacy has failed to produce a single regime or a single government capable of delivering victory. Maurras lived a long time, and he could see that this was just as true of France in 1940 as it had been in 1870: defeat by Germany proved it twice.

The Bonapartist regime of Louis Napoleon could not even keep the national territory intact. German seizure of Alsace and Lorraine could not be compensated for by French colonial expansion. Africans and Vietnamese could not be counted against the Frenchmen who now lived in the German Empire. Maurras was a realist in foreign policy to the extent that he saw clearly that only a successful revanchist war against Germany could restore the lost provinces. That is why the Dreyfus Affair meant so much to him: an attack on the integrity of French military justice was an attack on the army as the only French institution capable of lifting a finger to restore to France territory which was rightfully hers.

The Dreyfus Affair, and Maurras's contributions to it, have to be seen in the context of the soul-searching that went on in France after the disasters of the Franco-Prussian War and the *Commune*. The post mortems were numerous. Everybody started to look for sources of weakness and corruption in French national life, and, by the time all the fingers had been pointed at all the possible scapegoats, there was very little left that remained unscathed. Most of the details of the finger-pointing make tedious reading now. Suffice it to say that somebody sometime blamed the national catastrophes on the upper classes and the lower; on clericalism and anti-clericalism; on the left and the right; on republicanism and Bonapartism; on the press, on the political parties, on bankers, on Freemasons and on Jews, and, particularly wounding to the national vanity of the French, on alcoholism and a decline in the birth-rate: apparently Frenchmen were no longer capable of enjoying wine *and* women. Add these very generalised explanations of national decline to the spectacular scandals of the Third Republic (Wilson, Panama) and it all adds up to saying that there is not one honest man to be found in the whole of French politics, let alone one honest newspaper. With hindsight this panic about the state of the nation looks exaggerated, but contemporaries took it seriously enough.

None took it more seriously than Maurras. If the whole of official republican politics was corrupt then only the army remained pure, burning with the revanchist flame which would one day soon recapture the lost provinces of Alsace and Lorraine. Maurras already assumed with many other European conservatives that the left was fundamentally pacifist; a glance at the propaganda of the socialist Second International, in which the French were very active, showed that. The Second International, after all, was founded in 1889 to prevent a European war because it was likely to be a war of conscript armies forced into slaughtering proletarian comrades on the other side of the barricades. The French left were always sniping at the army, especially at compulsory military service. The right saw it as vital that the army's reputation was unsullied if it was to receive enough political and civilian support ever to defeat France's natural enemy, Germany. The army was already discredited by the defeat of 1870, and the socialists had always said that the officer class had not tried very hard against the Prussians in 1870 because they thought of the reds at home as the real enemy. It followed that the French army after 1870, and especially after 1871 when it suppressed the Paris *Commune* with a savagery which even the Prussians found hard to stomach, had to guard its reputation very jealously because it was so politically and morally vulnerable. Armies may march on their stomachs, but they remain effective through morale. What was going to happen to the morale of he troops if they continued to be branded as useless in the Franco-Prussian War and butchers of their fellow citizens in the *Commune*? The Dreyfus Affair threatened to re-open all the wounds incurred in the old battle between the French army and the socialist and republican left.

The affair began innocuously enough as a straightforward case of military espionage in 1894 when it was discovered that French military secrets were being passed to the Germans. A general staff captain, Alfred Dreyfus, was arrested, convicted by secret court martial and sent to Devil's Island. The army would probably have been quite content for the whole business to have been hushed up, but there had been a leak to the anti-Semitic press, in which there had been public pressure for a trial. There were always people in the army who thought that the verdict was unsound, and in civilian circles a small but determined Dreyfusard party, including Clemenceau and Zola, began to form. Zola published his famous open letter '*J'accuse*', in Clemenceau's newspaper *L'Aurore*, in which he claimed that there was a conspiracy to convict the Jew Dreyfus, in part at least to show that no *real* French officer could possibly be guilty of the treason which had undoubtedly been committed. And so the simple affair of military espionage became the famous Dreyfus Affair, which was to rumble on for ten years, split the political nation, and was not even really over in 1906 when Dreyfus was pardoned (though innocent), rehabilitated, promoted and awarded the Legion of Honour (fourth class).

For the anti-Dreyfusards Dreyfus's Jewishness was crucial. It showed that the real French army was still morally pure and therefore still capable of leading the crusade to recapture

Alsace and Lorraine. If *real* Frenchmen were passing military secrets to the Germans, then what hope was there for a regenerated France? This was especially important for a thinker like Maurras, who saw himself engaged in a struggle with the republican left for the nation's soul. We have become so used to the idea that patriotism is the property of the right wing in politics that it is easy to forget that in France there is a good deal to be said for the view that patriotism is the legitimate property of the republican left. The *patrie* of free and equal citizens is the ideological legacy of the French Revolution, and it was for the sake of that *patrie* that so many Frenchmen died in the revolutionary wars. Even Bonapartism could look populist from the point of view of a legitimist like Maurras: the Second Empire was a kind of plebiscitary despotism, upstart military rule legitimised by the popular will. This was uncomfortable for those who wanted to bring back the monarchy because it could so easily be argued that all France's great recent military victories had been won by other people and not by the king. French kings had won wars, but those wars could now seem very long ago. It was therefore imperative for the right to lay claim to their own particular brand of patriotism (which for convenience we will call 'nationalism'). The nationalism of the right invested a good deal of its political capital in the army's purity compared to all the other institutions of the republic. It therefore became an article of faith that the army could not itself be guilty; therefore the outsider, Dreyfus, must be guilty. It was that simple.

The Drefusards could not stomach the injustice done to Dreyfus under the Republic. If the Republic did not stand for justice for every French citizen, then what *did* it stand for? The anti-Dreyfusard answer to this was equally simple: Dreyfus had got justice, been found guilty and sentenced. Did justice mean that every accused person should be found innocent? The Dreyfusards countered by saying that the military justice which Dreyfus had been subjected to wasn't really justice at all. This put the anti-Dreyfusards onto what they thought of as solid ground. Where did the standards come from by which French justice could be judged and found wanting? Why, from a universal standard of justice, of course: this universal standard was foreign by definition and almost certainly Kantian and therefore German. Anybody with the slightest inkling of the meaning of French history of the past century knew the direction in which the Dreyfusard argument about universal justice was leading, and that was towards a re-run of the French Revolution. Not quite literally, perhaps, because there was a republic already in existence, but a similar divisiveness was bound to occur between those who were prepared to defend French institutions and those who held institutions up to the judgement of a chimerical universal justice. Dreyfusism was Enlightenment universalism revisited.

Universalism itself had changed because it now included socialism. The Second International had been making pacifist noises in the ten years before Dreyfus (and would continue to make them right up to August 1914). Nothing could be more predictable than that the socialist in France would join any attack against the army. The French left did not see the army as the avengers of national honour but rather as the repressors of the *Commune* and as a mechanism for dragooning French proletarians into slaughtering their German comrades in the International. From the point of view of a nationalist like Maurras, Marxism was just another of those foreign imports tailor-made to sap French vitality. When Maurras looked across the Rhine he saw a German Empire powerful enough not to have to worry about a stab in the back from its socialists, while in France he saw republicanism and socialists making common cause against an army which was just about the only national institution with any vitality left in it. This alliance between republicans and socialists was something new. Politicians of the left had spent much time since 1871 execrating the bourgeois republic of the *Commune* massacres, and the French working class had known since 1848 that the republic would never be theirs except as the result of a socialist revolution. For a long time the ideas of a bourgeois and a social republic simply did not mix. Now a kind of popular frontism before its time seemed likely to tie the French proletariat, or at least some of its leaders, into the Republic, which raised the spectre of the reds eventually being part of government.

Maurras's anti-Marxism went well beyond red-hating. He put his finger on Marxist economic determinism as the real danger because it could induce a kind of fatalism in the minds of anti-Marxists. Socialists everywhere were proclaiming that the future belonged to them. The proletariat was already in existence. All that was required was for that proletariat to become collectively conscious of its own strength, and revolution would be a formality. If the future belonged to the working class then what was the point of trying to push against the pricks? If the real determining forces in any society were economic, and if politics was just the froth on top, then anti-socialist politics could only be a doomed holding operation. If you thought that, it made perfectly good sense to do what some republicans were doing and try to ally with the left on the principle of 'if you can't beat them, join them'.

It was against this sense of fatalism that Maurras coined his famous slogan *la politique d'abord*. The phrase does not translate easily into English. 'Politics really matters' catches some of the force of Maurras's original. Forms of regime are a matter of political will and not the necessary result of long-term economic trends. (How, otherwise, could a bourgeois republic survive in a country of peasants?) Maurras recognises with Hegel that the problem which the French Revolution did not solve was the question of what form the state should take in the modern world. The whole of European political theory in the nineteenth and twentieth centuries (not to mention most of European politics) is a gloss on that theme. The mistake that most political theory makes is to answer the question in terms which are too general. Why should the solution to the regime problem be everywhere the same? The assumption underlying the thesis that the modern regime should be some kind of democratic or parliamentary republic is merely a piece of liberal futurology, while the socialist claim that after the bourgeois republic comes the dictatorship of the proletariat is a piece of futurology based on a piece of futurology. Both views are effectively determinist. Maurras, on the contrary, believes that politics has a certain autonomy. If the democratic republic can survive in a France which Maurras believes is monarchist at heart, then why should a monarchy have any difficulty in surviving and prospering?

Maurras on monarchy

Monarchism is Maurras's way of being radical without being fascist or Marxist. Maurras is a radical because he is a thoroughgoing reactionary who wants to reverse what his liberal, socialist and Marxist enemies would call the natural development of a modern society and polity. All progressives could agree that modernity meant the supercession of pre-capitalist economic relations by free buying and selling of labour in the market, and all progressives could agree that the natural political accompaniment of the inevitable victory of capitalist economic formations was some kind of bourgeois democratic parliamentary republic based on a widely enjoyed right of suffrage. From that point on, the progressives began to divide, because the left also wanted universal suffrage as a means to convert the bourgeois republic into a socialist republic which bourgeois liberals had good reason to fear, but liberals and socialists were at least talking the same language of modernity. No doubt liberals and socialists saw secularisation as the natural accompaniment of social and political modernisation, so that the least they could expect in a modern republic was separation of Church and state. A regime which legitimised itself as the expression of popular will did not need God's blessing: if God is *for* the republic, all well and good, but if not, then *vox populi, vox Dei*.

Maurras was ahead of his time in doubting the necessity of the whole progressive scenario. He does not see why a society should not be, in the language of the progressives, *incompletely* modern. Progressivism comes in too neatly tied a package. Again Maurras is instinctively anti-Marxist. He does not deny that the whole progressive ticket might one day become reality because the democratic republic is the ideal breeding ground for Marxism, but he cannot see any necessity at work here. Progressivism is something which some people *want* to happen and which other people allow to happen. No doubt it strengthens the progressive position to argue that history is on its side, but this Maurras dismisses as propaganda. Liberalism and Marxism are no more and no less necessary than monarchism. Economy may not be a matter of choice in the modern world, but politics still is.

It is no coincidence that Maurras was arguing his own version of political voluntarism while Lenin was arguing his. Lenin attacked those Russian socialists who came to be known as the Economist faction for thinking that the development of revolutionary class-consciousness in the proletariat was simply a matter of waiting for the development of Russian capitalism to reach the stage at which the working class would automatically develop its own revolutionary class-consciousness without any outside help from a professional revolutionary party. Maurras's attack on all the 'wait and see' schools of political thinking puts him in with stranger bedfellows than Lenin. The emerging fascist parties of the 1920s also hoped eventually to celebrate the 'triumph of the will'.

Maurras himself was never a fascist, because fascism and legitimist monarchism cannot go together. The disasters of Bonapartism taught Maurras to despise the rowdyism of Caesarist politics of all kinds. Fascists were johnny-come-latelies, toughs from out of town with no more genuine national pedigree than their natural street-fighting enemies, the communists. Communists and fascists both upset Maurras's innately classical sense of order. There was, however, a complication, because there was no getting away from the fact that fascism's enemies were Maurras's own enemies, and this made him an anti-anti-fascist. Fascists were anti-parliamentarists and anti-Semites, anti-liberals and anti-socialists, anti-internationalists and anti-pacifists, and Maurras himself was all of these things. As one would expect, he was more sympathetic to the clerical fascism of a General Franco than to the populism of Mussolini, and Maurras had more time for Latin fascism than for its northern counterpart in the Nazism of Hitlerite Germany. Whenever Maurras looked across the Rhine he saw those same restless Germanic tribes that had figured so prominently in the minds and policies of the ancient Romans. A resurgent Germany was always going to threaten the classical civilisation of France, a view which hadn't changed since Tacitus and which would probably never change. (Maurras had always regarded Rousseau as a marauding barbarian tribe of one.) When he looked at Hitler he saw the same spirit of turbulence, this time mediated through Wagner.

This vision of Nazism clouded Maurras's usually very clear political judgement. Nazism's turbulence necessarily led him to suppose that Nazism was disorderly, and, being disorderly, was something likely to be state-threatening, not state-strengthening. This was a view which put Maurras in the same boat as the members of the Third International, which until very late insisted on denying that fascism had much of a future. Maurras the aesthete and literary critic could only see an absurd pastiche of every kind of German romanticism decked out as a system of politics. Maurras's political friends tried in vain to get him to see Hitler as a particularly modern kind of political leader successfully dealing with problems, especially economic problems, which were never Maurras's forte, in a European context in which most other political leaders were failing. The Germans were following Hitler not because he promised to turn them all into little Siegfrieds but because he promised solutions to problems about which the governments of the Weimar Republic could only haver. Maurras realised very late that Nazi Germany threatened more than Jews and communists and joined the rising chorus for quicker rearmament, but it was rearmament for a war which, on Maurras's own account of the essential weakness of the Republic, France could not win. And so it proved in 1940.

Maurras never seems to have considered where a victory of Germany over France would leave him. In one sense Maurras was the victim of his own accurate futurology, a kind of French Churchill vulnerable to the charge of consorting with the enemy. Nothing was going to be easier, after France had been liberated in 1944, than to see Maurras, the scourge of the Republic, as being in some ill-defined sense part of the cause of the Republic's collapse in favour of Marshal Pétain after the defeat by Germany. Maurras's ideas could certainly be seen as the ideological basis of the Marshal's eventually collaborationist regime, but the circumstances which made the Vichy regime possible could hardly be blamed on a man who had never really been much more than the editor of a newspaper. The post-Liberation charges against Maurras in fact confirmed Maurras's own view of politics in a rather bizarre way. Maurras had always believed that politics was a matter of conviction and will, and that at bottom it was adherence to political ideas that counted. Books had made the French Revolution and the Republic and books could therefore undo it; so men like Maurras have therefore no grounds for complaint when their political enemies take the same view and blame great national disasters on intellectuals.

The question of Maurras's collaborationism is part of the larger question of how *Action Française* was ever going to get its programme implemented. The central problem which a Legitimist government in exile has to face is the problem of order. Legitimist monarchists always have to argue that it is their opponents who are the disorderly rabble, but this is always difficult to argue when these opponents are actually the government of the day as the republicans were in France. What, then, constitutes an 'orderly' way to disorder a government in place? Insurgency is out of the question because it is the means of opportunists of both the left and the right, and legitimate monarchy is supposed to be the opposite of opportunism. A monarchy wishing to return to the throne of its ancestors must find a legitimate way of doing so because the last thing it wants is to return to its own realm as a conqueror from beyond the national frontiers. (Unreconstructed Vichyites always saw de Gaulle as just another of France's conquerors, returning with a foreign army of invaders in 1944.) The only legitimate way for an exiled monarchy to return is at the invitation of the nation, which effectively means at the invitation of some, if not all, of the great national institutions. There was certainly a hope after 1870 that the king might be asked back by either the Chamber (where there was probably a royalist majority, or a majority which was not actively anti-royalist) or the army or both. That army was, after all, controlled by an officer corps not notorious for its republican sympathies and it was also the army that had put down the *Commune*. But times changed. The Chamber became more republican and so, after the Dreyfus Affair, did the army. The army was not exactly purged of its monarchist clericals, but their victory in the Dreyfus Affair made the republicans confident enough to promote republican officers to key posts, including posts in the military schools.

France's dearly bought victory in the Great War could be seen as a victory of left and right, the left claiming they had beaten off the challenge of Prussian militarism in the name of liberty and the rights of man, and the right claiming that France had avenged herself on the traditional enemy by the reacquisition of the lost provinces of Alsace and Lorraine. The nationalist right and the republican left enjoyed a brief honeymoon together after 1919, when both were swept along in a national orgy of patriotic self-congratulation. But it couldn't last, and it didn't. *Action Française* soon began to chant its anti-republican litany again but, as time went on, that litany began to produce different resonances. French politics might not have been changed much by the Great War but the politics of her continental neighbours were changing a great deal. Soon-to-be-beleaguered parliamentary republics appeared almost everywhere as a result of the treaties of settlement made after the Great War. These new republics were harassed by the radical right before they even had time to embed themselves in their own national cultures. This harassment was frequently fascist.

The fascist critique of liberal democracy was being cobbled together at the same time as *Action Française* were again taking up the anti-republican argument where they had left off in 1914. It could not help but occur to a disinterested listener that there was much in common between the arguments of *Action Française* and the arguments of the fascists, though at least to begin with there was a certain difference of tone. Fascism was raucous in a way that *Action Française* was not. But with time even this difference began to fade as *Action Française* pleaded its case with increasing urgency every year that the Third Republic managed to survive.

It is important to emphasise how consistent Maurras was. He changed his mind about nothing important from the time of the Dreyfus Affair to the day of his death. It was typical of him to describe his condemnation for collaboration after the Second World War as

'Dreyfus's revenge'. There comes a time when the only way to keep saying the same thing is to shout and then to bawl. A bawling *Action Française* was hard to distinguish from the fascist gangs of the 1930s and especially hard to distinguish from the imitation fascist gangs which sprang up in France. *Action Française* was peddling its own brand of monarchist dictatorship while the fascists were hawking their leadership principle, and this at a time when there was simply no chance of any of the great institutions of the French state inviting a pretender back to change the Republic into a monarchy once more. What chance, then, did *Action Française* have of ever coming to power except by methods indistinguishable from those which the fascists followed? In circumstances like these *Action Française* could easily be mistaken for the gang of street fighters it had always claimed not to be.

There was one other possibility. By the 1930s *Action Française* had known for a long time that their only chance of coming close to power was through a great national catastrophe. France had been changing its regime after great crises since 1789, so it might be *Action Française*'s turn at the next crisis, or the next crisis but one. However, these crises were supposed to be *internal* crises in the Republic and Maurras's own account of it were bound to happen sooner rather than later. But the Third Republic's capacity to survive its own crises was remarkable, and it was not until the defeat by the Germans in 1940 that the Republic finally threw in the towel. Maurras never seems to have considered what position an event like this would put him in. The Vichy regime, while not exactly royalist, had had in its leader, Marshal Pétain, a deeply Catholic anti-democratic reactionary trailing clouds of military heroism from Verdun. This was only second-best to restored monarchy, but it was a very good second-best. Better still, the Marshal was one of Maurras's admirers, and Vichy organised itself into more than a parody of some of the social and political ideals which Maurras had long held. Perhaps Vichy France never intended to be a client state of Germany, but that is what it turned out to be. Hence the final irony of Maurras's long career as an ideologue. He was punished for collaboration with Germany when anti-Germanism was a connecting thread of all his political thought. Thinking meticulously as ever Maurras does not seem to have realised that Frenchmen in their enthusiasm for purging the Vichyites were unlikely to pay much attention to the distinction between anti-anti-Nazism and pro-Germanism. Perhaps Maurras deserved better from a France which has always placed too high a value on political intelligence.

If there is a Maurrasian legacy then it shows more clearly in France's democratic politics than in the perennial right-wing lunatic fringe (though only time will tell whether a party like the National Front can ever be more than just a protest party). Gaullism and eventually Mitterrandism both based themselves on an analysis of the weakness of a French republican politics which in its way is profoundly Maurrasian. Democratic politics is more than a matter of universal suffrage and rival political parties. What successful democratic politics needs above everything else is majorities. Only majorities can produce strong political leadership, and only strong political leadership can make the institutions of state function in a way that makes the solution of great national problems possible. In the language of political science, France is no longer the great European example of 'institutional failure'. The French state no longer merely exists but actually works. That was what Maurras had always wanted, but he had never believed that it was possible through democratic means.

Of course, there were other ways besides Maurrasism for French democrats to learn that lesson, especially the living examples of British and American democracy. This adds the final irony: France may have learned and assimilated lessons from foreigners, a thing which Maurras's critique of Rousseau convinced him could never be.

THE CONSERVATIVE WORLD OF MICHAEL OAKESHOTT

Oakeshott calls himself a conservative but it is not easy to determine what kind of conservative he is. We look in vain in Oakeshott's political writings for a specific political doctrine, and there is nothing there that would help us to decide which side to come down on on any particular political issue. Oakeshott believes that there is such a thing as political *philosophy* which has got nothing to do with the world of political practice beyond *saying* that it has nothing to do with the world of political practice. Philosophy and the world are worlds apart.

This may seem to be a very negative viewpoint, but it has enormous implications for what we usually take 'political philosophy' or 'political theory' to be. The thinkers we include in 'the history of political theory' are often treated as if at least part of their claim to importance lies in the advice they give about the conduct of practical political life, and it is certainly the case that political actors – ancient tyrants, medieval popes, modern political movements – have always been keen to recruit the great names in philosophy to their sides. Philosophy appears to have prestige even in the political rough and tumble. Oakeshott does not, of course, deny that the great names in philosophy have been true philosophers, but he does think that philosophers have not always been very clear about the restricted nature of the true philosophical enterprise. Philosophers have often deserted their true calling in favour of the much more dubious profession of preaching. Philosophy is about knowledge and preaching is about practising what you preach, and philosophical knowledge is not knowledge of a kind which helps you to do any particular thing well. Philosophical knowledge does not speak directly to the world of practical affairs, and so when philosophers speak about practical affairs they do so as part of the world of practical affairs and not as philosophers.

Oakeshott is an Idealist thinker after the manner of Hegel, even though Hegel himself is not entirely free from the preachiness which Oakeshott thinks is the typical 'holiday excursion' of the philosophers, time off from philosophy proper. Like Hegel, Oakeshott thinks of philosophy as 'the thinking view of things', an attempt, which can never be complete, to understand the world. This understanding is of a particular kind, and the best way of explaining it is to contrast it with two other kinds of understanding from which it is different, and we might call these other kinds of understanding transcendental metaphysics and positivism. (These two categories do not exhaust all the possibilities of human understanding, and Oakeshott in fact takes the claim of 'practical understanding' very seriously though he thinks the claims made for it are often exaggerated, especially by 'practical' men who know what they like and will stand no nonsense.)

Transcendental metaphysics, of which Platonism is an outstanding example, is one of the possible philosophical reactions of a mind puzzled by the world of experience. All minds want to make sense of the world, and one of the things which makes the world difficult to understand is that it is always changing. The Platonist calls the changing world the world of Becoming, and he doubts whether any knowledge worth the name is possible about a changing world, on the grounds that what is true about that world today is unlikely to be true tomorrow. If knowledge is to be real, then it has to be knowledge which lasts, knowledge about Being rather than Becoming. Knowledge about Being still has to be knowledge *about* something, but it cannot be knowledge about the everyday, changing world. Transcendental metaphysics therefore posits the existence of a world which never changes and which is located somewhere beyond or above the world of ordinary experience. This world of Being not Becoming is the only world about which it is worth knowing anything. A world of Platonic Forms or 'ideal essences', intelligible only to exceptional and highly trained minds, is about as different from the everyday world as it is possible to be. Transcendental metaphysics effectively confines philosophy to the heavens, though philosophers like Plato have an irritating habit of claiming that those who understand the ghostly world of the Forms can also understand the everyday world perfectly and are therefore uniquely qualified to give men advice about how to live their lives (and even to force them to live them in accordance with ghostly precepts).

A positivist (and all the 'sciences' are positivist, including the 'social' sciences) thinks that transcendental metaphysics sidesteps questions about understanding the world. The Platonist, when asked to explain the world, cheats by inventing another, metaphysical world, and explains that. The metaphysician evades the question completely; he answers questions about a world which is not in question, and he often makes the absurd claim that understanding his own self-created world entitles him to tell truths about the ordinary world which are not available to anyone else. The positivist takes the ordinary world of experience for his own, and seeks to explain it as a collection of processes which work in regular ways. These regularities are worked up into empirically verifiable laws which constitute a growing body of scientific theory, and this body of scientific theory in its turn tells scientists what they should look for next. Science becomes a body of scientific ideas which enable scientists to go further in their search for the understanding of experience, and their understanding of further aspects of experience itself adds to a growing body of scientific ideas. However, like philosophers, scientists sometimes make unsustainable claims for their own expertise. They tend to make two in particular. The first is the claim that science, and science alone, confronts the 'real' world direct and without prejudice. The scientific mind, it is claimed, is open in a way no other mind is. It looks at nature *to see*; the scientific mind is a blank sheet waiting for nature to make its impressions on it. The scientific mind, it is sometimes claimed, really looks at nature as nature really is.

For Oakeshott, this is plain nonsense. The scientist looks at bits of nature with a body of scientific ideas already in his head, and he relates what he sees in nature to that body of ideas ('scientific theory'), which he then modifies or confirms depending on what he finds. The activity of doing science is as ideas-bound as any other human intellectual activity. It has to be said that the last thing Oakeshott is doing is attacking the scientific enterprise. It does not matter in the least to scientific practice that the working scientist thinks he is doing one thing when in fact he is doing another. Failure to understand the true nature of what one is doing does not of itself invalidate the activity being pursued. In the case of science, failure to understand the nature of the scientific enterprise can have no effect on the validity of the data of empirical experiment, but what failure to understand the nature of the activity can do is lead the scientist into making unsustainable general claims for scientific knowledge as compared to other kinds of knowledge claims. Scientists sometimes claim that scientific knowledge overrides all other kinds of knowledge, or that scientific knowledge can some-how adjudicate between other kinds of knowledge claims, whereas Oakeshott is concerned to show that science's claim to be 'knowledge in its own right' should be taken literally. A particular piece of scientific knowledge can only be part of other pieces of knowledge like itself. Knowledge 'in its own right' can't be knowledge about something else.

The claims for science become outrageous at the moment when the procedures of scientific method come to be seen as a generalistic procedure for solving any problem with which mankind is ever faced. The 'scientific mind', it is sometimes said, can approach and solve *any* kind of problem much better than *any* other kind of mind, including social and political problems. Scientific habits of mind, it is claimed, can comfortably inhabit any aspect or area of human experience. Science, in short, is a training for life. The effects of such a view may be felt at any particular level of political thinking or political practice. It can include a demand for more 'rigour' in the way political theorists pose their questions; it can include asking observers of political processes to collect more and more political data, and at the level of political practice it can consist of a plea for more scientists in the bureaucracy and more scientific advisers to politicians, especially to politicians in office because they are the ones who are continually called upon to solve problems. It is impor-tant to be clear exactly what is at issue here. What is being claimed is not just that scientists should be called in to advise governments about science itself; rather, it is that scientific training qualifies scientists to advise governments about the way to solve any kind of problem. (Margaret Thatcher was fond of saying that she wanted to be remembered not as the first woman prime minister but as the first scientist prime minister.)

Oakeshott will have none of this. Scientists might in fact be good solvers of political problems, but that has got nothing to do with their being scientists. Being a scientist consists of possessing a body of scientific ideas without which the practice of science is impossible. Doing science consists of testing those ideas ('experiment') and adding to them ('theorising'). Science (and this would include the 'soft' as well as the 'hard' sciences) is its own world of experience and cannot therefore have anything useful to say outside its own world. Some scientists are, no doubt, better at doing science than others. Some minds are sharper, or more systematic, or more open to new ideas, than others, and perhaps these are mental qualities useful outside science's own world, but there is nothing specifically *scientific* about these qualities. Scientists who do in fact end up as scientific advisors to statesmen are just particularly good examples of a type of 'scientific politician', men who have been successful political operators in the world of scientists. They, like the politicians whom they serve, have 'got on' in their own particular world by developing and using skills which are probably identical to the skills which the successful politicians possess. When a scientist advises political decision-makers, like speaks to like.

766

What is true of science is also, in its own way, true of philosophy. Oakeshott is keen to deprive governors and governing decisions of any bogus prestige they might be able to extract from science or philosophy. Politics, after all, happens in a culture, and different intellectual activities have high prestige in different cultures. In Western culture, it has always been useful in politics to be able to say that the 'latest' scientific philosophical thinking is 'on our side', therefore our side is the thinking man's side. Oakeshott demurs: neither science nor philosophy, properly conceived, can speak directly to the world of practice, including political practice.

Philosophy and the world of experience

Oakeshott calls the world of ordinary experience the world of 'practice'. Practice is only one of the 'modes' of experience. It consists of the pursuit of ordinary human ends or, as Aristotle would say, the pursuit of goods or things which men call good. Getting and spending, falling in and out of love, getting elected or failing to get elected, ruling and being ruled, are all parts of the world of practice. The world of practice does not exhaust the possibilities of experience, which means that, whether we know it or not, we can and do live simultaneously in several different worlds of experience. Oakeshott says that we can experience the world as practice, science, history or poetry, and it is important to stress that these different but simultaneous worlds are not experienced in any particular order. Quite the reverse. These are separate worlds with different 'voices' in the same conversation. What Oakeshott calls the 'conversation of mankind' is supposed to be conducted in a civilised way. It is a conversation, not a debate, and it certainly should not be a squabble. No single voice is expected to be heard above the others, and each voice must recognise that the other voices really have got something worth hearing to say. Voices in a conversation have to strike the right note, and it is easy to see what would introduce a raucous tone. This would occur at the moment when one voice claimed some kind of priority over another; that is, when one voice claimed to speak with authority about a world which was not its own. We have already come across one possible example of that in the case of the scientist who thinks that he is uniquely qualified to speak for everybody. Such a claim must be bogus because there is no single unified world of experience for the scientist to have knowledge of. A scientist must learn to listen to other voices because it is absurd for him to claim that what he knows is the only thing which can be known.

Why is philosophy not a voice in the conversation of mankind? Oakeshott invites us to see philosophy as being outside the conversation but at the same time listening carefully and benignly to it. Perhaps philosophy is best thought of as being older than the active participants in the conversation of mankind, and possessed of a wisdom which is not immediately available to them. It is a wisdom which comes from experience, but it is not wisdom which comes from experience of any particular world. On the other hand, philosophical experience is not limitless because it stops well short of trying to know the mind of God. Philosophy's job is to take a view of the world as a whole, which is just another way of saying that philosophy tries to make sense of the world by trying to see how the particular worlds of experience fit together. The problem with the worlds of particular experience – practice, science, poetry and history – is that they only have boundaries in a very restricted sense. These boundaries exist only in the mind of a detached but interested philosophical observer. For all other purposes the worlds of possible experience exist in the same intellectual space. They are superimposed on each other, but that superimposition does not exist in any systematic way. The worlds of experience as seen from the inside, that is *as* experience, have no particular coherence because they appear haphazardly to ordinary minds as different bits of different worlds of experience. This is especially true of minds which lack self-awareness, which probably means most minds. This does not mean that most people are confused; it may simply mean that clear-thinking but not necessarily self-reflective minds can move easily and without noticing from one world of experience to another.

As an Idealist after the manner of Hegel, Oakeshott takes a view of what minds are *for*. Like Hegel, Oakeshott believes that minds meet the world half-way. Mind is neither passive in the face of the world nor does it create an arbitrary world outside the self. Idealists are not positivists who believe that there is a world 'out there' waiting to be discovered. Rather, mind is to be seen as always trying to make sense of a world; that is to say, mind tries to find coherences in the world without the positivist's conviction that the coherence is 'out there' waiting to be turned into the elegant simplicity of a few scientific laws. All minds share the characteristic of having a picture of the world, but it is a picture they have painted themselves, and it is not a photograph. All minds are like that: childish minds; adults minds; self-aware minds and minds without a clue what self-awareness means. This is very far from saying that all minds are equally good at making things coherent and it is very far from saying that all minds are trying to make sense of the same things. All minds make more or less coherent worlds of experience, which is just another way of saying that minds (that is, human beings) find ways of coping in the world. Like the ancients, Oakeshott believes that each kind of human activity requires its own kind of knowledge. Doing anything, and especially doing anything well, requires understanding, though how that understanding is acquired is still an open question (and so is the question of whether everyone acquires the same knowledge in the same way). The worlds of practice, science, poetry and history are all more or less well-understood by those who live or work within them. This makes philosophy's job harder, because it means that philosophy is an invitation to those who already understand an activity to understand it in a new way. Philosophy's job is hard but it is important to remember that philosophy is not necessary to the competent management of life in any of its forms of experience. Any working scientist, for instance, knows that he can do science without ever having heard of the 'philosophy of science'.

The world of practice is the world in which most of us live. In the Oakeshottian scheme of things practice comes closest to what we mean by ordinary experience, but it is not quite what ordinary experience is usually taken to be. We have become used to contrasting the world 'as it is' and the world 'as it ought to be', and we have been encouraged to make this contrast by every great political thinker except Hegel. Philosophy has been trying to teach the world what it should be ever since philosophy was invented, so that nothing is easier than to contrast a philosophical world of 'oughts' with the sordid and humdrum business of

768

ordinary living. 'Oughts' are pictures of a much better world and sometimes of an ideal world, and these 'oughts' often prove to be very tough and they almost never die. 'Oughts' add up, and, as we would expect, the world becomes more cluttered up with 'oughts' as time goes on. Again, we might expect that a world which is changing rapidly would produce new 'oughts' rather quickly, and since the French Revolution this had indeed been the case. The twentieth-century world is awash with 'oughts'. Part of Oakeshott's purpose is to root these 'oughts' firmly in the world of practice. Properly speaking, these 'oughts' do not deserve whatever dignity they might acquire by claiming to be part of philosophy because they are not part of the philosophical enterprise at all.

We have already noticed that Oakeshott wags his finger at philosophers when they start to preach. Preaching is exhortation to change one's behaviour in the world of practice, and there is no difference in kind between the exhortations given to us by preachers and the exhortation we give to ourselves the whole time. We spend our whole lives telling ourselves to do *this* and not to do *that*. All human action is value-driven; otherwise it would simply be behaviour. The difference between different kinds of human action is often that in one case the pursuit of a value is highly explicit while in another case the judgement of value is only implicit. This latter comes close to what we ordinarily mean by 'habit', human action the value of which is no longer even remotely in question and may therefore not even be present in the actor's own mind. The world of practice is constituted by what we think we want to do and also what we think we ought to do, and there is not, at bottom, much to separate the two. What we think of as morality appears as a single set of 'oughts' among many such sets, moral goods among the other goods which men wish or choose to pursue.

What Oakeshott has done here is to sidestep the notorious 'fact/value' problem which has bedevilled moral and political philosophy in the twentieth century. Moralists have been pondering the connection, if any, between 'is' and 'ought' ever since Hume pointed out in the *Treatise of Human Nature* that 'is' statements and 'ought' statements are of such logically different types that no statement of value can come out of any statement of fact. What this means, for those prepared to take it seriously, is that the activity of doing moral philosophy can have no connection with the 'real' world at all. 'Oughts' live in a self-subsistent world apart, with no lever on the world of the ordinary experience of living. All moral philosophy can therefore do is either endlessly reiterate this simple logical truth, or become a kind of moral sociology in which value systems are plotted on a map, which somehow shows the relationship between the development of different value systems and the stages of the development of particular societies. (Hume's own theory of justice relies on just such a correlation.) That moral sociology effectively became the programme of nineteenth-century social science, in which it was generally recognised, if only implicitly, that systems of values cannot be universal. Human values in general came to be thought of as being group-specific, the values of a class, or of a nation, of a tribe, of a religion or of anything. This turned the traditional business of moral philosophy on its head. Humanity ceased to be seen as a single group chasing a system of universally shared values. Rather, the moral world came to be seen as a series of separate systems of moral values, each waiting for the appropriate human group to come along and take it for its own.

Oakeshott is therefore on very solid ground when he puts facts and values in the same world of practice. Hegel-like, he is recording what has been happening for the past two centuries in the world of ideas. Setting the record straight is useful because the rhetoric of morality has not always kept pace with the changes which have happened in the world of morality itself. People still have a tendency to speak of their own value systems *as if* they were universally valid, transcending all the barriers of space and time. People have never got out of the irritating habit of being hurt or outraged by the refusal of others to think morally like them. People still think of morality as the primary thing which people have in common, thus ignoring the obvious truth that it is the fact that people have lots of *other* things in common which enables them to share a common set of values in the first place.

The transition to politics

Oakeshott clearly does not overvalue the philosophical enterprise. Philosophy as he understands it is not necessary for life and philosophers have no particular claim to the respect of their fellow men. The philosophical enterprise is distinct from other enterprises in life, and Oakeshott thinks that to confuse 'philosophy' and 'life' in the sense of a 'philosophy of life' is bad for philosophy and would probably make life worse. To understand why this is so we have to turn again to the claims which have been made in the past for philosophical knowledge, or, indeed, for knowledge of any kind.

Ever since Plato, knowledge claims have tended to be rulership claims. The history of political thought is littered with the idea that the possession of particular kinds of knowledge constitutes a valid claim for the possessor of that knowledge to rule others. Political thinkers may disagree about what kind of knowledge is required. Right at the beginning, for instance, Aristotle disagreed with his erstwhile master Plato about the kind of knowledge which was required of the statesman, but they still agreed that a statesman was a statesman by virtue of the knowledge he possessed. Statesmen without the required knowledge were bogus and dangerous. Even a thinker with Machiavelli's reputation for brutal pragmatism thought that claims to rulership were based on a kind of knowledge which could be learned. And so matters have continued to our own day. Political leaders as far apart as Hitler and Mao Tse-tung have claimed to have privileged access to a source of political wisdom denied to others. Oakeshott is very concerned that we should understand that the knowledge claims which he advances for philosophy are worlds away from rulership claims.

What is true of philosophy in general is also true of political philosophy. The rulership claims which political philosophers have tended to see in political philosophy come about as the result of the elision of two meanings of the word 'higher'. If political philosophy is the 'highest' form of political knowledge, then it is often taken to follow that those who possess this 'highest' form of political knowledge ought to occupy the 'highest' positions in the state. Hence the rulership claim for political knowledge. Oakeshott detects a *non sequitur* here. He recognises that there are different levels of political knowledge, but he denies that the 'higher' the level, the greater the rulership claim. Oakeshott in fact probably thinks the reverse: the 'highest' form of knowledge about politics is of so 'elevated' a kind that it can have no lever on the world of practice of which politics is a part.

770

We do well to remind ourselves what an Idealist like Oakeshott thinks knowledge is. Like Hegel, Oakeshott thinks that minds try to make coherent pictures of the world. Knowledge advances its own knowledge claims to the extent that it is a coherent picture of its world. Ideas of the world, that is to say pictures of the world, have to make sense, and they make sense to the extent that the picture of the world contains all the right bits and that the bits fit together in the right way. Not everybody's world is the same world. Different worlds can be encompassed by mind. Simple minds living in simple worlds contain very little so they have very little to make sense of. Worlds become more 'abstract' the simpler they become, because they contain and make sense of only a few facts 'abstracted' from all the possible worlds of experience. If it were possible for a mind only to contain a single fact, then that would be the most 'abstract' mind of all, because the single fact which it contained would not be abstract in the sense of being related to anything else. A single fact is the ultimate abstract idea (it is an 'idea' because ideas are all that minds can contain).

Philosophical Idealism goes against the grain of ordinary language here. Those of us who are not Idealists have become accustomed to thinking that minds contain 'facts' and 'ideas' as if these were separate entities, mental events of qualitatively different kinds. We have also become accustomed to thinking of minds which contain a high proportion of 'ideas' as opposed to 'facts' as doing their thinking on a more 'abstract' level than minds which contain a high proportion of 'facts' as opposed to 'ideas'. Hence the popular idea of the philosopher as a man with his feet off the ground and his head in the clouds, not part of the world of mundane facts which he hardly seems to notice. Oakeshott rightly thinks this is nonsense. 'Abstract' thinking is not somehow 'out of this world'; rather, 'abstract' thinking is so rooted in a few facts abstracted from the 'real' world that it cannot see beyond itself to other possible worlds of experience. The difference between a philosophical mind and an ordinary mind is not of the 'head in the air' versus 'feet on the ground' kind. Rather, the philosophical mind tries to make coherence out of coherencies – that is, tries to make general sense out of worlds which already make sense to those who live and work within them. To do philosophy is to take a view of the *whole* of experience – that is, to make the possible worlds of experience make sense by seeing how they fit together. This activity is the reverse of 'abstract' in the ordinary sense because, rather than considering nothing about the world, it considers everything about all possible worlds. Philosophy consists of trying to make a kind of supercoherence, a coherence of all possible worlds, and it does this by refusing to take at their face value the different worlds of experiences' views of themselves.

Philosophy, then, 'makes sense' of different 'making-senses'. It cannot speak with authority in any particular world of experience. Philosophy properly conceived cannot do honest spadework in some corner of experience. Philosophy never commands. It may look 'down from above', but that is simply a metaphor. It might equally be said that it 'looks on the game from the touchline', or that philosophy sometimes acts as a referee. Philosophy does not speak with any authority about how particular experience games are to be played, but philosophy is sometimes allowed to cry 'Foul!' Philosophy blows its whistle when one player in the game infringes improperly on another. To revert to Oakeshott's own analogy of a conversation between different worlds of experience, a 'foul' would be committed when a voice from one world of experience tried to speak with authority about a world which is not its own. In Oakeshottian terms, this would amount to that form of bad manners which we call 'monopolising the conversation'. Unless it is stopped, the intrusive voice would turn the conversation into monologue, which is just another name for preaching.

Philosophy appears as the thinking view of things in general, where 'things in general' are to be understood as different worlds of experience. Of course, there is nothing to stop a philosophical mind reflecting on anything it pleases, and it doesn't much matter if that mind does or does not signal to itself that it is passing from philosophy properly conceived to reflection in a philosophical mood. It is, after all, the same mind, and mind may do as it pleases. Reflection about political life may occur at any level. It can be about political means to given ends, or it may attempt the more ambitious consideration of political ends themselves. Reflection about politics can arise from a variety of motives. Political thinkers may wish to see changes in existing political arrangements, and they may try to bring these about by generalising the data of political experience up to the level of a political doctrine, or again, political thinkers may construct just such a doctrine to show that existing political arrangements should remain as they are. The political reflections of a philosophical mind will tend to flow upwards, and the activity of political philosophy begins when reflection about politics reaches a certain level. The political philosopher begins with the world of political practice, but he always has other worlds in mind. Political philosophy tries to make the world of political experience coherent so that he can begin to explore the coherence of the world of politics with other worlds.

The rejection of ideology

A rejection of all political ideology is implicit in Oakeshott's view of the nature of political philosophy. It is not that he thinks that all the claims made by political ideologists are untrue, and it is not that he thinks that all political ideologists are somehow equivalents. Rather, what he is concerned to show is that the claims made on behalf of political ideologies are necessarily bogus. Ideologists all make one very simple mistake, or, to put it another way, all ideologists are founded on two propositions about the world, one of which is manifestly true and the other obviously shaky. Ideologists know (who doesn't?) that politics takes place in the same world as every other human activity. There is nothing particularly startling about this simple truth; it is true by definition, and you do not even have to know anything about the world to know it is true. Ideologists think that it follows from this simple truism that everything has a political 'dimension', and that therefore everything is 'part of politics'. 'Political' truths are therefore paraded by ideologists as general truths about the world.

Ideology politicises everything. In Oakeshottian terms, this means that political ideology mistakes the world of politics for the whole world of experience. Lots of things which ideologists say will no doubt be true because ideologists are not always altogether fools, and it does not follow that ideologists are confused about the little things because they are confused about the big things. The ideologist makes claims which are similar to those made by those pushy scientists who claim that only science can tell truths in and about the world of science. If a scientist tries to tell the truths about other worlds, either he is mistaken or he no longer acts as a scientist. There is, after all, no particular reason why a scientist should only be familiar with the world of science, and he may even strike out towards philosophy. The point is that being a scientist is no more a qualification for philosophy than it is a disqualification. A scientist is philosopher to the extent that he does philosophy, and the only possible source of confusion between the two activities of science and philosophy is that they could take place quite happily together in the same mind. The ideologist fails to realise that politics is only a little corner of the world of practice, and he extrapolates a view of the whole of experience from inside that little corner. It's as if you could get a view of a mountain range from deep inside one of its valleys.

Ideologists, then, politicise every possible world of experience. That accounts for the impulse towards ideology, and it also accounts for the content of ideologies. Ideologists pride themselves on their connection with 'philosophy' as they, but not Oakeshott, understand the term. Ideologues admire 'philosophy' for its 'originality' (a quality which Oakeshott never claims it has). Thinking is valued by ideologists because only thoughts can be new. The world of practice, the world we actually live in, is always old, or what is old about the world of practice always preponderates over what is new. What is 'new' always in some sense either is the 'product' of the old, or arrives in the world contaminated by it. Only thought can be free from the present and the past; only thought can practise a kind of chastity amid the temptations of a corrupt world. Only free thought can genuinely turn against the society it appears in because free thought is the only thing we can be certain is not part of a corrupted world.

Oakeshott makes short work of this absurdly over-inflated claim for thought. Like Hegel, Oakeshott denies that the past can ever really be over. Human beings are historical creatures because one of the things they carry about with them in their heads is an idea, that is to say a picture, of the past. A picture of the past, it might be said, is a constituent part of human personality. This picture of the past will, no doubt, vary from person to person in the sharpness of its detail and the comprehensiveness of its content, and different people will display very different degrees of awareness about having such a picture. People called 'historians' will have an acute professional awareness of how the past lives in the present, while ordinary people are likely only to be vaguely aware that the past appears to them as a present. Those who pride themselves on being plain and practical men would be especially hard to convince that they were, in some sense, 'living with the past', and they would be inclined to contrast the 'presentness' of their own practical lives with the history buffs who often seem to 'live in the past'. From an Oakeshottian point of view, the 'practical man' simply accepts the past in the present without knowing it, and, of course, it would not make much difference to the way he lives his life if he did know it. A certain rough and ready picture of the world and a certain everyday code of conduct will see him through. (If the practical man is also a Christian he will on Sunday, to an extent, desert his everyday views about the world by dressing himself up in his moral Sunday best. In church he will be invited to see his ordinary life in relation to eternity. For a moment he will seem to himself to be 'high-minded', but this will hardly affect what he does or thinks when he goes back to his ordinary life on Monday.)

The proof that ideological thought is not virgin lies in the content of ideologies themselves. No matter how hard ideologues try to say something new, observers have no difficulty in relating the content of ideologies to their own time. This applies to ideologies constructed in the past and it applies equally to the present. Ideologies are selective, so you would not expect them to contain everything that their contemporary world of ideas contains, but you would expect ideologies to incorporate ideas which are 'in the air'. There is a simple proof of this. In any given era you would expect competing ideologies to overlap considerably and the later an ideology appears the more you would expect it to contain within itself elements of other ideologies. There is more to this than straightforward criticism of one ideology by another. Rather, we would expect a fairly constant set of doctrinal positions to be scattered among various ideologies, and we would account for the rivalry between ideologies on the simple grounds that different ideologies cobble together the same doctrinal positions in different ways.

Though Oakeshott himself does not use it, anarchism would be an excellent example of an ideology which sets out to be 'new' but whose components can easily be identified as parts of other ideologies which anarchists despise. The anarchist critique of capitalist societies is often indistinguishable from the Marxist critique; the anarchist emphasis on individual autonomy is redolent of what J.S. Mill has to say about the sovereignty of the individual in *On Liberty*, and the anarchist distinction between 'artificial' communities based on force and 'natural' communities arising out of the well-springs of human nature contains more than an echo of the old conservatives' idea of the organic society. Even the central anarchist activity of state-bashing can be seen as a combination of the traditional liberal fear of the state and the worried conservative view of law and order as permanently fragile: anarchists tend to think that if you gave the state one final push it would collapse. The supposed 'originality' of anarchism turns out to be no more than giving a different twist to strands of argument which are readily available in the political culture in which anarchists think.

There is nothing 'wrong' with working up existing material into new arguments. This happens the whole time in the world of practice of which politics is a part. There is nothing especially 'political' about recasting old material into new-looking arguments. The world of practice, we should remind ourselves, is the everyday world of devising means to ends. The 'ends' of human conduct are not fixed. There is no list of 'fundamental human needs' waiting to be satisfied. The ends of human conduct are what we now call 'emergent'; that is to say, human ends *emerge* from the process of human conduct in the pursuit of other ends, and there is no reason in principle why the process of end-emergence should ever stop. All this means is that there is no foreseeable point at which what we call human conduct would stop, no point at which every conceivable human end has been attained. Human conduct looks as if it will go on to infinity. Crudely speaking, human beings can achieve their ends either by force or by force of argument (or a judicious blend of the two, as in 'threatening'). Most of human civilised life is conducted on the level of persuasion. There may often be veiled threats in the conduct of human affairs, as when we make someone an offer they can't refuse, but on the whole human conduct works through words, that is through good and bad arguments. Politics is simply a special case of human conduct in general: means are adduced to ends in political life, just as they are in life as a whole.

774

Political ends are emergent in the same sense that all human ends are emergent. People sometimes make rather dramatic claims about the nature of political life. 'Politics', they will say, 'is about power'; politics is a 'hot' activity – 'if you don't like heat, stay out of the kitchen'; political decisions are 'tough' decisions because politics is a tough business to be in, so that mere survival, as in the jungle, is an achievement in itself; and so on. The truth about most politics is less dramatic, because most of the time it's about words. (To convince yourself about this, all you have to do is to look at the sheer volume of the writings and collected speeches of great 'men of action', Oliver Cromwell, for instance, or Lenin.) Words are not a 'substitute' for 'political action' because most of the time words *are* political action. Oakeshott recognises all this perfectly well. Much of what passes for 'political thought' or 'political theory' is really indistinguishable from 'political action', and is therefore firmly rooted in the world of practice, not part of the world of philosophy at all. In other words, Oakeshott overvalues neither political thinking nor politics as part of the world of practice. Political thinking in particular is so much a part of the world in which it arises that it is ridiculous to think that political thought can be a lever on its own world. Political thought cannot be both a part of its own world and a view of its own world from outside demanding our particular attention. A view of the world which comes, so to speak, from inside that world's own head cannot have any independent 'philosophical' status as a critique of that world. Political ideologies which criticise their own world (and even those which do not) simply turn one part of the given world against another, so why should we take the critical part more seriously than the part being criticised? If both are the product of their own time, then what is there to choose between them?

The politics of the modern world may be ideological politics in the sense that ideology distinguishes modern from other kinds of politics, but it does not follow from that that ideological politics is the only kind of politics which is going on. Equally, it follows that ideological thinking about politics is not the only kind of political thinking available. An attack like Oakeshott's is, of course, an attack on ideological politics in all its forms, which effectively means that he rejects all of the noisier forms of politics in the modern world. Yet Oakeshott calls himself a conservative, and he is plainly a thinking man's conservative, so there must be a form of conservative thought which in Oakeshott's own terms is definitionally non-ideological.

Oakeshott's conservatism

The first question to ask about a thinking conservatism is: What is it thinking *about*? The answer must of course be: thinking about politics; but it must also be said that it is thinking about politics which is not ideologically conceived. Ideology is grand in its scope, so we might guess that thinking conservatively after the manner of Oakeshott is by comparison a much more modest enterprise. Politics in the modern world obviously happens for the most part in nation-states – that is to say, in communities with a certain past, with a certain social make-up and with a certain set of arrangements for making political decisions. All these are givens. Politics, in the famous Oakeshottian phrase, consists of 'attending to' these decision-making arrangements.

This 'attending to' is not so much vague as open, because it is not always easy to predict even in general terms what the business of politics will actually require political actors to do, and, given Oakeshott's often indirect way of approaching problems, it should come as no surprise to us that Oakeshott has a good deal to say about how politics should not be done. In a famous essay on *Political Education* (which was also his inaugural lecture as Professor of Political Science at the London School of Economics in 1951) Oakeshott treats us to a series of reflections on how political actors actually do politics, as a way into the question of how politics should be done.

As an Idealist, Oakeshott is committed to the view that an activity cannot be done at all without the actor's already having in his mind an idea of what the activity should be like. Oakeshott identifies two ways of looking at political activity, the empirical and the rationalist (and we should not be surprised to find that there is considerable similarity between the rationalist and ideological views of politics). These views are equally open to political actors and to those who study politics. Politics being part of the world of experience, it would make no sense for political scientists (Oakeshott would probably wince at the neologism) to arrive at an understanding of politics which was incomprehensible to those actively engaged in the political enterprise.

The view of politics as an empirical activity would have us believe that politics consists of waking up in the morning, asking: What would I like to do today? and doing it. Purely empirical politics would be a politics without preconceptions and without antecedents, government without policy. This is woefully inadequate as a description of political activity, because no human activity short of insanity is ever without patterns of consistency, and there is method even in madness. Why, then, point to an empirical view of politics at all? What use can it possibly have? The answer is that the empirical view of politics comes very close to describing what a certain kind of politician *thinks* he is doing. This kind of politician we sometimes call a 'pragmatist' because we think of him as a no-nonsense problem-solver. He will not be in the least interested in the 'clash of issues'. Politics for the empiricist will not be a matter of endless idle debating chatter as the issues are 'addressed'; rather, he will see the world of politics as presenting politicians with a series of problems to be solved, and he will see himself and be seen as a political technician more or less adept at solving them. And the word 'presenting' should be stressed. Problems 'present' themselves to government; government does not go looking for problems. The role of government in the empirical view of problems is what we would now call 'reactive' as distinct from 'proactive'. Government does not 'get in there first'; government waits to see what it will have to do and then does it. To the extent that the tasks of government are limited, though, it should be noted that the tasks of government are not limited in principle, because in principle there is no limit to the number of problems which a society could in fact press on its government. In practice this does not matter greatly, because it would probably be the case that government empirically conceived in Oakeshott's sense would be continually adept at problem-solving, so that such a government would have to be very unlucky indeed to be presented with so many problems at once that it was overwhelmed by them.

Politicians and governments may *think* that this is what they are doing, but Oakeshott thinks that it is plain to any observer that they do nothing of the kind. You can't negate the past and you can't act without an eye to the future. Being reactive over a period of time *is* to have a policy; this policy is based on a view of the role of government as the business of interim crisis management, and this view of the role of government reflects a view of the proper relationship between government and society: successful government will be government which solves problems as they arise from society so that the problems don't stack up to the extent that they threaten to overload the processes of government and cause it to blow a fuse and come to a stop. Again, the empirical view of politics takes a particularly instrumental view of governing institutions: it is not enough for governing institutions to exist and to perpetuate themselves. Governing institutions have to deliver the goods – problem-solving – so that implicit in the empirical view of politics is a set of failure criteria for government. The practitioner of empirical politics is operating on the basis of a view of the world even though he might deny it till he is blue in the face. Of course, it has to be said that it would probably make very little difference to his effectiveness as a political actor if he did acknowledge his own 'idealism' (though it might make the practical man of affairs a little less strident about his no-nonsense virtues).

The rationalist view of politics is the empirical view's polar opposite. The rationalist view consists of waking up in the morning and asking the question: What ought the world to be like?, and then devising means to make the world resemble the picture in your head of what it ought to look like. Specifically, the rationalist in politics asks: What are the best possible political arrangements?, and then sets about the business of setting them up. Oakeshott's objection to this type of politics is that it is a compound of an impossibility and a mistake. The rationalist style of politics is obviously based on the possibility of being able to think up *a priori* truths about politics which are the product of reason alone. This is the familiar over-claim which ideologists always make for political thinking. Oakeshott thinks that these apparently *a priori* rationalist truths always in fact come from reflection about a form of politics which already exists. Truly abstract and general political principles are a chimera because they always come out of what already exists, which is to say they form part of a tradition. It is an axiom for Oakeshott, in so far as he has axioms, that practice is always prior to doctrine. He writes:

> So far from a political ideology being the quasi-divine parent of political activity, it turns out to be its earthly step-child.

> (*Rationalism in Politics*)

The rationalist makes the mistake of thinking that he acts on a 'pure' view of the world when in fact he acts on the basis of an incomplete perception of the world masquerading as a disembodied corpus of political principles whose truth is independent of place and time.

There is, of course, no reason in principle why any particular political actor should consistently take an empirical or a rationalist view of politics. One of the messages of Oakeshott's political thought is that politics is 'messier' than either the empirical or rationalist views of it would have us believe, and it is easy to see why. Both the empiricist and the rationalist try in their different ways to pretend that the past does not exist in the present. The empiricist fails to realise that in fact he attends to precedents and has an eye to the future (a past which has yet to happen) while the rationalist refuses to see that his 'pure reason' has only a dubious claim to virginity.

If politics cannot be done in an empirical or a rationalist way – though attempts to do it these ways can cause a lot of trouble – then how is politics to be done at all? What is the recommended Oakeshottian way of 'attending to' the political arrangements of a political community which chance or choice has brought together? The business of 'attending to' has to be carried out in the full recognition that political communities have a history. Like all conservatives, Oakeshott has to confront the problem of change, and saying that political communities have a history is his way of recognising that the future is going to be different from the past. Conservatism is not so much hostile to change as a way of coping with it. Oakeshott recognises, like Aristotle, that men have two contradictory expectations about their political arrangements: that they expect them both to change and not to change. Political arrangements which change and change quickly can leave men bewildered because they may not know what to expect of them. On the other hand, political arrangements which refuse to change can very quickly begin to look ridiculous. Political arrangements which lagged behind their own changing society would lose their capacity to produce viable decisions so that the problems would begin to pile up.

The problem of government for Oakeshott, as for all other political thinkers, is to discover what kind of knowledge governments need in order to govern well. We already know a good deal about what Oakeshott considers to be bogus forms of political knowledge, and we would expect his own knowledge claims to be modest. And so they are. The business of government properly conceived consists of what Oakeshott famously calls the 'pursuit of intimations'. Intimations have to come from somewhere and they have to lead somewhere. They come from the practice of politics and they arise out of a sense of unease, a feeling that things are not quite right. This feeling itself arises from the mind's tendency to be uneasy in the face of incoherence. Human conduct is never deliberately arbitrary, which means that mind is forever seeking to render coherent that which has the appearance of incoherence. In practical life coherences emerges as recognisable patterns of utterance or conduct. In politics this can take the forms of precedent and policy, the realisation that certain measures taken in the past imply that a certain kind of action should be taken in the present and followed up in the future. Patterns of action are seldom, if ever, complete, and it is the condition of partly realised patterns of action that they speak to us about what they need to be complete. As Oakeshott puts it, the political life of any given society appears at once coherent and incoherent, patterned but incomplete, which intimates 'a sympathy for what does not fully appear'.

Political discourse will then be about what is latently present but not yet there, or, to put it another way, the discussion of statesmen will be about the right time and the right way of responding to the sympathy they feel for what does not fully appear. Intimations come to those who are already engaged in the practice of politics (though there is no reason in principle why they should be confined to practising politicians), but they do not come singly. An intimation is like a signal from the world, but one of the world's problems with the world is that it sends many signals and sometimes so many that, taken together, they constitute a noise. The art of politics lies in being able to hear the separate signals clearly and knowing which to respond to and which to ignore. Not being a rationalist, the states-man has no set of *a priori* criteria which tell him which or what kind of intimations he ought to pursue. Intimations can be divided into two rough and ready categories, those which proceed from the 'strongest' impulses of which human beings are capable and those which spring from the 'highest'. Interest and justice will press their claims strongly on the states-man's attention, and he does well to listen to both. He will certainly not listen to either exclusively, and he would be wise not to prefer the one consistently to the other.

Beyond that, the making of political decisions is a matter for a particular kind of politi-cal education. What does Oakeshott think an education in political practice would actually be like? Again, in his mildly maddening way, Oakeshott is much clearer about what a polit-ical education should *not* be like than he is about what it should be like. He is particularly at pains to distinguish real political education from the kind of bogus political education on offer in a political 'crib'. Cribs, as everybody knows, are substitutes for the real thing, and they are often the recource of those who have, for one reason or another, been denied access to the real thing. Real political skills cannot be learned 'out of a book', much less by correspondence course. Both of these methods are bogus because they assume that 'knowing' comes before 'doing', that there is a kind of 'technical' knowledge which can somehow be prior to the 'practical' knowledge which doing anything well requires. Oakeshott's attitude to the acquisition of appropriate knowledge is not a little tinged with snobbery. Political knowledge of a practical kind is knowledge acquired in a tradition. How, then, is this knowledge handed down? Oakeshott's answer is through a mixture of apprenticeship and connoisseurship. Practical knowledge is what the chef has and what the jumped-up kitchen porter who has read a cookery book definitely has not. Oakeshott is very far from denying that kitchen porters can ever become chefs. Quite the reverse. What he is denying is that the kitchen porter can ever become a chef until he has served an apprenticeship as a chef's assistant. Then, and only then, will the erstwhile kitchen porter realise that cookery books are only useful to those who already know how to cook and who can tell simply by tasting whether a dish is successful. Oakeshott cannot resist a dig here at a particular kind of left-wing sensibility:

> The Rationalist is like a shopkeeper who, having bought an estate, thinks that a correspondence course in estate management will give him all the knowledge necessary to control it and its tenantry, and the knowledge which belongs to a man who has been educated from his earliest years in the responsibilities and duties of a landowner is not (where it goes beyond the technique) knowledge at all, but nescience.
>
> (*Rationalism in Politics*)

Books about wine are useful only to those who are already connoisseurs or who are on their way to becoming so. The same must be true of any form of practical knowledge. Becoming a successful politician means serving one's time, getting to know one's way around, getting to know how to sniff the air, and if one has been born into a political family so much the better. What makes the Oakeshottian account of the acquisition of political knowledge doubly irritating to anti-conservatives is that he has turned a left-wing critique of political practice on its head. Critics of existing political practice have always really known that the way to become a political adept is to be or to become a political leader. It has never been much of a secret that the best way to become a successful king is to be born a prince into a royal family, and to experience kingship from the inside by trying the crown on from time to time. Intelligent political elites have always found ways of bringing up their successors, and since Burke English conservatives have had no doubt that their survival in the modern world depends in part on their being willing to welcome into the fold talents which it might be dangerous to leave unsocialised on the outside.

OAKESHOTT'S CONSERVATISM

It might seem from what has already been said that Oakeshott is just another defender of the ruling class after the manner of Burke, but this is not really the case. Oakeshott is fond of occasionally trailing his coat to irritate the left, but a moment's reflection is enough to tell us that he is a conservative with a very small 'c'. Oakeshott's political thought is about a way of doing politics which is meant to appeal to the right but by no means exclusively. In a famous essay, 'On Being a Conservative', Oakeshott refers to conservatism as a 'disposition'. He cannot call conservatism a political 'philosophy' because the philosophical enterprise, as he understands it cannot impinge directly on a world of practical experience, while even the more modest term political 'theory' has sometimes paraded itself in borrowed philosophical robes. A 'disposition' carries no intellectually pretentious overtones; it is suitably provisional and the reverse of dogmatic or didactic. An invitation to share that disposition might be given, though how general that invitation can be is an open question.

The conservative disposition arises from the perfectly ordinary human desire to live in a familiar world, while at the same time the mind tells us that the world in which we live changes. A familiar world is no guarantee of human happiness, but it is a world in which ordinary men can form their own projects with a reasonable chance of their being accomplished. A familiar world is capable of engaging our affections even if it is incapable of inspiring love. It is not necessarily always safe, but its dangers are well enough known for them to be avoided with everyday prudence. The feeling of familiarity works at every level and in every aspect of human living, so it can easily attach itself to a set of political arrangements.

An important part of a country's political arrangements is its governing institutions, and Oakeshott takes a very instrumental view of governing institutions. He does not, like Burke, see them through a gauze of misty veneration. For Oakeshott, institutions are sets of procedures which are put into operation to deal with the problems with which even the sleepiest of governments is confronted from time to time. The craft of politics, like any other craft, consists of manipulating a set of tools for a particular end. Learning to handle tools is what any apprenticeship amounts to, so a political apprenticeship is an education in how to make certain kinds of institution work. This must be done from the inside, and it must be done under the tutelage of masters. Political skills, then, are a valuable resource, and at no time are they to be prized more than in emergencies.

Like all conservatives, Oakeshott detects a noxious tendency to cry for changes in institutions during times of political emergency. Times of political emergency are times when governing institutions are presented with problems of a kind which they are not used to coping with. It is this confrontation with unfamiliar problems which leads enthusiasts to call for re-designed institutions to cope with them, whereas Oakeshott's view of the nature of governing institutions tells us that the last thing to do in a crisis is to start fooling around with institutional arrangements. After all, institutional procedures are the only thing a society in crisis has going for it. No doubt, these procedures have a history. They will have developed out of coping with problems presented to government in the past, so that old and trusted governing procedures may look a bit dated when they are applied to unfamiliar problems, but this datedness is probably more apparent than real. Part of any skill is skill at adaptation. In the ordinary course of things, no two problems requiring skilled attention are ever really the same, though they may not be very different. A craftsman adapts his skills all the time, though he may himself be unaware that he does this, which is just another way of saying that new skills are always being learned on the basis of the old. Oakeshott thinks that changes in political institutions happen in exactly the same way. Institutions learn by doing; that is, institutional procedures change by adaptation as they cope with unfamiliar problems. Familiar skills change in the process of coping with unfamiliar circumstances.

Understood in this highly instrumental way, it is easy to see where the revolutionary enthusiast goes wrong in his haste to re-design institutions. He wrongly supposes that only new procedures are adequate to solve new problems. He fails to see that the only sound basis for the development of new skills is the old. The only alternative is to start inventing institutions from scratch, which amounts to trying to invent skills on the basis of nothing. Skills just can't be invented, only developed. Hence the tendency of revolutionaries to 'terrible simplifications'. They see no craft mysteries in the business of government; rather they see governors cultivating self-serving mystique about government. This raises ancient radical hackles because it smells of the incense of the divine right of kings, the assertion that God mysteriously chose certain men called kings as the sole repositories of the wisdom of statecraft which was not communicable to ordinary mortals. In this the radical sees not statecraft but witchcraft, a monstrous fraud no less fraudulent because kings, like witches, often believe in their own vocation. Democrats ancient and modern have said often enough that the business of government is and ought to be adapted to the meanest human capacity, so that a child could do it. Radicals often say that the business of government has become needlessly complicated by those involved in it to guarantee their own indispensability. Oakeshott would reply that you only have to look at the shambles consequent upon revolutions to see how right he is about the nature of political institutions. Revolutionary government is really a contradiction in terms, because revolutionaries are always simulta- neously engaged in making new institutions and learning to work them. The first is impossible, because it amounts to inventing new skills which have then to be taught quickly to new would-be craftsmen, which is also impossible. No wonder that all revolutions are followed by reactions. In Oakeshott's terms there is nothing mysterious about this. It is simply a process in which revolutionaries realise that the new men aren't up to the highly skilled job of governing and so the revolutionaries are compelled to hand back some at least of the tasks of government to adepts of the old regime. This necessary return of the familiar shows open-minded men that revolutions are not worth the trouble they cause.

Oakeshott's contention that men wish to live in a familiar world goes beyond affection for a fireside, an old pipe and slippers. Oakeshott's Idealist view of mind as endlessly trying to make the world outside itself coherent can easily be restated as mind's continuous effort to hang onto familiarity in a changing world. Mind deals with new experience by fitting it into a picture of the world which it already has, and another way of putting that would be to say that mind strives to make the unfamiliar familiar by incorporating it into an already familiar landscape. Of course that familiar landscape alters in the process but it is at the same time still recognisably itself. Again, it is true that a time will come when so many alterations will have been made to mind's picture of the world that the whole picture will have altered, but the change will have been so gradual that at any one moment the familiar will far outweigh the unfamiliar. Growing up is like that. Children wait in vain for the *moment* when they will begin to feel 'grown up', and adults sometimes say they 'have never grown up' when they obviously have. All they mean is that in retrospect they cannot remember a moment at which the transition to adulthood occurred. It happened, so to speak, unawares. The only way to observe the change 'all at once' is not to see the child in its adolescent years, but to come upon it at twenty-one not having seen it since it was seven. Then the observer would be able to experience the change in a way which the child itself never can. The same thing is true about how a physical landscape changes. It changes imperceptibly before our eyes (if we are lucky, that is, to avoid the rationalist attentions of landscape redesigners), but if we return to a landscape unvisited since childhood our first reaction is often to exclaim: 'But it's changed!' This can be an unnerving experience. At the very least everything will look smaller, and this change of scale, coupled with all the other alterations, gives rise to a feeling of uneasiness which is very different from the feeling we get when confronted with a landscape in a foreign country which we have never seen before.

The familiar grown unfamiliar is among the most unsettling of human emotions. The familiar becomes both itself and not itself, like a friend altered by illness but not beyond recognition, or simply the common occurrence of meeting a friend who 'is not himself' today. (It is not for nothing that the old Latin word for friend is *familiar*.) When our familiar world changes too quickly we begin to feel like strangers in our own country, at home nowhere. We can easily see how Oakeshott's concern for the familiar relates to his critique of ideology. All ideologies are to a degree utopian. They are intended to estrange us from our own real existence by painting a picture of an ideal world in which 'human nature' really could be at home. For Oakeshott, this amounts to designing an abstract world for abstract men, a Procrustean bed for which everyone will have to be cut down to size in order to fit in. Real individuality inheres in people living their lives in a viable society the richness of whose history produces the genuine individuality which comes from diversity. How, Oakeshott reasonably asks, can we all be similar examples of 'human nature' and real individuals at the same time? The answer is that we can't. The promises of ideologies are therefore doubly false. They are false because they cannot deliver a future which is a negation of the past because the past always refuses to go away, and, even if an ideology could deliver its promised future, there would be so little real individuality that we would not even be able to recognise ourselves.

Oakeshottian conservatism means making the most of the given world. Conservatives are sometimes thought of as being attached to the past in some special sense which makes them downgrade the present, but Oakeshott would say that this is to misunderstand conservatism's own nature. A true conservative would no more like to live 'in the past' than he would like to live in a future utopia. Both would be another country. Better fence-mending in this world than pining for lost pasts and unattainable futures.

Oakeshott's modest claims for political thought make it hard to pin him down to any particular band in the political spectrum. Oakeshott's political thought cannot be a political philosophy, and it is not obvious in what sense it constitutes a political doctrine when one of its purposes is to arouse in us a suspicion of most of the claims which political doctrines make. Perhaps the best way of looking at Oakeshott's political thought is to see it as intended to encourage a particularly sceptical way of holding political doctrines. Oakeshott certainly does not think that his own political thought is capable of banishing political doctrines from the world. Political doctrines, we do well to remind ourselves, are part of the world of practice, and it is not thought's job to alter the world of practice much, let alone to abolish parts of it. The world of practice, however, being a world of change, can always be improved, and Oakeshott is not addressing his mild admonitions only to those who would call themselves political conservatives. Oakeshottianism could just as easily be a way of being a socialist as being a conservative. There is, after all, something called a socialist 'tradition' which is very self-conscious of itself as a tradition and which means that some socialists at least recognise a past as well as a present and a future. Movements calling themselves 'social-ist' often split into what outside observers call 'moderates' and 'extremists' or 'purists', and these last fit as neatly into Oakeshott's category of 'rationalists' as the former fit into his category of 'conservatives'. And anybody who has ever belonged to a political group which calls itself a 'movement' has been exasperated by how slowly it can be to get it to move.

Much the same thing could be said about Oakeshottianism at the level of government. Governments do have a tendency to act in a conservative way no matter what their political colouring. Governments of both the left and the right will always be accused by their own zealots of being aimless, lacking vision and having 'lost their way'. Oakeshott's message (if that is the right word) to governments accused of such things is that, provided they are keeping the state afloat, they understand their own business perfectly well.

NOTES ON SOURCES

Maurras's *Enquête sur la monarchie* is one of the few great political works never to have been trans-lated into English. Some Maurras is available in J.S. McClelland, ed., *The French Right: From De Maistre to Maurras*, (1971). M. Curtis, *Three Against the Third Republic: Sorel, Barres, Maurras* (1959), is a good place to start. E. Weber, *Action française* (1962), and R. Remond, *The Right in France from 1815 to de Gaulle* (1966), are standard. Oakeshott's *Experience and its Modes* (1933), is not easy to read. His *Rationalism in Politics and Other Essays* (1962), and *On Human Conduct* (1975), are easy to read but not always easy to understand.

32

THINKING ABOUT THINKING, AND THE LAPSE INTO DISCOURSES

Every history has to come to an end. These ends can be either symbolic or chronological, and it is often hard to make the two coincide. Symbolically, my history of political thought ends with Nietzsche, some time in the 1880s, and chronologically, with the supposed European bankruptcy of Marxism, some time in the 1980s. This takes some explaining. What it means is that Nietzsche's work already contains all the equipment necessary to a thoroughgoing, piece-by-piece dismantling of the whole enterprise of political theorising as traditionally conceived. However, in the beginning at least, almost nobody read Nietzsche, and those who did read him did not always read him very well, so that it took nearly another century for truths to be generally recognised which Nietzsche almost alone recognised in his own time.

By 'recognised' I mean something different from 'believed by everybody'. An inspired reading of Nietzsche before 1900 (one might almost say a 'futuristic' reading) could have put very exceptional readers on the same track as most of the advanced European thought of the next three or four generations, but, as things turned out, it was mainly from later voices that Europeans were to learn the things which were so fundamentally to undermine the intellectual foundations of their civilisation. Naturally enough, there were resistances. Attempts were made to shore up the rationalist and universalist tradition in which the European West had invested so much. In this sense, much of the political thought of the twentieth century either ignores late nineteenth- and early twentieth-century thinkers like Nietzsche, Sorel and Freud, or pretends they have not happened. Reading Maurras, for instance, or Oakeshott, you might never guess at the existence of highly sophisticated theories of unconscious motivation which make a real conundrum of the relationship between thought and life.

It is only with hindsight that we can see that, since the Enlightenment, a whole version of modernity hangs on the proposition that we can understand our own thoughts. Nothing is easier than forgetting how much enlightened thinking was about what we would now call the psychology of the individual. Enlightened radicalism dug down to the root by attempting to give an exact account of the thing we do our thinking *with*. No effort to understand the world could possibly engage the loyalty of rational men unless that understanding was built upon, or could be seen as an emanation from, an understanding of the human understanding itself. It is his account of human understanding, of how we know what we know, that makes Locke the outstanding figure of the early Enlightenment, and it can truly be said that all subsequent psychologies are either variants of Lockianism or implicit attacks upon it. The modest claims of Locke's own empirical epistemology were either exaggerated or built upon by later thinkers, so that by 1800 thinkers as far apart as Bentham and Godwin could believe that mind was no longer problematical, so that mind could confront the world as the world really was. There was still the niggle, which the Idealist philosophers were to make much of, that we can't know *things-in-themselves* but only our impressions of them, but that could not matter very much in the rougher and readier world of enlightened political thinking.

It may be that it was Enlightenment's claim to understand the world inside and outside the self which accounts for a certain smugness in Enlightenment's nineteenth- and twentieth-century followers. Perhaps the enlightened party and their Comtean and Spencerite progeny just could not see how circular their own basic argument was. What was inside took stock of what was outside, and vice versa; each confirmed the other in a never-ending series of careful experiential and experimental stages, mapping out the natural and moral worlds in a particularly knowing way. This was the route to progress, 'enormous, certain, slow'. The prescriptions for the improvement of the world which were supposed to come out of the acquisition of 'useful knowledge' were to be seen as just as necessary as their scientific under-pinnings, for in those happy days the naturalistic fallacy had yet to worry thinking men and women into moral funk.

The now famous 'revolt against positivism', or the 'revolt against science', which is supposed to have happened at the *fin de siècle*, can now be seen as an attack on the more outrageous claims made on science's behalf, rather than as an attack on the scientific enter-prise itself. What was at stake was not truth, but orthodoxy, where 'orthodoxy' stands for what we would call 'ideology'. Scientism had become ideological in the straightforward sense that it would countenance only a particular kind of knowledge, so that scientists already knew what kind of knowledge they were looking for, in much the same way as a prospector goes looking for gold and recognises it when he sees it.

The world of positivism was a tight world, and it can still surprise us that thinkers like Pareto, Sorel and Freud could think their ways out of it without formally repudiating the methods of science. Theirs was an attack upon the positivist worldview from the inside, cutting science down to size while using science's own procedures. Again, it has to be emphasised that it was scientific idolatry, and not twentieth-century science's more modest knowledge-claims, which was at issue here. Nietzsche did not know much science, but he had a very shrewd idea about the direction in which a particular branch of scientific rhetoric pointed. Science had had a potentially egalitarian thrust ever since the atomic theory of Democritus. If every process in the natural world could be explained as the effect of the movement of tiny particles all of the same fundamental kind, then anything which happened in the human world – that is, in societies and polities – could be explained through a parallel methodological individualism. Liberalism had already done this well before 1900, and the proof is that some liberals were already well ahead in the business of toning down liberalism's threateningly rugged individualism while Herbert Spencer was still alive and thinking.

Liberal individuals had come a long way from their Democritean origins. Now they lived in a world which could be understood as an extrapolation from themselves; the world was the individual writ large in a sense that had not made sense since Plato. Human evolution's crowning glory was a *homo sapiens* who could choose a social and political identity for him-self, and could love his neighbour as himself without needing to hear God's command. Purely rational intuition would set autonomous liberal man on reason's own path.

What that world-view could not stand was *fin de siècle*'s radical scepticism about the truthfulness of the statements which human beings make about the world and, especially, about themselves. Part of this scepticism came from what can be conveniently called 'the recovery of the unconscious', if by that we mean an increasingly explicit awareness of the unthinking causes of human behaviour. The unconscious was very different from what we might call 'things we have forgotten'; rather, the unconscious came to be seen as a dynamic set of wishes and drives whose relationship to the conscious was problematical because the conscious mind seemed not to want to know them. Part of mind's job was to keep the unconscious in its proper place, but dynamic unconscious energy had to find an outlet, and to do that it had to find ways round the obstacles which mind put in its way. The unconscious never takes the shortest path between two points. The unconscious is endlessly devious in a mechanically elaborate way. It tries to find a route past the mind's own censor, and it does this by sending its messages in codes which can be devilishly hard to break, though in principle they can always be broken.

This simplified account of Freud's view of mind can stand for the 'new' burgeoning psychology of the end of the nineteenth century. Freud added twists and turns of his own, and he was a great systematiser, but his account of the complications of mind speaks with the *fin-de-siècle* consensus. The truths of introspection were damned for ever. Confessional literature could no longer be trusted at all. Now, it was not so much that Rousseau was keeping something back in the *Confessions*, lying by omission; rather, it was that there were certain truths that he could not tell about himself because nobody else could tell those truths about themselves either. If statements about oneself were automatically suspect, then it followed as clearly as the night the day that statements about the world were doubly suspect, coming as they did from a highly suspect piece of mental equipment. People could no longer *really* mean what they said, because nothing very certain could be said about that part of them which was doing the saying. Speech and writing must still be *for* something, but that 'for something' could no longer be seen to be either truth-telling or the instrumental adjustment of means to ends. Thinking like this about thinking meant that the world was no longer rational in any sense that made sense. Enlightenment and the dreams of positivism were over if the understanding mind was no longer an open book.

Mistrust of thoughts came from more than one direction. Another of its main thrusts came out of social science of the positivist kind from exemplars as politically and culturally far apart as Durkheim and Pareto. Any social science which contrasted, however provisionally and implicitly, what people thought they were doing, or, better still, said they were doing, and what they actually did, undermined the status of thinking, speaking and writing. This was happening at the same time as the social sciences were beginning to bite hard on the concepts of culture and ideology. It was beginning to be made explicit that cultures were not arbitrary, while at the same time they could not be understood as extrapolations from the minds in which those cultures lived: cultures worked from the outside in, not from the inside out. The sociology of culture was not applied psychology; nor was it social psychology, the study of human interaction from the points of view people carry about with them in their own heads. 'Culture' and 'society' came increasingly to be seen as genuine 'things', with lives of their own, impinged on by other lives but not determined by them. The concept of ideology had already begun to map out the connections between patterns of thought and patterns of power. What could be more obvious, then, that all speech, all argument, all thought, was the outward surface of an inner will to power?

The will-to-power angle on thought by no means denied the power of thought in the world. The truth content of thought might no longer be the most important thing about it, but thought certainly *worked*. A century and a half before, Hume had said that all government rested on opinion. Now, that truth could be extended to cover all the power relations in a society: power that lasts covers itself in a set of rationalisations which lie ready to use when power is questioned. Nobody understood this better than the anarchists from Godwin to Kropotkin. The anarchists realised that, unless we are particularly unlucky, we don't very often confront head-on the institutions which control and direct our lives. We usually come across institutions at second-hand through implicit or explicit rationalisations for them. The world of politics, which is the sum of the world's power relations, is an extremely prolix world of interlocking justifications for the exercise of power by one over another. Politics consists of the tactical and strategic deployment of competing sets of justificatory words.

Sets of justificatory words have to *come from* something and have to be *aimed at* something, hence the sociology of knowledge. Sets of justifications – which we sometimes call ideologies – come from, or emerge on behalf of, power groups and have as their aim the longevity of a certain existing set of power relations. Ideological attacks on existing power relations in favour of others – what we sometimes call utopias – come from, or emerge on behalf of, out-groups wishing to become in-groups.

The will-to-power view of the relationship of thought to life is frank in its acceptance of the permanent plurality of languages and audiences. The clue to this shift, from the whole of mankind as an audience to particular audiences in separate theatres, is to be found in Nietzsche's own playful but deadly insistence that what he has to say is addressed only to three nameable contemporary fellow spirits. Although he writes in German, Nietzsche explicitly excludes the Germans from his audience, showing that he knows that it was the Germans who began to corral mankind up into its separate and latently hostile cultural laagers. We can already see the beginning of that process of ghettoisation in the works of Herder at the end of the German Enlightenment. I must emphasise 'beginning', because Herder in fact thought that there was *very little* which could not successfully make the transition from one culture or language to another. As a culture-critic (the word itself is not an altogether happy import from the German), Herder spent a lot of his energy trying to find ways to make other cultures and languages accessible to his native Germans. He also tried to explain francophone Germans to themselves and the Germans to others. None the less, Herder did put a high value, though not the very highest, on those aspects (Germans would call them 'inner' aspects) of a culture which do not travel well.

For Herder, that certain incommunicable 'something' (it invites the cliché) was only a fraction of the sum of human experience. It was especially important in aesthetics, and it was crucial to poetry, but in some quantifiable sense it was almost nothing when seen beside the huge weight of shareable human experience. Herder could still believe in Humanity with a capital 'H', by which he meant the sum total of human experience as it expressed itself in individual minds and separate cultures. Herder did believe in cultural hegemony, moments when discrete national cultures bound ahead of their rivals, but these moments of hegemony, properly understood, are the great educational opportunities of humankind. Nation really could speak unto nation, and could make almost everything it had to say understood. Cultural hegemony could be a source of national pride – witness the smugness of the French about 'their' Enlightenment – but, at its best, cultural hegemony was supposed to bring nations up to the start-line, ready to charge the armies of ignorance. There was always going to be something offensive about this. The armies of ignorance might not always appreciate the efforts that were being made on their behalf and rescue could always look suspiciously like invasion, especially if ignorance was wilful. The road to conquest is often paved with good intentions, and those intentions could become hopelessly entangled with national self-interest. What, then, could be more natural than that Enlightenment's critics should go a bit further down the Herder road and claim that only those things about a culture really mattered which could not pass unaltered across cultural, national, boundaries?

This was not Herder's fault, however much one might suspect that in his heart-of-hearts he was already half-way down the road to proclaiming the validity and indivisibility of all cultures, while at the same time denying that each culture was equally 'good'. Enlightenment pinned the idea of human progress on Herder right from the beginning, so Herder at least invited people to believe something which at first sight seems puzzling, namely that each culture has a unique integral character but that some are superior to others. The position is not, however, as contradictory as it might seem. The claim to superiority is a claim to under-standing: some cultures, and perhaps a single culture, are so favourably positioned that they can understand other cultures without those other cultures being able to understand them. If Herder did not entirely hold this position, then Fichte certainly did. Enlightenment's universalist message continues to be broadcast, but in an oddly perverted way. The claim is now being made that the privilege of universal understanding is, by definition, restricted to a particular national group, something that Enlightenment had always denied. The general lesson to be learned from Herder and Fichte is that henceforward it is to be recognised that mankind is no longer a single audience capable of hearing a single voice. There are many separate audiences 'out there', and they have to be addressed in so many different voices. Humanity in the oldest sense of all no longer exists, which in the language of social and political theorising means that there cannot be a single set of moral and political arguments about values which is capable of engaging and retaining the loyalty of all right-thinking men. The world begins to be seen as a group of groups, each one of which, or each one of which save one, is locked up in its own private world of values and language, and it is not very far from there to the currently fashionable notion that the world is a series of parallel discourses which will only meet at infinity.

The Fichtean claim to privileged understanding has not worn very well despite its having by no means been restricted to German nationalist thought. Take away all claims to a privileged understanding and you are already in an moral universe in which the only intellectually defensible enterprise is a non-judgemental comparative cultural anthropology – stamp-collecting masquerading as social science. In this scheme of things, all languages are intensely private: we may *think* we are hearing other voices, but all we are really hearing is noise. Either we talk only to ourselves or the rest is silence. (And that includes silencing the voice of non-judgemental comparative cultural anthropology itself, for how could that voice sustain its claim to be the single universal mediating discourse in the hostile world of untranslatable private languages?)

Nietzsche recognised all this in his own age's refusal to acknowledge its own truth that the intellectual world had been privatised. What enraged him was Europe's cowardly refusal to go beyond its own intellectual gentility: on the surface everyone pretended that what was happening wasn't really happening at all. Different knowledge-claims were simply the historical forms which the will to power just happened to take. All 'philosophies of history' were therefore shams. The world wasn't going in any particular direction. Perhaps the eternal recurrence of Eastern philosophy was right and we were stuck with the endless round of existence. But life might, after all, be fun, so round again!

Enlightenment might also appear to be indistinguishable from the class interest of an enlightened bourgeoisie. Perhaps nothing could have stopped this from happening. Enlightened political and social theorising was about principle above all, and there has always been something bourgeois-sounding about principle. If there is such a thing as a 'bourgeois spirit', then it is miles away from the aristocratic spirit that we find in radical aristocrats like Byron and Pushkin. Aristocracy is code, manner and sensibility; aristocratic radicalism can only be random outrage in action, Byron at Missolonghi, and part of its charm is that it is accidental and therefore fundamentally inexplicable: who *understands* Byron? Contrast this with the politics of bourgeois principle, which has the whole world for its audience and expects eventually to convince everybody. Critics of Enlightenment could easily see in the Enlightenment project a conspiracy to take over the world. Marxists would see Enlightenment, and especially its economics and sociology, as a part of 'bourgeois ideology', the self-interest of a class pretending to be the general interest of mankind.

However, Marxism itself still stuck to a version of enlightened universality translated into the world of sociology. The Marxist theory of ideology, and in particular the idea of 'false consciousness', certainly cast grave doubts on the possibility that all men could come to share the same belief-system, but Marxism added the twist that the fundamental fault did not lie in the available belief-systems. Rather the fault ran through the societies in which those belief-systems tried to universalise themselves. Different classes could not share the same belief-system on anything like straightforward terms. A society in which everybody, or nearly everybody, shared the same beliefs was certainly a possibility because it is part of the job of an ideology to try to universalise itself, but the world had known since Plato's *Republic* that justice was the interest of the stronger and that injustice pays. In Marxist terms, the only way that a whole society could share the same system of beliefs, without force or fraud, would be if that society could achieve the condition of classlessness, either by a miracle or by revolution.

For Marxists intellectual engineering begins with social engineering: you don't find the moral and political arguments to fit the group, you universalise the group to fit the arguments; hence the Marxist insistence that the proletariat can universalise itself because a universalised proletariat – it might just as well be called 'humanity' – is the only human group not to require its opposite in order to be itself. Universalise the proletariat and you see a group without sub-groups, where sub-groups define themselves as groups with dissident belief-systems. Just as Marxist politics looks forward to the end of politics traditionally conceived as the provisional adjustment of conflict, so Marxist moral sociology would be the end of sociologising as we know it, because the groups which sociology usually deals with would either cease to exist or exist palely and inactively, doing nothing much worth bothering about in noncompetitive social space.

Marxism, it is said, has not been notably successful in its twentieth-century attempts to abolish the sociology which Marxists would call 'bourgeois'. 'Dissidence' in the peoples' democracies of Eastern Europe used to be a code-word for the existence of societies and states crying out to be understood in the terms of the sociology of cantankerous and competing groups with different belief-systems. Communists tried rather half-heartedly to paper over the cracks with loose theoretical talk about 'non-dialectical' social contradictions and 'socialist' competition, but it was never very convincing. And so we come to our own world, where all we are being invited to see are barriers between human groups through which intelligible human utterance cannot pass. All language has become in some sense body language: it is said that people 'give off signals' when they are arguing, or that they speak a particular 'language', and these sets of signals and sets of words provide us with access to the real text. No specific argument, *my* argument or *your* argument, really matters. What does matter is being able to identify arguments as belonging to a particular type. This unmasking of arguments is all that needs to be done in order to demonstrate that the arguments themselves are problematical. Pinning particular arguments to a problematic leads, by a sleight of hand, to the further contention that all arguments are probably equally problematical, and this, in its turn, leads to a position in which it is held that there is, therefore (and the *non sequitur* is blatant), no reason why I should ever listen to any particular set of arguments at all. Or, to put the matter less nihilistically, any argument will do.

None of this might matter, were it not for the fact that people who think like this are often deeply convinced that the world is ruled through implicit or explicit arguments in defence of authority. This perception is not new. Thrasymachus said much the same thing, but the difference between Thrasymachus' world and ours is that Plato will never quite allow Thrasymachus to deny that true arguments exist *somewhere*. Perhaps that is what a 'real' Thrasymachus would have said, but we can't know that. Our problem is to disentangle the implications of this for a world which might be ruled through arguments, none of which can be said to be true in the sense of being capable of commanding the assent of everybody who understands them. If *all* moral and political arguments are *ipso facto* problematical, then what can arguments possibly *do*? The only answer can be that it is not very clear what arguments may usefully do beyond 'raising consciousness', where consciousness is about 'issues'. 'Raising consciousness' does not seem to amount to very much more than getting people worked up about 'issues'. And there is a real evasion in the word 'issues'. 'Issues', we are being told, are not the same as 'problems', because calling things 'problems' carries with it the implication that problems can be solved if we think about them properly, and that is to fall back into the old trap of Enlightenment. Raising consciousness about issues is the same as rallying the troops for an ideological war in which argumentative confrontations are the skirmishes and debates the set-piece battles.

This habit of preaching to the half-converted does fit in rather painlessly with an old way of looking at the practice of electoral politics and with a current way of looking at the state of Western liberalism. Practising politicians in systems of representative government have always known the difference between converting the opposition, on the one hand, and, on the other hand, getting out the vote. The political propaganda of electoral campaigning may sound as if it is meant for everybody, but in fact it is only or primarily meant to mobilise one's own supporters. The assumption made before elections by every political party is that they will win provided their supporters turn up at the polls. Converts may be made, but the art of electioneering is not importantly about conversion (I leave aside the vexed question of the 'floating voter'). So the fact that different groups are tucked hermetically up in their own 'worlds of discourse' might well go unnoticed simply because it cannot much affect the way representatives are chosen in liberal democracies. It does mean, however, that the system of representative government can have no rational foundation for at least some of the groups who choose to play the electoral game. Electoral politics will become meaningless, or at least precariously provisional, because the system of representative government can no longer have any rational justification. It is, so to speak, up to *other* groups to keep the system of electoral politics going.

Pluralism is the version of liberalism which suits moral sociology best. Discourse groups locked up in their own language worlds could continue to exist without attracting much notice in a robust civil society comprised of many well-organised interest groups with a strong sense of their own identity. In fact, to continue to exist at all discourse groups in pluralist societies would have to speak two different languages, one for internal use and another, 'public', language for external use in their relations with other groups which do not consider themselves to be discourse groups. Discourse groups would, of course, regard their use of public language as being purely tactical. The public language could not be used for telling cross-group truths, because truths of that kind, by definition, cannot exist for those who deny the existence of a public which can share those truths.

The question is: How long could ordinary interest groups and discourse groups continue to play the pluralist game together? It almost goes without saying that there could not possibly be any rational grounds which could conceivably convince discourse groups that pluralism was the best, or even a good, way of doing politics. (It is possible that a discourse group could come to think that pluralism was the best way, or the only good way, of doing politics, but that view of pluralism could come to an interest group only by coincidence.) Pluralism could only be kept in being by the enthusiasm for it engendered by other, non-discourse, interest groups. Discourse groups would continue to survive only as parasites on the emotional energy of others keeping pluralism in being.

Some pluralists, mainly American, talk as if pluralism will happen as long as there are groups to play it. This talk is especially plausible in cultures which make a fetish of poker-playing. Poker is a persuasive model for pluralism because the game of poker is in principle endless. Players may enter and leave the game at any time, but the game goes on. To sit down to play, all you need is an 'ante' – money, resources, 'capital' – and in principle you may leave the game at any time you wish. (I say 'in principle' because the game is subject to a certain code of good manners. Quitting while spectacularly 'ahead of the game' – that is, without giving opponents a chance of winning some of their money back – is almost always regarded as bad form, and so, too, is gloating.) This model exactly fits a civil society in which groups rise, decline and fall. In particular, it accounts for a high degree of social stability in a society which is constantly changing: some out-groups manage to raise the political ante and join the game, while some groups already in the game find they can no longer stand their losses and they quit.

Poker pluralism may appear to be able to accommodate discourse groups quite easily, especially when we remember that superfluous talk at the poker table is actively discouraged. Poker is played without there being much communication between neighbours. It is, of course, important to know how your neighbour plays the game, but that is all you have to know. This knowledge is to be inferred from how a player plays, and not from anything he says. Players will, therefore, be careful not to 'give anything away', so that, beyond the bare minimum, there does not have to be, and there should not be, any communication between the players at all. This begins to look very like a model of a society made up of non-communicating discourse groups, so the question has to be asked: What is there to prevent a society of non-communicating discourse groups from playing an endless game of pluralism? And a second question naturally arises: How could you tell the difference between an ordinary pluralism of communicating groups and an apparent pluralism of non-communicating discourse groups?

The answer to both of these questions is time. Non-communicating discourse groups could at the beginning insert themselves inconspicuously into a genuine pluralism of communicating groups. However, the discourse groups would cause a few eyebrows to be raised by their gruffness, and a little later it would begin to dawn on the other groups that the discourse groups were playing a different game. This dawning would arise in any number of different ways under the heading of 'not playing the game'. The most likely way for an awareness of strangeness to arise would be from an attitude to winning and losing. Like poker, pluralism is played according to a certain code of good manners. Playing the pluralist game properly means accepting that, for the most part, wins will be modest. In pluralism there are not supposed to be all that many big wins. Not getting everything you want, and appearing to be a good loser, is part of the game.

Eventually, the existence of strangers in the camp would become obvious from a shrillness in their voices. Non-communicating discourse groups do not really expect to convince others of the reasonableness of their causes. Shrillness would give way to sheer volume as the only strategy to make sense in a world in which nobody would really be listening. Ordinary pluralist groups would have no choice but to follow the discourse groups and turn up the volume too. In effect, they themselves would be forced into becoming discourse groups. Only two possibilities would then exist. Either everybody would go deaf, or, what amounts to much the same thing, everybody would realise that the only sane course would be to remain silent. Silence is non-communication. Non-communication is another word for incivility, and civility is one of the oldest words for politics. A silent world would be uncivil. This matters a great deal in a world which seems to be putting more and more faith in the capacity of international organisations to solve the world's problems. If the world is collapsing into discourse groups, then it follows that the worlds of political thought and action are moving in opposite directions.

NOTES

11 SOCIAL CONTRACT 1: THE HOBBESIAN VERSION

1 The idea that the state is always broke even in very rich societies is comparatively recent and probably arose out of the possibility of computing national wealth.

2 If he had heard of it, Hobbes would have liked the custom of Chinese emperors, who, to reward their serviceable subjects, ennobled them and their ancestors, not their descendants.

3 A more homely example of something analogous to the collapse of sovereignty happens every day at street crossings controlled by the little green and little red man. People wait in numbers for the little green man, but somebody usually crosses the street on red. Others immediately follow, because they do not like to see others stealing a march on them. The sovereign authority, as represented by the little red man (fear of punishment for jay-walking), collapses in the face of fear that neighbours will gain an advantage on you by getting to the shops first. This can even overcome the *real* fear of the traffic which is still coming past while the little red man is still trying to do his duty as the Sovereign's agent.

19 THE RISE OF LIBERALISM

1 It might be argued that the principle of corporate representation survived for as long as the suffrage was restricted to men only, the man voting, so to speak, as head of the household, and the whole household being represented through him.

23 MARXISM AND OTHER SOCIALISMS

1 There is a very simple test you can do on yourself to see whether Marx is right about this: the next time you go into a public art gallery, ask yourself why you are buying a reproduction of a painting if not out of a desire to possess the painting itself.

28 LIBERALISM'S SPECIAL ENEMIES: THE CROWD AND ITS THEORISTS

1   Not quite all: Tarde excludes the family.

30 FACISM, OR BEING REVOLUTIONARY WITHOUT BEING MARXIST

1   I am aware that to call Nazism 'fascist' without qualification is to rush into a minefield of theoretical controversy. I will be content if calling Nazism 'fascist' makes the reader begin to think of Nazism as a 'late' (and perhaps 'untypical') variant of fascism, and I will be pleased if the reader begins to realise how widespread fascism was in Europe before Hitler even became Chancellor in 1933. (I will be delighted if the reader stops thinking, if he does, that fascism is somehow only 'of the past'. There is plenty of it still around in our world.)
2   'The Mob' as a synonym for the Mafia shows that the late nineteenth-century usage is not quite dead.
3   I count myself among them.

31 CONSERVATISM

1   It need hardly be said that Maurras's is a distorted view of only one side of Rousseau's political thought.

INDEX